The Sage Handbook of Social Network Analysis

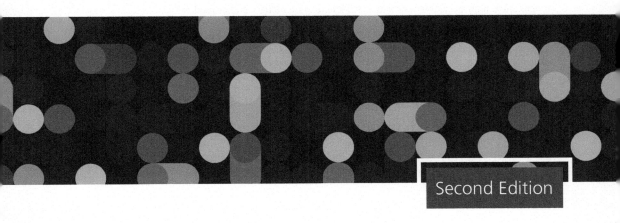

Second Edition

This new edition of *The Sage Handbook of Social Network Analysis* builds on the success of its predecessor, offering a comprehensive overview of social network analysis produced by leading international scholars in the field.

Brand new chapters provide both significant updates to topics covered in the first edition, as well as discussing cutting edge topics that have developed since, including new chapters on:

- General issues such as social categories, computational social science, and signed graphs;
- Applications in contexts such as socio-ecological systems, environmental policy, gender, ethnicity, cognition and social media and digital networks;
- Concepts, methods such as centrality, blockmodeling, multilevel network analysis, dynamic and spatial analysis, data collection;
- Statistical models such as exponential random graph models, relational event models, stochastic actor-oriented models, generative models and latent space models, and beyond.

By providing authoritative accounts of the history, theories and methodology of various disciplines and topics, the second edition of *The Sage Handbook of Social Network Analysis* is designed to provide a state-of-the-art presentation of classic and contemporary views, and to lay the foundations for the further development of the area.

PART 1: GENERAL ISSUES
PART 2: APPLICATIONS
PART 3: CONCEPTS AND METHODS

The Sage Handbook of Social Network Analysis

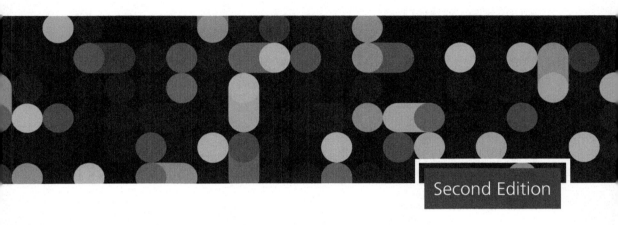

Second Edition

Edited by
John McLevey
John Scott and
Peter J. Carrington

Sage

1 Oliver's Yard
55 City Road
London EC1Y 1SP

2455 Teller Road
Thousand Oaks, California 91320

Unit No 323-333, Third Floor, F-Block
International Trade Tower Nehru Place
New Delhi – 110 019

8 Marina View Suite 43-053
Asia Square Tower 1
Singapore 018960

Editor: Umeeka Raichura
Editorial Assistant: Benedict Hegarty
Production Editor: Gourav Kumar
Copyeditor: Joy Tucker
Proofreader: Genevieve Friar
Indexer: KnowledgeWorks Global Ltd
Marketing Manager: Ben Griffin-Sherwood
Cover Design: Ginkhan Siam
Typeset by KnowledgeWorks Global Ltd
Printed in the UK

At Sage we take sustainability seriously. Most of our products are printed in the UK using responsibly sourced papers and boards. When we print overseas we ensure sustainable papers are used as measured by the Paper Chain Project grading system. We undertake an annual audit to monitor our sustainability.

Editorial Arrangement & Introduction © John McLevey, John Scott, Peter J. Carrington, 2024
Chapter 2 © Christina Prell and David R. Schaefer, 2024
Chapter 3 © Ronald Breiger and Robin Wagner-Pacifici, 2024
Chapter 4 © James A. Kitts, Helene Grogan and Kevin Lewis, 2024
Chapter 5 © Jan Fuhse and Ann Mische, 2024
Chapter 6 © Örjan Bodin, 2024
Chapter 7 © Tyler A. Scott, Mark Lubell and Gwen Arnold, 2024
Chapter 8 © Kayla de la Haye, 2024
Chapter 9 © Mario Diani, 2024
Chapter 10 © David Tindall, 2024
Chapter 11 © Elisa Bellotti, 2024
Chapter 12 © Rochelle Côté, 2024
Chapter 13 © Omar Lizardo, 2024
Chapter 14 © Sarah Shugars and Sandra González-Bailón, 2024
Chapter 15 © Matthew E. Brashears and Victoria Money, 2024
Chapter 16 © Donghyun Kang and James Evans, 2024
Chapter 17 © Marie Ouellet and Logan Ledford, 2024
Chapter 18 © Ian Kumekawa, 2024
Chapter 19 © Damon Centola, 2024
Chapter 20 © Thomas W. Valente, 2024
Chapter 21 © Anabel Quan-Haase, Lyndsay Foisey and Riley McLaughlin, 2024
Chapter 22 © Beate Völker, 2024
Chapter 23 © Lijun Song and Zhe Zhang, 2024
Chapter 24 © William K. Carroll, M. Jouke Huijzer and J.P. Sapinski, 2024
Chapter 25 © Christina Prell, James Hollway, Petr Matous and Yasuyuki Todo, 2024
Chapter 26 © M.G. Everett and S.P. Borgatti, 2024
Chapter 27 © James Moody and Peter J. Mucha, 2024
Chapter 28 © Lorien Jasny, 2024
Chapter 29 © Patrick Doreian, Anuška Ferligoj and Vladimir Batagelj, 2024
Chapter 30 © Pierson Browne, Tyler Crick and John McLevey, 2024
Chapter 31 © Brea Perry, Adam Roth and Mario Small, 2024
Chapter 32 © Emmanuel Lazega and Peng Wang, 2024
Chapter 33 © Johan Koskinen, 2024
Chapter 34 © Tom A.B. Snijders and Christian E.G. Steglich, 2024
Chapter 35 © Aaron Schecter and Noshir Contractor, 2024
Chapter 36 © Hardeep Kaur, Riccardo Rastelli, Nial Friel and Adrian E. Raftery, 2024
Chapter 37 © Filip Agneessens, 2024
Chapter 38 © Betina Hollstein, 2024
Chapter 39 © John R. Hipp, 2024
Chapter 40 © jimi adams and Miranda Lubbers, 2024
Chapter 41 © Robert W. Krause and Mark Huisman, 2024
Chapter 42 © Pierson Browne, Adam Howe, Yasmin Koop-Monteiro, Yixi Yang and John McLevey, 2024

Apart from any fair dealing for the purposes of research, private study, or criticism or review, as permitted under the Copyright, Designs and Patents Act, 1988, this publication may not be reproduced, stored or transmitted in any form, or by any means, without the prior permission in writing of the publisher, or in the case of reprographic reproduction, in accordance with the terms of licences issued by the Copyright Licensing Agency. Enquiries concerning reproduction outside those terms should be sent to the publisher.

Library of Congress Control Number: 2023945081

British Library Cataloguing in Publication data

A catalogue record for this book is available from the British Library

ISBN 978-1-5297-7961-5

Contents

Website for Colour Figures viii
About the Editors ix
About the Contributors x

1   Introduction   1
    John Scott, John McLevey and Peter Carrington

PART 1   GENERAL ISSUES

2   Introducing Social Network Analysis   19
    Christina Prell and David R. Schaefer

3   Social Networks and Social Categories   32
    Ronald Breiger and Robin Wagner-Pacifici

4   Social Networks and Computational Social Science   44
    James A. Kitts, Helene Grogan, and Kevin Lewis

5   Relational Sociology: Networks, Culture and Interaction   55
    Jan Fuhse and Ann Mische

PART 2   APPLICATIONS

6   Social-Ecological Networks: What Are They, Why Are They Useful And How Can I Use Them?   75
    Örjan Bodin

7   The Evolution of Environmental Policy Network Analysis   92
    Tyler A. Scott, Mark Lubell, and Gwen Arnold

8   Health Behaviours and Outcomes   116
    Kayla de la Haye

9   Political and Policy Networks   130
    Mario Diani

10   Social Movements and Collective Action   146
    David Tindall

11   Gender and Social Networks   162
    Elisa Bellotti

12	Why Can't We be Friends? Understanding Ethnic Relations Through Network Analysis *Rochelle Côté*	175
13	Culture and Networks *Omar Lizardo*	188
14	Semantic and Cultural Networks *Sarah Shugars and Sandra González-Bailón*	202
15	Cognition and Social Networks *Matthew E. Brashears and Victoria Money*	212
16	Scientific Networks *Donghyun Kang and James Evans*	225
17	Crime and Networks *Marie Ouellet and Logan Ledford*	243
18	Historical Network Analysis: Two Problems of Scale *Ian Kumekawa*	255
19	The Paradox of Behaviour Change and the Science of Network Diffusion *Damon Centola*	267
20	Network Interventions: Using Social Networks to Accelerate Diffusion of Innovations *Thomas W. Valente*	282
21	Social Media and Digital Networks *Anabel Quan-Haase, Lyndsay Foisey, and Riley McLaughlin*	297
22	Social Capital *Beate Völker*	309
23	Social Support *Lijun Song and Zhe Zhang*	322
24	Corporate Networks *William K. Carroll, M. Jouke Huijzer, and J. P. Sapinski*	336
25	International Trade Networks *Christina Prell, James Hollway, Petr Matous, and Yasuyuki Todo*	350

PART 3 CONCEPTS AND METHODS

26	Centrality *Martin G. Everett and Steve P. Borgatti*	363
27	Structural Cohesion and Cohesive Groups *James Moody and Peter J. Mucha*	376

28	Multimodal Social Network Analysis *Lorien Jasny*	392
29	Blockmodeling, Positions and Roles *Patrick Doreian, Anuška Ferligoj, and Vladimir Batagelj*	404
30	Inferential Network Clustering with Hierarchical Bayesian Stochastic Blockmodels *Pierson Browne, Tyler Crick, and John McLevey*	417
31	Personal Networks and Egocentric Analysis *Brea Perry, Adam Roth, and Mario Small*	439
32	Multilevel Network Analysis *Emmanuel Lazega and Peng Wang*	455
33	Exponential Random Graph Models *Johan Koskinen*	474
34	Network Dynamics *Tom A. B. Snijders and Christian E. G. Steglich*	501
35	Relational Event Models *Aaron Schecter and Noshir Contractor*	513
36	Latent Position Network Models *Hardeep Kaur, Riccardo Rastelli, Nial Friel, and Adrian E. Raftery*	526
37	Negative Ties and Signed Networks *Filip Agneessens*	542
38	Qualitative and Mixed Methods *Betina Hollstein*	562
39	Spatial Analysis of Social Networks *John R. Hipp*	575
40	Social Network Data Collection: Principles and Modalities *jimi adams and Miranda Lubbers*	587
41	Missing Network Data *Robert W. Krause and Mark Huisman*	599
42	Scientific Software for Network Analysis *Pierson Browne, Adam Howe, Yasmin Koop-Monteiro, Yixi Yang, and John McLevey*	610

Index   636

Website for Colour Figures

Full-colour versions of the figures in this Handbook can be found online at:

https://github.com/mclevey/SHSNAv2

About the Editors

Peter Carrington is Professor Emeritus of the University of Waterloo, Canada, where he worked as professor of sociology. His current research project, the Canadian Criminal Careers and Criminal Networks Study, combines his longstanding interests in social network analysis and in the development of crime and delinquency. His articles have appeared in various journals, including *Criminology*, *Journal of Quantitative Criminology*, *Journal of Mathematical Sociology*, *Social Networks* and *American Journal of Psychiatry*. He was editor of *Canadian Journal of Criminology and Criminal Justice* (2004–14) and was editor or co-editor of *Applications of social network analysis* (Sage, 2014), *The SAGE handbook of social network analysis, first edition* (Sage, 2011) and *Models and methods in social network analysis* (Cambridge University Press, 2005).

John McLevey is Associate Professor of Knowledge Integration and Sociology and Legal Studies at the University of Waterloo (Ontario, Canada) and the principal investigator of Netlab. His current research concentrates on (1) the multilevel network dynamics of cognition, affect, lifestyle, influence and diffusion; and (2) generative models of opinion dynamics, mis/disinformation and censorship, and political polarisation. He is the author of *Doing computational social science* (Sage, 2021) and co-author of *Industrial development and eco-tourisms* (Palgrave Macmillan, 2020) and *The face-to-face principle: science, truth, trust, and democracy* (Cardiff University Press, 2022). He recently co-edited special journal issues on social networks and anthropogenic climate change (*Social Networks*, 2023) and climate change, natural resource governance and energy futures (*Society and Natural Resources*, 2020). His current research is funded by the Social Sciences and Humanities Research Council of Canada.

John Scott is Emeritus Professor at Plymouth University, UK, where he was pro-Vice Chancellor for Research. He is an Honorary Visiting Professor at the University of Essex, the University of Exeter and Copenhagen University. He is an established author of 44 books on social networks, documentary research, economic sociology, social stratification and social theory. His most recent publications include *British social theory* (Sage, 2018), *British sociology: a history* (Palgrave, 2020), *The Emerald guide to Max Weber* (Emerald, 2019), and *The Emerald guide to Talcott Parsons* (Emerald, 2020). In social network analysis he was co-editor of *The SAGE handbook of social network analysis, first edition* (Sage, 2011, with Peter Carrington) and *Models and methods in social network analysis* (Cambridge University Press, 2005, with Peter Carrington and Stan Wasserman), and wrote *Social network analysis* (Sage, 1992; 4th ed., 2017).

About the Contributors

jimi adams is Professor of Health and Behavioral Sciences at the University of Colorado Denver. His work focuses on examining social networks to understand how infectious diseases and novel ideas spread. He is the author of *Gathering social network data* (Sage, 2019).

Filip Agneessens is an Associate Professor at the Department of Sociology and Social Research, University of Trento. He has published on a diversity of topics related to social networks, including measures of centrality, statistical models, ego-networks and social support, two-mode networks, negative ties, multilevel networks and issues related to data collection. With Martin Everett, he was a guest editor for a special issue on 'Advances in Two-mode Social Network Analysis' in the journal *Social Networks* and, with Nick Harrigan and Joe Labianca, he guest-edited a special issue on 'Negative and Signed Tie Networks'. Together with Steve Borgatti, Martin Everett and Jeff Johnson he co-authored the book *Analyzing social networks with R* (Sage, 2022).

Gwen Arnold is an Associate Professor in the Department of Environmental Science and Policy at University of California, Davis, where she co-directs the Center for Environmental Politics and Behavior. Her research interests concern energy policy, local governance, community resilience, policy entrepreneurship and theories of the policy process. She is an associate editor of *Policy Studies Journal*.

Vladimir Batagelj, PhD, is a Professor Emeritus of Discrete and Computational Mathematics from the University of Ljubljana, Slovenia. He is a Senior Researcher at the Department of Theoretical Computer Science of IMFM, Ljubljana, the Institute Andrej Marušič at University of Primorska, Koper, and NRU HSE International Laboratory for Applied Network Research, Moscow. His main research interests are in mathematics and computer science, combinatorics with emphasis on graph theory, algorithms on graphs and networks, combinatorial optimisation, algorithms and data structures, cluster analysis, symbolic data analysis, visualisation, social network analysis and applications of information technology in education. He is a co-author of the program Pajek for large network analysis and visualisation. He is an elected member of the International Statistical Institute. He co-authored books *Generalized blockmodeling* (Cambridge University Press, 2005), *Exploratory social network analysis with Pajek* (Cambridge University Press, 2005, 2011, 2018), *Understanding large temporal networks and spatial networks* (Wiley, 2014) and *Advances in network clustering and blockmodeling* (Wiley, 2020).

Elisa Bellotti is Senior Lecturer in Sociology and co-director of the Mitchell Centre for Social Network Analysis at the University of Manchester. She has published extensively on applications of social network analysis and mixed methods in sociological substantive fields, like criminal networks, scientific networks and personal networks. Her recent work focuses on gender aspects of social network formations and outcomes. She has written the book *Qualitative networks: mixed methods in sociological research* (Routledge, 2015) and co-authored the book *Social network analysis for egonets* (Sage, 2015).

Örjan Bodin is a Professor of Environmental and Sustainability Science at the Stockholm Resilience Centre at Stockholm University. He is studying different challenges and opportunities in governing and managing natural resources, and much of his research bridges the natural and social sciences. Together with Christina Prell, he edited the book *Social networks and natural resource management: uncovering the social fabric of environmental governance* (Cambridge University Press, 2011). In addition, he has contributed to over 100 publications that have appeared in top journals across a range of scientific disciplines.

ABOUT THE CONTRIBUTORS

Stephen P. Borgatti is the Gatton Endowed Chair of Management at the Gatton College of Business and Economics at the University of Kentucky. He has published extensively in management journals, as well as cross-disciplinary journals such as *Science and Social Networks*. He has published over 100 peer-reviewed articles on network analysis, garnering more than 80,000 Google Scholar citations. With Martin Everett, Steve is co-author of UCINET, a well-known software package for social network analysis, as well as founder of the annual LINKS Center workshop on social network analysis. He is also a 2-term past President of INSNA (the professional association for network researchers) and winner of their Simmel Award for lifetime achievement.

Matthew E. Brashears is a Professor of Sociology at the University of South Carolina. His research focuses on linking cognition to social network structure, studying the effects of error and error correction on diffusion dynamics, and using ecological models to connect individual behaviour to collective dynamics. His work has appeared in the *American Sociological Review*, the *American Journal of Sociology*, *Social Networks*, *Advances in Group Processes* and *Frontiers in Cognitive Psychology*, among others. He has received grants from the National Science Foundation, the Defense Threat Reduction Agency, the Army Research Institute, the Army Research Office and the Office of Naval Research.

Ronald Breiger is a Regents Professor and Professor of Sociology at the University of Arizona. He works in the areas of social network methods and theory, networks and culture, mathematical models and measurement in cultural and institutional analysis. With Eric Schoon, David Melamed and other colleagues he is formulating an innovative approach to regression modelling built on recognising the duality (co-constitution) of cases and variables. With Robin Wagner-Pacifici and the late John Mohr he has been exploring possibilities for a 'third way' of text analysis of public national security strategy documents, in between automated and human-centred readings. In 2022 he was named an inaugural recipient of the Progress in Mathematical Sociology Award of the American Sociological Association Mathematical Sociology Section (shared with Ronald Burt and Harrison White).

Pierson Browne is a PhD candidate in the Department of Sociology at the University of Waterloo. His research focuses on Bayesian inference, social network analysis, digital games, player studies and principled data processing.

William K. Carroll's research interests are in the political economy/ecology of corporate capitalism, social movements and social change, and critical social theory and method. Since 2015 he has co-directed the Corporate Mapping Project, an interdisciplinary initiative bringing scholars and activists together in research and knowledge mobilisation on the power and influence of fossil capital in Canada. He has been a member of the University of Victoria's Sociology Department since 1981 and was the founding Director of UVic's interdisciplinary programme in Social Justice Studies. Dr Carroll's books include *Regime of obstruction: how corporate power blocks energy democracy* (AU Press, 2021; free download here: www.aupress.ca/books/120293-regime-of-obstruction/), *The making of a transnational capitalist class* (Zed, 2010), *Organizing the 1%: how corporate power works* (Fernwood, 2018, with J.P. Sapinski), *Expose, oppose, propose: alternative policy groups and the struggle for global justice* (Zed, 2016), *A world to win contemporary social movements and counter-hegemony* (ARP, 2016, with Kanchan Sarker), *Corporate power in a globalizing world* (Oxford University Press, 2010) and *Corporate power and Canadian capitalism* (UBC Press, 1986).

Damon Centola is the Elihu Katz Professor of Communication, Sociology and Engineering at the University of Pennsylvania, where he is Director of the Network Dynamics Group and Senior Fellow at the Leonard Davis Institute of Health Economics. Before coming to Penn, Damon was a professor at MIT, and prior to that he was a fellow at Harvard University. Damon is a leading scholar on social networks and behaviour change. His work has received numerous scientific awards, including the Goodman Prize for Outstanding Contributions to Sociological Methodology in 2011; the James Coleman Award for Outstanding Research in Rationality and Society in 2017; and the Harrison White Award for Outstanding

Scholarly Book in 2019. He was a developer of the NetLogo agent-based modelling environment, and was awarded a US Patent for inventing a method to promote diffusion in online networks. Damon is a fellow of the Center for Advanced Study in the Behavioral Sciences at Stanford University. Popular accounts of Damon's work have appeared in the *New York Times*, *Washington Post*, *Wall Street Journal*, *Wired*, *TIME*, *The Atlantic*, *Scientific American* and *CNN*, among other outlets. His research has been funded by the National Science Foundation, the National Institutes of Health, the Robert Wood Johnson Foundation, the James S. McDonnell Foundation, the Templeton Foundation, the Hewlett Foundation and Facebook. Damon's speaking and consulting clients include Amazon, Apple, Cigna, General Motors, Microsoft, Ben & Jerry's, the US Army and the NBA, among others. He is a series editor for Princeton University Press and the author of *How behavior spreads: the science of complex contagions* (Princeton University Press, 2018), and *Change: how to make big things happen* (Little Brown, 2021).

Noshir Contractor is the Jane S. and William J. White Professor of Behavioral Sciences in the McCormick School of Engineering, the School of Communication and the Kellogg School of Management at Northwestern University. He investigates how social and knowledge networks form and perform. He is a Distinguished Scholar of the National Communication Association and a Fellow of the American Association for the Advancement of Science, the Association for Computing Machinery, the Network Science Society and the International Communication Association. He received the Simmel Award from the International Network for Social Network Analysis (INSNA), and the Lifetime Service Award from the Communication, Digital Technology, and Organization Division of the Academy of Management. He received the Distinguished Alumnus Award from the Indian Institute of Technology, Madras, where he received a Bachelor's degree in Electrical Engineering. He has a PhD from the Annenberg School of Communication at the University of Southern California.

Rochelle Côté is currently an Associate Professor of Sociology at Memorial University of Newfoundland and Labrador, Canada. Dr Côté's research and teaching explores the relationship between overarching institutions, sociocultural contexts, social networks, and ethnoracial inequality. Her research currently focuses on unpacking sources and consequences of ethnic and racial inequalities – from looking at the ways in which Indigenous people navigate their experiences of social mobility alongside connections to community and culture, to mapping and documenting the Indigenous history of cities, and impacts to ethnoracial network diversity and tolerance. Motivated by an interest in mixed methods and cross-national research, her work considers the experiences of Indigenous people, ethnic minorities and immigrants as they engage with society through participation in cultural, social and economic venues. Her work has appeared in such journals as *Social Networks*, *Social Problems*, *Demography*, *Sociology*, *Journal of Sociology* and *American Behavioral Scientist*, alongside various edited volumes.

Tyler Crick is a PhD candidate in Sociology at the University of Waterloo, where he is a member of Netlab under Dr John McLevey's supervision. His current research interests are focused on misinformation, with an emphasis on its production, conditions of dissemination and social impact. This research involves large-scale data analysis using methods from social network analysis, machine learning, Bayesian modelling and natural language processing. He has published papers using computational social science methods in the *Canadian Review of Sociology*, *Social Networks*, *The SAGE handbook of social media research methods* (Sage, 2016) and *The Routledge handbook of computational social science* (Routledge, 2021). He has provided consulting in these areas for Cardiff University's Crime and Security Research Institute, as well as a number of private consulting firms.

Mario Diani (PhD 1987, Turin) has been a Professor of Sociology at the University of Trento, Italy, since 2001. He also held chairs at the University of Strathclyde in Glasgow (1996–2001) and ICREA-Universitat Pompeu Fabra in Barcelona (2010–12). He has worked extensively on social movements as a particular form of network organising. Major works on this topic include *Green networks* (Edinburgh University Press, 1995), *Social movements and networks* (Oxford University Press, 2003, co-edited with

Doug McAdam), *The cement of civil society* (Cambridge University Press, 2015) and *Multimodal political networks* (Cambridge University Press, 2021, with D. Knoke, J. Hollway and D. Christopoulos).

Patrick Doreian's (University of Ljubljana and University of Pittsburgh) work has been involved primarily with the generation of new methods for analysing networks and applying them in many empirical contexts. Studying signed networks and police academy networks are included. More recently, he has been heavily involved in studying the US Supreme Court and the large network of allies of the Koch Brothers as these units attempt to shape US policies and shape public opinion.

James Evans (PhD 2004, Stanford) is the Max Palevsky Professor of Sociology at the University of Chicago and the Santa Fe Institute. He directs the Knowledge Lab and the Computational Social Science programs at Chicago, with research focusing on the collective system of thinking and knowing, ranging from the distribution of attention and the origin of ideas to processes of agreement, evolving certainty and the texture of human and machine understanding. He is especially interested in innovation and the role that social and technical institutions play in collective cognition and discovery. He supports the creation of novel observatories for human understanding and action through crowd sourcing, information extraction, the use of distributed sensors, computationally driven experiments and surveys, and complementary AI. His work uses machine learning, generative modelling, social and semantic network representations to explore knowledge processes, scale up interpretive and field methods and create alternatives to current discovery regimes. His work has been published in *Nature*, *Science*, *PNAS* and top social and computer science journals.

Martin G. Everett, DPhil is Professor of Social Network Analysis and co-director of the Mitchell Centre for Social Network Analysis at the University of Manchester. He has published extensively on social network analysis, has published over 100 peer-reviewed articles and consulted with government agencies as well as public and private companies. With Stephen Borgatti, Martin is co-author of UCINET, a well-known software package for social network analysis, and is co-editor of the journal *Social Networks*. He is also a past president of INSNA (the professional association for network researchers) and winner of their Simmel Award for lifetime achievement. He was elected an academician of the UK Academy of Social Sciences in 2004.

Anuška Ferligoj is Professor Emeritus at the University of Ljubljana and the scientific supervisor at the Laboratory for Applied Network Research at the NRU HSE in Moscow. Her research interests include multivariate analysis (clustering with constraints, multicriteria clustering) and social network analysis (blockmodelling, quality of network measurement). She has published over 100 papers, several book chapters and books. For the monograph co-authored with Patrick Doreian and Vladimir Batagelj, *Generalized blockmodeling* (Cambridge University Press, 2005), they obtained the Harrison White Outstanding Book Award 2007, given by the Mathematical Sociology Section at the American Sociological Association. She is a member of the European Academy of Sociology. In 2010, she received Doctor et Professor Honoris Causa at Eotvos Lorand University in Budapest.

Lyndsay Foisey is a doctoral candidate in Health Information Science (Faculty of Information and Media Studies and Faculty of Health Sciences) at Western University. She has authored over twenty peer-reviewed journal articles, book chapters, conference publications and white papers on health, digital technology and communications. She has received provincial and national-level awards for her doctoral work, including a federally funded grant to study public health messaging on social media during the Covid-19 pandemic in Canada. She has taught social media and health at the undergraduate level, as well as worked at research institutions and not-for-profit organisations across Canada.

Nial Friel is a Full Professor of Statistics at University College Dublin. He was previously a lecturer and then reader in statistics at the University of Glasgow. Prior to that he held post-doctoral positions at Queensland University of Technology, Cambridge University and Athens University of Economics and

Business. He was awarded a PhD in statistics from University of Glasgow in 1999. His research interests include Bayesian statistics; Monte Carlo methods; Statistical network analysis.

Jan Fuhse is Interim Professor of Sociology at Chemnitz University of Technology and Senior Lecturer (Privatdozent) at Humboldt University of Berlin (both in Germany). His research focuses on the theory of social networks, on social networks in inequality and interethnic relations, on constellations in political discourse and on the role of theory in the social sciences. Recent publications: *Social networks of meaning and communication* (Oxford University Press, 2022), 'How can theories represent social phenomena?' (*Sociological Theory*, 2022), 'Analyzing social networks in communication: a mixed methods study of a political debate' (*Quality and Quantity*, forthcoming), 'Networks from culture: mechanisms of tie-formation follow institutionalized rules in social fields' (with Neha Gondal, *Social Networks*, forthcoming).

Sandra González-Bailón is the Carolyn Marvin Professor of Communication at the Annenberg School, University of Pennsylvania, where she directs the Center for Information Networks and Democracy. Her research analyses how networks shape exposure to political information and how online behaviours inform algorithmic forms of curation. Her empirical research spans areas that include political engagement; protest participation; the coordination of information campaigns; and the consumption and diffusion of political content. She is the author of the book *Decoding the social world* (MIT Press, 2017) and co-editor of *The Oxford handbook of networked communication* (Oxford University Press, 2020). She has a PhD in Sociology from the University of Oxford.

Helene Grogan is a sociology PhD student at the University of Massachusetts Amherst. Her research focuses on the sociology of health, disability and social movements, with an emphasis on archival and computational methods.

Kayla de la Haye is an Associate Professor of Population and Public Health Sciences at the University of Southern California (USC), and scientist at the USC Center for Economic and Social Research, in Los Angeles. She works to promote health and prevent disease by applying social network analysis and systems science to key public health issues. Her research focuses on family and community social networks to promote healthy eating, nutrition security and prevent non-communicable diseases like obesity. She also explores the role of social networks in how families, teams and coalitions solve complex problems. She currently serves as Vice President of the International Network of Social Network Analysis (INSNA) and, in 2018, she received the INSNA Freeman Award for significant contributions to the study of social structure. She holds a PhD in psychology from the University of Adelaide, Australia.

John R. Hipp is a Professor in the departments of Criminology, Law and Society, and Sociology at the University of California Irvine. His research interests focus on how neighbourhoods change over time, how that change both affects and is affected by neighbourhood crime, and the role networks and institutions play in that change. He approaches these questions using quantitative methods as well as social network analysis. He has published substantive work in such journals as *American Sociological Review*, *Criminology*, *Journal of Quantitative Criminology*, *Social Forces*, *Social Problems*, *City and Community*, *Urban Studies* and *Journal of Urban Affairs*. He has published methodological work in such journals as *Sociological Methodology*, *Psychological Methods* and *Structural Equation Modelling*.

Betina Hollstein is Chair of Sociology at the University of Bremen. Her work is centred around personal networks, social inequality and methods of network research. She is especially interested in understanding network dynamics across the life course and network effects – for example, how personal networks affect the transition from school to work. In studying network processes and mechanisms, Betina Hollstein champions the use of qualitative approaches and mixed methods research designs (Cambridge University Press, 2014, ed. with Silvia Dominguez). Current projects tackle visual methods for network data collection and innovative combinations of qualitative methods and computational social sciences.

ABOUT THE CONTRIBUTORS

James Hollway is Associate Professor of International Relations and Political Science at the Graduate Institute of International and Development Studies, Geneva, and principal investigator of PANARCHIC. His research develops multilevel and dynamic network theories, methods, data and software to help understand the causes and consequences of actors' institutional and policy choices in empirical settings such as fisheries, freshwater, health and trade. His book *Multimodal political networks*, together with David Knoke, Mario Diani and Dimitris Christopoulos, was published with Cambridge University Press in 2021, with other networks pieces appearing in, among others, *Network Science*, *Social Networks*, *Sociological Methodology* and the *Journal of Conflict Resolution*.

Adam C. Howe completed his PhD studying climate change policy networks at the University of British Columbia in Vancouver. His research interests include environmental sociology and climate change governance, social movements and activism and computational social science. He has published on topics such as investigating the structural mechanisms that give rise to and shape policy networks, and how social structures (particularly policy networks) and media intersect to shape social influence and climate change governance. His work appears in academic journals including *Social Networks*, *Sociological Perspectives* and in the edited book *Protest public relations: communicating dissent and activism* (Routledge, 2020).

M. Jouke Huijzer is a PhD researcher at the Vrije Universiteit Brussel, Department of Political Science. He has an interest in the politics and contestation of contemporary capitalism. His research focuses on corporate and political elites and their ideas. He hopes his work will contribute to an understanding of how to foster social emancipation and bring about political change.

Mark Huisman is an Assistant Professor at the Department of Sociology of the University of Groningen. His previous work involved statistical methods for missing data, especially multiple imputation, both for survey and network data. His current research interests are latent variable path models and the analysis of causal relations.

Lorien Jasny is a computational social scientist in the Department of Politics at the University of Exeter. Her work focuses on the role of social networks in questions of public engagement, environmental management and community health. In her research Lorien explores two related themes – how the structure and dynamics of interorganisational networks affect policy change, and how the structure and dynamics of social and belief networks affect behavioural change. Substantively, she studies how people try to bring about societal change in response to political and environmental concerns. Methodologically, the need to grapple with these often complex phenomena requires the use and development of techniques for handling large, dynamic and relational datasets.

Donghyun Kang is a PhD candidate in Sociology and a member of the Knowledge Lab at the University of Chicago. His academic interest centres on advancing our understanding of social conditions and processes shaping the genesis, diffusion and demise of ideas and practices through which science and human knowledge evolve. He particularly seeks to extend and revisit insights from social studies of science and the sociology of knowledge, using statistical approaches and computational techniques ranging from natural language processing to network embedding models.

Hardeep Kaur is a PhD candidate in the School of Mathematics and Statistics at University College Dublin, Ireland. Her research focuses on developing new statistical models for complex network data. She is currently developing new models for the analysis of multivariate time series using latent complex network frameworks. Her study emphasises the significance of comprehending and interpreting the temporal and contemporaneous relationships among the network's constituent components.

James Kitts is Professor of Sociology and Founding Co-Director of the Computational Social Science Institute at the University of Massachusetts. He earned his PhD from Cornell University in 2001 and has held faculty appointments at Columbia University, Dartmouth College and the University of Washington. Bridging computational social science, sociology and public health, he has worked on methods to detect social interaction from audio signals using wearable sensors, has analysed the dynamics of patient transfers across hospitals, has modelled opinion polarisation on dynamic networks and now co-directs an NIH-funded longitudinal study of adolescent social networks and health behaviour. His work appeared in *American Sociological Review, American Journal of Sociology, Social Forces, Social Networks* and *Demography*. jameskitts.com/

Yasmin Koop-Monteiro is currently a PhD candidate in Sociology at the University of British Columbia (Vancouver, Canada). Her research interests include social network analysis, social movements and environmental sociology, with a special interest in human–nonhuman interactions. Yasmin's PhD thesis explores various factors believed to promote participation in animal rights advocacy, and considers how animal rights activists' social ties or encounters with animals (wild, companion and/or farmed) may contribute to engagement in low-, medium- and high-risk/cost activism.

Johan Koskinen is Lecturer in Statistics at Stockholm University, having previously held positions at the universities of Melbourne, Oxford and Linköping. He develops statistical models and inference for social networks and often works in close collaboration with subject area experts to infer underlying network processes for empirical data, preferably within a Bayesian framework. Together with colleagues in Melbourne he edited the 2013 book on *Exponential random graph models* (Cambridge University Press, 2012), which was awarded the Harrison White Book Award. He has contributed to the publicly available programs MPNet and RSiena, and has been active in delivering training in network analysis across the world. Of particular interest to him is imperfectly observed network data and computational methods for networks on different types of ties and nodes, in space and across time.

Robert W. Krause is an Assistant Professor of Management at the Gatton College Business and Economics at the University of Kentucky. He wrote his PhD thesis on 'Multiple imputation for missing network data' and has published several papers and tutorial articles on how to handle missing network data. His research focuses on developing, implementing and testing better missing data treatments in Bayesian ERGMs and Stochastic Actor-Oriented Models. He is a co-author of the Bergm package in R for the estimation of Bayesian ERGMs and regularly writes scripts and provides support for users of the RSiena package for the estimation of SAOMs. His applied work is varied and covers networks such as school classes, leadership structures in students and professionals, advice-seeking among former and graduate students, or board interlocks.

Ian Kumekawa is a Postdoctoral Prize Fellow in Economics, History and Politics at the Center for History and Economics at Harvard University and the coordinator of the Visualizing Historical Networks Project at Harvard. His research concerns the history of economic thinking, and networked histories of imperial statecraft and global capitalism in the 19th and 20th centuries. His book, *The first serious optimist: A.C. Pigou and the birth of welfare economics* (Princeton University Press, 2017), was a co-winner of the Joseph Spengler Prize and his work has appeared or is forthcoming in the *Historical Journal, Journal of Modern History* and *Modern Intellectual History*. His current projects focus on state capture and offshore capitalism in the 20th century.

Emmanuel Lazega is Professor of Sociology at Sciences Po, Paris, and a member of the Centre of the Sociology of Organizations (CSO-CNRS). His research interests are in the social rationality, relational infrastructures (single level or multilevel) and social mechanisms that help members of organisations manage the dilemmas of their collective agency. His most recent books are *Bureaucracy, collegiality and social change: redefining organizations with multilevel relational infrastructures* (Edward Elgar, 2020) and an edited volume with Tom A.B. Snijders and Rafael P.M. Wittek and twenty contributors, *Social networks and social resilience* (Edward Elgar, 2022). His work can be downloaded from www.elazega.fr

Logan Ledford is a doctoral candidate in criminal justice and criminology at Georgia State University. His interests include police stress and job satisfaction, police legitimacy, police networks and crime networks generally.

Kevin Lewis is an Associate Professor of Sociology at the University of California, San Diego. His research focuses on the formation and evolution of social networks, the principles of human interaction that produce global network patterns and the implications of these processes for the genesis and reproduction of inequality. To address these topics, he has analysed a number of large-scale network datasets – spanning topics from online dating to internet activism to college students' behaviour on Facebook – and his work has been published in a variety of sociological and interdisciplinary journals.

Omar Lizardo (He/Him) is the LeRoy Neiman Term Chair Professor in the Department of Sociology at the University of California, Los Angeles. He studies culture, cognition, networks, consumption, institutions, organisation and social theory. His work has appeared in such journals as *American Sociological Review*, *Social Forces*, *Sociological Theory*, *Theory and Society* and *Social Networks*. He currently serves on the editorial board of *Social Forces*, *Sociological Theory*, *Sociological Forum*, *Journal for the Theory of Social Behaviour* and *Poetics*. He is also a member of the Board of Reviewing Editors for the journal *Science* and an associate editor for *Discover Data*.

Miranda Lubbers is Professor in Social and Cultural Anthropology at the Autonomous University of Barcelona (Spain) and Director of the COALESCE Lab. She is an elected Acadèmia fellow of the Catalan Institution for Research and Advanced Studies (ICREA) and elected fellow of the European Academy of Sociology. Her research concerns the networked mechanisms of social cohesion, social exclusion and polarisation. Lubbers was awarded the European Research Council's Advanced Grant for the project 'A network science approach to social cohesion in european societies' (2021–6) and her other research projects are funded by the Volkswagen Foundation and the Spanish Ministry of Science and Innovation.

Mark Lubell is a Professor of Environmental Science and Policy at the University of California at Davis, where he also co-directs the Center for Environmental Policy and Behavior. He holds a PhD in Political Science from State University of New York at Stony Brook. Dr Lubell's research applies network theory and analysis to cooperation problems in the context of environmental governance. His research is published in political science, public policy, public administration and interdisciplinary environmental journals.

Petr Matous is Associate Professor in the School of Project Management, Faculty of Engineering, University of Sydney, and serves as Associate Head of School (Research) and Associate Dean (Indigenous Strategy and Service) at the University. He received his PhD in 2007 at the University of Tokyo where he previously spent most of his academic career. Dr Matous's research revolves around networks and interventions in socioenvironmental systems, searching for ways to leverage social networks in rural and marginalised communities for sustainability and resilience to disasters. He also enjoys consulting work for development organisations in South-East Asia. Petr teaches innovation, sustainability and SNA and holds the University of Tokyo Presidential Award and the University of Sydney Vice Chancellor's Award for Excellence.

Riley McLaughlin is a Graduate Research Assistant at Western University. She has an MA in Research for Policy and Evaluation and a BA with an honours specialisation in Sociology. Riley received Western's Undergraduate Summer Research Internship fellowship award to work with the Sociodigital Media Lab and now continues her work there. She also has experience working at various non-profit organisations, with a focus on equity, diversity and inclusion as well as policy development and evaluation. Much of her work surrounds social media use, digital literacy, systemic inequality and equitable policy making.

Ann Mische is an Associate Professor of Sociology and Peace Studies at the University of Notre Dame. Currently, she is working on a book on the role of futures thinking and foresight methodologies in social and political change efforts focused on democracy, development, peacebuilding and climate change. She is also working on a separate project on the political pathways of anti-partisan protest cycles in the global protest wave since 2008. Her first book, *Partisan publics: communication and contention across Brazilian youth activist networks* (Princeton University Press, 2008) examined civic and political networks of Brazilian youth activism during the re-democratisation period. She has also written theoretical articles on agency, culture, networks, temporality and social interaction. Her articles have appeared in the *American Journal of Sociology*, the *Annual Review of Sociology*, *Sociological Forum*, *Social Research*, *Poetics* and *Theory and Society*.

Victoria Money is a PhD candidate in the Sociology Department at the University of South Carolina. She is interested in how multiplex relationships and stigmatised identities impact network activation and structure, and how this relationship impacts health outcomes (physical and mental health, and cognitive flexibility). Her primary interest is in assessing how socially disadvantaged groups can optimise networks to attain long-term adherence to health-promoting behaviours. She has newly published work in *Social Psychology Quarterly*.

James Moody is Professor of Sociology at Duke University. He has published extensively in the field of social networks, methods and social theory with over 70 peer-reviewed papers and extensive consultation with industry and DoD and research grants from NSF, NIH and private foundations. His work focuses on the network foundations of social cohesion and diffusion, with an emphasis on building tools and methods for understanding dynamic social networks. He has published network papers on organisational performance, school racial segregation, adolescent health, disease spread, economic development and the development of scientific disciplines (among others). He is winner of INSNA's Freeman Award for scholarly contributions to network analysis and was named a Thomson Reuters 'Highly Cited Researcher'. He is founding director of the Duke Network Analysis Center, former editor of the *Journal of Social Structure* and co-founding editor of the open access journal *Socius*. people.duke.edu/~jmoody77/

Peter J. Mucha is the Jack Byrne Distinguished Professor in Mathematics at Dartmouth College. After a PhD in Applied and Computational Mathematics from Princeton and an applied mathematics instructorship at MIT, he held faculty positions at Georgia Tech and UNC–Chapel Hill. His current research includes a variety of topics in the mathematics of networks and data science, including network representations of data, community detection, network classification problems and modelling dynamics on and of networks. His group's activities are largely driven by interdisciplinary collaboration, applying tools of network analysis and data science across the physical, life and social sciences.

Marie Ouellet is an Assistant Professor in the Department of Criminal Justice and Criminology at Georgia State University. Her research focuses on delinquent groups, including how they emerge and evolve and how networks structure this process. She was recently awarded a National Science Foundation Early CAREER award to better understand how informal and formal relationships within police departments shape the diffusion of officer behaviours and attitudes.

Brea Perry is the Allen D. and Polly S. Grimshaw Professor in the Department of Sociology and Associate Director of the Irsay Family Institute for Sociomedical Sciences at Indiana University. Her areas of research include social networks, biosociology, social inequalities, ageing and medical sociology and mental health. In the social networks domain, she focuses largely on theory and methodology related to personal social networks (e.g., egocentric networks) and network dynamics. Brea was a recent National

Academy of Medicine Emerging Leaders in Health and Medicine Scholar (2019–22) and her work has been funded by NIH, NSF, the Russell Sage Foundation and the Spencer Foundation.

Christina Prell is an Associate Professor at the Faculty of Spatial Sciences at the University of Groningen. Her research focuses on the intersection of social networks and the environment. On the global scale, she studies how trade networks perpetuate climate change impacts and create winners and losers along global supply chains. On a more local or regional scale, she considers the role social networks play in developing adaptive strategies and/or shaping perceptions of climate change. She has published 40+ articles in peer-reviewed journals, and two books on the topic of social networks, one being a sole-authored book entitled, *Social Network Analysis: History, theory, and methodology* (Sage). Christina was a recent Fulbright-Austrian Scholar at the University of Klagenfurt, where she taught courses on coupled systems and social network analysis.

Anabel Quan-Haase is a Full Professor of Sociology and Information and Media Studies at Western University and Rogers Chair in Studies in Journalism and New Information Technology. She is the author of *Technology and society* (Oxford University Press, 2020), co-author of *Real-life sociology* (Oxford University Press, 2021), co-editor of the *Handbook of social media research methods* (Sage, 2022), and co-editor of the *Handbook of computational social science* (Routledge, 2022). Dr Quan-Haase has published over 100 peer-reviewed articles, book chapters and conference proceedings. She is past chair of the Communication, Information Technology and Media Sociology section of the American Sociological Association and past president of the Canadian Association for Information Science. Through her policy work she has cooperated with organisations such as the Benton Foundation, Canada's Digital Policy Forum, Federal Communications Commission (FCC), Library and Archives Canada and Media Smarts.

Riccardo Rastelli is Assistant Professor in Statistics at the School of Mathematics and Statistics, University College Dublin, Ireland. His work focuses on computational statistics, Bayesian statistics, biostatistics and how these topics intersect with the statistical analysis of network data.

Adrian E. Raftery is the Boeing International Professor of Statistics and Sociology, and an Adjunct Professor of Atmospheric Sciences at the University of Washington. He develops new statistical methods for problems in the social, environmental and health sciences. An elected member of the US National Academy of Sciences, he was identified as the world's most cited researcher in mathematics for the decade 1995–2005 by Thomson-ISI. He has supervised 32 PhD graduates, of whom 21 hold or have held tenure-track university faculty positions.

Adam R. Roth is Assistant Professor of Sociology at Oklahoma State University. His research addresses the importance of social context by exploring the types of communities, social networks and families within which people are embedded. His recent work has appeared in *Social Networks*, *Social Science and Medicine* and *Socius* and has been funded by the National Institutes of Health.

J.P. Sapinski is Associate Professor of Environmental Studies at Université de Moncton, located in Mi'kma'ki, the unceded land of the Mi'kmaq First Nation, in New Brunswick, Canada. He is interested in how the structures of capitalism and corporate power mediate the social metabolism between human societies and the ecosphere, and how we can transform and decolonise this relationship to make it just and sustainable.

David R. Schaefer is Professor of Sociology at the University of California, Irvine. His research investigates network formation and evolution, and their consequences for individual behaviours, identity and well-being. Recent projects have focused on ethnic-racial identity development among youth, how activity foci structure networks and how new network entrants develop relationships. He has focused predominantly on students in school settings (preschool, middle and high schools, college) and individuals incarcerated in prison. He was awarded the 2012 Freeman Award for significant contributions to the study of social structure by the International Network for Social Network Analysis.

Aaron Schecter is an Assistant Professor of Management Information Systems at the University of Georgia Terry College of Business. His research focuses on patterns of interaction among people in small groups, in online communities and through digital artefacts. He uses network methods, particularly relational event modelling, to identify these patterns and link them to different forms of performance. Current research interests include algorithmic decision making, human-algorithm teamwork and combining machine learning with social network data.

Tyler A. Scott is an Associate Professor in the Department of Environmental Science and Policy at the University of California, Davis (UCD), and co-director of the UCD Center for Environmental Policy and Behavior. Scott's research concerns the use of science in policy decisions, organisational strategy and innovation (particularly related to infrastructure), and coordination in complex institutional settings. His current research is supported by the US National Science Foundation and the US Department of Agriculture.

Sarah Shugars is an Assistant Professor of Communication at Rutgers University. Their research focuses on how everyday people talk about, engage with and collectively shape the modern world around them. Bringing together computational communication and deliberative democracy, they develop new text and network methods to examine the relational nature of public life, the linguistic modes through which people express themselves, and the technological affordances which shape digital discourse.

Mario L. Small is Quetelet Professor of Social Science at Columbia University. An elected member of the National Academy of Sciences, the American Academy of Arts and Sciences and the American Academy of Political and Social Sciences, Small has published award-winning articles, edited volumes and books on topics such as urban poverty, personal networks and the relationship between qualitative and quantitative methods. His latest books include *Someone to talk to: how networks matter in practice* (Oxford University Press, 2019) and the co-edited *Personal networks: classic readings and new directions in egocentric analysis* (Cambridge University Press, 2021).

Tom A.B. Snijders is Emeritus Professor of Statistics and Methodology in the Social Sciences at the University of Groningen and Emeritus Fellow of Nuffield College, University of Oxford. His research concentrates on social network analysis and multilevel analysis. His work on developing statistical methodology for network dynamics is implemented in the software package RSiena (Simulation Inference for Empirical Network Analysis) in the statistical system R. With Roel J. Bosker he wrote *Multilevel analysis; an introduction to basic and advanced multilevel modelling* (Sage, 2nd ed., 2012). Combining these two research strands, together with Emmanuel Lazega he edited *Multilevel network analysis for the social sciences: theory, methods, and applications* (Springer, 2016).

Lijun Song is an Associate Professor of Sociology and Medicine, Health and Society at Vanderbilt University. Her major research interests include social networks, medical sociology, mental health, social stratification (gender/sexuality, race/ethnicity and class), social psychology, marriage and family, and comparative historical sociology. Her work has appeared in such journals as *Social Forces*, *Journal of Health and Social Behavior*, *Society and Mental Health*, *Social Psychology Quarterly*, *Social Science and Medicine*, *Social Networks*, *Sociological Perspectives*, *American Behavioral Scientist* and *Chinese Sociological Review*. Her scholarship has been supported by the National Institutes of Health, the Andrew W. Mellon Foundation, the Ford Foundation and the Chiang Ching-kuo Foundation for International Scholarly Exchange. She has received two publication awards from the American Sociological Association: one from the Section on Asia/Asian America and the other from the Section on Sociology of Mental Health.

Christian E.G. Steglich is Associate Professor at the Sociology Department of the University of Groningen and Senior Lecturer at the Institute for Analytical Sociology of Linköping University. His published research focuses on statistical inference for social networks, in particular social influence processes. Current research interests are the modelling of macro- and meso-level entities by micro-level model specifications, and the analysis of networks derived from non-research data collection, such as population registers and social media.

David Tindall is a Professor in the Department of Sociology, at the University of British Columbia. He earned his PhD from the University of Toronto where he studied with Bonnie Erickson and Barry Wellman. A primary focus of his research has been upon contention over environmental issues. He has developed an ego social network model of micromobilisation for collective action related to environmentalism. He has also published extensively on climate change policy and discourse networks. His current research examines the role of social networks in facilitating action to address climate change, and compares and contrasts the roles of virtual and non-virtual social network ties. He has published numerous times in the journal *Social Networks*, and recently co-edited a special issue of the journal on social networks and anthropogenic climate change. Among numerous other publications, he is the lead author on 'Influence of social ties to environmentalists on public climate change perceptions' in the journal *Nature Climate Change*.

Yasuyuki Todo gained a PhD in Economics from Stanford University and has been a Professor at the Graduate School of Economics, Waseda University, Tokyo since 2014, after serving as the Department Head at the Department of International Studies, the University of Tokyo. His research fields are international economics, development economics and applied micro-econometrics, currently focusing on the role of social and economic networks in economic growth and resilience based on firm- and household-level data from various countries. He has published more than 60 academic papers in refereed journals including *Nature Sustainability*, *Ecological Economics*, *Research Policy* and *World Development*.

Beate Völker is the scientific director of the Netherlands Institute for the Study of Crime and Law Enforcement (NSCR) and Professor of Human Geography (Utrecht University). Her research interests focus on social networks, community and social capital, how people build such circles, whether and how they benefit, how they change through time and how they fail. She studied networks in various social contexts such as neighbourhoods, hospitals, prisons and work organisations. Her work is published in, among others, *Social Networks*, *Network Science*, *Advances in Life Course Research*, *European Sociological Review* and *Social Forces*.

Thomas W. Valente is a Professor in the Department of Population and Public Health Sciences, Keck School of Medicine, at the University of Southern California. He is the author of *Social networks and health: models, methods, and applications* (Oxford University Press, 2010); *Evaluating health promotion programs* (Oxford University Press, 2002); *Network models of the diffusion of innovations* (Hampton Press, 1995) and over 250 articles and chapters on social networks, behaviour change and programme evaluation. Valente uses social network analysis, health communication and mathematical models to implement and evaluate health promotion programmes. He is currently working on specifications for network models of diffusion and contagion with the R package NetdiffuseR. Valente is also well-known for his work developing network models of programme implementation and network interventions. Valente earned his BS in Mathematics from the University of Mary Washington, his MS in Mass Communication from San Diego State University and his PhD from the Annenberg School for Communication at USC. From 1991 to 2000 he was at the Bloomberg School of Public Health, Johns Hopkins University; in 2008, he was a Visiting Senior Scientist at NIH (NHGRI) for six months; and in 2010–11 he was a Visiting Professor at the École des Haute Études en Santé Publique (Paris/Rennes). Valente is co-editor (with Martin Everett) of *Social Networks*, and on the editorial board of the *Journal of Health Communication: International Perspectives*. Valente has received the Simmel Award from INSNA and the Rogers award from APHA; and mentoring awards at USC and JHU.

Robin Wagner-Pacifici is a University Professor at The New School. She has written five books on social, political and violent conflict and its termination. She is the author of: *The art of surrender: decomposing sovereignty at conflict's end* (University of Chicago Press, 2006); *Theorizing the standoff: contingency in action* (Cambridge University Press, 2000); *Discourse and destruction: the city of Philadelphia vs MOVE* (University of Chicago Press, 1994); *The Moro morality play: terrorism as social drama* (University of Chicago Press, 1986) and, most recently, *What is an event?* (University of Chicago Press, 2017). An ongoing collaboration analysing official national security texts draws from both hermeneutic and computational approaches to textual analysis has generated several publications, including the *Poetics* journal article, 'Graphing the grammar of motives in US national security strategies: cultural interpretation, automated text analysis and the drama of global politics' (co-authored with John W. Mohr, Ronald L. Breiger and Petko Bogdanov).

Peng Wang is an Associate Professor of Innovation Studies at the Centre for Transformative Innovation, Swinburne University of Technology. His research focuses on the development and applications of statistical models for social network structure and the associated outcomes. He leads the design and implementation of the MPNet suite of software packages for modelling multiplex and multilevel networks. He has publications in the research fields of public health, education, management, social-ecological systems, interlocking directorates, public policy and social network intervention evaluations. He serves on the Board of the Australian Network of Social Network Analysis (ANSNA) and was the president of ANSNA in 2022. He received the INSNA Freeman Award for significant contributions to the study of social structure in 2022.

Yixi Yang is a PhD candidate in the Department of Sociology at Memorial University of Newfoundland and Labrador, Canada. Her research interests include climate change communication, social networks, environmental sociology and environmental governance and movement in China.

Zhe Zhang is a PhD student in the Department of Sociology at Vanderbilt University. His research focuses on the social determinants of health and health disparities throughout the life course, with a particular interest in the roles of social relationships and social networks, stress/adversity and social/political contexts.

Introduction

John Scott, John McLevey and Peter Carrington

This new edition of *The SAGE handbook of social network analysis* aims to build on the success of its predecessor, bringing together in one place a comprehensive overview of social network analysis produced by leading international scholars in the field. We present authoritative accounts of its history, theories and methods, and a wide-ranging review of the various disciplines and topics to which it has made important contributions. Most of the topics covered in the first edition are included here, but in thoroughly revised or new chapters, many by new authors. We have also included chapters on a number of new topics that have experienced significant development since the first edition appeared, in order to ensure that the volume is completely up to date and so continues to meet the needs and expectations of our readers. In what follows, we provide a high-level overview of the development and growth of social network analysis and discuss several ideas that are foundational to the field.

The Development of Social Network Analysis

The idea of social structure has been central to sociological thought from its earliest days, but it was not until the early twentieth century that the idea of the social network began to be used as a metaphor in sociological analysis to represent the features of social structures.[1]

This was, perhaps, especially marked in German sociology, where there was a concern to understand the complex interweaving of social relations into 'figurations' and 'webs' of connections. Georg Simmel argued that 'society merely is the name for a number of individuals connected by interaction' (1950 [1917], p. 10), and that the task of sociology is to investigate the forms, or structure, of those interactions through 'geometrical abstraction' (Simmel, 1950[1917], pp. 21–22). He and his followers developed a 'social geometry' that emphasised the formal properties of these patterns of connection and introduced a novel terminology that referred to 'points' and 'lines' to understand actors and their social relations.

These formal ideas were first systematised by Helen Bott (1928), Jacob Moreno (1934) and Kurt Lewin (1936) in their studies in social psychology and psychotherapy. They were concerned with how the structures of small groups influenced the perceptions and action choices of their individual members. To this end, they treated a group as a 'field' or 'space' of activity that could be explored mathematically. Moreno and Helen Jennings referred to this approach as 'sociometry', or 'psychological geography' – the measurement and mapping of social relations – and invented the 'sociogram' as a way of visually representing social networks as patterns of points and lines. Sociometric investigations were undertaken in education (Jennings, 1948; Gronlund, 1959) and community studies (Lundberg & Lawsing, 1937; Lundberg & Steele, 1938). Later work in social psychology developed this as 'group dynamics' (Cartwright & Zander, 1953; Harary & Norman, 1953), an approach that was furthered at the University of Michigan and at the Tavistock Institute in London.

George Lundberg's insights into community relations had a wider impact through the work of Lloyd Warner in the studies, undertaken with Elton Mayo, of the Hawthorne electrical works in Chicago (Roethlisberger & Dickson, 1939). The Hawthorne researchers were inspired by the sociometric studies in seeking visual representations of social relations, but they were also directly influenced by the electrical wiring diagrams used in the Hawthorne factory and saw wiring networks as a model for representing group relations. Warner built on this early research in investigations into the community structures of American towns and cities. Influenced by the work of the British anthropologist Alfred Radcliffe-Brown, Warner looked at the structure of group relations in large communities and used network diagrams to represent their social structures. In his study of the New England town of Newburyport, carried out between 1930 and 1935, Warner presented large-scale community relations in matrix form, showing that group relations could be represented in mathematical terms and that these mathematical structures could be transformed into a visual representation. Central to Warner's concerns was an exploration of the formation of 'cliques' within large urban social networks (Warner & Lunt, 1941). In a justly famous commentary, George Homans (1950) used these matrix methods to re-analyse a small clique of women studied by Warner in the southern town of Natchez.

A crucial advance in social network analysis took place at the University of Manchester in the 1950s. A group of sociologists and social anthropologists working on African and European communities, and critical of the mainstream emphasis in American sociology on consensus and harmony, sought to place conflict and division at the centre of their analyses. They were strongly influenced by the 'structuralist' view of society that had been expounded by Radcliffe-Brown since the 1920s, his public lectures delivered in 1937 and 1940 referring explicitly to the 'network of social relations' and its 'social morphology' (Radcliffe-Brown, 1940, 1957). Working closely with the Manchester scholars, John Barnes and Elizabeth Bott allied this approach with the group dynamics being developed at the Tavistock Institute and with the work of Warner. In a Norwegian study, Barnes (1954) proposed that the metaphor of the network of relations be taken seriously as a way of exploring the warp and weft of community relations, and in a study of kinship in London, Bott (1955, 1956) employed ideas of connectedness and density in urban kinship relations. Under the influence of a systematic study by Siegfried Nadel (1957), the developing Manchester work on African communities was reported by Clyde Mitchell (1969b), who also provided one of the earliest summaries of a formal social network methodology (1969a). The role of kinship in social cohesion has been considerably extended and elaborated since those early works (White, 2011).

Simultaneously with the work of Mitchell and his associates was the work of a group of American researchers led by Harrison White, who had also begun to develop and apply formal, mathematical methods for social network analysis. Building on the work of Claude Lévi-Strauss (1969 [1949]) in collaboration with André Weil, White (1963a) used algebra to represent kinship structures. When White moved from Chicago to Harvard University, he formed a large and dynamic group of students and associates to develop a paradigm for network analysis (see Mullins, 1973, Chapter 10). These researchers included Joel Levine's (1972) work on corporate power as a multidimensional field, Nancy Lee's (1969) research on the role of communication networks in helping American women find doctors willing to perform an abortion prior to Roe v. Wade, Mark Granovetter's (1973, 1974) comparison of the role of 'strong' and 'weak' ties in searches for employment opportunities and Nick Mullins' (1973) network analysis of mid-20th-century American sociology. White himself worked with various colleagues on algebraic methods for representing and analysing systems of social positions and roles (Lorrain & White, 1971; Boorman & White, 1976; White et al., 1976). This group constituted a new generation of social network researchers who helped to spread social network analysis across the globe. White went on to formalise his approach in a classic, but complex text (2008; see also Azarian 2005).

One of the principal areas in which social network analysis has been applied is the investigation of corporate power and interlocking directorships (Carroll et al., this volume). Early studies by Paul Sweezy (1939[1953]) and others had adopted ad hoc techniques for drawing network diagrams of board-level connections, but it was not until the 1960s and 1970s that these suggestions were furthered as a result of the technical advances made by White and his associates. Joel Levine (1972) documented the clusters formed by particular banks and their directors, and a path-breaking paper by Jim Bearden and his colleagues (2002 [1975]) used the idea of centrality to explore the power and influence of banks in the American corporate world. Elsewhere, work led by Rob Mokken and Frans Stokman in the Netherlands (Helmers et al., 1975) became the basis for an investigation of transnational patterns (Fennema, 1982) and an international comparative investigation (Stokman et al., 1985; and see Scott & Griff, 1984). This was extended into a comparative investigation of intercorporate shareholding networks (Scott, 1986) and led to numerous studies in a variety of societies (see the reviews in Scott, 1997, and the comparative study edited by David & Westerhuis, 2014).

Another important area of application has been the investigation of community structure. Rooted in Warner's studies, it was again a number of researchers influenced by the developments at Harvard who pushed this area forward. Claude Fischer (1977) and Barry Wellman (1979) undertook work that completely reoriented the research area. Wellman carried out a series of investigations into the changing structure of friendship in the social integration of communal relations in a Canadian city. His particular concern was to investigate the changing ways in which people maintained contact with each other, and his thesis was that each individual has his or her own personal 'community', consisting of those to whom they are socially connected (Chua et al., 2011). Reconceptualising community as formed of personal networks, or egonets (Perry et al., this volume), liberated community study from its previous spatial bounds in the neighbourhood. Wellman was also an important early contributor to research on the impact of electronic communication on the structure and operation of interpersonal networks (Wellman & Hogan, 2006). This work led to the development of a now-thriving literature on social media and online communities (Quan-Haase, this volume), as well as networks of social support (Song & Zhang, this volume). It also influenced studies of 'social capital' (Völker, this volume), which developed from the varying works of Robert Putnam (2000) and Pierre Bourdieu (Bourdieu & Passeron, 1977[1970]). Nan Lin (2001) and Ronald Burt (2005; see also Lin et al., 2001) also made influential contributions to this literature.

The structuralist orientation of social network analysis put it at odds with concepts such as culture, identity and agency for much of the field's early history, but this started to change in the early 1990s. For example, White (2008 [1992]), Emirbayer (Emirbayer & Goodwin, 1994; Emirbayer, 1997; Emirbayer & Mische, 1998) and Mische (2003) began to theorise the foundations of a 'relational sociology' (Mische & Fuhse, this volume), building on White's approach to culture and identity. Other approaches to relational sociology (Donati, 2012) that utilise social network analysis have also developed, most markedly in the work of Nick Crossley (2010, 2021).

Beyond 'relational sociology', research at the intersection of networks, culture, language, cognition and affect has been thriving in recent years (Lizardo, this volume; Shugars & González-Bailón, this volume; Brashears & Money, this volume; Agneessens, this volume). This work, together with advances in modelling scientific (Kang & Evans, this volume) and socioecological networks (Bodin, this volume), has contributed to the development of methods and models for multimodal (Jasny, this volume) and multilevel networks (Lazega & Wang, this volume).

Numerous other applications have extended social network analysis beyond sociology and anthropology into other disciplines, such as history (Kumekawa, this volume), geography (Hipp, this volume), environmental science and policy (Bodin, this volume; Scott et al., this volume) and economics (Goyal, 2011). Network analysis has also been used to make important contributions to interdisciplinary research on subjects such as political and policy networks (Diani, this volume; Knoke, 1990; Knoke et al., 1996; Knoke, 2011), social movements (Tindall, this volume; Diani, 1995, 2011), gender and ethnicity (Bellotti, this volume; Côté, this volume), crime (Ouellet, this volume; Morselli, 2009; Arquilla & Ronfeldt, 2001), terrorism (van der Hulst, 2011), international trade (Prell et al., this volume) and the world political economy (Kick & Davis, 2001; Kick et al., 2011; Carroll et al., this volume), diffusion (Centola, this volume), the impact of peers on attitudes and behaviour (Kirke, 2006; An, 2011), health outcomes (de la Haye, this volume); and many other topics.

Since the late 1970s, there has been a huge increase in technical contributions to social network methodology and in its application (e.g., Burt 1982; Holland et al., 1983; Freeman et al., 1989; Wasserman & Faust, 1994; Wasserman & Galaskiewicz, 1994; Hoff et al., 2002; Brandes & Erlebach, 2005; Carrington et al., 2005; Butts, 2008; Snijders et al., 2010; Lusher et al., 2013). The importance of technical contributions in social network analysis (SNA) is evident when we take a high-level view of the field. For example, we analysed the latent topic structure of all publications in *Social Networks* by fitting a hierarchical Bayesian stochastic blockmodel to a bipartite network of journal articles and the words contained in their titles and abstracts (see Gerlach et al., 2018, for a discussion of network-based generative topic models, and Browne, Crick, and McLevey, this volume, for Bayesian stochastic blockmodels). Our analysis detected 26 latent topics (at the lowest level of the model), twenty of which are substantively interesting.[2]

Figure 1.1 is a visualisation of the hierarchical blockmodel, with word nodes clustered into latent topics on the right, and document nodes clustered based on their topic mixtures on the left. The hierarchical blockmodel is superimposed, with square blue nodes, over the original complex network. We focus on the lowest levels of the blockmodel, which are the blocks furthest to the right (topics) and left (document clusters) of the graph.

To interpret each latent topic, we read the full list of associated words, as well as the titles and abstracts of articles that prominently feature the topic, and the titles and abstract of documents belonging to document clusters that prominently feature the topic. We then assigned each a general label, computed the distribution of topics over all *Social Networks* publications, and aggregated the results for each year to examine change over time. Those results are shown in Figure 1.2, which compares the weight of each detected topic over time.

Our model results illustrate the importance of technical contributions to social network analysis since *Social Networks* was founded in the late 1970s. For example, we see technical work on network clustering, partitioning and dimensionality reduction (Moody & Mucha, this volume; Dorien et al., this volume; Browne, Crick, and McLevey, this volume); relational data collection, sampling and measurement (adams & Lubbers, this volume); statistical modelling, in particular exponential random graph models (Koskinen, this volume), stochastic actor-oriented models (Snijders & Steglich, this volume) and relational even models (Schecter & Contractor, this volume); as well as centrality and related measures (Everett & Borgatti, this volume). We also see topics representing developments in methods and models for negative ties and signed graphs (Agneessens, this volume), as well as multimodal (Jasny, this volume) and multilevel networks (Lazega & Wang, this volume); and models of diffusion, opinion dynamics and network interventions (Centola, this volume; Valente, this volume).

Some of these developments, at various points in SNA's history, are the result of interdisciplinary engagement between sociology and other social sciences, on the one hand, and physics and other natural sciences, on the other. While social network analysis has long had meaningful connections to physics (e.g., Harrison White earned two PhDs, one in theoretical physics, the other in sociology), both have unique approaches to doing network science (see Borgatti et al., 2009, for a high-level comparison of these two branches of network science, with an emphasis on differences in what constitutes a theoretical contribution), and the relationship between the two fields has been difficult at times.

For example, many in social network analysis were frustrated by the group of physicists who became interested in the properties of 'small world' networks following the publication of a paper by Duncan Watts and Steven Strogatz (1998), which built on Stanley Milgram's pioneering work on small worlds (1967; Travers and Milgram, 1969) and the literature on random networks that had grown up around this. Barabási (2002) and Watts (1999, 2003) suggested that these ideas could be applied to the social world, egregiously ignoring the work on social networks that had already been undertaken by sociologists, anthropologists, economists and political scientists. Despite this lack of awareness of prior research, their ideas have begun to contextualise established work on network structures and their development over time.

Freeman's (2004) history of social network analysis undertook a network analysis of citation patterns in research on social networks and showed that the work published by Barabási and Watts had rarely cited work by social scientists. It also disclosed, however, that social network analysts had been reluctant to engage with the work of the physicists. To some extent, the divide between social network analysis and network analysis in physics is still salient. Figure 1.3 is a visualisation of a citation network consisting of all network analysis articles published in *Social Networks* and *Physical Review E* (filtered to articles containing the word 'network' in the title or abstract), with physics publications shown in gold and social networks publications shown in black. The separation between the two fields is clear, but we should expect this given well-known disciplinary differences (Borgatti et al., 2009). Furthermore, the fact that these two approaches to network analysis are differentiated while still being densely connected is a promising sign for the evolving relationship between our fields.

In general, it seems the division between network analysis in the social sciences and physics is breaking down and we are seeing productive intellectual engagements within and across disciplinary bounds. Citations aside, Watts moved into sociology long ago, and sociologists have debated and built on his contributions (Freeman, 2011; Scott, 2011). More recently, the INSNA Sunbelt conference was held jointly with NetSci at Indiana University in 2021, and the interdisciplinary journal *Network Science* was founded in 2013 with

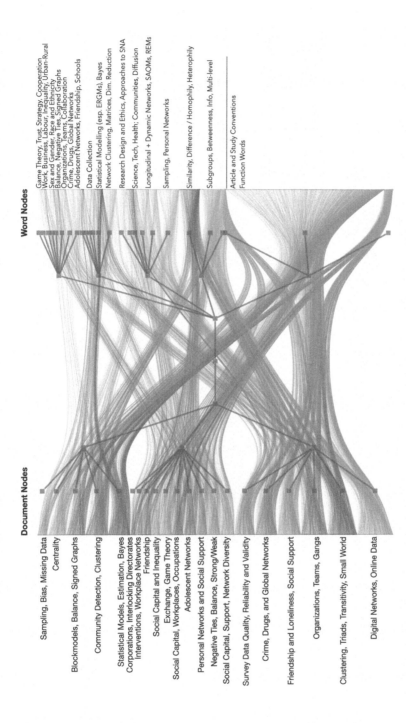

Figure 1.1 Visualisation of a hierarchical Bayesian stochastic blockmodel fit to the bipartite network of *Social Networks* articles and the words contained in their titles and abstracts. The nodes on the right are words, clustered into mixtures of latent topics. The nodes on the left are documents, clustered based on their latent topic mixtures

6 THE SAGE HANDBOOK OF SOCIAL NETWORK ANALYSIS

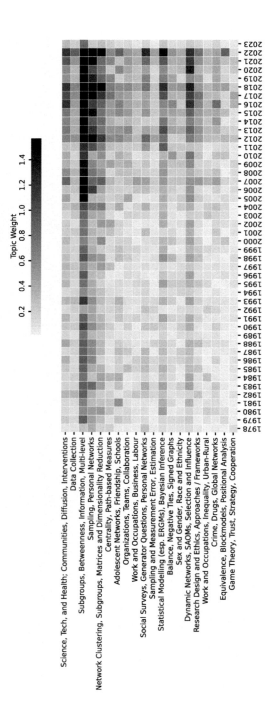

Figure 1.2 Changes in the topics covered by *Social Networks* publications over time

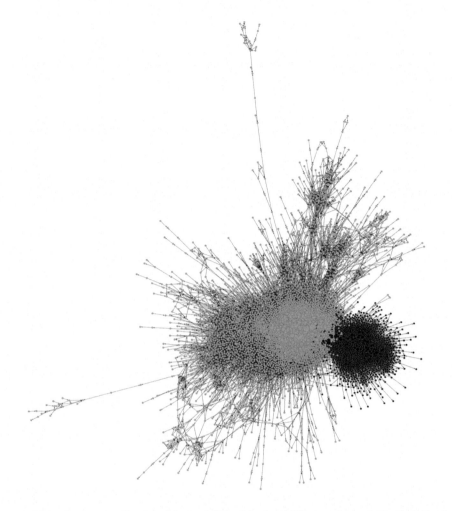

Figure 1.3 Citation network of articles published in *Social Networks* and *Physical Review E* (filtered to articles that contain 'network' in the title or abstract). Physics publications are shown in gold, and *Social Networks* publications in black

editors from both social and natural science disciplines (Brandes et al., 2013). Social network analysis can now be considered a sub-field – albeit a very large one – of a more general 'network science' (Newman et al., 2006; Newman, 2018 [2010]).

One area where the interdisciplinarity of network science has been especially productive is in modelling network dynamics (and, relatedly, dynamics on networks). Several major innovations have come from social network analysis (Stadtfeld et al., 2020; Snijders & Steglich, this volume; Schecter & Contractor, this volume; Centola, this volume), with some leading figures calling for the need to rethink foundational network concepts given the availability of timestamped streams of interactional data and extremely powerful computers (Kitts et al., this volume). Increased computing power has also greatly facilitated the development of generative approaches to network analysis, including stochastic actor-oriented models (Steglich & Snijders, 2022) and other approaches that utilise agent-based simulations, on the one hand, and Bayesian probabilistic modelling (for nearly all contemporary network models), on the other.

Social network analysis is not a distinct theoretical approach. It is, however, a general theoretical orientation, or paradigm, and its methods have been employed in the development of many specific social theories. We can also think of it as a scientific community, or 'invisible college' (Crane, 1972), with a recognisable intellectual lineage and clusters of researchers based in several centres and loosely linked by cross-cutting collaborations and inter-citations (Freeman, 2004). It is also a scientific institution, with dedicated journals (*Social Networks*, *Journal of Social Structure*, *Connections* and *Network Science*), introductory textbooks (e.g., Degenne & Forsé, 1999 [1994]; Hanneman & Riddle, 2005, 2011a, 2011b; Knoke & Yang, 2008; Prell, 2012; Crossley et al., 2015; Robins, 2015; Scott, 2017 [1991]; Borgatti et al., 2022), handbooks for scholars and practitioners (Wasserman & Faust, 1994; Carrington et al., 2005; Scott & Carrington 2011; Light & Moody, 2020, and this volume), dedicated and specialist computer software (Borgatti et al., 2022; Browne, Crick, and McLevey, this volume), an association (the International Network for Social Network Analysis) and a presence in other professional associations, such as the more recently formed NetSciSociety.

Since its take-off in the 1970s, the volume of published research in social networks has grown exponentially. To approximate this growth, we collected metadata on nearly 40,000 articles indexed in the *Web of Science* (as of January 2022) that cite at least one article published in *Social Networks*. Within that collection, we label an article as an SNA publication if 'network' appears in the abstract.[3] The results are shown in Figure 1.4, with the top subplot showing increases in the number of publications per year and the

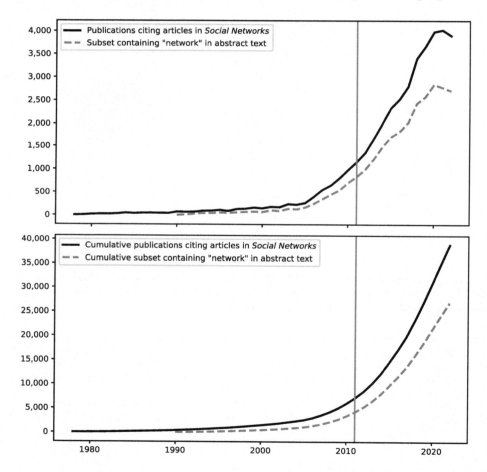

Figure 1.4 Growth of social network analysis over time. The top subplot shows the number of articles in the *Web of Science* that cite articles published in *Social Networks*, and the subset that also contain 'network' in the abstract. The bottom subplot shows cumulative growth

bottom subplot showing cumulative growth. The vertical line marks the publication of the first volume of this handbook in 2011, revealing how much the field has grown over twelve years. As of early 2023, we are approaching almost 2,500 new SNA articles published per year (likely higher), with over 25,000 publications in the field to date (likely higher). Neither the volume of published research nor the expansion of social network analysis into diverse subject areas (as previously discussed) show any signs of levelling off.

Central Ideas in Social Network Analysis

The mathematical ideas that underlie social network analysis are those of graph theory (Harary & Norman, 1953; Harary et al., 1965; Harary, 1969). This comprises a set of axioms and deductions about the relations between points and the lines connecting them that originated in Leonhard Euler's (1736) mathematical investigations of the famous problem of the seven bridges of Königsberg. Euler investigated whether it was possible to walk through all city areas and islands while crossing each river bridge just once. He converted this practical problem into an abstract model of points and lines in which the points represented the areas of the city and the lines represented the bridges, and demonstrated mathematically that the task is impossible. Euler's proof laid the foundations for studying networks of all kinds as graphs of points and lines.

Social network analysis, then, involves treating individuals and other social actors, such as groups and organisations as points or 'nodes', and their social relations as lines or 'edges'. The various theorems of graph theory can then be used to describe and explore features of the social network. This mathematical model formalises the initial insight depicted in Moreno's sociograms, and the theorems of graph theory provide a basis for analysing their formal properties. However, it is not necessary to draw a sociogram in order to use graph theoretical concepts and measures, as network data on any given social relationship can be recorded in matrices. A 'sociomatrix', for example, would have rows and columns in the matrix to represent individuals or other social actors, with the presence, absence, or strength of a social relationship between each pair of individuals recorded as a numerical entry in the cells of the matrix.[4]

Thus, the sociomatrix contains the same information as the corresponding sociogram: the rows or columns are its points and the contents of the cells are measures of the lines connecting them.

While it can be very difficult, and often impossible, to calculate the properties of a large sociogram by visual inspection, matrices can be analysed using mathematical techniques (and therefore computers) regardless of the size of the network. Matrix models of graphs, then, allow a wide range of real social networks to be analysed and compared.

Graph theory is concerned with the structural properties of the configuration of points and lines that comprises the graph. Several extensions of the concept of the graph have been useful in social network analysis. For example, the 'directed graph' or 'digraph' takes account of the 'direction' of a line, to represent asymmetric relations such as friendship choices made or the flow of influence or resources between one actor and another. The 'weighted' or 'valued' graph can take account of the intensity or strength of a relationship by assigning a numerical 'weight' or 'value' to a line. In the 'signed' graph, the lines have positive or negative signs, which can represent sentiments or attitudes, among other things (Agneessens, this volume). In the 'multigraph', points may also be connected by multiple lines, each labelled by direction and value to represent a different type of relationship. Points may also have discrete- or continuous-valued properties, representing the attributes of the actors represented by the points, as in conventional social analysis. In mathematics, the term 'network' is used to describe these extensions to the basic idea of a graph, in which the lines and/or points have properties such as direction, valence, weight, multiplicity, etc. Thus, social network analysis is the analysis of systems of social relationships – social structures – represented by mathematical networks.

Special techniques must generally be used to obtain or generate network data (adams & Lubbers, this volume). Network data can be difficult to obtain and can raise unique problems of measurement validity and reliability, as well as particular ethical issues (both themes which are represented in our topic models of social networks research). Getting accurate and complete data on connections among the members of even a moderately large population (e.g., more than a dozen or so) by interviews or questionnaires can be impractical or subject to major inaccuracies – as the number of potential connections increases with the square of the number of members. At least three possible solutions to this problem are commonly used. First, data on connections may be collected from all members of the population, accepting the likelihood of inaccuracies, especially the inability of respondents to report all their existing connections. Second, data may be collected from a (possibly random) sample of members, who may also identify members who are omitted from the sample, and (possibly) also on their connections. Both approaches are likely to result in missing data on connections, which should be, but often are not, dealt with by special techniques for inference to the population (Krause & Huisman, this volume). The second approach results in a set of 'ego-networks' or 'egocentric networks', each centred on the 'ego' who was sampled (Crossley et al., 2015; Perry et al., this volume). A third approach is to use already existing data on connections among the entire population, typically from archived organisational records. This method entirely avoids problems of inference from samples, and may also avoid inadvertent 'missing data', as long as the data that were originally collected are accurate.

While the emphasis in social network analysis has been on quantitative data and analyses, qualitative and mixed-methods approaches are also used, and indeed these characterised much of the foundational anthropological work in social network analysis, as well as a growing body of recent work (Domínguez & Hollstein, 2005; Hollstein, this volume).

Once a social structure can be represented mathematically, a network analyst can measure such simple features as the overall 'density' of the network and the relative 'centrality' (Everett & Borgatti, this volume) of its points. A sociological analysis gives these concepts a substantive interpretation. For example, centrality measures have typically been used as indicators of power, influence, popularity, or prestige. Other network analyses based on graph theory include the investigation of cliques and clusters of points, structural divisions within a social network being seen in terms of the existence of particularly dense or well-connected subgroupings; or, equivalently, in terms of particularly sparse or poorly connected areas of the network, representing points of potential cleavage (Moody & Mucha, this volume). Notions of local clustering, cleavage and centrality have allowed the investigation of intermediary or brokerage roles (Burt, 2005), as well as the development of methods for 'network reduction', in which large, complex networks are reduced to smaller, more manageable realisations (Doreian et al., 2014; Batagelj et al. this volume; Browne, Crick and McLevey, this volume).

Most social network research has involved 'one-mode' analysis, where the rows and columns of the data matrix represent the same set of points, or social actors. Increasingly, however, researchers have investigated 'two-mode' networks in which there are two distinct classes of points, and the lines exclusively connect points of one class with points of the other class (Jasny, this volume). These are also called 'affiliation' networks, because they have often been used to represent the affiliations of people with organisations, although many other applications are possible. Two-mode data are represented in a rectangular matrix, in which the rows represent one type of point and the columns represent the other type. For example, one class of points could be persons and the other type could be events in which they were involved, or organisations to which they belong. Each cell entry indicates whether the indexed person is related to the indexed event or organisation, or the strength, etc., of the relationship. Two-mode networks can easily be converted to one-mode networks with some loss of information, but among the most recent advances in social network analysis are the direct analysis of such features as centrality in two-mode networks (without first converting them to one-mode networks), and the extension of the concept of two-mode to multimode networks (Knoke et al., 2021; Jasny, this volume). The network-based topic models reported in this introduction, for example, are based on the direct analysis of bipartite networks of journal articles and words rather than one-mode projections of word co-occurrences.

Another recent extension of the basic network is the multilevel network, in which networks are hierarchically embedded in other networks; for example, the employees of an organisation form a workplace network, which in turn is embedded in the interorganisational network formed by relationships among several or many such organisations. Analysis of such structures combines insights and statistical models developed for social network analysis and for multilevel analysis of conventional multilevel attribute data (Lazega & Snijders, 2015; Lazega & Wang, this volume).

While graph theory and network theory are basic to social network analysis, other mathematical models have also been used to analyse specific aspects of network structure. The algebraic approach used by Harrison White and others looks not at the properties of individuals and groups but at the structural properties of the social positions (or 'statuses') occupied by individuals, and the performed roles that are associated with these positions (Lorrain & White, 1971; Boorman & White, 1976; Pattison, 2011). These so-called positional approaches, or 'blockmodels', use methods of matrix clustering to build on Homans' early work and show how networks can be decomposed into hierarchical positions of the kind documented by Nadel (1957). These approaches have led to various ways of measuring and analysing the 'structural equivalence' or 'substitutability' of individuals within social positions, and to algebraic modelling of systems of compound social roles, corresponding formally to the more familiar systems of compound kinship roles (mother's brother, wife's father, etc.) developed by ethnographers (Doreian et al., 2005; Doreian et al., this volume). Recent developments in this area include the development of probabilistic generative models based on the idea of 'stochastic equivalence' and are grounded in Bayesian inference and latent variable modelling (Browne, Crick and McLevey, this volume; see Blei (2014) on iterative data analysis with latent variable models).

As we have noted, networks larger than twenty or so points are difficult to draw accurately and legibly as sociograms. Multidimensional scaling was one of the earliest methods used to eliminate the random jumble of criss-crossing lines and so to order and display points in a way that retains spatial patterns inherent in relational data. Newer algorithms have greatly improved graph drawing, and researchers such as Batagelj and his colleagues (De Nooy et al., 2005; see also vlado.fmf.uni-lj.si/) and Krempel (2005, 2011) have been exploring alternative bases for network visualisation, including moving images of network change. Because network drawings are so useful for gaining an intuitive grasp of their structure, methods and software for network visualisation (or 'graph drawing') have received much attention from computer scientists (e.g., graphdrawing.org/symposia.html).

Many procedures for data analysis and statistical inference that are common in the social sciences (such as regression analysis, ANOVA and various tests of statistical significance within the Frequentist paradigm) cannot be applied in network analysis without modifications, as they rely on the assumption that observations are independent of one another. This violates the central idea of network analysis: interdependence. This is one reason why, as previously discussed, technical contributions to network methodology have been so prominent in the field. A body of statistical theory, methods and software has been steadily developing that enables valid description and inference from network data (van Duijn & Huisman, 2011; Robins, 2015, Chapter 10). Ove Frank (2011) has pioneered the investigation of inference from sampled network data, and conventional statistical models have been adapted for use with network data. Building on work by Frank and Strauss (1986), network statisticians have developed novel statistical techniques by generalising Markov graphs to a larger family of models (Wasserman & Pattison, 1996; Pattison & Wasserman, 1999; Robins et al., 1999; Lusher et al., 2013). The so-called exponential random graph model ('ERGM') resembles a logistic regression in which each pair of nodes in the graph is an 'observation', and the 'dependent variable' is the presence or absence of a connection between them. Solving the estimating equations for the parameters of the model provides estimates of the impact of such structural features of the graph as transitivity, reciprocity, etc., as well as of the attributes of the points. Most applications of the ERGM have been to simple graphs (i.e., with binary-valued edges), but methods and software have recently been developed to apply ERGMs to networks with weighted (valued) edges (Krivitsky, 2012; Huang & Butts, 2021; Krivitsky et al., 2021). ERGMs have become pervasive in contemporary network analysis. So much so that some feel ERGMs are being uncritically adopted as a kind of GLM for networks (see the discussion in Koskinen, this volume).

Until the beginning of this century, most social network analyses used cross-sectional data and static models. With the growing availability of longitudinal network data (especially multiwave panel data) and timestamped interaction data, new statistical models and methods for the analysis of change in networks over time have been developed. Agent-based computational methods have been used to explore processes of change in networks, relating structural transformations to the unanticipated consequences of individual-level decision making (Monge & Contractor, 2003; Steglich & Snijders, 2022). Knowledge of the rules under which agents make decisions and act can be used to predict broad patterns of change in network structure. Networks change because of the ways in which individual actions are constrained by the structural locations of actors and the wider structural properties of the network (Centola, this volume). Tom Snijders has developed a powerful approach to this problem in which networks develop through the continual iteration of actions, and in which small, incremental changes can accumulate to a tipping point at which nonlinear transformation in network structure occur (Snijders & van Duijn, 1997; Snijders, 2001, 2005; Snijders & Steglich, this volume). There are other widely used models, such as Relational Event Models (Butts, 2008; Schecter & Contractor, this volume), that are designed for timestamped interaction data.

CONCLUSION

In preparing this volume, we took the view that social network analysis is an evolving 'paradigm', rather than a theory or a method: that is, a way of conceptualising and analysing social life 'that guides the selection of the social behavior data that are studied, influences the way these data are organized for analysis, and specifies the kinds of questions addressed' (Leinhardt, 1977, p. xiii).

In the most general terms, social network analysis is a structural paradigm: it conceptualises social life in terms of structures of relationships among actors, prioritising them over the attributes of individual actors (cf. Breiger & Wagner-Pacifici, this volume). Harrison White's comment that 'subinfeudation reminds one of industrial decentralization' (1963b, p. 77) highlighted structural rather than categorical parallels, and illustrates the kinds of questions and insights that arise from their study: 'The same conundrums that baffled them baffle us. Just as William the Conqueror insisted on submission directly to himself from the chief vassals of his loyal lords ... so a wise President seeks loyalty of subcabinet officers directly to himself' (White, 1963b, p. 78).

A social science paradigm comprises a theory or theories, a methodology or set of commonly employed methods and a body of empirical research. This volume is organised around that tripartite division. Readers who are experienced in social network analysis can use this volume as a reference book, referring to particular chapters for up-to-date summaries of knowledge and indications of future trends, in a given topic area. Readers who are new to social network analysis may wish to begin with the introductory chapter by Prell and Schaefer before reading chapters on particular topics, and can start working with network data for the first time by following along with the introductory guide to network analysis software offered in Browne, Howe, Koop-Monteiro, Yang, and McLevey (this volume). Alternately, a newcomer to social network analysis who is interested in a particular topic, such as gender or social policy, or in applications of social network analysis in a particular discipline, such as history or criminology, may prefer to start with the corresponding substantive chapter, referring back to the introductory, conceptual and theoretical chapters as necessary.

In terms of theory, methods and substantive empirical work, this is an exciting time in social network analysis. The second edition of *The SAGE handbook of social network analysis* aims to be a one-volume state-of-the-art presentation of classic and contemporary views and to lay the foundations for the further development of the area.

Notes

1 Overviews of the history of social network analysis can be found in Freeman (2004), Prell (2012) and Scott (2017: Chapter 2).

2 The others consist of function words, as well as collections of words that are so common due to (a) their prevalence in nearly all SNA topics, or (b) article-writing conventions.

3 Of course, like all methods, this approach is imperfect. Our two-step approach is designed to avoid false positives due to the widespread use of 'network' as a metaphor, to differentiate between social network analysis and actor network theory, and so on. While this method may miss some social network analyses, we think the probability of a publication using social network analysis citing at least one article in *Social Networks* is very high. Among these articles, we consider any that contain 'network' to be an SNA publication.

4 Matrices are also used for other types of network data, such as bipartite, multilevel and multiplex networks.

REFERENCES

An, W. (2011). Models and methods to identify peer effects. In J. Scott and P.J. Carrington (Eds.), *The SAGE handbook of social network analysis*. Sage.

Arquilla, J., & Ronfeldt, D. (2001). *Networks and netwars: the future of terror, crime, and militancy*. Rand.

Azarian, G.R. (2005). *The general sociology of Harrison C. White*. Macmillan.

Barabási, A.-L. (2002). *Linked: the new science of networks*. Perseus.

Barnes, J.A. (1954). Class and committee in a Norwegian island parish, *Human Relations*, 7, 39–58.

Batagelj, V., Doreian, P., Ferligoj, A., & Kejzar, N. (2014). *Understanding large temporal networks and spatial networks: exploration, pattern searching, visualization and network evolution*. John Wiley & Sons.

Bearden, J., Atwood, W., Freitag, P., Hendricks, C., Mintz, B., & Schwartz, M. (2002 [1975]). The nature and extent of bank centrality in corporate networks. In J. Scott (Ed.), *Social networks*. Vol. 3. Sage, 2002. Originally presented at the Annual Meetings of the American Sociological Association, 1975.

Blei, D. (2014). Build, compute, critique, repeat: data analysis with latent variable models. *Annual Review of Statistics and Its Application*, 1(1), 203–232.

Boorman, S.A., & White, H.C. (1976). Social structure from multiple networks II: role structures. *American Journal of Sociology*, 81, 1384–1446.

Borgatti, S., Mehra, A., Brass, D., & Labianca, G. (2009). Network analysis in the social sciences. *Science, 323*(5916), 892–895.

Borgatti, S.P., & Lopez-Kidwell, V. (2011). Network theory. In J. Scott and P.J. Carrington (Eds.), *The SAGE handbook of social network analysis*. Sage.

Borgatti, S.P., Everett, M.G., Johnson, J.C., & Agneessens, F. (2022). *Analyzing social networks using R*. Sage.

Bott, E. (1955). Urban families: conjugal roles and social networks. *Human Relations, 8*, 345–384.

Bott, E. (1956). Urban families: the norms of conjugal roles. *Human Relations, 9*, 325–341.

Bott, H. (1928). Observation of play activities in a nursery school. *Genetic Psychology Monographs, 4*, 44–48.

Bourdieu, P., & Passeron, J.-C. (1977 [1970]). *Reproduction in economy and society*. Sage.

Brandes, U., & Erlebach, T. (Eds.) (2005). *Network analysis: methodological foundations*. Springer.

Brandes, U., Robins, G., McCranie, A., & Wasserman, S. (2013). What is network science? *Network Science, 1*(1), 1–15.

Buchanan, M. (2002). *Small world: uncovering nature's hidden networks*. Weidenfeld & Nicolson.

Burt, R.S. (1982). *Towards a structural theory of action*. Academic Press.

Burt, R.S. (2005). *Brokerage and closure: an introduction to social capital*. Oxford University Press.

Butts, Carter (2008). A relational event framework for social action. *Sociological Methodology, 38*(1), 155–200.

Carrington, P.J., Scott, J., & Wasserman, S. (Eds.) (2005). *Models and methods in social network analysis*. Cambridge University Press.

Cartwright, D., & Zander, A. (Eds.) (1953). *Group dynamics*. Tavistock.

Chua, V., Madej, J., & Wellman, B. (2011). Personal communities: the world according to me. In J. Scott and P.J. Carrington (Eds.), *The SAGE handbook of social network analysis*. Sage.

Crane, D. (1972). *Invisible colleges: diffusion of knowledge in scientific communities*. University of Chicago Press.

Crossley, N. (2010). *Towards relational sociology*. Routledge.

Crossley, N. (2021). A dependent structure of interdependence: structure and agency in relational perspective. *British Journal of Sociology, 56*(1), 166–182.

Crossley, N., Bellotti, E., Edwards, G., Everett, M.G., Koskinen, J., & Tranmer, M. (2015). *Social network analysis for ego-nets*. Sage.

Crossley, N., McAndrew, S., & Widdop, P. (Eds.) (2019). *Social networks and music worlds*. Routledge.

David, T., & Westerhuis, G. (Eds.) (2014). *The power of corporate networks. a comparative and historical perspective*. Routledge.

De Nooy, W., Mrvar, A., & Batagelj, V. (2005). *Exploratory social network analysis with Pajek*. Cambridge University Press.

Degenne, A., & Forsé, M. (1999 [1994]). *Introducing social networks*. Sage. Originally published as *Les réseaux sociaux. Une approche structurale en sociologie*. Armand Colin, 1994.

Donati, P. (2012). *Relational sociology: a new paradigm for the social sciences*. Routledge.

Diani, M. (1995). *Green networks: structural analysis of the Italian environmental movement*. Edinburgh University Press.

Diani, M. (2011). Social movements and collective action. In J. Scott and P.J. Carrington (Eds.), *The SAGE handbook of social network analysis*. Sage.

Domínguez, S., & Hollstein, B. (Eds.) (2014). *Mixed methods social networks research: design and applications*. Cambridge University Press.

Doreian, P., Batagelj, V., & Ferligoj, A. (2005). *Generalized blockmodeling*. Cambridge University Press.

Emirbayer, M. (1997). Manifesto for a relational sociology. *American Journal of Sociology, 103*, 281–317.

Emirbayer, M., & Goodwin, J. (1994). Network analysis, culture, and the problem of agency. *American Journal of Sociology, 99*, 1411–1454.

Emirbayer, M., & Mische, A. (1998). What is agency? *American Journal of Sociology, 103*, 962–1023.

Euler, L. (1736). Solutio problematis ad geometriam situs pertinentis [The solution of a problem relating to the geometry of position]. *Commentarii academiae scientiarum imperialis Petropolitanae, 8*, 128–140.

Fennema, M. (1982). *International networks of banks and industry*. Martinus Nijhof.

Fischer, C.S. (1977). *Networks and places: social relations in the urban setting*. Free Press.

Frank, O. (2011). Survey sampling in networks. In J. Scott and P.J. Carrington (Eds.), *The SAGE handbook of social network analysis*. Sage.

Frank, O., & Strauss, D. (1986). Markov graphs. *Journal of the American Statistical Association, 81*(395), 832–842.

Freeman, L.C. (2004). *The development of social network analysis: a study in the sociology of science*. Empirical Press.

Freeman, L.C. (2011). The development of social network analysis – with an emphasis on recent events. In J. Scott and P.J. Carrington (Eds.), *The SAGE handbook of social network analysis*. Sage.

Freeman, L.C., White, D.R., & Romney, A.K. (Eds.) (1989). *Research methods in social network analysis*. Transaction.

Gerlach, M., Peixoto, T., & Altmann, E. (2018). A network approach to topic models. *Science Advances, 4*(7).

Goyal, S. (2011). Social networks in economics. In J. Scott and P.J. Carrington (Eds.), *The SAGE handbook of social network analysis*. Sage.

Granovetter, M. (1973). The strength of weak ties. *American Journal of Sociology*, 78(6), 1360–1380.

Granovetter, M. (1974). *Getting a job*. Harvard University Press.

Gronlund, N.E. (1959). *Sociometry in the classroom*. Harper & Bros.

Hanneman, R.A., & Riddle, M. (2005). *Introduction to social network methods*. University of California, Riverside. faculty.ucr.edu/~hanneman/

Hanneman, R.A., & Riddle, M. (2011a). Concepts and measures for basic network analysis. In J. Scott and P.J. Carrington (Eds.), *The SAGE handbook of social network analysis*. Sage.

Hanneman, R.A., & Riddle, M. (2011b). Concepts and measures for basic network analysis. In J. Scott and P.J. Carrington (Eds.), *The SAGE handbook of social network analysis*. Sage.

Harary, F. (1969). *Graph theory*. Addison-Wesley.

Harary, F., & Norman, R.Z. (1953). *Graph theory as a mathematical model in social science*. Institute for Social Research.

Harary, F., Norman, R.Z., & Cartwright, D. (1965). *Structural models: an introduction to the theory of directed graphs*. Wiley.

Helmers, H.M., Mokken, R.J.R., Plijter, C., & Stokman, F.N. (1975). *Graven naar Macht. Op Zoek naar de Kern van de Nederlandse Economic*. Van Gennep.

Hoff, P., Raftery, A., & Handcock, M. (2002). Latent space approaches to social network analysis. *Journal of the American Statistical Association*, 97(460), 1090–1098.

Holland, P., Laskey, K.B., & Leinhardt, S. (1983). Stochastic blockmodels: first steps. *Social Networks*, 5(2), 109–137.

Homans, G. (1950). *The human group*. Routledge and Kegan Paul, 1951.

Huang, P., & Butts, C.T. (2021). Parameter estimation procedures for exponential-family random graph models on count-valued networks: a comparative simulation study. *arXiv*: 2111.02372. 3 November.

Jennings, H.H. (1948). *Sociometry in group relations*. American Council on Education.

Kick, E.L., & Davis, B.L. (2001). World-system structure and change: an analysis of global networks and economic growth across two time periods. *American Behavioral Scientist*, 44, 1561–1578.

Kick, E.L., McKinney, L.A., McDonald, S., & Jorgenson, A. (2011). A multiple-network analysis of the world system of nations, 1995–1999. In J. Scott and P.J. Carrington (Eds.), *The SAGE handbook of social network analysis*. Sage.

Kirke, D.M. (2006). *Teenagers and substance use*. Palgrave Macmillan.

Knoke, D. (1990). *Political networks*. Cambridge University Press.

Knoke, D. (2011). Policy networks. In J. Scott and P.J. Carrington (Eds.), *The SAGE handbook of social network analysis*. Sage.

Knoke, D., Diani, M., Hollway, J., & Christopoulos, D. (2021). *Multimodal political analysis*. Cambridge University Press.

Knoke, D., Pappi, F.U., Broadbent, J., & Tsujinaka, Y. (1996). *Comparing policy networks. labor politics in the US, Germany, and Japan*. Cambridge University Press.

Knoke, D., & Yang, S. (2008). *Network analysis*. 2nd ed. Sage.

Krempel, L. (2005). *Visualisierung komplexer Strukturen*. Campus Verlag.

Krempel, L. (2011). Network visualization. In J. Scott and P.J. Carrington (Eds.), *The SAGE handbook of social network analysis*. Sage.

Krivitsky, P.N. (2012). Exponential-family random graph models for valued networks. *Electronic Journal of Statistics*, 6, 1100–1128.

Krivitsky, P.N., Hunter, D.R., Morris M., & Klumb, C. (2021). ergm 4.0: new features and improvements. arXiv preprint. *arXiv*:2106.04997.

Lazega, E., & Snijders, T. (2015). *Multilevel network analysis for the social sciences: theory, methods and applications*. Springer.

Lee, N.H. (1969). *The search for an abortionist*. Chicago University Press.

Leinhardt, S. (Ed.) (1977). *Social networks: a developing paradigm*. Academic Press.

Lévi-Strauss, C. (1969 [1949]). *The elementary structures of kinship*. Rev. ed. R. Needham (Ed.). Beacon Press. Originally published as *Les Structures élémentaires de la Parenté*. Mouton, 1949.

Levine, J.H. (1972). The sphere of influence. *American Sociological Review*, 37, 14–27.

Lewin, K. (1936). *Principles of topological psychology*. Harper and Row.

Light, R., & Moody, J. (Eds.) (2020). *The Oxford handbook of social networks*. Oxford University Press.

Lin, N. (2001). *Social capital: a theory of social structure and action*. Cambridge University Press.

Lin, N., Cook, K.S., & Burt, R.S. (Eds.) (2001). *Social capital: theory and research*. Transaction.

Lorrain, F.P., & White, H.C. (1971). Structural equivalence of individuals in social networks. *Journal of Mathematical Sociology*, 1, 49–80.

Lundberg, G.A., & Lawsing, M. (1937). The sociography of some community relations. *American Sociological Review*, 2, 318–35.

Lundberg, G., & Steele, M. (1938). Social attraction-patterns in a village. *Sociometry*, 1, 375–419.

Lusher, D., Koskinen, J., & Robins, G. (2013). *Exponential random graph models for social networks: theory, methods, and applications*. Cambridge University Press.

Milgram, S. (1967). The small world problem. *Psychology Today*, 2, 60–67.

Mische, A. (2003). Cross-talk in movements: rethinking the culture-network link. In M. Diani & D. McAdam (Eds.), *Social movements and networks:*

relational approaches to collective action. Oxford University Press.

Mische, A. (2007). *Partisan publics: communication and contention across Brazilian youth activist networks*. Princeton University Press.

Mische, A. (2011). Relational sociology, culture, and agency. In J. Scott and P.J. Carrington (Eds.), *The SAGE handbook of social network analysis*. Sage.

Mitchell, J.C. (1969a). The concept and use of social networks. In J.C. Mitchell (Ed.), *Social networks in urban situations*. Manchester University Press.

Mitchell, J.C. (Ed.) (1969b). *Social networks in urban situations*. Manchester University Press.

Monge, P.R., & Contractor, N.S. (2003). *Theories of communication networks*. Oxford University Press.

Moreno, J.L. (1934). *Who shall survive?* Beacon Press.

Morselli, C. (2009). *Inside criminal networks*. Springer.

Mullins, N.C. (1973). *Theories and theory groups in American sociology*. Harper and Row.

Nadel, S.F. (1957). *The theory of social structure*. Free Press.

Newman, M. (2018 [2010]). *Networks: an introduction*. 2nd ed. Oxford University Press.

Newman, M., Barabási, A.-L., & Watts, D.J. (Eds.) (2006). *The structure and dynamics of networks*. CPrinceton University Press.

Pattison, P.E. (2011). Relation algebras and social networks. In J. Scott and P.J. Carrington (Eds.), *The SAGE handbook of social network analysis*. Sage.

Pattison, P., & Wasserman, S. (1999). Logit models and logistic regressions for social networks: II. Multivariate relations. *British Journal of Mathematical and Statistical Psychology*, 52, 169–193.

Prell, C. (2012). *Social network analysis: history, theory and methodology*. Sage.

Putnam, R.D. (2000). *Bowling alone: the collapse and revival of American community*. Simon & Schuster.

Radcliffe-Brown, A.R. (1940). On social structure. *Journal of the Royal Anthropological Institute of Great Britain and Ireland*, 70, 1–12.

Radcliffe-Brown, A.R. (1957). *A natural science of society*. University of Chicago Press.

Robins, G. (2015). *Doing social network research: network-based research design for social scientists*. Sage

Robins, G.L., Pattison, P., & Wasserman, S. (1999). Logit models and logistic regressions for social networks: III. Valued relations. *Psychometrika*, 64, 371–394.

Roethlisberger, F.J., & Dickson, W.J. (1939). *Management and the worker*. Harvard University Press.

Scott, J. (1986). *Capitalist property and financial power*. Wheatsheaf.

Scott, J. (1997). *Corporate business and capitalist classes*. Oxford University Press.

Scott, J. (2010). Social network analysis: developments, advances, and prospects. *Social Network Analysis and Mining*, 1, 1.

Scott, J. (2011). Social physics and social networks. In J. Scott and P.J. Carrington (Eds.), *The SAGE handbook of social network analysis*. Sage.

Scott, J. (2017 [1991]). *Social network analysis, fourth edition*. Sage.

Scott, J., & Carrington, P.J. (2011) (Eds.), *The SAGE handbook of social network analysis*. Sage.

Scott, J., & Griff, C. (1984). *Directors of industry*. Polity Press.

Simmel, G. (1950 [1917]). *Grundfragen der Soziologie (Individuum und Gesellschaft)*. Walter de Gruyter. Trans. and ed. Kurt Wolff (1950), *The sociology of Georg Simmel*. Free Press.

Snijders, T.A.B. (2001). The statistical evaluation of social network dynamics. In M.E. Sobel & M.P. Becker (Eds.), *Sociological methodology, 2001*. Basil Blackwell.

Snijders, T.A.B. (2005). Models for longitudinal network data. In P.J. Carrington, J. Scott and S. Wasserman (Eds.), *Models and methods in social network analysis*. Cambridge University Press.

Snijders, T.A.B. & van Duijn, M.A.J. (1997). Simulation for statistical inference in dynamic network models. In R. Conte, R. Hegelmann & P. Terna (Eds.), *Simulating social phenomena*. Springer.

Snijders, T.A.B., Gerhard G. Van de Bunt, and Christian EG Steglich. (2010) 'Introduction to stochastic actor-based models for network dynamics.' *Social networks* 32(1): 44-60.

Stadtfeld, C., Snijders, T.A.B., Steglich, C., & van Duijn, M. (2020). Statistical power in longitudinal network studies. *Sociological Methods and Research*, 49, 1103–1132.

Steglich, C., & Snijders, T.A.B. (2022). Stochastic network modeling as generative social science. In K. Gërxhani, N.D. de Graaf & W. Raub (Eds.), *Handbook of sociological science*. Edward Elgar.

Stokman, F., Ziegler, R., & Scott, J. (Eds.) (1985). *Networks of corporate power*. Polity Press.

Sweezy, P.M. (1939 [1953]). Interest groups in the American economy. In National Resources Committee, *The structure of the American economy*, Part 1, Appendix 13. Reprinted in P.M. Sweezy, *The present as history*. Monthly Review Press, 1953.

Van der Hulst, R.C. (2011). Terrorist networks: the threat of connectivity. In J. Scott and P.J. Carrington (Eds.), *The SAGE handbook of social network analysis*. Sage.

Van Duijn, M.A.J., & Huisman, M. (2011). Statistical models for ties and actors. In J. Scott and P.J. Carrington (Eds.), *The SAGE handbook of social network analysis*. Sage.

Travers, J., & Milgram, S. (1969). An experimental study of the small world problem. *Sociometry*, 32(4), 425–443.

Warner, W.L., & Lunt, P.S. (1941). *The social life of a modern community*. Yale University Press.

Wasserman, S., & Faust, K. (1994). *Social network analysis: methods and applications.* Cambridge University Press.

Wasserman, S., & Galaskiewicz, J. (Eds.) (1994). *Advances in social network analysis.* Sage.

Wasserman, S., & Pattison, P. (1996). Logit models and logistic regressions for social networks: I. An introduction to Markov random graphs and p*. *Psychometrika, 60,* 401–426.

Watts, D.J. (1999). *Small worlds: the dynamics of networks between order and randomness.* Princeton University Press.

Watts, D.J. (2003). *Six degrees: the science of a connected age.* W.W. Norton.

Watts, D.J., & Strogatz, S.H. (1998). Collective dynamics of 'small-world' networks. *Nature, 393,* 440–442.

Wellman, B. (1979). The community question: the intimate networks of East Yorkers. *American Journal of Sociology, 84,* 1201–1231.

Wellman, B., & Hogan, B. (2006). Connected lives: the project. In J. Purcell (Ed.), *Networked neighbourhoods.* Springer-Verlag.

White, D.R. (2011). Kinship, class, and community. In J. Scott and P.J. Carrington (Eds.), *The SAGE handbook of social network analysis.* Sage.

White, H.C. (1963a). *An anatomy of kinship.* Prentice-Hall.

White, H.C. (1963b). Uses of mathematics in sociology. In J.C. Charlesworth (Ed.), *Mathematics and the social sciences.* American Academy of Political and Social Science.

White, H.C. (2008 [1992]). *Identity and control.* 2nd ed. Princeton University Press. First edition published in 1992.

White, H.C., Boorman, S.A., & Breiger, R.L. (1976). Social structure from multiple networks I: Blockmodels of roles and positions. *American Journal of Sociology, 81,* 730–781.

PART 1
General Issues

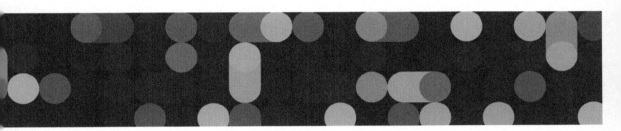

General Issues

Introducing Social Network Analysis

Christina Prell and David R. Schaefer

The world is filled with everyday experiences of social networks. One's friends, acquaintances and family members all comprise one's social network, and reflecting on how these networks shape daily life provides insights into fundamental notions guiding the field of social network analysis (SNA): people tend to trust those to whom they are strongly tied (e.g., family members), and people tend to have fewer strongly tied contacts than weakly tied ones (e.g., acquaintances).

SNA takes these intuitive, everyday notions of networks and formalises them through a combination of graph theory, statistics and matrix algebra. These analytical procedures are informed by social theories to test and explore various research questions regarding networks' impact on individuals and society, the drivers of network formation and/or change, and how networks and other factors co-evolve in relation to one another. This chapter introduces the novice to the field by introducing key terms, theories and the overall research process.

SETTING THE CONTEXT

Social network analysis has a rich history reaching back to the early 20th century. Historical accounts tend to agree that the field began via the collaborative efforts of Jacob Moreno and Helen Hall Jennings, in which the two scholars employed quantitative methods and sociograms to explore how social relations affected psychological well-being (Moreno & Jennings, 1934). Since then, scholars from a wide variety of disciplines (including mathematics, anthropology, sociology, psychology, ecology and computer science, to name a few), across several countries, have steadily contributed to the field, making contributions to theory, data gathering, visualisation and analysis techniques, modelling and simulation (for a more detailed history of the field, see Freeman, 2004; Prell, 2012; Scott, 2017). This colourful history suggests that SNA does not belong to any one discipline, but rather speaks to a wide variety of disciplines sharing a common interest in the role networks play in understanding aspects of the social (and increasingly non-social) world. This core interest in networks distinguishes SNA from more traditional, quantitative approaches that treat cases as independent from one another.

The main journals representing the field, which include *Social Networks*, *Connections*, *Journal of Social Structure* and *Network Science*, reflect this richness and diversity of disciplinary influences. Articles range from new analytical techniques, formal mathematical and/or simulation models, critical reviews of particular topics (e.g., small worlds or social capital), ethics, data gathering and applications to a variety of empirical settings. The main associations representing the field include the International Network of Social Network Analysis (www.insna.org), whose membership is more widely represented by social scientists, and the Network Science Society (netscisociety.net), whose membership is more widely represented by natural scientists. Recently, there have been efforts to bring these two communities together, for example, the Joint Sunbelt and NetSci Conference of 2021.

This breadth and range of topics and disciplines is similarly represented in the chapters found in this handbook. Although the field of SNA is quite wide and diverse, there are nonetheless some key, core concepts and terms that cut across the diversity of the field. In the next section, we offer a brief summary of some of these terms for the reader.

CORE CONCEPTS AND TERMS

Beginning with the most basic concept, a *social network* refers to a set of entities and the relationships connecting them. The *entities* found in a network typically refer to human ones, such as individual persons, organisations and/or nation states, yet they may also refer to non-human ones, such as fish, parcels of land, or words. Furthermore, network analysts vary in how they refer to these entities – using terms such as *actors*, *vertices*, or *nodes*, and thus newcomers to the field should expect to encounter these various terms for the same concept. For purposes of this chapter, the terms actors and nodes shall be used interchangeably. A final distinction, in relation to actors, is that of *ego* (the focal actor) and *alter* (an actor connected to ego).

The term *relation* refers to a particular type of relationship under investigation (e.g., friendship). Relationships are also referred to as *ties*, *connections* and *links* in the literature. Relations may be unilateral in nature, such as when one person offers advice to another, and such unilateral ties are referred to as *arcs*. A network composed of arcs is a *directed* or *asymmetrical* network. By contrast, when relations are inherently bilateral (e.g., marriage) then ties are called *edges*. A network composed of edges is referred to as an *undirected* or *symmetrical* network.

Relations can take many forms (Borgatti et al., 2009) including affective (e.g., friendship or trust), cognitive (e.g., perceived friendship), flows (e.g., trade or information), roles (teacher–student) and interactions (e.g., email exchanges). In addition, relations are classified as being states or events. *State relations* are stable and persist over time whereas *event relations* are transitory and consist of discrete incidents or interactions. State relations are often assumed to contain events that are not measured (e.g., one assumes friendship to contain many exchanges or encounters) and, similarly, one might aggregate events data to indicate a state relation (e.g., actors that socialise frequently together may be categorised as friends). When data are gathered on multiple relations (e.g., friendship, advice and email exchanges) among a set of nodes, such a network is considered a *multiplex*, *multilayer*, or *multi-relational* network.

Relations may also be characterised by their valence or strength. With valence, a *positive* relation may indicate friendship or trust, and a *negative* relation may indicate dislike or distrust. *Strength* of tie is often represented by the weight or value assigned to a tie. For example, given a range of values from 1 to 3, a tie assigned a value of 1 may indicate acquaintanceship, whereas a tie assigned a value of 3 may represent close intimacy. Although theoretically interesting, methods for analysing the value and valence of network data are less developed and, thus, network scholars often transform such data to a binary format of 1s and 0s before analysis. In such instances, careful thought is needed pertaining to the decision rules underlying such data transformations.

A scholar may gather relational data on a sample of individuals drawn from a larger population, in which case s/he is studying *ego networks*, also referred to as *personal networks* or *local networks*. Here, the sampled individuals (or egos) report on their contacts (alters), and may also report on their perception of the ties between those alters. When a scholar gathers relational data on an entire population, then s/he is studying *complete networks*, also known as *full* or *whole* networks. Most of the chapters in this volume (including this one) largely pertain to complete networks (although see Perry et al., this volume, on ego networks). In addition, there are entire books detailing the study of ego networks that readers may wish to explore (Crossley et al., 2022; Perry et al., 2018).

Configurations (or motifs) are particular patterns of connection among a set of nodes, such as those shown in Figure 2.1. They are used by network scholars to capture theoretical concepts, and may thus include or ignore information on the attributes of actors as needed. For example, a transitive triad configuration may reflect notions of subgroups (Freeman, 1992); a tie connecting nodes with the same nodal attributes may reflect ideas of homophily (McPherson et al., 2001); and a two-path configuration, with or without considerations

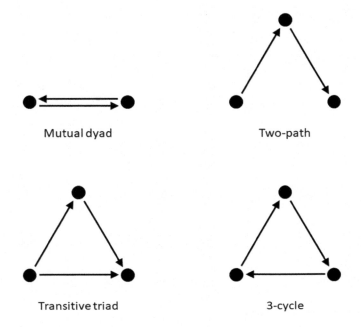

Figure 2.1 Examples of network configurations

for nodal attributes, may represent various forms of brokerage (Gould & Fernandez, 1989; Burt 2004). Later chapters (e.g., Koskinen, this volume; Steglich & Snijders, this volume; Schecter & Contracter, this volume) discuss the importance of network configurations for statistical modelling.

Up until this point, we have described complete networks as *one-mode networks*, defined as a set of nodes and ties between them. Yet complete networks may also take the form of a *two-mode* network (also called a *bipartite* or *affiliation* network). A two-mode network consists of two sets of nodes and the relationships between them (e.g., students and musical bands, with the 'like' relation linking students to bands). Combining one-mode and two-mode networks leads to *multimodal* networks, which consist of two (or more) different sets of nodes and their links between them. For example, a multimodal network of students (node set 1) and bands (node set 2) may consist of a one-mode friendship network among students, combined with a two-mode network of student preferences for particular bands. If this particular multimodal network also includes ties among the set of bands (e.g., who collaborates with whom), then one could also call this multimodal network a *multilevel* one, which consists of two node sets and the links between and within each one (Knoke et al., 2021). Readers may refer to Jasny (this volume) and Lazega and Wang (this volume) for further details. Finally,

one may have data on the same type of nodes and relations for multiple contexts, where ties between contexts are impossible or ignored. Such data can be conceptualised as a *multigroup* network (e.g., several schools and the networks of friendships within each). Figure 2.2 illustrates the differences between these different kinds of network formats.

THEORISING SOCIAL NETWORKS

While there is no overarching 'network theory', there are common principles that cut across a range of theories used by network analysts. Such principles include the *functions* of networks, networks' *levels of analysis* and the *causal role* of networks.

UNDERLYING MODELS OF NETWORK FUNCTION

Network function refers to the purpose of a network, and two common functions discussed in the literature include *flow* versus *structuralist functions* (see Borgatti & Foster, 2003). Flow models assume the main function of ties is enabling the

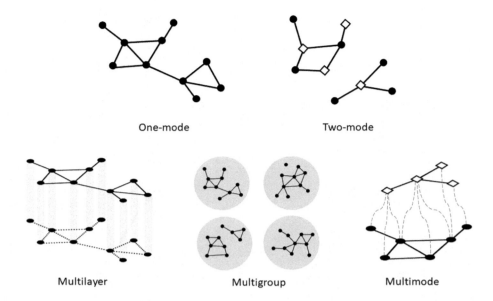

Figure 2.2 Different network formats

circulation of resources (such as information or commodities). One example of a flow model is *social influence theory*, which stipulates that behaviours and beliefs flow through a network, leading to actors becoming more similar to their socially tied peers (Friedkin & Johnsen, 2011). Structuralist models assume that the structural patterns of networks empower or constrain the choices and behaviours of actors. An example of a structuralist model is *structural holes* theory (Burt, 2004), which argues that actors positioned as brokers hold a strategic advantage over others, enabling them easier access to new information and ideas. Often, networks have both flow and structuralist functions. For example, roads in a transportation network enable the flow of traffic, and the structure of the road-system locks locations in Euclidean space, thus impacting actors' attempts to move from one location to the next.

Most studies either implicitly or explicitly adopt one (or both) of these views of network function. Having a clearer understanding of the assumptions one is making in relation to network functionality can improve the clarity of one's theoretical claims.

FORMULATING RESEARCH QUESTIONS

Research questions pertaining to networks can be discerned along two key dimensions. The first dimension pertains to the *causal role* of networks, where a distinction is made between explaining the outcomes of networks (i.e., networks act as *explanans*) and uncovering the drivers of networks (i.e., networks as *explanandum*). The second dimension pertains to a network's *level of analysis* – that is, the individual actor, dyad, subgroup, or network level.

Analytic approaches differ greatly based on the causal role of networks and their level of analysis, and thus clarifying research questions on these two dimensions is important for ascertaining a suitable method (Agneessens, 2020). The following sections offer several examples of research questions along these dimensions.

Networks as Explanans

Studies treating networks as explanans consider how network patterns predict outcomes for individuals, collectives, or the network as a whole. Questions on the individual level pertain to how a node's pattern of ties or its network position affects that node's outcomes. This includes (but is not limited to) research within the social capital tradition, where features of an actor's personal network – for example, the number of contacts, or level of closure, are linked to outcomes such as individual achievement (Burt, 2004) or social mobility (Lin, et al., 2011). Studies focusing on the position of individual nodes within a larger network structure, such as a core–periphery structure, may consider whether placement in one particular structural position (e.g., the core) yields more benefits or resource access than another (see, for example, Prell et al., this volume). Additional examples of networks-as-explanans research include the impacts of networks on (1) the kinds of interpersonal ties that form, for example, relations of imbalance and conflict, or, alternatively, trust and relational solidarity (Molm, 2010); (2) the speed and/or extent of diffusion processes (Centola, 2018); and (3) the relative effectiveness of residents monitoring and responding to threats (Sampson et al., 1997).

Networks as Explanandum

Turning to networks as explanandum leads to questions on the drivers of networks and network structure. Individual-level studies focus on explaining a node's position, such as its location in the core or otherwise, or explaining patterns of a node's personal network, such as an actor's degree centrality or heterogeneity of his/her alters. Examples of predictors for explaining individual-level networks include actor attributes (e.g., sociodemographics, perceptions, or personality traits), contextual factors (e.g., belonging to a church or political party), or the network structure itself (e.g., a node being embedded in a triad, see discussion on *endogeneity* below). Any of these predictors may shed light on why a node has acquired a particular network position or has a particular set of network patterns. In some cases, such predictors are also studied as outcomes of those same networks. For example, health may impact one's ability to socialise, but health may also be a consequence of being a central node in a network, as in the case of epidemics (Haas et al., 2010).

Research predicting higher-order network structures, such as dyads or triads, often pose the question of why ties are more (or less) likely to be found in a given configuration. For example, research shows that ties are more likely to form among actors who are physically or geographically proximate (Festinger et al., 1950), share common activities or *foci* (Feld, 1981) and/or share similar backgrounds, behaviours, or attitudes (i.e. the theory of homophily; McPherson et al., 2001). Another driver is network *endogeneity* – which refers to ties being present/absent in response to inherent structural tendencies of the network. Two common endogenous processes include *transitivity* (when a tie forms between two actors that already share a third actor in common) and the Matthew Effect (Merton, 1968), which refers to actors maintaining their popularity via sustaining ties and attracting new ones.

Other research focuses on explaining network topology – that is, the overall network structure or signature of a network. Mechanistic approaches emphasise formal theories for explaining stylised network structures, such as explaining small-world structures via local configurations like transitive triads and two-paths (Robins et al., 2005) or explaining scale-free networks via preferential attachment (Barabási & Albert, 1999). Here, little emphasis is placed on understanding empirical networks (Marin & Wellman, 2011) and relations tend to be conceptualised in simple, utilitarian terms (Prell & Lo, 2016). By contrast, macrostructural arguments reveal how empirically observed network structures, such as a polarised network, emerge from patterns found in the population, such as wealth or age distributions, associations between actor attributes, or sizes of subgroups (Blau, 1977; Mayhew, 1980). A key insight from these macrostructural studies is that the same topological outcomes may arise when actors are randomly paired, due to the population being structured in a particular way.

Finally, a growing body of literature focuses on the intertwined changes in both networks and actors' attributes over time. Such a co-evolutionary approach enables scholars to disentangle social selection processes from social influence (Snijders et al., 2010). Such work also reveals the relative strength of various processes (adams et al., 2022) and how emergent outcomes (such as inequality) may arise from these intertwined tendencies (DiMaggio & Garip, 2012).

SOCIAL NETWORK RESEARCH DESIGNS

There are a variety of different kinds of research designs for studying social networks (a more thorough discussion is provided by Robins, 2015). This chapter considers the two most common types found in the literature – complete versus ego network studies.

COMPLETE NETWORK STUDIES

When studying a complete network, a researcher assumes that the set of network members comprises the entire population of interest. Identifying the boundary of this network population can thus be a challenge (discussed below). In addition, gathering network data on all network members, especially in the case of surveys or structured interviews, can lead to respondent fatigue and potentially low response rates. Yet once data have been gathered, complete network studies offer a wide range of analytical possibilities, allowing researchers to test hypotheses at the ego, dyadic and higher levels. In addition, complete network studies capture the *absence* of ties, thus allowing for a wider exploration of relational phenomena. Finally, data are gathered on both the attributes and ties for all network members, which enables researchers to explore the various associations between actor attributes, ties, network configurations and the larger network structure.

PERSONAL OR EGO NETWORK STUDIES

Ego network studies gather and analyse data on a set of focal actors (egos) and their alters. Data are gathered (typically through surveys) from a sample of independent egos. The data include information on the ties between egos and their alters, the attributes of egos and alters and, in many cases, ties among the alters themselves. Network measures, such as density or cohesion, are then calculated on these ego networks and treated as ego attributes, thus enabling the use of standard regression techniques. Studies on social support (e.g., Faber & Wasserman, 2002), social movements (e.g., Tindall et al., 2021) and social capital (e.g., Hällsten et al., 2015) typically make use of ego network research designs.

Scholars may prefer adopting an ego-network research design, for example, when the population (network boundary) is unknown, when the research questions are limited to the individual (ego) level and/or when research aims include understanding ego network features across various contexts, as opposed to focusing only on the ties and actors within a prescribed boundary. However, there are some drawbacks to ego network studies, such as alters not being given a chance to comment on the tie reported by ego (which risks self-attribution bias). Please see Perry et al. (this volume) for more guidance on ego network studies.

STUDYING SOCIAL NETWORKS

Individual chapters in this handbook offer readers examples for studying social networks, yet newcomers to the field may wonder how to get started in constructing a research design of their own. This section offers a simple overview of some of the main considerations for studying complete networks (although some of the advice may apply to ego network studies as well).

GETTING STARTED: WHICH RELATIONS TO STUDY AND WHY

Designing a network study should begin with an understanding of the relevant literature and the unique nature of the research context. One should seek to identify which relations matter most for the research topic, context and theory, as not all relations are the same, and different relations can serve different functions (Borgatti & Foster, 2003). In some cases, a researcher has little control of which relation(s) can be measured, as in the case of secondary analysis of available social network data. Here, one must consider the appropriateness of research questions given the network at one's disposal and the suitability of the dataset for the researcher's aims.

DETERMINING THE NETWORK BOUNDARY

For complete network studies, generating a full list of network members relies on how researchers define the *network boundary* – that is, the criterion or criteria that determine network membership. Some contexts have clear boundaries, such as classrooms (Knecht et al., 2011) or organisations (Borgatti & Foster, 2003), yet a number of other empirical settings require more thought.

Laumann et al. (1983) developed criteria that many network analysts use for specifying the boundary. The *realist* approach involves actors declaring their own network membership, whereas a *nominalist* approach uses research objectives as the primary guide. Building on these two distinctions, the authors offer four additional criteria, each of which can be adopted by either a realist or nominalist approach. A *positional-attribute focus* defines a boundary by the presence or absence of an attribute; a *reputational focus* relies on informants to identify network members; a *social relations focus* identifies network members based on the presence or absence of certain social ties; and an *event-driven focus* identifies network members via their participation in certain activities or events.

Increasingly, scholars argue that boundary specification should primarily be based on a nominalist approach and, hence, be determined by theory and research questions (Borgatti & Halgin, 2011; Butts, 2008; Nowell et al., 2018; Robins, 2015; Scott, 2017). In some cases, however, a mixed approach is advisable, especially in more participatory research contexts in which stakeholders inform aspects of the research process, making boundary considerations a balance between the analysts' and stakeholders' objectives (Hauck et al., 2016; Nowell et al., 2018; Prell et al., 2021; Schiffer & Hauck, 2010).

MEASUREMENT AND DATA COLLECTION

Once relations and network members have been specified, a logical next step is designing measures for capturing relationships of interest. Here, we summarise common ways of measuring relationships and discuss some of the main trade-offs or concerns in terms of reliability or validity.

Name, Position and Resource Generators

The three generators discussed in this section are all aimed at eliciting names of contacts from an ego. These generators are typically included in surveys used for ego-network studies as the network boundary is unknown, thus requiring researchers to rely on a respondent's ability to recall (generate) a list of contacts. *Name generators* ask egos to nominate individuals (alters) with whom they share a particular kind of tie. For example, the 1985 General Social Survey contains a question asking respondents to nominate individuals *with whom they discussed important matters*. Name generators may fix the number of alters a respondent names (referred to as a *fixed-recall* generator) or allow respondents to nominate as many alters as they wish (a *free-recall* generator). Although fixed-recall approaches reduce respondent fatigue, they may only capture the strongest ties (Marsden, 1990), thus potentially omitting actors and ties important for the network. A *position generator* asks egos to name individuals in their personal networks who occupy a particular position, such as a lawyer or doctor (Lin & Dumin, 1986). Similarly, a *resource generator* asks respondents to list individuals that have particular skills or resources, such as fixing or loaning a car (Van Der Gaag & Snijders, 2005).

Once an ego has nominated a set of alters, additional information on alters may be gathered via *name interpreter questions*. For ego-network studies, name interpreter questions are the sole means for gathering alter attribute data. Similarly, *relationship-interpreter questions* can be used to gain additional information on the tie between two actors, such as the tie strength, relationship history, or a tie's meaning to the respondent (Kreager et al., 2017).

Research has shown that generators tend to be more reliable at capturing stronger or more stable ties than weaker and/or more short-term relations (Marsden & Campbell, 1984; Freeman et al., 1987). Studies have also shown that generator questions tend to capture approximately 50 per cent of the same data gathered via observation (Bernard et al., 1979; Bernard & Killworth, 1977; Killworth & Bernard, 2008). Taken together, when studying stable patterns of networks, relying on respondents' own views of their contacts is still justifiable (Robins, 2015).

Surveys using generators may likewise be used for complete network studies, yet a preferable method is the use of roster. Here, the survey contains a list of all network members (the roster), and each network member is asked to select names from the roster that meet some criteria (e.g., who is the respondent's collaborator or friend). The survey may then include additional relationship-interpreter questions, such as how often the respondent meets with that person and so on. Assuming that the survey is also gathering attribute and/or behavioural data from each respondent, name interpreter questions are no longer necessary (although *perceptions* of alters may be valuable information, depending on the research questions). When the network is large (i.e., the roster is quite long), researchers may prefer using a fixed-recall name generator as a means to reduce respondents' fatigue (i.e., the need to laboriously read through all names on the roster).

Other Measures and Data-gathering Strategies

Although gathering network data via surveys has a long tradition in social network analysis, there are additional ways for researchers to gather such data (see Chapter 40 for further details). These include participant-observation (Roethlisberger & Dickson, 1939); historical archives (e.g., Padgett & Ansell, 1993), electronic archives such as Twitter (e.g., Takhteyev et al., 2012), or simulation (e.g., Robins et al., 2005; Prell & Lo, 2016).

ORGANISING YOUR DATA: EDGELIST VERSUS SOCIOMATRIX

Once data collection is complete, data must be organised into a suitable format for analysis. This section covers two of the most common: edgelists and sociomatrices.

Edgelists

An edgelist organises network data into a table consisting of a minimum of two columns, where the first column contains the IDs of actors that send ties, and the second column holds the IDs of the recipients of ties. Figure 2.3 shows an example of an edgelist. Edgelists may contain additional columns to hold edge attribute information, such as tie strength, type of relation, or temporal information. One should be aware that edgelists only contain ties that are present in a network, which means those network members holding no ties (isolates) are omitted from the edgelist.

Matrix Representations

Network data can also be represented in matrix form. For a one-mode network this takes the form of a sociomatrix, which is a square, actor-by-actor matrix in which the cells of the matrix represent the presence or absence of a tie (1s or 0s, respectively) from the node in row i to the node in column j. The diagonal of the matrix is typically set to 0 if the relationship from an actor to itself is undefined or of little interest to the researcher. For weighted network data, the cells in the sociomatrix contain values indicating tie strength. For non-directed networks, the sociomatrix is symmetrical, meaning the cells above the diagonal hold the same value as those below the diagonal (i.e., cells i,j and j,i are the same value).

For two-mode networks, rows are used to represent one set of actors (mode A) and columns for the second set (mode B). The matrix structure for a multilevel network consists of two square sociomatrices for the two one-mode networks (e.g., mode A and mode B) and one affiliation matrix connecting mode A with B. These various A, B and AB networks would be organised into three separate matrices and analysed jointly (see Jasny, this volume, for guidance on multimodal and multilevel analyses). Finally, a multigroup network in matrix form would consist of one large square matrix in which the multiple groups would lay along the diagonal and coded values (e.g., a structural zeros) would populate the remaining cells, to indicate the absence of ties between groups.

Network data are easily transformed between edgelist and matrix representations. Matrix formats generally require more computer memory because they track all dyads, including those with null ties, whereas edgelists require less, as they only contain ties that are present. However, matrices are preferred for matrix algebra calculations used to produce various network measures (e.g., indegree and outdegree can be calculated by summing matrix columns or rows, respectively). Some software applications may require one format or the other.

Organising Data for Actor Attributes

Researchers are often interested in how nodal attributes are associated with network structure. Nodal attribute data are typically structured in traditional case-by-variable format. This means that multiple data objects (and data structures) are often used for analysis. Ultimately, however, any/all data objects need to conform to the analytical package being used, and thus attention is needed as to which formats are required.

Sender	Receiver
1	2
1	4
2	4
4	1
4	5
5	4

Receiver

	1	2	3	4	5
1	0	1	0	1	0
2	0	0	0	1	0
3	0	0	0	0	0
4	1	0	0	0	1
5	0	0	0	1	0

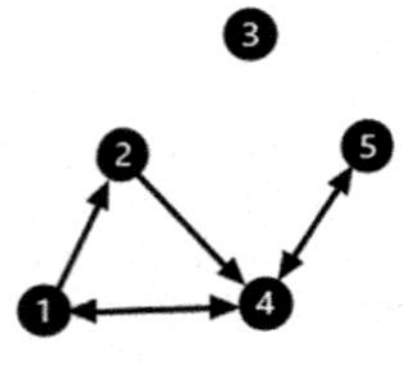

Sender

Figure 2.3 Network data organisation

SUMMARISING NETWORK DATA

This section mainly focuses on analyses for complete networks, beginning with descriptive measures. Network analysts use various descriptive measures (many covered in the chapters in this handbook) for acquiring a feeling for the shape and contours of the dataset, which in turn lay the groundwork for inferential analyses. A few common descriptive measures are found below.

Degree centrality captures how many ties a focal actor has and, for directed networks, it is distinguished between a node's incoming ties (i.e., indegree centrality) and its outgoing ties (i.e., outdegree centrality). Plotting the distribution of degree centrality scores is a common first step to understanding the differences in actors' level of connectivity. Everett and Borgatti (this volume) offer further centrality measures one may use for data exploration purposes.

Density refers to the portion of possible ties that are present in a given network, expressed as a proportion. Higher-density scores tend to reflect greater levels of cohesion. Density is useful to view alongside *network centralisation*, which measures the extent to which network ties are organised around a few actors and is also expressed as a proportion. For example, if both density and degree centralisation are (relatively) high, this may be interpreted as ties in the network being plentiful (all else being equal), yet unevenly distributed, in which case the cohesion of the network depends on the connectivity provided by a few central actors.

Other network summaries include the *dyad* and *triad censuses*, which count the frequencies of configurations such as those shown in Figure 2.1, among others (Holland & Leinhardt, 1970). Subgroup detection methods (Wasserman & Faust, 1994) and community detection algorithms (Porter et al., 2009), identify sets of more interconnected nodes that characterise social groupings. *Blockmodelling* assigns actors to sets or 'blocks' based on common patterns of relations (see Chapter 29 and Chapter 30, this volume). The chapters in this book will offer insights into many of these (and other) approaches.

Beyond descriptive network measures, analysts often visualise their network data in the form of a *graph* or, in the case of directed data, a *digraph*. Here, nodes are represented by a shape (typically a dot or circle) and the ties linking nodes are depicted as lines. Characteristics of nodes can also be displayed through the specification of nodal colour, shape, or size. For example, the centrality scores of actors are often conveyed via the size of nodes, while the colour or shape of nodes may represent an attribute such as gender or political affiliation. Typically, the placement of nodes in a graph is done via an algorithm such as a spring or high dimensional embedding technique (Battista et al., 1998; Brandes & Sedlmair, 2019). Alternatively, one may manually position nodes according to one's preferences, for example, grouping all nodes together that share a given colour or shape. Edge attributes can similarly be displayed, such as weighting lines to indicate tie strength, or using arrows to indicate tie directionality. Figure 2.4 is

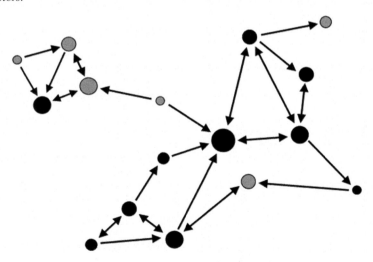

Digraph: nodes shaded by attribute and sized by indegree

Figure 2.4 Example of a digraph

an example of a digraph where node size reflects actors' indegree centrality (larger nodes indicating higher levels of centrality) and node colouring represents actors' gender.

INFERENCES AND HYPOTHESIS TESTING

Approaches to inferential network analysis range in complexity depending upon the nature of one's research question, coupled with the form of interdependence. Although interdependence is inherent to all network data, the form of interdependence varies, with implications for both measurement and inferential method. In some cases, interdependence between two actors can be handled via aggregation, as is typically the case with ego-network studies. Here, properties of an ego's local network (e.g., number of contacts, or level of constraint) are treated as an attribute of ego. Similarly, data gathered on independent, small groups (such as in social exchange experiments), may be summarised using group-level measures, such as the density for each group; and studies of multiple, independent networks (such as in a multigroup network studies) can treat network-level measures, such as density or centralisation, as attributes of the overall network. In all these examples, analysis can often rely upon conventional statistical approaches (e.g., OLS) that assume independent observations.

However, there are many instances where these summarisation strategies are not suitable. For example, predicting dyad-level outcomes with ego-centric network data can be complicated, given the interdependence of dyads (i.e., alters connected through a common ego), and thus one should consider methods like hierarchical models that nest dyads within egos (Perry et al., 2018). When using complete network data to answer questions about node-level outcomes, all units of analysis are potentially interdependent and, hence, network-autocorrelation models may be the best strategy (Leenders, 2002).

When complete networks are the outcome, one moves into the realm of *stochastic network models*. Here, one may be interested in explaining the features of a given network structure, change in network structure over time, or both. If data are cross-sectional, then the *exponential family of random graph model* (ERGM) is a widespread approach for network analysis (Robins et al., 2007). An ERGM represents network structure via a set of specified configurations representing the network properties of interest (e.g., mutuality, transitivity, homophily; see Figure 2.1). The model evaluates the likelihood of these various configurations, net of one another. If one is not interested in testing for configurations, and simply wishes to test the effect of one or more predictors on a dyadic outcome, then a permutation approach quadratic assignment procedure, or QAP (Krackhardt, 1987) or its extension, the multiple regression QAP, i.e. MRQAP (Dekker et al., 2007), is sufficient.

Another set of models capture change in networks over time. For example, *stochastic actor-oriented models* (SAOMs) (Snijders, 2001) model changes to network structure with network panel data consisting of two or more discrete time points of observation. Changes to the network are modelled via a utility function which assumes the viewpoint of an ego creating, maintaining or ending ties to other actors, given the structure of the network, and given the attributes/behaviours of ego and other actors. This utility function guides the estimation procedure, which simulates changes between (discrete) observations via a series of micro-steps that resemble a Markov chain. In addition to modelling change in network structure, SAOMs also include a function capturing change in actor behaviour (Steglich et al., 2010). Changes in network(s) and behaviour(s) are estimated simultaneously, allowing one to pursue questions regarding co-evolution and disentangling processes of social influence from selection (Steglich et al., 2010). The SAOM is flexible enough to handle changes in multiple networks, including one-mode and two-mode network co-evolution (Snijders et al., 2013).

A *dynamic ERGM* may also be used to estimate discrete change from one network observation to the next (Schaefer & Marcum, 2020). However, unlike the SAOM, ERGMs cannot model endogenous change in actor attributes and other co-evolutionary processes. Moreover, a key distinction between the dynamic ERGM and SAOM is that the latter represents actor tendencies to make particular network selection decisions (i.e., reciprocate an incoming tie, or add a tie that closes a triad) as opposed to the dynamic ERGM, which models the tendency to observe a given structure (i.e., a mutual dyad or transitive triad).

Finally, an emerging class of models focuses on the micro-dynamics of temporal interactions (i.e., networks of event data). The *relational event model* (REM) analyses patterns within data on dyadic events and their timing. The model can represent interactional dynamics like turn-taking, reciprocity and usurping at the moment-to-moment level, as well as cumulative effects across prior interactions (see Schecter & Contractor, this volume).

A NOTE ON ETHICS

The concern for the ethical issues unique to social networks has been growing and a recent special issue on this topic can be found in the journal

Social Networks (see October 2021, volume 67). A few of the main issues for a newcomer to the field are summarised here.

Anonymity is an ethical concern, especially for complete network studies, as respondents will typically see their own name and the names of other network members when completing the survey. This may make respondents uncomfortable, and thus an informed consent form should clearly address how participants' identity will be treated throughout the course of the study and after the study's completion. In addition, there is the risk of deductive disclosure. For example, if nodes in graphs are coloured or sized based on actor characteristics, then someone familiar with the context and/or the network may be able to deduce the identities of individuals or subgroups. To help decrease the likelihood of this occurring, one can avoid identifying individual nodes in the digraph, keep the research site anonymous (Robins, 2015) and keep the timeframe of the study general.

Another ethical issue pertains to how results will ultimately be used. For example, will results of an organisational network study potentially lead to some employees being treated differently because they are not as central to the network as others (Borgatti & Molina, 2005)? Similarly, researchers of criminal networks may be required to report to government officials any knowledge of criminal behaviours, and public health officials must often report incidents of infectious diseases, such as HIV and other STIs (adams, 2020). Again, what is critical here is informed consent: respondents should be made aware of how results will be used.

FINAL NOTES

This chapter touched on some of the main concepts, terms and research design considerations for newcomers to the field. Additional chapters in this handbook will increase readers' foundational knowledge base, and readers may wish to also explore the resources found on the website insna.org.

REFERENCES

adams, j. (2020). *Gathering social network data*. Sage.

adams, j., Lawrence, E.M., Goode, J.A., Schaefer, D.R., & Mollborn, S. (2022). Peer network processes in adolescents' health lifestyles. *Journal of Health and Social Behavior*, 63(1), 125–141.

Agneessens, F. (2020). Dyadic, nodal, and group-level approaches to study the antecedents and consequences of networks. In R. Light & J. Moody (Eds.), *The Oxford handbook of social networks* (pp. 188–218). Oxford University Press.

Barabási A., & Albert R. (1999). Emergence of scaling in random networks. *Science*, 286(5439), 509–512. doi.org/10.1126/science.286.5439.509

Battista, G.D., Eades, P., Tamassia, R., & Tollis, I.G. (1998). *Graph drawing: algorithms for the visualization of graphs*. Prentice Hall.

Bernard, H.R., & Killworth, P.D. (1977). Informant accuracy in social network data II. *Human Communication Research*, 4(1), 3–18. doi.org/10.1111/j.1468-2958.1977.tb00591.x

Bernard, H.R., Killworth, P.D., & Sailer, L. (1979). Informant accuracy in social network data IV: a comparison of clique-level structure in behavioral and cognitive network data. *Social Networks*, 2(3), 191–218. doi.org/10.1016/0378-8733(79)90014-5

Blau, P. (1977). *Inequality and heterogeneity: a primitive theory of social structure*. Free Press.

Bojanowski, M., & Corten, R. (2014). Measuring segregation in social networks. *Social Networks*, 39, 14–32.

Borgatti, S.P., & Foster, P.C. (2003). The network paradigm in organizational research: a review and typology. *Journal of Management*, 29(6), 991–1013. doi.org/10.1016/S0149-2063_03_00087-4

Borgatti, S.P., & Halgin, D.S. (2011). On network theory. *Organization Science*, 1–13.

Borgatti, S.P., Mehra, A., Brass, D.J., & Labianca, G. (2009). Network analysis in the social sciences. *Science*, 323(5916), 892–895. doi.org/10.1126/science.1165821

Borgatti, S., & Molina, J.L. (2005). Toward ethical guidelines for network research in organizations. *Social Networks*, 27, 107–117. doi.org/10.1016/j.socnet.2005.01.004

Brandes, U., & Sedlmair, M. (2019). Network visualization. In F. Biagini, G. Kauwermann & T. Meyer-Brandis (Eds.), *Network Science*. Springer.

Butts, C.T. (2008). Social network analysis: a methodological introduction. *Asian Journal of Social Psychology*, 11, 13–41.

Burt, R.S. (2004). Structural holes and good ideas. *American Journal of Sociology*, 110(2), 349–399. doi.org/10.1086/421787

Centola, D. (2018). *How behavior spreads*. Princeton University Press.

Crossley, N., Bellotti, E., Edwards, G., & Everett, M.G. (2022). *Social network analysis for ego-nets*. Sage. doi.org/10.4135/9781473911871

Dekker, D., Krackhardt, D., & Snijders, T.A. (2007). Sensitivity of MRQAP tests to collinearity and autocorrelation conditions. *Psychometrika*, 72(4), 563–581.

DiMaggio, P., & Garip, F. (2012). Network effects and social inequality. *Annual Review of Sociology*, 38, 93–118.

Eades, P. (1984). A heuristic for graph drawing. *Congressus Numerantium*, 42, 149–160.

Faber, A.D., & Wasserman, S. (2002). Social support and social networks: synthesis and review. In J.A. Levy & B.A. Pescosolido (Eds.), *Social networks and health* (Vol. 8, pp. 29–72). Emerald. doi. org/10.1016/S1057-6290(02)80020-1

Feld, S.L. (1981). The focused organization of social ties. *American Journal of Sociology*, 86(5), 1015–1035.

Festinger, L., Schachter, S., & Back, K. (1950). *Social pressures in informal groups: a study of human factors in housing*. Harper and Brothers.

Freeman, L.C. (1992). The sociological concept of 'group': an empirical test of two models. *American Journal of Sociology*, 98(1), 152–166. doi.org/10.1086/229972

Freeman, L.C. (2004). *The development of social network analysis: a study in the sociology of science*. Empirical Press. books.google.nl/books?id=VcxqQgAACAAJ

Freeman, L.C., Romney, A.K., & Freeman, S.C. (1987). Cognitive structure and informant accuracy. *American Anthropologist*, 89(2), 310–325. JSTOR.

Friedkin, N.E., & Johnsen, E.C. (2011). *Social influence network theory: a sociological examination of small group dynamics*. Cambridge University Press; Cambridge Core. doi.org/10.1017/CBO9780511976735

Gould, R.V., & Fernandez, R.M. (1989). Structures of mediation: A formal approach to brokerage in transaction networks. *Sociological Methodology*, 19, 89–126.

Haas, S.A., Schaefer, D.R., & Kornienko, O. (2010). Health and the structure of adolescent social networks. *Journal of Health and Social Behavior*, 51(4), 424–439. doi.org/10.1177/0022146510386791

Hällsten, M., Edling, C., & Rydgren, J. (2015). The effects of specific occupations in position generator measures of social capital. *Social Networks*, 40, 55–63. doi.org/10.1016/j.socnet.2013.06.002

Hauck, J., Schmidt, J., & Werner, A. (2016). Using social network analysis to identify key stakeholders in agricultural biodiversity governance and related land-use decisions at regional and local level. *Ecology and Society*, 21(2). doi.org/10.5751/es-08596-210249

Holland, P.W., & Leinhardt, S. (1970). A method for detecting structure in sociometric data. *American Journal of Sociology*, 76(3), 492–513. JSTOR.

Holland, P.W., & Leinhardt, S. (1972). Some evidence on the transitivity of positive interpersonal sentiment. *American Journal of Sociology*, 72, 1205–1209.

Killworth, P., & Bernard, H. (2008). Informant accuracy in social network data. *Human Organization*, 35(3), 269–286. doi.org/10.17730/humo.35.3.10215j2m359266n2

Knecht, A.K., Burk, W.J., Weesie, J., & Steglich, C. (2011). Friendship and alcohol use in early adolescence: a multilevel social network approach. *Journal of Research on Adolescence*, 21(2), 475. doi.org/10.1111/j.1532-7795.2010.00685.x

Knoke, D., Diani, M., Hollway, J., & Christopoulos, D. (2021). *Multimodal political networks*. Cambridge University Press.

Krackardt, D. (1987). QAP partialling as a test of spuriousness. *Social Networks*, 9(2), 171–186.

Kreager, D.A., Young, J.T., Haynie, D.L., Bouchard, M., Schaefer, D.R., & Zajac, G. (2017). Where 'old heads' prevail: inmate hierarchy in a men's prison unit. *American Sociological Review*, 82(4), 685–718.

Laumann, E., Marsden, P., & Prensky, D. (1983). The boundary specification problem in network analysis. *Applied Network Analysis: A Methodological Introduction*, 61.

Leenders, R.T.A. (2002). Modeling social influence through network autocorrelation: constructing the weight matrix. *Social Networks*, 24(1), 21–47.

Lewis, K. (2021). Digital networks: elements of a theoretical framework. *Social Networks*, doi.org/10.1016/j.socnet.2021.12.002

Lin, N., Cook, K., & Burt, R. (2011). *Social capital: theory and research*. Routledge.

Lin, N., & Dumin, M. (1986). Access to occupations through social ties. *Social Networks*, 8(4), 365–385.

Marin, A., & Wellman, B. (2011). Social network analysis: an introduction. *The SAGE handbook of social network analysis*. Sage.

Marsden, P. (1990). Network data and measurement. *Annual Review of Sociology*, 16, 435–463.

Marsden, P.V., & Campbell, K.E. (1984). Measuring tie strength. *Social Forces*, 63(2), 482–501. JSTOR. doi.org/10.2307/2579058

Mayhew, B.H. (1980). Structuralism versus Individualism: Part 1, shadowboxing in the dark. *Social Forces*, 59(2), 335–375. JSTOR. doi.org/10.2307/2578025

McPherson, M., Smith-Lovin, L., & Cook, J.M. (2001). Birds of a feather: homophily in social networks. *Annual Review of Sociology*, 27(1), 415–443. doi.org/10.1146/annurev.soc.27.1.415

Merton, R.K. (1968). The Matthew effect in science. *Science*, 159(3810), 56–63. doi.org/10.1126/science.159.3810.56

Molm, L.D. (2010). The structure of reciprocity. *Social Psychology Quarterly*, 73(2), 119–131.

Moreno, J.L., & Jennings, H. (1934). *Who shall survive? A new approach to the problem of human interrelations*. Nervous and Mental Disease Pub. Co.; /z-wcorg/

Nowell, B.L., Velez, A.-L. K., Hano, M.C., Sudweeks, J., Albrecht, K., & Steelman, T. (2018). Studying networks in complex problem domains: advancing methods in boundary specification. *Perspectives on Public Management and Governance*, 1–10.

Padgett, J.F., & Ansell, C.K. (1993). Robust action and the rise of the Medici, 1400–1433. *American Journal of Sociology*, *98*(6), 1259–1319. JSTOR.

Perry, B.L., Pescosolido, B.A., & Borgatti, S.P. (2018). *Egocentric network analysis: foundations, methods, and models*. Cambridge University Press; CambridgeCore. doi.org/10.1017/9781316443255

Porter, M.A., Onnela, J.P., & Mucha, P.J. (2009). Communities in networks. *Notices of the AMS*, *56*(9), 1082–1097.

Prell, C. (2012). *Social network analysis: history, theory, and methodology*. Sage.

Prell, C., & Lo, Y.-J. (2016). Network formation and knowledge gains. *Journal of Mathematical Sociology*, *40*(1), 21–52. doi.org/10.1080/0022250X.2015.1112385

Prell, C., Hesed, C.D.M., Johnson, K., Paolisso, M., Teodoro, J.D., & Van Dolah, E. (2021). Transdisciplinarity and shifting network boundaries: the challenges of studying an evolving stakeholder network in participatory settings. *Field Methods*, 1525822X20983983. doi.org/10.1177/1525822X20983984

Robins, G. (2015). *Doing social network research: network research design for social scientists* (18182721). Sage.

Robins, G., Pattison, P., Kalish, Y., & Lusher, D. (2007). An introduction to exponential random graph (p*) models for social networks. *Social Networks*, *29*(2), 173–191.

Robins, G., Pattison, P., & Woolcock, J. (2005). Small and other worlds: global network structures from local processes. *American Journal of Sociology*, *110*(4), 894–936. doi.org/10.1086/427322

Roethlisberger, F.J., & Dickson, W.J. (1939). *Management and the worker*. Harvard University Press.

Sampson, R.J., Raudenbush, S.W., & Earls, F. (1997). Neighborhoods and violent crime: a multilevel study of collective efficacy. *Science*, *277* (5328), 918–923. doi.org/10.1126/science.277.5328.918

Schaefer, D.R., & Marcum, C.S. (2020). Modeling network dynamics. In R. Light & J. Moody (Eds.), *The Oxford handbook of social networks* (pp. 254–287). Oxford University Press.

Schiffer, E., & Hauck, J. (2010). Net-Map: collecting social network data and facilitating network learning through participatory influence network mapping. *Field Methods*, *22*(3), 231–249. doi.org/10.1177/1525822X10374798

Scott, J. (2017). *Social network analysis: a handbook* (4th ed.). Sage.

Snijders, T.A.B. (2001). The statistical evaluation of social network dynamics. *Sociological Methodology*, *31*(1), 361–395.

Snijders, T.A.B., van de Bunt, G.G., & Steglich, C.E.G. (2010). Introduction to stochastic actor-based models for network dynamics. *Social Networks*, *32*(1), 44–60. doi.org/DOI: 10.1016/j.socnet.2009.02.004

Snijders, T.A., Lomi, A., & Torló, V.J. (2013). A model for the multiplex dynamics of two-mode and one-mode networks, with an application to employment preference, friendship, and advice. *Social Networks*, *35*(2), 265–276.

Steglich, C.E.G., Snijders, T.A.B., & Pearson, M. (2010). Dynamic networks and behavior: separating selection from influence. *Sociological Methodology*, *40*(1), 329–393.

Takhteyev, Y., Gruzd, A., & Wellman, B. (2012). Geography of Twitter networks. *Capturing Context: Integrating Spatial and Social Network Analyses*, *34*(1), 73–81. doi.org/10.1016/j.socnet.2011.05.006

Tindall, D.B., Howe, A.C., & Mauboulès, C. (2021). Tangled roots: personal networks and the participation of individuals in an anti-environmentalism countermovement. *Sociological Perspectives*, *64*(1), 5–36. doi.org/10.1177/0731121420908886

Van Der Gaag, M., & Snijders, T.A.B. (2005). The resource generator: social capital quantification with concrete items. *Social Networks*, *27*(1), 1–29. doi.org/10.1016/j.socnet.2003.10.001

Wasserman, S., & Faust, K. (1994). *Social network analysis: methods and applications*. Cambridge University Press.

Social Networks and Social Categories

Ronald Breiger and Robin Wagner-Pacifici

Categories are interesting because in important ways they are the 'opposite' of networks. This opposition, along with many productive efforts to overcome it, is at the core of several of the most influential foundational streams of contemporary social network research. In this chapter we critically review research on networks and categories as a general issue confronting social network analysis, and we point to challenges for future work in this area as well as some directions for meeting these challenges.

BACKGROUND

By the mid-1960s, Harrison White understood his research agenda as having both a positive thrust and a negative one. He saw the 'positive thrust' of his thinking as about *networks*, the relational space of social life. By contrast, White perceived 'the negative thrust' as the necessity of arguing 'against the attributes … and the associated panoply of variables … and statistical testing then and still predominant, despite [having] little phenomenological or causative depth', referring to the latter as conventional or 'categorical' social description and analysis (White, [1965] 2008b, pp. 1, 3). In the following decades White and his research group began to generate 'so much important theory and research focused on social networks that social scientists everywhere … could no longer ignore the idea' (Freeman, 2011, p. 27).

In an influential paper, White et al. (1976, p. 733) argued that in modern societies categorical boundaries for social relations have been fraying or dissolving (as seen, for example, in the increased importance of contracts, careers and social connections that cross-cut conventional status, community and class boundaries), whereas 'in our view, the major problem with postclassical social theory has been that its concepts remain wedded to categorical imagery'. Motivating much of the subsequent development of social network analysis has been an 'anticategorical imperative' (Emirbayer & Goodwin, 1994), rejecting 'the primacy of attributional categories and other substantives' (Emirbayer, 1997, p. 298) in favour of 'observable processes-in-relations' (White, 1997, p. 60).[1]

However, our story does not end, but only begins, with an assertion of a simple opposition between networks and categories. Things are not as straightforward as that. For example, as White recognised, networks themselves can be seen as ties among categories. The sociometric representation of a simple network – a table with one row (and the corresponding column) for each actor, and a 1 (or 0) in each cell indicating the presence (or absence) of a tie between them – 'can be regarded as formally similar to a cross tabulation …, with each person being regarded as a category and the relations being the items to be cross-tabulated' (White, 2008b, p. 2). 'Positions' in networks, sets of actors identified on the basis of having similar patterns of ties, are therefore analogous to aggregations of categories (Cheng & Park, 2020; Lin & Hung, 2022), an idea that Lorrain and White (1971) formalised early on as an algebra of categories. Likewise, a single category is a meaningless idea. 'To say category is to mean a system of categories' (White, 2008b, p. 4). Moreover, the individual actors who populate social networks may themselves be viewed as arising from intersections of social categories (Mützel & Kressin, 2021, pp. 221–222).[2]

In brief: alongside the oft-voiced slogan that networks and categories are 'opposites', two alternative visions – social networks as relations among intersecting categories and categories as systems of relations – have been at the root of a good deal of the development of social network analysis. These partially overlapping, partially conflicting visions have contributed to making social network analysis the many-splendored scientific endeavour that it is.

NETWORKS AND CATEGORIES AS A GENERAL ISSUE

We proceed by delineating several of the most influential ways of thinking about, modelling and criticising the relation of social networks and social categories.

Categories from Relations and Flows

John Mohr was a pioneering analyst who reoriented the methods of network analysis in order to explore collective cultural models (DiMaggio, 2020; see also Rawlings & Childress, 2021; Wagner-Pacifici & Breiger, 2020). In an early study of the welfare system in New York City as it operated in a period spanning the beginning of the twentieth century, Mohr (1994; Mohr & Duquenne, 1997) focused on categories by which welfare recipients were labelled in administrative records (working men, immigrant women, mothers, the blind, soldiers, tramps and so on). He analysed the network of profile similarity among these categories based on the services provided (job training, workhouse, reformatory, temporary shelter, fresh air vacation, etc.). Mohr aggregated the categories in order to identify what he referred to as discourse roles (identities subject to similar treatment; DiMaggio, 2020, p. 3). The network analysis identified a set of categorical labels (including soldiers, widows, sailors) for people who were seen to have earned entitlement (for having served their country, or for having been married), and a distinct set of categories of persons (including mothers, working boys, working girls, working women) who were argued to be tightly coupled to the domestic sphere (Mohr, 1994, p. 349). These aggregated categories (discourse roles), identified from the relational analysis, seemed to capture the underpinnings of the moral order of the welfare system studied (cf. Skocpol, 1992).

Mohr's work on discourse roles has been foundational for understanding categories on the basis of the social relations that comprise and link them. Stuhler (2021), who studies overtime change in categories by which refugees are portrayed in German news media, by constructing a network of categories from profiles of attributes used in discourse about each category, sets forth conceptual and methodological groundwork for a general approach to discourse role analysis.

Searching for the categories that emerge from discovered or postulated relational configurations has been consequential as well in other research domains. In the study of social mobility, how many categories should be used in constructing a mobility table, and which ones should they be? For example, should the category 'salaried professionals' be grouped with 'self-employed professionals', or alternatively with 'managers' within what might be identified as a salaried middle class, or (a third possibility) not grouped with any other category? Decisions such as these are fundamental, because the analyst ought to consider the classification itself as part of the model specification (Duncan, 1984). Like a social network, a mobility table portrays flows among categories. Most often, the categories are occupations, and the flows are counts of people who transit from an earlier to a later categorical status. It is possible to define a set of categories reflexively so as to make a given model for relationships among the categories (such a 'homogeneity' of mobility flow within and between the categories) work, as in models of Breiger (1981), Goodman (1981), Marsden (1985) and Cheng and Park (2020). Breiger and Mohr (2004) relate similar models for categorical data to the social network logic of structural equivalence.

Catness × Netness = Organisation

Consider a set of persons and their friendship ties. Some have friends of friends, some have more indirect ties of friendship (through longer chains of intermediaries) to others, and often the indirect friendship ties link pairs of persons who are (by a direct connection) friends. As the density of ties among a subset of persons in the net reaches some threshold, the subset will come to regard itself as having an identity (White, 2008b, p. 8). 'Most of the pairs in the subset may not be connected by the net relation in a given time, but because of the feeling of identity all relations will be regarded as present in a latent way,' and any person in the subset will feel free to 'mobilise' another such person (p. 8). This set of network actors has become what White termed a *catnet*, in that they jointly exhibit features of a network and a categorical identity as members of a friendship circle or clique. As a collective identity that induces a reductive simplification of the pattern of network ties, catnets can lower the costs of interaction (Krinsky & Mische, 2013, p. 11).

White understood that his catnet concept represented 'some retrenchment on my glib disdain for conventional, "categorical" as I called it, social description and analysis', bringing in culture (in the form of categorical identity) jointly with networks. Indeed, the catnet concept was 'my effort to square the circle of network truth with some categorical aspects of sociocultural reality' (White, 2008c, p. 2).

If there are overlapping networks of different types of tie (say, friendship and advising among the managers in a corporate law firm), the catnet may be identified as clumps of individuals who share a patterning of direct and indirect connections across the multiple networks. For example, as a general rule in the firm studied by Lazega and Pattison (1999), two advisors of the same manager may be friends with each other, whereas advisors of advisors are not friends.[3] White referred to this kind of structuring of direct and indirect relations, across multiple types of tie, as 'a theory held in that culture', in that it exists independently of the concrete network of connections (White, [1965] 2008b, p. 12). This is 'the cultural definition of a net' that White referred to as a *frame* (evidently borrowing and repurposing the latter term from Goffman, 1974). White further developed his thinking about catnets in the two editions of *Identity and control* (White, 1992, 2008a).

Charles Tilly had attended some of White's Harvard lectures in the mid-1960s, and the two were often in productive intellectual conversation. Tilly and White would, three decades later, become the two most eminent generators of intellectual excitement in the 'New York School' of social network analysis (Mische, 2011). Tilly began working out his own highly influential version of White's catnet concept in a book (Tilly, 1978) that became 'a kind of Ur-text in both social movement analysis and structural sociology' and that is 'probably the single most important text which has contributed to spreading White's insights well beyond the original network of White's students' (Santoro, 2008, p. 12). Tilly turned both categories and networks into variables in a two-dimensional diagram, theorising that 'the more extensive its common identity and internal networks, the more organised the group. CATNESS × NETNESS = ORGANIZATION' (Tilly, 1978, pp. 63–64, original emphasis).

John Scott's (2022) theory of structure and social action may be seen to pose interesting challenges for the concept of catnets. Scott distinguishes a deep structure of 'underlying' relations among categories of actors ('formational structures') from social interactions including, for example, companionship and antagonism ('figurational structures'). The distinction builds upon David Lockwood's discussion of system integration (the fit or coherence among the structural parts of a social system) and social integration (the extensiveness of social order among actors; Scott 2022, p. 73). With respect to these distinctions, the analytical gain from Tilly's approach to catnets was insight into the joint necessity of (categorical) identity and a density of network ties above some threshold in order to attain social movement mobilisation and organisation. The theoretical regress implicit in Tilly's version, as Santoro (2008, pp. 12–13) has noted, is the loss of White's distinctive perspective on framing – that is, the rule-like catenation of multiple types of tie that arise from network connections even as they are independent of the specific connections among a movement's members.

Categories as the Infrastructure for Networks

This is the opposite of the emphasis on categories being created by relations and flows. In important ways, social networks could not begin to be understood without recognising their rootedness in social categories. Perhaps the most fundamental move in social network analysis is to map a mathematical graph (or more generally, a network) onto some social phenomenon.[4] This requires specifying which social entities are to be mapped into the vertices of the network, which inevitably depends on categorical thinking (e.g., 'person' is a category of social entity, as are 'corporation', 'giraffe', 'city', 'gang' and so forth). The specification of the edges or connections in the network (which, in graph theory, are just pairs of vertices) requires no less categorical thinking, in the form of distinctions between types of relation such as 'friendship', 'director of', 'resource supplier', 'shares a gang tattoo with' and many others. As White (2008b, p. 2) asserts: 'Population is essentially a categorical concept; so the concept of net [network] is not in fact independent of cat [category].'

Identification of networks based on categorical distinctions used in documents (amicus briefs, in contrast to court decisions) reflect social movement as distinct from elite orientations in Espinoza-Kulick's (2020) study of the discursive framing of disputes over same-sex marriage. The nodes in this network study (such as 'dependent benefits' and 'religious liberty') reflect concepts and categories that are external to the networks while also shaping their structure. Similar shaping of networks by a wider and more encompassing set of social distinctions is studied in Krinsky's (2007) blockmodel analyses of contested language around the Mayor Rudolph Giuliani administration's implementation in New York City of workfare (which uses welfare recipients to do routine work once performed by unionised workers).

The idea is an old one. In his Latin dissertation, Emile Durkheim, a founder of sociology, traced his interest in social morphology to that of the eighteenth-century thinker, Montesquieu, who distinguished types of societies 'differ[ing] in the number, arrangement, and cohesion of their component parts' (Durkheim, [1892] 1960, pp. 26–27).[5] Montesquieu had identified various forms of political society, such as monarchy, aristocracy and republic. Durkheim protested that Montesquieu had distinguished these categories and named them, 'not on the basis of division of labor or the nature of their social ties, but solely according to the nature of their sovereign authority'. Durkheim criticised this as a failure to see 'that the essential is not the number of persons subject to the same authority, but the number bound by some form of relationship' (Durkheim, [1892] 1960, pp. 32, 38). The categories are animated by social relations, to be sure, but with equal certitude the social relations are shaped and constrained by the political structure (evidencing reciprocated ties in the city state of the republic, hierarchical ties in a monarchy; p. 27). In this way, categories can productively be analysed as providing an infrastructure for networks.

As Hanna and co-authors assert, when categories work, they are invisible. 'Categories themselves become a type of infrastructure: they are the ground upon which other structural and ideational elements are built' (Hanna et al., 2020, p. 504). With respect to social networks, DiMaggio (1992) argued for thinking of categorical attributes as typifications that may shape the evolution of network structures.

The early 'structuralist' developments in network analysis, including much 1970s work of Harrison White and co-authors, took for granted the categorical shaping of connections, even as they refused to theorise it (as explicated by Brint, 1992; DiMaggio, 1992; Mützel, 2009; Fuhse, 2022). Important strands of more contemporary work begin with 'the general idea that networks are patterned by categories' (Fuhse, 2022, p. 135).

Categories as relations among actors; actors as relations among categories

A special case of a network is a set of partially interconnected nodes where the nodes are actors and the relations connecting pairs of actors are the (number of) categories they share. For example, the actors might be white women in the racially segregated society of Nachez, Mississippi, in the 1930s, and the categories might be various social events attended by subsets of the actors (Davis et al., 1941). This 'Southern Women' dataset has been a foundational one for the development of social network analysis (Freeman, 2011). From this dataset the analyst may create two networks, a network among persons (persons are the nodes; the number of shared events among pairs of persons reflects the extent to which they share categories of cultural activity, such as a church supper or a club meeting), and a network among categories (events are the nodes; the number of persons attending each pair of events indexes similarity among events). These two networks are distinct but also mutually constitutive (Mützel & Breiger, 2020; Lerner & Lomi, 2022).

To take another example, the actors might be respondents to the Survey of Public Participation in the Arts, and the categories might be types of cultural activity (such as reading self-help books, reading romance stories, listening to country music, listening to bluegrass music), as in Lizardo's (2014) study. As described here, the nodes are actors, and the cultural similarity of two actors – a network tie between them – is some function of the extent to which they share types of cultural activity. Cluster analysis of the actors in this network can be helpful for understanding 'the ways that people use culture to make connections with one another' (DiMaggio, 1987, p. 442).[6] However, there is another network that turns 'inside out' the one just described. From the same data (linkages between survey respondents and the categories they participate in), we may construct a 'dual' network in which the nodes are the categories and the network tie between any two categories is the number of survey participants who engage in both types of activity. Cluster analysis of the categories can help identify cultural genres. Specifically, 'just as populations of persons can be partitioned into groups on the basis of the works of art they like, so populations of artworks can be partitioned into groups, or genres, on the basis of the persons who choose them' (DiMaggio, 1987, p. 445).

The above two networks are 'dual' to each other in that the nodes in one network become the relations in the other, and vice versa (Breiger, 1974). This duality principle has been of general interest in the development of social network analysis, allowing networks to be defined, not only in terms of who interacts with whom, but as consisting of ties between different levels, such as persons and cultural tastes (as illustrated above), persons and groups, authors and articles, organisations and practices, ingredients used in recipes and chemical compounds (leading to construction of a 'flavour network'; Ahn et al., 2011) and many more (Mützel & Breiger, 2020). Analyses of two-mode networks (Jasny, this volume) often aid the study of duality; for example, the 'flavour network' is built from a binary two-mode network where the modes are chemical compounds and recipe ingredients, and the network indicates which compounds comprise each ingredient.

The duality principle has also been generalised in significant ways that move beyond the original formalism. Multilevel systems of categories and actors have been conceptualised (Fararo & Doreian, 1984; Carley, 2003; Lee & Martin, 2018; Basov et al., 2020) and analysed as multilevel networks (Cornwell et al., 2003; Melamed et al., 2013; Wang et al., 2016; Martin & Lee, 2018). In particular, the general theoretical approach and related models developed by Lazega and colleagues theorise and examine the agency of actors at multiple levels simultaneously (Lazega, 2020); for example, scientists connected by co-authorship, cancer labs connected by the career mobility of individual scientists, as well as affiliations of scientists to labs (Lazega et al., 2008; Lazega & Snijders, 2016; Lazega & Wang, this volume). Mützel (2010) theorises and analyses the central role of ambiguity and multivocality in the making of categories that may serve to bridge cultural holes. Padgett and Powell (2012) and their collaborators develop a general theory, along with a series of empirical studies, which take as a fundamental principle that an organisation is the reproduction and recombination of persons and rules, while persons are collections and products of prior networks and their interaction rules. 'In other words, both organizations and people are shaped, through network co-evolution, by the history of each flowing through the other' (Padgett & Powell, 2012, p. 171).

Lerner and Lomi (2022) provide powerful generalisation of duality concepts by applying recently derived relational hyperevent models (RHEM; Lerner et al., 2021) to analyse the mutual constitution of individuals and their attendance at timestamped events. RHEM are explicitly designed to model networks of relational events with fine-grained time information. The RHEM model extends the applicability of duality concepts by incorporating explicit dynamic elements in the form of a time-ordered sequence of events in which individuals participate. Lerner and Lomi (2022) demonstrate how such modelling can support hypothesis testing about competing mechanisms driving participation in events.

How categories weaken and new categories emerge from networks

The anticategorical imperative that drives much social network analysis (Emirbayer & Goodwin, 1994) implies that networks often cross-cut existing categories. This emphasis on the degree of intersection among categories and dimensions of difference, such as race and income, owes much to the theory of Peter Blau (1977), although this intellectual heritage often goes unrecognised. Blau's 'central thesis' (p. 273) is that extensive intergroup relations depend on the degree of intersection. In turn, such cross-cutting implies the possibility that categorical boundaries may weaken, fray, or dissolve, as well as the prospect that new categories may be created.

The weakening of categories

A person who segregates one's social connections on the basis of one dimension, say occupational category (choosing to associate only with other sociologists, for example) may thereby increase one's network ties across another dimension, for example connecting with colleagues of diverse religious categories, if it is the case that members of that occupation are heterogeneous with respect to religion. Such 'multiform heterogeneity' (Blau, 1974, p. 622) compels people to have associates outside their own groups, 'because it makes ingroup relations simultaneously intergroup relations in terms of different [dimensions]'. Active identification with a category that crosses racial boundaries, for example identification with individuals who have gay, lesbian, or bisexual sexual identities, spurs an override of the rigidity of racial boundaries that otherwise dissuades interpersonal diversity and constrains network relations (Horowitz & Gomez, 2018).

In 'Beyond the binaries', a classic article subtitled 'Depolarizing the categories of sex, sexuality, and gender', Lorber (1996) argued that the sociologist's task should be to deconstruct the conventional categories of sexual and gender orientation, and to create 'new complex, cross-cutting constructs'. As the author recognised, this is a call for relational methodologies, including 'analysis of positions in a social network' (Lorber, 1996, p. 152). The standard or 'familiar' categories can be brought into a relational analysis 'to see whether the emergent network positions, attitude clusters, typical behavior, and subtexts are characteristic of those of different genders, races, ethnic groups, and classes' and then they can be related to power and the control of resources (Lorber, 1996, p. 152). When one term or category is defined only by its opposite, any resistance simply reaffirms the polarity. 'Introducing even one more term, such as bisexuality, forces a rethinking of the oppositeness of heterosexuality and homosexuality' (Lorber, 1996, p. 155).

Seeley (2014), building on network-analytic conceptualisation of Fuhse (2009; see also Fuhse, 2022), posits two ways in which such rethinking might be done. One approach would advance White's (2008a) later work that focuses on the centrality of narrative and stories for explaining and stabilising social networks and formations. 'Here, then, gender might easily be returned to White's theory and SNA generally not as an identity but as a constant thread running through most narratives and stories' (Seeley, 2014, p. 38). The second, related approach that Seeley recommends is to perform network analysis on observed expressions of masculinity and femininity without regard to the gender of the actors. 'For example, research on the interaction of service workers and customers could develop a coding scheme for expressions of masculinity and femininity applied at the statement level without regard for the speaker's gender' (Seeley, 2014, p. 39). The performance of masculinity and femininity could then be related to the social network position of actors without assuming that such expressions are rigidly bound to standard gender categories and gendered bodies. In brief, 'White, and SNA generally, would benefit from feminist poststructuralists' shift of the ontological status of gender from attributional to an aspect of narratives and stories' (Seeley, 2014, p. 38).

Emergence of New Categories

In Abbott's (1995) formulation, social actors create new categories by linking already-existing boundaries to produce new units. Boundaries come first, then entities. A new category, the occupation of social work, 'emerged when actors began to hook up the women from psychiatric work with the scientifically trained workers from the kindergartens with the non-church group in friendly visiting and the child workers in probation' (Abbott, 1995, p. 869). 'Hooking up' means connection of multiple sites of difference such that one side of each proto-boundary is defined as 'inside' the emergent entity (Abbott, 1995, p. 871). Abbott's is a compelling set of images which form a beginning for a comprehensive theory of the emergence of new categories. In work to be reviewed next, the topological metaphors in Abbott's article might find a formal network operationalisation that is up to the task of carrying forward this thinking.

Mützel (2022) demonstrates how semantic network analysis and topic modelling may be combined with qualitative research and applied to tens of thousands of scientific papers, corporate reports and newspaper stories to study the emergence of a new category. Interrelations between narratives from multiple network domains of science, biotech companies, finance and industry were brought together, through competitive, negotiated and collaborative mechanisms to form a new treatment category in the field of breast cancer therapeutics. In turn, this new categorisation induced a shift in the structure of the market for therapies, and ultimately the emergence of a new market.

By way of contrast, Jones et al. (2011) studied the emergence of the category of 'modern architecture' as what they call a 'de novo' category, one that does not yet have a code that defines it and is not a combination or transposition of already-existing categories. (On the distinction between category emergence and category creation, see Durand and Khaire, 2016.) Jones et al. use word co-occurrences to build networks of concepts, an approach akin to *map analysis* (Carley, 1997), a form of network textual analysis that enables identification of actors' meanings and symbolic systems. Jones et al. constructed two types of network based on written works of eminent architects and critics for each of three periods together spanning the years 1870 to 1975. One type of network was coded from a series of oppositions (such as modern–traditional, economic–artistic, engineer–architect) representing dyadic co-occurrences of the most relevant symbols used. The other type of network was based on 'artefact codes', operationalised as dyadic relations among material features that architects used in their exemplary buildings. Nodes consisted of building materials such as wood, brick, reinforced concrete, among others. The result was a study of institutional logics, defined as interrelated sets of material practices *and* symbolic constructions (Jones et al., 2011, p. 1526; see also Friedland & Arjaliès, 2021).

A research group led by Damon Centola has been developing a highly distinctive approach to modelling the network dynamics of category emergence (Puglisi et al., 2008; Guilbeault et al., 2021). What accounts for the finding from anthropological studies that large, independent societies consistently arrive at highly similar category systems across a range of topics? This is a question pursued by Guilbeault et al. (2021), who developed an online experimental platform enabling real-time observation of the formation of independently constructed category systems in both small and large populations. The researchers found that, in contrast to solitary individuals and small-scale groups, which produced highly divergent category systems, replicated studies in large populations with unique subjects converged on highly similar category systems. These results suggest to the authors that 'convergence in category formation across independent populations is significantly shaped by the communication networks in which people are embedded' (2021, p. 4). In particular, these researchers argue that communication networks in large-scale societies can filter lexical diversity in a way that produces convergent and replicable trajectories in category creation.

SOME NEAR-TERM CHALLENGES

As we hope to have illustrated, the relation between social networks and categories has been a rich wellspring of developments in social network analysis. The research questions and range of contributions to be made in this area are far from exhausted. In this concluding section we focus on identifying selected research questions and areas where we think advances would be significant for the field, and where existing contributions have made additional progress feasible.

A Relational Sociology of Race

Race has most often been treated as an attribute or a category in network studies.[7] Recent work (Fiel, 2021; Fuhse, 2022) is challenging this procedure along with its underlying assumptions, in ways similar to our review (above) of works by Lorber and Seeley in our section on the weakening of categories.

Fiel's agenda-setting discussion of the history of racial segregation in the US emphasises that segregation 'is not total separation, it is not inevitable or unchangeable, … it does not have mechanical causes or effects' and it exhibits 'a tenuous duality of separation and interdependence' (Fiel, 2021, p. 175). None of this is to assert that racial categories don't matter, or that they are decreasing in importance. Exactly to the contrary, 'total segregation would have severed mechanisms by which white people exploited and controlled black people' (2021, p. 154). It is precisely as an approach to understanding this kind of exploitation and control – 'dueling control efforts among categorical actors with malleable categorical identities' (Fiel, 2021, p. 153) – that we need a relational sociology, one that allows us to see segregation as 'a pattern of relations that is not only built on categorical identities but also is creating, maintaining, and molding those identities' (2021, p. 158).

With respect to the largely compatible approach of Fuhse, the perspective of relational sociology sees ethnic structures as resulting from the interplay of ethnic categories and social networks (Fuhse, 2022, p. 117). Referencing Tilly (1998), Fuhse observes that whether or not the categories reflect or transmit social inequality depends on social relationships and on the meanings and relational expectations attached to the categories (2022, p. 117). We may consider as one example of a quantitative application of relational theory Hedegard's (2013) correspondence analysis of the dual association of self-identified racial categories and musical tastes in Brazil.

In support of efforts to develop social science methods that incorporate aspects of critical race theory, such as Hanna et al.'s (2020) examination of frameworks for assessing algorithmic fairness, in which race is understood, not as an attribute, but rather as a structural, institutional and relational phenomenon, there is a prospect of developing a critical social network analysis (González Canché & Rios-Aguilar, 2015). González Canché and Rios-Aguilar show how Breiger's (1974) 'duality of persons and groups' can be used in a new way, to study networks among African American and Hispanic community college students in the US on the basis of shared college classes, finding 'peer effects' such that students in these groups benefit from interacting with peers in the same racial/ethnic group, in terms of the number of college courses completed. This repurposing of a conventional perspective, applying it to a research problem chosen for the light it can shine on a problem of inequality, is for its authors a move towards a 'critical' social network analysis (González Canché & Rios-Aguilar, 2015; see also Breiger, 2021).

Cognition, Concepts, Categories – and Networks

A highly promising and productive programme on theory and research on social classification is that of Michael Hannan and his research collaborators; see Hannan et al. (2019) for an extended statement; see also Goldberg et al. (2016). These authors have developed an approach according to which mental representations of concepts can be usefully viewed as probability distributions over positions in a semantic space. Categories are sets of objects (which may be persons, products, collective actions, or a wide variety of other phenomena) that someone categorises as an instance of a concept (Hannan et al., 2019, p. 97). Drawing on cognitive science, concepts are mental representations by which people classify the entities that they encounter (2019, pp. 1–13).

By formulating a geometry of concepts – a semantic space within which (for example) styles of rap music (club/dance, urban, party rap and so forth) are related to one another within a field defined by orthogonal quantitative dimensions (named, for example, 'swagger' and 'street violence') from a topic model applied to thousands of rap music lyrics, Hannan et al. (2019, pp. 40–46) are bringing relational modelling akin to network analysis to bear in their studies of concept and category structuring. In future work it should be possible to bridge this research and that of sociology of culture scholars who formalise semantic and social relations (Jones, 2021, p. 236).

More generally, a growing body of research (reviewed by Smith et al., 2020) indicates that cognitive processes influence many aspects of human social networks. Experimental studies of the ease of recalling relationships based on their categorisation (kin, social relational, activity type) suggest that category systems and normative rules for relations among categories may be responses to cognitive limitations (Brashears & Brashears, 2016).

Networks and categories as events

A theme that has emerged in the latter half of our review, largely implicit until now, is the desirability of furthering research on networks and categories with the aim of understanding them in many situations and contexts as eventful. For example, we have reviewed work on new categories emerging from contention (Abbott, Mützel), on gender categories as infrastructure for the active performance of gender (Lorber, Seeley) and on Fiel's vision, evidently influenced by that of Harrison White (2008a), of 'dueling control efforts among actors with malleable categorical identities' (Fiel, 2021, p. 153). In light of the instability of categories, we are in need of models that capture the endogenous change within categories and the implications of such change for shifting identities (Li, 2021). We would like to encourage more attention to an analytical shift away from 'groups' and other categories as simply taken-for-granted basic units of analysis and towards according greater attention to 'group-making' and 'grouping' activities such as 'classification, categorization, and identification, public and private, through which [such categories] are sustained from day to day' (Brubaker et al., 2004, p. 45; see also Wagner-Pacifici, 2010, p. 1356; Wagner-Pacifici, 2017).

When people speak to one another or engage in other forms of social connection in dyads or networks, they are involved in an active process of communication. In such communication, people typically refer either explicitly or implicitly to what conversation analysts have called 'membership categorisation devices' to situate and give meaning to their interactions. The membership categorisation device (Sacks, 1972) consists of any collection of membership categories and some rules of application. An example of a categorisation device is 'family'; its collection (in some particular instance) might be baby, mummy, daddy and so on. A rule of application might be that if the baby cries the mummy picks it up. People who interact (as well as analysts of social interaction) must often work with a network of overlapping categories. For example, 'baby' can be a member of the category 'family' and/or the category 'stage of life' (baby, teenager, young adult, …), or even sibling birth order (i.e., someone described as 'the baby of the family').

In eventful interaction, the participants actively negotiate meanings across such networks. Building on Sacks's concept, Whitehead (2009) studies how people 'categorise the categoriser'. An example is that a speaker's use of a racial category to explain someone else's action may provide 'a warrantable basis' for listeners to treat the speaker's own racial category as relevant for understanding and assessing the speaker's actions (Whitehead, 2009, p. 325).

We suggest that a near-term challenge is to formulate an approach by which the membership categorisation device can be studied beyond the realm of dyads or triads, within a full network of interaction. At the same time, we would encourage a reorientation of network analysis towards envisioning the eventful work that people do as they negotiate and contest the overlapping category systems that connect, constrain and/or liberate them.

Notes

1. Azarian (2005) provides a valuable introduction to and explication of much of Harrison White's sociology.
2. Mützel and Kressin (2021, pp. 221–222) focus on the contributions of a classical sociologist, Georg Simmel, who connects intersecting social circles to the development of individuality. A related image is that of Sorokin ([1927] 1959, p. 6), who paraphrased a proverb: 'Tell me to what social groups you belong and what function you perform within each of those groups, and I will tell you what is your social position in the human universe, and who you are as a socius.'
3. The question used to elicit names of 'advisors' asked each lawyer to think back over the past year, consider all the lawyers in the firm, and name those who provided professional advice, which was defined by means of examples such as 'mak[ing] sure that you are handling a case right, making a proper decision' and so forth, and explicitly excluded 'simply technical advice' (Lazega & Pattison, 1999, p. 88). In addition to advice and friendship (specified as ties to other lawyers with whom one socialised outside work), the researchers elicited a network of strong co-worker ties (e.g., being assigned the same case to work on).
4. This and the remaining sentences in this paragraph were strongly influenced by a personal communication from Peter J. Carrington, for which we are most grateful. DiMaggio (1992) makes some similar points.
5. This paragraph borrows from Breiger and Roberts (1998, p. 242).
6. Specifically, 'artworks lend themselves to multiple interpretations; their intended meanings may be sociologically less important than the ways in which they signify group affiliation' (DiMaggio, 1987, p. 442).
7. 'Ethnicity' is preferred to 'race' by some analysts, due to the difficulties in defining 'race'. We use 'race' with the explicit understanding that the contemporary research reviewed here problematises the definition. For example, Hanna et al. (2020) discuss 'subjective self-identification', 'the race you check on an official form or survey with constrained options', 'the race others believe you to be', 'the race you believe others assume you to be', among other potential indicators.

REFERENCES

Abbott, A. (1995). Things of boundaries. *Social Research*, *62*(4), 857–882.

Ahn, Y.-Y., Ahnert, S.E., Bagrow, J.P., & Barabási, A.-L. (2011). Flavor network and the principles of food pairing. *Scientific Reports*, *1*(196), 1–7.

Azarian, R. (2005). *The general sociology of Harrison C. White: chaos and order in networks*. Palgrave Macmillan.

Basov, N., Breiger, R., & Hellsten, I. (2020). Socio-semantic and other dualities. *Poetics*, *78*(1), 101433.

Blau, P.M. (1974). Presidential address: parameters of social structure. *American Sociological Review*, *39*(5), 615–635.

Blau, P.M. (1977). *Inequality and heterogeneity: a primitive theory of social structure*. Free Press.

Brashears, M.E., & Brashears, L.A. (2016). The enemy of my friend is easy to remember: balance as a compression heuristic. *Advances in Group Processses*, *33*, 1–31.

Breiger, R.L. (1974). The duality of persons and groups. *Social Forces*, *53*(2), 181–190.

Breiger, R.L. (1981). The social class structure of occupational mobility. *American Journal of Sociology*, *87*(3), 578–611.

Breiger, R.L. (2021). A concluding comment: toward a critical social network analysis. *Social Networks*, *67*, 74–75.

Breiger, R.L., & Mohr, J.W. (2004). Institutional logics from the aggregation of organizational networks: operational procedures for the analysis of counted data. *Computational and Mathematical Organization Theory*, *10*(1), 17–43.

Breiger, R.L., & Roberts Jr, J.M. (1998). Solidarity and social networks. In P. Doreian & T.J. Fararo (Eds.), *The problem of solidarity: theories and models* (pp. 239–262). Gordon and Breach.

Brint, S. (1992). Hidden meanings: cultural content and context in Harrison White's structural sociology. *Sociological Theory*, *10*(2), 194–208.

Brubaker, R., Loveman, M., & Stamatov, P. (2004). Ethnicity as cognition. *Theory and Society*, *33*(1), 31–64.

Carley, K.M. (1997). Extracting team mental models through textual analysis. *Journal of Organizational Behavior*, *18*(S1), 533–558.

Carley, K.M. (2003). Dynamic network analysis. In R.L. Breiger, K.M. Carley & P.E. Pattison (Eds.), *Dynamic social network modeling and analysis: workshop summary and papers* (pp. 133–145). National Academies Press.

Cheng, S., & Park, B. (2020). Flows and boundaries: a network approach to studying occupational mobility in the labor market. *American Journal of Sociology*, *126*(3), 577–631.

Cornwell, B., Curry, T.J., & Schwirian, K.P. (2003). Revisiting Norton Long's ecology of games: a network approach. *City and Community*, *2*(2), 121–142.

Davis, A., Gardner, B.B., & Gardner, M.R. (1941). *Deep South: a social anthropological study of caste and class*. University of Chicago Press.

DiMaggio, P. (1987). Classification in art. *American Sociological Review*, *52*(4), 440–455.

DiMaggio, P. (1992). Nadel's paradox revisited: relational and cultural aspects of organizational structure. In N. Nohria & R.G. Eccles (Eds.), *Networks and organizations: structure, form, and action* (pp. 118–142). Harvard Business School Press.

DiMaggio, P. (2020). Duality and relationality: the cultural matrix of John W. Mohr. *Poetics*, 101438.

Duncan, O.D. (1984). Foreword. In L.A. Goodman, *The analysis of cross-classified data having ordered categories*. Harvard University Press.

Durand, R., & Khaire, M. (2016). Where do market categories come from and how? Distinguishing category creation from category emergence. *Journal of Management*, *43*(1), 87–110.

Durkheim, É. (1960). *Montesquieu and Rousseau: forerunners of sociology*. University of Michigan Press.

Emirbayer, M. (1997). Manifesto for a relational sociology. *American Journal of Sociology*, *103*(2), 281–317.

Emirbayer, M., & Goodwin, J. (1994). Network analysis, culture, and the problem of agency. *American Journal of Sociology*, *99*(6), 1411–1454.

Espinoza-Kulick, A. (2020). A multimethod approach to framing disputes: same-sex marriage on trial in Obergefell v. Hodges. *Mobilization: An International Quarterly*, *25*(1), 45–70.

Fararo, T.J., & Doreian, P. (1984). Tripartite structural analysis: generalizing the Breiger–Wilson formalism. *Social Networks*, *6*(2), 141–175.

Fiel, J.E. (2021). Relational segregation: a structural view of categorical relations. *Sociological Theory*, *39*(3), 153–179.

Freeman, L.C. (2011). The development of social network analysis – with an emphasis on recent events. In J. Scott & P.J. Carrington (Eds.), *The SAGE handbook of social network analysis*. 1st ed. (pp. 26–39). Sage.

Friedland, R., & Arjaliès, D.-L. (2021). Putting things in place: institutional objects and institutional logics. In M. Lounsbury, D.A. Anderson & P. Spee (Eds.), *On practice and institution: new empirical directions* (pp. 45–86). Research in the Sociology of Organizations. Emerald.

Fuhse, J. (2009). The meaning structure of social networks. *Sociological Theory*, *27*(1), 51–73.

Fuhse, J. (2022). *Social networks of meaning and communication*. Oxford University Press.

Goffman, E. (1974). *Frame analysis: an essay on the organization of experience*. Harvard University Press.

Goldberg, A., Hannan, M.T., & Kovács, B. (2016). What does it mean to span cultural boundaries? Variety and atypicality in cultural consumption. *American Sociological Review*, *81*(2), 215–241.

González Canché, M.S., & Rios-Aguilar, C. (2015). Critical social network analysis in community colleges: peer effects and credit attainment. *New Directions for Institutional Research*, *2014*(163), 75–91.

Goodman, L.A. (1981). Criteria for determining whether certain categories in a cross-classification table should be combined, with special reference to occupational categories in an occupational mobility table. *American Journal of Sociology*, *87*(3), 612–650.

Guilbeault, D., Baronchelli, A., & Centola, D. (2021). Experimental evidence for scale-induced category convergence across populations. *Nature Communications*, *12*(327), 1–7.

Hanna, A., Denton, E., Smart, A., & Smith-Loud, J. (2020). Towards a critical race methodology in algorithmic fairness. *FAT* 2020: Proceedings of the 2020 Conference on Fairness, Accountability, and Transparency*. Association for Computing Machinery, 501–512.

Hannan, M.T., Le Mens, G., Hsu, G., Kovács, B., Negro, G., Pólos, L., Pontikes, E.G., & Sharkey, A.J. (2019). *Concepts and categories: foundations for sociological and cultural analysis*. Columbia University Press.

Hedegard, D. (2013). Finding 'strong' and 'soft' racial meanings in cultural taste patterns in Brazil. *Ethnic and Racial Studies*, *36*(5), 774–794.

Horowitz, A.L., & Gomez, C.J. (2018). Identity override: how sexual orientation reduces the rigidity of racial boundaries. *Sociological Science*, *5*, 669–693.

Jones, C. (2021). Review of Concepts and categories: foundations for sociological and cultural analysis. *Contemporary Sociology: A Journal of Reviews*, *50*(3), 234–236.

Jones, C., Maoret, M., Massa, F.G., & Svejenova, S. (2011). Rebels with a cause: formation, contestation, and expansion of the de novo category 'modern architecture', 1870–1975. *Organization Science*, *23*(6), 1523–1545.

Krinsky, J. (2007). *Free labor: workfare and the contested language of neoliberalism*. University of Chicago Press.

Krinsky, J., & Mische, A. (2013). Formations and formalisms: Charles Tilly and the paradox of the actor. *Annual Review of Sociology*, *39*, 1–26.

Lazega, E. (2020). *Bureaucracy, Collegiality and Social Change: Redefining Organizations with*

Multilevel Relational Infrastructures. Edward Elgar Publishing.

Lazega, E., & Pattison, P.E. (1999). Multiplexity, generalized exchange and cooperation in organizations: a case study. *Social Networks*, 21(1), 67–90.

Lazega, E., & Snijders, T.A.B. (2016). *Multilevel network analysis for the social sciences: theory, methods and applications*. Springer (Methodos Series).

Lazega, E., Jourda, M.-T., Mounier, L., & Stofer, R. (2008). Catching up with big fish in the big pond? Multi-level network analysis through linked design. *Social Networks*, 30(2), 159–176.

Lee, M., & Martin, J.L. (2018). Doorway to the dharma of duality. *Poetics*, 68, 18–30.

Lerner, J., & Lomi, A. (2022). A dynamic model for the mutual constitution of individuals and events. *Journal of Complex Networks*, 10(2), 1–30.

Lerner, J., Lomi, A., Mowbray, J., Rollings, N., & Tranmer, M. (2021). Dynamic network analysis of contact diaries. *Social Networks*, 66, 224–236.

Li, Z. (2021). Lexicon into categories: a semantic network approach. Paper presented at the Networks 2021 virtual conference (Sunbelt and NetSci), 5 July.

Lin, K.-H., & Hung, K. (2022). The network structure of occupations: fragmentation, differentiation, and contagion. *American Journal of Sociology*, 127(5), 1551–1601.

Lizardo, O. (2014). Omnivorousness as the bridging of cultural holes: a measurement strategy. *Theory and Society*, 43(3–4), 395–419.

Lorber, J. (1996). Beyond the binaries: depolarizing the categories of sex, sexuality, and gender. *Sociological Inquiry*, 66(2), 143–160.

Lorrain, F., & White, H.C. (1971). Structural equivalence of individuals in social networks. *Journal of Mathematical Sociology*, 1(1), 49–80.

Marsden, P.V. (1985). Latent structure models for relationally defined social classes. *American Journal of Sociology*, 90(5), 1002–1021.

Martin, J.L., & Lee, M. (2018). A formal approach to meaning. *Poetics*, 68, 10–17.

Melamed, D., Breiger, R.L., & West, A.J. (2013). Community structure in multi-mode networks: applying an Eigenspectrum approach. *Connections*, 33(1), 18–23.

Mische, A. (2011). Relational sociology, culture, and agency. In J. Scott & P.J. Carrington (Eds.), *The SAGE handbook of social network analysis*. 1st ed. (pp. 80–97). Sage.

Mohr, J.W. (1994). Soldiers, mothers, tramps and others: discourse roles in the 1907 New York City charity directory. *Poetics*, 22(4), 327–357.

Mohr, J.W., & Duquenne, V. (1997). The duality of culture and pactice: poverty relief in New York City, 1888-1917. *Theory and Society*, 26(2/3), 305–356.

Mützel, S. (2009). Networks as culturally constituted processes: a comparison of relational sociology and actor-network theory. *Current Sociology*, 57(6), 871–887.

Mützel, S. (2010). Koordinierung von Märkten durch narrativen Wettbewerb. *Kölner Zeitschrift für Soziologie und Sozialpsychologie*, 49(Sonderheft), 87–106.

Mützel, S. (2022). *Making sense: markets from stories in new breast cancer therapeutics*. Stanford University Press.

Mützel, S., & Breiger, R.L. (2020). Duality beyond persons and groups: culture and affiliation. In R. Light & J. Moody (Eds.), *The Oxford handbook of social networks* (pp. 392–413). Oxford University Press.

Mützel, S., & Kressin, L. (2021). From Simmel to relational sociology. In S. Abrutyn & O. Lizardo (Eds.), *Handbook of classical sociological theory* (pp. 217–238). Springer Nature.

Padgett, J.F., & Powell, W.W. (2012). *The emergence of organizations and markets*. Princeton University Press.

Puglisi, A., Baronchelli, A., & Loreto, V. (2008). Cultural route to the emergence of linguistic categories. *Proceedings of the National Academy of Sciences*, 105(23), 7936–7940.

Rawlings, C.M., & Childress, C. (2021). Measure Mohr culture. *Poetics*, 88(1), 1–6.

Sacks, H. (1972). On the analysability of stories by children. In J.J. Gumperz & D. Hymes (Eds.), *Directions in sociolinguistics: the ethnography of communication* (pp. 329–345). Holt, Rinehart & Winston.

Santoro, M. (2008). Framing notes: an introduction to 'catnets'. *Sociologica*, 1, 1–22.

Scott, J. (2022). *Structure and social action: on constituting and connecting social worlds*. Emerald.

Seeley, J.L. (2014). Harrison White as (not quite) poststructuralist. *Sociological Theory*, 32(1), 27–42.

Skocpol, T. (1992). *Protecting soldiers and mothers: the political origins of social policy in the United States*. Harvard University Press.

Smith EB, Brands RA, Brashears ME, et al. (2020). Social Networks and Cognition. *Annual Review of Sociology* 46(1), 159–174.

Sorokin, P.A. (1959). *Social and cultural mobility*. Free Press.

Stuhler, O. (2021). What's in a category? A new approach to discourse role analysis. *Poetics*, 88, 101568.

Tilly, C. (1978). *From mobilization to revolution*. Addison-Wesley.

Tilly, C. (1998). *Durable inequality*. University of California Press.

Wagner-Pacifici, R. (2010). Theorizing the restlessness of events. *American Journal of Sociology*, 115(5), 1351–1386.

Wagner-Pacifici, R.E. (2017). *What is an event?* University of Chicago Press.

Wagner-Pacifici, R., & Breiger, R. (2020). In appreciation of John Mohr. *Poetics*, *78*, 101436.

Wang, P., Robins, G., Pattison, P., & Lazega, E. (2016). Social selection models for multilevel networks. *Social Networks*, *44*, 346–362.

White, H. (1992). *Identity and control: a structural theory of social action*. Princeton University Press.

White, H. (1997). Can mathematics be social? Flexible representations for interaction process and its sociocultural constructions. *Sociological Forum*, *12*(1), 53–71.

White, H. (2008a). *Identity and control: how social formations emerge*. 2nd ed. Princeton University Press.

White, H. (2008b). Notes on the constituents of social structure: *Social Relations 10 -*, Spring '65. *Sociologica*, 1, 1–14.

White, H. (2008c). Preface: catnets forty years later. *Sociologica*, *1*, 1–4.

White, H., Boorman, S., & Breiger, R. (1976). Social structure from multiple networks. I. Blockmodels of roles and positions. *American Journal of Sociology*, *81*(4), 730–780.

Whitehead, K.A. (2009). 'Categorizing the categorizer': the management of racial common sense in interaction. *Social Psycholoogy Quarterly*, *72*(4), 325–342.

Social Networks and Computational Social Science[1]

James A. Kitts, Helene Grogan, and Kevin Lewis

A landmark article in *Science* (Lazer et al., 2009) presented computational social science (CSS) as a new domain for social science research based on novel data sources. This discussion highlighted how our locations, activities, interactions and transactions are increasingly monitored by sensors and location-aware devices, from transit cards and toll transponders to credit cards and security cameras. It also highlighted ubiquitous data collection on media consumption and interpersonal communication by telephone, email, or social media. This presentation of CSS included two branches that target distinct sources of relational data: first, those that study face-to-face networks using electronic devices; and, second, those that study computer-mediated social networks using email, social media and other telecommunication technology.[2] In either case, CSS encompasses the collection, processing and analysis of 'digital breadcrumbs' recorded through our everyday lives.

Researchers acknowledged from the start that these new data were relevant to scholarship on social networks, but the link from the new data to the body of conventional social network theory has often been absent, implicit, or unrigorous. This chapter extends recent efforts (Kitts, 2014; Kitts & Quintane, 2020; Lewis, 2022) to enrich the dialogue between the new CSS data sources and conventional social network concepts and theories. We will build on their analytic framework, which distinguishes four basic approaches to defining social ties as theoretical objects: *sentiments*, *role relations*, *social interaction* and *access*. Each of these four approaches represents a set of assumptions about the nature of social ties, which make it applicable to scope conditions for distinct domains of social network theory.

Classic theories of network dynamics often interpret social ties as interpersonal *sentiments*, which are thoughts or feelings directed from one social actor to others. Sentiments may be positive (liking, esteem, or trust), negative (hatred, disrespect, or distrust), or neutral (acquaintance, familiarity). In all of these cases, the 'tie' exists in the subjective thoughts or feelings of one actor towards another, so the resulting data are inherently directional and any tendency towards mutuality (e.g., shared feelings of liking or antipathy between two parties) is an empirical question.

Other classic social network research has measured social ties as *role relations*, socially recognised labels assigned to dyads (such as a friend, romantic partner, or family member), where the label represents distinct role expectations for the parties. These may go beyond dyads to represent shared involvement in a group that implies or imposes roles on members (such as teammates, officemates, housemates, or co-authors). These relations operate primarily as norms, expectations and repertoires for how actors behave towards one another within their roles (Kitts & Quintane, 2020; Fuhse & Gondal, 2022). For example, recent research on the meaning of friendship among adolescents (Kitts & Leal, 2021) shows that friendship is typically construed as *relational norms* (e.g., friends are expected to defend, help, or support one another, and to refrain from telling each other's secrets) as well as *structural expectations* (e.g., mutuality, transitivity, homophily). Role relations may also be directed, with norms and behavioural repertoires applying asymmetrically within the relation. For example, lawyers and clients, doctors and patients, or teachers and students follow particular scripts and respect particular expectations for role-related behaviour. Role relations are by definition socially recognised; the relationship exists insofar as the parties are aware of their roles and employ the associated behavioural repertoires. This social recognition makes role relations easy to measure, as researchers may simply ask individuals to identify their friends, or may obtain archival records of relationships such as co-authors of articles or co-sponsors of congressional bills.[3]

Research depicting network position as a source of power or social capital is often predicated on a definition of network ties as *access* to resources or information. Knowing the set of alters accessible to any given ego for a particular purpose (such as borrowing money or hearing about a job opportunity) allows a researcher to construct a graph of possible paths through which resources might flow among actors. This graph may support inferences about individuals based on their network position: an actor connected to others by shorter paths is assumed to have high-fidelity access to timely information, and an actor who is an intermediary on many paths of access among peers may derive power by controlling flows of resources. This work regards ties as providing opportunities for exchange or interaction, whether or not those opportunities are actually realised.

Increasingly, researchers measure actual social *interaction* as it occurs in relational behaviour between parties. Here they are concerned not with ties that could be activated, but where social contacts actually occur. Social interactions could be *directed*, as in giving a favour to a neighbour, sending a letter, or passing a syringe during drug use. Other forms of interaction are undirected by definition, as in sharing a dinner date or a phone conversation. Notably, interaction occurs in discrete social events at particular moments in time, which could at least in principle be represented as event histories (Kitts, 2014; de Nooy, 2015).

To make interaction data conformable with traditional network lenses, researchers have turned event histories into timeless abstractions, such as social ties. An easy way to interpret social interaction events as relationships is to collect self-reports of implicitly aggregated interactions, such as typical or most frequent interaction partners (Paluck & Shepherd, 2012). Another way is to directly measure timestamped interaction events and then aggregate those events over time and compare the count to a threshold, inferring that a 'tie' exists if at least k interaction events occurred on the time interval (Huberman et al., 2009). For example, more than a certain number of phone calls or emails in a month indicates a friendship. This implicit or explicit aggregation is a common way to turn timestamped event data into *ties* that are abstracted from time and thus conformable to our concepts and theories of social networks.

This typology reflects qualitatively distinct approaches to thinking about network ties, as reflected in separate literatures addressing different theories. This is not a taxonomy of types of empirical ties, but a typology of approaches to defining ties. We consider the general category of *sentiment* ties, for example, but other work (e.g., Genkin et al., 2022) makes important empirical distinctions between specific sentiments captured by name generator surveys.[4] We build on work (Kitts & Quintane, 2020) that has interrogated the mapping from data to theory across these four types of network concepts, revealing some of the perils of using data representing one network concept (such as role relations or interaction) to investigate theories developed for another network concept (such as sentiments or access). Data sources are often selected for convenience rather than for their applicability to a given theoretical question. Much of the early research in social network analysis used role relations because of the ease of measuring those relationships using surveys or archival data. For example, network theories of all kinds have been applied to self-reported data on friendships. As the advent of computational social science brought unprecedented availability of data on interaction events, recently researchers have used interaction data (often aggregating events over time) as a proxy measure for various kinds of relationships, again applying all varieties of network theory to aggregated interaction data.

We focus here on the particular promise of CSS data for social network theory, and advocate for thinking more deeply about how to grapple with timestamped event data streams, rather than merely aggregating them and calling them relationships. Network researchers have had a variety of options to collect timestamped event data: human coding of observational or archival materials (Fuhse,

2022), retrospective self-reports (Vörös et al., 2021), experience sampling (Meijerink-Bosman et al., 2022), or time diaries (Zhang et al., 2021). While these methods are essential to our toolkit, they are typically challenging, expensive and prone to human error. In the following sections, we will review some ways that physical sensors and online platforms are vehicles to collect massive amounts of timestamped relational data. These have focused primarily on social interaction but, as we will see, can also measure sentiments, role relations and access.

DETECTING FACE-TO-FACE NETWORKS WITH DEVICES: SENSORS, LOCATION-AWARE TECHNOLOGY AND ACTIVITY RECOGNITION

A wave of early research in computational social science employed sensors, sometimes embedded in wearable badges or in handheld devices such as mobile phones. These sensors are used to automatically detect relational phenomena, often in fine time grain and over spans of time and space that would be difficult to observe with the human eye. For example, Bluetooth, GPS, Wifi, infrared (IR) and radio frequency (RFID) sensors can be used to infer location, orientation, or proximity of devices. Other sensor platforms have employed microphones to detect audio signals, accelerometers or gyroscopes to measure movement and physiological sensors to observe such features as heart rate, skin conductance, or hormone levels. These capabilities have been deployed over a broad range of contexts, including student communities in schools (Bahulkar et al., 2017; Vörös et al., 2021), employees or members in organisations (Chaffin et al., 2017; Müller et al., 2019) and children in families (de Barbaro, 2019).

Sensor technology has been applied most often to study social interaction, as it allows researchers to automatically collect timestamped data on interaction behaviour *in situ*, as it naturally occurs in time and space. Smartphones and other location-aware devices allow us to infer interaction among parties by observing colocation (Flamino et al., 2021; Lee et al., 2013) or by observing shared mobility patterns (Cranshaw et al., 2010). Specifically, several studies have used Bluetooth, RFID, IR, or wifi sensors to detect physical proximity or colocation (Eagle et al., 2009; Malik, 2018; Salathé et al., 2010; Guclu et al., 2016) and interpreted these as instances of social interaction. To refine simple colocation as a proxy measure of social interaction, researchers have used signal strength (Sekara & Lehmann, 2014), device direction or mutual orientation using infrared or RFID (Jang et al., 2017), and interaction duration (Oloritun et al., 2013). Researchers have also used microphones in either smartphones or dedicated sensor platforms to detect face-to-face conversations (Poudyal et al., 2021; Demiray et al., 2020; Harari et al., 2020; Wyatt et al., 2011), deployed sensors in clothing to monitor breathing patterns and detect conversations (Ejupi & Menon, 2018; Rahman et al., 2011), and even deployed sensors in seat cushions to measure meetings (Wang et al., 2004).

Note that sensors do not directly detect relationships or even social interaction behaviour, but detect some lower-level physical phenomena, such as Bluetooth signal strength or audio frequency. Researchers then take this sensor-derived data stream as an indirect measure of some meso-level construct, such as proximity between persons, and further infer a higher-order network construct like a social relationship. It is important to note that for each of these there are conceptual leaps between the fundamental property being measured (e.g., signal strength), the interpretation of that property (e.g., physical proximity and/or face-to-face orientation) and the theoretical construct it represents (e.g., social interaction). Partly to address the weak links between rich sociological concepts and the low-level physical properties monitored by sensors, some studies have aimed to triangulate by combining multiple sensor measures to study patterns of proximity, spatial positioning and verbal behaviour (Olguin et al., 2009; Onnela et al., 2014; Parker et al., 2018; Zhang et al., 2018).

Recent research has sought to collect electronic trace data on affective states using sensors. Affect can be measured as two distinct dimensions: *valence*, ranging from negative to positive, and *arousal*, or the intensity of feeling as indicated by activation of the sympathetic nervous system. Most sentiment-related sensor research has used sensing technology to monitor arousal by measuring physiological reactions such as galvanic skin response, heart rate, or pupil dilation (Palaghias et al., 2016). The work on inferring arousal from biometric sensors has often left valence unmeasured. In some cases, valence may be inferred by the researcher from the situation, or may be experimentally manipulated by the investigator (Kim et al., 2004). Other work has combined sensor measures of arousal with a more conventional measure of valence such as a self-report time diary survey deployed either periodically (Zhang et al., 2021) or using experience sampling (Zhang et al., 2018). In rare cases, researchers have attempted to measure affective valence using sensors; for example, Black et al. (2013) used audio recordings of conversations between couples in counselling, with the goal of using specific audio features to automatically classify communication in terms of positive and negative affect.

Other approaches have used sensors to detect events or activities that have an assumed relationship with particular sentiments. For example, researchers may employ sensors to monitor non-verbal behaviour, such as using accelerometers to detect laughter (Hung et al., 2013) or posture and body movement (Dragon et al., 2008), using video recordings to analyse patterns in eye gaze, body posture, or facial expressions (Dragon et al., 2008; Schmid Mast et al., 2015), using radio frequency signals to analyse breathing patterns and heartbeat (Zhao et al., 2016), using microphones to analyse response latency in speech (Iyengar & Westwood, 2015) or other acoustic features of spoken voices (Gu et al., 2017; Rachuri et al., 2010; Black et al., 2013) and using infrared thermography to infer emotions from facial microexpressions (Clay-Warner & Robinson, 2015). Such measures are then taken to reflect a related affective state.

It is important to note that the above work using sensors to measure affect can serve as a proof of concept for measuring sentiments. However, even if the technology successfully measures affect, this typically applies to the individual rather than a dyad or relationship – that is, they are not generally network data. Whereas we could use traditional surveys to measure *interpersonal* sentiments, interpreting sensor measures of affect as directed at another specific person would require further analysis or contextual information. For example, we might analyse audio signals to detect features of a speaker's voice indicating arousal, but to derive meaningful sociometric inferences we may need to overlay these sentiments on more explicitly relational data, such as measures of social interaction. We might, for example, examine the *change* of speech features for a given speaker when interacting with particular conversation partners (Wyatt et al., 2008) and take those changes as evidence of relationships loaded with sentiments.

Sensors measure physical states at particular times and so cannot be used to directly detect or monitor socially constructed role relations. Researchers can use sensor measures of interaction behaviour or sentiments to infer or predict the existence of relations like friendship (Sekara & Lehmann, 2014), but the sensor measures alone do not directly detect friendship as a role relation. Similarly, Flamino et al. (2021) use hierarchical clustering of Bluetooth sensor proximity measures to infer undergraduate students' membership in groups, but strictly speaking these are only patterns of physical proximity in time; the sensors do not directly measure the role relation of group membership. Analysis of turn-taking patterns in classroom speech data would likely reveal the distinction between teacher and students. But the classification would be derived from our knowledge of relational norms for how teachers and students talk in class, not derived directly from the sensors. Similarly, sensor data have been combined with contextual data or knowledge of relational norms about how and when friends interact – such as characteristic locations and times of day for interaction – to predict friendships as self-reported in surveys (Eagle et al., 2009; Oloritun et al., 2013).

Sensors have not been widely used to study access. As location and physical proximity sensors are typically interpreted as revealing social interaction events, this assumed equivalence between sensed colocation and social interaction means that researchers cannot interpret colocation as opportunities or determinants of interaction. Instead, sensor measures of location and proximity could be used to model the opportunity structure for interaction at a particular moment, but this would require an independent measure of interaction to identify where this opportunity is realised in social behaviour. For example, combining sensor measures of colocation (such as Bluetooth, Wifi, or GPS localisation) with human observers of face-to-face conversations, one could examine the effects of physical location and proximity on patterns of realised face-to-face conversations. Researchers could replace human observers with sensor measures more finely tuned to detect face-to-face interaction, such as RFID or IR (Malik, 2018) or 'situated speech data' using audio sensors (Wyatt et al., 2011). Even if we can perfectly detect conversations and disambiguate them from colocation, it will be challenging to disentangle problems of endogeneity outside controlled laboratory settings. People may strike up conversations with others who happen to be standing nearby at cocktail parties or academic conferences, but they may also relocate themselves in the crowd to be near their regular or aspirational conversation partners – that is, the proximity may be a byproduct rather than a cause of the conversation.

Because sensor technology typically monitors properties that are quite remote from meaningful social network data, they are often used in tandem with more traditional network measures in order to aid interpretation. Some studies have combined surveys of affect with sensor measures of proximity and interaction to explore the relationship between social interaction and interpersonal sentiments (Zhang et al., 2018; Olguin et al., 2009). For example, Alshamsi et al. (2016) collect sensor (IR) traces from wearable badges to observe face-to-face communication (via a combination of proximity and facing), paired with logs of communication through mobile phones as a measure of social interaction, then combine both of those data sources with self-reported affect measured through experience sampling. This allowed them to analyse how different types of social contact correlated with positive and negative affect.

DETECTING COMPUTER-MEDIATED NETWORKS: SOCIAL MEDIA, TELECOMMUNICATION AND ONLINE LINKS

Our second focus is the collection of network data from computer-mediated contexts. In contrast to relational information that is inferred from wearable or fixed sensors, we are here referring to a class of data where network phenomena are not only recorded by but actually *enacted through* some kind of digital media (e.g., Facebook, Twitter, SMS, voice or video chat). Here, user activity on a platform leaves behind digital 'footprints' or 'breadcrumbs' that researchers may study. In many cases all objective features of the relational event itself are captured – for instance, exactly when a text message was sent and received as well as the entire contents of the message itself.

Understandably, the advent of online social network sites was accompanied by a great deal of enthusiasm and research (e.g., Lewis et al., 2008b; Mayer & Puller, 2008), already the focus of recent review essays (e.g., Lewis, 2022; Tindall et al., 2022). These platforms appeared to offer large-scale, error-free and naturally occurring network data that potentially surmounts obstacles of prior work on face-to-face networks. In the time since, network studies of computer-mediated communication have encompassed a wide variety of platforms such as Facebook (Bond et al., 2012), Twitter (Tremayne, 2014), Wikipedia (Piskorski & Gorbatâi, 2017), online dating sites (Lewis, 2016) and massively multiplayer online games (Pham et al., 2022). They have examined interpersonal phenomena ranging from emails (Kossinets & Watts, 2009) and text messages (Igarashi et al., 2005) to 'friendship' or 'follower' relations on a variety of different platforms. And the boundaries of these networks have been defined in a variety of different ways, such as all communications among employees at a given organisation (Srivastava et al., 2018) or all tweets that include a given hashtag (Papacharissi & Oliveira, 2012). The activities recorded by these digital breadcrumbs can also have any manner of relationship with offline behaviour – at times preceding it (as when two singles who met online have their first date), at times succeeding it (as when two undergraduates meet in class and exchange phone numbers) and at times occurring entirely without it (as with anonymous participants in an online support group).

As with sensor research, computer-mediated contexts are most commonly used to study social interaction behaviours. For example, researchers examine timestamped logs of emails (Kleinbaum et al., 2013; Kossinets & Watts, 2009), instant messages (Leskovec & Horvitz, 2008), tweets (Boutyline & Willer, 2017), phone calls (Eagle et al., 2010; Onnela et al., 2007; Raeder et al., 2011; Stadtfeld & Block, 2017) and electronic calendar meetings (Lovett et al., 2010). They also analyse a variety of behaviours enacted within online platforms for gaming (Pham et al., 2022), resource sharing (State et al., 2016), dating (Lin & Lundquist, 2013), crowdsourced editing (Crandall et al., 2008) and cultural evaluation (Goldberg et al., 2016). Using network analysis tools to study the structure of interactions in these data requires some strong equivalence assumptions, such as treating nodes as interchangeable and treating interaction events as interchangeable in order to focus on the shape of the contact network. In contrast to the nuances of face-to-face interaction, digital interactions might seem well suited to formal network analysis, as the underlying behaviours may appear simple and even binary (such as 'swiping left' or 'swiping right'), thus easily translated to the binary sociomatrices employed by social network analysts. Even so, these contexts often provide rich additional information that could be used to observe the content or quality of communication and relationships. For example, researchers could use digital media data to record tie 'strength', such as the total time spent in phone calls (Onnela et al., 2007) or automated collection of measures of interaction intensity, intimacy, reciprocal giving, emotional support and relational duration (Gilbert & Karahalios, 2009).

Data that draw on computer-mediated communication to study interpersonal sentiments necessarily focus on *enacted* sentiments rather than direct measurement of psychological states; the correspondence between the two (especially given the performative nature of many such actions) warrants much more attention than it has currently received. As with digital interaction, sentiment data may also raise problems of interpretation insofar as superficially similar evaluations can mean many different things (e.g., Sumner et al., 2017). Enacted emotional evaluations become still more complex to study insofar as they provide the gateway to behavioural interaction (for instance, if two people have to 'like' each other on a dating site before they can interact, someone might strategically 'like' a lot of people to maximise romantic opportunities). Further, often what is 'liked' (or 'disliked' or 'loved' or 'laughed at') is not another person per se but a photo, link, comment, or other digital artefact they have uploaded. Other examples of online sentiment data include situations where users rate one another (or specific transactions between them), such as on Amazon, Etsy, or Airbnb (e.g., Leskovec et al., 2010; State et al., 2016), or give each other 'gifts' or other goods through the platform (Park & Kim, 2017). A final opportunity to study emotional expressions online is to apply sentiment analysis or other natural language processing tools to text in messages or posts (Pozzi et al., 2016). Such methods have been applied to social media data to identify emotional expressions and reveal temporal patterns in moods (Dodds et al., 2011; Golder & Macy, 2011) and also to analyse dyadic similarity in users' sentiments towards social objects (Yang et al., 2017). Sentiment analysis of Facebook status updates (Coviello et al., 2014) allowed observation of emotional contagion on networks of Facebook contacts. The same tools can be applied to text sent from one actor to another to provide potentially rich and variegated measures of interpersonal sentiments.

On a variety of digital platforms (e.g., Facebook, Instagram, Twitter, LinkedIn), users may enter into formalised role relations, some of which parallel broader social categories of ties (e.g., 'friend') and others that are unique to digital space (e.g., 'follower'). As with offline relationships, these ties may be undirected or directed and are governed by norms and expectations associated with the role relations. Unlike offline role relations, these online relationships may be explicitly constrained by the technical requirements of the platform software. For example, Facebook 'friend' relations must be mutually reciprocated, and are therefore undirected by definition, while Twitter 'follower' relations are directed and may or may not be reciprocated. However, these norms and expectations are also embedded within particular platforms and may not coincide with broader cultural meanings (e.g., a 'Facebook friend' may not be someone's 'friend' offline). Additionally, whereas in the offline world there may be discordance in reporting role relations like friend or romantic partner, role relations online are typically hard-wired into the platform and observable without error or uncertainty. Further, whereas offline role relations entail relational norms and structural expectations, these may also be hard-wired into an online platform, where forms of interaction may be enabled only within certain kinds of relationships and disabled otherwise. In most cases, formal digital relationships also tend to persist until or unless they are actively terminated (whereas elsewhere role relations may fade unless they are actively renewed).

As with offline role relation data, these relations are often convenient to measure but may not correspond to theoretically motivated network concepts (sentiments, interaction, access). Given such ambiguous data on online relationships, scholars may use a variety of approaches to identify a subset of digital contacts that maps more closely to a social tie concept from conventional offline networks research. For example, Golder et al. (2007) make Facebook 'friends' more comparable to offline friendships by removing Facebook friends that are never observed to interact on the platform; Gilbert and Karahalios (2009) measure tie strength among Facebook friends by observing exchange of photos as well as public and private messages; and Wimmer and Lewis (2010) focus only on Facebook friends who have posted and tagged pictures of each other (and therefore have presumably spent time together offline). These approaches essentially add a measure of interaction to refine the definition of a role relation, blending the two network concepts together.

Kitts and Quintane (2020) point out that access networks are generally difficult to observe outside the laboratory, but well-defined online platforms may be an exception as digital media data present novel ways to study networks as access. For example, platform privacy settings may allow users to share or restrict profile information, updates, or direct messages to subsets of other users (or the public at large) and analysing these data allows us to see who has access to what information about peers (Anthony et al., 2017; Lewis et al., 2008a). For some platforms this is linked to role relations, as having a certain relationship with someone may be a prerequisite for accessing information about them or communicating with them. For instance, two people may have to be friends in order to post to each other's profile; two dating site users may have to mutually 'like' one another before they can directly communicate; or a user may have to 'follow' someone (and have this request approved) before they have the opportunity to view that person's post. Each of these provides the opportunity to rigorously measure channels of access to information or communication within a naturalistic setting, whereas direct investigation of access networks has been heretofore limited largely to experimental research (Centola, 2010). Although this approach contains a great deal of promise, there is one major caveat to keep in mind: these data on access are generally limited to a single platform. Just because two users cannot communicate on a given platform does not mean that they cannot communicate outside the platform. In this sense, it is a high bar to find interpersonal channels where the transmission of information is truly impossible. This is of course even more true for offline networks (where we typically observe only a small slice of access networks, fail to observe much interaction that actually occurred and never observe the potential interactions that failed to occur).

CONCLUSION

Computational social science methods employing physical sensors and digital media have offered timestamped data streams with great potential for the extension of social network research and theory. We have discussed these new data sources in light of four approaches to defining social ties: sentiments, role relations, interaction and access. We have shown that both types of CSS data lend themselves foremost to observing behavioural interactions, though there are emerging methods for using either sensors or digital media to observe affect, with applications to interpersonal sentiments. It is difficult to measure role relations and access using sensors, though digital media offer some promise in these areas.

In discussing these new sources of data, we have amplified recent calls for researchers to pay close attention to how the observed social ties or other relational data fit into standard network concepts (enabling them to be connected to social network theories). Within computational social science, particular theoretical questions may also apply better to either sensor or digital media data, as these approaches are not at all interchangeable. For example, most applications of sensors can yield only undirected data (e.g., shared conversations, colocation) so research that requires directed data, such as investigations of reciprocity dynamics, could more fruitfully draw on digital media data. Given that node-level data on individuals (personal traits, identities and attitudes) are rarely detectable by sensors, research that requires such node-level data – such as on homophily, social influence and diffusion – is difficult to pursue with a sensor approach unless individual-level data are collected by some other means. Some node-level data may be available within a digital media platform (often as part of a user's public profile, including postings of likes, favourites, or status updates) and this may support research on homophily or social influence. However, such generally public declarations may reflect a user's self-presentation to friends or other audiences rather than private opinions or other details as might be measured by a confidential survey.

Data collection using sensors is typically designed by the researcher in order to detect and monitor naturally occurring relational phenomena, as when a researcher deploys wearable badges on a population of college students. This approach is often expensive but highly customisable. Although online platforms may be set up by a researcher for experimental purposes (e.g., Centola, 2010) they are typically created by firms for commercial purposes and observed passively by researchers, allowing for observation of much larger populations but with less control. In some cases, the online platform design may manipulate networks in ways that interfere with research objectives. For example, an online social networking platform may recommend friends for users based on their similar interests or attitudes, or based on their shared relationships with third parties (friends of friends), confounding research on homophily or triad closure. More generally, online data face profound challenges that observed relationships and relational behaviour may not correspond to offline counterparts. So for researchers interested in making this link the opportunity to collect timestamped relational data for face-to-face relationships using sensors is a pathbreaking frontier. The advent of sensors and location-aware devices also opens an unprecedented opportunity to understand the relationship between social networks and physical space, which remains a blind spot for much research on online networks. We thus see particular promise for research in computational social science that integrates both approaches in dialogue with social network theory.

Notes

1   Research reported in this publication was supported by the National Institutes of Health (NICHD) under award number R01HD086259 to joint Principal Investigators James A. Kitts and John R. Sirard. The content is solely the responsibility of the authors and does not necessarily represent the official views of the funders.

2   The term 'computational social science' has been used to describe other communities as well as the two branches described in this chapter. The oldest body of work under the CSS umbrella (as represented in the four-volume 2010 Sage collection, *Computational Social Science*, edited by Gilbert) involves the use of computational models to simulate social processes and elucidate social theory, typically without any reference to empirical data. Second, recent work in CSS has applied

computational analytical methods (e.g., machine learning) aiming to detect, classify and predict patterns in social data of any kind, typically without any reference to theory. While acknowledging the work on computational theory and computational methods, we focus on the bodies of work targeting new data sources.

3 Note that many network scholars define social ties as relationships of this kind and then regard interaction, sentiments and access as properties or features of ties, rather than as ties themselves.

4 Other work has discussed a superficially similar typology of name generator questions on surveys, as ways of measuring an individual's 'personal network' for social support (Marin & Hampton, 2007). In that work, there is one underlying support network and there are four kinds of name generators (role relation, interaction, affective and exchange) that may be used to capture the true underlying support network. Their distinct aim is to find a minimal set of name generator questions that adequately represent the 'true' support network without the expense and burden of asking many questions.

REFERENCES

Alshamsi, A., Pianesi, F., Lepri, B., Pentland, A., and Rahwan, I. (2016). Network diversity and affect dynamics: the role of personality traits. *PLOS One*, 11, e0152358. doi: 10.1371/journal.pone.0152358

Anthony, D.L., Campos-Castillo, C., & Horne, C. (2017). Toward a sociology of privacy. *Annual Review of Sociology*, 43(1), 249–269.

Bahulkar, A., Szymanski, B.K., Chan, K., & Lizardo, O. (2017). Coevolution of a multilayer node-aligned network whose layers represent different social relations. *Computational Social Networks*, 4(1), 11.

Black, M.P., Katsamanis, A., Baucom, B.R., Lee, C.C., Lammert, A.C., Christensen, A., Georgiou, P.G., & Narayanan, S.S. (2013). Toward automating a human behavioral coding system for married couples' interactions using speech acoustic features. *Speech Communication*, 55(1), 1–21. doi.org/10.1016/j.specom.2011.12.003

Bond, R.M., Fariss, C.J., Jones, J.J., Kramer, A.D.I., Marlow, C., Settle, J.E., & Fowler, J.H. (2012). A 61-million-person experiment in social influence and political mobilization. *Nature*, 489, 295–298.

Boutyline, A., & Willer, R. (2017). The social structure of political echo chambers: variation in ideological homophily in online networks. *Political Psychology*, 38, 551–569.

Centola, D. (2010). The spread of behavior in an online social network experiment. *Science*, 329(5996), 1194–1197.

Chaffin, D., Heidl, R., Hollenbeck, J. R., Howe, M., Yu, A., Voorhees, C., & Calantone, R. (2017). The promise and perils of wearable sensors in organizational research. *Organizational Research Methods*, 20, 3–31. doi: 10.1177/1094428115617004

Clay-Warner, J., & Robinson, D.T. (2015). Infrared thermography as a measure of emotion response. *Emotion Review*, 7(2), 157–162.

Coviello, L., Sohn, Y., Kramer, A.D.I., Marlow, C., Franceschetti, M., Christakis, N.A., & Fowler, J.H. (2014). Detecting emotional contagion in massive social networks. *PLOS One*, 9(3), e90315.

Crandall, D., Cosley, D., Huttenlocher, D., Kleinberg, J., & Suri, S. (2008). Feedback effects between similarity and social influence in online communities. In *Proceedings of the 14th ACM SIGKDD International Conference on Knowledge Discovery and Data Mining* (pp. 160–168). ACM.

Cranshaw, J., Toch, E., Hong, J., Kittur, A., & Sadeh, N. (2010). Bridging the gap between physical location and online social networks. In *Proceedings of the 12th ACM International Conference on Ubiquitous Computing* (pp. 119–128). ACM.

de Barbaro, K. (2019). Automated sensing of daily activity: a new lens into development. *Developmental Psychobiology*, 61(3), 444–464.

de Nooy, W. (2015). Structure from interaction events. *Big Data and Society*, 2(2).

Demiray, B., Luo, M., Tejeda-Padron, A., & Mehl, M.P. (2020). Sounds of healthy aging: assessing everyday social and cognitive activity from ecologically sampled ambient audio data. In P.L. Hill & M. Allemand (Eds.), *Personality and Healthy Aging in Adulthood* (pp. 111–132). Springer.

Dodds, P.S., Harris, K.D., Kloumann, I.M., Bliss, C.A., & Danforth, C.M. (2011). Temporal patterns of happiness and information in a global social network: hedonometrics and Twitter. *PLOS One*, 6(12), e26752.

Dragon, T., Arroyo, I., Woolf, B.P., Burleson, W., El Kaliouby, R., & Eydgahi, H. (2008). Viewing student affect and learning through classroom observation and physical sensors. Paper presented at the International Conference on Intelligent Tutoring Systems.

Eagle, N., Macy, M., & Claxton, R. (2010). Network diversity and economic development. *Science*, 328(5981), 1029–1031.

Eagle, N., Pentland, A. S., & Lazer, D. (2009). Inferring friendship network structure by using mobile phone data. *Proceedings of the National Academy of Sciences*, 106(36), 15274–15278.

Ejupi, A., & Menon, C. (2018). Detection of talking in respiratory signals: a feasibility study using

machine learning and wearable textile-based sensors. *Sensors*, *18*(8), 2474.
Flamino, J., Szymanski, B.K., Bahulkar, A., Chan, K., & Lizardo O. (2021). Creation, evolution, and dissolution of social groups. *Scientific Reports*, *11*(1), 1–11.
Fuhse, J.A. (2022). Analyzing networks in communication: a mixed methods study of a political debate. *Quality and Quantity*, March, 1–24.
Fuhse, J.A., & Gondal, N. (2022). Networks from culture: Mechanisms of tie-formation follow institutionalized rules in social fields. *Social Networks*, January.
Genkin, M., Harrigan, N., Kanagavel, R., & Yap, J. (2022). Dimensions of social networks: a taxonomy and operationalization. *Social Networks*, *71*(2), 12–31.
Gilbert, E., & Karahalios, K. (2009). Predicting tie strength with social media. In *Proceedings of the SIGCHI Conference on Human Factors in Computing Systems* (pp. 211–220). ACM.
Gilbert, N. (2010). *Computational social science*. Sage.
Goldberg, A., Hannan, M.T., & Kovács, B. (2016). What does it mean to span cultural boundaries? Variety and atypicality in cultural consumption. *American Sociological Review*, *81*(2), 215–241.
Golder, S.A., & Macy, M.W. (2011). Diurnal and seasonal mood vary with work, sleep, and daylength across diverse cultures. *Science*, *333*(6051), 1878–1881.
Golder, S.A., Wilkinson, D.M., & Huberman, B.A. (2007). Rhythms of social interaction: messaging within a massive online network. In C. Steinfield, B.T. Pentland, M. Ackerman & N. Contractor (Eds.), *Communities and technologies* (pp. 41–66). Springer.
Gu, J., Gao, B., Chen, Y., Jiang, L., Gao, Z., Ma, X.,… & Jin, J. (2017). Wearable social sensing: content-based processing methodology and implementation. *IEEE Sensors Journal*, *17*(21), 7167–7176.
Guclu, H., Read, J., Vukotich, C.J., Galloway, D.D., Gao, H., Rainey, J.J., Uzucanin, A., Zimmer, S.M., & Cummings, D.A.T. (2016). Social contact networks and mixing among students in K-12 schools in pittsburgh, PA. *PLOS One*, 11, e0151139. doi: 10.1371/journal.pone.01 51139
Harari, G.M., Müller, S.R., Stachl, C., Wang, R., Wang, W., Bühner, M., Rentfrow, P.J., Campbell, A.T., & Gosling, S.D. (2020). Sensing sociability: Individual differences in young adults' conversation, calling, texting, and app use behaviors in daily life. *Journal of Personality and Social Psychology*, *119*(1), 204–228. Advance online publication. http://dx.doi.org/10.1037/pspp0000245
Huberman, B.A., Romero, D.M., & Wu, F. (2009). Social networks that matter: Twitter under the microscope. *First Monday*, *14*(1).
Hung, H., Englebienne, G., & Kools, J. (2013). Classifying social actions with a single accelerometer. In *Proceedings of the 2013 ACM International Joint Conference on Pervasive and Ubiquitous Computing* (pp. 207–210). ACM.
Igarashi, T., Takai, J., & Yoshida, T. (2005). Gender differences in social network development via mobile phone text messages: a longitudinal study. *Journal of Social and Personal Relationships*, *22*, 691–713.
Iyengar, S., & Westwood, S. J. (2015). Fear and loathing across party lines: new evidence on group polarization. *American Journal of Political Science*, *59*(3), 690–707.
Jang, H., Choe, S.P., Gunkel, S.N., Kang, S., & Song, J. (2017). A system to analyze group socializing behaviors in social parties. *IEEE Transactions on Human-Machine Systems*, *47*(6), 801–813.
Kim, K.H., Bang, S.W., & Kim, S.R. (2004). Emotion recognition system using short-term monitoring of physiological signals. *Medical and Biological Engineering and Computing*, *42*, 419–427.
Kitts, J.A. (2014). Beyond networks in structural theories of exchange: promises from computational social science. *Advances in Group Processes*, *31*, 263–298.
Kitts, J.A., & Leal, D.F. (2021). What is(n't) a friend? Dimensions of the friendship concept among adolescents. *Social Networks*, *66*, 161–170.
Kitts, J.A. & Quintane, E. (2020). Rethinking social networks in the era of computational social science. In R. Light & J. Moody (Eds.), *The Oxford handbook of social networks* (pp 71–97). Oxford University Press.
Kleinbaum, A.M., Stuart, T.E., & Tushman, M.L. (2013). Discretion within constraint: homophily and structure in a formal organization. *Organization Science*, *24*(5), 1316–1336.
Kossinets, G., & Watts, D.J. (2009). Origins of homophily in an evolving social network. *American Journal of Sociology*, *115*(2), 405–450.
Lazer, D., Pentland, A., Adamic, L., Aral, S., Barabási, A. L., Brewer, D., Brewer, D., Christakis, N., Contractor, N., Fowler, J., Gutmann, M., Jebara, T., King, G., Macy, M., Roy, D., & Van Alstyne, M. (2009). Computational social science. *Science*, *323*(5915), 721–723.
Lee, Y., Min, C., Hwang, C., Lee, J., Hwang, I., Ju, Y., Yoo, C., Moon, M., Lee, U., & Song, J. (2013). Sociophone: everyday face-to-face interaction monitoring platform using multi-phone sensor fusion. In *Proceedings of the 11th Annual International Conference on Mobile Systems, Applications, and Services* (pp. 375–388). ACM.
Leskovec, J., & Horvitz, E. (2008). Planetary-scale views on a large instant-messaging network. In *WWW '08: Proceedings of the 17th International*

Conference on World Wide Web (pp. 915–924). Beijing.
Leskovec, J., Huttenlocher, D., & Kleinberg, J. (2010). Signed networks in social media. In *Proceedings of the SIGCHI Conference on Human Factors in Computing Systems* (pp. 1361–1370). ACM.
Lewis, K. (2016). Preferences in the early stages of mate choice. *Social Forces*, 95(1), 283–320.
Lewis, K. (2022). Digital networks: elements of a theoretical framework. *Social Networks*.
Lewis, K., Kaufman, J., & Christakis, N. (2008a). The taste for privacy: an analysis of college student privacy settings in an online social network. *Journal of Computer-Mediated Communication*, 14, 79–100.
Lewis, K., Kaufman, J., Gonzalez, M., Wimmer, A., & Christakis, N. (2008b). Tastes, ties, and time: a new social network dataset using Facebook.com. *Social Networks*, 30, 330–342.
Lin, K.H., & Lundquist, J. (2013). Mate selection in cyberspace: the intersection of race, gender, and education. *American Journal of Sociology*, 119(1), 183–215.
Lovett, T., O'Neill, E., Irwin, J., & Pollington, D. (2010). The calendar as a sensor: analysis and improvement using data fusion with social networks and location. In *Proceedings of the 12th ACM International Conference on Ubiquitous Computing* (pp. 3–12). ACM.
Malik, M.M. (2018). Bias and beyond in digital trace data (doctoral dissertation, Carnegie Mellon University). reports-archive.adm.cs.cmu.edu/anon/isr2018/ abstracts/18-105.html
Marin, A., & Hampton, K.N. (2007). Simplifying the personal network name generator: alternatives to traditional multiple and single name generators. *Field Methods*, 19(2), 163–193.
Mayer, A., & Puller, S.L. (2008). The old boy (and girl) network: social network formation on university campuses. *Journal of Public Economics*, 92, 329–347.
Meijerink-Bosman, M., Back, M., Geukes, K., Leenders, R., & Mulder, J. (2022). Discovering trends of social interaction behavior over time: an introduction to relational event modeling. *Behavior Research Methods*, 1–27.
Müller, J., Fàbregues, S., Guenther, E.A., & Romano, M.J. (2019). Using sensors in organizational research – clarifying rationales and validation challenges for mixed methods. *Frontiers in Psychology*, 10, 1188.
Olguin, D.O., Waber, B.N., Taemie, K., Mohan, A., Ara, K., & Pentland, A. (2009). Sensible organizations: technology and methodology for automatically measuring organizational behavior. *IEEE Transactions on Systems Man and Cybernetics*, Part B 39, 43–55. doi: 10.1109/TSMCB.2008.2006638
Oloritun, R.O., Madan, A., Pentland, A., & Khayal, I. (2013). Identifying close friendships in a sensed social network. *Procedia-Social and Behavioral Sciences*, 79, 18–26.
Onnela, J.-P., Saramäki, J., Hyvönen, J., Szabó, G., Lazer, D., Kaski, K., Kertész, J., & Barabási, A.-L. (2007). Structure and tie strengths in mobile communication networks. In *Proceedings of the National Academy of Sciences*, 104, 7332.
Onnela, J.-P., Waber, B.N., Pentland, A., Schnorf, S., & Lazer, D. (2014). Using sociometers to quantify social interaction patterns. *Scientific Reports*, 4, 5604. doi: 10.1038/srep06278
Palaghias, N., Hoseinitabatabaei, S.A., Nati, M., Gluhak, A., & Moessner, K. (2016). A survey on mobile social signal processing. *ACM Computing Surveys (CSUR)*, 48(4), 57.
Paluck, E.L., & Shepherd, H. (2012). The salience of social referents: a field experiment on collective norms and harassment behavior in a school social network. *Journal of Personality and Social Psychology*, 103(6), 899.
Papacharissi, Z., & Oliveira, M.d.F. (2012). Affective news and networked publics: the rhythms of news storytelling on #Egypt. *Journal of Communication*, 62, 266–282.
Park, P.S., & Kim, Y.H. (2017). Reciprocation under status ambiguity: how dominance motives and spread of status value shape gift exchange. *Social Networks*, 48, 142–156.
Parker, J.N., Cardenas, E., Dorr, A.N., & Hackett, E.J. (2018). Using sociometers to advance small group research. *Sociological Methods and Research*. doi: 10.1177/0049124118769091
Pham, T.M., Korbel, J., Hanel, R., & Thurner, S. (2022). Empirical social triad statistics can be explained with dyadic homophylic interactions. *Proceedings of the National Academy of Sciences*, 119(6).
Piskorski, M.J., & Gorbatâi, A. (2017). Testing Coleman's social-norm enforcement mechanism: evidence from Wikipedia. *American Journal of Sociology*, 122, 1183–1222.
Poudyal, A., Van Heerden, A., Hagaman, A., Islam, C., Thapa, A., Maharjan, S.M., Byanjankar, P., & Kohrt, B.A. (2021). What does social support sound like? Challenges and opportunities for using passive episodic audio collection to assess the social environment. *Frontiers in Public Health*, 9.
Pozzi, F.A., Fersini, E., Messina, E., & Liu, B. (2016). *Sentiment analysis in social networks*. Morgan Kaufmann.
Rachuri, K.K., Musolesi, M., Mascolo, C., Rentfrow, P.J., Longworth, C., & Aucinas, A. (2010). EmotionSense: a mobile phones based adaptive platform for experimental social psychology research. In *Proceedings of the 12th ACM International Conference on Ubiquitous Computing* (pp. 281–290). September. ACM.
Raeder, T., Lizardo, O., Hachen, D., & Chawla, N.V. (2011). Predictors of short-term decay of cell

phone contacts in a large scale communication network. *Social Networks*, *33*(4), 245–257.

Rahman, M.M., Ali, A.A., Plarre, K., Al'Absi, M., Ertin, E., & Kumar, S. (2011). mconverse: inferring conversation episodes from respiratory measurements collected in the field. In *Proceedings of the 2nd Conference on Wireless Health* (p. 10). ACM.

Salathé, M., Kazandjieva, M., Lee, J.W., Levis, P., Feldman, M.W., and Jones, J.H. (2010). A high-resolution human contact network for infectious disease transmission. *Proceedings of the National Academy of Sciences of the United States of America*, *107*, 22020–22025. doi: 10.1073/pnas.1009094108

Schmid Mast, M., Gatica-Perez, D., Frauendorfer, D., Nguyen, L., & Choudhury, T. (2015). Social sensing for psychology: automated interpersonal behavior assessment. *Current Directions in Psychological Science*, *24*(2), 154–160.

Sekara, V., & Lehmann, S. (2014). The strength of friendship ties in proximity sensor data. *PLOS One*, *9*, e100915. doi: 10.1371/journal.pone.0100915

Srivastava, S.B., Goldberg, A., Manian, V.G., & Potts, C. (2018). Enculturation trajectories: language, cultural adaptation, and individual outcomes in organizations. *Management Science*, *64*, 1348–1364.

Stadtfeld, C., & Block, P. (2017). Interactions, actors, and time: dynamic network actor models for relational events. *Sociological Science*, *4*, 318–352.

State, B., Abrahao, B., & Cook, K. (2016). Power imbalance and rating systems. In *Proceedings of the 10th International AAAI Conference on Web and Social Media (ICWSM)*.

Sumner, E.M., Ruge-Jones, L., & Alcorn, D. (2017). A functional approach to the Facebook Like button: an exploration of meaning, interpersonal functionality, and potential alternative response buttons. *New Media and Society*, *20*(4), 1451–1469.

Tindall, D., McLevey, J., Koop-Monteiro, Y., & Graham, A. (2022). Big data, computational social science, and other recent innovations in social network analysis. *Canadian Review of Sociology*, *59*(2), 271–288.

Tremayne, M. (2014). Anatomy of protest in the digital era: a network analysis of Twitter and Occupy Wall Street. *Social Movement Studies*, *13*, 110–126.

Vörös, A., Boda, Z., Elmer, T., Hoffman, M., Mepham, K., Raabe, I.J., & Stadtfeld, C. (2021). The Swiss StudentLife study: investigating the emergence of an undergraduate community through dynamic, multidimensional social network data. *Social Networks*, *65*, 71–84.

Wang, J., Chen, G., & Kotz, D. (2004). A sensor-fusion approach for meeting detection. *Dartmouth Scholarship*, 3311. digitalcommons.dartmouth.edu/facoa/3311

Wimmer, A., & Lewis, K. (2010). Beyond and below racial homophily: ERG models of a friendship network documented on Facebook. *American Journal of Sociology*, *116*(2), 583–642.

Wyatt, D., Bilmes, J., Choudhury, T., & Kitts, J.A. (2008). Towards the automated social analysis of situated speech data. In *Proceedings of the 10th International Conference on Ubiquitous Computing* (pp. 168–171). ACM.

Wyatt, D., Choudhury, T., Bilmes, J., & Kitts, J.A. (2011). Inferring colocation and conversation networks from privacy-sensitive audio with implications for computational social science. *ACM Transactions on Intelligent Systems and Technology (TIST)*, *2*(1), 7.

Yang, D., Huang, C., & Wang, M. (2017). A social recommender system by combining social network and sentiment similarity: a case study of healthcare. *Journal of Information Science*, *43*(5), 635–648.

Zhang, A., Goosby, B., & Cheadle, J.E. (2021). In the flow of life: capturing affective socializing dynamics using a wearable sensor and intensive daily diaries. *Socius*, *7*, 1–15.

Zhang, Y., Olenick, J., Chang, C.-H., Kozlowski, S.W.J., & Hung, H. (2018). TeamSense: assessing personal affect and group cohesion in small teams through dyadic interaction and behavior analysis with wearable sensors. In *Proceedings of the ACM on Interactive, Mobile, Wearable and Ubiquitous Technologies*. ACM. *2*, 1–22. doi: 10.1145/3264960

Zhao, M., Adib, F., & Katabi, D. (2016). Emotion recognition using wireless signals. In *Proceedings of the 22nd Annual International Conference on Mobile Computing and Networking* (pp. 95–108). ACM.

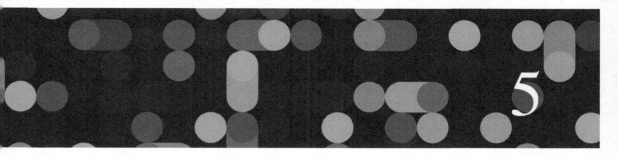

Relational Sociology: Networks, Culture And Interaction*

Jan Fuhse and Ann Mische

Network researchers have long grappled with the theoretical status of social networks (Granovetter, 1979). In the 1980s, existing theoretical paradigms like symbolic interactionism and rational choice theory sought to incorporate networks into their frameworks (Fine & Kleinman, 1983; Coleman, 1990). At the same time, some voices in the networks community proclaimed a new paradigm with social relations – rather than individuals, groups, attributes, or categories – as the fundamental unit of social analysis (Wellman, 1988). Social networks were assumed to form the centre stage in social life, contributing to diverse outcomes such as job attainment, social mobilisation and collective action, economic processes and the diffusion of information. This 'structuralist' vision of the social world implicitly underlies most network research and yields important insights.

In the 1990s, a small group of network researchers, theorists, historical sociologists and social movement scholars in New York City and elsewhere expanded on this perspective to develop a new way of thinking about social networks. This new approach builds on the dual premises (1) that social relations and networks do not exist as mere structural patterns, but that they are interwoven with *culture* (social categories, narratives, symbolic markers etc.) and (2) that they dynamically form and develop over the course of *interaction*.

This perspective takes some of the broader theoretical insights of network analysis and extends them to the realms of culture, history, politics, economics and social psychology.

The well-known Manifesto by Mustafa Emirbayer (1997) labeled the approach as 'relational sociology'. Since 2000, a wider understanding of relational sociology as a theoretical project has flourished, with diverse contributions from positions including symbolic interactionism, Elias's configurational sociology, critical realism, Bourdieu's field theory, or actor-network theory (Dépelteau, 2018). We leave aside most of this discourse with little connection to network research to focus on the specific North American version of relational sociology that developed around White and Tilly (Fuhse, 2020a). To demarcate it from other versions of relational sociology, we call it the *networks, culture and interaction* (NCI) approach to relational sociology. The NCI perspective diverges from other strands of relational sociology in its central emphasis on networks as patterns of relations based on processes of communication and meaning-making.

This chapter starts with an account of the emergence of this approach from its origins at Harvard University in the 1960s to 1980s to the intersecting networks and intense discussions in the New York area in the 1990s and 2000s. We go on to sketch other sites of conversation related to relational sociology and its proliferation into wider sociological and network research. The final part of the chapter gives a brief overview of the central conceptual elements of the approach.

Our chronicle of the emergence and development of this perspective draws on its own core concepts. Conversations in New York City in particular, but also in other hubs of the approach and dissemination to Europe, developed through personal network connections and in overlapping discussion forums related to networks and culture. These settings acted as 'publics' where diverse networks intersected, where junior and senior scholars interacted and where outside scholars brought in important impulses. As participants wrestled with the tensions generated in these conversations, they developed not a unified theory (important differences remain among them), but rather a shared focus on the meaningful construction of network relations and of their grounding in dynamic processes of interaction. In short, the NCI approach is itself an example of how networks of social relationships are infused with meaning, give rise to new cultural orientations and change over the course of interaction.

Budding Seeds: Structuralism and the Harvard Moment

Before the 1970s, network analysis was by and large an obscure speciality in the periphery of the social sciences. This changed with what Linton Freeman calls 'The Renaissance at Harvard' (2004, pp. 121ff). Trained physicist Harrison White was hired by Harvard University's Department of Social Relations in 1963. With his early works on kinship structures and vacancy chains, he established a focus on empirically observable network patterns, in opposition to the dominant 'grand' systems theory of Talcott Parsons. White assembled an impressive group of graduate students that went on to build prominent careers and to firmly establish network research on the sociological radar. These included Peter Bearman, Philipp Bonacich, Scott Boorman, Ronald Breiger, Kathleen Carley, Bonnie Erickson, Roger Gould, Mark Granovetter, Edward Laumann, David Stark, Barry Wellman and many others, with Charles Tilly and John Padgett as colleagues, and Paul DiMaggio, Mustafa Emirbayer and Margaret Somers as PhD students in the orbit around White.

White's own research with key collaborators Boorman and Breiger focused on the concept of structural equivalence and on developing the blockmodeling technique (White et al., 1976; Boorman & White, 1976). While blockmodeling remains largely true to a structuralist position, it does imply that networks are interwoven with cultural meaning, in particular with role categories and different types of relationships (Brint, 1992). Together, the work of White and his students and colleagues led to a notable increase in attention to social networks, transforming networks from an eccentric interest of a few mathematicians and technically oriented sociological outsiders to an established feature of the social world.

By the 1990s, this made for a mature field, with the publication of several handbooks and edited volumes as well as a specialised journal and a professional association. However, most network studies were highly formal and technical, making them relatively inaccessible to nonmathematical researchers. Cultural theorists tended to view network analysis as located squarely in the positivist camp, reducing cultural richness to 1s and 0s and lacking attention to processes of interpretation and meaning construction (Fuhse, 2009; Erikson, 2013).

At the same time, the subfield of cultural sociology in the United States was undergoing a rapid expansion and shift in orientation, moving beyond the study of artistic production to encompass practice and discourse more generally. While a handful of researchers in the late 1980s and early 1990s were starting to pioneer the use of network analytic techniques to study cultural and historical processes (Erickson, 1988, 1996; Carley, 1994; Bearman, 1993; Bearman & Stovel, 2000; Mohr, 1994; Gould, 1995), a sizeable gap remained between formal network analysis and cultural research (Pachucki & Breiger, 2010).

The Setting: Columbia and the New School

These streams converged in the mid-1990s in New York City as a cluster of scholars across several universities in the area engaged in a series of intensive exchanges related to networks, culture and historical analysis. One centre was Columbia University, where network researcher Ronald Burt pushed for the hiring of Harrison White in 1988, before moving to Chicago. White took on the directorship of the Paul F. Lazarsfeld Center for the Social Sciences, which sponsored a series of interdisciplinary workshops on topics including social networks, sociolinguistics, complex systems and political economy. These workshops brought in outside speakers while sponsoring graduate students and nurturing local research and debate.

A few miles to the South, the Graduate Faculty of the New School for Social Research was another lively hub of interdisciplinary discussion. In the mid-1980s, Charles and Louise Tilly were hired and joined a diverse faculty of critical theorists, poststructuralists and structurally oriented historical scholars. Debates were frequent and intense, pushing Tilly to re-examine the role of identities, narratives and discourse in theories of contentious politics (see below). In 1991, Harvard graduate Mustafa Emirbayer arrived at the New School as an assistant professor. Influenced by American pragmatism and the Durkheimian interpretive tradition, he and his fellow Harvard alum Jeff Goodwin (NYU) called for a systematic consideration of culture in network research (Emirbayer and Goodwin, 1994).

Harrison White began what might be called his 'cultural turn' in the early 1990s with his major theoretical statement, *Identity and Control* (1992, second thoroughly rewritten edition, 2008). White had been preoccupied since the 1970s with the lack of theoretical understanding of network ties, and specifically different 'types of ties' (as the units of blockmodel analysis and role algebras). In *Identity and Control*, he argues that network ties are generated and defined in 'stories' about the behaviour of identities in relation to each other ('efforts at control'), and these stories then structure future interaction (White, 1992, p. 67; see below). The new challenge for network analysis, White argues, is to understand the link between temporality, language and social relations.

The Deliberations

Many of these ideas were elaborated in White's ongoing graduate seminar on 'Identity and Control' at Columbia, as well as in student-organised workshops at the Lazarsfeld Center. These settings contributed to a series of papers on the relationship between language, time, publics, conversational 'situations' and social relations (White, 1995; Mische & White, 1998). These papers propose the notion of 'network domains' or 'netdoms,' to mark the intertwining of *net*works of social relations and *dom*ains of cultural forms (Mische & Chandler, 2019; Mische, 2021; see below).

Between 1993 and 1996, White organised a series of miniconferences at the Lazarsfeld Center around the themes of time, language, identities and networks. A broad range of outside scholars took part, with expertise across cultural, historical, organisational, psychological and network subfields (Mische, 2011). At one miniconference, Emirbayer was inspired to write a programmatic statement that systematised ideas that the group was discussing. The resulting 'Manifesto for a relational sociology' (Emirbayer, 1997) draws on pragmatist, linguistic and interactionist philosophies to call for a 'transactional' approach focusing on the dynamics of 'supra-personal' relations that connect and transcend individual entities. This widely cited article has become one of the rallying cries of the 'new relational' approach in sociology.

At the same time, Emirbayer was organising a study group on Theory and Culture at the New School that brought in graduate students and some faculty from the broader New York area (including the New School, Columbia, NYU, Princeton and CUNY), with a focus on pragmatist, cultural and relational scholarship. Several participants in the Theory/Culture group were also students of Charles Tilly at the New School, where they engaged in another essential public for the discussion of relational sociology: Tilly's Workshop on Contentious Politics. This workshop was started by Charles and Louise Tilly at Michigan in the 1970s, transplanted to the New School in the late 1980s and then relocated again when Tilly moved to Columbia in 1996. The famously democratic workshop drew in faculty and students from the greater New York region and many international scholars.

Tilly is widely known as a social movements scholar and historical sociologist. However, as an early Harvard colleague and life-long friend of Harrison White, he had already recognised the importance of networks in social movements in the 1970s (Tilly 1978). During the 1990s, Tilly was undergoing a transition from a mostly structuralist conflict-focused position to an emphasis on relational and conversational processes of meaning-making, such as boundary activation, identity formation and storytelling (Tilly, 2002; Diani, 2007; Tarrow, 2008; Krinsky & Mische, 2013). During this period, he published on the relational underpinnings of categorical inequality (1998), on the social construction of political identities in narratives (2002, 2006a) and on the historical invention and change of action repertoires of social movements (1995; Tilly & Wood, 2003). He termed the underlying perspective 'relational realism' in contrast to 'methodological individualism', 'phenomenological individualism' and 'holism'. In a series of broad statements, he described relational realism as 'the doctrine that transactions, interactions, social ties and conversations constitute the central stuff of social life' (2002, p. 72; see also Tilly 2006b, 2008; for a related perspective on 'relational realism', see Somers, 1993, 1998). This perspective became a cornerstone of the contentious politics approach, advanced with Doug McAdam and Sidney Tarrow (McAdam et al., 2001).

In 1996, Tilly moved to Columbia University, consolidating its position as a hub for relational sociology. Historical sociologist Karen Barkey had joined in 1988, publishing a major study on the role of networks in the bureaucratic transformation of the Ottoman Empire (1994; Barkey & van Rossem, 1997). Francesca Polletta finished several important works while at Columbia on relational and communicative processes of deliberation and storytelling in political protest (Polletta, 2002, 2006). David Stark arrived from Cornell in 1997, bringing a focus on network combinatorics in political and economic transitions. Duncan Watts was a postdoctoral fellow in 1997–1998 and joined the faculty in 2000, contributing mathematical expertise and complex thinking on network patterns. And in 1999, Peter Bearman came to Columbia from the University of North Carolina, strengthening the Harvard contingent of empirical network researchers.

A strong generation of PhD students studied with varying combinations of White, Tilly, Emirbayer, Bearman, Barkey and Stark during the 1990s and 2000s, participating in cross-cutting workshops and study groups in the New York milieu. From the New School, these included Javier Auyero, Chad Goldberg, Ann Mische and Mimi Sheller. Sheller (2000), for example, examines linguistic markers and social networks in black antislavery counter-publics in Haiti and Jamaica. Auyero (2001) draws heavily on Tilly's notion of 'relational mechanisms' in his work on networks, performance and popular protest in Latin America. Chad Goldberg (2007) worked with Emirbayer and Tilly in studying the relational reconstruction of the citizenship discourse through struggles over class, race and welfare rights.

Columbia students from that time include Delia Baldassari, Matthew Bothner, Emily Erikson, Jorge Fontdevila, David Gibson, Frédéric Godart, Hennig Hillmann, John Krinsky, Jennifer Lena, Sophie Mützel, Paolo Parigi, Tammy Smith, Matthias Thiemann, Leslie Wood, Balazs Vedres and many more. Many of them combine networks and discourse in one way or another, such as Krinsky's (2007) study of discourse, relations and contentious events in welfare-to-work programmes in New York City, Bearman and Parigi's study (2004) of the relationship between social networks and conversational topics, and Hillman's (2008) study of mediation across multiple elite networks before the English civil war.

In short, the New York area in the 1990s and 2000s was a rich hub of conversation that reformulated the link between networks, culture and social interaction. The 'publics' convened across these universities combined a complex web of overlapping personal ties (colleagueship, co-authorship, dissertation advising, workshop participation and study group membership) with frequent cross-fertilisation by visiting scholars. The emerging perspective straddled structuralist and interpretivist positions, stressing the mutual constitution of networks and discourse, the communicative nature of social ties and the interplay between multiple relations in social action.

NETWORKED CONVERSATIONS

In 2008, Tilly died after a long struggle with cancer. White retired from Columbia in 2011 and moved to Tucson, Arizona. While this dissolved some of the publics in and around New York City, it did not end the theoretical conversations, and New York was not the only place where they thrived. In this section, we sketch additional hubs of relational sociology that developed out of Harvard, in conversation with the New York publics and through the movement of its participants to universities elsewhere.

Chicago

In 1984, White's and Breiger's colleague John Padgett moved from Harvard to the University of Chicago, where he started a long-term research project on the political, economic and familial networks in Renaissance Florence. The first paper from the project accounts for the rise of the Medici family in Florence out of their favourable network position at the intersection of economic credit ties and family alliances (Padgett & Ansell, 1993). While this can be seen as the consequence of projecting identities in networks (Emirbayer & Goodwin, 1994), Padgett is less interested in the interplay between networks and culture than in the development of organisational forms – as in the emergence of the partnership form in Florentine banking (Padgett and McLean 2006). In his book with Walter Powell, Padgett lays out a general theory of how social networks arise in the process of communication, and how different kinds of networks relate to each other to breed organisational innovation (Padgett & Powell, 2012).

In addition to Padgett, Andrew Abbott, Karin Knorr Cetina and Roger Gould (before his move to Yale and early death in 2000) were frequent interlocutors with the approach around White, making Chicago a lively hub in the relational sociology network. Several Chicago PhDs from the 1990s and 2000s have made important contributions, including Chistopher Ansell, who examined the role of symbolic networks in cross-sectoral mobilisation (1997), as well as Paul McLean and Daniel McFarland (discussed below). In 2008, John Levi Martin – former colleague of McLean and Mische at Rutgers – arrived at the University of Chicago to strengthen the relational sociological contingent. In addition to his early quantitative work on the interplay of network structures and culture in urban communes, Martin gave key theoretical impulses with his theory of large-scale social structures out of micro-network patterns (2009) and with his revised version of field theory (2003, 2011).

Tucson, Arizona

In 1981, White's former student and collaborator Ronald Breiger moved to Cornell University. He frequently participated in the New York workshops before transferring to the University of Arizona at Tucson in 2000. There he joined network scholars Joseph Galaskiewicz, Lynn Smith-Lovin and Miller McPherson. Breiger contributed the concept of 'duality' to relational sociology with a highly influential mathematical formulation of the Simmelian idea that individuals and groups mutually define each other in affiliation networks (1974). Later, he used the concept of duality to point out that actors and their sociocultural practices are also dual, building on Bourdieu (Breiger, 2000, cf. Mohr & Duquênne, 1997). These considerations apply to the general interplay between networks of affiliations and the cultural meanings associated with them (Mützel & Breiger, 2020). Breiger continues exploring the implications and use of a diverse set of cutting-edge methods such as computational text analysis, multiple correspondence analysis, and qualitative comparative analysis, as well as conventional regression analysis.

Important studies linking culture and networks come from Breiger's student, Omar Lizardo, who joined the University of Notre Dame and then UCLA. Lizardo analyses how cultural tastes influence network tie formation (2006), and draws on Breiger's notion of 'duality' to measure cultural omnivorousness (2015). He also collaborated with Stephen Vaisey in a study of how moral values (as deep-seated cultural schemas) shape friendship networks (Vaisey & Lizardo, 2009).

Yale

White's second blockmodelling collaborator, Scott Boorman, moved to Yale University in 1976, soon joined by Paul DiMaggio. While DiMaggio is best known for his work in neo-institutionalism with Walter Powell (1983), he has published extensively on the role of social networks in social inequality (DiMaggio, 1987) and in social fields (1986, 1991). DiMaggio's research is influenced by the sociology of Pierre Bourdieu, highlighting the importance of symbolic practices and cultural capital. DiMaggio went on to work at Princeton and since 2016 at New York University. Two noteworthy DiMaggio students from Yale are Helmut Anheier and John Mohr (see below).

Eiko Ikegami (another Harvard alumna) frequently joined the New York discussions from Yale in the 1990s before moving to the New School of Social Research in 1999. Her research on historical creativity, social relations and aesthetic publics in Japan firmly joins networks and culture (1995, 2005). Emily Erikson was hired by Yale in 2010; her research focuses on the role of networks in historical economics, such as trade patterns in the Indian Ocean (Erikson & Bearman, 2006). She also contributes to recent discussions on relational sociology with her distinction between formalism and relationalism in network research (2013).

Santa Barbara and 'Measuring Culture'

After studying at Yale with DiMaggio, John Mohr joined the University of California at Santa Barbara, where he worked until his untimely death in 2019. Mohr pioneered the analysis of cultural networks between symbols or categories in archival material, using formal techniques such as blockmodeling and Galois lattices (1994, 1998; Mohr & Duquênne, 1997). Like DiMaggio, he draws heavily on Bourdieu to interpret cultural networks as institutionalised 'meaning structures' in social fields. As we discuss below, this move towards a 'cultural network analysis' has deeply influenced relational sociology, connecting it to two important sites of theoretical and methodological development. One site is the budding field of computational social science, which frequently analyses textual data with regard to systematic network patterns (see below). In an important collaboration with Breiger and cultural sociologist Robin Wagner-Pacifici, Mohr et al. (2013; 2015) envision a 'computational hermeneutics' that first explores text data in quantitative automation before zooming in on qualitative interpretation.

The second site consists of discussions around the measurement of culture that Mohr spearheaded since the 1990s through a series of conferences and symposia (with Ann Swidler, Roger Friedland and others). In 2013 Mohr helped assemble a group of prominent junior scholars to discuss the use of diverse methods in the cultural analysis of persons, objects and relations (Mohr & Ghaziani, 2014; Mohr et al., 2020). The *Measuring Culture* project reinforces the now widespread recognition that culture can be studied with both interpretive-qualitative and formal-quantitative methods. In alignment with this approach, two prominent Mohr students, Clayton Childress and Craig Rawlings, use formal network analysis and other methods to study interconnections between networks and culture. They have examined interactional dynamics of meaning-making in book groups (Rawlings & Childress, 2019) and sensory interpretation (Rawlings and Childress 2021); as well as the relational dynamics of book prize evaluations (Childress et al., 2017).

Rutgers and Notre Dame

Another hub in close proximity to New York City sprang up at Rutgers University with the hiring of three junior relational sociologists. John Levi Martin arrived from Berkeley in 1997, joined two years later by Paul McLean from Chicago and Ann Mische from the New School. Together, they brought a research focus on networks and culture using both quantitative and qualitative methods. They supervised a younger cohort of relational sociologists including King-To Yeung, Neha Gondal and Sourabh Singh. McLean continues to work at Rutgers, with his overview book *Culture in Networks* (2017), a major resource for introducing students to the approach.

The double hire of Mische and David Gibson (who both studied with White, along with Tilly and Bearman respectively) by the University of Notre Dame in 2013 made their sociology department another relational sociology hub. Omar Lizardo was at Notre Dame at the time, along with cultural sociologists Lyn Spillman, Erika Summers-Effler and Terry McDonnell, leading to lively discussions about networks, culture and interaction. Notre Dame hosted the 2015 gathering of the *Measuring Culture* group that laid the groundwork for the 2020 book.

Duke

In the 2000s, the sociology department at Duke University established itself as a major centre for social network analysis, slowly acquiring a relational sociological tilt. Miller McPherson and Lynn Smith-Lovin arrived from Arizona in 2002. In 2006, Bearman's student James Moody was hired, followed by Stephen Vaisey in 2011 and Christopher Bail in 2015. Bail had developed a strong interest in social networks and the spread of ideas in political discourse at Harvard University. He is now a leading computational social scientist studying political polarisation, particularly with regard to online communication (Bail, 2015, 2021). In 2018, the department hired Mohr's student Craig Rawlings, who engaged in several collaborations on network and interactions with Moody and McFarland (now at Stanford). Notable students from Duke include Ryan Light and Achim Edelmann.

Europe

Since 2000 the NCI approach has branched out vigorously to Europe, often through European graduate students returning to their home countries. Examples are Henning Hillmann (from Columbia through Stanford to Mannheim), Sophie Mützel (from Columbia to Berlin and later Lucerne, Switzerland) and Frédéric Godart (Columbia to INSEAD, Paris). Three Germans, Achim Edelmann (from Duke), Matthias Thiemann and Philipp Brandt (both from Columbia) are located at SciencePo in Paris. Mexican Victor Corona (from Columbia) is now based in Barcelona. Reza Azarian (Uppsala) and Jan Fuhse (Berlin) converged into relational sociology with research visits to Columbia. Nick Crossley (Manchester) developed his own version of relational sociology (2011) based on a pragmatist-interactionist vision of social structure, partly in dialogue with the approach around White (see below). Crossley's empirical work on the emergence of punk and post-punk in the UK demonstrates the importance of close-knit networks of interaction for cultural creativity (2015).

Together, these European connections signal that the NCI approach to relational sociology is no longer confined to North America, but more broadly recognised and diffused internationally. The publics where the approach is discussed and elaborated include international journals and book publications, as well as conferences as in Berlin 2008 (organised by Fuhse and Mützel) or at Stanford 2017 (organised by Amir Goldberg and Daniel McFarland).

KEY THEMES

Our overview of the development of relational sociology focused more on personal connections and institutional affiliations than on ideas. In the following, we provide short discussions of key themes in the networks, culture and interaction approach. We focus (1) on the conceptualization of networks and ties as co-constituted with stories, categories and identities, (2) on the analysis of culture itself as networked, and (3) on how networks inform agency, publics and fields.

Networks and Ties

The key move of White's *Identity and Control* (1992, 2008a) is to lay out a phenomenological conception of social networks. These are no longer regarded as acultural patterns of edges between nodes. Instead, networks are patterns of meaning, of identities linked to each other in stories. Both key terms of network research are reconceptualised in terms of meaning:

- *Nodes* become identities constructed at various levels of generality (White 2008a, pp. 9–12). A node is no longer just the intersection of lines in a network graph (as in structuralism), or an isolated heroic actor bringing about social processes (as in rational choice). Rather, an identity is a projection point very much shaped by its network environment.
- *Edges* are now symbolically constructed relationships between identities, and this construction takes the form of stories about how they relate to each other (Tilly, 2002). These stories recount events or episodes ('Alan brought roses for Sue on Valentine's Day') and define the relationship between identities.

Overall, social networks acquire a 'phenomenological reality' (White, 1992, p. 65); they become 'meaning structures' (Fuhse, 2022, pp. 26–71) that structure the interaction within and across them.

Story

The concept of 'story' is not really defined in the first edition of *Identity and Control* (White 1992, p. 68). Tilly gives a more concise rendering with his concept of 'standard stories', later taken up by White in the revision of *Identity and Control* (2008a, pp. 29f). According to Tilly, 'standard stories' are the predominant kind of narratives in the social world (2002, pp. 8f, 26ff, 2006b). They recount events as springing from the autonomous actions and motivations of individuals, rather than from external circumstances. A story about the doings of a set of characters symbolically relates them to each other, which sets the scene for their future interaction, thereby constructing time as well as relations.

The notion of story adds both symbolic construction and dynamics to network ties. These are evolving, rather than static, on the basis of changing narratives about relationships. White adds that stories classify events into behaviours typical for kinds of relationships: 'types of story-tie' (2008a, p. 31). For example, the bringing of roses is typical for romantic relationships (or for dating behaviours) and will be classified as such. The stories told about identities and their relations to each other build on culturally shared interpretations of how actors relate to each other. Individual behaviour is carefully monitored for the kinds of relationships it fits into, and behaviour is designed to signal particular kinds of relationships (McLean, 1998). This parallels the focus on the 'relational work' that goes into building culturally meaningful ties and exchanges in recent economic sociology (Zelizer, 2012; Wherry, 2016; Bandelj, 2020).

White's notion of 'identities' signals that not only individuals become enmeshed in networks. Tilly's focus on political constellations requires that we include collective and corporate actors like insurgent groups, political parties, or states (2002). For these 'political identities' to form, actors tell stories about them and their relations to each other, making them projection points for expectations and future interaction. In his theory of social inequality, Tilly points to stories around social categories like gender or race as constituting and legitimising these collectivities (1998, pp. 63f, 102f). Tammy Smith reconstructs two different sets of stories around ethnic boundaries in Istria and New York City (2007). These map different sets of social relationships between people involved, while also reinforcing them symbolically.

Social Categories and Collective Identities

In an early, long unpublished set of notes, White formulates the concept of 'catnet' to capture how social categories contribute to the ordering of social ties (2008b, pp. 8ff). The category symbolically separates an inside from outside, fostering dense ties between members of the same category, while cross-category ties thin out. This results in 'catnets': networks of increased internal density bounded by *cat*egories. In his early work, Tilly (1978) extends this concept to political mobilisation, arguing that populations are only able to mobilise around common causes if they show these dual features of catnets: 'catness' (identifying with a social category) and 'netness' (internal connectivity; 1978, pp. 62ff). His later theory of 'durable inequality' builds on the same ordering of social networks by categories, such as ethnic categories (Tilly, 1998). This allows groups to 'hoard opportunities' since outsiders are symbolically represented as different and barred from access to resources. Gould's account of the Paris Commune offers an expansion of Tilly's mobilisation argument. Here, the collective identity allowing for the mobilisation of insurgents as 'Parisians' builds on increased interpersonal and neighbourhood connectivity, supplanting work-based ties (Gould, 1995, pp. 13–18, 200–206). 'Catness' depends on 'netness'.

The notion of *structural equivalence* and its analysis in blockmodeling rest on a wider notion of the interplay of categories and networks (White et al., 1976). Structurally equivalent positions in networks do not necessarily show internal connectivity. For instance, clients in a patronage structure have few ties among themselves, but they are structurally equivalent in their ties to their patrons. This means that social categories can contribute to the symbolic ordering of networks in terms of structural equivalence, even without 'netness'. Blockmodeling identifies structurally equivalent positions across multiple types of ties, such as awareness, friendship, admiration, or conflict. Role categories concatenate and stabilise multiple types of ties across the same network population (McLean, 2017, pp. 90–95; Fuhse 2022, pp. 135–138). One example is the gender category, producing different network structures in romantic ties (mostly cross-category), friendships (same-gender cliques) and family ties (along gendered kinship categories; Fuhse, 2022, pp. 185–192).

Netdoms and Culture

Typical sets of stories about relationships and social categories help constitute the realm of shared symbolic forms frequently summarised as 'culture' (McLean, 2017, pp. 34–42; Mohr et al., 2020). Relational sociology does not conceptualise culture as an integrated layer encompassing society. Instead, culture is tied to networks on different scales, many of them much below the level of nation states. Symbolic forms emerge, disseminate, change and wither in the course of interaction, making networks of interaction the habitats of culture. Small groups develop their own unique culture, often in opposition to other groups or to wider society (Eliasoph & Lichterman, 2003; Fine, 2012; Crossley, 2015). Even relationships in the smallest contexts of interaction come with their own culture of rituals, nicknames and stories (Wood, 1982).

Instead of invoking the tricky notion of 'culture', White and Mische term the symbolic forms specific to a network context as its 'domain' (White, 1995; Mische & White, 1998). Domains include 'story sets, symbols, idioms, registers … that characterize a particular specialized field of interaction' (Mische & White, 1998, p. 702). The repeated interaction in a close-knit network brings about specific cultural forms that differ from those around them. This 'network culture' (Yeung, 2005) then forms the basis of the interaction in the group, organising social relationships and their patterns (Gondal & McLean, 2013).

If networks bring about different cultures, and if networks are symbolically ordered, then different networks show distinct ways of relating and resulting network patterns. Yeung (2005) explores this in his study of cultural patterns in urban communes with very different understandings of the story-tie or relationship label 'love'. Using the same data, Rawlings (2020; see also Rawlings & Friedkin, 2017) draws on network balance theories to show how differently structured interpersonal relations within groups contribute to emotional and attitudinal shifts over time, and how these shifts are mediated by local authority relations.

Cultural Networks

The NCI approach has come to regard culture itself as patterned in networks in a way that is amenable to formal analysis (Mohr, 1998; Fuchs, 2001a; DiMaggio, 2011; Edelman & Mohr, 2018; Fuhse et al., 2020; Light & Cunningham, 2020). Symbolic forms are related systematically to each other, as when attitudes, symbols or concepts frequently co-occur. Pioneering work in this regard was carried out by Harvard alumna Kathleen Carley, beginning with her early work extracting culture from texts (Carley, 1994; Carley & Kaufer, 1993). Carley goes beyond conventional content analysis by examining relations between concepts, writing that 'the meaning of a concept for an individual is embedded in its relationship to other concepts in the individual's mental model' (Carley & Palmquist, 1992, p. 602). The networks of relations between concepts can be analysed using network analytic measures such as density, consensus and conductivity.

John Mohr is another pioneer in the formal analysis of cultural networks, using blockmodelling and Galois lattices to examine relations between discourse and practice in changing institutional fields. Using a cultural adaptation of Breiger's notion of 'duality', Mohr studies the dual association between social categories of 'needy' people and poverty relief services (Mohr, 1994; Mohr & Duquênne, 1997), as well as the relational logic of affirmative action categories and practices (Mohr & Lee, 2000; Breiger & Mohr, 2004). Several other researchers have used the idea of duality to map cultural elements. John Levi Martin (2000) examines the dual association between symbolic representations of animals and job occupations in a children's book. Ann Mische and Philippa Pattison (2000) propose a tripartite version of lattice analysis to examine intersections among organisations, projects and events in Brazilian protests. Yeung's study (2005) uses Galois lattices to map relations between meanings attributed to persons and relationships.

More recent work on cultural networks focuses on reconstructing word patterns from quantitative analysis of archival texts (natural language processing, NLP). In line with Carley's early work, this is still mostly done through co-occurrence analysis, where words are connected based on frequency of co-appearance in texts – for example, within sentences or 'moving windows' of a set number of words (Evans & Aceves, 2016). The resulting word networks are then examined with regard to communities of sets of words with increased connectivity (Rule et al., 2015; Fuhse et al., 2020). A related method is topic modeling, which allows for words to appear in relation to various topics, depending on their probability of co-occurrence with other words (DiMaggio et al., 2013; McFarland et al., 2013b; Mohr & Bogdanov, 2013). Recent advances include word embeddings, where concepts such as 'rich' and 'poor' or 'man' and 'woman' are examined with regard to similarities in words around them (Kozlowski et al., 2019; Stoltz & Taylor, 2021).

These studies rely on a 'bag of words' approach, disregarding grammatical sentence structure. Another approach focuses on the grammatical roles of terms in sentences, for example, examining which subjects frequently occur with what verbs and objects (Franzosi, 2004). Tilly (1997) uses semantic grammars to show how categories of actors are linked by kinds of actions (e.g., claim, attack, control, cheer) in newspaper reports on claim-making in Britain (see also Tilly & Wood, 2003; Wada, 2004). Using natural language processing techniques such as named entity analysis and part-of-speech tagging, Mohr and his co-authors (2013) trace actors, their attributed actions and their 'grammars of motives' in their analysis of National Security Strategy documents. These early studies still rely on hand or automated coding of actors and actions, rather than automated parsers detecting actual sentence structures. Oscar Stuhler (2021, 2022) – a student of DiMaggio, Fuhse and Martin – applies automated dependency parsers to detect systematic grammatical relations between 'discourse roles' in Mohr's sense.

Overall, this line of work has established cultural networks between symbols alongside networks of social relationships as important subjects of the NCI approach. One challenge is to reflect upon the differences between these kinds of networks, and to study their interplay with each other, as in the work on sociosemantic networks (Roth & Cointet, 2010; Basov & Brennecke, 2017; Fuhse et al., 2020).

Interaction

Another advance concerns the role of social interaction processes. White's first edition of *Identity and Control* (1992) still focused mostly on relatively stable patterns in the whirlwinds of the social world. In later writings, he turned to the role of micro-events in these sociocultural structures. The main focus was on '*switchings*' – events that cross borders between network domains, connecting them to each other momentarily and provoking irritations and 'fresh meanings' (White, 1995; Mische & White, 1998). Switchings build on the inherent uncertainty of social processes in that no social context can control entirely what is going on. But they also recreate uncertainty by generating fresh connections and meanings (White et al., 2007; Godart & White, 2010; Fontdevila et al., 2011; White et al., 2013; see also Kirchner & Mohr, 2010).

While White considers switchings ubiquitous, they seem to denote a particular phenomenon in social life, rather than social processes in general. In contrast, Emirbayer and Tilly elaborate on the concept of *transactions* (from Charles Dewey and Arthur Bentley) as a general term for relational processes and events in the social world. Emirbayer defines relational sociology as starting from transaction as a 'dynamic, unfolding process'; the individuals or other social units involved 'derive their meaning, significance, and identity from the (changing) functional roles they play within that transaction' (1997, p. 287). In the same vein, Tilly writes of 'interpersonal transactions as the basic stuff of social processes' that bring about identities, social boundaries and network ties (2006a, pp. 6f).

Nick Crossley prefers the concept 'interaction' as the basis for social networks and culture, building on pragmatism and symbolic interactionism (2011, pp. 28–35). For him, a social relationship is 'the lived trajectory of iterated bouts of interaction between actors', bringing about a 'common ground' between them, a 'shared but perhaps tacit "definition of the situation"'. This ties processes in networks to the subjective orientations of actors involved, as the basis for dynamic processing of meaning between them. Fuhse (2022, pp. 235–273) draws on Luhmann's concept of communication to conceptualise the processual unfolding of meaning, with social relationships and networks as one structure of expectations emerging in that process. Like Emirbayer's and Tilly's 'transactions', this emphasises the supra-personal nature of social processes, disregarding subjective motivations and orientations as secondary. Fuhse's perspective leads to a methodological focus on the relational implications of communicative events, which can be studied using conversation analysis and interactional sociolinguistics, as in his analysis of relational positioning in a televised political debate (Fuhse, 2023).

Relational sociologists have produced a number of empirical studies on interactional processes in networks, including McLean's (1998, 2007) analysis of relational self-presentation in patronage-seeking letters in Florence and McFarland's (2001, 2004; Diehl & McFarland, 2012) work on classroom disruptions. Recent studies by McFarland and his collaborators include minute examination of potential formation of new relationships in speed-dating (McFarland et al., 2013a) and the network embeddedness of written notes between high school students (McFarland and Wolff, 2022). These studies combine attention to network relations, cultural discourse and unfolding interactions with the focus on identity presentation and situational positioning from Erving Goffman (Diehl & McFarland, 2010; Diehl, 2019).

Ann Mische and David Gibson also work empirically on social processes in networks. Mische (2003, 2008) qualitatively examines how interactions among movement leaders are informed and channelled by affiliations within and across organisations. Gibson (2003, 2005) analyses turn-taking patterns in managerial meetings quantitatively with regard to formal organisational roles and personal relationships. He argues for the fruitful combination of relational sociology with conversation analysis, showing the analytic leverage gained from quantifying interactional processes and subjecting them to formal analysis. This becomes more important with new developments in computational social science that work with timestamped process-generated communication data rather than cross-sectional surveys (Kitts & Quintane, 2020; Lewis, forthcoming).

Agency

The notion of *agency* became important in relational sociology in the 1990s, but remained contested between different strands of the movement. Coined by critical realist Roy Bhaskar in the 1970s, the term was propagated in sociology by British social theorists Anthony Giddens and Margaret Archer in the 1980s. Emirbayer and his co-authors provided a pragmatist-informed elaboration of the concept in the 1990s (Emirbayer & Goodwin, 1994; Emirbayer & Mische, 1998), although not all relational sociologists are comfortable with the term.

Critics hold that the concept of agency one-sidedly stresses unpredictability and human freedom, adding little to the sociological business of systematic modelling and explanation. In this vein, Stephan Fuchs (2001b, p. 27) claims: 'Assuming that whatever an actor actually did, he or she could have done otherwise does not explain what the actor actually did. Free will and agency are moral concessions, not social facts.' This may have led a number of key authors to avoid the term. White, Padgett and Tilly aim at improving on network structuralist models – that is, to increase their explanatory value. That means looking for systematic connections, not claiming unpredictability for the sake of human free will. According to Ian Burkitt (2016, pp. 335f), agency should not be seen as individual, but as anchored in 'webs of interdependence' with others. He argues against the structure/agency dualism of Bhaskar, Giddens and Archer by pointing out that social relationships (as the basic unit of social structures in network thinking) constitute 'the very structure and form of agency'.

Strands of relational sociology informed by pragmatism and social phenomenology move away from defining agency in terms of free will or unpredictability, noting that agency does not necessarily entail novel or unexpected outcomes, and stressing the embeddedness of agency in temporal-relational contexts. Emirbayer and Mische (1998) argue that agency appears in routinised, problem-solving and imaginative forms of action, and discuss how temporal orientations might be influenced by degrees of relational complexity. Other relational sociologists focus less on internal and intersubjective orientations than on situational and historical contingency, albeit strongly conditioned by relational contexts. David Gibson (2000) argues for the 'conversational agency' of individuals who can influence interactional flows within situational constraints, contingent on reactions by others. As Emily Erikson (2013, pp. 233–234) notes, 'relationalist' approaches stress that 'the ambiguity, complexity and flux of any one position requires interpretation of circumstances, through which agency is expressed'. John Scott (2022) draws on network and interactionist approaches to consider how relationally embedded actors 'act back' on social structures, generating opportunities and constraints. While debate remains among relational sociologists about the extent of individual free will, the NCI approach is firmly grounded in a relational (rather than individualist) perspective on agency.

Publics

The notion of network 'publics' is another conceptual elaboration of the NCI approach, also building on the work of Erving Goffman. According to White and colleagues (White, 1995; Mische & White, 1998), publics consist of forums or encounters where actors otherwise embedded in separate network domains are temporarily brought together. Within the bubble of publics, participants experience a momentary sense of connectedness due to suspension of surrounding ties. Such publics can range from silent encounters in elevators to cocktail parties, carnivals, or protest rallies. All of these involve provisional equalisation of relationships and decoupling from stories and relations around them, which nevertheless may threaten to disrupt the situation (Mische & Chandler, 2019). In publics, actors construct identities in relation to each other, as when party guests mingle and socialise, telling stories that cast themselves and others in a particular light.

As Ikegami (2000, 2005) notes in her study of aesthetic public in modern Japan, publics are not only spaces of interaction between individuals, but also intersections of otherwise separate networks. Emirbayer and Sheller (1999) explore the network composition of publics as interstitial locations for the exchange of ideas (see also Sheller 2000). Smilde (2004) shows how popular street protests provide relational contexts for bridging social networks and expanding discourse. Mische (2008) examines youth activist publics during Brazil's democratic reconstruction. As activists move between different organisational networks (student, religious, partisan, professional, NGO), they suppress, segment and combine dimensions of their multiple identities as they create new styles of civic and political intervention.

Fields

The notion of social *fields* is closely aligned with relational sociology, although it encompasses diverse analytical approaches. Research on fields has been strongly influenced by Pierre Bourdieu, who uses the term to denote large-scale sociocultural patterns like the state, the economy, science, education or art (Mohr, 2013). DiMaggio and Powell (1983) use the concept to describe the mutual orientation, adaptation and behavioural patterns among organisations. DiMaggio and his students Anheier and Mohr draw on network analysis to examine the social and cultural patterns in fields (Anheier et al., 1995; DiMaggio, 1986; Mohr, 1994). The field concept has been central to recent work in relational sociology (Martin, 2003, 2011; Powell et al., 2005; Emirbayer & Johnson, 2008; Bottero & Crossley, 2011).

Like Bourdieu and neo-institutionalist theory, the NCI perspective on fields starts from the mutual orientation of actors in a field of interaction, where scarce resources are contested (be it money, power, or prestige; Martin, 2003, 2011; Fligstein & McAdam, 2012). Like Bourdieu, it envisions fields as characterised by social and cultural patterns, involving social relations, on the one hand, and a common understanding of symbolic boundaries and the institutionalised 'rules of the game', on the other (Bourdieu & Wacquant, 1992). However, Bourdieu considers social relations chiefly in the sense of classificatory schemas and unequal distributions of economic, cultural, symbolic and social capital. The NCI approach, in contrast, studies the social structure of fields in intersubjective and meaning-laden networks of social ties between actors (de Nooy, 2003; Powell et al., 2005; Crossley & Diani, 2019; Bottero, 2009; Mohr, 2013; Fuhse, 2020b).

Rather than reserving the concept of fields for macro-social spheres, research grounded in the NCI perspective is more flexible in focus. Fields can be found on various levels, such as charity organisations in New York City (Mohr, 1994), artists in Cologne, Germany (Anheier et al., 1995), art museums in the US (DiMaggio, 1991), psychiatric contention in the UK (Crossley, 2005), sexual encounters (Martin & George, 2006), the allocation of prestige in the 'racial field' (Emirbayer & Desmond, 2015) or the field of rival approaches within relational sociology (Fuhse, 2020). Relational sociology uses the field concept as an analytical tool for examining a range of empirical phenomena in which actors mutually orient and compete for resources, and in which social relations form and shared cultural understandings emerge.

CONCLUSION

The networks, culture and interaction approach to relational sociology as profiled here falls short on many criteria that we usually associate with established sociological theories. Its intellectual leader – Harrison White – is less discussed than other recent major figures like Bourdieu, Latour, or Luhmann, and substantially less cited. It does not have an established and widely adopted set of theoretical concepts and arguments. For most authors (Tilly, Padgett, DiMaggio, Martin, to name a few), it is not entirely clear to what extent they form part of the approach, or rather pursue their own theoretical enterprises.

Nevertheless, we hold the NCI approach to be one of the most important movements since 1990 within both North American sociology and interdisciplinary network research. In spite of internal differences, relational sociologists have given important impulses to both. For North American sociology, they further advanced the idea that social networks form an integral and, in many ways, central layer of the social world. Networks are essential not only for social mobility, but also for the mobilisation and success of social movements, for political regime change, for the institutionalisation and salience of social categories, for artistic and intellectual creativity, in classrooms and manager meetings, and in large-scale historical change.

Social networks are no longer seen only as formal methodological tools, but also as a particular phenomenon with a specified substance and form. Networks are not static structures, but patterns of relationships interwoven with forms of meaning: stories, identities, expectations, roles, institutions, social categories and models of relationships. These ideas are less codified than in other approaches, but they are widely disseminated and form part of the general understanding of social structures in the discipline.

The interplay of social networks with meaning or culture has also become popular within network research. Here, it serves as a counterpoint to the formal structuralist, graph theoretical understanding of networks that unites diverse researchers from physics to education science. In particular, 'network physicists' like Albert-László Barabási, Mark Newman and Duncan Watts have pushed for a renewed interest in abstract formal modelling of a wide range of empirical patterns as networks (Freeman, 2004, pp. 164–167). The NCI approach has challenged these trends not by dismissing them, but by calling for revision of the prevalent structuralist stance. Social networks are imbued with meaning and should be studied in their interplay with culture.

Consequently, networks are not the same everywhere: technical, neurological, social and symbolic networks can be studied with the same tools, but they show different structures. For instance, recent network research argues that uniform patterns (e.g., small-world, scale-free) can be found in all kinds of networks, and have similar underlying processes of tie formation (homophily, transitivity, preferential attachment etc.). Such 'network mechanisms' (Rivera et al. 2010) have been identified in a range of networks with sophisticated techniques like exponential random graph or stochastic actor-oriented models, but not everywhere to the same extent. Scientific citations seem driven by preferential attachment, friendship by homophily, reciprocity and transitivity, and sexual contacts chiefly by heterophily and absence of transitivity. The NCI approach accounts for these differences by pointing to the context-dependent cultural expectations attached to different kinds of social relationships (Fuhse and Gondal, forthcoming; Gondal, 2022). This leads to diverse network patterns, rather than uniform structures.

The NCI approach has contributed to methodological as well as theoretical advances. As we have noted above, relational sociology is well placed to inform and inspire research in computational social science, particularly with regard to networks of symbols in natural language processing. Another push is for inclusion of qualitative methods geared at interpretation of meaning in networks (Crossley, 2010; Fuhse & Mützel, 2011). Many key studies of relational sociology draw on a mix of qualitative methods and formal analysis (Tilly, 1995; McFarland, 2001, 2003; McLean, 2007; Mische, 2008; Crossley, 2015; Edelman, 2018). Recent advances include Desmond's (2014) discussion of 'relational ethnography' and approaches that complement natural language processing with qualitative interpretation (Nelson, 2020). Overall, relational sociology inspires work using a wide range of methods (Mohr et al., 2020).

In spite of several attempts at an overall framework (White, 2008a; Crossley, 2011; Padgett & Powell, 2012; Fuhse, 2022), the NCI approach to relational sociology remains an *assemblage of interrelated ideas*, rather than a well-integrated theoretical perspective. Its strength lies less in providing a coherent worldview than in inspiring empirical research at the intersection of networks, culture and interaction. In doing so, it *corrects and complements structuralist network research* rather than trying to overturn it. Formal network structuralism has been quite successful in investigating a wide range of social phenomena. While criticising the reduction of social structures to formal patterns, the NCI perspective does not oppose this approach; rather it wants to arrive at models that better capture the relationally constituted and meaning-infused processes of the social world.

Note

* This updated version of the original 2011 chapter by Mische ("Relational Sociology, Culture and Agency") is a fully collaborative effort with equal contributions by the two co-authors.

REFERENCES

Anheier, H., Gerhards, J., & Romo, F. (1995). Forms of capital and social structure in cultural fields: examining Bourdieu's social topography. *American Journal of Sociology*, 100, 859–903.

Ansell, C.K. (1997). Symbolic networks: the realignment of the French working class, 1887–1894. *American Journal of Sociology*, 103, 359–90.

Auyero, J. (2001). *Poor people's politics: Peronist networks and the legacy of Evita*. Duke University Press.

Bail, C.A. (2015). *Terrified: how anti-Muslim fringe organizations became mainstream*. Princeton University Press.

Bail, C.A. (2021). *Breaking the social media prism: how to make our platforms less polarizing*. Princeton University Press.

Bandelj, N. (2020). Relational Work in the Economy. *Annual Review of Sociology*, 46, 251–72.

Barkey, K. (1994). *Bandits and bureaucrats: the Ottoman route to state centralization*. Cornell University Press.

Barkey, K., & van Rossem, R. (1997). Networks of contention: villages and regional structure in the seventeenth century Ottoman Empire. *American Journal of Sociology*, 102(5), 1345–82.

Basov, N., & Brennecke, J. (2017). Duality beyond dyads: multiplex patterning of social ties and cultural meanings. *Research in the Sociology of Organizations*, 53, 87–112.

Bearman, P. (1993). *Relations into rhetorics: local elite social structure in Norfolk, England: 1540–1640*. American Sociological Association, Rose Monograph Series. Rutgers University Press.

Bearman, P.S., & Parigi, P. (2004). Cloning headless frogs and other important matters: conversation topics and network structure. *Social Forces*, 83(2), 535–57.

Bearman, P.S., & Stovel, K. (2000). Becoming a Nazi: models for narrative networks. *Poetics*, 27, 69–90.

Boorman, S., & White, H. (1976). Social structure from multiple networks. II. Role structures. *American Journal of Sociology*, 81, 1384–1446.

Bottero, W. (2009). Relationality and social interaction. *British Journal of Sociology*, 60, 399–420.

Bottero, W., & Crossley, N. (2011). Worlds, fields and networks: Becker, Bourdieu and the structures of social relations. *Cultural Sociology*, 5, 99–119.

Bourdieu, P., & Wacquant, L. (1992). *Invitation to reflexive sociology*. Polity.

Breiger, R.L. (1974). The duality of persons and groups. *Social Forces*, 53, 181–190.

Breiger, R.L. (2000). A tool kit for practice theory. *Poetics*, 27.

Breiger, R.L. & Mohr, J.W. (2004). Institutional logics from the aggregation of organizational networks: operational procedures for the analysis of counted data. *Computational and Mathematical Organization Theory*, 10, 17–43.

Brint, S. (1992). Hidden meanings: cultural content and context in Harrison White's structural sociology. *Sociological Theory*, 10, 194–208.

Burkitt, I. (2016). Relational agency: Relational Sociology, agency and interaction. *European Journal of Social Theory* 19(3), 322–339.

Carley, K. (1994). Extracting culture through textual analysis. *Poetics*, 22, 291–312.

Carley, K., & Palmquist, M. (1992). Extracting, representing and analyzing mental models. *Social Forces*, 70, 601–636.

Carley, K., & Kaufer, D. (1993). Semantic connectivity: an approach for analyzing symbols in semantic networks. *Communication Theory*, 3, 183–213.

Childress, C., Rawlings, C.M., & Moeran, B. (2017). Publishers, authors, and texts: The process of cultural consecration in prize evaluation. *Poetics*, 60, 48–61.

Coleman, J.S. (1990). *Foundations of social theory*. Belknap.

Crossley, N. (2005). The field of psychiatric contention in the UK, 1960–2000. *Social Science and Medicine*, 62, 552–563.

Crossley, N. (2010). The social world of the network. combining qualitative and quantitative elements in social network analysis. *Sociologica*, 4(1), 1–34.

Crossley, N. (2011). *Towards relational sociology*. Routledge.

Crossley, N. (2015). *Networks of sound, style and subversion: the punk and post-punk worlds of Manchester, London, Liverpool and Sheffield, 1975–1980*. Manchester University Press.

Crossley, N., & Diani, M. (2019). Networks and fields. In D.A. Snow, S.A. Sould, H. Kriesi & H.J. McCammon (Eds.), *The Wiley Blackwell companion to social movements*. 2nd ed. (pp. 151–166). John Wiley and Sons.

de Nooy, W. (2003). Fields and networks: correspondence analysis and social network analysis in the framework of field theory. *Poetics*, 31, 305–327.

Dépelteau, F. (Ed.) (2018). *The Palgrave handbook of relational sociology*. Palgrave.

Desmond, M. (2014). Relational ethnography. *Theory and Society*, 43(5), 547–579.

Diani, M. (2007). Review essay: the relational element in Charles Tilly's recent (and not so recent) work. *Social Networks*, 29, 316–323.

Diehl, D. (2019). Language and interaction: applying sociolinguistics to social network analysis. *Quality and Quantity*, 53, 757–774.

Diehl, D., & McFarland, D. (2010). Toward a historical sociology of social situations. *American Journal of Sociology*, 115(6), 1713–1752.

Diehl, D., & McFarland, D. (2012). Classroom ordering and the situational imperatives of routine and ritual. *Sociology of Education*, 85(4), 326–349.

DiMaggio, P. (1986). Structural analysis of organizational fields. *Research on Organizational Behavior*, 8, 335–370.

DiMaggio, P. (1987). Classification in art. *American Sociological Review*, 52, 440–455.

DiMaggio, P. (1991). Constructing an organizational field as a professional project: US art museums, 1920–1940. In W.W. Powell & P. DiMaggio (Eds.), *The new institutionalism in organizational analysis* (pp. 267–292). University of Chicago Press.

DiMaggio, P. (2011). Cultural networks. In J. Scott & P. Carrington (Eds.), *The Sage handbook of social network analysis* (pp. 286–301). Sage.

DiMaggio, P., Nag, M., & Blei, D. (2013). Exploiting affinities between topic modeling and the sociological perspective on culture: application to newspaper coverage of US government arts funding. *Poetics*, 41, 570–606.

DiMaggio, P., & Powell, W. (1983). The iron cage revisited: institutional isomorphism and collective rationality in organizational fields. *American Sociological Review*, 48(2), 147–160.

Edelmann, A. (2018). Culturally meaningful networks: on the transition from military to civilian life. *Theory and Society*, 47(3), 327–380.

Edelmann, A., & Mohr, J.W. (2018). Formal studies of culture: issues, challenges and current trends. *Poetics*, 68, 1–9.

Eliasoph, N., & Lichterman, P. (2003). Culture in interaction. *American Journal of Sociology*, 108, 735–794.

Emirbayer, M. (1997). Manifesto for a relational sociology. *American Journal of Sociology*, 103, 281–317.

Emirbayer, M., & Desmond, M. (2015). *The racial order*. University of Chicago Press.

Emirbayer, M., & Goodwin, J. (1994). Network analysis, culture, and the problem of agency. *American Journal of Sociology*, 99, 1411–1454.

Emirbayer, M., & Johnson, V. (2008). Bourdieu and organizational analysis. *Theory and Society*, 37, 1–44.

Emirbayer, M., & Mische, A. (1998). What is agency? *American Journal of Sociology*, 103, 962–1023.

Emirbayer, M., & Sheller, M. (1999). Publics in history. *Theory and Society*, 28, 145–197.

Erickson, B.H. (1988). The relational basis of attitudes. In B. Wellman & S.D. Berkowitz (Eds.), *Social Structures a Network Approach* (pp. 99–121). Cambridge University Press.

Erickson, B.H. (1996). Culture, class, and connections. *American Journal of Sociology*, 102, 217–251.

Erikson, E. (2013). Formalist and relationalist theory in social network analysis. *Sociological Theory*, 31, 219–242.

Erikson, E., & Bearman, P. (2006). Malfeasance and the foundations for global trade: the structure of English trade in the East Indies, 1601–1833. *American Journal of Sociology*, 112, 195–230.

Evans, J., & Aceves, P. (2016). Machine translation: mining text for social theory. *Annual Review of Sociology*, 42, 21–50.

Fine, G.A. (2012). *Tiny publics: a theory of group action and culture*. Russell Sage Foundation.

Fine, G.A. & Kleinman, S. (1983). Network and meaning: an interactionist approach to structure. *Symbolic Interaction*, 6, 97–110.

Fligstein, N., & McAdam, D. (2012). *A theory of fields*. Oxford University Press.

Fontdevila, J., Opazo, P., & White, H. (2011). Order at the edge of chaos: meanings from netdom switchings across functional systems. *Sociological Theory*, 29(3), 178–198.

Franzosi, R. (2004). *From words to numbers: narrative, data, and social science*. Cambridge University Press.

Freeman, L.C. (2004). *The development of social network analysis: a study in the sociology of science*. Empirical Press.

Fuchs, S. (2001a). *Against essentialism*. Harvard University Press.

Fuchs, S. (2001b). Beyond agency. *Sociological Theory*, 19(1), 24–40.

Fuhse, J.A. (2009). The meaning structure of social networks. *Sociological Theory*, 27, 51–73.

Fuhse, J. (2020a). The field of relational sociology. *Digithum*, 26, 1–10.

Fuhse, J. (2020b). Relational Sociology of the Scientific Field: Communication, Identities, and Field Relations. *Digithum*, 26, 1–14.

Fuhse, J. (2022). *Social networks of meaning and communication*. Oxford University Press.

Fuhse, J. (2023). Analyzing social networks in communication: a mixed methods study of a political debate. *Quality and Quantity* 57, 1207–1230.

Fuhse, J., & Gondal, N. (forthcoming). Networks from culture: mechanisms of tie formation follow institutionalized rules in social fields. *Social Networks*.

Fuhse, J., & Mützel, S. (2011). Tackling connections, structure and meaning in networks: quantitative and qualitative methods in sociological network research. *Quality and Quantity*, 45, 1067–1089

Fuhse, J., Stuhler, O., Riebling, J., & Martin, J.L. (2020). 'Relating social and symbolic relations in quantitative text analysis: a study of parliamentary discourse in the Weimar Republic. *Poetics, 78,* 101363.

Gibson, D. (2000). Seizing the moment: the problem of conversational agency. *Sociological Theory, 18,* 368–382.

Gibson, D. (2003). Participation shifts: order and differentiation in group conversation. *Social Forces, 81,* 1135–1181.

Gibson, D. (2005). Taking turns and talking ties: network structure and conversational sequences. *American Journal of Sociology, 110*(6), 1561–1597.

Godart, F.C., & White, H.C. (2010). Switchings under uncertainty: the coming and becoming of meanings. *Poetics, 38*(6), 567–586.

Goldberg, C.A. (2007). *Citizens and paupers: relief, rights, and race, from the Freedmen's Bureau to Workfare.* University of Chicago Press.

Gondal, N. (2022). Multiplexity as a lens to investigate the cultural meanings of interpersonal ties. *Social Networks, 68,* 209–217.

Gondal, N., & McLean, P. (2013). What makes a network go round; exploring the structure of a strong component with exponential random graph models. *Social Networks, 35*(4), 499–513.

Gould, R. (1991). Multiple networks and mobilization in the Paris commune, 1871. *American Sociological Review, 56,* 716–729.

Gould, R.(1995). *Insurgent identities: class, community, and insurrection in Paris from 1848 to the commune.* University of Chicago Press.

Granovetter, M. (1979). The Theory-Gap in Social Network Analysis. In P.W. Holland and S. Leinhardt (Eds.), *Perspectives on Social Network Research;* New York: Academic Press.

Hillmann, H. (2008). Mediation in multiple networks: elite mobilization before the English civil war. *American Sociological Review, 73,* 426–454.

Ikegami, E. (1995). *The taming of the samurai: honorific Individualism and the Making of Modern Japan.* Harvard University Press.

Ikegami, E. (2000). A sociological theory of publics: Identity and culture as emergent properties in networks'. *Social Research* 67: 989–1029.

Ikegami, E. (2005). *Bonds of civility: aesthetic publics and the political origins* of Japanese publics. Cambridge University Press.

Kirchner, C., & Mohr, J.W. (2010). Meanings and relations: an introduction to the study of language, discourse and networks. *Poetics, 38*(6), 555–566.

Kitts, J., & Quintane, E. (2020). Rethinking social networks in the era of computational social science. In R. Light & J. Moody (Eds.), *The Oxford handbook of social networks* (pp. 71–97). Oxford University Press.

Kozlowski, C.A., Taddy, M., & Evans, J.A. (2019). The geometry of culture: analyzing the meanings of class through word embeddings. *American Sociological Review, 84*(5), 905–949.

Krinsky, J. (2007). *Free labor: workfare and the contested language of neoliberalism.* University of Chicago Press.

Krinsky, J., & Mische, A. (2013). Formations and formalisms: Charles Tilly and the paradox of the actor. *Annual Review of Sociology, 39,* 1–26.

Lewis, K. (forthcoming). Digital networks: elements of a theoretical framework. *Social Networks.*

Light, R., & Cunningham, J. (2020). Networks of culture, networks of meaning: two approaches to text networks. In R. Light & J. Moody (Eds.), *The Oxford handbook of social networks* (pp. 414–431). Oxford University Press.

Lizardo, O. (2006). How cultural tastes shape personal networks. *American Sociological Review, 71,* 778–807.

Lizardo, O. (2015). Omnivorousness as the bridging of cultural holes: a measurement strategy. *Theory and Society, 43,* 395–419.

Martin, J.L. (2000). What do animals do all day? On the totemic logic of class bodies. *Poetics, 27,* 195–231.

Martin, J.L. (2003). What is field theory? *American Journal of Sociology,* 109, 1–49.

Martin, J.L. (2009). *Social structures.* Princeton University Press.

Martin, J.L. (2011). *The explanation of social action.* Oxford University Press.

Martin, J.L., & George, M. (2006). Theories of sexual stratification: toward an analytics of the sexual field and a theory of sexual capital. *Sociological Theory, 24*(2), 107–132.

McAdam, D., Tarrow, S., & Tilly, C. (2001). *Dynamics of contention.* Cambridge Studies in Contentious Politics. Cambridge University Press.

McFarland, D.A. (2001). Student resistance: how the formal and informal organization of classrooms facilitate everyday forms of student defiance. *American Journal of Sociology, 107*(3), 612–678.

McFarland, D.A. (2004). Resistance as a social dram: a study of change-oriented encounters. *American Journal of Sociology, 109*(6), 1249–1318.

McFarland, D.A., Jurafsky, D., & Rawlings, C. (2013a). Making the connection: Social bonding in courtship situations. *American Journal of Sociology, 118*(6), 1596–1649.

McFarland, D.A., Ramage, D., Chuang, J., Heer, J., Manning, C.D., & Jurafsky, D. (2013b). Differentiating language usage through topic models. *Poetics, 41*(6), 607–625.

McFarland, D.A., & Wolff, T. (2022). Writing into relationships. *Social Networks,* 71, 96–114.

McLean, P. (1998). A frame analysis of favor seeking in the Renaissance: agency, networks, and political culture. *American Journal of Sociology, 104,* 51–91.

McLean, P. (2007). *The art of the network: strategic interaction and patronage in Renaissance Florence.* Duke University Press.

McLean, P. (2017). *Culture in networks.* Polity.

Mische, A. (2003). Cross-talk in movements: rethinking the culture-network link. In: M. Diani & Doug McAdam (Eds.), *Social movements and networks: relational approaches to collective action* (pp. 258–280). Oxford University Press.

Mische, A. (2008). *Partisan publics: communication and contention across Brazilian youth activist networks*. Princeton University Press.

Mische, A. (2011). Relational sociology, culture, and agency. In J. Scott & P. Carrington (Eds.), *The Sage handbook of social network analysis* (pp. 80–97). Sage.

Mische, A. (2021). On parachutes and lion-taming. In M. Small, Mario, B. Perry & B. Pescosolido (Eds.), *Personal networks: classic readings and new directions* (pp. 199–270). Cambridge University Press.

Mische, A., & Chandler, M.J. (2019). Narratives, networks and publics. In J.R. Hall, M.-C. Lo & L. Grindstaff (Eds.), *Routledge handbook of cultural sociology, 2nd edition* (pp. 278–287). Routledge.

Mische, A., & Pattison, P. (2000). Composing a civic arena: publics, projects, and social settings. *Poetics*, 27, 163–194.

Mische, A., & White, H.C. (1998). Between conversation and situation: public switching dynamics across network domains. *Social Research*, 65, 695–724.

Mohr, J. (1994). Soldiers, mothers, tramps, and others: discourse roles in the 1907 New York City charity directory. *Poetics*, 22, 327–357.

Mohr, J. (1998). Measuring meaning structures. *Annual Review of Sociololgy*, 24, 345–370

Mohr, J. (2013). Bourdieu's relational method in theory and in practice'. In F. Dépelteau & C. Powell (Eds.), *Applying relational sociology* (pp. 101–135). Palgrave.

Mohr, J.W., Bail, C.A., Frye, M., Lena, J.C., Lizardo, O., McDonnell, T.E., Mische, A., Tavory, I., & Wherry, F.F. (2020). *Measuring culture*. Columbia University Press.

Mohr, J., & Bogdanov, P. (2013). Introduction – topic models: what they are and why they matter. *Poetics*, 41(6), 545–569.

Mohr, J.W., & Duquênne, V. (1997). The duality of culture and practice: poverty relief in New York City, 1888–1917. *Theory and Society*, 26, 305–356.

Mohr, J.W., & Ghaziani, A. (2014). Problems and prospects of measurement in the study of culture. *Theory and Society*, 43, 225–246.

Mohr, J.W., & Lee, H.K. (2000). From affirmative action to outreach: discourse shifts at the University of California. *Poetics*, 28(1), 47–71.

Mohr, J.W., Wagner-Pacifici, R., & Breiger, R.L. (2015). Toward a computational hermeneutics. *Big Data and Society*, 2(2), 1–8.

Mohr, J.W., Wagner-Pacifici, R., & Breiger, R.L., & Bogdanov, P. (2013). Graphing the grammar of motives in National Security Strategies: cultural interpretation, automated text analysis and the drama of global politics. *Poetics*, 41, 670–700.

Mützel, S. (2009). Networks as culturally constituted processes: A comparison of relational sociology and actor-network theory. *Current Sociology*, 57(6), 871–887.

Mützel, S., & Breiger, R.L. (2020). Duality beyond persons and groups: culture and affiliation. In R. Light & J. Moody (Eds.), *The Oxford handbook of social networks* (pp. 392–413). Oxford University Press.

Nelson, L.K. (2020). Computational grounded theory: a methodological framework. *Sociological Methods and Research*, 49(1), 3–42.

Pachucki, M.A., & Breiger, R.L. (2010). Cultural holes: beyond relationality in social networks and culture. *Annual Review of Sociology*, 36, 205–224.

Padgett, J.F., & Ansell, C.K. (1993). Robust action and the rise of the Medici, 1400–1434. *American Journal of Sociology*, 98, 1259–1319.

Padgett, J.F., & McLean, P.D. (2006). Organizational invention and elite transformation: the birth of partnership systems in Renaissance Florence. *American Journal of Sociology*, 111, 1463–1568.

Padgett, J.F., & Powell, W.W. (2012). *The emergence of organizations and markets*. Princeton University Press.

Polletta, F. (2002). *Freedom is an endless meeting: democracy in American social movements*. University of Chicago Press.

Polletta, F. (2006). *It was like a fever: storytelling in protest and politics*. University of Chicago Press.

Powell, W., White, D., Koput, K., & Owen-Smith, J. (2005). Network dynamics and field evolution: the growth of inter-organizational collaboration in the life sciences. *American Journal of Sociology*, 110(4), 1132–1205.

Rawlings, C.M. (2020). 'Cognitive Authority and the Constraint of Attitude Change in Groups. *American Sociological Review* 85(6): 992-1021.

Rawlings, C.M., & Childress, C. (2019). Emergent meanings: reconciling dispositional and situational accounts of meaning-making from cultural objects. *American Journal of Sociology*, 124(6), 1763–1809.

Rawlings, C.M., & Childress, C. (2021). Schemas, interactions, and objects in meaning-making. *Sociological Forum*, 36, 1446–77.

Rawlings, C.M., & Friedkin, N.E. (2017). The structural balance theory of sentiment networks: elaboration and test. *American Journal of Sociology*, 123(3), 510–548.

Rivera, M., Soderstrom, S., & Uzzi, B. (2010). Dynamics of dyads in social networks: assortative, relational, and proximity mechanisms. *Annual Review of Sociology*, 36, 91–115.

Roth, C., & Cointet, J.-P. (2010). Social and semantic coevolution in knowledge networks. *Social Networks*, 32(1), 16–29.

Rule, A., Jean-Philippe Cointet, J.-P., & Bearman, P. (2015). Lexical shifts, substantive changes, and continuity in state of the union discourse, 1790–2014. *Proceedings of the National Academy of Sciences*, *112*, 10837–10844.

Scott, J. (2022). *Structure and social action: on constituting and connecting social worlds*. Emerald.

Sheller, M. (2000). *Democracy after slavery: black publics and peasant radicalism in Haiti and Jamaica*. Macmillan.

Smilde, D. (2004). Popular publics: street protest and plaza preachers in Caracas. *International Review of Social History*, *49*, 179–195.

Smith, T.A. (2007). Narrative boundaries and the dynamics of ethnic conflict and conciliation. *Poetics*, *35*, 22–46.

Somers, M.R. (1993). Citizenship and the place of the public sphere: law, community, and political culture in the transition to democracy. *American Sociological Review*, *58*(5), 587–620.

Somers, M.R. (1998). We're no angels: realism, rational choice, and relationality in social science. *American Journal of Sociology*, *104*(3), 722–784.

Stoltz, D. & Taylor, M. (2021). Cultural cartography with word embeddings. *Poetics*, *88*, 101567.

Stuhler, O. (2021). What's in a category? A new approach to discourse role analysis. *Poetics*, *88*, 101568.

Stuhler, O. (2022). Who does what to whom? Making text parsers work for sociological inquiry. *Sociological Methods and Research*, *51*(4), 1580–1633.

Tarrow, S. (2008). Charles Tilly and the practice of contentious politics. *Social Movement Studies*, *7*(3), 225–246.

Tilly, C. (1978). *From mobilization to revolution*. Addison-Wesley.

Tilly, C. (1995). *Popular contention in Great Britain, 1758–1834*. Harvard University Press.

Tilly, C. (1997). Parliamentarization of popular contention in Great Britain, 1758–1834. *Theory and Society*, *26*, 245–273

Tilly, C. (1998). *Durable inequality*. University of California Press.

Tilly, Charles (2002). *Stories, identities, and political change*. Rowman & Littlefield.

Tilly, C. (2006a). *Identities, boundaries, and social ties*. Paradigm.

Tilly, C. (2006b). *Why?* Princeton University Press.

Tilly, C. (2008). *Explaining social processes*. Paradigm.

Tilly, C., & Wood, L. (2003). Contentious connections in Great Britain, 1828–34. In M. Diani & D. McAdam (Eds.), *Social movements and networks: relational approaches to collective action* (pp. 147–172). Oxford University Press.

Vaisey, S., & Lizardo, O. (2009). Can cultural worldviews influence network composition? *Social Forces*, *88*, 1595–1618.

Wada, T. (2004). '.Event analysis of claim making in Mexico: H.how are social protests transformed into political protests? *Mobilization*, *9*(3), 241–257.

Wellman, B. (1988). Structural analysis: From method and metaphor to theory and substance. In B. Wellman & S.D. Berkowitz (Eds.), *Social Structures a Network Approach* (pp. 19–61). Cambridge University Press.

Wherry, F.F. (2016). Relational accounting: a cultural approach. *American Journal of Cultural Sociology*, *4*(2), 131–156

White, H.C. (1992). *Identity and control: a structural theory of social action*. Princeton University Press.

White, H.C. (1995). Network switchings and Bayesian forks: reconstructing the social and behavioral sciences. *Social Research*, *62*, 1035–1063.

White, H.C. (2008a). *Identity and control: how social formations emerge*. Princeton University Press.

White, H.C. (2008b). Notes on the constituents of social structure: *Sociology of Religion*, 10, Spring '65. *Sociologica*, *1*, 1–14.

White, H., Boorman, S., & Breiger, R. (1976). Social structure from multiple networks. I. Blockmodels of roles and positions. *American Journal of Sociology*, *81*, 730–780.

White, H.C., Godart, F.C., & Corona, V.P. (2007). 'Mobilizing identities: Uncertainty and control in strategy'. *Theory, Culture and Society* 24(7–8): 181–202.

White, H.C., Godart, F.C., & Thiemann, M. (2013). Turning points and the space of possibles: A relational perspective on the different forms of uncertainty. In F. Dépelteau & C. Powell (Eds.), *Applying relational sociology*. Palgrave Macmillan.

Wood, J. (1982). Communication and relational culture: bases for the study of human relationships. *Communication Quarterly*, *30*(2), 75–83.

Yeung, K.-T. (2005). What does love mean? Exploring network culture in two network settings. *Social Forces*, *84*(1), pp. 391–420.

Zelizer, V. (2012). How I became a relational economic sociologist and what does that mean? *Politics and Society*, *40*(2), 145–174.

PART 2
Applications

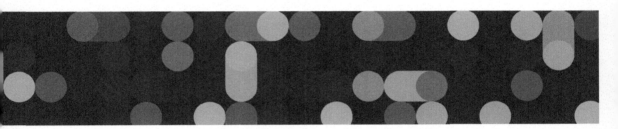

6

Social-Ecological Networks: What Are They, Why Are They Useful And How Can I Use Them?

Örjan Bodin

INTRODUCTION

People and nature are irrevocably linked. Without the natural environment and the ecosystem services it provides, there would be no people (Alcamo & Bennett, 2003). And, conversely, the natural environment as we know it today is largely shaped by people and societies (Haberl et al., 2014). This has even led to the proposition of defining the time from when humans started to significantly impact the earth as a new geographic epoch named the Anthropocene (Waters et al., 2016). Regardless of whether the current state of affairs warrant the definition of a new geographical epoch, it stands clear that our abilities to sustain both thriving human societies and healthy ecosystems inevitably depends on how links between societies and ecosystems are formed, shaped and acted upon. The 'essences' of these links are diverse, ranging from extraction of natural resources for human use and consumption such as logging and agriculture production, to more cultural and emotional links capturing how human cognition and well-being benefits from spending time in the natural environment (Bowler et al., 2010). The existence of these numerous links, which implies interdependencies, has spurred scholars and practitioners to conceptualise our world as an interdependent *social-ecological system* (SES; e.g., Berkes & Folke, 1998). From this follows that our abilities to govern people and nature in sustainable ways requires us to develop a better understanding of the causes and consequences of the complex patterns of interdependencies connecting people and ecosystems within and across scales (Bodin et al., 2019a).

Both human societies (e.g., groups, communities, states) and the natural environment have long been described, understood and analysed as networks. This book with its focus on social networks is devoted to the former, whereas in the environmental sciences network models have been used at least since the 1970s to understand species interactions such as predation and symbiosis (Bascompte et al., 2003; May, 1972; Pimm, 1982) as well as species dispersals and movements across landscapes and beyond (Urban & Keitt, 2001). Within the environmental sciences, such network models have increased our understanding of, for example, community ecology – that is, how species coexist (or not) through competition and collaboration within certain geographical boundaries, to how species populations are able to sustain themselves (or not) in a fragmented landscape where habitats are geographically scattered within a matrix of largely inhospitable land (Urban & Keitt, 2001). However, in spite of the prominence of network thinking both within the environmental and social sciences, and the increasing realisation of the importance of the complex patterns of interdependencies connecting the social and ecological domains of reality, it was only relatively recently that social and ecological network models were combined and integrated into social-ecological networks (Janssen et al., 2006). In a social-ecological network, human actors and ecological components are typically defined as different sets (or levels) of nodes, and links are defined within these levels (social-to-social and ecological-to-ecological) and across these levels (social-to-ecological), thereby constituting a multilevel network (Fig. 6.1, and Wang et al., 2013; Lazega & Wang, this volume). The conceptualisation of a social-ecological network is not hard-wired to any specific type of actor or ecological component. Instead, it can accommodate very different conceptualisations of nodes and links, as will be elaborated below.

Although social-ecological network models obviously do not provide the ultimate solution to the huge quest of developing better understanding of human–nature interdependencies, they nonetheless deliver a certain set of benefits.

From rhetoric to concretisation. Although the arguments behind seeing humans and nature as irrevocably interdependent are plenty and convincing, the question on how to move from this realisation to concretisation in research and practice is encumbered with numerous challenges. These challenges are largely shared with the challenges associated with interdisciplinary social and natural science research, and derives from, for example, different epistemologies, methods, traditions and ways of theorising among different scientific disciplines (Schlüter et al., 2022).

Although constructing a social-ecological network model does not 'solve' these issues in an instant, it provides a way to find some common ground. Network thinking helps providing a uniform language that is spoken across disciplines, thereby reducing the risk for misunderstanding and misconceptions when engaging in interdisciplinary endeavours (Janssen et al., 2006). Further, it provides a means to explicate the essence of human–nature interdependencies – that is, it provides a model that accommodates all types of interdependencies in one single model without requiring either side, social or ecological, to reduce or fundamentally alter the ways network models have already been used within their respective research fields (Cumming et al., 2010).

Advance understanding of how social-ecological interdependencies are formed and shaped. Social-ecological interdependencies do not emerge by chance. They are the results of conscious and unconscious decisions made by actors of various kinds, and emerge when ecosystems respond to various human activities, such as extraction of resources such as timber or water, or the introduction of chemicals, such as pesticides, and alien species. Thus, the very formation and evolution of patterns of interdependencies can be understood as manifestations of different social, ecological and social-ecological processes (Bodin et al., 2016). Hence, a social-ecological network interpreted in this way is equivalent to a social selection model, where the aim of the research is to understand why social ties are formed in a community of actors (e.g., homophily, resource availability, power). In terms of causality, a social-ecological network is here understood as the outcome: the dependent

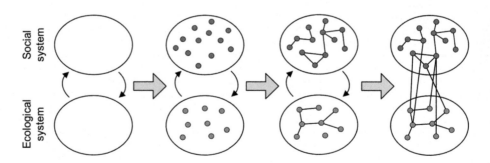

Figure 6.1 A social-ecological system as a social-ecological network. To the right, no details about the social and ecological (sub)systems are provided, but the figures to the right display an increasing level of resolution. The rightmost figure encapsulates individual social nodes (actors in a broad sense), their social relationships, ecological nodes (ecological components), their biophysical interdependencies and, finally, the interdependencies connecting to actors with the ecological components. Adapted from Bodin et al., 2016, in accordance with the CC BY 4.0 license (creativecommons.org/licenses/by/4.0/)

variable. And the possible causes, be they social, ecological or social-ecological, are at focus for the research.

What to expect from certain patterns of social-ecological interdependencies. By analysing network structures, we are able to discern possible causes in terms of underlying processes including how and why people interact, their aims and motivations, their perceptions of risks and rewards and more. However, these emerging structures will affect what comes after. In this sense, a network perspective resonates with Giddens' structuration theory, in which a social network sets the conditions for agency and represents the outcome of agents' behaviour at the same time (Bodin et al., 2020; Giddens, 1984). A social-ecological network takes this perspective of 'weak structuralism' further by accounting for both the actors and the environments, and how they interdepend. Thus, by taking the structure of a social-ecological network into account, different outcomes can be better understood and theorised (Barnes et al., 2019; 2020; Bodin & Tengö, 2012). In fact, many theories that relate to the management and governance of the environment directly or indirectly lend themselves to a social-ecological network formalism, as will be elaborated further down. For example, if two actors extract resources from a common ecological component – that is, they compete – common pool resource theories state that their ability to sustainably manage the shared ecological component increases if they communicate and use that social tie to agree on certain harvest restrictions (Ostrom, 1990). In network terms, this means that if the triangle formed between two actors (social nodes) and one ecological component (ecological node) is fully connected, the abilities to manage for sustainability increases (Barnes et al., 2019; Bodin et al., 2014).

Making environmental governance research more environmental (and vice versa). Environmental governance is here used as a short name for various research streams across disciplines that study the governance of the environment. This research naturally relies heavily on scholarship across many social science disciplines such as political science and sociology, but it also embraces interdisciplinary approaches accommodating social-ecological systems thinking and the environmental sciences more broadly. Notwithstanding the rapidly increasing interest in, and the increasing relevance of, environmental governance research, it is still struggling to bridge the natural and social sciences (e.g., Koontz & Thomas, 2006). The social-ecological network approach makes an important contribution to this quest. It accommodates interdisciplinary research that embraces a holistic perspective of governance as a collective endeavour that engages many different types of actors that interact across many different venues (cf. action situations, forum, platforms, collaborate institutions) in learning, deliberating, collaborating, competing and making decisions in how to develop policies in regard to different aspects and components of the natural environment (Lubell, 2013; cf. McGinnis, 2011). Such a comprehensive multi-actor, multi-venue and multi-environmental policy perspective of present-time governance structures and processes lends itself very well to a multilevel social-ecological network conceptualisation (Leventon et al., 2017; Morrison et al., 2023).

CONSTRUCTING SOCIAL-ECOLOGICAL NETWORKS[1]

The abilities of any model to advance understanding of the study object relies on how well it has been constructed. This naturally also applies to social-ecological network models. Concretely, this involves making informed choices of what defines nodes and links. A major challenge in relation to defining 'traditional' social or ecological networks is that a social-ecological network encompasses nodes of very different types, and the choices of what constitutes a social node depends on choices on what constitutes an ecological node (and vice versa). And these choices depend on what types of social-ecological interdependencies are at focus, which in turn depends on the empirical context and the theoretical underpinnings of the study. Finally, all these choices depend on the research questions – that is, the scientific objectives of the study. From this follows that some level of pre-understanding of the study object is generally needed before the analysts can be well positioned to start defining relevant nodes and links. Further, it is immensely helpful to start from a position where some theoretically and empirically grounded assumptions about factors likely being of importance in addressing the research questions are already laid out (cf. Guerrero et al., 2020). This suggests that social-ecological network studies benefit from the application of multiple methods, and it is often advisable to initiate the research by the use of qualitative methods such as explorative literature reviews and stakeholder interviews, and possibly also by directly engaging the stakeholders in the research process (co-production, or action research; see, e.g., Jasny et al., 2021; Norström et al., 2020). Further, iteratively and continually (re)defining nodes and links as the understanding of the study object develops could also be an integral part of the research process.

While acknowledging there is no one-size-fits-all solution in constructing a social-ecological network model that is able to adequately represent the study object in a way that enables empirically grounded theoretical advancements, the following steps and suggestions are provided as a guideline.

Step 1: what social-ecological interdependencies are at focus?

A feasible starting point is to define what kind of relationships between humans and the environment are of key interest in a given study. These relationships (interdependencies) could be based on direct extractions such as when actors withdraw resources from the natural environment through logging, mining or fishing (Barnes et al., 2019; Bodin & Tengö, 2012). In this case, a social-ecological link would encapsulate an actor (social node) utilising an ecological component (ecological node) for resource extraction. Similarly, jurisdictional and institutionalised competence, authority and/or ownership could be defined as the social-ecological interdependencies of key interest. Other and broader types of social-ecological interdependencies could also be defined – for example, the utilisation of different ecosystem services, including cultural and emotional services, provided by the natural environment (Felipe-Lucia et al., 2021). Further, the social-ecological interdependencies could be less directly linked to specific geographically, temporally, or functionally defined components of the natural environment. For example, when actors engage in policy development aiming to safeguard lakes and water streams in a drainage basin from excessive pollution or overuse, the relationships connecting the actors and the ecological (or eco-hydrological) components of the drainage basin are often somewhat diluted across the entire drainage basin. In such cases it might be more appropriate to define the social-ecological interdependencies as links between actors and specific environmental *policy issues* (Hedlund et al., 2021b; Metz et al., 2020).

Step 2: what is an actor (social node), and how do actors interact with each other?

The most straightforward conceptualisation of social nodes would be the actors of relevance given the type(s) of social-ecological interdependencies at focus (step 1). An actor could be an individual, household, or an organisation of some sort. In many cases it could, however, be more sensible to define a social node as an institution – that is, as a set of rules and norms to regulate certain behaviours; a policy document; or a specific jurisdictional and/or political entity (e.g., Ekstrom & Young, 2009). Links among the social actors should subsequently be defined based on the social structures and processes at play that are assumed to be relevant in regards to the chosen social-ecological relationships, and could include collaboration, competition, learning, influence and power. It is important to define those links in terms of impact: these social relationships should be expected to have an effect on the actors' behaviours in relation to how they utilise their social-ecological relationships (and vice versa). If that would not be the case, these links would carry no or little meaning in trying to understand how the social network influences, or is being influenced, by social-ecological interdependencies.

Step 3: what is an ecological component, and how do these components interact?

If following the previous steps, defining an ecological node often comes naturally. It sits on the opposite end to the social actor on the defined social-ecological link. If social-ecological interdependencies are defined based on direct resource extraction and/or utilisation, an ecological node could be defined as a localised fish population or a habitat patch in a landscape (e.g., Bodin et al., 2016). Broader spanning conceptualisations of social-ecological interdependencies typically imply that ecological nodes should take a more 'aggregated' form. They could, as stated above, be defined as functions or services provided by nature (Felipe-Lucia et al., 2021), and/or as the specific policy issues actors engage in when trying to address environmental problems (Hedlund et al., 2021a). Again, it is important to consider the potential impact the social actors could have on the ecological component. If the impact of an actors' behaviours on the ecological component is negligible, for example a single fishing vessel's ability to affect the status of a tuna fish population that spans the globe, it makes little sense to define the vessel as a social actor and the global tuna fish stock as an ecological node. In such case, it may make more sense to define the actor as a country's entire fishing fleet since at that level of aggregation, a social actor can have a significant effect on the status of the tuna population. This example illustrates that defining the social and the ecological nodes need to go hand in hand.

As for the social links, ecological links should also be defined in terms of impact. In other words, what happens to one ecological node (which could be a consequence of how an actor utilises its link to that node) should have consequences for the status of other (connected) ecological nodes. Further, the links connecting the ecological nodes could either represent a 'scientific' assessment of relevant ecological interdependencies, or represent actors' perceptions about how ecological nodes are interdependent (Bodin et al., 2019a). If the focus of the research is to primarily understand how actors behave and make decisions, the definition of ecological nodes and links should ideally coincide with the actors' 'mental models' of the natural environment (Hamilton et al., 2019) since those mental models would constitute a basis for their actions. Conversely, if the focus is to understand how resource uses affect environmental outcomes, the definition of ecological nodes and links should primarily derive from biophysical realities and not from actors' perceptions of such (Hamilton et al., 2019).

Step 4: Revisit the previous steps

As stated, it is often advisable to adopt an iterative process in defining (and analysing) social-ecological networks as the understanding and knowledge about the study object increase. The same applies to these steps. By going through these steps iteratively, one might not only arrive at a more well-defined social-ecological network model given the research objectives, one might also come to realise that a full-fledged social-ecological model is not needed. In fact, these four steps aim to develop what has been called a *fully articulated* social-ecological network model (Sayles et al., 2019). A fully articulated social-ecological network model articulates not only social and ecological nodes, but also all types of interdependencies connecting these nodes (within and across these levels). In many cases, a less comprehensive model could very well suffice. Maybe there is no apparent need, given the study context and the empirical realities, to account for interdependencies between ecological nodes and/or links between social actors? Or maybe it could suffice to only study the social network of the governing actors, or the network of ecological components? Conversely, maybe there is a need to add more complexity to the model – for example, by adding a third level (network), or by modelling actors, venues and ecological components as three separate but interdependent networks (cf. Lubell, 2013).

Less comprehensive models make the data-gathering processes less resource demanding, although obviously at the expense of details and future abilities to fully account for how humans and nature interdepend. More comprehensive models clearly present challenges in terms of data gathering as well in the subsequent analyses. In a recent review, the authors provide compelling arguments that anyone interested in pursuing a social-ecological network approach should consider the value of less comprehensive models since they could, in many cases, strike a more favourable balance between explanatory power and the need for extensive and often hard-to-get data (Kluger et al., 2020).

ANALYSING SOCIAL-ECOLOGICAL NETWORKS

Defining what should constitute the social-ecological networks under investigation requires a large amount of intellectual labour. Gathering the required data will also involve significant efforts. Data gathering is, however, not covered in this chapter since applicable methods and techniques to gather the needed data are, in general, no different from when conducting 'standard' social and environmental network-centric studies. Methods to define and empirically assess aggregated and/or more 'anthropocentric' forms of ecological nodes and links might, however, not necessarily be easily accessible 'off-the-shelf'. To give some guidance in that matter, a subsequent section of this chapter presents an example of a study where the ecological nodes were defined as different policy issues.

The acquired social-ecological network model, however, only constitutes the start for further analyses. In other words, the objective with the research is rarely just to define and measure the social-ecological network, but rather to use that model to address its research questions. Thus, what comes next is to conduct network analysis. Again, this does not necessarily differ from other types of network-centric studies, although the multilevel structure of the network model calls for some considerations. Fortunately, in recent years and across different scientific disciplines, significant methodological and theoretical developments of multi-level network analyses have taken place. The same applies to multilayered network analysis, although multilayered models assume that the representation of nodes are the same across all different layers although the links in each layer are defined differently (the reader is advised that there are some terminological inconsistencies in scholarly literatures, and sometimes multilayer means multilevel, and vice versa; see, e.g., Maciejewski & Baggio, 2021). Thus, no detailed descriptions of analytical techniques are covered here, rather the aim of this and the subsequent section is to provide some guidance in choosing appropriate methods given the objective of the research.

A fundamental question is whether the research aims to explain why the observed social-ecological network has come to be, or if the aim is to understand the consequences (outcomes) of an observed social-ecological network (cf. dependent versus independent variable). Being clear on such casual reasoning is of great importance for theory developments (Schlüter et al., 2019). Having said that, I acknowledge that causal paths are often complex and entangled through feedback loops, thus distinguishing causes from effects using only observational data is a very challenging task. Further, the analytical methods are often the same for both types of questions, although the interpretation of the results is likely different. Notwithstanding these difficulties, the value of being clear on causal assumptions is still immense (Bodin et al., 2019a).

Generally, one can distinguish methods aiming to assess global structural properties of a network (macro) versus methods aiming to explain the formation of links (micro). The former is often used when the objective is to explain the outcome of a network, whereas the latter is often associated with understanding what caused the formation of the observed network. An example of the former is whether certain network characteristics such as network density and betweenness centralisation are associated with certain communal or network-level outcomes such as the use of destructive fish gears (Gorris et al., 2019), and an example of the latter is whether two organisations working with biological conservation are more prone to form a collaborative relationship if they are engaged in conservation efforts within the same geographical area (defined as vegetation cluster) (Guerrero et al., 2015). To generalise, if the objective is to understand the outcome of a certain social-ecological network, it is greatly beneficial to gather data from different but comparable cases (Barnes et al., 2019), and/or to gather longitudinal data from one case (see, e.g., Barnes et al., 2022) since one instance of a social-ecological network could be seen as just one single data point. Given the time and efforts needed to gather data from multiple cases, single-case studies still prevail in the scholarly social-ecological network literature (Sayles et al., 2019). Further, not all studies are easily categorised as either focused on the global network structure or on the specific reasons why certain nodes are connected or not. Complex causation implies assumptions of 'compounded causalities' where micro- and macro-level characteristics of the network interact through feedback mechanism (Bodin et al., 2019a).

Assessing global characteristics of a social-ecological network is similar to assessing commonly used global characteristics of single-level networks, such as network density, degree centralisation and level of clustering/fragmentation. The multilevel nature of the network does, however, complicate the issue. Since the network actually consists of three different networks, which of these networks, if not all, should be weighted in these analyses, and how? Actually, to date, very few published studies are assessing such commonly used global network properties across all three networks simultaneously (however, see Baggio et al., 2016, for an example of a *multilayered* social-ecological network study partly focusing on global network characteristics). Rather, focus has been set on describing social-ecological networks through statistical approaches focused on revealing the occurrences (frequencies) of certain micro-level social-ecological network structures (often called *configurations* in the social network literature, or *motifs* in the environmental sciences; Milo et al., 2002; Moreno & Jennings, 1938). Hence, the global structure of a social-ecological network is assessed either as a quite simplistic count of certain social-ecological configurations that are then compared to a large set of randomised networks (cf. conditional uniform random graph), or by the use of multilevel exponential random graph models (Bodin et al., 2016; Wang et al., 2013; Lazega & Wang, this volume).

The use of multilevel exponential random graph models (ML-ERGM) serves as a good example of how a specific method is used both for explaining network links and to assess the global properties of a social-ecological network. It should be noted that a key benefit of ML-ERGM is that the social and ecological networks can be treated as different, but still interdependent. Hence, it is possible to, for example, distinguish between different tie formation processes in the social and the ecological networks (although I acknowledge this is an area where more work is warranted). Thus, it is up to the analyst to interpret the analytical results from the ML-ERGM as either the dependent or the independent variable. This chapter's section demonstrating some applications illustrates how both interpretations have been applied in previous research.

Although there is a huge scholarly and practical interest in understanding how certain network-level outcomes are shaped by certain network structures, such as abilities to collectively address global challenges such as climate change that requires different actors to find agreeable ways to work together, many outcomes are materialising at the level of individual nodes (social actor and/ or ecological components). In network terminology, this is equivalent to explain nodal attributes as being an effect of how the nodes are situated within the network. Here, one can differentiate between descriptive metrics capturing individual nodes' positions and roles in the network based on, for example, their degrees or betweenness centralities, and more intricate statistical methods aiming to better account for interdependencies that are inherent in network data (see, e.g., Guerrero et al., 2020). The former typically first assesses these network metrics for each node, and then runs a regression analysis to see if these metrics relate to the nodal attribute of interest (i.e., the outcome). The regression could be based on ordinary linear regression, or using regression analyses where different permutation techniques are applied to better assess statistical significance while accounting for data interdependencies (see, e.g., Robins et al., 2012). Whether the use of descriptive metrics is adequate in any given case depends on assumptions about causalities, the aim of the research and if any possible statistical imperfections are seen as acceptable or not.

The autologistic actor attribute model (ALAAM) uses ideas and techniques from the ERGM family of models (Daraganova & Robins, 2013; Koskinen, this volume), and provides a statistically robust model in explaining nodal attributes in cases where it is difficult to justify disregarding network interdependencies, and/ or when the focus of the research is to explicitly investigate the effect of any such interdependencies. The computer program MPnet uses ALAAM to support analyses of nodal attributes in multilevel networks (Wang et al., 2014). ALAAM has recently been applied in a study of a tropical island in Papua New Guinea with the objective to understand if and why certain households are better able to adapt and/or transform as a response to climate change, based on how the households are situated in a social-ecological network (Barnes et al., 2020). Other studies are forthcoming that use autoregressive networks models adapted to a multilevel network structure to examine if certain multilevel structures are associated with more effective responses at the level of individual actors' responding to wildfire disasters (Bodin et al., 2022).

Finally, as indicated above, different 'off-the-shelf' network analytical methods can and have been applied to social-ecological network studies, such as simulations, behavioural experiments, stochastic actor-oriented models; often in combination with other methods (quantitative and qualitative). Analysing a social-ecological network is thus not fundamentally different from analysing other types of networks, although they need to be understood and theorised for what they are. Hence, the full palette of old, new and forthcoming analytical methods can potentially be applied to this type of research, although the meaning of and the interpretations of analytical results naturally needs to be framed within relevant theoretical and empirical contexts.

APPLICATIONS

Reasoning about conceptualisations, methods and analytical approaches and about social-ecological network models only takes us so far. With the objective to further describe how social-ecological network models can be used to research human–nature interdependencies, a few example studies are presented below. They are primarily selected to illustrate different analytical approaches, study contexts and conceptualisations. However, in no way do they provide an exhaustive view of this research field.

Preservation of forest patches in Madagascar

This example represents one of the first empirical studies using a social-ecological network model. The context is an agricultural landscape in southern Madagascar, which is part of a region characterised by high levels of biodiversity and endemism (Bodin & Tengö, 2012). Agriculture represents the main income source for most people living in this low-income area. The landscape is dominated by small fields and pastures, but it also includes many small forest patches ranging in size from <1 to more than 90 ha. The forest patches provide important services to the inhabitants, ranging from microclimate regulation through crop pollination to ancestral burying grounds and sites for ceremonies. In spite of strong pressure for land, they have been quite well preserved over considerable time.

The inhabitants are settled in the landscape in accordance with clan affiliations, and the clans are managing different forest patches (management here implies making use of the forest patches, but also upholding the taboo systems that restrict access to the patches). The different clans interact socially in different ways and of importance here are *kinship* relations, which capture shared ancestry, agreed kinship, or historical dependencies that are manifested in forest-related ceremonies such as burials. Ethnographical studies revealed these relationships to be of importance for how the clans manage their forest patches. The forest patches, together with the larger surrounding forests, are interconnected through species dispersals (i.e., the movement of organisms across the patches). Dispersal is, according to metapopulational theory, important to maintain the small forest patches over time (Lindenmayer, 2018). In describing this study context as a social-ecological network, the clans were defined as social nodes, kinship relations as social links, forest patches as ecological nodes and possibilities for dispersal of plant seeds as ecological links (the dispersal possibilities were based on geographical distances, and the distance threshold was set to represent how far the endemic ring-tailed lemur was assumed to disperse seeds across the patches) (Figure 6.2).

The overarching research question of this study was to seek explanations why the clans, as a community, have been reasonably successful in preserving their forest patches in spite of increased pressure for land. Theories related to common pool resource management were at focus (Ostrom, 1990), and of particular interest was if the social relationships among the clans contributed to this outcome. The analytical approach was based on investigations of whether and how often certain social-ecological configurations were present in

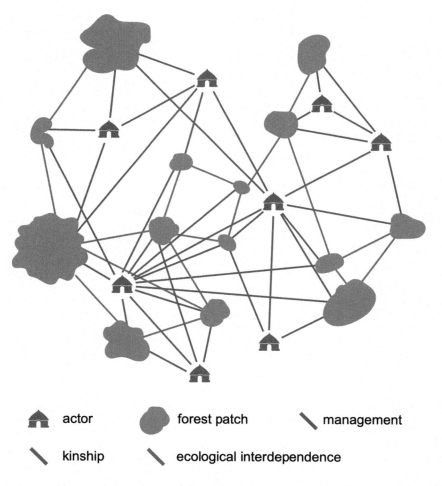

Figure 6.2 The studies' agricultural landscape described as a social-ecological network (illustration from Bodin et al., 2019a)

the network. The study investigated a high number of configurations, but, for simplicity, only four are presented here (Figure 6.3). These four configurations represent two pairs of configurations, and for each pair one of them was deemed, based on common pool resource theories, as more favourable for forest management. The occurrences of these four configurations were assessed and compared to their occurrences in a large set of randomised networks (with the same number and types of nodes and links as in the empirical network). If any of the empirical counts were outside the frequency distributions drawn from the random networks by >95 per cent or < 5 per cent, these empirical estimates were considered significant.

The results were very much in accordance with the theoretical expectations, and thus suggest that clan relationships that are 'well aligned' with the patterns in which the clan are managing the forest patches, and the patterns in which the patches themselves are interconnected, contributed to the collective ability of the clans to preserve the patches over time.

This rather simplistic analytical approach (relating the empirical estimates to estimates drawn from a large set of conditional uniform random graphs) was compared to the analytical results from a multilevel exponential random graph model and, in this particular case, the overarching results largely remained the same (Bodin et al., 2016).

The capacity of households in a local fishing community to adapt to climate change

This study focuses on understanding how different households' positions within a social-ecological network relate to their capacity to adapt to climate change (Barnes et al., 2020). The studied households constitute all households living on a small tropical island in Papua New Guinea, where fishing and harvesting of marine resources is the dominate activity supporting livelihoods and providing income. Adaptive capacity was defined on

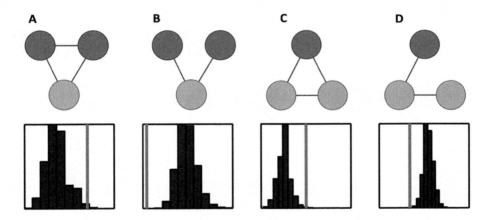

Figure 6.3 The selected social-ecological configurations, and their occurrences compared to the distributions drawn from 10,000 random networks. The two configurations to the left (A, B) represent a setting where two clans are sharing a common forest patch. In the leftmost configuration (A), the clans have a social relation, whereas in the other one (B), they do not. Assuming a social relationship helps the clans to better mitigate possibly competing interest for the same forest patch, the leftmost configuration (A) is deemed as better suited for preservation of the forest patch. The two configurations to the right (C, D) represent settings where a clan is managing one or both of two interconnected forest patches. Assuming a clan that is managing both patches would be better suited to take into account any side effects deriving from how they choose to manage one (or both) of the patches, the configuration to the left (C) is deemed as better suited for forest preservation. The dark gray in the histograms underneath each configuration represent the frequency distributions of the respective configuration drawn from the random networks, whereas the light gray represent the frequencies in the empirical network

a household level based on a range of indicators, such as assets owned, access to credit, use of multiple fishing gears, education level, past experience and involvement in decision-making processes. Each household was defined as a social actor. Social-to-ecological links were defined based on what fish species were mainly targeted by a given household, and the fish species targeted for fishing were defined as ecological nodes. Social relations were defined as communicative relationships among both men and women across households, including close friendships and fishing-related information exchange relationships, since the assumption was that these relationships have a significant impact on fishing practices on a daily and longer-term basis. Finally, ecological links were defined based on trophic interactions – that is, who eats whom – since this type of relationship has a strong effect on local fish population sizes. Drawing from a range of different theories related to adaptation and social organisation and using previous insights, the study defined five different social-ecological configurations that were theoretically assessed as determinants of adaptive capacity (Figure 6.4). Several other configurations were investigated, but these related to the social network only, and are therefore not included here.

The results from the study reinforce some pre-existing insights and theories, as well as challenging others. For example, it was found that closed social-ecological structures involving two interdependent ecological nodes (Figure 6.4, C and D) were significantly related to having taken action in light of climate impacts. Specifically, they found that configuration C (Figure 6.4) was positively significant for predicting for transformative action, and D (Figure 6.4) was negatively significant for predicting adaptive action. The authors argue that these configurations are related to different types of learning and the internalisation of ecological feedbacks. The study thus further strengthens the social-ecological network perspective as a credible approach in both testing and extending insights and theories about human–nature interdependencies and consequences thereof. This study furthermore differs from the Madagascar study in several ways. Besides the very different social-ecological context and the differences in how nodes and links were defined and empirically assessed, the aim was to explain why certain households (nodes) were more adaptive than others (i.e., the outcomes were assessed on the node and not the network level). Further, the analyses were based on a multilevel ALAAM, thus the analyses were better able to tackle the many intrinsic challenges associated with statistical analyses of

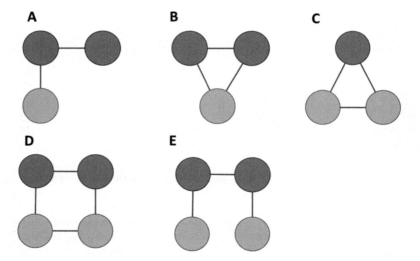

Figure 6.4 Five different social-ecological configurations that were assessed as potential determinants of households' adaptive capacities to respond to climate change. B and C are the same as in the previous example. A captures whether households targeting many fish species have more or fewer social links than other households. D can be interpreted as a variant of B, but here the two socially connected households target separate but interdependent fish species. Configuration E can thus be seen as opposite to D in the sense that the socially connected households target independent fish species

interdependent network data. Both studies do, however, make extensive use of complementing data and methods to assess outcomes, and to build and justify the conceptualisation of the social-ecological network models that were developed and analysed for each respective case.

Ecological components as policy issues, and beyond

As indicated earlier, in many cases the ecological domain of the social-ecological systems perspective does not easily lend itself to a series of ecologically well-defined components – given that the ecological components should represent something the actors are directly engaged with, and can have a measurable impact on. The water governance study presented here illustrates such a case, and shows how a social-ecological network perspective could still be useful in understanding human–nature interdependencies in a broad sense.

Governance of water resources represents a challenge that prevails across the world, and has drawn considerable scholarly interest (Özerol et al., 2018). Water governance at the level of the drainage basin often takes place through cross-boundary collaborative governance, thereby creating a polycentric, intertwined governance system that divides responsibility between multiple units on the national, regional and local scale. Likewise, the system of hydrologically interconnected water streams, lakes and wetlands implies that contaminates as well as water-dwelling species will be distributed across the basin. Although such setting resembles a 'networked system', it can nonetheless be quite challenging to pinpoint exactly which actor is managing what specific water resource. Instead, it might be more relevant to focus on which water-related policy issues the various governing actors are mostly engaged with. A policy issue is here understood as separable yet often interdependent challenges associated with a broader environmental problem actors perceive, organise around and take action on (Hedlund et al., 2021b; Metz et al., 2020).

The water council Mälarens vattenvårdsförbund operating within the drainage basin around Lake Mälaren and Lake Hjälmaren, mid-Sweden, were at focus for the study (Hedlund et al., 2021b). The council gathers a diverse set of local and regional governmental, nongovernmental and private actors with the objective to address a broad range of policy issues related to water governance through collaboration. The key research objective with the study was to understand why any two actors in the council would choose to collaborate directly with each other. Since water governance relies heavily on collaboration, it is imperative to understand what motivates any two actors to form a collaborative relationship. The overarching hypothesis in this study was that the ways in which the actors in the council engage with policy issues also influences their choices of collaborating partners.

A set of sixteen different policy issues, as well as their mutual interdependencies, were identified using methodological and empirical 'triangulation' (Hedlund et al., 2021a). This task involved identifying a set of environmental targets and, through 'backward engineering', linking these targets with specific policy issues. This process also involved identifying intervening factors in the causal chains[2] linking the policy issues to the environmental targets (Figure 6.5A). Any two or more policy issues sharing a common intervening factor would thus be considered interdependent (Figure 6.5B/C). In this way, a network of interdependent policy issues was created. This network therefore represents the 'universe' of policy issues the actors in the council engage with.

With the objective to understand what drives the formation of collaborative relationships among the actors, a social-ecological network model was created. The individual members representing their organisations in the council were defined as the social nodes (the actors), and their collaborative relationships as the social links. The policy issues and their interdependencies represented the ecological network. Finally, the specific policy issues the different actors mostly engage with were captured by links going across the social and the ecological networks. Hence, even though the network model follows the conceptualisation of a social-ecological network, it is likely better described as an actor–policy issue network. This also illustrates that the social-ecological network model can be applied to different kinds of settings where humans interact with the environment, but not necessarily only in settings where actors interact directly with some specific and solely biophysically defined components of the environment. Another example of a similar conceptualisation of a social-ecological network can be found in recent studies of wildfire crisis mitigation, where the social-ecological network model is used to capture how different actors situated in the headquarters of the crisis mitigation operation enterprise engage with specific but interdependent operational tasks, such as evacuation and clearance of roads and other means of transportation (Bodin & Nohrstedt, 2016; Bodin et al., 2019b). Conceptualising ecosystem services and their interdependencies presents another avenue where the social-ecological network model can be useful (Felipe-Lucia et al., 2021). Finally, in a study of community-based obesity prevention interventions, a social network of actors engaged

A. Causal pathways

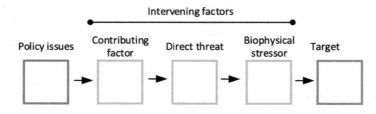

B. Common intervening factors

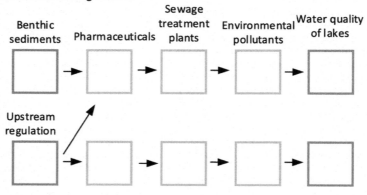

C. Policy issue interdependence

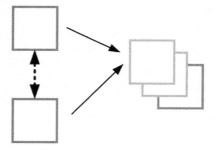

Figure 6.5 (A) illustrates a causal pathway linking a policy issue to an environmental target through different intervening factors. (B) Shows an example of two causal paths sharing a common intervening factor. The policy issue treatment of benthic sediments (upper path) involves measures to reduce the amount of pharmaceuticals in sediment, which in turn relates to implementing improvements in sewage treatment plants. Sewage treatment effectiveness in turn affect the amount of environmental pollutants that are released into the water streams, which relates to the environmental target water quality of lakes. The policy issue upstream regulation by the source (lower path) involves instigating measures to increase the amount of pharmaceuticals that are properly discarded by households, manufacturers, and health care providers, which reduces the amount of pharmaceuticals that contaminate the bottom sediment. Thus, pharmaceuticals represented a shared intervening factor, thereby making the two policy issues interdependent, as illustrated by the dotted line in (C). Adapted from Hedlund et al., 2021a

in the interventions was integrated with a network model depicting a causal loop diagram of obesity drivers, thereby effectively forming a multilevel network model conceptually identical to a social-ecological network model (McGlashan et al., 2019). This model was then used to investigate how the intricacies in the web of obesity drivers affected how the actors collaborate.

Using ML-ERGM, the water governance study described here investigated the prevalence of a series of actor–policy issue configurations. These configurations largely overlapped, structurally, with the social-ecological configurations investigated in the previous two study examples. However, here the objective was to seek explanations why a social link was formed. Therefore, all other types of links were considered externally determined (i.e., 'fixed'), and the only type of link that was modelled in the ML-ERGM was the social.[3] Interviews with the actors confirmed this being a valid assumption, as the respondents deemed social links being more 'fluid' than the other types of links. Interdependencies between policy issues are largely externally determined vis-à-vis the actors' whereabouts, and the ways in which actors engage with policy issues are largely determined by their organisational affiliation and interests. Although links connecting actors with policy issues are also to some extent fluid, the processes that steer actors' choices of which policy issues to engage with are most likely operating at a slower pace than the processes that steer their choices of collaborating partners.

The analytical results revealed that the patterns in which actors engage with policy issues, and how these issues interdepend, do affect their choices of collaborating partners. The results also demonstrated that the influence of actor–policy issue entanglements operate in tandem with social drivers such as homophily and the tendency to form relationships with the chair of the council. Interestingly, the results showed that the specific actor–policy issue configurations that were identified as stimulating collaboration were not always the ones that, from a theoretical point of view, seemed most suitable in succeeding with the governing objectives. Most notably, the actors, all else equal, hesitated to collaborate with other actors that were engaged with interdependent policy issues (i.e., the coefficient of the 'closed square' configurations linking two actors and two policy issues was negative and significant, cf. Figure 6.4, D).

Ways forward

As this chapter has hopefully conveyed, there has been much progress in using social-ecological network models to further our understanding of human–nature interdependencies and their consequences on our abilities to sustainably govern nature and society. In spite of these developments, this line of research is still largely in its infancy (or perhaps it has moved towards the toddler state). Hence, there is still lots that can and needs to be done to take this further. I argue a very important venue for future research is to continue to elaborate the very conceptualisation of social-ecological networks as adequate and informative representations of social-ecological systems. Moving beyond just advocating for the importance of complex human–nature interdependencies to actually conducting empirically and theoretically grounded in-depth interdisciplinary investigations is still posing a big challenge for scholars and practitioners. Current social-ecological network research has mostly scratched the surface, and I envision there are many novel conceptualisations and applications of this modelling approach that lie ahead of us. This in particular applies in relation to the task of describing the natural environment in an 'anthropocentric' form, like ecosystem services, environmental policy issues, or ecosystem functions (cf. Ekstrom & Young, 2009). These methodological developments also need to co-evolve with interdisciplinary theory developments (Sayles et al., 2019). Central to this quest is to continue reasoning about cause and effect. Is the modelled social-ecological network a cause or an effect? I would argue it is both, but depending on the research questions, the underlying theories and contextual understanding, it can be considered as either/or. Being clearer on these assumptions in any given study is a first but important step (Bodin et al., 2019a).

Further, a very interesting venue for future studies would be to explicitly investigate social and ecological feedback mechanisms, applying a dynamic perspective where the social-ecological network is studied through time (cf. Snijders & Steglich, this volume), in concert with investigations on both individual- and system-level outcomes of various kinds. Finally, since social-ecological systems are very complex study objects where causal pathways can be entangled in complex ways (complex causalities, see, e.g., Schlüter et al., 2022), I argue it is often beneficial to apply multiple methods in an effort to disentangle those pathways through triangulation (in particular, I think mixing qualitative and quantitative methods can be very fruitful).

In addition to these methodological and theoretical developments, there is a need to further develop the analytical machinery suitable for multilevel social-ecological network analyses. One key issue is to pave the way for adding additional networks to the multilevel network model. For example, in the ecology of games framework that is gaining traction in the environmental governance literatures, focus is set on three types of entities: actors, venues and issues (Lubell, 2013). This conceptualisation lends itself very well to a three-level network model – that is, a social-ecological network model but with three separate albeit interconnected networks. Although there are certainly ways to use currently available analytical methods and software packages to conduct three or more level analyses, these analyses typically need to be done off 'the beaten track', thus making it more difficult for people less immersed in sophisticated statistical methods such as ERGM to analyse their models. And I would also argue there are possible applications of three or more-level network analyses that strictly cannot be done without further developments.

I also think there is a need to consider more descriptive whole-network measures of social-ecological networks, equivalent to off-the-shelf metrics such as degree centralisations and levels of fragmentation on single-level networks. Such metrics can be very useful when comparing multiple networks and, if tied closely to relevant theories,[4] they could be very informative. Perhaps a bit surprising, very few if any social-ecological network studies have, to date, done much in this respect. Thus, there are plenty of opportunities to break new ground.

Furthermore, as stated earlier, not all analyses of social-ecological networks necessarily need to take into account all types of links and nodes. Although the information contained within a fully articulated social-ecological network model exceeds what can be accommodated in a simpler model, not all research questions require that high level of information content (Kluger et al., 2020). Thus, a cost–benefit perspective could favour a simpler model over a more complicated one since the cost of acquiring empirical social and ecological data is typically high.

In summary, the social-ecological network modelling approach has established itself as a creditable and informative tool that fits well within the wider social-ecological systems research toolbox (Maciejewski & Baggio, 2021). It has contributed to new and important insights about if and how human–environment interdependencies relate to human behaviours and decision-making vis-à-vis the natural environment. The modelling approach is still rather new, and much work remains to be done in terms of model conceptualisations, associated interdisciplinary (and disciplinary) theory developments and analytical approaches. I thus encourage anyone interested in studying human–nature interdependencies and environmental governance and science more generally to contribute to these developments, in particular if also interested in network thinking and network analysis.

Notes

1 Many of the suggestions in this section draw heavily from previous work, in particular Bodin and Tengö (2012) and Bodin et al. (2019a).
2 Although the term *causal chain* is used, not all relationships among the identified intervening factors are strictly causal. Relationships among intervening factors also encompass associations, such as when two factors represent 'two sides of the same coin'.
3 This was, however, to a varying extent also the case in the previous two example studies since their objectives were to understand how the existence of social links affects the actors' behaviour in regards to how they managed and utilised their ecological components.
4 I acknowledge that different multilevel network measures and metrics have been developed in recent years, but their relevance to social-ecological networks and associated theories remain vague.

REFERENCES

Alcamo, J., & Bennett, E.M. (2003). *Ecosystems and human well-being: a framework for assessment.* Island Press.

Baggio, J.A., BurnSilver, S.B., Arenas, A., Magdanz, J.S., Kofinas, G.P., & De Domenico, M. (2016). Multiplex social ecological network analysis reveals how social changes affect community robustness more than resource depletion. *Proceedings of the National Academy of Sciences*, 113(48), 13708–13713. doi.org/10.1073/pnas.1604401113

Barnes, M.L., Bodin, Ö., McClanahan, T.R., Kittinger, J.N., Hoey, A.S., Gaoue, O.G., & Graham, N.A.J. (2019). Social-ecological alignment and ecological conditions in coral reefs. *Nature Communications*, 10(1), 2039. doi.org/10.1038/s41467-019-09994-1

Barnes, M.L., Jasny, L., Bauman, A., Ben, J., Berardo, R., Bodin, Ö., Cinner, J., Feary, D.A., Guerrero, A.M., Januchowski-Hartley, F.A., Kuage, J.T., Lau, J.D., Wang, P., & Zamborain-Mason, J. (2022). 'Bunkering down': how one community is tightening social-ecological network structures in the face of global change. *People and Nature*, August 2021, 1–17. doi.org/10.1002/pan3.10364

Barnes, M.L., Wang, P., Cinner, J.E., Graham, N.A.J., Guerrero, A.M., Jasny, L., Lau, J., Sutcliffe, S.R., &

Zamborain-Mason, J. (2020). Social determinants of adaptive and transformative responses to climate change. *Nature Climate Change*. doi.org/10.1038/s41558-020-0871-4

Bascompte, J., Jordano, P., Melián, C.J., & Olesen, J.M. (2003). The nested assembly of plant–animal mutualistic networks. *Proceedings of the National Academy of Sciences of the United States of America*, *100*(16), 9383–9387.

Berkes, F., & Folke, C. (1998). *Linking social and ecological systems*. Cambridge University Press.

Bodin, Ö., Alexander, S.M., Baggio, J., Barnes, M.L., Berardo, R., Cumming, G.S., Dee, L., Fischer, A.P., Fischer, M., Mancilla-Garcia, M., Guerrero, A., Hileman, J., Ingold, K., Matous, P., Morrison, T.H., Nohrstedt, D., Pittman, J., Robins, G., & Sayles, J.S. (2019a). Improving network approaches to the study of complex social–ecological interdependencies. *Nature Sustainability*, *2*(7), 551–559. doi.org/10.1038/s41893-019-0308-0

Bodin, Ö., Crona, B., Thyresson, M., Golz, A.-L., & Tengö, M. (2014). Conservation success as a function of good alignment of social and ecological structures and processes. *Conservation Biology*, *28*(5), 1371–1379. doi.org/10.1111/cobi.12306

Bodin, Ö., Guerrero, A. M., Nohrstedt, D., Baird, J., Summers, R., Plummer, R., & Jasny, L. (2022). Choose your collaborators wisely: addressing interdependent tasks through collaboration in responding to wildfire disasters. *Public Administration Review*, *82*(6), 1154–1167. doi.org/10.1111/puar.13518

Bodin, Ö., Mancilla García, M., & Robins, G. (2020). Reconciling conflict and cooperation in environmental governance: a social network perspective. *Annual Review of Environment and Resources*, *45*(1), 471–495. doi.org/10.1146/annurev-environ-011020-064352

Bodin, Ö., & Nohrstedt, D. (2016). Formation and performance of collaborative disaster management networks: evidence from a Swedish wildfire response. *Global Environmental Change*, *41*, 183–194. doi.org/10.1016/j.gloenvcha.2016.10.004

Bodin, Ö., Nohrstedt, D., Baird, J., Summers, R., & Plummer, R. (2019b). Working at the 'speed of trust': pre-existing and emerging social ties in wildfire responder networks in Sweden and Canada. *Regional Environmental Change*, *19*(8), 2353–2364. doi.org/10.1007/s10113-019-01546-z

Bodin, Ö., Robins, G., Mcallister, R. R. J., Guerrero, A. M., Crona, B., Tengö, M., & Lubell, M. (2016). Theorizing benefits and constraints in collaborative environmental governance: a transdisciplinary social-ecological network approach for empirical investigations. *Ecology and Society*, *21*(1), 40. doi.org/10.5751/ES-08368-210140

Bodin, Ö., & Tengö, M. (2012). Disentangling intangible social–ecological systems. *Global Environmental Change*, *22*, 430–439. doi.org/10.1016/j.gloenvcha.2012.01.005

Bowler, D.E., Buyung-Ali, L.M., Knight, T.M., & Pullin, A.S. (2010). A systematic review of evidence for the added benefits to health of exposure to natural environments. *BMC Public Health*, *10*(1), 456. doi.org/10.1186/1471-2458-10-456

Cumming, G.S., Bodin, Ö., Ernstson, H., & Elmqvist, T. (2010). Network analysis in conservation biogeography: challenges and opportunities. *Diversity and Distributions*, *16*, 414–425. doi.org/10.1111/j.1472-4642.2010.00651.x

Daraganova, G., & Robins, G. (2013). Autologistic actor attribute models. In D. Lusher, J. Koskinen & G. Robins (Eds.), *Exponential random graph models for social networks: theory, methods and applications* (pp. 102–108). Cambridge University Press,.

Ekstrom, J.A., & Young, O.R. (2009). evaluating functional fit between a set of institutions and an ecosystem. *Ecology and Society*, *14*(2), 16.

Felipe-Lucia, M.R., Guerrero, A.M., Alexander, S.M., Ashander, J., Baggio, J.A., Barnes, M. L., Bodin, Ö., Bonn, A., Fortin, M.-J., Friedman, R.S., Gephart, J.A., Helmstedt, K.J., Keyes, A.A., Kroetz, K., Massol, F., Pocock, M.J.O., Sayles, J., Thompson, R.M., Wood, S.A., & Dee, L.E. (2021). Conceptualizing ecosystem services using social–ecological networks. *Trends in Ecology and Evolution*, 1–12. doi.org/10.1016/j.tree.2021.11.012

Giddens, A. (1984). *The constitution of society: outline of the theory of structuration*. Polity Press.

Gorris, P., Glaser, M., Idrus, R., & Yusuf, A. (2019). The role of social structure for governing natural resources in decentralized political systems: insights from governing a fishery in Indonesia. *Public Administration*, *97*(3), 654–670. doi.org/10.1111/padm.12586

Guerrero, A. M., Barnes, M., Bodin, Ö., Chadès, I., Davis, K.J., Iftekhar, M.S., Morgans, C., & Wilson, K.A. (2020). Key considerations and challenges in the application of social-network research for environmental decision making. *Conservation Biology*, *34*(3), 733–742. doi.org/10.1111/cobi.13461

Guerrero, A.M., Bodin, Ö., McAllister, R.R.J., & Wilson, K.A. (2015). Achieving social-ecological fit through bottom-up collaborative governance: an empirical investigation. *Ecology and Society*, *20*(4), 41. doi.org/10.5751/ES-08035-200441

Haberl, H., Erb, K.-H., & Krausmann, F. (2014). Human appropriation of net primary production: patterns, trends, and planetary boundaries. *Annual Review of Environment and Resources*, *39*(1), 363–391. doi.org/10.1146/annurev-environ-121912-094620

Hamilton, M., Salerno, J., & Fischer, A.P. (2019). Cognition of complexity and trade-offs in a wildfire-prone social-ecological system. *Environmental Research Letters*, *14*(12), 125017. doi.org/10.1088/1748-9326/ab59c1

Hedlund, J., Bodin, Ö., & Nohrstedt, D. (2021a). assessing policy issue interdependencies in environmental governance. *International Journal of the Commons*, *15*(1), 82. doi.org/10.5334/ijc.1060

Hedlund, J., Bodin, Ö., & Nohrstedt, D. (2021b). Policy issue interdependency and the formation of collaborative networks. *People and Nature*, *3*(1), 236–250. doi.org/10.1002/pan3.10170

Janssen, M.A., Bodin, Ö., Anderies, J.M., Elmqvist, T., Ernstson, H., McAllister, R.R.J., Olsson, P., & Ryan, P. (2006). Toward a network perspective of the study of resilience in social-ecological systems. *Ecology and Society*, *11*(1), 15.

Jasny, L., Sayles, J., Hamilton, M., Roldan Gomez, L., Jacobs, D., Prell, C., Matous, P., Schiffer, E., Guerrero, A.M., & Barnes, M.L. (2021). Participant engagement in environmentally focused social network research. *Social Networks*, *66*, 125–138. doi.org/10.1016/j.socnet.2021.01.005

Kluger, L.C., Gorris, P., Kochalski, S., Mueller, M.S., & Romagnoni, G. (2020). Studying human–nature relationships through a network lens: a systematic review. *People and Nature*, February, pan3.10136. doi.org/10.1002/pan3.10136

Koontz, T.M., & Thomas, C.W. (2006). What do we know and need to know about the environmental outcomes of collaborative management? *Public Administration Review*, *66*(1), 111–121. doi.org/10.1111/j.1540-6210.2006.00671.x

Leventon, J., Schaal, T., Velten, S., Dänhardt, J., Fischer, J., Abson, D.J., & Newig, J. (2017). Collaboration or fragmentation? Biodiversity management through the common agricultural policy. *Land Use Policy*, *64*, 1–12. doi.org/10.1016/j.landusepol.2017.02.009

Lindenmayer, D. (2018). Small patches make critical contributions to biodiversity conservation. *Proceedings of the National Academy of Sciences*, *116*(3), 201820169. doi.org/10.1073/PNAS.1820169116

Lubell, M. (2013). Governing institutional complexity: the ecology of games framework. *Policy Studies Journal*, *41*(3), 537–559. onlinelibrary.wiley.com/doi/10.1111/psj.12028/full

Maciejewski, K., & Baggio, J. (2021). Network analysis. In R. Biggs, A. de Vos, R. Preiser, H. Clements, K. Maciejewski & M. Schlüter (Eds.), *The Routledge handbook of research methods for social-ecological systems* (pp. 321–331). Routledge.

May, R.M. (1972). Will a large complex system be stable? *Nature*, *238*, 413–414.

McGinnis, M.D. (2011). Networks of adjacent action situations in polycentric governance. *Policy Studies Journal*, *39*(1), 51–78. doi.org/10.1111/j.1541-0072.2010.00396.x

McGlashan, J., Haye, K. De, Wang, P., & Allender, S. (2019). Collaboration in complex systems: multilevel network analysis for community-based obesity prevention interventions. *Scientific Reports*, July, 1–10. doi.org/10.1038/s41598-019-47759-4

Metz, F., Angst, M., & Fischer, M. (2020). Policy integration: do laws or actors integrate issues relevant to flood risk management in Switzerland? *Global Environmental Change*, *61*, June 2019, 101945. doi.org/10.1016/j.gloenvcha.2019.101945

Milo, R., Shen-Orr, S., Itzkovitz, S., Kashtan, N., Chklovskii, D., & Alon, U. (2002). Network motifs: simple building blocks of complex networks. *Science*, *298*(5594), 824–827. doi.org/10.1126/science.298.5594.824

Moreno, J.L., & Jennings, H.H. (1938). Statistics of social configurations. *Sociometry*, *1*, 342–374.

Morrison, T.H., Bodin, Ö., Cumming, G.S., Lubell, M., Seppelt, R., Seppelt, T., & Weible, C. M. (2023). Building blocks of polycentric governance. *Policy Studies Journal*, forthcoming.

Norström, A.V., Cvitanovic, C., Löf, M.F., West, S., Wyborn, C., Balvanera, P., … Österblom, H. (2020). Principles for knowledge co-production in sustainability research. *Nature Sustainability*. doi.org/10.1038/s41893-019-0448-2

Ostrom, E. (1990). *Governing the commons: the evolution of institutions for collective action*. Cambridge University Press.

Özerol, G., Vinke-de Kruijf, J., Brisbois, M.C., Casiano Flores, C., Deekshit, P., Girard, C., Knieper, C., Mirnezami, S.J., Ortega-Reig, M., Ranjan, P., Schröder, N.S.J., & Schröter, B. (2018). Comparative studies of water governance: a systematic review. *Ecology and Society*, *23*(4), art43. doi.org/10.5751/ES-10548-230443

Pimm, S.L. (1982). *Food webs*. Chapman and Hall.

Robins, G., Lewis, J.M., & Wang, P. (2012). Statistical network analysis for analyzing policy networks. *Policy Studies Journal*, *40*(3), 375–401.

Sayles, J.S., Mancilla Garcia, M., Hamilton, M., Alexander, S.M., Baggio, J.A., Fischer, A. P., Ingold, K., Meredith, G.R., & Pittman, J. (2019). Social-ecological network analysis for sustainability sciences: a systematic review and innovative research agenda for the future. *Environmental Research Letters*, *14*(9), 093003. doi.org/10.1088/1748-9326/ab2619

Schlüter, M., Caniglia, G., Orach, K., Bodin, Ö., Magliocca, N., Meyfroidt, P., & Reyers, B. (2022). Why care about theories? Innovative ways of theorizing in sustainability science. *Current Opinion in Environmental Sustainability*, *54*, 101154. doi.org/10.1016/j.cosust.2022.101154

Schlüter, M., Orach, K., Lindkvist, E., Martin, R., Wijermans, N., Bodin, Ö., & Boonstra, W. J. (2019). Toward a methodology for explaining and theorizing about social-ecological phenomena. *Current Opinion in Environmental Sustainability*, *39*, 44–53. doi.org/10.1016/j.cosust.2019.06.011

Urban, D.L., & Keitt, T. (2001). Landscape connectivity: a graph-theoretic perspective. *Ecology*, *82*(5), 1205–1218.

Wang, P., Robins, G., Pattison, P., & Lazega, E. (2013). Exponential random graph models for multilevel networks. *Social Networks*, *35*(1), 96–115.

Wang, P., Robins, G., Pattison, P., & Koskinen, J.H. (2014). *MPNet: program for the simulation and estimation of (p*) exponential random graph models for multilevel networks*. sna.unimelb.edu.au/PNet

Waters, C.N., Zalasiewicz, J., Summerhayes, C., Barnosky, A.D., Poirier, C., Gałuszka, A., ... Wolfe, A.P. (2016). The Anthropocene is functionally and stratigraphically distinct from the Holocene. *Science*, *351*(6269). doi.org/10.1126/science.aad2622

The Evolution of Environmental Policy Network Analysis[1]

Tyler A. Scott, Mark Lubell, and Gwen Arnold

INTRODUCTION

Network analysis has become one of the most important methodological approaches for research on environmental policy and governance. By network analysis, we mean both theoretical ideas related to networks and the application of empirical network analysis methods. This chapter uses a bibliometric approach to identify the key research communities involved in environmental policy network analysis, trace the critical path of citations over time and summarise key research questions and findings of the literature.

Why have networks become so important in environmental policy research? The overarching reason is that environmental policy involves many types of interdependence, which is an essential idea in network analysis. Interdependence occurs when the decisions, outputs and outcomes experienced by one actor or component of a system are conditional on the experiences of other actors or components of the system. In network science, the components of the system are usually depicted as 'nodes' of different types connected by 'edges' that capture some type of social or biophysical process or relationship that jointly influences connected nodes. The various theoretical approaches to environmental policy network analysis develop hypotheses about the types of social processes occurring in the system and how they might be operationalised in the context of an empirical network analysis.

Networks are fundamental in two core social processes considered in environmental policy: collective/social learning and cooperation. Collective learning, as defined by Gerlak and Heikkila (2011), involves the collective dissemination, assessment and translation of knowledge and the emergence of collective products such as shared ideas or policies. Similarly, Pahl-Wostl (2009) describes how interactions among governance actors generate different levels of social learning. By definition, such learning requires connections between individuals (and organisations), hence the primacy of network concepts and network analysis for understanding this process. A classic example is the importance of 'weak ties' (Granovetter, 1973) that bridge disparate communities. Ties spanning such 'structural holes' (Burt, 1992) are conduits of new information and ideas.

Cooperation may emerge when two or more actors can achieve joint benefits through coordinated actions. Despite these benefits, cooperation may not occur because each actor has an incentive to 'free-ride' on the effort of others, particularly when that effort is individually costly; as in a prisoner's dilemma, there is a conflict between individual and collective benefits. The terms 'collaboration' and 'coordination' are colloquially used as synonyms for cooperation, although from a technical game theory perspective, coordination problems have a different pay-off structure (Berardo & Scholz, 2010) and scholars often categorise these different terms as referring to different gradations or intensities of collective action (e.g., Margerum, 2011). Networks are instrumental for cooperation because network structures can create social capital supporting norms of reciprocity, reputation formation and social sanctioning (Lubell & Scholz, 2001; Pretty & Ward, 2001; Ingold & Leifeld, 2016). Networks also illuminate political dimensions of cooperation, such as the structure of policy coalitions (Sabatier & Jenkins-Smith, 1993) and homophilic tendencies in partner selection (Gerber et al., 2013).

We next describe the bibliometric analysis we use to further dissect the environmental policy network analysis literature and trace the 'critical path' of its evolution over time. The bibliometric results help us offer a detailed synthesis of the different traditions of research within environmental policy network analysis. Our analysis focuses on the epistemological role that networks play in different communities of research, and how the literature has evolved from general to more specific applications with branches into interdisciplinary approaches. We also believe that bibliometric analysis is a compelling empirical approach for any literature review, and our code is publicly available at the link in footnote 1.

THE 'CRITICAL PATH' FOR ENVIRONMENTAL POLICY NETWORK SCHOLARSHIP

We implement a bibliometric analysis of the key communities and the 'critical path' of citations over time. Similar bibliometric approaches are used by Van Holt et al. (2016) and Lucio-Arias and Leydesorff (2008). Critical path analysis (CPA) represents the structural backbone of a body of literature by identifying influential work that 'cites many who cited critical others and is cited by many who in turn are highly cited' (Van Holt et al., 2016). By incorporating both citations and literature cited, CPA traces the trajectory of a field over time.

Methods

To start, we queried Clarivate's Web of Science (WoS) database to develop a sample of the scientific literature and establish network boundaries. WoS is a global citation database indexing all academic journals and cited references. Our query sought literature at the intersection of governance, networks and the environment. This includes: (1) public administration (PA) and policy literature focused on social networks germane to environmental governance, though potentially not explicitly referencing environmental topics; and (2) environmental policy and management literature that concerns social networks. Specifically, the query returned: (1) *any* article using the phrases 'governance networks', 'network governance', or 'policy networks' in the title, abstract, or keywords; and (2) any article using the phrases 'natural resource' or 'environmental management' *and* one of 'social network' or 'network analysis'.[2]

This query (conducted on 15 February 2022) returned 4,166 results. We filtered the sample to include only works published in English and classified in WoS as an original research journal article, as opposed to book chapters, letters, reviews, corrections and editorial material. Of these exclusions, reviews are the most noteworthy. For instance, Bodin and Crona's (2009) review article in *Global Environmental Change* is the fourth-most cited piece in the query. However, review articles do not present primary research. The purpose of a review article – summarising extant literature – does not reflect the assumptions about the data-generating process which underlie critical path analysis.

The WoS database indexes citations made by each publication in the query. We performed a series of cleaning and filtering steps on these citations (documented in the public Github code repository associated with this chapter) to disambiguate references[3] and remove citations to non-academic products (e.g., UN, Organisation for Economic Co-operation and Development (OECD) reports). Finally, we retain only works cited five or more times by publications in the query sample. The result is a citation matrix with 2,932 rows (remaining query results) and 3,247 columns (works cited five or more times by the 2,932 publications). This matrix represents a citation network, with values of 1 representing a citation link between two publications.

Next, we identify communities in this matrix using the Louvain method for community detection (Blondel et al., 2008), which identifies the optimal number of clusters that maximises total modularity, or the strength of division in the network.

Louvain clustering identified thirteen clusters of publications. However, clusters 10 through 13 are small (just three to ten publications each) and close inspection revealed that these isolated clusters contain work that is not germane to environmental governance or policy networks. Thus, we drop these four clusters, and retain the nine larger clusters that are relevant to the analysis at hand.

To characterise the scholarly community each cluster represents, we apply rapid automatic keyword extraction (RAKE) (Wijffels, 2021) to the text of abstracts for each community. RAKE is an unsupervised learning method that identifies key phrases based on frequency, colocation and co-occurrence of words. Each phrase receives a RAKE score, with higher values indicating a stronger keyword. Because phrases – rather than single words – tend to be more evocative about the nature of a citation community, we retain phrases of two or more words, and then present the top three phrases (by RAKE score) for each cluster.[4]

The nine clusters, their associated keywords and the three papers from each cluster *in our sample query* that are cited the most *by papers in the sample query* are summarised in Table 7.1.

Finally, we calculate the critical path in the citation network (Batagelj, 2003) by: (1) identifying all source nodes (node with zero incoming ties, i.e., the most recent publications that have no citations themselves) and sink nodes (nodes with no outgoing ties, generally older publications not contained in the query sample that are cited by papers in the sample); (2) identifying the search path count (SPC) of every tie that counts how many times a given tie is traversed by all possible paths from every source to every sink; and (3) identifying the citation chain with the highest overall traversal count total. This results in a single path, only branching at the very beginning and end (several sources and sinks are effectively tied since they contribute the same amount to overall traversal counts).

Table 7.1 Detected communities in the citation network

Cluster	# members (in query + cited work)	RAKE derived keywords	Top three papers in the cluster most highly cited by other papers in the query sample
1	1,189	net. manage.+social capital+PA	Klijn et al. (2010a) Klijn et al. (2010b) Provan & Kenis (2008)
2	1,218	SNA+policy nets.+policy community	Börzel (1998) Dowding (1995) Marsh & Smith (2000)
3	1,243	nat. res. manage.+SES+SNA	Bodin et al. (2006) Newig et al. (2010) Prell et al. (2009)
4	673	SNA+ACF+climate change	Berardo & Scholz (2010) Schneider et al. (2003) Weible & Sabatier (2005)
5	1,294	civil society+policy nets.+gov. network	Klijn & Skelcher (2007) Sørensen & Torfing (2005) Sørensen & Torfing (2009)
6	76	network gov.+policy nets.+policy makers	Campbell et al. (2014) Milat et al. (2013) Pirson & Turnbull (2011)
7	190	policy nets.+educ. policy+network gov.	Ball (2009) Ball (2016) Kretchmar et al. (2014)
8	58	social. inf. sys.+virtual pol. nets.+policy capacity	McNutt (2008) McNutt & Pal (2011) Rethemeyer (2007)
9	52	ecol. net. analysis+renew. energy+policy makers	Bodini & Bondavalli (2002) Domènech & Saurí (2010) Monaco & Ulanowicz (1997)

Results

Figure 7.1 displays the main communities embedded in the corpus of research related to environmental policy. Citations between papers in the different communities are aggregated to the community level – darker, thicker lines indicate more citations. For clarity, tie totals less than the average tie total between communities are omitted. Roughly speaking, there are three types of communities: (1) large and specialised towards the environment (e.g., cluster #3, 'nat. res. Manage.+social-ecological systems (SES)+SNA'); (2) large and oriented towards general network theory (e.g., cluster #1, 'net. manage.+social capital+PA'); and (3) smaller, peripheral communities picked up in the query that have overlapping theoretical and methodological ideas but related to different policy areas (e.g., cluster #7 concerns education policy, cluster #8 contains research about virtual networks and cluster #9 is somewhat of a 'grab bag' of other topics related to the environment and networks such as trophic networks and energy infrastructure).

The large and environmentally specialised communities include natural resource management and SES scholarship (cluster #3), as well as SNA applied to theories of the policy process such as the Advocacy Coalition Framework (ACF) in environmental contexts (cluster #4). The SES community is more interdisciplinary, with connections to ecological and other biophysical sciences, while the policy process community is more squarely housed within the disciplines of public administration, political science and policy sciences. The research in these communities emphasises environmental policy cases, using network science theory and empirical approaches to characterise and assess interdependencies crucial to outcomes.

Cluster-level citation network

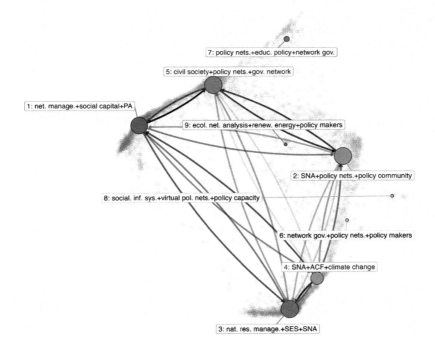

*node size = # papers in cluster
**edge darkness = # citations between clusters
***edges with # papers < mean edge value omitted

Figure 7.1 Cluster-level citation network

The large and general network communities include clusters (clusters #1 and #5) focused on network management and a cluster (#2) developing network typologies, typically illustrating them by comparative analysis across countries and sectors. The network management clusters are more centred on public administration topics, such as management strategies and resources (e.g., social capital) needed for network effectiveness. The core premise of this work is that delivering public benefits requires cooperation among multiple, diverse stakeholders rather than administration by just one centralised government agency (Sørensen & Torfing, 2009; Klijn et al., 2010a; Provan & Kenis, 2008). The network typology cluster focuses on how the structure, function and processes of policy networks vary across policy sectors and institutional settings (Dowding, 1995; Marsh & Smith, 2000). This comparative network research also spends some time examining how European versus American scholars conceptualise the role of networks (Börzel, 1998).

The small and more peripheral communities are more heterogeneous and appear to play a role in translating core network methods and theoretical concepts into even more specialised and auxiliary topics. For example, two peripheral communities link to other policy sectors, health policy (cluster #7) and information technology (cluster #8).

These sectors are similar to the environmental domain in that they also feature multi-actor policy systems and, in some cases, they have direct substantive overlap with environmental policy (e.g., environmental health). Climate change is only a prominent topic for one cluster, despite being the most important environmental collective action problem facing the Earth – supporting the contention that climate change has not received enough attention from the policy sciences (Keohane, 2015; Javeline, 2014).[5] Additionally, some research communities are only partially captured by our query: for instance, social capital is a very important general idea for environmental policy research, but much of the massive literature on social capital is outside of the bounds of our focused query.

Figure 7.2 shows the growth in these communities over time. The first thing to note is that all the communities are growing – network science applied to public policy and environmental policy is a vibrant and evolving field. Second, the large and general communities (cluster #1, #2 and #5) are accelerating rapidly. Not only are they foundational to the more specialised applications to environmental policy, but the general nature of their ideas and methods has a large range of applications, producing a multiplier effect in the literature. The natural resource management/SES community (cluster #3) is the fastest growing more

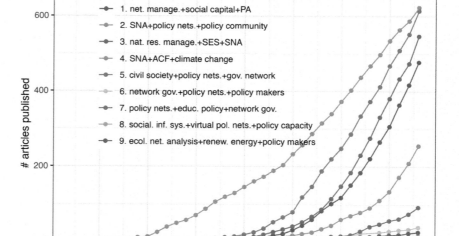

Figure 7.2 Cumulative count of articles by cluster in sample

specialised topic, likely because it is relatively new and capitalises on the interdisciplinary nature of network science along with the widespread recognition that effective environmental governance requires considering both the natural and social components of a system and how they interact. At the same time, the more specialised environmental policy process research (e.g., cluster #4) continues to be a going concern within the policy sciences.

The critical path analysis (Figure 7.3) is a sharper example of how the contrasts of periphery/core and general/specialised shape the evolution of the literature. In Figure 7.3, the dark, bolded arrows and larger labels bookended with '*' symbols denote the critical path. We then add: (1) highly cited source nodes (newer research that is picked up by the query but not cited by the query) and sink nodes (older research that is cited by work in the query but not itself picked up in by the query) for the critical path; and (2) additional noteworthy pieces that cite work on the critical path to provide added context. These pieces are selected as follows. For the first non-sink node on the critical path (Van Waarden, 1992), we identify the top two most highly cited papers *in the query sample* which cite that node. We then exclude those two papers and repeat the exercise successively for each node on the path.

Of the nine clusters identified in the sample, only four are represented in the critical path figure. The root of the critical path is mainly composed of the more generalised communities applying network theory across policy domains and countries, primarily using qualitative and descriptive methods. These communities are the source of some very general ideas about networks, like the notion that actors are arrayed in complex, fluid, issue-specific structures (Heclo, 1978) or that

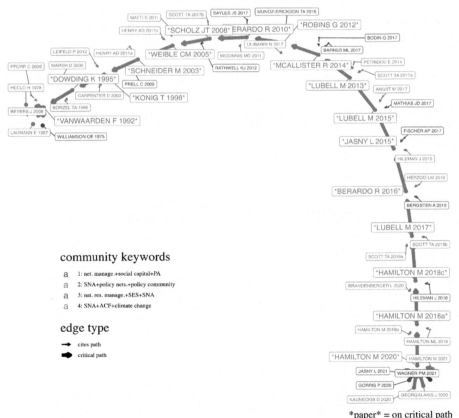

Figure 7.3 Critical path and most cited papers citing the path

understanding policy dynamics requires analysing power dynamics affecting participant bargaining (Dowding, 1995). These insights are then carried forward and translated into some of the more specialised communities that evolve over time. As the literature advances, the community that comprises much of the critical path applies network science insights to recognised theories of the policy process such as the Advocacy Coalition Framework, Institutional Collective Action Framework and collaborative and polycentric governance theories. At the periphery of the critical path is research on social-ecological systems, which is accelerating over time but has an interdisciplinary component that draws it away from the critical path and towards other communities.

Overall, the community detection and critical path analysis suggest that environmental policy network analysis may follow a similar evolutionary pattern as any domain of research or knowledge. It has a wellspring in general theoretical and methodological approaches, for example, early works on the critical path focused on policy network theory and what Bodin et al. (2011) call the 'binary metaphorical' approach – a concern with the presence or absence of networks and the implications of these non-hierarchical, non-market structures. Gradually, we observe a transition into a more specialised context of quantitative network analysis. That specialised context creates a strong lineage or branch of research that continues motivating science and a core research community over time. The main lineage is surrounded by a peripheral set of interdisciplinary research, which serves as a kind of a porous boundary for idea exchange that fuels the evolution of the main lineage and its impact on the broader scientific enterprise.

Before proceeding, let's address two questions: (1) why are papers on the critical path not necessarily the most highly cited papers in the sample query?; and (2) why are certain clusters not, or barely, represented on the critical path (and why is the critical path primarily composed of the fifth-largest cluster)? To the first question: papers on the critical path cite other papers which cite critical works and are cited by works which become highly cited (Van Holt et al., 2016). Thus, while a highly cited paper is more likely to be on the critical path than another paper, all else equal, it is the extent to which a paper acts as a conduit between the influential work of others that determines its presence on the critical path. With respect to the second question, consider the nature of the bibliometric query generating the initial sample: the query captured segments of two different primary bodies of literature focused on social/organisational networks: public administration and policy and environmental science and management. The critical path analysis is based on publications in the sample and publications cited by works in the sample. Thus, cross-over publications straddling this divide are advantaged in the critical path analysis because they are likely to cite and be cited by work in both bodies of literature. Thus, works such as Provan and Milward's (2008) paper in the *Journal of Public Administration and Theory* (JPART) and Prell et al.'s (2009) *Society and Natural Resources* article, which are the first and third most highly cited works in the entire sample, respectively, are not on the critical path. Both articles are central in their respective disciplines, but do not exhibit strong cross-over behaviour in terms of citing, and being cited by, work that is highly influential in both scholarly communities. We can extend this same logic to the clusters in general: papers on the critical path are likely to have membership in clusters bridging the two literature bodies, like the 'SNA [social network analysis] + ACF [Advocacy Coalition Framework] + climate change' cluster, which involves scholars who largely focus on environmental cases but publish in general-audience public administration and policy outlets such as *Public Administration Review* (e.g., Lubell et al., 2017), *Policy Studies Journal* (e.g., Weible & Sabatier, 2005) and the *American Journal of Political Science* (e.g., Berardo & Scholz 2010). The critical path estimate is in part shaped by the initial query and sample selection, and so provides a lens for understanding the evolution of environmental policy network scholarship but is certainly not the last word on the most influential work in the field.

CORE RESEARCH THEMES IN ENVIRONMENTAL POLICY NETWORK SCHOLARSHIP

This section describes the key research questions, methods and important findings from groups of literature identified in the cluster and critical path analyses. Our sample frame captures network-focused elements of several broader research communities: institutional theory, public administration and environmental governance. Rather than representing the backbone of a single large research domain, the critical path charts the ongoing convergence and co-evolution of these different communities. Thus, while we mostly constrain discussion to papers and associated research traditions shown in Figures 7.1 and 7.3, we also discuss several large bodies of scholarship from which modern policy network scholarship emerged, but which are not represented on the critical path. In the sample query literature, we identify three general, often interrelated roles for network-related concepts in institutional theory, public administration and environmental governance: (1) networks as an organising principle; (2) networks as a methodological tool; and (3) networks as an approach for mapping and modelling complex systems. These categories reflect the epistemological role networks play in different veins of research, which provides a high-level distinction that goes beyond a particular theory or model type (Bodin et al., 2011; Alexander & Armitage, 2015).

Networks as Institutional Arrangement: Comparative Networks and Network Management

The first category of work conceptualises networks as an institutional arrangement, fundamentally different from markets or hierarchies, which organises the behaviours of actors in political systems, organisations and policy sectors. Examples of this stream of work are represented in the bibliometric analysis by elements of clusters #1 ('network management+social capital+public administration'), #2 (SNA+policy nets.+policy community) and #5 ('civil society+policy networks+governance network'). The fundamental idea in this work is that public service delivery and policy implementation increasingly occur through networks of organisations rather than a formally structured hierarchy. Hence, we observe Williamson's (1973) work on 'Markets and hierarchies' as an antecedent sink node for the critical path. Williamson shared the Nobel Prize in economics with Elinor Ostrom[6] and pioneered the analysis of how transaction costs influence the organisation of economic exchange. This work is a foundational precursor for network governance scholarship because it sets the stage for considering how the attributes of a transaction (i.e., asset specificity, uncertainty, frequency) influence how actors structure their economic relationships.

The comparative network studies in this category of work focus on how the structure, function and processes of policy networks vary across political and issue contexts. For political science researchers from both Europe and the United States, this research community tends to focus on comparisons at the macro-political institutional scale. For instance, Heclo (1978) introduced the foundational concept of 'issue networks' within the United States executive branch, and Rhodes and Marsh (1992) extended this idea into comparative analysis across corporatist and pluralist systems. Van Waarden (1992) identifies seven dimensions of policy networks that vary across classic comparative politics descriptions of political systems such as clientelism and pluralism. Work in this vein compares sectors as well as political systems; in one early quantitative analysis, Lauman and Knoke (1987) compare network structures across the health and energy sectors.

The early comparative network scholarship used a wide range of conceptual definitions of networks, which motivated scholars to develop more simplified typologies. For example, Börzel (1998) simplified the 'Babylonian' proliferation of policy network concepts into two schools of thought, policy networks as 'interest intermediation' versus a 'specific form of governance'. Interest intermediation extends the idea of issue networks, describing the relationships between various types of interest groups and state actors (Beyers et al., 2008). In contrast, the idea of networks as a 'specific form of governance' refers to arrangements where public service delivery or other governance tasks occur within a multi-organisational structure.

The network management literature in this category focuses on how the delivery of public services depends on relationships among multiple organisations with different roles and resources (Klijn et al., 2010a; Provan & Kenis, 2008). In the spirit of Williamson, the effectiveness of different network management strategies depends on the policy context, such as the number of actors and levels of trust. This strategic management focus is also closely intertwined with the concept of *new public management* (NPM) which emerged in the 1980s as an efficiency-oriented framework emphasising 'businesslike' practices in public administration. Contracting, outsourcing and other practices captured under the umbrella of NPM create the 'hollow state' (Milward & Provan, 2000) in which network governance is required (Sørensen & Torfing, 2009; Klijn et al., 2010a). Thus, while the NPM term itself has fallen out of fashion, contracting (Brunjes, 2022; Amirkhanyan & Lambright, 2017; Brown et al., 2018), public–private partnerships (Bertelli, 2019) and business-oriented practices (Mergel et al., 2021) remain core considerations in public management – hence the steady rise in work related to public administration and network management (cluster #1) and civil society[7] and network governance (cluster #5) shown in Figure 7.1.

The research in these communities is influential because it develops general concepts that can be applied in any policy context, and in fact many of the empirical studies are in non-environmental sectors. Methodologically, these studies are mostly qualitative and descriptive, relying on comparative case studies (Moynihan, 2009) and set-theory approaches (Raab et al., 2015) (although not shown in the figures, both publications in cluster #1) to understand macro-level dynamics such as how contexts relate to effectiveness. Many of the most prominent works in this cluster are not structurally explicit – that is, they do not measure and model specific ties between specific actors (e.g., Sørensen & Torfing, 2009). Rather, networks are used metaphorically to describe relationships among governmental and nongovernmental actors and how relational dynamics shape decision-making (Dowding, 1995). The evolution and continued relevance of comparative and network management literature is exemplified by Wagner et al. (2021), who analyse which mode of network governance best describes the Irish climate change policy network at the national level. This piece likewise demonstrates the ongoing methodological evolution of this literature by using sophisticated statistical methods, such as conditional uniform random graph tests, to show how the network is centralised around key government actors.

Networks as Method: Collaborative Governance, Institutional Collective Action and Advocacy Coalitions

The second high-level throughline we observe is research that uses networks as a methodological tool for understanding relational phenomena in three theories of the policy process: collaborative governance, institutional collective action (ICF) and advocacy coalition frameworks. These theories are mostly a subset of cluster #4 (SNA + ACF + climate change), which dominates the critical path. As shown in the critical path (Figure 7.4), work in cluster #2 (SNA + policy networks + policy community) is a clear antecedent of this methodology-focused work. Dowding (1995) foreshadowed this transition by writing that 'policy network analysis began as a metaphor, and may only become a theory by developing along the lines of sociological network analysis' (1995, p. 136). The focus on SNA by this cluster is rooted in the fact that the relational concepts posed by these policy process theories exhibit 'hyperdyadic dependence' (Cranmer & Desmarais, 2016) – that is, relationships are influenced by surrounding relationships along with individual-level attributes. Network graph models such as exponential random graph models (ERGMs) account for interdependence in ways modelling dyadic data such as logistic regression does not (Robins et al., 2012). In the remainder of this section, we describe the collaborative governance, ICA and ACF work shown in Figures 7.1 and 7.3.

For collaborative governance scholarship, the critical path and highly cited works that cite work on the path show a series of innovative applications of quantitative network analysis. Schneider et al. (2003) demonstrate that networks involved with the collaborative National Estuary Program are more likely to span boundaries between science and policy, levels of government and across interest groups. Linking network structure to individual attributes, Scholz et al. (2008) find a correlation between network centrality and the extent to which National Estuary Program participants engage in collaborative activities. Ulibarri and Scott (2017) use exponential random graph models to demonstrate correspondence between network structures and levels of collaboration as measured via qualitative assessment and process tracing. Lubell (2015) hypothesises that collaborative governance forums embedded in polycentric governance systems create networks that spread social capital across the system. Hamilton and Lubell (2018) provide evidence that joint participation in collaborative governance builds actor-level networks, particularly locally. Jasny and Lubell (2015) extend the concept of network brokerage to policy subsystems in which organisations participate in multiple policy forums to quantify the homogeneity and heterogeneity of different collaborative partnerships.

The empirical network research on collaborative governance supports two basic conclusions. First, collaborative governance institutions influence network structures in ways generally consistent with cooperation (i.e., more reciprocity) and learning (i.e., more boundary spanning). Second, some network structures appear linked to more collaborative attitudes/behaviours and policy influence. However, the dearth of longitudinal data makes it difficult to untangle the causal feedbacks among institutions, networks and behaviour which surely co-evolve over time. Furthermore, like most research on environmental policy, there is limited evidence of how collaborative governance and networks influence environmental outcomes (Scott, 2015).

The ICA literature applies a similar network-oriented logic, focusing specifically on levels of collaboration and collective action among governments. The basic premise is that governments experience interdependencies in attempts to produce or provide services for citizens. These interdependencies occur horizontally (e.g., a city that charges residents fees for rubbish collection could incentivise residents to dump their rubbish in a neighbouring city), vertically (e.g., a state environmental agency's decision not to issue a permit to a local developer could prevent a city from achieving its economic development goals), or functionally (e.g., a decision by a city public works department to charge for rubbish collection could result in more waste being deposited down drains, creating additional work for the city's water treatment facility) (Yi et al., 2018). Governments may attempt to solve these problems by contracting, partnering, or otherwise collaborating with one another (e.g., jurisdictions could develop and implement a regional waste management strategy). As the literature evolved, it expanded to include governmental and nongovernmental actors at a range of geographic scales (Kim et al., 2022).

ICA is rooted in neo-institutional economic theory, arguing that policy networks are more likely to form when the benefits to actors of engagement outweigh the transaction costs of searching for partners, negotiating relationships and monitoring and enforcing any formal or informal social agreements (Kim et al., 2020). This approach posits that actors will choose the type of network relationship (e.g., an informal consultation process versus a legally codified, mandated joint venture, among many others) that minimises their transaction costs, given the level of risk involved in the activity. A joint activity is risky to the extent that a partnership may fail to produce desired coordination, may saddle an actor with responsibilities or burdens they perceive as unfair, or open up opportunities for a partner to defect, taking advantage of the actor's willingness to collaborate and free-riding on the actor's efforts (Jung et al., 2019b; Jung et al., 2019a).

Arguably the most important vein of ICA work develops Berardo and Scholz's (2010) risk hypothesis, building an explicit bridge to network science via the application of social network analysis and linkages to network theorising about bonding and bridging capital (Burt, 1992). The basic premise is that when collaboration is risky due to the possibility of non-cooperating actors defecting and imposing costs on others, actors will prefer to form strong, mutually reinforcing 'bonding' ties to monitor policy defection. When there is less risk because the dilemma primarily concerns finding a solution that helps achieve shared goals, actors will prefer weak 'bridging' ties linking otherwise unconnected actors, thereby increasing access to new information which could point to a solution (Berardo, 2014). The logic of this hypothesis has recently been evaluated in more complex networks, wherein different types of nodes are connected (Berardo, 2014; Lubell & Robins, 2022). Contextual factors, such as the stability of political institutions and the occurrence of focusing events, affect network partner preference and choice (Berardo & Lubell, 2016; Olivier & Berardo 2022) and how these dynamics manifest over time (Angst & Hirschi, 2017; Jung et al., 2019b).

Finally, the Advocacy Coalition Framework (ACF) literature uses quantitative network methods to understand coalition formation and conflict in policy subsystems (e.g., US climate change policy, California groundwater policy). The ACF assumes relational interdependence in how policy coalitions form based on shared beliefs and collective action to achieve common goals. Networks are the 'glue' of advocacy coalitions, enabling actors with similar belief systems to effectively coordinate and reinforce their beliefs. ACF theorists maintain that actors forge relationships based on shared beliefs and those beliefs are then reinforced within these relationships, as well as through conflict with those holding opposing policy preferences. Social network analytical tools are frequently used to measure and model characteristics of advocacy coalitions, including their size and boundaries and ties among participants (Ingold & Leifeld, 2016).

The central ACF assumption of shared beliefs is often measured as *belief homophily*, a term deriving from social network analysis and describing the tendency of actors with similar attributes to form ties with one another. The ACF *belief homophily hypothesis* – that actors choose coalition partners based on shared beliefs – has received substantial empirical attention from scholars, who have found support for it in the context of transportation and land use planning policy in California (Henry, 2011; Henry et al., 2011) and Ontario (Heinmiller & Pirak, 2017), energy development in Canada (Howe et al., 2021), forest policy in South Africa (Malkamäki et al., 2021) and climate and energy policy in Colorado (Elgin & Weible, 2013).

Beyond shared beliefs, factors such as the pursuit of powerful allies and pre-existing social relationships are also shown to motivate coalition formation (Henry, 2011; Howe et al., 2021; Malkamäki et al., 2021). An emerging area of enquiry is whether, at least under some conditions or in some settings, coalition formation is driven not by shared beliefs but rather other factors, such as social trust and resource-seeking (Calanni et al., 2015; Möck, 2021; Sapat et al., 2019). Important frontiers in environmental policy network scholarship include how coalitions evolve over time (Henry et al., 2020), how governance structures can affect coalition partner preference (Henry, 2021) and typologising advocacy coalitions based on structure, composition and/or behaviour (Weible et al., 2020).

Networks to Model Complexity: Polycentricity and Social-ecological Systems

The final overarching theme we observe in the bibliometric analysis is network and environmental governance scholarship that uses network approaches to measure and model complex systems. Whether focused on multilevel institutional arrangements or connections within and between institutional and ecological features, this work uses network analysis to quantify and assess the overall structure of these systems and underlying dynamics that shape system structure and function. The primary community representing this research focus is cluster #3, 'natural resource management+SES+SNA'.

The foundations of this systems-oriented community in environmental network governance scholarship are in the Nobel Prize-winning work of Elinor Ostrom (1990) on polycentricity and governance of common-pool resources (CPRs). A system is polycentric when it contains multiple formally independent centres of decision-making (Ostrom et al., 1961). These centres may function independently or consider one another when making choices, potentially engaging in collaboration, competition, or other types of relationships. Elinor Ostrom used the IAD framework to probe CPR management. She examined how decision-making of resource users jointly determines outcomes for resources like groundwater, considering how choices about boundaries, appropriation, monitoring and enforcement affect social costs users experience, incentives for free-riding and biophysical outcomes (e.g., aquifer overdraft, sustainable fishing). This work showed that successful CPR governance is built upon interpersonal networks wherein iterated interactions among users build trust, shared norms and language, and mutual understanding of goals, and common knowledge about the resource system.

Although early polycentricity and IAD scholarship did not explicitly integrate network theory or use network analysis for empirical research, this is changing. Carlsson (2000) explicitly connected IAD with policy network scholarship, theorising policy networks as instances of collective action which can be typologised according to IAD elements of contextual setting: rules, norms and associated incentives, and biophysical attributes. More recently, Herzog et al. (2021) used social network analytics to test ACF- and IAD-related hypotheses concerning interactions among organisations and agencies involved in water management in a German watershed. Analysing the polycentric system that has evolved around climate adaptation in the Lake Victoria region of Africa, Hamilton and Lubell (Hamilton & Lubell, 2019) explored how organisations' perceptions of the multiple decision-making forums in which they could participate was affected by network measures of bridging versus bonding social capital. One key idea is that the environmental policy process emerges from networks of interaction among many different types of policy actors or 'stakeholders': governmental agencies, nongovernmental organisations, advocacy groups, private sector businesses, research institutions and many others. These actors operate at different levels of geographic scale ranging from local to global (Cash et al., 2006).

The critical path cuts through a periphery of research related to social-ecological networks that analyses links within and between social and ecological nodes (Bodin et al., 2017; Barnes et al., 2017; Bergsten et al., 2019). Social-ecological networks are peripheral to the critical path because they are an interdisciplinary approach that involves ecologists and other biophysical scientists, who often collaborate with some of the core researchers in the more disciplinary path around public administration and political science. However, social-ecological network analysis forms a distinct, large and quickly growing community within our sample.

A unifying theme of social-ecological network research is a quest for structural features of networks that are expected to improve 'institutional fit' and reduce 'scale mismatch' (Sayles & Baggio, 2017). The presence of certain social-ecological motifs is posited to increase institutional fit. The most important hypothesis is that institutional fit is enhanced if two social actors form collaborative ties when jointly interested in one or more ecological nodes. The foundational analysis of Bodin and Tengö (2012) show that Madagascar forest users sharing forest resources are more likely to have collaborative ties relative to a random network. Bodin (2017) expands on the idea of institutional fit to identify the social-ecological network building blocks (i.e., motifs) that signal horizontal and vertical coordination in multilevel systems. Barnes et al. (2017, 2020) extends this analysis, theorising the 'closed' motifs enable adaptation, while more 'open' motifs linking to new resources or actors may facilitate system transformation.

The concept of institutional fit closely relates to the idea of scale mismatch, where the geographic scale of governance does not match the geographic scale of associated ecological processes, and networks can potentially bridge across scale (Ostrom, 1990; Young, 2002). Using urban ecosystems in Stockholm, Sweden, as a case study, Ernstson et al. (2010) argue that the tendency of networks to develop around local resources inhibits cross-scale brokerage, implying a role for collaborative governance in investing in developing boundary-spanning relationships. In Quebec, governmental and nongovernmental organisations played a crucial bridging role in connecting localities sharing ecosystems services but otherwise lacking horizontal networks (Rathwell & Peterson, 2012). Sayles and Baggio (2017) find a similar dearth of cross-scale networks in the context of anadromous fish restoration in Washington State. In three different Australian case studies, McAllister et al. (2017; 2015; 2014) identify incentives for collaboration among local actors, while noting that transaction costs limit cross-scale interactions and imply a role for centralised governmental actors in reducing scale mismatch and enhancing regional cooperation.

Social-ecological network research faces two crucial challenges: over-determination and linking to outcomes. First, while various network structural features are theorised as 'fingerprints' of specific micro-level social processes such as cooperation, there is often no direct micro-level observation, and multiple social processes could produce any particular structural feature. Second, while improving institutional fit and reducing scale

Table 7.2 Summary of key themes in environmental policy network research

	Research questions	Methods	Findings
Networks as institutional arrangement			
Network governance	How do networks influence coordination among multiple actors for public service delivery?	Qualitative and descriptive	The effectiveness of different types of network strategies depends on policy context
Policy network typologies	What are the basic structures, functions and processes of networks?	Qualitative and descriptive	Network structure varies across issue types and macro-political institutions, and government actors are typically central
Networks as methods			
Collaborative governance	How do collaborative governance institutions and networks co-evolve?	One- and two-mode networks, descriptive and some statistical models	Collaborative governance institutions enable boundary-spanning networks
Institutional collective action	How do networks respond to risks from different types of collective action problems?	One- and two-mode networks, descriptive and some statistical models	Closed network structures useful for cooperation, open networks structures for learning/coordination
Advocacy coalition framework	How do networks influence coalition formation?	One- and two-mode networks, descriptive and some statistical models	Actors with similar belief systems will form networks
Networks to model complexity			
Polycentric governance	How do networks facilitate social processes across policy forums in multilevel systems?	One- and two-mode networks, descriptive and some statistical models	Horizontal and vertical policy networks enable learning, cooperation and conflict resolution across the multiple forums that constitute polycentric governance systems
Social-ecological systems	How do networks influence alignment between social and ecological processes?	Multilevel, social-ecological networks	Networks potentially improve institutional fit and mitigate scale mismatch, but transaction costs limit cross-scale relationships

mismatch are logically related to an improved capacity to manage interdependent resources, there is very limited empirical evidence linking those network features to environmental outcomes (Sayles & Baggio, 2017). One exception is Barnes et al. (2019), which provides evidence that social-ecological alignment is correlated with positive ecological conditions in coral reefs.

CONCLUSION

Environmental policy network analysis is a quickly growing and important field of research because the interdependencies involved with environmental policy are closely aligned with the theoretical and empirical foundations of network analysis. Network methods enable empirical analysis of interdependencies that goes beyond the typical assumptions of individual-level models. Because many of the same cooperation and learning problems are found throughout public policy and public administration, environmental policy network analysis is rooted in and contributes to the broader fields of network governance and network typologies. Environmental policy network analysis is a testbed for core theories of the policy process.

The research communities that are present in the environmental policy network literature, as well as the evolution of its critical path, suggest some general features about the organisation of scientific knowledge. There are some large and general research communities that apply network theory and methods across many policy domains and provide a foundation for more specialised communities focused specifically on environmental policy. At the periphery of the critical path is an emerging interdisciplinary thread of research, directly linking social network ideas with the structure of ecological systems. Various smaller splinter groups apply these ideas in even more specialised domains.

Communities within the environmental policy network literature are differentiated by how they consider the epistemological role of networks. Networks can be viewed as an institutional arrangement that structures relationships among actors at different scales of a social system, ranging from local service delivery to macro-level political dynamics. Networks are used as a methodological approach to capture fundamentally relational phenomena occurring in policy systems, such as coalition building. Finally, networks are used to describe complex systems, including the fit or misfit between social and ecological patterns of interdependencies.

Environmental policy network analysis is substantively important. Researchers are addressing some of the most important issues facing global society, such as climate change. Policy networks are useful points of contact with real-world policy makers, who enjoy thinking about their position in networks. For policy makers, network analysis is often a useful 'policy therapy' because they can talk with researchers about how to navigate complex institutional arrangements and social-ecological systems (Lubell & Morrison). However, environmental policy network researchers still have a long road to travel before we can be confident in delivering strong applied recommendations that consistently link network structure to improved environmental policy outputs and outcomes.

Notes

1 Full color figures, as well as all data and code necessary to replicate the results of this analysis are available at github.com/tylerascott/consumnes
2 We added one query restriction, excluding any paper mentioning 'policy networks' and 'artificial intelligence' (AI), because in AI terminology, the phrase 'policy network' refers to a graph linking actions and states. Thus a query for the phrase 'policy network' returns a large segment of literature on reinforcement learning and other AI topics.
3 Examples include rectifying cases where the same source is referenced in slightly different ways (e.g., Ostrom, 1990, *Governing the commons* and Ostrom, 1990, *Gov. the commons*) and where the same source is referenced by different articles using either the author's first name or first initial (e.g., Williamson, Oliver and Williamson, O.).
4 A few additional notes about how cluster keywords are identified: (1) we filter out candidate phrases that occur in less than 10 per cent of abstracts in the cluster; (2) we omit duplicative keywords, so that if 'policy network' and 'policy networks' are both top ranks only one is retained; and (3) for one of the smaller clusters, we removed the suggested keyword 'Elsevier Ltd', which is mistakenly appended to some abstracts in WoS.
5 Admittedly, the bibliometric query we used in WoS does not directly target climate change-focused work. To the extent that studies concerning climate change and governance networks are distinct from the environmental governance literature more generally (e.g., by using phrases such as 'environmental governance' or 'natural resources'), some climate-focused work might have been excluded.

6   Ostrom's work is of course highly cited by papers picked up in the sample query, but is not part of the initial sample results. This is because while Ostrom's work directly relates to natural resource governance, it is not explicitly about networks. For instance, networks and network analysis are not mentioned in the title, abstract, or other metadata associated with Ostrom's seminal 1990 book, *Governing the commons: the evolution of institutions for collective action*.
7   The term 'civil society' in this case refers to organisations that are not associated with the government.

REFERENCES

Alexander, S.M., & Armitage, D. (2015). A social relational network perspective for MPA science. *Conservation Letters*, 8(1), 1–13.

Amirkhanyan, A.A., & Lambright, K.T. (2017). *Citizen participation in the age of contracting: when service delivery trumps democracy*. Routledge.

Angst, M., & Hirschi, C. (2017). Network dynamics in natural resource governance: a case study of Swiss landscape management. *Policy Studies Journal: The Journal of the Policy Studies Organization*, 45(2), 315–336.

Ball, S.J. (2009). Privatising education, privatising education policy, privatising educational research: network governance and the 'competition state'. *Journal of Education Policy*, 24(1), 83–99.

Ball, S.J. (2016). Following policy: networks, network ethnography and education policy mobilities. *Journal of Education Policy*, 31(5), 549–566.

Barnes, M., Bodin, Ö., Guerrero, A., McAllister, R., Alexander, S., & Robins, G. (2017). The social structural foundations of adaptation and transformation in social–ecological systems. *Ecology and Society*, 22(4). doi.org/10.5751/ES-09769-220416.

Barnes, M.L., Bodin, Ö., McClanahan, T.R., Kittinger, J.N., Hoey, A.S., Gaoue, O.G., & Graham, N.A.J. (2019). Social-ecological alignment and ecological conditions in coral reefs. *Nature Communications*, 10(1), 2039.

Barnes, M.L., Wang, P., Cinner, J.E., & Graham, N.A.J. (2020). Social determinants of adaptive and transformative responses to climate change. *Nature Climate Change*. www.nature.com/articles/s41558-020-0871-4

Batagelj, V. (2003). Efficient algorithms for citation network analysis. *arXiv [cs.DL]*. arXiv. arxiv.org/abs/cs/0309023

Berardo, R. (2014). Bridging and bonding capital in two-mode collaboration networks. *Policy Studies Journal: The Journal of the Policy Studies Organization*, 42(2), 197–225.

Berardo, R, & Lubell, M. (2016). Understanding what shapes a polycentric governance system. *Public Administration Review*, 76(5), 738–751.

Berardo, R., & Scholz, J.T. (2010). Self-organizing policy networks: risk, partner selection, and cooperation in estuaries. *American Journal of Political Science*, 54(3), 632–649.

Bergsten, A., Jiren, T.S., Leventon, J., Dorresteijn, I., Schultner, J., & Fischer, J. (2019). 'Identifying Governance Gaps among Interlinked Sustainability Challenges.' *Environmental Science & Policy* 91 (January): 27–38.

Bertelli, A.M. (2019). Public goods, private partnerships, and political institutions. *Journal of Public Administration Research and Theory*, 29(1), 67–83.

Beyers, J., Eising, R., & Maloney, W. (2008). Researching interest group politics in Europe and elsewhere: much we study, little we know? *West European Politics*, 31(6), 1103–1128.

Blondel, V.D., Guillaume, J.-L., Lambiotte, R., & Lefebvre, E. (2008). Fast unfolding of communities in large networks. *Journal of Statistical Mechanics*, 10, P10008.

Bodini, A., & Bondavalli, C. (2002). Towards a sustainable use of water resources: a whole-ecosystem approach using network analysis. *International Journal of Environment and Geoinformatics*. www.researchgate.net/profile/Antonio-Bodini-2/publication/249919992_Towards_a_sustainable_use_of_water_resources_A_whole-ecosystem_approach_using_network_analysis/links/6131e61bc69a4e4879768612/Towards-a-sustainable-use-of-water-resources-A-whole-ecosystem-approach-using-network-analysis.pdf

Bodin, Ö. (2017). Collaborative environmental governance: achieving collective action in social-ecological systems. *Science*, 357(6352). doi.org/10.1126/science.aan1114.

Bodin, Ö., & Crona, B. (2009). The role of social networks in natural resource governance: what relational patterns make a difference? *Global Environmental Change: Human and Policy Dimensions*, 19(3), 366–374.

Bodin, Ö., Crona, B., & Ernstson, H. (2006). Social networks in natural resource management: what is there to learn from a structural perspective. *Ecology and Society*, 11(2), r2.

Bodin, Ö., Ramirez-Sanchez, S., Ernstson, H., & Prell, C. (2011). A social relational approach to natural resource governance. In Ö. Bodin & C. Prell (Eds.), *Social networks and natural resource management: uncovering the social fabric of environmental governance* (pp. 3–28). Cambridge University Press.

Bodin, Ö., Sandström, A., & Crona, B. (2017). Collaborative networks for effective ecosystem-based management: a set of working hypotheses. *Policy Studies Journal*, 45(2), 289–314.

Bodin, Ö., & Teng, M. (2012). Disentangling intangible social-ecological systems. *Global Environmöental Change: Human and Policy Dimensions*, 22(2), 430–439.

Börzel, T.A. (1998). Organizing Babylon: on the different conceptions of policy networks. *Public Administration*, 76(2), 253–73.

Brandenberger, L., Ingold, K., Fischer, M., Schläpfer, I., & Leifeld, P. (2022). Boundary Spanning through engagement of policy actors in multiple issues. *Policy Studies Journal: The Journal of the Policy Studies Organization*, 50(1), 35–64.

Brown, T.L., Potoski, M., & Van Slyke, D.M. (2018). Complex contracting: management challenges and solutions. *Public Administration Review*, 78(5), 739–747.

Brunjes, B.M. (2022). Your competitive side is calling: an analysis of Florida contract performance. *Public Administration Review*, 82(1), 83–101.

Burt, R.S. (1992). *Structural holes: the structure of social capital competition*. Harvard University Press.

Calanni, J.C., Siddiki, S.N., Weible, C.M., & Leach, W.D. (2015). Explaining coordination in collaborative partnerships and clarifying the scope of the belief homophily hypothesis. *Journal of Public Administration Research and Theory*, 25(3), 901–927.

Campbell, C., Corson, C., Gray, N.J., MacDonald, K.I., & Brosius, P. (2014). Studying global environmental meetings to understand global environmental governance: collaborative event ethnography at the Tenth Conference of the Parties to the …. *Environmental Politics*. direct.mit.edu/glep/article-abstract/14/3/1/14685

Carlsson, L. (2000). Policy networks as collective action. *Policy Studies Journal: The Journal of the Policy Studies Organization*, 28(3), 502–520.

Carpenter, D., Esterling, K., & Lazer, D. (2003). The strength of strong ties: a model of contact-making in policy networks with evidence from US health politics. *Rationality And Society*, 15(4), 411–440.

Cash, D., Adger, W.N., Berkes, F., Garden, P., Lebel, L., Olsson, P., Pritchard, L., & Young, O. (2006). Scale and cross-scale dynamics: governance and information in a multilevel world.' *Ecology and Society*, 11(2). www.ecologyandsociety.org/vol11/iss2/art8/main.html

Cranmer, S.J., & Desmarais, B.A. (2016). A critique of dyadic design. *International Studies Quarterly: A Publication of the International Studies Association*, 60(2), 355–362.

Domènech, L., & Saurí, D. (2010). Socio-technical transitions in water scarcity contexts: public acceptance of greywater reuse technologies in the metropolitan area of Barcelona.' *Resources, Conservation and Recycling*, 55(1), 53–62.

Dowding, K. (1995). Model or metaphor? A critical review of the policy network approach. *Political Studies*, 43(1), 136–158.

Elgin, D.J., & Weible, C.M. (2013). A stakeholder analysis of Colorado climate and energy issues using policy analytical capacity and the Advocacy Coalition Framework. *Review of Policy Research*, 30(1), 114–133.

Ernstson, H., Barthel, S., Andersson, E., & Borgstrom, S.T. (2010). Scale-crossing brokers and network governance of urban ecosystem services: the case of Stockholm. *Ecology and Society*, 15(4), 28.

Fischer, A.P., & Jasny, L. (2017). Capacity to adapt to environmental change: evidence from a network of organizations concerned with increasing wildfire risk. *Ecology and Society*. www.consecol.org/vol22/iss1/art23/

Georgalakis, J. (2020). A disconnected policy network: the UK's response to the Sierra Leone ebola epidemic. *Social Science and Medicine*, 250, February, 112851.

Gerber, E.R., Henry, A.D., & Lubell, M. (2013). Political homophily and collaboration in regional planning networks. *American Journal of Political Science*, 57(3), 598–610.

Gerlak, A.K., & Heikkila, T. (2011). Building a theory of learning in collaboratives: evidence from the Everglades Restoration Program. *Journal of Public Administration Research and Theory*, 21(4), 619–644.

Granovetter, M.S. (1973). The strength of weak ties. *American Journal of Sociology*, 78(6), 1360–1380.

Hamilton, M. (2018). Understanding what shapes varying perceptions of the procedural fairness of transboundary environmental decision-making processes.' *Ecology and Society*, 23(4). www.jstor.org/stable/26796881

Hamilton, M., Fischer, A.P., & Jasny, L. (2021). Bridging collaboration gaps in fragmented environmental governance systems. *Environmental Science and Policy*, 124, October, 461–470.

Hamilton, M., Hileman, J., & Bodin, Ö. (2020). Evaluating heterogeneous brokerage: new conceptual and methodological approaches and their application to multi-level environmental governance networks. *Social Networks*. www.sciencedirect.com/science/article/pii/S0378873319301364

Hamilton, M.L., & Lubell, M. (2018). Collaborative governance of climate change adaptation across spatial and institutional scales. *Policy Studies Journal: The Journal of the Policy Studies Organization*, 46(2), 222–247.

Hamilton, M.L., & Lubell, M. (2019). Climate change adaptation, social capital, and the performance of polycentric governance institutions. *Climatic Change*, 152(3), 307–326.

Hamilton, M., Lubell, M., & Namaganda, E. (2018). Cross-level linkages in an ecology of climate change adaptation policy games. *Ecology and Society*, 23(2). www.jstor.org/stable/26799099

Heclo, H. (1978). Issue networks and the executive establishment. In A. King (Ed.), *The New American Political System* (pp. 87–124). American Enterprise Institute.

Heinmiller, T., & Pirak, K. (2017). Advocacy coalitions in Ontario land use policy development. *Review of Policy Research*, 34(2), 168–185.

Henry, A.D. (2011). Ideology, power, and the structure of policy networks. *Policy Studies Journal: The Journal of the Policy Studies Organization*, 39(3), 361–383.

Henry, A.D. (2021). Evaluating collaborative institutions by segregation and homophily in policy networks. *Public Administration*, December. doi.org/10.1111/padm.12800

Henry, A.D., Dietz, T., & Sweeney, R.L. (2020). Coevolution of networks and beliefs in US environmental risk policy. *Policy Studies Journal: The Journal of the Policy Studies Organization* (n/a). doi.org/10.1111/psj.12407

Henry, A.D., Lubell, M., & McCoy, M. (2011). Belief systems and social capital as drivers of policy network structure: the case of California regional planning. *Journal of Public Administration Research and Theory*, 21(3), 419–444.

Herzog, L., Ingold, K., & Schlager, E. (2021). Prescribed by law and therefore realized? Analyzing rules and their implied actor interactions as networks. *Policy Studies Journal: The Journal of the Policy Studies Organization*, psj.12448, August. doi.org/10.1111/psj.12448

Herzog, L.M., & Ingold, K. (2019). Threats to common-pool resources and the importance of forums: on the emergence of cooperation in CPR problem settings. *Policy Studies Journal: The Journal of the Policy Studies Organization*, 47(1), 77–113.

Hileman, J., & Bodin, Ö. (2019). Balancing costs and benefits of collaboration in an ecology of games. *Policy Studies Journal: The Journal of the Policy Studies Organization*, 47(1), 138–158.

Hileman, J., & Lubell, M. (2018). The network structure of multilevel water resources governance in Central America. *Ecology and Society*, 23(2). www.jstor.org/stable/26799107

Howe, A.C., Tindall, D.B., & Marck C. J. Stoddart, M.C.J. (2021). Drivers of tie formation in the Canadian climate change policy network: belief homophily and social structural processes. *Social Networks*, July. doi.org/10.1016/j.socnet.2021.06.004

Ingold, K., & Leifeld, P. (2016). Structural and institutional determinants of influence reputation: a comparison of collaborative and adversarial policy networks in decision making and implementation. *Journal of Public Administration Research and Theory*, 26(1), 1–18.

Jasny, Lorien, & Mark Lubell. 2015. Two-mode brokerage in policy networks. *Social Networks* 41 (May): 36–47.

Jasny, L., Sayles, J., Hamilton, M., Gomez, L.R., Jacobs, D., Prell, C., Matous, P., Schiffer, E., Guerrero, A.M., & Barnes, M.L. (2021). Participant engagement in environmentally focused social network research. *Social Networks*, 66, July, 125–138.

Javeline, D. (2014). The most important topic political scientists are not studying: adapting to climate change. *Perspectives on Politics*, 12(2), 420–434.

Jung, K., Song, M., & Feiock, R. (2019a). Isolated and broken bridges from interorganizational emergency management networks: an institutional collective action perspective. *Urban Affairs Review*, 55(3), 950–975.

Jung, K., Song, M., & Park, H.J. (2019b). The dynamics of an interorganizational emergency management network: interdependent and independent risk hypotheses. *Public Administration Review*, 79(2), 225–235.

Kauneckis, D., & Martin, D. (2020). Patterns of adaptation response by coastal communities to climate risks. *Coastal Management: An International Journal of Marine Environment, Resources, Law, and Society*, 48(4), 257–274.

Keohane, R.O. (2015). The global politics of climate change: challenge for political science. *PS, Political Science and Politics*, 48(1), 19–26.

Kim, S.Y., Swann, W.L., & Feiock, R.C. (2020). Collective learning and institutional collective action in fragmented governance. In J. Glückler, G. Herrigel & M. Handke (Eds.), *Knowledge for Governance* (pp. 351–373). Springer.

Kim, S.Y., Swann, W.L., Weible, C.M., Bolognesi, T., Krause, R.M., Park, A.Y.S., Tang, T., Maletsky, K., & Feiock, R.C. (2022). Updating the institutional collective action framework. *Policy Studies Journal: The Journal of the Policy Studies Organization*, 50(1), 9–34.

Klijn, E.-H., Steijn, B., & Edelenbos, J. (2010a). The impact of network management on outcomes in governance networks. *Public Administration*, 88(4), 1063–1082.

Klijn, E.-H., Edelenbos, J., & Steijn, B. (2010b). Trust in governance networks its impacts on outcomes. *Administration and Society*, 42(2), 193–221.

Klijn, E.-H., & Skelcher, C. (2007). Democracy and governance networks: compatible or not? *Public Administration*, 85(3), 587–608.

König, T., & Bräuninger, T. (1998). The formation of policy networks: preferences, institutions and actors' choice of information and exchange relations. *Journal of Theoretical Politics*, 10(4), 445–471.

Kretchmar, K., Sondel, B., & Ferrare, J.J. (2014). Mapping the terrain: teach For America, charter school reform, and corporate sponsorship. *Journal of Education Policy*, 29(6), 742–759.

Laumann, E.O., & Knoke, D. (1987). *The organizational state: social choice in national policy domains*. University of Wisconsin Press.

Leifeld, P., & Schneider, V. (2012). Information exchange in policy networks. *American Journal of Political Science*, 56(3), 731–744.

Lubell, M. (2013). Governing institutional complexity: the ecology of games framework. *Policy Studies Journal*, 41(3), 537–559.

Lubell, M. (2015). Collaborative partnerships in complex institutional systems. *Current Opinion in Environmental Sustainability*, 12, February, 41–47.

Lubell, M., Mewhirter, J.M., Berardo, R., & Scholz, J.T. (2017). Transaction costs and the perceived effectiveness of complex institutional systems. *Public Administration Review*, 77(5), 668–680.

Lubell, M., & Robbins, M. (2022). Adapting to sea-level rise: centralization or decentralization in polycentric governance systems? *Policy Studies Journal: The Journal of the Policy Studies Organization*, 50(1), 143–175.

Lubell, M., & Scholz, J.T. (2001). Cooperation, reciprocity, and the collective-action heuristic. *American Journal of Political Science*, 45(1), 160–178.

Lucio-Arias, D., & Leydesdorff, L. (2008). Main-path analysis and path-dependent transitions in HistCite™-based historiograms. *Journal of the American Society for Information Science and Technology*, 59(12), 1948–1962.

Lubell, Mark, and Tiffany H. Morrison (2021). Institutional navigation for polycentric sustainability governance. *Nature Sustainability*, 4(8), 664–671.

Malkamäki, A., Wagner, P.M., Brockhaus, M., Toppinen, A., & Ylä-Anttila, T. (2021). On the acoustics of policy learning: can co-participation in policy forums break up echo chambers? *Policy Studies Journal: The Journal of the Policy Studies Organization*, 49(2), 431–456.

Margerum, R.D. (2011). *Beyond consensus: improving collaborative planning and management*. MIT Press.

Marsh, D., & Smith, M. (2000). Understanding policy networks: towards a dialectical approach. *Political Studies*, 48(1), 4–21.

Mathias, J.-D., Lade, S., & Galaz, V. (2017). Multilevel policies and adaptive social networks: a conceptual modeling study for maintaining a polycentric governance system. *International Journal of the Commons*, 11(1), 220.

Matti, S., & Sandström, A. (2011). The rationale determining advocacy coalitions: examining coordination networks and corresponding beliefs. *Policy Studies Journal*, 39(3), 385–410.

McAllister, R., Robinson, C., & Brown, A. (2017). Balancing collaboration with coordination: contesting eradication in the Australian plant pest and disease biosecurity system. *International Journal of the Commons*. www.thecommonsjournal.org/articles/701/

McAllister, R.R.J., McCrea, R., & Lubell, M. (2014). Policy networks, stakeholder interactions and climate adaptation in the region of South East Queensland, Australia. *Regional Environmental Change*, 14(2), 527–539.

McAllister, R.R.J., Taylor, B.M., & Harman, B.P. (2015). Partnership networks for urban development: how structure is shaped by risk. *Policy Studies Journal: The Journal of the Policy Studies Organization*, 43(3), 379–398.

McGinnis, M.D. (2011). Networks of adjacent action situations in polycentric governance. *Policy Studies Journal*, 39(1), 51–78.

McNutt, K.M. (2008). Policy and politics on the web: virtual policy networks and climate change. *Canadian Political Science Review*, 2(1), 1–15.

Mcnutt, K., & Pal, L.A. (2011). 'Modernizing government': mapping global public policy networks. *Governance*, 24(3), 439–467.

Mergel, I., Ganapati, S., & Whitford, A.B. (2021). Agile: a new way of governing. *Public Administration Review*. onlinelibrary.wiley.com/doi/abs/10.1111/puar.13202

Milat, A.J., Laws, R., King, L., Newson, R., Rychetnik, L., Rissel, C., Bauman, A.E., Redman, S., & Bennie, J. (2013). Policy and practice impacts of applied research: a case study analysis of the New South Wales Health Promotion Demonstration Research Grants Scheme 2000–2006. *Health Research Policy and Systems/BioMed Central*, 11(1), 5.

Milward, H.B., & Provan, K.G. (2000). Governing the hollow state. *Journal of Public Administration Research and Theory*, 10(2), 359–380.

Möck, M. (2021). Patterns of policy networks at the local level in Germany. *Review of Policy Research*, 38(4) 454–477.

Monaco, M.E., & Ulanowicz, R.E. (1997). Comparative ecosystem trophic structure of three US mid-Atlantic estuaries. *Marine Ecology Progress Series*, 161, 239–524.

Moynihan, D.P. (2009). The network governance of crisis response: case studies of incident command systems. *Journal of Public Administration Research and Theory*, 19(4), 895–915.

Muñoz-Erickson, T.A., & Cutts, B.B. (2016). Structural dimensions of knowledge–action networks for sustainability. *Current Opinion in Environmental Sustainability*, 18, February, 56–64.

Newig, J., Günther, D., & Pahl-Wostl, C. (2010). Synapses in the network: learning in governance networks in the context of environmental management. *Ecology and Society*, 15(4), 24.

Olivier, T., & Berardo, R. (2022). Birds of a feather fight together: forum involvement in a weakly institutionalized ecology of policy games. *Policy Studies Journal: The Journal of the Policy Studies Organization*, 50(1), 176–198.

Ostrom, E. (1990). *Governing the commons: the evolution of institutions for collective action*. Cambridge University Press.

Ostrom, V., Tiebout, C.M., & Warren, R. (1961). The organization of government in metropolitan areas: a theoretical inquiry. *The American Political Science Review*, 55(4): 831–842.

Pahl-Wostl, Claudia. 2009. "A Conceptual Framework for Analysing Adaptive Capacity and Multi-Level Learning Processes in Resource Governance Regimes." Global Environmental Change: Human and Policy Dimensions 19 (3): 354–65.

Petridou, E. (2014). Theories of the policy process: contemporary scholarship and future directions. *Policy Studies Journal: The Journal of the Policy Studies Organization*, 42, April, S12–32.

Pforr, C. (2006). Tourism policy in the making: an Australian network study. *Annals Of Tourism Research*, 33(1), 87–108.

Pirson, M., & Turnbull, S. (2011). Corporate governance, risk management, and the financial crisis: an information processing view. *Corporate Governance An International Review*, 19(5), 459–470.

Prell, C., Hubacek, K., & Reed, M. (2009). Stakeholder analysis and social network analysis in natural resource management. *Society and Natural Resources*, 22(6), 501–518.

Pretty, J., & Ward, H. (2001). Social capital and the environment. *World Development*, 29(2), 209–227.

Provan, K.G., & Kenis, P. (2008). Modes of network governance: structure, management, and effectiveness. *Journal of Public Administration Research and Theory*, 18(2), 229–252.

Raab, J., Mannak, R.S., & Cambré, B. (2015). Combining structure, governance, and context: a configurational approach to network effectiveness. *Journal of Public Administration Research and Theory*, 25(2), 479–511.

Rathwell, K.J., & Peterson, G.D. (2012). Connecting social networks with ecosystem services for watershed governance: a social-ecological network perspective highlights the critical role of bridging organizations. *Ecology and Society*, 17(2). www.jstor.org/stable/26269043

Rethemeyer, R.K. (2007). Policymaking in the age of internet: is the internet tending to make policy networks more or less inclusive? *Journal of Public Administration Research and Theory*, 17(2), 259–284.

Rhodes, R.A.W., & Marsh, D. (1992). New directions in the study of policy networks. *European Journal of Political Research*, 21(1–2), 181–205.

Robins, G., Lewis, J.M., & Wang, P. (2012). Statistical network analysis for analyzing policy networks. *Policy Studies Journal*, 40(3), 375–401.

Sabatier, P.A., & Jenkins-Smith, H.C. (1993). *Policy change and learning: an advocacy coalition framework*. Westview.

Sapat, A., Esnard, A.-M., & Kolpakov, A. (2019). Understanding collaboration in disaster assistance networks: organizational homophily or resource dependency? *American Review of Public Administration*, 49(8), 957–972.

Sayles, J.S., & Baggio, J.A. (2017). Social–ecological network analysis of scale mismatches in estuary watershed restoration. *Proceedings of the National Academy of Sciences*. www.pnas.org/content/pnas/114/10/E1776

Schneider, M., Scholz, J.T., Lubell, M., Mindruta, D., & Edwardsen, M. (2003). Building consensual institutions: networks and the national estuary program. *American Journal of Political Science*, 47(1), 143–158.

Scholz, J.T., Berardo, R., & Kile, B. (2008). Do networks solve collective action problems? Credibility, search, and collaboration. *Journal of Politics*, 70(2), 393–406.

Scott, T.A. (2015). Does collaboration make any difference? Linking collaborative governance to environmental outcomes. *Journal of Policy Analysis and Management*, 34(3) 537–566.

Scott, T.A., & Greer, R.A. (2019). Polycentricity and the hollow state: exploring shared personnel as a source of connectivity in fragmented urban systems. *Policy Studies Journal: The Journal of the Policy Studies Organization*. onlinelibrary.wiley.com/doi/abs/10.1111/psj.12289

Scott, T.A., & Thomas, C.W. (2017a). Unpacking the collaborative toolbox: why and when do public managers choose collaborative governance strategies? *Policy Studies Journal*, 45(1), 191–214.

Scott, T.A., & Thomas, C.W. (2017b). Winners and losers in the ecology of games: network position, connectivity, and the benefits of collaborative governance regimes. *Journal of Public Administration Research and Theory*, 27(4), 647–660.

Scott, T.A., & Ulibarri, N. (2019). Taking network analysis seriously: methodological improvements for governance network scholarship. *Perspectives on Public Management and Governance*, January. doi.org/10.1093/ppmgov/gvy011

Sørensen, E., & Torfing, J. (2005). The democratic anchorage of governance networks.' *Scandinavian Political Studies*, 28(3), 195–218.

Sørensen, E., & Torfing, J. (2009). Making governance networks effective and democratic through metagovernance. *Public Administration*, 87(2), 234–258.

Ulibarri, N., & Scott, T.A. (2017). Linking network structure to collaborative governance. *Journal of Public Administration Research*. academic.oup.com/jpart/article-abstract/27/1/163/2629285

Van Holt, T., Johnson, J.C., Moates, S., & Carley, K. (2016). The role of datasets on scientific influence within conflict research. *PLOS One*, *11*(4), e0154148.

Van Waarden, F. (1992). Dimensions and types of policy networks. *European Journal of Political Research*, *21*(1–2), 29–52.

Wagner, P.M., Torney, D., & Ylä-Anttila, T. (2021). Governing a multilevel and cross-sectoral climate policy implementation network. *Environmental Policy and Governance*, *31*(5), 417–431.

Weible, C.M., Ingold, K., Nohrstedt, D., Henry, A.D., & Jenkins-Smith, H.C. (2020). Sharpening advocacy coalitions. *Policy Studies Journal: The Journal of the Policy Studies Organization*, *48*(4), 1054–1081.

Weible, C.M., & Sabatier, P.A. (2005). Comparing policy networks: marine protected areas in California. *Policy Studies Journal*, 33(2), 181–201.

Wijffels, J. (2021). Udpipe: tokenization, parts of speech tagging, lemmatization and dependency parsing with the 'UDPipe' 'NLP' toolkit. CRAN.R-project.org/package=udpipe

Williamson, O.E. (1973). Markets and hierarchies: some elementary considerations. *American Economic Review*, *63*(2), 316–325.

Yi, H., Suo, L., Shen, R., Zhang, J., Ramaswami, A., & Feiock, R.C. (2018). Regional governance and institutional collective action for environmental sustainability. *Public Administration Review*, *78*(4), 556–566.

Young, O.R. (2002). *The institutional dimensions of environmental change: fit, interplay, and scale.* MIT Press.

APPENDIX

Table A7.1   Paper-based representation of literature clusters grouped in Figure 7.1

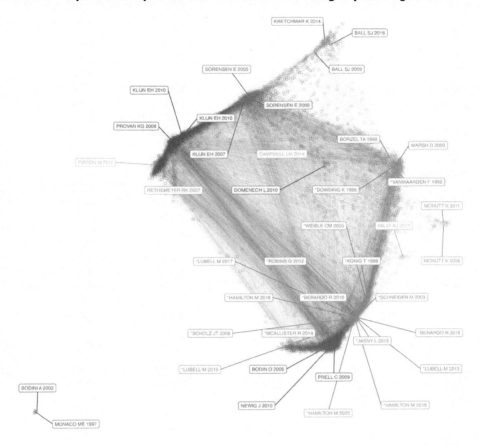

[] = on critical path
other labeled nodes = top cited work in cluster

Table A7.2 Papers on the identified critical path

Cluster keywords	Citation	Title
1: net. manage.+social capital+PA	(Williamson, 1973)*	Markets and hierarchies: some elementary considerations
2: SNA+policy nets.+policy community	(Heclo, 1978)*	Issue networks and the executive establishment
4: SNA+ACF+climate change	(Laumann & Knoke, 1987)*	The organisational state: social choice in national policy domains
2: SNA+policy nets.+policy community	(Van Waarden, 1992)	Dimensions and types of policy networks
2: SNA+policy nets.+policy community	(Dowding, 1995)	Model or metaphor? A critical review of the policy network approach
2: SNA+policy nets.+policy community	(König & Bräuninger, 1998)	The formation of policy networks: preferences, institutions and actors' choice of information and exchange relations
4: SNA+ACF+climate change	(Schneider et al., 2003)	Building consensual institutions: networks and the National Estuary Program
4: SNA+ACF+climate change	(Weible & Sabatier, 2005)	Comparing policy networks: marine protected areas in California
4: SNA+ACF+climate change	(Scholz et al., 2008)	Do networks solve collective action problems? Credibility, search, and collaboration
4: SNA+ACF+climate change	(Berardo & Scholz, 2010)	Self-organizing policy networks: risk, partner selection, and cooperation in estuaries
4: SNA+ACF+climate change	(Robins et al., 2012)	Statistical network analysis for analyzing policy networks
4: SNA+ACF+climate change	(Lubell, 2013)	Governing institutional complexity: the ecology of games framework
4: SNA+ACF+climate change	(McAllister et al., 2014)	Policy networks, stakeholder interactions and climate adaptation in the region of South East Queensland, Australia
4: SNA+ACF+climate change	(Jasny & Lubell, 2015)	Two-mode brokerage in policy networks
4: SNA+ACF+climate change	(Lubell, 2015)	Collaborative partnerships in complex institutional systems
4: SNA+ACF+climate change	(Berardo & Lubell, 2016)	Understanding what shapes a polycentric governance system
4: SNA+ACF+climate change	(Lubell et al., 2017)	Transaction costs and the perceived effectiveness of complex institutional systems
4: SNA+ACF+climate change	(Hamilton et al., 2018)	Cross-level linkages in an ecology of climate change adaptation policy games
4: SNA+ACF+climate change	(Hamilton & Lubell, 2018)	Collaborative governance of climate change adaptation across spatial and institutional scales
3: nat. res. manage.+SES+SNA	(Georgalakis, 2020)**	A disconnected policy network: the UK's response to the Sierra Leone ebola epidemic
4: SNA+ACF+climate change	(Hamilton et al., 2020)	Evaluating heterogeneous brokerage: new conceptual and methodological approaches and their application to multilevel environmental governance networks

(Continued)

Table A7.2 Papers on the identified critical path (*Continued*)

Cluster keywords	Citation	Title
4: SNA+ACF+climate change	(Kauneckis & Martin, 2020)**	Patterns of adaptation response by coastal communities to climate risks
4: SNA+ACF+climate change	(Hamilton et al., 2021)**	Bridging collaboration gaps in fragmented environmental governance systems
3: nat. res. manage.+SES+SNA	(Jasny et al., 2021)**	Participant engagement in environmentally focused social network research
1: net. manage.+social capital+PA	(Wagner et al., 2021)**	Governing a multilevel and cross-sectoral climate policy implementation network

these are books, not articles, that are prominent 'sink' nodes for the critical path, meaning that these works were cited by articles in the query sample but were not contained in the query sample (hence why these books remain even though only articles were retained from the query)

**these* are source nodes which initiate the critical path, meaning that these articles were picked up in the sample query but were not cited by any other work in the sample query

Table A7.3 Highly cited papers that cite papers on the critical path as shown in Figure 7.3

Cluster keywords	Citation	Title
2: SNA+policy nets.+policy community	(Börzel, 1998)	Organizing Babylon: on the different conceptions of policy networks
2: SNA+policy nets.+policy community	(Marsh & Smith, 2000)	Understanding policy networks: towards a dialectical approach
4: SNA+ACF+climate change	(Carpenter et al., 2003)	The strength of strong ties: a model of contact-making in policy networks with evidence from us health politics
2: SNA+policy nets.+policy community	(Pforr, 2006)	Tourism policy in the making: an Australian network study
2: SNA+policy nets.+policy community	(Beyers et al., 2008)	Researching interest group politics in Europe and elsewhere: much we study, little we know?
3: nat. res. manage.+SES+SNA	(Prell et al., 2009)	Stakeholder analysis and social network analysis in natural resource management
4: SNA+ACF+climate change	(Henry et al., 2011)	Belief systems and social capital as drivers of policy network structure: the case of California regional planning
4: SNA+ACF+climate change	(Henry, 2011)	Ideology, power, and the structure of policy networks
4: SNA+ACF+climate change	(Matti & Sandström, 2011)	The rationale determining advocacy coalitions: examining coordination networks and corresponding beliefs
4: SNA+ACF+climate change	(McGinnis, 2011)	Networks of adjacent action situations in polycentric governance
4: SNA+ACF+climate change	(Leifeld & Schneider, 2012)	Information exchange in policy networks

(*Continued*)

Table A7.3 Highly cited papers that cite papers on the critical path as shown in Figure 7.3 (*Continued*)

Cluster keywords	Citation	Title
3: nat. res. manage.+SES+SNA	(Rathwell & Peterson, 2012)	Connecting social networks with ecosystem services for watershed governance: a social-ecological network perspective highlights the critical role of bridging organizations
4: SNA+ACF+climate change	(Petridou, 2014)	Theories of the policy process: contemporary scholarship and future directions
3: nat. res. manage.+SES+SNA	(Muñoz-Erickson & Cutts, 2016)	Structural dimensions of knowledge-action networks for sustainability
4: SNA+ACF+climate change	(Angst & Hirschi, 2017)	Network dynamics in natural resource governance: a case study of Swiss landscape management
3: nat. res. manage.+SES+SNA	(Barnes et al., 2017)	The social structural foundations of adaptation and transformation in social-ecological systems
3: nat. res. manage.+SES+SNA	(Bodin et al., 2017)	Collaborative networks for effective ecosystem-based management: a set of working hypotheses
3: nat. res. manage.+SES+SNA	(Fischer & Jasny, 2017)	Capacity to adapt to environmental change: evidence from a network of organizations concerned with increasing wildfire risk
3: nat. res. manage.+SES+SNA	(Mathias et al., 2017)	Multilevel policies and adaptive social networks - a conceptual modeling study for maintaining a polycentric governance system
3: nat. res. manage.+SES+SNA	(Sayles & Baggio, 2017)	Social-ecological network analysis of scale mismatches in estuary watershed restoration
4: SNA+ACF+climate change	(Scott & Thomas, 2017b)	Winners and losers in the ecology of games: network position, connectivity, and the benefits of collaborative governance regimes
4: SNA+ACF+climate change	(Scott & Thomas, 2017a)	Unpacking the collaborative toolbox: why and when do public managers choose collaborative governance strategies?
4: SNA+ACF+climate change	(Ulibarri & Scott, 2017)	Linking network structure to collaborative governance
4: SNA+ACF+climate change	(Hamilton, 2018)	Understanding what shapes varying perceptions of the procedural fairness of transboundary environmental decision-making processes
3: nat. res. manage.+SES+SNA	(Hileman & Lubell, 2018)	The network structure of multilevel water resources governance in Central America

(*Continued*)

Table A7.3 Highly cited papers that cite papers on the critical path as shown in Figure 7.3 (*Continued*)

Cluster keywords	Citation	Title
3: nat. res. manage.+SES+SNA	(Bergsten et al., 2019)	Identifying governance gaps among interlinked sustainability challenges
4: SNA+ACF+climate change	(Hamilton & Lubell, 2019)	Climate change adaptation, social capital, and the performance of polycentric governance institutions
4: SNA+ACF+climate change	(Herzog & Ingold, 2019)	Threats to common-pool resources and the importance of forums: on the emergence of cooperation in CPR problem settings
4: SNA+ACF+climate change	(Hileman & Bodin, 2019)	Balancing costs and benefits of collaboration in an ecology of games
4: SNA+ACF+climate change	(Scott & Ulibarri, 2019)	Taking network analysis seriously: methodological improvements for governance network scholarship
4: SNA+ACF+climate change	(Scott & Greer, 2019)	Polycentricity and the hollow state: exploring shared personnel as a source of connectivity in fragmented urban systems
4: SNA+ACF+climate change	(Brandenberger et al., 2022)	Boundary spanning through engagement of policy actors in multiple issues

Health Behaviours and Outcomes

Kayla de la Haye

INTRODUCTION

Our understanding of what contributes to good health, and what factors put people at risk for poor health, has changed a lot over the past decades. A good example of this comes from the Alameda County Study, based in California. In the 1960s, researchers working on this study began looking for explanations of poor health beyond infectious diseases, which had been a leading cause of death for much of the century. This study was seminal in establishing that *lifestyles* and *health habits* like sleep, diet, exercise, alcohol intake and smoking impact whether or not people became ill, and how long they live (Belloc & Breslow, 1972). In the decades that followed, researchers started asking new types of questions, like 'do social connections impact people's health', revisiting the Alameda County Study data for answers. They found compelling evidence that social factors *did* impact health. Over and above people's healthy or unhealthy habits, their social networks, church participation and marital status also helped to explain whether or not they were healthy or ill (Housman & Dorman, 2005). Today, 'social determinants of health' (or SDOH), which are a range of 'non-medical' factors that influence health outcomes including social, community and broader structural contexts, are viewed as a *primary driver of health outcomes and health disparities across groups*, by major health organisations like the World Health Organizations (WHO) and the US Centers for Disease Control (US Department of Health and Human Services; WHO, 2022).

Another seminal study alerting us to the importance of social factors to health examined the relationship between social connections and mortality. This meta-analysis of almost 150 international studies arrived at two striking conclusions: first, people with stronger social relationships have a 50 per cent increased chance of survival compared to people with weaker relationships; and second, that social connections may matter *more* to our risk for disease and death than smoking, exercise, alcohol intake and obesity (Holt-Lunstad et al., 2010). This provided additional compelling evidence that we must pay attention to people's social networks if we want to improve their health.

There is a wealth of research and theories to help us understand *why* social connections are so important to human health and well-being. Currently, there remains a need and opportunity to develop a richer understanding of how social connections are intertwined with health, and how they can be leveraged to promote good health, using social network analysis and theory (SNA/T)

(Valente & Pitts, 2017). This chapter describes why SNA/T is a useful framework for better understanding the often-complex relationships between social networks and health. Some of the key mechanisms through which social networks impact health, and how health in turn, impacts our social networks, are also reviewed. Finally, this chapter looks to directions for future research and how this field can be applied to improve the health of people and groups, particularly those who experience the greatest inequities in poor health.

WHY STUDY SOCIAL NETWORKS IF YOU WANT TO UNDERSTAND OR IMPROVE HEALTH?

The adoption of a social network framework has been a natural progression for researchers interested in social influences on health. This is because social ties, and importantly *the broader structure and or patterning of these social ties* (i.e., social networks), are important milieus that shape exposure to contagious diseases, as well as exposure to resources, information, innovations, behavioural norms and stigma, which in turn can influence health behaviours and outcomes. Social networks can be sources of social influence for both healthy or unhealthy behaviours and habits, and can be a source of, or barrier to, social support and social capital. And when an individual is motivated to change their health behaviours, social networks can help to promote, or impede, this change. In other words, social networks do not have an inherently good or bad impact on health. Rather, it is the *characteristics and functions* of these networks that matter to health outcomes.

Historically, the study of social influences on health has focused on individuals' beliefs about their social context broadly. For example, *perceived norms* are often a central tenet of theories of health behaviour (Ajzen, 1991), and reflect what an individual thinks are the typical health behaviours of people they know. It is assessed by questions like 'do most people in your peer group exercise regularly?' ('peer group' could be replaced by other referent groups like 'family', 'friends,' or 'co-workers'; and 'exercise regularly' could be replaced by other health behaviours, like 'binge drink', 'smoke cigarettes', or 'get annual vaccinations'). Research has shown that what people perceive to be 'the norm' often influences their behaviour, such that people prefer to align their own behaviours so that they are *similar to* the behaviours of important people in their life. For example, if an individual thinks that their family and friends *do not* exercise – that is, this isn't 'what their family and friends typically do' – it is less likely they will become regular exercisers.

Social influence has also been studied among *pairs* or *small groups* of people, often in a laboratory setting. Many of these research studies tested if study participants would copy or imitate the health behaviours of other people in the laboratory. For example, some of these studies had a study 'confederate' (i.e., a person who is on the research team) pretend that they were a research participant, but they were actually instructed to model a particular health behaviour in front of other 'real' participants during the experiment. Although the 'real' research participants are not told about the confederate or this research goal (rather, they are often deceived and told the purpose of the research is something else, like taking a test), the research participant often copies the behaviour of the confederate. For example, in one study, young adults drank more alcohol in a 'bar lab' when exposed to a confederate who drank more alcohol versus a confederate who drank less alcohol (Larsen et al., 2009). This body of evidence shows that social influence can have a powerful impact on health behaviours, even among people who just met (Turner, 1991).

So why do we need SNA/T to better understand social influences on health? A benefit of SNA/T is that it provides a framework that goes beyond the study of social influence from an individual or dyad (interpersonal) perspective, which can be reductionist and lose valuable information about people's complex, real-life social contexts. Rather, SNA/T allows us to measure, map out and better examine *emergent properties* of the social systems in which people are embedded. This includes properties like whether a social network is densely or sparsely connected, if social influences are homogeneous or different across different network members, or how resources and social capital are distributed across a network (described in more detail below). Finally, we can study how these social network phenomena impact people's health.

TYPES OF SOCIAL NETWORKS THAT ARE RELEVANT TO HEALTH

Social networks refer to social structures that are made up of social actors (for this chapter, we focus on human social actors; either individuals or groups/organisations) and the web of relationships among these actors. The types of relationships and thus social networks that may be relevant to health issues are very diverse: it could include family/kinship relationships among members of a community, friendship ties among school students, advice and help-seeking among friends and colleagues, sexual contact networks in a city, sharing or liking other's content on social media platforms, and even collaboration between organisations or government entities (Valente, 2010).

The types of social networks that are relevant to health are broad *because the factors that shape people's health are broad*. Very few, if any, health decisions or behaviours are driven solely by a simple set of individual characteristics, like an individual's knowledge about whether the decision or behaviour is likely to be 'good' or 'bad' for their health. Most health behaviours and outcomes are influenced by social-ecological factors (Bronfenbrenner, 1977; Sallis et al., 2015). This means that health behaviours and outcomes are typically shaped by multiple individual factors like genetics, beliefs, emotions and finances, and they are also influenced by factors at other 'levels'. These levels include the social context and social networks, organisations, community and broader policy and structural environments that also directly or indirectly influence health. In other words, many health outcomes are at least in part, socially and structurally determined. The social networks that influence individuals, families and groups, as well as the social networks that shape the other levels of ecological influences, such as social networks within and across organisations, coalitions, governments and industry that have a role in shaping our environments, all matter to health.

Some examples of the breadth of research on social networks and health includes:

- studies documenting how infectious disease, like HIV, hepatitis and Covid-19, is transmitted through contact networks (Klovdahl et al., 1994; Rolls et al., 2012; Saraswathi et al., 2020);
- research finding evidence of 'social contagion' of obesity, smoking, happiness, vaccine uptake and health decisions through networks of family, friends and acquaintances (Bruine de Bruin et al., 2019; Centola, 2010; de la Haye et al., 2019b; Fowler & Christakis, 2008; Zhang et al., 2018);
- studies of how support from one's social network impacts cancer survival (Kroenke, 2018; Nausheen et al., 2009);
- research finding that physician's social networks impact the health care practices they adopt (Coleman et al., 1957; Fattore et al., 2009);
- mapping social networks among policy makers and other influential stakeholders to understand how they impact the implementation of health policy or initiatives (Oliver et al., 2012; Shearer et al., 2014; Valente et al., 2019).

THE SNA TOOLKIT: WHY IT'S UNIQUE AND USEFUL FOR HEALTH RESEARCH

A social network approach to health research can help to formulate research questions and hypotheses about how social networks and health are connected, and it can serve as a tool to measure and analyse social structures so that these research questions can be tested. SNA provides a suite of methods, both quantitative and qualitative, and descriptive and inferential (described in several chapters in this book), to measure and understand social networks. In *health* research, SNA/T is commonly applied for two broad objectives:

- to understand the impact of social networks on health decisions, behaviours and outcomes;
- to design health interventions that use social networks to improve health outcomes for individuals or groups, and to impact health practice and policy.

Social network theory (SNT) is premised on the notion that people/social actors are embedded within webs of social relationships, and that social actors and their social networks are *interdependent*, meaning they influence one another (Borgatti & Ofem, 2010). Examples of prominent social network theories that have been applied to health research include network diffusion theory (Rogers, 2003; Valente, 2005), strength of weak ties theory (Granovetter, 1983) and small world theory (Milgram, 1967; Watts & Strogatz, 1998).

When applied to health behaviours and outcomes, social network theory emphasises that social networks can shape the health of people and groups, and that social networks, in turn, may be shaped by health factors (Valente & Pitts, 2017). As a result, it is valuable to study these phenomena together to understand how they are connected and co-evolve, instead of studying or addressing them in isolation.

Social network analysis (SNA) makes it possible to measure and assess how patterns of relationships within social networks are related to, and potentially influence, social actor's health behaviours and outcomes. The *types* of social networks (e.g., contact networks, friendship networks) and the *features* of social networks (e.g., the network size, density, or composition) that are of interest will depend on: (1) the health issue in question, (2) the population of interest and (3) the social phenomena that are hypothesised to be relevant to that issue and population (e.g., social contact, support provision, access to social capital, social contagion).

Depending on the research questions and study design, the types of measures used to capture information on social relationships and networks might include: (1) surveys that use 'name generators' that ask survey participants to report on their social ties; (2) observational or ethnographic studies where networks are observed and recorded by the researcher; (3) mining secondary data on social connections via phone, email, or social media records, or other records of social interaction; (4) or passive collection of social interaction through mobile technology and sensors that capture peoples' movement and mobility, or social interaction with others wearing a sensor (Robins, 2015).

The research question will also drive the type of social network *study design* that is selected. Two commonly applied SNA methods are (1) personal (egocentric) and (2) complete (sociocentric).

In *personal* or *'egocentric' social network studies*, the goal is to measure social networks from an individual's perspective, and the social ties and structures that surround this focal individual (McCarty et al., 2019) (also see Chapter 31, Perry et al., this volume). The focal individual is often referred to as the 'ego', with their social ties called 'alters'. These social ties might include family, romantic partners, friends, neighbours, co-workers and relationships with community members through faith-based organisations, or schools. In health studies, researchers often ask about alters with whom the ego discusses 'health matters' (Perry & Pescosolido, 2010). Personal network methods are commonly applied in health research that involves studying *samples* of individuals from a population; a common approach in observational studies, health surveillance surveys and trials testing health interventions. In these types of study designs, the sampled participants in the study are often assumed to be independent of one another (i.e., *not* socially connected), rather than a part of a bounded social group.

There are many rich examples of health research that has applied personal (egocentric) network methods, and a few are summarised here.

- Research by Dhand and colleagues has investigated how patients' personal networks are linked to their health-seeking behaviours and patient outcomes. They have found that patients with small, close-knit personal networks of highly familiar contacts – that is, networks with high *constraint* – had *longer* delays in getting to the hospital after a stroke; narrowing a very time-sensitive window for effective treatment (Dhand et al., 2019). They proposed that these close-knit, constrained networks may offer less variety of opinions and fewer people willing to speak up and tell the ego (patient) to get to the hospital quickly. In another study, among patients with multiple sclerosis, those embedded in personal networks with greater network constraint had *worse* physical functioning compared to those with more open networks (Levin et al., 2020). Based on this research, they have started to develop tools that would help doctors map their patients' social network to inform treatment strategies (Dhand et al., 2018).
- Personal social networks have been found to matter to mental and cognitive health. For example, among adults with a new and serious mental illness, those who were able to activate relationships within their personal networks involving communication and support, and those embedded within networks that had a more 'pro-medical' culture, had better quality of life and other health indicators one year later (Perry & Pescosolido, 2015). In another study of Alzheimer's disease among older adults, those with personal social networks that were characterised as having more social bridging – meaning larger social networks, lower network density and more weak ties and non-kin ties – had better cognitive outcomes over time (Perry et al., 2021).
- Studies that have measured the personal networks of homeless youth in the United States have found that their networks entail complex and 'multiplex' relationships (i.e., relationships with multiple dimensions) of support provision *and* shared risk. These multiplex relationships could have competing effects on their health. Homeless youth were found to primarily receive social support from family, sex partners and social contacts who were housed, but support provision also depended upon other network characteristics, such as the number of people in their social networks who were also homeless (de la Haye et al., 2012). Homeless youth also engaged in risky health behaviours with members of their personal networks, and they were more likely to drink or use drugs with alters

who occupied influential social roles, such as opinion leaders, popular social ties *and* people in their networks who provided them with support (Green et al., 2013).

In studies of *complete* or *'sociocentric'* social networks, the goal is to move away from the social networks of individuals, towards understanding the entire social network among a defined group of people. This group may be students in a school, employees within an organisation, users of an online media platform, or even all residents of a village or community. This approach focuses on getting a complete picture or 'census' of all the relationships among group members by gathering data on the social relationships (and often individual attributes) from all (or most) people in the group. Examples of health research that has applied this sociocentric approach, include the following.

- Several large studies have been designed to investigate how peer and friendship networks influence the health of children and adolescents, by studying sociocentric networks among students in classrooms or schools. Examples include the National Longitudinal Study of Adolescent to Adult Health (Add Health) in the United States (Harris et al., 2019) and TRAILS (*Tracking adolescents' individual lives survey*) in the Netherlands (*TRAILS*, 2022), among others. These studies generally aim to enroll most students in a classroom or school into the study and do this at multiple schools so that they can study several complete school social networks. They have used surveys to gather data from students about their social connections, asking them questions like 'Name the students in your school who are your best friends.' This study design has the advantage of collecting self-report or objective health characteristics from all participating students in the class or school (instead of relying on data about 'perceived behaviour' of friends), such as students' substance use, weight status, or mental health, in addition to social network data. Analyses of these data have generated a wealth of knowledge about peer network effects on health behaviours. For example, studies have found that adolescents are more likely to drink alcohol, smoke cigarettes, use marijuana and exercise if their school friends do that particular behaviour (Alexander et al., 2001; de la Haye et al., 2013; Mundt, 2011; Osgood et al., 2013; Simpkins et al., 2013). This research has also documented that a student's position in their school peer networks can matter to their health behaviours: for example, the 'in-degree' or number of friendships nominations a student receives, indicative of their popularity as a friend, has been associated with their substance use and smoking (Moody et al., 2011; Valente et al., 2005).
- Some of these studies of peer networks in classrooms and schools also employed longitudinal designs, where they measured social networks and individual health characteristics at multiple time points/study waves (see Figure 8.1 as an example). This allowed researchers to test hypotheses about peer network and health behaviour *dynamics*, meaning how networks

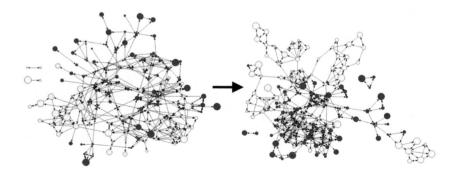

Figure 8.1 Friendship network and body mass index (BMI) in one grade 8 school cohort (N = 156 students), measured at two time points: (1) the start of the school year, and (2) the end of the school year (de la Haye et al., 2011).

Note: light nodes = girls, dark nodes = boys, node size = BMI, ties = best friend nominations.

and health influence each other over time. This research has found, for example, that youth are more likely to *select* friends who are similar to them in terms of health behaviours, like smoking (Mercken et al., 2010). And even though this social selection leads to initial similarities in these behaviours among friends, there is also evidence that friends go on to influence each other so that they become *more alike* in their health behaviours over time (Mercken et al., 2010; Veenstra et al., 2013). The extent to which social selection or social influence are operating appears to depend on the setting, characteristics of the population (e.g., gender), and type of health behaviour. Nonetheless, these social selection and influence processes are often found to work together, as social networks evolve, to have a profound influence on child and adolescent health.

- Some researchers have attempted to collect complete or sociocentric network data from all (or many) residents in a village or community. The Framingham Heart Study is one example of this type of study, which starting in 1948 enrolled about one fifth of all 28,000 residents of Framingham, a small city in the north east of the United States (Andersson et al., 2019). These residents (and new cohorts) continue to be tracked 70+ years later. Data was collected about participants' family and social connections, and this has been the focus of several studies documenting the importance of social networks on people's health trajectories over their lifespan. This research has shown that obesity, smoking and happiness cluster and 'spread through' social networks (Christakis & Fowler, 2007; Christakis & Fowler, 2008; Fowler & Christakis, 2008).

- Other examples of complete social network studies come from rural communities across the globe. One such study is based in Mbarara, Uganda, whose 1,600+ adult residents participated in a research study on HIV (Takada et al., 2019). Seven per cent of adults in this community were HIV positive. Social network data was collected from all adult participants, and researchers found that socially connected residents tended to be similar in their HIV-related stigma, and that residents had lower stigma if someone they were socially connected to was HIV positive. Based on these findings, the researchers made several recommendations for leveraging social networks to reduce HIV-related stigma (Takada et al., 2019), which is a barrier to treatment and better health outcomes.

Social Network Structures

Regardless of the approach used to sample and measure social networks, the goal of social network analysis is typically to understand the observed social structures, and how they relate to the health of individuals or the group. These social structures are particular patterns of ties, or interesting 'structural signatures' that emerge from social relationships, which provide insight into social functions and processes that matter to health. A few examples of structural signatures that are of interest to health are summarised in Table 8.1.

Descriptive and Statistical Analysis of Social Network Data

Descriptive statistics of social network structures or social actors' positions in a network, like those defined in Table 8.1, are often of interest to health researchers and practitioners. In personal network studies researchers might examine if an ego's network density, transitivity, or constraint predicts their health outcomes (e.g., if more network density is associated with better mental health). In sociocentric network studies, researchers might examine if social actor's popularity (e.g., in-degree centrality) is associated with health behaviours (e.g., if popularity is associated with smoking).

SNA also goes beyond the description of network structures and provides ***statistical methods*** to test research hypotheses. For example, to test if actors who share a network tie have statistically significant similarity in a health behaviour or outcome (i.e., more similarity than would be expected by chance), like weight status, substance use, or vaccination uptake. Or one can test if characteristics of actors' social ties significantly predict their health outcomes. Because the network perspective assumes that individuals and relationships in a network are interdependent, traditional statistical models that assume data are *independent* are often not appropriate for studies of complete social networks. Therefore probabilistic network models have been developed that account for dependencies inherent in network data. These include dependencies between actors who share a tie, as well as more complex dependencies based on broader social structures that are important network building blocks (Robins & Pattison, 2005). For example, social actors are often more likely to have a social connection, such as friendship, if they share a common friend (a process referred to as transitivity).

Table 8.1 Examples of structural features of social networks that are of interest in health research

Structural feature	Tie configuration	Description
Size		The number of actors in a network
Reciprocity		The extent to which ties in the network are reciprocated (mutual) or unreciprocated (not mutual)
Multiplexity		Combinations of different social connections between a pair of actors
Centrality		The extent to which an actor is central in the network, based on their direct and indirect ties. This is often evaluated based on an actor's in-degree (in-degree centrality), and the extent to which they are connected to other high-degree nodes. Actors who have many connections to others may be viewed important opinion leaders or hubs for diffusion/contagion
Density		The extent to which a network is sparsely or densely connected. Network density is defined as the ratio of observed ties to the number of possible ties in the network
Transitivity		This reflects the clustering of ties in a social network, and specifically the extent to which two paths in the network (i.e., a tie from node A to node B, and a tie from node B to node C) are closed (i.e., there is a tie from node A to node C). In a friendship network, this means 'a friend of a friend is a friend' (i.e., shared friendship)
Homophily		The extent to which ties in the network are observed among social actors who share the same/similar characteristics

Note: In the images of tie configurations, 'nodes' represent social actors and lines or arrows represent social ties.

Models for *longitudinal* social network data also provide a sophisticated and useful approach to understand health and social network dynamics, and tease apart mechanisms of social selection, social influence and other possibly confounding processes (Robins, 2015; Snijders et al., 2017; Veenstra et al., 2013). Specifically, these methods allow researchers to isolate factors that predict the formation of social ties (e.g., friendship choices) from among a set of social actors, while simultaneously testing for network and confounding effects that predict changes in individual attributes (e.g., health beliefs, behaviours, or outcomes). These tools have been useful in testing hypotheses about social influence, diffusion and contagion, and growing our understanding and theory of social network dynamics as they relate to individual and population health.

Example: Modelling the Dynamics of Peer Social Networks and Obesity

Although the family context has often been a central focus for understanding and addressing childhood obesity, peer and school contexts become increasingly important as children develop. Social network studies are providing new insights into peer effects on childhood obesity. For example, studies of adolescent peer networks show that obesity and related health behaviours, including eating and physical activity, are associated with social network structures. Obesity risk has been found to 'cluster' in youth social networks, whereby friends tend to be similar in weight status and weight-related behaviours (de la Haye et al., 2010). Similarities in obesity risk among friends can also grow stronger over time (Shoham et al., 2015; Simpkins et al., 2013; Trogdon et al., 2008; Valente et al., 2009).

There is some evidence that these phenomena are explained by peer network influences, where adolescents' diet, physical activity and ultimately weight status are influenced by the behaviours and characteristics of their friends. Friends may directly influence each other's lifestyle behaviours (Salvy et al., 2012), or influence each other's weight norms, such as their perceptions of a healthy weight (Maximova et al., 2008). However, social network research has also shown that the clustering of obesity in youth peer networks is also explained by social selection. In particular, youth tend to select and form friendships with peers who are similar to them in weight status, and this is in part due to weight-based stigma (de la Haye et al., 2017; de la Haye et al., 2011; Schaefer & Simpkins, 2014; Simpkins et al., 2013). Although youth with overweight have been found to be unbiased in terms of befriending peers with overweight or not, non-overweight youth often avoid befriending peers who are overweight. As a result, youth with overweight often befriend one another, and have fewer friends, locating them in more peripheral positions in their peer networks (de la Haye et al., 2011; Schaefer & Simpkins, 2014; Simpkins et al., 2013; Strauss & Pollack, 2003). This is likely to have negative consequences for the health of youth with overweight.

SOCIAL NETWORK MECHANISMS AND FUNCTIONS LINKED TO HEALTH

The spread of ideas, innovations, behaviours and diseases through social networks – frequently referred to as *diffusion* or *social contagion* – is often a focus of research linking social networks and health. This includes research on the interpersonal spread of pathogens and contagious disease through contact networks, as well as the diffusion and contagion of health beliefs, behaviours and even health conditions like obesity and happiness through social ties and networks (Christakis & Fowler, 2007; Valente, 2010; Zhang & Centola, 2019). This research often investigates the role of network structures and characteristics of social ties and social actors that enable or constrain social contagion.

Social contagion is one of many social functions that play out within social networks that matter to health. *Social influence* is a related but distinct concept, referring specifically to changes in behaviour that are due to peoples' perceptions of others. For example, several theories of health behaviour emphasise that perceived social norms – our perceptions about what others typically do (descriptive norms) and what we think others expect us to do (injunctive norms) – shape our intentions and adoption of health behaviours (Ajzen, 1991). There are many studies of social networks that document that the 'average' or typical behaviour of one's social ties can influence an individual's behaviour. For example, studies of peer influence on adolescent substance use, physical activity, eating behaviours and delinquent behaviours have found that youth tend to change their behaviour so that it is more aligned with the average behaviour of the friends to whom they are directly connected in their peer network (Montgomery et al., 2019). Thus, depending on the health behaviours of our social connections, social networks can be a source of healthy or unhealthy social influences on health.

Social networks may or may not be sources of *social support*, which also impacts people's health (Holt-Lunstad & Uchino, 2015). Social support encompasses the resources and assistance exchanged through interpersonal relationships, which influences health through several mechanisms. For example, social support can practically assist someone in adopting a health behaviour when social contacts provide money or other needed resources (i.e., instrumental or tangible support) that make it easier to do a behaviour. This type of support could help someone get to a visit with their doctor, adhere to their medications, or engage in exercise. Access to other types of social support, like emotional or belonging support, can reduce stress and increase self-efficacy, in turn reducing barriers to adopting healthy behaviours. This type of support can also provide a 'buffering mechanism' for stressful life events, where the receipt of this support makes it less likely people will turn to unhealthy coping strategies, like substance use (Uchino et al., 1996). There have been many studies that examine how the provision of social support within social networks impacts health, generating evidence that these phenomena are often complex but matter to both mental and physical health (de la Haye et al., 2019a; Song et al., 2011). A related social network function is *social capital*, referring more specifically to the norms for the exchange and distribution of resources through social networks (Pitkin Derose & Varda, 2009). And *social isolation* and the resulting lack of social connection and support can literally 'get under the skin', impacting epigenetic processes that are related to inflammation and viral suppression, making people more physiologically prone to illness (Cole, 2013). Conversely, *social integration*, signalling the presence of social ties and participation in a broad range of relationships, has been consistently shown to benefit health (Holt-Lunstad et al., 2010).

Another social network mechanism that has a profound impact on health and well-being is *social undermining, aggression and stigma*. For example, social network phenomena have been found to explain bullying among children and youth (Veenstra & Huitsing, 2021), which has profound long-term impacts on their mental health and well-being. And social networks can play a key role in contributing to, and buffering against, experiences of racism and discrimination (Goldman, 2022; Leahy & Chopik, 2020), a key social determinant of health.

Among social actors that are organisations or entities like coalitions or governments, the structure of social relationships that involve *interorganisational collaboration*, such as communication, advice seeking and resource sharing, have been found to impact the adoption of organisational practices that matter to health (Valente et al., 2007).

SOCIAL NETWORKS AND SNA/T ARE POWERFUL TOOLS IN HEALTH INTERVENTIONS

Given the evidence that social networks influence health through multiple mechanisms, a logical next step is to identify ways that social networks can be integrated into health interventions. However, the implementation of network intervention strategies into major health initiatives is certainly not common. One reason may be that the historically dominant view of health and health behaviours, as being largely driven by individual decisions and thus rooted in personal responsibility, has generated a toolbox of evidence-based interventions that seek to change individual factors, like knowledge, beliefs and attitudes.

There are a wealth of opportunities to develop health interventions that include 'network intervention' strategies or components (Valente, 2012). These interventions might include strategies that attempt to change social networks, or leverage social network structures or functions, so that they better support the desired health behaviour or outcome. In a 2012 paper, Valente outlined four distinct types of network interventions.

1 *Individual*, where individual people/social actors are selected for the intervention based on some social network characteristic. For example, selecting highly connected individuals in the network to receive an intervention because they have the potential to spread new healthy ideas or behaviours to many others.
2 *Segmentation*, where certain groups of people that are connected in a social network are selected for the intervention. For example, a well-connected group of friends who engage in risky health behaviours may be recruited to participate together in a group-based intervention.
3 *Induction*, where the intervention strategies encourage or enhance interactions among members of a social network so that information or intervention effects can spread. For example, interventions that use 'snowball methods' for recruitment, where intervention participants are encouraged to invite their family or friends to also enroll in the intervention, and so on.
4 *Alteration*, where intervention strategies explicitly seek to change social networks by adding or deleting specific social ties. For example, interventions that match participants with a 'buddy' or 'peer mentor' are adding a network tie who is trained to provide positive social influence and social support.

A recent review of the literature on social network interventions for health identified almost 40 studies, conducted between 1996 and 2018, that included social network intervention strategies (Hunter et al., 2019). Many were interventions focused on substance use or sexual health. A meta-analysis of these studies led the authors to conclude that social network intervention strategies are effective in both short-term and long-term health behaviour change, including positive effects for sexual health outcomes, alcohol misuse, diabetes risk factors, smoking cessation and well-being (Hunter et al., 2019). They also concluded that interventions that included social network intervention strategies were more effective than those that did not. These results, as well as findings from other reviews (e.g., Spencer-Bonilla et al., 2017; Webel et al., 2010), make a strong case that more health interventions should move beyond individual-level approaches, and design and test intervention components that are focused on social networks.

One example of research that has applied social network methods to understand and address health issues is focused on social networks and health within family systems. This research bridges egocentric and sociocentric methods, as it often relies on multiple family members reporting on social interactions and relationships within their family to map 'family networks'. These studies have explored patterns of communication, advice seeking, social support and social undermining within multigenerational family and kin systems, and examined how the structural signatures of these networks relate to the health of individuals or the family as a whole. For example, research by Koehly and colleagues has found that family social networks structures help us understand communication about family health history (e.g., family history of heart disease or breast cancer) and family genetic and genomic risk information (e.g., genetic test results) (Ashida et al., 2009; Koehly et al., 2009). This research group has also shown that interventions that engage multiple family members with information about their family health history can help to activate supportive and helpful *changes* to family social networks, which in turn assist family members in adopting health behaviours that can reduce their risk for these familial diseases (e.g., exercise, healthy eating, smoking cessation) (e.g., de Heer et al., 2016).

Overall, it is likely that social networks have an important but untapped potential to bolster health interventions and outcomes. More on network interventions is covered in Valente, in Chapter 20 of this volume.

CONCLUSIONS

This chapter has described many important insights that have been gained by using social network theory and analysis to understand and improve health phenomena. Some of these insights are listed here.

- *Social networks are related to a wide range of health behaviours and outcomes*, including diet and exercise, alcohol and substance use, health screening and vaccination, mental health, chronic disease, infectious disease and health-related quality of life. Thus, social networks matter to behaviours relevant to the early prevention of disease (primary prevention) as well as those associated with health screening and treatment (secondary and tertiary prevention) and, ultimately, health outcomes.
- *The social network structures and functions that matter to health are complex.* There are many different mechanisms that operate through social networks that can impact health, from social contagion and influence, to social support and social undermining. How people are impacted by these processes can depend on their position in the network, the type of network ties they are embedded in and the broader structure and ecological context of the network.
- *The dynamics of social networks and health, as they unfold over time, are important to understand.*

Effects of social networks on health are not a one-way street. Often people and their health experiences shape how networks form and evolve, and these networks in turn influence the health of individuals, and the health and health differences of groups. This may create feedback loops that are critical to address to promote good health.

- *Social network interventions are promising but underutilised.* Studies that leverage or change social networks as part of intervention strategies have proven to be effective, and there is a wealth of opportunity to develop and test more network interventions for health.

There are also opportunities in new or budding areas of research that could advance our knowledge about health and the development of initiatives to promote good health. Some examples are listed here.

- We need more research to understand the role that social networks play in influencing systematic differences and inequities in the health of priority populations, such as people with low incomes or communities of colour.
- Using new technologies, like mobile sensors, which capture rich, real-time and granular information about social contacts and social ties, will likely generate new insights into temporal processes and mechanisms that link social networks and health.
- There are opportunities to apply SNA/T in implementation science, which seeks to understand and improve how evidence-based health practices and interventions are adopted and used, so that they translate to real-world health improvements. Barriers that prevent or slow the uptake of effective health interventions are often rooted in social phenomena.
- We need to bridge research that focuses on social networks of people and groups, with research on the social networks of organisations and governments whose activities play a key role in shaping the contexts and environments that influence health. Interventions that leverage both levels of social networks may be especially powerful in creating systemic change across social-ecological factors, which is needed for sustained improvements in public health.

In sum, the expansion of research and interventions focused on social networks and health will no doubt strengthen our knowledge and strategies to improve health and well-being.

REFERENCES

Ajzen, I. (1991). The theory of planned behavior. *Organizational Behavior and Human Decision Processes, 50*, 179–211.

Alexander, C., Piazza, M., Mekos, D., & Valente, T. (2001). Peers, schools, and adolescent cigarette smoking. *Journal of Adolescent Health, 29*, 22–30. doi.org/10.1016/S1054-139X(01)00210-5

Andersson, C., Johnson, A.D., Benjamin, E.J., Levy, D., & Vasan, R.S. (2019). 70-year legacy of the Framingham Heart Study. *Nature Reviews Cardiology, 16*(11), 687–698. doi.org/10.1038/s41569-019-0202-5

Ashida, S., Koehly, L.M., Roberts, J.S., Chen, C.A., Hiraki, S., & Green, R.C. (2009). Disclosing the disclosure: factors associated with communicating the results of genetic susceptibility testing for Alzheimer's Disease. *Journal of Health Communication, 14*(8), 768–784. doi.org/10.1080/10810730903295518

Belloc, N.B., & Breslow, L. (1972). Relationship of physical health status and health practices. *Preventive Medicine, 1*(3), 409–421. doi.org/10.1016/0091-7435(72)90014-X

Borgatti, S.P., & Ofem, B. (2010). Social network theory and analysis. In Alan J. Daly (Ed.), *Social Network Theory and Educational Change* (pp. 17–29). Harvard Education Press.

Bronfenbrenner, U. (1977). Toward an experimental ecology of human development. *American Psychologist, 32*, 513–531. doi.org/10.1037/0003-066x.32.7.513

Bruine de Bruin, W., Parker, A.M., Galesic, M., & Vardavas, R. (2019). Reports of social circles' and own vaccination behavior: a national longitudinal survey. *Health Psychology, 38*(11), 975–983. doi.org/10.1037/hea0000771

Centola, D. (2010). The spread of behavior in an online social network experiment. *Science, 329*, 1194–1197. doi.org/10.1126/science.1185231

Christakis, N.A., & Fowler, J.H. (2007). The spread of obesity in a large social network over 32 years. *New England Journal of Medicine, 357*, 370–379. doi.org/10.1056/NEJMsa066082

Christakis, N.A., & Fowler, J.H. (2008). The collective dynamics of smoking in a large social network. *New England Journal of Medicine, 358*, 2249–2258. doi.org/doi:10.1056/NEJMsa0706154

Cole, S.W. (2013). Social regulation of human gene expression: mechanisms and implications for public health. *American Journal of Public Health, 103 Suppl 1*, S84–92. doi.org/10.2105/AJPH.2012.301183

Coleman, J., Katz, E., & Menzel, H. (1957). The diffusion of an innovation among physicians. *Sociometry, 20*, 253–270.

de Heer, H.D., de la Haye, K., Skapinsky, K., Goergen, A.F., Wilkinson, A.V., & Koehly, L.M. (2016). Let's move together: a randomized trial of the impact of family health history on encouragement and co-engagement in physical activity of Mexican-origin parents and their children. *Health Education and Behavior, 44*(1), 141–152. doi.org/10.1177/1090198116644703

de la Haye, K., Bell, B., & Salvy, S.J. (2019a). The role of maternal social networks on the outcomes of a home-based childhood obesity prevention pilot intervention. *Journal of Social Structure, 20*(3), 7–28. doi.org/10.21307/joss-2019-004

de la Haye, K., Dijkstra, J.K., Lubbers, M.J., van Rijsewijk, L., & Stolk, R. (2017). The dual role of friendship and antipathy relations in the marginalization of overweight children in their peer networks: the TRAILS study. *PLOS One, 12*(6), e0178130. doi.org/10.1371/journal.pone.0178130

de la Haye, K., Green, H.D., Kennedy, D.P., Pollard, M.S., & Tucker, J.S. (2013). Selection and influence mechanisms associated with marijuana initiation and use in adolescent friendship networks. *Journal of Research on Adolescence, 23*, 474–486. doi.org/10.1111/jora.12018

de la Haye, K., Green, H.D., Kennedy, D.P., Zhou, A., Golinelli, D., Wenzel, S.L., & Tucker, J.S. (2012). Who is supporting homeless youth? Predictors of support in personal networks. *Journal of Research on Adolescence, 22*(4), 604–616. doi.org/10.1111/j.1532-7795.2012.00806.x

de la Haye, K., Robins, G., Mohr, P., & Wilson, C. (2010). Obesity-related behaviors in adolescent friendship networks. *Social Networks, 32*, 161–167. doi.org/10.1016/j.socnet.2009.09.001

de la Haye, K., Robins, G., Mohr, P., & Wilson, C. (2011). Homophily and contagion as explanations for weight similarities among adolescent friends. *Journal of Adolescent Health, 49*, 421–427. doi.org/10.1016/j.jadohealth.2011.02.008

de la Haye, K., Shin, H., Vega Yon, G.G., & Valente, T.W. (2019b). Smoking diffusion through networks of diverse, urban American adolescents over the high school period. *Journal of Health and Social Behavior, 60*(3), 362–376. doi.org/10.1177/0022146519870521

Dhand, A., Luke, D., Lang, C., Tsiaklides, M., Feske, S., & Lee, J.-M. (2019). Social networks and risk of delayed hospital arrival after acute stroke. *Nature Communications, 10*(1), 1206. doi.org/10.1038/s41467-019-09073-5

Dhand, A., White, C.C., Johnson, C., Xia, Z., & De Jager, P.L. (2018). A scalable online tool for quantitative social network assessment reveals potentially modifiable social environmental risks. *Nature Communications, 9*(1), 3930. doi.org/10.1038/s41467-018-06408-6

Fattore, G., Frosini, F., Salvatore, D., & Tozzi, V. (2009). Social network analysis in primary care: the impact of interactions on prescribing behaviour. *Health Policy*, *92*(2), 141–148. doi.org/10.1016/j.healthpol.2009.03.005

Fowler, J.H., & Christakis, N.A. (2008). Dynamic spread of happiness in a large social network: Longitudinal analysis over 20 years in the Framingham Heart Study. *BMJ*, *337*, a2338. doi.org/10.1136/bmj.a2338

Goldman, A.W. (2022). Everyday discrimination in later life: a social network approach. *Social Science Research*, *104*, 102670. doi.org/10.1016/j.ssresearch.2021.102670

Granovetter, M. (1983). The strength of weak ties: a network theory revisited. *Sociological Theory*, *1*, 201–233. doi.org/10.2307/202051

Green, H.D., de la Haye, K., Tucker, J.S., & Golinelli, D. (2013). Shared risk: who engages in substance use with American homeless youth? *Addiction*, *108*(9), 1618–1624. doi.org/10.1111/add.12177

Harris, K.M., C.T. Halpern, E.A. Whitsel, J.M. Hussey, L. Killeya-Jones, J. Tabor, & S.C. Dean. (2019). Cohort profile: The National Longitudinal Study of Adolescent to Adult Health (Add Health). *International Journal of Epidemiology*, 48(5):1415–1425 doi.org/10.1093/ije/dyz115.

Holt-Lunstad, J., Smith, T.B., & Layton, J.B. (2010). Social relationships and mortality risk: a meta-analytic review. *PLOS Medicine*, *7*, e1000316. doi.org/10.1371/journal.pmed.1000316

Holt-Lunstad, J., & Uchino, B. (2015). Social support and health. In K. Glanz, B.K. Rimer, & K. Viswanath (Eds.), *Health Behavior: Theory, Research, and Practice*. John Wiley & Sons.

Housman, J., & Dorman, S. (2005). The Alameda County Study: a systematic, chronological review. *American Journal of Health Education*, *36*(5), 302–308. doi.org/10.1080/19325037.2005.10608200

Hunter, R.F., de la Haye, K., Murray, J.M., Badham, J., Valente, T.W., Clarke, M., & Kee, F. (2019). Social network interventions for health behaviours and outcomes: a systematic review and meta-analysis. *PLOS Medicine*, *16*(9), e1002890. doi.org/10.1371/journal.pmed.1002890

Klovdahl, A.S., Potterat, J.J., Woodhouse, D.E., Muth, J.B., Muth, S.Q., & Darrow, W.W. (1994). Social networks and infectious disease: the Colorado Springs study. *Social Science and Medicine*, *38*(1), 79–88. doi.org/10.1016/0277-9536(94)90302-6

Koehly, L.M., Peters, J.A., Kenen, R., Hoskins, L.M., Ersig, A.L., Kuhn, N.R., Loud, J.T., & Greene, M.H. (2009). Characteristics of health information gatherers, disseminators, and blockers within families at risk of hereditary cancer: implications for family health communication interventions. *American Journal of Public Health*, *99*, 2203–2209. doi.org/10.2105/AJPH.2008.154096

Kroenke, C.H. (2018). A conceptual model of social networks and mechanisms of cancer mortality, and potential strategies to improve survival. *Translational Behavioral Medicine*, *8*(4), 629–642. doi.org/10.1093/tbm/ibx061

Larsen, H., Engels, R.C.M.E., Granic, I., & Overbeek, G. (2009). An experimental study on imitation of alcohol consumption in same-sex dyads. *Alcohol and Alcoholism*, *44*(3), 250–255. doi.org/10.1093/alcalc/agp002

Leahy, K.E., & Chopik, W.J. (2020). The effect of social network size and composition on the link between discrimination and health among sexual minorities. *Journal of Aging and Health*, *32*(9), 1214–1221. doi.org/10.1177/0898264320908982

Levin, S.N., Riley, C.S., Dhand, A., White, C.C., Venkatesh, S., Boehm, B., Nassif, C., Socia, L., Onomichi, K., Leavitt, V.M., Levine, L., Heyman, R., Farber, R.S., Vargas, W.S., Xia, Z., & De Jager, P.L. (2020). Association of social network structure and physical function in patients with multiple sclerosis. *Neurology*, *95*(11), e1565–e1574. doi.org/10.1212/wnl.0000000000010460

Maximova, K., McGrath, J.J., Barnett, T., Loughlin, J.O., Paradis, G., & Lamber, M. (2008). Do you see what I see? Weight status misperception and exposure to obesity among children and adolescents. *International Journal of Obesity*, *32*, 1008–1015.

McCarty, C., Lubbers, M.J., Vacca, R., & Molina, J.L. (2019). *Conducting Personal Network Research: a Practical Guide*. Guilford.

Mercken, L., Snijders, T.A.B., Steglich, C., Vartiainen, E., & de Vries, H. (2010). Dynamics of adolescent friendship networks and smoking behavior. *Social Networks*, *32*, 72–81. doi.org/10.1016/j.socnet.2009.02.005

Milgram, S. (1967). The small world problem. *Psychology Today*, *2*(1), 60–67.

Montgomery, S.C., Donnelly, M., Bhatnagar, P., Carlin, A., Kee, F., & Hunter, R.F. (2019). Peer social network processes and adolescent health behaviors: a systematic review. *Preventive Medicine*, 105900. doi.org/10.1016/j.ypmed.2019.105900

Moody, J., Brynildsen, W.D., Osgood, D.W., Feinberg, M.E., & Gest, S. (2011). Popularity trajectories and substance use in early adolescence. *Social Networks*, *33*, 101–112. doi.org/10.1016/j.socnet.2010.10.001

Mundt, M.P. (2011). The impact of peer social networks on adolescent alcohol use initiation. *Academic Pediatrics*, *11*(5), 414–421. doi.org/10.1016/j.acap.2011.05.005

Nausheen, B., Gidron, Y., Peveler, R., & Moss-Morris, R. (2009). Social support and cancer progression: a systematic review. *Journal of Psychosomatic*

Research, 67(5), 403–415. doi.org/10.1016/j.jpsychores.2008.12.012

Oliver, K., Everett, M., Verma, A., & de Vocht, F. (2012). The human factor: re-organisations in public health policy. *Health Policy*, 106(1), 97–103. doi.org/10.1016/j.healthpol.2012.03.009

Osgood, D.W., Ragan, D.T., Wallace, L., Gest, S.D., Feinberg, M.E., & Moody, J. (2013). Peers and the emergence of alcohol use: Influence and selection processes in adolescent friendship networks. *Journal of Research on Adolescence*, 23(3), 500–512. doi.org/10.1111/jora.12059

Perry, B.L., McConnell, W.R., Peng, S., Roth, A.R., Coleman, M., Manchella, M., Roessler, M., Francis, H., Sheean, H., & Apostolova, L.A. (2021). Social networks and cognitive function: an evaluation of social bridging and bonding mechanisms. *The Gerontologist*, 62(6), 865–875. doi.org/10.1093/geront/gnab112

Perry, B.L., & Pescosolido, B.A. (2010). Functional specificity in discussion networks: the influence of general and problem-specific networks on health outcomes. *Social Networks*, 32(4), 345–357. doi.org/10.1016/j.socnet.2010.06.005

Perry, B.L., & Pescosolido, B.A. (2015). Social network activation: the role of health discussion partners in recovery from mental illness. *Social Science and Medicine*, 125, 116–128. doi.org/10.1016/j.socscimed.2013.12.033

Pitkin Derose, K., & Varda, D.M. (2009). Social capital and health care access: a systematic review. *Medical Care Research and Review*, 66(3), 272–306. doi.org/10.1177/1077558708330428

Robins, G. (2015). *Doing Social Network Research: Network-based Research Design for Social Scientists*. Sage.

Robins, G., & Pattison, P. (2005). Interdependencies and social processes: dependence graphs and generalized dependence structures. In P.J. Carrington, J. Scott, & S. Wasserman (Eds.), *Models and Methods in Social Network Analysis* (pp. 192–214). Cambridge University Press.

Rogers, E.M. (2003). *Diffusion of Innovations* (5th ed.). Free Press.

Rolls, D.A., Daraganova, G., Sacks-Davis, R., Hellard, M., Jenkinson, R., McBryde, E., Pattison, P.E., & Robins, G.L. (2012). Modelling hepatitis C transmission over a social network of injecting drug users. *Journal of Theoretical Biology*, 297, 73–87. doi.org/10.1016/j.jtbi.2011.12.008

Sallis, J.F., Owen, N., & Fisher, E. (2015). Ecological models of health behavior. In K. Glanz, B.K. Rimer, & K. Viswanath (Eds.), *Health Behavior: Theory, Research, and Practice* (Vol. 5, pp. 43–64). Jossey-Bass.

Salvy, S.-J., de la Haye, K., Bowker, J.C., & Hermans, R.C.J. (2012). Influence of peers and friends on children's and adolescents' eating and activity behaviors. *Physiology and Behavior*, 106, 369–378. doi.org/10.1016/j.physbeh.2012.03.022

Saraswathi, S., Mukhopadhyay, A., Shah, H., & Ranganath, T.S. (2020). Social network analysis of Covid-19 transmission in Karnataka, India. *Epidemiology and Infection*, 148, e230. doi.org/10.1017/S095026882000223X

Schaefer, D.R., & Simpkins, S.D. (2014). Using social network analysis to clarify the role of obesity in selection of adolescent friends. *American Journal of Public Health*, 104(7), 1223–1229. doi.org/10.2105/ajph.2013.301768

Shearer, J.C., Dion, M., & Lavis, J.N. (2014). Exchanging and using research evidence in health policy networks: a statistical network analysis. *Implementation Science*, 9(1), 126. doi.org/10.1186/s13012-014-0126-8

Shoham, D.A., Hammond, R., Rahmandad, H., Wang, Y., & Hovmand, P. (2015). Modeling social norms and social influence in obesity. *Current Epidemiology Reports*, 2(1), 71–79. doi.org/10.1007/s40471-014-0032-2

Simpkins, S.D., Schaefer, D.R., Price, C.D., & Vest, A.E. (2013). Adolescent friendships, BMI, and physical activity: untangling selection and influence through longitudinal social network analysis. *Journal of Research on Adolescence*, 23(3), 537–549. doi.org/10.1111/j.1532-7795.2012.00836.x

Snijders, T., Steglich, C., & Schweinberger, M. (2017). Modeling the coevolution of networks and behavior. In K. van Montfort, J. Oud, & A. Satorra (Eds.), *Longitudinal Models in the Behavioral and Related Sciences* (pp. 41–71). Routledge.

Song, L., Son, J., & Lin, N. (2011). Social support. In J. Scott & P.J. Carrington (Eds.), *The Sage Handbook of Social Network Analysis* (pp. 116–128). SAGE.

Spencer-Bonilla, G., Ponce, O.J., Rodriguez-Gutierrez, R., Alvarez-Villalobos, N., Erwin, P. J., Larrea-Mantilla, L., Rogers, A., & Montori, V.M. (2017). A systematic review and meta-analysis of trials of social network interventions in type 2 diabetes. *BMJ Open*, 7(8), e016506. doi.org/10.1136/bmjopen-2017-016506

Strauss, R.S., & Pollack, H.A. (2003). Social marginalization of overweight children. *Archives of Pediatrics and Adolescent Medicine*, 157, 746–752. doi.org/10.1001/archpedi.157.8.746

Takada, S., Nyakato, V., Nishi, A., O'Malley, A.J., Kakuhikire, B., Perkins, J.M., Bangsberg, D.R., Christakis, N.A., & Tsai, A.C. (2019). The social network context of HIV stigma: population-based, sociocentric network study in rural Uganda. *Social Science and Medicine*, 233, 229–236. doi.org/10.1016/j.socscimed.2019.05.012

TRAILS (Tracking adolescents' individual lives survey) (2022). www.trails.nl/en/hoofdmenu/over-trails

Trogdon, J.G., Nonnemaker, J., & Pais, J. (2008). Peer effects in adolescent overweight. *Journal of Health Economics*, *27*, 1388–1399. doi.org/10.1016/j.jhealeco.2008.05.003

Turner, J.C. (1991). *Social Influence*. Thomson Brooks/Cole.

Uchino, B.N., Cacioppo, J.T., & Kiecolt-Glaser, J.K. (1996). The relationship between social support and physiological processes: a review with emphasis on underlying mechanisms and implications for health. *Psychological Bulletin*, *119*, 488–531. doi.org/10.1037/0033-2909.119.3.488

US Department of Health and Human Services (n.d.) *Healthy People 2030*. health.gov/healthypeople/objectives-and-data/social-determinants-health

Valente, T.W. (2005). Network models and methods for studying the diffusion of innovations. In P.J. Carrington, J. Scott, & S. Wasserman (Eds.), *Models and Methods in Social Network Analysis* (pp. 78–116). Cambridge University Press.

Valente, T.W. (2010). *Social Networks and Health. Models, Methods, and Applications*. Oxford University Press.

Valente, T.W. (2012). Network interventions. *Science*, *337*, 49–53. doi.org/10.1126/science.1217330

Valente, T.W., Chou, C.P., & Pentz, M.A. (2007). Community coalitions as a system: effects of network change on adoption of evidence-based substance abuse prevention. *American Journal of Public Health*, *97*(5), 880–886. doi.org/10.2105/AJPH.2005.063644

Valente, T.W., Fujimoto, K., Chou, C.-P., & Spruijt-Metz, D. (2009). Adolescent affiliations and adiposity: a social network analysis of friendships and obesity. *Journal of Adolescent Health*, *45*, 202–204. doi.org/10.1016/j.jadohealth.2009.01.007

Valente, T.W., & Pitts, S.R. (2017). An appraisal of social network theory and analysis as applied to public health: Challenges and opportunities. *Annual Revue of Public Health*, *38*, 103–118. doi.org/10.1146/annurev-publhealth-031816-044528

Valente, T.W., Pitts, S., Wipfli, H., & Vega Yon, G.G. (2019). Network influences on policy implementation: evidence from a global health treaty. *Social Science and Medicine*, *222*, 188–197. doi.org/10.1016/j.socscimed.2019.01.008

Valente, T.W., Unger, J.B., & Johnson, C.A. (2005). Do popular students smoke? The association between popularity and smoking among middle school students. *Journal of Adolescent Health*, *37*, 323–329.

Veenstra, R., Dijkstra, J.K., Steglich, C., & Van Zalk, M. (2013). Network-behavior dynamics. *Journal of Research on Adolescence*, *23*, 399–412. doi.org/10.1111/jora.12070

Veenstra, R., & Huitsing, G. (2021). Social network approaches to bullying and victimization. In P.K. Smith & J. O'Higgins Norman (Eds.), *The Wiley Blackwell Handbook of Bullying* (Vol. 1). Wiley.

Watts, D.J., & Strogatz, S.H. (1998). Collective dynamics of 'small-world' networks. *Nature*, *393*(6684), 440–442. doi.org/10.1038/30918

Webel, A.R., Okonsky, J., Trompeta, J., & Holzemer, W.L. (2010). A systematic review of the effectiveness of peer-based interventions on health-related behaviors in adults. *American Journal of Public Health*, *100*(2), 247–253. doi.org/10.2105/ajph.2008.149419

World Health Organization (WHO) (2022). *Social determinants of health*. www.who.int/health-topics/social-determinants-of-health#tab=tab_1

Zhang, J., & Centola, D. (2019). Social networks and health: new developments in diffusion, online and offline. *Annual Review of Sociology*, *45*(1), 91–109. doi.org/10.1146/annurev-soc-073117-041421

Zhang, S., de la Haye, K., Ji, M., & An, R. (2018). Applications of social network analysis to obesity: a systematic review. *Obesity Reviews*, *19*(7), 976–988. doi.org/10.1111/obr.12684

Political and Policy Networks

Mario Diani

This chapter views political networks as multimodal entities consisting of at least three fundamental elements. Of them, individuals and organisations have agentic capacities; the third one, events, does not have agency, yet events represent a fundamental component of the political process in their own right. Broadly conceived, 'events' include policy decisions as well as protest rallies or revolutionary episodes, but also instances of symbolic production. The first two sections are devoted to individual political actors, starting with citizens' networks and then moving to elite networks. The third section looks at different forms of political organising, differentiating in particular between coalitional dynamics between political organisations and the role of community networks in supporting political action. The fourth section is devoted to policy networks, followed by one addressing network approaches to political discourse. While it is important to recognise that all networks consist of structures of meaning, this section focuses in particular on some methodological approaches to the analysis of discourse. The chapter concludes with a brief assessment of possible future developments.

Keywords: polarisation; elite networks; network organisations; collective action; semantic networks; discourse analysis; diffusion; policy networks; coalitions; community networks.

POLITICAL AND POLICY NETWORKS

Mario Diani, University of Trento

Applications of network analytic tools to the study of politics have grown exponentially in the last decades. While in the 1990s it was still possible to attempt a synthesis of the literature within the boundaries of a single book (Knoke, 1990), this has now become more reasonably a matter for a handbook (see e.g. Victor et al., 2017a). It's certainly not a manageable task for a single chapter. Accordingly, my presentation of the field will be necessarily very partial. It will focus largely on works that have appeared since the early 2010s in the most prominent outlets. Even so, important lines of enquiry will be omitted or only partially covered (including research in my own field of contentious politics: on this, see Tindall, this volume).

The organising principles behind this chapter are quite simple. First, I refer to a classic view of politics as the complex of activities aiming at the selection of political personnel and the formulation and implementation of policy (see, e.g., Pizzorno, 1970). Second, I move from the recognition that 'Deciding what are (and are not) nodes and edges in a political network is the most fundamental theoretical action an analyst must take' (Patty & Penn, 2017, p. 148). More specifically, political networks can be regarded as multimodal entities consisting of at least three fundamental elements. Two of them, individuals and organisations, have agentic capacities; the third one, events, do not have agency, strictly speaking, yet they represent a fundamental component of the political process in their own right (see, e.g., Knoke et al., 2021). Here, events are broadly conceived, including policy decisions as well as protest rallies or revolutionary episodes, but also instances of symbolic production.

The presentation of materials in this chapter reflects this tripartite conceptualisation. Two sections are devoted to individual political actors, starting with citizens' networks and then moving to elite networks. The third section looks at different forms of political organising, differentiating in particular between coalitional dynamics between political organisations and the role of (broadly defined) community networks in supporting political action. The fourth section is devoted to policy networks, followed by one addressing network approaches to political discourse. While it is important to recognise that all networks consist of structures of meaning (Fuhse, 2022; Mische, 2011; White, 2008), this section focuses in particular on some methodological approaches to the analysis of discourse. The chapter concludes with a brief assessment of possible future developments.

INDIVIDUAL NETWORKS

Networks and Participation

Interpersonal networks have long been identified as a major factor shaping the formation of political opinions and patterns of participation among the citizenry (Knoke, 1990, Chapter 2). Recent research has expanded on earlier lines, as well as adding new perspectives to its agenda. 'Classic' themes certainly include the extent to which the structure of interpersonal networks may reinforce polarisation among citizens, or instead reduce it. Paradoxically, the demise of 20th century's major ideological narratives, coupled with growing individualism, seems to have reduced people's ability to debate potentially divisive issues. In particular, studies of the US public have found people with strong partisan views to be increasingly excluding from their discussion networks family and friends with diverging opinions, in contrast to people with weaker partisan allegiances (Bello & Rolfe, 2014); the implications for the democratic process, originating from people's tendency to selectively disclose their political attitudes, have also been discussed (Cowan & Baldassarri, 2018).

The recognition of growing differentiation in personal discussion networks has also prompted a reassessment of name generators – the tools conventionally used to identify the composition of personal networks (Cowan & Baldassarri, 2018; Eveland et al., 2018). Drawing upon different large-scale survey experiments, Sokhey and Djupe (2014) have taken into account, in order to create more specific political name generators, factors such as the variation in the role of people's alters, the characteristics of their ties and the specific *political* nature of *social* exchanges. Kmetty and Tardos (2022) have proposed a 'Party nexus position generator' in order to better test levels of homophily in ego networks, defined in terms of alters' partisan allegiances.

Unsurprisingly, exchanges on social media have attracted considerable attention. The role of social media platforms in polarising public opinion has been repeatedly analysed, particularly in reference to American politics (Bail, 2021; Benkler et al., 2018). Taking a comparative angle, an analysis of interactions on Twitter between followers of political parties in sixteen democratic countries suggests considerable variation in levels of polarisation, and highlights the difficulty of drawing generalisations about the polarising impact of social media from studies based on single countries. In particular, polarisation seems to be highest in two-party systems, lowest in multi-party systems with proportional voting. This is consistent with findings from a study of how the three US presidential debates of 2016 were live tweeted: even on Twitter, partisan identification strongly shaped exchanges (Zheng & Shahin, 2020). The recurring question of whether online relations reflect offline ones has also been addressed in the context of political networks. Using data collected in an experimental setting, Bisbee and Larson (2017) have found 'strong, robust similarity between online and offline relationships'.

Network structure also affects various forms of political participation. The role of networks as predictors of involvement in grassroots activism has consistently attracted scholarly interest (see Tindall, this volume). Some recent contributions on routinised forms of participation have translated into the electoral sphere questions addressed in reference to public opinion. An experiment conducted in the UK found heterogeneous households to be more receptive of campaign efforts from the outside than homogeneous households; accordingly, discussion rather than behavioural contagion might be the strongest driving force behind electoral participation (Foos & de Rooij, 2017). The amount of political competence in one's network has been found to be positively correlated not only with participation in elections but also with willingness to engage with different viewpoints (McClurg, 2006).

Diffusion Mechanisms

The exploration of personal networks, both online and offline, has identified two broad classes of mechanisms for the diffusion of ideas, motivations and practices. One has to do with the role of opinion leaders and influencers; the other, with the structural properties of specific communities. We are indebted to Damon Centola (2018) for a most comprehensive assessment of their interplay, drawing upon computational social science tools. Examining diffusion processes that refer to both political (in particular, policy and social movement diffusion) and non-political dynamics, Centola robustly qualifies the general assumption that weak ties and central roles in networks are the sole determinants of diffusion. He points at the decisive role of dense, reinforcement networks as important facilitators of individual decisions to adopt innovation.

Empirically, the same dynamics have often been explored jointly in the study of specific settings. A study of network ties within a local community in Australia (Alexander, 2015) showed the amount and breadth of political connections to be an important predictor of political involvement. However, involvement in community affairs does not necessarily depend on the diffusion of inputs from local leaders. Field experiments conducted in Northern Ghana suggest, for example, that the structure of local networks might reflect citizens' consolidated practices rather than mechanisms of social influence (Atwell & Nathan, 2021).

Studies conducted in non-Western settings have repeatedly cast doubts on the universal strength of the correlation between community integration and generation of public goods. A large-scale study of family networks in 15,000 villages of the Philippines suggests, for example, that the provision of public goods and levels of political competition is higher in communities with more fragmented social networks (Cruz et al., 2020). A number of field experiments on the word-of-mouth diffusion of information in Ugandan villages found that ethnic homogeneity and network density do not necessarily covariate in accounting for quicker information diffusion: face-to-face mechanisms of diffusion operated more effectively in settings that were ethnically homogeneous; however, network density was higher in heterogeneous communities (Larson & Lewis, 2017).

It is worth pointing out that central roles within communication networks are not restricted to 'formal' experts but can be taken up by a much broader set of people. Such roles are all the more important, the more communication processes are characterised by biased information and misleading messages. In such contexts, experiments have suggested that better-informed participants in discussion networks are both less subject to influence by biased sources and more able to sustain their claims over time (Huckfeldt et al., 2014). At the same time, it would be naive to see networks only as counterbalancing the negative effects of mass media communication; network structures may also hamper the diffusion of trustworthy messages and amplify media bias (Siegel, 2013). Care is also needed when exploring the relation between actors' traits, network position and perceived influence; for example, a study of Twitter exchanges on Brexit shows that network centrality does not necessarily correlate with self-perceptions of impact over a discussion network (Winter et al., 2021).

What Shapes Personal Political Networks?

While attention has focused on networks as independent variables, affecting patterns of individual political participation and their efficacy, attention has also been paid to the factors that account for their size and shape. In doing so, analysts have been driven by concerns similar to those behind the search for political name generators – that is, the need to recognise that not all alters are involved in the same ties, and that the connections conducive to political participation do not necessarily overlap with those that facilitate exchanges on private matters, or leisure-time activities. For example, surveys conducted in fifteen countries between 2012 and 2018 found most political networks to fall between three and six alters, with heavily skewed distributions both within and across countries (Eveland & Shen, 2021).

Other studies have looked at the relationship between network properties, political attitudes and class. Data from Sweden showed networks to have a strong class profile, with the interaction between class and networks shaping the structure of the political space: 'while we maintain that class differences in political attitudes are anchored in employment relations and the work situation, we argue that the class profile of personal networks calibrates political divides' (Lindh et al., 2021, p. 698).

ELITE NETWORKS

The centrality of elites in associational networks and the resulting disproportionate amount of social capital that they control is a well-documented fact. Comparative studies have also pointed at how cross-country variations in associational social capital are correlated to broader inequality structures in different societies (Pichler & Wallace, 2009). For example, a study of the connections between individuals and corporations involved in the 2008 financial crisis exposed 'an extensive array of ties among corporate executives, members of Congress, elite universities, banks, and other financial institutions', which in turn prompted an interpretation of the financial crisis through 'the lens of class inequality' (Perrucci, 2011).

The relationship between business and political elites has attracted special attention (see Carroll et al., this volume). While the dominant approach has been to focus on how business interests shape politics (see, e.g., Knoke & Kostiuchenko, 2017), attention has also been paid to how business networks are affected by politics. A historical *network analysis* of the relationship between firms and parties in the Hungarian economy (Stark & Vedres, 2012) showed director interlocks to be largely shaped by firms' affiliation with specific political camps. This was not a direct legacy of state socialism but rather of electoral competition. The influence of the state on elite networks seems more limited than one might expect even in heavily centralised systems like China. On the one hand, a study of the co-appearances of senior Chinese Community Party (CCP) officials at *political* events (Huhe et al., 2021) highlights the mechanisms behind the appointments of specific elite members to the leading small groups (LSGs) of the CCP Central Committee and the Central Government. On the other hand, however, direct government control over the elites, especially business elites, is far from complete. A study of interlocking memberships in newly established foundation boards (Ma & DeDeo, 2018) shows a complex picture. The widespread presence of government officials on the boards of nonprofit organisations is compensated by their limited role on the boards of the most powerful foundations. In the latter, business elite networks prevail. As a general conclusion, 'rather than a core–periphery structure centered around government officials, the Chinese nonprofit world appears to be a multipolar one of distinct elite groups, many of which achieve high levels of independence from direct government control' (Ma & DeDeo, 2018, p. 291).

Network studies have repeatedly highlighted the internal complexity and the significant variations in the role that different sections of the elites play in different specific settings. In Chile for example, pragmatic technocrats and academics without partisan identities seem to play a key role in presidential advisory committees, regardless of which coalition is ruling in an ideologically divided polity (Cisternas & Vásquez, 2018). Network analysis has also been applied to explore the role of technical bureaucrats in promoting international collaboration, making up for reduced commitment from states (Alcaniz, 2016). Exponential random graph models (henceforth, ERGM) illustrated patterns of transgovernmental collaboration across the three main regions of the Global South on nuclear energy, science and technology, and environmental protection issues.

A network perspective has also proved useful to assess elite transformation over time. Rather than reflecting stable configurations of power, elite composition may be at times subject to drastic structural variations. A systematic mapping of the Trump administration's networks showed, for instance, alongside some strong continuities, also significant differences in terms of *political* affiliations, ties to different sectors of the corporate elite and disconnection from previous policy planning circles (De Graaff & Van Apeldoorn, 2021; also see Van Apeldoorn & De Graaff, 2014). An analysis conducted from a *political* field theory perspective showed networks of Indian politicians in the 1970s to be deeply shaped by conflicting conceptions about the meaning of politics rather than by elite solidarity (Singh, 2016).

The role of elites in local and urban settings has long been a subject of investigation (see, e.g., Laumann & Pappi, 1976). Several network studies have addressed this issue paying special attention to patron–client relations. A study of neighbourhood councillors in the municipality of Naples, Italy, pointed at the importance of those relatively minor political figures as bridges between voters and influential political patrons. In this councillors took up a role that was previously played primarily by traditional political parties (Brancaccio, 2011). Another study of politicians at the district level, conducted in New York City, looked at contracts allocated by city council members to nonprofit organisations. Researchers differentiated between patronage dynamics, 'characterized by exclusive and long-lasting relationships between a council member and his/her local constituency and a partnership dynamic characterized by citywide relationships that are short-lived and fostered by organisational differentiation and embeddedness' (Marwell et al., 2020, p. 1561). Focusing on the link between voters and political parties, a study of the networks of 199 political brokers and 701 randomly sampled voters conducted in Mahamot, Philippines, in 2016 suggested that patrons adopted different monitoring strategies depending on the density of local social ties: 'where village social networks are dense, brokers prefer to target voters who have many ties in the network because their votes are easiest to monitor. Where networks are sparse, brokers target intrinsically reciprocal voters whose behavior they need not monitor' (Ravanilla et al., 2021, p. 795). The importance of centrality in non-political networks for local political brokerage has also been highlighted in studies of deprived urban communities in Argentina (Szwarcberg, 2012).

The degeneration of patronage roles into explicitly corrupt practices has also been repeatedly addressed with network analytic tools. A core–periphery exploration of political and business actors involved in 7,000 public construction tenders in Laval, Canada, between 1996 and 2013 pointed at the constant core position of firms suspected of bid-rigging activities (Reeves-Latour & Morselli, 2017). At the parliamentary level, network analysis showed that bribery in the 105th US Congress (2005–2006) was not the result of individual misdemeanour. They represented instead a particular version of corporate crime (Peoples & Sutton, 2015). Of course, analyses pointing at the damaging role of elites for democracy have not been restricted to corruptive practices. A study of political dynasties in the Philippines has illustrated the ability of family networks to circumvent legal and constitutional innovations designed to limit their political influence (Mendoza et al., 2020). Another study, drawing upon evidence about the 1991 coup in Haiti, has highlighted the role of elite networks in promoting the demise of democratically elected governments, testing a model according to which coups are a source of rents for elites (Naidu et al., 2021).

Significant attention has also been paid to the structure of public discourse and at the role of elites within public communication networks. A study of two of Canada's largest political Twitter communities (Dubois & Gaffney, 2014) found that different metrics identify different sets of influential players. In particular, standard centrality measures underlined the influence of members of 'the traditional political elite (media outlets, journalists, politicians) … whereas measures considering the quality of messages and interactions provide a different group of influencers, including political commentators and bloggers' (Dubois & Gaffney, 2014, p. 1260). Along similar lines, an analysis of Twitter exchanges on climate change and internet governance identified differences in framing between nongovernmental organisations and citizen media, on one side, and *political* actors and traditional media, on the other (Stier et al., 2018). Political elites are often at the core of discursive coalitions that form and re-form on the web. A study of the online social networks of Members of Parliament (MPs) and Members of the European Parliament (MEPs) in the United Kingdom between 2015 and 2016 has provided the context to test a new tool, *multiplex community affiliation clustering* (MCAC: Weaver et al., 2018, p. 201). While party affiliations have been found to drive most of those coalitions, both specific events and intra-party tensions seemed to undermine the solidity of partisan cleavages.

Overall, analyses of online communication at different levels have questioned its capacity to bridge partisan divides. An analysis of online interactions between mayors of the 100 largest US cities suggested tie formation is driven by political marketing considerations rather than genuine attempts to exchange best practices (Wukich, 2022). An exploratory analysis of the network ties of elite, moderate blogs in relation to and in comparison with elite, partisan blogs in the US in 2007 suggested that:

weak-tie connections enabled moderate blogs to bridge all ideological blog networks more comprehensibly and expansively than partisan blog networks. Unfortunately, the bridging effect of weak-tie connections provided less internal and external cohesion within the moderate blog network when compared to both partisan blog networks. Moderate blogs had low intragroup (within group) and intergroup (between group) cohesion: moderate blogs not only linked less internally but received fewer, reciprocal linkages from partisan blog networks.

(Meraz, 2013, p. 191)

MODES OF COORDINATION AND ORGANISING

Shifts in patterns of organising within collective action fields have attracted considerable attention.

Claims about a diminishing role for formal organisations in favour of looser forms of coordination, made possible by new communication technology (Bennett & Segerberg, 2013), have been complemented by analyses emphasising the multiplicity of 'modes of coordination' operating within any collective action field (Diani, 2015). Network analytic tools have contributed to two main, partially intersecting, lines of research, one focusing on the structure of informal 'political communities' (Knoke et al., 2021), the other on the mechanisms behind interorganisational networks in broad coalitions (Byrd & Jasny, 2010; Simpson, 2015).

Among the former, activist communities have attracted considerable attention, especially in reference to the role of computer mediated communication (CMC; see Earl & Kimport, 2011; Tufecki, 2017). The spread of CMC has significantly contributed to the consolidation and resilience of activist networks in repressive regimes. Apart from the already mentioned case of the Middle East and North Africa (MENA) regimes, studies have highlighted the contribution of micro-blogging services to the spread of issue networks in China (Huang & Sun, 2014) or the role of ideological differences in shaping the Cuban oppositional blogosphere and rendering it distant not only from the regime-controlled but also the US-controlled media sources (Vicari, 2015, p. 201).

CMC has also played a key role in facilitating the spread of radical movements that might have a limited access to the polity and to established media because of their extreme positions. The bulk of research has been devoted to right-wing, racist networks. A comparative analysis of Facebook pages of extreme right parties and organisations in several Western European countries shows political opportunities to affect, although not determine, different network structures and the positions occupied within them by political parties (Klein & Muis, 2019). Facebook pages (in particular, pages devoted to anti-shelter initiatives) have also been used to map the structures of anti-immigrant mobilisations in Germany (Hoffmann, 2020). Results suggest different 'modes of coordination' (Diani, 2015) to characterise networks in different regions of the country. Finally, Twitter exchanges between far-right individuals across France, Germany, Italy and the UK have provided the data to map connections between far-right organisations (Froio & Ganesh, 2019). Even in such a case, however, evidence has pointed at the persisting relevance of national borders and of parties over movement organisations in the construction of extremist discourse, and at the limited role of social media in creating transnational spaces.

The contribution of CMC to the integration and coordination of otherwise disconnected sectors of public opinion has also been repeatedly highlighted for 'progressive' movements, especially in reference to the 2011 events that included the Occupy and Indignados campaigns as well as the 2011 revolts in Egypt and Tunisia (González-Bailón & Wang, 2016; Lotan et al., 2011). Increasingly, attention has turned to the specific structural properties of protest communities. Based on a *network analysis* of nearly 2.4 million tweets and a *content analysis* of a subset of 5,126 of those tweets, Ogan and Varol (2017) explored the structure of the protest community that mobilised around the Gezi park conflict in Turkey in 2013. They differentiated between leadership roles and information exchanges and identified, in reference to the structure of the communication networks, sectors of public with similar behaviours.

Fragmentation was a distinct property of the 2011 movements. Looking at possible overlaps of the communities behind Twitter exchanges on Occupy and Indignados suggested that networks of exchanges between activists, sympathisers and concerned publics persisted to be heavily fragmented, and that brokerage roles were the preserve of a minority (González-Bailón & Wang, 2016). The role of brokers as linkages between different, and sometimes distant, sectors of the population has often been explored in terms of the combination of online and offline networks. In her exploration of the 2011 Egyptian revolution, Deena Abul-Fottouh (2018; Abul-Fottouh & Fetner, 2018) has shown social movement coalition theories to perform similarly well to account for brokerage in both online and offline activism. In a different context, an analysis of Twitter exchanges on the occasion of the '#not1more' protest campaign against immigrant deportations in the United States has pointed at the important presence of clusters of committed organisers located in specific cities (van Haperen et al., 2018). A crucial theoretical issue for the analysis of online communities has been the identification of the network topologies that are most conducive to their activation – namely, to the convergence of individualised acts such as tweeting a message or endorsing a call for action into some kind of coordinated action. A comparison of different topological models challenges the presumed efficiency of centralised network structures (Piedrahita et al., 2018).

At the same time, SNA has kept contributing to the analysis of offline relational structures. Some studies of radical collective action have found structural patterns to be shaped by environmental conditions. For example, an investigation of a banned Islamist network in the UK suggested that its structure changed from a fairly centralised one to 'a more decentralized "small-world-like" network featuring clusters of local activists connected through multiple bridges ... as its environment became increasingly hostile' (Kenney et al., 2017, p. 2208). Conversely, an exploration of an extreme right terrorist organisation in Turkey showed its core–periphery structure, usually deemed unsuitable for a *dark network*, proved sustainable in light of the significant tolerance with which authorities looked at that organisation (Demiroz & Kapucu, 2012). Strong embeddedness of activist networks in non-political, daily-life social networks has actually been found to play an important role in supporting Palestinian resistance organisations in a hostile environment like Lebanon in the 1980s (Parkinson, 2013). Of course, the combination of online and offline networks, as well as of political and non-political ones, has not been limited to radical forms of politics. Other explorations have looked at network multiplexity to account for the interdependence of cultural and political networks – for example, in the case of artistic collectives in European cities (Basov, 2020; Basov et al., 2021; Basov & Kholodova, 2021).

While the mobilising role of informal communities has been increasingly emphasised, a massive amount of collective action is still coordinated through sustained coalition work between a multiplicity of organisations. The mechanisms behind interorganisational networks have attracted considerable attention. Some reflect organisational properties, such as the number of resources available to organisations, their membership and staff size, the degree of formalisation, etc. (Box-Steffensmeier et al., 2018; Diani, 2015). Others relate to ideological differences between prospective allies, that may render sustained cooperation difficult to achieve (see, e.g., Kanellopoulos et al., 2016, in reference to the Greek anti-austerity campaigns). Differences about strategic and ideological preferences may affect the tightness of coalitions as well as their ultimate chances of survival (Taraktaş, 2022). Finally, we should not discard the role of CMC in facilitating alliances and social movement emergence on a large territorial scale. For example, an analysis of hyperlinks between social form websites illustrates the mechanisms of identity building in the global social justice movement (also see Ackland & O'Neil, 2011; Vicari, 2014).

Whether we are referring to informal networks of advocacy organisations or to more established policy networks, the activation of alliances reflects the combined influence of previous social relations and homophily mechanisms (Diani, 2015, Chapter 3; Leifeld & Schneider, 2012). At the same time, the impact of different organisational properties and orientations on the structure of alliance networks is heavily dependent on shifts in political opportunities. The persistent salience of dominant cleavages and the degrees of openness of political opportunities have been found to significantly affect alliance patterns in collective action fields. Examples include networks of environmental groups in Italy and Northern Ireland (Cinalli, 2003; Diani, 1995), of voluntary charitable organisations in Italy and Poland (Bassoli & Theiss, 2014) and of ethnic groups in France and Switzerland (Eggert, 2014), as well as broader sectors of civic organisations in British cities (Diani, 2015).

Coalition building is particularly problematic in authoritarian regimes. Analyses of the Egyptian uprising of 2011 have pointed at the role of strong networks connecting members of the opposition in Cairo as crucial factors in mobilising new generations of actors and facilitating the coordination of multiple actors in joint campaigns (Wackenhut, 2020). In contexts when authority is not crumbling, like contemporary China, civic associations that manage to combine some degree of autonomy with relatively strong vertical linkages with authorities (e.g., seniors' associations) seem to be best equipped to mediate between the state and aggrieved citizens. Such hybrid relational models enable organisations to engage in both cooperation and contention (Lu & Tao, 2017).

Despite the tendency to neatly differentiate social movement organisations from established members of the polity such as interest groups or parties, coalition networks routinely include both. Blockmodelling and centrality analysis have been applied to the exploration of those networks in a number of contexts, using different data sources. Each has strong and weak points. Newspaper reports allow for the exploration of network evolution, although the identification of less conspicuous actors is difficult. For example, accounts of 1797 protest campaigns in Mexico between 1964 and 2000 highlighted the growing role of some actors – especially single-issue NGOs – alongside the persistence of others (Wada, 2014). While unlikely to provide a diachronic perspective, fieldwork involving systematic mapping of civic organisations may help analysts to capture the role of less conspicuous yet active grassroots groups that make up the fabric of civil society in specific local settings – see, for example, explorations of civic networks in the UK and South Africa (Diani, 2015; Diani et al., 2018). Individual-level data from cross-sectional surveys, used from a two-mode perspective, may also prove useful. Although they cannot provide insights on the position of specific organisations, they may contribute to the exploration of flows of ties between organisational types. For example, comparative research on the connections between unions, other organisations of the 'formal institutional sphere', such as parties and professional associations, and the organisations of the 'informal civil sphere' has shown the configuration of those networks to matter for the defence of welfare rights (also see Knoke et al., 2021, Chapter 5; Lee, 2016).

POLICY NETWORKS

The study of policy networks has stimulated a number of methodological explorations, the implications of which may be extended to other substantive applications of SNA. Most efforts have focused on different strategies for the statistical modelling of networks. Robins et al. (2012) have compared quadratic assignment procedure (QAP), ERGM and stochastic actor-oriented models (SAOMs), focusing in particular on ERGMs. While their discussion has largely been conceptual, other studies have drawn upon specific datasets to illustrate pros and cons of different approaches. For example, an exploration of data from a climate change policy network (Ingold & Fischer, 2014) has been used to compare different approaches to network modelling – QAP, ERGMs and latent space network models (Cranmer et al., 2017). The relative weight assigned by different researchers to the modelling of dependencies or to assessing the impact of covariates has been identified as a key factor behind choosing ERGMs over alternative models.

Moving to substantive issues, parliamentary policy making has attracted considerable attention, particularly in reference to the US Congress. Two-mode data, mostly in the form of co-sponsorship of bills, have provided the evidence to explore several substantive dynamics. Looking at the period between 1973 and 2016, Neal (2020) found polarisation to have increased over time, along party affiliation lines, in both its weak version (corresponding to absence of ties between competing coalitions) and strong version (corresponding to negative ties). Partisan identity was also found to be a stronger source of homophily than gender or other sources of identity in the relations between Congress representatives (Neal et al., 2022). A longitudinal perspective, if in reference to a shorter time span (2013–2015), has also been used to investigate mechanisms of reciprocity in the joint presentation of bills (Brandenberger, 2018).

Ties developed through legislative collaborations have been analysed as either dependent or independent variables. One example of the former has looked at five congressional terms to explore the determinants of legislative effectiveness. Legislators' social connections, in particular alumni connections, have been identified as an important predictor alongside more political variables such as congressional seniority or legislative leadership (Battaglini et al., 2020). As for the latter, legislative collaboration has been treated as one of the determinants of other forms of political activity, such as representatives' joint promotion of press events (Desmarais et al., 2015b) or collaboration in election campaigns (Box-Steffensmeier et al., 2020), alongside partisan affiliation. Co-sponsorship of bills has also been used to explore the internal structure of major political parties. Using data from the lower chamber of the Italian Parliament from 1972–1977, and viewing parties as 'organised networks of formal and informal relationships', Parigi and Sartori (2014) looked at both the Christian Democrat and the Communist party structures. They differentiated in particular between strong (repeated co-sponsorships) and weak (one-off initiatives) ties to explore the impact of major cleavages on MPs' relational patterns.

Mechanisms of policy diffusion have long been analysed from a network perspective. A diffusion network of 187 policies across US states from 1960–2009 was constructed, driven by the assumption that some states adopting certain policies would encourage other states to adopt them (Desmarais et al., 2015a). Data were analysed with a specific algorithm, NetInf, and the resulting estimates were then validated in reference to media sources. The analysis identified capacity, political homophily and geographic proximity as major drivers of policy adoption. Another study explored the impact of digital communication over the diffusion of democracy across 189 countries between 2000 and 2010 (Rhue & Sundararajan, 2014). Data on digital access in different countries were combined with data on geographic, migration and trade networks to estimate the probability of the adoption of democratic practices. A stochastic actor-oriented model suggested that 'mobile technologies have a unique and persistent impact on the emergence and increase in civil liberties' (Rhue & Sundararajan, 2014, p. 51). Network tools have also driven research on the diffusion of specific health measures. For example, a project identified a network of 238 organisations and individuals involved in the promotion of misoprostol, a specific drug for postpartum haemorrhage promoted by the World Health Organization (WHO). Findings suggested 'strong interdependency between the funding bodies, civil society organisations, researchers and clinician organisations' (Millard et al., 2015, p. 190).

Policy networks have proved to be key domains in which to explore dynamics of political power. ERGMs have often been applied to explore power dynamics in relation to the constitution of such networks, and the reproduction of power inequalities within them. An exploration of networks explicitly designed from a participatory perspective in Ghana, Senegal and Uganda showed that they were dominated by donor and research organisations, to the detriment of farm interests and civil society groups. This was the result of organisations' reputation or social networking activities (Henning et al., 2019). ERGMs were also applied to ten *political* decision-making processes in Switzerland in order to identify the mechanisms – intended and unintended – behind reputational power (Fischer & Sciarini, 2015). The analysis pointed at the embeddedness of actors in the same collaboration networks as a significant factor distorting perceptions of other actors as powerful. Studies of policy influence should not just pay attention to policy entrepreneurs' leadership skills and the amounts of social capital that they are able to mobilise. A review of available literature on British road policy since the 1980s also pointed at the possibility that once influential individuals retain their ability to affect the policy process through playing advisory roles. This in turn might help to explain relative continuity in a policy network over time (Witting & Dudley, 2020). Christopoulos also explored political entrepreneurs' positions in a number of different policy domains. He developed a model of exceptional agency that takes into account structural constraints alongside agents' attributes. He also expanded this approach to include multimodal data (Christopoulos, 2006; Christopoulos & Ingold, 2015; Knoke et al., 2021, Chapter 3).

DISCOURSE NETWORKS

The analysis of the cultural elements of politics (discourses, beliefs, value systems, representations) has hugely benefited from the growing application of SNA tools. They have enabled analysts to trace the connections between ideas, concepts, symbols and thus to identify the structure of the rhetorical forms through which political positions are communicated and ultimately legitimated. One general strength of network analyses of political culture lies in their dynamic, temporal structure. Because of their reliance on documentary sources (at least in most cases), whether of the printed or digital form, the evolution of arguments and positions can be traced over time. So can the networks of political actors who share certain rhetorical forms at specific points in time.

The two-mode tends to be the dominant network format in these analyses. It usually connects sources of a message (individuals, political organisations, media) with specific symbols, cultural elements, or utterances. Different approaches have been devised to this purpose. Some have looked at the structure of more stable and less contingent cultural elements, such as belief systems. Others have focused on the structure of discourses about specific issues or events.

Some scholars have relied primarily on standard survey data, in which modes consisted of individuals and their responses to batteries of items, to map belief systems. Some have used White's entailment theory (White, Burton, & Brudner, 1977) to explore connections of beliefs among climate change protestors (Jasny & Fisher, 2022). Others have applied relational class analysis (Goldberg, 2011) to twenty waves of ANES-American National Election Studies between 1984 and 2004 has shown 'networks of interconnected political beliefs' within the American public to be largely differentiated across different social groups (Baldassarri & Goldberg, 2014).

In their own version of *belief network analysis*, Boutyline and Vaisey (2017) have calculated network metrics such as shortest-path betweenness and centralisation for data from the 2000 wave of American National Election Studies (ANES). They have also broken the analysis down into 44 subpopulations to explore for variation of belief structures across different social groups, reaching a different conclusion. In another study, waves 1 and 10 of the 2008–2009 ANES Panel Study have been used to explore how time shapes the structure of belief networks for different populations (Fishman & Davis, 2021). Apart from finding variable support for the hypothesis that belief structures are linked to political knowledge, they have failed to find correlations between centrality scores of specific beliefs and their relevance for other beliefs. Along similar lines, DellaPosta (2020) has looked at 44 years of the US General Social Survey (GSS) to document the rising polarisation of belief systems among the US public. He has shown polarisation to stem not only from the radicalisation of explicitly political beliefs, but from the crystallisation of specific combinations of different styles of social and cultural behaviour into non-communicating subsectors of the population.

The use of diachronic data partially addresses one of the major criticisms raised at survey data, namely, their inability to account for time variations in the structure of networks of cultural elements and their adopters. To that purpose, approaches based on the analysis of available documents seem more powerful. One example along these lines is *discourse network analysis*. Leifeld (2017) has developed an integrated approach to the exploration of discourse networks that looks at both 'the configuration of actors and the structure of the contents of a debate' (Leifeld, 2017, p. 304), focusing on three levels: 'coalition formation (clustering at the actor level), framing (clustering at the level of concepts), and issue attention cycles (temporal clustering of statements)' (Leifeld, 2017, p. 304).

Leifeld's tool (www.philipleifeld.com/software/software.html) has proved fruitful to the exploration of several policy debates and conflicts. Focusing on media sources, some have looked at discursive coalitions around conflicts such as software patents and intellectual property rights (Haunss, 2013) or environmentally damaging urban projects (Nagel & Satoh, 2019); others have looked at the role of policy actors and moral justifications in debates on climate change in different national contexts (Kukkonen et al., 2021; Wagner & Payne, 2017). Minutes of parliamentary debates have also proved major sources of data. For example, policy debates on agri-food technologies in the European Parliament have been reconstructed to explore the relative weight of emotional and science-based arguments (Vogeler et al., 2021).

ANTMN (acronym for *analysis of topic model networks*) provides another approach to discourse network analysis (Walter & Ophir, 2019). It consists of three steps. First, it identifies frame elements using topic modelling. Second, it identifies a network structure, in which topics are nodes connected by valued edges, representing the strength of the association between topics given their co-occurrence over documents. Third, it relies on community detection techniques to cluster together these topics into coherent frames. Applications of this approach have included coverage of candidates in Senate races, of foreign nations and of epidemics (Walter & Ophir, 2019) as well as the symbolic role of peripheral territories in international disputes such as that between the US and North Korea (Fabregat & Kperogi, 2021).

Network analytic techniques have also proved useful for the analysis of cultural elements within specific populations, and for the identification of their internal complexity. In particular, they have challenged the idea that traits of political culture are relatively stable (or have to be in order to work). This has been done in reference to both conventional and contentious politics. For example, statements by parties in the media during electoral campaigns in the Netherlands have been analysed using concepts like structural balance and transitivity in order to capture variation in the two-mode network of issue positions and parties (Kleinnijenhuis & de Nooy, 2013).

Moving to contentious politics, and also drawing upon data from press sources, Ghaziani & Baldassarri (2011) have built networks of themes around the organisation of four LGBT marches in the US. They have used measures of topic eigenvector centrality and brokerage to show (a) how themes evolved over time and (b) how a set of ideas that remained fixed in the conversation played the role of 'cultural anchors' in enabling different actors to stick together and share some coherent worldview without renouncing their differences. With a pronounced historical perspective, Nelson (2021) has combined SNA and computational text analysis to examine women's movement discourse in the 19th and 20th century in New York and Chicago. She has highlighted the role of broader local political cultures in securing the continuity of different feminist discourses in the two cities over time.

CONCLUSIONS

It is difficult to identify common trends and lines of development, given the vastity of the topic. Generally speaking, one can share a recent assessment of the field that pointed at six challenges: tackling the issue of endogeneity; dealing with missing data and sampling issues; understanding how to use big data; paying more attention to network evolution over time; strengthening the link between network analysis and social scientific theorising on political processes; developing the analysis of multiplex networks (Victor et al., 2017b, pp. 24–27). Some of these challenges, while crucial, do not seem to be distinctive to the political networks field: in particular, how to deal with the possibility that unobservable factors influence both network formation and the outcomes of social action, or how to treat missing data, represent problems shared across the SNA research community (see, e.g., Battaglini et al., 2022; Cheng & Lee, 2017; Huisman, 2014). As for the persistent need to link more strongly SNA and theorising of politics, it is certainly promising that some of the most sophisticated recent attempts to theorise social networks have come from scholars with a strong substantive interest in political processes (see, e.g., Crossley, 2011; Fuhse, 2022; also see Kitts et al., this volume). Efforts have also been made by political sociologists not specialising in social networks to adapt network concepts to established political theories, such as in the field of power (see, e.g., Janoski & Jonas, 2021).

Among these challenges, looking not only at multiplex but also at multimodal networks seems particularly relevant. There are several reasons behind the growing attention paid to multimodal data. They offer a more nuanced understanding of the political process, as connections are not only between actors but between events, speeches, symbols. They also enable us to gather more data through unobtrusive measures, and especially data on diachronic processes. On this ground there is substantial progress to be made. Most of the contributions introduced in this chapter actually refer to one-mode or two-mode networks. However, it is also possible to think of three-mode or multimode networks in which different elements combine in more complex patterns. Following some pathbreaking attempts (e.g., Fararo & Doreian, 1984; Melamed et al., 2013), efforts have been made to expand analyses of the political process that account for the interdependence of individuals, organisations and events. Some works have illustrated substantive applications of basic methods (e.g. Knoke et al. 2021), others have focused on the development of sophisticated methodological tools (Dickison et al., 2016; Lazega & Snijders, 2016; see also Jasny, this volume; Lazega & Wang, this volume).

Finally, while the increase in the use of big data in political analysis appears inevitable (Lazer & Wojcik, 2017; Robles-Morales & Córdoba-Hernández, 2019), attention to the quality of data should not be restricted to that sphere. The use of data triangulation in the network analysis of politics should indeed receive more attention. While quantitative tools are essential to identify basic patterns between increasingly high numbers of actors, a sound interpretation of those patterns needs to massively draw upon qualitative data (e.g., from field work) as well as institutional data (Alcaniz, 2016; Diani, 2015; Haunss, 2013; also see Hollstein, this volume).

REFERENCES

Abul-Fottouh, D. (2018). Brokerage roles and strategic positions in Twitter networks of the 2011 Egyptian revolution. *Policy and Internet*, *10*(2), 218–240. doi.org/10.1002/poi3.169

Abul-Fottouh, D., & Fetner, T. (2018). Solidarity or schism: ideological congruence and the Twitter networks of Egyptian activists. *Mobilization: An International Quarterly*, *23*(1), 23–44. doi.org/10.17813/1086-671X-23-1-23

Ackland, R., & O'Neil, M. (2011). Online collective identity: the case of the environmental movement. *Social Networks*, *33*(3), 177–190. doi.org/10.1016/j.socnet.2011.03.001

Alcaniz, I. (2016). *Environmental and nuclear networks in the Global South: how skills shape international cooperation*. Cambridge University Press.

Alexander, D. (2015). It's not what you know it's who you know: political connectedness and political engagement at the local level. *Journal of Sociology*, *51*(4), 827–842. doi.org/10.1177/1440783312474082

Atwell, P., & Nathan, N. L. (2021). Channels for influence or maps of behavior? A field experiment on social networks and cooperation. *American Journal of Political Science*, *66*(3), 696–713. doi.org/10.1111/ajps.12586

Bail, C. (2021). *Breaking the social media prism: how to make our platforms less polarizing*. Princeton University Press. doi.org/10.1515/9780691216508

Baldassarri, D., & Goldberg, A. (2014). Neither ideologues nor agnostics: alternative voters' belief system in an age of partisan politics. *American Journal of Sociology*, *120*(1), 45–95. doi.org/10.1086/676042

Basov, N. (2020). The ambivalence of cultural homophily: field positions, semantic similarities, and social network ties in creative collectives. *Poetics*, *78*, 101353. doi.org/10.1016/j.poetic.2019.02.004

Basov, N., de Nooy, W., & Nenko, A. (2021). Local meaning structures: mixed-method sociosemantic network analysis. *American Journal of Cultural Sociology*, *9*(3), 376–417. doi.org/10.1057/s41290-019-00084-9

Basov, N., & Kholodova, D. (2021). Networks of context: three-layer socio-cultural mapping for a Verstehende network analysis. *Social Networks*, *69*, 84–101. doi.org/10.1016/j.socnet.2021.03.003

Bassoli, M., & Theiss, M. (2014). Inheriting divisions? The role of Catholic and leftist affiliation in local cooperation networks: the case of Italy and Poland. In S. Baglioni & M.G. Giugni (Eds.), *Civil society organizations, unemployment, and precarity in Europe* (pp. 175–203). Palgrave.

Battaglini, M., Patacchini, E., & Rainone, E. (2022). Endogenous social interactions with unobserved networks. *The Review of Economic Studies*, *89*(4), 1694–1747. doi.org/10.1093/restud/rdab058

Battaglini, M., Sciabolazza, V.L., & Patacchini, E. (2020). Effectiveness of connected legislators. *American Journal of Political Science*, *64*(4), 739–756. doi.org/10.1111/ajps.12518

Bello, J., & Rolfe, M. (2014). Is influence mightier than selection? Forging agreement in political discussion networks during a campaign. *Social Networks*, *36*, 134–146. doi.org/10.1016/j.socnet.2013.06.001

Benkler, Y., Faris, R., & Roberts, H. (2018). *Network propaganda: manipulation, disinformation, and radicalization in American politics*. Oxford University Press.

Bennett, L., & Segerberg, A. (2013). *The logic of connective action*. Cambridge University Press.

Bisbee, J., & Larson, J. M. (2017). Testing social science network theories with online network data: an evaluation of external validity. *American Political Science Review*, *111*(3), 502–521. doi.org/10.1017/S0003055417000120

Boutyline, A., & Vaisey, S. (2017). Belief network analysis: a relational approach to understanding the structure of attitudes. *American Journal of Sociology*, *122*(5), 1371–1447.

Box-Steffensmeier, J.M., Campbell, B.W., Christenson, D.P., & Navabi, Z. (2018). Role analysis using the ego-ERGM: a look at environmental interest group coalitions. *Social Networks*, *52*, 213–227. doi.org/10.1016/j.socnet.2017.08.004

Box-Steffensmeier, J.M., Campbell, B.W., Podob, A.W., & Walker, S.J. (2020). I get by with a little help from my friends: leveraging campaign resources to maximize congressional power. *American Journal of Political Science*, *64*(4), 1017–1033. doi.org/10.1111/ajps.12528

Brancaccio, L. (2011). Among leaders and territories: the political networks of the district councillors in Naples. *Quality and Quantity*, *45*(5), 1127. doi.org/10.1007/s11135-011-9495-0

Brandenberger, L. (2018). Trading favors: examining the temporal dynamics of reciprocity in congressional collaborations using relational event models. *Social Networks*, *54*, 238–253. doi.org/10.1016/j.socnet.2018.02.001

Byrd, S.C., and Jasny, L. (2010. Transnational Movement Innovation and Collaboration: Analysis of World Social Forum Networks. *Social Movement Studies*, 9, 355–72. https://doi.org/10.1080/14742837.2010.522305.

Centola, D. (2018). *How behavior spreads: the science of complex contagions*. Princeton University Press.

Cheng, W., & Lee, L. (2017). Testing endogeneity of spatial and social networks. *Regional Science and Urban Economics*, *64*, 81–97. doi.org/10.1016/j.regsciurbeco.2017.03.005

Christopoulos, D. (2006). Relational attributes of political entrepreneurs: a network perspective. *Journal of European Public Policy*, *13*(5), 757–778. doi.org/10.1080/13501760600808964

Christopoulos, D., & Ingold, K. (2015). Exceptional or just well connected? Political entrepreneurs and brokers in policy making. *European Political Science Review*, *7*(3), 475–498. doi.org/10.1017/S1755773914000277

Cinalli, M. (2003). Socio-politically polarized contexts, urban mobilization and the environmental movement: a comparative study of two campaigns of protest in Northern Ireland. *International Journal of Urban and Regional Research*, *27*(1), 158–177.

Cisternas, C., & Vásquez, J. (2018). Comisiones Asesoras Presidenciales en Chile: Entre la expertise y la pluralidad de actores sociales [Presidential Advisory Boards in Chile: between expertise and the plurality of social actors]. *European Review of Latin American and Caribbean Studies*, *106*, 1–22. doi.org/10.32992/erlacs.10349

Cowan, S.K., & Baldassarri, D. (2018). 'It could turn ugly': Selective disclosure of attitudes in political discussion networks. *Social Networks*, *52*, 1–17. doi.org/10.1016/j.socnet.2017.04.002

Cranmer, S.J., Leifeld, P., McClurg, S.D., & Rolfe, M. (2017). Navigating the range of statistical tools for inferential network analysis. *American Journal of Political Science*, *61*(1), 237–251. doi.org/10.1111/ajps.12263

Crossley, N. (2011). *Towards relational sociology*. Routledge.

Cruz, C., Labonne, J., & Querubín: (2020). Social network structures and the politics of public goods provision: evidence from the Philippines. *American Political Science Review*, *114*(2), 486–501. doi.org/10.1017/S0003055419000789

De Graaff, N., & Van Apeldoorn, B. (2021). The transnationalist US foreign-policy elite in exile? A comparative network analysis of the Trump administration. *Global Networks*, *21*(2), 238–264. doi.org/10.1111/glob.12265

DellaPosta, D. (2020). Pluralistic collapse: the 'oil spill' model of mass opinion polarization. *American Sociological Review*, *85*(3), 507–536. doi.org/10.1177/0003122420922989

Demiroz, F., & Kapucu, N. (2012). Anatomy of a dark network: the case of the Turkish Ergenekon terrorist organization. *Trends in Organized Crime*, *15*(4), 271–295. doi.org/10.1007/s12117-012-9151-7

Desmarais, B.A., Harden, J.J., & Boehmke, F.J. (2015a). Persistent policy pathways: inferring diffusion networks in the American states. *American Political Science Review*, *109*(2), 392–406. doi.org/10.1017/S0003055415000040

Desmarais, B.A., Moscardelli, V.G., Schaffner, B.F., & Kowal, M.S. (2015b). Measuring legislative collaboration: the Senate press events network. *Social Networks*, *40*, 43–54. doi.org/10.1016/j.socnet.2014.07.006

Diani, M. (1995). *Green networks: a structural analysis of the Italian environmental movement*. Edinburgh University Press.

Diani, M. (2015). *The cement of civil society: studying networks in localities*. Cambridge University Press.

Diani, M., Ernstson, H., & Jasny, L. (2018). 'Right to the city' and the structure of civic organizational fields: evidence from Cape Town. *Voluntas*, *29*, 637–652.

Dickison, M.E., Magnani, M., & Rossi, L. (2016). *Multilayer social networks*. Cambridge University Press.

www-cambridge-org.ezp.biblio.unitn.it/core/books/multilayer-social-networks/39383306D9843313057CECEBF7B9BF26

Dubois, E., & Gaffney, D. (2014). The multiple facets of influence: identifying political influentials and opinion leaders on Twitter. *American Behavioral Scientist*, 58(10), 1260–1277. doi.org/10.1177/0002764214527088

Earl, J., & Kimport, K. (2011). *Digitally enabled social change activism in the internet age*. MIT Press.

Eggert, N. (2014). The impact of political opportunities on interorganizational networks: a comparison of migrants' organizational fields. *Mobilization: An International Quarterly*, 19(4), 369–386. doi.org/10.17813/maiq.19.4.d5p65x6563778xv6

Eveland, W.P., Appiah, O., & Beck: A. (2018). Americans are more exposed to difference than we think: capturing hidden exposure to political and racial difference. *Social Networks*, 52, 192–200. doi.org/10.1016/j.socnet.2017.08.002

Eveland, W.P., & Shen, F. (2021). Cross-national variation in political network size, distribution, and prediction. *Social Networks*, 66, 100–113. doi.org/10.1016/j.socnet.2021.01.003

Fabregat, E., & Kperogi, F.A. (2021). The 'other' in the bowels of the hegemon: US media portrayals of Guam during the United States–North Korea tension. *International Journal of Media & Cultural Politics*, 17(2), 119–137. doi.org/10.1386/macp_00043_1

Fararo, T.J., & Doreian, P. (1984). Tripartite structural analysis: generalizing the Breiger-Wilson formalism. *Social Networks*, 6, 141–175.

Fischer, M., & Sciarini, P. (2015). Unpacking reputational power: intended and unintended determinants of the assessment of actors' power. *Social Networks*, 42, 60–71. doi.org/10.1016/j.socnet.2015.02.008

Fishman, N., & Davis, N.T. (2021). Change we can believe in: structural and content dynamics within belief networks. *American Journal of Political Science*, n/a(n/a). doi.org/10.1111/ajps.12626

Foos, F., & de Rooij, E. A. (2017). All in the family: partisan disagreement and electoral mobilization in intimate networks: a spillover experiment. *American Journal of Political Science*, 61(2), 289–304. doi.org/10.1111/ajps.12270

Froio, C., & Ganesh, B. (2019). The transnationalisation of far right discourse on Twitter: issues and actors that cross borders in Western European democracies. *European Societies*, 21(4), 513–539. doi.org/10.1080/14616696.2018.1494295

Fuhse, J. (2022). *Social networks of meaning and communication*. Oxford University Press.

Ghaziani, A., & Baldassarri, D. (2011). Cultural anchors and the organization of differences: a multi-method analysis of LGBT marches on Washington. *American Sociological Review*, 76(2), 179–206. doi.org/10.1177/0003122411401252

Goldberg, A. (2011). Mapping Shared Understandings Using Relational Class Analysis: The Case of the Cultural Omnivore Reexamined. *American Journal of Sociology*, 116, 1397–1436. https://doi.org/10.1086/657976.

González-Bailón, S., & Wang, N. (2016). Networked discontent: the anatomy of protest campaigns in social media. *Social Networks*, 44, 95–104.

Haunss, S. (2013). *Conflicts in the knowledge society: the contentious politics of intellectual property*. Cambridge University Press.

Henning, C., Aßmann, C., Hedtrich, J., Ehrenfels, J., & Krampe, E. (2019). What drives participatory policy processes: grassroot activities, scientific knowledge or donor money? A comparative policy network approach. *Social Networks*, 58, 78–104. doi.org/10.1016/j.socnet.2019.03.001

Hoffmann, M. (2020). Exploring the Facebook networks of German anti-immigration groups. PhD dissertation. University of Trento.

Huang, R., & Sun, X. (2014). Weibo network, information diffusion and implications for collective action in China. *Information, Communication and Society*, 17(1), 86–104. doi.org/10.1080/1369118X.2013.853817

Huckfeldt, R., Pietryka, M.T., & Reilly, J. (2014). Noise, bias, and expertise in political communication networks. *Social Networks*, 36, 110–121. doi.org/10.1016/j.socnet.2013.02.003

Huhe, N., Gallop, M., & Minhas, S. (2021). Who are in charge, who do I work with, and who are my friends: a latent space approach to understanding elite coappearances in China. *Social Networks*, 66, 26–37. doi.org/10.1016/j.socnet.2021.01.002

Huisman, M. (2014). Imputation of missing network data: some simple procedures. In R. Alhajj & J. Rokne (Eds.), *Encyclopedia of social network analysis and mining* (pp. 707–715). Springer. doi.org/10.1007/978-1-4614-6170-8_394

Ingold, K., & Fischer, M. (2014). Drivers of collaboration to mitigate climate change: an illustration of Swiss climate policy over 15 years. *Global Environmental Change*, 24, 88–98. doi.org/10.1016/j.gloenvcha.2013.11.021

Janoski, T., & Jonas, A. (2021). A synthetic theory of political sociology: bringing social networks and power dependence to power resources theory in city politics. *Sociology White Papers*. uknowledge.uky.edu/sociology_reports/5

Jasny, L., and Fisher, D.R. (2022). How Networks of Social Movement Issues Motivate Climate Resistance. *Social Networks*, February, S0378873322000181. https://doi.org/10.1016/j.socnet.2022.02.002.

Kanellopoulos, K., Kostopoulos, K., Papanikolopoulos, D., & Rongas, V. (2016). Competing modes of coordination in the Greek anti-austerity campaign, 2010–2012. *Social Movement Studies*, *16*, 101–118. doi.org/10.1080/14742837.2016.1153464

Kenney, M., Coulthart, S., & Wright, D. (2017). Structure and performance in a violent extremist network: the small-world solution. *Journal of Conflict Resolution*, *61*(10), 2208–2234. doi.org/10.1177/0022002716631104

Klein, O., & Muis, J. (2019). Online discontent: comparing Western European far-right groups on Facebook. *European Societies*, *21*(4), 540–562. doi.org/10.1080/14616696.2018.1494293

Kleinnijenhuis, J., & de Nooy, W. (2013). Adjustment of issue positions based on network strategies in an election campaign: a two-mode network autoregression model with cross-nested random effects. *Social Networks*, *35*(2), 168–177. doi.org/10.1016/j.socnet.2011.03.002

Kmetty, Z., & Tardos, R. (2022). Party nexus position generator. *Social Networks*, *70*, 112–125. doi.org/10.1016/j.socnet.2021.11.011

Knoke, D. (1990). *Political networks*. Cambridge University Press.

Knoke, D., Diani, M., Christopoulos, D.C., & Hollway, J. (2021). *Multimodal political networks*. Cambridge University Press.

Knoke, D., & Kostiuchenko, T. (2017). Power structures of policy networks. In J.N. Victor, A.H. Montgomery & M. Lubell (Eds.), *The Oxford handbook of political networks* (pp. 91–113). Oxford University Press.

Kukkonen, A., Stoddart, M.C., & Ylä-Anttila, T. (2021). Actors and justifications in media debates on Arctic climate change in Finland and Canada: a network approach. *Acta Sociologica*, *64*(1), 103–117. doi.org/10.1177/0001699319890902

Larson, J.M., & Lewis, J.I. (2017). Ethnic networks. *American Journal of Political Science*, *61*(2), 350–364. doi.org/10.1111/ajps.12282

Laumann, E.O., & Pappi, F.U. (1976). *Networks of collective action*. Academic Press.

Lazega, E., & Snijders, T.A.B. (Eds.). (2016). *Multilevel network analysis for the social sciences*. Springer.

Lazer, D., & Wojcik, S. (2017). Political networks and computational social science. In J.N. Victor, A.H. Montgomery & M. Lubell (Eds.), *The Oxford handbook of political networks* (pp. 115–130). Oxford University Press. doi.org/10.1093/oxfordhb/9780190228217.013.40

Lee, C.-S. (2016). *When solidarity works*. Cambridge University Press.

Leifeld, P. (2017). Discourse network analysis: policy debates as dynamic networks. In J.N. Victor, A.H. Montgomery & M. Lubell (Eds.), *The Oxford handbook of political networks* (p. 301/326). Oxford University Press.

Leifeld, P., & Schneider, V. (2012). Information exchange in policy networks. *American Journal of Political Science*, *56*(3), 731–744. doi.org/10.1111/j.1540-5907.2011.00580.x

Lindh, A., Andersson, A.B., & Volker, B. (2021). The missing link: network influences on class divides in political attitudes. *European Sociological Review*, *37*(5), 695–712. doi.org/10.1093/esr/jcab010

Lotan, G., Graeff, E., Ananny, M., Gaffney, D., Pearce, I., & Boyd, D. (2011). The revolutions were tweeted: information flows during the 2011 Tunisian and Egyptian revolutions. *International Journal of Communication*, *5*, 1375–1405.

Lu, Y., & Tao, R. (2017). Organizational structure and collective action: lineage networks, semiautonomous civic associations, and collective resistance in rural China. *American Journal of Sociology*, *122*(6), 1726–1774.

Ma, J., & DeDeo, S. (2018). State power and elite autonomy in a networked civil society: the board interlocking of Chinese non-profits. *Social Networks*, *54*, 291–302. doi.org/10.1016/j.socnet.2017.10.001

Marwell, N.P., Marantz, E.A., & Baldassarri, D. (2020). The microrelations of urban governance: dynamics of patronage and partnership. *American Journal of Sociology*, *125*(6), 1559–1601. doi.org/10.1086/709250

McClurg, S.D. (2006). The electoral relevance of political talk: examining disagreement and expertise effects in social networks on political participation. *American Journal of Political Science*, *50*(3), 737–754. doi.org/10.1111/j.1540-5907.2006.00213.x

Melamed, D., Breiger, R.L., & West, J. (2013). Community structure in multi-mode networks. *Connections*, *33*(1), 18–23.

Mendoza, R.U., Banaag, M.S., Hiwatig, J.D., Yusingco, M.H.L., & Yap, J.K. (2020). Term limits and political dynasties in the Philippines: unpacking the links. *Asia-Pacific Social Science Review*, *20*(4), 88–99.

Meraz, S. (2013). The democratic contribution of weakly tied political networks: moderate political blogs as bridges to heterogeneous information pools. *Social Science Computer Review*, *31*(2), 191–207. doi.org/10.1177/0894439312451879

Millard, C., Brhlikova, P., & Pollock, A. (2015). Social networks and health policy: the case of misoprostol and the WHO model essential medicine list. *Social Science and Medicine*, *132*, 190–196. doi.org/10.1016/j.socscimed.2015.03.011

Mische, A. (2011). Relational sociology, culture, and agency. In P. Carrington & J. Scott (Eds.), *The Sage handbook of social network analysis* (pp. 80–97). Sage.

Nagel, M., & Satoh, K. (2019). Protesting iconic megaprojects: a discourse network analysis of the evolution of the conflict over Stuttgart 21. *Urban*

Studies, 56(8), 1681–1700. doi.org/10.1177/0042098018775903

Naidu, S., Robinson, J.A., & Young, L.E. (2021). Social Origins of Dictatorships: Elite Networks and Political Transitions in Haiti. *American Political Science Review*, *115*(3), 900–916. doi.org/10.1017/S0003055421000289

Neal, Z.P. (2020). A sign of the times? Weak and strong polarization in the US Congress, 1973–2016. *Social Networks*, *60*, 103–112. doi.org/10.1016/j.socnet.2018.07.007

Neal, Z.P., Domagalski, R., & Yan, X. (2022). Homophily in collaborations among US House Representatives, 1981–2018. *Social Networks*, *68*, 97–106. doi.org/10.1016/j.socnet.2021.04.007

Nelson, L.K. (2021). Cycles of conflict, a century of continuity: the impact of persistent place-based political logics on social movement strategy. *American Journal of Sociology*, *127*(1), 1–59. doi.org/10.1086/714915

Ogan, C., & Varol, O. (2017). What is gained and what is left to be done when content analysis is added to network analysis in the study of a social movement: Twitter use during Gezi Park. *Information, Communication and Society*, *20*(8), 1220–1238. doi.org/10.1080/1369118X.2016.1229006

Parigi, P., & Sartori, L. (2014). The political party as a network of cleavages: disclosing the inner structure of Italian political parties in the seventies. *Social Networks*, *36*, 54–65. doi.org/10.1016/j.socnet.2012.07.005

Parkinson, S.E. (2013). Organizing rebellion: rethinking high-risk mobilization and social networks in war. *American Political Science Review*, *107*(3), 418–432. doi.org/10.1017/S0003055413000208

Patty, J.W., & Penn, E.M. (2017). Network theory and political science. In J.N. Victor, A.H. Montgomery & M. Lubell (Eds.), *The Oxford handbook of political networks* (pp. 147–171). Oxford University Press.

Peoples, C., & Sutton, J. (2015). Congressional bribery as state-corporate crime: a social network analysis. *Crime, Law and Social Change*, *64*(2/3), 103–125. doi.org/10.1007/s10611-015-9584-4

Perrucci, R. (2011). 'Too big to fail': a network perspective. *International Journal of Contemporary Sociology*, *48*(2), 251–278.

Pichler, F., & Wallace, C. (2009). Social capital and social class in Europe: the role of social networks in social stratification. *European Sociological Review*, *25*(3), 319–332. doi.org/10.1093/esr/jcn050

Piedrahita, P., Borge-Holthoefer, J., Moreno, Y., & González-Bailón, S. (2018). The contagion effects of repeated activation in social networks. *Social Networks*, *54*, 326–335. doi.org/10.1016/j.socnet.2017.11.001

Pizzorno, A. (1970). An introduction to the theory of political participation. *Social Science Information*, *9*(5), 29–61. doi.org/10.1177/053901847000900503

Ravanilla, N., Haim, D., & Hicken, A. (2021). Brokers, social networks, reciprocity, and clientelism. *American Journal of Political Science*, *66*(2). doi.org/10.1111/ajps.12604

Reeves-Latour, M., & Morselli, C. (2017). Bid-rigging networks and state-corporate crime in the construction industry. *Social Networks*, *51*, 158–170. doi.org/10.1016/j.socnet.2016.10.003

Rhue, L., & Sundararajan, A. (2014). Digital access, political networks and the diffusion of democracy. *Social Networks*, *36*, 40–53. doi.org/10.1016/j.socnet.2012.06.007

Robins, G., Lewis, J.M., & Wang, P. (2012). Statistical network analysis for analyzing policy networks. *Policy Studies Journal*, *40*(3), 375–401. doi.org/10.1111/j.1541-0072.2012.00458.x

Robles-Morales, J.M., & Córdoba-Hernández, A.M. (2019). *Digital political participation, social networks and big data: disintermediation in the era of Web 2.0*. Springer Nature.

Siegel, D.A. (2013). Social networks and the mass media. *American Political Science Review*, *107*(4), 786–805. doi.org/10.1017/S0003055413000452

Simpson, C.R. (2015). Multiplexity and Strategic Alliances: The Relational Embeddedness of Coalitions in Social Movement Organisational Fields. *Social Networks*, *42*, 42–59.

Singh, S. (2016). Appreciating field theory's insights into politics: an empirical illustration using the case of emergency in India (1975-77). *Theory and Society*, *45*(2), 107–142. doi.org/10.1007/s11186-016-9266-y

Sokhey, A.E., & Djupe, P.A. (2014). Name generation in interpersonal political network data: results from a series of experiments. *Social Networks*, *36*, 147–161. doi.org/10.1016/j.socnet.2013.02.002

Stark, D., & Vedres, B. (2012). Political holes in the economy: the business network of partisan firms in Hungary. *American Sociological Review*, *77*(5), 700–722. doi.org/10.1177/0003122412453921

Stier, S., Schünemann, W.J., & Steiger, S. (2018). Of activists and gatekeepers: temporal and structural properties of policy networks on Twitter. *New Media and Society*, *20*(5), 1910–1930. doi.org/10.1177/1461444817709282

Szwarcberg, M. (2012). Revisiting clientelism: a network analysis of problem-solving networks in Argentina. *Social Networks*, *34*(2), 230–240. doi.org/10.1016/j.socnet.2011.12.003

Taraktaş, B. (2022). Tolerable disagreements: collective action capacity and shape of coalitions. *Social Networks*, *68*, 15–30. doi.org/10.1016/j.socnet.2021.04.002

Tufecki, Z. (2017). *Twitter and teargas: the power and fragility of networked protest*. Yale University Press.

van Apeldoorn, B., & de Graaff, N. (2014). Corporate elite networks and US post-Cold War grand strategy from Clinton to Obama. *European Journal of International Relations*, *20*(1), 29–55. doi.org/10.1177/1354066111433895

van Haperen, S., Nicholls, W., & Uitermark, J. (2018). Building protest online: engagement with the digitally networked #not1more protest campaign on Twitter. *Social Movement Studies*, *17*(4), 408–423. doi.org/10.1080/14742837.2018.1434499

Vicari, S. (2014). Networks of contention: the shape of online transnationalism in early twenty-first century social movement coalitions. *Social Movement Studies*, *13*(1), 92–109. doi.org/10.1080/14742837.2013.832621

Vicari, S. (2015). Exploring the Cuban blogosphere: discourse networks and informal politics. *New Media and Society*, *17*(9), 1492–1512. doi.org/10.1177/1461444814529285

Victor, J.N., Montgomery, A.H., & Lubell, M. (Eds.). (2017a). *The Oxford handbook of political networks*. Oxford University Press.

Victor, J.N., Montgomery, A.H., & Lubell, M. (2017b). The emergence of the study of networks in politics. In J.N. Victor, A.H. Montgomery & M. Lubell (Eds.), *The Oxford handbook of political networks* (pp. 3–57). Oxford University Press.

Vogeler, C.S., Schwindenhammer, S., Gonglach, D., & Bandelow, N.C. (2021). Agri-food technology politics: exploring policy narratives in the European Parliament. *European Policy Analysis*, *7*, 324–343. doi.org/10.1002/epa2.1114

Wackenhut, A.F. (2020). Revisiting the Egyptian uprising of 2011: exploring the role of relational networks within the Cairo-based political opposition. *Social Problems*, *67*(2), 342–357. doi.org/10.1093/socpro/spz014

Wada, T. (2014). Who are the active and central actors in the 'rising civil society' in Mexico? *Social Movement Studies*, *13*(1), 127–157. doi.org/10.1080/14742837.2013.860876

Wagner, P., & Payne, D. (2017). Trends, frames and discourse networks: analysing the coverage of climate change in Irish newspapers. *Irish Journal of Sociology*, *25*(1), 5–28. doi.org/10.7227/IJS.0011

Walter, D., & Ophir, Y. (2019). News frame analysis: an inductive mixed-method computational approach. *Communication Methods and Measures*, *13*(4), 248–266. doi.org/10.1080/19312458.2019.1639145

Weaver, I.S., Williams, H., Cioroianu, I., Williams, M., Coan, T., & Banducci, S. (2018). Dynamic social media affiliations among UK politicians. *Social Networks*, *54*, 132–144. doi.org/10.1016/j.socnet.2018.01.008

White, D.R., Burton, M.L., & Brudner, L.A. (1977). Entailment Theory and Method: A Cross-Cultural Analysis of the Sexual Division of Labor. *Behavior Science Research*, *12*, 1–24. https://doi.org/10.1177/106939717701200101.

White, H. (2008). *Identity and control: how social formations emerge*. Princeton University Press.

Winter, S., Neubaum, G., Stieglitz, S., & Ross, B. (2021). #Opinionleaders: a comparison of self-reported and observable influence of Twitter users. *Information, Communication and Society*, *24*(11), 1533–1550. doi.org/10.1080/1369118X.2019.1705374

Witting, A., & Dudley, G. (2020). A long-term perspective on entrepreneurial strategies and their impact on British road policy. *European Policy Analysis*, *6*(1), 58–76. doi.org/10.1002/epa2.1070

Wukich, C. (2022). Connecting mayors: the content and formation of Twitter information networks. *Urban Affairs Review*, *58*(1), 33–67. doi.org/10.1177/1078087420947182

Zheng, P., & Shahin, S. (2020). Live tweeting live debates: how Twitter reflects and refracts the US political climate in a campaign season. *Information, Communication and Society*, *23*(3), 337–357. doi.org/10.1080/1369118X.2018.1503697

Social Movements and Collective Action

David Tindall

INTRODUCTION

In contemporary societies social movement protest seems ubiquitous. Meyer and Tarrow have referred to this situation as the 'social movement society' (Meyer & Tarrow, 1998).[1] As this chapter will describe, much social movement activity involves social network processes of some sort (such as mobilisation through personal ties, coalition formation among previously existing groups, or the diffusion of social movement ideas and tactics).

In recent years, a number of high-profile social movement mobilisations have captured the media and the public's attention, such as the millions of youth who are concerned about the climate crisis who participated in climate strikes and related protests as part of Fridays for Future. Herrmann et al. (2022) describe how these protests were fostered by the social media platform Instagram. In the US, a pattern of police killings of unarmed African Americans led to mass protests in support of Black Lives Matter (BLM). Hong and Peoples (2021) have studied how social ties with African Americans affected whites' participation in the BLM movement. In the early 2010s mass anti-government protests arose in Arab countries such as Tunisia, Libya, Egypt, Yemen, Syria and Bahrain. These protests came to be known as the Arab Spring, and were one of the earliest high-profile cases where virtual social networks were recognised as being an important factor in the uprisings (Tufekci & Wilson, 2012; Norris, 2012). In the 2010s and early 2020s several waves of pro-democracy protests occurred in Hong Kong. Shen et al. (2020) investigated the extent to which some of these protests were facilitated by social media. In the US, in the latter part of the 2010s there were multiple waves of protest against the Trump administration, a phenomenon that became known as 'The Resistance' (Fisher, 2019). One component of this protest was mobilisation in support of women's rights, including a recurring event referred to as the Women's March. As Fischer et al. describe (2017), participants often became involved in the Women's March through personal social networks, or were mobilised through social media. All of these protests involved some aspect of social networks (such as personal networks, or interactions over social media) as an important part of the mobilisation process.

This chapter begins by examining several definitions of collective action and social movements, then describes an ego-network model of micro-mobilisation. Next the chapter briefly discusses meso-level networks and fields, and then provides an overview of virtual social networks in the context of social movements and compares them with non-virtual networks. The chapter next provides an overview of some key methodological considerations for research on social networks and social movements, and the concluding section presents a variety of analytical considerations.

WHAT ARE SOCIAL MOVEMENTS?

In the scholarly literature, collective action refers to groups of people acting in unison to pursue a common goal. Such phenomena are referred to as collective action when they are relatively informal and non-routine – which generally excludes activities that take place in the context of corporations or governments. When collective action is directed towards achieving or resisting social change, it is referred to as a social movement (or in the latter case, a counter-movement; Meyer & Staggenborg, 1996). There are a variety of definitions of social movements. McCarthy and Zald (1977, pp. 1217–1218) define social movements as: 'a set of opinions and beliefs in a population which represents preferences for changing some elements of the social structure and/or reward distribution of a society'. Diani (1992; 2003a; 2004; Diani & Bison 2004) has argued that social movements are a distinct social process, which actors engaged in collective action: '1. are involved in conflictual relations with clearly identified opponents; 2. are linked by dense informal networks; 3. share a distinct collective identity' (della Porta & Diani, 2006, p. 20).

Diani's definition makes social network relations a key aspect in his definition. Della Porta and Diani (2006, p. 30) further distinguish social movements from other types of phenomena:

> These include collective actions oriented to non-conflictual goals, such as in the field of charity work ... coalitions mobilizing on specific issues or events for instrumental reasons ... political organizations such as parties and traditional interest groups (section 1.2.4); and protest repertoires.

Other scholars have noted that social movements share characteristics with other phenomena, and it might be analytically useful to refer to this larger class of phenomena as *contentious politics*. Tarrow (2011, p. 6) argues: 'Contentious politics occurs when ordinary people – often in alliance with more influential citizens and with changes in public mood – join forces in confrontation with elites, authorities, and opponents.'

Some critics (including New Social Movement Scholars) have questioned the centrality of authorities, and opposition to them, as being essential to defining social movements. For example, David Snow has criticised the contentious politics perspective, noting that there are other forms that social movements can take beyond directly challenging governments and corporations (Snow, 2002, p. 24).

What many definitions of social movements have in common is the notion that participants are connected relationally. Tindall and Robinson (2015) have pushed this insight further in the context of analysis at the unit of the individual, by using social network relations as one criterion for defining membership in a movement. Taking this approach yields some interesting, and somewhat counterintuitive, conclusions – such as the notion that membership in social movements may be overestimated in popular perceptions.

HOW CAN WE THINK RELATIONALLY ABOUT SOCIAL MOVEMENTS?

Traditional approaches to social network analysis tended to focus on individuals or groups as nodes, and social relationships or types of interactions as the lines or ties. In the realm of social movements this might mean looking at individual adherents of a social movement and their social relationships with others affiliated with the movement (Tindall & Robinson, 2017). Conversely, an analyst interested in studying things at the meso level might examine the nature of relationships among social movement organisations (Diani, 2015).

Ron Breiger's introduction of the idea of the duality of persons and groups (1974) enables social network scholars to combine these levels of analysis, and conversely to focus on one of them vis-à-vis the other mode. Over time, social network scholars have increasingly studied other types of nodes, such as discourse nodes (Leifeld, 2017), or ecosystem elements (Bodin et al., 2006). Scholars studying social networks can utilise network thinking when considering the mechanisms involved in micromobilisation, such as the ways in which collective identification intervenes between network embeddedness and movement participation (Tindall, 2002).

SOCIAL NETWORKS AND MICROMOBILISATION

A significant amount of work has been done on social networks and micromobilisation (Snow et al., 1980; McAdam, 1986; Klandermans & Oegema, 1987; Kitts, 2000; Passy & Giugni, 2001; Tindall, 2002). Figure 10.1 provides a visualisation of a synthesis of theoretical ideas and empirical findings regarding networks and micromobilisation.[2] There are three main components to the diagram. The (main) top component presents a path diagram illustrating a number of elements of micromobilisation, and the relations among them. A second component illustrates tie decay over time. As elaborated below, tie decay is an empirical fact, and a key process in the model. A third component notes that there are trends above the level of the individual that affect tie formation and dissolution, such as variations in the wave of protest or the intensity of social movement campaigns over time (Tindall, 2007; Tarrow, 2011; Tindall et al., 2022).

Let's start with the first component of the path model (top left side of the diagram). This shows that individual participation in a social movement is positively affected by one's embeddedness through social ties with other movement participants. The more friendship and family ties (strong ties) and acquaintanceship ties (weak ties) one has to people affiliated with a movement, the more active one is in the movement (Tindall, 2002). There are a variety of processes in this relationship. The more ties one has, the more opportunities there are for communication and the more frequently one communicates about social movement issues (Tindall, 2002, 2004). This includes substantive information about the movement, and information about movement events such as protest demonstrations (Kitts, 2000).

The more ties one has to other members of the movement, the more highly one tends to identify as a member of the movement (Tindall, 2002). This is partly due to the process of social comparison, as individuals compare and contrast themselves with others in their network (Gartrell, 1987; Tindall, 2002).

Also, the more ties one has to other members of the movement, the more often one receives requests to participate in movement events. These network effects can underlie both initial recruitment to participate in an event and ongoing movement participation (Tindall, 2002, 2004; Fisher, 2019).

The intervening variables identified in Figure 10.1 all have positive effects on level of activism: the more requests one receives to participate the more likely one is to participate, the more frequently one talks with other movement participants about movement issues the more likely one is to participate, and the more an individual identifies as a member of a movement the more active they will tend to be (Tindall, 2002; Tindall & Robinson, 2017).

The solid lines in the diagram are the posited main direction of causal influence. However, it is possible for reciprocal processes to occur (Tindall, 2004; Tindall et al., 2021). Most saliently, while having network ties may generate activism among individuals, the more actively a person participates in a movement, the greater the number of other movement participants they meet, and the more embedded they become in the movement. In Figure 10.1, this particular reciprocal relationship is illustrated twice – within each time slice, and across time slices. While it is somewhat redundant, this relationship is visualised to emphasise that within a time slice the relationship could start with either activism (started by non-network factors) or with network ties. Also, the process is replicated over time, and the more active one is, the more ties one is likely to make.

Other reciprocal influences identified in Figure 10.1 include the following. While individuals who identify more with a movement will become more active, it is also the case that individuals who are more active will reflect on their action and this will shape their collective identification. While those who talk more frequently about movement events and issues will identify more with the movement, it is also the case that those who identify more strongly with a movement will be more motivated to discuss issues, and thus will talk about them more frequently. Finally, while having more ties to movement participants leads to higher levels of collective identity, via social comparison processes, it is also the case that those with higher levels of movement identity will be more motivated to form new social ties with others involved in the movement (Tindall, 2002).

The second component of Figure 10.1 illustrates how ties tend to decay over time (Burt, 2000). Empirical research has documented that ties dissolve over time, albeit at different rates and probabilities (Wellman et al., 1997; Tindall, 2004). This is a counter-force to the relations in the path model that described how different micromobilisation mechanisms tend to reinforce tie formation. In other words, without tie decay, the number of ties that movement participants have could continue to grow indefinitely. Clearly, this is an untenable assumption. A related issue, and one that merits further attention in the social network scholarship on movements, is the issue of latent ties (Morgan et al., 1996; Mariotti & Delbridge, 2012). This refers to the notion that some ties don't necessarily disappear, but rather they become inactive and thus latent (Mariotti & Delbridge, 2012). But when urgent social movement events and campaigns arise, such ties can potentially become reactivated for remobilisation.

SOCIAL MOVEMENTS AND COLLECTIVE ACTION 149

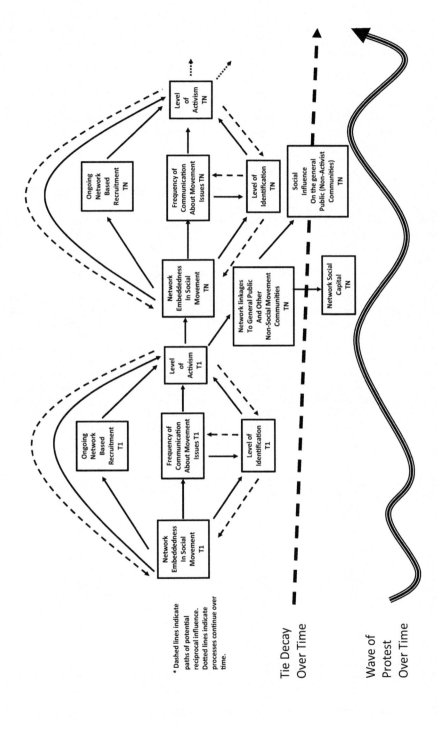

Figure 10.1 An Ego-Network-Model of Micromobilization in Low Cost/Risk Social Movement Activism*

Social movements are dynamic, and marked by increases and decreases in the intensity of protest, interactions with various foes and allies, and subject to dissipating altogether. Consequently, tie formation and dissolution also vary with the cycle of protest. When movement activity is intense, collective identities connected to the movement become more salient, and individuals are more motivated to form ties and/or interact with other movement participants. When movement activity is less intense, movement identities become less salient, and some ties become inactive and/or latent (Mariotti & Delbridge, 2012). Figure 10.1 illustrates the fact that various social network processes related to social movements, including tie formation/dissolution/activation/inactivation, identity salience and participation, vary with the intensity with the cycle or wave of protest.

Some scholars have described social movement organisations and other civil society organisations, and civic engagement, as important aspects of social capital (Foley & Edwards, 1999). Diani (1997) proposed a novel observation on the relationship between social movements and social capital, and noted that during the process of mobilisation and campaigning many social movement participants interact with those outside the movement, and hence create a form of network social capital that might serve as a useful resource in the future. Tindall et al. (2012) drew on this insight in studying environmental movement participants in Canada. They found that the more active individuals were in the movement, the greater the diversity of their ties to people in different occupations outside the movement. Tindall and Piggot (2015) further studied ties between environmental movement participants and members of the general public. They found that members of the general public who did not belong to an environmental organisation, but who did have social ties to movement organisation members, were significantly more likely to have a plan to deal with climate change. They interpret this as a form of collective social capital resulting from social influence through social network ties. These various social capital outcome effects are illustrated in the right-lower quadrant of Figure 10.1.

MESO-LEVEL NETWORKS AND FIELDS

While personal networks play an important role in the micromobilisation of individuals into social movements (and certain forms of collective action), ties at the meso level among organisations are at the heart of social movement phenomena (Diani, 1995, 2015). This is because social movements are inherently a form of collective phenomena, and social movement organisations (SMOs) often play a key role in contentious politics. Further, SMOs are typically linked to other SMOs as well as other organisations, and these networks often operate in a coordinated fashion (Carroll & Ratner, 1996; Heaney & Rojas, 2008; Andrews & Edwards, 2005; Brulle, 2021). As Diani (2011, p. 226) notes, large-scale collective action has tended to be organised in networks, and the network nature of social movements has been emphasised

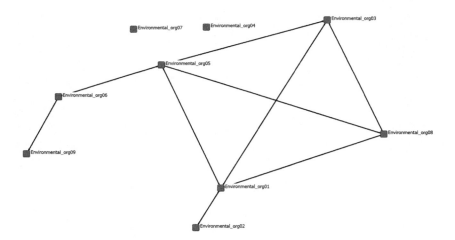

Figure 10.2 Communication Amongst Environmental Groups in a Climate Change Policy Network

by social movement scholars (Diani & McAdam, 2003; Krinsky & Crossley, 2014). Often these social networks are informal. Ties among organisations are sometimes conceptualised as the overlap of organisational exchanges. Figure 10.2 shows a communication network among environmental SMOs involved in climate change policy discourse and actions. Another approach focuses on individual activists and their multiple memberships. Figure 10.3 shows connections among Canadian environmental organisations via their shared members. Interorganisational ties can also be based on participation in joint campaigns, or joint events. Figure 10.4 shows a simulated two-mode network of social movement activists by protest events.

Diani has developed the most theoretically sophisticated approach to understanding meso-level networks in social movements. He set out to understand interorganisational relations in social movements and related phenomena, and has introduced the concept of 'modes of coordination' to

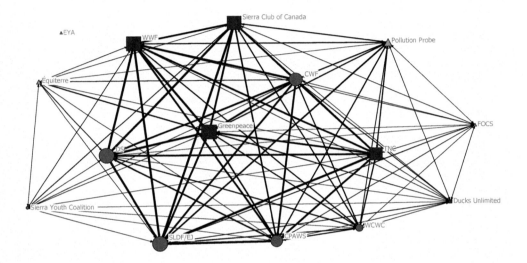

Figure 10.3   Ties Amongst Canadian Environmental Social Movement Organizations vis a vis Joint Memberships

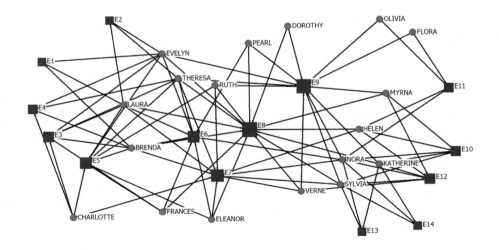

Figure 10.4   Activists by Protest Events

classify the different ways in which organisations are related to one another in meso-level networks. He asserts that 'looking at modes of coordination will enable us to capture the distinctiveness of social movements as a particular form of collective action, while locating them firmly within broader civil society dynamics' (2015, p. 5). Diani's classification scheme makes social network characteristics central to understanding overlapping but different types of phenomena:

> [W]e propose to look at modes of coordination as consisting of different combinations of two relational dimensions, corresponding to mechanisms of resource allocation and mechanisms of boundary definition. Sometimes, collective action is mainly coordinated within the boundaries of specific organizations, with few interorganizational exchanges and no, or limited, solidarity and identification between organizations. In fact, social movement processes are most likely to be found in situations characterized by extensive networks of resource allocation and diffuse feelings of solidarity that exceed the boundaries of any specific group (Diani 1992, 1995; Diani and Bison 2004). Other combinations of the same dimensions define two additional modes of coordination: a coalitional mode features dense networks of resource allocation but weak identities, while a subcultural/communitarian mode consists of sparse resource exchanges but relatively strong identities and broader boundary definitions.

(p. 5)

In his empirical analyses, Diani examines organisational, coalitional and social movement modes of coordination in two cities. At the meso level of analysis, several social movement scholars have developed versions of 'field theory' that set out to explain the actions of social movement actors vis-à-vis one another, and also synthesise a number of other elements of social movements such as culture, identities and political opportunities. Diani's (2015) work is one contribution to field theory (see also Diani, this volume); another has been provided by Fligstein and McAdam (2012).

VIRTUAL NETWORKS AND SOCIAL MOVEMENTS

Social movement scholars have been interested in information communication technology (ICTs) and digital social networks for several decades (Diani, 2000; Earl & Kimport, 2011; Bennett & Segerberg, 2013; Pavan, 2017; Tufekci, 2017; Earl, 2018). As a category, ICTs potentially cover a number of things. Because of its contemporary importance we will focus mostly on social media below.

Virtual social networks have garnered a great deal of attention in social movement research as well as other substantive domains for several different reasons. First, they constitute a potentially 'game changing' technology for social movement actors, and this is inherently interesting. Second, they are also a relatively quick and easy source of data, and usually take fewer resources to research than collecting data through more traditional social science research methods such as surveys, interviews, ethnographies, or human observation.

In both the social network literatures on personal networks and community (Wellman et al., 2020) and the social movements literature (Diani, 2000; Earl & Kimport, 2011; Tindall et al., 2021) there have been debates about the extent to which social media and other ICTs change things substantially, or whether they are merely new tools that complement previously existing phenomena (Hampton & Wellman, 2018).

For instance, in the context of social movements, biographical availability (the extent to which things like having a full-time job or child care responsibilities) is thought to constrain participation, and to be related to the costs and risks of participation (McAdam, 1986; Tindall, 2002). But for some types of activism, the web may bring down costs, so biographical availability may not be a barrier to the same extent.

In the past two decades, alternative media have become more important to social movements (Earl & Kimport, 2011; Bennett & Segerberg, 2013; Tufekci, 2017; Tindall et al., 2021) and, to the extent that social movement actors are linked together through the web and related media, we can think of the internet as comprising a social network dimension of activism.

Social media can greatly reduce the costs and increase the efficiency of organising (Diani, 2000), and some commentators have argued that new media technologies have the potential to 'level the playing field' (Earl et al., 2013) between social movement actors and their opponents.

Social media like Facebook and Twitter simultaneously serve several functions. In particular: (1) like mainstream media, they serve as a source of information; (2) like the telephone, they serve as a tool for communication; and (3) ties among users create a quasi-social network.

Social media can provide information about events, and about substantive and ideological issues. This can be done more efficiently – such as by providing links to URLs, or by attaching videos. 'Traditional' social network scholars have argued that there are important linkages between social network structures and communication processes. Social media are also a tool of communication (Diani, 2000), within dyads (and across larger structures) and in terms of broadcasting messages. Within dyads and larger structures, alters can be tagged on posts and they can also direct message. Thus, in some ways social media function like texting on mobile phones, or writing emails. But they are more powerful in terms of broadcasting and dissemination to indirect alters. A third function of social media is to provide a digital embodiment of social ties between actors, and consequently social networks among larger sets of actors. Some scholars have questioned whether ICTs enable new forms of social networks (Diani, 2000), or if they are more like the telephone – and supplement existing social networks (Hampton & Wellman, 2018). Others have argued that they fundamentally change things (or have the potential to) in the realm of social movements (Earl & Kimport, 2011; Tufekci, 2017).

In the context of social media, network ties can be operationalised in several ways (Tindall et al., 2021, 2022) depending upon the features provided by the platform in question. We will use Twitter as an example. Users can follow other users. Thus 'follow' and 'follower' can be considered indicators of out-ties and in-ties. On Twitter users can also tag one another in the content of their tweets. This is a potential indicator of out-ties and in-ties. Users can also share tweets – another possible indicator of ties. Also, as in the case of other forms of media, users can be linked by use of the same 'discourse elements'. This latter type of indicator is not inherent in the platforms, but requires some separate coding and analysis (Leifeld, 2017; McLevey, 2022). There is not yet a consensus on the comparability of social media ties to relational ties that are not based purely on virtual links, though this is a problem that scholars are wrestling with. Further, there are debates about the extent to which there is overlap between online and offline ties (Wellman et al., 2020; Tindall et al., 2022). It is also important to note that these various forms of linkage might also be indicators of oppositional or negative ties (Tindall et al., 2021), and such interactions might actually be part of a process that fuels polarisation.[3]

Various scholars have explored the importance of strong ties and weak ties in the context of social movements (McAdam, 1986; Tindall, 2002; Gould, 2003). As Marsden has noted, the best indicators of tie strength are indicators of social closeness (Marsden & Campbell, 1984, 2012). However, in research on non-virtual social networks, researchers often use relationship status as a proxy for tie strength (Tindall & Wellman, 2001; Tindall, 2002), with ties to close friends and family members being indicative of strong ties, and acquaintanceship ties being indicative of weak ties. In such research, weak and strong ties are often seen as involved in different processes. Because weak ties stretch further in social space, and people have many more of them, they are more likely to be sources of novel information (Granovetter, 1973; Tindall, 2002) and are often important for low-risk forms of activism. Strong ties, by contrast, are more likely to be important for social influence and social support (McAdam, 1986).

Many contemporary studies of social movements and social networks rely solely on analysis of social media data (partly because of the ease of data collection). In such situations it is difficult to accurately assess tie strength. Various suggestions have been made to address this problem, following from earlier research on non-virtual networks. Some suggestions for strong ties include: reciprocation of following, reciprocation of tagging, reciprocation of sharing, frequency of interaction and documenting the existence of Simmelean ties (Krackhardt, 1999). Yet, it is not clear that these are indicators of emotional closeness – the core of the Granovetter (1973) measure of strong ties (though Granovetter himself used other indicators).

Ties that are not strong (as indicated by one of the methods listed above) are often assumed to be weak ties. But again, it is not clear that this is the same as a Granovetter weak tie. For example, one commonly used survey operationalisation of a weak tie is someone a person knows, with whom they could hold a casual conversation (Tindall et al., 2021). Many social media ties involve connections to users that do not meet this criterion's threshold.

Never the less, like non-virtual ties, social media ties can facilitate network-based social psychological processes. For example, some social media functions can provide an indicator of the numbers of others who support or participate in a movement, and from the individual perspective affect the 'tipping point' or threshold for influencing one's participation (Granovetter, 1978; Macy, 1990; Centola, 2018). Social media enhances the possibility of providing reference points for self–other comparison for the formation of collective identities (Gartrell, 1987; Tindall, 2002).

METHODOLOGICAL CONSIDERATIONS

A well-known methodological issue for social network studies is the boundary specification problem (Laumann, 2006). Borgatti et al. (2018) offer a summary of different types of sampling strategies. They identify two basic approaches: *nominal/etic* (researcher-defined networks) and *realist/emic* ('natural' groups). Which of these approaches a researcher might take depends on a variety of considerations, including what information is available, the size of the group and research objectives (Tindall et al., 2021). One challenge with studying social movements, especially mass movements, is that they are often very large, and usually there is no 'membership list' of the entire movement. Thus, certain types of standard approaches are difficult to undertake. If a researcher is interested in studying a small group, they might adopt an ethnographic approach and, after making some initial contacts, utilise snowball sampling. If they are interested in conducting a census of the group, they might continue this until no new targets are revealed. Very often, social movement scholars organise their research around social movement organisations. Sometimes it is possible (directly or indirectly) to obtain access to lists of members and supporters to utilise as a sampling frame. When this happens, the researcher could use standard social survey sampling techniques. In the former instance, researchers might use a 'realist approach' and rely on informants to tell them who is 'part' of the movement. In the latter case, researchers might use a nominal definition of membership in an SMO as an indicator of being within the boundary of the domain of the study. Challenges remain; for example, some people consider themselves parts of movements but do not belong to an SMO. Such individuals might get missed if SMO membership lists were used for sampling. Some SMOs are informal, and thus don't have membership lists. Some people might seem to be part of a movement because of referral by others through snowball sampling, but they might not identify as a member of the movement themselves. Addressing the boundary specification problem requires some substantive knowledge, and reflection on the part of the researcher.

Common forms of data collection on social movements (Diani, 2002; Tindall et al., 2021) include:

1 surveys of individuals or groups;
2 interviews with leaders and other activists;
3 systematic observation at protest events;
4 ethnography involving observation and field notes;
5 archival methods such as use of organisational records;
6 collection of digital data such as data scrapped from websites, or retrieved from social media sites such as Twitter.

Diani (2002) provides an overview of methodological considerations about social movements and social network analysis. McLevey (2022) provides details on collecting and managing digital data, such as those obtained from social media platforms. (See also Tindall et al., 2021.)

Borgatti et al. (2018) discuss different types of dyadic phenomena that can constitute relations. While not specific to social movement research, they are all relevant and include:

1 co-occurrences (e.g., joint membership in an organisation);
2 social relations (e.g., role relations);
3 interactions (e.g., communications);
4 flows (e.g., actors connected via the flow of information).

Likewise, Diani (2002) describes the following types of social movement relations:

1 ties representing alliances among organisations;
2 ties linking organisations to involvement in single-issue campaigns;
3 links among organisations based on the number of joint campaigns they participate in;
4 ties linking different events to one another via the SMOs that participate in them.

Like other social network phenomena, analysts studying social movements can focus on whole networks, or on ego-networks. The choice depends in part on the availability of data and in part on the objectives of the researcher. For example, if a researcher is mostly interested in relations among organisations, in many instances collecting whole network data would be feasible. (Figure 10.2 provides a graph of the communication networks among Canadian environmental social movement organisations who are part of the Canadian climate change policy network.) But here, it depends on the scale and level of the data. For example, unless a study was based on available data of some sort (such as digital data), doing a whole network study of all organisations around the globe involved in the environmental movement would likely not be possible. In the case of individuals, whole networks studies of individuals in movements is usually either impractical or impossible due to the size of the network and the impracticality of asking systematic network questions about all actors, the unavailability of membership lists, or barriers to accessing movement participants. One solution is to study such phenomena either at smaller scales or by sampling. An example of the former might be to focus on the participants in a particular social movement organisation. For example, Figure 10.5 provides a graph of the working relationships among members of a small youth environmental social movement organisation.

Another example might be to conduct a random sample of an organisation, and collect ego-network data (Tindall et al., 2021).

Some practical solutions to collecting ego-network data with members of movement organisations include: (1) using summary count measures of ties to people with certain types of roles (e.g., friends, family and acquaintances affiliated with an organisation); and (2) providing a matrix question asking respondents about their affiliations with particular organisations (Tindall et al., 2021).

In matrix terms, one-mode networks are networks where the row nodes and the column nodes are the same actors. Two-mode networks are matrices where the row actors and the column nodes are different types of actors. When two-mode data are collected on, say, ties of individuals to organisations, the data can be manipulated to create a two-mode graph of individuals by organisations (as illustrated in Figure 10.6) or to create an individuals by individuals graph (via organisations), or an organisations by organisations graph (via individuals, as illustrated in Figure 10.3).

DISCUSSION: ANALYTICAL CONSIDERATIONS

This concluding section will briefly discuss a variety of analytical considerations. Many of these apply to social network analysis in general, and thus will be applicable to other substantive problems as well as social movements. But, as described below, there are some unique features of social movements to bear in mind.

A general problem faced by social network analysts is the problem of selection versus influence. In the case of an individual involved in the environmental movement this might be translated as: did they choose to form ties with other environmentalists because of a pre-existing concern about environmental issues, or did they become influenced by their pre-existing ties to environmental movement participants and chose to become an environmental activist? More work needs to be done on untangling this issue. While social networks are certainly important to micromobilisation and other processes, the correlation between social network ties to activists and activism is likely at least partly a function of selection. Fortunately, there are new statistical tools to try to address this issue. Ideally, longitudinal approaches can be undertaken, and stochastic actor-oriented models employed (such as SIENA, Snijders et al., 2010). Also, previously, exponential random graph models, which can get some leverage at distinguishing influence and selection effects, were available only for whole network data. But new statistical models have been developed for ego-network data (Krivitsky & Morris, 2017).

Social tie formation can happen in a variety of ways, including as a result of strategic intention, or as an accidental byproduct of other processes. Certain streams of the social capital literature emphasise the former (Lin, 2002), and see actors as rationally investing in network social capital. It is less clear that most movement ties are formed

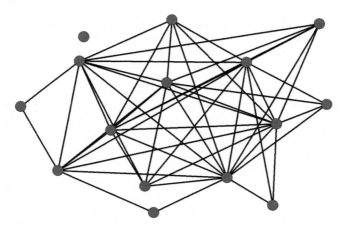

Figure 10.5 "Worked with" Relations Amongst a Youth Environmental Social Movement Organization

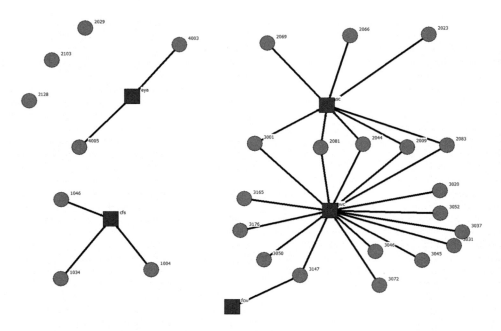

Figure 10.6 Two-Mode Network: Individuals by Organizations in the British Columbia Wilderness Preservation Movement

in the same way – though, it does seem likely that movement organisers act strategically at times in creating links among others, and between organisations (Diani, 2003b).

Quantitative social network researchers tend to be interested in general patterns and models. For example, how is network centrality correlated with social movement participation (Tindall, 2002)? Often such general patterns are thought to potentially hold across a variety of cases (e.g. McAdam, 1986; Tindall, 2002). Such approaches are referred to as *nomothetic*. By contrast, some researchers are interested in all of the specific details of a case, and not necessarily interested in generalising beyond that case. These types of approaches are common in historical analysis, and are referred to as *idiographic* approaches. Idiographic approaches are often qualitative, and focus more on description and meaning. For instance, Aldon Morris describes some of the key individuals and organisations involved in the civil rights movement in the US, and their relations with one another (Morris, 1986). Mixed methods approaches have the potential of supporting both strategies (Dominguez & Hollstein, 2014; Stoddart et al., 2015; Tindall et al., 2021). Researchers could be more reflective and explicit about their adoption of nomothetic versus idiographic approaches.

As briefly noted earlier, in recent years network scholars have become increasingly interested in non-agent nodes. Methodologically, two-mode (Breiger, 1974) and multimode network approaches enable the modelling of agent and non-agent nodes in the same analysis (Knoke et al., 2021). Diani (2004) has called for more attention being placed on spatial aspects of social movement studies. Integrating non-agent nodes would be one way of doing this. Modelling of non-agent nodes is common in socio-ecological network studies (Bodin et al., 2006). Here, non-human nodes such as ecosystem elements and animals are included with the model along with human agents. Discourse network analysis is another way of modelling non-agent nodes such as discourse themes. Figure 10.7 provides a discourse network of ties among Canadian environmental groups and among environmental concerns based on joint affiliations of members (among the groups, and with different environmental concerns).

Stoddart et al. (2015) provide an analysis that models human agents (including social movement actors) and non-human nodes (environmental themes) in a comparative analysis of two environmental disputes. Social movement scholars could make more use of these techniques.

Multilevel network models (Lazega & Snijders, 2015; Knoke et al., 2021) involve models where

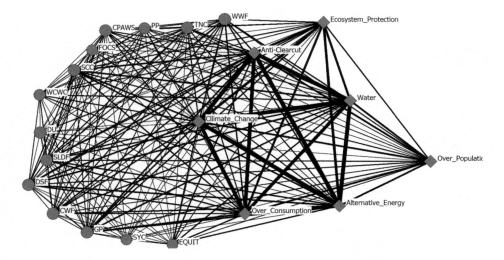

Figure 10.7   Organizational Affiliations and Environmental Concerns Via Members

smaller levels of units are nested within larger ones. Social movements are a compelling phenomenon for such applications. For example, consider the following four levels: the social movement sectors, different social movements, social movement organisations, and individuals (activists, bystanders).

As noted earlier, social movements are dynamic phenomena and consequently provide opportunities and challenges for the development of dynamic models. Longitudinal approaches, especially with the use of panel data, are among the best approaches for trying to understand network dynamics and causal mechanisms. Relatively little quantitative longitudinal research has been done on this topic from a survey perspective. In one study, Tindall (2004) analysed panel data from environmental movement participants on social network ties and levels of identification and participation over time. Some work has been done using other approaches. Wang and Soule (2012) have analysed tactical diffusion through a network formed via SMO collaboration in protest events. Stevens and Crossley (2014) studied the inner circle of the Irish Republican Army using autobiographical accounts. A number of researchers have taken advantage of digital data to examine network dynamics online, including Wang et al., 2013; Liu, 2016; Steinert-Threlkeld, 2017; Wang et al., 2021. In addition to examining changes in ties and level of participation, future research might also try to undertake multimode and multilevel analyses, and examine how changes in ties are related to other aspects of social movement dynamics such as waves of protest.

A final analytical point is to note that there are multiple pathways to micromobilisation, and potentially multiple pathways to other social movement outcomes of interest. In recent years a number of social network researchers have become interested in integrating qualitative comparative analysis (QCA) into social network research (e.g., Breiger, 2009). There are a number of different implications of this development. One is the observation that there are sometimes multiple pathways to particular outcomes (Ragin, 2008). For example, a number of studies have examined micromobilisation using regression techniques, and have estimated the effect of social network ties on social movement participation for the average actor (e.g., McAdam, 1986; Tindall, 2002). QCA approaches would allow for the possibility that some people become mobilised through personal networks, others through other means (e.g., perhaps media appeals). Analyses focusing on multiple pathways might help researchers to understand the relationship between virtual and non-virtual social network ties, and the extent to which they are complementary or distinct aspects of micromobilisation.

Notes

1   The author would like to thank Mark Shakespear and Victor Lam, for their assistance with the preparation of the chapter, and the following people for helpful feedback on an earlier draft: Catherine Corrigall-Brown, Antti Gronow,

Yasmin Koop-Monteiro, Mark Shakespear, Howard Ramos, Neil McLaughlin, Adam Howe, Guy Stecklov, Moses Boudourides, Valerie Berseth and Jennifer Earl.

2   Note: a somewhat different model of micromobilisation through networks is described in Centola (2018), and also in Centola's chapter in this volume.

3   On social movements, oppositional ties and ties to non-movement actors, see McAdam and Paulsen (1993); Tindall et al. (2021).

REFERENCES

Andrews, K., & Edwards, B. (2005). The organizational structure of local environmentalism. *Mobilization: An International Quarterly*, *10*(2): 213–234.

Bennett, W.L., & Segerberg, A. (2013). *The logic of connective action: digital media and the personalization of contentious politics*. Cambridge University Press.

Bodin, Ö., Crona, B.I., & Ernstson, H. (2006). Social networks in natural resource management: what is there to learn from a structural perspective? *Ecology and Society*, *11*(2), r2.

Borgatti, S.P., Everett, M.G., & Johnson, J.C. (2018). *Analyzing social networks* (2nd ed.). Sage.

Breiger, R.L. (1974). The duality of persons and groups. *Social Forces*, *53*(2), 181–90.

Breiger, R.L. (2009). On the duality of cases and variables: correspondence analysis (CA) and qualitative comparative analysis (QCA). In D. Byrne & C.C. Ragin (Eds.), *The Sage handbook of case-based methods* (pp. 243–59). Sage.

Brulle, R.J. (2021). Networks of opposition: a structural analysis of US climate change countermovement coalitions 1989–2015. *Sociological Inquiry*, *91*(3), 603–624.

Burt, R.S. (2000). Decay functions. *Social Networks*, *22*(1), 1–28.

Carroll, W.K., & Ratner, R.S. (1996). Master framing and cross-movement networking in contemporary social movements. *Sociological Quarterly*, *37*(4), 601–625.

Centola, D. (2018). *How behavior spreads: the science of complex contagions*. Princeton University Press.

della Porta, D., & Diani, M. (2006). *Social movements: an introduction* (2nd ed.). Blackwell.

Diani, M. (1992). The concept of social movement. *Sociological Review*, *40*(1), 1–25.

Diani, M. (1995). *Green networks: a structural analysis of the Italian environmental movement*. Edinburgh University Press.

Diani, M. (1997). Social movements and social capital: a network perspective on social movement outcomes. *Mobilization: An International Journal*, *2*, 129–147.

Diani, M. (2000). Social movement networks virtual and real. *Information, Communication and Society*, *3*(3), 386–401.

Diani, M. (2002). Network analysis. In B. Klandermans & S. Staggenborg (Eds.), *Methods of social movement research* (pp. 173–200). University of Minnesota Press.

Diani, M. (2003a). 'Leaders' or brokers? Positions and influence in social movement networks. In M. Diani & D. McAdam (Eds.), *Social movements and social networks: relational approaches to collective action* (pp. 105–122). Oxford University Press.

Diani, M. (2003b). Networks and social movements: a research programme. In M. Diani & D. McAdam (Eds.), *Social movements and social networks: relational approaches to collective action* (pp. 299–319). Oxford University Press.

Diani, M. (2004). Networks and participation. In S.A. Soule, D.A. Snow, & H. Kriesi (Eds.), *The Blackwell companion to social movements* (pp. 339–359). Blackwell.

Diani, M. (2011). Social movements and collective action. In J. Scott and P.J. Carrington (Eds.), *The SAGE handbook of social network analysis* (pp. 223–35). Sage.

Diani, M. (2015). *The cement of civil society*. Cambridge University Press.

Diani, M., & Bison, I. (2004). Organizations, coalitions, and movements. *Theory and Society*, *33*(3–4), 281–309.

Diani, M., & McAdam, D. (2003). *Social movements and networks: relational approaches to collective action*. Oxford University Press.

Dominguez, S., & Hollstein, B. (Eds.) (2014). *Mixed methods social networks research: design and applications*. Cambridge University Press.

Earl, J. (2018). Technology and social media. In D.A. Snow, S.A. Soule, H. Kriesi & H.J. McCammon (Eds.), *The Wiley Blackwell companion to social movements* (2nd ed.) (pp. 289–305). Wiley Blackwell.

Earl, J., & Kimport, K. (2011). *Digitally enabled social change: activism in the internet age*. MIT Press.

Earl, J., Hurwitz, H.M., Mesinas, A.M., Tolan, M., & Arlotti, A. (2013). This protest will be tweeted: Twitter and protest policing during the Pittsburgh G20. *Information, Communication and Society*, *16*(4), 459–478.

Fisher, D.R. (2019). *American resistance: from the women's march to the blue wave*. Columbia University Press.

Fisher, D.R., Dow, D.M., & Ray, R. (2017). Intersectionality takes it to the streets: mobilizing across diverse interests for the women's march. *Science Advances*, *3*(9), eaao1390.

Fligstein, N., & McAdam, D. (2012). *A theory of fields*. Oxford University Press.

Foley, M.W., & Edwards, B. (1999). Is it time to disinvest in social capital? *Journal of Public Policy*, *19*(2), 141–73.

Gartrell, C.D. (1987). Network approaches to social evaluation. *Annual Review of Sociology*, *13*, 49–66.

Gould, R.V. (2003). Why do networks matter? Rationalist and structuralist interpretations. In M. Diani & D. McAdam (Eds.), *Social movements and networks: relational approaches to collective action* (pp. 233–257). Oxford University Press.

Granovetter, M.S. (1973). The strength of weak ties. *American Journal of Sociology*, *78*(6), 1360–1380.

Granovetter, M.S. (1978). Threshold models of collective behavior. *American Journal of Sociology*, *83*(6), 1420–1443.

Hampton, K.N., & Wellman, B. (2018). Lost and saved ... again: the moral panic about the loss of community takes hold of social media. *Contemporary Sociology*, *47*(6), 643–651.

Heaney, M.T., & Rojas, F. (2008). Coalition dissolution, mobilization, and network dynamics in the US antiwar movement. *Research in Social Movements, Conflicts and Change*, *28*, 39–82.

Herrmann, C., Rhein, S., & Dorsch, I. (2022). # Fridaysforfuture: What does Instagram tell us about a social movement? *Journal of Information Science*, 1–17.

Hong, P.M, & Peoples, C.D. (2021). The ties that mobilize us: networks, intergroup contact, and participation in the Black Lives Matter movement. *Analyses of Social Issues and Public Policy*, *21*(1), 541–56.

Kitts, J.A. (2000). Mobilizing in black boxes: social networks and participation in social movement organizations. *Mobilization*, *5*(2), 241–57.

Klandermans, B., & Oegema, B. (1987). Potentials, networks, motivations, and barriers: steps towards participation in social movements. *American Sociological Review*, *52*(4), 519–531.

Knoke, D., Diani, M., Hollway, J., & Christopoulos, D. (2021). *Multimodal political networks*. Cambridge University Press.

Krackhardt, D. (1999). The ties that torture: Simmelian tie analysis in organizations. *Research in the Sociology of Organizations*, *16*(1), 183–210.

Krinsky, J., & Crossley, N. (2014). Social movements and social networks: introduction. *Social Movement Studies*, *13*(1), 1–21.

Krivitsky, P.N., & Morris, M. (2017). Inference for social network models from egocentrically sampled data, with application to understanding persistent racial disparities in HIV prevalence in the US. *Annals of Applied Statistics*, *11*(1), 427–455.

Laumann, E.O. (2006). A 45-year retrospective on doing networks. *Connections*, *27*(1), 65–90.

Lazega, E., & Snijders, T.A.B. (2015). *Multilevel network analysis for the social sciences: theory, methods and applications*. Springer.

Leifeld, P. (2017). Discourse network analysis. In J.N. Victor, A.H. Montgomery, & M. Lubell (Eds.), *The Oxford handbook of political networks* (pp. 301–326). Oxford University Press.

Lin, N. (2002). *Social capital: a theory of social structure and action*. Cambridge University Press.

Liu, W. (2016). How Twitter connects to the information sources network over time in the Occupy Wall Street social movement. *Social Media Studies*, *2*(2), 111–21.

Macy, M.W. (1990). Learning theory and the logic of critical mass. *American Sociological Review*, *55*(6), 809–26.

Mariotti, F., & Delbridge, R. (2012). Overcoming network overload and redundancy in interorganizational networks: the roles of potential and latent ties. *Organization Science*, *23*(2), 511–28.

Marsden, P.V., & Campbell, K.E. (1984). Measuring tie strength. *Social Forces*, *63*(2), 482–501.

Marsden, P.V., & Campbell, K.E. (2012). Reflections on conceptualizing and measuring tie strength. *Social Forces*, *91*(1), 17–23.

McAdam, D. (1986). Recruitment to high-risk activism: the case of Freedom Summer. *American Journal of Sociology*, *92*, 64–90.

McAdam, D., & Paulsen, R. (1993). Specifying the relationship between social ties and activism. *American Journal of Sociology*, *99*(3), 640–667.

McCarthy, J.D., & Zald, M.N. (1977). Resource mobilization and social movements: a partial theory. *American Journal of Sociology*, *82*(6), 1212–1241.

McLevey, J. (2022). *Doing computational social science: a practical introduction*. Sage.

Meyer, D.S., & Staggenborg, S. (1996). Movements, countermovements, and the structure of political opportunity. *American Journal of Sociology*, *101*(6), 1628–60.

Meyer, D.S., & Tarrow, S. (1998). A movement society: contentious politics for a new century. In D.S. Meyer and S. Tarrow (Eds.), *The social movement society: contentious politics for a new century* (pp. 1–28). Rowman and Littlefield.

Morgan, D.L., Neal, M.B., & Carder, P. (1996). The stability of core and peripheral networks over time. *Social Networks*, *19*(1), 9–25.

Morris, A.D. (1986). *Origins of the civil rights movements*. Free Press.

Norris, P. (2012). Political mobilization and social networks: the example of the Arab Spring.

In N. Kersting (Ed.), *Electronic emocrdacy* (pp. 55–76). Barbara Budrich.

Passy, F., & Giugni, M. (2001). Social networks and individual perceptions: explaining differential participation in social movements. Paper presented at the Sociological Forum.

Pavan, E. (2017). The integrative power of online collective action networks beyond protest: exploring social media use in the process of institutionalization. *Social Movement Studies*, 16(4), 433–46.

Ragin, C.C. (2008). *Redesigning social inquiry: fuzzy sets and beyond*. Wiley Online Library.

Shen, F., Xia, C., & Skoric, M. (2020). Examining the roles of social media and alternative media in social movement participation: a study of Hong Kong's Umbrella movement. *Telematics and Informatics*, 47, 101303.

Snijders, T.A.B., Van de Bunt, G.G., & Steglich, C.E.G. (2010). Introduction to stochastic actor-based models for network dynamics. *Social Networks*, 32(1), 44–60.

Snow, D.A. (2002). Social movements as challenges to authority: resistance to an emerging conceptual hegemony. Authority in Contention CBSM Workshop, University of Notre Dame, Notre Dame, Indiana. 14–15 August.

Snow, D.A., Zurcher Jr, L.A., & Ekland-Olson, S. (1980). Social networks and social movements: a microstructural approach to differential recruitment. *American Sociological Review*, 45(5), 787–801.

Steinert-Threlkeld, Z.C. (2017). Longitudinal network centrality using incomplete data. *Political Analysis*, 25(3), 308–28.

Stevenson, R., & Crossley, N. (2014). Change in covert social movement networks: the 'inner circle' of the provisional Irish Republican Army. *Social Movement Studies*, 13(1), 70–91.

Stoddart, M.C.J., Ramos, H., & Tindall, D.B. (2015). Environmentalists' media-work for Jumbo Pass and the Tobeatic Wilderness, Canada: combining text-centred and activist-centred approaches to news media and social movements. *Social Movement Studies*, 14(1), 75–91.

Stryker, S. (2000). Identity competition: key to differential social movements. In S. Stryker, T.J. Owens & R.W. White (Eds.), *Self, identity, and social movements* (pp. 21–40). University of Minnesota Press.

Tarrow, S.G. (2011). *Power in movement: social movements and contentious politics* (3rd ed.). Cambridge University Press.

Tindall, D.B. (2002). Social networks, identification, and participation in an environmental movement: low–medium cost activism within the British Columbia Wilderness Preservation Movement. *Canadian Review of Sociology*, 39(4), 413–452.

Tindall, D.B. (2004). Social movement participation over time: an ego-network approach to micro-mobilization. *Sociological Focus*, 37(2), 163–184.

Tindall, D.B. (2007). From metaphors to mechanisms: critical issues in networks and social movements research. *Social Networks*, 29(1), 160–169.

Tindall, D.B., Cormier, J., & Diani, M. (2012). Network social capital as an outcome of social movement mobilization: using the position generator as an indicator of social network diversity. *Social Networks*, 34(4), 387–395.

Tindall, D.B., Howe, A.C., & Mauboulès, C. (2021). Tangled roots: personal networks and the participation of individuals in an anti-environmentalism countermovement. *Sociological Perspectives*, 64(1), 5–36.

Tindall, D.B., McLevey, J., Koop-Monteiro, Y., & Graham, A. (2022). Big data, computational social science, and other recent innovations in social network analysis. *Canadian Review of Sociology/Revue canadienne de sociologie*, 59(2), 271–288.

Tindall, D.B., & Piggot, G. (2015). Influence of social ties to environmentalists on public climate change perceptions. *Nature Climate Change*, 5(6), 546–549.

Tindall, D.B., & Robinson, J.L. (2015). The concept of social movement and its relationship to the social movement society: an empirical investigation. In H. Ramos & K. Rodgers (Eds.), *Protest and politics: the promise of social Movement societies* (pp. 208–30). UBC Press.

Tindall, D.B., & Robinson, J.L. (2017). Collective action to save the temperate rainforest: social networks and environmental activism in Clayoquot Sound. *Ecology and Society*, 22(1), 40.

Tindall, D.B., Stoddart, M.C.J., McLevey, J., Jasny, L., Fisher, D.R., Earl, J., & Diani, M. (2021). On movements: the opportunities and challenges of studying social movement ego-networks: online and offline. In M.L. Small, B.L. Perry, B.A. Pescosolido & E.B. Smith (Eds.), *Personal networks: classic readings and new directions in ego-centric analysis* (pp. 696–717). Cambridge University Press.

Tindall, D.B. and Wellman, B., (2001). Canada as social structure: social network analysis and Canadian sociology. *Canadian Journal of Sociology/Cahiers canadiens de sociologie*, 26(3), 265–308.

Tufekci, Z. (2017). *Twitter and tear gas: the power and fragility of networked protest*. Yale University Press.

Tufekci, Z., & Wilson, C. (2012). Social media and the decision to participate in political protest: observations from Tahrir Square. *Journal of Communication*, 62(2), 363–379.

Wang, C., Wang, P., & Zhu, J.J.H. (2013). Discussing Occupy Wall Street on Twitter: longitudinal network analysis of equality, emotion, and stability of public discussion. *Cyberpsychology, Behavior, and Social Networking*, *16*(9), 679–85.

Wang, D.J., & Soule, S.A. (2012). Social movement organizational collaboration: networks of learning and the diffusion of protest tactics, 1960–1995. *American Journal of Sociology*, *117*(6), 1674–1722.

Wang, L., Yang, A., & Thorson, K. (2021). Serial participants of social media climate discussion as a community of practice: a longitudinal network analysis. *Information, Communication and Society*, *24*(7), 941–959.

Wellman, B., Wong, R.Y.-L., Tindall, D., & Nazer, N. (1997). A decade of network change: turnover, persistence and stability in personal communities. *Social Networks*, *19*(1), 27–50.

Wellman, B., Quan-Haase, A., & Harper, M.R. (2020). The networked question in the digital era: how do networked, bounded, and limited individuals connect at different stages in the life course? *Network Science*, *8*(3), 291–312.

11

Gender and Social Networks

Elisa Bellotti

INTRODUCTION

The scope of this chapter is to review the contributions that social network analysis has made to the study of gender, together with an evaluation of the potentials that a social network perspective can offer to this area of research.

In what follows, and in line with classic feminist work (Butler, 1990), gender is defined as the socially constructed feminine and masculine characteristics typically attributed to men and women, and is distinguished from sex, as bodily endowments (Oakley, 1972, p. 1). Microstructural and interactionist theories played an important role in showing how gender constructions emerge out of interactions, crystallise in collective norms and behavioural expectations, and reinforce structural opportunities and constraints that men and women, as well as people who do not identify in binary categories, face in their lives. While recognising the importance of social networks in forming, reproducing and challenging gender norms and stereotypes, such theories rarely evaluate the social network mechanisms that produce them. Social network scholars instead largely use gender as an exogenous category to characterise social networks, but do not typically distinguish between gender performativity and sexual biological characteristics, and rarely make gender as the main focus of social network theory (Fuhse, 2022).

In the first section of the chapter, I review the microstructural and interactionist approaches to the study of gender with the aim of identifying the gaps where a social network theory of gender may sit, and the contributions it may make.

The theoretical review is followed by three subsections that summarise the main results of social network scholars' studies of gender: socialisation and school environments, personal networks and foci of activities, organisational and business settings. I excluded studies where social networks are only metaphorically discussed but not empirically measured, studies where gender is only added as a variable but not discussed in the results, and studies that focus on online networks and social media, as I am interested in the construction and performance of gender in face-to-face interactions and offline institutional and organisational settings.

The reviewed work highlights how gender inequalities are formed and reproduced within social networks, and how these inequalities generate, over time, disparities and biases. Gender inequalities are defined as any observed difference between people of different gender (Traag & Waltman, 2020). Gender disparity instead refers to any difference between people indirectly caused by their gender, while gender biases are differences between people that are directly affected by their gender. Initial inequalities, even small and unconscious, can lock people into social network configurations and relational styles that become progressively harder to disentangle. As these differences ingrain in our daily lives, mounting constraints or accumulated opportunities become the basis of disparities that sediment over time (Smith-Lovin & McPherson, 1993), in the sense that men and women may not be directly discriminated but inevitably end up in different regions of social networks, with different opportunities and constraints. Inequalities and disparities can also produce biases, where gender stereotypes become so cemented in collective beliefs that directly affect women and men's lifelong possibilities.

Understanding how inequalities, disparities and biases are formed is useful because I am not only interested in discriminations that affect women against men. My aim is to identify differences in network formation and outcomes that distinguish male and female mechanisms of social interacting, and the consequences that these mechanisms have on masculine and feminine behaviour, as well as on opportunities and constraints that men and women face in their lives. Gender differences can affect men especially when they engage in traditionally feminine roles, as well as people who do not recognise their gender identity within the binary system of masculine and feminine. They also intersect with other forms of inequalities related to class, ethnicity, religion, age, or different body abilities (Saltzman Chafetz, 1988). There are, however, very few social network studies that have tackled LGBT and intersectional inequalities (Erosheva et al., 2016), leaving the stage open for future research.

The three domains that constitute the next three sections are the ones where research has mainly concentrated, although they are not considered exhaustive of all the scientific production on social networks and gender. Some notable new areas are emerging – for example, the study of gender in criminal networks (Carrington, 2016; Smith, 2019; Diviák et al., 2020). These are briefly touched upon in the discussion, which also offers an attempt to summarise the network mechanisms that contribute to the formation and evolution of gendered social structures, as well as the effects and consequences that these structures have in shaping gender performances within social networks. Conclusions identify the limits of the reviewed literature and the potential venues for future research.

GENDER AS A SOCIAL CONSTRUCTION AND THE ROLE OF SOCIAL NETWORKS

Gender discussion was first brought to the core of social research and activism by the 1970s second wave of Feminism (Saltzman Chafetz, 1999) which focused on three key arguments: that gender, as a social construction, is distinguished from – and not determined by – the biological characteristics of sex; that gender, as socially constructed, produces expectations in regards of roles stereotypically covered by men and women; and that role expectations are hierarchically organised, so stereotypical male roles are retained in higher statuses compared to female ones. Status expectations inform gender performances: when interacting with men, women often find themselves in lower ranks; they perceive higher ranks as masculine and they experience lack of legitimacy when they happen to cover these roles. Likewise, when interacting with women men often find themselves in higher ranks, perceive lower ranks as feminine and are likely to be devalued when covering typically feminine roles.

Lopata (1994, 1999) extends the reflection on gender expectations embedded in social roles by exploring how individuals enact such roles within their social circles. Roles are 'sets of patterned, mutually interdependent, social relations between a person and a social circle involving negotiated duties and obligations, rights and privileges' (Lopata, 1999, p. 230): the more circles a person embeds into, the more possibilities are to differentiate the gender performance. The diversification of social circles also produces higher burdens as demands on individuals multiply (Lopata, 1994): people may get frustrated for their inadequate performances, social circles can make conflicting demands and expectations can be contradictory or inconsistent. Lopata (1994, 1999) thus offers a clear link between gender roles and social network theory, but she does not formalise her conjectures in elementary network structures that could explain, for example, how networks with high closure may reinforce gender expectations, or how highly segregated networks could increase possibilities for multiple performances or contradicting demands.

Lopata's performative take on social roles links microstructural theories with interactionist theories, which focus on how interaction processes produce and reproduce gender identities in everyday life. Such interactive work is at the core of West and Zimmerman's seminal article (1987), which challenges the idea of individuals as passively obliging to gender expectations embedded in social roles. According to West and Zimmerman (1987), social interactions require people to constantly characterise themselves and others by attributing gender identities, which carry gender normative expectations of appropriateness. In doing gender, people reaffirm or challenge such normative expectations, holding themselves and others accountable for their gender-appropriate behaviour (West & Fenstermaker, 1993). This interactive process of negotiation of gender norms explains why definitions of masculinity and femininity may vary in time and social contexts.

The same interactive process also explains why traditional gender expectations are resistant to change: while people may negotiate gender norms in everyday interactions, the types of expectations that individuals experience are constrained by the tendency of humans to typify situations, simplify social contexts and interpret actions and responses using previous interactions (Mead, 1934; Stryker, 2002). Goffman defines the act of role-performing as scripted in interaction orders (1983) which provide social organisation of experience, or, as he calls it, 'social ritualization' (Goffman, 1983, p. 3). For performances to be recognised and supported they need to at least partially follow expected, culturally accepted interactive orders (Goffman, 1961, 1983). Gender, in this view, is one of the primary frames with which we categorise people and we organise social relations (Ridgeway, 2009).

Interactionist theories, and especially ethnomethodology, proposed the concept of network accountability (Schwalbe, 2016) that links the relational work people do in affirming and challenging gender definitions to the importance of social networks. When deciding on a course of action, people consider how others will likely perceive their behaviours, so they anticipate potential future needs to provide legible accounts. In most circumstances, people are unaware of this management (Hollander, 2013, p. 4): accounts become explicit when interactive partners perceive that the other somehow violates the socially accepted norms regulating their behaviour. In these situations, accountability becomes a means of social control, as not only actors will call each other to account for their behaviour but they may also invoke others to implement negative consequences of breaking behavioural norms. Teachers reproaching kids for what they consider an inappropriate way of dressing at school may threaten them by calling them in front of the principal or by calling the family, invoking the concerted effort of the social network around the kids in holding them accountable for their behaviour.

Network accountability works in any type of interactive situation, and because gender categories are a primary frame that we use to make sense of social relations (Ridgeway, 2009), people are held accountable for their performance as a man or a woman in virtually any activity they carry on (West & Zimmerman, 1987, p. 136). These normative requirements of what constitutes an appropriate gender behaviour vary, but resistance to them, as in being evaluated gender-inappropriate, carry consequences that can go from disapproval, to stigma, to violence. By behaving appropriately, people 'sustain, reproduce, and render legitimate the institutional arrangements that are based on sex categories' (West & Zimmerman, 1987, p. 146).

This brief and inevitably partial review of microstructural and interactionist theories of gender gives us some key conceptual materials to untangle the complex dynamics by which gender inequalities emerge and reproduce in societies. Network accountabilities explain how individuals learn, from a very early age, to interact appropriately according to the gender they are assigned at birth, and how their gender expectations are usually reinforced in the social circles they interact with. Gendered expectations explain why certain roles tend to be occupied predominantly by men or women, therefore becoming more and more characterised by gender stereotypes that make it increasingly difficult for other genders to be considered for such roles.

How do social networks contribute to these complex dynamics of gender inequalities? Social network scholars distinguish between theories of social networks and network theories (Borgatti & Lopez-Kidwell, 2014). Theories of social networks identify social mechanisms that pattern social network configurations: people tend to interact with others similar to them, they tend to reciprocate friendly or hostile behaviour in similar manners, they tend to treat friends of friends in amicable ways, etc. If men and women are socialised from a very early age to display masculine and feminine traits (Gansen & Martin, 2018), we can expect gender performances to facilitate the formation of networks that are typical masculine or feminine. If men and women occupy different network positions, we can expect their social circles to differentiate, and the opportunities and demands placed upon men and women to vary accordingly. Gender-segregated positions may impact the possibilities for men and women to form social networks that are either gender homophilous or gender diverse: male teachers would find it difficult to interact with other male teachers simply because there are not enough of them, and female executive managers would find it difficult to interact with other female executive managers for the same reason (Ibarra, 1992, 1997). The lack of men or women in specific types of roles reinforce the stereotypes that such roles are typically gendered, making it difficult for excluded genders to identify with them.

Social network theories instead identify the potential outcomes that network configurations produce. People embedded in highly connected networks may share the same norms and values but may also experience higher levels of concerted accountability, or as Coleman (1990) calls it, social control; people liaising across non-overlapping social circles may be exposed to novel ideas (Burt,

1992); and people interacting with others in higher ranks may obtain benefits (Burt, 1998). If men and women, over their lifetime, build different social networks, then we should expect that they obtain different outcomes. Such outcomes also produce different opportunities and constraints for network formation, maintenance and dissolution, which further generate differentiated outcomes.

The interplay between network formations and outcomes bears important consequences for gender inequalities. As we have seen in the introduction, gender inequalities only assume that differences exist between men and women: if we observe different network formations, and different network outcomes, we may conclude that variations in outcomes depend, all else being equal, on the different ways that men and women build their networks. If women and men were to develop similar network structures, their outcomes would be equally similar. As men and women progressively find themselves embedded in different network structures, the inequalities accumulate over their lifetime, making it increasingly difficult to modify such structures. We could also observe that despite network similarities, women and men obtain different outcomes. In this case we can assume that gender disparities or biases are in place. Disparities may be due to intervening factors that differentiate outcomes despite similar network structures – for example, in cases where women similarly occupy favouring brokerage positions in networks, but their roles are not acknowledged and rewards not granted (Brands & Kilduff, 2014). Biases may occur when all else being equal, women – or men – are still discriminated in their outcomes. Such discriminations can be explicit, like in countries where women are legally banned from certain activities; or implicit, like in hiring processes where male applicants are rated more competent despite their applications being identical to those of women (Moss-Racusin et al., 2012).

WHO DO YOU PLAY WITH? GENDER, SCHOOLS AND SOCIAL NETWORKS

The most conspicuous scientific production on gender and social networks focuses on the gendered paths of socialisations in schools. Here the first sign of gender differentiation in children's peer relation is the increasing gender separation. From the age of three children show preferences for playing with peers of the same gender and the tendency increases steadily all the way through adolescence. Studies with preschool children as well as middle childhood and early adolescence suggest that boys have more integrated social networks than girls in that their friends are more likely to be friends with one another, resulting in boys playing in larger groups than girls (Kirke, 2009; see Rose & Rudolph, 2006, for a review).

The social network mechanisms that may produce larger groups for boys have received notable attention, although studies are rare. Eder and Hallinan (1978) observe the dynamics of triadic structures of friendship relations in five US fifth-grade classrooms (ten to eleven years old) over a school year. They look at the triads (with at least three kids involved – A, B and C), where there is a reciprocal tie between B and C and no ties to A. They define exclusive triads the ones in which, over time, neither B nor C send a tie to A; and nonexclusive triads the ones where over time at least one of B or C (or both) send a tie to A. Overall, they find that nonexclusive triad are significantly more likely in boys, who seem to be more willing to nominate new friends as well as to respond positively to a friendship offer, while girls increasingly show propensity for exclusive dyads. These tendencies explain why over time girls tend to reduce the number of friendship triads and reverse to dyadic relationships, while boys are more likely to add inclusive triads progressively producing larger groups.

Gender also intersects with hierarchies in structuring school friendship networks. Hallinan and Kubitschek (1990) show that if a student is more popular than a peer in a transitive triplet, the popular student is likely to change from transitive to intransitive friendship choices in order to drop the friendship tie with the less popular kid. Again, studies noted gender differences by which boys seem to have greater shared understanding about which group members are more popular, therefore developing better-defined hierarchies than girls (Omark et al., 1975; Savin-Williams, 1979).

It is difficult to advance clear explanations for these gendered tendencies towards homophily, hierarchy and intransitivity. Psychological studies have largely investigated gender differences in individuals' relational style showing that overall girls tend to care more about their dyadic friendship, spend more time in social conversation and adopt connection-oriented goals, whereas boys focus more on agentic goals, including their own dominance in the peer group and prefer games which require more participants than the ones selected by girls (see Rose & Rudolph, 2006, for a review).

Are these differences driving the evolution social network configurations, making boys more inclusive and girls more exclusive in their friendship choices, and friendship circles more gender homophilous? As we will see in the next section, adults' social networks are equally gender homophilous, and women are more likely to carry the responsibility of emotional work within families and friends. Boys and girls learn relational styles from their families, styles that are also extensively reproduced in the media. These initially small and unconscious differences in what is considered as appropriate gender behaviour are likely to be reinforced in school networks: the more the individuals' social-cognitive style in relationships are reinforced in gender segregated groups, the more boys tend to be more inclusive and girls more exclusive, meaning that over time they end up in very different social circles (Smith-Lovin & McPherson, 1993).

If research on the gender influence on network formation and evolution seems to agree on the existence of different ways in which boys and girls develop their network configurations, research on network outcomes is far more inconclusive. Some studies investigate the relationship between friendship nominations in schools and academic achievements, finding that boys and girls are differently influenced in their academic achievements by their friends' school performances (Kretschmer et al., 2018; Shin & Ryan, 2014; Raabe et al., 2019), although in Chow et al. (2018) gender differences are not significant.

Another line of research focuses on social network configurations and individual risk behaviour. As friendship groups become less gender homophilous with age, research shows that boys are the ones mostly responsible in influencing both their male and female friends in drinking and smoking (Deutsch et al., 2014; Mercken et al., 2010; Pearson & Michell, 2000). Lorant and Nicaise (2015) instead associate the influence over drinking not so much to the gender of the influencer, but to the gendered nature of the social context. They look at Belgian university students and find that in engineering degrees, where females are scarce, highly central women are more prone to binge drinking, possibly to convey a more masculine social identity and avoid marginalisation. Likewise in psychology degrees, where males are scarce, highly central men avoid binge drinking, possibly to conform to more feminine environments where drinking is not particularly diffused. Jacobs and colleagues' review (2016) concludes that there is inconsistent evidence of influence of social networks over risk behaviours, as some studies find either boys or girls to be more susceptible of influence, other studies find no gender differences at all and others that differences are due to the type of substance abuse.

Similar inconsistent results emerge from studies of aggressive behaviours in social networks, where aggressiveness is related to network hierarchies. In a study of twelve- to fourteen-year-old US students, Faris and Felmlee (2011) note that the more the friendship nominations students receive, the more aggressive towards their peers they are, with the exception of those individual at the very bottom and at the very top of the network hierarchies, who display significantly less aggressive traits. Molano and Jones (2018), looking at a younger cohort of US kids (eight years old) find similar results for boys but not for girls, suggesting that female aggression in higher ranks may develop at a later age. More interestingly, both studies found significant effects of cross-gender relationships on reducing aggressions, although when these relationships are rare (Faris & Felmlee, 2011) or when boys attain higher levels of centrality within a context of mostly female peers (Molano & Jones, 2018) aggressions increase.

Not only adolescents select friends with similar level of physical aggression, but they are also influenced in increasing or reducing aggressive behaviours by how aggressive their friends are, although studies disagree on whom, between boys and girls, is most susceptible to being influenced and who influences more (Sentse et al., 2014; Shin, 2017; Zhang et al., 2020). The study of DeLay and colleagues (2018) on homophobic aggressions bears importance for the study of gender identity and performativity as it shows significant evidence that over time adolescents internalise the homophobic messages they receive from peers and incorporate them into their perception and performance of their own gender identity.

The studies reviewed in this section span from early childhood to university, although most of them concentrate on teenagers. The wide age range makes it difficult to compare results, but at the same time it allows conjecture about how gender norms and social networks evolve during youth. These studies also use very similar name generators, concentrating on close friendship: while we know that friendship can be interpreted differently in different contexts (Fischer, 1982) and that it is not exhaustive of children's relationships, we can at least consider results more comparable than if studies observed completely different types of relationships. Studies that directly observe interactions rather than asking children to report on their relationship were at the forefront of pioneering work in social network analysis (Wellman, 1926; Chevaleva-Janovskaja, 1927; Bott, 1928; Hubbard, 1929) but are now rarer (see, for example, Stehlé et al., 2013), although they should be encouraged as they are more reliable (Hagman, 1933; Bernard & Killworth, 1977) and avoid the issue of women being better than men in recalling social relationships (Brashears et al., 2016). Finally, studies span across different countries (North America, South America, Europe, Scandinavia, Russia, Middle East) and over the last four decades. Geographical and contextual factors, like historical events, cultural stereotypes and social and economic backgrounds are likely to play a role that we cannot account for in this review.

GENDERED PERSONAL NETWORKS, LIFE COURSE AND FOCI OF ACTIVITIES

While children tend to interact most exclusively in same-gender groups, peer homophily relaxes during pubertal timing when friendship groups open up to romantic and sexual relationships (Hill & Lynch, 1983). Sexual relationships are – still – largely dominated by the norms of heterosexuality (Foucault, 1976; Butler, 1990; Fuhse, 2022) which organises the mating conventions by dividing people in two binary and mutually exclusive genders. These conventions have important consequences for the configurations of social networks because heterosexual relationships are usually intransitive and generate tree-like structures, with the unwritten rule that discourages 'dating your ex-partner's ex' (Bearman et al., 2004). While adolescent peer groups open up to cross-gender ties, by the time romantic couples stabilise, friendship relationships reverse to homophilous ties to avoid the suspicion of possible extra-conjugal sexual interests (Fuhse, 2022; Booth & Hess, 1974; Fischer & Oliker, 1983).

If heterosexual love prescribes norms of cross-sex interactions, the gendered division of labour typical of the modern and bourgeoise heterosexual marriage dramatically impacts the structural opportunities and constraints of men and women's personal networks. Social contexts are organised around foci of activities – workplaces, voluntary organisations, hangouts, families, etc. (Feld, 1981) – and constitute the major settings for establishing and cultivating personal relations (Blau, 1977; Fischer, 1982). Social contexts provide the structural opportunities of interactions, but also segregate these opportunities, as we only have limited emotional and temporal resources to maintain relationships (Roberts et al., 2009; Chua, 2013).

Research on personal networks mostly focuses on the structure and composition of networks at various stages of individuals' lifetimes, with few longitudinal studies (Bidart & Lavenu, 2005; Lubbers et al., 2010). Classic works collected information on personal networks from representative samples of the US populations, and those datasets have been subsequently re-analysed with a gender lens. Fischer and Oliker (1983), in their re-analysis of Fischer (1982), observe that women's personal networks shrink in size when they marry, while married men's networks grow with an increased number of co-workers. Such differences are not simply explained by the tendency of women to withdraw from the labour force when they have children, because childless employed men still name more co-workers than childless employed women, and the friends of working women are less likely to have been met at work and more likely to have been met through husbands. The effects of marriage on the size and composition of personal networks, according to Fischer and Oliker (1983), is more likely to be affected by the division of housework, which dramatically reduces the time available for sociability for working women but increases it for working men. It is true that parenthood forces women out of employment much more than men, therefore depriving them of a social context whereby to develop personal relationships, but even for those who keep their jobs, their opportunities to socialise are constrained by household and caring responsibilities.

Bott (1957), in her study of married couples in mid-20th century in London, finds that the degree of segregation of conjugal roles is also related to the degree of connectedness of the couple's social network. Those families with close-knit networks tend to have a high degree of segregated conjugal roles, as in independent and complementary activities performed by husband and wives, while those with loose-knit networks tend to have more shared activities and interchangeable tasks. Bott attributes these differences to the diminishing informal social control that loose-knit networks exercise on couples that are freer to negotiate their conjugal roles within their own couples and allow partners to interact in different social circles (1957, pp. 101–105).

Another widely researched aspect of gender differences in personal networks focuses on the resources such networks provide. We have already seen in Fischer and Oliker (1983) that women tend to name comparatively fewer co-workers than men. Other studies suggest that their personal networks tend to involve more kin and neighbours (Fischer, 1982; Marsden, 1987; Wellman, 1985; Dunbar & Spoors, 1995; Bastani, 2007; Moore, 1990) and that their social circles, especially when they look after children, comprise mainly other women – mothers, teachers, carers, nurses, etc. (Fischer, 1982; Fischer & Oliker, 1983; Wellman, 1985; Chua, 2013). The different composition of personal networks has been associated with the different type of support men and women receive, as well as to different levels of demands networks pose to individuals. Haines and Hurlbert (1992) re-analyse data collected by Fischer (1982) in northern California and look at the amount of instrumental, companionship and emotional support men and women receive from their networks, as well as the associated levels of stress. Along with other notable differences, they found that women with larger networks, especially when married, report higher levels of stress mainly related to family's and friends' demands.

These results suggest that women tend to be overburdened in larger networks which demand instead of offering support, in line with Lopata's argument (1994) on the negative effects that women may experience when they diversify their social circles. This reading is reinforced by several studies indicating that women are the primary source of emotional support for their husbands, but not vice versa (Wellman, 1990; Campbell et al., 1986; Lowental & Hanen, 1968); that women are named as helpers between 30 per cent and 50 per cent more times than men (Kessler et al., 1985); that women are more aware of and responsive to the crises that occur in people they know (Kessler & McCleod, 1984); and that women provide their friends with personal favours, emotional support and informal counselling more than men (Flaherty & Richman, 1989). As women are left with the burden of emotional work, the more ties they have, the more demands are placed on them, especially when they have husbands and children to care for, and the more they end up reducing the burden by cutting off relationships.

Women's personal networks also differ in terms of the variety of jobs their contacts do, and therefore on the type of jobs they may get access to (van Tubergen et al., 2016). Campbell (1988) interviewed 186 employed men and women in North Carolina and found that men knew more people in diverse occupations than women, results that were also confirmed in McDonald and Mair (2010) and van Tubergen and Volker (2015). McDonald (2011) also shows that by having smaller networks with less diverse occupational profiles, women receive significant fewer jobs leads, and end up trapped in horizontally segregated networks of female-dominated careers. Lubbers et al. (2019) note that men have more acquaintances in their networks, and that these acquaintances are more likely to provide support in finding a job, in line with Granovetter's theory (1973) of the role of weak ties in job searches.

As women have unequal access to the variety of social contexts in which relationships are formed, over time their personal networks reproduce these gender inequalities. Women end up relegated in regions of networks which are rich in information about family, children and households, while men dominate regions where resources about career, money and social mobility are abundant (Smith-Lovin & McPherson, 1993). These patterns have important consequences for women's positions in business and organisational networks and their access to leadership roles, which we will discuss in the next section. They are also important because they set examples for younger generations: boys and girls grow up in families where mothers and fathers navigate different – and gender homophilous – social circles, engage in different activities and provide – or obtain – different types of social support. While boys will be more likely to mimic their fathers' tendency to engage in larger and varied networks with fewer relational demands, girls will learn from their mothers to provide emotional support, to reduce the burden of emotional work by narrowing the size of networks and to reproduce these relational styles in their preferences over dyadic relationships and intransitive triads.

GENDER IN BUSINESS AND ORGANISATIONS: WHO RULES?

The last area of research that has extensively contributed to exploring gender differences in social networks is organisational studies, where scholars specifically investigate if gender inequalities are driven by the different network structures women may build, or if despite similar structures women still obtain unequal returns (see Woehler et al., 2021, for a review).

In a seminal work on the workflow, communication and friendship between employers of a newspaper publishing company, Brass (1985) finds that while women are central in the female network, they are peripheral in the male one. As the male network exercises more influence in promotion processes, women are promoted less, while when women occupy positions equally central to the ones of men, they enjoy the same influential power. Brass's work (1985) highlights an important feature of organisational networks: as in the case of schools, women and men interact in highly homophilous and segregated networks, where men occupy hierarchically higher positions of influence. Women's segregation is what causes differences in outcomes, so if women were to modify their networks, they would also obtain higher returns.

In her study of an advertising and public relations agency, Ibarra (1992) similarly finds that while women chose homophilous ties for expressive support and heterophilous ties for instrumental support, men chose homophilous ties for both types of support. She argues, in a subsequent paper

(Ibarra, 1997), that differences in network structures are induced by the lack of women in leadership positions: as people benefit from instrumental ties with colleagues who are hierarchically higher than them, women are forced to seek these ties with men, who instead can choose from a wider pool of both homophilous and upreaching ties.

Burt (1998) suggests an alternative explanation for the tendency of women to instrumentally rely on men. He compares the career trajectories of women and men who achieve early promotions in a large US firm and finds that while men are promoted when they occupy brokerage roles, women do better in networks of highly interconnected contacts. Successful women do not gain direct advantages from brokerage but borrow it from their male sponsors whom they are closely related to. In other words, men and women are favoured by different organisational network configurations, and according to Burt this is due to the lack of legitimacy and credibility women have in large organisations. His findings are reinforced by Brands and Kilduff's results (2014) that show how women are systematically misassigned to their brokerage positions, and when their brokerage roles are acknowledged women are usually regarded as lacking feminine traits. These findings are in line with the theoretical discussion over gender expectations and social roles. The fewer women occupy positions in organisations, and the less they advance to prestigious roles, the more these positions and roles are associated with masculine stereotypes therefore inhibiting the advancement of female candidates.

When we look at men and women at the very top of elite and business networks instead, gender differences in network structures seem to fade away. In studying political elites in Sweden, for example, Edling and colleagues (2013) observe that while women are numerically underrepresented, those who actually make it into these tight circles are not significantly less centrally placed nor less likely to occupy brokerage positions, and the sex heterogeneity of their networks is not significantly different to men's. Similar results are found in Hawarden and Marsland (2011) who compare the networks of directors of the top Fortune global firms, while Yang and colleagues (2019) found that both male and female students recruited for leadership positions are usually highly central in the school-wide network, but women also need an inner circle of predominantly female contacts who provide informal support.

Qualitative studies, however, warn against the conclusions that men and women at the top of hierarchies enjoy similar networks and more importantly show that sitting on executive boards of top firms does not automatically translate in equal returns. The female expatriate senior managers interviewed by Linehan (2001), for example, lament the lack of networking opportunities for female managers, who are excluded from the 'old boys' network' created in informal contexts. They spoke of male bonding and business discussions that take place after work hours, when women with families return to their child care duties. In the rare cases in which women set up their own female networking programme they are met with derogatory comments – 'it's hen time'– and suspicions of male-bashing intents, but they also run the risk of reproducing once again those gender-segregated networks that isolate them from where decisions are made (Linehan, 2001, p. 409).

Ridgeway (2009) associates the disparities of women's outcomes, in terms of professional success, to the hierarchical structure of organisational networks and their gender compositions. She argues that in organisations with flat hierarchies and mixed gender compositions women achieve outcomes equal to men because the gender frame by which women are stereotypically assigned to lower ranks is less salient. The same flat hierarchies, however, disadvantage women in male-dominated contexts, where gender stereotypes are more relevant and the informal work structure facilitates the emergence of a 'boys' club' atmosphere. In such male-dominated contexts women do better when hierarchies are well defined, because formal rules and gender equality policies level out, to some extent, gender stereotypes.

DISCUSSION: THE CO-EVOLUTION OF GENDER AND NETWORKS

In this chapter I reviewed prominent studies that look at the intersections between social networks and gender in the most important institutional settings of everyday lives, namely schools, families and working environments. One aspect that clearly emerges is the co-evolution of social network configurations and gendered cultural and social expectations over the lifetime. From a very early age men and women favour interactions within same-sex groups. In these groups they share and reinforce feminine and masculine relational styles which appear to be associated with different ways boys and girls negotiate inclusion and hierarchies in friendship groups. The co-evolution of interactive styles and network configurations reproduces gender segregation and pushes boys and girls towards different regions of social networks.

Once men and women move into adult life, they carry with them the gender dispositions they performed in schools, together with the gendered network configurations they are familiar with. The hegemonic heterosexual kinship structures relegate them once again in gender-homophilous circles. More importantly, the hierarchical structure of family roles overloads women with emotional work, caring responsibilities and the burden of the second shift (Hochschild & Machung, 2003). Despite recent changes in the discourses that portray masculine family roles as more attentive to parenting and housework (Dermott, 2008), and changes in the policies that endorse women's access and resilience in the labour market (UN, 2011; HM Government, 2019), women's personal networks are still much more limited in the opportunities they offer compared to the ones of men, and much more constraining in terms of the demands they impose on women. Here it is important to note that the hegemonic association of caring responsibilities as female duties also affect men who do step up in parenting roles. Brooks and Hodkinson (2020) show how the social networks of fathers with primary or equal responsibility for the care of their young children considerably lack contact with other parents. Fathers' isolation is due to their feeling 'out-of-place' in many daytime public spaces; their fear of being judged because of their gender; and the difficulty of meeting other fathers with caring responsibility.

Where we seem to observe a limited effect of the growing number of women in the labour market, and of gender equality policies, is in organisational structures. Here networks are still predominantly gender segregated, and higher ranks mostly preclude women: in male-dominated contexts formal means of facilitating women's access to higher ranks can reduce gender inequalities (Burt, 1998), while where the mixed gender composition increases, the differences in network structures and outcomes seem to naturally level out, although again gender intersects with hierarchies in enabling or hampering women's success. In those cases in which women reach the top tiers they seem to enjoy similar networks, but as there are very few women in such high-flying positions it is difficult to systematically compare their social networks and gender-relational styles to the ones of men. There is relatively good evidence that in positions of equal formal authority men and women interact in similar manners with either same-gender or cross-gender subordinates (Johnson, 1994; Eagly & Johnson, 1990). However, when they lead, women seem to be more democratic and participatory than men, and if they behave in directive and autocratic styles they tend to be evaluated more negatively than men (Eagly et al., 1992).

An interesting area of research emerges from studies that look at the role of women in criminal activities. Informal markets are clearly exempt from gender equalities policies and these predominantly masculine environments seem to relegate women to the margins of criminal networks, from which positions they need to rely on influential men to exercise and maintain their power (Diviák et al., 2020; Smith, 2019). Research on trends in crime shows how gender segregation, as in the exclusion of females from collaborations with males, is particularly strong in robbery, assault and minor theft, but it is lower than expected in most violent crimes, drug trafficking and especially in sex crimes against children, where women are of particular value to their male co-offenders (Carrington, 2016, p. 628).

Looking at covert networks generates interesting insights in the study of gender roles, as women may occupy less central and more segregated position in networks, yet they may be strategic for the crime procedural processes thanks to their relative invisibility. Research on the role of women in mafia-type organisations, for example, suggests the term 'submerged centrality' (Principato & Dino, 1997) to describe the temporary delegation of power that mafia leaders grant to their female family members when they are incarcerated or on the run (Siebert, 2007). Yet again, the opportunities that mafia-type organisations offer to women seem to be related to the higher or lower hierarchical structure of the criminal network, as well as its patriarchal attitude (Allum & Marchi, 2018) and the gender-based division of labour within the criminal group (Savona & Natoli, 2007; Zhang et al., 2007).

CONCLUSIONS AND FUTURE WORK

The gender inequalities highlighted in this chapter accumulate over the lifetime, creating and reproducing implicit disparities and explicit biases in what is expected from men and women, and consequently in how we evaluate male and female behaviours (Ridgeway, 2009). Social network theory offers the possibility of looking at gender inequalities as they play out in network structures. Longitudinal analysis of school networks allows observation of how networks' configurations and gender-relational styles co-evolve. Personal network surveys across representative samples of the population give indications of network structure, composition and available resources for different social groups, identifying pockets of vulnerability and social exclusion where gender intersects with low income, older age, migration or hard-to-reach populations. Systematic comparison of organisational structures and gendered outcomes is useful to test the efficacy of gender policies and to tailor them according to more or less homophilous and hierarchical network configurations.

The theoretical and empirical work social network scholars have conducted so far has produced more questions than answers, so it is time that we tackle these questions more systematically. Could we expect, for example, that by favouring more mixed-gender environments from an early age gender stereotypes might weaken? Would we see different patterns of network formations by discouraging relational styles that seem to produce gendered ways of resolving intransitivity? Would an equal share of emotional and caring work improve women's participation in the labour force, and consequently a more equal distribution of leadership roles?

To answer these questions, collecting further evidence can be a valuable option, especially when data are old or confined to specific countries. It is the case that large-scale personal network surveys are still rare. The ones available are either dated (Burt, 1985; Wellman, 1979; Fischer, 1982) or focus only on core discussion networks (Grossetti, 2007; Boase & Ikeda, 2012; Fischer, 2021), with the exception of Lubbers et al. (2019). We need up-to-date information of personal networks that extend beyond core networks, but we also need studies that measure social networks in low-income countries and for diverse groups of the population, to see how gender intersects with macro-cultural factors like class, ethnicity, or non-binary gender identities.[1]

We should also capitalise on the large amount of social network data already collected, for which the information on gender is available. Several studies, both in schools and in organisations, collect details on various types of relationships: close friendship, advice, negative ties, acquaintances and the like. A comparative analysis of how gender interplays with social networks in different types of relationships would offer valuable insights, for example, on how men and women resolve relational conflicts, and how network configurations emerge and modify when same-sex ties and cross-sex ties intersect with multiplex ties. Meta-analysis of social networks in schools and organisations may also reveal interesting patterns that go beyond the microstructural and interactionist dynamics, linking those to the social, cultural and economic background of the data. A multi-level approach that takes into account hegemonic gender cultures, gender equality policies, local indexes of inequalities and other general macro-structures could better specify the opportunities and constraints women and men face in their lives, the networks they form and sustain, and the resources and support these networks provide.

Note

1 Some datasets are now available, which can be analysed from a gender perspective, see Published social network surveys and software (raffaelevacca.github.io).

REFERENCES

Allum, F., & Marchi I. (2018). Analyzing the role of women in Italian mafias: the case of the Neapolitan Camorra. *Qualitative Sociology*, 41, 361–380.

Bastani, S. (2007). Family comes first: men's and women's personal networks in Tehran. *Social Networks*, 29(3), 357–374.

Bearman, P., Moody, J., & Stovel, K. (2004). Chains of affection: the structure of adolescent romantic and sexual networks. *American Journal of Sociology*, 110(1), 44–91.

Bernard, H.R., & Killworth, P.D. (1977). Informant accuracy in social network data II. Human communication research. *Human Organization*, 4(1), 3–18.

Bidart, C., & Lavenu, D. (2005). Evolutions of personal networks and life events. *Social Networks*, 27(4), 359–376,

Blau, P. (1977). *Inequality and heterogeneity*. Free Press.

Boase, J., & Ken'ichi, I. (2012). Core discussion networks in Japan and America. *Human Communication Research*, 38(1), 95–119

Booth, A., & Hess, E. (1974). Cross-sex friendship. *Journal of Marriage and the Family*, 36(1), 38–46.

Borgatti, S., & Lopez-Kidwell, V. (2014). Network theory. In J. Scott & P.J. Carrington (Eds.), *The Sage handbook of social network analysis* (pp. 40–54). Sage.

Bott, E. (1957). *Family and social network*. Tavistock.

Bott, H. (1928). Observation of play activities in a nursery school. *Genetic Psychology Monographs*, 4, 44–88.

Brands, R.A., & Kilduff, M. (2014). Just like a woman? Effects of gender-biased perceptions of friendship network brokerage on attributions and performance. *Organization Science*, 25(5), 1530–1548.

Brashears, M.E., Hoagland, E., & Quintane, E. (2016). Sex and network recall accuracy. *Social Networks*, 44, 74–84.

Brass, D.J., 1985, Men's and women's networks: a study of interaction patterns and influence in an organization. *Academy of Management Journal*, 28(2), 327–343.

Brooks, R., & Hodkinson, P. (2020). Out-of-place: the lack of engagement with parent networks of caregiving fathers of young children. *Families, Relationships and Societies*, 9(2), 201–216.

Burt, R.S. (1985). General Social Survey network items. *Connections*, *8*, 119–123.

Burt, R.S. (1992). *Structure holes*. Harvard University Press.

Burt, R.S. (1998). The gender of social capital. *Rationality and Society*, *10*(1), 5–46.

Butler, J. ([1990] 2007). *Gender trouble*. Routledge.

Campbell, K.E. (1988). Gender differences in job-related networks. *Work and Occupations*, *15*(2), 179–200.

Campbell, K.E., Marsden, P., & Hurlbert, J. (1986). Social resources and socioeconomic status. *Social Networks*, *8*, 97–117.

Carrington, P. (2016). Gender and age segregation and stratification in criminal collaborations. *Journal of Quantitative Criminology*, *32*, 613–649.

Chevaleva-Janovskaja, E. (1927). Groupements spontanés d'enfants à l'age préscolaire. *Archives de Psychologie*, *20*, 219–223.

Chow, A., Kiuru, N., Parker, P.D., Eccles, J.S., & Salmela-Aro, K. (2018). Development of friendship and task values in a new school: friend selection for the arts and physical education but socialization for academic subjects. *Journal of Youth and Adolescence*, *47*(9), 1966–1977.

Chua, V. (2013). Categorical sources of varieties of network inequalities. *Social Science Research*, *42*(5), 1236–1253.

Coleman, J.S. (1990). *The foundations of social theory*. Belknap Press.

DeLay, D., Lynn Martin, C., Cook, R.E., & Hanish, L.D. (2018). The influence of peers during adolescence: does homophobic name calling by peers change gender identity? *Journal of Youth and Adolescence*, *47*(3), 636–649.

Dermott, E. (2008). *Intimate fatherhood: a sociological analysis*. Routledge.

Deutsch, A.R., Steinley, D., & Slutske, W.S. (2014). The role of gender and friends' gender on peer socialization of adolescent drinking: a prospective multilevel social network analysis. *Journal of Youth and Adolescence*, *43*(9), 1421–1435.

Diviák, T., Coutinho, J.A., & Stivala, A.D. (2020). A man's world? Comparing the structural positions of men and women in an organized criminal network. *Crime, Law and Social Change*, *74*(5), 547–569.

Dunbar, R.I., & Spoors, M. (1995). Social networks, support cliques, and kinship. *Human Nature*, *6*(3), 273–290.

Eagly, A.H., & Johnson, B.T. (1990). Gender and the emergence of leaders: a meta-analysis. *Psychological Bulletin*, *108*, 233–256.

Eagly, A.H., Makhijani, M.G., & Klonsky, B.G. (1992). Gender and the evaluation of leaders: a meta-analysis. *Psychological Bulletin*, *111*, 543–588.

Eder, D., & Hallinan, M. (1978). Sex differences in children's friendships. *American Sociological Review*, *43*, 237–250.

Edling, C., Farkas, G., & Rydgren, J. (2013). Women in power: sex differences in Swedish local elite networks. *Acta Sociologica*, *56*(1), 21–40.

Erosheva, E.A., Kim, H.-J., Emlet, C., & Fredriksen-Goldsen, K.I. (2016). Social networks of lesbian, gay, bisexual, and transgender older adults. *Research on Aging*, *38*(1), 98–123.

Faris, R., & Felmlee, D. (2011). Status struggles: network centrality and gender segregation in same- and cross-gender aggression. *American Sociological Review*, *76*(1), 48–73.

Feld, S. (1981). The focused organization of social ties. *American Journal of Sociology*, *86*(5), 1015–1035.

Fischer, C.S. (1982). *To dwell among friends*. University of Chicago Press.

Fischer, C.S. (2021). From the Northern California Community Study, 1977–1978, to the University of California, Berkeley, Social Networks Project, 2015–2020. In B. Pescosolido & E. Smith (Authors) & M. Small & B. Perry (Eds.), *Personal networks: classic readings and new directions in egocentric analysis* (pp. 227–239). Cambridge University Press.

Fischer, C.S., & Oliker, S.J. (1983). A research note on friendship, gender and the life cycle. *Social Forces*, *62*(1), 124–133.

Flaherty, J., & Richman, J.A. (1989). Gender differences in the perception and utilization of social support: theoretical perspectives and an empirical test. *Social Science and Medicine*, *28*(12), 1221–1228.

Foucault, M. ([1976] 1978). The history of sexuality. Volume 1: an introduction. Pantheon.

Fuhse, J. (2022). *Social networks of meanings and communication*. Oxford University Press.

Gansen, H.M., & Martin, K.A. (2018). Becoming gendered. In B.J. Risman, C.M. Froyum & W.J. Scarborough (Eds.), *Handbook of the sociology of gender*. Springer.

Goffman, E. (1961). *Encounters*. Bobbs-Merrill Co.

Goffman, E. (1983). The interaction order: American Sociological Association, 1982 Presidential Address. *American Sociological Review*, *48*(1), 1–17.

Granovetter, M.S. (1973). The strength of weak ties. *American Journal of Sociology*, *78*(6), 1360–1380.

Grossetti, M. (2007). Are French networks different? *Social Networks*, *29*(3), 391–404.

Hagman, E.P. (1933). The companionships of preschool children. *University of Iowa Studies in Child Welfare*, *7*, 10–69.

Haines, V.A., & Hurlbert, J.S. (1992). Network range and health. *Journal of Health and Social Behavior*, *33*(3), 254–266.

Hallinan, M.T., & Kubitschek, W.N. (1990). The formation of intransitive friendships. *Social Forces*, *69*(2), 505–519.

Hawarden, R.J., & Marsland, S. (2011). Locating women board members in gendered director networks. *Gender in Management: An International Journal*, *26*(8), 532–549.

Hill, J.P., & Lynch, M.E. (1983). The intensification of gender-related role expectations. In J. Brooks-Gunn & A.C. Peterson (Eds.), *Girls at puberty* (pp. 201–228). Plenum.

HM Government (2019). *Gender equality at every stage: a roadmap for change*. Government Equalities Office. www.gov.uk/government/publications/gender-equality-at-every-stage-a-roadmap-for-change

Hochschild, A.R., & Machung, A. (2003). *The second shift*. Penguin.

Hollander, J.A. (2013). 'I demand more of people': accountability, interaction, and gender change. *Gender and Society*, 27, 5–29.

Hubbard, R.M. (1929). A method of studying spontaneous group formation. In D.S. Thomas (Ed.), *Some new techniques for studying social behavior* (pp. 76–85). Teachers College, Columbia University, Child Development Monographs.

Ibarra, H. (1992). Homophily and differential returns: sex differences in network structure and access in an advertising firm. *Administrative Science Quarterly*, 37(3), 422–447.

Ibarra, H. (1997). Paving an alternative route: gender differences in managerial networks. *Social Psychology Quarterly*, 60(1), 91–102.

Jacobs, W., Goodson, P., Barry, A.E., & McLeroy, K.R. (2016). The role of gender in adolescents' social networks and alcohol, tobacco, and drug use: a systematic review. *Journal of School Health*, 86(5), 322–333.

Johnson, C. (1994). Gender, legitimate authority, and leader-subordinate conversations. *American Sociological Review*, 59, 122–135.

Kessler, R.C., & McCleod, J.D. (1984). Sex differences in vulnerability to undesirable life events. *American Sociological Review*, 49, 620–631.

Kessler, R.C., McCleod J.D., & Wethington E. (1985). The costs of caring: a perspective on the relationship between sex and psychological distress. In I.G. Sarason & B.R. Sarason (Eds.), *Social support: theory, research and applications*. Martinus Nijhof.

Kirke, D. (2009). Gender clustering in friendship networks: some sociological implications. *Methodological Innovations*, online, 23–36.

Kretschmer, D., Leszczensky, L., & Pink, S. (2018). Selection and influence processes in academic achievement: more pronounced for girls? *Social Networks*, 52, 251–260.

Linehan, M. (2001). European female expatriate careers: critical success factors. *Journal of European Industrial Training*, 25(8), 392–418.

Lopata, H.Z. (1994). *Circles and settings: role changes of American women*. Suny University Press.

Lopata, H.Z. (1999). Gender and social roles. In C.J. Saltzman (Ed.), *Handbook of sociology of gender*. Kluwer Academic/Plenum.

Lorant, V., & Nicaise, P. (2015). Binge drinking at university: a social network study in Belgium. *Health Promotion International*, 30(3), 675–683.

Lowental, M., & Hanen, C. (1968). Interaction and adaptation: intimacy as a critical variable. *American Sociological Review*, 33, 390–400.

Lubbers, M.J., Molina J.L., Lerner, J., Brandes, U., Ávila, J., & McCarty, C. (2010). Longitudinal analysis of personal networks: the case of Argentinean migrants in Spain. *Social Networks*, 32(1), 91–104.

Lubbers, M.J., Molina, J.L., & Valenzuela-García, H. (2019). When networks speak volumes: Variation in the size of broader acquaintanceship networks. *Social Networks*, 56, 55–69.

Marsden, P.V. (1987). Core discussion networks of Americans. *American Sociological Review*, 52(1), 122–31.

McDonald, S., 2011, What's in the 'old boys' network? Accessing social capital in gendered and racialized networks. *Social Networks*, 33(4), 317–330.

McDonald, S., & Mair, C.A. (2010). Social capital across the life course: age and gendered patterns of network resources. *Sociological Forum*, 25, 335–359.

Mead, G.H. (1934). *Mind, self, and society*. University of Chicago Press.

Mercken, L., Snijders, T.A.B., Steglich, C. Vertiainen, E., & de Vries, H. (2010). Smoking-based selection and influence in gender-segregated friendship networks: a social network analysis of adolescent smoking. *Addiction*, 105(7), 1280–1289.

Molano, A., & Jones, S.M. (2018). Social centrality and aggressive behavior in the elementary school: gender segregation, social structure, and psychological factors. *Social Development*, 27(2), 415–430.

Moore, G. (1990). Structural determinants of men's and women's personal networks. *American Sociological Review*, 55(5), 726–35.

Moss-Racusin, C.A., Dovidio, J.F., Brescoll, V.L., Graham, M.J., & Handelsman, J. (2012). Science faculty's subtle gender biases favour male students. *Proceedings of the National Academy of Sciences of the United States of America*, 109(41), 16474–16479.

Oakley, A. (1972). *Sex, gender and society*. Maurice Temple Smith.

Omark, R.R., Omark, M., & Edelman, M. (1975). Formation of dominance hierarchies in young children. In T.R. Williams (Ed.), *Psychological anthropology* (pp. 289–316). Mouton.

Pearson, M., & Michell, L. (2000). Smoke rings: social network analysis of friendship groups, smoking and drug-taking. *Drugs: Education, Prevention and Policy*, 7(1), 21–37.

Principato, T., & Dino, A. (1997). *Mafia Donna: le vestali del sacro e dell'onore*. Flaccovio editore.

Raabe, I.J., Boda, Z., & Stadtfeld, C. (2019). The social pipeline: how friend influence and peer exposure widen STEM gender gap. *Sociology of Education*, 92(2), 105–123.

Ridgeway, C.L. (2009). Framed before you now it. *Gender and Society*, 23(2), 145–160.

Roberts, S.G.B., Dunbar, R.I.M., Pollet, T.V., & Kuppens, T. (2009). Exploring variation in active network size: constraints and ego characteristics. *Social Networks*, 31(2), 138–146.

Rose, A.J., & Rudolph, K.D. (2006). A review of sex differences in peer relationship processes: potential trade-offs for the emotional and behavioral development of girls and boys. *Psychological Bulletin*, 132(1), 98–131.

Saltzman Chafetz, J. (1988). *Feminist sociology: an overview of contemporary theories*. F.E. Peacock.

Saltzman Chafetz, J. (1999). The varieties of gender theories in sociology. In J. Saltzman Chafetz (Ed.), *Handbook of sociology of gender*. Kluwer Academic/Plenum.

Savin-Williams, R.C. (1979). Dominance hierarchies in groups of early adolescents. *Child Development*, 50, 923–935.

Savona, E., & Natoli, G. (2007). Women and other mafia type criminal organizations. In G. Fiandaca (Ed.), *Women and the mafia: female roles in organized crime structures*. Springer.

Schwalbe, M. (2016). Overcoming aprocessual bias in the study of inequality: parsing the capitalist interaction order. *Studies in Symbolic Interaction*, 46, 95–122.

Sentse M., Kiuru N., Veenstra, R., & Salmivalli, C. (2014). A social network approach to the interplay between adolescents' bullying and likeability over time. *Journal of Youth and Adolescence*, 43(9), 1409–1420.

Shin, H. (2017). Friendship dynamics of adolescent aggression, prosocial behavior, and social status: the moderating role of gender. *Journal of Youth and Adolescence*, 46(11), 2305–2320.

Shin, H., & Ryan, A.M. (2014). Friendship networks and achievement goals: an examination of selection and influence processes and variations by gender. *Journal of Youth and Adolescence*, 43(9), 1453–1464.

Siebert, R. (2007). Donne di mafia. Affermazione di un pseudo-soggetto femminile. Il caso della Bndrangheta. In G. Fiandaca (Ed.), *Women and the Mafia: female roles in organized crime structures*. Springer.

Smith, C. (2019). *Syndicate women: gender and networks in Chicago organized crime*. University of California Press.

Smith-Lovin, L., & McPherson, J.M. (1993). You are who you know: a network approach to gender. In P. England (Ed.), *Theory on gender/feminism on theory*. Aldine De Gruyter.

Stehlé, J., Charbonnier, F., Picard, T., Cattuto, C., & Barrat, A. (2013). Gender homophily from spatial behavior in a primary school: a sociometric study. *Social Networks*, 35, 604–613.

Stryker, S. (2002). Traditional symbolic interactionism, role theory, and structural symbolic interactionism: the road to identity theory. In J.H. Turner (Ed.), *Handbook of sociological theory*. Springer.

Traag, V., & Waltman, L. (2020). *The causal intricacies of studying gender bias in science*. Leiden Madtrics.

UN (2011). *Gender equality policy*. UN, Human Rights. genderequalitypolicy_september2011.pdf (ohchr.org)

Van Tubergen, F., & Volker, B. (2015). Inequality in access to social capital in the Netherlands. *Sociology*, 49(3), 521–538.

Van Tubergen, F., Ali Al-Modaf, O., Almosaed, N.F., & Said Al-Ghamdi, M.Ben (2016). Personal networks in Saudi Arabia: the role of ascribed and achieved characteristics. *Social Networks*, 45, 45–54.

Wellman, B. (1926). The school child's choice of companions. *Journal of Educational Research*, 14:126–132.

Wellman, B. (1979). The community question: the intimate networks of East Yorkers. *American Journal of Sociology*, 84, 1201–1231.

Wellman, B. (1985). Domestic work, paid work and network. In S. Duck and D. Perlman (Eds.), *Understanding personal relationships: an interdisciplinary approach* (pp. 159–191). Sage.

Wellman, B. (1990). Different strokes from different folks: community ties and social support. *American Journal of Sociology*, 96, 558–588.

West, C., & Fenstermaker, S. (1993). Power, inequality, and the accomplishment of gender: an ethnometodological view. In P. England (Ed.), *Theory on gender/feminism on theory* (pp.151–174). Aldine De Gruyter.

West, C., & Zimmerman, D. (1987). Doing gender. *Gender and Society*, 1, 125–151.

Woehler, M.L., Cullen-Lester, K.L., Porter, C.M., & Frear, K.A. (2021). Whether, how, and why networks influence men's and women's career success: review and research agenda. *Journal of Management*, 479(1), 207–236.

Yang, Y., Chawla, N.V., & Uzzi, B. (2019). A network's gender composition and communication pattern predict women's leadership success. *Proceedings of the National Academy of Sciences of the United States of America*, 116(6), 2033–2038.

Zhang, M., Liu, H., & Zhang, Y. (2020). Adolescent social networks and physical, verbal, and indirect aggression in China: the moderating role of gender. *Frontiers in Psychology*, 11, 658.

Zhang, S.X., Chin, K., & Miller, J. (2007). Women's participation in Chinese transnational human smuggling: a gendered market perspective. *Criminology*, 45(3), 699–732.

12

Why Can't We Be Friends? Understanding Ethnic Relations Through Network Analysis

Rochelle Côté

INTRODUCTION

This chapter will take the position that the study of race and ethnic relations is in part about the study of power, discrimination and intolerance stemming from perceived differences of physical, cultural and religious traits (see Satzewich, 2021, for comprehensive discussion). In general, researchers have taken to identifying and categorising systems of hierarchy and inequality that exist between and across ethnoracial groups, documenting the impact on a range of outcomes – immigration and incorporation, health, education, employment/entrepreneurship, civic participation and social support to name a few. Social network analysis distinguishes itself as a method and set of theoretical perspectives that link individual and group outcomes to the structure (and content) of the networks in which they belong. It can provide an important key not only to defining and broadening our understanding of systems of ethnoracial inequality, but to also decolonising the way we view ethnic groups in general. While interethnic contact and relationships are discussed as one such important mechanism to minimising inequality, studies typically focus on self-report, observational or experimental data around contact to draw conclusions (Christ & Wagner, 2013; Pettigrew & Tropp, 2006). This chapter will review the literature and work in this area, and show how network analysis is making important methodological and theoretical contributions to mapping and understanding contact between ethnoracial groups and its outcomes. The discussion will focus on the potential strength of network analysis as a component of decolonising the way research is being done in this space.

Contact between ethnic groups that is personal, positive, voluntary and of equal status that includes shared goals leads to positive orientations towards other groups, and also encourages people to interact and share experiences that ideally decrease racism and intolerance in society (Allport, 1954; Dixon & Rosenbaum, 2004; Sigelman et al., 1996). Past work has focused on strong ties such as close friends to consider change in ethnoracial attitudes, with little evidence showing that changes occur within this paradigm (Putnam, 2000). Further, broad and diverse interethnic contact and interactions are seen as a way of reducing prejudice and as a hallmark of successful assimilation of ethnic minorities and immigrants into host societies (Allport, 1954; Gordon, 1964). In this vein, the causes and consequences of cultivating interethnic contact and relationships is one focus of work and debate around ethnic inequality.

'Birds of a feather ...' is a common expression that explains a great deal about the way individuals organise themselves within and between groups. Individuals prefer to surround themselves with people who are like them, who enjoy similar activities and ways of thinking about the world (McPherson et al., 2001). Research continues to show that racial and ethnic homophily features in the way that individuals (and groups) connect and interact with each other (Leszczensky & Pink, 2019; McPherson et al., 2001). This should not be surprising – common interests, occupation, education, gender, culture and religion are all ways in which individuals look to form lasting connections with others (McPherson et al., 2001). Are ethnicity and race really any different?

This becomes problematic, however, when ethnicity and race are used to craft boundaries that exclude and devalue particular groups, cementing discriminatory, racist practices that disadvantage individuals from getting ahead. Groups will practice homophily to draw boundaries to protect and keep resources and opportunities out of the reach of outgroup members (Wilson, 1987; 1996b; Wimmer, 2004). In the context of ethnic relations, boundaries increase difficulties minorities have with incorporating into societies, finding employment and advancing, the creation of enclave economies, making friends and marrying, or even in how social support is sought. Key to these conversations is network analysis – whether the focus looks to the structure of individual or group networks with respect to density, size, strength of ties, presence of structural holes, or characteristics of contacts, and a focus on how gender, class and race (or interactions between) impact the kinds of resources and opportunities accessed. Studies who fail to account for the role of social networks are missing important information about societal outcomes when it comes to conversations about inequality, immigrants, ethnic minorities and Indigenous Peoples.

MEASURING INTER-GROUP CONTACT: NETWORK STRUCTURE AND CONTENT

Studies of racial and ethnic inequality have increasingly incorporated network methods in a variety of ways that consider the impact of respondent race and ethnicity as well as the ethnoracial structure and content of ties on a host of outcomes (Laumann, 1966; Verhaeghe & Li, 2015). If the ethnoracial background of the respondent is associated with unequal outcomes, it would seem obvious that the ethnoracial backgrounds of the people we know are equally responsible for perpetuating unequal outcomes. While the significance of measuring actor race and/or ethnic background has been a part of surveys for a significant amount of time, measuring the racial and/or ethnic composition of networks has been variably embraced. Whether it is argued that time, funding or preference constraints are responsible for the way in which network data is collected, identifying racial and ethnic background of network ties is still not standard practice. If studies aim to look at how the structure and composition of networks is contributing to inequality, ethnicity and/or race of network members needs to be included.

Name and position generators are two ways in which the ethnoracial structure and composition of whole and egocentric networks are measured. In my own work and the work of others, these methods have been used to research tolerance of ethnic minorities (Côté et al., 2015; Côté & Erickson, 2009; Dovidio et al., 2003; Kuhn, 2004), unequal access to health services and information (Marquez et al., 2014; Song, 2011), entry and mobility in the labour market (McDonald et al., 2009), access to opportunities in and out of educational institutions (Muller et al., 2010; Mayer & Puller, 2008), status attainment (Cross & Lin, 2008) and underlying causes of migration (Coombs, 1978/79). For a broader discussion of network data collection methods, please also see Adams and Lubbers, this volume, and Perry et al., this volume.

Name generators

When whole network studies are not possible, whether because the population is not known or too large, or the time and expense of collecting this data too burdensome, egocentric studies are an alternative method of data collection. Irrespective of the type of study, name generators are a widely used method to determine the structure and content of networks, and have incorporated interpreter questions to better understand the 'who' of network ties (Burt, 1984; Marsden, 1987; Marsden et al., 2019; Stoyanova, 2008). One great example of this type of work as it relates to ethnicity/race stems from the US General Social Survey (Smith et al., 2019), which asks respondents to list the five people they discuss important matters with (Figure 12.1). A follow-up question then asks individuals to indicate the ethnoracial background of each contact. The benefit of this method is that alters are matched to their ethnicity or race, allowing researchers to accurately describe the ethnoracial composition of respondent networks. It also allows for accurate diagramming and mapping of individual networks, when follow-up questions ask for ties between alters.

An often-cited drawback of this method is that respondents are more likely to list alters who are

```
                                    -53-
                                                              BEGIN DECK 11
    127.  From time to time, most people discuss important matters with other
          people.  Looking back over the last six months - who are the people
          with whom you discussed matters important to you?  Just tell me their
          first names or initials.  IF LESS THAN 5 NAMES MENTIONED, PROBE, Anyone
          else?  ONLY RECORD FIRST 5 NAMES.

          LIST ALL NAMES IN ORDER ACROSS THE TOP OF THE MATRIX ON FACING PAGE.
          THEN WRITE NAMES 2-5 DOWN THE SIDE OF THE MATRIX.

    132.  Is (NAME) Asian, Black, Hispanic,    Asian..................1       36/
          White or something else?             Black..................2
          ASK FOR EACH NAME.                   Hispanic...............3
                                               White..................4
                                             · OTHER..................5
                                               REFUSED................7
                                               DON'T KNOW.............8
```

Figure 12.1 Name generator and interpreter (*US General Social Survey*)

Source: 1985 *US General Social Survey* (Smith et al., 2019). gss.norc.org/documents/quex/1985%20GSS%20Quex.pdf

strong ties, with whom they share stronger ties, and alters who are more densely connected in the network (Marin, 2004). With respect to having an idea of the true range and diversity of ties (both strong and weak), name generators can limit information and understanding. Research also shows that the number of interracial friendships changes with the number and type of questions asked, with a name generator eliciting the fewest reported contacts (Smith, 2002).

A second example of ways in which data on the ethnoracial composition of networks has been collected through the use of name generators, is through the *National Longitudinal Study of Adolescent Health* (Add Health) (Carolina Population Centre, 2001). Individuals are asked to nominate up to five male and five female friends, with a series of follow-up questions asked about each (Figure 12.2). In addition to detailed information about egocentric networks, the data can be used to build a whole network through the combining of adolescents in school contexts in the US. Respondents are asked about their ethnicity/race, and data is extrapolated to the network through friendship nominations.

Position Generators

The position generator method originally started with a measure that looked to integrate class understandings of inequality – the distribution of resources across middle- and working-class occupations. Originally developed by Lin and Dumin (1986), the position generator asks respondents to select occupations from a list in which they know someone. This was extended in Erickson (2004) to include gender distribution across occupations, asking respondents whether they knew a man and a woman in each of a list of working-class occupations. In a study of Indigenous entrepreneurs, Côté (2012) added ethnoracial categories, where respondents indicated if they knew someone Indigenous, white and non-Indigenous/non-white across a series of occupations (see Figure 12.3). The measure also accounts for class and gender composition of ties, as well as strength of tie with the use of very close, somewhat close and acquaintance role relationship categories (see Wellman et al., 2006, for discussion of strength of ties measure).

Past work tells us that ethnicity/race matter in terms of access to resources and opportunities that impact economic, social and political outcomes of discriminated ethnoracial classes. It is imperative that studies using network analysis attend to ethnicity/race in their network measures for richer understandings of how and why individual network patterns vary.

While debate around the use of the position generator has at times been contentious, occupational position generators have been validated across many contexts and populations. A wealth of work now shows that they reliably and consistently measure diversity in social networks (for examples, please see Côté, 2012; Côté et al., 2019; Lin et al., 2001; Miething et al., 2017; Verhaeghe et al., 2013). Position generators lend themselves well to surveys (and interviews) in that they take less time than name generator questions, can elicit a greater number of data points that can be used

4. Are you of Hispanic or Spanish origin?			S4	num 1
63664	0	no (skip to Q.6)		
15542	1	yes (go to Q.5)		
5751	8	I don't know. (skip to Q.6)		
10	9	multiple response		
5151	!	missing		
5. What is your background?			S5	num 2
5959	1	Mexican/Mexican American		
945	2	Chicano/Chicana		
1229	3	Cuban		
1525	4	Puerto Rican		
3104	5	Central/South American		
1817	6	other Hispanic		
69383	97	legitimate skip		
560	98	I don't know.		
287	99	multiple response		
5309	!	missing		
First Female Friend			FF1AID	num 8
47266		AID of nominated friend		
10907	77777777	nominated friend doesn't go to sister or sample school		
3251	88888888	nominated friend goes to sister school- not on list		
252	99959995	out-of-range identification number used for nomination		
4682	99999999	nominated friend goes to sample school- not on list		
23760		did not nominate a friend		

Figure 12.2 Respondent question and name generator (Add Health Longitudinal

Source: 1999 *National Longitudinal Study of Adolescent Health* (Carolina Population Centre, 2001). addhealth.cpc.unc.edu/

to measure diversity and can make assumptions about the meaning of that diversity based on the class, gender and ethnoracial compositions of a respondent's network.

A drawback of this method depends on how the position generator is used, and if it is more important to link ethnicity/race with a specific tie, or whether it is more important to look at the general effect of ethnic diversity on a particular outcome. Figure 12.3 shows one example of how a position generator has been used to create a measure of ethnoracial diversity across occupations (an indicator of social class position). Interactions cannot be created however, with strength of tie or with gender of a tie in this case, as each cell is treated as an independent variable, limiting the kinds of measures this data can create.

ETHNIC INEQUALITY AS A FUNCTION OF MIGRATION, CONTACT AND TOLERANCE

Current research output considering the variable experiences of ethnoracial groups as a product of network structure and content is an increasingly rich field of enquiry. Whether the experiences of ethnoracial minorities, immigrants, and/or Indigenous Peoples, research has looked at how the

Do you know a …	Very close	Somewhat close	Acquainted only	Male	Female	Indigenous	White	Non-Indigenous/ Non-White
A. Tribal council member	1	2	3	4	5	6	7	8
B. Hereditary or elected chief	1	2	3	4	5	6	7	8
C. Store clerk/cashier	1	2	3	4	5	6	7	8
D. Community Economic Development Officer	1	2	3	4	5	6	7	8
E. Casino worker	1	2	3	4	5	6	7	8
F. Venture capitalist	1	2	3	4	5	6	7	8
G. Hairstylist	1	2	3	4	5	6	7	8
H. Lawyer	1	2	3	4	5	6	7	8
I. Janitor	1	2	3	4	5	6	7	8
J. Computer programmer	1	2	3	4	5	6	7	8
K. Electrician	1	2	3	4	5	6	7	8
L. Sales manager	1	2	3	4	5	6	7	8
M. Policeman or policewoman	1	2	3	4	5	6	7	8
N. Entrepreneur	1	2	3	4	5	6	7	8
O. School teacher	1	2	3	4	5	6	7	8
P. Physician	1	2	3	4	5	6	7	8
Q. Mechanic	1	2	3	4	5	6	7	8
R. Human resources manager	1	2	3	4	5	6	7	8
S. Restaurant worker	1	2	3	4	5	6	7	8
T. Journalist/editor in media	1	2	3	4	5	6	7	8
U. Gardener/landscaper	1	2	3	4	5	6	7	8
V. Accountant	1	2	3	4	5	6	7	8
W. Farm laborer	1	2	3	4	5	6	7	8
X. Bank loan officer	1	2	3	4	5	6	7	8
Y. Enlisted military personnel	1	2	3	4	5	6	7	8
Z. Professor	1	2	3	4	5	6	7	8
AA. Tailor, dressmaker	1	2	3	4	5	6	7	8
BB. Government official	1	2	3	4	5	6	7	8

Figure 12.3 Occupational position generator

Source: Côté, R. *The Making of success: indigenous entrepreneurship in and around Phoenix*. Supported through Government of Canada, Social Sciences and Humanities Research Council Post-Doctoral Fellowship, 2011–2013.

structure and content of networks contribute to our understanding of access to opportunities, friendship and information, as well as newcomer incorporation and integration.

Migration, Assimilation and Transnationalism

One particular area of research focuses on the immigrant experience, paths of international migration, modes of incorporation and integration into host societies, and maintenance of transnational connections to countries of origin. Bilecen et al. (2018) rightly point out that while a great deal of work around migration has touched on the importance of networks, social network analysis has been somewhat missing from the conversation. Significant work recognises the importance of friends and relatives in predicting patterns of labour market participation, choice of destination and in how immigrants assimilate into host societies, but without the use of SNA (Boyd, 1989; Massey et al., 1993; Portes & Rumbaut 2001; Shah & Menon, 1999; Waldinger 2005).

More than can be reviewed here in this chapter, but making a significant contribution to this area, Bilecen et al. (2018) co-edit a special issue in *Social Networks* that brings together studies of international migration using network analysis. A particularly leading-edge application of SNA illuminates trends of geographical and spatial migrant distribution graphically and over time (Danchev & Porter, 2018; Hooghe et al., 2008; Windzio 2018). With the use of social-spatial modelling, Danchev and Porter (2018) identify the range of global, local and glocal networks of migration, breaking down data by decade to show trends over time. While theories have suggested that a significant amount of migration is between geographically close and/or distant, disconnected states, their findings show that immigration increasingly follows transnational paths – long-distance migration with individuals maintaining ties to home countries, friends and families.

Transnational ties are known to impact several aspects of the migration experience, which network analysis is uniquely valuable at documenting – entrepreneurial activities, flows of social and economic support and other forms of participation in home countries after migration (Bilecen & Cardona, 2018; Chen & Tan, 2009; Keck & Sikkink, 1998; Kornieko et al., 2018; Poros, 2001; Portes et al., 2002; Sommer & Gamper, 2018). The documentation and acknowledgement of the retention of transnational ties is a departure from conventional assumptions about immigrant experience – that they 'give up' their home culture and connections in favour of melting into the culture and connections of the country they have arrived in. Network analysis is helping us understand how the process of immigration plays out, by attending to connections beyond those to dominant populations in host societies.

Interethnic Contact, Friendship and Support

Gordon (1964) theorised that assimilation into host societies was inevitable, and perhaps even without conflict. With people from northern Europe and the UK moving into the US, it was not hard to think this was the case – race, ethnicity and cultures matched, ensuring somewhat smooth passage and transition. Unfortunately, the thinking of the day did not take into account the experiences of forced assimilation of Indigenous Peoples and African Americans, nor the experiences of immigrants from non-northern European countries. With mid-20th-century immigration policies in North America opening to increased entry for groups from Asia, Latin America, the Middle East and other parts of Europe, the ethnic and racial landscape was changing significantly.

The work of Zhou (1997), Portes and Zhou (1993), Waters (1990) and others shows clearly that Gordon's assumed path of upward social mobility and expected transition to middle classness was not only blocked for immigrants from these other parts of the world, but also for non-White members of US society. Feelings of threat reinforced boundaries meant to protect in-group resources and opportunities from new immigrants and members of discriminated racial classes (Blumer, 1958; King & Wheelock, 2007; Western, 2002). Academically, economically and politically, the question then became how to break down boundaries, discrimination and racism, and carve a path for minority groups to incorporate and thrive. Facilitating and increasing contact between ethnoracial groups is considered a mechanism to make this happen.

Can tolerance, openness and acceptance to new cultures and groups – an appreciation even of multiculturalism – be fostered at an early age, through exposure to friends with diverse, positive attitudes towards minorities? In other words, does contact with the right ideas make a difference, or is there something more to it? Friends are known to be an important resource when it comes to learning about social norms and attitudes, suggesting that contact with new ideas from the right people can promote new attitudes (Kuhn, 2004). In a study of junior high students in Sweden, Van Zalk et al. (2013) show that adolescents are significantly influenced by their networks of peers – friends' levels of tolerance predict increases in respondents' tolerance and vice versa.

Similar findings in the US and Sweden suggest that tolerance spreads inconsistently across adolescent networks of peers. Whereas accepting behaviours spread from students through their close friends to acquaintances, tolerant attitudes spread inconsistently across adolescent peer networks. (Bayram Özdemir & Özdemir, 2020; Hjerm et al., 2018; Paluck, 2010). While networks of friends who are tolerant are important, perhaps it is not enough (or merely one factor) in achieving generalised tolerance that consists of positive behaviour and attitudes towards racial and ethnic minorities. More than contact with ideas is required.

A more careful reading of the contact hypothesis states that positive feelings towards a group grow as contact with members of that group increases, provided that the contact is of the right kind. Positive orientations flow from contact between ethnoracial groups that is voluntary, positive, personal and of equal status (Dixon

& Rosenbaum, 2004; Erickson & Nosanchuk, 1998; Sigelman et al., 1996). This kind of contact encourages people to interact, cooperate, share valued experiences, come to like each other and learn positive things about each other. If people have the right kind of contact with other groups, their orientations towards those groups should become more positive.

Studies of possible effects of contact on positive attitudes often look at strong ties such as friends or family members (see Gravelle, 2018, for example). As Putnam (2000) and others point out, however, contact with a small number of close people is considered too specific to lead to change in generalised orientations towards whole social groups. If one has a best friend who is a member of an ethnic minority, one can easily classify that friend as unique, valuing that friend while devaluing the group. Researchers argue that tolerance flows from widespread interethnic contact through a diverse spectrum of social experiences that include both acquaintance and strong ties (Dovidio et al., 2003; Putnam, 2000).

The generalised contact hypothesis implies that there is greater tolerance among people with diversified social networks, and among those who participate in rich, diverse social settings such as voluntary associations and metropolitan areas. Diversity is not of a singular kind, there are many kinds which bring different kinds of contact experiences and different effects on tolerance. New contexts are opportunities for friend selection, but how does choice work? In group contexts where minority group members are a rarity, racial minorities are more likely to pursue friendships with other members of their racial group (Mehra et al., 1998). Boundary work from majority group members and minority group individual preferences towards homophily are reasons behind this outcome.

In the Canadian context, research shows that the kind of network diversity matters – respondents' networks that are diverse with middle-class contacts are also more tolerant of ethnic minorities and immigrants, than those with networks that are diverse with working-class contacts (Côté & Erickson, 2009; Côté et al., 2015). Middle classness is known to be a strong predictor of tolerance, where social networks diverse in middle-class ties presumably cultivate tolerance through contact with diverse ideas, educational backgrounds, social class and ethnoracial backgrounds (Andersen & Fetner, 2008; Andersen & Milligan, 2009).

A Swiss study further suggests that, in general, contact with immigrants mediates views that see immigration as a threat to economic participation and Swiss culture (Freitag & Rapp, 2013). But they note that not all social interactions have this effect – in particular, regular workplace interactions may be more likely to overcome intolerant attitudes (Freitag & Rapp, 2013). A second study in Iraq shows that people who spend time and interact in ethnically diverse spaces are more likely to cultivate interethnic friendships and have higher levels of trust towards other ethnic groups (Rydgren et al., 2013).

A novel application of network analysis and the contact hypothesis considers the impact of genetic ancestry testing (GATs) on the ethnoracial diversity of White Americans' social networks (Roth et al., 2022). Findings show that those individuals who take a GAT report less ethnically diverse networks afterward. Follow-up analyses suggest that it is less about individuals becoming increasingly homophilous in their network choices, and more about actively questioning the ethnicity/race of people in their networks. In this way, the ability to measure network diversity is contributing to our understanding of the social construction of race and ethnicity, and perhaps the deconstruction of barriers.

Spatial Distribution and the Racialisation of Neighbourhoods

In some country contexts, neighbourhoods constrain interethnic contact through segregation, racialising spaces and limiting opportunities for meaningful contact between groups. If interethnic contact is so incredibly important to increasing tolerance and decreasing discrimination, looking at the contexts that constrain opportunities for contact is very important. Oliver (1988) signalled the emergence of network analysis as a tool to fundamentally rethink the way we view and discuss racialised neighbourhoods. Rather than trying to compare (and evaluate) the organisation of Black communities based on modes of organisation of White communities, this chapter looked at the social organisation of Black neighbourhoods compared to each other, offering a fresh perspective on structure and defining features. Sampling the core networks of respondents from three neighbourhoods across Los Angeles, Oliver was able to identify the various types and relational contexts of network ties, as well as the spatial distribution of ties, density and the multiplex and reciprocal nature of network ties. Contrary to theories of the day that talked about Black neighbourhoods as dysfunctional and 'lost' (see Wellman, 1979, and Wellman & Leighton, 1979, for review of this thesis), findings show black neighbourhoods that are elaborately organised, spatially diverse, containing rich networks of social support and sociality (Oliver, 1988).

Other work has followed, considering the effect of neighbourhood racial segregation on interracial friendships and interactions, and access to health resources and social support, employment, income and educational opportunities (Alesina & La Ferrara, 2005; Borjas, 1995; Diez Roux & Mair, 2010; Prestby et al., 2019). Relying on Add Health network data, Mouw and Entwisle (2006) unpack the effect of residential segregation on racial friendship segregation in schools. Characteristic of networks in the US, there is a significant effect of racial segregation in schools and an accompanying significant effect of racial homophily when choosing friends (Lazersfeld & Merton, 1954; Logan et al., 2002; McPherson et al., 2001; Quillian & Campbell, 2003; Orfield & Lee, 2004; Rickles & Ong, 2001).

Schools, while embedded within neighbourhoods, are sites with increased opportunities for sociability and interethnic contact and friendships. Network analysis has been used to further consider schools as sites for developing interethnic friendships. Moody (2001) points out that specific organisational features of schools in the US that can impact the level of racial friendship segregation. Mirroring tenets of the contact hypothesis, findings show that situations in which contact is status equal and requires individuals to act together are more likely to encourage interracial friendships (Moody, 2001). In a study of adolescent school friendships, Mouw and Entwisle (2006) show that there are both direct and indirect impacts of distance on friendship formation, showing importantly that the structure of networks impacts friendship formation, over and above a straight relationship of distance between two people. Perhaps counterintuitively, there is no significant effect of spatial proximity on within-school racial friendship segregation.

A Note on Social Support and Interethnic Relationships

When it comes to social support and our reliance on strong ties, network analysis has documented our preference for racially similar contacts (Marsden, 1987; Vega et al., 1991). In a study of social support systems for elderly New Yorkers, Cantor et al. (2004) determined that Whites have more diverse and proximally distant networks, compared with Blacks and Latinos. Elder Black and Latino respondents are more likely to have less inclusive networks composed mainly of kin living nearby. Building on this work, Ajrouch et al. (2001) use a life-course perspective to look at the differences between the networks of Blacks and Whites. Consistent with past work on network size differences (Cantor et al., 1994; Roschelle, 1997; Wilson, 1996a), Ajrouch et al. (2001) find that smaller networks with more kin and frequent contact are associated with the networks of Blacks irrespective of age. If race and ethnicity impact access to health information and care, ethnoracially homophilous networks for minorities can impact health outcomes (Marquez et al., 2014; Song, 2011).

Looking to contexts in Europe, Baerveldt et al. (2007) consider the prevalence of interethnic ties for emotional support in the networks of Dutch alongside Turkish, Moroccan and Surinamese migrants to the Netherlands. Their research shows differences across these four groups, where Dutch and Turkish respondents rely more so on intraethnic ties for support, with Moroccan and Surinamese respondents looking more often across ethnic groups and relying more on interethnic ties for support. Jasinskaja-Lahti et al. (2006) consider the impact of ethnic versus host support networks on the well-being and perceived discrimination of three immigrant groups to Finland. This study shows strong support for the role of active interactions with host country networks and its function for the psychological well-being of immigrants.

Alongside identifying different classes of structured migrant networks, Djundeva and Ellwardt (2020) show that Polish migrants in the Netherlands are most lonely when they have small, homophilous networks that lack role diversity – different kinds of relationships within their communities. Exploring the social networks of Polish immigrants to London, Ryan et al. (2008) provide a great exploration of the types of support and resources available through social networks. Their findings reveal that immigrants rely on a host of networking strategies, with some most reliant on co-ethnic ties. These individuals have a greater likelihood of becoming ensconced in ethnic enclaves and seemed to be generally more distrustful of wider society than others who had diverse networks with a mix of ties from both country of origin and host countries.

NETWORK ANALYSIS AND THE (DE)COLONIAL PROJECT

The start of this chapter notes that the field of ethnic relations is in part about the study of inequalities based on perceptions about physical traits, culture and religion that make up our understandings of race and ethnicity. Social scientists try to understand ethnoracial inequalities as a product of these perceptions, where one area of research documents how the structure and content of contact between ethnoracial groups impacts these inequalities through increased tolerance, understanding and acceptance.

A critical look at this space shows that studies tend to – more often than not – default to perspectives and research that prioritise colonial understandings of ethnic relations. Studies focus on ties between dominant and minority populations, where the dominant population is typically characterised as White and of European descent. Research looks at how ethnic minorities relate to and are accepted by them. Studies of transnational ties tend to focus on one-way support, from host to home societies, and Western nations to the global south. In this, much work perpetuates a colonial understanding of relationships between countries and populations. Work that shows the richness of co-ethnic networks and reciprocal ties in providing support is helping to shift the way research looks at assimilation – showing ethnic minorities and immigrants that have rich and diverse networks within their own communities, or perhaps ties to other ethnic minorities. While the importance of dominant group, interethnic ties cannot be dismissed when it comes to instrumental outcomes like access to employment outside one's own community, documenting networks is providing evidence of how ethnoracial minorities are perhaps choosing how and when they engage in interethnic contact and relationships.

As a method, network analysis is well placed to assist in pursuing questions that challenge conventional and colonial understandings of ethnic minorities and their networks. As one example, Leonard et al. (2008) find that members of smaller ethnic groups are just as well connected as members of larger ethnic groups, challenging the theory that members of smaller ethnic groups tend to focus on relationships within their own community, and are less well connected. Contemporary theories and research tend to focus and perpetuate understandings of ethnic minorities as groups that are deprived, assimilated and 'have-nots'. This is no truer than with Indigenous Peoples, and the abundance of research that focuses on the real and perceived damage within communities (Tuck, 2009). My work challenges the assumption that economically successful Indigenous people have assimilated away from connections to their own Indigenous communities and culture, by mapping the diversity of entrepreneurial networks across ethnoracial groups (Côté, 2012). Teves and Fischer (2008) show that rural Andean societies have extensive social, cultural and economic networks that build on traditional knowledge, economic and power relations linking local, national and international communities.

With the changing landscape of academia, the increasing prevalence of non-white faculty members and students, and the resulting integration of non-Western knowledge and perspectives into research, there are demands for increasingly sophisticated methods and applications to decolonise research. Quinless (2022) argues for the inclusion of network studies in the form of work around social capital, to unpack understandings of Indigenous health and wellness. Resources embedded in network ties can facilitate access to information and support around health care, where network studies can be used to show how Indigenous perspectives around health improve outcomes, and support the further control of Indigenous communities over their own health systems (Hodge et al., 2011). Horsethief (2012) uses network analysis to show how Ktunaxa Nation is revitalising their language through internally generated community efforts to do so, and focusing on the strength and resilience within the community and their networks. Abizaid et al. (2016) study the sharing of seeds across three Peruvian communities where they prioritise the understanding of Indigenous ways of farming that focus on kin relations, the size of communities and the flow of seeds through networks, again prioritising different ways of thinking, and the strength that exists within and across these communities. I would argue that mapping networks is important to look at how power flows through ties and is used as a mechanism to discriminate, but to also build resilience in ethnic communities (Ledogar & Fleming, 2008).

Future directions should consider the utility and power of network analysis in continuing to decolonise our understanding of the lived experiences of ethnoracial groups in society. Explorations of international migration patterns, the evolving nature of transnational systems of support and trade, modes of incorporation and the nature of social support, are all fruitful directions for continued work. While interethnic contact is important to understand in terms of how ethnically diverse societies navigate racism and intolerance, how co-ethnic ties continue to build resilience and fill important roles around social support is also important to understanding the lived experiences of different ethnoracial groups. Network analysis can play an important role in navigating both.

REFERENCES

Abizaid, C., Coomes, O.T., & Perrault-Archambault, M. (2016). Seed sharing in Amazonian indigenous rain forest communities: a social network analysis in three Achuar villages, Peru. *Human Ecology*, *44*(5), 577–594.

Adams, J. and M. Lubbers. (2022). Social network data collection: Principles and modalities. Ajrouch, K.J., Antonucci, T.C., & Janevic, M.R. (2001). Social networks among blacks and whites: the interaction between race and age. *Journals of Gerontology Series B: Psychological Sciences and Social Sciences*, *56*(2), S112–S118.

Alesina, A., & Ferrara, E.L. (2005). Ethnic diversity and economic performance. *Journal of Economic Literature*, *43*(3), 762–800.

Allport, G.W. (1954). *The nature of prejudice*. Doubleday.

Andersen, R., & Fetner, T. (2008). Economic inequality and intolerance: attitudes toward homosexuality in 35 democracies. *American Journal of Political Science*, *52*(4), 942–958.

Andersen, R., & Milligan, S. (2009). Inequality and intolerance: Canada in cross-national perspective. In E.G. Grabb & N. Guppy (Eds.), *Social inequality in Canada: patterns, problems, and policies* (5th ed.; pp. 390–408). Prentice Hall.

Baerveldt, C., Zijlstra, B., De Wolf, M., Van Rossem, R., & Van Duijn, M.A. (2007). Ethnic boundaries in high school students' networks in Flanders and the Netherlands. *International Sociology*, *22*(6), 701–720.

Bayram Özdemir, S., & Özdemir, M. (2020). The role of perceived inter-ethnic classroom climate in adolescents' engagement in ethnic victimization: for whom does it work? *Journal of Youth and Adolescence*, *49*(6), 1328–1340.

Bilecen, B., & Cardona, A. (2018). Do transnational brokers always win? A multilevel analysis of social support. *Social Networks*, *53*(May), 90–100.

Bilecen, B., Gamper, M., & Lubbers, M.J. (2018). The missing link: social network analysis in migration and transnationalism. *Social Networks*, *53*(May), 1–3.

Blumer, H. (1958). Race, prejudice as a sense of group position. *Pacific Sociological Review*, *1*, 3–7.

Bonacich, E. (1972). A theory of ethnic antagonism: the split labor market. *American Sociological Review*, *37*(5), 547–559.

Borjas, G.J. (1995). The economic benefits from immigration. *Journal of Economic Perspectives*, *9*(2), 3–22.

Boyd, M. (1989). Family and personal networks in international migration: recent developments and new agendas. *International Migration Review*, *23*(3), 638–670.

Burt, R.S. (1984). Network items and the general social survey. *Social Networks*, *6*(4), 293–339.

Cantor, M.H., Brennan, M., & Sainz, A. (1994). The importance of ethnicity in the social support systems of older New Yorkers: a longitudinal perspective (1970–1990). *Journal of Gerontological Social Work*, *22*, 95–128.

Carolina Population Centre (2001). *National Longitudinal Study of Adolescent Health*. University of North Carolina at Chapel Hill.

Chen, W., & Tan, J. (2009). Understanding transnational entrepreneurship through a network lens: theoretical and methodological considerations. *Entrepreneurship Theory and Practice*, *33*(5), 1079–1091.

Christ, O., & Wagner, U. (2013). Methodological issues in the study of intergroup contact: towards a new wave of research. In G. Hodson & M. Hewstone (Eds.), *Advances in intergroup contact* (pp. 233–261). Psychology Press.

Coombs, G. (1978/79). Opportunities, information networks and the migration-distance relationship. *Social Networks*, *1*, 257–276.

Côté, R.R. (2012). Networks of advantage: urban Indigenous entrepreneurship and the importance of social capital. In D. Newhouse, K. Fitzmaurice, T. McGuire-Adams & D. Jette (Eds.), *Well-being in the urban Aboriginal community* (pp. 73–101). Thompson Educational.

Côté, R.R., Andersen, B. & Erickson, B.H. (2015). Social capital and ethnic tolerance: the opposing effects of diversity and competition. In Y. Li (Ed.), *The handbook of research methods and applications on social capital* (pp. 91–106). Edward Elgar.

Côté, R.R., Huang, X., Huang, Y., & Western, M. (2019). Immigrant network diversity in the land of the fair go. *Journal of Sociology*, *55*(2), 199–218.

Côté, Rochelle and Bonnie H. Erickson (2009) 'Untangling the Roots of Tolerance: How Forms of Social Capital Shape Attitudes toward Ethnic Minorities and Immigrants', *American Behavioral Scientist* 52(12): 1664–89.

Cross, J.L.M., & Lin, N. (2008). Access to social capital and status attainment in the United States: racial/ethnic and gender differences. In N. Lin & B.H. Erickson (Eds.), *Social capital: an international research program* (pp. 364–379). Oxford University Press.

Danchev, V., & Porter, M.A. (2018). Neither global nor local: heterogeneous connectivity in spatial network structures of world migration. *Social Networks*, *53*, 4–19.

Diez Roux, A.V., & Mair, C. (2010). Neighborhoods and health. *Annals of the New York Academy of Sciences*, *1186*(1), 125–145.

Dixon, J.C., & Rosenbaum, M.S. (2004). Nice to know you? Testing contact, cultural, and group threat theories of anti-black and anti-Hispanic stereotypes. *Social Science Quarterly*, *85*(2), 257–280.

Djundeva, M., & Ellwardt, L. (2020). Social support networks and loneliness of Polish migrants in the

Netherlands. *Journal of Ethnic and Migration Studies, 46*(7), 1281–1300.

Dovidio, J.F., Gaertner, S.L., & Kawakami, K. (2003). Intergroup contact: the past, present and future. *Group Processes and Intergroup Relations, 6*(1), 5–21.

Erickson, B.H., & Nosanchuk, T.A. (1998). Contact and stereotyping in a voluntary association. *Bulletin de Méthodologie Sociologique, 60*(1), 5–33.

Erickson, Bonnie (2004) 'The Distribution of Gendered Social Capital in Canada', pp. 34–52 in Henk Flap and Beata Völker (eds) *Creation and Returns of Social Capital: A New Research Program*. London: Routledge.

Freitag, M., & Rapp, C. (2013). Intolerance toward immigrants in Switzerland: diminished threat through social contacts? *Swiss Political Science Review, 19*(4), 425–446.

Gordon, M.M. (1964). *Assimilation in American life: the role of race, religion, and national origins*. Oxford University Press.

Gravelle, T.B. (2018a). Friends, neighbours, townspeople and parties: explaining Canadian attitudes toward Muslims. *Canadian Journal of Political Science, 51*(3), 643–664.

Hjerm, M., Eger, M.A., & Danell, R. (2018). Peer attitudes and the development of prejudice in adolescence. *Socius, 4*, 1–11.

Hodge, F., Pasqua, A., Marquez, C., & Geishirt-Cantrell, B. (2011). Utilizing traditional story-telling to promote wellness in American Indians communities. *Journal of Transcultural Nursing, 13*(1), 6–11.

Hooghe, M., Trappers, A., Meuleman, B., & Reeskens, T. (2008). Migration to European countries: a structural explanation of patterns, 1980–2004. *International Migration Review, 42*(2), 476–504.

Horsethief, C. (2012). *Emergent complex behavior in social networks: examples from the Ktunaxa speech community*. ProQuest.

Jasinskaja-Lahti, I., Liebkind, K., Jaakkola, M., & Reuter, A. (2006). Perceived discrimination, social support networks, and psychological well-being among three immigrant groups. *Journal of Cross-Cultural Psychology, 37*(3), 293–311.

Keck, M., & Sikkink, K. (1998). *Activists beyond borders: advocacy networks in international politics*. Cornell University Press

King, R.D., & Wheelock, D. (2007). Group threat and social control: race, perceptions of minorities and the desire to punish. *Social Forces, 85*(3), 1255–1280.

Kornienko, O., Agadjanian, V., Menjívar, C., & Zotova, N. (2018). Financial and emotional support in close personal ties among Central Asian migrant women in Russia. *Social Networks, 53*(May), 125–135.

Kuhn, H.P. (2004). Adolescent voting for right-wing extremist parties and readiness to use violence in political action: parent and peer contexts. *Journal of Adolescence, 27*(5), 561–581.

Laumann, E.O. (1966). *Prestige and association in an urban community: an analysis of an urban stratification system*. Bobbs-Merrill.

Lazarsfeld, P.F., & Merton, R.K. (1954). Friendship as a social process: a substantive and methodological analysis. *Freedom and Control in Modern Society, 18*(1), 18–66.

Ledogar, R.J., & Fleming, J. (2008). Social capital and resilience: a review of concepts and selected literature relevant to Aboriginal youth resilience research. *Pimatisiwin, 6*(2), 25.

Leonard, A.S., Mehra, A., & Katerberg, R. (2008). The social identity and social networks of ethnic minority groups in organizations: a crucial test of distinctiveness theory. *Journal of Organizational Behavior: The International Journal of Industrial, Occupational and Organizational Psychology and Behavior, 29*(5), 573–589.

Leszczensky, L., & Pink, S. (2019). What drives ethnic homophily? A relational approach on how ethnic identification moderates preferences for same-ethnic friends. *American Sociological Review, 84*(3), 394–419.

Lin, N. (2001). A network theory of social capital. In J. van Deth & G. Wolleb (Eds.), *Handbook on social capital*. Oxford University Press.

Lin, N., & Dumin, M. (1986). Access to occupations through social ties. *Social Networks, 8*(4), 365–385.

Lin, N., Fu, Y.C., & Hsung, R.M. (2001). Measurement techniques for investigations of social capital. In N. Lin, K. Cook & R.S. Burt (Eds.), *Social capital: theory and research* (pp. 57–81). Walter de Gruyter.

Logan, John R., Jacob Stowell, and Deirdre Oakley. "Choosing Segregation: Racial Imbalance in American Public Schools, 1990-2000." (2002).

Marin, A. (2004). Are respondents more likely to list alters with certain characteristics? Implications for name generator data. *Social Networks, 26*(4), 289–307.

Marquez, B., Elder, J.P., Arredondo, E.M., Madanat, H., Ji, M., & Ayala, G.X. (2014). Social network characteristics associated with health promoting behaviors among Latinos. *Health Psychology, 33*(6), 544.

Marsden, P.V. (1987). Core discussion networks of Americans. *American Sociological Review*, 122–131.

Marsden, P.V., Fekete, M., & Baum, D. (2019). Contributions of the general social survey to egocentric network research. Presented at a workshop on Personal Networks: Frontiers of Ego-Network Analysis. December.

Massey, D.S., Arango, J., Hugo, G., Kouaouci, A., Pellegrino, A., & Taylor, J.E. (1993). Theories of international migration: a review and appraisal. *Population and Development Review*, *19*(3), 431–466.

Mayer, A., & Puller, S.L. (2008). The old boy (and girl) network: social network formation on university campuses. *Journal of Public Economics*, *92*(1–2), 329–347.

McDonald, S. (2011). What's in the 'old boys' network? Accessing social capital in gendered and racialized networks. *Social Networks*, *33*(4), 317–330.

McDonald, S., & Day, J.C. (2010). Race, gender, and the invisible hand of social capital. *Sociology Compass*, *4*(7), 532–543.

McDonald, S., Hamm, L., Elliott, J.R., & Knepper, P. (2016). Race, place, and unsolicited job leads: how the ethnoracial structure of local labor markets shapes employment opportunities. *Social Currents*, *3*(2), 118–137.

McDonald, S., Lin, N., & Ao, D. (2009). Networks of opportunity: gender, race, and job leads. *Social Problems*, *56*(3), 385–402.

McPherson, M., Smith-Lovin, L., & Cook, J.M. (2001). Birds of a feather: homophily in social networks. *Annual Review of Sociology*, *27*(1), 415–444.

Mehra, A., Kilduff, M., & Brass, D.J. (1998). At the margins: a distinctiveness approach to the social identity and social networks of underrepresented groups. *Academy of Management Journal*, *41*(4), 441–452.

Miething, A., Rostila, M., & Rydgren, J. (2017). Access to occupational networks and ethnic variation of depressive symptoms in young adults in Sweden. *Social Science and Medicine*, *190*, 207–216.

Mouw, T., & Entwisle, B. (2006). Residential segregation and interracial friendship in schools. *American Journal of Sociology*, *112*(2), 394–441.

Moody, J. (2001). Race, school integration, and friendship segregation in America. *American Journal of Sociology*, *107*(3), 679–716.

Muller, C., Riegle-Crumb, C., Schiller, K.S., Wilkinson, L., & Frank, K.A. (2010). Race and academic achievement in racially diverse high schools: opportunity and stratification. *Teachers College Record*, *112*(4), 1038–1063.

Oliver, M.L. (1988). The urban black community as network: toward a social network perspective. *Sociological Quarterly*, *29*(4), 623–645.

Olzak, S., & Nagel, J. (Eds.) (1986). *Competitive ethnic relations*. Academic Press.

Orfield, G., & Lee, C. (2004). 'Brown' at 50: king's dream or 'Plessy's' nightmare? Civil Rights Project at Harvard University.

Paluck, E.L. (2010). Peer pressure against prejudice: a high school field experiment examining social network change. *Journal of Experimental Social Psychology*, *47*, 350–358.

Perry, P., A. Roth and M. Small. forthcoming. Personal networks and Egocentric Analysis. *Sage handbook of social network analysis*. J. McLevey, P. Carrington, and J. Scott (Eds.) Sage Publications, Thousand Oaks, CA.

Pettigrew, T.F. (2008). Future directions for intergroup contact theory and research. *International Journal of Intercultural Relations*, *32*, 187–199.

Pettigrew, T.F., & Tropp, L.R. (2006). A meta-analytic test of intergroup contact theory. *Journal of Personality and Social Psychology*, *90*(5), 751.

Poros, M.V. (2001). The role of migrant networks in linking local labour markets: the case of Asian Indian migration to New York and London. *Global Networks*, *1*(3), 243–260.

Portes, A., Haller, W.J., & Guarnizo, L.E. (2002). Transnational entrepreneurs: an alternative form of immigrant economic adaptation. *American Sociological Review*, 278–298.

Portes, A., & Rumbaut, R.G. (2001). *Legacies: the story of the immigrant second generation*. University of California Press.

Portes, A., & Zhou, M. (1993). The new second generation: segmented assimilation and its variants. *Annals of the American Academy of Political and Social Science*, *530*(1), 74–96.

Prestby, Timothy, Joseph App, Yuhao Kang, and Song Gao. "Understanding neighborhood isolation through spatial interaction network analysis using location big data." *Environment and Planning A: Economy and Space* 52, no. 6 (2020): 1027–1031.

Putnam, R.D. (2000). *Bowling alone: the collapse and revival of American community*. Simon & Shuster.

Quillian, L., & Campbell, M.E. (2003). Beyond black and white: the present and future of multiracial friendship segregation. *American Sociological Review*, *68*(4), 540–566.

Quinless, J.M. (2022). *Decolonizing data: unsettling conversations about social research methods*. University of Toronto Press.

Rickles, Jordan, and Paul M. Ong. 2001. "Relationship between School and Residential Segregation at the Turn of the Century." The Ralph and Goldy Lewis Center for Regional Policy Studies,The School of Public Policy Social Research, UCLA. http://www.sppsr.ucla.edu/lewis/metroamerica/segl.htm

Roschelle A.R. (1997). *No more kin: exploring race, class, and gender in family networks*. Sage.

Roth, W.D., Côté, R., & Eastmond, J. (2022). Bridging boundaries? The effect of genetic ancestry testing on ties across racial groups. *Social Problems*. January.

Ryan, L., Sales, R., Tilki, M., & Siara, B. (2008). Social networks, social support and social capital: the experiences of recent Polish migrants in London. *Sociology*, *42*(4), 672–690.

Rydgren, J., Sofi, D., & Hällsten, M. (2013). Interethnic friendship, trust, and tolerance: findings from two north Iraqi cities. *American Journal of Sociology*, *118*(6), 1650–1694.

Satzewich, V. (2021). *'Race' and ethnicity in Canada: a critical introduction*. 5th ed. Oxford University Press.

Shah, N.M., & Menon, I. (1999). Chain migration through the social network: experience of labour migrants in Kuwait. *International Migration*, *37*(2), 361–382.

Sigelman, L., Bledsoe, T., Welch, S., & Combs, M.W. (1996). Making contact? Black–white social interaction in an urban setting. *American Journal of Sociology*, *101*(5), 1306–1332.

Smith, T.W. (2002). Measuring inter-racial friendships. *Social Science Research*, *31*(4), 576–593.

Smith, T.W., Davern, M., Freese, J., and Morgan, S.L. (2019). *General social surveys, 1972–2018*. National Science Foundation. NORC.

Sommer, E., & Gamper, M. (2018). Transnational entrepreneurial activities: a qualitative network study of self-employed migrants from the former Soviet Union in Germany. *Social Networks*, *53*, 136–147.

Song, L. (2011). Social capital and psychological distress. *Journal of Health and Social Behavior*, *52*(4), 478–492.

Stoyanova, S.Y. (2008). Factors influencing the choice of friends: analysis of Bulgarian friendship networks. *Portularia: Revista de Trabajo Social*, *8*, 93–109.

Teves, L., & Fischer, E. (2008). Social network analysis in the context of Andean local groups: the textile producers of the Calchaquí Valleys. www.researchgate.net/profile/Laura-Teves/publication/228501041_Social_Network_Analysis_in_the_Context_of_Andean_Local_Groups_The_Textile_Producers_of_the_Calchaqui_Valleys1/links/53d97c8e0cf2a19eee87e00a/Social-Network-Analysis-in-the-Context-of-Andean-Local-Groups-The-Textile-Producers-of-the-Calchaqui-Valleys1.pdf

Tuck, E. (2009). Suspending damage: a letter to communities. *Harvard Educational Review*, *79*(3), 409–428.

Van Zalk, M.H.W., Kerr, M., Van Zalk, N., & Stattin, H. (2013). Xenophobia and tolerance toward immigrants in adolescence: cross-influence processes within friendships. *Journal of Abnormal Child Psychology*, *41*(4), 627–639.

Vega, W., Kolody, B., Valle, R., & Weir, J. (1991). Social networks, social support, and their relationship to depression among immigrant Mexican women. *Human Organization*, *50*(2), 154–162.

Verhaeghe, P.P., Putte, B.V.D., & Roose, H. (2013). Reliability of position generator measures across different occupational lists: a parallel test experiment. *Field Methods*, *25*(3), 238–261.

Verhaeghe, P.P., & Li, Y. (2015). The position generator approach to social capital research: measurements and results. In Y. Li (Ed.), *Handbook of research methods and applications in social capital*. Edward Elgar.

Waldinger, R. (2005). 12 networks and niches: the continuing significance of ethnic connections. In G. Loury, T. Modood & S. Teles (Eds.), *Ethnicity, Social Mobility, and Public Policy: Comparing the USA and UK* (pp. 342–362). Cambridge University Press.

Waters, M.C. (1990). *Ethnic options: choosing identities in America*. University of California Press.

Wellman, B. (1979). The community question: the intimate networks of East Yorkers. *American Journal of Sociology*, *84*(5), 1201–1231.

Wellman, B., Hogan, B., Berg, K., Boase, J., Carrasco, J.A., Côté, R., & Tran, P. (2006). Connected lives: the project. In P. Purcell (Ed.), *Networked neighbourhoods* (pp. 161–216). Springer.

Wellman, B., & Leighton, B. (1979). Networks, neighborhoods, and communities: approaches to the study of the community question. *Urban Affairs Quarterly*, *14*(3), 363–390.

Western, B. (2002). The impact of incarceration on wage mobility and inequality. *American Sociological Review*, *67*, 526–546.

Wilson, W.J. (1987). *The truly disadvantaged*. University of Chicago Press.

Wilson W.J. (1996a). The meaning and significance of race: employers and inner-city workers. In W.J. Wilson (Ed.), *When work disappears: the world of the new urban poor* (pp. 111–146). Alfred A. Knopf.

Wilson, W.J. (1996b). *When work disappears: the world of the new urban poor*. Alfred A. Knopf.

Wimmer, A. (2004). The making and unmaking of ethnic boundaries: a multilevel process theory. *American Journal of Sociology*, *113*(4), 970–1022.

Windzio, M. (2018). The network of global migration 1990–2013: using ERGMs to test theories of migration between countries. *Social Networks*, *53*, 20–29.

Zhou, M. (1997). Segmented assimilation: issues, controversies, and recent research on the new second generation. *International Migration Review*, *31*(4), 975–1008.

Culture and Networks

Omar Lizardo

INTRODUCTION

There is something paradoxical about 'culture networks' as a field of study. On the one hand, the area is coherent and visible enough to have been the subject of numerous chapter-length reviews in the last decade or so (Breiger & Puetz, 2015; Mützel & Breiger, 2020; Pachucki & Breiger, 2010; Rule & Bearman, 2015), including programmatic treatments by Paul DiMaggio (2011) and Ann Mische (2011) in the previous edition of this handbook.[1] However, it is still being determined what exactly the field of culture and network studies is as a scholarly domain of practice. Some (Breiger & Puetz, 2015, p. 557) refer to it 'as a research specialty in its own right' – a somewhat optimistic assessment – but others see it, at least implicitly, more as a cluster of studies united by thematic similarities and substantive emphases across various distinct sub-areas in sociology and the social sciences more generally (DiMaggio, 2011; Mische, 2011; Rule & Bearman, 2015). These include, *inter alia*, studies of artistic, collaboration, civil society and creative networks, or the formal modelling of certain cultural elements, such as text, practices, language, concepts, narratives and events, as a network of elements, or the study of the meaningful bases of interaction and relationship formation in social networks via cultural change and the construction of identities and boundaries. Nevertheless, something is missing in these previous treatments: a general sense of whether, beyond *topical* intersections of culture and networks or the study of interesting empirical phenomena, there exists a general *theoretical* or conceptual basis uniting the field.

In this chapter, I argue that the answer to this last question is affirmative. I broadly follow Borgatti & Lopez-Kidwell's (2011) approach – see also Borgatti & Halgin (2011) – in the previous edition of this volume to define the parameters of network theory in the case of the study of culture and networks. I will not review specific pieces of empirical research clustered according to thematic criteria loosely concerned with the culture-networks linkage. Instead, I organised particular strands of the literature according to underlying theoretical *ur*-models, explicitly stating their assumptions and critical empirical implications and showing how analysts deploy them for analytic and explanatory purposes. Thus, the chapter's primary goal is to outline the *theoretical foundations* of work linking culture and networks. As such, my review of specific research will be highly selective; the point is not to exhaustively consider the large number of studies that have been conducted across the thematic areas mentioned earlier. Instead, I will select specific *exemplars* (in Kuhn's sense) in which the core theoretical imagery is showcased or significantly developed.

The central claim is that just like the seemingly cluttered landscape of network theorising turns out to be organised by a surprisingly small number of underlying theoretical models – only two in Borgatti & Lopez-Kidwell's (2011) accounting – much of the work on the culture-networks linkage is also organised by a surprisingly compact set of theoretical images. Only two in my accounting. First, a vision of the interplay between personal culture and network ties built on the *constructural* imagery (Carley, 1991), in which the continuous exchange of cultural information helps people form, construct and maintain social connections while defining sociocultural affinities and boundaries. Second, a vision of the link between people and broader social categories, public culture, groups, cultural objects, genres, knowledge and the like, animated by the *cultural holes* imagery (Pachucki & Breiger, 2010). Here linkages between people and other social entities in multimode networks define distributions of positions – for people and objects – in dually constituted 'sociocultural' and 'culturosocial spaces' (Lee & Martin, 2018; Puetz, 2017). Together, the constructural and cultural holes imageries, as well as their recent developments and refinements, form the theoretical backbone of research in culture and networks.

The rest of the chapter is organised into two major sections, covering the constructural and cultural holes models, their main variations and core applications. I close with a brief section discussing the argument's implications for future work.

THE CONSTRUCTURAL IMAGERY

Constructuralism and Network Ecologies

Carley's Constructural Model
I begin by considering what, to my knowledge, was the first formal theory of the dynamic coupling of culture and networks: Kathleen Carley's (1991) *constructural model*, one of the *ur*-models from which a whole swath of research on culture and networks derives. Because it was initially stated as a formal computational model, we do not need to work too hard to uncover the fundamental premises of the model. In the constructural imagery, agents exchange 'pieces' of culture (e.g., facts, information, beliefs, tastes, preferences and the like) when they interact. As a result of interacting, agents become more culturally similar. Moreover, agents' cultural similarity increases the chance of future interaction as the probability of two actors interacting at any given occasion is a positive function of their shared culture.

There is independent theoretical reasoning and quite a lot of empirical work that supports each of the constructural model's premises (considering this work, however, is outside the scope of this chapter). The key idea is that the three processes define a positive feedback loop connecting cultural exchange to the 'tie strength' between people (Granovetter, 1973; Marsden & Campbell, 1984), which becomes indexed to their relative cultural similarity compared to that they have with other actors in the system. The more people interact, the more culture they exchange, and the more their dyadic ties strengthen, which leads to future bouts of interaction and dyadic cultural exchange. As Carley (1991) noted in the initial statement of the theory, a plausible equilibrium, all else equal, is for all actors to reach maximum cultural similarity with one another and thus form a fully connected clique in terms of their interaction probabilities. Of course, complications can be introduced to the model to account for the apparent fact of cultural differentiation and differential probabilities of interaction in large-scale systems, inclusive of the capacity for actors to 'lose' (e.g., forget) cultural knowledge (Mark, 1998a) and the emergence of non-interactive 'actants' (books or other information archives such as the World Wide Web) from which individuals can extract cultural knowledge not available via face-to-face interaction with others (Carley, 1995). Carley's basic constructural imagery thus provides the basis for several more recent developments in theorising the link between culture and social networks and linking theory to empirical evidence.

Mark's Cultural Ecology Model
The first model of the culture and networks linkage explicitly built on the constructural imagery is Mark's (2003) network ecology model (NEM) – see also Mark (1998b) for a precursor. Mark departs from the evident observation that cultural tastes, opinions and beliefs are segregated into distinct 'niches' of socio-demographic space. Here Mark draws on McPherson's (2004) socio-demographic niche theory, which builds on earlier insights from Blau's (1977) macrostructural theory conceptualising social space as a multidimensional space. People's position in this 'Blau space', whose axes are composed of 'dimensions of association', continuous, ordinal and nominal (such as age, gender, race, occupational prestige and the like), shape the chances people will form network connections.

The basic principle here is that of *homophily* (McPherson et al., 2001), such that the probability of two being tied in a social network is a function of the number of socio-demographic characteristics they share translates to a distance gradient in Blau space. People close to one another are more likely to be connected.

In the NEM, connectivity is a conduit via which cultural tastes, opinions and beliefs are transmitted via imitation and social influence. The suggested mechanism is that acquiring cultural tastes is best envisioned as a 'local bandwagon' process of network-based imitation or contagion. Because the distribution of network ties in Blau space is 'lumpy' (with people concentrated along areas that maximise similarity), so will the distribution of tastes, which will concentrate along particular 'niches' (particular areas of Blau space). For instance, rock and roll will be more likely to be found in the Blau space area marked by relatively high education, occupational prestige, older age and white ethnoracial identity. Mark's NEM uses the constructural imagery to provide a formal model of how this process of concentration of tastes along socio-demographic can be realised via routine interaction, thus explaining why tastes and opinions cluster in specific 'cultural niches' and why at any one moment, we are liable to find systematic correlations between socio-demographic position and cultural tastes (Bourdieu, [1979]1984).

More recent work by DellaPosta et al. (2015) uses insights from the NEM to explain the association between cultural tastes and practices and presumably (e.g., logically) unrelated attitudes and beliefs such as political liberalism and conservatism. The basic idea is that once relatively small correlations between politics and lifestyle begin to obtain (even if for contingent reasons), and political ideology becomes a fundamental dimension of association in Blau's sense, arbitrary linkages between politics, tastes and lifestyle practices can be amplified via the twin mechanisms of homophily and personal influence. Accordingly, local bandwagon processes segregate conservatives and liberals in distinct cultural niches, reifying political boundaries by the standard mechanisms of relational segregation and selective interaction.

Conversion and Matching

Lizardo's Culture Conversion Model

If Mark's cultural ecology model theorised how social-structural biases led to the social segregation of cultural tastes (thus relying on half of the two-sided dynamic process of conversion emphasised by Carley), Lizardo's (2006) *culture conversion model* (CCM) examined the obverse process; how cultural tastes can lead to the biased formation of social network ties. Lizardo's CCM synthesised three key theoretical strands in the literature that, at the time, had developed separately, despite each addressing critical processes and mechanisms linking culture and social networks. The first was, of course, Carley's constructural theory (Carley, 1991). The second consisted of micro-interactionist approaches to theorising the functions of culture consumption in modern artistic classification systems linking cultural consumption to Simmelian sociability and the creation of bounded solidarities via the mobilisation of cultural capital in 'interaction rituals' (DiMaggio, 1987). The third was Bourdieu's (1986) imagery of the interconvertibility of the three forms of capital (social, economic and cultural). The basic idea is that cultural resources, particularly the possession of embodied abilities to consume certain forms of culture, should lead people to differentially cumulate and maintain social network ties (such that people with a wide variety of tastes should maintain more extensive social networks). The CCM thus stands in contrast to models postulating a one-directional arrow of causation (or conversion) going exclusively from network ties to cultural tastes, like Mark's NEM.

Moreover, according to the CCM, consumption of 'asset-specific' cultural goods (e.g., requiring esoteric or difficult-to-acquire cultural knowledge) should have *restricted conversion value*, leading mainly to creating and maintaining networks of strong ties and local solidarities. On the other hand, consumption of cultural goods that are less asset-specific, such as popular culture with which most people are familiar, should have *generalised conversion value*, leading to the formation and maintenance of ego networks rich in weak ties. 'Omnivorous' consumption of both types of culture should lead to more extensive networks containing weak and strong ties. Using data from the culture and network modules of the US General Social Survey (GSS), Lizardo found strong support for the general outlines of the CCM. The more cultural activities people consume, the more extensive their reported ego networks are. Highbrow culture – a type of asset-specific culture – increased the volume of strong ties, while consumption of popular culture increased the volume of weak ties. Omnivores who engage in both forms of culture can thus wield complementary resources, enjoying the advantages of bridging (with their weak ties) and bonding (with their strong ties).

Subsequent work has elaborated Lizardo's culture conversion model conceptually while providing partial empirical support for its key predictions. For example, Schultz & Breiger (2010) rework Lizardo's original distinction between 'asset-specific' and 'non-asset-specific' culture to align with Granovetter's (1973) classic distinction between weak and strong ties. According to Schultz and Breiger, popular culture endowed with generalised conversion can best be considered *weak culture*. Like weak ties in Granovetter's theory, weak culture turns out to be strong because it allows people to form social ties, however fleeting, linking to others in distant positions in social space. In addition, they show, using US GSS data, that the more mild positive cultural preferences a people have (e.g., 'likes' instead of 'likes very much'), the more likely it is that they perceive the US to be 'united' (rather than divided). In short, weak culture leads to the perception of a potential for interaction across critical social divides, an unexpected implication of the culture conversion imagery, with critical implications for contemporary issues like cultural and political polarisation (DellaPosta et al., 2015).

Vaisey and Lizardo's Cultural Matching Model

Vaisey & Lizardo's (2010) *cultural matching model* (CMM) also builds on the constructural imagery linking culture to social network ties. According to the CMM, cultural tastes, values and preferences affect social networks mainly by serving as the underlying basis for *homophily* (thus reversing the causal arrow postulated by Mark's NEM). In this way, tastes, and other internalised cultural aptitudes, preferences and practices can have an independent causal effect in shaping social networks because people use the match between their tastes and others to *self-select* into particular social ties (Shalizi & Thomas, 2011). Moreover, the degree of cultural match between two people also determines whether certain social relationships stick over time or instead selectively die off, thus linking cultural matching at the dyadic level with processes of tie-decay at the network level (Burt, 2000; Martin & Yeung, 2006). Using longitudinal data from the US National Study of Youth and Religion, Vaisey and Lizardo find that, compared to those who express more communitarian cultural worldviews, adolescents abiding by individualist-expressivist cultural worldviews are more likely to maintain social ties with other adolescents who engage in substance use. In contrast, those abiding by a more individualist-utilitarian worldview are more likely to keep social ties with those who volunteer.

Other empirical work supports critical predictions of the CMM. For instance, Friemel (2012/17) shows that shared cultural tastes promote tie-formation among adolescents, with similar results using college-aged populations in the domain of musical taste reported by Lomi and Stadtfeld (2014), Vlegels (2014, pp. 71ff) and Hachen et al. (2022). Edelmann and Vaisey (2014), using data from the Cambridge College Network Dataset, a longitudinal sample of graduate students in England, extend the CMM to consider not just substantive matches in terms of tastes and worldviews but also matching in terms of *abstentions* or dislikes. Just like people can match their avowed cultural tastes and practices, they can match according to what they do not or refuse to do; refusals are as important as choices (Bourdieu, [1979]1984). Consistent with the extended CMM, Edelmann & Vaisey find that mutual consumption of the same musical genres and common non-consumption systematically affects network ties, increasing the odds that two students will sustain a network connection over time.

Lewis and Kaufman's Generalised Conversion Model

The most sustained elaboration of the conversion and matching models, theoretically and empirically, is that developed by Lewis and Kaufman (2018). Lewis and Kaufman synthesise the conversion and matching ideas into a generalised conversion model (GCM) while also considering variations in the local cultural ecology to specify the notions of weak and strong culture. Lewis and Kaufman's GCM offers various conceptual advances over previous formulations of the link between culture and networks based on the constructural imagery. First, they endogenise Schultz and Breiger's idea of weak and strong culture to what they refer to as the local cultural ecology. Rather than using exogenous criteria to determine what counts as weak or strong culture (e.g., broad labels such as highbrow or popular), they note that what counts as weak or strong culture will depend on the distribution of tastes and aptitudes in the local cultural environment. Second, they distinguish between different culture conversion and matching mechanisms and show how they can operate in tandem.

First, there is the *dyadic conversion* of cultural into social capital, whereby people exploit commonalities in cultural tastes and aptitudes specific to the focal dyad to form and sustain relationships. Second, there is a *generalised conversion* process, whereby particular forms of taste and cultural consumption lead people to form more ties with others (increasing the acquaintance volume). Finally, there is *cultural matching*, where similarities in entire cultural profiles – including, following Edelmann and Vaisey, both active engagements and abstentions – increase the chances of people creating social connections with similar others. Using stochastic actor-based models for longitudinal network data on a unique Facebook dataset – the 'tastes, ties and time' data collected during the platform's early days in the US (Lewis et al., 2008) – Lewis & Kaufman find support for all three conversion mechanisms. Notably, the more tastes two students shared, the more likely they were to become Facebook friends, especially if those tastes were 'specialised' to the local cultural ecology. In the same way, individuals who displayed typical tastes in the local cultural ecology were more likely to accumulate a larger volume of acquaintances via the generalised conversion mechanism.

Constructuralism 2.0: associative diffusion

In a recent paper, Goldberg and Stein (2018) propose an *associative diffusion model* (ADM) of the way culture and networks interact. The ADM's argument is deceptively simple but ultimately far-reaching. According to Goldberg and Stein, culture does not diffuse like a 'virus' in social networks; people do not pick up *single* beliefs, attitudes, tastes, or styles from their contacts. Instead, cultural practices, beliefs and attitudes are embedded in a relational network of meanings. That is, there is a 'cultural network' that dictates 'what goes with what' that is analytically independent of the network dictating who is tied to whom (a key point of difference with the constructural imagery). In contrast to constructuralism, the ADM uses recent advances in conceptualising culture as schemas (Goldberg, 2011) and schemas as an analytically distinct network of cognitive associations between cultural items that can differ across people. Thus, there are as many cultural networks as there are agents, and what diffuses between people when they interact are the *relations* between elements. In this way, the ADM can be considered the constructural model 2.0.

Accordingly, we must distinguish the diffusion of cognitive associations between elements (this is what Goldberg and Stein refer to as 'associative diffusion') or the cognitive representation of 'what goes with what' each agent carries with them from the specific attitudes (e.g., like/dislike, adoption/refusal, endorsement/non-endorsement) specific people take towards the given practice or attitude. If we allow for associations between elements to be the unit of diffusion, then specific attitudes of adoption/non-adoption towards those elements can be derived as a process of soft-constraint optimisation on the part of people (formalising the idea of cognitive consistency between preferences), allowing them to harmonise their attitudes towards particular objects, with the way they believe those cultural elements are linked.

For instance, a person may know that caviar is connected to champagne, which in turn is connected to foie gras, while having a negative attitude towards the latter and a favourable preference for the first two. What diffuses via social networks are the pairwise links between these elements, and these links are strengthened (reinforced) the more people are exposed to these associations (e.g., caviar and champagne) when interacting with others (alternatively, associations that are not reinforced in interaction decay over time). Each time a person is exposed to a given cultural association, the strength between the two is 'updated' in the cultural network, meaning people harmonise their attitudes towards the things they think are related, much like people need to 'balance' their sentiments across triadic structures in interpersonal sentiment networks (Davis, 1963). Thus, the person who thinks caviar is strongly related to both champagne and foie gras but who hates foie gras must either start liking foie gras more or liking champagne and caviar less.

The ADM thus links the idea of schemas as a network of cultural elements to interaction, social construction and learning processes and implements this dynamic in an elegant computer simulation. One pay-off is that the ADM can show that the core phenomenon those who study diffusion believe requires structural segregation at the network level (attitude or taste polarisation) can emerge via associative diffusion mechanisms even when social structures are not segregated (e.g., fully connected or high-density networks), a situation where 'virus-type' diffusion models – such as Mark's network ecology model – would predict convergence rather than cultural niche divergence. This is a significant result because it attests to the robustness of the cultural polarisation phenomenon even in the face of structural conditions that network ecology models would predict would make it impossible, while also showing that a critical boundary condition of these models – pre-existing relational segregation – is not necessary for the emergence of cultural differentiation. The ADM also complicates 'network-based' solutions to the polarisation issue premised on creating links or increasing exposure between people with opposed attitudes and worldviews, as suggested in recent empirical work (Bail et al., 2018).

THE CULTURAL HOLES IMAGERY

As DiMaggio (2011) noted more than a decade ago, research on 'cultural networks' has become a central organising hub linking work on creativity, collaboration, group identity, symbolic boundaries and the relational constitution of meanings in the sociology of culture, and network imagery is a natural way to unify this otherwise disparate array of work on a variety of substantive areas. Mützel & Breiger (2020) note that much of this work was united by the *duality* between two or more entities in (multimode) cultural networks. Nevertheless, while hinting at an underlying theoretical model, the overall idea of cultural networks and the more specific idea of duality are more like general frameworks helpful in organising a variety of empirical work around loosely related thematic areas. Is there an underlying theoretical model that can be seen as doing the bulk of the explanatory work? I propose that there is such a model centred on the notion of *cultural holes* (Pachucki & Breiger, 2010).

Cultural Holes as a Model for Cultural Networks

In contrast to the constructural (or associative diffusion) model, there has never been a formalisation of the cultural holes model.[2] However, surveying the use of the idea in recent work is not difficult. The cultural holes argument can be seen as a steady-state macro-level implication of the constructural model but applicable to social systems at scale. In this case, differentiation and insulation generate discontinuities in the cultural distribution of knowledge across people (Reay, 2010), thus creating 'gaps' in the cultural structure, represented by 'patterned absences of relations' among cultural items (Breiger, 2010, p. 39). This contrasts with the small group, where the steady-state equilibrium of the constructural process is for everyone to end up knowing everything everyone else knows. Second, as Carley (1991) noted, there is a link between this imagery and that of duality since the cultural distribution of knowledge can be modelled as a two-mode network of people by 'pieces' of cultural information. Projecting the network into a person-by-person one-mode weighted network in the way proposed by Breiger (1974), we end up with the cultural similarity between people, as discussed earlier.

Conversely, projecting the original two-mode network into an item-by-item one-mode network gives us the cultural relatedness of the items, such that two cultural items are strongly related if they are likely to be known by the same people and weakly related if they are unlikely to be known by the same people. We can thus define a 'cultural ego network' at the agent level, with the person connected to all the cultural items they know – the link between the items being the weight of their linkage in their respective one-mode network projection, perhaps suitably corrected for the statistical likelihood of observing a weighted link of a specific size (Neal, 2014). Computing Burt's ([1992]2009) ego-network efficiency among the alters (cultural items) of the cultural ego network gives us one way of measuring the extent to which agents bridge cultural holes (Lizardo, 2014).

In essence, the cultural holes argument links the cultural distribution of pieces of cultural knowledge in a given social system to define the 'position' of a given agent in the 'sociocultural' structure (Lee & Martin, 2018). Most research using this approach links the positional status of agents or items to various outcomes, much like previous work on sociometric holes (Burt, 2004). Note, however, that this 'agent-centric' approach to studying cultural holes, although natural and intuitive, is not the only one we can take. Given duality, it is possible to be interested in the item-by-item 'culturosocial structure' itself (Lee & Martin, 2018) and study cultural holes from a 'culture-centric' perspective – for instance, by looking at which cultural items are likely to be 'bridges' (e.g., mediating between clusters of weakly connected items). In this respect, the cultural holes argument presupposes a 'mutual alignment' between agent and culture-centric perspectives (Puetz, 2017). Following this lead, analysts have taken both agent- and culture-centric routes in analysing cultural holes.

Agent-Centric Approaches to the Study of Cultural Holes

Cultural Holes, Omnivorousness and taste

A natural application of the cultural holes argument from an agent-centric perspective is to *specify* phenomena that have been recalcitrant to analytic treatment in other fields. One particularly promising arena is the sociological study of cultural taste and consumption (Bourdieu, [1979]1984). This area has come to be populated by a host of concepts meant to denote 'openness' and 'cosmopolitanism' as a modern marker of being a 'tolerant' person with a taste for diversity and varieties of cultural experiences (Ollivier, 2008). These include, in addition to the eponymous 'cosmopolitanism', such constructs as 'cultural omnivorousness' (Peterson & Kern, 1996). For example, suppose we view cultural taste as 'pieces' of cultural knowledge. In that case, the natural thing is to see the cosmopolitan 'cultural omnivore' as one who bridges cultural holes via their consumption choices.

Lizardo (2014) follows this approach, noting that the cultural omnivore can be considered an agent with an 'efficient' cultural ego network relative to cultural tastes. That is, omnivores select non-redundant genres, with redundancy defined as the extent to which the audience of any one genre chosen overlaps with that of other genres also chosen – building on the logic of Burt's structural holes argument. From this perspective, omnivorousness refers to bridging cultural holes in a space defined by cultural genres by choosing sets of genres whose audiences display relatively low overlap. After proposing an intuitive way to capture this tendency, combining Breiger's (1974) projection approach with a variation of Burt's metrics for structural holes, Lizardo shows that the socio-demographic markers traditionally associated with cultural omnivorousness when measured as the sheer quantity of choices differ in systematic ways from those linked to omnivorousness when measured in terms of bridging cultural holes. In more recent work, Puetz (2021) extends the cultural holes argument concerning aesthetic engagement to the realm of friendship preferences, showing that people who bridge cultural holes when it comes to their musical taste choices are also more likely to express a preference for friends who are 'creative' and 'cultured' as compared to people who make cultural choices that commonly go together.

Cultural Holes and the Categorical Imperative

Silver et al. (2022) deploy the cultural holes argument to shed light on the 'categorical imperative', namely the often-noted phenomenon that actors (both individual and corporate) who cross categorical boundaries are penalised in market settings. Like the above, this work shows that recent work on 'categories' in organisation and management studies (Goldberg et al., 2016a; Kovács & Hannan, 2015) can most profitably be specified with the cultural holes framework. The basic idea is that when audiences (regulators, critics, customers) are faced with actors who present themselves in multiple categories (e.g., a brewery that is also an ice creamery), they are confused and infer that a 'jack of all trades is probably master of none', or more accurately not as masterful as one with a focused (e.g., singular) identity (Hannan, 2010). From this perspective, bridging cultural holes in a category system is likely to be deleterious to actors in competitive fields. By contrast, Silver et al. (2022) argue that rather than an unconditional negative link, the connection between cultural-hole-spanning, creativity, and success is likely to take something closer to an inverted u-shape, especially in fields that reward innovation and creativity. Too much focus on a single genre category (lack of cultural-hole bridging) is seen by audiences hungry for novelty as conventional and boring. However, spanning cultural holes across considerable categorical distances is likely to trigger the various deleterious mechanisms mentioned earlier, with audiences left befuddled at bizarre or non-standard genre combinations.

To test their proposal, Silver et al. examined data from close to 3 million bands listed in Myspace in the late aughts. They use the music genre categories selected by each band and compute the categorical distance between genre labels based on co-occurrence patterns from the one-mode (genre-by-genre) projection of the original band-by-genre two-mode network. They find that indeed, across three musical 'worlds' – high-level clusters of genres labelled 'Rock', 'Hip Hop' and 'Niche' (see also Silver et al., 2016) – there is an inverted u-relationship between cultural-hole bridging and popularity (as measured by the number of views, fans and digital 'plays' of their music). Bands with highly focused identities (failing to bridge cultural holes) and bands who span cultural holes across very distant categories are less popular than bands who combine categories at a moderate distance from one another. Thus, *moderate* cultural-hole bridging is the key to success in this empirical case. While this is the predominant tendency in the data, Silver et al. also find systematic variation in this empirical pattern by musical world.[3] In some musical worlds, like Hip Hop, the predominant pattern is closer to a 'dual innovation' model, with peaks in popularity at both a moderate and an extreme label of cultural-hole bridging. Some musical worlds reward creativity and unconventionality, but most follow the tendency to reward cultural-hole bridging up to a point, after which the 'categorical imperative' kicks in.[4]

Cultural Holes versus Structural Holes

Silver et al.'s work proposes a systematic link between cultural-hole bridging, creativity and success; Choi's (2018) recent work examines this issue directly. Choi uses the cultural holes argument to study the origins of ideational creativity among members of the IT department of a medium-sized tech company in South Korea. The topic of 'good ideas' has been studied before using sociometric network models like Burt's structural holes (Burt, 2004). The primary finding here is that people who bridge sociometric structural holes are likelier to have 'good ideas' than those who live in social worlds in which their contacts are connected. The presumed mechanism is that structural holes provide the potential to access otherwise disconnected ideas by others. Thus, structural brokers are better positioned to synthesise these separate pieces of information into more original and creative insights.

Choi (2018) reasons that the structural holes model is an indirect 'one step removed' version of a more basic cultural holes model. That is, structural brokers have better ideas because they are *cultural brokers*; the direct operative mechanism concerns not the position of the person in a sociometric network of personal relations but a person's position in a cultural network composed of local ideational frames. Regarding creativity, the cultural holes argument partially supersedes the structural holes one (or, at the very least, provides a more direct mechanism leading to the same outcome). To test this hypothesis, Choi first measured the most prevalent local frames in the company using a free-text elicitation strategy from which higher-level frames were coded and extracted, using an 'idea tournament' approach based on Salganik's Wiki survey method (Salganik & Levy, 2015).[5]

In this setup, participants anonymously submitted ideas to improve the company. Then, the ideas were (also anonymously) rated by others using pairwise comparisons between two randomly selected ideas at a time. Ideas that were more likely to 'win' when compared to other randomly selected ideas were deemed the most creative. The frame extraction approach resulted in a two-mode network of people by cultural frames. Cultural brokers are thus people who hold cultural frames not likely held by the same others. Choi found that, indeed, cultural brokers are more likely to have ideas considered creative by others, even after adjusting for sociometric brokerage (which also leads to ideas being considered more creative) and relative cultural fit (the likelihood of holding frames that are also likely to be held by others).

Choi's finding that bridging cultural holes has a direct effect on creativity *even after statistically adjusting* for bridging sociometric structural holes is consistent with recent work arguing and showing that sociometric bridging (structural holes) is analytically distinct from cultural bridging (cultural holes) and thus has independent effects on key outcomes. For instance, Graham et al. (2022) analyse large-scale scientific co-authorship data across 25 scientific fields. They use computational linguistic techniques to measure each scientist's diversity of information based on the terms and concepts used in their publication's title, abstract and keywords and the articles they cite in their work. They find only weak correlations between sociometric position in the co-authorship network and ego's direct and indirect access to information diversity, showing that bridging structural holes does not automatically translate into bridging cultural holes.

Graham et al.'s findings dovetail with those of Goldberg et al. (2016b), who also use computational linguistic techniques to measure the extent to which people exhibit 'culturally fit' (e.g., use language that is similar to their communication partners in a directed email network) within an organisation. They find that bridging structural holes and having high cultural fit lead to more beneficial outcomes (e.g., better performance reviews and lower chances of involuntary exit) when considered independently. However, precisely because the link between position in the cultural and sociometric networks is relatively weak, the two dimensions can also be considered *jointly* (e.g., one effect moderating the other). When this is done, the results indicate that structural holes help but only for those who culturally fit the organisation ('assimilated brokers'). Notably, the results suggest that bridging cultural holes is *sufficient* for experiencing comparatively successful outcomes. People with high levels of sociometric constraint but who stand out culturally from others in the organisation – integrated non-conformists – do systematically better compared to those who have access to structural holes but do not bridge cultural holes ('disembedded actors').

Finally, work by de Vaan et al. (2015) shows that the argument distinguishing cultural from structural bridging extends beyond individuals to explain the creative success of teams. While previous work on creative teams (e.g., Uzzi & Spiro, 2005) focuses mainly on structural network position – and is thus forced to infer cultural bridging from structural bridging – de Vaan et al. develop separate measures of each for creative teams of video game developers. Furthermore, they show that it is a *combination* of structural and cultural bridging that best explains creative success – as measured by critical acclaim teams composed of groups (defined as subsets of creators who have worked together in the past) that share members with other groups within the team ('structural folding') *and* groups that bridge cultural holes by spanning large cultural distances relative to other groups (as defined by the distance in product space of previously created games created) are the most likely to come up with both novel (category-atypical compared to previous entries) *and* acclaimed cultural products.

Culture-Centric Approaches to the Study of Cultural Holes

Cultural Consumption Networks

Sokolova and Sokolov (2020) set out to study cultural holes by building a culture-centric network of literary authors based on patterns of fiction books co-borrowing from the municipal library network in St Petersburg, Russia. Authors are strongly connected to the extent that there is significant overlap between the sets of people who read them. Sokolova and Sokolov's primary goal is to ascertain whether institutionally consecrated objects (or objects consumed by high-status people) – which in Lizardo's original definition would count as 'asset-specific' or 'strong' culture in Schultz & Breiger's (2010) sense – can themselves bridge cultural holes in a culture-centric network. They find, contrary to the idea that institutional "consecration" (in Bourdieu's sense) renders high-status cultural goods 'niche', that the most consecrated authors are also the ones most likely to bridge cultural holes – as given by Burt's constraint measure and betweenness centrality – and the same goes for authors more likely to be read by college-educated audiences. These results are consistent with Lewis & Kaufman's (2018) warnings regarding the *relativity* of exogenous markers of the status of cultural goods, as the latter have no logical link to whether they serve as strong or weak culture since these last speak to *formal properties* of such goods within a local ecology. Sokolova and Sokolov's study shows that in a context where consecrated and high-status works are generally valued, they behave very much like we would expect 'popular culture' would; as bridges within the cultural network.

Cultural Holes in Text Networks

Perhaps the most exciting recent advance in the culture-centric analysis of cultural holes is Stoltz & Taylor's (2019) proposal to measure 'discursive holes' in-text similarity networks. The recent rise of computational social science has brought a slew of techniques to analyse large-scale text data. However, almost all the now well-established methods yield some weighted text-to-text network where the edge weight is based on the similarities – and, by implication, the distances – between each pair of texts. Although each analytic technique – for example, topic models, word-vector embeddings – produces a different criterion for similarity, every text analyst deals with such a network. For instance, Stoltz & Taylor note that topic models yield a two-mode matrix of texts by topic, where the row entry for text is the probability that text i engages topic j (with the probabilities summing to one row-wise). This argument can be generalised to the analysis of two-mode network data more generally beyond texts since every one-mode projection is, in fact, a potential similarity (or distance) matrix across the nodes in each mode (Everett & Borgatti, 2013). Following this insight, Stoltz & Taylor use a measurement strategy developed for agent-centric cultural analysis but deploy it in the culture-centric level of texts in discursive fields. They thus propose a measure of 'textual spanning' (cultural-hole bridging) for particular texts based on a simple idea: within a discursive field defined by a textual similarity space, *texts bridge cultural (discursive) holes when they are similar to texts that are themselves dissimilar*. Stoltz and Taylor go on to show that this approach to measure cultural-hole spanning generates insights about the positionality of texts in discursive space that are occluded by using standard 'medial' or 'radial' centrality measures based on the weighted path distance (like betweenness and closeness).

Cultural Holes, Atypicality and Categorical Diversity

While not couched in explicit network terms, Goldberg et al.'s (2016a) approach to analysing cultural boundaries is based on the fundamental cultural holes imagery. Importantly, their approach can be interpreted as engaging in agent- and culture-centric analysis simultaneously by defining agent-centric properties relevant to cultural-hole bridging using culture-centric ones.[6] The critical difference is that rather than departing from a *two*-mode network of people by cultural objects chosen, they develop concepts and metrics linked to a *three*-mode network of people, objects and the *category labels* applied to those objects (e.g., by audiences like critics, consumers, or websites). The key observation from the perspective of the cultural holes model is that sets of objects in a given cultural domain (e.g., movies, cuisines, art and the like) and sets of labels (Action, Cambodian, Cubist and the like) can bridge cultural holes by spanning wide distances in label space. People, in turn, can bridge cultural holes by choosing categorically distinct objects *or* objects that bridge across category labels.

For instance, we can begin by constructing a two-mode object-by-label network – where object i is linked to label j if that label is applied to that object (Kovács & Hannan, 2015). We can then use variations of Breiger's (1974) projection approach to define a one-mode label-by-label network (Everett & Borgatti, 2013). In this network, strongly related labels have significant overlaps between the set of objects each label is applied. On the other hand, category labels are weakly related when the overlap between their object sets is relatively small (Silver et al., 2022). In this way, the weighted label-to-label network encodes the relative *similarity* of each pair of labels. By implication, this network also encodes inter-label distance since, as Hannan and Kovács (2015) note, similarities between labels are an inverse function of distance in some conceptual space (Gardenfors, 2014). Strongly related labels are close, while weakly related labels are far. Accordingly, we can construct a derivative label-to-label network where the weighted links are given by pairwise distances, using some suitable mathematical transformation of the original pairwise similarities.

Given that each object is assigned a set of labels, we can then aggregate or average the pairwise distances of the labels assigned to each object. According to this metric, atypical objects will receive high scores, while typical objects will receive lower scores. This is another way of saying that *atypical objects bridge cultural holes across labels*. We can also use the inter-label distance information to define an object-by-object network. The weighted link between objects is given by the average similarity between the two sets of labels assigned to the objects incident to each edge. The inter-object network thus encodes the relative *categorical distinctiveness* between each pair of objects, with categorically non-distinct objects clustering together and categorically distinct objects falling in separate communities. As with labels, we can generate a derivative inter-object network by transforming inter-object similarities into distances.

With this information in hand, we can loop back to the agent's perspective and define a person's *taste for atypicality* by aggregating or averaging the atypicality scores of the objects they choose (as encoded in a two-mode network of people by objects chosen).[7] Thus, *agents can bridge cultural holes by selecting atypical objects*, namely objects bridging culture holes in label space.[8] However, there is a second way to define an agent's penchant for bridging cultural holes in their consumption choices. Similarly, we can define a person's *taste for variety* by aggregating or averaging the pairwise distances of the objects they choose. Thus, *agents can bridge cultural holes by selecting categorically distinct (sets of) objects*. As Goldberg et al. (2016a) show, these two agent-centric ways of bridging cultural holes are conceptually and empirically distinct, as the atypicality of an object relative to the set of labels it is assigned is not definitionally linked to its categorical distinctiveness relative to other objects.

Importantly, tastes for variety and atypicality are empirically distinct from the sheer numerical *quantity* of objects chosen – what has been referred to in the literature as 'omnivorousness by volume' (Lizardo, 2014). In the case of atypicality, for instance, a person can bridge cultural holes even when selecting a single (e.g., highly atypical) object – 'univores' are therefore capable of bridging cultural holes. Alternatively, a person can select many categorically non-distinct objects, thus failing to bridge in the variety sense – quantitative 'omnivores' are therefore not guaranteed to bridge cultural holes. Because they are distinct, agents may have a high or low taste for atypicality combined with a high or low taste for variety, yielding three ways to bridge cultural holes. For instance, people can choose (or like) categorically a small set of indistinct atypical objects ('mono-mixer'), a large set of categorically distinct typical objects ('poly-purist'), or a large set of categorically distinct atypical objects ('poly-mixer').

While being a poly-mixer may seem like the ultimate way to bridge cultural holes, Goldberg et al. (2016a) provide suggestive evidence that the 'high-status' omnivore who populates much work in the sociology of taste (see Jarness & Friedman, 2017) is a person who bridges cultural holes in the variety sense, but who *refuses* to do so in the atypicality sense. These poly-purist omnivores decide instead to 'police' categorical boundaries (e.g., by downgrading atypical objects), thus sharpening the typicality of objects and increasing opportunities for cultural-hole spanning in their preferred sense.

CONCLUDING REMARKS

We opened the chapter by considering whether 'culture and networks' is a research speciality, a research cluster, or something else. I noted that the answer to these questions depends on the degree of unity we seek. On the one hand, we can be content with a rather superficial thematic unity based on topics and substantive emphases. On the other hand, we can seek a deeper unity based on the underlying theoretical models – or, more loosely, as referred to here, 'imageries' – analysts rely on to develop theories, formalisation, measures and hypotheses in their work. I argue that such underlying unity does exist in the field and is centred around two underlying *ur*-models: constructuralism and cultural holes. I showed how research using this imagery has progressed by addressing a coherent set of problems and issues and by extending theoretical models and claims to speak to the limitations of previous formulations.

Constructuralism

For instance, regarding constructuralism, Mark built his network ecology model on partial constructuralist insights, and Lizardo's conversion model developed the constructuralist strand left behind in the network ecology formulation.

Subsequently, Lewis and Kaufman responded to weaknesses in the conversion approach, generalising and distinguishing between various conversion mechanisms while linking to the larger cultural ecology. Finally, Goldberg and Stein's associative diffusion model develops the somewhat rudimentary cognitive foundations of original constructuralism by incorporating insights from the schematic construction of cultural meaning while incorporating cognitive consistency mechanisms into the interactionist constructionist imagery. The ADM thus moves beyond the limitations of network ecology, constructuralism and conversion models, all of which are tied to limiting conceptions of piecemeal cultural diffusion. The cutting edge of future work in this area thus lies in further integration between social network, interactionist, cultural and cognitive mechanisms in processes of cultural creation, transmission and diffusion and in generating observable patterns of cultural niche creation, maintenance and dissolution – for example, in the vein of Fuhse (2021), Goldberg & Stein (2018) and de Vaan et al. (2015). Importantly, this will require more sophisticated models of how culture is internalised and processed by people embedded in social network structures and subject to interactional constraints and asymmetries (Arseniev-Koehler & Foster, 2020; Foster, 2018; Lizardo, 2021). Additionally, we will have to keep firmly in sight the double emphasis of constructuralism as both a theory of what networks *do* and a theory of *where networks come from*.[9]

Cultural Holes

Research on cultural holes has also developed rapidly since Pachucki & Breiger (2010) introduced the idea, with accompanying innovations in measures, formalisation and the range of substantive applications. I argued here, however, that behind the thematic unity of the various studies, and even above and beyond the underlying conception of 'duality', there is an underlying theoretical imagery, linking agents and cultural objects (broadly defined) to mutually defining positions in a field (Puetz, 2017). As we saw, the cultural holes models can even be seen as a positional, comparative-statics-cousin to constructuralism's cognitive interactionism since both models share a common strand in Breiger's (1974) duality idea.

Accordingly, the cultural holes argument relates the agent's and object's position in sociocultural and cultural-social structures to various substantive outcomes (e.g., creativity, spanning, cosmopolitanism, vision) of interest to the analyst. In this particular way, the cultural holes argument has been interpreted and used similarly to its sociometric 'structural holes' cousin. As we saw, however, a key implication of recent work in this area is that cultural and structural hole bridging must be kept analytically distinct; one cannot be inferred from the other as has been the practice of assuming that structural brokers are also cultural brokers (Goldberg et al., 2016b; Graham et al., 2022). The cultural holes model is distinct from its sociometric cousin because it conceives the 'position' people occupy in sociocultural space as driven by analytically distinct (but coupled) dynamics from those driving the construction and the dissolution of sociometric ties. Recent advances in measuring culture from free-form text data using computational linguistic techniques have thus helped clarify the empirical contribution that people's position in the cultural information space has on key outcomes, as distinct from their 'structural' position in a network of social ties.

Another advantage of treating the idea of cultural holes as an underlying *ur*-model is that we can then integrate work that, while not nominally claiming to belong to this camp, *formally* does so, like work on categories, cognition and category-spanning in organisation and management studies (Goldberg et al., 2016a; Hannan et al., 2019; Silver et al., 2022); this is something that would have been impossible had we remained at the more surface level of commonalities based on explicit concepts or formal modelling procedures. Nevertheless, as work using the cultural holes imagery moves forward, more explicit formalisation of the cultural holes argument, perhaps a *deepening* of the idea of cultural holes in a more dynamic vein (e.g., towards temporal two-mode networks), such as by more explicit use of dynamic computational models and simulation – à la constructuralism and associative diffusion – seems to be called for, since most work in the cultural holes approach uses static measures of position. In the same way, an *extension* of the cultural holes imagery outside fields where it has been exploited the most (e.g., cultural production and consumption), such as knowledge production in science (Vilhena et al., 2014), or entrepreneurship and innovation – as with Choi's study mentioned earlier – would help stretch the paradigm and lead to further conceptual and empirical development.

Notes

1. The field has also been covered in a monograph-length publication by McLean (2016).
2. Of course, Breiger (1974) formalised the idea of *duality* in his classic paper, which is central to the cultural holes argument.

3 See unconventionality.github.io/
4 Socio-demographic and political-economic characteristics of the metro area also moderate the strength of the inverted-u relationship between cultural-hole bridging and success without violating the general pattern.
5 See www.allourideas.org/
6 See Kovàcs (2010) and Lizardo (2018) for related approaches.
7 Goldberg et al. (2016a) distinguish 'sampling' an object from 'liking' an object (technically defining a two-mode multigraph with 'sampling' and 'liking' edges between people and objects), but that is a complication that is not relevant to our purposes.
8 In the same way, community detection on the inter-object network yields clusters of categorically similar objects separated from other sets of categorically dissimilar ones.
9 That is, constructuralism functions as both a 'network theory' and a 'network theory of networks' in Borgatti and Halgin's (2011) sense.

REFERENCES

Arseniev-Koehler, A., & Foster, J.G. (2020). Machine learning as a model for cultural learning: teaching an algorithm what it means to be fat. *arXiv*. doi.org/10.31235/osf.io/c9yj3

Bail, C.A., Argyle, L.P., Brown, T.W., Bumpus, J.P., Chen, H., Hunzaker, M.B.F., Lee, J., Mann, M., Merhout, F., & Volfovsky, A. (2018). Exposure to opposing views on social media can increase political polarization. *Proceedings of the National Academy of Sciences of the United States of America*, *115*(37), 9216–9221.

Blau, P.M. (1977). A macrosociological theory of social structure. *the American Journal of Sociology*, *83*(1), 26–54.

Borgatti, S.P., & Halgin, D.S. (2011). On network theory. *Organization Science*, *22*(5), 1168–1181.

Borgatti, S.P., & Lopez-Kidwell, V. (2011). Network theory. In J. Scott & P. J. Carrington (Eds.), *The Sage handbook of social network analysis* (pp. 40–54). Sage.

Bourdieu, P. ([1979]1984). *Distinction: a social critique of the judgement of taste* (R. Nice, trans.). Harvard University Press. (Original work published 1979.)

Bourdieu, P. (1986). The forms of capital. In J. Richardson (Ed.), *Handbook of theory and research for the sociology of education* (pp. 241–258). Greenwood Press.

Breiger, R.L. (1974). The duality of persons and groups. *Social Forces: A Scientific Medium of Social Study and Interpretation*, *53*(2), 181–190.

Breiger, R.L. (2010). Dualities of culture and structure: seeing through cultural holes. In J. Fuhse & S. Mützel (Eds.), *Relationale Soziologie: Zur kulturellen Wende der Netzwerkforschung* (pp. 37–47). VS Verlag für Sozialwissenschaften.

Breiger, R.L., & Puetz, K. (2015). Culture and networks. In J.D. Wright (Ed.), *International encyclopedia of social and behavioral sciences* (Vol. 5, pp. 557–562). Elsevier.

Burt, R.S. (2000). Decay functions. *Social Networks*, *22*(1), 1–28.

Burt, R.S. (2004). Structural holes and good ideas. *American Journal of Sociology*, *110*(2), 349–399.

Burt, R.S. ([1992]2009). *Structural holes: the social structure of competition*. Harvard University Press.

Carley, K.M. (1991). A theory of group stability. *American Sociological Review*, *56*(3), 331–354.

Carley, K.M. (1995). Communication technologies and their effect on cultural homogeneity, consensus, and the diffusion of new ideas. *Sociological Perspectives*, *38*(4), 547–571.

Choi, Y. (2018). *Cultural brokerage and creativity: how individuals' bridging of cultural holes affect creativity*. Columbia University Press. doi.org/10.7916/D88K8T0B

Davis, J. A. (1963). Structural balance, mechanical solidarity, and interpersonal relations. American Journal of Sociology, 68(4), 444–462.

DellaPosta, D., Shi, Y., & Macy, M. (2015). Why do liberals drink lattes? *American Journal of Sociology*, *120*(5), 1473–1511.

de Vaan, M., Stark, D., & Vedres, B. (2015). Game changer: the topology of creativity. *American Journal of Sociology*, *120*(4), 1144–1194.

DiMaggio, P. (1987). Classification in art. *American Sociological Review*, *52*(4), 440–455.

DiMaggio, P. (2011). Cultural networks. In J. Scott & P. J. Carrington (Eds.), *The Sage handbook of social network analysis* (pp. 286–310). Sage.

Edelmann, A., & Vaisey, S. (2014). Cultural resources and cultural distinction in networks. *Poetics*, *46*, 22–37.

Everett, M.G., & Borgatti, S.P. (2013). The dual-projection approach for two-mode networks. *Social Networks*, *35*(2), 204–210.

Foster, J.G. (2018). Culture and computation: steps to a probably approximately correct theory of culture. *Poetics*, *68*, 144–154.

Friemel, T.N. (2012/17). Network dynamics of television use in school classes. *Social Networks*, *34*(3), 346–358.

Fuhse, J. (2021). *Social networks of meaning and communication*. Oxford University Press.

Gardenfors, P. (2014). *The geometry of meaning: semantics based on conceptual spaces*. MIT Press.

Goldberg, A. (2011). Mapping shared understandings using relational class analysis: the case of the cultural omnivore reexamined. *American Journal of Sociology*, *116*(5), 1397–1436.

Goldberg, A., Hannan, M.T., & Kovács, B. (2016a). What does it mean to span cultural boundaries? Variety and atypicality in cultural consumption. *American Sociological Review*, *81* (2), 215–241.

Goldberg, A., Srivastava, S.B., Manian, V.G., Monroe, W., & Potts, C. (2016b). Fitting in or standing out? The tradeoffs of structural and cultural embeddedness. *American Sociological Review*, *81*(6), 1190–1222.

Goldberg, A., & Stein, S.K. (2018). Beyond social contagion: associative diffusion and the emergence of cultural variation. *American Sociological Review 83*(5), 897–932.

Graham, A.V., McLevey, J., Browne, P., & Crick, T. (2022). Structural diversity is a poor proxy for information diversity: evidence from 25 scientific fields. *Social Networks*, *70*, 55–63.

Granovetter, M.S. (1973). The strength of weak ties. *American Journal of Sociology*, *78*(3), 1360–1380.

Hachen, D., Wang, C., Sepulvado, B., & Lizardo, O. (2022). Generators or diffusers? Examining differences in the dynamic coupling of context and social ties across multiple types of foci. *Social Networks*. doi.org/10.1016/j.socnet.2022.02.004

Hannan, M.T. (2010). Partiality of memberships in categories and audiences. *Annual Review of Sociology*, *36*(1), 159–181.

Hannan, M.T., Le Mens, G., Hsu, G., Kovács, B., Negro, G., Pólos, L., Pontikes, E., & Sharkey, A.J. (2019). *concepts and categories: foundations for sociological and cultural analysis (The Middle Range Series)* (Illustrated ed.). Columbia University Press.

Jarness, V., & Friedman, S. (2017). 'I'm not a snob, but …': class boundaries and the downplaying of difference. *Poetics*, *61*, 14–25.

Kovács, B. (2010). A generalized model of relational similarity. *Social Networks*, *32*(3), 197–211.

Kovács, B., & Hannan, M. (2015). Conceptual spaces and the consequences of category spanning. *Sociological Science*, *2*, 252–286.

Lee, M., & Martin, J.L. (2018). Doorway to the dharma of duality. *Poetics*, *68*, 18–30.

Lewis, K., & Kaufman, J. (2018). The conversion of cultural tastes into social network ties. *American Journal of Sociology*, *123*(6), 1684–1742.

Lewis, K., Kaufman, J., Gonzalez, M., Wimmer, A., & Christakis, N. (2008). Tastes, ties, and time: a new social network dataset using Facebook.com. *Social Networks*, *30*(4), 330–342.

Lizardo, O. (2006). How cultural tastes shape personal networks. *American Sociological Review*, *71*(5), 778–807.

Lizardo, O. (2014). Omnivorousness as the bridging of cultural holes: a measurement strategy. *Theory and Society*, *43*(3–4), 395–419.

Lizardo, O. (2018). The mutual specification of genres and audiences: reflective two-mode centralities in person-to-culture data. *Poetics*, *68*, 52–71.

Lizardo, O. (2021). Culture, cognition, and internalization. *Sociological Forum*, *36*, 1177–1206.

Lomi, A., & Stadtfeld, C. (2014). Social networks and social settings: developing a coevolutionary view. *Kölner Zeitschrift Für Soziologie Und Sozialpsychologie*, *66*(1), 395–415.

Mark, N.P. (1998a). Beyond individual differences: social differentiation from first principles. *American Sociological Review*, *63*(3), 309–330.

Mark, N.P. (1998b). Birds of a feather sing together. *Social Forces: A Scientific Medium of Social Study and Interpretation*, *77*(2), 453–485.

Mark, N.P. (2003). Culture and competition: homophily and distancing explanations for cultural niches. *American Sociological Review*, *68*(3), 319–345.

Marsden, P.V., & Campbell, K.E. (1984). Measuring tie strength. *Social Forces: A Scientific Medium of Social Study and Interpretation*, *63*(2), 482.

Martin, J.L., & Yeung, K.-T. (2006). Persistence of close personal ties over a 12-year period. *Social Networks*, *28*(4), 331–362.

McLean, P. (2016). *Culture in networks*. John Wiley & Sons.

McPherson, J.M. (2004). A Blau space primer: prolegomenon to an ecology of affiliation. *Industrial and Corporate Change*, *13*(1), 263–280.

McPherson, J.M., Smith-Lovin, L., & Cook, J.M. (2001). Birds of a feather: homophily in social networks. *Annual Review of Sociology*, *27*(1), 415–444.

Mische, A. (2011). Relational sociology, culture, and agency. In J. Scott & P. J. Carrington (Eds.), *The Sage handbook of social network analysis* (pp. 80–97). Sage.

Mützel, S., & Breiger, R. (2020). Duality beyond persons and groups. In R. Light & J. Moody (Eds.), *The Oxford handbook of social networks* (pp. 392–413). Oxford University Press.

Neal, Z. (2014). The backbone of bipartite projections: inferring relationships from co-authorship, co-sponsorship, co-attendance and other co-behaviors. *Social Networks*, *39*, 84–97.

Ollivier, M. (2008). Modes of openness to cultural diversity: humanist, populist, practical, and indifferent. *Poetics*, *36*(2–3), 120–147.

Pachucki, M.A., & Breiger, R.L. (2010). Cultural holes: beyond relationality in social networks and culture. *Annual Review of Sociology*, *36*(1), 205–224.

Peterson, R.A., & Kern, R.M. (1996). Changing highbrow taste: from snob to omnivore. *American Sociological Review*, *61*(5), 900–907.

Puetz, K. (2017). Fields of mutual alignment: a dual-order approach to the study of cultural holes. *Sociological Theory*, *35*(3), 228–260.

Puetz, K. (2021). Taste boundaries and friendship preferences: insights from the formalist approach. *Poetics, 86*, 101551.

Reay, M. (2010). Knowledge distribution, embodiment, and insulation. *Sociological Theory, 28*(1), 91–107.

Rule, A., & Bearman, P. (2015). Networks and culture. In L. Hanquinet & M. Savage (Eds.), *Routledge international handbook of the sociology of art and culture* (pp. 161–173). Routledge.

Salganik, M.J., & Levy, K.E.C. (2015). Wiki surveys: open and quantifiable social data collection. *PLOS One, 10*(5), e0123483.

Schultz, J., & Breiger, R.L. (2010). The strength of weak culture. *Poetics, 38*(6), 610–624.

Shalizi, C.R., & Thomas, A.C. (2011). Homophily and contagion are generically confounded in observational social network studies. *Sociological Methods and Research, 40*(2), 211–239.

Silver, D., Childress, C., Lee, M., Slez, A., & Dias, F. (2022). Balancing categorical conventionality in music. *American Journal of Sociology, 128*(1), 224–286.

Silver, D., Lee, M., & Childress, C.C. (2016). Genre complexes in popular music. *PLOS One, 11*(5), e0155471.

Sokolova, N., & Sokolov, M. (2020). Does popular culture bridge cultural holes? A study of a literary taste system using unimodal network projections. *Poetics, 83*, 101472.

Stoltz, D.S., & Taylor, M.A. (2019). Textual spanning: finding discursive holes in text networks. *Socius, 5*, 2378023119827674.

Uzzi, B., & Spiro, J. (2005). Collaboration and creativity: the small world problem. *American Journal of Sociology, 111*(2), 447–504.

Vaisey, S., & Lizardo, O. (2010). Can cultural worldviews influence network composition? *Social Forces, 88*(4), 1595–1618.

Vilhena, D., Foster, J., Rosvall, M., West, J., Evans, J., & Bergstrom, C. (2014). Finding cultural holes: how structure and culture diverge in networks of scholarly communication. *Sociological Science, 1*, 221–238.

Vlegels, J. (2014). *Network dynamics in the cultural system*. Ghent University. biblio.ugent.be/publication/5785476/file/5785490

Semantic and Cultural Networks

Sarah Shugars and Sandra González-Bailón

1. INTRODUCTION

When Queen Victoria chose to wear white to her wedding in 1840, she seeded a lasting connection in Western minds. While Western brides had previously worn a variety of colours, the Queen's colour choice sparked a fashion trend which quickly evolved into a cultural standard. The concept of 'wedding dress' now immediately evokes the concept of 'white'. There is no inherent, natural reason why these concepts must be connected to one another; this connection was instead forged through a process of imitation and social diffusion that ultimately crystallised into a cultural norm.

There are many such connections we could draw between ideas, beliefs and other types of cultural constructs. These connections might be observed through tangible artefacts – that is, words, images, or videos – or they may primarily exist as latent conceptual ties – that is, as assumptions, associations, or justifications. Despite this diversity in scope, there is a great deal of conceptual and methodological similarity in the analysis of these socially constructed networks. As with other types of networks, a key decision is which constructs are to be included as nodes, and what type of 'connection' the edges represent. In the case of semantic and cultural networks, both can be understood as socially constructed networks in which tangible or intangible cultural artefacts are connected to one another according to some meaningful measure. By 'cultural artefacts' we mean information units – words, ideas, beliefs, images – whose meanings are co-created and used by individuals to communicate or otherwise navigate a shared culture.

As we discuss in this chapter, these socially constructed structures include conceptual and knowledge networks – for example, networks of ideas; networks of words and meanings; and networks of images, audio, or video (a more nascent research area). What all these networks have in common is that the nodes are culturally created artefacts and the edges capture socially conceived connections between those artefacts. If 'white' and 'wedding dress' are connected, it is because someone once put them together, and this co-occurrence became more frequent over time, to the point that the connection became reified in the collective imagination. This example also highlights the importance of the cultural frame of reference: in China, for instance, wedding dresses are predominantly red, a colour which symbolises good luck and happiness.

2. WHY STUDY SEMANTIC AND CULTURAL NETWORKS?

We usually think of social networks as models describing relationships between social actors, such as individuals, organisations, or countries. However, social network analysis (SNA) is more broadly understood as the structural examination of social systems (Freeman, 2004): the goal isn't merely to understand how actors are connected to one another, but to shed insight into why actors form connections and the implications of these social embeddings. The study of socially constructed networks – such as semantic and cultural networks – is deeply germane to this goal: studying cultural artefacts and the perceived connections between them has the potential to build understanding into how people interpret, represent and communicate their realities. These models can therefore allow researchers to examine why actors engage in certain behaviours and interactions and to further interrogate the collective implications of those actions.

The study of semantic and cultural networks can, for example, cast light into the biases of a given society. When semantic networks tell us that the word 'programmer' is more closely connected to the word 'male' than to the word 'female' (Bolukbasi et al., 2016) or when the concept of 'gender' is defined as a binary, thus hiding other identities, we are uncovering important information about a society, its structure and its collective understanding of the world. In other words, semantic and conceptual networks help us make tangible the biases, values and associations of the society that generated them. This is particularly important since advances in machine learning and data analysis increase the potential to exacerbate the biases embedded in these socially constructed networks (Mehrabi et al., 2021). Identifying a gendered connotation to the word 'programmer' tells us something relevant about a culture. But when automated tasks of information retrieval or machine translation leverage the data contained in semantic networks, it not only reinforces existing social biases; it also creates the illusion that these semantic connections are not merely socially constructed but a reflection of some natural truth. Uncovering these connections for what they are (i.e., socially constructed meaning) is a crucial step in deploying these automated tasks responsibly.

Socially constructed networks can also serve as powerful tools for mapping processes of human problem solving and meaning-making. For example, the education one might receive in an MBA or other professional programme is not typically about memorising a list of facts, but is more richly geared towards learning a profession's approach to reasoning and decision-making (Shaffer et al., 2009; Shavelson, 1974). This is why case studies can be such a useful pedagogical tool – rather than learning discrete, isolated facts, students develop generalised knowledge by learning to weigh relevant trade-offs between connected ideas and approaches (Flyvbjerg, 2006). Notably, this is an inherently networked understanding of the learning process (Lynn & Bassett, 2020) – it's not just about the ideas (nodes), but also about the connections (or edges) bringing those ideas together. As students learn their profession's understanding of those connections, they are better able to address the novel problems they encounter.

These examples also allow us to introduce some of the challenges of working with semantic and cultural networks. Human processes such as learning, remembering, reasoning, arguing, explaining and communicating are often *implicitly* networked, but may not be explicitly so. In many cases, *both* the nodes and the edges are socially constructed and, therefore, are latent network properties that researchers need to infer. In the analysis of semantic networks, for instance, nodes might be easily defined as 'words' which can be directly observed; but this does not solve important conceptual issues: for instance, should homographs (i.e., words which share a spelling but not a meaning) be considered as the same node? What about words which are spelled differently but share the same meaning? Might some nodes be multiword phrases rather than single unigrams? What rules do we use for determining which words are connected? Must they be within the same span? The same sentence? The same paragraph? All of these are questions researchers must consider within the context of their data and their research question. In other words, when examining culturally constructed networks, researchers must give careful thought to how they conceptualise and operationalise their basic units of analysis (nodes and edges), and they should be mindful of the many degrees of freedom that go into their observations and measurements.

While the challenges of measuring and analysing socially constructed networks may at first seem overwhelming, it is important to remember that many of these issues also exist within other areas of SNA as well. Arguably, when the nodes in a social network are actors, the definition of the population is more concrete, as long as network boundaries are clearly delineated. Yet, the connections between those actors are often open to interpretation and may at times be intangible as well. An observed tie in a social network may represent a concrete interaction such as an email exchange, a transfer of funds, or being physically proximate with a radio frequency identification (or RFID) badge; but these ties may equally be intangible: feelings of trust, having memorable conversations, or perceiving someone as a leader. Furthermore, ties may mean different things even if their measurement is equivalent: ties to a spouse, a dear friend, or a sibling may be equally strong (in terms of frequency of contact) but different in terms of emotional, supportive, or informational value; likewise, after years of absence some social ties may be permanently severed while others can be effortlessly reconnected. Just as there are important conceptual questions when studying semantic and cultural networks, there are similarly deep conceptual questions in actor-driven SNA that require careful consideration.

The challenges faced by researchers aiming to study semantic and cultural networks are therefore neither new nor unique. The difference is not that these networks of cultural artefacts are inherently more ineffable than other forms of social networks; rather there has simply been less time spent collectively grappling with and navigating these conceptual concerns. While scholars have raised questions about semantic and cultural networks for nearly as long as they have been examining actor-driven social networks, it is only relatively recently that computational tools have made the study of these networks tractable and scalable, raising the stakes of failing to examine the implicit biases and assumptions embedded in cultural artefacts and their relations.

In what follows, we first provide a brief overview of the philosophical and theoretical background to existing work in this area. We then discuss recent research organised along two distinct strands: networks of concepts, beliefs and knowledge; and networks of cultural artefacts such as text and images. We then provide some practical advice to help scholars navigate the methodological decisions and available computational tools.

3. THEORETICAL BACKGROUND

Some of the earliest work in SNA focused not on measuring naturally occurring social network structures, but on studying how networks of communication patterns affected group problem solving and performance (Bavelas, 1950; Guetzkow & Simon, 1955). In a series of lab-based studies, the arrangement of a social network was assumed to be imposed as a formal organisational structure. The process of interest, then, was the degree to which information could flow across this organisational network. In other words, could agents who themselves had access only to partial information collectively reach optimal outcomes through strategic knowledge sharing? While this line of work went on to form an important foundation for SNA studies in organisational and management science (Burt, 2004; Lazer & Friedman, 2007; Mason & Watts, 2012; Riedl et al., 2021), it is notable here for its early attention to the interconnected roles of human language, cognition and social ties. Networks of social relationships don't simply exist on their own, they serve as critical pathways for information sharing and meaning-making – social processes which themselves can generate cultural artefacts which in turn can be understood as having meaningful network structure.

In focusing his research on the effectiveness of different social structures, Bavelas intentionally chose to disregard 'the nature of the communication' itself (Bavelas, 1950) – aiming to design simple tasks in which the complexity of the ideas communicated or the language used to communicate would not exert undue influence on a group's ability to successfully share disparate information. For example, in one experiment described by Bavelas, each subject received a card with five geometric symbols taken from a pool of six possible symbols. By passing messages through their designated network structure, each subject had to determine which symbol was uniquely shared across all cards. Interestingly, even when the appropriate pathways for communication were available, relevant information was not always communicated flawlessly. This suggests that the process of information sharing is not only subject to the structure of social ties, but is likely also affected by the complexity of the exchanged ideas and the language used to communicate. If errors can occur in a relatively straightforward symbol-passing task, they may be more likely to occur when messages are more complex. Indeed, this is essentially the premise of the children's game Telephone, in which a starting player whispers a phrase to another player and the message is passed down the line until it is inevitably jumbled through this process of iterated exchange. Furthermore, social ties may not merely be conduits for communication, but communication itself may serve to forge and maintain social ties – again, emphasising the need to take these cultural constructs into account (Doerfel & Moore, 2016).

Given the complexity of natural language and real-world knowledge-sharing tasks, work in linguistics, computational linguistics and linguistic philosophy has long tackled the related question of what information exchange actually looks like. Consider, for example, the simple model of human communication proposed by Cohen (1987). At minimum, communication requires a dyadic interaction between a single Speaker and a single Hearer. The Speaker sends an information signal, and the Hearer interprets that information signal. While this signal could be as simple as a written series of geometric shapes – as in the lab studies of Bavelas (1950) – a common but more complex message could take the form of an 'argument'. That is, we might imagine the Speaker transmits some message with the goal of convincing the Hearer of some piece of information contained within that message. The Speaker's job is to construct the message in such a way as to be interpretable, and the Hearer's job is to interpret that message to understand the argument the Speaker is making. For such an exchange to be successful, both the Speaker and the Hearer must share a common set of rules for encoding and decoding any transmitted message: they must share a language which dictates the message's structure.

While the 'social network' in this model may be trivial – two actors who are assumed to communicate freely and share information in good faith – the simplicity of the social dimension allows for closer scrutiny of the linguistic dimension. Specifically, the key insight offered here is that in order for this process of argument encoding and decoding to be successful, the argument itself must have a predictable structure (Shannon, 1948).

This is a very old idea which dates back at least as far as Aristotle, who described how a major premise ('All men are mortal') may be connected to a minor premise ('Socrates is a man') in order to deductively reach a valid conclusion ('Socrates is mortal') (Mill, 1882). This is an inherently networked understanding of argument structure: these statements do not stand on their own, but are connected in such a way as to justify the final conclusion. This networked approach to argument structure has continued through modern linguistic philosophy (Toulmin, 1958; Walton et al., 2008) and has most recently served as the basis for machine learning approaches for argument detection and argument mining (Feng & Hirst, 2011; Habernal & Gurevych, 2015; Mochales & Moens, 2011; Palau & Moens, 2009; Stab & Gurevych, 2014).

Importantly, the mere presence of argument structure is not enough to ensure successful communication. In order for a Hearer – either human or algorithmic – to accurately interpret the argument of a Speaker, they must be able to both interpret the individual statements made and to recognise the connections between those statements (Cohen, 1987). Observable linguistic cues may help a Hearer identify connections and detect argument structure (Cohen, 1987; Mochales & Moens, 2011), but it takes a process of cognition or memory retrieval in order to assess the meaning or veracity of each individual statement. After all, an argument which begins with the premise that 'all men are *im*mortal' and concludes with the claim that 'Socrates is *im*mortal' would have the same *structure* as an argument in which all men are assumed to be mortal. A Hearer aiming to determine which of these statements to believe would therefore need some means of assessing the true relationship between the concept of 'men' and the concept of 'mortality'.

4. COGNITIVE, CONCEPTUAL AND BELIEF NETWORKS

In this sense, knowledge itself can be understood as having a network structure. In making sense of the world, humans do more than simply accrue long lists of declarative facts (Dorsey et al., 1999). We *organise* our knowledge, understanding concepts through their relationships with other concepts and leveraging those connections in order to efficiently store and retrieve information (Collins & Loftus, 1975; Collins & Quillian, 1969; Dorsey et al., 1999). Importantly, these connections reflect a diversity of types of knowledge, including natural facts (i.e., men are mortal) and cultural norms (i.e., wedding dresses are white). People may not always be explicitly aware that they are making or using network structures in their cognitive processes, but humans are remarkably adept at learning these network structures and identifying the resulting patterns (Lynn & Bassett, 2020). This suggests that networked-based models can be valuable for studying a range of cognitive processes. The chapter 'Cognition and Social Networks' (Brashears & Money, this volume) offers a more in-depth analysis of how networks help us uncover the logic of cognitive processes. Here, we focus on those processes as they intersect with the generation of cultural meaning and communicative practices.

Scholars have therefore taken different approaches to conceptualising and operationalising networks related to diverse cognitive processes including reasoning, remembering, arguing and learning. One line of work in public opinion, for example, has leveraged survey methods to infer mass ideology – that is, belief systems of connected political attitudes (Baldassarri & Goldberg, 2014; DellaPosta et al., 2015; Boutyline & Vaisey 2017; DellaPosta, 2020; Fishman & Davis, 2021). In these networks, the nodes are beliefs, measured as responses to survey policy questions (i.e., attitude towards gay marriage, affirmative action, or defence spending), and the edges are undirected ties measuring correlation, proximity, or covariance (i.e., clustering in those beliefs). Analysis of these structures allows identifying longitudinal trends in public opinion. For instance, increasing density in these networks or changes in the centrality of nodes suggest shifts in public opinion that cannot be captured by just looking at changes in support around individual policy items. The analysis of belief networks also helps identify subpopulations – it helps separate groups of people depending on how similar their belief structures are. It can also help identify organising heuristics that guide how people filter the information they encounter. Emerging work in this area has further built upon survey methods to not only measure the belief nodes, but to also measure the edges – directly asking respondents about the connections they see, or don't see, between their policy stances and their social ideals.

One of the benefits of using survey instruments to elicit beliefs is that they make tangible what exists only in the mind of a subject; they also help extrapolate those beliefs to entire populations. Belief networks help track shifts in public opinion and mass belief systems, which in turn can contribute to the study of political rhetoric, policy framing and issue salience (Yang & González-Bailón, 2016). Opinion surveys, however, are only useful for the items included in the survey, which may not represent the whole range of beliefs deemed important to subjects themselves. The explosion of digital data has given rise to new computational opportunities to be creative with the measurement of these networks. For instance, we can now analyse large-scale textual data that includes political news coverage, transcripts of political statements and debates, and social media posts and commentary from the public (Yang & González-Bailón, 2016). This ever-expanding corpus of written expression is enlarging the territory we can map with belief networks. But digital technologies also allow us to go beyond written communication.

Communication is essential to share information, ideas, or beliefs, and it makes use of all sorts of cultural artefacts capable of conveying information from one person to another. When asked for their opinion, a person might use words to describe their views (Shugars, 2020) but there are other forms of expressing that opinion. For instance, when aiming to educate, a person may use a combination of written, audio, or visual information to teach (Shavelson, 1974). When working in groups, individuals may take cues from each other to converge to a common way of speaking (Saint-Charles & Mongeau, 2017). In other words, as we aim to complete a task, seek to educate, or simply communicate with one another, we generate observable trace data in the form of interconnected cultural artefacts that manifest themselves beyond words. In the digital age, these artefacts also leave a digital trail that can be more easily parsed for measurement and analysis.

These observable trace data may then be used to meaningfully infer a subject's underlying conceptual network structure – or, in other words, their mental models (Carley & Palmquist, 1992). For instance, while we can't directly observe someone's political reasoning, we can observe the language they use when explaining or justifying their views. This opens up opportunities for inferring conceptual network structure from free response text or other documents in which people share political opinions (Atteveldt, 2008; Axelrod, 1976; Shugars, 2020).

Words themselves are cultural artefacts which represent or communicate some underlying concept. In this sense, observed words can be interpreted as representations of the latent concepts they seek to express – concepts which can then be treated as nodes in a conceptual network structure. Edges between these concepts can be understood based on observed co-occurrence within some designated span, or based on the grammatical structure of a text itself – after all, grammar is fundamentally a cultural tool aimed at signalling to a Hearer how expressed concepts are logically connected (Cohen, 1987; Shugars, 2021).

Once these conceptual networks are constructed, researchers can determine the degree to which an individual's network exhibits certain structural properties – such as connectivity, density, or clustering. Existing work suggests these structural properties may be meaningfully correlated with personality measures – providing a means to examine *how* people reason about political topics separately from the *content* of those reasons (Shugars, 2021). Changes in the structural properties of conceptual networks also signal shifts in mass opinion and the boundaries in political conflict (Yang & González-Bailón, 2016). The substantive meaning of those changes, of course, is contingent on measurement.

Inferring network structure from text requires making first several important methodological choices. In the context of conceptual networks, for example, not every word necessarily represents a unique or meaningful concept – some words may serve to represent the same concept while others contain no real meaning. Identifying this second type of word can be accomplished through the use of stopword lists or by simply excluding the parts of speech typically associated with stopwords (i.e., articles, conjunctions). Determining which words refer to the same concept, on the other hand, requires a measure of word similarity – a measure which would then allow 'similar' words to be clustered together and interpreted as the same concept or node (Shugars, 2021).

One popular means of determining word similarity comes in the form of word embeddings, which themselves are based on a networked understanding of linguistic structure. When linguist Robert Firth observed that 'you shall know a word by the company it keeps' (Firth, 1957), he was implicitly making an argument for inferring semantic networks from text: a word (node) is connected (edge) to nearby words, and those connections *convey meaningful information* about the word itself. We might imagine some Hearer – either human or computer – 'learning' a word's meaning by seeing it used in context many times. Semantic knowledge bases (Navigli & Ponzetto, 2012; Speer & Havasi, 2012) are premised on this idea – collecting large corpora of text in order to build near-complete, multilingual semantic networks. These knowledge bases can then serve as an 'encyclopaedic dictionary' (Navigli & Ponzetto, 2012) in which a user can determine a word's varied meanings by examining that word's (node's) connected words and concepts. More recently, this semantic network idea has served as the foundation for word embeddings (Devlin et al., 2019; Levy & Goldberg, 2014; Mikolov et al., 2013). This *natural language processing* (NLP) technique 'embeds' words in high-dimensional space, representing each word as a vector and calculating those vectors in such a way that words which appear in similar contexts are represented by similar vectors. Using extremely large corpora such as Wikipedia (Devlin et al., 2019) or Google News (Mikolov et al., 2013) these mathematical representations of words allow for meaningful insight into word meanings, connections and biases.

5. NETWORKS OF CULTURAL ARTEFACTS

Text, images and other forms of cultural expression are therefore another key focus of research in the analysis of socially constructed networks. Instead of trying to gauge intangible constructs or cognitive concepts, this stream of research centres on communication and what is revealed through communication processes. For instance, the combination of NLP and network analysis tools has allowed researchers to identify cultural bridges in how advocacy organisations engage with the public in social media (Bail, 2016). The nodes in this network are advocacy groups, and the weighted edges between these organisations measure the overlap of nouns and noun phrases in the posts they publish on social media. A measure of 'cultural betweenness' is then calculated for each organisation (using betweenness centrality), which allows testing the hypothesis that organisations that build more cultural bridges (i.e., organisations with high centrality scores because they connect typically unrelated themes) get more engagement from their audiences.

In another recent study, semantic networks are used to analyse the evolution of American politics as reflected in the presidents' State of the Union addresses over the 1790–2014 period (Rule et al., 2015). Methodologically, this research builds and analyses networks of words co-occurring over time, which reveals evolving semantic neighbourhoods for specific terms (i.e., 'ideals' or 'constitution'). These terms are, again, obtained using NLP techniques. Proximity scores are then computed to measure the relatedness of each pair of those terms, based on their co-occurrence in the same paragraph in a document published at a specific time. A community detection algorithm is then used to identify cohesive subsets of words; the clusters that emerge are treated as discursive categories. The temporal analysis of these networks and the discursive categories they reveal (and how they change over the centuries) allows for the identification of historical transitions in the evolution of American political thought.

More generally, this research is an example of how semantic networks allow us to extract not just mental models (as discussed in the previous section) but also culture from texts (Carley, 1994; Carley & Kaufer, 1993). Research looking at narrative structures offers another example of how to use network analysis to reveal symbolic representations across domains – autobiographical discourse (Bearman & Stovel, 2000), literature (Franzosi, 1998, 2004), or historical analysis (Bearman et al., 1999). Networks, in this case, encapsulate a sequence of events, as connected by people reflecting on their personal growth (or devolution); by writers in crafting their stories; or by historians in making sense of the past. Nodes in these networks represent events, and the ties help map how these events are encased chronologically or in narrative time.

Most of this research relies on text, or symbolic categories derived from text, but there is no reason why other forms of cultural expression, like images, could not be used. While this is an incipient area of research, advances in computer vision techniques have allowed the development of new measurement tools for large-scale analysis of images (Williams et al., 2020; Chen et al., 2021). Visual communication has become ever more central in digitally mediated interactions, and the automated analysis of images allows scaling up thematic coding and the extraction of units of meaning (i.e., objects, people, affect) that constitute the building blocks of networks. Although there is not a lot of research applying network tools to the analysis of images (i.e., how they co-appear, or how they cluster in terms of their visual features), we anticipate this will become a rising area of interest.

6. THE SOCIAL CONSTRUCTION OF SEMANTIC AND CULTURAL NETWORKS

The analysis of cultural networks aims to uncover symbolic connections intrinsic to culture and mental models of the world; but the research process is itself a social construction to the extent that it depends on choices and subjective decisions. There are two key questions in this process: (1) how to delimit the research domain (i.e., how to delimit the corpora and sampling frame); and (2) how to operationalise key constructs (i.e., what counts as a tie in the network). In this section, we outline the steps involved in the analysis of semantic and cultural networks, offering both a summary of the research discussed so far and an entry-point guide to research design in this area.

Figure 14.1 offers a schematic representation of the basic steps involved in the analysis of semantic networks. At the outset, there is the data collection stage, where the corpora of documents or artefacts to be analysed is defined; sampling procedures are executed; and the identification and extraction of units of meaning are performed. These units of meaning can be words, categories, or actors (or any other social construct), and they constitute the building blocks of the networks that are then assembled in step 2. The key decision in this step is how to define the edges in the network. Connections can signal affiliation ties (as when certain actors are linked to certain concepts); they can signal co-occurrence (with stronger ties connecting, say, words that co-appear more frequently); or they can signal a sequence in a larger narrative (as when concepts evolve in historical discourse). Once the network is assembled, the key decision is how to extract the most relevant information from that structure. Past research has used statistics like density, centrality, or structural constraint to identify meaningful changes in public discourse over time or the actors in more advantageous positions to influence the public or enact

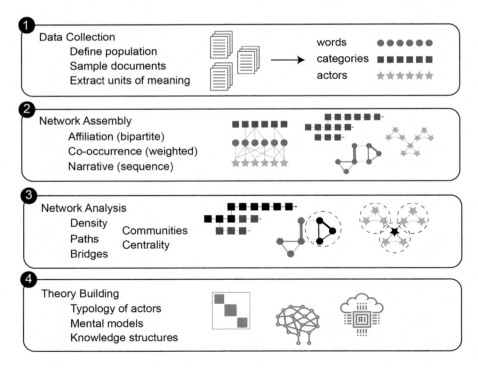

Figure 14.1 Schema of four analytical steps in semantic network research

change. Ultimately the purpose of these analyses is to improve our theoretical understanding of belief and cultural systems, and map knowledge structures as they relate to actions and behaviour – and, increasingly, to automate decisions and AI technologies.

The idea that humans store and retrieve information in a relational way (i.e., using network structures) has served as an important theoretical model for work in artificial intelligence (Collins & Loftus, 1975; Shapiro & Rapaport, 1987). A researcher can teach a computer to 'reason' by supplying or iteratively 'teaching' it appropriately structured knowledge, as inferred from human logic. For example, both a human and a computer can accurately determine that the statement 'a canary can fly' is true – if they have the additional, connected knowledge that (1) a canary is a bird and (2) birds can fly (Collins & Quillian, 1969). While observing a human's process for determining the truth of this statement can be challenging, a 'conceptual network' coded into a computer *can* be directly observed. Furthermore, such semantic network retrieval has been shown to be an efficient way to allow computers to make meaningful inference given new information (Navigli & Ponzetto, 2012; Shapiro & Rapaport, 1987; Speer & Havasi, 2012). For example, given the additional piece of information that a hawk is a bird, a computer with a networked knowledge base could correctly determine that hawks can fly, despite not being directly taught that flight is a property of hawks.

The intimate connection between human reasoning structures and the observable artefacts of human communication has fuelled further advances in machine learning and artificial intelligence. Indeed, the 'data mining' of modern machine learning is premised on the idea that meaningful patterns can be found within human-generated data – even within so-called 'unstructured' data such as text, images, audio and video. While the data of these cultural artefacts is 'unstructured' insofar as it does not come ready-made into a tidy data table, the fact that algorithms are able to detect and identify meaningful patterns suggests that these data are, in fact, structured in some sense of the word. Of course, the impact that cultural stereotypes and biases have on the structuring of the data can only be analysed through the data itself and a critical inspection of the data generation mechanisms (O'Neil, 2016; Buolamwini & Gebru, 2018; Kearns & Roth, 2020). When an algorithm learns that 'white' and 'wedding dress' are associated concepts, the algorithm is really learning is a social construction, not an ontological property of the world. And while this may be an innocuous association, many others can be more harmful and generate downstream consequences if not properly interrogated prior to the deployment of AI tools. This is an area of theoretical development that will only become more relevant as AI technologies expand their reach and their societal impact becomes more salient.

To sum up, the process of analysing semantic and cultural networks requires answering four interrelated questions: What is the process to be studied? What is the simplest way of modelling this process? What can be observed and what must be inferred? And what is the theoretical motivation driving the work?

7. CONCLUSION

The analysis of semantic and cultural networks adds an important layer to the analysis of interpersonal communication by capturing cognitive and symbolic interdependencies that shape meaning – and therefore behaviour. Beyond advancing fundamental research, uncovering the information contained in these structures also facilitates the development of machine learning and AI tools deployed in a range of social settings (from search engines to targeted recommendations). The theoretical value of research in this area is, consequently, extending to all the domains in which these technologies are being applied. An already burgeoning area of research, we anticipate the analysis of symbolic and conceptual networks will become even more popular in the next few years as it absorbs a wider range of cultural artefacts created and stored in digital form.

REFERENCES

Atteveldt, W. van (2008). *Semantic network analysis: techniques for extracting, representing, and querying media content*. BookSurge

Axelrod, R. (1976). *Structure of decision: the cognitive maps of political elites*. Princeton University Press.

Bail, C.A. (2016). Combining natural language processing and network analysis to examine how advocacy organizations stimulate conversation on social media. *Proceedings of the National Academy of Sciences, 113*(42), 11823–11828. doi.org/10.1073/pnas.1607151113

Baldassarri, D., & Goldberg, A. (2014). Neither ideologues nor agnostics: alternative voters' belief system in an age of partisan politics. *American Journal of Sociology, 120*(1), 45–95. doi.org/10.1086/676042

Bavelas, A. (1950). Communication patterns in task-oriented groups. *Journal of the Acoustical Society of America*, 22, 725.

Bearman, P., Faris, R., & Moody, J. (1999). Blocking the future: new solutions for old problems in historical social science. *Social Science History*, 23(4), 501–533.

Bearman, P.S., & Stovel, K. (2000). Becoming a Nazi: a model for narrative networks. *Poetics*, 27(2), 69–90. doi.org/10.1016/S0304-422X(99)00022-4

Bolukbasi, T., Chang, K.-W., Zou, J.Y., Saligrama, V., & Kalai, A.T. (2016). Man is to computer programmer as woman is to homemaker? Debiasing word embeddings. *Advances in Neural Information Processing Systems*, 29. proceedings.neurips.cc/paper/2016/hash/a486cd07e4ac3d270571622f-4f316ec5-Abstract.html

Boutyline, A., & Vaisey, S. (2017). Belief network analysis: a relational approach to understanding the structure of attitudes. *American Journal of Sociology*, 122(5), 1371–1447. www.journals.uchicago.edu/doi/abs/10.1086/691274

Buolamwini, J., & Gebru, T. (2018). Gender shades: intersectional accuracy disparities in commercial gender classification. Paper presented at the Conference on Fairness, Accountability and Transparency.

Burt, R.S. (2004). Structural holes and good ideas. *American Journal of Sociology*, 110(2), 349–399.

Carley, K. (1994). Extracting culture through textual analysis. *Poetics*, 22(4), 291–312. doi.org/10.1016/0304-422X(94)90011-6

Carley, K.M., & Kaufer, D.S. (1993). Semantic connectivity: an approach for analyzing symbols in semantic networks. *Communication Theory*, 3(3), 183–213. doi.org/10.1111/j.1468-2885.1993.tb00070.x

Carley, K., & Palmquist, M. (1992). Extracting, representing, and analyzing mental models. *Social Forces*, 70(3), 601–636. doi.org/10.2307/2579746

Chen, Y., Sherren, K., Smit, M., & Lee, K.Y. (2021) Using social media images as data in social science research. *New Media and Society*, 14614448211038761. doi.org/10.1177/14614448211038761

Cohen, R. (1987). Analyzing the structure of argumentative discourse. *Computational Linguistics*, 13(1–2), 11–24.

Collins, A.M., & Loftus, E.F. (1975). A spreading-activation theory of semantic processing. *Psychological Review*, 82(6), 407.

Collins, A.M., & Quillian, M.R. (1969). Retrieval time from semantic memory. *Journal of Verbal Learning and Verbal Behavior*, 8(2), 240–247. doi.org/10.1016/S0022-5371(69)80069-1

DellaPosta, D. (2020). Pluralistic collapse: the 'oil spill' model of mass opinion polarization. *American Sociological Review*, 85(3), 507–536. journals.sagepub.com/doi/abs/10.1177/0003122420922989

DellaPosta, D., Shi, Y., & Macy, M. (2015). Why do liberals drink lattes? *American Journal of Sociology*, 120(5), 1473–1511. www.journals.uchicago.edu/doi/abs/10.1086/681254

Devlin, J., Chang, M.-W., Lee, K., & Toutanova, K. (2019). BERT: pre-training of deep bidirectional transformers for language understanding. *ArXiv:1810.04805 [Cs]*. arxiv.org/abs/1810.04805

Doerfel, M.L., & Moore, P.J. (2016). Digitizing strength of weak ties: understanding social network relationships through online discourse analysis. *Annals of the International Communication Association*, 40(1), 127–148. doi.org/10.1080/23808985.2015.11735258

Dorsey, D.W., Campbell, G.E., Foster, L.L., & Miles, D.E. (1999). Assessing knowledge structures: relations with experience and posttraining performance. *Human Performance*, 12(1), 31–57.

Feng, V.W., & Hirst, G. (2011). Classifying arguments by scheme. *Proceedings of the 49th Annual Meeting of the Association for Computational Linguistics: Human Language Technologies*, 987–996. www.aclweb.org/anthology/P11-1099

Firth, J.R. (1957). *Studies in linguistic analysis*. Wiley-Blackwell.

Fishman, N., & Davis, N.T. (2021). Change we can believe in: structural and content dynamics within belief networks. *American Journal of Political Science*. doi.org/10.1111/ajps.12626

Flyvbjerg, B. (2006). Five misunderstandings about case-study research. *Qualitative Inquiry*, 12(2), 219–245. doi.org/10.1177/1077800405284363

Franzosi, R. (1998). Narrative analysis-or why (and how) sociologists should be interested in narrative. *Annual Review of Sociology*, 24, 517–554.

Franzosi, R. (2004). *From words to numbers narrative, data, and social science*. Cambridge University Press. www.cambridge.org/us/academic/subjects/sociology/sociology-general-interest/words-numbers-narrative-data-and-social-science, www.cambridge.org/us/academic/subjects/sociology/sociology-general-interest

Freeman, L. (2004). *The development of social network analysis*. Empirical Press.

Guetzkow, H., & Simon, H.A. (1955). The impact of certain communication nets upon organization and performance in task-oriented groups. *Management Science*, 1(3–4), 233–250.

Habernal, I., & Gurevych, I. (2015). Exploiting debate portals for semi-supervised argumentation mining in user-generated web discourse. *Proceedings of the 2015 Conference on Empirical Methods in Natural Language Processing*, 2127–2137.

Kearns, M., & Roth, A. (2020). *The ethical algorithm*. Oxford University Press.

Lazer, D., & Friedman, A. (2007). The network structure of exploration and exploitation. *Administrative Science Quarterly*, 52(4), 667–694.

Levy, O., & Goldberg, Y. (2014). Dependency-based word embeddings. *Proceedings of the 52nd*

Annual Meeting of the Association for Computational Linguistics (Volume 2: Short Papers), 302–308. doi.org/10.3115/v1/P14-2050

Lynn, C.W., & Bassett, D.S. (2020). How humans learn and represent networks. *Proceedings of the National Academy of Sciences*, *117*(47), 29407–29415. doi.org/10.1073/pnas.1912328117

Mason, W., & Watts, D.J. (2012). Collaborative learning in networks. *Proceedings of the National Academy of Sciences*, *109*(3), 764–769. doi.org/10.1073/pnas.1110069108

Mehrabi, N., Morstatter, F., Saxena, N., Lerman, K., & Galstyan, A. (2021). A survey on bias and fairness in machine learning. *ACM Computing Surveys*, *54*(6), Article 1151, 1–35. doi.org/10.1145/3457607

Mikolov, T., Chen, K., Corrado, G., & Dean, J. (2013). Efficient estimation of word representations in vector space. *ArXiv Preprint ArXiv:1301.3781*.

Mill, J.S. (1882). *A system of logic, ratiocinative and inductive* (8th ed.). Harper & Brothers, Project Gutenberg. www.gutenberg.org/files/27942/27942-h/27942-h.htm

Mochales, R., & Moens, M.-F. (2011). Argumentation mining. *Artificial Intelligence and Law*, *19*(1), 1–22.

Navigli, R., & Ponzetto, S.P. (2012). BabelNet: the automatic construction, evaluation and application of a wide-coverage multilingual semantic network. *Artificial Intelligence*, *193*, 217–250.

O'Neil, C. (2016). Weapons of math destruction: how big data increases inequality and threatens democracy. Penguin/Random House. books.google.com/books?id=60n0DAAAQBAJ

Palau, R.M., & Moens, M.-F. (2009). Argumentation mining: the detection, classification and structure of arguments in text. *Proceedings of the 12th International Conference on Artificial Intelligence and Law*, 98–107.

Riedl, C., Kim, Y.J., Gupta, P., Malone, T.W., & Woolley, A.W. (2021). Quantifying collective intelligence in human groups. *Proceedings of the National Academy of Sciences*, *118*(21), e2005737118. doi.org/10.1073/pnas.2005737118

Rule, A., Cointet, J.-P., & Bearman, P.S. (2015). Lexical shifts, substantive changes, and continuity in State of the Union discourse, 1790–2014. *Proceedings of the National Academy of Sciences*, *112*(35), 10837–10844. doi.org/10.1073/pnas.1512221112

Saint-Charles, J., & Mongeau, P. (2017). Social influence and discourse similarity networks in workgroups. *Social Networks*. doi.org/10.1016/j.socnet.2017.09.001

Shaffer, D.W., Hatfield, D., Svarovsky, G.N., Nash, P., Nulty, A., Bagley, E., Frank, K., Rupp, A.A., & Mislevy, R. (2009). Epistemic network analysis: a prototype for 21st-century assessment of learning. *International Journal of Learning and Media*, *1*(2), 33–53.

Shannon, C.E. (1948). A mathematical theory of communication. *Bell System Technical Journal*, *27*(3), 379–423.

Shapiro, S.C., & Rapaport, W.J. (1987). SNePS considered as a fully intensional propositional semantic network. In N. Cercone & G. McCalla (Eds.), *The knowledge frontier* (pp. 262–315). Springer.

Shavelson, R.J. (1974). Methods for examining representations of a subject-matter structure in a student's memory. *Journal of Research in Science Teaching*, *11*(3), 231–249.

Shugars, S. (2020). Reasoning together: network methods for political talk and normative reasoning. PhD thesis. Northeastern University.

Shugars, S. (2021). *The structure of reasoning: inferring conceptual networks from short text*. doi.org/10.17605/OSF.IO/PNWD8

Speer, R., & Havasi, C. (2012). Representing general relational knowledge in ConceptNet 5. *LREC*, 3679–3686.

Stab, C., & Gurevych, I. (2014). Identifying argumentative discourse structures in persuasive essays. *Proceedings of the 2014 Conference on Empirical Methods in Natural Language Processing (EMNLP)*, 46–56. www.aclweb.org/anthology/D14-1006

Toulmin, S.E. (1958). *The uses of argument*. Cambridge University Press.

Walton, D.N., Reed, C., & Macagno, F. (2008). *Argumentation schemes*. Cambridge University Press.

Williams, N.W., Casas, A., & Wilkerson, J.D. (2020). Images as data for social science research: an introduction to convolutional neural nets for image classification. Cambridge University Press.

Yang, S., & González-Bailón, S. (2016). Semantic networks and applications in public opinion research. In M. Lubell, A.H. Montgomery & J.N. Victor (Eds.), *Handbook of political networks*. Oxford University Press.

Cognition and Social Networks

Matthew E. Brashears and Victoria Money

INTRODUCTION

In 1922 Georg Simmel published 'Die Kreuzung sozialer Kreise',[1] in which he explored how the intersection of memberships in groups, and involvements with others, could play a key role in defining the individual's sense of self and life opportunities. This essay is one of the foundational early works in what would eventually become the thriving field of social network analysis (SNA), and explains why Georg Simmel is viewed as one of the field's founding thinkers. But what is less often recognised is that Simmel began his essay by examining thought, asserting, 'The difference between thinking in its advanced and its primitive form is shown in the different motives which determine the association of ideas' (Simmel [1955]1964, p. 127). He continued to develop an argument that sophisticated thought about concepts only occurs when those concepts are seen as nexuses of ideas, rather than as entities whole and complete in themselves, essentially arguing that thought is a network process. It is only after developing this notion that he turns to the typical substance of SNA, arguing that, 'The development which takes place among ideas finds an analogue in the relationship of individuals to each other' (Simmel [1955]1964, p. 127). In essence, as goes the mind, so goes the network.

One should be reluctant to cite classic thinkers unironically, as it risks giving the impression that no progress has been made since their seminal contributions, but we raise Simmel's work for two reasons. First, to show that researchers have long perceived a close association between the cognitive process in human brains, on the one hand, and the structure of interpersonal bonds in human groups on the other. Since the very inception of the field, there has always lurked the notion that, in some way, mind and network are inextricably linked. This notion has only grown stronger over the decades as both the structure and operation of social networks and of the brain, have been illuminated by painstaking research. At heart, both mind and society are now seen as networks, of neurons/functional areas and persons/institutions respectively, vindicating Simmel's early insight.

But there is a second insight to be had here: whereas Simmel analogised his new ideas about social relationships to the operation of the mind, in effect making social interaction appear to be an outgrowth of cognition, there is growing evidence that the size and power of the human brain is an outgrowth of our social networks. Put differently, humans are not social because we are so smart, but are instead smart specifically because we are so social. It is then no coincidence that Simmel found the operation of our minds to be such a good model for the function of our social worlds, as our brains appear to have been shaped specifically to confront the demands of building, maintaining and exploiting social networks.

In this chapter, we will explore how research has uncovered, and continues to reveal, the deep connections between cognition and social networks. These connections do not run simplistically from our brains to our networks, as if humans were clockwork mechanisms made of meat, but comprise a complex, interdependent system. We begin by introducing the context that makes the rest comprehensible: the critical role of sociality in human evolution. We then review the progress that has been made in showing how mind and brain are linked in modern times. Finally, we will point to key new domains for future research that can help fill the substantial gaps remaining in our knowledge.

THE EVOLUTION OF MINDS

Humans have long viewed themselves as uniquely intelligent, going so far as to make this the defining trait of our scientific name, *Homo Sapiens* (i.e., 'the wise man'). Yet, this high intelligence also represents a problem. While the brain accounts for approximately 3 per cent of an adult human's body mass, it consumes 20–25 per cent of our metabolic resources (Dunbar, 1992). Put differently, a fifth to a quarter of all calories that we consume are devoted solely to maintaining our large and powerful brains. Moreover, these calorific demands are largely constant regardless of level of activity; whether awake or sleeping, working on a paper or watching reality television, our brains are always consuming 20–25 per cent of the calories that we consume. This raises an unavoidable question: if the brain is so expensive to develop and maintain, why was its evolution favoured?

A number of answers to this question have been proposed, each with their own drawbacks. An obvious initial answer might be that our powerful brains are adaptive because they have allowed us to fashion complex tools and exert control over the world around us. This argument is correct, insofar as we have developed high technology that provides us with advantage,[2] but the impact of this advantage has only really been felt since the rise of anatomically modern humans approximately 250,000 years ago. In order for a trait to be favoured it must be advantageous at the time of selection (i.e., evolution is not forward-looking), and therefore while our ability to create powerful tools is clear, this ability emerged from our high intelligence, rather than acted as a primary driver of it. A second argument is that greater, and more reliable, access to high-calorie foods (e.g., meat, nuts) provided the fuel for the growth of the brain (Clutton-Brock & Harvey, 1980). This ecological hypothesis focuses on the ability to locate and harvest high-calorific foods, given the necessity of their consumption for brain growth and functionality. Although this ability utilises innovation and intelligence, its relationship to brain size among primates is not universal or linear (Dunbar & Shultz, 2017), and thus its ability to explain human intelligence is unclear. Additionally, access to such resources represents a necessary, but not sufficient, condition for the growth of hominid brains. In other words, just because rich resources are accessible, it does not necessarily follow that a species will respond by increasing in intelligence, rather than by, for example, increasing in population size.

Other arguments present various physical challenges that high intelligence allows a species to overcome, such as identifying/predicting when time-limited resources (e.g., ripe fruit) will be available or engaging in extractive foraging (Clutton-Brock & Harvey, 1980; Melin et al., 2014; Parker, 2015). These arguments all have their advantages but suffer from a common issue: most of these problems do not require high levels of general intelligence. For example, extractive foraging is the process of removing a food item from an otherwise inedible matrix, such as chimpanzees (*Pan Troglodytes*) 'fishing' for termites, or humans preparing and consuming artichokes. The argument is thus that highly intelligent species are better able to engage in extractive foraging than are less intelligent species, and subsequently become dependent on the high calorific values these foods provide. The difficulty is that most of these tasks are relatively stable over time and therefore can be solved quite handily by either evolutionary adaptation (e.g., starfish are well-adapted to extract clams from their inedible shells), or by learning (e.g., it is unnecessary for me to figure out how to prepare artichokes if someone else can show me). Given that many species are capable of learning new behaviours without necessarily being highly intelligent (although mimicry is a cognitively complex task; see: Byrne, [1995]2006), it does not appear that these physical challenges are sufficient to explain the development of high general intelligence.[3]

The *social brain hypothesis* (Dunbar, 1998; Dunbar & Schultz, 2017; Humphrey, 1976) sidesteps the difficulties outlined above by arguing that our intelligence is essentially 'Machiavellian', providing advantages to individual humans who are able to socially outmanoeuvre members of their own group. Social life provides many advantages for a species, including shared defence, cooperative food gathering and shared child rearing. But at the same time social living creates challenges: individuals are constantly surrounded by others who prefer the same food, shelter and mating opportunities that they do themselves. As such, social living helps protect one from many external dangers but at the cost of increasing the intensity of competition with conspecifics. Successful social living demands the individual find a balance between group success, which is essential for survival, and individual success, allowing one to propogate one's own genes or the genes of one's kin. The social brain hypothesis asserts that the most intelligent individuals in a group will be most successful at balancing these demands and will leave the most offspring as a result. If intelligence is at least partly genetic, the next generation will be slightly more intelligent on average than the one that came before. But unlike physical challenges, the difficulty of the social challenge increases in proportion to mean intelligence (i.e., striking a successful balance always depends on the competition), and therefore no matter how intelligent a species becomes, there is always an adaptive benefit to being smarter than the rest of the group. In short, humans became so smart because we encountered a challenge that increased in proportion to the intelligence that we used to overcome it.

If the social brain hypothesis is correct, then we should expect to see a connection between some aspect of brain size and the size or structure of social networks. Robin Dunbar (1992) evaluated this proposition by examining the relationship between primary group size and the neocortical ratio (i.e., neocortex volume divided by the remaining volume of the brain) for 38 primate genuses, ranging from *Avahi* (i.e., certain lemurs) to *Pan* (i.e., chimpanzees and bonobos, our closest extant non-human relatives). He identified a positive correlation between neocortical ratio and primary group size and used it to predict that human primary groups should contain roughly 150 individuals. This estimate has come to be known as 'Dunbar's Number' and subsequent research has supported Dunbar's model and, by extension, the social brain hypothesis: there is a general relationship between neocortical ratio and network size in primates, as well as humans, even with the addition of numerous controls (e.g., Barton, 1996; Kudo & Dunbar, 2001; Dunbar, 1993, 1995, 2018; Gonçalves et al., 2011). Additional work supports a strong link between cognitive ability and network size (Stiller & Dunbar, 2007) as well as cognitive limits on sociability (Roberts et al., 2009).[4] Moreover, recent research indicates that network recall is robust even in the face of cognitive declines associated with Alzheimer's disease or dementia (Roth et al., 2021), suggestive of the deep connections between social networks, on the one hand, and memory and cognition, on the other. Additionally, the shift from solitary nocturnal living to social diurnal living increased social interaction frequency and complexity, with corresponding exponential brain growth in humans (Shultz et al., 2011). Ample evidence supports a link between the growth of our brains and the growth of our networks.

The social brain hypothesis is a compelling argument for the evolution of human intelligence, but in many ways it fails to make specific predictions about either brain or network structure. For example, larger brains are not invariably more powerful than smaller brains, and even quite simple neural networks can be capable of sophisticated processing in the right circumstances. For example, *Portia*, a genus of jumping spider that preys on other spiders, appear to be able to plan ahead, learn from trial-and-error experience and actively deceive prey items (Wilcox & Jackson, 1998), albeit while requiring longer processing times than humans. Likewise, not all networks are equivalent. Many birds, fish and ungulates live in sometimes enormous flocks, schools and herds without necessarily exhibiting particularly high levels of intelligence. The networks of these flocks, schools and herds may be large, but they are also structurally quite simple, and thus present a limited cognitive challenge. Modern research on networks and cognition thus fills a critical void by, among other things, casting light on the cognitive networks involved in processing social stimuli, as well as the network structures that pose the greatest challenge, and thus are most strongly connected to human intelligence.

NEURAL REPRESENTATIONS OF SOCIAL INFORMATION

In order for humans to act in relation to social information it is necessary that they encode this information (i.e., enter it into the brain), process it (i.e., perform computational operations on it) and then extract responses; the social must be imprinted into the neural. Part of what makes this process so interesting is its level of abstraction. Social cognition requires observing and tracking social interactions, making inferences about the intentions and behaviours of others, and deriving predictions about likely future actions in response to one's own actions. It is not enough to see two people together, or to directly interact with an associate; humans must also *imagine* what these interactions mean or what other people may believe. As a result, social problems are highly complex and solving them should require an ensemble of neural systems. These needs are served in part via exaptation, or the repurposing of the brain's circuitry to support multiple purposes.

Social neuroscience has identified brain regions that appear to involve 'co-opted' circuity that serves multiple purposes, frequently by handling both social and non-social information (Parkinson & Wheatley, 2013, 2015). A good example, identified via functional magnetic resonance imaging (fMRI), links linguistic representations of both spatial and social distance. Spatial distance – the simple Euclidean distance between points in physical space – is surely familiar to readers and requires no description. However, distance-based metaphors for social relations (e.g., 'close friends', 'distant family') are common both in colloquial speech as well as in the academic literature (e.g., Straits, 2000). Unsurprisingly, social distance as a theoretical construct has received substantial attention as it may help to both explain and predict cooperation or conflict between two individuals or two groups. While the metaphor of social distance enjoys wide acceptance, its definition and operationalisation appears to be highly variable in the social and behavioural sciences. Definitions presented in the literature range from a willingness to accept and interact with others to varying degrees (Smith et al., 2014), to perceived compatibility (Yamakawa et al., 2009), to the degree of perceived distinctiveness between the self and other (Bar-Anan et al., 2007) and to above or below baseline rates of association between groups (Brashears, 2008, 2015; Marsden, 1988). In addition to being highly variable, and somewhat nebulous, it is important to note that these definitions do not pertain to subjective emotional closeness. While the metaphor often treats social distance as analogous to the 'strength' of a tie between two persons (e.g., 'close' versus 'distant' friends), the measures have much more to do with the judgements of compatibility or similarity. Likewise, the work measuring social distance via realised patterns of interaction between groups is unavoidably mixing felt closeness with realised ties.[5] Within social neuroscience, social distance is most frequently interpreted as perceptions of compatibility rather than as emotional closeness. Nonetheless, there are exceptions, such as research showing that network proximity is highly correlated with neural similarity (Parkinson et al., 2018); individuals who are more closely positioned in a network exhibit more similar patterns of neural activation in response to identical stimuli. In this case, social distance is operationalised in terms of the geodesic between two nodes in a network, rather than the more common perceived similarity, which is more clearly linked to the likelihood of compatibility for cooperation or relationship formation.[6] Structural homophily, or the tendency for individuals with similar traits to associate with each other because wider forces sort them into the same contexts (McPherson et al., 2001), suggests that network proximity ought to be positively related to actual and perceived similarity, but it is nonetheless important to note that the term 'social distance' can be applied to widely varying operationalisations.

A variety of methods have been used for assessing the potential overlap of spatial and social cognitive processes such as between physical and social distance. Methods have included pictures of random individuals (Yamakawa et al., 2009) and terms used to represent distinct and similar others (Bar-Anan et al., 2007), which were then used alongside terms and images of physical objects. Social terms such as 'friend' and 'stranger' appear to be spatially represented (i.e., activate neural circuitry known to be involved in processing distance) when evaluating how distal the term is from the self; 'friend' was characterised as proximal whereas 'stranger' was described as distal based on visual representations (Bar-Anan et al., 2007). When evaluating social compatibility between random others and the self (social distance), the intraparietal regions of the brain, known to be associated with self-referential distance from an object, were found to be active (Yamakawa et al., 2009). This research demonstrates that neural systems used for processing physical space are also employed to represent social space; perceived similarity and compatibility is considered close just as proximal physical objects are regarded as close. Or, put another way, some relationships feel subjectively 'close' while others feel subjectively 'distant' because our brains exhibit parallel patterns of activation for close objects and close others. The ability to use networks in the brain for multiple purposes, such as processing both concrete and abstract information, may have facilitated the growth of complex social relations over time. In evolutionary terms, it was also adaptive as it avoided the need to develop entirely new brain regions with correspondingly larger metabolic demands.

Similar exaptation processes may be at work in the processing of aversive stimuli, including pain. For example, Eisenberger (2012) summarises a research programme demonstrating that social and physical pain are tightly coupled. To study this relation, Eisenberger et al. (2003) placed subjects in an fMRI machine and asked them to play a simple ball-passing game with two simulated individuals via a computer monitor. At a programmed moment, the interactants began to pass the ball between themselves, excluding the subject. Examination of the activation patterns resulting from this social exclusion reveals them to be quite similar to activation patterns experienced in response to painful stimuli. Moreover, the degree of activation of these systems was correlated with the strength of the self-reports of discomfort due to social exclusion. It appears that social exclusion can realistically be said to 'hurt' because both social and physical pain are processed by the same neural systems, and subjective awareness of social discomfort is associated with the level of neural activation.

Social pain also extends to an individual's ability to empathise with the pain of others, and how the perceived closeness to another modulates neural activity. Much like the similarity between spatial and social distance, the imagined pain of oneself and the imagined pain of a loved-one provokes more neural activity compared to when the brain processes the imagined pain of a stranger (Cheng et al., 2010). This is not, however, isolated to close associates such as loved-ones but is also seen when witnessing the imagined pain of racial in-group members (Xu et al., 2009) and phylogenetically similar non-human primates (Rae Westbury & Neumann, 2008). Increased perceived similarity appears to invoke heightened empathy; when processing pain, the more similar the other is to the self, the more likely the other's pain will produce a substantial neurological reaction. Thought to be an evolutionary byproduct of imitation, a form of social learning paramount to survival, empathy promotes other prosocial behaviours such as cooperation (Barclay & Van Vugt, 2014). It does so by allowing an individual to relate to and identify with another's emotions (de Waal, 2014). However, this research demonstrates that empathy is not automatic or universal, as the brain receives, encodes and recalls information differently based on similarity or relationship type. A great many social and political issues may be partly rooted in the fact that the brain makes the pain of similar others more intense, or real, than the pain of less similar others. Finally, recent research reveals that patterns of neural activation are similar between experiences of cognitively dissonant information and affectively imbalanced structures (Chiang et al., 2020). This indicates that the neural response to information that appears contradictory is similar to the response to social relations that are discordant (e.g., when the friend of a friend is an enemy). The neural fingerprints of something that 'doesn't make sense' applies whether the something is pieces of information or patterns of imbalanced social relations.

Beyond revealing important clues about our evolutionary history, exaptation is important because it can exert a durable influence on how humans come to grips with their world. The feeling that some individuals are 'closer' than others, and our ability to empathise closely with them, is easy to understand when one realises that the same neural structures are responsible for processing both physical and social distance. This in turn influences and facilitates relationship and group formation necessary for survival. Likewise, our sense that some interactions are painful makes sense in light of the knowledge that the same neural structures are used to process both physical and social discomfort. This repurposing of the same brain region for multiple purposes likely has subtle downstream effects; for example, the language that feels natural for describing relations, and the way in which we understand their similarities and differences, may well be rooted in their common locus of processing in the brain. These effects can be quite meaningful for even scientific understanding of network processes. For example, both classic (e.g., Granovetter, 1973) and more modern (Aral & Van Alstyne, 2011) models of network ties implicitly treat relationships as if they vary on a single strength-like dimension that is analogous to distance, even though there is good reason to think that network relations differ along at least three separate dimensions (Brashears & Quintane, 2018). While human social behaviour is complex and not entirely a direct result of evolved mechanisms, the underlying neural structures we use to process social problems are the basic tools of social existence, and their operation colours every other perception we make, inference we derive and action we execute.

A great deal can be learned about social cognition by studying neural activation, but this is not the only approach. An alternative method is to study the behaviour of the brain in order to understand the heuristics it employs to process and respond to information, much as we can study the algorithms used by computers without having to focus directly on the hardware. Below we present a framework for integrating a variety of studies on cognition and networks before reviewing literature relevant to various states in this framework.

COGNITION IN SOCIAL NETWORKS

The brain is obviously relevant to social networks, but it is equally obvious that no individual's cognitions are solely responsible for even a single dyad, much less higher order structures. So how do we bridge the gap between the brain (micro) and the social world (macro)? A strong framework for translating cognitive activity into concrete behaviours and, by extension, realised networks can be found in Smith et al. (2012). They conceptualise a series of stages through which individuals move, first populating the mental representation of a social space, and then winnowing it as thought translates to action. First, there is the *potential network*, consisting of all of the individuals that a person knows. This type of person information is retained in long-term memory, but the capacity of long-term memory greatly exceeds the capacity of working memory (i.e., we have more information stored in our brains than we can actively think about at any one time). As such, when reasoning about a particular situation, humans will draw from the potential network to populate the *cognitively activated network*, or the specific known others who are brought to mind for a given situation. This activation can be either deliberate, such as when we try to imagine all of the guests someone might want for their surprise party, or can be highly automatic, such as when all household members become available in the mind when thinking about a problem at home. Having activated a network in the mind, individuals will then select which associates they wish to contact or involve in a given situation, producing the *mobilised network*. This stage thus comprises decision-making about who to interact with as well as action execution. And finally, individuals who allow themselves to be activated by the individual (i.e., respond favourably to being contacted) constitute the *realised network*.[7] While these four stages are important, the analytically meaningful element for our purposes are the transitions: the process of extracting the cognitively activated network from the potential network, the process of choosing the mobilised network from the activated network, and finally the reactions of others to mobilisation attempts that translate the mobilised network into the realised network.

In order for a human to think about networks it is necessary for networks to enter the brain and the mind. The social brain hypothesis argues that this is a critically important process; it is by learning to think about social networks that humans in effect learned to think at all. By extension, the more social information one can hold in working memory, shifting it from the potential network to the cognitively activated network, the more sophisticated one's social reasoning may become. Yet, this task is far more onerous than one might guess.

At a bare minimum, group living requires that the individual manage his or her own relations with other group members. This is effectively the level achieved by organisms living in herds or flocks, who shape their behaviour based on the actions of their neighbours only. But in order for humans to be truly successful, we must track the relations between our associates. Yet, tracking this information can be highly expensive given that the number of such relationships grows rapidly as group size increases. A group of size n includes $n(n-1)$ possible relations among all members.[8] As a result, in a group of ten one would need to track as many as 90 different relationships, only nine of which include oneself (i.e., are direct). An increase in group size from ten to fifteen would produce a linear change in the number of direct relations from nine to fourteen, as well as a super-linear increase in the number of indirect relations from 81 to 196. In short, even relatively small groups (in human terms) contain potentially very large amounts of social information to be absorbed, tracked and exploited. And, critically, even small increases in group size result in unavoidable and dramatic increases in the cognitive demands on the organism. Moreover, it is not enough to simply track the existence of relationships between others, but we must also model the thoughts, knowledge and intentions of those others. The ability to do so is known as possessing a 'theory of mind', and nested levels of this ability (e.g., What I think you believe about another person's knowledge and beliefs) is known as 'intentionality' (Stiller & Dunbar, 2007). While the existence of sophisticated theory of mind in our extant primate relatives is often questionable (e.g., Cheney & Seyfarth, 2008), we know humans can and do perform this trick: simply understanding the behaviours and actions of characters in a TV drama requires that viewers track the relations between, and knowledge and intentions of, other individuals. Indeed, whereas non-humans often appear to struggle to mentally represent the thoughts and intentions of a single other, humans engage in multiple levels of this process essentially for entertainment. While useful, this capability nonetheless requires that the brain be capable of encoding, storing and recalling even more information.

The dramatic increase in information processing as networks grow points to a potential drawback in Dunbar's Number. If a fixed amount of neocortical volume[9] is needed to store each new relationship, increases in group size should quickly add up to unsupportably large increases in required brain mass and calorific intake. Dunbar's model (Dunbar, 1992, eq. 1) avoids this challenge by assuming that as the neocortex grows it also becomes more efficient,[10] but no explanation is provided for how this is achieved. Moreover, research (e.g., Bernard et al., 1987; McCarty et al.,

2001; DiPrete et al., 2011; Killworth et al., 1990) suggests that humans likely maintain more core ties than predicted by Dunbar's Number, requiring an even greater increase in neocortical efficiency. How are humans able to achieve the necessary increases in neocortical efficiency without exceeding their physical limitations?

Prior research has demonstrated that human social recall is often superior to recall of other types of information. Network structures containing social information (e.g., people connected through friendship ties) are recalled more accurately than identical non-social networks (e.g., locations linked by roads) (e.g., Janicik & Larrick, 2005; Simpson et al., 2011; Van Kreveld & Zajonc 1966). However, it does not appear that the networks recalled by humans necessarily match observable interactions. Comparisons of observed interaction to recalled interaction (e.g., Bernard & Killworth, 1977) show mismatches at the dyadic (i.e., person-to-person; Bernard and Killworth, 1977), triadic (i.e., three-person group; Killworth et al., 1979, 1980) and clique (i.e., larger saturated group; Bernard et al. 1979, 1980) levels. Yet humans are quite good at remembering typical patterns of interaction and overall group structure (Freeman et al., 1988, 1989; Freeman & Romney, 1987; Freeman et al., 1987). In other words, it appears that humans are not remembering the interactions but are remembering a larger pattern of information into which those interactions can be fit.

Patterns of information into which specific facts can be inserted, or schemas, are well established aspects of human cognition useful for accelerating the learning process (e.g., Bartlett, 1932; Brewer & Treyens, 1981; Martin, 1993; Neisser, 1967). The earliest work showing its relevance to social networks (De Soto, 1960) found that subjects recalled hierarchical relations more quickly when the relations matched the implicit schema (e.g., when nodes linked by asymmetric directed edges were 'influenced by' rather than 'friends with' other nodes). Subsequent research has reinforced this early finding (Fischer, 1968; Picek et al., 1975; Sentis & Burnstein, 1979; Walker, 1976; see also Welch-Ross & Schmidt, 1996). Individuals recall networks composed of kinship (Brewer & Yang, 1994), context (Brewer & Garrett, 2001) and geographic location (Brewer & Garett, 2001; Killworth & Bernard, 1982) schemas more quickly and more accurately. However, schemas also function as 'compression heuristics' (Brashears, 2013), permitting humans to store network information in simpler, easier to recall structures.

Compression heuristics are rules that allow social networks to be reconstructed from partial information, permitting us to discard recall of specific connections in favour of particular rules. For example, if triadic closure is common in networks, then successfully recalling that two edges in a triad are present allows one to infer that the third should also be present. And given that the same edge may be involved in multiple triads, a relatively small number of edges can be reconstructed into a fairly substantial network. Research shows that triads and kin relations function as compression heuristics (Brashears, 2013; Brashears et al., 2016), that while network recall is flexible, the default unit of relationship encoding appears to be the triad (Brashears & Quintane, 2015), that females exhibit a significant advantage in network recall relative to males (Brashears et al., 2016) and that affective balance operates as a compression heuristic (Brashears & Brashears 2016). Moreover, a simple mechanistic model shows that human network recall behaviour is highly consistent with this compression logic (Omodei et al., 2017). It therefore appears that humans achieve high levels of recall efficiency not by increasing the capability of our neocortex, but by using tricks to rebuild full networks from partial information when needed. By extension, this suggests that humans are able to manage larger amounts of information when transitioning from the potential network to the cognitively activated network by, in part, relying on compression heuristics to simplify the recall task.

The finding that humans use compression heuristics helps to account for the earlier mismatch between observed interactions and reported interactions. Individuals use interactions that they observe, or participate in, to shape the particular compression heuristic that they will apply to that group. Having done so, the details of the interaction and, by extension, the network are discarded. When subsequently asked to report about the network, individuals use the encoded heuristic to reconstruct the network and then make their reports from the reconstruction. Mismatches between observed and reported interactions therefore are partly attributable to portions of the reconstructed network that are heuristic consistent as recalled, but are heuristic inconsistent as experienced. Additionally, because many compression heuristics are widely applicable across many different networks (e.g., affective balance), individuals will exhibit similar tendencies to commit specific types of recall errors (e.g., recalling kin networks as less affectively balanced than non-kin networks; see Brashears & Brashears, 2016). If social networks are the result of social actions, and action is shaped by the sometimes inaccurate recall provided by the use of compression heuristics, then we can and should expect that the heuristics used by individuals will, over time, help to shape the structure of the network.

Selection of potential network members for cognitive activation can be deliberate (i.e., the result of effortful processing) or automatic (i.e., the result of subconscious processes in the brain), and both are vulnerable to influence by priming. Priming occurs when the presentation of certain stimuli makes subsequent memory recall or processing more likely; for example, wearing a swimsuit as opposed to a sweater has been shown to activate gendered stereotypes and diminish math test performance among females but not males (Fredrickson et al., 1998). Priming can exert an influence over who is thought of and, by extension, what actions are taken and support realised. Moreover, priming effects are both subtle, in that even limited prior stimuli may be sufficient to shape cognitive reactions (see Brashears et al., 2016) and ubiquitous (e.g., sex and gender are one of the most immediately noticed, and activated, social features; Ridgeway & Correll, 2004; Ridgeway & Smith-Lovin, 1999). Prior research has found that when exposed to social exclusion, individuals tend to activate denser social networks (O'Connor & Gladstone, 2018), seemingly withdrawing into a safer space relative to when they have not experienced exclusion and show more willingness to be adventurous. Unsurprisingly, the same effect is observed when individuals experience positive versus negative emotion generally (Shea et al., 2015). We also see this pattern with interpersonal power, which has been found to influence the accuracy of network recall, though the literature is unclear on precisely how. Prior research has found that formal power has no impact on recall accuracy (Krackhardt, 1990), that power leads to decreased recall accuracy (Casciaro, 1998) and that high power leads to decreased awareness of absent relations relative to those that are present (Simpson et al., 2011). More recent research has found that power enhanced network recall accuracy, albeit primarily for the most task-relevant interactions, and generated positive workplace outcomes (Marineau et al., 2018). Regardless of the ultimate resolution of this empirical debate, the key insight is that temporary and durable primes can influence the social information that is transferred from the potential network into the cognitively activated network. There are a variety of ways this can be measured, such as the 'jump ratio' (Sun & Smith, 2018; Sun et al., 2021), which quantifies the difference between the order in which individuals are recalled and their proximity to each other in the network. Priming respondents to use an ineffective schema should produce increases in the jump ratio.

While cognition is of central importance, mobilisation relies on actions and realisation relies upon the decisions and actions of others. Much as no man is an island, no social cognitive process is complete without the responses of others. Work on the connection between cognitive processes and the responses of others to contact attempts is still in its infancy, but nonetheless there are some studies that cast light on this process. For example, Brashears et al. (2020) combined multiple experiments into a synthetic sample to examine the impact of master statuses (e.g., race, sex, age), personality traits (i.e., the Big Five personality traits), network recall accuracy and working memory capacity on ego-network size and structure. This effort thus attempted to examine the role of cognitive features, emotional/motivational features and concrete socially relevant characteristics in generating realised social networks. Perhaps the most salient result was that, overall, any one feature (e.g., recall accuracy) was rarely associated with more than one, or a few, outcomes (e.g., racial diversity or network density). Possibly the most consistent predictor was extraversion, which reliably predicted larger networks with higher reported density. However, prior research has found that higher levels of extraversion are associated with decreased levels of network recall accuracy (Brashears et al., 2016), suggesting that the denser networks reported by extraverts may not be as dense as they claim. Additionally, it is interesting to note that a motivational characteristic we might expect to produce increased network size (i.e., extraversion) is associated with decreased success in mentally tracking the structure of a network. This implies that extraverts may experience higher levels of network turnover, as they rapidly add associates but prove insufficient to the task of managing the resulting social complexity.

Other research points more directly to features that impact the transition from mobilised to realised networks. For example, O'Connor and Gladstone (2018) show that more physically attractive individuals both exhibit a greater preference for advantageous brokerage positions in networks, and report possessing networks that are sparser than do less attractive individuals. Greater levels of attractiveness by definition makes one more desirable as an associate across many types of interaction. Therefore, these preferences and outcomes suggest that more attractive persons are more accustomed to being able to translate their mobilised networks into realised networks, and adopt networking behaviour to match. In a second paper (Gladstone & O'Connor, 2018) the same authors found that individuals exhibiting brokerage behaviour expected of persons who bridge over structural holes are viewed as less trustworthy than non-brokers. This suggests that individuals who have the cognitive ability to act as network bridges, and who further take action to fill this role, may in many cases experience greater difficulty in transforming their mobilised networks into realised networks. Finally, research on trait neuroticism shows that individuals high in neuroticism exhibit reluctance to occupy better-connected network positions, as well as inspire aversion in others (Gladstone et al., 2019). Thus, neuroticism, an emotional/motivational characteristic, influences both the transition from cognitively activated network to mobilised network (i.e., the decision about whether to attempt to occupy a position) as well as the transition from mobilised to realised network (i.e., whether others respond favourably to the contact attempt). In short, while the transition from mobilised to realised network is outside of the full control of a single individual, it nevertheless appears that a number of individual traits may be meaningful in predicting the success, or failure, of mobilisation attempts.

CONCLUSION

At the start of this chapter, we pointed out how cognition and social networks have been intertwined since the beginning of the field. Far more than a simple metaphor, research has shown that cognitive processes are deeply relevant to developing and maintaining social networks. Our cognitive and motivational features impact every phase of network activity, from imagining a network, to choosing how a network should be used, to succeeding (or not) in making those choices manifest as reality. Additionally, we have examined a rich body of research suggesting that high intelligence, perhaps the single most defining characteristic of *homo sapiens*, evolved specifically to help us manoeuvre in the face of social, rather than physical, challenges. In a very real sense, we are smart because we are social. In studying the social networking strategies of modern humans, we cast light upon the history of our neurological evolution. The mental capacities and strategies that enable success in formal organisations (e.g., corporations) are likely the same tools that supported success in hunter-gatherer bands, and by understanding one, we understand the other.

As we close this chapter we make a plea, not simply for more research into the connections between networks and cognition, but for research into the role of networks in supporting a higher, more abstract kind of cognition. Joel Podolny (2001) has famously noted that social networks serve as pipes, supporting the movement of information, and as prisms, shaping the impressions and judgements of others. But we want to amplify earlier work (Brashears & Gladstone, 2016) in asserting that we should add a third P to Podolny's scheme: that social networks can function as processors. Dense, redundant sections of a network function to retransmit the same information between nodes, aiding individual recall via repetition while converting the entire structure into a sort of memory storage device. Structurally non-redundant, high-capacity ties operate like a long-distance data bus, shunting information between different portions of the network. Errors, and efforts to correct errors, in information passing over network ties will systematically transform the contents of networks (Brashears & Gladstone, 2016). When what enters one side of a network is different from what emerges from the other side, and the changes in between are systematic rather than random, we are forced to conclude that we are not only dealing with a social network, but with an information-processing structure composed of human beings and the links between them. Does this mean that social networks 'think'? Can they be 'aware' in some fundamental sense? Are the moods of crowds, the morale of military units, or the attitudes of nations partly a result of distributed cognition occurring at the level of the network? The idea is, at present, a mélange of speculation and science fiction. Yet, the more we learn about the connection between networks and cognition, the closer together we find them to be bound. And if networks and thought are inextricably bound together as we delve towards the micro, into the brain itself, then perhaps so too they are bound together as we rise towards the macro. In the future, we hope that researchers will unravel not simply how networks influence thought, and how thoughts influence networks, but how networks themselves are thinking.

Notes

1 Literally, 'The intersection of social circles', but many readers will be more familiar with Reinhard Bendix's translation, 'The web of group-affiliations'. Henceforth, all quotations from Simmel rely on Bendix's translation.
2 In a time of anthropogenic climate change, it has become obvious that it may also prove to be a disadvantage.
3 Though it may be critical to the development of high sensory motor intelligence (e.g., Melin et al. 2014).

4   This finding may have more to do with how humans recall alters in network surveys than with factors that determine the size or structure of actual networks (see Bell et al., 2007; Marin 2004).
5   This is a particular issue in that much of this stream of research is based on the 'important matters' name generator, which identifies alters based both on their importance as well as their expertise (Perry & Pescosolido, 2010; Small, 2013; but see also Brashears, 2014).
6   This may be in the form of maintained frequency of interaction for previously established relationships.
7   By implication, an individual who is contacted by another begins this process in the second stage as the contact will cause a cognitively activated network to manifest in the mind. The decision about whether, and how, to respond corresponds to the mobilised network stage. However, the realised network stage is overlapping with the prior stage; given that they are responding to a contact initiated by another, we may assume that a decision to accept the contact will cause a realised tie to come into being (i.e., a potential tie will be activated).
8   This assumes that relations can be asymmetric (e.g., person A considers person B to be a friend while person B does not view person A the same way). We make such an assumption both because asymmetry is observed in real social networks and because symmetry would not substantially alter the conclusions.
9   We focus on the neocortex in this discussion because it is the key variable in Dunbar's Number, but the argument generalises to any explanation that links the size of the brain to social network size.
10 According to the model, if the neocortical ratio of an organism increases from 0.96 to 3.22 (i.e., across the range of extant non-human primates from *Avahi* to *Pan*) the estimated number of direct ties that organism could maintain would increase by roughly 64 while the number of indirect ties it could track would increase by approximately 4,250. A further rise in its neocortical ratio to 4.1 (i.e., equivalent to *homo sapiens*) would increase the estimated number of direct ties the organism could manage by approximately 83 and the number of indirect ties it could track by roughly 17,600. Put differently, the model indicates that the smaller increase in neocortical ratio from *Pan* to *Homo* (i.e., +0.88) would produce a more substantial gain in the ability to track and manage social relations than would the larger increase in neocortical ratio from *Avahi* to *Pan* (i.e., +2.26). Dunbar's model requires that as the neocortex gets *bigger* every cubic centimetre of it must also get *better* at processing social information.

REFERENCES

Aral, S., & Van Alstyne, M. (2011). The diversity-bandwidth trade-off. *American Journal of Sociology, 117*, 90–171.

Bar-Anan, Y., Liberman, N., Trope, Y., & Algom, D. (2007). Automatic processing of psychological distance: evidence from a stroop task. *Journal of Experimental Psychology: General, 136*(4), 610–22. doi: 10.1037/0096-3445.136.4.610

Barclay, P., & van Vugt, M. (2014). The evolutionary psychology of human prosociality. In D.A. Schroeder & W.G. Graziano (Eds.), *The Oxford handbook of prosocial behavior* (pp. 37–60). Oxford University Press.

Bartlett, F.C. (1932). *Remembering: a study in experimental and social psychology.* Cambridge University Press.

Barton, R.A. (1996). Neocortex size and behavioural ecology in primates. *Proceedings of the Royal Society of London. Series B: Biological Sciences, 263*, 173–177.

Bell, D.C., Belli-McQueen, B., & Haider, A. (2007). Partner naming and forgetting: recall of network members. *Social Networks, 29*, 279–299.

Bernard, H.R., & Killworth, P.D. (1977). Informant accuracy in social network data II. *Human Communication Research, 4*, 3–18.

Bernard, H.R., Killworth, P.D., & Sailer, L. (1979). Informant accuracy in social network data IV: a comparison of clique-level structure in behavioral and cognitive network data. *Social Networks, 2*, 191–218.

Bernard, H.R., Killworth, P.D., & Sailer, L. (1980). Informant accuracy in social network data IV: a comparison of clique-level in behavioral and cognitive network data. *Social Science Research, 11*, 30–66.

Bernard, H.R., Shelley, G.A., & Killworth, P. (1987). How much of a network does the GSS and RSW dredge up?' *Social Networks, 9*, 49–61.

Brashears, M.E. (2008). Gender and homophily: differences in male and female association in Blau space. *Social Science Research, 37*, 400–415.

Brashears, M.E. (2013). Humans use compression heuristics to improve the recall of social networks. *Nature Scientific Reports, 3*, 1513.

Brashears, M.E. (2014). 'Trivial' topics and rich ties: the relationship between discussion topic, alter role, and resource availability using the 'important matters' name generator. *Sociological Science, 1*, 493–511.

Brashears, M.E. (2015). A longitudinal analysis of gendered association patterns: homophily and social distance in the general social survey. *Journal of Social Structure, 16*, 3. www.cmu.edu/joss/content/abstracts.html#1603

Brashears, M.E., & Brashears, L.A. (2016). The enemy of my friend is easy to remember: balance as a compression heuristic. In S.R. Thye & E.J. Lawler (Eds.), *Advances in Group Processes* (pp. 1–31). Emerald.

Brashears, M.E., Brashears, L.A., & Harder, N.L. (2020). Where you are, what you want, and what you can do: the role of master statuses, personality traits, and social cognition in shaping ego network size, structure, and composition. *Network Science*, 8, 356–380.

Brashears, M.E., & Gladstone, E. (2016). Error correction mechanisms in social networks can reduce accuracy and encourage innovation. *Social Networks*, 44, 22–35.

Brashears, M.E., Hoagland, E., & Quintane, E. (2016). Sex and network recall accuracy. *Social Networks*, 44, 74–84.

Brashears, M.E., & Quintane, E. (2015). The microstructures of network recall: how social networks are encoded and represented in human memory. *Social Networks*, 41, 113–26

Brashears, M.E., & Quintane, E. (2018). The weakness of tie strength. *Social Networks*, 55, 104–115.

Brewer, D.D., & Garrett, S.B. (2001). Evaluation of interviewing techniques to enhance recall of sexual and drug injection partners. *Sexually Transmitted Diseases*, 28, 666–77

Brewer, D.D., & Yang, B.L. (1994). Patterns in the recall of persons in a religious community.' *Social Networks*, 16, 347–379.

Brewer, W.F., & Treyens, J.C. (1981). Role of schemata in memory for places. *Cognitive Psychology*, 13, 207–30.

Byrne, R. ([1995]2006). *The thinking ape: evolutionary origins of intelligence*. Oxford University Press.

Casciaro, T. (1998). Seeing things clearly: social structure, personality, and accuracy in social network perception. *Social Networks*, 20, 331–351.

Cheney, D.L., & Seyfarth, R.M. (2008). *Baboon metaphysics: the evolution of a social mind*. University of Chicago Press.

Cheng, Y., Chen, C., Lin, C.P., Chou, K.H., & Decety, J. (2010). Love hurts: an FMRI study. *NeuroImage*, 51(2), 923–929. doi: 10.1016/j.neuroimage.2010.02.047

Chiang, Y.-S., Chen, Y.-W., Chuang, W.-C., Wu, C.-I., & Wu, C.-T. (2020). Triadic balance in the brain: seeking brain evidence for Heider's structural balance theory. *Social Networks*, 63, 80–90.

Clutton-Brock, T.H., & Harvey, P.H. (1980). Primates, brains and ecology. *Journal of Zoology*, 190, 309–323.

De Soto, C.B. (1960). Learning a social structure. *Journal of Abnormal and Social Psychology*, 60, 417–421.

de Waal, F.B.M. (2014). Prosocial Primates. In D.A. Schroeder & W.G. Graziano (Eds.), *The Oxford handbook of prosocial behavior* (pp. 61–85). Oxford University Press.

DiPrete, T.A., Gelman, A., McCormick, T., Teitler, J., & Zheng, T. (2011). Segregation in social networks based on acquaintanceship and trust. *American Journal of Sociology*, 116, 1234–1283.

Dunbar, R.I. (1992). Neocortex size as a constraint on group size in primates. *Journal of Human Evolution*, 22, 469–493.

Dunbar, R.I. (1993). Coevolution of neocortical size, group size and language in humans. *Behavioral and Brain Sciences*, 16, 681–694.

Dunbar, R.I. (1995). Neocortex size and group size in primates: a test of the hypothesis. *Journal of Human Evolution*, 28, 287–296.

Dunbar, R.I.M. (1998). The social brain hypothesis. *Evolutionary Anthropology*, 6(5), 178–190. doi: 10.1002/(SICI)1520-6505(1998)6:5<178::AID-EVAN5>3.0.CO;2-8

Dunbar, R.I.M. (2018). The anatomy of friendship. *Trends in Cognitive Sciences*, 22, 32–51.

Dunbar, R.I.M., & Shultz, S. (2017). Why are there so many explanations for primate brain evolution? *Philosophical Transactions of the Royal Society of London. Series B, Biological Sciences*, 372, 20160244.

Eisenberger, N.I. (2012). The neural bases of social pain: evidence for shared representations with physical pain. *Psychosomatic Medicine*, 74, 126–135.

Eisenberger, N.I., Lieberman, M.D., & Williams, K.D. (2003). Does rejection hurt: an fMRI study of social exclusion. *Science*, 302, 290–292.

Fischer, C.T. (1968). Social schemas: response sets or perceptual meanings? *Journal of Personality and Social Psychology*, 10(1), 8–14.

Fredrickson, B.L., Noll, S.M., Roberts, T.-A., Quinn, D.M. & Twenge, J.M. (1998). That swimsuit becomes you: sex differences in self-objectification, restrained eating, and math performance. *Journal of Personality and Social Psychology*, 75(1), 269–284.

Freeman, L.C., Freeman, S.C., & Michaelson, A.G. (1988). On human social intelligence. *Journal of Social and Biological Structures*, 11, 415–425.

Freeman, L.C., Freeman, S.C., & Michaelson, A.G. (1989). How humans see social groups: a test of the Sailer–Gaulin models. *Journal of Quantitative Anthropology*, 1, 229–238.

Freeman, L.C., & Romney, A.K. (1987). Words, deeds and social structure: a preliminary study of the reliability of informants. *Human Organization*, 46, 330–334.

Freeman, L.C., Romney, A.K., & Freeman, S.C. (1987). Cognitive structure and informant accuracy. *American Anthropologist*, 89: 310–25.

Gladstone, E.C., & O'Connor, K. (2018). Smart but shifty: trust and the contingent appeal of brokers.

Academy of Management Proceedings, 2013. doi.org/10.5465/ambpp.2013.17438abstract

Gladstone, E., O'Connor, K.M., & Taylor, W. (2019). The push and pull of network mobility: how those high in trait-level neuroticism can come to occupy peripheral network positions. Behavioral Sciences, 9, 69. doi.org/10.3390/bs9070069

Gonçalves, B., Perra, N., & Vespignani, A. (2011). Modeling users' activity on twitter networks: validation of Dunbar's number. PLOS One, 6, e22656.

Granovetter, M.S. (1973). The strength of weak ties. American Journal of Sociology, 78, 1360–1380.

Humphrey, N.K. (1976). The social function of intellect. In P.P.G. Bateson & R.A. Hinde (Eds.), Growing points in ethology (pp. 303–317). Cambridge University Press.

Janicik, G.A., & Larrick, R.P. (2005). Social network schemas and the learning of incomplete networks. Journal of Personality and Social Psychology, 88, 348–364.

Killworth, P.D., & Bernard, H.R. (1979). Informant accuracy in social network data III: a comparison of triadic structure in behavioral and cognitive data. Social Networks, 2, 19–46

Killworth, P.D., & Bernard, H.R. (1982). A technique for comparing mental maps. Social Networks, 3, 307–312.

Killworth, P.D., Johnsen, E.C., Bernard, H.R., Shelley, G.A., & McCarty, C. (1990). Estimating the size of personal networks. Social Networks, 12, 289–312.

Krackhardt, D. (1990). Assessing the political landscape: structure, cognition, and power in organizations. Administrative Science Quarterly, 35, 342–369.

Kudo, H., & Dunbar, R.I. (2001). Neocortex size and social network size in primates. Animal Behaviour, 62, 711–22.

Marin, A. (2004). Are respondents more likely to list alters with certain characteristics? Implications for name generator data. Social Networks, 26, 289–307.

Marineau, J.E., Labianca, G.(J.), Brass, D.J., Borgatti, S.P., & Vecchi, P. (2018). Individuals' power and their social network accuracy: a situated cognition perspective. Social Networks, 54, 145–161.

Marsden, P.V. (1988). Homogeneity in confiding relations. Social Networks, 10, 57–76.

Martin, C.L. (1993). New directions for investigating children's gender knowledge. Developmental Review, 13, 184–204.

McCarty, C., Killworth, P.D., Bernard, H.R., Johnsen, E.C., & Shelley, G.A. (2001). Comparing two methods for estimating network size. Human Organization, 60, 28–39.

McPherson, M., Smith-Lovin, L., & Cook, J.M. (2001). Birds of a feather: homophily in social networks. Annual Review of Sociology, 27, 415–444.

Melin, A.D., Young, H.C., Mosdossy, K.N., & Fedigan, L.M. (2014). Seasonality, extractive foraging, and the evolution of primate sensorimotor intelligence. Journal of Human Evolution, 71, 77–86.

Neisser, U. (1967). Cognitive psychology. Appleton-Crofts.

O'Connor, K.M., & Gladstone, E. (2018). Beauty and social capital: being attractive shapes social networks. Social Networks, 52, 42–47.

Omodei, E., Brashears, M.E., & Arenas, A.. (2017). A mechanistic model of human recall of social network structure and relationship affect. Scientific Reports, 7, 17133.

Parker, S.T. (2015). Re-evaluating the extractive foraging hypothesis. New Ideas in Psychology, 37, 1–12.

Parkinson, C., Kleinbaum, A.M., & Wheatley, T. (2018). Similar neural responses predict friendship. Nature Communications, 9(1). doi: 10.1038/s41467-017-02722-7

Parkinson, C., & Wheatley, T. (2013). Old cortex, new contexts: re-purposing spatial perception for social cognition. Frontiers in Human Neuroscience, 7(October),1–7. doi: 10.3389/fnhum.2013.00645

Parkinson, C., & Wheatley, T. (2015). The repurposed social brain. Trends in Cognitive Sciences, 19(3), 133–141. doi: 10.1016/j.tics.2015.01.003

Perry, B.L., & Pescosolido, B.A. (2010). Functional specificity in discussion networks: the influence of general and problem-specific networks on health outcomes. Social Networks, 32, 345–357.

Picek, J.S., Sherman, S.J., & Shiffrin, R.M. (1975). Cognitive organization and coding of social structures. Journal of Personality and Social Psychology, 31(4), 758–768.

Podolny, J.M. (2001). Networks as the pipes and prisms of the market. American Journal of Sociology, 107, 33–60.

Rae Westbury, H., & Neumann, D.L. (2008). Empathy-related responses to moving film stimuli depicting human and non-human animal targets in negative circumstances. Biological Psychology, 78(1), 66–74. doi: 10.1016/j.biopsycho.2007.12.009

Ridgeway, C.L., & Correll, S.J. (2004). Unpacking the gender system: a theoretical perspective on gender beliefs and social relations. Gender and Society, 18, 510–531.

Ridgeway, C.L., & Smith-Lovin, L. (1999). The gender system and interaction. Annual Review of Sociology, 25, 191–216.

Roberts, S.G., Dunbar, R.I., Pollet, T.V., & Kuppens, T. (2009). Exploring variation in active network size: constraints and ego characteristics. Social Networks, 31, 138–146.

Roth, A.R., Peng, S., Coleman, M.E., Finley, E., & Perry, B.L. (2021). Network recall among older adults with cognitive impairments. Social Networks, 64, 99–108.

Sentis, K.P., & Burnstein, E. (1979). Remembering schema-consistent information: effects of a balance schema on recognition memory. *Journal of Personality and Social Psychology, 37*(12), 2200–2211.

Shea, Catherine T., Tanya Menon, Edward B. Smith, and Kyle Emich. (2015). "The Affective Antecedents of Cognitive Social Network Activation." Social Networks 43:91–99. doi: 10.1016/j.socnet.2015.01.003.

Shultz, S., Opie, C., & Atkinson, Q.D. (2011). Stepwise evolution of stable sociality in primates. *Nature, 479*(7372), 219–223.

Simmel, G. ([1955]1964). *Conflict and the web of group-affiliations*. Free Press.

Simpson, B., Markovsky, B., & Steketee, M. (2011). Power and the perception of social networks. *Social Networks, 33*, 166–171.

Small, M.L. (2013). Weak ties and the core discussion network: why people regularly discuss important matters with unimportant alters. *Social Networks, 35*, 470–483.

Smith, E.B., Menon, T., & Thompson, L. (2012). Status differences in the cognitive activation of social networks. *Organization Science, 23*, 67–82.

Smith, J.A., McPherson, M., & Smith-Lovin, L. (2014). Social distance in the United States: sex, race, religion, age, and education homophily among confidants, 1985 to 2004. *American Sociological Review, 79*(3), 432–456.

Stiller, J., & Dunbar, R.I.M. (2007). Perspective-taking and memory capacity predict social network size. *Social Networks, 29*(1), 93–104. doi: 10.1016/j.socnet.2006.04.001

Straits, B.C. (2000). Ego's important discussants or significant people: an experiment in varying the wording of personal network name generators. *Social Networks, 22*, 123–140.

Sun, H., Brashears, M.E., & Smith, E.B. (2021). Network representation capacity: how social relationships are represented in the human mind. In M. Small, B. Perry & B. Pescosolido (Eds.), *Personal networks: frontiers of ego network analysis* (pp. 651–672). Cambridge University Press.

Sun, H., & Smith, E.B. (2018). Cognitive search and social networks. *Academy of Management Proceedings*.

Van Kreveld, D., & Zajonc, R.B. (1966). The learning of influence structures. *Journal of Personality, 34*, 205–223.

Walker, C.J. (1976). The employment of vertical and horizontal social schemata in the learning of a social structure. *Journal of Personality and Social Psychology, 33*(2), 132–141.

Welch-Ross, M.K., & Schmidt, C.R. (1996). Gender-schema development and children's constructive story memory: evidence for a developmental model. *Child Development, 67*(3), 820–835.

Wilcox, R.S., & Jackson, R.R. (1998). Cognitive abilities of araneophagic jumping spiders. In R.P. Balda, I.M. Pepperberg & A.C. Kamil (Eds.), *Animal Cognition in Nature* (pp. 411–434). Academic Press.

Xu, X., Zuo, X., Wang, X., & Han, S. (2009). Do you feel my pain? Racial group membership modulates empathic neural responses. *Journal of Neuroscience, 29*(26), 8525–29. doi: 10.1523/JNEUROSCI.2418-09.2009

Yamakawa, Y., Kanai, R., Matsumura, M., & Naito, E. (2009). Social distance evaluation in human parietal cortex.' *PLOS One, 4*(2). doi: 10.1371/journal.pone.0004360

Scientific Networks

Donghyun Kang and James Evans

INTRODUCTION

The operation of science hinges on and evolves with connections between scientists, institutions, capital, concepts and culture. Consider the dense interactions between students' cultural and social backgrounds and the mentors that bring them into science; conversations between scientists and staff engaged in the business of teaching and research; dependencies between research methods they use and research activities in which they engage; linkages between scientific artefacts and intellectual property they produce; relationships between the universities, journals and other institutions that sponsor and host them; and connections between the worlds of technology, labour and commerce influenced by them. These complex interdependencies not only invite network analytic representations, but they have catalysed network innovations relevant to many other sectors of social life.[1]

In science, networks have been used to characterise and investigate patterns of scientific collaboration (Barabási et al., 2002; de Solla Price, 1963; Newman, 2001), recognition (Wang et al., 2013), contexts of discovery and consensus (Belikov et al., 2022; Wu et al., 2019), contents of scientific claims (Goh et al., 2007; Ozgür et al., 2008) and the diffusion of research products into the world (Ahmadpoor & Jones, 2017; Marx & Fuegi, 2020; Yin et al., 2021). In this chapter, we provide an overview of scientific networks across related fields including the sociology of science, science studies and actor-network theory, informatics and scientometrics, complex systems, and the rapidly emerging multidisciplinary field, the science of science, in which computational techniques are applied to large-scale data about the research enterprise for scientific insight and public benefit (Fortunato et al., 2018; Wang & Barabási, 2021; Zeng et al., 2017).

Specifically, we will review network research that considers complex linkages between the multitude of different scientific actors, institutions and entities that constitute the scientific enterprise. We connect this research to the scientific outcomes they produce, ranging from discovery to diffusion and impact, and ultimate epistemic certainty. We also survey the range of emergent network representations through which connections between scientific entities have been modelled, from simple, pairwise networks to multimode and high-dimensional hypergraphs to continuous network embeddings. We show how each of these representations captures different aspects of scientific production and its consequences. Discrete representations trace material action and interaction, while continuous approximations capture the probability of future (inter)action. Together the precision of recent network modelling approaches has allowed analysts to optimise science funding (Sattari et al., 2022), maximise the impact of scientific discovery (Larivière et al., 2015), facilitate innovation and robust science (Belikov et al., 2022) and not only predict (Wang et al., 2013), but also quantitatively analyse and forecast at large scales many aspects of science previously accessible only to qualitative and small-scale investigation (Fortunato et al., 2018; Sinatra et al., 2016; Wang & Barabási, 2021). We conclude by suggesting the ways in which this work can and should expand our approach to the analysis of social networks in other domains of life where the things and their interconnection may not always be traced by detailed data, but nevertheless exist and operate through complex interconnection.

Big Scientific Data

The deluge of scientific publications and metadata available in digital form offers us an unprecedented opportunity to understand the relational structure of science, assisted by conceptualisation and tools from the network approach. Scientific publications historically inscribed the first scientific network explored at scale (de Solla Price, 1965; Garfield, 1955; White, 2011), providing bibliometric information that enabled analysis of citation links between papers, and collaboration networks between scientists. We hope to convince the reader, however, that for the analysis of scientific networks to achieve its promise of modelling and generative prediction, emerging representations and analyses must simultaneously cover complex interactions between social agents, institutions and scholarly artefacts connected through diverse channels of communication, interaction and ultimate influence. We acknowledge that this view reflects a picture of science advanced by Latour (1987), Callon (1984) and scholars in the actor-network tradition (Callon et al., 1986) in that we seriously consider the important roles played by non-human nodes within the complex social system of science in society. This approach also echoes and generalises the notion of social duality (Breiger, 1974), extending it to the myriad scientific actors and entities that together weave science as a social fabric. Ignoring the diversity of entities and relations will dramatically limit the degree to which modelling them can produce highly descriptive and predictive models of the scientific system.

ENTITIES AND IDENTITIES IN SCIENTIFIC NETWORK(S)

People and Social Institutions

Scientific networks comprise many types of entities and identities. Scientists represent a driving force in these networks. They engage in scientific activities that produce and consume the goods and services of science. Scientists apply for funding, collect data, conduct analysis, present the results of research at conferences, write papers, evaluate manuscripts for publication and proposals for funding, and they read articles when posted or published. Contemporary scientists affiliate with research institutions, including research universities, government-funded research centres and commercial companies. More intimate social networks of scientists form informal *invisible colleges* – dense communities of researchers actively engaged with each other through various communication channels (Crane, 1972; de Solla Price, 1961). Scientists in research universities are typically employed within departments, which reproduce disciplinary boundaries (Jacobs, 2014) by teaching and certifying students, then employing PhD graduates (Abbott, 2001; Jacobs & Frickel, 2009). Research centres outside departments also play an important role in fostering interactions and collaborations between scientists that transcend department boundaries (Biancani et al., 2014).

From World War II, contemporary scientific research has also become tightly interconnected across broader institutional environments. These include national innovation systems (Nelson & Rosenberg, 1993) organised by governments and funded with tax revenue, as well as international market systems supported by industry (Etzkowitz & Leydesdorff, 1997). Funding agencies include national institutions such as the National Science Foundation (NSF) in the United States, multinational funding schemes like the European Research Council (ERC) and increasingly important private foundations such as the Gates Foundation in the United States, the Wellcome Trust in Britain and the Novo Nordisk Foundation in Europe. Those funders' resource allocation methods shape competition and collaboration patterns (Sattari et al., 2022). They can also influence local and national research cultures (Kim, 2022; Shi & Rao, 2010) by prioritising and incentivising distinct configurations of values. Beyond governmental agencies, industry hires scientists and sponsors scientific research, yielding additional players and layers of interaction, extending scientific networks more deeply into economy and society (Evans, 2010a;

Powell et al., 1996; Sohn, 2021). Different combinations of institutional and contextual settings lead to structured trajectories of global scientific development (Miao et al., 2022).

Scientific artefacts

Diverse 'scientific artefacts' reside within scientific networks. Data is collected and analysed. Methods and protocols are developed and documented. Computer programs are written and distributed through public repositories. Manuscripts are crafted and shared through preprints or peer-reviewed journal articles; patents are applied for exclusive intellectual rights. Those are the synthetic outputs of scientific activities. We can further consider more granular subcomponents engaged with by scientists, such as theoretical claims, the concepts within them, and even chemical compounds and molecular structures. Such components of large, synthetic scientific artefacts like research papers are themselves 'small', disaggregated scientific artefacts.

Scientific artefacts constitute a second mode of 'things' in scientific networks, and they link with one another through their own complex networks of interdependence. Papers cite other papers, patents reference other patents, and software formally calls other software for operation. Each of one of these networks can be rendered in different ways to answer distinctive questions. Citation networks linking scientific publications, the topic of nearly seven decades of scientometric investigation (de Solla Price, 1965), are most commonly viewed and analysed as a directed acyclic graph.[2] They may also be analysed in terms of bibliographic coupling, how much two papers share references (Kessler, 1963), or co-citation, how frequently two papers are cited together in future work (Small, 1973).

The tradition of sociology of science has focused on the social and institutional factors at play in science (Merton, 1973), while scientometric approaches have focused more attention on the networks tracing scientific collaboration (Beaver & Rosen, 1978) and document-to-document references (Garfield et al., 1978). We emphasise that scientific concepts, natural or artificial entities, and the scientific claims that assemble or index them give rise to a complex networked world suggested by philosophers of science (Quine, 1951). Actor-network theory depicts them as in multiplex connection across levels with those people, institutions and places animate them (Latour, 1987). These intertwined relationships can be extracted from published scientific texts, which showcase accepted structures (Foster et al., 2015; Shi et al., 2015). Established entity relationships constrain future ties and condition future combinations (Callon et al., 1986).

Putting them all together

Putting all the elements of science together, we conceive a complex system of heterogeneous entities – scientists, staff, research institutions, students, funding agencies and scientific artefacts, large and small – linked by myriad multilevel relations through which they recursively influence and constrain one in producing (and reproducing) science, as depicted in Figure 16.1.

Increasingly detailed, large-scale data on the intermixture of networked entities offers an observatory through which network analysts may probe answers to questions about the complex functioning of science. Implications drawn from the analysis of complex networks linking scientific entities would contribute not only to the understanding of science, but to social science and network theory more generally. For example, probing interactions between co-authorship and citation (Martin et al., 2013) provides evidence demonstrating the nuanced role of reciprocity. Examining citation networks and content simultaneously can advance our insights on the diffusion process of knowledge and practice (Gerow et al., 2018). Linking the co-authorship structure to peer review can reveal how network structure shapes cognitive bias in evaluation (Teplitskiy et al., 2018). Thus, we underscore that scientific networks are multimodal 'social' networks of humans and non-humans (Latour, 1987; Pachucki & Breiger, 2010), which construct a field in which scientists and the accumulated history of scientific things and relations co-constitute many of the emergent properties of science (Bourdieu, 1975; Camic, 2011; Foster et al., 2015).

ANALYSING SIMPLE SCIENTIFIC NETWORKS

Co-authorship Networks

While research collaboration can take place in diverse formats, including informal discussion and data sharing,[3] co-authorship has been conceived as the most visible and well-documented indicator of research collaboration (Milojević, 2010). In co-authorship networks, two authors are

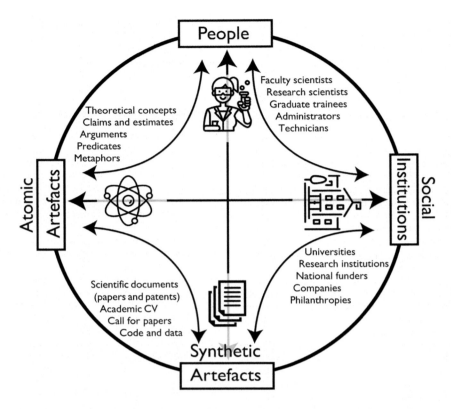

Figure 16.1 Schema of divergent things typically involved in multilevel scientific networks

typically considered connected when they appear as authors in a publication record. Some approaches use author orders to construct directed networks of authors (Kim & Diesner, 2015), but co-authorship networks are usually represented as an undirected network of all collaborating researchers weighted by the number of papers they co-authored within a given time span.

Network scientists' seminal work in the early 2000s opened up large-scale analyses of the network of co-authorship. Newman's (2001) work revealed its 'small world' structure (Milgram, 1967; Watts & Strogatz, 1998) from co-authorship networks of scientists in biomedicine, high-energy physics and computer science. Barabási et al. (2002) investigated the evolutionary pattern of co-authorship networks from mathematics and neuroscience in the 1990s and proposed dynamic generative models that could reproduce network characteristics (e.g., connectivity, diameter, clustering coefficient) from the observed data. Notably, one of the earliest modularity-based community detection algorithms was first showcased with the co-authorship network of researchers affiliated with the Sante Fe Institute between 1999 and 2000 (Girvan & Newman, 2002). We refer to Kumar (2015) for a comprehensive overview of studies specifically focusing on co-authorship networks.

One important, longstanding challenge in co-authorship analysis has been to disambiguate scientists' identities. Challenges come when long or complex names are alternatively translated (e.g., those with non-Latin characters) and a single person is treated as multiple authors, or when multiple authors have similar or identical names and are treated as the same person. Contemporary large-scale databases of scientific networks (e.g, Microsoft Academic Graph, Open Alex, IRIS UMETRICS, PubMed Knowledge Graph) provide name-disambiguated author IDs per publication, but they suffer from both challenges. Author-name disambiguation at scale continues to be an active area of research for improving the efficiency and quality of scientific data (D'Angelo & van Eck, 2020; Kim & Owen-Smith, 2021).

Name disambiguation is particularly challenging for the comparative analysis of national scientific systems. For social network analysis,

Type I error (linking multiple people into a single identity) will artificially inflate network density, while Type II error (allowing the same person to have multiple identities) will artificially produce greater network sparsity. The population of scientists with popular Korean names will induce greater Type I error, and the population of scientists with variously translated German names will induce greater Type II error, potentially making it erroneously appear that Korean science is more densely integrated, suggesting that one might need alternative algorithms or thresholds for calibrated comparison. Furthermore, the best algorithm will depend on its analytical function in research.

The precise hypothesis will also shape whether biasing towards Type I or II error is more desirable to construct a conservative test. For example, consider an analysis that seeks to demonstrate how co-authorship distance between a reviewer and author increases the likelihood of accepting that paper for publication (Teplitskiy et al., 2018). For such an analysis, using a disambiguation algorithm with Type I error would be more epistemologically desirable than Type II, because it would add noise to the test (suggesting that some people are close who are not) and demonstrate that the estimated effect represents a lower bound, and is almost certainly higher in actuality. These principles all carry over to the disambiguation of other entities such as institutions mentioned within article metadata or concepts within article content.

Citation Networks

The scientific enterprise builds on prior work. A research article references relevant previous scientific work, which inscribes directed networks of papers linked via citation. Citation networks are, by nature, temporal. In-degree centrality for papers from citation networks – or citation counts – has long been an essential subject of study for scientometric analysis (de Solla Price, 1965; Garfield, 1955). The early vision of Eugene Garfield, the scientometric pioneer who created the Web of Science, was to aid scientists' search for literature (Mingers & Leydesdorff, 2015), and paper citations have come to play a crucial role in research impact evaluation (Wang & Barabási, 2021).

The most straightforward and popular network measurement for citation networks is the in-degree centrality, or a papers' citation counts. Skewness in the distribution of citation counts across different fields has been well documented (Fortunato et al., 2018). Analyses show that heavy-tailed citation distributions follow power law distributions (de Solla Price, 1965; Radicchi et al., 2008), universal to any degree distribution observed from network data (Newman et al., 2011). Cumulative advantage, often summarised as a 'rich-get-richer' phenomenon, has been modelled with the process of preferential attachment (Barabási & Albert, 1999). Research articles may experience a burst of scientific attention long after their first appearance by deviating from a typical cycle of scientific attention as 'sleeping beauties', which has been successfully measured as the convexity of their degree distribution over time (Ke et al., 2015; Van Raan, 2004).

Scholarly journals have also represented an important unit of analysis within citation networks. *Journal impact factor* (JIF), which was famously devised by Eugene Garfield (1972), has become widespread over the past decades. This characterises a journal by the average citation counts per paper published during a given prior period. While JIF only considers first-order relations, a new generation of journal-level metrics harnesses network centrality measures that account for high-order connections. Most prominently, the Eigenfactor indicator (Bergstrom, 2007; Bergstrom et al., 2008) uses an approach similar to Bonacich's power centrality (Bonacich, 1987) and Google's more recent PageRank algorithm (Page et al., 1999) to place more weight on a citation from highly cited journals.

Citation impact has become important for research evaluation, researcher promotion and institutional funding allocation with its visibility. As a result, citation counts have become a metric that researchers maximise in their own selection of projects and institutions maximise in their selection of researchers. This fixation on citation impact has led to unintended consequences (Hicks et al., 2015) by incentivising scientists to make choices that inexpensively maximise it while driving down its correlation to generalised research quality (Campbell, 1979; Goodhart, 1975; Lucas, 1976). Research demonstrates that scientists are rewarded by publishing in fashionable areas of science where citations are abundant (Foster et al., 2015; Rzhetsky et al., 2015), making their work relevant for citation by other contemporary researchers working on those topics. This has contributed to log-jams in science where scientists crowd together along the scientific frontier (Azoulay et al., 2018), driving down the relationship between short-term impact and long-term influence.

Against this backdrop, alternative citation-based measures have been proposed to reveal the distinct character of scholarly work beyond simple popularity in the scientometric literature. Two recent, prominent metrics of novelty and disruption have arisen that highlight work generating new combinations and directions (McMahan & McFarland, 2021), whereby new scientific ideas and approaches supplant the old (Lin et al., 2022). Novelty has been assessed in many ways (Foster et al., 2021), but one high-profile approach models how research draws upon unusual combinations of prior research in crafting their own contributions (Uzzi et al., 2013), which we detail in the following section. Disruption models how research comes to eclipse the prior work on which it builds (Figure 16.2), becoming recognised as a new scientific direction (Funk & Owen-Smith, 2017; Wu et al., 2019). The latter metric, disruption, helps to reveal how exponential growth in the volume of scientific publications often decreases the rate of disruptive work, ossifying the established canon (Chu & Evans, 2021; Park et al., 2021).

Insofar as citations reflect scientific attention, citation networks will remain as a crucial ingredient for research evaluation, but this poses opportunities for the network analysis of citations to reduce the gaming of citations by generating credible models and metrics that capture diverse values underlying robust and useful science.

Analyses based on citation networks also capture collective properties of the scientific enterprise. Shwed and Bearman (2010) repurposed a modularity maximisation algorithm for community detection to trace how scientific debates (e.g., smoking is carcinogenic; vaccination causes autism) unfold. By measuring the level of fragmentation in research communities from citation networks with modularity, they showed that the decline of modularity over time captures the increase of scientific consensus. McMahan and McFarland (2021) studied the degree to which review articles shifted the academic discourse. By analysing citations and co-citation patterns of original research mentioned in authoritative reviews, they showed that review articles poach citations from the articles they review, but drive new attention to work that spans research boundaries, and so reshape future academic discourse.

ANALYSING COMPLEX SCIENTIFIC NETWORKS

In the previous section, we narrowed our scope to scientific networks containing a single type of node and relation – either co-authorship between scientists or citations between papers. We proceed to survey studies of scientific networks with heterogeneous entities, attributes and relationships that generate interactions shaping scientific networks in action. Not all that we introduce here construct a formal network representation or model, but they identify phenomena that can only be understood by simultaneously incorporating these heterogeneous entities into account and pose targets for future formalisation.

Networks of Scientists and Scientific Activities

Studies have shown that networks of scientists and their attributes influence problem selection, productivity, research impact, evaluation and the degree of reproducibility in scientific claims.

A. Science of Team Science

With the undisputed trend of team science (Leahey, 2016) and the increasing availability of data on team compositions, how different scientific team configurations shape research outputs has received extensive attention in studies of scientific networks. The most robust conclusions to date regard the relationship between team size and contribution. Analysing nearly 20 million papers' citation trajectories, Wuchty et al. (2007) showed that scientific articles produced by teams tend to accrue more citations than solo-authored papers. Another analysis on 28 million scientific articles published between 1900 and 2011 demonstrated the positive relationship between team size and number of citation papers garner

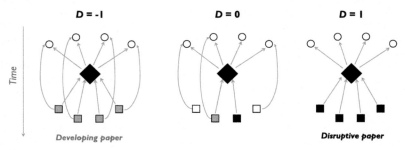

Figure 16.2 Disruption metric (from Wu et al., 2019)

(Larivière et al., 2015). By contrast, Wu et al. (2019) showed that small teams are more likely to produce disruptive research than large teams (Funk & Owen-Smith 2017). Papers produced by large teams tend to receive more citations more quickly insofar as they develop on recent, popular work.

Other studies use network analysis to interrogate the relationship between team structure and impact. One study measured the freshness of team members by calculating the fraction of new versus repeat collaborators, then demonstrated an inverted-u-shaped relationship between team freshness and paper citation impact (Liu et al., 2022). Studies using contributorship data disclosed from the open-access *PLOS* journals captured distinct clusters of tasks, for instance, technical and conceptual work (Larivière et al., 2016), and different types of researchers like specialists, team players and versatiles (Lu et al., 2020). Xu et al. (2022) developed a measure to capture the hierarchy of teams from contributorship information, then showed that flat teams with less hierarchy are more likely to produce novel and disruptive research. Relatedly, Walsh et al. (2019) demonstrated a positive association between level of division of labour – hierarchy in teams – and rate of retraction in biomedical research. As more scientific journals require authors to submit contributorship information with manuscripts as metadata, we expect that our understanding of the relationship between team structure, research activities and research outcomes will be enhanced.

B. Network of Scientists and Productivity, Evaluation, Replicability

The role of 'star scientists' in shaping scientific networks has been variously explored and documented. Analysing the productivity of scientists affiliated with more than 250 evolutionary biology departments, Agrawal et al. (2014) reported that hiring a star scientist (who ranked in the top 10 per cent of citations received before arrival) boosted short- and long-term productivity of other scientists in the same department by almost 50 per cent, suggesting strong peer effects. Azoulay et al. (2010) took the inverse route and estimated the effect of premature death among eminent life scientists could lead to a 5–8 per cent reduction in co-authors' published productivity. This increases non-collaborator's productivity and funding streams within the subfield, however, by lowering the entry barrier associated with a prominent gatekeeper (Azoulay et al., 2019). Rawlings et al.'s (2015) analysis of collaboration networks among faculty at Stanford University demonstrated that intellectual cohesion and integration measured in citation networks among faculty members occurred around star scientists.

How scientists' connections with industry relates to their research activities has also emerged as an important topic in social network research. This has become more prominent as a topic as industry supports additional science and in transitions towards a 'knowledge economy' (Etzkowitz & Leydesdorff, 1997). Studies examining research on the plant model organism *Arabidopsis thaliana* suggest that the collaboration of academic and industrial scientists nudged academic scientists towards theoretically novel and untraditional research (Evans, 2010a), while industry sponsorship reduced sharing of research materials with competing labs, raising the level of secrecy (Evans, 2010b). Bikard et al. (2019) exhibited that academic scientists who collaborate with industry paradoxically produce more scientific papers but fewer patents than their counterparts without industry sponsors. Analysing faculty activity from a Spanish university, D'Este et al. (2019) reported that interdisciplinary researchers engage in industry interactions more actively than those firmly rooted within disciplines.

Networks of collaborating researchers are consequential for scientific evaluation. In the context of Spain, Zinovyeva and Bagues (2015) showed that connections between promotion committees for full professorship and candidates (PhD advisor–advisee mentorship, colleagues, co-authors) produced bias favouring those with connections. Similarly, Bagues et al. (2019) documented how professional connections convey relevant information about scholarly qualification evaluation in Italy. A study analysing neuroscience manuscripts submitted to *PLOS One* from Teplitskiy et al. (2018) found that reviewers tend to assign more positive scores for manuscripts written by authors close in co-authorship networks, not only due to reciprocity, but from disagreements stemming from different 'schools of thought'.

Studies have also shown that replicability of particular scientific claims can be predicted from the network structure of scientists. The likelihood of published claims regarding drug–gene interactions decreases when the research communities that generate them are densely connected and centralised through overlapping co-authorship (Danchev et al., 2019). Another study on the replicability of published gene–gene interactions found that claims supported by socially and institutionally independent research groups tend to be more robust and replicable (Belikov et al., 2022).

Heterogeneous Networks of Scientific Artefacts

In the last section, we explore topics that have largely been investigated paper-to-paper citation and author collaboration networks using simple graph representations. Here we expand our scope to networks of scientific artefacts containing multiple types of entities – including concepts, materials, methods, claims, papers, journals, disciplines and more.

A. Measuring Novelty and Interdisciplinarity

Like other domains of creative activity, novelty is a crucial aspect of scientific knowledge. Novelty arises when something previously unseen emerges or is introduced into the system. The network perspective allows us to refigure our assessments of novelty in science such that rather than treating objects as categorically new or old (e.g., a novel molecule), we may treat them as more or less new based on linkages between existing entities (e.g., novel atoms and bonds that make the molecule, Foster et al., 2021).

Guided by the theory of recombinant novelty (Fleming, 2001; Fleming & Sorenson, 2004), Uzzi et al. (2013) proposed a measurement of *novelty* based on the relative infrequency of co-cited journal pairs, which we briefly discussed early in the analysis of citation networks. This approach draws on the intuition that if a paper cites a pair of rarely co-cited journals, it signals the novel recombination of knowledge within them. Their analysis, based on Web of Science data, revealed that scientific papers that both have higher 'conventionality' (median combination rate) and higher 'tail novelty' (top ten percentile combination rate) are likely to accrue outsized citations. This suggests the importance of novelty and conventionality in achieving outsized attention and impact. Work from Foster et al. (2015) constructed networks of chemicals from biomedical abstracts and demonstrated that biomedical scientists are more likely to conservatively establish chemical interactions, but that they venture to explore novel chemical relationships more than might be expected if they were only seeking to maximise expected citations, which are more likely to result in blockbuster citations and awards.

Interdisciplinarity has received extensive attention as a critical source of novel ideas that provoke scientific progress (Klein, 1990; National Academy of Sciences, 2005). Although disciplinary boundaries are not always clear-cut, journal-level categories provided by bibliometric databases have been widely used to delineate intellectual boundaries. One popular measurement for interdisciplinarity (Porter et al., 2007) utilises subject categories assigned by the Web of Science to measure the level of intellectual diversity observed within a focal paper's references (Stirling, 2007). Many other studies have investigated the effect of interdisciplinarity in various contexts. Yegros-Yegros et al. (2015) show an inverted u-shape relationship between interdisciplinarity and paper citations. Leahey et al. (2017) demonstrate that interdisciplinary research is high risk with low productivity caused by cognitive challenges in collaboration and peer review, but more likely results in high-impact research.

B. Harvesting More Signals from Texts

Papers and journals constitute a crucial platform in scientific networks at the higher level, but entities observed within scientific documents allow construction of more fine-grained scientific entity networks with heterogeneous nodes and links.

Citation network analysis rarely distinguishes types of citations. Dramatic advances in the development of natural language processing techniques have enabled citation to be classified by intention at scale (Cohan et al., 2019), which can lead to enriched insight regarding scientific networks. Using the full corpus of papers from the *Journal of Immunology* (1998–2007), Catalini et al. (2015) showed that only 2.4 per cent of citations were negative, critically engaging with prior work; they also demonstrated that papers cited negatively experienced long-term citation disadvantage. Building on larger-scale scientific textual and citation resources, recent work has enabled classification at much larger scales (Cohan et al., 2019; Jurgens et al., 2018), and analysis from Cui et al. (2022) shows that the rate of criticism is tightly tethered to the scientific age of authors on the research team, and increases collectively as fields age.

Information inscribed in articles in textual form provides crucial ingredients to capture and analyse networked scientific components, including all objects present within a field-specific ontology – diseases, chemicals and species for biomedical science; cosmological phenomena, instrumentation and particles for the physical sciences (Shi & Evans, 2023); or even all heterogeneous words present in article data and metadata (Callon et al., 1986). By counting unique phrases from scientific publications, Milojević (2015) showed the growth of scientific papers and larger scientific teams is inversely correlated with their 'cognitive extent' or the diameter of their semantic content.

Formalising the concept of cultural holes (Pachucki & Breiger, 2010) with information-theory,

Vilhena et al. (2014) show that academic jargon specific to scholarly communities reduces its accessibility to neighbouring fields. Graham et al. (2022) challenge extant theory of structural holes in which structure diversity is assumed to capture information advantages (Burt, 1992, 2004). They show that scientific co-authorship bridging structural holes does not necessarily converge with diverse keyword combinations. An examination of the relationship between the ambiguity of language and the structure of subsequent citation networks demonstrated that greater ambiguity resulted in less fragmented citation networks, suggesting that semantic ambiguity inspired follow-on papers to engage more actively with them and each other (McMahan & Evans, 2018).

C. Scientific Networks Reaching to Other Social Domains

The reach of scientific networks extends to other domains in contemporary society. Interplays between scientific publications and technology patents have received marked attention as university-affiliated scientists frequently apply for patents, and industry scientists publish academic papers (Marx & Fuegi, 2020). Ahmadpoor and Jones (2017) demonstrated how the worlds of scientific publications and patents are fruitfully linked through citations. These indicate the proximity or distance of different fields from the 'dual frontier' separating the publication from commercialisation. Other work examines further channels through which science diffuses into society. A study examining the interface between scientific work and Wikipedia showed that articles published in open-access journals are 50 per cent more likely to be cited by relevant Wikipedia pages, amplifying the diffusion of free information (Teplitskiy et al., 2017). Another analysis studied the citation of scientific articles on Covid-19 by policy documents during the pandemic, revealing how policy documents systematically identify high-quality scientific articles and cite them to inform policy (Yin et al., 2021). These studies show the scope of the scientific networks is not necessarily limited to specialised systems of knowledge production but spans other networked spheres of social life.

Gender in Scientific Networks

The role of gender has become a central topic in studying the scientific system. Work in the sociology of science has documented the low publication rate of women scientists relative to their male counterparts (Long, 1990; Xie & Shauman, 1998). This gap, attributed to unequal domestic duties (Hochschild & Machung, 2012) and discrimination (Loder, 1999), has declined over time, but differences have persisted in traditionally male-dominant fields such as physics, mathematics and computer science (Holman et al., 2018). Gender disparity has also manifested in citation inequality. Bibliographic analysis from Larivière et al. (2013) revealed that papers with female names on the first or last author position tend to garner fewer citations than those enlisting male names as first or last author. Another study triangulating administrative, bibliometrics and survey data demonstrated that women in scientific teams are less likely to become recognised as authors than their male peers (Ross et al., 2022).

Gender discrimination may be direct as well as indirect. Analysis of US dissertations showed that dissertation writers who engaged with research topics typically associated with women's research subjects were less likely to become faculty advisors (Kim et al., 2022). Recent work by an overlapping Stanford team on the same dataset (Hofstra et al., 2020) demonstrated that demographically underrepresented students – women and minorities – innovate at higher rates than majority students, but their novel contributions are discounted and less likely to earn them academic positions. A lack of diversity is not only critical for the generation of research novelty, but also the construction of diverse impacts. Koning et al. (2021) show that although women are less likely to invent biomedical technology, when they do, they are more likely to generate innovations relevant to women's health. Moreover, large-scale analysis on the relationship between team-level gender diversity and the novelty and impact of research demonstrated that research papers in medicine produced by mixed-gender teams are more likely to post higher novelty and receive more citations (Yang et al., 2022), suggesting the importance of gender diversity in advancing scientific work. These findings highlight how disparities in representation and recognition pose missed opportunities for advancing science.

TOWARDS CONTINUOUS REPRESENTATIONS OF SCIENTIFIC NETWORKS

Hypergraph Representation of Scientific Networks

Traditional network modelling strategies utilise a pairwise adjacency matrix to trace interactions with a simple graph in which an edge represents a particular type of connection between node pairs. Under this formalism, an edge may connect only two entities. Hypergraph representations generalise pairwise graphs with hyperedges that can represent interactions or connections encompassing any number of entities. Many interactions and relationships in scientific networks can be modelled natively as a hypergraph. For example, co-authorship networks can be naturally represented as a hypergraph with hyperedges including all scientists listed as authors on a paper (Ko et al., 2022). Hypergraphs can be projected onto simple graphs, with a hyperedge represented by a fully connected clique, but this adds structure that may not exist (e.g., if three people attended the 5,000-person American Sociological Association meeting, should they be connected?).

Shi et al. (2015) conceptualised scientific entities appearing within biomedical papers – authors, chemicals, diseases and methods – as a multimodal hypergraph, such that a hyperedge inscribed entities appearing together in a paper. Exploring the hypergraph constructed from millions of publications indexed by MEDLINE with random walks, this work revealed remarkably short distances between biomedical entities and temporally evolving connections, such as the role of methods in bridging and weaving scientific networks together. Other work demonstrated that by including authoring scientists within the hypergraph of science, alongside scientific entities such as materials and properties, the direction of scientific discovery can be dramatically improved. This is because the density of random walks across the hypergraph from properties to materials (e.g., Bi_2Te_3 is thermo-electric) are proportional to their cognitive availability as inferences insofar as there are scientists present to imagine, research and publish them (Sourati & Evans, 2021).

Neural Embedding for Large-Scale Scientific Networks

Social network analysts historically considered only the topology of social networks, and not their intrinsic geometry. At the limit, a graph with n nodes would require up to $n-1$ Euclidean dimensions to represent geometrically, so geometric embedding was not perceived as reducing the complexity of network data. The Johnson–Lindenstrauss theorem (1984), however, proved that networks can be represented with minimal distortion in far fewer (~log n) dimensions. The rise of autoencoders, or neural network models that automatically learn to embed data from one representation into another, alongside improvements in high-performance computing have

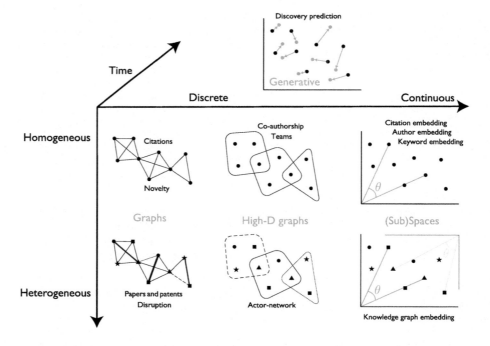

Figure 16.3   Diagram of native representations used in scientific network analysis

enabled analysts to efficiently and practically place social networks into much lower dimensional geometric representations (Chamberlain et al., 2017; Nickel & Kiela, 2017).

These neural embedding techniques have proven remarkably successful in constructing continuous, dimensionalised vector spaces for unstructured entities sharing contexts in many domains, from text and images to networks. Graph or network embedding models are considered 'low-dimensional' techniques relative to the number of nodes in a network (e.g., 300 dimensions versus 300,000 nodes) because they reduce this very high-dimensional node space, in the same way that word embeddings successfully reduce the dimensionality inscribed by vocabulary size. Nevertheless, in comparison with two- or three-dimensional spaces common in network visualisations (Mrvar & Batagelj, 2016), these spaces may also be considered 'high dimensional' in that they produce much more complex and accurate associations, as demonstrated by many recent analyses (Bolukbasi et al., 2016; Caliskan et al., 2017; Garg et al., 2018; Kozlowski et al., 2019).

Successful and efficient neural embeddings demonstrated their performance in natural language processing by implementing the distributional semantics hypothesis (Harris, 1954), summarised by the British linguist Firth as 'a word is characterized by the company it keeps' (1957). Word embedding models such as Word2vec (Mikolov et al., 2013), created to identify semantic similarity, were soon generalised to efficiently project networked entities onto low-dimensional metric spaces that characterised their path distances with minimal distortion.

A pioneering neural embedding model was the DeepWalk algorithm, which borrowed the skip-gram architecture from Word2vec (Perozzi et al., 2014). Various network embedding techniques have been subsequently proposed such as LINE (Tang et al., 2015) and Node2Vec (Grover & Leskovec, 2016), which powerfully characterise networks and have come to dominate performance for the prediction of missing or future links (Wang et al., 2022). As such, neural models have become a major approach that capitalises on large-scale network data and a capability to encode sparse discrete network representations into dense continuous vector representations (Cui et al., 2019) that approximate and scale results from matrix factorisation (Levy & Goldberg, 2014; Qiu et al., 2018). Scientific networks have been important test beds for many approaches to social network embedding. For instance, the Metapath2vec model (Dong et al., 2017) proposed a strategy to generate random walks that consider the multiplicity of node types in observed heterogeneous networks,

which improves performance for nodal type classification and clustering for papers, scientists and venues in computer science. Embedding models such as HIN2vec (Fu et al., 2017) attempted to encode heterogeneous relationships such as papers to authors and papers to conferences in a complex embedding space.

Network embedding techniques have been deployed to investigate complex latent structures inferred from interdependent entities in science. Applying the DeepWalk and Node2vec models to the paper citation network from Microsoft Academic Graph, Peng et al. (2021) trained a 100-dimensional vector model for ~20,000 scientific periodicals. They then deployed it to analyse structures of scientific disciplines and captured substantive dimensions of sciences such as 'soft–hard' and 'social–biological'. Lin et al. (2022) show that the novelty score initially proposed by Uzzi et al. (2013) can be reformulated, more efficiently computed and dynamically updated with a neural embedding approach. Shi and Evans (2023) generalised graph embedding to the embedding of scientific hypergraphs in order to assess article novelty-based published combinations least probable under the most probable embedding model. They demonstrate that by using hypergraphs instead of standard, simple graphs, they double their prediction papers will become hits (within the top 10 per cent of citations).

Curvature in Continuous Embeddings for Hierarchical Scientific Networks

Euclidean space is constrained by the triangle inequality such that for any three sides of a triangle, $a + b > c$. This forces transitivity, such that friends of friends must be friends. Despite the resonance of this principle with social psychological theories of intimate networks like Heider's balance theory (Heider, 1958), this property makes it difficult to represent large-scale scientific networks that manifest substantial hierarchy and intransitivity (Feld, 1981). Social network theories that focus on the importance of bridging ties, including the 'strength of weak ties' (Granovetter, 1973) and 'structural holes' (Burt, 1992, 2004), highlight the importance of violating transitivity for the flow of information and advantage. Social network actors with higher betweenness centrality (Freeman, 1977) uniquely own more ties and bridge more structural holes. They represent knowledge brokers by connecting people disconnected from each other. In social systems, broken triads accumulate into the hierarchy of power structures, which allow for the division and aggregation of labour, scaling-up institutions to coordinate complex social action.

Hyperbolic geometry, assuming constant, negative curvature and allowing triangle inequality, is a strong candidate for modelling these asymmetric structures. Because of the expanded area or 'ruffled edge' of hyperbolic space, two nodes can simultaneously be close to the same central, bridging node and far from one another. Statistical physicists first proposed the use of a Poincaré disk to embed complex social networks (Krioukov et al., 2010; Papadopoulos et al., 2012). By embedding university-level collaboration and semantic networks from scientific publications into Poincaré disks (Nickel & Kiela, 2017), Linzhuo et al. (2020) reveal that networks of increasingly collaborative scientists lead to contractions in the space of scientific ideas, paradoxically reducing collective sources of diversity for the future. Chami et al. (2019) developed deep graph convolutional neural networks to generalise convolutional neural networks (CNNs), developed for machine vision, to the context of hierarchical graphs. By incorporating hyperbolic geometry to each network layer, with learnable curvature, they capture the hierarchical structure characteristic of scientific networks, dramatically improving prediction of masked PubMed citation links.

Embedding networks in continuous and curved geometric spaces abstracts away from the discrete nodes and edges that detail social interaction. Rather than conceiving of them as replacements or even efficient summaries of social and scientific networks, we argue that such embeddings generatively model the probability of future interactions (Burchard et al., 2022). Network regions embedded in positive curvature manifest dense thickets of ties in which information pools and cycles; regions embedded in negative curvature are characterised by sparse ties representing ridges over which information spreads and flows, as in cross-disciplinary scientific innovation. In this way, curvature combines local and global perspectives, providing a continuous characterisation of network structure.

The literature on network embeddings is growing rapidly, suggesting novel network analysis and prediction tasks with its improved predictive power. We expect readers will see many advances in network embedding techniques, which will provide exciting opportunities to represent and analyse scientific networks – or any networked data at scale – through network embedding. These approaches enable the simulation of context-sensitive networked futures with greater resolution than previously imagined.

DISCUSSION

In this chapter, we provide an overview of research on scientific networks. As we illustrate, the diversity of social and scientific 'things' in networks have become more widely traceable with the wealth of digitised scientific data and increased computing power. Studies on complex scientific networks provide new evidence of network mechanisms (Graham et al., 2022; Vilhena et al., 2014). They also provide insight and generate predictions that facilitate scientific discovery, promote innovation and ensure robust scientific findings (Sourati et al., 2022). Simulations on scientific networks, resolved through neural graph embeddings, enable us to improve how we design, evaluate, incentivise and improve science, society's primary engine of innovation and economic growth (Jones & Summers, 2020).

We conclude this chapter with a list of principles (Box 16.1) regarding representations and analysis for scientific networks as a practical guide for readers enthusiastic about diving into the science of networks and networks of science.

Box 16.1 (Some) Principles for Scientific Networks Analysis and Representations

- Simple pairwise graph representations of scientific networks are powerful tools for descriptive and exploratory analysis of small and sparse scientific networks.
- Analysts should recall that single-mode network representations in scientific networks (e.g., scientific collaboration) are often constructed from projection of multimodal or high-dimensional relationships into a single mode (e.g., co-authorship on a scientific paper).
- Citations reflect scientific attention, and citation networks will remain as a crucial ingredient for research evaluation, which poses opportunities for citation analysis to reduce the gaming of citations by generating credible models and metrics that capture diverse values for science.

- Scientific networks may include heterogeneous entities and relationships, encompassing scientists, institutions, artefacts and concepts within and across levels of analysis, all of which may meaningfully be conceived as engaged in 'social' interaction.
- Network heterogeneity helps the analyst imagine, theorise and discover latent patterns and associations otherwise undetectable, like complex combinatorial novelty.
- Entity disambiguation (e.g., names of scientists) and resolution directly influence network density; for a conservative test, they should bias away from the anticipated network effect.
- Network representations reduce the dimensionality of their subject matters, such that shifting representations (e.g., scientists as edges instead of nodes; labelled subjects as nodes instead of attributes, a citation act as a node instead of an edge, distances calculated over multimodal hypergraphs rather than their single-mode projections), can reveal robust patterns inaccessible within their traditional representations.
- Static network measures are effective for the analysis of sparsely connected networks, like co-authorship; but dynamic processes like random walks or network embeddings are required for the analysis of densely connected networks, like networks of scientific content.
- Discrete network representations trace realised network interactions; continuous network embeddings trace the probability of future network interactions.

Notes

1 Citation network models from de Solla Price (1965) became one important way of conceiving and modelling the World Wide Web.
2 For an exception, see Evans (2010b).
3 See Lewis et al. (2012) for more discussion.

REFERENCES

Abbott, A. (2001). *Chaos of disciplines*. University of Chicago Press.

Agrawal, A., McHale, J., & Oettl, A. (2014). *Why stars matter* (No. 20012). National Bureau of Economic Research.

Ahmadpoor, M., & Jones, B.F. (2017). The dual frontier: patented inventions and prior scientific advance. *Science*, 357(6351), 583–587.

Azoulay, P., Fons-Rosen, C., & Zivin, J.S.G. (2019). Does science advance one funeral at a time? *American Economic Review*, 109(8), 2889–2920.

Azoulay, P., Graff-Zivin, J., Uzzi, B., Wang, D., Williams, H., Evans, J A., Jin, G.Z., Lu, S.F., Jones, B.F., Börner, K., Lakhani, K.R., Boudreau, K.J., & Guinan, E.C. (2018). Toward a more scientific science. *Science*, 361(6408), 1194–1197.

Azoulay, P., Graff Zivin, J.S., & Wang, J. (2010). Superstar extinction. *Quarterly Journal of Economics*, 125(2), 549–589.

Bagues, M., Sylos-Labini, M., & Zinovyeva, N. (2019). Connections in scientific committees and applicants' self-selection: evidence from a natural randomized experiment. *Labour Economics*, 58, 81–97.

Barabási, A.-L., & Albert, R. (1999). Emergence of scaling in random networks. *Science*, 286(5439), 509–512.

Barabási, A.-L., Jeong, H., Néda, Z., Ravasz, E., Schubert, A., & Vicsek, T. (2002). Evolution of the social network of scientific collaborations. *Physica A: Statistical Mechanics and Its Applications*, 311(3–4), 590–614.

Beaver, D.D., & Rosen, R. (1978). Studies in scientific collaboration. *Scientometrics*, 1(1), 65–84.

Belikov, A.V., Rzhetsky, A., & Evans, J. (2022). Prediction of robust scientific facts from literature. *Nature Machine Intelligence*, 4(5), 445–454.

Bergstrom, C.T. (2007). Eigenfactor: measuring the value and prestige of scholarly journals. *College and Research Libraries News*, 68(5), 314–316.

Bergstrom, C.T., West, J.D., & Wiseman, M.A. (2008). The Eigenfactor™ metrics. *Journal of Neuroscience*, 28(45), 11433–11434.

Biancani, S., McFarland, D.A., & Dahlander, L. (2014). The semiformal organization. *Organization Science*, 25(5), 1306–1324.

Bikard, M., Vakili, K., & Teodoridis, F. (2019). When collaboration bridges institutions: the impact of university-industry collaboration on academic productivity. *Organization Science*, 30(2), 426–445.

Bolukbasi, T., Chang, K.-W., Zou, J.Y., Saligrama, V., & Kalai, A.T. (2016). Man is to computer programmer as woman is to homemaker? Debiasing word embeddings. *Advances in Neural Information Processing Systems*, 4349–4357.

Bonacich, P. (1987). Power and centrality: a family of measures. *The American Journal of Sociology*, 92(5), 1170–1182.

Bourdieu, P. (1975). The specificity of the scientific field and the social conditions of the progress of reason. *Social Sciences Information. Information Sur Les Sciences Sociales*, 14(6), 19–47.

Breiger, R.L. (1974). The duality of persons and groups. *Social Forces*, 53(2), 181–190.

Burchard, J., McCormick, T., & Evans J.A. (2022). The geometry of social life: discrete networks and curved manifolds as social interaction and constraint. Working paper. December.

Burt, R.S. (1992). *Structural holes: the social structure of competition*. Harvard University Press.

Burt, R.S. (2004). Structural holes and good ideas. *American Journal of Sociology*, 110(2), 349–399.

Caliskan, A., Bryson, J.J., & Narayanan, A. (2017). Semantics derived automatically from language corpora contain human-like biases. *Science*, 356(6334), 183–186.

Callon, M. (1984). Some elements of a sociology of translation: domestication of the scallops and the fishermen of St Brieuc Bay. *Sociological Review*, 32(1_suppl), 196–233.

Callon, M., Rip, A., & Law, J. (1986). *Mapping the dynamics of science and technology: sociology of science in the real world*. Springer.

Camic, C. (2011). Bourdieu's cleft sociology of science. *Minerva*, 49(3), 275–293.

Campbell, D.T. (1979). Assessing the impact of planned social change. *Evaluation and Program Planning*, 2(1), 67–90.

Catalini, C., Lacetera, N., & Oettl, A. (2015). The incidence and role of negative citations in science. *Proceedings of the National Academy of Sciences*, 112(45), 13823–13826.

Chamberlain, B.P., Clough, J., & Deisenroth, M.P. (2017). Neural embeddings of graphs in hyperbolic space. In *arXiv [stat.ML]*. arXiv. arxiv.org/abs/1705.10359

Chami, I., Ying, R., Ré, C., & Leskovec, J. (2019). Hyperbolic graph convolutional neural networks. *Advances in Neural Information Processing Systems*, 32, 4869–4880.

Chu, J.S.G., & Evans, J.A. (2021). Slowed canonical progress in large fields of science. *Proceedings of the National Academy of Sciences of the United States of America*, 118(41), e2021636118.

Cohan, A., Ammar, W., van Zuylen, M., & Cady, F. (2019). Structural scaffolds for citation intent classification in scientific publications. In *arXiv [cs.CL]*. arXiv. arxiv.org/abs/1904.01608

Crane, D. (1972). *Invisible colleges: diffusion of knowledge in scientific communities*. University of Chicago Press.

Cui, H., Wu, L., & Evans, J.A. (2022). Aging scientists and slowed advance. In *arXiv [cs.DL]*. arXiv. arxiv.org/abs/2202.04044

Cui, P., Wang, X., Pei, J., & Zhu, W. (2019). A survey on network embedding. *IEEE Transactions on Knowledge and Data Engineering*, 31(5), 833–852.

Danchev, V., Rzhetsky, A., & Evans, J.A. (2019). Meta-research: centralized scientific communities are less likely to generate replicable results. *eLife*, 8, e43094.

D'Angelo, C.A., & van Eck, N.J. (2020). Collecting large-scale publication data at the level of individual researchers: a practical proposal for author name disambiguation. *Scientometrics*, 123(2), 883–907.

de Solla Price, D.J. (1961). *Science since Babylon*. Yale University Press.

de Solla Price, D.J. (1963). *Little science, big science*. Columbia University Press.

de Solla Price, D.J. (1965). Networks of scientific papers: the pattern of bibliographic references indicates the nature of the scientific research front. *Science*, 149(3683), 510–515.

D'Este, P., Llopis, O., Rentocchini, F., & Yegros, A. (2019). The relationship between interdisciplinarity and distinct modes of university-industry interaction. *Research Policy*, 48(9).

Dong, Y., Chawla, N.V., & Swami, A. (2017). metapath2vec: scalable representation learning for heterogeneous networks. *Proceedings of the 23rd ACM SIGKDD International Conference on Knowledge Discovery and Data Mining*, 135–144.

Etzkowitz, H., & Leydesdorff, L. (1997). *Universities and the global knowledge economy: a triple helix of university-industry relations*. papers.ssrn.com/abstract=3404823

Evans, J.A. (2010a). Industry induces academic science to know less about more. *American Journal of Sociology*, 116(2), 389–452.

Evans, J.A. (2010b). Industry collaboration, scientific sharing, and the dissemination of knowledge. *Social Studies of Science*, 40(5), 757–791.

Feld, S.L. (1981). The focused organization of social ties. *American Journal of Sociology*, 86(5), 1015–1035.

Firth, J.R. (1957). A synopsis of linguistic theory, 1930–1955. In *Studies in linguistic analysis*. Blackwell.

Fleming, L. (2001). Recombinant uncertainty in technological search. *Management Science*, 47(1), 117–132.

Fleming, L., & Sorenson, O. (2004). Science as a map in technological search. *Strategic Management Journal*, 25(89), 909–928.

Fortunato, S., Bergstrom, C.T., Börner, K., Evans, J.A., Helbing, D., Milojević, S., Petersen, A.M., Radicchi, F., Sinatra, R., Uzzi, B., Vespignani, A., Waltman, L., Wang, D., & Barabási, A.-L. (2018). Science of science. *Science*, 359(6379).

Foster, J.G., Rzhetsky, A., & Evans, J.A. (2015). Tradition and innovation in scientists' research strategies. *American Sociological Review*, 80(5), 875–908.

Foster, J.G., Shi, F., & Evans, J. (2021). Surprise! Measuring novelty as expectation violation. In *SocArXiv*. doi.org/10.31235/osf.io/2t46f

Freeman, L.C. (1977). A set of measures of centrality based on betweenness. *Sociometry*, *40*(1), 35–41.

Funk, R.J., & Owen-Smith, J. (2017). A dynamic network measure of technological change. *Management Science*, *63*(3), 791–817.

Fu, T.-Y., Lee, W.-C., & Lei, Z. (2017). Hin2vec: explore meta-paths in heterogeneous information networks for representation learning. *Proceedings of the 2017 ACM on Conference on Information and Knowledge Management*, 1797–1806.

Garfield, E. (1955). Citation indexes for science. *Science*, *122*(3159), 108–111.

Garfield, E. (1972). Citation analysis as a tool in journal evaluation. *Science*, *178*(4060), 471–479.

Garfield, E., Malin, M.V., & Small, H. (1978). Citation data as science indicators. In Y. Elkana, J. Lederberg, R.K. Merton, A. Thackray, & H. Zuckerman (Eds.), *Toward a metric of science: the advent of science indicator* (pp. 179–208). John Wiley & Sons.

Garg, N., Schiebinger, L., Jurafsky, D., & Zou, J. (2018). Word embeddings quantify 100 years of gender and ethnic stereotypes. *Proceedings of the National Academy of Sciences of the United States of America*, *115*(16), E3635–E3644.

Gerow, A., Hu, Y., Boyd-Graber, J., Blei, D.M., & Evans, J.A. (2018). Measuring discursive influence across scholarship. *Proceedings of the National Academy of Sciences of the United States of America*, *115*(13), 3308–3313.

Girvan, M., & Newman, M.E.J. (2002). Community structure in social and biological networks. *Proceedings of the National Academy of Sciences of the United States of America*, *99*(12), 7821–7826.

Goh, K.-I., Cusick, M.E., Valle, D., Childs, B., Vidal, M., & Barabási, A.-L. (2007). The human disease network. *Proceedings of the National Academy of Sciences of the United States of America*, *104*(21), 8685–8690.

Goodhart, C. (1975). Problems of monetary management: the UK experience in papers in monetary economics. *Monetary Economics*, *1*.

Graham, A.V., McLevey, J., Browne, P., & Crick, T. (2022). Structural diversity is a poor proxy for information diversity: evidence from 25 scientific fields. *Social Networks*, *70*, 55–63.

Granovetter, M.S. (1973). The strength of weak ties. *American Journal of Sociology*, *78*(6), 1360–1380.

Grover, A., & Leskovec, J. (2016). node2vec: scalable feature learning for networks. *KDD: Proceedings/International Conference on Knowledge Discovery and Data Mining. International Conference on Knowledge Discovery and Data Mining*, *2016*, 855–864.

Harris, Z.S. (1954). Distributional structure. *Word and World*, *10*(2–3), 146–162.

Heider, F. (1958). *The psychology of interpersonal relations*. John Wiley & Sons.

Hicks, D., Wouters, P., Waltman, L., de Rijcke, S., & Rafols, I. (2015). Bibliometrics: the Leiden Manifesto for research metrics. *Nature*, *520*(7548), 429–431.

Hochschild, A., & Machung, A. (2012). *The second shift: working families and the revolution at home*. Penguin.

Hofstra, B., Kulkarni, V.V., Galvez, S.M.-N., He, B., Jurafsky, D., & McFarland, D.A. (2020). The diversity–innovation paradox in science. *Proceedings of the National Academy of Sciences of the United States of America*, *117*(17), 9284–9291.

Holman, L., Stuart-Fox, D., & Hauser, C.E. (2018). The gender gap in science: how long until women are equally represented? *PLOS Biology*, *16*(4), e2004956.

Jacobs, J.A. (2014). *In defense of disciplines: interdisciplinarity and specialization in the research university*. University of Chicago Press.

Jacobs, J.A., & Frickel, S. (2009). Interdisciplinarity: a critical assessment. *Annual Review of Sociology*, *35*(1), 43–65.

Johnson, W.B., & Lindenstrauss, J. (1984). Extensions of Lipschitz mappings into a Hilbert space. *Contemporary Mathematics*, *26*(1), 189–206.

Jones, B.F., & Summers, L.H. (2020). *A calculation of the social returns to innovation* (No. 27863). National Bureau of Economic Research.

Jurgens, D., Kumar, S., Hoover, R., McFarland, D., & Jurafsky, D. (2018). Measuring the evolution of a scientific field through citation frames. *Transactions of the Association for Computational Linguistics*, *6*, 391–406.

Ke, Q., Ferrara, E., Radicchi, F., & Flammini, A. (2015). Defining and identifying Sleeping Beauties in science. *Proceedings of the National Academy of Sciences of the United States of America*, *112*(24), 7426–7431.

Kessler, M.M. (1963). Bibliographic coupling between scientific papers. *American Documentation*, *14*(1), 10–25.

Kim, J., & Diesner, J. (2015). Coauthorship networks: a directed network approach considering the order and number of coauthors. *Journal of the Association for Information Science and Technology*, *66*(12), 2685–2696.

Kim, J., & Owen-Smith, J. (2021). ORCID-linked labeled data for evaluating author name disambiguation at scale. *Scientometrics*, *126*(3), 2057–2083.

Kim, L., Smith, D.S., Hofstra, B., & McFarland, D.A. (2022). Gendered knowledge in fields and academic careers. *Research Policy*, *51*(1), 104411.

Kim, S.Y. (2022). To boost South Korea's basic science, look to values, not just budgets. *Nature*, *606*(7913), 229–229.

Klein, J.T. (1990). *Interdisciplinarity: history, theory, and practice*. Wayne State University Press.

Ko, J., Kook, Y., & Shin, K. (2022). Growth patterns and models of real-world hypergraphs. *Knowledge and Information Systems*, *64*(11), 2883–2920.

Koning, R., Samila, S., & Ferguson, J.-P. (2021). Who do we invent for? Patents by women focus more on women's health, but few women get to invent. *Science*, *372*(6548), 1345–1348.

Kozlowski, A.C., Taddy, M., & Evans, J.A. (2019). The geometry of culture: analyzing the meanings of class through word embeddings. *American Sociological Review*, *84*(5), 905–949.

Krioukov, D., Papadopoulos, F., Kitsak, M., Vahdat, A., & Boguñá, M. (2010). Hyperbolic geometry of complex networks. *Physical Review. E, Statistical, Nonlinear, and Soft Matter Physics*, *82*(3 Pt 2), 036106.

Kumar, S. (2015). Co-authorship networks: a review of the literature. *Aslib Journal of Information Management*, *67*(1), 55–73.

Larivière, V., Desrochers, N., Macaluso, B., Mongeon, P., Paul-Hus, A., & Sugimoto, C.R. (2016). Contributorship and division of labor in knowledge production. *Social Studies of Science*, *46*(3), 417–435.

Larivière, V., Gingras, Y., Sugimoto, C.R., & Tsou, A. (2015). Team size matters: collaboration and scientific impact since 1900. *Journal of the Association for Information Science and Technology*, *66*(7), 1323–1332.

Larivière, V., Ni, C., Gingras, Y., Cronin, B., & Sugimoto, C.R. (2013). Bibliometrics: global gender disparities in science. *Nature*, *504*(7479), 211–213.

Latour, B. (1987). *Science in action: how to follow scientists and engineers through society*. Harvard University Press.

Leahey, E. (2016). From sole investigator to team scientist: trends in the practice and study of research collaboration. *Annual Review of Sociology*, *42*(1), 81–100.

Leahey, E., Beckman, C.M., & Stanko, T.L. (2017). Prominent but less productive: the impact of interdisciplinarity on scientists' research. *Administrative Science Quarterly*, *62*(1), 105–139.

Levy, O., & Goldberg, Y. (2014). Neural word embedding as implicit matrix factorization. *Advances in Neural Information Processing Systems*, *27*.

Lewis, J.M., Ross, S., & Holden, T. (2012). The how and why of academic collaboration: disciplinary differences and policy implications. *Higher Education*, *64*(5), 693–708.

Lin, Y., Evans, J.A., & Wu, L. (2022). New directions in science emerge from disconnection and discord. *Journal of Informetrics*, *16*(1), 101234.

Linzhuo, L., Lingfei, W., & James, E. (2020). Social centralization and semantic collapse: hyperbolic embeddings of networks and text. *Poetics*, *78*, 101428.

Liu, M., Jaiswal, A., Bu, Y., Min, C., Yang, S., Liu, Z., Acuña, D., & Ding, Y. (2022). Team formation and team impact: the balance between team freshness and repeat collaboration. *Journal of Informetrics*, *16*(4), 101337.

Loder, N. (1999). Gender discrimination 'undermines science'. *Nature*, *402*(6760), 337–337.

Long, J.S. (1990). The origins of sex differences in science. *Social Forces*, *68*(4), 1297–1316.

Lucas, R.E. (1976). Econometric policy evaluation: a critique. *Carnegie-Rochester Conference Series on Public Policy*, *1*, 19–46.

Lu, C., Zhang, Y., Ahn, Y.-Y., Ding, Y., Zhang, C., & Ma, D. (2020). Co-contributorship network and division of labor in individual scientific collaborations. *Journal of the Association for Information Science and Technology*, *71*(10), 1162–1178.

Martin, T., Ball, B., Karrer, B., & Newman, M.E.J. (2013). Coauthorship and citation patterns in the Physical Review. *Physical Review. E, Statistical, Nonlinear, and Soft Matter Physics*, *88*(1), 012814.

Marx, M., & Fuegi, A. (2020). Reliance on science: worldwide front-page patent citations to scientific articles. *Strategic Management Journal*, *41*(9), 1572–1594.

McMahan, P., & Evans, J. (2018). Ambiguity and engagement. *American Journal of Sociology*, *124*(3), 860–912.

McMahan, P., & McFarland, D.A. (2021). Creative destruction: the structural consequences of scientific curation. *American Sociological Review*, *86*(2), 341–376.

Merton, R.K. (1973). *The sociology of science: theoretical and empirical investigations*. University of Chicago Press.

Miao, L., Murray, D., Jung, W.-S., Larivière, V., Sugimoto, C.R., & Ahn, Y.-Y. (2022). The latent structure of global scientific development. *Nature Human Behaviour*, *6*(9), 1206–1217.

Mikolov, T., Sutskever, I., Chen, K., Corrado, G.S., & Dean, J. (2013). Distributed representations of words and phrases and their compositionality. *Advances in Neural Information Processing Systems*, *26*.

Milgram, S. (1967). The small-world problem. *Psychology Today*, *2*(1), 60–67.

Milojević, S. (2010). Modes of collaboration in modern science: beyond power laws and preferential attachment. *Journal of the American Society for Information Science and Technology*, *61*(7), 1410–1423.

Milojević, S. (2015). Quantifying the cognitive extent of science. *Journal of Informetrics*, *9*(4), 962–973.

Mingers, J., & Leydesdorff, L. (2015). A review of theory and practice in scientometrics. *European Journal of Operational Research*, *246*(1), 1–19.

Mrvar, A., & Batagelj, V. (2016). Analysis and visualization of large networks with program package

Pajek. *Complex Adaptive Systems Modeling*, *4*(1), 1–8.

National Academy of Sciences (2005). *Facilitating interdisciplinary research*. National Academies Press.

Nelson, R.R., & Rosenberg, N. (1993). National innovation systems: a comparative analysis. In R.R. Nelson (Ed.), *Technical innovation and national systems* (Vol. 1, pp. 3–21). Oxford University Press.

Newman, M.E.J. (2001). The structure of scientific collaboration networks. *Proceedings of the National Academy of Sciences of the United States of America*, *98*(2), 404–409.

Newman, M.E.J., Barabási, A.-L., & Watts, D.J. (2011). *The structure and dynamics of networks*. Princeton University Press.

Nickel, M., & Kiela, D. (2017). Poincaré embeddings for learning hierarchical representations. *Advances in Neural Information Processing Systems*, *30*, 6338–6347.

Ozgür, A., Vu, T., Erkan, G., & Radev, D.R. (2008). Identifying gene-disease associations using centrality on a literature mined gene-interaction network. *Bioinformatics*, *24*(13), i277–i285.

Pachucki, M.A., & Breiger, R.L. (2010). Cultural holes: beyond relationality in social networks and culture. *Annual Review of Sociology*, *36*(1), 205–224.

Page, L., Brin, S., Motwani, R., & Winograd, T. (1999). *The PageRank citation ranking: bringing order to the Web*. ilpubs.stanford.edu:8090/422

Papadopoulos, F., Kitsak, M., Serrano, M.Á., Boguñá, M., & Krioukov, D. (2012). Popularity versus similarity in growing networks. *Nature*, *489*(7417), 537–540.

Park, M., Leahey, E., & Funk, R. (2021). The decline of disruptive science and technology. In *arXiv [cs.SI]*. arXiv. arxiv.org/abs/2106.11184

Peng, H., Ke, Q., Budak, C., Romero, D.M., & Ahn, Y.-Y. (2021). Neural embeddings of scholarly periodicals reveal complex disciplinary organizations. *Science Advances*, *7*(17).

Perozzi, B., Al-Rfou, R., & Skiena, S. (2014). DeepWalk: online learning of social representations. *Proceedings of the 20th ACM SIGKDD International Conference on Knowledge Discovery and Data Mining*, 701–710.

Porter, A.L., Cohen, A.S., David Roessner, J., & Perreault, M. (2007). Measuring researcher interdisciplinarity. *Scientometrics*, *72*(1), 117–147.

Powell, W.W., Koput, K.W., & Smith-Doerr, L. (1996). Interorganizational collaboration and the locus of innovation: networks of learning in biotechnology. *Administrative Science Quarterly*, *41*(1), 116.

Qiu, J., Dong, Y., Ma, H., Li, J., Wang, K., & Tang, J. (2018). Network embedding as matrix factorization: unifying DeepWalk, LINE, PTE, and node2vec. *Proceedings of the Eleventh ACM International Conference on Web Search and Data Mining*, 459–467.

Quine, W.V. (1951). Main trends in recent philosophy: two dogmas of empiricism. *Philosophical Review*, *60*(1), 20–43.

Radicchi, F., Fortunato, S., & Castellano, C. (2008). Universality of citation distributions: toward an objective measure of scientific impact. *Proceedings of the National Academy of Sciences of the United States of America*, *105*(45), 17268–17272.

Rawlings, C.M., McFarland, D.A., Dahlander, L., & Wang, D. (2015). Streams of thought: knowledge flows and intellectual cohesion in a multidisciplinary era. *Social Forces*, *93*(4), 1687–1722.

Ross, M.B., Glennon, B.M., Murciano-Goroff, R., Berkes, E.G., Weinberg, B.A., & Lane, J.I. (2022). Women are credited less in science than men. *Nature*, *608*(7921), 135–145.

Rzhetsky, A., Foster, J.G., Foster, I.T., & Evans, J.A. (2015). Choosing experiments to accelerate collective discovery. *Proceedings of the National Academy of Sciences of the United States of America*, *112*(47), 14569–14574.

Sattari, R., Bae, J., Berkes, E., & Weinberg, B.A. (2022). The ripple effects of funding on researchers and output. *Science Advances*, *8*(16), eabb7348.

Shi, F., & Evans, J. (2023). Surprising combinations of research contents and contexts are related to impact and emerge with scientific outsiders from distant disciplines. *Nature Communications*, *14*(1), 1641. Chicago

Shi, F., Foster, J.G., & Evans, J.A. (2015). Weaving the fabric of science: dynamic network models of science's unfolding structure. *Social Networks*, *43*, 73–85.

Shi, Y., & Rao, Y. (2010). China's research culture. *Science*, *329*(5996), 1128.

Shwed, U., & Bearman, P.S. (2010). The temporal structure of scientific consensus formation. *American Sociological Review*, *75*(6), 817–840.

Sinatra, R., Wang, D., Deville, P., Song, C., & Barabási, A.-L. (2016). Quantifying the evolution of individual scientific impact. *Science*, *354*(6312).

Small, H. (1973). Co-citation in the scientific literature: a new measure of the relationship between two documents. *Journal of the American Society for Information Science*, *24*(4), 265–269.

Sohn, E. (2021). How local industry R&D shapes academic research: evidence from the agricultural biotechnology revolution. *Organization Science*, *32*(3), 675–707.

Sourati, J., Belikov, A., & Evans, J. (2022). Data on how science is made can make science better. *Harvard Data Science Review*, *4*(2).

Sourati, J., & Evans, J. (2021). Accelerating science with human versus alien artificial intelligences. In *arXiv [cs.AI]*. arXiv. arxiv.org/abs/2104.05188

Stirling, A. (2007). A general framework for analysing diversity in science, technology and society. *Journal of the Royal Society Interface*, *4*(15), 707–719.

Tang, J., Qu, M., Wang, M., Zhang, M., Yan, J., & Mei, Q. (2015). LINE: large-scale information network embedding. *Proceedings of the 24th International Conference on World Wide Web*, 1067–1077.

Teplitskiy, M., Acuna, D., Elamrani-Raoult, A., Körding, K., & Evans, J. (2018). The sociology of scientific validity: how professional networks shape judgement in peer review. *Research Policy*, *47*(9), 1825–1841.

Teplitskiy, M., Lu, G., & Duede, E. (2017). Amplifying the impact of open access: Wikipedia and the diffusion of science. *Journal of the Association for Information Science and Technology*, *68*(9), 2116–2127.

Uzzi, B., Mukherjee, S., Stringer, M., & Jones, B. (2013). Atypical combinations and scientific impact. *Science*, *342*(6157), 468–472.

Van Raan, A.F.J. (2004). Sleeping beauties in science. *Scientometrics*, *59*(3), 467–472.

Vilhena, D., Foster, J., Rosvall, M., West, J., Evans, J., & Bergstrom, C. (2014). Finding cultural holes: how structure and culture diverge in networks of scholarly communication. *Sociological Science*, *1*, 221–238.

Walsh, J.P., Lee, Y.-N., & Tang, L. (2019). Pathogenic organization in science: division of labor and retractions. *Research Policy*, *48*(2), 444–461.

Wang, D., & Barabási, A.-L. (2021). *The science of science*. Cambridge University Press.

Wang, D., Song, C., & Barabási, A.-L. (2013). Quantifying long-term scientific impact. *Science*, *342*(6154), 127–132.

Wang, X., Bo, D., Shi, C., Fan, S., Ye, Y., & Yu, P.S. (2022). A survey on heterogeneous graph embedding: methods, techniques, applications and sources. *IEEE Transactions on Big Data*. par.nsf.gov/servlets/purl/10341014

Watts, D.J., & Strogatz, S.H. (1998). Collective dynamics of 'small-world' networks. *Nature*, *393*(6684), 440–442.

White, H.D. (2011). Scientific and scholarly networks. In J. Scott & P.J. Carrington (Eds.), *The Sage handbook of social network analysis* (1st ed., pp. 271–285). Sage.

Wu, L., Wang, D., & Evans, J.A. (2019). Large teams develop and small teams disrupt science and technology. *Nature*, *566*(7744), 378–382.

Wuchty, S., Jones, B.F., & Uzzi, B. (2007). The increasing dominance of teams in production of knowledge. *Science*, *316*(5827), 1036–1039.

Xie, Y., & Shauman, K. A. (1998). Sex differences in research productivity: new evidence about an old puzzle. *American Sociological Review*, *63*(6), 847–870.

Xu, F., Wu, L., & Evans, J. (2022). Flat teams drive scientific innovation. *Proceedings of the National Academy of Sciences of the United States of America*, *119*(23), e2200927119.

Yang, Y., Tian, T.Y., Woodruff, T.K., Jones, B.F., & Uzzi, B. (2022). Gender-diverse teams produce more novel and higher-impact scientific ideas. *Proceedings of the National Academy of Sciences of the United States of America*, *119*(36), e2200841119.

Yegros-Yegros, A., Rafols, I., & D'Este, P. (2015). Does interdisciplinary research lead to higher citation impact? The different effect of proximal and distal interdisciplinarity. *PLOS One*, *10*(8), e0135095.

Yin, Y., Gao, J., Jones, B.F., & Wang, D. (2021). Coevolution of policy and science during the pandemic. *Science*, *371*(6525), 128–130.

Zeng, A., Shen, Z., Zhou, J., Wu, J., Fan, Y., Wang, Y., & Stanley, H.E. (2017). The science of science: from the perspective of complex systems. *Physics Reports*, *714*, 1–73.

Zinovyeva, N., & Bagues, M.F. (2015). The role of connections in academic promotions. *American Economic Journal: Applied Economics*, *7*(2), 264–292.

17

Crime and Networks

Marie Ouellet and Logan Ledford

INTRODUCTION

Networks have been central to criminological thinking since its origins. Subcultural and social learning theories call attention to dense connections between deviant peers in promoting delinquency (Cloward & Ohlin, 1960; Sutherland, 1947). Social bond and strain theories emphasise the role of prosocial relationships in tethering individuals to conventional society (Hirschi, 1969). Contemporary social disorganisation and collective efficacy theories contend with the role of social cohesion in shaping local crime rates (Sampson et al., 1997; Sampson, 2006).

By formalising relational constructs, networks help shape a wide and diverse scholarship about the etiology of crime and delinquency. Criminologists use network methods to answer questions as broad as peer influence in adolescence and the diffusion of gun violence to human trafficking and drug exchanges on the dark web. The centrality of networks to a wide range of crime issues emphasises the need to take stock of recent advances.

This chapter charts the growth of network analysis within criminology, focusing on some of the earliest pieces to introduce network methods to the field and then details major innovations since these landmark studies. We identify key developments in the area of peer effects, criminal organisations, gangs, co-offending and neighbourhood networks. We conclude with a discussion of more recent applications of networks to the study of crime that are generating insight into prison structures, police misconduct and digital crimes.

TAKING STOCK OF NETWORKS WITHIN CRIMINOLOGY

Figure 17.1 plots the number of publications using network methods to study crime, as recorded in the Dimensions scholarly database.[1,2] The first decade of the 21st century shows slow growth in the number of studies using network methods to study crime, consistent with past assessments (Carrington, 2011). However, starting in the early 2010s this began to shift, with a notable increase in the number of studies, although this has tapered off slightly in the past few years. While using a single database provides conservative estimates of the volume of scholarly work, these results suggest network methods are starting to take hold in criminology.

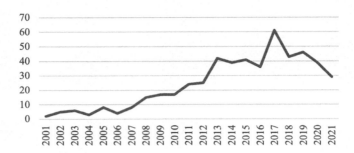

Figure 17.1 Publications using network data to study crime and delinquency

We also take stock of how these publications are connected by mapping the citation network, where the nodes represent manuscripts and the edges manuscripts that cite one another. We assess the structure of the citation network by using the Louvain community detection method (Blondel et al., 2008), which divided the network into eight research communities. The largest community consisted primarily of papers examining peer effects on delinquency. Two other large communities captured a wide array of papers exploring crime's social organisation. The fourth large community comprised papers examining spatial networks and gang networks. The fifth large community consisted mainly of papers examining co-offending networks. We draw from these communities to structure our review of key developments within the study of networks and crime.

PEER EFFECTS AND DELINQUENCY

More than 35 years ago, Krohn (1986) introduced network analysis to a wider criminology audience to advance the study of peer effects and delinquency. He identified network structure, including density and multiplexity, as key to whether individuals conform to the delinquency of their peers. Haynie (2001), one of the first to test this proposition, examined whether the structure of friendship networks corresponded with adolescent delinquency. Her analysis of nearly 13,000 adolescents across 120 schools suggested Krohn's (1986) predictions were robust. Not only did friends' self-reported delinquency impact respondents' delinquency, but the structure of friendship networks moderated this link.

Since these landmark studies, the application of network methods to study peer effects has taken off within criminology. Indeed, peer effects are core to network thinking, examining how an individual's social context impacts attitudes, beliefs and behaviours. Within criminology, the study of peer effects has primarily relied on school-based surveys, which are used to ascertain student friendship networks, and what we focus on here. For instance, McGloin and Shermer (2009) show that individuals who are central to their deviant friendship network are more likely to engage in delinquency. Moody et al. (2011) find that instability in an individual's centrality within their friendship network increases status-seeking behaviours, including substance use. Young et al. (2011) demonstrate that denser friendship networks increase individuals' ability to assess friends' delinquency levels.

Network studies also find variation in susceptibility to deviant peers. Burk et al. (2007) show that peer effects are greatest when friendships are reciprocated, and among friends who spend more time with one another (see Haynie & Osgood, 2005). Others show that the reach of peers extends beyond immediate social circles. For instance, Payne and Cornwell (2007) find that 'friends of friends' shape delinquency, and Bond and Bushman (2017) show 'friends of friends of friends of friends' impact violence. Peer effects tend to be more pronounced for females than males in shaping delinquency (Haynie et al., 2014; McGloin & Shermer, 2009; McMillan et al., 2018). Peer effects decline with age, with older youth less likely to adjust their delinquent behaviours to their friends (Ragan, 2020). Peer effects are also stronger for individuals low in impulsivity; youth who are more likely to seek immediate rewards are less influenced by their friends (McGloin & Stickle, 2011; Thomas & McGloin, 2013).

An impressive body of work using network methods to study peer effects has accumulated over the more than 35 years since Krohn (1986) lauded its benefits to criminologists.[3] However, a key turning point for studies of peer effects occurred only in the past decade: the development of dynamic network models. These advances enabled scholars to shed light on a key question occupying criminologists for more than half a century: whether peer effects could be explained by individual tendencies to select into delinquent groups (Gottfredson & Hirschi, 1990). From this perspective, delinquency is not a consequence of deviant peers (influence) but rather deviant peers are a consequence of delinquency (selection).

The development of dynamic network models proved to be a key innovation for teasing out whether peer effects should be rejected in favour of selection-based mechanisms by simultaneously modelling selection effects and peer effects (Snijders et al., 2010). Indeed, the rapid adoption of dynamic network models permitted a meta-analysis. Gallupe et al.'s (2019) findings largely put to rest a core criminological debate, showing 'people are both influenced by the offending of their peers and select into friendships based on similarity in offenders' (p. 329). This work highlights that selection and influence effects are complementary rather than distinct processes that should be pitted against one another (Thornberry, 1987).

SOCIAL ORGANISATION OF CRIME

Networks also took root among criminologists studying the social organisation of crime. A key driver of this tradition was Morselli (2005, 2009), who challenged the common stereotype of organised crime as a hierarchical structure. In applying network methods, he showed that organised crime tended to be built around more flexible and decentralised structures (Bouchard & Morselli, 2014; Campana, 2016). Indeed, more often, the network position of actors drove success and key roles within an organisation (Morselli & Tremblay, 2004), rather than official designations as 'leaders' within a group (Campana, 2016; Morselli et al., 2017).

Morselli showed that the structural features of crime mattered also for the fate of the group. Inspired by the work of Baker and Faulkner (1993) on price fixing-conspiracies, Morselli and colleagues (2007) showed how network structure could expose or protect criminal groups from risk. Termed the 'security–efficiency trade-off', they argued that criminal groups must contend with the decision to organise into more secure and decentralised structures to elude detection or more efficient and centralised structures to mobilise resources. They showed profit-oriented groups adopted efficient structures to gain a competitive edge, whereas ideological-oriented groups assumed secure structures to evade enforcement.

The security–efficiency trade-off prompted a host of work on illicit organisations, including their vulnerability to disruption (Duijn et al. 2014; Duxbury & Haynie, 2019; Malm & Bichler, 2011), the formation of ties between illicit actors (Bright et al., 2019) and adaptations to law enforcement pressure (Ouellet et al., 2017). Innovatively, Duxbury and Haynie (2019) used agent-based models to test whether network structure impacted criminal organisations' ability to recover from disruption. They found secure network structures were more resilient to attacks and quicker to recover following the removal of central actors. However, efficient networks were better equipped to restore the number of network components and the size of the largest component, or features more closely associated with 'hierarchy and constant offending' (p. 330).

Another closely related body of work shows how illicit networks transform across shifting legal contexts. Smith (2019) drew from detailed archival records spanning more than three decades to examine organised crime networks in Chicago before and after the prohibition of alcohol. She found that the ban of alcohol transformed organised crime networks, with higher profits leading the network to evolve into a more hierarchical structure, organised around central actors. This growth exacerbated social inequalities and further embedded corrupt actors. Under prohibition, women were sidelined to the network's periphery (Smith, 2019), whereas political actors maintained central positions (Joseph & Smith, 2021).

Studies examining the social organisation of crime from a network perspective pull from a variety of sources to uncover the structural features of illicit groups, including court documents, law enforcement records, biographies and social media data. The detailed data has permitted studies to move beyond descriptive accounts detailing the decentralised and opportunistic structure of illicit organisations to dynamic studies exploring the mechanisms that allow these organisations to evolve (e.g., Bright et al., 2019). However, much of what we know about the social organisation of crime hinges on a few case studies, and comparative case studies or representative samples tend to be rare. Looking across the social organisation of crime, triangulating data sources, could be beneficial for extending insight into crime's organisation.

GANGS, COHESION AND SUBGROUPS

The idea of treating gangs and gang violence as a network phenomenon has become increasingly popular over the past decade, shifting networks to the forefront of gang explanations and approaches to curb gang violence.

The use of network methods to map gang conflict can be traced back to the work of Kennedy et al. (1997). Responding to a gang violence problem in Boston, they used law enforcement data to map gangs' conflict networks – their rivalries to other gangs – and then identified the most central gangs within this network as targets for intervention. Tita and colleagues (2003) extended the use of network interventions to gangs in Los Angeles, demonstrating how gangs' conflict networks provided a promising approach for reducing gang violence. In Chicago, Papachristos (2009) mapped the network structure of gang violence, where the nodes were gangs and the edges instances of lethal violence between gangs. He showed that the gang violence network exhibited a stable structure over time, and that prior conflict between gangs increased the likelihood of retaliation (also see Lewis & Papachristos, 2020; Niezink & Campana, 2022; Papachristos et al., 2013). The use of network methods to map gang conflict has also proved to have broader implications for better focusing law enforcement interventions (Bichler et al., 2019), and mitigating the effects of gang violence on non-gang members (Wood & Papachristos, 2019).

One key challenge for gang scholars has been to incorporate a broader set of networks between gangs, including the alliances and allegiances that underpin many conflicts. Descormiers and Morselli (2011) represent one of the first studies to map both the network of gang alliances and rivalries among Montreal-based gangs. They find that rivalries and alliances are not mutually exclusive categories; rather gangs were often embedded in conflicts with the very same gangs they considered allies. Later work has shown these alliances play important roles within organised crime groups, bridging organisations and providing access to opportunities beyond group boundaries (Calderoni et al., 2017; Coutinho et al., 2020; Malm et al., 2011).

Studies of gang networks also test the role of cohesion in structuring a group's delinquency. Klein and Crawford (1967) pioneered the application of network methods to test whether cohesion impacted a group's delinquency levels. Mapping the interactions between 576 gang members across four gang clusters, they found the most cohesive gangs also had the highest levels of delinquency. Hughes (2013) also examined variation in delinquency and cohesion using information from 248 gang members in Chicago from the early 1960s. Measuring gang cohesion as the mean number of friends each member had within the gang, she found that cohesion negatively predicted a group's violence but not their overall delinquency levels.

Cohesion has long been central to the study of criminal groups; however, a key challenge for researchers aiming to uncover the role of cohesion, and other elements of group structure on collective outcomes, is that rarely do researchers have access to a roster of all group members or their interactions. Knowledge of active group members is seldom recorded and may even be unknown among its membership (Bouchard & Konarski, 2014; Hashimi & Bouchard, 2017; Ouellet & Bouchard, 2018), a problem that increases with group size. Early work on gang cohesion highlights the extensive efforts required to collect network data, drawing from multi-year projects with researchers embedded in gang interactions.

Recently, scholars have turned to network methods as a promising avenue to delineate the boundaries of criminal groups. Community detection methods help uncover pockets of densely connected actors within networks. Kreager et al. (2011) used community detection methods to delineate friendship groups embedded in a school network, and then tested how groups' or communities' network structure, including their cohesion, shaped their delinquency. Similarly, Ouellet and colleagues (2019a) applied community detection methods to identify criminal groups embedded in law enforcement data, and showed how the groups' cohesion impacted their survival. Notably, they found that gang members with the same affiliation tended to be sorted into the same communities. These studies highlight ways forward; however, more work to validate communities using network methods with ground truth is needed.

NEIGHBOURHOOD NETWORKS

In many ways network thinking permeates the study of space and place within criminology. Spatial models of crime routinely incorporate information about crime in adjacent and nearby areas. Network methods recognise the rich tradition of treating neighbourhoods as dependent entities, but extends the focus to social proximity as the source of dependence in addition to spatial proximity. The closer coupling of networks with spatial criminology has led to transformative research in this area, recasting how we see neighbourhoods within their broader social networks.

Browning and colleagues introduced *eco-networks* as a measure to evaluate whether clustering in neighbourhood residential networks impacts local crime rates. Eco-networks are measured by first specifying a bipartite network where the two sets of nodes are the residents and the locations residents visit in their daily routines (grocery stores, workplaces, child care). Eco-network intensity is then assessed as the extent to which residents' shared activity locations overlap. Neighbourhoods with higher eco-network intensity experience higher rates of youth delinquency, substance use (Browning et al., 2015), and overall rates of violent and property crimes (Browning et al., 2017b; Browning et al., 2017a).

Another line of neighbourhood network research applies simulation approaches to model residents' social ties. Hipp and colleagues (2013) simulated social ties as a function of the spatial distance of households. Closer households are presumed to be more likely to have formed ties than those farther apart. From the simulated network, they then measured the structural features of each neighbourhood at the block level, including its mean degree, density and the extent to which residential ties extend beyond the neighbourhood boundaries. Neighbourhoods with a higher mean degree and whose residential ties did not extend beyond the neighbourhood boundaries had lower violent and property crime levels. In contrast, neighbourhoods with greater population density were associated with higher violent and property crime.

Papachristos and colleagues extend the scope of spatial network studies, assessing how co-offending partnerships that span neighbourhood boundaries shape crime diffusion. In their neighbourhood co-offending networks, nodes are neighbourhoods and edges the extent to which offenders who reside in different neighbourhoods co-offend (see Schaefer, 2012). Bastomski and colleagues (2017) find that many of Chicago's neighbourhoods are connected through crime and that neighbourhoods highly embedded in the co-offending network have higher homicide rates. Papachristos and Bastomski (2018) demonstrate how neighbourhood homicide rates are better explained by neighbourhoods' *socially* adjacent neighbours – neighbourhoods connected through co-offending ties – than their *spatially* adjacent neighbours.

Other work focuses on how residential travel between neighbourhoods shape crime rates. Graif and colleagues (2017; 2021) reconstructed the Chicago inter-neighbourhood commuting network by linking neighbourhoods through residents' daily commutes. The commuting network is drawn from survey data and then used to establish the extent to which neighbourhoods are the recipient of commuting ties from disadvantaged areas. Neighbourhoods with greater exposure to disadvantaged ties within their everyday commuting networks had higher local crime rates; although more recent work has shown this varies across contexts and crimes (Kelling et al., 2021). Others have shown that where an offender commits their crime is dependent on the larger pattern of visitor flows, mirroring larger neighbourhood mobility patterns (see Boivin & D'Elia, 2017; Song et al., 2019).

Geo-coded Twitter data offers another measure of neighbourhood networks and their relationship with crime rates. Levy et al. (2020) show that the patterns with which residents visit other neighbourhoods impact city homicide rates. Across 37 of the largest US cities they assess the extent to which residents of a neighbourhood travel to other neighbourhoods with high levels of disadvantage and receive residents from neighbourhoods with low levels of disadvantage. They find the everyday travel routines of residents to and from disadvantaged areas within a city help explain homicide rates. Sampson and Levy (2020) extend this analysis to 50 of the largest US cities and calculate a city's equitable mobility score, as the 'extent to which residents of each neighborhood in a city travel to all other neighborhoods in that city equally' (p. 80), finding that cities where residents restrict their travel patterns to select neighbourhoods tend to have higher homicide rates.

Like many areas in criminology, digital technologies are transforming the study of crime and providing promising avenues to study mobility patterns. On the one hand, the use of these impressive datasets highlights how criminal mobility creates social channels that shape how crime moves within a city. On the other, these studies often aggregate this granular data to the neighbourhood or city level. One area ripe for exploring is integrating the individual back into these places to better understand the people responsible for creating and sustaining these larger network structures that shape crime rates.

CO-OFFENDING NETWORKS

The study of co-offending cross-cuts much of the research investigating crime and networks. Co-offending networks are typically extracted from police records where individuals are linked through co-participation in the same event, such as a field report or arrest. The ability to extract large networks of co-offenders from arrest records has made it a versatile data source to better understand a variety of crime phenomena.

One of the first scholars to see the potential of police records was Sarnecki's (1990, 2001) examination of a youth co-offending network in Sweden. He showed how seemingly independent arrest events could be connected together through a series of shared co-offences. This finding extended much of the earlier insight that crime is often committed in the company of others (Shaw & McKay, 1942). Since Sarnecki's seminal work, studies of co-offending networks have examined the formation of co-offending ties, their stability and consequences for criminal behaviour.

One body of research on co-offending networks identifies the features of suitable co-offending partners (Campana, 2016; McCuish et al., 2015; Smith & Papachristos, 2016), including what leads individuals to return to the same co-offending partners in future crimes (Charette & Papachristos, 2017; McGloin et al., 2008). McCuish et al. (2015) find that individuals recruited to be a partner for a homicide event were selected from the core gang membership, but turned to non-gang members for less serious crimes, suggesting that when the stakes are higher, fellow gang members provide more trustworthy partners. Smith and Papachristos (2016) show co-offending partnerships are more likely to form between trusted ties, including individuals with mutual ties in common, and multiplex relationships. Charette and Papachristos (2017) find prior history of offending together and belonging to the same gang increased the likelihood of re-activating a co-offending tie. Notably, individuals who have a co-offending partner in common are more likely to maintain their co-offending partnership, particularly if that partner commits similar offences. Conversely, victimisation severed co-offending ties, with peers' violent victimisations decreasing the odds of maintaining a co-offending partnership.

Co-offending networks also help understand individual offending pathways and victimisation risk. For instance, McGloin and Piquero (2010) find that being embedded in non-redundant co-offending networks, where not all your associates are connected, increases offending versatility. Lantz and Ruback (2017) show how co-offending networks introduce affiliates to crime opportunities. They find that when repeat victimisations are committed by someone other than the original perpetrator, it often involves someone within their co-offending network. A series of papers using co-offending data find victimisation risk is highest among individuals directly or indirectly connected to other victims (Green et al., 2017; Papachristos et al., 2012; Papachristos & Wildeman, 2012; Papachristos et al., 2015), to gang members (Papachristos et al., 2015) and, in particular, gang members with access to firearms (Roberto et al., 2018).

The most recent extension to studies of co-offending networks has been attending to the dynamic nature of co-offending data. Niezink and Campana (2022) demonstrate how relational event models can be used to tease out the longitudinal order of co-offending events. Using data on organised-crime-related events recorded by a UK police agency, they find a history of co-offending increased the likelihood of 'future victimization at the hands of the co-offenders by slightly more than 56 times' (p. 14). Further, females and individuals who belong to the same organised crime group experienced higher victimisation risks, as well as those who had perpetrated violent crimes against others in the past.

Together, these studies highlight the important role of co-offending data to tap into a broad range of issues. Police data permits analyses of large samples of individuals; however, it imposes artificial boundaries on networks, only accounting for individuals who were detected and recorded as coming in contact with the police (see Campana & Varese, 2022). Further, analyses of co-offending networks tend to rely on one-mode projections of bipartite networks (offender by event matrices). However, collapsing the data in this way loses information about the event and may result in biased measures. Recent work has aimed to simultaneously capture the dependence of individuals and events jointly (Nieto et al., 2022), which could shed insight into the links between individuals and the crime events in which they participate.

NEW DIRECTIONS

This section highlights recent applications of network methods that draw from unique sources and apply innovative methods to tap into broader issues within the criminal justice system and illicit marketplaces.

Prison Networks

Social ties have long been central to explanations of the social order of prisons; however, only recently have network methods been used to map prisons' informal systems.

Leading much of this work is Kreager and colleagues who designed a network survey to reconstruct relationships between inmates. Asking inmates who they 'get along with', 'trust' and view as 'powerful or influential', they explored the structure of prison networks across a series of studies. They show the most influential and powerful inmates are those with longer tenure on the unit, and who are more central to the inmate social structure, brokering between groups (Kreager et al., 2017; Kreager et al., 2021; Schaefer et al., 2017; Young & Haynie, 2020). Further, who inmates get along with predicts who they trust and view as more powerful and influential within the prison (Kreagar et al., 2021; Young & Haynie, 2020). Lastly, they observe important differences across sexes and contexts. For example, males did not describe any relationships as negative; however, negative ties structured much of females' interactions in prison, including with more powerful and influential inmates (Kreager et al., 2021; also see Sentse et al., 2021, for differences in international contexts).

Using longitudinal network methods, Schaefer and Kreager (2020) examined the get along and mentor relationships to identify whether processes that lead to tie formation change or remain stable across 58 members of a prison-based therapeutic community. Results show that preference for tie formation changed across inmates' tenure in prison. Early in one's stay, propinquity (cell mate) and entrainment (mentor and prior acquaintance) played a role in relationship formation; however, later on in one's tenure, the strength of these processes decreased. Similarly, racial homophily was strongest at unit entry, with racial processes dissolving by the end of their stay.

Other work focuses on how incarceration shifts the networks of formerly imprisoned individuals. Volker et al. (2016) compared inmate social ties before and after release from prison in the Netherlands. Focusing on core discussion partners, they find that longer incarceration periods increase the likelihood of relationship dissolution. Rengifo and DeWitt (2019), comparing the networks of individuals who had and had not been incarcerated, find that a history of incarceration is associated with weaker ties, characterised by shorter duration and less multiplexity.

Police Networks

The increasing attention being called to police violence has led network scholars to investigate the role of police networks in shaping deviance. Much like the use of police records to reconstruct co-offending networks, this work primarily relies on complaint records housed by law enforcement agencies to map officers' misconduct networks. Here, misconduct networks capture officers who are linked as co-complainants within the same misconduct report.

Mapping the networks of police misconduct within the Chicago Police Department, Wood and colleagues (2019) show that problematic officers are highly connected. Extending this work, Jain and colleagues (2002) use machine-learning techniques to identify communities of problematic officers within the misconduct network. They detect groups of officers who are jointly involved in misconduct with one another, and find these groups disproportionately accounted for the department's use of force complaints, officer-involved shootings and city settlements. Others have shown that misconduct networks have implications for an officer's future behaviours. Zhao and Papachristos (2020) show that officers positioned as brokers within misconduct networks are more likely to discharge their firearms, and Ouellet et al. (2019b) find officers with greater exposure to peers who use force are more likely to engage in these same behaviours (see Quispe-Torreblanca & Stewart, 2019).

More recently, studies of police networks show the importance of mapping officer networks beyond their deviant ties. Simpson and Kirk (2021) draw from 911 call data to map officers' networks based on co-responses to the same calls. Using this data, they find null peer effects for misconduct; officers with greater exposure to deviant peers did not have higher rates of future misconduct. Ouellet et al. (2020) recently relied on network surveys to map friendship and mentorship networks within departments, offering a promising way to extend discussions of organisational deviance.

Digital Networks

As crime moves into the digital realm, network methods have proved a useful way to generate insight into online crimes. Studies applying network methods to online crimes have primarily relied on digital trace data collected from forums and illicit marketplaces (Décary-Hétu et al., 2012), law enforcement records, including seized harddrives (Dupont, 2012) and wiretaps (Leukfeldt et al., 2017).

Online marketplaces hosted on the clear and dark web provide centralised platforms for vendors and clients to exchange illicit products relatively anonymously. Because product listings and transactions are often archived on these websites, they provide access to near population-level data on illicit exchanges. These data can be leveraged to reconstruct transaction networks of illicit markets, comprising exchanges between buyers and sellers. Reconstructing the transaction network of one online drug market, Duxbury and Haynie (2018a) found buyers frequently returned to the same vendors, and this loyalty was responsible for creating distinct communities of buyers and vendors in the network. Further, when buyers made more than one purchase, they tended to return to the same seller – even when other sellers offered a cheaper alternative. Similar to an on-the-ground drug trafficking operation, trust plays an instrumental role in actor decision-making (Duxbury & Haynie, 2018b; Norbutas, 2018; Norbutas et al., 2020). Indeed, longitudinal examinations of transaction networks on illicit online marketplaces have shown network processes, including closure, shape prices (Duxbury & Haynie, 2021).

Digital trace data has also been used to inform law enforcement interdictions. Duxbury and Haynie (2018b) simulated best practices for fragmenting online trafficking networks, finding highly active portions of the network are relatively difficult to disrupt, though removing vendors that span structural holes in the network results in the largest amount of network damage to the online market. This largely parallels Duxbury and Haynie's (2019) recommendation for offline networks as well, where simply selecting the most connected or active individuals may not cause a major disruption in the network, but purposefully removing vendors that occupy positions critical to the flow of information and resources creates more network disruption.

CONCLUSION

Although criminology was slower to seize network methods than other fields (Carrington, 2011; Papachristos, 2011), the past decade has experienced rapid advances and seen its application to understand a wide range of criminal phenomena. In criminology, applications of network methods have progressed from descriptive analyses to sophisticated modelling of crime networks. Scholars are repurposing traditional administrative records to extract relational data and drawing from computational social science techniques to harness archived network data, providing unprecedented insight into the structures of crime.

Our review reveals that studies approaching crime from a network perspective have led to major advances; however, we also want to highlight a key area for moving forward. Many of the studies detailed in this review reconstruct networks from large data sources, including sociometric data from surveys, law enforcement reports and digital records. However, aside from some notable exceptions, there is a paucity of qualitative data to understand the meaning and contextual information behind these relationships. A call to incorporating qualitative interviews and contextual data into criminology network studies is not novel (see Campana & Varese, 2022). However, with advance of large digital datasets, qualitative data can contextualise and provide narratives to the relationships that are being uncovered. In turn, these observations can help underpin the mechanisms that are driving relationships and lead to new theoretical insights. Although interviews may be limited when individuals are not aware of the entire criminal network, one area where they may be particularly useful, is returning to ego-network analysis (see Perry et al., this volume). Combining ego-network research with interview data presents a promising avenue to complement the growth in digital data and contextualise findings extracted from administrative records.

Notes

1. Dimensions is accessible at: www.dimensions.ai/
2. Search performed on 1 December 2022 using the search terms: ('network analysis' OR 'network method') AND (crime OR delinquency) from 2001 to 2022 within the criminology and sociology research fields. The search produced 2,803 publications containing our key word. 510 papers were retained, explicitly using network data and methods to study crime and delinquency.
3. See Carrington (2011) for a more extensive treatment of peer effects.

REFERENCES

Baker, W.E., & Faulkner, R.R. (1993). The social organization of conspiracy: illegal networks in the heavy electrical equipment industry. *American Sociological Review*, 58(6), 837–860.

Bastomski, S., Brazil, N., & Papachristos, A.V. (2017). Neighborhood co-offending networks, structural embeddedness, and violent crime in Chicago. *Social Networks*, 51, 23–39.

Bichler, G., Norris, A., Dmello, J.R., & Randle, J. (2019). The impact of civil gang injunctions on networked violence between the bloods and the crips. *Crime and Delinquency*, 65(7), 875–915.

Blondel, V.D., Guillaume, J.-L., Lambiotte, R., & Lefebvre, E. (2008). Fast unfolding of communities in large networks. *Journal of Statistical Mechanics*, P10008.

Boivin, R., & D'Elia, M. (2017). A network of neighborhoods: predicting crime trips in a large Canadian city. *Journal of Research in Crime and Delinquency*, 54(6), 824–846.

Bond, R.M., & Bushman, B.J. (2017). The contagious spread of violence among US adolescents through social networks. *American Journal of Public Health*, *107*(2), 288–294.

Bouchard, M., & Morselli, C. (2014). Opportunistic structures of organized crime. In L. Paoli (Ed.), *The Oxford handbook of organized crime* (pp. 288–302). Oxford University Press.

Bouchard, M., & Konarski, R. (2014). Assessing the core membership of a youth gang from its co-offending network. In C. Morselli (Ed.), *Crime and networks* (pp. 81–96). Routledge.

Bright, D., Koskinen, J., & Malm, A. (2019). Illicit network dynamics: the formation and evolution of a drug trafficking network. *Journal of Quantitative Criminology*, *35*(2), 237–258.

Browning, C.R., Calder, C.A., Boettner, B., & Smith, A. (2017a). Ecological networks and urban crime: the structure of shared routine activity locations and neighborhood-level informal control capacity. *Criminology*, *55*(4), 754–778.

Browning, C.R., Calder, C.A., Soller, B., Jackson, A.L., & Dirlam, J. (2017b). Ecological networks and neighborhood social organization. *American Journal of Sociology*, *122*(6), 1939–1988.

Browning, C.R., Soller, B., & Jackson, A.L. (2015). Neighborhoods and adolescent health-risk behavior: An ecological network approach. *Social Science and Medicine*, *125*, 163–172.

Burk, W.J., Steglich, C.E., & Snijders, T.A. (2007). Beyond dyadic interdependence: actor-oriented models for co-evolving social networks and individual behaviors. *International Journal of Behavioral Development*, *31*(4), 397–404.

Calderoni, F., Brunetto, D., & Piccardi, C. (2017). Communities in criminal networks: a case study. *Social Networks*, *48*, 116–125.

Campana, P. (2016). The structure of human trafficking: lifting the bonnet on a Nigerian transnational network. *British Journal of Criminology*, *56*(1), 68–86.

Campana, P., & Varese, F. (2022). Studying organized crime networks: data sources, boundaries and the limits of structural measures. *Social Networks*, *69*, 149–159.

Carrington, P.J. (2011). Crime and social network analysis. In J. Scott & P.J. Carrington (Eds.), *The Sage handbook of social network analysis* (pp. 236–255). Sage.

Charette, Y., & Papachristos, A.V. (2017). The network dynamics of co-offending careers. *Social Networks*, *51*, 3–13.

Cloward, R.A., & Ohlin, L.E. (1960). *Delinquency and opportunity: a theory of delinquent gangs*. Free Press.

Coutinho, J.A., Diviák, T., Bright, D., & Koskinen, J. (2020). Multilevel determinants of collaboration between organized criminal groups. *Social Networks*, *63*, 56–69.

Décary-Hétu, D., Morselli, C., & Leman-Langlois, S. (2012). Welcome to the scene: a study of social organization and recognition among warez hackers. *Journal of Research in Crime and Delinquency*, *49*(3), 359–382.

Descormiers, K., & Morselli, C. (2011). Alliances, conflicts, and contradictions in Montreal's street gang landscape, *International Criminal Justice Review*, *21*(3), 297–314.

Duijn, P.A., Kashirin, V., & Sloot, P.M. (2014). The relative ineffectiveness of criminal network disruption. *Scientific Reports*, *4*(1), 1–15.

Dupont, B. (2012). Skills and trust: a tour inside the hard drives of computer hackers. SSRN 2154952

Duxbury, S.W., & Haynie, D.L. (2018a). The network structure of opioid distribution on a darknet cryptomarket. *Journal of Quantitative Criminology*, *34*(4), 921–941.

Duxbury, S.W., & Haynie, D.L. (2018b). Building them up, breaking them down: topology, vendor selection patterns, and a digital drug market's robustness to disruption. *Social Networks*, *52*, 238–250.

Duxbury, S.W., & Haynie, D.L. (2019). Criminal network security: an agent-based approach to evaluating network resilience. *Criminology*, *57*(2), 314–342.

Duxbury, S.W., & Haynie, D.L. (2021). Network embeddedness in illegal online markets: endogenous sources of prices and profit in anonymous criminal drug trade. *Socio-Economic Review*, 1–26.

Gallupe, O., McLevey, J., & Brown, S. (2019). Selection and influence: a meta-analysis of the association between peer and personal offending. *Journal of Quantitative Criminology*, *35*(2), 313–335.

Gottfredson, M.R., & Hirschi, T. (1990). *A general theory of crime*. Stanford University Press.

Graif, C., Freelin, B.N., Kuo, Y.-H., Wang, H., Li, Z., & Kifer, D. (2021). Network spillovers and neighborhood crime: a computational statistics analysis of employment-based networks of neighborhoods. *Justice Quarterly*, *38*(2), 344–374.

Graif, C., Lungeanu, A., & Yetter, A.M. (2017). Neighborhood isolation in Chicago: violent crime effects on structural isolation and homophily in inter-neighborhood commuting networks. *Social Networks*, *51*, 40–59.

Green, B., Horel, T., & Papachristos, A.V. (2017). Modeling contagion through social networks to explain and predict gunshot violence in Chicago, 2006 to 2014, *JAMA Internal Medicine*, *177*(3), 326–333.

Hashimi, S., & Bouchard, M. (2017). On to the next one? Using social network data to inform police target prioritization, *Policing: An International Journal of Police Strategies and Management*, *40*(4), 768–782.

Haynie, D.L. (2001). Delinquent peers revisited: does network structure matter? *American Journal of Sociology*, 106(4), 1013–1057.

Haynie, D.L., Doogan, N.J., & Soller, B. (2014). Gender, friendship networks, and delinquency: a dynamic network approach, *Criminology*, 52(4), 688–722.

Haynie, D.L., & Osgood, D.W. (2005). Reconsidering peers and delinquency: how do peers matter? *Social Forces*, 84(2), 1109–1130.

Hipp, J.R., Butts, C.T., Acton, R., Nagle, N.N., & Boessen, A. (2013). Extrapolative simulation of neighborhood networks based on population spatial distribution: do they predict crime? *Social Networks*, 35(4), 614–625.

Hirschi, T. (1969). *Causes of delinquency*. University California Press.

Hughes, L.A. (2013). Group cohesiveness, gang member prestige, and delinquency and violence in Chicago, 1959–1962. *Criminology*, 51(4), 795–832.

Jain, A., Sinclair, R., & Papachristos, A.V. (2022). Identifying misconduct-committing officer crews in the Chicago police department. *PLOS One*, 17(5): e0267217.

Joseph, J., & Smith, C.M. (2021). The ties that bribe: corruption's embeddedness in Chicago organized crime. *Criminology*, 59(4), 671–703.

Kelling, C., Graif, C., Korkmaz, G., & Haran, M. (2021). Modeling the social and spatial proximity of crime: domestic and sexual violence across neighborhoods. *Journal of Quantitative Criminology*, 37(2), 481–516.

Kennedy, D.M., Braga, A.A., & Piehl, A. (1997). Mapping gangs and gang violence in Boston. In D. Weisburd & T. McEwan (Eds.), *Crime mapping and crime prevention* (pp. 219–262). Justice Press.

Klein, M.W., & Crawford, L.Y. (1967). Groups, gangs, and cohesiveness. *Journal of Research in Crime and Delinquency*, 4(1), 63–75.

Kreager, D.A., Rulison, K., & Moody, J. (2011). Delinquency and the structure of adolescent peer groups. *Criminology*, 49(1), 95–127.

Kreager, D.A., Young, J.T., Haynie, D.L., Bouchard, M., Schaefer, D.R., & Zajac, G. (2017). Where 'old heads' prevail: inmate hierarchy in a men's prison unit. *American Sociological Review*, 82(4), 685–718.

Kreager, D.A., Young, J.T., Haynie, D.L., Schaefer, D.R., Bouchard, M., & Davidson, K.M. (2021). In the eye of the beholder: meaning and structure of informal status in women's and men's prisons. *Criminology*, 59(1), 42–72.

Krohn, M.D. (1986). The web of conformity: a network approach to the explanation of delinquent behavior. *Social Problems*, 33(6), s81–s93.

Lantz, B., & Ruback, R.B. (2017). A networked boost: burglary co-offending and repeat victimization using a network approach. *Crime and Delinquency*, 63(9), 1066–1090.

Leukfeldt, E.R., Kleemans, E.R., & Stol, W.P. (2017). Cybercriminal networks, social ties and online forums: social ties versus digital ties within phishing and malware networks. *British Journal of Criminology*, 57(3), 704–722.

Levy, B.L., Phillips, N.E., & Sampson, R.J. (2020). Triple disadvantage: neighborhood networks of everyday urban mobility and violence in US Cities. *American Sociological Review*, 85(6), 925–956.

Lewis, K., & Papachristos, A.V. (2020). Rules of the game: exponential random graph models of a gang homicide network. *Social Forces*, 98(4), 1829–1858.

Malm, A., & Bichler, G. (2011). Networks of collaborating criminals: assessing the structural vulnerability of drug markets. *Journal of Research in Crime and Delinquency*, 48(2), 271–297.

Malm, A., Bichler, G., & Nash, R. (2011). Co-offending between criminal enterprise groups. *Global Crime*, 12(2), 112–128.

McCuish, E.C., Bouchard, M., & Corrado, R.R. (2015). The search for suitable homicide co-offenders among gang members. *Journal of Contemporary Criminal Justice*, 31(3), 319–336.

McGloin, J.M., & Piquero, A.R. (2010). On the relationship between co-offending network redundancy and offending versatility. *Journal of Research in Crime and Delinquency*, 47(1), 63–90.

McGloin, J.M., & Shermer, L.O.N. (2009). Self-control and deviant peer network structure. *Journal of Research in Crime and Delinquency*, 46(1), 35–72.

McGloin, J.M., & Stickle, W.P. (2011). Influence or convenience? Disentangling peer influence and co-offending for chronic offenders. *Journal of Research in Crime and Delinquency*, 48(3), 419–447.

McGloin, J.M., Sullivan, C.J., Piquero, A.R., & Bacon, S. (2008). Investigating the stability of co-offending and co-offenders among a sample of youthful offenders. *Criminology*, 46(1), 155–188.

McMillan, C., Felmlee, D., & Osgood, D.W. (2018). Peer influence, friend selection, and gender: how network processes shape adolescent smoking, drinking, and delinquency, *Social Networks*, 55, 86–96.

Moody, J., Brynildsen, W.D., Osgood, D.W., Feinberg, M.E., & Gest, S. (2011). Popularity trajectories and substance use in early adolescence. *Social Networks*, 33(2), 101–112.

Morselli, C. (2005). *Contacts, opportunities, and criminal enterprise*. University of Toronto Press.

Morselli, C. (2009). *Inside criminal networks*. Springer.

Morselli, C., Giguère, C., & Petit, K. (2007). The efficiency/security tradeoff in criminal networks. *Social Networks*, 29(1), 143–153.

Morselli, C., Paquet-Clouston, M., & Provost, C. (2017). The independent's edge in an illegal drug distribution setting: Levitt and Venkatesh revisited. *Social Networks*, *51*, 118–126.

Morselli, C., & Tremblay, P. (2004). Criminal achievement, offender networks and the benefits of low self-control. *Criminology*, *42*(3), 773–804.

Nieto, A., Davies, T., & Borrion, H. (2022). 'Offending with the accomplices of my accomplices': evidence and implications regarding triadic closure in co-offending networks. *Social Networks*, *70*, 325–333.

Niezink, N., & Campana, P. (2022). When things turn sour: a network event study of organized crime violence. *Journal of Quantitative Criminology*. April. doi.org/10.1007/s10940-022-09540-1

Norbutas, L. (2018). Offline constraints in online drug marketplaces: an exploratory analysis of a cryptomarket trade network. *International Journal of Drug Policy*, *56*, 92–100.

Norbutas, L., Ruiter, S., & Corten, R. (2020). Believe it when you see it: dyadic embeddedness and reputation effects on trust in cryptomarkets for illegal drugs. *Social Networks*, *63*, 150–161.

Ouellet, M., & Bouchard, M. (2018). The 40 members of the Toronto 18: group boundaries and the analysis of illicit networks. *Deviant Behavior*, *39*(11), 1467–1482.

Ouellet, M., Bouchard, M., & Charette, Y. (2019a). One gang dies, another gains? The network dynamics of criminal group persistence. *Criminology*, *57*(1), 5–33.

Ouellet, M., Bouchard, M., & Hart, M. (2017). Criminal collaboration and risk: the drivers of Al Qaeda's network structure before and after 9/11. *Social Networks*, *51*, 171–177.

Ouellet, M., Hashimi, S., Gravel, J., & Dabney, D. (2020). The promise of a network approach for policing research. *Justice Quarterly*, *37*(7), 1221–1240.

Ouellet, M., Hashimi, S., Gravel, J., & Papachristos, A.V. (2019b). Network exposure and excessive use of force: investigating the social transmission of police misconduct. *Criminology and Public Policy*, *18*(3), 675–704.

Papachristos, A.V. (2009). Murder by structure: dominance relations and the social structure of gang homicide. *American Journal of Sociology*, *115*(1), 74–128.

Papachristos, A.V. (2011). The coming of a networked criminology? In J. MacDonald (Ed.), *Measuring crime and criminality* (pp. 101–140). Transaction.

Papachristos, A.V., & Bastomski, S. (2018). Connected in crime: the enduring effect of neighborhood networks on the spatial patterning of violence. *American Journal of Sociology*, *124*(2), 517–568.

Papachristos, A.V., Braga, A.A., & Hureau, D.M. (2012). Social networks and the risk of gunshot injury. *Journal of Urban Health*, *89*(6), 992–1003.

Papachristos, A.V., Braga, A.A., Piza, E., & Grossman, L.S. (2015). The company you keep? The spillover effects of gang membership on individual gunshot victimization in a co-offending network. *Criminology*, *53*(4), 624–649.

Papachristos, A.V., Hureau, D.M., & Braga, A.A. (2013). The corner and the crew: the influence of geography and social networks on gang violence. *American Sociological Review*, *78*(3), 417–447.

Papachristos, A.V., & Wildeman, C. (2012). Social networks and risk of homicide victimization in an African American community. SSRN 2149219

Papachristos, A.V., Wildeman, C., & Roberto, E. (2015). Tragic, but not random: the social contagion of nonfatal gunshot injuries. *Social Science and Medicine*, *125*, 139–150.

Payne, D.C., & Cornwell, B. (2007). Reconsidering peer influences on delinquency: do less proximate contacts matter? *Journal of Quantitative Criminology*, *23*(2), 127–149.

Quispe-Torreblanca, E.G., & Stewart, N. (2019). Causal peer effects in police misconduct. *Nature Human Behaviour*, *3*(8), 797–807.

Ragan, D.T. (2020). Similarity between deviant peers: developmental trends in influence and selection. *Criminology*, *58*(2), 336–369.

Rengifo, A.F., & DeWitt, S.E. (2019). Incarceration and personal networks: unpacking measures and meanings of tie strength. *Journal of Quantitative Criminology*, *35*(2), 393–431.

Roberto, E., Braga, A.A., & Papachristos, A.V. (2018). Closer to guns: the role of street gangs in facilitating access to illegal firearms. *Journal of Urban Health*, *95*(3), 372–382.

Sampson, R.J. (2006). How does community context matter? Social mechanisms and the explanation of crime rates. In P.H. Wikström & R.J. Sampson (Eds.), *The explanation of crime: context, mechanisms, and development* (pp. 31–60). Cambridge University Press.

Sampson, R.J., & Levy, B.L. (2020). Beyond residential segregation: mobility-based connectedness and rates of violence in large cities. *Race and Social Problems*, *12*(1), 77–86.

Sampson, R.J., Raudenbush, S.W., & Earls, F. (1997). Neighborhoods and violent crime: a multilevel study of collective efficacy, *Science*, *277*(5328), 918–924.

Sarnecki, J. (1990). Delinquent networks in Sweden. *Journal of Quantitative Criminology*, *6*(1), 31–50.

Sarnecki, J. (2001). *Delinquent networks: youth co-offending in Stockholm*. Cambridge University Press.

Schaefer, D.R. (2012). Youth co-offending networks: an investigation of social and spatial effects. *Social Networks*, *34*(1), 141–149.

Schaefer, D.R., Bouchard, M., Young, J.T., & Kreager, D.A. (2017). Friends in locked places: an investigation of prison inmate network structure. *Social Networks*, *51*, 88–103.

Schaefer, D.R., & Kreager, D.A. (2020). New on the block: analyzing network selection trajectories in a prison treatment program. *American Sociological Review*, *85*(4), 709–737.

Sentse, M., Kreager, D.A., Bosma, A.Q., Nieuwbeerta, P., & Palmen, H. (2021). Social organization in prison: a social network analysis of interpersonal relationships among Dutch prisoners. *Justice Quarterly*, *38*(6), 1047–1069.

Shaw, C.R., & McKay, H.D. (1942). *Juvenile delinquency and urban areas*. University of Chicago Press.

Simpson, C.R., & Kirk, D.S. (2022). Is police misconduct contagious? Non-trivial null findings from Dallas, Texas. *Journal of Quantitative Criminology*, 1–39.

Small et al. (2020)

Smith, C.M. (2019). *Syndicate women: gender and networks in Chicago organized crime*. University of California Press.

Smith, C.M., & Papachristos, A.V. (2016). Trust thy crooked neighbor: multiplexity in Chicago organized crime networks. *American Sociological Review*, *81*(4), 644–667.

Snijders, T.A.B., van de Bunt, G.G. & Steglich, C.E.G. (2010). Introduction to stochastic actor-based models for network dynamics. *Social Networks*, *32*, 44–60.

Song, G., Bernasco, W., Liu, L., Xiao, L., Zhou, S., & Liao, W. (2019). Crime feeds on legal activities: daily mobility flows help to explain thieves' target location choices. *Journal of Quantitative Criminology*, *35*(4), 831–854.

Sutherland, E. (1947). *Principles of criminology*. J.B. Lipincott.

Thomas, K.J., & McGloin, J.M. (2013). A dual-systems approach for understanding differential susceptibility to processes of peer influence. *Criminology*, *51*(2), 435–474.

Thornberry, T.P. (1987). Toward an interactional theory of delinquency. *Criminology*, *25*(4), 863–892.

Tita, G.E., Riley, K.J., Ridgeway, G., Grammich, C., Abrahamse, A.F., & Greenwood, P. (2003). *Reducing gun violence: results from an intervention in East Los Angeles*. RAND Press.

Volker, B., De Cuyper, R., Mollenhorst, G., Dirkzwager, A., van der Laan, P., & Nieuwbeerta, P. (2016). Changes in the social networks of prisoners: a comparison of their networks before and after imprisonment. *Social Networks*, *47*, 47–58.

Wood, G., & Papachristos, A.V. (2019). Reducing gunshot victimization in high-risk social networks through direct and spillover effects. *Nature Human Behaviour*, *3*(11), 1164–1170.

Wood, G., Roithmayr, D., & Papachristos, A.V. (2019). The network structure of police misconduct. *Socius*, *5*, 2378023119879798.

Young, J.T., Barnes, J., Meldrum, R.C., & Weerman, F.M. (2011). Assessing and explaining misperceptions of peer delinquency. *Criminology*, *49*(2), 599–630.

Young, J.T., & Haynie, D. (2020). Trusting the untrustworthy: the social organization of trust among incarcerated women. *Justice Quarterly*, *39*(3), 553–584.

Zhao, L., & Papachristos, A.V. (2020). Network position and police who shoot. *The ANNALS of the American Academy of Political and Social Science*, *687*(1), 89–112.

18

Historical Network Analysis: Two Problems of Scale

Ian Kumekawa

INTRODUCTION

Historians have long documented dense networks of family, friendship, commerce and politics. In the late 19th century, classical historians in Germany (Klebs et al., 1897–1898) spent years producing a massive study of the connections of Roman elites, collected under the title *Prosopographia Imperii Romani*. By the mid-20th century, prosopography – 'the investigation of the common background characteristics of a group of actors in history by means of a collective study of their lives' (Stone, 1971, p. 46) – was firmly established in Anglophone historiography. Ronald Syme (1939) deployed the technique to analyse the Roman Revolution. Lewis Namier (1964) used the approach on 18th-century British members of parliament. Prosopography flourished among historians of ancient and mediaeval Europe; there are online prosopographies of the Later Roman Empire (Martindale, 1971–1993), Anglo-Saxon England and Church of England clergy, among many others (Modern History Research Unit, n.d.). Starting in the 1970s, historians in Germany (Reinhard, 1979) were even using formal network analysis to study early and pre-modern groups. Scholars in neighbouring disciplines also made pioneering use of historical data to map networks (see, e.g., Padgett & Ansell, 1993; Bearman, 1993).

But only in the past two decades has the metaphor of the network come to occupy a central position in historical writing (Brewer, 2021; Ferguson, 2017; Davison, 2019; Ahnert et al., 2021). At the same time that historians have taken a 'network turn', increasingly sophisticated and accessible digital tools have allowed scholars to probe historical questions in new ways. At the intersection of these two trends lies a growing body of scholarship that deploys visualisations and computational analyses of networks. As of September 2021, the bibliography of Historical Network Research projects, maintained on the Community of Historical Network Research website (Historical Network Research Community, n.d.), boasted 1,037 entries. It is a diverse field, covering a multitude of subjects and genres of history: from social and economic, to business and family, to cultural and intellectual. There is no one methodological standard, nor a single goal shared by historical network analyses. Nor is there a standard tool. Some historians work with networks in python or using D3.js, a JavaScript library. Others use out-of-the-box platforms, especially Gephi, Cytoscape, Pajek and Palladio, the last developed by the Stanford Digital Humanities Lab between 2013 and 2016 with historians in mind.

In short, the expanding literature dealing with historical networks resists easy categorisation. The field is exciting not least because it is diverse and dynamic. Historians have deployed network visualisation and analysis to investigate a vast range of topics in divergent ways. Some have used networks as interactive indices of their own work: a map of the connections laid out in an accompanying text. Others have leveraged them to explore a dataset in an open-ended way. Still others have wielded them as arguments, rhetorical tools to advance a particular interpretation of the past. While some have used increasingly standardised quantitative methods to parse data, others have relied on 'visual network analysis' (Decuypere, 2020), effectively the qualitative evaluation of a graph.

There are several reasons why historians have turned towards networks. Historians (like everyone else) have been barraged by countless references to the 'networked society', the 'network age', even the 'global network revolution' (Ferguson, 2017, p. 12). At the same time, newly accessible and manipulable sources of data have pushed the frontiers of possible research using digital methods. More fundamentally, networks speak to a theme that has long obsessed historians: the interaction between the individual and the social. From undergraduate courses onwards, historians are taught to consider the relative importance of agents (human or otherwise) and structures in understanding the past. Networks are so alluring because they can render both structures and agents in a single analytical plane.

The promise of historical networks is that they can help solve two problems of scale that have long plagued historians. The first problem – summarised by Ann Blair (2010) as 'too much to know' – is one of quantities of knowledge or information. Historians have long understood (Edelstein et al., 2017) that connections between people matter, but holding a large number of connections in one's head is a daunting if not impossible task. Networks, especially searchable digital networks, can help researchers and 'readers' make sense of a pile of information; a network can serve as a graphical index to an argument about the past, a diagram, or finding aid. As Blair (2010) and others (Rosenberg, 2003; Putnam, 2016) have noted, such a tool is hardly new. Nor is the phenomenon of information overload. But the ease with which historians can collect and aggregate information is new. Networks and other analytics can help the historian keep track and make sense of the information they collect.

The other problem of scale that networks can solve concerns the relationship between an individual person and a larger community, polity, or zeitgeist. Networks hold the potential to put the macro and the micro into the same field of view. In the past, historians struggled to simultaneously analyse individual and group. Cliometricians of the 1960s focused on the forest rather than the trees. Italian microhistorians, by contrast, focused on individual trees, often to check and correct sweeping characterisations of the forest. Networks unite the goals and processes of the cliometricians and microhistorians: they enable seamless movement from individual to social structure and back again, without loss of definition or granularity.

This chapter is organised around these two problems of scale and the ways that historians have deployed networks to confront them. The first section addresses how historians have leveraged networks to bridge the gap between the individual and the group. The second covers how historians used networks to process and categorise information, available at unprecedented scales.

BRIDGING MICRO AND MACRO

The first way in which networks confront a problem of scale is by relating the individual to the social. Like other scholars, historians have been drawn to analyse and visualise collections of people, not as static things, but as articulated complexes: *as* networks. Doing so helps historians understand how the group itself behaved, how it evolved and what it meant. The Republic of Letters Project at Stanford, for instance, used a correspondence network to grapple with a diffuse scholarly community as a whole. Ruth Ahnert and Sebastian Ahnert (2015) mapped the composition of English Protestant networks during the reign of the Catholic Mary I in order to understand how the community survived the period. Martin Grandjean (2019) explored the internal structure of League of Nations officials to trace how bureaucratisation affected intellectual cooperation. Historians have also used network analysis to sort groups into suborders, finding unexpected new constituencies. For instance, by plotting collaboration between 16th-century Mughal court artists, Yael Rice (2017) found that, contrary to previous understanding, schools of artists were not rigid, but rather fluid and overlapping. This fluidity, Rice posited, contributed to the 'production of a new, synthetic style' (abstract).

These studies work by relating a set of individuals to a wider group. In the studies mentioned so far, the intellectual pay-off concerns the group itself. But the pay-off may also be greater insight about a particular individual. This is typically true in the case of so-called *ego-networks*, networks of a single individual (or group of individuals), though, as John Brewer (2021) noted, such networks also offer explanatory insight about dissemination and contagion. Dan Edelstein and Biliana Kassabova's study (2020) of Voltaire's letters, for instance, is a geographic network of many correspondents, but is ultimately *about* Voltaire himself. Similarly, work on the letters of John Locke (Willan, 2016) and Benjamin Franklin (Arcenas, 2016) are *about* Locke and Franklin.

Like scholars in neighbouring disciplines (Giddens, 1976), historians debate the relative importance of structures and agents, but generally agree that narrating the past depends on *both* structures *and* agents (Sewell, 2005). Similarly, although historical network analyses often yield conclusions that pertain either to the group or the individual, they work by relating the two. In fact, network analyses are unusually useful tools because they can help historians maintain simultaneous focus on individual and group. For historians, networks hold the elusive promise of moving between micro and macro without loss of definition or, put another way, of bringing structure and agent together (see Lemercier, 2015; Marx, 2016). This is important because one of the past century's chief historiographical questions has concerned how historians relate individuals to large social, political, or economic phenomena. With networks, especially digitised and indexed ones, historians can do just that. Network visualisations 'reveal the general shape of things, orders of magnitude, and large-scale trends; they also draw our attention to microhistories that we might otherwise have missed' (Edelstein et al., 2017, pp. 408–409).

At the turn of the 20th century, the academic discipline of history was effectively a study of 'great men', whether princes, philosophers, or scientists. It was clear to contemporary historians how great individuals related to historical change; history moved at their behest, as a result of their choices and actions. But in the mid-20th century, a new wave of historians – particularly those influenced by Marxian class analysis – began shifting the focus of historical enquiry towards less storied individuals: individuals who needed to be recovered, as British social historian E.P. Thompson (1963) wrote, from 'the condescension of posterity' (p. 12).

Thompson and other social historians attended to historical actors who were neither rich nor famous, but who collectively (at least according to Marxian thinking) were the drivers of history. Studying a whole 'class' of people posed challenges. It was one thing to rescue a handful of individuals from the condescension of history – to treat them with the attention previously only lavished on the rich and famous – but it was another to attend to the motivations, backgrounds, thoughts and acts of a group of hundreds, thousands, or even millions.

Despite the challenges, a group of social historians in France clustered around the journal *Annales d'histoire économique et sociale* set themselves this goal. Prewar luminaries of the *Annales* school, among them Lucien Febvre and Marc Bloch, stressed the importance of narrating history over a long time horizon, '*la longue durée*'. Doing so allowed them to attend to deep and durable structures. But *Annalistes* – especially after World War II – equally aspired to uncover and understand emotional or psychological mentalities (*mentalités*) of past eras (Debating the longue durée, 2015).

Getting inside the mind of one or two individuals was hard enough, but collecting data on the mentalities of hundreds of thousands of people, most of whom left few traces in the archival record, proved monumentally difficult. Faced with a choice between attending to large numbers of people and capturing richly textured sentiments, *Annales* historians in the 1960s and 1970s prioritised numbers. They dispatched legions of graduate students around France in search of information that could be counted and collated: information that was 'structurally numerical' (Furet, 1971, p. 158). The collection of such information – baptism, marriage and death records from local parishes, tax rolls from municipal archives – formed the basis of many social and economic studies. Often using punch cards and the new field of 'cliometrics', the historians analysed the reams of collected information (Ladurie, 1981). *Annales* school historians turned to social, economic and demographic data as determinant of *mentalités* themselves. Indeed, the massive data collection drives were premised on a conviction that it was possible to discern *mentalités* in 'their most repetitive and least personal expressions' (Chartier, 1982, p. 30; Hunt, 1986, pp. 216–217).

By the 1980s, that conviction was showing cracks. As Lynn Hunt (1986) rhetorically asked, 'is serial analysis of wills, iconographic themes, or book production the best method for getting at this collective mentality?' (p. 216). If reality were materialist, then the sources of reality had to be material too: vital records, notarial accounts and tax records. But focusing on such sources risked abandoning the interpretative mission of investigating mentalities.

Around the same time, in the 1970s and 1980s, a group of historians especially concentrated in Italy was turning to a different way of relating the individual to large-scale historical transformations. Instead of collecting and collating massive datasets, these historians focused on telling highly detailed stories about specific individuals or localities: 'microhistories'. As Francesca

Trivellato (2011) noted, microhistorians used 'the micro-scale of analysis in order to test the validity of macro-scale explanatory paradigms' (section II). The *Annalistes* (with their emphasis on the *longue durée*) were set on macrohistory: on making stylised claims about very large subjects. Microhistorians took a different course. As Giovanni Levi (1992, in Trivellato, 2011) put it, 'Microhistory tries not to sacrifice knowledge of individual elements to wider generalisation, and in fact it accentuates individual lives and events' (section III). For microhistorians, the genre's focus allowed for 'a more penetrating and honest approach to empiricism and objectivity'. It also allowed for an uncompromising insistence on individual agency. If the *Annalistes* prioritised structure over agency, microhistorians did the opposite.

The decades after the fall of the Berlin Wall saw a gradual retreat of microhistory, or at least a relative advance of macro-scaled histories. As Trivellato (2011) and others (Bayly et al., 2006; Osterhammel and Petersson, 2009; Conrad, 2017) recognised, a new global order guaranteed by a single hegemon called forth new *global* histories. Big was back in, not just in terms of the size of the historical question or geographic reach, but also in terms of *kinds* of data. The internet opened vast new possibilities. It inspired historians to think about new connections and networks, and enabled them to easily search and collect information. The digitisation of troves of books and documents inspired immense excitement and optimism (e.g., Armitage and Guldi, 2014) about the prospects of big data in history. To many, big data seemed a good place to find answers to big questions.

Over the last decade, big data has aroused both suspicion and scrutiny from the historical community. As Edelstein et al. (2017) summarised the criticisms, the accessibility of big datasets 'conjures up the worrisome specter of digitally savvy sorcerer's apprentices who, thanks to new databases, "cite anything and construe nothing"' (p. 402). Data without analysis is empty. Bad or insufficient analysis is a constant lurking threat. And, perhaps most worryingly, historians might be tempted away from the hard work of thoughtful qualitative interpretation and to move too quickly and uncritically into the world of facts and figures.

But as historians have shown over the last decade, not only is it possible to approach data (especially networked data) rigorously and thoughtfully, doing so can also bring together the aspirations of both the macrohistorical *Annalistes* and the microhistorical scholars of the 1970s and 1980s. In mapping a way to reconcile the values of microhistorians with the ambitions of a rising wave of scholars interested in 'global history', Francesca Trivellato (2011) pointed to networks. In her own work, Trivellato explored how Livorno's Jewish community inhabited and responded to entangled local and global contexts. 'Family alliances, the Sephardic diaspora, all Jews, the city of Livorno and the grand duchy of Tuscany, the Mediterranean, the Atlantic, and the Indian Ocean, other trading communities and the political economy of state powers … all intersect with one another simultaneously' (section VII).

Trivellato identified Emma Rothschild's *The inner life of empires* (2011) as another work that transcended conventional divisions between micro and global history. Following eleven siblings of an 18th-century Scottish family, *The inner life* showed how a tight-knit family network reached around the world: from the Scottish Lowlands to upstate New York, Pensacola, Bengal and Grenada. One Johnstone sibling was a close associate of Adam Smith, another was a notorious slave owner in the West Indies, a third returned to Scotland from India with an enslaved woman named Bell (alias Belinda). Through these stories, the book offered an ant's-eye window onto global transformations of the 18th and early 19th century: the abolition of the slave trade, colonisation, the expansion of overseas finance, even the Enlightenment itself. *The inner life of empires* was inspired by Italian microhistory, but it offered 'a new kind of microhistory', one that connected 'micro- and microhistories by the history of the individuals' own connections' (Rothschild, 2011, p. 269).

In her subsequent project, Rothschild more consciously united the ambitions of the Italian microhistorians of the 1980s with those of the French founders of the *Annales* school. As Rothschild put it, the project was inspired by 'the spirit of the new economic history to which Marc Bloch once looked forward, in which the "political," the "economic," and the "religious" would be intertwined, in contrast to a ("bloodless") history of "a world without individuals"' (Bloch, 1949, p. 79, cited in Rothschild, 2021, p. 10). Working with 'the traditional sources' of *Annaliste* social history: church parish and civil records as well as notarial documents from the French city of Angoulême, Rothschild (2014) demonstrated how poor and illiterate artisans were connected to a wider world. The network visualisations produced by her team at Harvard (*Angoulême in 1764*) highlight microhistories within a greater network of the 4,089 individuals who appeared in the city's parish records during a pivotal year in the mid-18th century. Written work picks up where the network visualisations end: connecting the stories to the wider narratives of French, Atlantic and imperial history in the 18th, 19th and 20th centuries.

Rothschild explicitly recognised the potential of networks to bridge the macro and micro divide.

But she is not alone in deploying networks to pair microhistorical narrative with macrohistorical framing. The *'Verflechtung'* (entanglement) theory deployed by German historians including Wolfgang Reinhard (2005) starting in the 1970s similarly linked micro to macro. So too did sociologists (Alexander et al., 1987). In the early 2000s, French historians including Paul-André Rosental (2002) and Claire Lemercier (2005) described networks as offering a 'meso' level of analysis that could link individual choice with structural dynamics.

More recently, historians have used networks to map if not a mentality, then at least a shared imaginary. Rachel Midura (2021) analysed network routes printed in early modern itinerary books to get a handle on a pre-cartographic spatial imaginary. Midura outlined a geography of the itinerary books, but the real pay-off was about the imagined geographies as understood by people in Early Modern Europe. Working with digitised datasets of 17th-century British 'newsbooks', or early newspapers, Yann Ciarán Ryan (2018) also reconstructed an imagined geography. By analysing the 'dispatch locations' for news items that appeared in London newsbooks, Ryan traced the 'geography of news' and recovered the 'sense of place' that newsbook readers might have experienced.

Historians have also used network analysis to identify individuals within groups who played particular functions as intermediaries or social hubs. In work on state surveillance in the Tudor state papers, Ruth Ahnert and Sebastian Ahnert showed (2019) how a combination of simple metrics like betweenness and degree might be used to 'predict' whether particular individuals sent or received letters held in the Tudor state papers were conspirators or spies. Ahnert and Ahnert turn techniques typically deployed by 21st-century state surveillance apparatuses on communications metadata to a historical dataset, but they also tell the particular stories of individuals living in Tudor England using traditional archival methods. Then, the authors used a similar process to detect and investigate people that Tudor state surveilled. That is, not only did Ahnert and Ahnert use social network analysis to identify particular kinds of individuals, they also used the methods to detect a pattern in the machinations of the state apparatus.

TOO MUCH TO THINK ABOUT: NETWORKS AS QUESTIONS AND ANSWERS

Networks bring together the macro and the micro, the individual and the social. In this way, they unite scales of enquiry. But they also bridge scales of enquiry in a different methodological way. By allowing historians to engage with information at both a granular and aggregated level, they help historians make sense of vast troves of information. And historians are awash in information. The internet has opened new archives, search patterns and research methods. Moreover, through digitisation, archivists and librarians have translated existing containers of information into forms that can be manipulated in new ways. Because of increasingly accessible digital tools, it is ever easier to process swaths of knowledge as 'data' (Davison, 2019; Edelstein et al., 2017).

Networks have proved useful and popular ways of grappling with a mass of information for both authors and for readers. Dan Edelstein and Biliana Kassabova (2020) describe the process of working with networks as 'defamiliarising' the historian and provoking new research questions. For Martin Grandjean (2017), visualising complex networks is an 'exploratory process' (p. 17). Even small datasets with dozens of nodes contain quantities of information that are difficult to hold in one's head. Information in a network format, especially one that is searchable, can serve an indexical function, helping historians keep track of the connections and homologies encountered in the course of research. Plotting connections between individuals featured in one's own work might serve as a reminder that someone who appears in chapter 1 had the same teacher as someone who appears in chapter 4. The network form can help historians develop narrative threads and patterns. As research tools, networks are 'knowledge generators' – 'graphical forms that support combinatoric calculation' (Drucker, 2014, pp. 105–116).

But, more than knowledge, networks (especially visualisations) are useful for provoking questions. There is no one definitive way to visualise a network. The same dataset can be run through any number of layout or sorting algorithms, with widely varying results. Because many pieces of software that digital humanists use to create visualisations have built-in layout algorithms, it is relatively easy for scholars to create impressive-looking graphs. There is both opportunity and danger lurking in this ease. Networks carry great interpretive power, but historians need to think through and understand the parameters of their presentation, starting with the choice of software (Venturini et al., 2021; Davison, 2019).

Still, with sufficient understanding, the indeterminateness of networks transforms from a liability to an asset. Putting data in networked form can help generate unexpected results and productive confusion. In fact, as Tommaso Venturini, Mathieu Jacomy and Pablo Jensen (2021) note: 'the same ambiguity that makes network charts unfit for hypothesis confirmation … makes them invaluable for exploratory data analysis' (p. 2). The inherent 'ambiguity' of a network visualisation reflects the 'messiness' (p. 9) of historical reality itself. To the reader who understands that a network visualisation is merely *a* representation, not *the* representation, the messiness of a network visualisation can be a useful reminder that it is part of an interpretive process.

In creating a geo-coded representation of Voltaire's correspondence network, Edelstein and Kassabova (2020) noticed that Voltaire exchanged very few letters with correspondents in England: a surprising result, given the centrality of England in the historiography of Voltaire's life. Though eager to explain this result, the authors realised that the graph could only pose, rather than answer, the question: 'all it [the graph] can do is reveal a discrepancy between what the historiography tells us and what is actually in this correspondence. To understand the meaning of this discrepancy, we have to move beyond the map' (pp. 38–39). The visualisation inspired a more traditional close-reading of texts that pushed Edelstein and Kassabova towards a substantial revision in the traditional thinking about the place of England in Voltaire's thought. As Martin Grandjean (2019) wrote (in French), as a research tool, a social network 'can be a judicious way to take a new look at a corpus' (pp. 2–3) and an impulse to conduct further investigation using other methods.

Those investigations are often quantitative but may also be qualitative. Researchers may gain insight about a network by fiddling with layout, sizing and colouring parameters in network visualisation software to ascertain if patterns emerge to the naked eye. Clusters, for instance, may indicate subgroups; elongated shapes may indicate polarisation. Venturini et al. (2021) and others (Eumann, 2016) suggest that this process – termed 'visual network analysis' (Decuypere, 2020) – is about searching for legibility. They narrate their own deployment of visual network analysis on a dataset containing connections between 6,381 jazz musicians culled from Wikipedia. Their result, after 'many trials and errors, and a lot of backs and forth between different visual variables and their parameterization', was a visualisation of 'the development of the jazz musical language: from *Dixieland* and *Swing* to *Bepop, Hard Bop, Post-Bop* and finally to *Free jazz* and *improvisation*' (Venturini et al., 2021, p. 7). In short, after considerable experimentation, the team produced a visualisation of the standard story of jazz's evolution.

A visualisation can be a powerful rhetorical (and pedagogical) tool in demonstrating a narrative. Though it is often useful to obtain findings that seem to confirm to our intuitions or to prior, unsubstantiated beliefs (Ahnert et al., 2021, p. 32), historians need to tread carefully when it comes to interpretation. It is easy and often tempting to create an analysis, especially a visualisation, that confirms existing suspicions.

Historians must be alive to the danger of confirmation bias, especially when seeking to use networks to prove a point or 'test a hypothesis' (Lemercier & Zalc, 2019, p. 107). Testing hypotheses often depends on quantitative social network analysis (So & Long, 2013; Sheehan, 2005). Historians dealing with large datasets typically employ computational approaches – whether 'macroanalytics' or 'cultural analytics' – to get a handle on the hundreds, thousands, or hundreds of thousands of lines of data in their corpus (Jockers, 2013). It is not coincidental that the language of 'hypothesis' and 'test' evokes scientific procedure. There is a 'correct' answer to the question of 'which node in this network has the greatest eigenvector centrality', a metric for measuring 'proximity to power' or influence (Ahnert & Ahnert, 2019, p. 31).

Many scholars worry that network graphs, especially those accompanied by empirical analyses like 'betweenness' or 'eigenvector centrality' appear to present fact as opposed to interpretation. For historian Kate Davison (2019), 'networks have an implicit positive bias that needs to be acknowledged and mitigated' (p. 476). Network visualisations and analyses have authors, with subjective biases. To quote information scholar Johanna Drucker (2017), 'no matter how sophisticated the algorithms, they are all based on models designed as interpretive acts' (p. 629). Network visualisations and analyses are similarly created. At each stage of working with networks, historians make choices that affect the result of any analytics or visualisation.

Quantitative analysis is, at most, only part of the task of a historian. In fact, it falls in the midst of the historical process. Before applying quantitative tools, the historian must determine the size and scope of the network under examination. They must 'clean' and 'code' the data. And after identifying the nodes with greatest eigenvector or betweenness centrality, the historian faces a much more important task: to interpret what those nodes mean, to evaluate competing hypotheses and to determine the certainty with which any claim might be tendered. In their investigation of the Tudor state papers, Ahnert and Ahnert (2019) identified people with relatively high betweenness and low degree. This was a *technical* task; but the identification was worth little without the subsequent interpretation: that these people were often conspirators and double agents.

All graphs start with data. Coming from the Latin verb *dare* (to give), 'data' are understood to be given. But data 'has no truth' (Rosenberg, 2013, p. 18). It may be right or wrong, misleading or incomplete. Indeed, data may not even be given. Drucker (2014) has insisted that 'all data is *capta*' (p. 129), not given, but taken: a product of interpretation. Certainly, bundling data into 'sets' is an interpretive act. A dataset is an object that researchers create, often from limited source materials (Gitelman, 2013; Rollinger, 2020; Grandjean, 2017). In order to be usable in network analysis, data either must be constructed or cleaned: a process that often constitutes a huge part of the time and effort involved in setting up a network. As information scholars Katie Rawson and Trevor Muñoz (2019) have pointed out, the widespread use of the term 'cleaning' suggests that the process is neutral, a black box not worth great attention. But cleaning is a vital authorial task, especially in the digital humanities, where conventions on data preparation are less codified than in neighbouring disciplines. Standardising names and connections, even determining what was a typographical error, are all interpretive choices that can have significant impact on the final analysis.

The fact that 'cleaning' is often figured as a black box has aroused deep suspicions. As Rawson and Muñoz point out, over the last two decades, scholars working in the humanities have been increasingly determined to recover narratives and stories that have been left out of canonical accounts. Thus, insofar as cleaning makes data less 'messy', it cuts against the grain of one of the strongest trends in historical scholarship of the 21st century. As Ahnert et al. (2021) note, both the humanist and the scientist who use networks 'produce results that are seductive in their elegance and simplicity' (p. 5). The negative image of simplicity is loss. Historians, trained to be critical of sources, bridle at any simple model that smooths out detail and nuance.

Still, it is the role of the historian to make such decisions. When historians collect information, whether from books, archives, or people, they inevitably translate that information into a more immediately usable form. A published article or book presents some pieces of information and not others; just as a dataset categorises and organises, so too does a monograph. But there are differences between this older type of 'cleaning' and the 'cleaning' of large datasets. In cleaning a large dataset, there is a heightened danger of systematically omitting or distorting voices from the past; historians can silence whole swaths of people with a single keystroke.

As with other kinds of historical work, at every step in the process of working with networks, historians must weigh and evaluate detail and nuance. They must parse roles and relationships from the historical record. Calibrating the right degree of specificity is vital. The greater the specificity of the edge, the more information the historian has to work with. More material enables more interesting and penetrating questions (Lemercier & Zalc, 2019, p. 107). For instance, in reconstructing a network of people who aided Jews in Nazi Germany, Marten Düring (2015; 2016) took care in defining the relationships between individuals. Düring distinguished between forms of support that were rendered (e.g., food, money, lodging, contacts, or emotional support) and elaborated on the specific nature of the assistance. But more information also often means greater reliance on digital network tools to make sense of patterns. For Düring (2015), determining how to code the types of relations between individuals was 'one of the first and most difficult challenges' (n.p.) in visualising his data. Careful consideration and transparent justification are vital, even in family networks where relationships are formalised and often assumed (Lemercier, 2005). The best studies (e.g., Schor, 2011) of networks methodically set out rationales for coding and differentiating linkages and individuals.

If determining the internal structure of the dataset poses challenges, so too does determining the dataset's overall scope. Many boundaries are arbitrary, subjective, or temporally defined. Borders move. Cultural mores shift. The extent of a particular community or sect are often the products of active policing by historical actors. The decision to restrict data to a particular region or group of people may reify existing hierarchies and divisions. One way that historians have met this challenge is by using boundaries that emerge as actors' categories or as already settled in source material. Lemercier and Zalc (2019) noted the potential for charting 'relationships *as seen through a particular source* (or several), whereas the dream of reconstructing the "complete" networks of all relations of people in the past is doomed to fail' (p. 109).

Even reconstructions based on a single (or a few) texts depend on authorial decisions about selection criteria and representativeness. Some follow Lemercier and Zalc's advice and use the content of a particular historical source or repository to define a group. For instance, in their work on espionage and surveillance of the Tudor state, Ahnert and Ahnert (2019) used the 132,747 digitised letters in an online database. Others have drawn the boundaries of a group in a more ad hoc manner, according to their own expert opinion. Yael Rice (2017) chose to examine the artists who collaborated to produce three illustrated manuscripts.

The fact that the historical record is inherently incomplete and systematically privileges some voices over others, should temper any claim that historical social network analysis yields absolutely 'correct' or 'true' conclusions. In short, historical results derived from quantitative analyses rely on interpretive choices, just as results from qualitative analyses. They are, as Claire Lemercier (2015) has aptly noted, useful 'abstractions'. They can, as translated by the author, 'do justice to the diversity of reality without falling into the abyss of infinite observation of irreducible forms' (p. 24). There are strategies and best practices for quantitatively analysing network data and several guides for thinking through such strategies. Lemercier and Zalc (2019) is an excellent guide for those setting out; so too is the Historical Network Research Community (*Tools, blogs & tutorials*, n.d.) and others (Graham et al., 2016; Düring et al., 2016, section 3). Martin Grandjean (2021) has produced a series of videos on the subject that are accessible on YouTube. Yet while it is possible to fall short of those practices – to analyse 'badly' or 'incorrectly' – the same can be said of tried-and-true qualitative practices long deployed by historians, even those practices that are much less rigorously defined. Formal network analyses are incredibly powerful tools for the historian. They can, as Lemercier (2015) wrote, enable historians to 'go beyond the loose "relational turn" of the last decades, so that we not only change our vocabulary, but actually produce new results' (paragraph 2). They can provide clear and concrete answers to discrete questions. But they are only instruments to an end, not ends in themselves.

Recognising networks as such is a prerequisite to presenting them in a responsible manner. Johanna Drucker (2011) has asserted that all 'graphical tools are a kind of intellectual Trojan horse … they pass as unquestioned representations of "what is"'. 'In actuality,' Drucker contended, 'they are arguments made in graphical form' (p. 1). Many historians have understood the rhetorical potential of network visualisations. Variously described as a 'demonstration visualisation' (Grandjean, 2021) or 'argumentative' network (Meirelles, 2016), many networks explicitly are intended to convince the reader (or viewer) of a historical argument.

Take for example Emma Rothschild's (2014) visualisation of the 83 individuals who signed a prenuptial marriage contract of a poor illiterate woman in Angoulême in 1764. One of Rothschild's principal contentions was that provincial France in the years before the French Revolution was not so isolated or unworldly as has long been assumed. The reason 83 people signed a prenup was that the bride was the daughter of a recently deceased man who was reported to have made a fortune in the slave economy of the West Indies. A network visualisation (see Figure 18.1) of the 83 people, shaded according to their contact with regions outside metropolitan France, made this point clear. The visualisation did not, in and of itself, advance an argument independent of the argument in the text; in fact, the text described the visualisation in some detail. But the visualisation carried rhetorical power. It summarised and represented the contentions of several pages of text all at once. The shaded nodes immediately conveyed the prevalence of experience with the world outside France; the image of a network evoked connectivity.

The network was itself an explicit argument. It is a way of summarising and quickly conveying a massive amount of information, research and thinking. The network is a picture worth far more than a thousand words; it is a representation of a dataset incorporating hundreds of people and thousands of connections. It offers readers a key to interpreting an otherwise overwhelming quantity of information. But it is only optimally useful when paired with other, more traditional modes of exposition and research. Networks can help historians manipulate and present a small amount of information on a great number of entities. But they equally invite the historian to delve deeper, using traditional archival and analytical methods. Applying the lessons and values of contemporary historical practice to the process of network visualisation and analysis calls for conscientious self-reflection. The results of network analysis are 'never definitive, and always require further verification' (Edelstein et al., 2017, p. 409). That verification comes from historical expertise, time in the archives and hard interpretive work. Only by moving between individual source and whole corpus can historical network research really pay dividends.

CONCLUSIONS

Today, there is a robust scholarly community working specifically on historical network research. The *Journal of Historical Network Research*, published by the University of Luxembourg launched in 2017. An overlapping group of scholars also maintains a widely used website for the Historical Network Research Community. That site hosts an extensive bibliography of historical projects employing network research as well as a library of tutorials and instructions for research design and presentation. Another group, Res-Hist, based in France under the chief-editorship of Claire Lemercier, has similarly served as a centre of new work. So too have

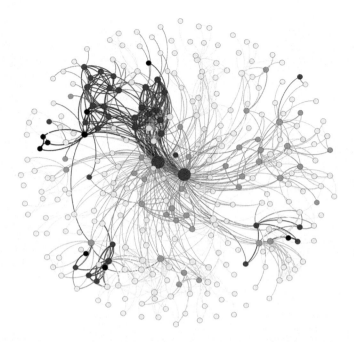

Figure 18.1 The darkest nodes represent individuals who travelled outside France. The dark grey nodes indicate those with a family member who had lived outside France. The individuals with the intermediate grey colour had one of the following attributes: a relative had been contractors to the army or navy; they or a household member had been selected for the militia in 1758; or they were immediate neighbours of someone who had lived outside France. For a colourised version, see histecon.fas.harvard.edu/visualizing/angouleme/83.html

the Visualizing Historical Networks group at Harvard and the Center for Spatial and Textual Analysis at Stanford.

For all the potential of networks, there remains a good deal of trepidation, if not scepticism, about them within the wider historical scholarly community. In the past five years, there have been several notable efforts to convince historians of networks' utility. In *The network turn*, for instance, Ahnert et al. (2021) exhorted historians to work with networks and in so doing to collaborate with scholars across disciplines. In *Quantitative methods in the humanities*, Claire Lemercier and Claire Zalc (2019) devoted a chapter to urging historians to take up networks. These exhortations would be unnecessary if not for resistance.

Networks are powerful tools and humanists have a role to play shaping how they are used and understood in popular culture: as metaphors and organisational frameworks, rather than as absolute or incontestable representations of reality (Ahnert et al., 2021). At the same time, historians must be careful not to dismiss networks as mere infographics or purely subjective illustrations. Concerns about the 'surveillance capitalism' (Zuboff, 2018) of large technology companies and fears about incursion of state security agencies into the privacy of people around the world are grounded in the assumption that such surveillance is highly efficacious. Many of the surveillance techniques involve network modelling. This is the starting point for Ahnert and Ahnert's work on Tudor surveillance; if the NSA can use networked communications metadata to identify individuals of interest, so too can historians. Clearly, networks are powerful instruments. Clearly, they can tell us something about the past. It falls to historians to determine what that something means. For networks are not ends in themselves, but rather, in Kate Davison's (2019) words, 'useful addition[s] to the historian's toolkit' (p. 482). As the editors of a handbook on historical network research (Düring et al., 2016) put it (in German), 'the successful projects of recent years depend on the mutual interaction between network analysis and traditional research methods'. They provide 'no hard facts about the past' and are to be deployed with 'corresponding caution' (p. 6).

This chapter has argued that networks help historians confront two problems of scale: the scale of available information, and the scale of historical analysis. Put another way, networks can help historians bridge the gap between individualised research and huge, diffuse quantities of information. Networks also let historians bridge the gap between the individual and social. They might also allow us to bridge a third methodological gap: between quantitative and qualitative methods: scientific and humanistic norms.

Academic scholarship works through networks. Historical scholarship is no exception. Historical scholarship itself, as a literature, is also a network: an ever-expanding corpus or cumulative library of interrelated observations, interpretations and commentaries on the past. Each new work in historical network research contributes to this library, offering a particular way of conceptualising the past.

Not all historians must (or should) work with networks. But because networks are valuable tools – like languages or archival skills – it is important that historical network research be accessible to a general historical audience so that it can enter the mainstream of historical thinking and research. Bringing networks into the mainstream is a shared responsibility. Authors need to be transparent about their data and reflective about their methodological choices. Certainly, any historian interested in taking up any research or expository tool ought to think through the limitations of the medium. Drucker (2014) has set out a programme of humanistic methods of visualisation that stresses 'a kind of visual fuzzy logic or graphical complexity' (pp. 130–135) with permeable edges, dotted and broken lines and non-uniform dots and points. To this, historians might add an emphasis on the active voice. A network is not simply analysed; rather, someone analyses it.

But perhaps there is a further, more diffuse requirement for accessibility: the education of historians in network methods and the assumptions that underlie them (Rieder & Röhle, 2017). As Julia Flanders and Fotis Jannidis (2019) pointed out, the increased accessibility of digital tools has widened the gap between the *use* of data modelling techniques, and the deep understanding, or 'technical expertise necessary to uncover and intervene in the modelling that animates our digital systems' (p. 6). This goes for both authors and readers. For transparency to work, a certain threshold level of disciplinary literacy is required. Historians need to set themselves the task of learning networks like they learn languages or other research skills. In popular consciousness, networks have become the domain of scientists, but scholars working in the humanities should be involved in bringing the 'metaphorical dimension' of networks into public view. Thinking of the network as a metaphor 'helps us pay attention to the role of human interpretation' (Ahnert et al., 2021, p. 22). Drucker (2014) has held that we are still in 'the incunabula period of information design' (p. 176). The future is to be won. And historians cannot afford to distance themselves from the quantitative or the networked.

REFERENCES

Ahnert, R., & Ahnert, S. (2015). Protestant letter networks in the reign of Mary I: A quantitative approach. *ELH*, *82*(1), 1–33.

Ahnert, R., & Ahnert, S. (2019). Metadata, surveillance and the Tudor state. *History Workshop Journal*, *87*(1), 27–51.

Ahnert, R., Ahnert, S., Coleman, C.N., & Weingart, S.B. (2021). *The network turn: Changing perspectives in the humanities.* Cambridge University Press.

Alexander, J.C., Giesen, B., Münch, R., & Smelser, N.J. (Eds.) (1987). *The micro–macro link.* University of California Press.

Angoulême in 1764 (2021). Visualizing Historical Networks, Center for History and Economics. histecon.fas.harvard.edu/visualizing/angouleme/index.html

Arcenas, C.R. (2016). *Benjamin Franklin Papers.* Mapping the Republic of Letters republicofletters.stanford.edu/publications/franklin/

Armitage, D., & Guldi, J. (2014). *The history manifesto.* Cambridge University Press.

Bayly, C.A., Beckert, S., Connelly, M., Hofmeyr, I., Kozol, W., & Seed, P. (2006). AHR conversation: on transnational history. *American Historical Review*, *111*(5), 1441–1464.

Bearman, P. (1993). *Relations into rhetorics: Local elite social structure in Norfolk, England, 1540–1840.* Rutgers University Press.

Blair, A. (2010) *Too much to know: managing scholarly information before the modern age.* Yale University Press.

Brewer, J. (2021). Networks. In A. Grafton, A.S. Goeing, P. Duguid & A. Blair (Eds.), *Information: a historical companion* (pp. 620–627). Princeton University Press.

Brooke, J., & Namier, L (Eds.) (1964). *The house of commons, 1754–1790* (3 volumes). Boydell & Brewer.

Chartier, R. (1982). Intellectual history or sociocultural history? The French trajectories. In D. La Capra & S.L. Kaplan (Eds.), *Modern European intellectual history: reappraisals and new perspectives* (pp. 13–46). Cornell University Press.

Conrad, S. (2017). *What is global history?* Princeton University Press.

Davison, K. (2019). Early modern social networks: antecedents, opportunities, and challenges. *American Historical Review*, 124(2), 456–482.

Debating the longue durée (2015). *Annales: Histoire, Sciences Sociales*, 70(2).

Decuypere, M. (2020). Visual network analysis: a qualitative method for research sociomaterial practice. *Qualitative Research*, 20(1), 73–90.

Drucker, J. (2011). Humanities approaches to graphical display. *Digital Humanities Quarterly*, 5(1). www.digitalhumanities.org/dhq/vol/5/1/000091/000091.html

Drucker, J. (2014). *Graphesis: visual forms of knowledge production.* Harvard University Press.

Drucker, J. (2017). Why distant reading isn't. *Publications of the Modern Language Association of America*, 132(3), 628–635.

Düring, M. (2015). From hermeneutics to data to networks: data extraction and network visualization of historical sources. *The Programming Historian 4.* doi.org/10.46430/phen0044

Düring, M. (2016). *Verdeckte soziale Netzwerke im Nationalsozialismus. Die Entstehung und Arbeitsweise von Berliner Hilfsnetzwerken für verfolgte Juden.* De Gruyter Oldenburg.

Düring, M., Eumann, U., Stark, M., & von Keyserlingk, L. (Eds.). (2016). *Handbuch historische Netzwerkforschung: Grundlagen und Andwendungen.* Lit Verlag.

Edelstein, D., Findlen, P., Ceserani, G., Winterer, C., & Coleman, N. (2017). Historical research in a digital age: reflections from the mapping the republic of letters project. *American Historical Review*, 122(2), 400–424.

Edelstein, D., & Kassabova, B. (2020). How England fell off the map of Voltaire's enlightenment. *Modern Intellectual History*, 17(1), 29–53.

Eumann, U. (2016). Heuristik. Hypothesenentwicklung und Hypotesentest. In M. Düring, U. Eumann, M. Stark & L. von Keyserlingk (Eds.), *Handbuch historische Netzwerkforschung: Grundlagen und Andwendungen* (pp. 113–123). Lit Verlag.

Ferguson, N. (2017). *The square and the tower: networks and power, from the freemasons to facebook.* Penguin.

Flanders, J., & Jannids, F. (Eds.) (2019). *The shape of data in the digital humanities.* Routledge.

Furet, F. (1971). Quantitative history. *Daedalus*, 100(1), 151–167.

Giddens, A. (1976). *New rules of sociological method.* Hutchinson.

Gitelman, L. (Ed.) (2013). *'Raw data' is an oxymoron.* MIT Press.

Graham, S., Milligan, I., & Weingart, S. (2016). *Exploring big historical data: the historian's macroscope.* Imperial College Press.

Grandjean, M. (2017). Structures complexes et organisations internationales. Preprint, halshs.archives-ouvertes.fr/halshs-01610098

Grandjean, M. (2019). Les réseaux de la cooperation intellectuelle. La Société des Nations comme actrice des échanges scientifiques et culturels dans l'entre-deux-guerres. Doctoral dissertation, Université de Lausanne. halshs.archives-ouvertes.fr/tel-01853903

Grandjean, M. (2021). *Introduction to social network analysis: basics and historical specificities.* 14 May. www.martingrandjean.ch/introduction-to-social-network-analysis/

Historical Network Research Community (n.d.). historicalnetworkresearch.org/

Hunt, L. (1986). French history in the last twenty years: the rise and fall of the Annales paradigm. *Journal of Contemporary History*, 21(2), 209–224.

Jockers, M. (2013). *Macroanalysis: digital analysis and literary history.* University of Illinois Press.

Klebs, E., von Rohden, P., & Dessau, H. (1897–1898). *Prosopographia Imperii Romani saec I. II. III.* Apud Georgium Reimerum.

Ladurie, E.L.R. (1981). History that stands still. In E.L.R. Ladurie, *The mind and method of the historian* (pp. 1–27). University of Chicago Press.

Lemercier, C. (2005). Analyse de réseaux et histoire. *Revue d'histoire modern et contemporaine*, 52(2), 88–112.

Lemercier, C. (2015). Formal network methods in history: why and how? In G. Fertig (Ed.), *Social networks, political institutions, and rural societies* (pp. 281–310). Brepols.

Lemercier, C., & Zalc, C. (2019). *Quantitative methods in the humanities: an introduction.* University of Virginia Press.

Levi, G. (1992). On microhistory. In P. Burke (Ed.), *New perspectives on historical writing* (pp. 93–113). Pennsylvania State University Press.

Martindale, J.R. (1971–1993). *The prosopography of the later Roman empire*, 3 volumes. Cambridge University Press.

Marx, C. (2016). Forschungsüberblick zur historischen Netzwerkforschung: Zwischen Anaysekatagorie und Metapher. In M. Düring, U. Eumann, M. Stark & L. von Keyserlingk (Eds.), *Handbuch historische Netzwerkforschung: Grundlagen und Andwendungen* (pp. 63–84). Lit Verlag.

Meirelles, I. (2019). Visualizing information. In J. Flanders & F. Jannidis (Eds.), *The shape of data in the digital humanities: modeling texts and text-based resources* (pp. 167–177). Routledge.

Midura, R. (2021). Itinerating Europe: early modern spatial networks in printed itineraries, 1545–1700. *Journal of Social History*, 54(4), 1023–1063.

Osterhammel, J., & Petersson, N.P. (2009). *Globalization: a short history.* Princeton University Press.

Padgett, J., & Ansell, C. (1993). Robust action and the rise of the Medici, 1400–1434. *American Journal of Sociology*, 98(6), 1259–1319.

Modern History Research Unit (n.d.). *Prosopography Research.* prosopography.history.ox.ac.uk/directory.htm

Putnam, L. (2016). The transnational and the text-searchable: digitized sources and the shadows they cast. *American Historical Review*, 121(2), 377–402.

Rawson, K., & Muñoz, T. (2019). Against cleaning. *Debates in the Digital Humanities 2019*. dhdebates.gc.cuny.edu/read/untitled-f2acf72c-a469-49d8-be35-67f9ac1e3a60/section/07154de9-4903-428e-9c61-7a92a6f22e51

Reinhard, W. (1979). *Freunde und Kreaturen: 'Verflechtung' als Konzept zur Erforschung historischer Führungsgruppen: Römische Oligarchie um 1600.* E. Vögel.

Reinhard, W. (2005). Kommentar: Mikrogeschichte und Makrogeschichte. In H. von Tiessen & C. Windler (Eds.), *Nähe in der Ferne: Personale Verflechtung in den Aussenbeziehungen der Frühen Neuzeit* (pp. 135–144). Duncker & Humblot.

Rice, Y. (2017). Workshop as network: a case study from Mughal South Asia. *Artl@s Bulletin*, Article 4.

Rieder, B., & Röhle, T. (2017). Digital methods from challenges to Bildung. In M.T. Schäfer & K. van Es (Eds.), *Datafied society: studying culture through data* (pp. 109–124). American University Press.

Rollinger, C. (2020). Prolegomena: problems and perspectives of historical network research and ancient history. *Journal of Historical Network Research*, 4, 1–35.

Rosenberg, D. (2003). Early modern information overload. *Journal of the History of Ideas*, 64(1), 1–9.

Rosenberg, D. (2013). Data before the fact. In L. Gitelman (Ed.), *'Raw data' is an oxymoron* (pp. 15–40). MIT Press.

Rosental, P.-A. (2002). Pour une analyse mésoscopique des migrations. *Annales de démographie historique*, 104(2), 145–160.

Rothschild, E. (2011). *The inner life of empire: an eighteenth-century story.* Princeton University Press.

Rothschild, E. (2014). Isolation and economic life in eighteenth-century France. *American Historical Review*, 119(4),1055–1082.

Rothschild, E. (2021). *An infinite history: the story of a family in France over three centuries.* Princeton University Press.

Ryan, Y.C. (2018). More difficult from Dublin than from Dieppe. *Media History*, 24(3–4), 458–476.

Schor, A. (2011). *Theodoret's people: social networks and religious conflicts in late Roman* University of California Press.

Sewell, W.H. (2005). *Logics of history: social theory and social transformation.* University of Chicago Press.

Sheehan, B. (2005). Myth and reality in Chinese financial cliques in 1936. *Enterprise and Society*, 6(3), 452–491.

So, R.J., & Long, H. (2013). Network analysis and the sociology of modernism. *boundary 2*, 40(2), 147–182.

Stone, L. (1971). Prosopography. *Daedalus*, 100(1), 46–79.

Syme, R. (1939). *The Roman Revolution.* Oxford University Press.

Thompson, E.P. (1963). *The making of the English working class.* Victor Gollancz.

Tools, blogs & tutorials (n.d.). Historical Network Research Community. historicalnetworkresearch.org/external-resources/

Trivellato, F. (2011). Is there a future for Italian microhistory in the age of global history? *California Italian Studies*, 2(1), doi.org/10.5070/C321009025

Venturini, T., Matthieu J., & Jensen, P. (2021). What do we see when we look at networks: visual network analysis, relational ambiguity, and force-directed layouts. *Big Data and Society*, 1–16.

Willan, C. (2016). *'John Locke likes this': an ego-network analysis of Locke's letters.* Mapping the Republic of Letters. republicofletters.stanford.edu/publications/locke/

Winterer, C. (2012). Where is America in the Republic of Letters? *Modern Intellectual History*, 9(3), 597–623.

Zuboff, S. (2018). *The age of surveillance capitalism: the fight for a human future at the new frontier of power.* Public Affairs.

The Paradox of Behaviour Change and the Science of Network Diffusion

Damon Centola

The modern science of networks and social diffusion emerged as a solution to an unexpected puzzle – why do people resist change when they are given good reasons for changing; and yet embrace change when they have no apparent reasons for doing so? The most obvious source of change – new information (e.g., about the safety of vaccines) – often fails to produce behaviour change, and in many cases even backfires, making people more resistant to change than they had been before (Centola, 2021a). The same is true for another obvious source of change – incentives (e.g., financial rewards for submitting to a medical exam). Providing people with rewards that encourage a behaviour (or punishments that discourage it) often fails to produce the desired change in behaviour, and can also trigger well-known backfire effects (e.g., with smoking behaviour).

Perhaps one of the earliest and best examples of this puzzle comes from the bizarre history of hybrid corn. Hybrid corn would eventually become one of the most successful change campaigns in US history – going from utter nonexistence (0 per cent adoption among US farmers) in 1928 to universal adoption (100 per cent of US farmers) within twenty years. The interesting part of this story is that this conversion happened despite the marketing efforts that supported it. Starting in 1929, marketing companies bombarded the American Mid-West, Iowa in particular, with advertisements, incentives, pamphlets, door-to-door visits, informational sessions and free trials, promoting the use of hybrid corn. By 1931, over 70 per cent of Iowa farmers had heard about the innovation. Informational awareness was achieved. But only 1 per cent of farmers had adopted it. For the vast majority of famers, hybrid corn was viewed as 'weird' – an innovation subject to extensive rumours and speculation within the farmers' word of mouth networks; suspicions that were ostensibly confirmed by the innovation's conspicuous lack of adoption in the community. By 1933, marketers conceded failure. But then a small number of farmers started experimenting with the technology, and talking with their neighbours about their experiences. Those neighbours tried the new corn, and shared their advice and insights with their other neighbours. And, so on. Within a decade, 100 per cent of Iowa farmers were using hybrid corn. And then 100 per cent of the nation.

This adoption process, and the questions it raised for the standard view of mass marketing and behaviour change, initiated the dawn of systematic research on social diffusion. Social theorists began to appreciate that whenever these questions arose, the explanation for both resistance and acceptance could often be traced back to invisible influences within people's social networks. In the same way that informational campaigns and financial incentives were (and still are) seen as economic tools – or 'mechanisms' – for explaining and controlling human decision-making, starting in the 1930s and 1940s, social networks also began to be explored as a 'social mechanism' that could underwrite and control vast patterns of human behaviour (Ryan & Gross, 1943).

Throughout the 1940s and 1950s, early explorations of these network applications become increasingly mathematical and experimental, and ranged broadly across the fields of psychology, sociology, organisational studies, biology and neuroscience. The two most enduring concepts discovered during this early boom in the 1950s were 'path length' and 'centrality' (complemented by related concepts such as 'clustering' and 'community structure') (Newman, 2010). Today, the measures of path length and centrality still dominate nearly all networks thinking in the study of diffusion, underwriting nearly every approach to understanding the diffusion of social change.

PATH LENGTH*

The study of communication networks and behaviour change dates back to the mid-20th century (Bavelas, 1950). Early network researchers identified the key network measure of average shortest 'path length' – that is, the shortest number of 'steps' between the nodes in a graph – as the controlling topological feature governing the efficiency of the spread of information through a population (Solomonoff & Rapoport, 1951; Rapoport, 1953; Rapoport & Horvath, 1961). Over the next several decades, this research matured into several important insights about the informational pathways that mediate the transmission of social learning within neighbourhoods (Blau & Schwartz, 1984), within organisations (Granovetter, 1973; Burt, 1992) and even across nations (Milgram, 1967).

A major leap forward in thinking about social networks and diffusion came from Granovetter's (1973) work on strong and weak ties. Granovetter's idea is powerful and clear. It hinges on his elegant distinction between 'strong' ties and 'weak' ties. Your close friends and family are your trusted strong ties. They make up your inner social circle. Your casual acquaintances – the people you meet at a conference, in a class, or on vacation – are your weak ties. They make up your outer circle – the random connections in your orbit. And because they exist outside your usual orbit, they connect you to new people with whom you would likely never intersect otherwise.

Granovetter observed that when two people have a strong connection to a third person, they are also likely to have a connection with one another. This means that a person's strong ties tend to be located within 'closed triads' – that is, social triangles in the network. Viewed from the *relational* perspective of each individual, strong ties are the most important links in the social network. They are proximate, trusted and familiar, and therefore the most influential for diffusion. However, from the *bird's eye* perspective of the entire network, strong ties also tend to be bunched together in redundant clusters of interlocking triangles. Consequently, for a contagion to spread from one part of a network to another across strong ties, it has to travel through lots of clustered neighbourhoods to get there.

Weak ties, by contrast, are relationally the least important contacts in each person's ego-network. People connected by weak ties are often not very similar to each other, nor do they typically interact frequently or substantively. Subjectively, they are often the least noticeable features of a person's social landscape.

However, Granovetter observed that this is also what makes them so important for diffusion. The fact that weak ties are not embedded in the network of strong relations gives them a tremendous structural power. While strong ties tend to be clustered into triangles of shared friends, weak ties branch randomly throughout a population. A key feature of Granovetter's insight is that structure, not affect, plays the major role in diffusion. Once affect is removed, the purely structural effect of adding weak ties to a network is to create shortcuts that link distant regions together.

A key lesson from this work was that weak ties, also known as 'cross-cutting ties' (Blau & Schwartz, 1984), across communities or organisational units (Burt, 1992), could reduce the 'simple path length' of a network (i.e., 'degrees of separation' between people), and thereby accelerate the spread of information among them (Centola & Macy, 2007; Centola, 2022a). However, more recent breakthroughs discussed below show that the measure of path length is not a fixed quantity for a network. Topology changes as the contagions that spread across it change – the shortest (simple) path length for the spread of information is not the same as the shortest (complex) path length for the spread of behaviour change (Guilbeault & Centola, 2021). Below, I show you how these complementary measures of *simple path length* and *complex path length* offer powerful tools for building network strategies to initiate innovation diffusion campaigns and social movements. To appreciate the importance of these advances, we first need to delve

---

* Section adapted from Centola (2018) and Centola (2022a).

into the second major network property governing social diffusion – *centrality*.

CENTRALITY**

In 1948, social scientists Paul Lazarsfeld, Bernard Berelson and Hazel Gaudet published a watershed study that placed network 'centrality' into the centre of the picture of political influence. The accepted view of the day was that broadcast media dominated the political sphere, reaching out to the electorate and influencing voting behaviour. *The people's choice* showed otherwise. Lazarsfeld et al. illustrated that it was people – friends, neighbours and family members – who were the primary channels through which people learned about political candidates.

Their real discovery was that mass media still mattered, but surprisingly the way that media signals reached most people was through their social networks. Lazarsfeld et al.'s new insight was that although media signals were broadcast across the continent, they only landed on a small fraction (perhaps 5 per cent) of individuals. These individuals acted as secondary channels of influence and dissemination for political messages. These rare people were dubbed 'opinion leaders' – the human relay stations that political influence travelled through to go from mainstream media to the public.

This insight initiated a new scientific investigation into the topic of opinion leaders, and the question of just how influential they really were for the spread of everything from political opinions to consumer goods. Nearly a decade later, the resulting study by Elihu Katz and Paul Lazarsfeld, *Personal influence* (1955), was an instant classic. It was landmark analysis of who the opinion leaders were, and how they influenced people.

The impact of *Personal influence* is partly due to the fact that it is a surprisingly subtle and detailed exploration of social influence. Katz and Lazarsfeld's analysis primarily focused on 800 women from Dectur, Illinois, and the features of their personalities and relationships that facilitated the flow of information from the mass media through their community. Katz and Lazarsfeld's study (1955) revealed that features of social status mattered for influence, but so did the groups that people belonged to, the friends and neighbours they were close to, and their perceived expertise on certain topics. In short, the patterns of influence were complex.

But one thing was clear. The influence of mass media was not a straight shot from broadcast towers to consumer behaviour. More often than not, Katz and Lazarsfeld found that a small group of people gave a disproportionate fraction of their attention to the media. And, those people became the most relevant sources of influence for their peers. Within their social circles, these opinion leaders were the key players in disseminating media messages.

For Katz and Lazarsfeld, opinion leaders are not people like Oprah Winfrey. Rather, Oprah's media empire would be considered a channel of broadcast communication. Katz and Lazarsfeld's insight was that media signals travelled in steps – from broadcast towers to the opinion leaders, and from opinion leaders to the public. According to this 'two-step flow' model, broadcast signals reached most of the public by being filtered through well-connected people in their social networks – their sister-in-law, or their friendly colleague – who were the primary receivers of media messages, and the primary vehicles through which those messages were then disseminated to everyone else.

The two-step flow model was only one part of Katz and Lazarsfeld's investigation. They also developed nuanced, but unfinished accounts of what makes certain people influential, and how that influence can hold sway across contexts, or vary across topics. These questions have since become productive areas of research for other sociologists (Lazarsfeld & Merton, 1954; Davis & Greve, 1997; Katz, 1957; Reagans & McEvily, 2003; Centola, 2011). But these are not the insights for which Katz and Lazarsfeld's (1955) study became famous. Rather, it was the key idea of the opinion leader that captured people's imagination. The hypothesis that a small number of people pay disproportionate attention to media, and therefore have disproportionate influence in disseminating it, became a focal point for a generation of communication scholars who continued to explore the two-step flow model.

But it was the *second* step in the two-step model that interested most people. Was it true that a small number of people could influence everyone else? Who are these influential people? How can product advertisers and political campaigns target them? These questions animated the work of generations of sociologists, political scientists, organisational scholars, marketing professionals, and, most recently, network scientists. Many of the subtleties of Katz and Lazarsfeld's original work (1955) were eventually refined into a single idea – articulated by Malcolm Gladwell's ominous phrase, 'the law of few' (2000). The idea is that there are a few special people out there and, if you can find them, they are the key to disseminating a new idea, product or candidate to everyone else.

**Section adapted from Centola (2021b).

Enter social media, and the birth of the modern 'influencer'.

Today, the notion of the opinion leader is not what it once was. The most significant reason for this is the unprecedented diversity of people's media diets, and the near ubiquity with which people are exposed to niche, almost personalised, media sources. The original question that Katz and Lazarsfeld set out to answer – regarding the influence of mass media on consumer behaviour – is less fashionable today, largely because institutions like 'the Media' (and 'the News') have ceased to exist as they once did. But Katz and Lazarsfeld's crucial insights into opinion leaders have endured. This is because Katz and Lazarsfeld looked beyond the influence of the media into the fundamental structure of social relations that controls the spread of personal influence. It thus remains a guiding force in contemporary research on social networks. The question that animates much of today's scientific work on social influence is a reformulated version of the question that motivated Katz and Lazarsfeld's original investigation (1955): 'How do new ideas, information and innovations become widely accepted by spreading through people's social networks?'

Generations of research building on Katz and Lazarsfeld's ideas have pushed scientific thinking beyond a psychological focus on the individual-level attributes of influencers (like people's personality, charisma or attractiveness) to the structural insight that was nascent within the Katz and Lazarsfeld's original work – the idea that there is a social structure that mediates the process through which social contagions spread from one person to the next. This idea led to the discovery of measurable patterns within social networks – much like Simmel's idea of the 'web of group affiliations' (Simmel, 1955) and the later 'strength of weak ties' (Granovetter, 1973) – that help to explain how new ideas and behaviours propagate through a society. A central feature of this approach is the insight that a small number of individuals are located at key points in the network structure, which makes them essential for the rapid dissemination of social contagions.

Today, this concept of 'structural position' is a core principle of the field of network science. From a networks perspective, the notion of opinion leaders – or 'influencers' – boils down to the essential question of which network positions have the most power for spreading new ideas. The classic answer is 'centrality' (Newman, 2010). The idea is that people at the centre of a social network are the individuals who are best positioned to spread social contagions to everyone else. A narrow reading of Katz and Lazarsfeld (1955), and a charitable reading of Gladwell (2000), unifies all of this research on the problem of personal influence, stretching back over three-quarters of a century, into a single analytical insight: the people at the centre of the social network *are* the influencers.

The most popular methods for identifying central individuals in a social network are: (1) 'degree centrality' (individuals with the most connections); (2) 'betweenness centrality' (individuals through which most paths must travel, going from one part of a network to another); and (3) 'eigenvector centrality' (individuals whose neighbours are highly connected). In the study of personal networks, these three measures are often collapsed down into a single metric – *viz.*, who is the most highly 'connected' individual? That person, or those people are considered to be the influencers.

SIMPLE AND COMPLEX CONTAGIONS***

Today, this long and important tradition in the study of personal influence has become so refined that it has uncovered a new and unexpected puzzle. This puzzle emerges from the fact that much of the contemporary work on opinion leaders, influencers and network centrality has been crystallised into the core insight that social innovations spread by propagating from the *core* of the network to the *periphery* – that is, it spreads from highly connected people at the 'centre' of the social network, to the less connected people at the periphery of the network. The puzzle is that this widely accepted theory of the dynamics of social influence does not match up with the most current data on how social innovations – ranging from new technologies to progressive social movements – actually spread through social networks (State & Adamic, 2015; Romero et al., 2011; Steinert-Threkeld, 2017; Traag, 2016; Sprague & House, 2017; Mønsted et al., 2017; Centola, 2018; Guilbeault et al., 2018a; Beaman et al., 2016).

The solution to this puzzle reveals the role of personal networks in the flow of social innovations, and the surprising implications for the modern notion of the 'influencer'. The solution starts with an overlooked distinction between *simple contagions*, like simple information and familiar ideas, which spread from a single contact; and *complex contagions*, like changes in workplace culture, or the adoption of innovative technologies, which

---

***Section adapted from Centola (2022b).

typically require reinforcement from several peers before people are willing to adopt them (Centola & Macy, 2007; Centola et al., 2007; Centola, 2010, 2015). The differences between simple and complex contagions have striking implications for how personal networks control the spread of innovations, the dispersion of ideas, the adoption of inventions, the growth of social movements, the success of political campaigns and the uptake of new health behaviours (Steinert-Threkeld, 2017; Traag, 2016; Sprague & House, 2017; Guilbeault et al., 2018a).

There are four key sources of resistance that create complexity in the process of social spreading (Centola & Macy, 2007; Centola, 2018). Each one is a barrier to adoption. Identifying whether an innovation will encounter any or all of these barriers reveals whether an innovation will be simple or complex.

1. *Social coordination*: If the value of an innovation or behaviour depends on coordinating with other people who adopt it – i.e., the greater the number of adopters the more useful the innovation – then it requires social reinforcement to spread. Think of Twitter or Facebook.
2. *Legitimacy*: For some behaviours, the more people who adopt them, the greater the expectation is that others will approve of the decision to adopt, and the lower the risk is of embarrassment or sanction. Think of wearing a new fashion.
3. *Credibility*: It often happens that adopters act as sources of social proof for an innovation. The more people who adopt a behaviour, the more likely it is that the behaviour is worth the cost or the effort it takes to adopt it – and the lower risk is of wasting time or resources on it. Think of the decision to adopt a new diet, or an expensive new digital technology.
4. *Emotional excitement*: Some innovations and behaviours are appealing only when people are emotionally energised by one another. Think of joining a protest like Black Lives Matter.

These four barriers to adoption – the need for coordination, legitimacy, credibility, or emotional excitement – may occur individually or together. All of them can be overcome by social reinforcement. For instance, innovative social media tools like Facebook and Twitter spread through peer networks that enable people to coordinate with their friends in their decision to adopt the new technologies (Ugander et al., 2012; Toole et al., 2011). The growth of political uprisings and social movements like the Arab Spring also require social reinforcement because people need to believe that a movement is legitimate before they will be willing to add their voice to the chorus (Steinert-Threkeld, 2017). Similarly, the spread of new workplace gender norms typically requires coordinated support from a 'critical mass' of peers before it will succeed in creating a new 'norm' (Kanter, 1977; Childs & Krook, Dahlerup, 2006). More generally, everything from the spread of memes like the Ice Bucket Challenge in the US, to the growth of environmental technologies like household solar panel installations in Europe, are all complex contagions that require social reinforcement in order to spread successfully.

The most significant consequence of the distinction between simple and complex contagions is that it transforms our understanding of how the structure of social networks impacts the dynamics of social contagion. Granovetter's superb (1973) study of the strength of weak ties shows that 'weak' acquaintanceship relations tend to link randomly across a network, bridging long social distances, while 'strong' intimate friendship and family relations tend to be clustered together, creating many 'triadic' friend-of-friend ties. Once Granovetter developed this strikingly clear conception of the large-scale structure of social networks, he inferred that long-distance acquaintanceship ties are more valuable for the process of social diffusion than trusted friendship ties. As he put it, 'whatever is to be diffused can reach a larger number of people, and traverse a greater social distance (i.e., path length), when passed through weak ties rather than strong' (1973, p. 1366). The crucial concept in Granovetter's analysis is path length: the number of steps in the shortest path from one individual to another. Because weak ties span long social distances, they shorten the path length between everyone in the network. The more weak ties there are, the shorter the path length between people becomes – and the faster that new ideas, innovations and social movements can spread from one person to everyone else.

But complex contagions change everything. For a complex contagion, a single link across a social network is not sufficient to spread an innovation from one person to another. The 'bridge' across the social network created by a weak tie is a narrow bridge – composed of a single link, as shown in Figure 19.1. Because the spread of complex contagions requires social reinforcement from multiple contacts, an effective bridge across the network must be a wide bridge – composed of multiple ties. Wide bridges are the essential network structure needed to spread complex contagions. And, they are typically associated with strong ties rather than weak.

Strong ties naturally create wide bridges because they are clustered together, creating stable pathways

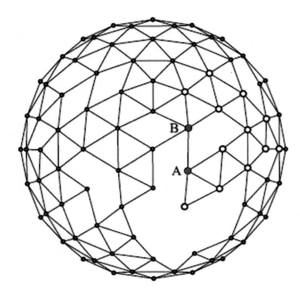

Figure 19.1 Example of a simple path from node A to B, composed of a single 'narrow bridge' (i.e., one 'step' in the network between the grey nodes), compared to a complex path from A to B, composed of wide bridges (nine 'steps' in the network, shown by white highlighted nodes)

for spreading complex contagions from one community to another. This is why so many innovations (from farming equipment to Twitter membership) have historically been found to spread 'spatially' or 'geographically' – because spatial and geographic networks are typically composed of strong ties that form wide bridges (Centola & Macy, 2007; Centola, 2018; Hagerstrand, 1970; Toole et al., 2011; Centola, 2021a). But wide bridges need not be geographically constrained. They can also span long geographic distances. On social media sites like Facebook, the emergence of 'virtual' wide bridges among vast networks of peers enables social reinforcement to propel the spread of complex contagions. As you will see below, social movements ranging from the Arab Spring to the growth of support for same-sex marriage are complex contagions that have spread across social media networks by using reinforcing network pathways. Remarkably, these networks bear a stronger resemblance to the strong-tie network pathways through which the Civil Rights Movement took hold (McAdam & Paulsen, 1993) and pre-industrial technologies spread (Hagerstrand, 1970), rather than the weak tie networks through which information and viruses typically expand (Centola, 2018, 2021a; Guilbeault et al., 2018a).

For nearly a century, network concepts such as distance, influence and centrality have been developed under the assumption that social dynamics follow the principles of simple contagion, for which each weak tie constitutes a bridge across the network. But a narrow bridge is not a viable path for a complex contagion (Centola, 2022b), which means that the distance between people (i.e., the number of steps between them in the social graph) is different for a simple contagion than for a complex contagion. So, how do we measure a network's path length? And, what does it mean for predicting the spread of social innovations? This chapter will show you how the findings on complex contagions have changed our conception of social networks, impacting everything from how we measure social distance to how we develop strategies for social change.

Most notably, these theoretical advances and empirical discoveries reveal that the classic model of social influence in which the highly connected 'influencer' is the source of social change assumes that all contagions are simple. However, social innovations that are risky or require social coordination are typically complex. For instance, innovative technologies like Facebook and Twitter usually depend on people coordinating with multiple peers before they are willing to adopt (Ugander et al., 2012; Toole et al., 2011). Similarly, successful political campaigns and social movements, like support for marriage equality and the #MeToo movement, are also complex contagions (State & Adamic, 2015; Traag, 2016; Steiner-Threkeld, 2017; Mønsted et al., 2017). People need to believe that a movement is legitimate before they are willing to add their voice to the chorus supporting it. Changes in workplace culture and the growth of new social norms concerning gender relations within organisations also spread through the dynamics of complex contagion (Kanter, 1977; Centola et al., 2018). In fact, the only social contagions that actually spread in the way that the classic model describes – from highly connected influencers at the core of the social network to the modestly connected members network periphery – are familiar ideas, simple information and infectious diseases. That is, simple contagions. Social innovation, however, is a whole other thing.

THE SURPRISING LIMITS OF CENTRALITY

To see why highly central people – whom I will refer to hereafter as 'influencers' – do not actually play the dominant role in initiating change, we will examine the spread of an innovative technology through the personal work networks of tech industry managers with varying levels of social connectedness.

Consider a C-level manager at a Fortune 500 company who is extremely well connected. This manager has hundreds of professional contacts, which makes it very easy for her to discover innovative ideas floating around in the vast network that surrounds her. She may be among the first people to find out about an innovative new process-centred management approach, such as *total quality management* (TQM). Although the TQM approach may seem unorthodox to her colleagues and peers, the Fortune 500 manager is nevertheless in an excellent position to be among the leaders in its adoption, responsible for spreading the innovative idea to her large network of connections.

Let's compare this Fortune 500 manager to another manager who is at a small startup company. This manager has many fewer professional connections – perhaps only a few dozen – and thus she has much less access to all of the new management innovations that may be percolating through various parts of the social network. Because the startup manager is less connected, she has much less power to spread any innovative ideas that she discovers. Consequently, the startup manager appears to be much less important than the Fortune 500 manager for spreading an innovative organisational practice like TQM.

However, while highly connected influencers, or 'hubs' in the social network, have access to many people in the community – and thus are excellent vehicles for spreading innovations to lots of people – they are also susceptible to peer influences from lots of people. For innovations that are risky or require legitimacy, the influence from a single adopter is typically weighed against the countervailing influences from all of a person's peer contacts who have not adopted the innovation. When risk or legitimacy are involved, the non-adopters in a person's social network weigh against the decision to adopt. Before adopting a costly or unfamiliar innovation, each manager must also consider the signals coming from all of these countervailing influences.

The Fortune 500 manager has the natural advantage that her vast network of contacts will lead her to discover the innovation early on, before it has become widely adopted. When considering her decision to adopt, her ability to make early discoveries also means that any innovative practices she encounters will not yet be adopted by the vast majority of her contacts. In this light, she needs to consider several things before making the decision to adopt. First, she needs to know if there is enough evidence to support the claim that a new management practice would be successful at her type of company, at her scale and in her sector. Without seeing peer institutions successfully implement the innovative practice, it would be a gamble to invest in making a large organisational change to an unproven management practice. Second, if she decides to adopt TQM before most of her peers and competitors do, will that decision be seen as savvy or reckless by her more conservative colleagues? That is, will she incur negative reputation effects from adopting an innovation that has not yet been validated by her peer community? Third, and perhaps most importantly, what are the potential reputation effects that she will suffer if the decision to adopt this innovation is a bad one? Because she is so well connected, she is a highly visible actor and thus she is subject to scrutiny from lots of people. If she waits to adopt until the innovation becomes accepted among several of her peer institutions, and many of her contacts have endorsed it, then she cannot be held personally accountable for her decision, given that it had become an industry norm. If the innovation then fails, this failure can be attributed to a collective error rather than to an individual one. By contrast, if she adopts the innovation upon her first exposure to it, as an early mover she will be individually accountable for any failures that come as a result of that decision. For all of these reasons, the Fortune 500 manager may wait until there is substantial social confirmation for the innovative management practice before she will be willing to adopt it.

By contrast, the startup manager is in a different position. She may have all the same concerns as her Fortune 500 colleague; however, she has a much smaller network of countervailing influences to consider. Early exposure to an innovative practice from just a few sources of reinforcement will have a much greater impact on her decision-making since this small number of contacts constitutes a much larger fraction of her professional network. For the startup manager, even a modest level of social reinforcement for the innovation may constitute a strong enough social signal for her to consider the innovation seriously. In addition, the startup manager is not subject to the same level of scrutiny as the Fortune 500 manager, nor is she as pressured by the same scale of reputation effects that might serve to inhibit her from being willing to be an early adopter. For the startup manager, as compared to the Fortune 500 manager, the greater relative impact of a few early adopters, along with her exposure to fewer countervailing influences, make her much more likely to be an early adopter of the innovative practice.

The strategic implication is that innovations may spread far more effectively by percolating through 'peripheral' clusters of less connected actors, rather than by trying to spread through highly connected network hubs. For simple contagions, hubs are excellent spreaders because of their vast access to the social network, which makes it very easy for them to become infected with new ideas early on in a spreading process. It also allows them to rapidly spread their infection to their large number of contacts. However, both of these advantages for spreading viral content – that is, early exposure and a large number of contacts – work against the spread of complex contagions.

For complex contagions, early detection of an innovation by hubs also means that most of the hubs' contacts will not have adopted the innovation. Moreover, because a hub is so visible, she is also likely to be very cautious before adopting an unproven innovation. Far from being the initial seed that launches the diffusion of an innovation, a highly connected Fortune 500 manager may be among the last people to adopt an innovative management practice.

Ironically, hubs in the social network may often be a roadblock for spreading particularly novel innovations. In order for 'game changing' innovations (that is, innovations that are particularly unfamiliar, unusual, or disruptive) to spread effectively, they typically need to follow peripheral pathways composed of clustered networks of interlocking managers at smaller firms who can build a critical mass for the innovation. The historic growth of innovative technologies such as Facebook, Twitter and Skype (Ugander et al., 2012; Toole et al., 2011; Karsai et al., 2016; Bakshy et al., 2009) have all shown that the need for social reinforcement means that diffusion will be most effective through peripheral channels of overlapping social ties. Once an innovation starts to catch on and spread through these peripheral channels, it can gain enough traction in the network to activate a substantial fraction of adopters. Once enough of the hub's contacts finally adopt, there will be enough reinforcement in the Fortune 500 manager's network to convince her that this innovation is credible and that she should adopt it, too. In other words, once an innovation finally takes off, that's when the highly connected leaders typically adopt it (Centola 2018, 2019).

The fatal mistake often made by entrepreneurs and marketers trying to spread innovations is to misread the rapid growth in the uptake of an innovation that *causes* a Fortune 500 manager's adoption, as the *result* of the Fortune 500 manager's adoption.

This fallacy comes from an obvious (but unscientific) observation. This observation is that the moment of increased growth that marks the sharp acceleration in the spread of an innovation (often referred to the 'elbow' in the growth curve) happens around the same time that highly connected people start adopting. The fallacy is that these highly connected adopters are the *cause* of that growth. It is certainly true that growth rates increase dramatically around the same time that the Fortune 500 managers start adopting. However, the massive acceleration in adoption that coincides with the Fortune 500 manager's adoption is not the *cause* of the innovation's success. Quite the opposite. The growing success of the innovation is the cause of the highly connected manager's willingness to adopt it. The fallacy is to think that targeting social connectors will jump-start a successful diffusion campaign.

The evidence from research on complex contagions (Toole et al., 2011; Wang et al., 2019; Centola, 2018) shows that the most successful strategy for spreading an innovation, particularly an unusual or costly one, is to target peripheral communities of moderately connected individuals, who are much better positioned to grow a groundswell of support. Once this groundswell grows large enough, it can then capture the attention of a Fortune 500 manager. By the time highly connected hubs start adopting an innovative practice, the innovation has typically gained enough support that it has already begun a period of rapid, widespread growth throughout the population.

The more innovative an idea is, the more important this fact about personal networks becomes. For innovations that are unfamiliar or disruptive, success comes from targeting social networks that can provide social reinforcement for a new idea. These social networks can be thought of as 'incubators', which can grow expanding pockets of support for an innovation.

Ironically, the reason that incubators in the network periphery can be so effective for sparking successful innovation diffusion is the exact opposite reason that highly connected hubs are so appealing. Hubs are appealing because they provide massive amounts of social exposure for an innovation. We might intuitively expect that increased exposure would lead to increased spreading. This is certainly true for simple contagions. However, for complex contagions, peripheral network channels are successful precisely because they protect potential adopters from being overwhelmed by exposure to too many countervailing influences from the non-adopters in the population. It is this protection that is essential for spreading an innovative idea.

INFLUENCER 'BACKFIRE' EFFECTS

'The law of the few' is a notion that has become widely accepted partly because there are lots of situations for which it works amazingly well. For instance, many people know the now-infamous (and apocryphal) story of Gaetan Dugas, the highly sexually active flight attendant who claimed to have had over 2,500 sexual partners; and whose promiscuity was thought to have played a significant role in the early spread of HIV/AIDS.

For medical scientists who study the spread of diseases, the notion of highly connected influencers offers an essential insight into how social networks trigger epidemics like HIV/AIDS and Covid-19 – and the pivotal role that highly connected people can play. Of course, this idea goes far beyond epidemiology. It has also helped to animate our imaginations when it comes to thinking about the spread of unusual cultural fads, the best strategies for developing our professional networks and the social contours that define major historical events.

But this imagination is precisely the problem. The spread of social innovations – within organisations and within our society – does not actually resemble the spread of a virus. It is the generalisation from simple contagions to complex contagions that is problematic. The problem is not simply that this generalisation has led to failures. The problem is that it can lead to backfire. Highly connected social stars within personal networks may not only *not help* innovations to succeed, they can inadvertently *undermine* any future attempts at innovation.

Why? Because exposure is not always a good thing. For simple contagions, exposure equals awareness, which translates into adoption. An effective strategy for creating awareness will always be to increase the connectedness of the adopters. This assumption does not generalise to many complex contagions.

For example, let's assume that a highly connected social star has effectively spread the word about an innovation. Everyone knows about it. But what happens if no one adopts it? Because of the popularity of the influencer who is spreading the word, the awareness campaign may have been *too* successful. Here's why. A successful awareness campaign not only makes people aware of the product, it also makes people aware that *everyone else* is aware of it. An effective word of mouth campaign includes not just information about the innovation, but also information about the fact that the innovation is well known.

What does it signal about an innovation if everyone knows about it – and everyone knows that everyone else knows about it – and yet everyone also knows that no one has adopted it? The countervailing influences from a large number of peers – who are known to be aware of an innovation *and* who have also elected not to adopt it – provide evidence for everyone else that the innovation is undesirable. The non-adopters offer an implicit social signal about the illegitimacy of the innovation. Before the awareness campaign succeeded, an innovation may simply have been seen as contentious or unfamiliar. The challenge for spreading this kind of unknown innovation is simply that it may not yet be seen as credible or legitimate. Things are different after an awareness campaign succeeds. If awareness of the innovation has been widely diffused, but the innovation itself has still has not caught on, then there is a much bigger problem. The sea of non-adopters *confirms* the innovation's illegitimacy. The problem now is that *it appears that* the innovation has been deliberately and publicly rejected by everyone.

The implicit social signal suggests that the innovation may carry a social stigma. This perception of stigma is created by the success of the influencer's awareness campaign, combined with the utter failure of their adoption campaign. This pinpoints the crucial difference between *awareness* and *acceptance*. For simple contagions, these two are treated as the same thing. For a complex contagion, they can be different, and that difference can have crucial backfire effects if innovators succeed at creating awareness but fail to create acceptance.

Consider Google's failed attempt to bring Google Glass to market. There was widespread awareness of Glass (we all knew about it), combined with widespread awareness of its lack of acceptance as a product (we all know that it failed). This created a negative social stigma, not just around the product, but also around the company. This stigma became such a significant impediment for the company, that it prevented Google's future attempts to reboot the product line. Google and other companies are now struggling to figure out how to make similar kinds of products grow in the soil that Google's early efforts have inadvertently salted.

The distinction between awareness and acceptance offers a valuable lesson for any diffusion strategy that would attempt to use a 'kitchen sink' approach to the spread of innovations – in which all network strategies are attempted simultaneously. One important reason not to use a simple contagion strategy – such as the activation of highly connected influencers – to spread a complex contagion is that successfully creating tremendous awareness for an innovation, while simultaneously failing to create corresponding levels of acceptance for it, can backfire. The result is not a *small gain* in adopters. But a *large loss* in public opinion about the company and the product line. Awareness without acceptance can create a well-known, but socially stigmatised innovation.

The downside of a highly successful awareness campaign is that everyone remembers the product. And, if it fails, everyone also remembers how badly it failed. Future attempts to spread similar innovations are likely to face even greater barriers to adoption than the initial innovation. A better strategy for spreading a novel or unfamiliar innovation is to target the network periphery, where support for the innovation can grow slowly, gaining acceptance in the social network without the unwieldy burden of widespread awareness.

COMPLEX CENTRALITY

A recent series of studies showing the ineffectiveness of highly connected influencers for spreading change – particularly, for the spread of unusual or contentious ideas on social media – have also highlighted that there are specific locations in the network periphery that are surprisingly effective for spreading these innovations (Bakshy et al., 2009; Barberá et al., 2015; Steinert-Threkeld, 2017). To identify these locations, my colleague and I tested a series of different models of innovation diffusion on 74 empirically collected large social networks (Guilbeault & Centola, 2021), with the goal of discovering the essential locations for initiating diffusion. Strikingly, the results converged on a new kind of centrality – *complex centrality* – which consistently identified the most influential individuals in the social network for spreading social innovations.

The key to complex centrality is that it pinpoints network clusters that are located at the intersection of 'wide bridges' between social groups. When we think of links between communities in a network, we typically imagine these links as a single 'bridge tie' from one group to the other. But a single tie is a very narrow bridge. Only a simple contagion can spread across it. For social innovations to effectively spread across communities, there must be wide bridges – composed of multiple overlapping ties – that can provide social reinforcement for a new idea to propagate from one group to the next (Centola & Macy, 2007; Centola 2015). We discovered that the locations in the social network that are most effective for spreading innovations are the social clusters located at the intersection of these wide bridges.

Figure 19.2 shows that from the perspective of simple contagions and narrow bridges, complex centrality appears to identify locations in the periphery of the social network, while traditional measures like degree centrality and percolation centrality identify individuals who are located near the centre of the standard visualised layout. However, from the point of view of social influence, complex centrality identifies the social clusters (a focal node and its neighbours) that are the most influential positions in the network for spreading behaviour change.

The social clusters (called *bridging groups*) identified by complex centrality are disproportionately influential because they are the most centrally located *groups* in the entire social network (Centola, 2015, 2021a). Crucially, however, the individual members of these social clusters are not central to the network. The individual members of bridging groups are not highly connected influencers, nor are they enterprising information brokers. In fact, individually, the members of these social clusters are languishing in the periphery, indistinguishable from anyone else. They are unlikely even to know that they occupy a special location in the network. But collectively, they are the most influential members of the network.

The influence of these social clusters comes from the fact that they sit at the intersection of wide bridges. Collectively, the members of a bridging group have more wide bridges to diverse parts of a social network than any other social cluster in the population. Bridging groups combine the *strength* of social reinforcement with the *accessibility* of boundary-spanning wide bridges – a rare and effective combination for diffusion (Guilbeault & Centola, 2021).

A recent study of peer influence on Chinese social media showed how effective these network locations can be (Wang et al., 2019; Centola,

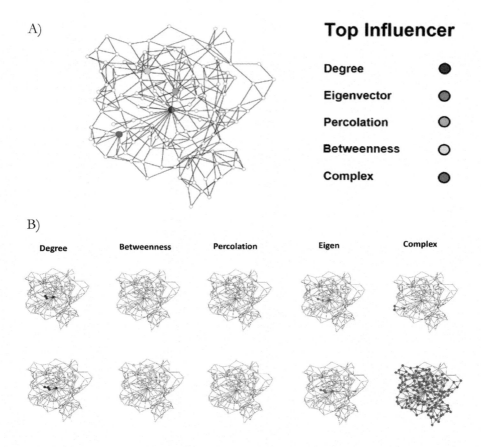

Figure 19.2 Diffusion using different measures of centrality to target influencers. Panel A shows the network locations associated with each measure of centrality and influence. In Panel B, the top row shows the initial seeding for triggering a behaviour change cascade through the network. The bottom row of Panel B shows the corresponding efficacy of each location for spreading a complex contagion (see Guilbeault & Centola, 2021, for complete details)

2019). This study compared the spreading patterns generated by highly connected network influencers (with more than 100,000 connections) to spreading patterns generated by regular users who were clustered amid wide bridges in the network periphery. When media content was a simple contagion, it spread most effectively from the highly connected influencers.

But when media content was politically charged, or pertained to normative topics, then highly connected influencers were only able to spread messages to their direct contacts. Beyond the influencer's immediate social circle, social contagions tended to die a quick death. For this kind of content, social clusters in the network periphery, composed of moderately connected users, significantly increased the spread of the messages – allowing media content to reach as much as five times farther into the population than when it came from highly connected influencers.

Strikingly, these locations in the network periphery are among the *least* effective places for initiating the spread of simple contagions. For viral diffusion, network redundancy and lower connectedness slows down the spreading process. However, these peripheral social clusters are ideal for initiating the spread of a social innovation. In these network locations, change agents can coordinate with each other and with others to accelerate the growth of a critical mass (Guilbeault & Centola, 2021).

CONCLUSION

Over the last several decades, the maturation of the early tools for social diffusion research into the contemporary field of network science has reinvigorated centuries-old problems of collective behaviour, collective rationality and collective intelligence, revealing hundreds of novel theoretical and applied problems for researchers working at this interdisciplinary frontier. I will conclude by highlighting a problem of immediate social and political significance – cultural bias – which has recently been illuminated using novel network-based analyses of how the structure of influence within social networks may control the growth (or decay) of cultural biases.

One sphere of social life in which influencers can be influential (and dangerously so) is in the spread of ideas and opinions that reinforce existing biases. Online and offline, when communities are organised homophilously, along the lines of shared political, social or cultural beliefs, then ideas that reinforce a community's existing beliefs are often simple contagions. They are easy to understand and easy to spread. Within political echo chambers, highly connected influencers at the centre of the conversation can easily spread misinformation that plays to a group's biases (Becker et al., 2017; Becker et al., 2019; Guilbeault et al., 2018b; Guilbeault & Centola, 2021).

By contrast, contentious ideas that challenge a group's biases are complex contagions. These ideas face strong opposition, and thus are not likely to emerge from highly connected individuals facing a sea of countervailing influences. New ideas that challenge the status quo emerge more commonly from the moderately connected network periphery – where everyone's voice is equally heard, and where new ideas can be reinforced among peers and protected from too many countervailing influences (Samuelson & Zeckhauser, 1988; Steinert-Threkeld, 2017; Centola, 2018).

This reveals an important asymmetry in the 'influence of the influencer'. A highly connected or authoritative person can effectively spread ideas that reinforce a community's existing biases, but they will not be very effective for spreading beliefs and behaviours that run contrary to people's biases. This asymmetry in the influence of influencers – namely, they're good for spreading simple contagions, but poor at spreading complex contagions – is particularly consequential for disadvantaged communities. The potential danger this poses for online influences has become particularly salient in the discussion about health misinformation among communities that are distrustful of mainstream health care.

A generation of research on underserved communities, in particular African-American and Latina women, has found that the members of these communities report disproportionate levels of distrust towards mainstream medical care (Kennedy et al., 2007). And, not without cause – for example, involuntary sterilisation programmes in the 1950s and 1960s (Kluchin, 2009). As a result, highly connected influencers in these communities can be effective for spreading messages that amplify people's distrust of current preventive health measures (Blankenship et al., 2018), such as birth control, vaccination and Covid-19 prevention measures. These biases may also make these communities disproportionately susceptible to malicious anti-vaccination campaigns that use highly connected, and well-disguised, social media 'bots' to spread misinformation (Broniatowski et al., 2018).

The power of influencers to spread misinformation about topics such as vaccination, birth control and Covid-19 precautions can further exacerbate health inequities, making communities that are already distrustful of mainstream health care increasingly vulnerable to suffering negative, but preventable health outcomes. The asymmetry in the network dynamics of simple and complex contagions means that in order to be effective, public health campaigns cannot succeed simply by spreading information (Centola, 2018, 2021b). If new preventive health advice challenges a community's existing biases, then successful information-spreading may not only fail, but also lead to *backfire*. Just like Google Glass, if everyone knows about the newly propagated health advice (and everyone knows that everyone knows about it), but everyone also knows that no one in their community has adopted it, then the success of the *informational* campaign may inadvertently manufacture social proof against behaviour change. An important direction for future research is to discover new ways that public health dissemination can be approached *not* as a problem of *awareness*, but as one of *acceptance*. Dissemination campaigns that face these challenges can succeed by finding ways to target reinforcing ties among people in the network periphery – that is, using complex centrality – which can minimise countervailing influences, and mobilise a challenge to biased expectations about health care and health advice.

REFERENCES

Ancona, D.G., & Caldwell, D. (1992). Bridging the boundary: external activity and performance in organizational teams. *Administrative Science Quarterly, 37*, 634–665.

Bakshy, E., Karrer, B., & Adamic, L. (2009). Social influence and the diffusion of user-created content. In *Proceedings of the 10th ACM Conference on Electronic Commerce* (pp. 325–334). Association of Computing Machinery.

Barberá, P., Wang, N., Bonneau, R., Jost, J.T., Nagler, J., Tucker, J., & González-Bailón, S. (2015). The critical periphery in the growth of social protests. *PLOS One, 10*, e0143611.

Bavelas, A. (1950). Communication patterns in task-oriented groups. *Journal of the Acoustical Society of America, 22*(6), 725–730.

Beaman, L., Benyishay, A., Fatch, P., & Magruder, J. (2016). Making networks work for policy: evidence from agricultural technology adoption in Malawi. *Impact Evaluation Report 43*. International Initiative for Impact Evaluation.

Becker, J., Brackbill, D., & Centola, D. (2017). Network dynamics of social influence in the wisdom of crowds. *Proceedings of the National Academy of Sciences, 114*(26), E5070–E5076.

Becker, J., Porter, E., & Centola, D. (2019). The wisdom of partisan crowds. *Proceedings of the National Academy of Sciences, 116*(22), 10717–10722.

Blankenship, E.B., Goff, M.E., Yin, J., Tse, Z.T.H., Fu, K.-W., Liang, H., Saroha, N., & Fung, I.C.-H. (2018). Sentiment, contents, and retweets: a study of two vaccine-related twitter datasets. *Permanent Journal, 22*, 17–138.

Blau, P., & Schwarz, J.E. (1984). *Crosscutting social circles*. Academic Press.

Broniatowski, D.A., Jamison, A.M., Qi, S.H., AlKulaib, L., Chen, T., Benton, A., & Quinn, S.C. (2018). Weaponized health communication: Twitter bots and Russian trolls amplify the vaccine debate. *American Journal of Public Health, 108*(10), 1378–1384.

Burt, R.S. (1992). *Structural holes: the social structure of competition*. Harvard University Press.

Campbell, E., & Salathé, M. (2013). Complex social contagion makes networks more vulnerable to disease outbreaks. *Scientific Reports, 3*, 1905.

Centola, D. (2010). The spread of behavior in an online social network experiment. *Science, 329*(5996), 1194–1197.

Centola, D. (2011). An experimental study of homophily in the adoption of health behavior. *Science, 334*(6060), 1269–1272.

Centola, D. (2015). The social origins of networks and diffusion. *American Journal of Sociology, 120*(5), 1295–1338.

Centola, D. (2018). *How behavior spreads*. Princeton University Press.

Centola, D. (2019). Influential networks. *Nature Human Behavior, 3*, 1–2.

Centola, D. (2021a). *Change: how to make big things happen*. Little, Brown & Co.

Centola, D. (2021b). Influencers, backfire effects and the power of the periphery. In B.L. Perry, B. Pescosolido, E. Smith & M.L. Small (Eds.), *Personal networks: classic readings and new directions in ego-centric analysis*. Cambridge University Press.

Centola, D. (2022a). Trends in cognitive sciences. *Network Science of Collective Intelligence, 26*(11), 923–941.

Centola, D. (2022b). Complex contagion. In G. Manzo (Ed.), *Research handbook on analytical sociology*. Edward Elgar (Elgar Advanced Introduction Series).

Centola, D., Becker, J., Brackbill, D., & Baronchelli, A. (2018). Experimental evidence for tipping points in social convention. *Science, 360*(6393), 1116–1119.

Centola, D., Eguíluz, V.M., & Macy, M.W. (2007). Cascade dynamics of multiplex propagation. *Physica A, 374*(1), 449–456.

Centola, D., & Macy, M. (2007). Complex contagions and the weakness of long ties. *American Journal of Sociology, 113*(3), 702–734.

Centola, D., & van de Rijt, A. (2015). Choosing your network: social preferences in an online health community. *Social Science and Medicine, 125*, 19–31.

Davis, G., & Greve, H.R. (1997). Corporate elite networks and governance changes in the 1980s. *American Journal of Sociology, 103*(1), 1–37.

Drude Dahlerup, (2006) "The Story of the Theory of Critical Mass," *Politics and Gender* 2, 4, 511–522.

Gladwell, M. (2000). *The tipping point: how little things can make a big difference*. Little, Brown.

Granovetter, M. (1973). The strength of weak ties. *American Journal of Sociology, 78*(6), 1360–1380.

Granovetter, M., & Soong, R. (1988). Threshold models of diversity: chinese restaurants, residential segregation, and the spiral of silence. *Sociological Methodology, 18*, 69–104. doi:10.2307/271045

Guilbeault, D., Becker, J., & Centola, D. (2018a). Complex contagions: a decade in review. In Y.Y. Ahn & S. Lehmann (Eds.), *Complex spreading phenomena in social systems*. Nature.

Guilbeault, D., Becker, J., & Centola, D. (2018b). Social learning and partisan bias in the interpretation of climate trends. *Proceedings of the National Academy of Sciences, 115*(39), 9714–9719.

Guilbeault, D., & Centola, D. (2020). Networked collective intelligence improves dissemination of scientific information regarding smoking risks. *PLOS One, 15*(2): e0227813.

Guilbeault, D., & Centola, D. (2021). Topological measures for identifying and predicting the spread of complex contagions. *Nature Communications, 12*, 4430.

Hansen, M.T. (1999). The search-transfer problem: the role of weak ties in sharing knowledge across organization subunits. *Administrative Science Quarterly, 44*(1), 82–111.

Howe, L., & Monin, B. (2017). Healthier than thou? 'Practicing what you preach' backfires by increasing anticipated devaluation. *Journal of Personality and Social Psychology*, *112*(5), 735.

Kanter, R.M. (1977). *Men and women of the corporation*. Basic Books.

Karsai, M., Iñiguez, G., Kikas, R., Kaski, K., & Kertész, J. (2016). Local cascades induced global contagion: how heterogeneous thresholds, exogenous effects, and unconcerned behaviour govern online adoption spreading. *Scientific Reports*, 27178. doi.org/10.1038/srep27178

Katz, E. (1957). The two-step flow of communication: an up-to-date report on an hypothesis. *Public Opinion Quarterly*, *21*, 61–78.

Katz, E., & Lazarsfeld, P. (1955). *Personal influence*. Free Press.

Kennedy, B.R., Mathis, C.C., & Woods, A.K. (2007). African Americans and their distrust of the health care system: healthcare for diverse populations. *Journal of Cultural Diversity*, *14*(2), 56–60.

Kluchin, R. (2009). *Fit to be tied: sterilization and reproductive rights in America, 1950–1980*. Rutgers University Press.

Krackhardt, D. (1999). The ties that torture: Simmelian tie analysis in organizations. *Research in the Sociology of Organizations*, *16*(1), 183–210.

Lazarsfeld, P., Berelson, B., & Gaudet, H. (1948). *The people's choice*. Duell, Sloan & Pearce.

Lazarsfeld, P.F., & Merton, R.K. (1954). Friendship as a social process: a substantive and methodological analysis. *Freedom and Control in Modern Society*, *18*(1), 18–66.

Manzo, G., Gabbriellini, S., Roux, V., & Nkirote M'Mbogori, F. (2018). Complex contagions and the diffusion of innovations: evidence from a small-n study. *Journal of Archaeological Method and Theory*, *25*(4), 1109–1154.

McAdam, Doug, and Ronnelle Paulsen. (1993). "Specifying the Relationship between Social Ties and Activism." *American Journal of Sociology*, *99*(3), 640–667.

Milgram, S. (1967). The small world. *Psychology Today*, *2*, 60–67.

Mønsted, B., Sapieżyński, P., Ferrara, E., & Lehmann, S. (2017). Evidence of complex contagion of information in social media: an experiment using Twitter bots. *PLOS One*, *12*(9), e0184148.

Newman, M. (2010). *Networks: an introduction*. Oxford University Press.

Padgett, J.F., & Ansell, C.K. (1993). Robust action and the rise of the Medici, 1400–1434. *American Journal of Sociology*, *98*(6), 1259–1319.

Page, E. (2007). *The Difference: How the Power of Diversity Creates Better Groups, Firms, Schools, and Societies*. Princeton University Press.

Rapoport, A. (1953). Spread of information through a population with socio-structural bias. I. assumption of transitivity. *Bulletin of Mathematical Biophysics*, *15*, 523–533.

Rapoport, A., & Horvath, W. (1961). A study of a large sociogram. *Behavioral Science*, *6*, 279–291.

Reagans, R., & McEvily, B. (2003). Network structure and knowledge transfer: the effects of cohesion and range. *Administrative Science Quarterly*, *48*(2), 240–267.

Romero, D.M., Meeder, B., & Kleinberg, J. (2011). Differences in the mechanics of information diffusion across topics: idioms, political hashtags, and complex contagion on Twitter. *Proceedings of the 20th International Conference on World Wide Web* (pp. 695–704). Association of Computing Machinery.

Ryan, B., & Gross, N.C. (1943). The diffusion of hybrid seed corn in two Iowa communities. *Rural Sociology*, *8*(1), 15–24.

Samuelson, W., & Zeckhauser, R. (1988). Status quo bias in decision making. *Journal of Risk and Uncertainty*, *1*, 7–59.

Sarah Childs and Mona Lena Krook. (2008) "Critical Mass Theory and Women's Political Representation," *Political Studies 56*, 725–736.

Simmel, G. (1955). *Conflict and the web of group affiliations*. Free Press.

Solomonoff, R., & Rapoport, A. (1951). Connectivity of random nets. *Bulletin of Mathematical Biophysics*, *13*, 107–17.

Sprague, D., & House, T. (2017). Evidence for complex contagion models of social contagion from observational data. *PLOS One*, *12*(7), e0180802.

State, B., & Adamic, L. (2015). The diffusion of support in an online social movement: evidence from the adoption of equal-sign profile pictures. *Proceedings of the 18th ACM Conference on Computer Supported Cooperative Work and Social Computing* (pp. 1741–1750). Association of Computing Machinery.

Steinert-Threlkeld, Z.C. (2017). Spontaneous collective action: peripheral mobilization during the Arab Spring. *American Political Science Review*, *111*(2), 379–403.

Su, Y., Zhang, X., Liu, L., Song, S., & Fang, B. (2016). Understanding information interactions in diffusion: an evolutionary game-theoretic perspective. *Frontiers of Computer Science*, *10*(3), 518–531.

Toole, J.L., Cha, M., & González, M.C. (2012). Modeling the adoption of innovations in the presence of geographic and media influences. *PLOS One*, *7*(1), e29528.

Torsten Hagerstrand, (1968). *Innovation Diffusion as a Spatial Process* (Chicago: University of Chicago Press).

Traag, V. (2016). Complex contagion of campaign donations. *PLOS One*, *11*(4), e0153539.

Ugander, J., Backstrom, L., Marlow, C., & Kleinberg, J. (2012). Structural diversity in social contagion. *Proceedings of the National Academy of Sciences*, *109*(16), 5962–5966.

Vaan, M. de, Vedres, B., & Stark, D. (2015). Game changer: the topology of creativity. *American Journal of Sociology*, *120*(4), 1144–1194.

Wang, X., Yan, L., & Xiao, J. (2019). Anomalous structure and dynamics in news diffusion among heterogeneous individuals. *Nature Human Behavior*, *3*, 1–10.

Zhang, J., & Centola, D. (2019). Social networks and health: new developments in diffusion, online and offline. *Annual Review of Sociology*, *45*(1), 91–109.

Zhao, L., & Garip, F. (2021). Network diffusion under homophily and consolidation as a mechanism for social inequality. *Sociological Methods and Research*, *50*(3), 1150–1185.

Network Interventions: Using Social Networks to Accelerate Diffusion of Innovations

Thomas W. Valente

NETWORK INTERVENTIONS

Existing evidence indicates that network-informed interventions and programmes are more effective than non-networked ones. Most behaviour change programmes think about networks and usually acknowledge that they are important components of programme design and/or delivery. Yet most programmes do not explicitly account for networks in their design, delivery and/or evaluation. Network data enable us to improve behaviour change programmes without substantially increasing costs or revising existing approaches. Indeed, network-based interventions are usually more cost-effective than non-network ones because of their stronger impacts and because local buy-in and delivery are enhanced. The field of network interventions is not new, and versions of these activities were first attempted decades ago. Recent innovations in theoretical, methodological, computational and social developments, however, have increased the application, need and feasibility for network interventions.

Social networks are important influences on many individual, organisational, community and societal behaviours. Evidence that people's friends, family members, colleagues and other relationships shape social norms and act as important messengers for information, sources of support, and behaviour change has come from decades of empirical research. Much of the evidence on the influence of networks relies on diffusion of innovations theory (Rogers, 2003; Valente, 1995; Valente, & Rogers, 1995). Diffusion research has shown that social networks influence behaviours in a number of ways and can be conducted at multiple levels such as individual, organisational and transnational (Valente et al., 2015).

Network interventions are purposeful and planned efforts to use social networks or social network data to generate social influence, accelerate behaviour change, improve performance or quality and/or achieve desirable outcomes among individuals, communities, organisations, or populations (Valente, 2012). Such interventions leverage network data to inform and implement strategic, tactical and operational choices on how best to deliver information, persuasive messages and other actions to improve desired outcomes. The accumulated evidence to date indicates that network interventions can be very effective in enacting change at individual and organisational levels and can be used to augment the success of other communication approaches when used synergistically.

In one sense, nearly all interventions are network interventions. When we promote public health, or health care services or new products, we are trying to get people to connect to things that they have not yet connected to. Often, we are intentionally trying to get people to talk about new products and engage with other people around some new topic or idea. Network interventions add more precision to this broad and general concept that behaviour change is a human communication process and that we can use data about that communication to determine the right people to engage, and better ways to sustain that engagement.

Focus on who not what. Part of the problem with existing behaviour and sociocultural change programmes is that we focus too much energy on trying to create standardised one-size-fits-all programmes that have manuals and rigidly set procedures that are expected to be adhered to with high fidelity. There is increasing recognition that highly standardised, complex and costly programmes may be difficult to adopt and implement, and that planned adaptations may be needed to 'fit' local conditions and contexts (Allen et al., 2018). A standardised programme that must be followed in a certain way or has certain core components or theoretically informed elements that make it effective cannot be modified 'on the fly' if the barriers to behaviour change have changed. Or, more importantly, if the settings under which the original programme was created are different than the ones where the programme is being delivered, then a mismatch between programme objectives and local needs will exist. Before describing network interventions, however, there are four principles which guide all behaviour change programmes but are particularly relevant in the context of network interventions.

Four principles. Several caveats regarding network interventions are warranted. First, network interventions are not agnostic or impartial, but depend on the goals and objectives that initiate the intervention. For example, when the goal is to disrupt disease transmission, the intervention will be based on different tactics than an intervention with the goal of accelerating the adoption of disease-prevention measures. Specifically, to slow the spread of infectious diseases, one can either fragment the disease transmission network or create a more cohesive network to accelerate the uptake of preventive measures. Thus, the goal is the same, but the means to get there varies.

Second, scientific theory regarding how individuals or organisations change or can be changed is critically important for choosing the right type of network intervention and the correct mix of promotional elements and educational materials (for instance, how much training of change agents is needed, what type of ancillary media should be used and so on) (Damschroder, 2020). A well-articulated theory of the behaviour under study will enable better interpersonal- and impersonal-messaging. Thus, it can be critical to understand the motivations and barriers to change, and the theory may directly suggest intervention approaches.

Third, the interventionist should use the network as a delivery vehicle and be prepared to use network information to learn from the community to better serve and address community or organisational needs. That is, rather than thinking of network interventions as a lever to be pushed to generate behavioural spread, a so-called social engineering approach, networks also function bi-directionally to learn from the community what is working and how the behaviour change process is proceeding and refine or adapt as needed.

Fourth, in part stemming from principle three, network interventions are iterative such that one doesn't deploy the intervention and walk away assuming it will work. The iterative nature means monitoring deployment becomes important as changes to activities may need to be made; people may change; or their enthusiasm for engaging in change may wane. Thus, the interventionist should be ready to change approaches, activities and even potentially messaging as new information emerges from the intervention and by learning from the network.

TAXONOMY OF NETWORK INTERVENTIONS

Network interventions have four strategies that capitalise on network data to develop planned change programmes. The four strategies are (Table 20.1) (1) identifying individuals (called 'nodes' within the network) who are selected on the basis of some network property; (2) segmentation, in which the intervention is directed towards and delivered within groups of people; (3) induction, in which excitation of the network occurs such that interactions between people (links in the network) are activated; and (4) alteration, interventions that change the network. These four strategies are listed in order of increasing complexity, though not necessarily according to their efficiency. The strategies, tactics, and some of the operational choices are listed in Table 20.1.

Behaviour change programmes operate at three levels, strategic, tactical and operational. Strategy is the broadest level which informs the approach the intervention team intends to take. Each strategy has multiple tactical alternatives. For example, many programmes identify individuals to act as 'programme champions', people recruited to promote behaviour change. Tactically, however,

Table 20.1 Taxonomy of network interventions

Strategy	Tactic	Operationalisation
Individual	Opinion leaders	Centrality degree, closeness, betweenness, etc.
	Key players	Positive vs negative
	Bridges	Inverse constraint, VF bridging, EV bridging
	Peripherals	Isolates, pendants, marginals
	Low threshold	Calculated on proportion or count
Segmentation	Groups	Components, cliques, communities
	Positions	Structural equivalence, hierarchies, blockmodelling
Induction	Word-of-mouth	Random excitation
	Snowball/sequenced	Respondent-driven sampling, outreach
	Matching	Leaders first, groups first, optimise leaders and groups
Alteration	Add or delete nodes	Optimal place for new members, vitality centrality
	Add or delete edges	On cohesion, other metrics
	Rewire	On network (e.g., small world), other network metrics, on behaviour

the individuals who are identified might be existing opinion leaders, or they might be bridging individuals, low-threshold ones, etc. Further, for each tactic there may be multiple network definitions or algorithms of the concept. For example, opinion leaders are often defined as individuals who are most central in a network, yet there are at least dozens of different definitions and formulas used to measure and identify the most central nodes in a network (Schoch, n.d.).

The network in Figure 20.1 consists of 35 people from different departments and will be used to illustrate some of the network intervention concepts presented here. We can see that there are some central individuals in the network such as persons 23, 6, 22 and 28, and there is a disconnected group of three people connected to one another and two isolates. There seems to be some clustering of the node shapes suggesting that who knew whom is based partly on being in the same department. There is a subgroup of squares centred around person 2, and some other peripheral nodes extending out from the core group such as persons 5, 8, 4, 15, 9 and 14.

The network in Figure 20.1 is small in order to clearly present network intervention alternatives and many early network interventions, used relatively small networks such as classrooms ($n \approx 30$ people); organisations ($n \approx 100$); schools ($n \approx 2,000$), but more recent studies have used online communities with thousands of members.

The R code for the analysis presented in this chapter is available from the author.

INDIVIDUAL STRATEGY

Opinion leaders. Before discussing opinion leader interventions, a note about terminology. Change agents are often recruited from outside an organisation/community and tasked with accelerating the dissemination of information and behavioural influences. Opinion leaders come from within the organisation/community and are tasked with accelerating the diffusion of the innovation. Brokers act as go-betweens often between different organisations/communities with the intent creating agreement on action plans. Champions are people who promote a product or practice and may be change agents or opinion leaders. Network opinion leaders are often defined as peer opinion leaders and/or popular opinion leader (POLs).

In the most basic network intervention, network data are used to identify individuals to act as POLs. The most frequent intervention of this type is the use of opinion leaders (Kelly et al., 2006; Starkey et al., 2009; Valente & Pumpuang, 2007). At least twenty published studies have used nominations by members of the social network to identify leaders to promote behaviour change. Most of the

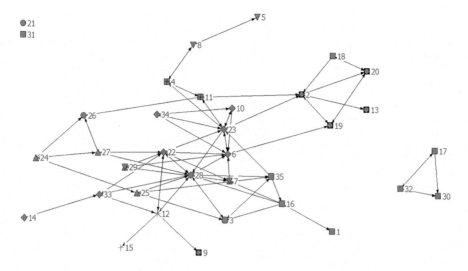

Figure 20.1 Network of 35 people connected on the relation who knows whom. Nodes are shaped by department. Graph made with Netdraw (Borgatti, 2002)

studies were randomised control trials designed to increase the uptake of evidence-based medical practices. In all cases, those who received the most nominations up to some threshold, the top 10–15 per cent, were identified as leaders (nodes 2, 6, 22, 23 and 28).

What makes POLs so effective? One basic reason is that by nature of their position in the network they can influence many other individuals. The network in Figure 20.1 has 94 ties or an overall density of 8 per cent. The average number of ties (whether outgoing or incoming) is 2.69. The top five members, the potential POLs, have 35 incoming ties, or 37.2 per cent of the total. In contrast, five average (in terms of in-degree) individuals have 13.45 incoming ties, or 14.3 per cent of the total. Thus, POLs have 2.60 more ties than average members. Consequently, if the POLs are the first adopters, they create much more potential for interpersonal influence and observational learning. Still further, should the first adopters be those on the periphery, two isolates and three with one incoming tie, there would be almost no interpersonal influence potential.

As mentioned earlier there are many other mathematical algorithms available to identify central nodes based on different conceptions of centrality (Freeman, 1979; Schoch, n.d.). Centrality closeness nodes (nodes 6, 15, 23, 26 and 28) can reach everyone else in fewer steps than other nodes. Centrality betweenness nodes occupy critical gate-keeping positions by calculating the frequency nodes lie on the shortest path connecting other nodes (nodes 2, 6, 22, 23 and 28, coincidentally the same as in-degree). Other centrality measures (e.g., eigenvector, power, information, flow, etc.) might be used depending on the goals and objectives of the programme. Although in this network the same or similar nodes have the highest centrality scores, others have created networks with as few as nine nodes and nine ties in which the nodes with highest scores on three different centrality measures are different (Brandes & Hilenbrand, 2014).

Borgatti suggested that the most critical nodes for behaviour change programmes can be identified by finding those who most optimally span the network (Borgatti, 2006). Furthermore, Borgatti observed that the most central nodes can sometimes be linked to the same people; thus, using the number of links a node has to identify key players may not identify the best nodes to disseminate information or, if removed, fragment the network most efficiently. The KeyPlayer software was developed to identify opinion leaders or people that would be the best seeds for spreading a behaviour (nodes 2, 5, 22, 32 and 35) and those best for disrupting its spread (nodes 2, 16, 22, 23 and 28).

An extension to the key player approach called *strategic players* (Ott et al., 2018) extends opinion leader ideas by identifying important people that are proximate (in network terms) to those whose behaviour we wish to change, and also far removed (in network terms) from those who may oppose the behaviour change. As the authors state, strategic players are people who 'are (1) able to influence those individuals who are part of the target population and are most receptive to intervention;

and (2) are not embedded with ties that are likely to be behaviorally antagonistic to the intervention or that would compromise the optimal evaluation of intervention efficacy' (Ott et al., 2018, p. 98). The authors demonstrate the different nodes identified when using strategic rather than key players.

Bridges. Leaders may not always be the best change agents. Leaders have a vested interest in the status quo, whereas bridging individuals (who link non- or loosely connected groups) may be more amenable to change and may be in a better position to change others. For example, when diffusion between groups is expected to be difficult, bridging individuals may be more effective change agents than highly central people (opinion leaders). Bridging nodes can be important to identify because if they can be inoculated, it can stem the flow of disease from one group to another. Bridging individuals may be preferred as change agents when the behaviour or policy is controversial or not likely to be well accepted initially. They may also be critical if the network is fragmented, and the intervention is designed to bring groups together.

Bridging nodes can be identified in at least three ways. Burt (2005) has shown persuasively that occupying a bridging position in a network is associated with advantages for certain outcomes such as job promotion and compensation. Burt developed a measure of constraint, which indicates the extent a person's network is closed around the focal node. Bridging is measured by calculating constraint and taking its inverse. The nodes with highest inverse constraint are coincidentally the same as the ones highest on in-degree. Two other sociometrically based bridging measures exist to identify different bridgers: the Valente and Fujimoto (2010) measure identifies nodes 4, 6, 19, 20 and 23; and the Everett and Valente (2016) one identifies nodes 2, 4, 8, 11 and 23.

Low-threshold adopters. Low-threshold change agents could be recruited to create early momentum for the change and accelerate the time to reach a critical mass or tipping point. Low-threshold adopters are individuals willing to adopt a new idea or innovation (e.g., a new behaviour) earlier than their peers (Valente, 1996). Calculating thresholds enables researchers to identify early adopters who are early relative to the system but late relative to their network; and conversely those who are later adopters but early relative to their network. These late low-threshold adopters are late adopters due to their position in the network rather than being resistant to peer influence. Low-threshold change agents would be good recruits to initiate a new diffusion cascade. Identifying low-threshold adopters as change agents, however, would require some prior knowledge of their behavioural adoption of a related innovation.

Marginals. People on the margins of the community or organisation may also be identified by change programmes because they are potentially excluded from services or the positive supports derived from community participation, not for their ability to persuade others. Individuals on the periphery of a network learn about new ideas or practices later than their more-integrated peers and hence may suffer disadvantages from their exclusion. For example, in two classic studies of diffusion of innovation through social networks, social isolates were significantly less likely to adopt new farming practices or modern methods of contraception (Valente, 1995). In some cases, peripheral individuals may be important to identify, as they are often the source of new ideas and innovations because they have contacts with other communities and/or are free from the social pressure to conform. Potential peripheral recruits include nodes 18, 17, 32, 21 and 31.

A logical extension to these individual identification tactics would be to combine them. For example, one might identify those highest on in-degree then recruit as champions those with the lowest thresholds; or cross-tabulate the top 20 per cent on in-degree and in-closeness centrality selecting those that meet both conditions. One might also consider an opinion leader strategy while simultaneously identifying isolates or marginals who are likely to be omitted from the flow of communication.

SEGMENTATION STRATEGY

Groups. In contrast to individual approaches in which certain individuals are recruited to be change agents, segmentation approaches identify groups of people to change at the same time. For example, companies often introduce new procedures at separate locations sequentially rather than having all locations adopt the new procedures simultaneously. In some cases, due to the interdependent nature of the innovation or behaviour change process, or system-wide contextual changes needed to facilitate change, adoption by a whole group at once can be an effective strategy.

People often view themselves as members of a community of practice with established norms and processes that can only change when the whole group changes (Meltzer et al., 2010; Wenger et al., 2002). For example, a new workflow practice or technology standard may be difficult to adopt unless the entire group agrees to use the system at the same time. Communication technologies such as fax machines, texting and social media/networking increase in value as more users adopt the technology or standard (Katz & Shapiro, 1985; Markus, 1987).

Community detection algorithms have been created to partition social networks into mutually exclusive groups and calculate an index indicating how well the groups represent the overall network structure (Girvan & Newman, 2002; Newman & Girvan, 2004). The mutually exclusive groups in the example data are (1) 4, 5, 8, 11 and 26; (2) 2, 13, 18, 19 and 20; (3) 24 and 27; (4) 6, 7, 10, 22, 23, 29 and 34; (5) 14 and 33; (6) 3, 16, 25, 28 and 35; (7) 9, 12 and 15; and (8) 17, 30 and 32. Nodes 1, 21 and 31 are in communities by themselves. Interventions can be delivered to the groups separately or sequentially.

A group structure that occurs in many inter- and intra-organisational networks is a core–periphery structure in which core members are densely connected to one another and peripheral members are connected to the core but not to each other (Borgatti & Everett, 1999). Mobilising networks that have a core–periphery structure may be accomplished by focusing resources on the core members or by ensuring that the core members have sufficient resources or diversity to achieve network goals (Valente et al., 2008). For example, community coalitions are often composed of hundreds of organisations and/or individuals, yet the core working group may consist of no more than twenty organisations. Understanding who is part of this core and their distribution of assets is critical to coalition success.

Positions. Segmentation may also be designed to identify nodes that occupy the same roles in the organisation or community (Doreian et al., 2005; Doreian et al., this volume). For example, a new sales product might be communicated differently to the sales and technical teams based on what is relevant to the roles they occupy. Similarly, in human service organisations, employees may be divided into positions such as line-service personnel, programme managers and programme directors. There are numerous definitions of positional equivalence in networks such as regular equivalence, automorphic equivalence, structural equivalence, etc.

INDUCTION STRATEGY

Induction interventions stimulate or encourage peer-to-peer interaction to create cascades in information/behavioural diffusion. The induction strategy differs from individual and segmentation by purposively trying to excite or enliven network activity. These tactics purposively activate communication or exchange of resources along the network ties.

Word of mouth (WOM). WOM interventions stimulate interpersonal communication to persuade others to adopt the new behaviour. Media marketing campaigns are often designed to generate buzz about their products, with the goal of increased sales (Rosen, 2009) and frequently encourage users to recommend products to their friends and family (Aral & Walker, 2011). Often referred to as 'going viral', these interventions do not necessarily use network data, but they depend on widespread diffusion among the network for their effects. Many online purchase sites such as Stub Hub provide an option in which a purchase can be automatically posted to one's social media accounts so those contacts learn about the purchase.

Respondent-driven sampling (RDS, or snowball-type methods). Research has shown that the success of WOM is a function of the network position of initial adopters and the incentives to recruit others (Pickard et al., 2010). RDS is a form of snowball sampling in which individuals recruit others to participate in a study (for instance, a clinical trial) or receive an intervention (Heckathorn, 1997). In RDS, an initial set of people who are members of the community or population to be influenced are selected and identified as 'seeds'. These seeds then recruit members of their social networks who subsequently encourage additional people to participate and so on. Researchers can use coupons or cards to track who recruited whom. Additionally, researchers must decide on the number of seeds to start with and how many others each seed can be expected to, or allowed to, recruit.

RDS is quite effective at connecting with hard-to-reach individuals who might not otherwise receive services. This is achieved by initiating recruitment with people who are members of this marginalised group. One of the initial studies applying RDS to the recruitment of injection drug users (IDUs) showed that an unbiased sample of IDUs could be recruited within three to five waves of recruitment (Heckathorn, 1997). This tactic enables researchers to generalise their study results to a broader group of IDUs and ensures that interventions for IDUs reach everyone they are intended to reach.

Network outreach. Network outreach is similar to RDS, except that the network seeds recruit members of their personal networks to participate in an intervention together, in which the behaviour change messages can be delivered to the entire group. Network outreach is expected to be more effective than individual interventions because the motivations and lessons (such as preparation of healthy food) are delivered in a group context, and the group can model and reinforce the positive behaviour change (Latkin et al., 2009). One of the main challenges with network outreach interventions is getting participants to recruit their network and have them consistently participate in the intervention to effectively shift and maintain social norms around the behaviour.

Optimal leader–group matching. The group segmentation technique and the network outreach approach both rely on assembling groups. These approaches can be further enhanced with network data by defining groups and choosing leaders at the same time. Valente and Davis (1999) proposed a technique in which leaders are identified, say, on in-degree, and then individuals assigned to the leaders they nominated or are closest to sociometrically. In a similar vein, Buller and colleagues identified groups first and then selected leaders from within the groups (Buller et al., 1999). This tactic has three different operational choices: (1) identify leaders first and build groups around them, (2) identify groups first (e.g., with a community detection algorithm) and choose leaders from within the groups, or (3) attempt to maximise both leader identification and group construction.

Two randomised studies created school-based substance abuse prevention programmes using network analysis matching leaders to groups (Valente et al., 2003; Valente et al., 2007). In both cases, the effects were dependent on contextual factors (who delivered the programme and the social context of delivery). Figure 20.2 illustrates the leader identification with optimal matching. In the smoking prevention study (Valente et al., 2003), optimal leader/learner matching was compared to leaders identified the same way but with groups constructed randomly. Results showed that the network optimisation method was effective at reducing tobacco use uptake yet was differentially effective depending on the version of the smoking prevention curriculum being implemented (there were two versions being compared). In other words, there was an interaction between network implementation method and the curriculum.

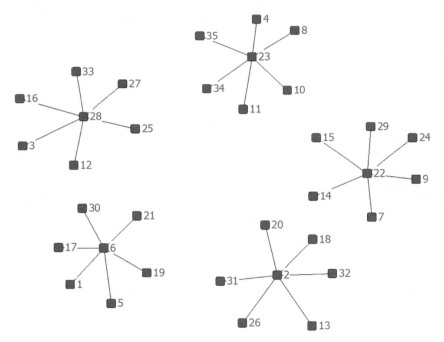

Figure 20.2 The network in Figure 20.1 reconfigured with the five nodes highest on in-degree (2, 6, 22, 23 and 28) paired with those who nominated them or those to whom they are closest sociometrically (fewer steps apart). Note, in this example, most people are assigned to a leader they are directly connected to, or two steps removed. Seven individuals (1, 5, 17, 21, 30, 31 and 32) are isolates or unreachable to the leaders so are assigned randomly

Buller and others created a healthy diet induction intervention by identifying cliques in a large organisation (N ≈ 2,000) and selecting opinion leaders within the cliques (Buller et al., 2000; Buller et al., 1999). The combination of different group segmentation and leader-identification techniques provides a few dozen operational variations of this tactic. This tactic, and its operational variants, seems likely to be one of the more effective network interventions to be deployed because it combines strategies one and two. In addition, optimality algorithms can be used to optimise both leader selection and group composition.

ALTERATION STRATEGY

Strategies one through three generally assume a static network (or ignore network dynamics). Many interventions deliberately alter the network to improve efficiency. Three different tactics might be considered: (1) adding/deleting nodes, (2) adding/deleting links, or (3) rewiring the network on some criteria such as making it a small-world network, a scale-free one, or matching users with non-users.

Adding/deleting nodes. Adding nodes is an important and longstanding behaviour change approach with outside change agents, expert consultants and community health workers or lay health advisors (LHAs, or peers who share similar characteristics from the community) (Shelton et al., 2017) being deployed in many settings. Many studies have effectively used LHAs, who are community members trained in behaviour change techniques, to impact change (Thomas et al., 1998). These LHAs fan out into the community, often going door-to-door, to inform individuals and groups about health and other topics to promote behaviour change. LHAs may sometimes work within their existing social networks or approach members of their community at their homes, churches, places of business, or in public areas. Politicians and advocacy groups often mount 'get out the vote' campaigns consisting of door-to-door appeals, which have been shown to increase voter participation and diffuse to other household members (Nickerson, 2008).

Support groups, such as Alcoholics Anonymous, are often used to add new people to a person's network to facilitate behaviour change. Node-addition interventions often create connections randomly, yet it is probably preferable to add nodes to the network selectively on the basis of network position. New individuals should be added to a network to bridge disconnected or loosely connected groups.

Node-deletion interventions remove nodes that occupy critical positions in a network (Borgatti & Everett, 2006; Koschützki et al., 2005). Nodes are then ranked on the degree to which their removal changes a network statistic. Node-deletion interventions have been embraced by anti-terrorist agencies to degrade terrorist networks (Roberts & Everton, 2011). Removing critical nodes from sexual contact networks is an effective way for public health agencies to reduce disease spread and protect communities. In such cases, it is not always physical node removal but rather the use of protective behaviours (such as condom use, mask wearing) that inhibits transmission by the node. The five nodes whose removal would decrease cohesion (increase the average path length) the most are 6, 22, 23, 25 and 28. Other network metrics can be used to determine which nodes are most critical based on different network metrics – for example, which nodes when removed affect network centralisation or modularity the most.

Link addition/deletion. As with node deletion, network measures can be used to determine optimal ties to add or remove (Valente & Fujimoto, 2010). Networks can be modified so that they have increased redundancy of the paths that connect individuals or how individuals connect to resources (Lin et al., 2006). For example, a nine-month study conducted in a global consulting agency revealed two distinct subgroups in the organisation that did not communicate with one another. The intervention created linkages between the two subgroups so that members throughout the organisation knew the resources and assets available throughout the entire organisation, not just within their own subgroup (Cross et al., 2002).

Link deletion or addition analysis can be conducted by calculating a network metric such as average path length (APL) then systematically removing each link, re-calculating APL and putting the difference in a matrix. Similarly, every non-link in the network could be added and the resulting change in APL also stored in the matrix. This creates a matrix of change scores in which link deletions are negative numbers and link additions positive ones.

Rewiring. Finally, networks can be rewired to increase efficiency or improve performance based on certain goals. For example, teachers often randomise classroom networks so that ability levels are randomly distributed in the network. As with node and link changes, the researcher can also maximise the network on one or several metrics. Rewiring may also be conducted to connect individuals with different attributes (e.g., a buddy system). Connecting existing users with non-users enables new users to have a ready source of information and support. Changing network structure is probably more difficult than using existing network structures (induction), because networks are often formed for a myriad of individual, relational, attitudinal and/or environmental reasons. Consequently, it may be challenging to create new ties or delete existing ones though such approaches would undoubtedly tell us a lot about human behaviour.

Egocentric network interventions. Network data can also be collected from individuals about their immediate contacts who are not identified by the researcher. Egocentric network data are those in which respondents/participants are asked to name their friends or some other relation, and then asked a series of questions about those named (Perry et al., 2018; Small & Perry, this volume). Egocentric interventions can be of several types. First is to ask the participant to articulate their networks on several relations such as family, friends, colleagues, acquaintances and so on. Then to have the participant indicate those who are positive influences and provide energy, those who provide negative influences and those who are neutral. In substance use studies, it is natural to ask whom do you consume drugs with and who refrains? Pilot studies have shown these interventions to be promising (Kennedy et al., 2016; Knopf et al., 2014).

SELECTING AN INTERVENTION

Selecting an appropriate network intervention depends on many factors, including the type and character of available network data, the type of behaviour change being promoted, the nature of the intervention or innovation, and the environmental or situational context. Network data can be derived from many sources, including archived communications (such as phone, email, text messaging and listserv postings), participant observations, published sources (such as corporate board membership) and survey data (adams & Lubbers, this volume). Due to the plethora of network data sources, studies may vary considerably in their ability to assess the validity and reliability of the data. Indeed, an objective standard for what constitutes a social relation may or may not exist, depending on the type of the social relation.

Three main factors affect network intervention selection: (1) the existing network, its structure (if there is one) and characteristics; (2) characteristics of the behaviour change being advocated; and (3) theoretical mechanisms that drive the behaviour and/or those through which behaviour change would occur. In many settings one or all these factors may be unclear, or they may be clear for some people/groups but not others. It is strongly recommended to conduct formative research, which is often qualitative or mixed-methods in nature, to get to know the community, the key actors, stakeholders and the cultural/political issues and social context that may affect programme success and widespread uptake. There are tools, researchers and best-practice guides on ways to collect network data using qualitative techniques (Hollstein et al., 2020; Hollstein, this volume; Yousefi Nooraie et al., 2020).

Network characteristics. The first step in selecting a network intervention is to determine if network data are available or accessible. The network data may indicate there is no network to work with and thus one must be constructed and specified. Building networks is difficult and time-consuming. To do so, a charismatic and approachable leader from within the community needs to be identified and given the resources to recruit and engage others to work with them. Often the first step in this process is to build a coalition and one that broadly represents different constituencies such as government, education, media, law enforcement, faith-based communities, etc.

Behaviour/product characteristics. Characteristics of the behaviour being studied also affect intervention choice. A programme designed to spread information of a readily accepted idea can rely on easily identified opinion leaders, whereas one that requires complex organisational and personal changes may need network alteration (rewiring) and/or inductive matching of opinion leaders. Interdependent behaviours are those that increase in value as more people adopt them. For example, Facebook becomes more appealing as more of one's friends use this service. Interdependent behaviours often have slow initial uptake because there are few advantages to being an early adopter. Thus, interdependent innovations benefit from segmentation strategies, induction matching, or rewiring so that the interdependence can be explicitly addressed.

Prevalence of the behaviour, the proportion of users, can also affect intervention choice. At high levels of prevalence (greater than 60–75 per cent), network interventions can be used to find individuals who have not yet adopted the behaviour in question, perhaps due to their network position. At low prevalence (less than 15 per cent), network interventions can identify whether early users are leaders and thus are well positioned to accelerate behaviour spread or whether they are on the periphery and hence likely to be slowly imitated. Intermediate prevalence, between 25 and

75 per cent, creates challenges because it is unclear if interventions will be cost-effective. Again, the main consideration here is how the existing adopters are distributed within the network: are they all in one group and hence is diffusion likely to be stalled? Is there some individual characteristic associated with adoption which explains the prevalence rate and its distribution?

Perceived political support or acceptability of the new behaviour can also influence intervention strategy. For example, in a study of public health officials in the 1960s, Becker showed that opinion leaders were early adopters of measles immunisation programmes that were culturally compatible with the public health establishment at the time, but these same leaders were later adopters of diabetes screening, which was perceived to be less compatible and riskier to adopt (Becker, 1970). Thus, the interventionist needs to 'read the tea leaves' and understand whether there is support for the new idea or whether there are political, cultural, or social barriers that will inhibit change.

This point bears repeating as the extent to which the behaviour change being promoted is consistent and compatible with past practices affects how difficult the change is likely to be. Innovations have been characterised as continuous such that they only require minor modification to adopt or discontinuous in that they require new ways of operating and thinking. The more radical, that is, discontinuous, the change, the harder it is likely to be to achieve. Battilana and Casciaro studied 68 organisational change efforts in the British National Health System and discovered that radical changes were more likely to be successful by change agents with high brokerage (ties across various groups) (Battilana & Casciaro, 2012). Conversely, change agents with networks low in brokerage, high in closure, were more successful when the organisational change was less radical.

In general, behaviours that are likely to be readily accepted by the network are likely to be adopted early by leaders. Controversial change processes will need to invest in network feedback and employ segmentation tactics to reduce resistance. Programmes perceived as being driven by a central authority are usually resisted. Resistance to change and susceptibility to change are influenced by many non-network factors as well. It is critical for programme staff to develop an extensive understanding of the variables that influence adoption (Michie & West, 2021).

If the barriers to change are technical then networks identifying experts are necessary (advice networks); when the barrier is cultural trust networks become critical (discussion). This can be a very important distinction as it is critical to match the network to the problem. If, on the one hand, research shows that the behaviour is not being adopted due to a lack of knowledge or not knowing how to do the new behaviour, then networks which identify the required expertise are critical. On the other hand, if the barrier is cultural or people do not know what to do, then networks which identify trusted messengers are critical.

Future research/practice. At least two research areas should be of both theoretical and practical importance: (1) measuring generative mechanisms and (2) social media applications. Implementing network interventions may have the side benefit of enabling researchers to understand how influence spreads through networks. That is, by creating experimental conditions such as a networked opinion leader intervention, the researcher is setting in motion social influences that should be detectable via data analytic procedures. Individuals directly connected to OLs should report earlier behaviour change than those indirectly connected which should be earlier than those not connected (Stoebenau & Valente, 2003).

Social and electronic media will play a role in any intervention. Young et al. (2021) observed that the current misinformation epidemic is largely driven by social media and states that 'network problems require network solutions(e1)'. In that essay the authors use the taxonomy in Table 20.1 to propose online strategies to (1) recruit champions, (2) segment users into groups, (3) induce virality and (4) alter network dynamics. In addition, a new strategy, redesigning existing social network platforms, is put forward as a way to address the root problem.

EXISTING EVIDENCE

Existing evidence on the effectiveness of various network intervention strategies and tactics is quite varied, being extensive for some (e.g., network-identified peer opinion leaders) and absent for many others (i.e., recruiting low-threshold champions, or segmentation based on position). Nonetheless it is important to document what is known about the effectiveness of various network interventions. The caveat to this evidence, however, is that many network interventions are implemented in business or other organisations, communities and schools for which there is no documentation.

Network-identified peer opinion leaders. The diffusion model has long recognised that OLs are important influences on the diffusion process (Rogers & Cartano, 1962). Once OLs adopt an innovation it sends a signal to the rest of the community that the behaviour is normative and likely to spread. Because OLs are, by definition, connected to more people than others in the network, their adoption increases exposure to the behaviour by a considerable amount. Thus, getting OLs to adopt and champion innovations is a wise strategy/tactic choice and one that has been used repeatedly.

Valente and Pumpuang (2007) reviewed the different ways OLs have been identified and used for behaviour change programmes. They argued that many of the methods used such as self-identification or programme-identification were less valid and reliable than the social network ones. Hundreds of studies were reviewed, and twenty studies identified, that used network analysis to select OLs to promote behaviour change. Many of these interventions were in medical settings, and all addressed health behaviours. All were effective, but because they were conducted in many varied settings such as treating kidney disease, acute myocardial infarction, or promoting HIV preventive behaviours, the evidence for the effectiveness of the approach did not accumulate.

By 2011, Flodgren and colleagues (2011) were able to conduct a systematic review in which they identified eighteen studies that used network-identified OLs. The overall risk difference (RD) across the studies was 0.12, or a 12-percentage point improvement in compliance. The risk difference is a difference of differences – that is, the difference in intervention group scores minus the difference in control group scores. The results varied slightly ranging from 9–14 per cent. In some studies, the OL condition was compared to a control group and in others it was compared to other interventions. This review provided clear-cut evidence for the effectiveness of network-identified opinion leaders for practice change.

Hunter and colleagues (2019) synthesised the evidence base on social network interventions for health behaviour change in a systematic review and meta-analysis. The systematic review included 37 studies involving 53,891 participants, conducted between 1996 and 2018 from eleven countries. Participants from included studies had a mean age 32.4 years [SD 12.7] and 45.5 per cent were female. A range of health outcomes were included such as sexual health, weight loss, diet, physical activity, smoking cessation, well-being, alcohol/other substance misuse, diabetes markers and mammography screening. Social network interventions showed a significant intervention effect compared with comparator groups for sexual health outcomes.

From the meta-analysis, the pooled odds ratio (OR) was 1.46 (95 per cent confidence interval [CI] 1.01–2.11; I 2 = 76%) for sexual health outcomes at ≤6 months and OR 1.51 (95 per cent CI 1.27–1.81; I 2 = 40%) for sexual health outcomes at >6–12 months. Intervention effects for drug risk outcomes at each time point were not significant. There were also significant intervention effects for some other health outcomes including alcohol misuse, well-being, change in haemoglobin A1c (HbA1c) and smoking cessation. However, it was not appropriate to pool data on these other behaviours in a meta-analysis due to clinical and measurement heterogeneity. For sexual health outcomes, prespecified subgroup analyses were significant for intervention approach ($p < 0.001$), mean age of participants ($p = 0.002$) and intervention length ($p = 0.05$), indicating that these are important aspects to consider when designing social network interventions. The study concludes that the evidence suggests that social network interventions are associated with positive health behaviours and outcomes. The study also highlights the role that social network interventions have in successfully reaching, retaining and changing the behaviour of at-risk populations, including MSM, people who inject drugs and other priority populations (e.g., low-income or minority populations).

NETWORKS FOR PROGRAMME IMPLEMENTATION

Thus far, network approaches for intervention development and selection have been the focus, but network theory and techniques can be applied more broadly to the diagnostics, implementation and monitoring of behaviour change programmes as well. Taking a network view of the implementation process highlights the many ways that network tools can be useful to inform programme implementation. It also helps identify and focus on who (e.g., which network members) is engaged in the process at every stage.

Programme implementation can be considered a developmental process, a transition through known stages (Aarons et al., 2011). Here, we use a four-stage model of the implementation process, similar to those used in evaluation frameworks and in the diffusion of innovations. The four stages are: (1) exploration or needs assessment; (2) adoption or programme design; (3) programme implementation; and (4) sustainment and monitoring. Table 20.2 summarises the research questions, common network measures used, concepts and outcomes when applying network analysis methods to these programme implementation stages.

Table 20.2 Network analyses procedures for each stage of implementation

	Stage of implementation			
	Exploration (needs assessment)	Adoption (programme design)	Implementation	Sustainment and monitoring
Research question	Who is recruited to design the intervention?	Are community leaders/opinion leaders engaged as change agents?	What are the implications of structural and individual metrics for programme improvement?	Do central individuals and/or organisations remain involved and committed?
Programme question	Who defines the needs?	Who delivers the intervention and what is the social network of its receipt?	What is the network position of early adopters/users?	Does the network exhibit changes conducive to continued programme success?
Measures	Density Isolates/marginals Groups By attributes	Opinion leaders Strategies: (1) individuals; (2) segmentation; (3) induction; and (4) alteration	Density Isolates Symmetry Groups Centralisation Transitivity/cohesion	Density Leaders/central nodes Contagion Advocacy
Concept	Network ethnography	Network interventions	Network diagnostics	Network surveillance
Outcomes	Document network position and structure of those providing input into problem definition	Select network properties of intervention design	Use network data to inform and modify intervention delivery	Ensure continued programme use by important network nodes
Citation		Valente, 2012	Gesell et al., 2013	Iyengar et al., 2011

CONCLUSION

This chapter has provided an introduction to network interventions. Most behaviour change programmes are network interventions, but few have explicitly incorporated network data and methods into their design and delivery. The argument here is that there are theoretical and intuitive reasons to do so. Important principles were stated regarding the role of programme goals/objectives; the use of behaviour theory; and the admonition to be prepared to learn from the network as well as induce change.

Table 20.1 provided a taxonomy for classifying interventions along strategic, tactical and operational dimensions. Four strategies: (1) individual identification, (2) segmentation, (3) induction and (4) alteration were reviewed. An empirical network presented in Figure 20.1 was used to illustrate each. A broader lens was then applied to the topic by presenting some language and thoughts for using social networks for programme implementation.

The implementation perspective highlights the usefulness of network analysis for the entire continuum of behaviour change programmes from goal-setting to sustainment. Finally, the chapter also reviewed the evidence on the effectiveness of network interventions which shows that these approaches are highly effective. The continued application of network theory and data to accelerate diffusion of innovations and promote behaviour change will likely return large dividends in terms of how networks influence behaviours; and how scientists can contribute to better health and social outcomes.

ACKNOWLEDGEMENTS

Support for this work was provided by NIH grant number grant #R01-DA051843 from the National Institute of Drug Abuse, the National Institutes of Health (NIH).

REFERENCES

Aarons, G.A., Hurlburt, M., & Horwitz, S.M. (2011). Advancing a conceptual model of evidence-based practice in implementation in public mental health and child welfare systems. *Administration and Policy in Mental Health and Mental Health Services Research, 38*, 4–23.

Allen, J.D., Shelton, R.C., Emmons, K.M., & Linnan, L. (2018). Fidelity and its relationship to implementation effectiveness, adaptation, and dissemination. In R.C. Brownson, G.A. Colditz & E.K. Proctor (Eds.), *Dissemination and implementation research in health: translating science to practice* (2 ed., pp. 267–284). Oxford University Press.

Aral, S., & Walker, D. (2011). Creating social contagion through viral product design. *Management Science, 57*, 1623–1639.

Battilana, J., & Casciaro, T. (2012). Change agents, networks, and institutions: a contingency theory of organizational change. *Academy of Management Journal, 55*, 381–398.

Becker, M.H. (1970). Sociometric location and innovativeness: reformulation and extension of the diffusion model. *American Sociological Review, 35*, 267–282.

Borgatti, S.P. (2002). *NetDraw: graph visualization software*. Analytic Technologies.

Borgatti, S. (2005). *KeyPlayer*. Analytic Technologies.

Borgatti, S.P. (2006). Identifying key players in a social network. *Computational and Mathematical Organization Theory, 12*, 21–34.

Borgatti, S.P., & Everett, M.G. (1999). Models of core/periphery structures. *Social Networks, 21*, 375–395.

Borgatti, S.P., & Everett, M.G. (2006). A graph-theoretic perspective on centrality. *Social Networks, 28*, 466–484.

Brandes, U., & Hilenbrand, J. (2014). Smallest graphs with distinct singleton centers. *Network Science, 2*, 416–418. doi:10.1017/nws.2014.25

Buller, D., Buller, M.K., Larkey, L., Sennott-Miller, L., Taren, D., Aickin, M., Wentzel, T. M., & Morrill, C. (2000). Implementing a 5-a-day peer health educator program for public sector labor and trades employees. *Health Education and Behaviour, 27*, 232–240.

Buller, D.B., Morrill, C., Taren, D., Aickin, M., Sennott-Miller, L., Buller, M.K., Larkey, L., Alatorre, C., & Wentzel, T.M. (1999). Randomized trial testing the effect of a peer education at increasing fruit and vegetable intake. *Journal of the National Cancer Institute, 91*, 1491–1500.

Burt, R.S. (2005). *Brokerage and closure: an introduction to social capital*. Oxford University Press.

Cross, R., Borgatti, S., & Parker, A. (2002). Making invisible work visible: using social network analysis to support human networks *California Management Review, 44*(2), 25–46.

Damschroder, L.J. (2020). Clarity out of chaos: use of theory in implementation research. *Psychiatry Research, 283*, 112461.

Doreian, P., Batagelj, V., & Ferligoj, A. (2005). *Generalized blockmodeling*. Cambridge University Press.

Everett, M., & Valente, T. (2016). Bridging, brokerage, and betweenness. *Social Networks, 44*, 202–208.

Flodgren, G., Parmelli, E., Doumit, G., Gattellari, M., O'Brien, M.A., Grimshaw, J., & Eccles, M.P. (2011). Local opinion leaders: effects on professional practice and health care outcomes. *Cochrane Database of Systematic Reviews*, CD000125.

Freeman, L. (1979). Centrality in social networks: conceptual clarification. *Social Networks, 1*(3), 215–239. www.sciencedirect.com/science/article/B6VD1-46BHRKM-C/2/d1d517b2d1da847cd2c9d1f30e5621e8

Gesell, S., Barkin, S., & Valente, T.W. (2013). Social network diagnostics: a tool for monitoring group interventions. *Implementation Science, 8*, 116.

Girvan, M., & Newman, M.E.J. (2002). Community structure in social and biological networks. *Proceedings of the National Academy of Science, 99*, 7821–7826.

Heckathorn, D. (1997). Respondent-driven sampling: a new approach to the study of hidden populations. *Social Problems, 44*, 174–199.

Hollstein, B., Töpfer, T., & Pfeffer, J. (2020). Collecting egocentric network data with visual tools: a comparative study. *Network Science, 8*, 223–250.

Hunter, R.F., de la Haye, K., Murray, J.M., Badham, J., Valente, T.W., Clarke, M., & Kee, F. (2019). Social network interventions for health behaviours and outcomes: A systematic review and meta-analysis. *PLOS Medicine, 16*(9), e1002890. doi.org/10.1371/journal.pmed.1002890

Iyengar, R., Van den Bulte, C. & Valente, T.W. (2011). Opinion leadership and contagion in new product diffusion. *Marketing Science, 30*, 195–212.

Katz, M., & Shapiro, C. (1985). Network externalities, competition, and compatibility. *American Economic Review, 75*, 424–440.

Kelly, J.A., Amirkhanian, Y.A., Kabakchieva, E., Vassileva, S., Vassilev, B., McAuliffe, T.L., DiFranceisco, W.J., Antonova, R., Petrova, E., Khoursine, R.A., & Dimitrov, B. (2006). Prevention of HIV and sexually transmitted diseases in high risk social networks of young Roma (Gypsy) men in Bulgaria: randomised controlled trial. *British Medical Journal, 333*, 1098.

Kennedy, D.P., Hunter, S.B., Osilla, K.C., Maksabedian, E., Golinelli, D., & Tucker, J.S. (2016). A computer-assisted motivational social network intervention to reduce alcohol, drug and HIV risk behaviours among Housing First residents. *Addiction Science* and *Clinical Practice*, *11*(4). doi: 10.1186/s13722-016-0052-y

Knopf, A., Agot, K., Sidle, J., Naanyu, V., & Morris, M. (2014). 'This is the medicine:' a Kenyan community responds to a sexual concurrency reduction intervention. *Social Science and Medicine*, *108*, 175–184. doi:10.1016/j.socscimed.2014.01.039

Koschützki, D., Lehmann, K.A., Peeters, L., Richter, S., Tenfelde-Podehl, D., & Zlotowski, O. (2005). Centrality indices. In U. Brandes & T. Erlebach (Eds.), *Network analysis: methodological foundations*. Springer-Verlag.

Latkin, C A., Donnell, D., Metzger, D., Sherman, S., Aramrattna, A., Davis-Vogel, A., Quan, V.M., Gandham, S., Vongchak, T., Perdue, T., & Celentano, D.D. (2009). The efficacy of a network intervention to reduce HIV risk behaviours among drug users and risk partners in Chiang Mai, Thailand and Philadelphia, USA. *Social Science and Medicine*, *68*, 740–748.

Lin, Z., Zhao, X., Ismail, K., & Carley, K.M. (2006). Organizational design and restructuring in response to crises: lessons from computational modeling and real world cases. *Organizational Science*, *17*, 598–618.

Markus, M.L. (1987). Toward a critical mass theory of interactive media: universal access, interdependence and diffusion. *Communication Research*, *14*, 491–511.

Meltzer, D., Chung, J., Khalili, P., Marlow, E., Arora, V., Schumock, G., & Burt, R. (2010). Exploring the use of social network methods in designing healthcare quality improvement teams. *Social Science and Medicine*, *71*, 1119–1130.

Michie, S., & West, R. (2021). Sustained behaviour change is key to preventing and tackling future pandemics. *Nature Medicine*, *27*, 749–752.

Newman, M.E.J., & Girvan, M. (2004). Finding and evaluating community structure in networks. *Physics Review, E 69*, 1–16.

Nickerson, D. (2008). Is voting contagious? Evidence from two field experiments. *American Political Science Review*, *102*, 49–57.

Ott, M.Q., Light, J.M., Clarrk, M.A., & Barnett, N.P. (2018). Strategic players for identifying optimal social network intervention subjects. *Social Networks*, *55*, 97–103. doi:10.1016/j.socnet.2018.05.004

Perry, B., Pescosolido, B.A., & Borgatti, S.B. (2018). *Egocentric network analysis: foundations, methods, and models*. Cambridge University Press.

Pickard, G., Rahwan, I., Pan, W., Cebrian, M., Crane, R., Madan, A., & Pentland, A. (2010). Time critical social mobilization: the DARPA network challenge winning strategy. arxiv.org/abs/1008.3172v1

Roberts, N., & Everton, S. (2011). Strategies for combating dark networks. *Journal of Social Structure*, *12*(2).

Rogers, E.M. (2003). *Diffusion of innovations (5th ed.)*. Free Press.

Rogers, E.M., & Cartano, D.G. (1962). Methods of measuring opinion leadership. *Public Opinion Quarterly*, *26*, 435–441.

Rosen, E. (2009). *The anatomy of buzz revisited: real-life lessons in word-of-mouth marketing*. Doubleday.

Schoch, D. (n.d.). schochastics.net/sna/periodic.html

Shelton, R., Dunston, S., Leoce, N., Jandorf, L., Thompson, H., & Erwin, D. (2017). Advancing understanding of the characteristics and capacity of African American lay health advisors in community-based settings. *Health Education and Behaviour*, *44*, 153–164. doi.org/10.1177/1090198116646365

Starkey, F., Audrey, S., Holliday, J., Moore, L., & Campbell, R. (2009). Identifying influential young people to undertake effective peer-led health promotion: the example of A Stop Smoking In Schools Trial (ASSIST). *Health Behaviour Research*, *24*, 977–988.

Stoebenau, K., & Valente, T.W. (2003). Using network analysis to understand community-based programs: a case study from Highland Madagascar. *International Family Planning Perspectives*, *29*, 167–173.

Thomas, J., Eng, E., Clark, M., Robinson J, & C.B. (1998). Lay health advisors: sexually transmitted disease prevention through community involvement. *American Journal of Public Health*, *88*, 1252–1253.

Valente, T. (2012). Network interventions. *Science*, *337*, 49–53.

Valente, T.W. (1995). *Network models of the diffusion of innovations*. Hampton Press.

Valente, T.W. (1996). Social network thresholds in the diffusion of innovations. *Social Networks*, *18*, 69–89.

Valente, T.W., Coronges, K., Stevens, G., & Cousineau, M. (2008). Collaboration and competition in a children's health initiative coalition: a network analysis. *Evaluation and Program Planning*, *31*, 392–402.

Valente, T.W., & Davis, R.L. (1999). Accelerating the diffusion of innovations using opinion leaders. *Annals of the American Academy of the Political and Social Sciences*, *566*, 55–67.

Valente, T.W., Dyal, S.P., Chu, K.C., Wipfli, H., & Fujimoto, K. (2015). Diffusion of innovations theory applied to global tobacco control treaty ratification. *Social Science and Medicine*, *145*, 89–97.

Valente, T.W., & Fujimoto, K. (2010). Bridges: locating critical connectors in a network. *Social Networks*, *32*, 212–220.

Valente, T. W., Hoffman, B.R., Ritt-Olson, A., Lichtman, K., Johnson, C.A. (2003). The effects of a social network method for group assignment strategies on peer led tobacco prevention programs in schools. *American Journal of Public Health*, 93, 1837–1843.

Valente, T.W., & Pumpuang, P. (2007). Identifying opinion leaders to promote behaviour change. *Health Education and Behaviour*, 34, 881–896.

Valente, T.W., & Rogers, E.M. (1995). The origins and development of the diffusion of innovations paradigm as an example of scientific growth. *Science Communication: An Interdisciplinary Social Science Journal*, 16, 238–269.

Valente, T.W., Sussman, S., Unger, J., Ritt-Olson, A., Okamoto, J. & Stacey, A. (2007). Peer acceleration: effects of a network tailored substance abuse prevention program among high risk adolescents. *Addiction*, 102, 1804–1815.

Wenger, E., McDermott, R., & Snyder, W. (2002). *Cultivating communities of practice: a guide to managing knowledge*. Harvard Business School Press.

Young, L., E., Sidnam-Mauch, E., Twyman, M., Wang, L., Xu, J. J., Sargent, M., Valente, T. W., Ferrara, E., Fulk, J., & Monge, P. (2021). Disrupting the COVID-19 Misinfodemic with Network Interventions: Network Solutions for Network Problems. *American Journal of Public Health*, 111, 514–519.

Yousefi Nooraie, R., Sale, J.E., Marin, A., & Ross, L.E. (2020). Social network analysis: an example of fusion between quantitative and qualitative methods. *Journal of Mixed Methods Research*, 14, 110–124.

21

Social Media and Digital Networks

Anabel Quan-Haase, Lyndsay Foisey, and Riley McLaughlin

INTRODUCTION

Social media has become a dominant force in society, affecting many spheres of life including socialisation, politics, health, work and entertainment. Social media is generally understood as web-based and mobile services that individuals, communities and organisations can use to collaborate, connect, interact and build community by enabling them to create, co-create, modify, share and engage with content (user- or bot-generated) (Nau et al., 2022). While social media was already widespread in Global North and Global South countries prior to the Covid-19 pandemic, the pandemic has further broadened social media's adopter base and global influence (Vally & Helmy, 2022). The loss of control felt during the pandemic resulted in many individuals turning to social media as a coping mechanism (Gioia et al., 2021), with many adopting novel entertainment-oriented services such as TikTok. The pandemic also revealed the many problematic aspects associated with social media use, with much disinformation spreading rapidly across networks (Nazar & Pieters, 2021), which undermined public health organisations' efforts to contain the virus (Malik et al., 2021). As social media continues to dominate the information and media landscapes of digital societies, there is an urgent need for rigorous study.

Social network analysis (SNA), with its focus on social ties and their embeddedness in social structure, is becoming an increasingly fruitful theoretical lens and methodological approach towards the study of social media and digital networks (Quan-Haase & McCay-Peet, 2016). Social media contains rich and complex data about how people interact, exchange information and are connected to one another, companies, institutions and sources of information. This allows for the application of many different types of network approaches that rely on relational data. Not only are the data from social media relational in nature, but they are also naturalistic and thereby 'capture practices as far as possible that are independent of the actions and interests of the researcher' (Potter & Shaw, 2018, p. 187). This provides a naturalistic examination of digital social networks, overcoming many of the methodological biases that limit network data obtained from self-report techniques. Commonly utilised self-report techniques such as surveys and interviews are problematic data collection methods because they rely on a respondents' memory of a social relation and are subject to biases such as recall, name identification errors (Barnett et al., 1993) and social rank (Griffiths et al., 2022). Thus, social media data being rich, complex and naturalistic allow for novel and exciting areas of social network investigation.

There are a multitude of reasons why SNA is well suited for the study of social media and digital networks. First, social media comprise large numbers of users and their interconnections, and SNA scales well. In a paper testing whether Twitter is more geared towards news dissemination or social connectivity, Kwak et al. (2010) collected data from 41.7 million Twitter profiles and 1.47 billion relations between profiles. Their analysis showed that with sufficient computing power, network theories can be tested with large data sets. Second, SNA can provide a wide range of insights into social media and digital networks because of its focus on network structure, dyadic relations and egocentric approaches. This chapter outlines past research that has applied SNA at all these levels. SNA, for example, has provided important insights into the network structure of influencers involved in social activism and how these central actors can serve as bridges to otherwise disconnected networks. Finally, SNA is advantageous because of its focus on how resources flow in a network. This allows scholars to examine and visualise how resources such as information, influence and social support spread within and across networks. This type of analysis can be particularly relevant when it comes to examining the rapid diffusion of misinformation and disinformation and its social and political impact. This type of analysis has also provided much insight into the spread of false health claims during the Covid-19 pandemic.

The aim of this chapter is to demonstrate the application of SNA to the study of social media and digital networks through a review of key concepts and selected past studies. The chapter examines the application of SNA to three core areas of social media and digital network study: friendship networks, health communities and digital activism. For each of the three areas, the chapter examines how SNA has provided new understandings and outlines new directions for research. We then focus on methodological challenges, including inequalities in expertise, boundary specification, and the type of actors in the network. Finally, we outline often overlooked ethical challenges that arise in the application of SNA to the study of social media and digital networks including aggregation and disaggregation, data archiving and consent.

THE APPLICATION OF SNA TO THE STUDY OF SOCIAL MEDIA AND DIGITAL NETWORKS

In this section, we explore the application of SNA to three core areas. First, we discuss how our understanding of friendship ties in a digital society has evolved from applying SNA to the study of the role of social media in creating, maintaining and strengthening ties. Second, we explore the network structure of digital health communities and review past studies using SNA as a tool to measure health outcomes and examine influencers. Finally, we look at how SNA can be used to study digital activism networks and their reach.

Digital Friendship Ties and Networks

Social media has provided new opportunities to study longstanding questions about friendship ties, as digital trace data provide direct insight into how friendship networks are created, maintained and strengthened. Since Granovetter's (1973, 1983) seminal work on the importance of weak ties, an ongoing debate has focused on how actors establish different types of ties. A key argument stresses the potential of social media platforms to help actors maintain large, loosely coupled networks of weak ties (Wellman et al., 2020). Research on Facebook suggests that social media is beneficial because numerous weak ties can be maintained cheaply and easily (Ellison et al., 2007). These weak ties often bridge to otherwise disconnected networks that can provide valuable resources (Wellman et al., 2020).

Yet, research has questioned the value of digital engagement for supporting strong ties. Research looking at Facebook engagement has noted that one-click acknowledgements such as likes are not meaningful to strengthen relations but rather represent 'social snacking' behaviours. These types of engagement do not satisfy a person's need for belonging and do not strengthen social relations (Hall, 2020). Pennington and Hall (2021) found that engagement on Facebook did not increase feelings of closeness among friends or lead to their decline. Rather, the extent of engagement reflected the closeness of the relationship, with close friends communicating often on Facebook and through different mechanisms. Research examining the benefits of Facebook connections suggests that not all engagement on Facebook has the same social benefits. Those who use Facebook more actively for dyadic communication, such as sending a direct message to a friend, reported greater relational closeness (McEwan et al., 2014) and more social benefits (Carpenter et al., 2018). This suggests that while social media can support large and diverse networks, not all communication has the same social impact and the communication mostly maintains ties rather than forms new ties.

The network approach has also substantively contributed to shedding light on how social media and digital networks signal a need for, facilitate the exchange of and provide social support. Social support is defined as aid exchanged with social ties – both tangible and intangible resources (Berkman, 1984; Song et al., 2011). Facebook and other social media were found as key to signalling a need for support to one's network. For instance, Rozzell et al. (2014) found that Facebook helped signal a need for social support to both close and non-close ties, increasing the availability of supportive ties, providing access to more types of support through varied ties and expediting access through real-time communication. A study collecting data from East York, Toronto (Ontario, Canada), found that exchanging companionship through social media was more often with friends than with kin, with whom companionship was exchanged more frequently in person or via phones (Quan-Haase et al., 2022). In the East York study, social media was also found to be relied upon to stay in touch with friends who were geographically dispersed. This suggests that the prominence of social media for the exchange of support is contextual depending on such dyadic factors as the role relation and the physical distance. Digital networks, despite their many benefits, can also undermine the exchange of social support. Users of Facebook often feel stressed and exhausted as a result of managing numerous and diverse social ties and their needs (Lo, 2019). Hampton (2016) refers to this as the 'cost of caring'. Social media, through its constant stream of updates, can signal the need for help and tire out those offering support, in turn leading to a decrease in support being offered (Rains et al., 2016).

In sum, SNA applications and social media data have led to novel insights into friendship formation and maintenance and have also elucidated the topology of the network. The studies show the value of social media for maintaining large, loosely coupled networks, while highlighting potential detrimental social impacts. This work has demonstrated the relevance of social media to the signalling and exchange of social support. This work has sparked much methodological development in computational approaches that can examine social networks at scale, test theories with subsets and draw from observational data (Engel et al., 2022).

Health communities

With a large proportion of North Americans using popular social media platforms (Pew Research Center, 2021; Mai & Gruzd, 2022), online health communities are commonplace. Participation in these communities has benefits for patients, caregivers and health professionals including better treatment options, research, health behaviour change, knowledge sharing and emotional and informational support (Zhou, 2018). SNA is a useful tool to investigate many relevant research questions about online health communities.

SNA can provide understandings not only on the impact of a person's position and role in the network, but also on subsequent health behaviour change outcomes (Xu & Cavallo, 2021). For example, differing positions in a network can impact access to resources, such as information and social support. Liu et al. (2022) found that when obtaining informational support in online health communities, the breadth of connections measured via weak ties was more important than the depth of connections measured via strong ties. By analysing online health communities, SNA can further our understanding of 'group or community interactions to determine what kinds of actors and ties make up the network; what exchange of information, social support, socializing, play, or other resources form the basis of the community; and what roles and cliques emerge that provide structure to the community' (Gruzd & Haythronthwaite, 2013, p. 2).

SNA research has also focused on the centrality of actors in a network and how this affects health behaviour change. For example, in their work on smoking cessation, Zhao et al. (2016) found that users with higher centrality scores in an online health community had much improved smoking cessation rates. This research also demonstrated that even those who were peripheral to the network had higher rates of smoking cessation than those who did not participate at all (Zhao et al., 2016). In their twelve-week pilot study, Xu and Cavallo (2021) used SNA to examine the network characteristics of a weight-loss group on Facebook in relation to behavioural and psychological outcomes. It was found that weight loss was associated with an increase in the number of comments, posts and reactions made by participants. Further, the number of comments received by a participant significantly predicted changes in psychological outcomes such as self-efficacy. It was also reported that the density of the network (i.e., how tightly connected a participant was to other actors in the network) weakly predicted changes in a participant's perceived social support. Thus, SNA can provide insight regarding participant engagement of health communities on social media, allowing researchers to assess engagement rates for participants to achieve positive health outcomes.

SNA has conceptualised and investigated the role of central actors (Quan-Haase & McCay-Peet, 2016). The concepts and measures from SNA can be applied to the study of influencers, those social media users who have large followings and occupy central positions in terms of in-degree centrality in directional networks found on such platforms as Instagram, Twitter, and TikTok. The role of influencers in public health campaigns has garnered much academic interest, in particular their impact on the flow of health mis/information. Moukarzel et al. (2021) used SNA to identify influencers during a global breastfeeding campaign on Twitter. They found that influencers were largely members of the scientific community, but some were non-experts. Based on their analysis of the network, the non-expert influencers acted as a bridge between the scientific community and other Twitter users.

In their study of the structure of the Twitter community group #hcsmca (Health Care Social Media Canada), Gruzd and Haythonthwaite (2013) used SNA to identify that influential group members overlapped in high in-degree centrality values (i.e., mentioned by others in the group/ retweeted/replied to) and out-degree centrality (i.e., how often they mentioned others/replied to others). In doing so, the authors were able to identify the structure of the community, influencers and community leaders. Malova (2021) paired semantic analysis with SNA to study the interaction patterns and emerging topics of discussion regarding Covid-19 vaccines among Twitter users, and reported a general vaccine hesitancy among the identified networks. Similarly, Seymour et al. (2015) used SNA to study the connectedness of anti-fluoride communities on Facebook. The authors found that three groups selected at random were highly connected with strong ties. These studies highlight how SNA can be useful for public health surveillance on social media, and how to target community influencers and combat misinformation.

SNA is a promising theoretical lens and methodological approach to the study of online health communities. However, there remain some limitations to its application in research, including a lack of research on SNA, health communities and newer social media platforms such as TikTok. TikTok is currently one of the most popular social media platforms, with 67 per cent of teens using the platform (Pew Research Center, 2022). Recent descriptive studies were published regarding health influencers and their impact on TikTok (Das & Drolet, 2021; Winzer et al., 2022). Future studies should include TikTok to improve our understanding of how health communities might function and the characteristics of networks on the newer platforms. SNA can be particularly useful to analyse how misinformation diffuses during large-scale crises, such as the Covid-19 pandemic. More research is needed in this area to support public health policy and health message dissemination.

Digital Activism Networks

Social media and the networks it fosters have revolutionised opportunities for activism, including increased awareness of a cause and rapid, large-scale mobilisation online and offline (Kavada, 2015). This section will review three contributions of SNA to the study of activism networks. We will start with how SNA can visualise the topology of digital activism networks showing who is engaging with a digital activism network and how they are connecting with other actors. Next, we discuss how SNA can provide insights into the reach of a social movement and its interconnectedness. Finally, we will examine how SNA informs our understanding of the flow of information within and across activism networks.

Since the work on small-group interaction by Moreno (1953), the visualisation of networks has been a key component of SNA. A key advantage is that visualisations can draw directly on data available on social media platforms, which give a direct look at where and how connections exist without contending with the problems inherent in self-report studies (Isa & Himelboim, 2018; Priadana & Tahalea, 2021). For example, Ma and Zhang (2022) used SNA to examine and display the digital activism network that developed on Sina Weibo in 2018 around China's #MeToo movement. In the visualisation, the size of a node represents how interconnected an individual is based on their out-degree centrality score (Ma & Zhang, 2022). To further enhance the visualisation, groups of individuals who operated closely together were colour coded to represent clusters (Ma & Zhang, 2022). To examine how clusters were interconnected, the authors computed the betweenness centrality of nodes. Based on the visualisation and scores on various network measures, Ma and Zhang (2022) developed a framework comprised of three categories. The first category, a provoking public, describes individuals who post content frequently, but do not share others' posts. Second, a bridging public, which refers to those who share posts from others, but do not post content. The final category identified was that of a powerful public, which describes individuals who engage in both types of behaviours. The two examples discussed demonstrate that in utilising SNA techniques, we can learn about the topology of activism networks, the role of central individuals in the network and the relevance of nodes that serve as interconnectors or bridges between clusters.

SNA is also used to investigate the reach and density of activism networks. For example, SNA shed light on the Occupy Wall Street movement, demonstrating how the network structure benefited the movement but also created challenges. Researchers tracked how individuals accessed and engaged with social media content such as livestreamed meetings or information posts online as well as how they spread that information and became more involved with the movement (Kavada, 2015). Challenges arose because members operated as a loosely connected network with no hierarchical structure, giving members autonomy (Savio, 2015). While the movement was able to expand rapidly, poor coordination among members weakened the movement's message and ultimately its ability to effect long-term social change (Savio, 2015). The analysis of the network structure of the Occupy Wall Street movement shows that it had great reach but low levels of interconnectedness. The individual actors operating within a digital network can also influence the reach and interconnectedness of digital activism networks (Isa & Himelboim, 2018). Some scholars distinguish between actors based on how involved they are in a given social movement and how much power or influence they have over others (Isa & Himelboim, 2018). A social movement with more invested members and more powerful members will have greater reach and interconnectedness.

This type of research has demonstrated that digital activism networks are decentralised (DeLuca et al., 2012). Decentralisation can improve the reach of digital activism networks while making them less interconnected (De Luca et al., 2012). This means that all members of the social movement are generally considered equal and there is no given leader who dictates their goals and actions (Kavada, 2015). To some extent, this allows the movement to grow organically and encourages as much membership as possible no matter one's location or ability to physically meet other members (DeLuca et al., 2012). However, this can also make the movement much less effective when it comes to lobbying policy makers, government leaders, or generally furthering their cause (Kavada, 2015).

SNA can also be used to track how information flows through digital activism networks (Ma & Zhang, 2022; Isa & Himelboim, 2018). Individual actors can greatly influence the network that a social movement operates within digitally, and SNA can be an effective way to study how these actors communicate with one another (Isa & Himelboim, 2018). As with reach and interconnectedness, the types of individuals operating within a digital activism network can influence information diffusion (Isa & Himelboim, 2018; Ma & Zhang, 2022). Isa and Himelboim (2018) used SNA to map how individuals within the #FreeAJStaff movement used Twitter to communicate about the arrests of journalists in Egypt. Their work documented that there were a few key actors who had significantly more engagement in the network and acted as mediators of the discussion (Isa & Himelboim, 2018). The network expanded outward from these mediators to reach others who had fewer connections but were still involved in the movement. Ma and Zhang's (2022) study described how information travels across a social movement by distinguishing between types of social actors. Those who are more invested in the movement post more of their own information that is then shared by others (Ma & Zhang, 2022). Those who have less intricate knowledge of the social movement but are still interested in the cause can still contribute to information flow by sharing posts (Ma & Zhang, 2022).

SNA has proven to be a fruitful tool for the study of digital activism. We discussed three core areas and provided examples of how SNA has been applied to gain new insights. This section shows that SNA's ability to visualise digital activism networks, assess their reach and interconnectedness and inform information diffusion has allowed researchers to gain new insights into who is involved in social movements and how they contribute to the network. Future research could use longitudinal studies to address how digital activism networks change over time.

METHODOLOGICAL CONSIDERATIONS AND CHALLENGES

SNA can provide much-needed insight into social media and digital networks (Ahmed et al., 2022). However, numerous methodological challenges also exist. Some relate to challenges that are common across all SNA studies and require novel solutions within the social media ecosystem. Other challenges are unique to social media data. One key challenge relates to the need for expertise in both SNA theory and methods and social media studies. While scholars often have expertise in one domain, they lack sufficient know-how in the other. This calls for building interdisciplinary research teams that can bring to bear technical competency with domain-specific understandings (Quan-Haase et al., 2022). Another challenge that arises is the need for not only computational skills to collect relational data from social media platforms, but also computational resources for data archiving and analysis. For example, the study discussed above by Kwak et al. (2010) that analysed 41.7 million Twitter profiles and 1.47 billion relations required substantial computational resources. This creates new inequalities in research, as only those scholars that have a combination of technical skills, SNA training and computational resources can conduct SNA studies at scale (Lutz, 2022). This limits scholars without these resources to small-scale, qualitative SNA studies. One area of development that is promising is the introduction of open source tools that facilitate data collection and analysis and can leverage the playing field (Ahmed et al., 2022; Gruzd et al., 2022). Yet, Lutz (2022) cautions that 'while free and open source tools exist to carry out the research effectively, the inequalities arise in the quality of training, mentoring, and capacities for self-development in these areas' (p. 684). Thus, issues of research opportunity continue to be central to this area of study.

Another common problem in SNA is boundary specification. While this is a frequent SNA methodological challenge, it is further exacerbated in SNA studies of social media. Boundary specification describes the need to delimit which social actors to include in a study (Laumann et al., 1989). In SNA, two types of approaches are commonly applied: the *realist* and the *nominalist* approach. In the realist approach, the social actors' perception of who is a member of the network is used to specify the boundary. This approach assumes that actors construct their social realities and thus can identify the boundaries of their own networks. By contrast, in the nominalist approach, the nature of the research problem delimits the boundary of the network. With social media data, the realist approach of asking social actors directly is not feasible because of the scale of the data. As a result, the nominalist approach is commonly utilised.

Within the nominalist approach, many social media and digital network studies employ hashtags to delimit the network boundary. For example, in a study of the online debate around informational self-determination and the legal framework of the General Data Protection Regulation (GDPR), the hashtag #RTBF (**R**ight **T**o **B**e **F**orgotten) was utilised to collect the network data (Yang et al., 2016). This was a useful proxy for data collection, allowing to identify actors that participated in the debate and determine the structure of the network including central players. There are, however, several problems with the use of hashtag approaches for boundary specification. One problem is that hashtags are organically created and used in the community and therefore multiple hashtags can be used in relation to a single topic. In the example, #RTBF was not the only hashtag used to discuss the topic of informational self-determination. Additional hashtags had to be added for data collection purposes including #2beforgotten and #righttobeforgotten. Only through careful observation of the communication patterns of the Twitter community could these additional hashtags be identified.

Another problem with using hashtags for boundary specification is that a single hashtag can serve multiple purposes and thus be utilised by unrelated networks, again reflecting the organic nature of hashtag use. In the case of the #RTBF study, Yang et al. (2016) had to disambiguate the network focused on debates around informational self-determination with the network focused simultaneously on the Eurovision 2015 Song Contest, a popular European song contest. Similarly, hashtag approaches have been criticised for excluding important voices in a network where hashtags emerge organically and where some actors may choose to use alternative hashtags as a political statement (Bruns & Burgess, 2015). Thus, the use of hashtags as a proxy for specifying a network boundary is a sound approach, but needs to carefully consider key methodological concerns.

The final consideration outlined in this section relates to the actors in a social network. SNA research makes an important assumption about actors, namely that all actors in a network are homogeneous – often referred to as a one-mode network. For example, a network may examine the social ties that connect children in a classroom (Chow et al., 2021). With the majority of SNA research drawing on self-report data via interviews or surveys, it is rarely a concern to have to include additional types of actors – a two-mode network. Yet on social media, actors are user accounts, making it difficult to verify a user's identity. Not only that, user accounts often represent organisations, institutions, or the media rather than single individuals. On Instagram, accounts are often brands, with some brands like Nike, Victoria's Secret and Chanel having millions of followers. Moreover, some accounts are neither individuals nor organisations at all, but rather bots who interact with the network to varying degrees but can influence its topology (Ferrara et al., 2016; Khaund, 2021). This conundrum necessitates more careful consideration in the interpretation of SNA findings.

ETHICAL CONSIDERATIONS AND DILEMMAS

This final section examines ethical considerations and dilemmas that are central to the application of SNA to the study of social media and digital networks. While only a few core issues can be addressed here, more extensive resources are available, such as a report from the Association of Internet Researchers (Franzke et al., 2020) and a newly added section on ethics in the *Sage handbook of social media research methods* (Quan-Haase & Sloan, 2022). Depending on the type of SNA project, different ethical concerns apply as not all projects rely on data collected directly from social media. In fact, many SNA projects have relied on self-report data about an actor's social ties and their reliance on social media (Quan-Haase et al., 2022), thereby going via the traditional route of obtaining approval from the Research Ethics Board. For example, in the study discussed earlier on the composition of networks, Ellison et al. (2007) conducted a survey of undergraduate students to learn the extent that Facebook helps to maintain bridging and bonding ties. In these cases, ethics is straightforward as a project would undergo a formal review process, and often require an information letter and informed consent.

Ethics becomes more contested in cases where scholars rely on publicly available relational data. In these studies, the assumption is that social media content is part of the public domain, making it available for research purposes. Yet, Williams et al. (2017) found among a sample of British Twitter users that 16 per cent were 'quite' or 'very concerned' about researchers employing their Twitter data. In fact, over half of respondents expected researchers would seek consent prior to collecting data from users, and three-quarters (76 per cent) expected their data to be anonymised (Williams et al., 2017). This confirms what boyd and Crawford (2012) have warned about all along: that 'researchers are rarely in a user's imagined audience' (p. 673). It also demonstrates that there is an expectation of consent and anonymity on the part of users as is often found in traditional research. Yet scholars rarely take ethics into consideration in studies relying on social media data. Zimmer and Proferes (2014) found that only 4 per cent of 382 cross-disciplinary studies of Twitter data discussed ethics. This shows that there is a disconnect between the ethical practices of researchers and the expectations of social media users.

Users may be less apprehensive if researchers only report aggregate and anonymised data (Bishop & Gray, 2017; Dubois et al., 2020). This may be particularly relevant to SNA research, as network studies on questions of composition or topology commonly rely on aggregation. Yet, aggregating social media data comes with risks that need consideration. A key problem is variability across actors and subgroups that can be lost in aggregation and masks social or political inequalities (Lerman, 2018). A network example discussed by Lerman (2018) looks at the aggregation effect on the spread of information. Lerman argues that when we look at how repeated exposures to hashtags affect a user's likelihood to use that hashtag at an aggregate level, multiple exposures 'inoculate' the user, decreasing the likelihood that information will be shared. When we disaggregate the data based on the volume of information users are exposed to based on their connectivity, we can see how frequent exposure to content increases the likelihood of sharing that content. Lerman (2018) shows how data aggregation may address concerns with ethics, but can lead to wrong conclusions. If subgroups are sufficiently large, disaggregation should not lead towards exposing single users and thus still protect privacy.

Much egocentric network research or community network research depends on knowing the identity of the actors, making anonymisation an ineffective strategy to protect users' privacy. An example is the study of Barry Wellman's egocentric network to examine questions of network interconnectivity and clustering (Gruzd et al., 2011). In this case, all nodes were identified, and the structure of the network was interpreted in relation to who was connected to whom. While Barry Wellman's egocentric network article was published with identifiable information, often journals request nodes be anonymised. In the study discussed above on the Twitter network that emerged during the debate around information self-determination (Yang et al., 2016), reviewers insisted that all nodes be anonymised. In the study, many nodes represented corporations, news organisations and policy think tanks, and thus the request for anonymity did not seem justified. But there were also privacy advocates and private citizens in the network, who may have expectations of privacy. This example shows that decisions around anonymisation are complex and depend on external factors. The anonymity requirement can reduce the insights gained from a study, as often contextual information such as the position of an actor in the network acquires social relevance in relation to who they are. But the right for users to remain anonymous in a political debate is then weighed against the public interest in gaining new knowledge. Currently, large-scale networks are often presented anonymously, but as research in this area continues to evolve, better guidelines are needed as to what contexts call for anonymity.

In sum, SNA as applied to social media data and digital networks shares similar ethical challenges to other types of SNA research including the need to aggregate data and anonymise nodes in a network. It also grapples with additional ethical questions that require more nuanced understandings of the sensitivity of information collected, the user population from which information is drawn, the purpose of the research question and who is collecting the information (Hollingshead et al., 2022b). This means that ethics cannot be approached monolithically (Quan-Haase & Ho, 2020), but rather users' perceptions and expectations of privacy and anonymity are contextually situated (Nissenbaum, 2011).

CONCLUSIONS

This chapter provides an overview of the application of SNA to the study of social media and digital networks. With more users across larger age groups adopting social media and joining digital networks (Pew Research Center, 2021), this is a promising and rapidly growing area of scholarship.

From our review of friendship ties, we learned that social media is an important tool in creating, maintaining and strengthening friendship ties. But we also learned that social media could tilt the balance between weak and strong ties and can create additional 'cost of care' related with supporting large and diverse networks. Future research can additionally focus on differences across the life course. While digital media supports friendship exchanges across the life course (Quan-Haase et al., 2022), adolescents rely on social media to connect with friends. In fact, two-thirds of respondents indicated that social media was their preferred way to communicate with friends (Rideout & Robb, 2018). Nonetheless, the study of friendship networks via social media data is not straightforward. Friendship networks are often dispersed across multiple platforms, making it difficult to gain a full picture through piecemeal approaches. Another challenge is that some friendship networks may have a larger offline presence and thus critical information may be missed if data is exclusively gained online. Thus, the study of friendship ties and networks continues to require a holistic approach that combines multiple data sources and a clear understanding of what kinds of research questions can be addressed with what kinds of data (Hollingshead et al., 2022a).

We found that health research can benefit from the application of SNA. Recent evidence has found that when health community members engage with others in the network, they are more likely to experience positive health outcomes (Xu & Cavallo, 2021). SNA can provide robust data on participants' engagement rates, allowing researchers to make inferences on associated health outcomes and ensure network success. We also learned that social media influencers play an important role in health communities, particularly regarding the dissemination of mis/information. The reviewed studies highlight how SNA can be useful for public health surveillance on social media, and how to target community influencers and combat misinformation during global pandemics such as the Covid-19 pandemic. While SNA is a promising tool, certain challenges exist including participation rates and a lack of research on newer social media platforms such as TikTok. Health communities on social media are a critical source of support for some; however, online support group participation remains a relatively small proportion of social media users.

Our review of digital activism networks suggests that social media has made it easier for social movements to have greater reach and widespread mobilisation (Kavada, 2015). We have learned that SNA research is well suited to the study of digital activism networks, as it can effectively visualise digital activism network topologies, describe their reach and interconnectedness and inform information diffusion across social movements. SNA techniques have allowed researchers to gain new insights into who influences social movements and how social movements gain widespread mobilisation across the globe. Future research can look at how the digital activism networks associated with social movements change over time and what may influence these changes.

As scholars continue to apply SNA concepts, theories and techniques to social media and digital network studies, they need to take into consideration a range of emerging research challenges. This chapter focused on social media services in general, but often relied on examples based on Twitter and Facebook data. This has been a repeated criticism of much scholarly work. Twitter and Facebook data are easily obtained and contain links via @mentions and hashtags that facilitate SNA research. In the future, SNA research needs to diversify and develop techniques that are applicable to other services.

Scholars also need to reflect on the ethics of their SNA work. What ethical care do scholars need to take when conducting social media research with younger age groups joining social media sites (McClain, 2022)? For example, are parental permissions needed as is the case in traditional research with minors to access, analyse and store these data? Or, can scholars assume that because the data is public and ephemeral, it is acceptable to include in an SNA study? Another important consideration is what Lutz (2022) has referred to as the inequalities that underlie social media research, including SNA research. Lutz proposes that the following inequalities are central: unequal access to social media data, unequal opportunities for digital methods skills development and unequal opportunities to leverage digital methods analyses for career development. Moving forward, SNA scholars need to make a commitment to wider access to data, a more equal distribution of skills and equal access to data analysis and visualisation of tools.

ACKNOWLEDGEMENT

This research was funded by a Social Sciences and Humanities Research Council of Canada (SSHRC) Grant.

REFERENCES

Ahmed, W., Meier, H., & Smith, M. (2022). NodeXL: Twitter social media network insights in just a few clicks. In A. Quan-Haaase & L. Sloan (Eds.), *The handbook of social media research methods* (2nd ed.). Sage.

Barnett, G.A., Danowski, J.A., & Richards, W.D. (1993). Communication networks and network analysis: a current assessment. *Progress in Communication Sciences*, *12*, 1–20.

Berkman, L.F. (1984). Assessing the physical health effects of social networks and social support. *Annual Review of Public Health*, *5*(1), 413–432.

Bishop, L., & Gray, D. (2017). Ethical challenges of publishing and sharing social media research data. In K. Woodfield (Ed.), *The ethics of online research* (Vol. 2, pp. 159–187). Emerald.

boyd, d., & Crawford, K. (2012). Critical questions for big data. *Information, Communication and Society*, *15*(5), 662–679. doi.org/10.1080/1369118X.2012.678878

Bruns, A., & Burgess, J. (2015). Twitter hashtags from ad hoc to calculated publics. In N. Rambukkana (Ed.), *Hashtag publics: the power and politics of discursive networks* (pp. 13–28). Peter Lang.

Carpenter, J., Green, M., & Laflam, J. (2018). Just between us: exclusive communications in online social networks. *Journal of Social Psychology*, *158*(4), 405–420. doi.org/10.1080/00224545.2018.1431603

Chow, J.C., Broda, M.D., Granger, K.L., Deering, B.T., & Dunn, K.T. (2021). Language skills and friendships in kindergarten classrooms: a social network analysis. *School Psychology*. doi.org/doi.org/10.1037/spq0000451

Das, R.K., & Drolet, B.C. (2021). Plastic surgeons in TikTok: top influencers, most recent posts, and user engagement. *Plastic and Reconstructive Surgery*, *148*(6), 1094e–1097e. doi.org/10.1097/PRS.0000000000008566

DeLuca, K.M., Lawson, S., & Sun, Y. (2012). Occupy Wall Street on the public screens of social media: the many framings of the birth of a protest movement. *Communication, Culture and Critique*, *5*(4), 483–509.

Dubois, E., Gruzd, A., & Jacobson, J. (2020). Journalists' use of social media to infer public opinion: the citizens' perspective. *Social Science Computer Review*, *38*(1), 57–74.

Ellison, N.B., Steinfield, C., & Lampe, C. (2007). The benefits of Facebook 'friends:' social capital and college students' use of online social network sites. *Journal of Computer-Mediated Communication*, *12*(4), article 1. jcmc.indiana.edu/vol12/issue4/ellison.html

Engel, U., Quan-Haase, A., Liu, X., & Lyberg, L. (2022). Introduction to the handbook of computational social science. In U. Engel, A. Quan-Haase, X. Liu, & L. Lyberg (Eds.), *The handbook of computational social science*. Routledge.

Ferrara, E., Varol, O., Davis, C., Menczer, F., & Flammini, A. (2016). The rise of social bots. *Communications of the ACM*, *59*(7), 96–104.

Franzke, aline shakti, Bechmann, A., Zimmer, M., Ess, C., & Association of Internet Researchers (2020). *Internet research: ethical guidelines 3.0*. aoir.org/reports/ethics3.pdf

Gioia, F., Fioravanti, G., Casale, S., & Boursier, V. (2021). The effects of the fear of missing out on people's social networking sites use during the Covid-19 pandemic: the mediating role of online relational closeness and individuals' online communication attitude. *Frontiers in Psychiatry*, *12*, 620442.

Granovetter, M.S. (1973). The strength of weak ties. *American Journal of Sociology*, *78*, 1360–1380.

Granovetter, M.S. (1983). The strength of weak ties: a network theory revisited. *Sociological Theory*, *1*(1), 201–233.

Griffiths, K., Stretton, J., & Dalgleish, T. (2022). Memory bias for social hierarchical information is modulated by perceived social rank. *Memory*, *30*(5), 650–657. doi.org/10.1080/09658211.2022.2029902

Gruzd, A. & Haythronthwaite, C. (2013). Enabling communities through social media. *Journal of*

Medical Internet Research, 15(10), e248. Doi: 10.2196/jmir.2796

Gruzd, A., Mai, P., & Kampen, A. (2022). Using Netlytic to analyze Twitter conversation about the 2014 Euromaidan revolution in Ukraine. In A. Quan-Haase & L. Sloan (Eds.), *The handbook of social media research methods* (2nd ed., pp. 467–475). Sage.

Gruzd, A., Wellman, B., & Takhteyev, Y. (2011). Imagining Twitter as an imagined community. *American Behavioral Scientist, 55*(10), 1294–1318. abs.sagepub.com/content/55/10/1294.short

Gruzd, A. & Haythronthwaite, C. (2013). Enabling communities through social media. *Journal of Medical Internet Research, 15*(10), e248. Doi: 10.2196/jmir.2796

Hall, J.A. (2020). *Relating through technology: everyday social interaction*. Cambridge University Press.

Hampton, K.N. (2016). Persistent and pervasive community. *American Behavioral Scientist, 60*(1), 101–124. doi.org/10.1177/0002764215601714

Hollingshead, W., Quan-Haase, A., & Blank, G. (2022a). Representation and bias in social media research: quantitative and qualitative approaches to sampling. In A. Quan-Haase & L. Sloan (Eds.), *The handbook of social media research methods* (2nd ed., pp. 79–90). Sage.

Hollingshead, W., Quan-Haase, A., & Chen, W. (2022b). Ethics and privacy in computational social science: a call for pedagogy. In U. Engel, A. Quan-Haase, L. Lyberg, & X. Liu (Eds.), *The handbook of computational social science*. Routledge.

Isa, D., & Himelboim, I. (2018). A social networks approach to online social movement: social mediators and mediated content in #freeAJstaff twitter network. *Social Media+ Society, 4*(1), 2056305118760807.

Kavada, A. (2015). Creating the collective: social media, the Occupy Movement and its constitution as a collective actor. *Information, Communication and Society, 18*(8), 872–886. doi.org/10.1080/1369118X.2015.1043318

Khaund, T. (2021). *Leveraging social network analysis and supervised machine learning to study coordination in online information campaigns*. University of Arkansas at Little Rock.

Kwak, H., Lee, C., Park, H., & Moon, S. (2010). What is Twitter, a social network or a news media? *International World Wide Web Conference Committee (IW3C2)*, 591–600. doi.org/10.1145/1772690.1772751

Laumann, E.O., Marsden, P.V, & Prensky, D. (1989). The boundary specification problem in network analysis. In L.C. Freeman, D.R. White, & A.K. Romney (Eds.), *Research methods in social network analysis* (pp. 61–87). George Mason University Press.

Lerman, K. (2018). Computational social scientist beware: Simpson's paradox in behavioral data. *Journal of Computational Social Science, 1*(1), 49–58.

Liu, M. Zou, X., Chen, J. & Ma, S. (2022). Comparative analysis of social support in online health communities using a word co-occurrence network analysis approach. *Entropy, 24*, 174. Doi: 10.3390/e24020174

Lo, J. (2019). Exploring the buffer effect of receiving social support on lonely and emotionally unstable social networking users. *Computers in Human Behavior, 90*, 103–116.

Lutz, C. (2022). Inequalities in social media use and their implications for digital methods research. In A. Quan-Haase & L. Sloan (Eds.), *The handbook of social media research methods* (2nd ed., pp. 679–690). Sage.

Ma, L., & Zhang, Y. (2022). Three social-mediated publics in digital activism: a network perspective of social media public segmentation. *Social Media+ Society, 8*(2), 20563051221094776.

Mai, P. & Gruzd, A. (2022). The State of Social Media in Canada 2022. Social Media Lab Toronto Metropolitan University. DOI: 10.6084/m9.figshare.21002848

Malik, A., Khan, L.M., & Quan-Haase, A. (2021). Public health agencies outreach through Instagram during Covid-19 pandemic: crisis and emergency risk communication perspective. *International Journal of Disaster Risk Reduction, 61*(July), 102346. doi.org/doi.org/10.1016/j.ijdrr.2021.102346

Malova, E. (2021). Understanding online conversations about Covid-19 vaccine on Twitter: vaccine hesitancy amid the public health crisis. *Communication Research Reports, 38*(5), 346–356. doi.org/10.1080/08824096.2021.1983424

McClain, C. (2022). How parents' views of their kids' screen time, social media use changed during Covid-19. www.pewresearch.org/fact-tank/2022/04/28/how-parents-views-of-their-kids-screen-time-social-media-use-changed-during-covid-19/

McEwan, B., Fletcher, J., Eden, J., & Sumner, E. (2014). Development and validation of a Facebook relational maintenance measure. *Communication Methods and Measures, 8*(4), 244–263.

Moreno, J. (1953). *Who shall survive? Foundations of sociometry, group, psychotherapy and sociodrama*. Beacon.

Moukarzel, S., Rehm, M., Caduff, A., Del Fresno, M., Perez-Escamilla, R., & Daly, A.J. (2021). Real-time Twitter interactions during World Breastfeeding Week: a case study and social network analysis. *PLOS One, 16*(3). doi.org/10.1371/JOURNAL.PONE.0249302

Nau, C., McCay-Peet, L., & Quan-Haase, A. (2022). Defining social media and asking social media research questions: how well applies the Swiss army knife metaphor? In A. Quan-Haase & L. Sloan (Eds.), *The handbook of social media research methods* (2nd ed., pp. 40–53). Sage.

Nazar, S., & Pieters, T. (2021). Plandemic revisited: a product of planned disinformation amplifying the Covid-19 'infodemic.' *Frontiers in Public Health*, *9*. www.frontiersin.org/articles/10.3389/fpubh.2021.649930

Nissenbaum, H. (2011). A contextual approach to privacy online. *Daedalus*, *140*, 32–48. doi.org/doi.org/32-48.10.1162/DAED_a_00113

Pennington, N., & Hall, J.A. (2021). Does Facebook-enabled communication influence weak-tie relationships over time? A longitudinal investigation into mediated relationship maintenance. *Communication Monographs*, *88*(1), 48–70.

Pew Research Center (2021). *Social media fact sheet*. www.pewresearch.org/internet/fact-sheet/social-media/

Pew Research Center (2022). *Teens, social media and technology 2022*. www.pewresearch.org/internet/2022/08/10/teens-social-media-and-technology-2022/

Potter, J., & Shaw, C. (2018). *The Sage handbook of qualitative data collection*. Sage. doi.org/10.4135/9781526416070

Priadana, A., & Tahalea, S.P. (2021). Hashtag activism and message frames: social network analysis of Instagram during the Covid-19 pandemic outbreak in Indonesia. *Journal of Physics: Conference Series*, *1836*(1), 12031.

Quan-Haase, A., Harper, M.-G., & Wellman, B. (2022). The role of communication technology across the life course: a field guide to social support in East York. *Journal of Social and Personal Relationships*, *38*(2), 3497–3517. doi.org/10.1177/02654075211056898

Quan-Haase, A., & Ho, D. (2020). Online privacy concerns and privacy protection strategies among older adults in East York, Canada. *Journal of the Association for Information Science and Technology*, *71*, 1089–1102.

Quan-Haase, A., & McCay-Peet, L. (2016). Social network analysis. In K.J. Bruhn & R.T. Craig (Eds.), *International encyclopedia of communication theory and philosophy*. Wiley.

Quan-Haase, A., McLaughlin, R., & McCay-Peet, L. (2022). Building social media interdisciplinary research teams across academia, industry, and community: motivations, challenges, and policy frameworks. In A. Quan-Haase & L. Sloan (Eds.), *The handbook of social media research methods* (2nd ed., pp. 40–53). Sage.

Quan-Haase, A., & Sloan, L. (2022). *The handbook of social media research methods* (2nd ed.). Sage.

Rains, S.A., Brunner, S.R., & Oman, K. (2016). Self-disclosure and new communication technologies: the implications of receiving superficial self-disclosures from friends. *Journal of Social and Personal Relationships*, *33*(1), 42–61.

Rideout, V., & Robb, M.B. (2018). *Social media, social life: teens reveal their experiences*. www.commonsensemedia.org/sites/default/files/research/report/2018-social-media-social-life-executive-summary-web.pdf

Rozzell, B., Piercy, C.W., Carr, C.T., King, S., Lane, B.L., Tornes, M., Johnson, A.J., & Wright, K.B. (2014). Notification pending: online social support from close and nonclose relational ties via Facebook. *Computers in Human Behavior*, *38*, 272–280.

Savio, G. (2015). Coordination outside formal organization: consensus-based decision-making and occupation in the Occupy Wall Street movement. *Contemporary Justice Review*, *18*(1), 42–54.

Seymour, B., Getman, R., Saraf, A., Zhang, L.H., & Kalenderian, E. (2015). When advocacy obscures accuracy online: digital pandemics of public health misinformation through an antifluoride case study. *American Journal of Public Health*, *105*(3), 517–523. doi.org/10.2105/AJPH.2014.302437

Song, L., Son, J., & Lin, N. (2011). Social support. In P. Carrington & J. Scott (Eds.), *The Sage handbook of social network analysis*. Sage. doi.org/10.4135/9781446294413

Vally, Z., & Helmy, M. (2022). The association between psychological burden related to Covid-19 and addictive social media use: testing the mediational role of anxious affect. *PLOS One*, *17*(7), e0271332.

Wellman, B., Quan-Haase, A., & Harper, G.M. (2020). The networked question in the digital era: how do networked, bounded, and limited individuals connect at different stages in the life course? *Network Science*, *8*(1), 1–22. doi.org/doi.org/10.1017/nws.2019.28

Williams, M.L., Burnap, P., & Sloan, L. (2017). Towards an ethical framework for publishing Twitter data in social research: taking into account users' views, online context and algorithmic estimation. *Sociology*, *51*(6), 1149–1168.

Winzer, E., Naderer, B., Klein, S., Lercher, L., & Wakolbinger, M. (2022). Promotion of food and beverages by German-speaking influencers popular with adolescents on TikTok, YouTube and Instagram. *International Journal of Environmental Research and Public Health*, *19*(17). doi.org/10.3390/ijerph191710911

Xu, R. & Cavallo, D. (2021). Social network analysis of the effects of a social media-based weight loss intervention targeting adults of low socioeconomic status: A single-arm intervention trial. *Journal of Medical Internet Research*, *23*(4): e24690. DOI: 10.2196/24690

Yang, S., Quan-Haase, A., & Rannenberg, K. (2016). The changing public sphere on Twitter: network structure, elites, and topics of the #righttobeforgotten. *New Media and Society*. doi.org/1461444816651409

Zhao, J., Freeman, B., & Li, M. (2016). Can mobile phone apps influence people's health behavior change? An evidence review. *Journal of Medical Internet Research*, *18*(11), 71–82. doi.org/dx.doi.org/10.2196/jmir.5692

Zhao, Y., Da, J., & Yan, J. (2021). Detecting health misinformation in online communities: Incorporating behavioural features into machine learning based approaches. *Information Processing & Management*, *58*(1), 102390. Doi: doi.org/10.1016/j.ipm.2020.102390

Zhou, J. (2018). Factors influencing people's personal information disclosure behaviors in online health communities: a pilot study. *Asia-Pacific Journal of Public Health*, *30*(3), 286–295. doi.org/10.1177/1010539518754390

Zimmer, M., & Proferes, N.J. (2014). A topology of Twitter research: disciplines, methods, and ethics. *Aslib Journal of Information Management*, *66*(3), 250–261.

Social Capital

Beate Völker

To have friends is to have power: for they are strengths united.

(Hobbes, 1651, p. 66)

Social capital can be characterized as outdated, up to date, or ahead of its time.

(Ostrom & Ahn, 2009, p. 31)

INTRODUCTION

Without any doubt people need all kind of resources to get ahead or to secure their living conditions. In what follows the theory of social capital is highlighted as one of the resources that people need to pursue a good life. The value of social capital is comparable to the value of human, financial, or cultural capital. After discussing the phenomenon, different theoretical accounts will be reviewed and the state of the art in research into social capital and, in particular, its measurement is described. Finally, some new developments and open questions are sketched.

THE 'SOCIAL CAPITAL' PHENOMENON

In recent years, research into social capital has grown enormously (see Figure 22.1) and social capital research has a prominent place in many different fields, ranging from economics to anthropology, cognitive neuroscience to sociology, and from management studies to human geography. Social capital research questions touch upon issues related to politics and policies, organisational performance, education, individual health and well-being, neighbourhood functioning and belonging to a group. Furthermore, the great variety of methods that scientists have at their disposal are employed in social capital research: quantitative social surveys, qualitative in-depth interviews, observations, field experiments and lab experiments. In short, there are not many research topics that span such a number of fields and methodological approaches as social capital research.

Next to this, a range of phenomena that are crucial for a society's functioning and for social fabric such as social participation, involvement and social cohesion relate to social capital. Social capital is of value for individuals and collectives

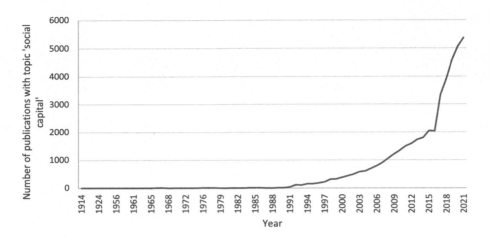

Figure 22.1   Papers on 'social capital' (topic search in web of science)

(see below) and plays a role in practically all domains of life and society.

The growth in attention to the phenomenon is probably due to several seminal contributions in the late 20th century, such as those by Bourdieu (1981), Coleman (1988, 1990) and Putnam (1993). However, and perhaps even more important, after decades of welfare in Western countries, it became clear that social inequality persists or even grows, although access to housing, work, education and the health system was generally improved. Despite the modernist and universalistic norms about the 'right person in the right place', certificates and diplomas still were not the only explanation for success. A person's social network matters; relationships can provide all kind of advantages. Having a good life depends not only on what you know but on who you know and by whom you are known. This fact sets the stage for research into social capital – actually, a criticism of modern societies, showing that the way to meritocracy is much farther and more complex than widely believed. Differently put, on the level of a society, the importance of individual social capital can be considered as an unintended byproduct of the increase of educational certificates in the 20th century: more accessibility and equality, on the one hand, are, on the other hand, associated with more conscious 'networking', with the goal of distinguishing oneself from the rest. Hence, although often discussed as an ingredient of social cohesion, social capital – in particular, social capital on the individual level – plays a significant role in the reproduction of social inequality.

THEORETICAL ACCOUNTS OF SOCIAL CAPITAL

There is not a single integrative theory on social capital but there are several conceptualisations and distinctions, which differ in their degree of elaboration and comprehensiveness. One should have in mind, however, that social capital relates to the different levels of aggregation in society: micro- as well as macro-level. Micro-level social capital focuses on individuals, their networks and the benefits that can be achieved through these relationships. Macro-level, or collective, social capital is located on the level of communities, such as organisations, neighbourhoods, or countries. Because individuals can enjoy this social capital often even without having invested in its creation, collective social capital is a public good that warrants the functioning of the community. Stated differently, individual social capital differences relate most straightforward to social inequality and collective social capital differences to social cohesion.

While Bourdieu's (1986) account on social capital is on individual social capital, Putnam's (1993, 2000) work is on collective social capital. The James Coleman acknowledges both sides.

Individual Social Capital

The theoretical account of social capital on the individual level is a neo-Weberian view on social resources. Max Weber (1922) coined the different types of capital, thereby extending the Marxist view that focused solely on economic capital. According to Weber, not only economic or financial capital but also symbolic and political capital help a person to get ahead in society. Later, the idea of social capital, which implies that knowing the right people helps to get ahead, had been added by modern sociologists. Bourdieu (1981) was among the first who wrote explicitly about social capital. His view was close to the Marxist perspective in the sense that he stressed that social capital safeguards and even reproduces class boundaries and creates exclusive networks. According to Bourdieu, the fundamental types of capital in societies are economic, cultural and social, and they are convertible into each other. For example, financial capital can be transformed to cultural capital, if it is used for buying art, books, or music instruments. Social capital can be transformed to economic capital when it helps to attain a position in society with a high salary. Next to possibilities of conversion, Bourdieu (1986) and later Coleman (1988) assumed that social capital can increase the returns of other forms of capital. For example, the returns of a good education are better if one has also contact with people in high positions.

Bourdieu and Coleman differ in their conceptualisation of social capital in the sense that Bourdieu puts greater emphasis on power inequalities. For Bourdieu, the major role of social capital in a society is the reproduction of status and class. It is a zero-sum game: some people have access to social capital because they are in the right position, but others have not and the advantages of some always come with a price for others. Taking this view very strict, this implies that investment in social capital does not guarantee its emergence and returns.

Coleman (1990) chose another point of departure for his account on social capital. Unlike Bourdieu, he placed the idea of social capital at the crossroads of two intellectual traditions: the sociological view of an actor guided by norms in a social context and the economic view of an actor, who attempts to maximise utility – independent of others' interests and of their mutual relationships (Völker, 2021). The former is the prototype of the 'oversocialised' actor in the sociological Durkheimian tradition (Granovetter, 1985), who has no internal trigger for actions but who is fully guided by external forces. The latter represents the 'undersocialised' actor in the economic tradition, who is solely guided by the motivation to maximise utility. This latter conceptualisation, however, lacks the acknowledgment of the influence of contexts, social institutions and social structures in general, and it ignores an actor's embeddedness in relations and networks. Coleman employed the economic principle of rational action in the analysis of social structures while accounting for the interdependencies between individual actors and their social environment. Indeed, social theory according to Coleman should include both traditions and social capital theory is a conceptual tool for such an integrative theoretical endeavour. In other words, the idea of social capital aligns with the integration of social structure and individual agency, by perceiving individual actions driven by utility goals but restricted by the surrounding structures and the rules therein.

Investment, Property Rights and Institutions

Investment

Both influential authors, Bourdieu and Coleman, acknowledged the role of exchanges and *investment* in social relationships in the creation of social capital. Social transactions create obligations, which are informally agreed upon or which are warranted by the institutions of a society.

Bourdieu considered the network of a person as the product of investment, when he wrote:

> In other words, the network of relationships is the product of investment strategies, individual or collective, consciously or unconsciously aimed at establishing or reproducing social relationships that are directly usable in the short or long term, i.e., at transforming contingent relations, such as those of neighbourhood, the workplace, or even kinship, into relationships that are at once necessary and elective, implying durable obligations subjectively felt (feelings of gratitude, respect, friendship, etc.) or institutionally guaranteed (rights).
>
> (Bourdieu, 1986, p. 248)

Coleman (1990) wrote about 'credit slips' to indicate the indebtedness and obligations related to favours or support one received in the past. An investment creates the credit slip warranting refund in the future.

Notably, the assumption that actors invest in their relationships in order to receive benefits in the future has many implications. First, investment decisions depend on the expected value of a relationship in the future. If there is no or only a short 'shadow of the future' (Axelrod, 1984; Boissevain, 1974), one cannot expect to get something in return. The same holds when social capital quickly decays (Burt, 2000a; Taylor, 1974, p.

9) – that is, if the discount rate is high. For example, it is unlikely that the credit slip that resulted from having done a little favour to a person holds its value for years. If it is not renewed, social capital loses its value.

Furthermore, investment in social capital cannot come about without *reciprocity assumptions* and norms. If there is no norm prescribing that favours should be returned – no matter whether this is in a generalised or personalised way – investments in relationships will not pay back. The time lag between investment in a relationship and the benefits that one can get in returns underlines the importance of trust in the specific relationship as well as in the stable existence of the world and social institutions. Trust emerges in closed or dense social structures (see below), where actors are all connected with each other. In such a structure, misbehaviour (opportunistic behaviour) can be effectively sanctioned (Coleman, 1990).

It is argued furthermore that people might not be picky in their investment decision, they simply invest heavily in social capital whenever possible, because they do not know their future and do not want to be caught on the wrong side (Flap, 2004; Glaeser, 2001; Glaeser et al., 2002). It should be noted, however, that social capital is not always acquired through investment. Bourdieu (1981) noted that social capital can also be inherited. Furthermore, relations can emerge instantly or are initiated through formal rules.

Property rights

Social capital is a capital good since it substantially facilitates the achievement of individual goals that cannot be achieved otherwise or only at much higher costs. However, in line with the perception of an actor who is simultaneously depending on a social structure and driven by their own interests, an individual is not fully in control of their social capital. One of the peculiarities of social capital is that the *property rights* for that resource are constrained: one cannot dispose of social capital alone.

> Social capital is defined by its function. It is not a single entity, but a variety of different entities having two characteristics in common: they all consist of some aspect of social structure, and they facilitate certain actions of individuals who are within the structure.
>
> (Coleman, 1990, p. 302)

The conceptualisation of shared property rights of social capital builds upon arguments of the economist Loury (1977, 1987), who coined the idea that social relationships represent a resource for the individual and emphasised that this kind of resource – social capital – is embedded in the relationships that a person has. This embeddedness distinguishes social capital from other forms of capital – in particular, from economic and human capital. People possess their money and their educational degrees, and they decide for themselves and independently how they are going to spend them. For social capital to become effective at least two people are involved. While financial or human capital have the character of private goods, the shared property rights indicate that social capital has in some respects a public good character (see below).

Institutions

Returns to investment – that is, the value of social capital – are not universal but depend on the *institutions* and the culture in a society. Institutions steer social behaviour and influence the creation of social capital as well as the returns (Völker & Flap, 2001). In societies, where all kinds of help are provided by the government, people might not feel the need to invest in their relationships, or, if they invest, the same returns are not brought about. In other words, if people are confronted with problems that are not solved by the institutions of a society, it can be expected that they create social capital and solve the issues themselves. Returns to investment in social capital are particularly large if no standardised, alternative ways are available to achieve a better life, or secure living conditions. Consequently, welfare states might weaken social capital. Empirical evidence for this straightforward idea, the so-called 'crowding out' hypothesis, is, however, scarce and findings are mixed, at best. Studies differ significantly in data used and measurements of social capital (see Van Oorschot & Arts, 2005; Kumlin & Rothstein, 2005: Kääriäinen & Lehtonen, 2006; see also the early account by Litwak & Szeleny, 1969, who study how technological developments on the societal level influence social network structures). The relation between state institutions, cultures and individual social capital is still open to deeper investigation.

Social Capital in the Structure of a Network

The individual approach to social capital requires a *network* as well as the *ability* and the *willingness* of the network members to provide help (see Flap & Völker, 2013; Völker, 2021).

There is, in addition, social capital in the *structure* of a network (Burt, 1992, 2000b). Both, Bourdieu (1981) and Coleman (1990) imply that a dense network provides social capital. Dense networks lower all kinds of cost, interaction, information and monitoring. Furthermore, dense networks can sanction opportunistic behaviour and the abuse of trust (Raub & Weesie, 1990; Buskens & Raub, 2002). Closure in Bourdieu's view refers to exclusive membership in groups with clear demarcated boundaries (Bourdieu & Wacquant, 1986).

An alternative perspective on high connectivity and closure providing social capital is brought up by Burt (1992). He built upon the idea of the 'strength of weak ties', elaborated earlier by Granovetter (1973). Granovetter studied how people attained their labour market position and found that relations that were relatively distant from the focal actor played an important role in this process. Because weak ties are in the position to provide unique and new information, they can be very beneficial – hence, they are strong. In a network with an actor having two strong ties with two otherwise unconnected alters (see Figure 22.2, network to the left), the likelihood that these alters also establish a tie is high. As the network at the right side in Figure 22.2 shows, this results in network closure. This tendency for closure comes into being for a number of reasons (Granovetter, 1973). The two members of the network have a higher meeting chance because of their strong tie to the same actor. Furthermore, they are probably similar to each other because the focal actor probably chose them because they are similar to her and homophily is a strong explanation for network formation (McPherson et al., 2001).

Weak ties do not have that tendency to enhance network closure but are bridges to other social circles. This finding coined the term that became famous: the 'strength of weak ties'. Burt (op. cit.) elaborated this idea of bridges and argued that the benefits of such ties do not rest in the characteristic of being weak, but in being a bridge. A weak tie that does not constitute a bridge does not provide social capital. In other words, if a weak tie is not a bridge, it is not strong.

Figure 22.3 illustrates the closed, highly connected network structure (left network in the figure) and the open network, where the focal actor in the middle has contacts that are not connected (network at the right side in the figure). While in the closed network, everyone's behaviour can be monitored, no such control exists in the open network structure. Furthermore, the actor in the middle of the open network is in an advantaged position since she receives information from everyone. This information is probably unique, as the network members have no contact with each other. Also, the focal actor in the middle can play the network members off against each other; they all depend on her (cf. Emerson, 1962).

Hence, the first network (left in the figure) is an idealised version of a social structure that consists of coinciding social groups whose members are highly connected with each other; they constitute a closed network (cf. Simmel, 1955b, p. 147). This type of network consists of relations that are strong, stable and multiplex. The strength of this kind of network structure is that it promotes a sense of belonging, cooperation, mutual support and trust (Coleman, 1988, p. 103, 1990, p. 306 passim). Its weakness is that it limits individual freedom and autonomy (see, e.g., Coser, 1984, p. 223). Because of the closure and the focus on group membership rather than individuality, the network is also associated with in-group favouritism and out-group rejection (cf. Levine & Campbell, 1972; Hewstone, 1989; Oakes et al., 1994). The third network has a radial or spoke structure (see Granovetter, 1973; Pescosolido & Rubin, 2000) in which an individual is the only link between multifarious other individuals or groups that do not intersect. Relations in this type of structure are typically uniplex, weak and temporary. In such a network the proportion of indirect ties is highest, and the proportion of direct ties is lowest. This is the network structure that is a social capital asset 'in its own right', according to Burt (1992, p. 3). Also, freedom and flexibility are at a maximum

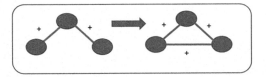

Figure 22.2 Network closure in networks of strong ties

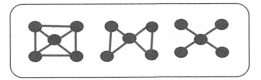

Figure 22.3 Paradigmatic network structures

and there is the least group pressure. The weakness of this network structure, however, is that it only provides limited social support, constructive feedback and help in structuring reality, constructing a stable identity, or becoming oriented towards other individuals or influences (cf. Maryanski & Turner, 1992). Promotions of common goods, cooperative efforts together with others, are not facilitated through by such a network structure.

Another network structure, in the middle of the figure, lies between the closed network and the more open network. This type of a network is also discussed in the literature (Krackhardt, 1999), although it has received much less attention. In this structure, a focal actor is a bridge between two otherwise unconnected but internally dense social networks. This personal network consists of cross-cutting social circles (Simmel, 1890, 1955a; also referred to as bow-tie structure, Krackhardt, 1999), with an individual at the intersection of different groups. Simmel (1890, p. 53) argues that this type of network structure strengthens an individual's identity and alleviates conflicts because people constantly integrate diverse group interests and demands. An individual at the intersection of these circles is assumed to have more freedom of choice, an open mind, high level of autonomy, increased tolerance of strangers and greater knowledge of the world (cf. Popper, 1945; Laumann, 1973; Coser, 1975, 1991, p. 25; Blau, 1993, p. 75). A liability of this network structure is that it can lead to anomia, double bind situations, and apathy, and cognitive and emotional conflicts (cf. Krackhardt, 1999; Pescosolido & Rubin, 2000, p. 57).

Although it is plausible that social capital can relate to different network structures, it should, however, not be forgotten that the consequences of these network structures for individual social capital depend also on the content of the relationships (Podolny & Baron, 1997). Relations among people who are entangled in hateful or negative networks do not constitute social capital, although some network positions will be still more advantageous than others. In this case, such a structural advantage might be having the power to harm others, or having a position that protects from being harmed.

Studying such paradigmatic structures can illustrate the difference between *bridging* social capital and *bonding* social capital. Bonding social capital is the relations that are important for 'getting through'; bridging social capital helps to get ahead. Woolcock (1998) added the idea of *linking* social capital, referring to contacts among people in different power positions (see also Poortinga, 2012).

Social Capital at the Collective Level

As already mentioned, there is a collective good aspect to social capital (Coleman, 1990). Putnam (1993) conceives social capital explicit as a characteristic of the macro/meso levels such as neighbourhoods, organisations, regions, or countries. He examined why the Italian South lagged so far behind the North and argued that the voluntary organisations and civic traditions in the North promoted networks of trust. People associated with each other in their various memberships could force the government to stick to agreements and prevent from corruption. This way, local democracy is strengthened, and economic growth can take place. In the Italian South corruption and patronage hampered collective action and democracy. In Putnam's account, social capital contributes to the functioning of the social fabric by increasing the cost of defecting and it fosters reciprocity norms (Putnam, 1993, p. 173). Importantly, social capital effects, in Putnam's view, are abundant. Lower crime rates, better health, better school performance, in his view, all go hand in hand with more social capital (Putnam, 2000). According to Putnam (1993, p. 35), social capital refers to 'features of social organizations, such as networks, norms and trust that facilitate action and cooperation for mutual benefit'.

The research on social capital in this vein focuses mostly on community health and a communitarian approach to social capital. Indeed, it has been shown that collective social capital – that is, a functioning neighbourhood community – promotes health (Mohnen et al., 2011; Veenstra et al., 2005) and feelings of well-being and safety.

However, structural network aspects are only rarely theorised in the collective approaches to social capital, although connections at the macro level must be, in one way or another, an aggregate of individual networks. How this aggregation works and how cohesion on a macro level emerges is usually not the focus of research on community social capital. A person's network and its structure do not seem regarded as important. Moore et al. (2006) recognised this and argued that the full potential of social capital is overlooked in this way. Network approaches and their relationship to social capital seem to be 'lost in translation' (Moore et al., 2006, p. 729) because the focus is dominated by the communitarian approach and the micro level not understood. Sight had been lost of the original intention to model social capital as a mediator between income levels and health.

Crucial for social capital being a collective good is that one can enjoy its benefits, even without having invested in the social capital creation. Putnam (2007) emphasises that it is exactly this aspect that makes networks in, for example, neighourhoods very important.

> I am able to be in Uppsala, Sweden, confident that my home is being protected by all that social capital, even though – and this is the moment for confession – I actually never go to the barbecues and cocktail parties. In other words, I benefit from those social networks even though I am not actually in them myself. In the language of economics, social networks often have powerful externalities.
>
> (Putnam, 2007, p. 138)

A similar example of collective social capital was given by Coleman (1990, p. 310). If people agreed to monitor their neighbourhood at night, not only would residents benefit from this form of social capital but so also would a stranger, who would be safe walking through the streets at night.

It should be taken into account, though, that viewing social capital as a collective or public good implies that the dilemma of public goods applies (Olson, 1965). Underinvestment in social capital will occur, since those who invest 'capture only a small part of the benefits' (Coleman, 1988, p. S119). This might explain why social capital on a collective level is often too small, or that people hesitate to build it up, because they do not trust that everyone will invest. Solutions to the public good problem (see Yamagishi & Sato, 1986; Cowen, 2008; Elliot & Golub, 2019) could help to develop this aspect of social capital further. This could also reopen anew the discussion about the relation between social capital and institutions (see above).

THE DARK SIDE OF SOCIAL CAPITAL

As already mentioned above, social relations are double-edged; they can provide support and confirm each other's identity or block development chances or actively harm (Moore et al., 2009; Moerbeek & Need, 2003). Obviously, network closure can have negative consequences (Portes, 2014; Portes & Landolt, 1996). Labianca and Brass (2006) even argued that the consequences of negative ties on performance might be more significant than the consequences of 'sweet' social capital.

More systematically, social capital can become 'sour' in several respects (Portes, 1998; Portes & Sensenbrenner, 1993). Social capital can enforce people to *actively harm* others and create a vicious circle of hateful acts and vengeance. Instead of having credit slips for doing something good, people might feel that having a credit slip implies having power and being able to extort own favours. Reciprocity here implies total dependency and paying the debt by doing harm. This is greatly illustrated in the opening scene of the movie *The Godfather* (1972, directed by Francis Coppola). The Godfather was asked by an acquaintance to take revenge on two boys who assaulted his daughter but were set free by the judge. The Godfather finally agreed, but stated at the end of the scene: 'Some day and that day may never come, I'll call upon you to do a service for me.'

Another example for the dark side of social capital is that *investments that are not returned* will turn social capital into sour social capital. This is the case when one has helped in many situations but never got anything in return. Also, and as mentioned above, social capital can decay if the time lag is too long and/or if the initial investment was not very large, and it is not renewed. Decay of social capital can result in withholding resources.

Furthermore, another uninvited aspect of social capital is that *social relationships themselves can have undesirable consequences* – for example, if individuals are locked in their networks and do not explore alternative relationships that might provide far better opportunities or help – such as a network of peers that encourages unhealthy or asocial behaviour. Another example of that type of social capital effect is the finding that many women stay in an abusive relationship (Rusbult & Martz, 1995).

Relationships also can represent sour social capital if they ascribe to norms that are in *conflict with a society's norms*, such as criminal clans and the Mafia. Such structures can undermine the functioning of a state but stabilise a system of patronage and corruption (Gambetta, 1993).

As already argued, a dense and cohesive network can be a mixed blessing for an individual in such a structure since it restricts freedom. For individuals outside such a structure, consequences might also be harmful. Almost by definition, *a cohesive structure implies exclusion*. Durlauf (2002) argued, therefore, that the decline of social capital might be not such a problem as sometimes assumed.

As for the creation of social capital, the creation of sour social capital can be influenced and enhanced by social structures. For example, a structure of extreme competition hampers investment in ties and promotes blocking life chances. Also, a structure where people are forced into dense networks without having choices probably promotes negative relationships. The major 'sour' aspect of social capital, however, rests in its particularity – the fact that social capital is at odds with treating all subjects equally. This was implied in Max Weber's (1922) plea for impersonal transactions and bureaucracy: he wanted to overcome particularism. Since social capital research shows that universalism fails, sour consequences may be inevitable at the micro-level as well as on macro level.

IS SOCIAL CAPITAL 'CAPITAL'?

The concept of social capital has been heavily criticised for being vague. Coleman's conception, most explicitly, has been critiqued because of the definition through its function (see above): if a person benefits from a social resource, embedded in a relation to someone else, this is considered as social capital. Furthermore, as mentioned in the section above, criticism is also formulated because of the focus on desirable consequences, although social capital also implies exclusion (Durlauf, 2002).

Another interesting discussion is on the question whether social capital is 'capital' at all or whether that one should better speak of 'resources' (Arrow, 1999). To an extent, this is a matter of which label is attached and, consequently, often will not significantly affect what researchers do. Depending on the theoretical elaboration, the idea of social capital can be close to other capital goods or more loosely related. However, there are several characteristics of social capital that make it similar to other forms of capital – and distinguish it from social resources or social support (see Robison et al., 2002; also Song & Zhang, this volume). The most important similarities between social capital and other forms of capital rest in ideas of: (1) investment and production; (2) decay/discount; and (3) convertibility.

(1) As to the idea of investment and production, although social capital can be inherited from parents or from the community to which a person belongs, social capital is created through investment in relationships. There is a favour or an act of help at the beginning of the emergence of social capital. Such an act is an investment that hopefully creates returns. As in investment in financial goods, one can fail, circumstances can change and the investment is lost. Like other investments, social capital investments can be actively withdrawn; if there are no returns expected any more, people will disinvest. If investments create returns, however, social capital is a commodity used in the production of other goods and services and increases future production (Smithson, 1982). This idea is not implied in resources or support.

(2) Concerning decay or discount, as described above; like a qualification attained decades ago, social capital decays through time if it is not renewed (Taylor, 1974). Like other goods, social capital needs maintenance. Getting a new job or moving to another place can make it difficult to maintain social capital; also an act of help provided years ago will no longer be considered as important. This argument is, likewise, not implied in social support elaborations.

(3) Finally, like financial capital, social capital can be used and converted into other forms of capital: a friend who can give advice in matters of work will also try to help when asked for help to find a house. Such convertibility is discussed in the context of social capital approaches but not in social resource ideas.

Obviously, there are also similarities between social capital, social resources and social support. However, the argument made here is that the idea of 'capital' is theoretically richer and inspires more fundamental research questions than the other concepts.

MEASUREMENT OF SOCIAL CAPITAL

Measuring social capital is a special case in measuring egocentric networks (see Perry et al., this volume). When aiming to measure social capital, it is important that one always has in mind that measuring a network does not imply measuring social capital. Network measurements, like the number of friends or the number of people with whom one has contact in the neighbourhood, are only a rough proxy for social capital. To date, measurements for social capital are still not always comparable across studies, although some instruments are rather well established.

Measuring Individual Social Capital

One important method for measuring social capital on the individual level is the so-called exchange method (Fischer, 1982; Fischer et al., 1977). This involves two stages of enquiry into people's interactions (exchanges) with others, such as lending money, helping with odd jobs, giving advice, or talking about important matters. Respondents mention the network members important for these different exchanges by their names or initials. In the second stage, these names are interpreted by asking what kind of relationship they have, how long they have known each other, how often they see each other, where they met, how close they are and so forth. Questions are also asked regarding the potential resources of the alters such as occupation and education, sometimes even income. Via this measurement, information about the presence, willingness and resources – that is, the ability of the alters to help – is collected.

Note that many of these name generator measurements differ in aspects that might not seem very important at first but actually make studies incomparable. For example, the time frame given in the questions is a source of differences – should respondents mention the people they have spoken to about important matters during the last two weeks, recent months or 'usually'? Furthermore, the network boundaries set are also important and differ across studies: are respondents allowed to mention three, five, or more network members? Differences in the wordings of these questions will lead to differences measured in network sizes.

The other established instrument is the so-called position generator (Lin & Dumin, 1986; Lin & Erickson, 2008; Lin, 2001). Respondents get a list with positions, usually occupational positions, and they are asked whether they know a person in such a position and whether they are friend, family, or acquaintance. The positions are sampled from the occupational prestige ladder. Once more, information on presence, willingness and capability of the network members is gathered. This instrument is very popular; it is straightforward, not expensive and established in many studies. As to the comparison of position generator measurements across studies, the same holds as for name generator measurements. How is 'knowing' a person described? Is it just a person one regularly sees in the street but never speaks to? Or is it a person one knows on a first-name basis? The number of positions will also matter, of course, as well as the kind of positions. Usually, researchers sample positions in higher, middle and lower social strata. It is yet to be studied whether the absolute prevalence of certain positions in a given area affects the delineated network. For example, in some regions doctors or lawyers are scarce; hence the chance of knowing a person in such a position is low.

Other measurements of networks, such as the summation method (Marsden, 2005) and the scale up methods (Laga et al., 2021) are in principle also applicable to measurement of social capital, but they are generally used for measuring network size and composition. They could however with slight adaptions provide interesting instruments for measuring individual social capital.

Measuring Collective Social Capital

Collective social capital is measured differently from individual social capital. It consists usually of enquiries into trust, shared norms and cohesion. In this regard the actor is still considered externally driven, which is exactly what Coleman (1988) aimed to leave behind in his account on social capital. A popular measurement is the question whether people trust others in general, or whether they are wary of others. Also, memberships are sometimes counted or whether people help each other in each neighbourhood.

General Measurement Issues

A general issue when measuring social capital is that one needs to decide whether the instrument should focus on 'access' or on 'use' of social capital, as well as whether 'actual' or 'hypothetical' help is important in the research. For example, the position generator method exclusively focuses on 'accessing' others; it does not tell whether one has made *use* of the resources. Furthermore, it makes a difference whether it is asked for the persons who *has helped* getting a job or for the persons one *would ask* for help in case one looks for a job. All these different measurements imply different conclusions in the research (see Völker, 2021). Figure 22.4 illustrates these different approaches and shows how survey questions differ depending on the chosen approach. These differences must

	Access	Use
Actual	Do you know a lawyer?	Whom did you ask for help in your recent legal conflict?
Hypothetical	Do you know someone who could help you in case you have a legal conflict?	Whom would you ask for help in a legal conflict?

Figure 22.4 Dimensions of measuring social capital with example survey questions

Source: (This figure is adapted from Völker, 2021).

be taken into account when designing a network data collection (see adams and Lubbers on network data collection *in this volume*).

CLOSER: IS SOCIAL CAPITAL DECLINING IN CONTEMPORARY SOCIETIES?

Putnam (2000) as well as Coleman (1990, 1993) allege that social capital in Western societies has declined since the 1960s. Putnam argues that, among other factors, this is probably due to technological innovation (modern communication technologies, which influence and weaken interactions) and also female labour market participation, causing women to be less active in schools and voluntary associations (an assumption which is not confirmed by empirical research). For Coleman (1988), the physical presence of adults in the household and a strong bond with the children are the conditions for the creation of social capital.

> The man's removal from the household left one adult there, but the women's leaves none. … One way of describing the loss for children is to say that the removal of women from the household curtails many of those daily activities of which child rearing is a byproduct.
>
> (Coleman, 1990, p. 587)

Such explanations, however, do not take into account that in modern societies many new forms of networks, togetherness and family compositions have come into being. It should not be underestimated that the new forms of how people live together will also create new forms of social capital. So far, evidence for the decline of social capital is mixed at best. Modern technology clearly affects weaker ties, and people nowadays can easily establish new links. The implications for social capital benefits through these links are subjects for future study.

CONCLUSION AND FUTURE DIRECTIONS

Social capital research is ongoing and the value of social capital for various domains of people's lives has been demonstrated by many empirical studies. This contribution aimed to set out important principles of social capital theories but also to point at some open questions and possible directions where interesting and important future research could be developed. Among others, rigorous studies into investment and returns, decay, aggregation from micro to macro level would probably help to understand social capital phenomena better and answer questions that are still open. Also, new forms of social capital and whether they come at the cost of older forms are worth to be studied. Online networks also entail social capital and how this type of social capital relates to social capital in the offline world – whether it is the same, whether it compensates or supplements, is not yet fully understood (Wellman et al., 2001).

Yet another important research question is the balance between exclusion and social capital/ cohesion, mentioned above. Can balance be achieved between the two; that is, is it possible that the growth of social capital does not come with exclusion, or is there an optimum? How does this look and how does it differ across settings?

New areas for social capital research probably entail, as in many other fields, interdisciplinary cooperation. Social capital questions relate very well to other disciplines, as stated in the beginning. Often, however, networks are still studied as a phenomenon, but the question why these network exist or who benefits from such a structure is not analysed. Social capital arguments can help to understand networks; hence all disciplines that study networks could use the arguments of social capital theory.

Social capital research can also benefit from methodological development. New digital techniques will allow more and quicker data collection and analysis and it will generate different types of data. New and other sources of data will become available. Techniques to collect data will become more advanced than they are nowadays. It is not clear so far how social capital questions can be studied with big data and in highly digitalized environments (Völker 2021). Data on opportunity structures for meeting in specific contexts will become more and more available through register data and micro data bases (Prins, 2017). These sources can help to understand the limits for network formation, but not the resulting networks and social capital benefits, since they do not measure actual relationships.

In any case, novel data sources constitute important future research sites for social capital studies. Think also of, for example, networks and social capital in literary novels (Völker & Smeets, 2020), networks of animals (Krause et al., 2009; Faust, 2011) or archaeological networks (Amati et al., 2018).

To conclude, social capital research enriches network research as it gives networks a theoretical meaning. It is a flourishing research tradition and is likely to remain so in the coming decades.

REFERENCES

Amati, V., Shafie, T., & Brandes, U. (2018). Reconstructing archaeological networks with structural holes. *Journal of Archaeological Method and Theory*, 25(1), 226–253.
Arrow, K.J. (1999). Observations on social capital. In P. Dasgupta and I. Serageldin (Eds.), *Social capital: a multifaceted perspective* (pp. 3–5). World Bank.
Axelrod, R. (1984). *The evolution of cooperation*. Basic Books.
Blau, J. (1993). *Social contracts and economic markets*. Plenum Press.
Boissevain J.F. (1974). *Friends of friends*. Blackwell.
Bourdieu, P. (1981). Le capital social. *Actes de la recherche en sciences sociales*, 31, 2–3.
Bourdieu, P. (1986) The forms of capital. In J. Richardson (Ed.), *Handbook of theory and research for the sociology of education* (pp. 241–258). Greenwood.
Burt, R. (1992). *Structural holes: the social structure of competition*. Harvard University Press.
Bourdieu P and Wacquant LJ (1992) *An Invitation to Reflexive Sociology*. University of Chicago press.
Burt, R.S. (2000a). Decay functions. *Social Networks*, 22(1), 1–28.
Burt, R. (2000b). The network structure of social capital. *Research in Organizational Behavior*, 22, 345–423.
Burt, R. (2002). The social capital of structural holes. *The New Economic Sociology: Developments in an Emerging Field*, 148, 90.
Buskens, V., & Raub, W. (2002). Embedded trust: control and learning. *Advances in Group Processes*, 19, 167–202, Emerald.
Coleman, J. (1988). Social capital in the creation of human capital. *American Journal of Sociology*, 95, S95–120.
Coleman, J. (1990). *The foundation of social theory*. Belknap Press.
Coleman, J. (1993). The rational reconstruction of society: 1992 presidential address. *American Sociological Review*, 58, 1–15.
Coser, R. (1975) The Complexity of Roles as a Seedbed of Individual Autonomy. In L. A. Coser (ed), *The Idea of Social Structure. Papers in Honor of Robert K. Merton*. Harcourt Brace, pp. 237–263.
Coser, R. (1984). The greedy nature of Gemeinschaft. In W.W. Powel & R. Robbins (Eds.), *Conflict and consensus* (pp. 221–239). Free Press.
Coser, R. (1991). *In defense of modernity: complexity of social roles and individual autonomy*. Stanford University Press.
Cowen, T. (2008). Public goods. In D.R. Henderson (Ed.), *The concise encyclopedia of economics* (pp. 197–199). Liberty Fund.
Durlauf, S. (2002). On the empirics of social capital. *Economic Journal*, 112(483), F459–F479.
Elliott, M., & Golub, B. (2019). A network approach to public goods. *Journal of Political Economy*, 127(2), 730–776.
Emerson, R.M. (1962). Power-dependence relations. *American Sociological Review*, 27, 31–41.
Faust, K. (2011). Animal social networks. In J. Scott & P.J. Carrington (Eds.), *The Sage handbook of social network analysis* (pp. 148–166). Sage.
Flap, H. (2004). Creation and returns of social capital. In H. Flap & B. Völker (Eds.), *Creation and returns of Social Capital* (pp. 3–24). Routledge.
Flap, H., & Völker, B. (2013). Social capital. In R. Wittek, V. Nee & T. Snijders (Eds.), *Handbook of rational choice social research* (pp. 220–251). Stanford University Press.
Fischer, C. (1982). *To dwell among friends*. University of Chicago Press.
Fischer, C.S., Jackson, R.M., Stueve, C.A., Gerson, K., McCallister Jones, L., & Baldassare, M. (1977). *Networks and places: social relations in the urban setting*. Free Press.
Gambetta, D. (1993). *The Sicilian Mafia: the business of private protection*. Harvard University Press.
Glaeser, E. (2001). The formation of social capital. *Canadian Journal of Policy Research*, 2(1), 34–40.
Glaeser, E.L., Laibson, D., & Sacerdote, B. (2002). An economic approach to social capital. *Economic Journal*, 112(483), F437–F458.
Granovetter, M. (1973). The strength of weak ties. *American Journal of Sociology*, 78, 1360–1380.
Granovetter, M. (1985). Economic action and social structure: the problem of embeddedness. *American Journal of Sociology*, 91(3), 481–510.
Hewstone, M. (1989). Changing stereotypes with disconfirming evidence. In D. Bar-Tal, C.F. Graumann, A.W. Kruglanski, & W. Stroebe (Eds.), *Stereotyping and prejudice: changing conceptions* (pp. 207–223). Springer.
Hobbes, T. (1651[1965]). *Leviathan*. Clarendon Press.
Kääriäinen, J., & Lehtonen, H. (2006). The variety of social capital in welfare state regimes: a comparative study of 21 countries. *European Societies*, 8(1), 27–57.
Krackhardt, D. (1999). The ties that torture: Simmelian tie analysis in organizations. *Research in the Sociology of Organizations*, 16, 183–210.
Krause, J., Lusseau, D., & James, R. (2009). Animal social networks: an introduction. *Behavioral Ecology and Sociobiology*, 63(7), 967–973.
Kumlin, S., & Rothstein, B. (2005). Making and breaking social capital: the impact of welfare-state institutions. *Comparative Political Studies*, 38(4), 339–365.
Labianca, G., & Brass, D.J. (2006). Exploring the social ledger: negative relationships and negative asymmetry in social networks in organizations. *Academy of Management Review*, 31(3), 596–614.

Laga, I., Bao, L., & Niu, X. (2021). Thirty years of the network scale-up method. *Journal of the American Statistical Association, 116*(535), 1548–1559.

Laumann, E.O. (1973) Bonds of Pluralism: The Form and Substance of Urban Social Networks. New York: John Wiley and Sons.

Levine, R.A., & Campbell, D.T. (1972). Ethnocentrism: theories of conflict, ethnic attitudes, and group behavior. Wiley.

Lin, N. (2001). *Social capital: a theory of social structure and action*. Cambridge University Press.

Lin, N., & Dumin, M. (1986). Access to occupations through social ties. *Social Networks, 8*, 365–385.

Lin, N., & Erickson, B.H. (Eds.) (2008). *Social capital: an international research program*. Oxford University Press.

Litwak, E., & Szelenyi, I. (1969). Primary group structures and their functions: kin, neighbors, and friends. *American Sociological Review*, 465–481.

Loury, G. (1977). A dynamic theory of racial income differences. In P.A. Wallace & A. Le Mund (Eds.), *Women, minorities, and employment discrimination* (pp. 153–188). Lexington.

Loury, G. (1987). Why should we care about group inequality? *Social Philosophy and Policy, 5*, 249–271.

Marsden, P. V. (2005). Recent developments in network measurement. *Models and methods in social network analysis, 8*, 30.

Maryanski, A., & Turner, J.H. (1992). *The social cage: human nature and the evolution of society*. Stanford University Press.

McPherson, M., Smith-Lovin, L., & Cook, J. (2001). Birds of a feather: homophily in social networks. *Annual Review of Sociology, 27*(1), 415–444.

Moerbeek, H.H.S. (2001). *Friends and foes in the occupational career: the influence of sweet and sour social capital on the labour market*. Thesis.

Moerbeek, H. H., & Need, A. (2003). Enemies at work: can they hinder your career?. *Social Networks, 25*(1), 67–82.

Mohnen, S.M., Völker, B., Flap, H., Subramanian, S.V., Groenewegen, P.P. (2011). The influence of social capital on individual health: is it the neighbourhood or the network? *Social Indicators Research, 121*(1 SI), 195–214.

Moore, S., Haines, V., Hawe, P., & Shiell, A. (2006). Lost in translation: a genealogy of the 'social capital' concept in public health. *Journal of Epidemiology and Community Health, 60*(8), 729–734.

Moore, S., Daniel, M., Gauvin, L., & Dubé, L. (2009). Not all social capital is good capital. *Health and Place, 15*(4), 1071–1077.

Oakes, P.J., Haslam, S.A., & Turner, J.C. (1994) *Stereotyping and social reality*. Blackwell.

Olson, M. (1965). *The logic of collective action: public goods and the theory of groups*. Harvard University Press.

Ostrom, E., & Ahn, T.K. (2009). The meaning of social capital and its link to collective action. In G. Tinggard Svendsen & G. Lind Haase Svendsen (Eds.), *Handbook of social capital: the troika of sociology, political science and economics* (pp. 17–35). Edward Elgar.

Pescosolido, B.A., & Rubin, B.A. (2000). The web of group affiliations revisited: social life, postmodernism and sociology. *American Sociological Review, 65*, 52–76.

Podolny, J., & J. Baron, J. (1997). Resources and relationships: social networks and mobility in the workplace. *American Sociological Review, 62*, 673–693.

Poortinga, W. (2012). Community resilience and health: the role of bonding, bridging, and linking aspects of social capital. *Health and Place, 18*(2), 286–295.

Popper, K.R. (1945). *The open society and its enemies*. Routledge and Kegan Paul.

Portes, A. (1998). Social capital: its origins and applications in modern sociology. *Annual Review of Sociology, 24*, 1–24.

Portes, A. (2014). Downsides of social capital. *Proceedings of the National Academy of Sciences, 111*(52), 18407–18408.

Portes, A., & Landolt, P. (1996). The downside of social capital. *American Prospect, 26*, 18–22.

Portes, A., & Sensenbrenner, J. (1993). Embeddedness. and immigration: notes on the social determinants of economic action. *American Journal of Sociology, 98*, 1320–1350.

Prins, K. (2017). *Population register data, basis for the Netherlands' population statistics*. Statistics Netherlands.

Putnam, R. (1993). *Making democracy work: civic traditions in modern Italy*. Princeton University Press.

Putnam, R. (2000). *Bowling alone: the collapse and revival of American community*. Simon & Schuster.

Putnam, R.D. (2007). E pluribus unum: diversity and community in the twenty-first century the 2006 Johan Skytte Prize Lecture. *Scandinavian Political Studies, 30*(2), 137–174.

Raub, W., & Weesie, J. (1990). Reputation and efficiency in social interactions: an example of network effects. *American Journal of Sociology, 96*(3), 626–654.

Robison L., Schmid, A., & Siles, M. (2002). Is social capital really capital? *Review of Social Economy, 60*(1), 1–21.

Rusbult, C.E., & Martz, J.M. (1995). Remaining in an abusive relationship: an investment model analysis of nonvoluntary dependence. *Personality and Social Psychology Bulletin, 21*(6), 558–571.

Simmel, G. (1890) *Über soziale Differenzierung*. Duncker & Humblot.

Simmel, G. (1955a). *Conflict and the web of group affiliations*. Free Press.

Simmel, G. (1955b). Die Ausdehnung der Gruppe und die Ausbildung der Individualität. In H.J. Dahme & O. Rammstedt (Eds., 1983), *Georg Simmel. Schriften zur Soziologie* (pp. 53–60). Suhrkamp.

Smithson, C.W. (1982). Capital: a factor of production. In D. Greenwald (Ed.), *Encyclopedia of economics* (pp. 111–112). McGraw-Hill.

Taylor, M. (1974). *Anarchy and cooperation*. Wiley.

Van Oorschot, W., & Arts, W. (2005). The social capital of European welfare states: the crowding out hypothesis revisited. *Journal of European Social Policy*, *15*(1), 5–26.

Veenstra, G., Luginaah, I., Wakefield, S., Birch, S., Eyles, J., & Elliott, S. (2005). Who you know, where you live: social capital, neighbourhood and health. *Social Science and Medicine*, *60*(12), 2799–2818.

Völker, B. (2021). Three decades of research into social capital: achievements, blind spots and future directions. In M. Small, B. Perry, B. Pescosolido & E. Smith (Eds.), *Personal networks: classic readings and new directions in egocentric analysis* (pp. 296–322). Cambridge University Press.

Völker, B., & Flap, H. (2001). Weak ties as a liability: the case of East Germany. *Rationality and Society*, *13*, 397–428.

Völker, B., and Smeets, R. (2020). Imagined social structures: mirrors or alternatives? A comparison between networks of characters in contemporary Dutch literature and networks of the population in the Netherlands. *Poetics*, *79*, 101379.

Weber, M. ([1922]1978) *Economy and society*. University of California Press.

Wellman, B., Haase, A.Q., Witte, J., & Hampton, K. (2001). Does the internet increase, decrease, or supplement social capital? Social networks, participation, and community commitment. *American Behavioral Scientist*, *45*(3), 436–455.

Woolcock, M. (1998). Social capital and economic development: toward a theoretical synthesis and policy framework. *Theory and Society*, *27*(2), 151–208.

Yamagishi, T., & Sato, K. (1986). Motivational bases of the public goods problem. *Journal of Personality and Social Psychology*, *50*(1), 67.

23

Social Support

Lijun Song and Zhe Zhang

Social support is a network-based phenomenon and concept rooted in classic sociological work. Comte ([1852]1875, p. 314), who coined the term 'sociology', states that 'all mental action depends on social support'. Seminal work by Durkheim, Simmel and Tönnies recognises the importance of support from social ties. Despite the long recognition, social support was not given systematic research attention until the mid-1970s for its protective role for health (Caplan, 1974; Cassel, 1976; Cobb, 1976; Dean & Lin, 1977; Kaplan et al., 1977; Lin et al., 1979). Dean and Lin (1977, p. 408) foresee it as 'the most important concept for future study'. The five decades-long literature on social support is dominated by health topics and establishes social support as a 'fundamental cause' of health (Link & Phelan, 1995; for reviews, see Crocker et al., 2017; Song, 2019; Song et al., 2011; Thoits, 2011; Turner & Turner, 2013; Uchino et al., 2012; see Figure 23.1).

Despite its substantial popularity and voluminous development, 'social support' still stimulates debates on its conceptualisation and operationalisation. It is confounded with other network-based concepts without clear differentiation. Its double-edged – protective and harmful – function for health has been given unbalanced attention. In comparison to its salubrious function, its deleterious function has received less scrutiny. Empirical results on its health returns are abundant but not always consistent. We begin this chapter by clarifying the definition and typology of social support. We then turn to its distinction from other network-based concepts, theorise their relationships with each other through a pair of competing theories (social resource versus social cost) and summarise empirical findings (Lin, 1983, 1986a, 2001; Song, 2020; Song & Pettis, 2020; Song et al., 2021). We further explain its double-edged function using this pair of theories, identify its diverse roles for health and, for the purpose of generalisability and representativeness, selectively review studies of nationally representative data of the general population, unless noted otherwise. We conclude with future research directions.

CONCEPTUALISATION OF SOCIAL SUPPORT: DEFINITION AND TYPOLOGY

Social support has diverse conceptualisations. Many of them suffer from two shortcomings that endanger its unique and broad theoretical value: lack of precision and functionalist health protection assumption (Song, 2019; Song et al., 2011). Imprecise definitions lead to broad, inconsistent

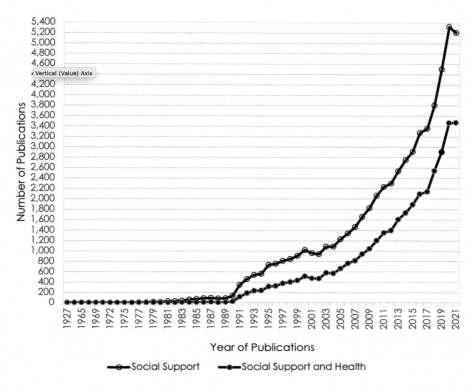

Figure 23.1 Journal articles with 'social support' and 'social support' and 'health' in topic (Social Sciences Citation Index, 1900–2021)

and invalid operationalisations and measurements, and mixed and inconclusive findings. Some do not explain the meaning of support (Cassel, 1976; Lin et al., 1979). Some explain the meaning of support using more upstream (e.g., social interaction, integration, relations, ties and bonds) or downstream (e.g., meaning) concepts (Caplan, 1974; Cobb, 1976; Pearlin et al., 1981; Thoits, 2011). Some constrain support to be a direct 'interpersonal transaction' between one provider and one recipient (House, 1981; Kahn & Antonucci, 1980; Shumaker & Brownell, 1984) and ignore support chains involving indirect ties (Lin et al., 1978). Some nail down the nature of social support as an exchange (Shumaker & Brownell, 1984), and neglect the existence of nonreciprocal support (George, 1986; Rook, 1987). Some recognise only strong tie-based support or argue against social networks as support sources to include strangers as support providers (Lin, 1986a; Shumaker & Brownell, 1984; Thoits, 1995). Support comes from both strong and weak ties, and strangers (including those in cyberspace) exemplify extremely weak ties (Granovetter, [1974]1995;

Lin et al., 1978; Wellman, 1981; Wellman et al., 1996; Small, 2017). Finally, some list a few types of support and neglect other types (Berkman, 1984).

The other shortcoming some definitions share is the functionalist health protection assumption, based on which social support is defined by its protective health effect, especially its stress-buffering role (e.g., Caplan 1974; Cobb, 1976; Cohen & McKay, 1984; House et al., 1988; Kaplan et al., 1977; Lin & Ensel, 1989; Pearlin et al., 1981; Shumaker & Brownell, 1984; Thoits, 1995). Some scholars hold this assumption partly because social support emerged as a post hoc speculative explanation for the salubrious effects of relational factors found in human and animal studies in the 1970s, and partly because health scholars are primarily interested in disease prevention and health promotion. This assumption has four problems. First, it mixes social support with its consequences and falls into the trap of functionalist tautology, which makes operationalisation and measurement difficult and renders hypothesis testing impossible (Lin, 2001). Second, this assumption recognises social support only when people have needs to meet and ignores its presence in other situations. People not looking for jobs can receive job information (Granovetter, [1974]1995; Lin & Ao, 2008). Third, this assumption simplifies the complexity and variability of social support and weakens its theoretical breadth and depth. Social support is a neutral concept. It is not always supportive or effective and sometimes is null and even harmful (Barrera, 1986; Turner & Turner, 2013). Furthermore, this assumption reserves the theoretical utility of social support only for health consequences and ignores its non-health consequences. It serves as a major mechanism, but the exact term 'social support' is missing in some network-based theories (e.g., social capital, structural hole and weak ties) on social stratification and economic sociology (Burt, 1992; Coleman, 1990; Granovetter, [1974]1995).

A strict, neutral, network-based and tie- and type-unbounded definition is required to overcome these two shortcomings. Based on the review, we favour the concise definition of social support as *the aid or help from social networks*. This definition narrows down social support to one specific operationalisable aspect of relational content, leaves the door open for its involved ties and complex typology, separates it from its preceding network-based determinants and other aspects of relational contents, eliminates the functionalist health protection assumption, and releases its full potential theoretical value for examining health and non-health outcomes.

Social support has multifaceted forms and is typologisable on at least six dimensions. In terms of its contents, it is emotional (liking, love, empathy), instrumental (goods and services), informational (information about the environment), or appraisal (information relevant to self-evaluation) (House, 1981). In terms of role relationships, social support comes from kin versus non-kin or primary versus secondary group members (Dean & Lin, 1977; Kahn & Antonucci, 1980). In terms of tie strength, social support comes from strong (or close) versus weak ties (Granovetter, [1974]1995; Lin et al., 1978; Wellman, 1981). In terms of its contexts, social support is routine (within an ordinary situation) versus non-routine (within a crisis) (Lin, 1986c). In terms of its reality and virtuality, it is offline versus online (Drentea & Moren-Cross, 2005; Song & Chang, 2012; Wellman et al., 1996). In terms of its directions, it is receiving (flowing from network members or alters to individuals or egos), providing (flowing from ego to alters), or exchanging (flowing reciprocally between ego and alters) (House, 1981; Wellman, 1981). In terms of its subjectivity or objectivity, it is perceived versus objective (actual, received, or enacted) (Caplan, 1979; Barrera, 1986). Received support can be further typologised on two dimensions. In terms of its solicitation, it is solicited (sought and obtained) versus unsolicited (obtained without seeking) (Barrera, 1986; Eckenrode & Wethington, 1990). In terms of its visibility, it is visible or explicit versus invisible or unnoticed (Bolger et al., 2000; Thoits, 2011). A cross-tabulation following these typologies produces already 3,840 forms of support. In the rest of this chapter, we focus more on receiving support as providing and exchanging support is given less attention in the literature. We centre on support from diverse alters. The literature on family support and caregiving is reviewed elsewhere (Roth et al., 2015; Umberson & Thomeer, 2020).

DISTINCTION AND NETWORK CONTINGENCY OF SOCIAL SUPPORT

The distinction between social support and other related network-based concepts is blurred. Some put social networks and social integration under the rubric of social support or subsume social support together with social networks, social cohesion and social integration under the umbrella of social capital (Coleman, 1990; Elliott, 2000; Lin et al., 1999; Putnam, 2000; Roxburgh, 2006; Turner, 1999). Such entangled conceptualisations jeopardise the unique theoretical utility of these concepts and confound their causal relationships with each other.

The above rigorous definition of social support helps distinguish social support from other related network-based concepts (Lin, 2008; Song, 2011, 2019; Song & Lin, 2009; Song et al., 2010; Song et al., 2011). A social network is 'a specific set of linkages among a defined set of persons, with the additional property that the characteristics of these linkages as a whole may be used to interpret the social behavior of the persons involved' (Mitchell, 1969, p. 2). Social networks are not a theory but a perspective from which network-based theories and concepts are derived (Pescosolido, 2006a). Social cohesion is the degree of social bonds and social equality within social networks, indicated by trust, norms of reciprocity and the lack of social conflict (Kawachi & Berkman, 2000; Sampson et al., 1997). Social integration is the extent of participation in social networks, indicated by engagement in social roles and activities and cognitive identification with alters (Brissette et al., 2000; Moen et al., 1989; Song, 2013). Social capital is resources embedded in social networks, which can be operationalised as alters' resources or status (accessed status) (Lin, 2001). Among diverse theoretical approaches to social capital, we adopt Lin's strict network-based approach to distinguish social capital from other network-based concepts (Burt, 2019; Song & Chen, 2021).

Conceived from a social network perspective, social support is separated from its structural contexts including the other three network-based concepts (House et al., 1988; Lin et al., 1999; Song, 2011; Song & Lin, 2009). In the theoretical causal chain (see Figure 23.2), social cohesion is most upstream followed by social integration, social capital and social support. This chain can be theorised by extending a pair of competing theories or models: social resource versus social cost. Social resource theory emphasises the protective function of social resources (resources embedded in social networks) (Lin, 1983, 1986a, 2001; Song, 2011, 2019; Song & Lin, 2009). To extend this theory, we expect the linkages between these four network-based concepts to be positive. The more cohesive the network norm, the more active ego's network participation, the greater the pool of alters' resources ego accumulates and the greater the quality and quantity of social support alters are willing or able to provide. In contrast, social cost theory highlights the detrimental function of social costs (costs embedded in social networks) and predicts the linkages between these four network-based concepts to be negative (Song, 2015a, 2015b, 2020; Song, Frazier, & Pettis, 2018; Song & Pettis, 2020; Song et al., 2021). When the network norm of reciprocity becomes unbearably burdensome, ego's motivation in social integration decrease, and ego's accumulation of social capital and receipt of social support decline. Furthermore, from a longitudinal and life course perspective, network-based concepts are dynamic and their relationships with each other are dynamic and reciprocal over time (Dean & Lin, 1977; Fischer & Beresford, 2015; Perry & Pescosolido, 2012). The satisfying versus unsatisfying receipt and use of social support reinforce or undermine the degree of social integration, the availability of social capital and the strength of social cohesion.

The literature on the network contingency of social support provides more evidence for social resource theory than for social cost theory. Social integration in general generates social support. As for perceived support, social integration (network size, number of face-to-face contacts, number of proximal ties, having a confidant relationship and direct contacts with children, friends and relatives) is positively associated with perceived instrumental and emotional support in a community study of older adults (Seeman & Berkman, 1988). Restricted (versus diverse) social network groups are negatively associated with perceived support among older adults (Harasemiw et al., 2018). The number of friends is positively associated with four types of perceived support, whereas results on the number of relatives and acquaintances are inconsistent (Lubbers et al., 2019). Both face-to-face and mediated contact are positively associated with perceived support (Patulny & Seaman, 2017). The frequency of church attendance is positively associated with perceived support from church members (Nooney & Woodrum, 2002). Network size generates no more perceived friend support after exceeding thirteen friends among adolescents (Falci & McNeely, 2009). As for received support, people with bigger networks or higher degrees of social participation are more likely to receive unsolicited job information or seek health information from friends or relatives (Lin & Ao, 2008; Song & Chang, 2012). The frequency of church attendance is positively associated with received support from church members among African American adults (Taylor & Chatters, 1988). The frequency of religious attendance is positively associated with four out of thirteen types of received support and with the variety of received support indirectly via network size in a community of adults (Ellison & George, 1994). A community study

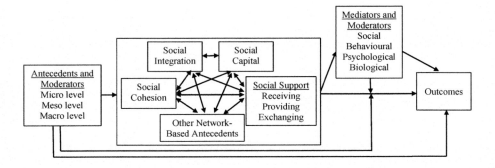

Figure 23.2 A conceptual model of the diverse roles of social support

measures perceived and received instrumental and expressive support and three indicators of social integration (participation in community organisations, the number of weekly contacts and having an intimate relationship) (Lin et al., 1999). The first indicator of social integration is directly positively associated with received instrumental support and indirectly positively associated with all four types of support via its second indicator and with perceived and received instrumental support via its third indicator. The three similar indicators of social integration are all positively associated with four types of support in Taiwan (Son et al., 2008). Network size is positively associated with exchanging emotional support in a community study (Plickert et al., 2007).

The association between social capital (as accessed status) and social support depends on the routine versus crisis situations. Accessed occupational status is positively associated with the receipt of unsolicited job leads or perceived support (Lin & Ao, 2008; Verhaeghe et al., 2012). Accessed educational status is positively associated with seeking health information from friends or relatives (Song & Chang, 2012). Knowing people at the highest organisational levels is positively associated with received influence-conferring support but not with received task or personal support among employees of a company (McGuire & Bielby, 2016). Having more educated alters is negatively associated with received informal recovery support in two communities after a hurricane (Beggs et al., 1996). Individuals with less education may possess disaster-relevant occupational skills.

The positive association between social cohesion and social support varies. Thinking of dense (closer ties between alters) versus sparse networks positively predicts perceived support in an experimental study (Lee et al., 2020). Dense networks are positively associated with perceived emotional (but not instrumental) support only among men in a community study (Haines & Hurlbert, 1992). Living in countries with more generalised trust is positively associated with perceived support from sources beyond family and friends, especially for the Roma, across twelve European countries (Sendroiu & Upenieks, 2020).

In addition, other network features (e.g., tie contents, role relationships, tie strength, homophily or heterophily, and physical access) also shape social support. In a community study, the average number of contents per tie decreases perceived instrumental support only for women, whereas the proportion of kin among alters increases perceived instrumental support only for men (Haines & Hurlbert, 1992). In another community study, parents and adult children offer more emotional aid, services and financial aid; siblings supplement the provision of services; extended kin is least supportive and less companionable (Wellman & Wortley, 1990). Also, stronger ties supply wider support and offer more emotional aid, small services and companionship; homophilous ties by employment status offer small services and financial aid; heterophilous ties by age provide small services; physically accessible ties tend to provide services. Same-faith ties are more likely to offer received support (Merino, 2014). Stronger ties are positively associated with three forms of received support among employees of a company (McGuire & Bielby, 2016). A community study reports positive associations between giving and receiving three forms of support (Plickert et al., 2007). Also, giving one type of support is associated with getting other types of support in turn. Being a neighbour, a parent, or an adult child is positively associated with exchanging support of major and minor services.

SOCIAL SUPPORT AND HEALTH

The double-edged health consequences of social support can be explained through the pair of competing theories: social resource versus social cost. Social resource theory dominates the social support and health literature. Based on the health protection assumption, it expects social support to protect health (Lin, 1983, 1986a, 2001). Possible psychosocial mechanisms include advancing status, enhancing healthy norms and lifestyles, decreasing stress exposure, reinforcing psychological resources and positive psychological reactions, improving access to health care, and boosting the immune system (Berkman et al., 2000; Lin, 1986b; Lin & Ao, 2008; Lin et al., 1979; House et al., 1988; Pearlin et al., 1981; Song, 2020; Song et al., 2021; Thoits, 2011; Uchino et al., 2012).

Social support also has detrimental consequences on which an integrative perspective is necessary but missing. The recently proposed social cost theory helps integrate our understanding of such consequences (Song et al., 2021). According to this theory, social support can damage health as detrimental social costs. Multiple psychosocial mechanisms are possible: the misfit between the attributes (e.g., amount, timing, source and content) of social support and recipients' needs and situations; recipients' negative perception of social support as unhelpful, unwanted and even destructive especially when social support is miscarried by providers (e.g., overprotection, interference and imposition); burdensome obligations for recipients to repay the help and upsetting over-reciprocating or over-benefitting exchanges; harmful upward or negative social comparison; reduced psychological resources and negative psychological feelings; stressful reactions and risky behaviours (Barrera, 1986; Bolger & Amarel, 2007; Coyne et al., 1988; Eckenrode & Wethington, 1990; Fisher et al., 1982; Rook, 1987; Shinn et al., 1984; Song, 2014; Song & Chen, 2014).

From a social causation perspective, social support plays four roles in the production of health: main/direct, indirect, mediating and moderating or interaction effects (see Figure 23.2; Dean & Lin, 1977; House et al., 1988; Lin, 1986b; Lin & Ensel, 1989; Pearlin et al., 1981). First, as social resource theory and social cost theory respectively predict, social support adds a unique explanatory power to the etiology of health and protects or harms health directly net of other determinants. Second, it prevents or causes disease indirectly through the aforementioned psychosocial mechanisms. A pair of competing hypotheses (stress prevention versus stress induction) expect social support to protect or damage health through deterring or inducing the occurrence of stressors (Dean & Lin, 1977; Lin, 1986b; Lin et al., 1979; Pearlin et al., 1981). Third, social support acts as an intermediate factor linking its precursors to health. As mentioned earlier, some upstream network-based factors influence health via social support. A pair of competing hypotheses (support mobilisation versus deterioration) expects stressors to trigger the mobilisation of or weaken the availability of social support (Dean & Lin, 1977; Lin et al., 1979; Eckenrode & Wethington, 1990). Finally, social support interacts with other determinants to mitigate or exacerbate their health effects. The most examined interaction-effect hypothesis is the stress-buffering hypothesis (Cassel, 1976; Cobb, 1976; Dean & Lin, 1977; Kaplan et al., 1977; Pearlin et al., 1981; Wheaton, 1985). Four matching propositions hypothesise the interaction between social support and the attributes of ties or recipients' purposes and needs. The tie-purpose matching proposition expects social support from strong and homophilous ties to improve expressive actions and that from weak and heterophilous ties to advance instrumental actions (Lin, 1983). The stressor-buffer matching proposition argues that different types of support buffer the effects of different types of stressors (Cohen & McKay, 1984; Cutrona, 1990). The source-type matching proposition states that significant others and experientially similar others provide different types of support to meet different needs (Thoits, 2011). The support-need matching proposition maintains that social support is protective when meeting recipients' needs but is less so or even harmful otherwise (Song & Chen, 2014).

From a social selection perspective, health influences the availability and activation of social support (Tausig, 1986; Pescosolido, 2006b; Thoits, 1995). There are two possibilities. On the one hand, poor health may provoke the recognition and mobilisation of social support because of higher needs for help. On the other hand, poor health may produce lower social support because of its constraint on social interaction.

The foregoing theories and hypotheses apply to receiving support. As for providing support, it protects health through fostering psychological resources, maintaining network ties and improving immune functioning (Crocker et al., 2017; Krause et al., 1999). It can also damage health via various forms of costly burdens (e.g., social, financial, psychological, emotional, physical, and time) (George, 1986; Song et al., 2021). As for exchanging support, it is protective when being reciprocal but less so or even harmful when being under-benefitting or over-benefitting (Rook, 1987).

Receiving support, especially perceived support, has been given most research attention and its diverse protective roles are well documented. Perceived support protects health independently. Perceived support from family, friends and spouse protects against risks of inflammation (Yang et al., 2014). Perceived support from family and friends is consistently associated with self-rated health across 139 countries (Kumar et al., 2012). The positive effect of parent and friend support decay on depression is stronger than the negative effect of parent and friend support growth among adolescents (Cornwell, 2003). Perceived care from parents and friends reduces depression among adolescents (Carter et al., 2015). Perceived friend support increases the receipt of both flu vaccinations and cancer screenings among husbands, and wives' perceived friend support increases husbands' receipt of prostate cancer screening (Han et al., 2019). Perceived emotional and instrumental support is negatively associated with four forms of psychological distress (Ross & Van Willigen, 1997). Perceived emotional support has a direct protective effect on three health outcomes (Ferraro & Koch, 1994). Among community studies, two out of four types of perceived support enhance cognitive functioning among older adults, and perceived emotional support does so for women only (Pillemer & Holtzer, 2016). Perceived emotional support has a direct protective effect on three health outcomes (Ferraro & Koch, 1994). Perceived instrumental support from family, friends and the partner protects against postpartum depression (Reid & Taylor, 2015). Perceived support from family or friends lowers the mortality risk of men but not women among older Mexican Americans (Hill et al., 2016).

Perceived support also plays an indirect or moderating role. It indirectly reduces depression via decreasing economic strain and increasing mastery (Pearlin et al., 1981). It and support satisfaction buffer the stressor–depression relationship (Landerman et al., 1989). Perceived support from the spouse and friends buffers the depression effects of different stressors (Jackson, 1992).

Perceived support protects health both directly and indirectly. It reduces psychological distress directly for men and indirectly for women via mastery (Gadalla, 2009). Perceived emotional support from family and friends is negatively associated with the risk of undiagnosed and uncontrolled hypertension, respectively, partly via health care utilisation among older adults (Cornwell & Waite, 2012). In a community study, mothers' perceived instrumental support is positively associated with children's overall health partly via mothers' economic security and well-being (Turney, 2013). In another community study, current support (the number of close friends, the number of close relatives and received socioemotional and instrumental assistance) has a negative effect on current depression and an indirect effect on subsequent depression via current depression (Aneshensel & Frerichs, 1982).

Perceived support plays both main and mediating roles. It explains away the effect of religious participation on depression among adolescents (Petts & Jolliff, 2008). It partially positively mediates the effect of accessed status on self-rated health (Verhaeghe et al., 2012). Parents' perceived support is negatively related to the risks of two out of seven health problems and partly explains third- and-higher-generation racial/ethnic disparities in health among children (Hamilton et al., 2011). Perceived support from family and friends partly mediates the association between fertility trajectories and depression (Grundy et al., 2020). The mediating effect of perceived support on the relationships between social network structures and depression varies by types of support and marital status among older adults (Harasemiw et al., 2019). Perceived care from peers, parents and teachers is all negatively associated with depression and mediates the effect of same-sex attraction and the same pattern applies to perceived care from parents and teachers in the prediction of suicidal tendencies among adolescents (Teasdale & Bradley-Engen, 2010). Perceived friend support is negatively associated with depression and mediates the ill effects of small but not large networks among adolescents (Falci & McNeely, 2009). Among community studies, neighbourhood disadvantage decreases depression through enhanced perceived support (Kim et al., 2010). Adverse childhood experiences are positively associated with adult mental health impairment partly via lower adult perceived support (Jones et al., 2018). Perceived support from partners, relatives, friends and co-workers has main negative effects on depressive symptoms and major depressive disorder and mediates some effects of gender, age, marital status and socioeconomic status (SES) (Turner & Lloyd, 1999; Turner & Marino, 1994). Extraversion protects against depression only for persons who have forewarning of the spousal death with perceived emotional support from friends and relatives as a mediator among older adults (Pai & Carr, 2010).

Perceived support plays both main and moderating roles. It decreases depression and buffers the effect of community SARS exposure among older adults (Wang et al., 2021). Perceived support from family and friends protects mental health and buffers the effect of unemployment (Milner et al., 2016). In comparison to moderate support, high support is most protective of mental health among long-term immigrants, and low support is most detrimental for recent immigrants (Puyat, 2013). Among community studies, perceived co-worker support has a negative effect on depression and is a stress buffer only for men, whereas perceived partner support exerts a negative effect on depression for both gender groups (Roxburgh, 2006). Companionship exerts a negative effect on distress and serves as a stress buffer (Haines & Hurlbert, 1992). Perceived emotional support reduces depressive symptoms and protects physical health, but only for residents of higher-SES neighbourhoods (Elliott, 2000). Perceived emotional support from family, friends and the spouse or partner has a stronger positive association with physical health and self-reported health in Tokyo (a support-approving cultural context) than in the United States, especially for those facing more stressors and having low neuroticism (Park et al., 2013). Perceived instrumental and partner support reduces maternal depression and is a stress buffer (Manuel et al., 2012).

Perceived support plays three protective roles simultaneously as reported in three community studies. It has a negative effect on depression, mediates some positive effects of marriage and education, and interacts in a complementary manner with the level of control (Ross & Mirowsky, 1989). Social support (community support, network support, confidant support and instrumental-expressive support) decreases depression directly and indirectly via suppressing current stressors and mediates the effect of prior stressors (Lin, 1986b). It exerts a negative effect on psychological distress, mediates the effect of personality only for the black community and has an indirect negative effect via personal control only for the white community (Lincoln et al., 2003).

A few studies examine the protective impacts of both perceived and received support. When married adults experience stressors, perceived support has a negative effect on psychological distress and received spouse support does so indirectly via perceived support (Wethington & Kessler, 1986). In a longitudinal online study, received offline (rather than perceived online) support is positively associated with life satisfaction (Trepte et al., 2015). Perceived emotional support and received instrumental support exert negative effects on depression, perceived emotional support mediates the effect of bonding relationships, and received instrumental support mediates the effects of belonging, bonding and binding relationships in a community study (Lin et al., 1999).

Receiving support also plays diverse detrimental roles. Perceived support from family and friends increases two out of six inflammatory markers in the United States but not in Taiwan (Glei et al., 2012). Perceived emotional support from friends increases the hazard of death (Yang et al., 2020). Received support is negatively associated with depression, and God-as-a-problem-solver buffers and exacerbates the stressor–depression relationship respectively among those receiving low and high support (Rainville & Krause, 2020). Receipt of prayer is positively associated with depression for those with a low religious salience (Upenieks, 2020).

The double-edged function of receiving support can co-exist. The association between receipt of unsolicited job leads and depression is more positive for those in better-off financial situations but less so or even negative for those facing more economic strains in the United States and this positive association is indirect through financial dissatisfaction in urban China (Song, 2014; Song & Chen, 2014). In contrast to the protective effects of support from parents and teachers, higher peer support increases depression among adolescents (Meadows, 2007). Perceived instrumental and emotional support and received emotional support from the spouse has negative effects on depression, whereas received emotional support has a positive effect (Son et al., 2008).

A few studies focus on older adults. Perceived support from family is negatively associated with cognitive functioning, partially mediates the effects of neighbourhood attributes and protects cognitive functioning for women but not for men (Lee & Waite, 2018). Perceived support (attachment, reassurance of worth and social integration) has a positive association with mental health, whereas perceived support as reliable alliance does the opposite; perceived support as reassurance of worth has a positive association with physical health, whereas perceived support as attachment does the opposite (Stephens et al., 2011). Increases in received emotional support enhance cognitive performance partly via reduced loneliness, especially for much older adults, whereas increases in received instrumental support lead to worse cognitive functioning (Ellwardt et al., 2013). Perceived care support increases survival rates, whereas received financial and medical support does the opposite (Feng et al., 2015).

In comparison to receiving support, providing support and its double-edged health effects receive less attention. Providing emotional support is positively associated with self-reported health for both men and women, and also mediates the positive health effect of religious practice, but only for men, among the elderly (Krause et al., 1999). Providing tangible, informational and emotional support is positively associated with depression indirectly through negative interaction (Liang et al., 2001). Providing financial and instrumental support is associated with worse health in central and southern Europe but not in northern Europe (Craveiro, 2017).

Finally, exchanging support affects health. Under-benefitting and over-benefitting are negatively and positively associated with depression, respectively (Liang et al., 2001). Reciprocal (versus under- and over-benefitting) instrumental (rather than emotional) support protects against risks of all-cause mortality (Chen et al., 2021). Receiving emotional support is positively related to depressive and somatic symptoms in over-benefitting exchanges but negatively in reciprocal exchanges (Nahum-Shani et al., 2011). A shift from reciprocal support to over-benefitting is positively associated with depression among women but negatively among men (Väänänen et al., 2008).

CONCLUSION

Scholars have made significant advances in exploring the substance and dimensions of social support, developing its diverse measurement instruments and examining its diverse roles for health inequalities. Future research is still needed to achieve a more coherent and comprehensive understanding of social support.

Social support is a distinctive, neutral, network-based concept. It has diverse definitions, some of which lack precision, confound it with other network-based concepts, or limit its application to health outcomes. Rather than going as far as

Barrera (1986) who proposes the abandonment of the general concept of social support, we suggest a rigorous strategy to define social support by its precise neutral nature (aid from social networks). This definition separates social support from its structural (especially network-based) preconditions and functional consequences, recognises its values in bridging health and non-health research fields and helps reduce the inconsistency in its measurements and empirical results (Song, 2019). This definition also helps enhance the application of social network analysis to social support research. Social integration receives much more attention as a precursor of social support. Future studies should measure more diverse network-based concepts jointly and examine their relationships with each other in a causal sequence. One urgent task is to examine how divergent types of social support interplay with network-based antecedents. The caveat is that social support should be captured more accurately through aid-related rather than general network instruments.

Social support is an empirical concept. Its double-edged function in the production of health inequalities receives imbalanced attention and requires the combination of two theoretical concepts: social resource and social cost. Social resource theory has been well examined and widely confirmed. A huge body of literature demonstrates the protective function of social support. In contrast, its detrimental function is examined and demonstrated in fewer studies. Social cost theory can help synthesise and integrate its adverse consequences. The two theories will form a balanced and comprehensive framework and stimulate future research to examine simultaneously the double-edged consequences of social support. 'When one looks only for supportive ties, one finds only supportive ties' (Wellman, 1981, p. 179). Similarly, when one looks only for protective support, one likely finds only protective support.

Social support is a multidimensional concept. There is a bigger literature on receiving support than on providing or exchanging support. Within this literature, there are more studies on perceived than received support, on emotional and instrumental than other contents of support and on support from family and friends than that from other alters. Different kinds of support come from disparate network-based preconditions. Perceived and emotional support has more consistent explanatory power in the prediction of health, especially mental health. Unsolicited support and over-benefitting exchanges are promising directions for us to disentangle the mixed health consequences of received support. Considering the inconsistent results, various types and measures of support from diverse types of alters need to be simultaneously subjected to empirical examination to distinguish their different network-based antecedents and compare their health effects.

Social support is more than a stress buffer and plays diverse roles for health inequalities from the social causation perspective: main/direct, indirect, mediating and moderating. Its main and moderating roles receive more attention than its mediating and indirect roles. There is more confirming evidence on its main role. It interacts with not only diverse forms of stressors but also various psychosocial factors (e.g., age, gender, immigration status, SES, religious belief, subjective well-being, neighbourhood and societal contexts, personality and psychological resources). It mediates the effects of many psychosocial factors (e.g., age, gender, sexuality, race/ethnicity, marital status, upstream or precedent network attributes, stressors, well-being, personality and psychological resources). It affects health indirectly via diverse pathways (e.g., neighbourhood attributes, social interaction, social support at later times, stressors, subjective well-being, psychological resources and health care utilisation). Future studies should explore these roles simultaneously. The aforementioned matching hypotheses need systematic examination. More cross-society comparative research is also needed to clearly map the institutional contingency of the social support–health relationship.

Finally, social support is dynamic over time. The majority of empirical studies are cross-sectional. Their results are subject to questions in terms of robustness and causality. How social support and its changes may be in reciprocal causal relationships with the changes of other network-based terms remains underexplored. The social selection perspective or how health influences social support also receives limited attention. Refined longitudinal national research designs are needed to disentangle the complicated causality puzzles.

REFERENCES

Aneshensel, C.S., & Frerichs, R.R. (1982). Stress, support, and depression: a longitudinal causal model. *Journal of Community Psychology*, 10, 363–376.

Barrera, M. Jr (1986). Distinctions between social support concepts, measures, and models. *American Journal of Community Psychology*, 14, 413–445.

Beehr, T.A., Bowling, N.A., & Bennett, M.M. (2010). Occupational stress and failures of social support: when helping hurts. *Journal of Occupational Health Psychology*, 15(1), 45–59.

Beggs, J.J., Haines, V.A., & Hurlbert, J.S. (1996). Situational contingencies surrounding the receipt of informal support. *Social Forces, 75,* 201–222.

Berkman, L. F. (1984) Assessing the physical health effects of social networks and social support. *Annual Review of Public Health,* 5(1), 413–32.

Berkman, L.F., Glass, T., Brissette, I., & Seeman, T.E. (2000). From social integration to health: Durkheim in the new millennium. *Social Science and Medicine, 51,* 843–857.

Bolger, N., & Amarel, D. (2007). Effects of social support visibility on adjustment to stress: experimental evidence. *Journal of Personality and Social Psychology, 92*(3), 458–475.

Bolger, N., Zuckerman, A., & Kessler, R.C. (2000). Invisible support and adjustment to stress. *Journal of Personality and Social Psychology, 79*(6), 953.

Brissette, I., Cohen, S., & Seeman, T.E. (2000). Measuring social integration and social networks. In S. Cohen, L.G. Underwood & B.H. Gottlieb (Eds.), *Social support measurement and intervention* (pp. 53–85). Oxford University Press.

Burt, R.S. (1992). *Structural holes: the social structure of competition.* Harvard University Press.

Burt, R.S. (2019). Nan Lin and social capital. In R.S. Burt, Y. Bian, L. Song & N. Lin (Eds.), *Social capital, social support and stratification: an analysis of the sociology of Nan Lin* (pp. 4–36). Edward Elgar.

Caplan, G. (1974). *Support systems and community mental health.* Behavioral.

Caplan, R.D. (1979). Social support, person-environment fit, and coping. In L.A. Ferman & J.P. Gordus (Eds.), *Mental health and the economy* (pp. 89–138). W.E. Upjohn Institute for Employment Research.

Carter, J.S., Dellucci, T., Turek, C., & Mir, S. (2015). Predicting depressive symptoms and weight from adolescence to adulthood: stressors and the role of protective factors. *Journal of Youth and Adolescence, 44*(11), 2122–2140.

Cassel, J. (1976). The contribution of the social environment to host resistance. *American Journal of Epidemiology, 104,* 107–123.

Chen, E., Lam, P.H., Finegood, E.D., Turiano, N.A., Mroczek, D.K., & Miller, G.E. (2021). The balance of giving versus receiving social support and all-cause mortality in a US national sample. *Proceedings of the National Academy of Sciences, 118*(24).

Cobb, S. (1976). Social support as a moderator of life stress. *Psychosomatic Medicine, 38,* 300–314.

Cohen, S., & McKay, G. (1984). Social support, stress and the buffering hypothesis: a theoretical analysis. In A. Baum, S.E. Taylor & J.E. Singer (Eds.), *Handbook of psychology and health* (pp. 253–267). Lawrence Erlbaum.

Coleman, J.S. (1990) *Foundations of social theory.* Belknap Press of Harvard University Press.

Comte, A. ([1852]1875). *System of positive polity.* Longmans.

Cornwell, B. (2003). The dynamic properties of social support: decay, growth, and staticity and their effects on adolescent depression. *Social Forces, 81*(3), 955–982.

Cornwell, E.Y., & Waite, L.J. (2012). Social network resources and management of hypertension. *Journal of Health and Social Behavior, 53*(2), 215–231.

Coyne, J.C., Wortman, C.B., & Lehman, D.R. (1988). The other side of support: emotional overinvolvement and miscarried helping. In B.H. Gottlieb (Ed.), *Marshaling social support: formats, processes, and effects* (pp. 305–330). Sage.

Craveiro, D. (2017). The role of personal social networks on health inequalities across European regions. *Health and Place, 45,* 24–31.

Crocker, J., Canevello, A., & Brown, A.A. (2017). Social motivation: costs and benefits of selfishness and otherishness. *Annual Review of Psychology, 68*(1), 299–325.

Cutrona, C.E. (1990). Stress and social support: in search of optimal matching. *Journal of Social and Clinical Psychology, 9*(1), 3–14.

Dean, A., & Lin, N. (1977). The stress-buffering role of social support: problems and prospects for systematic investigation. *Journal of Nervous and Mental Disease, 165,* 403–417.

Drentea, P., & Moren-Cross, J.L. (2005). Social capital and social support on the web: the case of an internet mother site. *Sociology of Health and Illness, 27*(7), 920–943.

Eckenrode, J., & Wethington, E. (1990). The process and outcome of mobilizing social support. In S. Duck & R.C. Silver (Eds.), *Personal relationships and social support* (pp. 83–103). Sage.

Elliott, M. (2000). The stress process in neighborhood context. *Health and Place, 6,* 287–299.

Ellison, C.G., & George, L.K. (1994). Religious involvement, social ties, and social support in a Southeastern community. *Journal for the Scientific Study of Religion, 33,* 46–61.

Ellwardt, L., Marja, A., Dorly D., & Nardi, S. (2013). Does loneliness mediate the relation between social support and cognitive functioning in later life? *Social Science and Medicine, 98,* 116.

Falci, C., & McNeely, C. (2009). Too many friends: social integration, network cohesion and adolescent depressive symptoms. *Social Forces, 87*(4), 2031–2061.

Feng, Z., Jones, K., & Wang, W.W. (2015). An exploratory discrete-time multilevel analysis of the effect of social support on the survival of elderly people in China. *Social Science and Medicine, 130,* 181.

Ferraro, K.F., & Koch, J.R. (1994). Religion and health among black and white adults: examining social support and consolation. *Journal for the Scientific Study of Religion, 33,* 362–375.

Fischer, C.S., & Beresford, L. (2015). Changes in support networks in late middle age: the extension of gender and educational differences. *Journals of Gerontology Series B: Psychological Sciences and Social Sciences*, 70(1), 123–131.

Fisher, J.D., Nadler, A., & Whitcher-Alagna, S. (1982). Recipient reactions to aid. *Psychological Bulletin*, 91(1), 27–54.

Gadalla, T.M. (2009). Determinants, correlates and mediators of psychological distress: a longitudinal study. *Social Science and Medicine*, 68(12), 2199–2205.

George, L.K. (1986). Caregiver burden: conflict between norms of reciprocity and solidarity. In K.A. Pillemer & R.S. Wolf (Eds.), *Elder abuse: conflict in the family* (pp. 67–92). Auburn House.

Glei, D.A., Goldman, N., Ryff, C.D., Lin, Y.-H., & Weinstein, M. (2012). Social relationships and inflammatory markers: an analysis of Taiwan and the US. *Social Science and Medicine*, 74(12), 1891–1899.

Granovetter, M. ([1974]1995). *Getting a job: a study of contacts and careers*. Harvard University Press.

Grundy, E.M.D., Read, S., & Väisänen, H. (2020). Fertility trajectories and later-life depression among parents in England. *Population Studies*, 74(2), 219–240.

Haines, V.A., & Hurlbert, J.S. (1992). Network range and health. *Journal of Health and Social Behavior*, 33, 254–266.

Hamilton, E., Cardoso, J.B., Hummer, R.A., & Padilla, Y.C. (2011). Assimilation and emerging health disparities among new generations of US children. *Demographic Research*, 25, 783–818.

Han, S.H., Kim, K., & Burr, J.A. (2019). Social support and preventive healthcare behaviors among couples in later life. *The Gerontologist*, 59(6), 1162.

Harasemiw, O., Newall, N., Mackenzie, C.S., Shooshtari, S., & Menec, V. (2018). From social integration to social isolation: the relationship between social network types and perceived availability of social support in a national sample of older Canadians. *Research on Aging*, 40(8), 715–739.

Harasemiw, O., Newall, N., Mackenzie, C.S., Shooshtari, S., & Menec, V. (2019). Is the association between social network types, depressive symptoms and life satisfaction mediated by the perceived availability of social support? A cross-sectional analysis using the Canadian longitudinal study on aging. *Aging and Mental Health*, 23(10), 1413–1422.

Hill, T.D., Uchino, B.N., Eckhardt, J.L., & Angel, J.L. (2016). Perceived social support trajectories and the all-cause mortality risk of older Mexican American women and men. *Research on Aging*, 38(3), 374.

House, J.S. (1981) *Work stress and social support*. Addison-Wesley.

House, J.S., Umberson, D., & Landis, K.R. (1988). Structures and processes of social support. *Annual Review of Sociology*, 14, 293–318.

Jackson, P.B. (1992). Specifying the buffering hypothesis: support, strain, and depression. *Social Psychology Quarterly*, 55, 363–378.

Jones, T.M., Nurius, P., Song, C., & Fleming, C.M. (2018). Modeling life course pathways from adverse childhood experiences to adult mental health. *Child Abuse and Neglect*, 80, 32.

Kahn, R.L., & Antonucci, T.C. (1980). Convoys over the life course: attachment roles and social support. In P.B. Baltes & O.G. Brim (Eds.), *Life-span development and behavior*, Vol. 3 (pp. 253–286). Academic Press.

Kaplan, B.H., Cassel, J.C., & Gore, S. (1977). Social support and health. *Medical Care*, 15, 47–58.

Kawachi, I., & Berkman, L. (2000). Social cohesion, social capital and health. In L.F. Berkman & I. Kawachi (Eds.), *Social epidemiology* (pp. 174–190). Oxford University Press.

Kim, J. (2010). Neighborhood disadvantage and mental health: the role of neighborhood disorder and social relationships. *Social Science Research*, 39(2), 260.

Krause, N., Ingersoll-Dayton, B., Liang, J., & Sugisawa, H. (1999). Religion, social support, and health among the Japanese elderly. *Journal of Health and Social Behavior*, 40, 405–421.

Kumar, S., Calvo, R., Avendano, M., Sivaramakrishnan, K., & Berkman, L.F. (2012). Social support, volunteering and health around the world: cross-national evidence from 139 countries. *Social Science and Medicine*, 74(5), 696.

Landerman, R., George, L.K., Campbell, R.T., & Blazer, D.G. (1989). Alternative models of the stress buffering hypothesis. *American Journal of Community Psychology*, 17, 625–41.

Lee, D.S., Stahl, J.L., & Bayer, J.B. (2020). Social resources as cognitive structures: thinking about a dense support network increases perceived support. *Social Psychology Quarterly*, 83(4), 405–422.

Lee, H., & Waite, L.J. (2018). Cognition in context: the role of objective and subjective measures of neighborhood and household in cognitive functioning in later life. *The Gerontologist*, 58(1), 159.

Liang, J., Krause, N.M., & Bennett, J.M. (2001). Social exchange and well-being: is giving better than receiving? *Psychology and Aging*, 16(3), 511–523.

Lin, N. (1983). Social resources and social actions: a progress report. *Connections*, 6(2), 10–16.

Lin, N. (1986a). Conceptualizing social support. In N. Lin, A. Dean & W. Ensel (Eds.), *Social support, life events and depression* (pp. 17–30). Academic Press.

Lin, N. (1986b). Modeling the effects of social support. In N. Lin, A. Dean & W. Ensel (Eds.), *Social support, life events and depression* (pp. 173–209). Academic Press.

Lin, N. (1986c). Epilogue: in retrospect and prospect. In N. Lin, A. Dean & W. Ensel (Eds.), *Social support, life events and depression* (pp. 333–342). Academic Press.

Lin, N. (2001) *Social capital: a theory of social structure and action*. Cambridge University Press.

Lin, N., & Ao, D. (2008). The invisible hand of social capital: an exploratory study. In N. Lin & B. Erickson (Eds.), *Social capital: advances in research* (pp. 107–132). Oxford University Press.

Lin, N., Dayton, P., & Greenwald, P. (1978). Analyzing the instrumental use of relations in the context of social structure. *Sociological Methods and Research*, 7(2),149–166.

Lin, N., & Ensel, W.M. (1989). Life stress and health: stressors and resources. *American Sociological Review*, 54, 382–399.

Lin, N., Ensel, W.M., Simeone, R.S., & Kuo, W. (1979). Social support, stressful life events, and illness: a model and an empirical test. *Journal of Health and Social Behavior*, 20, 108–119.

Lin, N., Ye, X., & Ensel, W.M. (1999). Social support and depressed mood: a structural analysis. *Journal of Health and Social Behavior*, 40, 344–359.

Lincoln, K.D., Chatters, L.M., & Taylor, R.J. (2003). Psychological distress among black and white Americans: differential effects of social support, negative interaction and personal control. *Journal of Health and Social Behavior*, 44, 390–407.

Link, B.G., & Phelan, J.C. (1995). Social conditions as fundamental causes of disease. *Journal of Health and Social Behavior*, Extra Issue, 80–94.

Lubbers, M.J., Molina, J.L., & Valenzuela-García, H. (2019). When networks speak volumes: variation in the size of broader acquaintanceship networks. *Social Networks*, 56, 55.

Manuel, J.I., Martinson, M.L., Bledsoe-Mansori, S.E., & Bellamy, J.L. (2012). The influence of stress and social support on depressive symptoms in mothers with young children. *Social Science and Medicine*, 75(11), 2013–2020.

McGuire, G.M., & Bielby, W.T. (2016). The variable effects of tie strength and social resources: how type of support matters. *Work and Occupations*, 43(1), 38.

Meadows, S.O. (2007). Evidence of parallel pathways: gender similarity in the impact of social support on adolescent depression and delinquency. *Social Forces*, 85(3), 1143–1167.

Merino, S.M. (2014). Social support and the religious dimensions of close ties. *Journal for the Scientific Study of Religion*, 53(3), 595.

Milner, A., Krnjacki, L., Butterworth, P., & LaMontagne, A.D. (2016). The role of social support in protecting mental health when employed and unemployed: a longitudinal fixed-effects analysis using 12 annual waves of the HILDA cohort. *Social Science and Medicine*, 153, 20.

Mitchell, J.C. (1969). The concept and use of social networks. In J.C. Mitchell (Ed.), *Social networks in urban situations* (pp. 1–50). Manchester University Press.

Moen, P., Dempster-McClain, D., & Williams, R.M. (1989). Social integration and longevity: an event history analysis of women's roles and resilience. *American Sociological Review*, 54(4), 635–647.

Nahum-Shani, I., Bamberger, P.A., & Bacharach, S.B. (2011). Social support and employee well-being: the conditioning effect of perceived patterns of supportive exchange. *Journal of Health and Social Behavior*, 52(1), 123–139.

Nooney, J., & Woodrum, E. (2002). Religious coping and church-based social support as predictors of mental health outcomes: testing a conceptual model. *Journal for the Scientific Study of Religion*, 41, 359–368.

Pai, M., & Carr. D. (2010). Do personality traits moderate the effect of late-life spousal loss on psychological distress? Social relationships and health. *Journal of Health and Social Behavior*, 51(2), 183–199.

Park, J., Kitayama, S., Karasawa, M., Curhan, K., Markus, H.R., Kawakami, N., Miyamoto, Y., Love, G.D., Coe, C.L., & Ryff, C.D. (2013). Clarifying the links between social support and health: culture, stress, and neuroticism matter. *Journal of Health Psychology*, 18(2), 226–235.

Patulny, R., & Seaman, C. (2017). 'I'll just text you': is face-to-face social contact declining in a mediated world? *Journal of Sociology*, 53(2), 285–302.

Pearlin, L.I., Menaghan, E.G., Lieberman, M.A., & Mullan, J.T. (1981). The stress process. *Journal of Health and Social Behavior*, 22, 337–356.

Perry, B.L., & Pescosolido, B.A. (2012). Social network dynamics and biographical disruption: the case of 'first-timers' with mental illness. *American Journal of Sociology*, 118(1), 134–175.

Pescosolido, B.A. (2006a). Sociology of social networks. In C.D. Bryant & D.L. Peck (Eds.), *21st century sociology: a reference book* (pp. 208–217). Sage.

Pescosolido, B.A. (2006b). Of pride and prejudice: the role of sociology and social networks in integrating the health sciences. *Journal of Health and Social Behavior*, 47(3), 189–208.

Petts, R.J., & Jolliff, A. (2008). Religion and adolescent depression: the impact of race and gender. *Review of Religious Research*, 49(4), 395–414.

Pillemer, S.C., & Holtzer, R. (2016). The differential relationships of dimensions of perceived social support with cognitive function among older adults. *Aging and Mental Health*, 20(7), 727–735.

Plickert, G., Côté, R.R., & Wellman, B. (2007). It's not who you know, it's how you know them: who exchanges what with whom? *Social Networks*, 29, 405–429.

Putnam, R.D. (2000). *Bowling alone: the collapse and revival of American community*. Simon & Schuster.

Puyat, J.H. (2013). Is the influence of social support on mental health the same for immigrants and non-immigrants? *Journal of Immigrant and Minority Health*, 15(3), 598–605.

Rainville, G.C., & Krause, N. (2020). Attributing problem-solving to God, receiving social support, and stress-moderation. *Journal for the Scientific Study of Religion*, 59(3), 476–483.

Reid, K.M., & Taylor, M.G. (2015). Social support, stress, and maternal postpartum depression: a comparison of supportive relationships. *Social Science Research*, 54, 246.

Rook, K.S. (1987). Reciprocity of social exchange and social satisfaction among older women. *Journal of Personality and Social Psychology*, 52(1), 145–154.

Ross, C.E., & Mirowsky, J. (1989). Explaining the social patterns of depression: control and problem solving – or support and talking? *Journal of Health and Social Behavior*, 30, 206–219.

Ross, C.E., & Van Willigen, M. (1997). Education and the subjective quality of life. *Journal of Health and Social Behavior*, 38, 275–297.

Roth, D., Fredman, L., & Haley, W.E. (2015). Informal caregiving and its impact on health: a reappraisal from population-based studies. *The Gerontologist*, 55(2), 309–319.

Roxburgh, S. (2006). 'I wish we had more time to spend together …': the distribution and predictors of perceived family time pressures among married men and women in the paid labor force. *Journal of Family Issues*, 27, 529–553.

Sampson, R.J., Raudenbush, S.W., & Earls, F. (1997). Neighborhoods and violent crime: a multilevel study of collective efficacy. *Science*, 277(5328), 918–924.

Seeman, T.E., & Berkman, L.F. (1988). Structural characteristics of social networks and their relationship with social support in the elderly: who provides support? *Social Science and Medicine*, 26, 737–749.

Sendroiu, I., & Upenieks, L. (2020). The contextual effect of trust on perceived support: evidence from Roma and non-Roma in East-Central Europe. *British Journal of Sociology*, 71(4), 702–721.

Shinn, M., Lehmann, S., & Wong, N.W. (1984). Social interaction and social support. *Journal of Social Issues*, 40(4), 55–76.

Shumaker, S.A., & Brownell A. (1984). Toward a theory of social support: closing conceptual gaps. *Journal of Social Issues*, 40(4), 11–36.

Small, M.L. (2017). *Someone to talk to*. Oxford University Press.

Son, J., Lin, N., & George, L.K. (2008). Cross-national comparison of social support structures between Taiwan and the United States. *Journal of Health and Social Behavior*, 49, 104–118.

Song, L. (2011). Social capital and psychological distress. *Journal of Health and Social Behavior*, 52(4), 478–492.

Song, L. (2013). Institutional embeddedness of network embeddedness in the workplace: Social integration at work and employee's health across three societies. *Research in the Sociology of Work*, 24 (Networks, Employment and Inequality), 323–356.

Song, L. (2014). Is unsolicited support protective or destructive in collectivistic culture? Receipt of unsolicited job leads in urban China. *Society and Mental Health*, 4(3), 235–254.

Song, L. (2015a). Does knowing people in the positional hierarchy protect or hurt? Social capital, comparative reference group, and depression in two societies. *Social Science & Medicine*, 136-137, 117–127.

Song, L. (2015b). Does knowing people in authority protect or hurt? Authoritative contacts and depression in urban China. *American Behavioral Scientist*, 59(9), 1173–1188.

Song, L. (2019). Nan Lin and social support. In R.S. Burt, Y. Bian, L. Song & N. Lin (Eds.), *Social capital, social support and stratification: an analysis of the sociology of Nan Lin* (pp. 78–106). Edward Elgar.

Song, L. (2020). Social capital, social cost, and relational culture in three societies. *Social Psychology Quarterly*, 83(4), 443–462.

Song, L., & Chang, T.-Y. (2012). Do resources of network members help in help seeking? Social capital and health information search. *Social Networks*, 34(4), 658–669.

Song, L., & Chen, W. (2014). Does receiving unsolicited support help or hurt? Receipt of unsolicited job leads and depression. *Journal of Health and Social Behavior*, 55(2), 144–160.

Song, L., & Chen, Y. (2021). Social capital and health. In W.C. Cockerham (Ed.), *The Wiley Blackwell companion to medical sociology* (pp. 192–214). Blackwell.

Song, L., Frazier, C., & Pettis, P.J. (2018). Do network members' resources generate health inequality? Social capital theory and beyond. In S. Folland and E. Nauerberg (Eds.), *Elgar Companion to Social Capital and Health* (pp. 233–253). Edward Elgar.

Song, L., & Lin, N. (2009). Social capital and health inequality: evidence from Taiwan. *Journal of Health and Social Behavior*, 50(2), 149–163.

Song, L., & Pettis, P.J. (2020). Does whom you know in the status hierarchy prevent or trigger health limitation? Institutional embeddedness of social capital and social cost theories in three societies. *Social Science and Medicine*, 257, 111959.

Song, L., Pettis, P.J., Chen, Y., & Goodson-Miller, M. (2021). Social cost and health: the downside of social relationships and social networks. *Journal of Health and Social Behavior*, 62(3), 371–387.

Song, L., Son, J., & Lin, N. (2010). Social capital and health. In W.C. Cockerham (Ed.), *The Wiley Blackwell companion to medical sociology* (pp. 184–210). Blackwell.

Song, L., Son, J., & Lin, N. (2011). Social support. In J. Scott & P.J. Carrington (Eds.), *The Sage handbook of social network analysis* (pp. 116–128). Sage.

Stephens, C., Alpass, F., Towers, A., & Stevenson, B. (2011). The effects of types of social networks, perceived social support, and loneliness on the health of older people: accounting for the social context. *Journal of Aging and Health*, *23*(6), 887–911.

Tausig, M. (1986). Prior history of illness in the basic model. In N. Lin, A. Dean & W. Ensel (Eds.), *Social support, life events and depression* (pp. 267–280). Academic Press.

Taylor, R., & Chatters, L. (1988). Church members as a source of informal social support. *Review of Religious Research*, *30*, 193–203.

Teasdale, B., & Bradley-Engen, M.S. (2010). Adolescent same-sex attraction and mental health: the role of stress and support. *Journal of Homosexuality*, *57*(2), 287–309.

Thoits, P.A. (1995). Stress, coping, and social support processes: where are we? What next? *Journal of Health and Social Behavior*, Extra issue, 53–79.

Thoits, P.A. (2011). Mechanisms linking social ties and support to physical and mental health. *Journal of Health and Social Behavior*, *52*, 145–161.

Trepte, S., Dienlin, T., & Reinecke, L. (2015). Influence of social support received in online and offline contexts on satisfaction with social support and satisfaction with life: a longitudinal study. *Media Psychology*, *18*(1), 74–105.

Turner, J.B., & Turner, R.J. (2013). Social relations, social integration, and social support. In C.S. Aneshensel, J.C. Phelan & A. Bierman (Eds.), *Handbook of the sociology of mental health (2nd edition)* (pp. 341–356). Springer.

Turner, R.J. (1999). Social support and coping. In A.V. Horwitz & T.L. Scheid (Eds.), *A Handbook for the study of mental health: social contexts, theories, and systems* (pp. 198–210). Cambridge University Press.

Turner, R.J., & Lloyd, D.A. (1999). The stress process and the social distribution of depression. *Journal of Health and Social Behavior*, *40*, 374–404.

Turner, R.J., & Marino, F. (1994). Social support and social structure: a descriptive epidemiology. *Journal of Health and Social Behavior*, *35*, 193–212.

Turney, K. (2013). Perceived instrumental support and children's health across the early life course. *Social Science & Medicine*, *95*, 34–42.

Uchino, B.N., Bowen, K., Carlisle, M., & Birmingham, W. (2012). Psychological pathways linking social support to health outcomes: a visit with the 'ghosts' of research past, present, and future. *Social Science and Medicine*, *74*(7), 949.

Umberson, D. and Thomeer, M.B. (2020). Family matters: research on family ties and health, 2010 to 2020. *Journal of Marriage and Family*, *82*(1), 404–419.

Upenieks, L. (2020). The influence of close ties on depression: does network religiosity matter? *Journal for the Scientific Study of Religion*, *59*(3), 484–508.

Väänänen, A., Buunk, A.P., Kivimäki, M., Vahtera, J., & Koskenvuo, M. (2008). Change in reciprocity as a predictor of depressive symptoms: a prospective cohort study of Finnish women and men. *Social Science and Medicine*, *67*(11), 1907–1916.

Verhaeghe, P.-P., Pattyn, E., Bracke, P., Verhaeghe, M., & Van De Putte, B. (2012). The association between network social capital and self-rated health: pouring old wine in new bottles? *Health and Place*, *18*(2), 358–365.

Wang, H., Stokes, J.E., & Burr, J.A. (2021). Depression and elevated inflammation among Chinese older adults: eight years after the 2003 SARS epidemic. *The Gerontologist*, *61*(2), 273.

Wellman, B. (1981). Applying social network analysis to the study of social support. In B.H. Gottlieb (Ed.), *Social networks and social support* (pp. 171–200). Sage.

Wellman, B., Salaff, J., Dimitrova, D., Garton, L., Gulia, M., & Haythornthwaite, C. (1996). Computer networks as social networks: collaborative work, telework, and virtual community, *Annual Review of Sociology*, *22*(1), 213–238.

Wellman, B., & Wortley, S. (1990). Different strokes from different folks: community ties and social support. *American Journal of Sociology*, *96*, 558–588.

Wethington, E., & Kessler, R.C. (1986). Perceived support, received support, and adjustment to stressful life events. *Journal of Health and Social Behavior*, *27*, 78–89.

Wheaton, B. (1985). Models for the stress-buffering functions of coping resources. *Journal of Health and Social Behavior*, *26*, 352–364.

Yang, T.-C., Sun, F., & Choi, S.E. (2021). Rural residence and mortality in later life: exploring the role of social integration and social support from a longitudinal perspective. *Population, Space and Place*, *27*(1).

Yang, Y.C., Schorpp, K., & Harris, K.M. (2014). Social support, social strain and inflammation: evidence from a national longitudinal study of US adults. *Social Science and Medicine*, *107*, 124.

Corporate Networks

William K. Carroll, M. Jouke Huijzer, and J. P. Sapinski

INTRODUCTION

Although systematic network analyses mapping the social organisation of business power date from the 1970s (Fennema & Heemskerk, 2018), scholars have explored the relations that link corporations and their directors into corporate elites and intercorporate networks for over a century. Otto Jeidels's (1905) path-breaking study of the relationship of German banks to industry discovered 1,350 interlocking directorates between the six biggest banks and industry (Fennema & Schijf, 1978, p. 298). This chapter reviews the empirical work that followed from Jeidels, emphasising the period since the 1970s, when social scientists turned to network analysis to represent elite and intercorporate relations.

Corporations are governed by boards of directors, elected at annual meetings of shareholders on the basis of one share, one vote – a system that favours owners of large blocs of shares – whether the shares are held by persons, other corporations, or institutional investors. Individuals sitting on two boards concurrently hold *interlocking directorships* with the companies, linking them at the level of governance. For individuals, interlocking directorships enhance contacts, influence and prestige. For firms, interlocking directorates may enable coordination of business strategies within an interlocked group. There is a *duality* in networks of directors and the corporate boards on which they sit (Breiger, 1974). These affiliation networks simultaneously draw together persons and corporations, and they can be fruitfully analysed on either level. The study of these networks is relevant to a number of issues, including economic organisation and the structure of capitalist classes (Scott, 1985a, p. 2).

Each corporate directorate is typically composed of both executives (insiders) and outside directors who do not hold executive positions in the firm. Individuals who hold interlocking directorships in large corporations include those with only outside directorships as well as executives of firms with which they are principally affiliated. In either case, 'their directorships spread throughout the economy, and they form a corporate or business elite' (Scott, 1991, p. 182). An elite, however, is more than a set of advantaged individuals; it refers to 'those who occupy the most powerful positions in structures of domination' (Scott, 2008, p. 33). As hierarchical organisations, large corporations are structures of domination par excellence. However, a corporate elite is different from a capitalist class, though the former, in its coordinated agency as an 'organised minority' (Brownlee, 2005), may be the 'leading edge' of the latter. 'An economic elite,' says Scott (2008, p. 37), 'is an inter-organizational group of people who hold positions of dominance in business organizations and who may, under certain circumstances, have certain additional powers available to them.' Interlocks figure heavily in creating or reflecting these circumstances. Just as interlocking directorships furnish the basis for a more or less cohesive corporate elite, interlocking directorates create relations between companies that add up to an intercorporate network.

It was not always so. Although elites and dominant classes have existed for millennia, corporate elites and intercorporate networks are creatures of advanced capitalism, going back to the merger movements of the late 19th and early 20th centuries that created, in world capitalism's core, today's large corporations or their predecessors (Stanworth & Giddens, 1975). Jeidels's (1905) pioneering work influenced Rudolf Hilferding's ([1910]1981) conception of finance capital as the symbiotic relation between money capital and industrial capital, which theorised the new power structure. On the one hand, banks needed an outlet to invest their accumulated capital; on the other, only the largest banks could provide sufficient capital to finance industry's massive scale of production. The system was managed by a small circle of finance capitalists whose corporate affiliations linked banks with top industrial corporations. In the United States, the first reference to interlocking directorates comes from the Pujo Committee, a congressional investigation set up in 1912 to address the growing concerns about bank power undermining market competition (Scott, 1997, p. 106). Another investigation directed by Paul Sweezy in the 1930s was the first to delineate several 'interest groups' in the US economy, based on ownership and directorate interlocking (Sweezy, 1953, pp. 166–167).

Concerns with concentration of power found another expression in C. Wright Mills's (1956) theory of the power elite, as well as in the work of Canadian sociologist John Porter (1956). Both invoked social networks more as metaphor than as research method. Mills argued that corporate interlockers, along with shareholders whose investments span many sectors, come to embrace class-wide interests, transcending specific firm-based interests (Mills, 1956, p. 123). Interlocks offer to these elites a potential for exchanging views, consolidating the corporate world by unifying the outlook and policy of the propertied class (Mills, 1956). Porter shared Mills's concerns about the threat to democracy posed by concentration of economic power. His study of interlocks in Canada revealed a strong relationship between banks and industrial corporations, as bankers sat on industrial boards and vice versa (Porter, 1956, p. 211). The classic work of G. William Domhoff (1967) also treated social networks more as metaphor than method. Domhoff's key contribution was to extend the analysis of interlocking to organisations that are part of the policy-planning process, such as business associations and think tanks.

POWER STRUCTURE RESEARCH AND THE TURN TO NETWORK ANALYSIS

The groundwork having been laid in the 1950s and 1960s, 'power structure research' came into its own in the 1970s (Domhoff, 1980), as researchers articulated an alternative to pluralist readings of economic and political power. The debate revolved mainly around the question of the unity and cohesiveness of the corporate elite. Against the pluralist position that market competition precludes elite unity, network analysis revealed elite cohesion and the capacity for political action.

At the level of individual directors, common participation in civic and political organisations (social clubs, foundations, universities, business associations and forums) as well as on corporate boards was found to foster social cohesion (Domhoff, 1974; Koenig & Gogel, 1981). Useem (1984) identified, as the 'dominant segment' of the capitalist class, an 'inner circle' of corporate interlockers, directors of multiple firms who possess greater wealth than single-firm directors, have more connections to financial institutions and show a higher degree of social cohesion and political influence. Elite cohesion, moreover, was shown to have biographical depth. Studies in the United Kingdom indicated that most corporate directors share an increasingly homogeneous background of privilege and inherited wealth (Stanworth & Giddens, 1975). For power structure researchers, corporate interlocking, layered upon personal networks that reach back to common social backgrounds, promoted a common worldview (Koenig & Gogel, 1981), the basis for elite consensus and for concerted political agency.

The findings of power structure researchers also challenged the managerialist position that saw a separation of ownership and control in the evolution of the modern corporation. As ownership became dispersed among many shareholders, control of the firm was claimed to pass into the hands of disinterested managers (Berle & Means, 1932), reducing corporate directors (and interlocks) to no more than window-dressing (Koenig et al., 1979). Power structure researchers questioned managerialism on several counts. On the level of corporations, Zeitlin (1974) showed that, for most cases, personal shareholding has been replaced by bank and insurance company shareholding, catapulting the latter, not managers, into controlling positions. On the individual level, Pfeffer (1987) argued that managers' goals accord with their organisations' goals, especially in the case of corporations where top executives directly benefit from the firm's profitability through the shares they hold.

Studies such as these affirmed that corporations are embedded in a system of power through interlocking directorates and other relations which shape corporate decisions. The research agenda moved beyond the 'aggregative' methods of classic elite analysis, of pluralist political science and of managerialism alike, which studied attributes of individuals or corporations but did not systematically examine the relations among them. In contrast, network analysis highlights the relations between units and the ways in which units (whether directors or corporations) are themselves shaped by their positions in systems of interrelations (Berkowitz, 1980).

Debates Within the Study of Interlocks

As network analysis of interlocks burgeoned, internal debates grew within the field. The main debates of the 1980s were between interorganisational approaches and a 'class hegemony' approach that emphasised the integrative function of interlocks for leading members of a dominant class. The former developed along two lines. Viewing corporations as formal organisations and corporate networks as interorganisational fields (Palmer, 1987), some researchers drew on the sociology of formal organisation, as in Allen's (1974) claim that interlocks issue from attempts by organisations to reduce environmental uncertainties by co-opting elites from other organisations (cf. Pennings, 1980; Pfeffer, 1987). Although this analytic lens afforded insights on how organisational imperatives shape networks, in assimilating the corporation to the broader category of formal organisation, its specificity as a key institution of advanced capitalism was lost. Issues of class, power and capital accumulation have not been taken up by interorganisational researchers, even though these are arguably central to this field of study.

Other researchers took an *intercorporate* view. In this perspective, interlocks are instrumental means in the accumulation and control of capital. Earlier researchers, often affiliated with old left parties, had taken up this approach, basing their work on Hilferding's view of finance capital as an integration of the financial and industrial forms of capital, placing big banks in central positions within a power structure segmented into 'financial groups' of aligned corporations (Park & Park, [1962]1973; Perlo, 1957). Mintz and Schwartz employed this approach in their study of the power structure of American business. Observing that 'large investments create a common fate; both lender and borrower depend heavily upon successful use of capital' (1985, p. 183), they analysed how, by controlling flows of capital, banks shape industrial structure, directing capital towards the most profitable or promising lines of investment. In this system of financial hegemony, the largest banks are 'vehicles for the class control of the economy' (1985, p. 254), and their central position in the interlock network reflects their hegemonic role as mediators of intraclass competition and meeting points for finance capitalists. Bank-centred interlocks provide the information necessary to financial hegemony – the broad scan across sectors of the business community. But at the individual level the same interlocks help constitute an elite of finance capitalists: 'a cohesive group of multiple directors tied together by shared background, friendship networks and economic interests, who sit on bank boards as representatives of capital in general' (1985, p. 254).

Finally, the class hegemony perspective saw corporations as 'units in a class controlled apparatus of appropriation' (Soref & Zeitlin, 1987, p. 58). In this view, decision-making takes place within a wider network of individual members of the dominant class, whose particular interests are crystallised not in individual corporations but in control groups (families or financial cliques), and whose general class interests are reinforced by the manifold weak ties of interlocking outside directors. Analysis focused on directors as members of the upper class, on the internal class structure, including the relations between the industrial and financial fractions of the capitalist class, and on how firms connect through individual board members or corporate and family ownership. Interlocks were viewed as expressions of class cohesion, enabling integration of potentially contradictory interests of the richest families, whose investments span different sectors (Soref & Zeitlin, 1987, p. 60). In the class hegemony perspective, interlocks provide channels of communication between individual directors, facilitating a common worldview among them (Koenig & Gogel, 1981), and giving the 'inner circle' of interlockers access to a broad resource base from which to exert their hegemony in and beyond the economy (Useem, 1984).

Useem's (1984, p. 77) finding that interlockers formed an inner circle representing the 'leading edge of business political activity' inspired research on campaign donations in the US by Mizruchi (1992), Burris (2001, 2005) and Heerwig and Murray (2019). Burris (2005, p. 278) demonstrated that 'the effect of ... directorship ties on political cohesion [measured as donations to the same presidential candidates] are stronger by several magnitudes than the effects of shared characteristics, like common industry or geographic proximity'. Yet, Burris also (2001) warned that the behaviour of individual business leaders differs from corporate donations. Murray (2017) finds that transnational interlocks can also foster political cohesion at a national level within the US.

Class-hegemony perspectives have also informed research on interlocking directorates between corporations and organisations such as interest groups, government committees, charities, foundations, universities, sports associations and cultural institutions. This type of research has been conducted, for instance, in France (Comet, 2019), the US (Burris, 2008), Canada (Carroll, 2004), Denmark (Ellersgaard et al., 2019) and at the transnational level (Carroll & Sapinski, 2010). While patterns of integration vary, a key finding is that, whereas national corporate interlocking networks seem in decline in most countries (see below), ties to policy planning organisations are, as Burris (2008, p. 3) has put it, 'substantively meaningful and relatively stable at the dyadic level'.

Corporate directors not only seek to influence politics; political actors also deliberately connect to the corporate world. A groundbreaking study by Stark and Vedres (2012) on corporate networks in post-Communist Hungary (1987–2001) demonstrated how, after the regime change, firms tended to cluster around certain political parties. When parties were in government they 'moved forcefully to place their politicians on corporate boards'; when they were in opposition they endeavoured to maintain those ties (2012, p. 718). Over the course of a single decade, Hungary turned into a 'politicised economy' as a fifth of all firms had a politician serving on one of their boards.

Network approaches, whether interorganisational, intercorporate or class-hegemonic, broke from the limitations of 'aggregative' approaches to corporate elites and intercorporate relations (Berkowitz, 1980). Many authors have stressed the complementarity between network approaches (Koenig & Gogel, 1981; Scott, 1985b; Stokman et al., 1988). In combination, they depict corporate interlocks as 'traces of power' (Helmers et al., 1975, cited in Fennema & Schijf, 1978) of two sorts: the instrumental power associated with the accumulation of capital and the expressive power associated with class hegemony (Carroll, 2004; Sonquist & Koenig, 1975). This raises a key question, succinctly posed by Mark Mizruchi: what do interlocks do?

What Do Interlocks Do?

In an extensive review of literature, Mizruchi (1996) considered the causes and consequences of corporate interlocks, noting both corporate and individual-level factors. For instance, interlocks can be mechanisms of co-optation or monitoring, as when a bank sends one of its officers to the board of one of its clients. Firms may invite prestigious directors on their boards to enhance their own reputations and contacts, and individual decisions to serve on multiple boards can be influenced by the prestige brought by the position, the remuneration and the possibilities of making useful personal contacts (Mizruchi, 1996, p. 277). Any one explanation accounts for only a subset of all interlocks (Mizruchi, 1996, p. 274); hence, the precise significance of a given interlock is highly context-dependent.

In this regard, Scott's (1991, p. 184) observation that 'power in intercorporate networks is based on at least three distinct kinds of intercorporate relation: personal, capital and commercial' has purchase. Commercial relations simply link buyers and sellers, but personal and capital relations are the main control relations surrounding corporations. Personal relations include interlocking directorships as well as kinship and friendship ties. Capital relations 'are the links between business agents that result from shareholdings and from the granting and withholding of credit' (p. 184). Interlock networks comprise only one type of relation in a multilayered formation. Of particular significance in decoding interlocks as 'traces of power' is the tendency, highlighted in the concept of finance capital, for interlocking directorships to be undergirded by capital relations (Scott, 2003, p. 159), including, in different contexts, intercorporate ownership, family control of multiple firms, institutional shareholding and the credit relations through which banks exercise allocative power vis-à-vis borrowers.

COMPARATIVE AND TRANSNATIONAL PERSPECTIVES

By the 1980s, a vast body of empirical research, much of it centred on the United States, had yielded many detailed insights on the structure of intercorporate networks and corporate elites. What was lacking, however, was a comparative-historical perspective that could broaden and deepen knowledge beyond the tacit positing of the United States as the norm.

Comparative Perspectives

It was in this context that John Scott (1985a) produced the second edition of his *Corporations, classes and capitalism*, just as an international research group published *Networks of corporate power*, comparing intercorporate networks across ten countries (Stokman et al., 1985). These works began to broaden interlock research through cross-national comparison.

Scott (1985b) noted that the capital relations that undergird interlock networks entail two forms of power: strategic control over specific corporations by means of concentrated blocs of shares and allocative power over capital flows, exercised by financial institutions. Distinct patterns of economic development and corporate law had produced national variants of these forms. In the German network of 'oligarchic bank hegemony' banks were dominant in both capital allocation and control. In the postwar Japanese system, strategic and allocative power were also combined in discrete, bank-centred enterprise groups whose members held large blocs of shares in each other. In France, Belgium and Italy, a 'Latin model', organised around the extensive shareholdings of rival holding companies, imparted 'a granular, group structuring of the economy' (Scott, 1985a, p. 136). In the Anglo-American system of 'polyarchic financial hegemony', consolidated during the post-World War II boom, large financial institutions held powerful allocative positions opposite industrial firms while institutional investors held blocs of shares that enabled them to function collectively as 'constellations of interests', exercising a constraining strategic power upon corporate management. The 'polyarchic' character of the Anglo-American system made for an interlock network centralised around major banks and insurance companies, with little to no fractioning of the network into discrete groups (Scott, 1985a, pp. 129–260). With continuing growth in all advanced capitalist countries of depersonalised, institutional investment, Scott saw 'a common move towards bank hegemony of a loosely structured kind' (Scott, 1985a, p. 227).

A stream of comparative research flowed in the wake of these initiatives, and by the time Scott (1997) issued a completely rewritten compendium he was able not only to refine his earlier categories of variant patterns, but to add the 'post-Communist pattern' of collusive business organisation in Eastern Europe and the 'Chinese pattern' of corporate cooperation based on fraternal inheritance. More recent comparative studies include Maclean et al.'s (2006) investigation of business elites and corporate governance in France and the United Kingdom, which contrasted the thinness of the British network with the extensive involvement of wealthy families and the state in corporate France. Paul Windolf's (2002) study of interlock networks in Europe and the United States offered further details on the organisation of big business in advanced capitalism but also analysed post-socialist networks in Eastern Europe. Windolf's analysis of the economic annexation of the former German Democratic Republic by the West German capitalist class – a process that produced an East German network of companies 'legally and economically dependent upon western interests' (2002, p. 163) – raised the larger question of how, in a globalising world, corporate power is configured on world capitalism's semi-periphery.

Three decades after the appearance of *Networks of corporate power*, David and Westerhuis (2014) edited a volume whose findings showed that observed declines in elite cohesion in the US and elsewhere reflected changing institutional arrangements rather than a decline of bank power, raising the issue of how national-level mechanisms interact with global-level dynamics. Sketching out such an analysis, Scott (2012, p. 20) explained that globalisation of share ownership integrates national economies within a transnational market in which pension funds, banks and holding companies from the core economies are major participants: 'As a result, an increasing number of enterprises have found themselves subject to the substantial influence, if not control, of shareholding interests that are international in character.'

Interlocks in the Semi-periphery

Since the beginning of the new century research into interlocking directorates has 'virtually exploded' (Burris, 2005, p. 249) as scholars map national and regional corporate networks in the economic core and periphery. As a result there is a growing body of research on board interlocks in Latin America, Asia and a number of African countries.

Patterns across regions vary to some degree. Ilya Okhmatovskiy's (2005) study of the Russian interlock network evidenced a reversal of the dominant pattern of financial hegemony found in core countries. In the aftermath of the 1998 financial crisis, Russian banks, previous leaders in converting public assets into capital but unable to access foreign capital, yielded their centrality to giant industrial firms whose resource exports generated deep pools of capital, on which the banks themselves came to depend. The study supported the concept of finance capital as an integration of financial and industrial forms, but showed how, when financial institutions are weak, a few industrial concerns can act as the coordinating centres of financial-industrial groups (2005, p. 452).

In Latin America, Cárdenas (2016) found that more cohesive networks develop in countries with higher market openness, facilitating big business to speak with one voice when governments negotiate trade deals. Naudet and Dubost (2017) draw the same conclusions in India. Similarly, in Thailand, Peng et al. (2001) found firms that were 'internationalising' tended to be well-connected in interlock networks. In a pioneering study on the contradictions and interlinkages between the indigenous and foreign bourgeoisie in Kenya, Nicola Swainson (1980) found that local business empires connected to foreign capital, politicians and businessmen (indigenous and European) through board interlocks. She noted a high degree of 'Africanisation' in the early 1970s as many African capitalists had developed their indigenous business empires, and concluded that it would be 'misleading' to assume that 'an indigenous capitalist class can develop only as an appendage of foreign capital' (1980, p. 208). Going further, Cox and Rogerson (1985) found the South African indigenous capitalist class organised, during late-stage Apartheid, geographically in two axes, corresponding to English and Afrikaaner capital.

The economic ascent of China has provoked interest in the Chinese elite although most early work focused on career paths and social background characteristics. Keller (2016) demonstrated the value of network analysis of party elites and corporate directors, compared to the study of factions, in dissecting Chinese power structures. De Graaff (2014, 2020) has tracked the increasing transnationalisation of China's corporate elite but found in a recent study that Chinese firms connect to European firms via a mere handful of 'exceptionally big linkers' (De Graaff & Valeeva, 2021).

Transnational Networks

Meanwhile, with the ongoing globalisation of corporations, network analysis of corporate organisation also went global. Key issues informing this strand of analysis have been (1) whether a shift is underway from national interlocks contained within countries to transnational interlocks between firms based in different countries and (2) the spatial distribution of transnational interlocking. These questions, the second of which we take up later, are crucial to an understanding of the *global* intercorporate network and the *global* corporate elite.

Fennema (1982) made the earliest attempt to analyse a transnational corporate network. Mapping the network before and after the generalised international recession of 1973–1974, he documented the consolidation of a Euro-North American component but found very few ties extending beyond that heartland of postwar capitalism. Later, Carroll and Fennema (2002) picked up the thread, comparing Fennema's (1982) 1976 network with data for 1996. They reported only a modest increase in transnational interlocking alongside the persistence of national networks, suggesting strong path dependencies reproducing patterns of national corporate-elite organisation discerned by Scott (1997).

Research tracking the 500 leading corporations in the world from 1996 to 2006 found a proliferation of transnational interlockers and a decline in national networkers, particularly in Japan, whose complement of leading corporations plummeted during the 1990s. The transnationalists have profuse ties to each other as well as to various national segments; thus, 'in the inner circle of the global corporate elite, transnationalists and national networkers intermingle extensively, "national" and "supranational" spaces intersect, and whatever common interest takes shape is likely to blend "national" and "transnational" concerns' (Carroll, 2009, p. 308; Carroll, 2010).

Most recently, increases in computing power and the emergence of sizable online databases have enabled *big data* approaches and new insights into regional and global corporate communities. In a pioneering article, Heemskerk and Takes (2016) applied community detection to a global network comprising the largest 1 million firms, aggregated by country, to make an empirical assessment of the degree to which emerging economies integrate into the global capitalist order. They found interlock relations to be clustered in eight communities of about ten to 30 countries that are either geographically proximal or share similarities in terms of language or culture. Their analysis suggests 'a *multi-level structure* where, in between the national and the transnational, discernible regional clusters play a fundamental role in the network architecture' (Heemskerk and Takes, 2016, p. 112, emphasis in original).

The application of big data approaches to the study of interlocks comes with significant issues regarding data quality (Heemskerk et al., 2017) and triggers new questions on how to demarcate samples of relevant corporations. Corporate network researchers have typically worked with samples of the largest 100 or 500 corporations. Huijzer and Heemskerk (2021) argued that, although the largest firms are most likely to occupy central positions, a significant number of smaller firms also occupy the network core. Firm size may not be the most relevant criterion; hence 'any future study on the topic should carefully consider which demarcation is most meaningful for the purpose of the research and how such demarcation may or may not impact the robustness of the results' (Huijzer and Heemskerk, 2021, p. 16). More fundamentally, an old question arises, dating back to the seminal work of Berkowitz et al. (1978) on how to demarcate a single corporation. Businesses have been internationalising and transforming from single firms to a so-called 'nexus of contracts' (Davis, 2013) comprising many, even thousands, of partly or wholly owned subsidiaries. It is increasingly difficult to delineate a single corporation and to consider which boards are relevant.

KEY ISSUES

Across the last several decades, researchers have used an eclectic combination of techniques to map corporate networks at different scales and over various time frames. In this section we consider how three analytic issues have been addressed – the duality of corporate networks, questions of temporality and network dynamics and questions of spatiality.

The Duality of Interlock Networks

As we saw earlier, interlock networks can be fruitfully analysed as interpersonal (corporate elite) or as intercorporate configurations. Although both approaches illuminate social organisation, each reveals only one facet of an inherently dualistic structure (Breiger, 1974), reducible neither to an elite of directors nor to a network of faceless corporations (Carroll, 1984, p. 249). The challenge has been to devise ways of representing interlock networks as configurations of both individual directors and the corporations they direct.

One approach has been to examine the network in two parallel analyses, as an interpersonal network of directors, linked to each other by virtue of their common corporate affiliations, and as an intercorporate network of interlocking directorates. Analysing the US network, Bearden and Mintz (1987, p. 204) discovered 'parallels in structure between the corporate and director networks', with regional organisation, the merger of institutional and class interests and the unifying role of big linkers occurring on both levels, and with bank boards serving as key sites in both the director network and the corporate network. Davis and colleagues (2003) also pursued parallel analyses in their small-world study of change in the US corporate network between 1982 and 1999. Although the mean degree of contacts decreased in both the interpersonal and intercorporate networks, at both levels the structure remained a small world, due to the integrative impact of both linchpin boards and linchpin directors: nodes whose ties across clusters create shortcuts that shrink the social space of the network.

Alternatively, the two levels can be considered in a single analysis of the interpersonal network by assigning to directors, as contextual variables, the attributes of the firms with which they are principally affiliated. Applying this approach to the Canadian network, Carroll (1984) found that industrial and financial firms controlled in Canada were strongly over-represented at the centre of the director network and in its principal cliques. The cliques were substantially organised around intercorporate ownership relations, supporting the conclusion that the Canadian corporate power structure revolves around 'groups of interlocked capitalists who own and manage supra-corporate blocs of finance capital' (p. 265).

Researchers have also addressed the issue of duality directly by analysing corporate affiliations as two-mode networks, thereby keeping both levels in view. Levine and Roy (1979) pioneered this approach with their 'rubber-band' model, simultaneously clustering directors and corporations on either side of a set of elastic board affiliations. Alexander (2003, p. 235) explored the boardroom networks of Australian directors in an intricate two-mode analysis at 1976 and 1996. He notes that both the interpersonal and intercorporate network have a common *infrastructure*, which provides the resources for network connectivity and simultaneously shapes both levels of the network. For instance, if directors tend to clump together on the same boards, as in a configuration built around corporate groups, the network will contain extensive redundancy, with the same directors linking the same boards in a system of 'tight' interlocks that will dampen the spread of contacts in the interpersonal network. In the Australian case, although the density of intercorporate relations increased only slightly from 1976 to 1996, redundancy in the infrastructure decreased substantially, which increased the interpersonal network's density and drew many more boards into the dominant component.

Recently, scholars have focused on the case of Denmark to examine the dynamics of board appointments and elite cohesion. Valeeva et al. (2020) used a 'relational event modelling approach' in which each appointment counts as an 'event' to identify both firm-level (sector, size) and individual-level predictors ('popularity', gender, nationality) of board appointments. Similarly, Ellersgaard et al. (2019) distinguished no less than ten 'pathways to the power elite' in terms of individual career paths, but they also considered which organisations were most important to which particular types of career paths.

Temporality

Corporate networks arise and persist in the broad sweep of history, and researchers have explored the temporality of these formations using a variety of approaches. The most basic longitudinal research design depicts network structure at two or more moments, and interprets patterns of continuity and change in view of social and historical processes that are known to have occurred in the interim (e.g., Allen, 1974; Bunting & Barbour, 1971; Piédalue, 1976). More recently, Barnes and Ritter (2001) tracked the thickening and then thinning of the American corporate network at four points from 1962 to 1995, and Barnes (2017), using the same data but examining the interpersonal network, explored multiple dimensions of the American corporate elite's small world. By assessing how much the addition of extra-corporate affiliations decreased mean geodesic distances among directors, Barnes documented the decline of cultural ties (e.g., to museum boards) but a steady increase in the integrative role of affiliations with policy planning organisations. In line with Useem (1984), these trends depict a corporate elite becoming less concerned with maintaining social or civic ties and more politically mobilised (cf. Carroll, 2004; Murray, 2006).

Although successive cross-sections allow researchers to pinpoint when major structural changes occur, they do not afford much basis for discerning the dynamics of change. The groundbreaking work of Helmers et al. (1975) showed that in the Netherlands in the 1960s interlocks between financial institutions and industrial corporations had a high probability of being restored after retirement, resignation, or death of a director. Several studies have employed restoration of broken ties as an indicator of the importance of an interlock to the participating firms. Ornstein (1984) found that of the 5,354 interlocks among large corporations in Canada broken at some point during the first three postwar decades, interlocks carried by executives in one of the interlocked firms, and interlocks that were part of a multiple-interlock relation or a relation of intercorporate ownership between firms, were substantially more likely to be restored. Richardson (1987) used cross-lagged correlations to show that in the Canadian network the profitability of industrial firms in 1963 predicted the restoration of their interlocks with financial institutions five years later, in a 'circular and self-sustaining process' that reinforced companies' original profit position, supporting the theory of finance capital as capital integration.

Palmer's study (1987) of broken ties in the American network found a low rate of restoration, particularly for non-executive interlocks. He concluded that although some interlocks facilitate formal intercorporate coordination, many of them are expressions of class hegemony, as interactions among leading directors and executives create 'a loose, but nonetheless very real system of coordination in which firms are instruments of inner circle policy' (p. 70). Stearns and Mizruchi (1986), however, in a panel study that tracked 22 major industrial corporations over three decades, found evidence of 'functional reconstitution' in which an industrial firm's broken tie to a financial institution is restored by an interlock to a different financial institution. This suggests that the incidence of purposive, strategic interlocking is higher than that estimated by the 'direct' restoration of broken ties. In a complementary investigation, event-history analysis of emergent interlocks showed that although firms with decreasing solvency and profitability were likely to appoint executives in financial institutions to their boards, all corporations were more likely to make such appointments during upswings in the business cycle, as capital needs expand. Both the specific situation facing a firm and the general context for capital accumulation appear to influence the creation of a financial-industrial interlock (Mizruchi & Stearns, 1988).

Network Dynamics

Although extensive sociological research on corporate networks has been set within the power-structure tradition, some of the most innovative analyses of temporality have explored practices only indirectly related to this central problematic. Galaskiewicz and Wasserman (1981), in a study of a regional corporate network, used Markov chains to model network processes. Focusing on the probability of establishing a linkage and the probability of an asymmetric (executive) linkage becoming reciprocated (or vice versa), they found that norms of reciprocity are not operative in corporate interlock networks, as they are in other interorganisational relations – consistent with the idea that interlocks carried by corporate insiders tend to be relations of influence and power. Diffusion of innovation analysis has also proven useful in tracking network effects on speed of adaptation and patterns of prevalence of corporate governance practices. Davis and Greve's (1997) study of the adoption of poison pills and golden parachutes in the American network (1980–1986), marking a shift to 'investor capitalism', is iconic. They showed how, amid the takeover waves of the 1980s, poison pills spread rapidly through board-to-board diffusion processes 'in which firms adopted to the extent that their contacts had done so', but parachutes spread slowly, on the basis of geographical proximity rather than interlocking directorates (p. 29).

Development of actor-oriented modelling by Tom Snijders and his colleagues (Snijders, this volume; Steglich et al., 2006) has opened new possibilities for systematic analysis of network dynamics. As applied to intercorporate networks, this approach accounts for the changing pattern of interfirm relations by estimating the underlying rational choices of network actors. For instance, Van de Bunt and Groenewegen's (2007) study of collaborative agreements among genomic companies found that firms prefer to start partnerships with high-status (well-connected) companies and with companies that are already members of the same (two-clique) groups as the focal firm. Actor-oriented modelling offers intriguing opportunities to explore how local, context-dependent corporate decisions shape macro-configurations.

The career trajectories of directors and executives present yet another dynamic in the life of corporate networks. In their study of pathways to corporate management in the United States, Useem and Karabel (1986) found that individuals who become members of the elite's inner circle are those with the greatest amount of both 'scholastic' (elite education) and 'social' (upper-class background) capital. The core of the elite, the segment most engaged in class-wide leadership, tends to be recruited through mechanisms emphasised in Bourdieu's (1984) generalised theory of capital. In a longitudinal study of Dutch corporations over two decades (1960–1980), Stokman et al. (1988) tracked the careers of the 105 big linkers whose typical career pattern involved entering the network as an executive, acquiring several outside directorships, then first retiring from the executive position and later exiting from the network altogether. As directorates recruit outside directors from a pool of executives of other large firms, and as executives move through this career sequence, the network is reproduced in its duality – partly on the basis of 'permanent economic and financial relations between companies', partly through recruitment processes that cause '*global* stability of the structure of the network, together with *local* instability of dyadic relations' (p. 203, emphasis original).

Finally, qualitative approaches have highlighted the contingent, historical and contextual character of network temporality. Glasberg's (1987) case studies of the assertion of financial hegemony in restructuring insolvent corporations through such mechanisms as stock dumping are of great relevance to the current era of financialised capitalism. Equally apposite is Brayshay and colleagues' (2006) study of 'power geometries' in the rescue of Hudson's Bay Company (HBC) by the Bank of England during the Great Depression. These researchers began from the biography of a single person, Patrick Ashley Cooper, appointed governor of the HBC in 1931 and a director of the Bank of England in 1932, who thereupon assembled a remarkable set of international business contacts. By tracing Cooper's network in depth, through archival documents, Brayshay et al. constructed a rich longitudinal account of the corporate network and wide range of business- and policy-related practices it enabled. Significantly, Cooper's embeddedness extended well beyond the boardrooms of London. Indeed, among his core group of special confidants were many people who had no overlapping corporate affiliations with him. Thus, 'a full reconstruction of an economic actor's array of contacts requires research beyond the stylized mapping of corporate networks' (Brayshay et al., 2006, p. 996). Such qualitative depth can illuminate specific mechanisms of social power, corporate control and capital accumulation.

Spatiality

The spatial organisation of business networks has preoccupied researchers since the consolidation of power structure analysis in the 1970s. The outstanding study from that era is Sonquist and Koenig's (1975) clique analysis of the American network circa 1969. Geocoding each corporation by the city of its headquarters, they mapped a network of 32 overlapping cliques and their satellites, most of which were based in particular cities, with New York hosting the largest and most central group. Mintz and Schwartz (1981, p. 863) soon demonstrated the special position of New York as 'the base of a national network of corporate interlocks, uniting regional clusters into a loosely integrated whole'. Green's (1983, 1993) subsequent studies of the interurban network of corporate interlocks and of institutional stock ownership revealed a regionalised network dominated by the cities in which major financial institutions have their headquarters: New York and, secondarily, Chicago, Boston, Los Angeles and San Francisco.

Later, Kono and his colleagues (1998) examined the relationship between spatial propinquity of corporate headquarters and corporate interlocking. Firms based in cities with exclusive upper-class clubs tended to interlock with each other, suggesting that 'the local capitalist class social organization made possible by the colocation of corporate headquarters and upper-class clubs may be an instrument by which corporate elites manage their organizational environments, gaining information, trusted contacts, and access to national networks of elites' (Kono et al., 1998, p. 904).

More recently, the geography of corporate networks has been explored at a global level. In a study of the global corporate elite (1996–2006) mentioned earlier, Carroll (2010) found a highly regionalised network, most of whose members are embedded in national networks, with transnational interlocking mainly integrating corporate Europe or linking across to North America. Moreover, the growing cohesiveness of corporate Europe and the thinning of the American network shifted the global network's centre of gravity, registering the success, from a business standpoint, of European integration, along with the decline of American hegemony.

Several investigations have reached similar conclusions by charting corporate interlocking in the network of global cities. Using interlock data from 1996, aggregated by city of head office, Carroll (2007) found an interurban network in which Paris, London and New York are particularly central, along with other cities of northeast North America and northwest Europe – the heartland of an Atlantic ruling class, in Van der Pijl's (1984) estimation. A comprehensive analysis by Heemskerk et al. (2016) examined over 8 million interlocking directors between 18 million firms, aggregated by city of head office. Using a community detection algorithm, they demonstrated that geographic proximity is but one factor shaping corporate communities. Communities often span multiple countries, sometimes reflecting language and ethnic connections, as in the links between Portuguese and Brazilian firms. Such analyses not only demonstrate the importance of key cities as loci of corporate command; they also offer an alternative, in spatialising the global network, to the ambiguous national-transnational binary (see Burris & Staples, 2012). Also affirmed in this line of research is the general observation that the global corporate elite, the global intercorporate network and the world city network compose a core–periphery structure in which the global North continues to dominate.

NEW DIRECTIONS

While research on corporate networks was initially centred upon an economic class divide, a growing body of research takes up climate justice as well as board diversity. Regarding the latter, Kogut et al. (2014, p. 900) found that in Norway, which mandates a quota of 40 per cent women on boards, '[l]ow numerical quotas are sufficient ... to generate a network of highly central and influential women directors'. Yet, across Scandinavia, 'increasing board diversity does not necessarily break up networks, but can actually reinforce them' (Edling et al., 2012, p. 199); indeed, African-American and women directors tend to interlock extensively, enhancing network cohesiveness (Hillman et al., 2002; Heemskerk & Fennema, 2014). However, in the global network, (white) women and ethnic minorities are underrepresented at the core (Young et al., 2020). Still, following Cinzia Arruzza et al. (2019), one can ask whether more women on corporate boards helps overcome a system that can be seen as patriarchal in itself.

Lastly, another recent strand of research uses interlocking directorships to map the field of climate and energy politics. De Graaf (2011, 2012, 2020) finds that Southern-based state-owned and private oil companies have become more integrated in the early 21st century, indicating a rise in power of the global South, with increasing links between the Chinese and global economic elite. Within the global climate policy-planning network, interlocks between policy groups and corporations highlight climate policy as a key area of corporate influence (Sapinski, 2015, 2016). Examining Canada as a petro-state, Carroll (2017) delineates a highly cohesive network of fossil-fuel companies extensively interlocked with Toronto-based financial corporations, confirming the close interdependence of 'fossil capital' and financial capital (Carroll et al., 2018; Hudson & Bowness, 2021). Interestingly, oil firms also insert themselves into so-called 'clean-growth' networks assumed to support energy transition, suggesting these networks adapt to the evolution of policy issues (Graham, 2021).

CONCLUSION

Corporate network research has come a long way since Jeidels's groundbreaking work. If in the past few decades the methods of analysis have grown in sophistication, corporate elites and intercorporate networks have hardly remained static in their organisational features. The research literature reviewed above records major structural changes, often catalysed by economic crises that provoke massive capital reorganisations and, sometimes, new regulatory frameworks. This dynamic has great relevance to the contemporary scene where economic crises are recurring and ecological disaster is imminent. Meanwhile, the increasing concentration of wealth in the hands of a few *big tech* giants along with the growth of giant corporations on the semi-periphery presents another possible source of recomposition in networks of corporate power. For corporate elites and intercorporate networks, both national and global, what is certain is that change is here to stay.

REFERENCES

Alexander, M. (2003). Boardroom networks among Australian company directors, 1976 and 1996. *Journal of Sociology, 39*(3), 231–251.

Allen, M.P. (1974). The structure of interorganizational elite cooptation: interlocking corporate directorates. *American Sociological Review*, (3), 393–406.

Arruzza, C., Bhattacharya, T., & Fraser, N. (2019). *Feminism for the 99 percent*. Verso.

Barnes, R.C. (2017). Structural redundancy and multiplicity within networks of US corporate directors. *Critical Sociology, 43*(1), 37–57.

Barnes, R.C., & Ritter, E.R. (2001). Networks of corporate interlocking : 1962–1995. *Critical Sociology 27*(2), 192–220.

Bearden, J., & Mintz, B. (1987). The structure of class cohesion : the corporate network and its dual. In M.S. Mizruchi and M. Schwartz (Eds.), *Intercorporate relations: the structural analysis of business* (pp. 187–207). Cambridge University Press.

Berkowitz, S.D. (1980). Structural and non-structural models of elites : a critique. *Canadian Journal of Sociology, 5*(1), 13–30.

Berkowitz, S.D., Carrington, P.J., Kotowitz, Y., & Waverman, L. (1978). The determination of enterprise groupings through combined ownership and directorship ties. *Social Networks, 1*(4), 391–413.

Berle, A.A., & Means, G.C. (1932). *The modern corporation and private property*. Harcourt, Brace & World.

Bourdieu, P. (1984). *Distinction: a social critique of the judgement of taste*. Trans. R. Nice. Harvard University Press.

Brayshay, M., Cleary, M., & Selwood, J. (2006). Power geometries : social networks and the 1930s multinational corporate elite. *Geoforum, 37*(6), 986–998.

Breiger, R.L. (1974). The duality of persons and groups. *Social Forces, 53*(2), 181–190.

Brownlee, J. (2005). *Ruling Canada: corporate cohesion and democracy*. Fernwood.

Bunting, D., & Barbour, J. (1971). Interlocking directorates in large American corporations, 1986–1964. *Business History Review, 45*(3), 317–335.

Burris, V. (2001). The two faces of capital : corporations and individual capitalists as political actors. *American Sociological Review, 66*(3), 361–381.

Burris, V. (2005). Interlocking directorates and political cohesion among corporate elites. *American Journal of Sociology, 111*(1), 249–283.

Burris, V. (2008). The interlock structure of the policy-planning network and the right turn in US state policy. *Research in Political Sociology, 17*, 3–42.

Burris, V., & Staples, C.L. (2012). In search of a transnational capitalist class : alternative methods for comparing director interlocks within and between nations and regions. *International Journal of Comparative Sociology, 53*(4), 323–342.

Cárdenas, J. (2016). Why do corporate elites form cohesive networks in some countries, and do not in others? Cross-national analysis of corporate elite networks in Latin America.' *International Sociology, 31*(3), 341–363.

Carroll, W.K. (1984). The individual, class, and corporate power in Canada. *Canadian Journal of Sociology, 9*(3), 245–268.

Carroll, W.K. (2004). *Corporate power in a globalizing world: a study in elite social organization*. Oxford University Press.

Carroll, W.K. (2007). Global cities in the global corporate network. *Environment and Planning A, 39*(10), 2297–2323.

Carroll, W.K. (2009). Transnationalists and national networkers in the global corporate elite. *Global Networks, 9*(3), 289–314.

Carroll, W.K. (2010). *The making of a transnational capitalist class*. Zed.

Carroll, W.K. (2017). Canada's carbon-capital elite : a tangled web of corporate power. *Canadian Journal of Sociology, 42*(3), 225–260.

Carroll, W.K., & Fennema, M. (2002). Is there a transnational business community? *International Sociology, 17*(3), 393–419.

Carroll, W.K., & Sapinski, J.P. (2010). The global corporate elite and the transnational policy-planning network, 1996 – 2006 : a structural analysis. *International Sociology, 25*(4), 501–538.

Carroll, W., Graham, N., Lang, M.K., Yunker, Z., & McCartney, K.D. (2018). The corporate elite and the architecture of climate change denial : a network analysis of carbon capital's reach into civil society. *Canadian Review of Sociology*, *55*(3), 425–450.

Comet, C. (2019). How does the inner circle shape the policy-planning network in France? *Socio-Economic Review*, *17*(4), 1021–1041.

Cox, B.A., & Rogerson, C.A. (1985). The corporate power elite in South Africa: interlocking directorships among large enterprises. *Political Geography Quarterly*, *4*(3), 219–234.

David, T., & Westerhuis, G. (Eds.) (2014). *The power of corporate networks: a comparative and historical perspective*. Routledge.

Davis, G.F. (2013). After the corporation. *Politics and Society*, *41*(2), 283–308.

Davis, G.F., & Greve, H.R. (1997). Corporate elite networks and governance changes in the 1980s. *American Journal of Sociology*, *103*(1), 1–37.

Davis, G.F., Yoo, M., & Baker, W.E. (2003). The small world of the American corporate elite, 1982–2001. *Strategic Organization*, *1*(3), 301–326.

De Graaff, N. (2011). A global energy network? The expansion and integration of non-triad national oil companies. *Global Networks*, *11*(2), 262–283.

De Graaff, N. (2012). Oil elite networks in a transforming global oil market. *International Journal of Comparative Sociology*, *53*(4), 275–297.

De Graaff, N. (2014). Global networks and the two faces of Chinese national oil companies. *Perspectives on Global Development and Technology*, *13*(5–6), 539–563.

De Graaff, N. (2020). China Inc. goes global : transnational and national networks of China's globalizing business elite. *Review of International Political Economy*, *27*(2), 208–233.

De Graaff, N., & Valeeva, D. (2021). Emerging Sino–European corporate elite networks. *Development and Change*, *52*(5), 1147–1173.

Domhoff, G.W. (1967). *Who Rules America?* Prentice-Hall.

Domhoff, G. William. (1974). *The Bohemian Grove and other retreats: a study in ruling-class cohesiveness*. Harper & Row.

Domhoff, G.W. (Ed.) (1980). *Power structure research*. Sage.

Edling, C., Hobdari, B., Randoy, T., Stafsudd, A., & Thomsen, S. (2012). Testing the 'old boys' network : diversity and board interlocks in Scandinavia. In B.M. Kogut (Ed.), *The small worlds of corporate governance* (pp. 183–202). MIT Press.

Ellersgaard, C.H., Lunding, J.A., Henriksen, L.F., & Larsen, A.G. (2019). Pathways to the power elite : the organizational landscape of elite careers. *Sociological Review*, *67*(5).

Fennema, M. (1982). *International networks of banks and industry*. M. Nijhoff.

Fennema, M., & Heemskerk, E. (2018). When theory meets methods : the naissance of computer assisted corporate interlock research. *Global Networks*, *18*(1), 81–104.

Fennema, M., & Schijf, H. (1978). Analysing interlocking directorates : theory and methods. *Social Networks*, *1*(4), 297–332.

Galaskiewicz, J., & Wasserman, S. (1981). A dynamic study of change in a regional corporate network. *American Sociological Review*, *46*(4), 475–484.

Glasberg, D. (1987). The ties that bind? Case studies in the significance of corporate board interlocks with financial institutions. *Sociological Perspectives*, *30*(1), 19–48.

Graham, N. (2021). *Forces of production, climate change, and Canadian fossil capitalism*. Brill.

Green, M.B. (1983). The interurban corporate interlocking directorate network of Canada and the United States : a spatial perspective. *Urban Geography*, *4*(4), 338–354.

Green, M.B. (1993). A geography of institutional stock ownership in the United States. *Annals of the Association of American Geographers*, *83*(1), 66–89.

Heemskerk, E., & Fennema, M. (2014). Women on board : female board membership as a form of elite democratization. *Enterprise and Society*, *15*(2), 252–284.

Heemskerk, E.M., & Takes, F.W. (2016). The corporate elite community structure of global capitalism. *New Political Economy*, *21*(1), 90–118.

Heemskerk, E.M., Takes, F.W., Garcia-Bernardo, J., & Huijzer, M.J. (2016). Where is the global corporate elite? A large-scale network study of local and nonlocal interlocking directorates. *Sociologica*, *10*(2).

Heemskerk, E.M., Young, K., Takes, F., Cronin, B., Garcia-Bernardo, J., Popov, V., Winecoff, W.K., Henriksen, L.F., & Laurin-Lamothe, A. (2017). The promise and perils of using big data in the study of corporate networks : problems, diagnostics and fixes. *Global Networks*, *18*(1), 3–32.

Heerwig, J.A., & Murray, J. (2019). The political strategies and unity of the American corporate inner circle : evidence from political donations, 1982–2000. *Social Problems*, *66*(4), 580–608.

Helmers, H.M., Mokken, R.J., Plijter, R.C., & Stokman, F.N. (1975). *Graven naar Macht. Op zoek naar de kern van de Nederlandse ekonomie*. Van Gennep.

Hilferding, R. ([1910]1981). *Finance capital: a study of the latest phase of capitalist development*. Trans. M. Watnick & S. Gordon. Routledge & K. Paul.

Hillman, A.J., Cannella, A.A., & Harris, I.C. (2002). Women and racial minorities in the boardroom :

how do directors differ? *Journal of Management*, 28(6), 747–763.

Hudson, M., & Bowness, E. (2021). Finance and fossil capital : a community divided? *The Extractive Industries and Society*, 8(2).

Huijzer, M.J., & Heemskerk, E.M. (2021). Delineating the corporate elite : inquiring the boundaries and composition of interlocking directorate networks. *Global Networks*, 21(4), 791–820.

Jeidels, O. (1905). Das Verhältnis der deutschen Grossbanken zur Industrie mit besonder Berücksichtigung der Eisenindustrie (Relation of the German big banks to industry with special reference to the iron industry). *Staats- und sozialwissenschaftliche Forschungen*, 24(2), 1–271.

Keller, F.B. (2016). Moving beyond factions : using social network analysis to uncover patronage networks among Chinese elites. *Journal of East Asian Studies*, 16(1), 17–41.

Koenig, T., & Gogel, R. (1981). Interlocking corporate directorships as a social network. *American Journal of Economics and Sociology*, 40(1), 37–50.

Koenig, T., Gogel, R., & Sonquist, J. (1979). Models of the significance of interlocking corporate directorates. *American Journal of Economics and Sociology*, 38(2), 173–186.

Kogut, B., Colomer, J., & Belinky, M. (2014). Equality at the top of the corporation : assessing possible worlds of mandated quotas. *Strategic Management Journal*, 35(6), 891–902.

Kono, C., Palmer, D., Friedland, R., & Zafonte, M. (1998). Lost in space : the geography of corporate interlocking directorates. *American Journal of Sociology*, 103(4), 863–911.

Levine, J.H., & Roy, W.S. (1979). A study of interlocking directorates : vital concepts of organization. In P.W. Holland & S. Leinhardt (Eds.), *Perspectives on social network research* (pp. 349–378). Academic Press.

Maclean, M., Harvey, C., & Press, J. (2006). *Business elites and corporate governance in France and the UK*. Palgrave Macmillan.

Mills, C.W. (1956). *The power elite*. Oxford University Press.

Mintz, B., & Schwartz, M. (1981). Interlocking directorates and interest group formation. *American Sociological Review*, 46, 851–69.

Mintz, B., & Schwartz, M. (1985). *The power structure of American business*. University of Chicago Press.

Mizruchi, M.S. (1992). *The structure of corporate political action*. Harvard University Press.

Mizruchi, M.S. (1996). What do interlocks do? An analysis, critique, and assessment of research on interlocking directorates. *Annual Review of Sociology*, 22, 271–298.

Mizruchi, M.S., & Stearns, L.B. (1988). A longitudinal study of the formation of interlocking directorates. *Administrative Science Quarterly*, 33(2), 194–210.

Murray, G. (2006). *Capitalist networks and social power in Australia and New Zealand*. Ashgate.

Murray, J. (2017). Interlock globally, act domestically : corporate political unity in the 21st century. *American Journal of Sociology*, 122(6), 1617–1663.

Naudet, J., & Dubost, C.-L. (2017). The Indian exception : the densification of the network of corporate interlocks and the specificities of the Indian business system (2000–2012). *Socio-Economic Review*, 15(2), 405–434.

Okhmatovskiy, I. (2005). Sources of capital and structures of influence : banks in the Russian corporate network. *International Sociology*, 20(4), 427–457.

Ornstein, M.D. (1984). Interlocking directorates in Canada : intercorporate or class alliance? *Administrative Science Quarterly*, 29(2), 210–231.

Palmer, Donald. (1987). The dual nature of corporate interlocks. In M. Schwartz (Ed.), *The structure of power in America: the corporate elite as a ruling class* (pp. 60–74). Holmes and Meier.

Park, L., & Park, F. ([1962]1973). *Anatomy of Big Business*. James Lewis & Samuel.

Peng, M.W., Au, K., & Wang, D.Y.L. (2001). Interlocking directorates as corporate governance in Third World multinationals : theory and evidence from Thailand. *Asia Pacific Journal of Management*, 18(2), 161–181.

Pennings, J.M. (1980). *Interlocking directorates: origins and consequences of connections among organizations' boards of directors*. Jossey-Bass.

Perlo, V. (1957). *The empire of high finance*. International.

Pfeffer, J. (1987). A resource dependence perspective on interorganizational relations. In M. S. Mizruchi & M. Schwartz (Eds.), *Intercorporate relations: the structural analysis of business* (pp. 22–55). Cambridge University Press.

Piédalue, G. (1976). Les groupes financiers au Canada 1900–1930 : Étude préliminaire. *Revue d'histoire de l'Amérique française*, 30(1), 3–34.

Porter, J. (1956). Concentration of economic power and the economic elite in Canada. *Canadian Journal of Economics and Political Science*, 22(2), 199–220.

Richardson, R.J. (1987). Directorship interlocks and corporate profitability. *Administrative Science Quarterly*, 32(3), 367–386.

Sapinski, J.P. (2015). Climate capitalism and the global corporate elite network. *Environmental Sociology*, 1(4), 268–279.

Sapinski, J.P. (2016). Constructing climate capitalism: corporate power and the global climate policy-planning network. *Global Networks*, 16(1), 89–111.

Scott, J. (1985a). *Corporations, classes, and capitalism* (2nd ed.). St Martin's Press.

Scott, J. (1985b). Theoretical framework and research design. In F.N. Stokman, R. Ziegler & J. Scott (Eds.), *Networks of corporate power: a comparative analysis of ten countries* (pp. 1–19). Polity Press.

Scott, J. (1991). Networks of corporate power: a comparative assessment. *Annual Review of Sociology, 17*, 181–203.

Scott, J. (1997). *Corporate business and capitalist classes*. Oxford University Press.

Scott, J. (2003). Transformations in the British economic elite. *Comparative Sociology, 2*(1), 155–173.

Scott, J. (2008). Modes of power and the re-conceptualization of elites. In M. Savage & K. Williams (Eds.), *Remembering elites* (pp. 27–43). Blackwell.

Scott, J. (2012). Capital mobilization, transnational structures, and capitalist classes. In G. Murray & J. Scott (Eds.), *Financial elites and transnational business: who rules the world?* (pp. 1–26). Edward Elgar.

Sonquist, J.A., & Koenig, T. (1975). Interlocking directorates in the top US corporations: a graph theory approach. *The Insurgent Sociologist, 5*(3), 196–230.

Soref, M., & Zeitlin, M. (1987). Finance capital and the internal structure of the capitalist class in the United States. In M.S. Mizruchi & M. Schwartz (Eds.), *Intercorporate relations: the structural analysis of business* (pp. 56–84). Cambridge University Press.

Stanworth, P., & Giddens, A. (1975). The modern corporate economy: interlocking directorships in Britain, 1906–1970. *Sociological Review, 23*(1), 5–28.

Stark, D., & Vedres, B. (2012). Political holes in the economy: the business network of partisan firms in Hungary. *American Sociological Review, 77*(5), 700–722.

Stearns, L.B., & Mizruchi, M.S. (1986). Broken-tie reconstitution and the functions of interorganizational interlocks: a reexamination. *Administrative Science Quarterly, 31*(4), 522–538.

Steglich, C.E.G., Snijders, T.A.B., & West, P. (2006). Applying SIENA: an illustrative analysis of the coevolution of adolescents' friendship networks, taste in music, and alcohol consumption. *Methodology, 2*, 48–56.

Stokman, F.N., van der Knoop, J., & Wasseur, F.W. (1988). Interlocks in the Netherlands: stability and careers in the period 1960–1980. *Social Networks, 10*, 183–208.

Stokman, F.N., Ziegler, R., & Scott, J. (Eds.) (1985). *Networks of corporate power: a comparative analysis of ten countries*. Polity Press.

Swainson, N. (1980). *The development of corporate capitalism in Kenya 1918–77* (Vol. 1). Heinemann.

Sweezy, P.M. (1953). *The present as history: essays and reviews on capitalism and socialism*. Monthly Review Press.

Useem, M. (1984). *The inner circle: large corporations and the rise of business political activity in the US and UK*. Oxford University Press.

Useem, M., & Karabel, J. (1986). Pathways to top corporate management. *American Sociological Review, 51*(2), 184–200.

Valeeva, D., Heemskerk, E.M., & Takes, F.W. (2020). The duality of firms and directors in board interlock networks: a relational event modeling approach. *Social Networks, 62*, 68–79.

Van de Bunt, G.G., & Groenewegen, P. (2007). An actor-oriented dynamic network approach: the case of interorganizational network evolution. *Organizational Research Methods, 10*, 463–482.

Van der Pijl, K. (1984). *The making of an Atlantic ruling class*. Verso.

Windolf, P. (2002). *Corporate networks in Europe and the United States*. Oxford University Press.

Young, K.L., Goldman, S.K., O'Connor, B., & Chuluun, T. (2020). How white is the global elite? An analysis of race, gender and network structure. *Global Networks, 21*(2), 365–392.

Zeitlin, M. (1974). Corporate ownership and control: the large corporation and the capitalist class. *American Journal of Sociology, 79*(4), 1073–1119.

International Trade Networks

Christina Prell, James Hollway,
Petr Matous, and Yasuyuki Todo

The global economy is a complex, interdependent system, consisting of actors at different levels and scales, linked through a variety of economic activities, agreements and flows (Kali & Reyes, 2007; Snyder & Kick, 1979; Morin et al., 2017). To better understand these complex interrelationships, scholars have increasingly turned to the analytical tools and methods found in social network analysis (Granovetter, 1985; Hafner-Burton et al., 2009; Lloyd et al., 2009; Mahutga & Smith, 2011). Early examples include the use of blockmodelling techniques as a means to ascertain countries' positions within the global economy or 'world system' (e.g., Snyder & Kick, 1979; Breiger, 1981; and see review by Lloyd et al., 2009). Here, questions pertaining to country-level outcomes and between-country differences were explored via ascertaining the positional blocks in which countries were situated, as well as the overall topology (i.e., blockmodel) of the global network. As new network measures and analytical procedures developed, along with datasets at increasing levels of resolution, scholars expanded their enquiries to consider a wider range of questions pertaining to the role of network structure in understanding economic and trade processes. Key to these new developments was the causal role played by networks, and how various processes theorised in the literature could be captured via specified network configurations.

This chapter focuses on international trade and, closely aligned with trade, the international trade agreements. We offer an overview and summary of past and current network studies focusing on international trade and trade agreements at different levels of aggregation. We first introduce readers to the kinds of trade relations reviewed in this chapter, their levels of aggregation, and examples of publicly available datasets. We then introduce readers to empirical network studies on global trade, distinguishing these studies according to questions pertaining to network topology (or global network structure); the mechanisms that give rise to network topology; the topologies or impacts of networks; and how network structure co-evolves alongside nodal attributes such as wealth or democracy.

TRADE RELATIONS AND LEVELS OF AGGREGATION

The trade networks reviewed in this chapter may be distinguished between commodity trade networks and preferential trade agreement (PTA) networks. Commodity trade networks consist of flows of goods and services from one actor (e.g., country, sector, or firm) to another. These flows may be analysed as valued or binary ties (see Chapter 2). As valued ties, a given commodity relation represents the amount of trade (usually in some currency) sent from one actor to another. If analysts wish to treat these ties binarily, then they must transform them from valued ties according to some threshold. Choosing a threshold criterion is an important decision, and scholars should justify their chosen threshold with care. Sensitivity analyses exploring different threshold criteria may be performed to give readers confidence that results are not an artefact of the particular threshold chosen (e.g., Prell & Feng, 2016) or, alternatively, to purposefully explore when a description of the trade network structure might change based on a different threshold value (Kali & Reyes, 2007).

Preferential trade agreement (PTA) networks are generally studied at the country level, and consist of countries' bilateral and/or plurilateral agreements established to govern commodity flows. Since bilateral trade agreement networks are mutual by design (i.e., both countries are participating in the agreement), these PTA networks are studied as undirected one-mode networks. Yet countries may also participate in plurilateral PTAs – that is, agreements among and between larger regional groupings (or blocks) of countries. In such a scenario, countries and their affiliations to plurilateral PTAs may be organised and studied as two-mode (bipartite) networks. Finally, scholars are increasingly advocating combining one-mode bilateral PTA networks among countries together with two-mode networks of countries and their affiliations to plurilateral PTAs to create an interlocking, multilevel network (Hollway, 2022). By doing so, analysts are better able to maintain the structural information found in a dataset consisting of both kinds of agreements (Knoke et al., 2021).

Commodity and PTA relations may be studied in conjunction but, more often, these relations are studied separately. In addition, whereas PTA relations are generally constrained to the country level of analysis, commodity relations may be studied at the country, sector and firm levels.

Table 25.1 below offers an overview of these two kinds of relations at different levels of aggregation. In addition, examples of datasets for each relation are provided.

CLASSIFYING TRADE NETWORK STUDIES: ASKING QUESTIONS ABOUT STRUCTURE AND CAUSALITY

As with other network studies, research questions pertaining to trade networks differ according to the causal nature given to networks (see Chapter 2). Networks can be positioned as the predictor of outcomes (networks as explanans), the outcome of particular drivers (networks as explanandum), or a variable that co-evolves with actors' attributes. This is likewise true of trade networks. In some cases, however, trade network scholars are less interested in explanation and more interested in describing structural features of a given trade network – for example, the network's topology.

In this section, we use these distinctions pertaining to the variety of network-related research questions to organise the trade network literature. We begin with studies that seek to describe the overall topology of trade networks, and then move into studies focusing on networks as explanans versus explanandum and, finally, questions pertaining to co-evolution. In doing so, we note that many studies ask research questions that incorporate two or more of these distinctions (e.g., asking for a description but also an explanation of a network's topology).

Table 25.1 Overview of relations studied by trade network scholars

Level	Relation	Example datasets
Country	Commodities	IMF trade statistics data
	Preferential trade agreements	WTO Regional Trade Agreements Database (rtais.wto.org)
Sector	Commodities/goods	EORA, GTAP (Guan et al., 2020), World input–output database (www.rug.nl/ggdc/valuechain/wiod/)
Firm	Commodities	FactSet supply chain relationships (Kashiwagi et al., 2021; Hyun et al., 2020), Compustat Global

Questions About Network Topology

Studies pertaining to a network's topology seek to describe that topology using descriptive network measures and/or simple digraphs. Such measures include (but are not limited to) degree distributions, density, network size, level of centralisation, and blockmodels. For example, the average degree and/or centralisation of global trade networks have been used to describe the level of economic integration of the overall global economy – that is, a flattening of differences between the economic haves and have-nots (Kali & Reyes, 2007; Kim & Shin, 2002). Elsewhere, network measures have been used to ascertain whether trade networks approximate ideal, stylised networks, such as scale-free networks, which focus on the degree distribution of a network, or small-world network structures, which refer to networks characterised by a high degree of clustering and short average path length (Hearnshaw & Wilson, 2013; Wiedmer & Griffis, 2021; Wilhite, 2001). Such studies link with discussions in complexity science and physics identifying topological regularities shared among networks (e.g., Barabási & Réka, 1999) rather than features unique to particular research contexts. Another idealised structure often investigated by trade scholars is that of a core and a periphery (see Text box 25.1). Here, analysts use blockmodelling techniques to identify the extent to which trade networks resemble a core–periphery structure – that is, one in which a few, highly connected countries occupy the core, leaving the vast majority of countries positioned in the peripheral block, isolated from one another and holding only a few ties with the core (Clark, 2010; Mahutga & Smith, 2011; Prell et al., 2014; Snyder & Kick, 1979). Finally, some trade network scholars have begun theorising how certain trade network topologies, such as a core–periphery or small-world structure, might correspond to robustness, resilience, and responsiveness (Hollway, 2022). In doing so, a number of these studies include additional international relations alongside trade ones to ascertain the network structure (Kick et al., 2022).

Textbox 25.1 Trade networks as a world system

The world systems perspective (WSP) was popularised by Immanuel Wallerstein (1974), who argued that nation-states could be organised according to a hierarchical model, consisting of wealthy, developed *core* countries that produce capital-intensive commodities and dominate the rules of trade, and *peripheral* countries that focus on low-skill, labour-intensive production and are dependent on the core. A number of political economy scholars have since translated this hierarchical model into network terms, arguing that the intuitive ideas found in the WSP regarding the interconnectivity of countries and their positions within this global system could be made more explicit by harnessing network tools. As such, various positional-role analysis and blockmodelling techniques (see Chapter 29 this volume) have been used to assess the extent to which the topology of a given, empirical trade network resembles that of an idealised core–periphery blockmodel, one in which the actors in the core comprise a dense, cohesive block and those in the peripheral are tied to the core, but not to one another. Such a stylised topology is shown in the table below, in which 1s indicate ties and 0s otherwise (within-country ties, expressed on the diagonal, have been ignored). In addition, an example of a core–periphery structure is also displayed, next to the matrix, as a graph.

	A	B	C	D	E	F
A	–	1	1	1	0	0
B	1	–	1	0	0	0
C	1	1	–	1		1
D	1	0	1	–	0	0
E	0	1	0	0	–	0
F	0	0	1	0	0	–

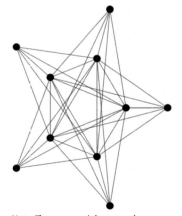

Note: The core–periphery graph was generated using migraph (Hollway, 2021).

In identifying the block positions of countries in a trade network, scholars have used these block positions to explain a variety of country-level outcomes. For example, studies have found that countries positioned in the core tend to experience higher levels of development, including economic growth (Bollen, 1983; Clark, 2010; Mahutga & Smith, 2011; Nemeth & Smith, 1985; Snyder & Kick, 1979; Van Rossem, 1996), higher levels of democracy (Bollen, 1983; Clark, 2012), lower mortality rates (Jorgenson & Burns, 2004; Prell et al., 2015), and less environmental degradation (Burns et al., 1997; Prell et al., 2014; Prell & Feng, 2016; Prew, 2010). Trade scholars have also identified some of the micro processes and network configurations that give rise to this core–periphery structure. For example, longitudinal studies on commodity trade and PTA networks have linked transitivity (or similarly triadic closure) to core–periphery structures (Manger et al., 2012; Prell & Feng, 2016). Countries with ties to a shared third party form a tie with one another as a means to prevent the third party from maintaining a strategic advantage over the otherwise disconnected two parties (Manger et al., 2012). A similar set of findings was found in studies making use of ERGMs for explaining core–periphery structures in PTA networks (Lee & Bai, 2013; Smith & Sarabi, 2022). Another micro tendency linked to core–periphery topology pertains to countries' GDP per capita wealth. Here, countries with similar GDP per capita have been shown to have the tendency of forming or maintaining trade ties with each other over time (Prell & Feng, 2016; Prell et al., 2017). Such a finding supports WSP arguments that wealthy countries tend to form an internally cohesive block among themselves (Clark, 2010; Mahutga & Smith, 2011).

Explaining Networks and Network Structure (Networks as Explanandum)

Increasingly, scholars are moving beyond describing a trade network's topology to consider what drives that topology or other structural features. Key to this discussion is the role played by micro processes or network configurations – small-scale patterns of connections among nodes (Chapter 2). Here, specific configurations are chosen to test for hypothesised tendencies – for example, that trade ties embedded in transitive triads are more likely to be observed than otherwise, or that countries are more likely to form export ties with geographically closer, wealthier countries. Given that such hypothesised tendencies tend to be intertwined, researchers employ stochastic network models designed to handle the interdependencies of network data to test the prevalence, or likelihood, of these specified tendencies, net of one another (see Stadtfeld & Amati, 2021). Such models include exponential random graph models (ERGMs) (Koskinen, this volume), which are typically used on cross-sectional complete network data and test the presence/likelihood of ties (a tie-based model), and stochastic actor-oriented models (SAOMs) (Snijders and Steglich, this volume), which model the co-evolution of networks and nodal attributes as a continuous time process, between discreet waves of observed data, from the view point of the actor (an actor-based model).

An important distinction in specifying network configurations as explanatory variables is whether or not the configuration can be considered *endogenous* – that is, when the presence of ties are driven by inherent structural tendencies of the network, such as the tendency to reciprocate a tie, or *exogenous* – that is, when the presence of a tie is explained by actor or network covariates, such as wealth or geographical distance, and these attributes themselves are assumed to result from mechanisms not included in the model.

Endogenous network configurations. Studies have identified a number of endogenous configurations that explain the presence of trade-related ties (and thus the structure of the network) based on the presence or absence of other such ties. One key endogenous driver is that of *triadic closure* or *transitivity*. For example, Textbox 25.1 mentions studies linking transitivity to the formation of a core–periphery structure, and a number of PTA studies have found support for transitivity overtime (Kinne, 2014; Manger et al., 2012; Manger & Pickup, 2016; Milewicz et al. 2018).

Transitivity is also an endogenous driver found in interfirm networks (Todo & Matous, 2016; Uzzi & Lancaster, 2003) and economic networks more generally (Jackson & Rogers, 2005). For example, Earnest & Wilkinson (2018) found that partners of partners are more likely to be trusted (especially in case of firms that rely on unique inputs or that face high switching costs), and this in turn leads to the formation of interfirm ties at the triadic level, giving rise to a clustered topology.

Another endogenous driver to tie formation is that of *preferential attachment* – the tendency of popular nodes to attract further ties. Preferential attachment has been identified in a number of interfirm studies as a predictor of tie presence (Ahuja et al., 2009; Ahuja et al., 2011; Gulati & Gargiulo, 1999; Madhavan et al., 1998; Matous & Todo, 2016; van de Bunt & Groenewegen, 2007). Goto et al. (2015) found preferential attachment to be an important driver explaining interfirm topological structures such as clustering and scale-freeness, and Koskinen and Lomi (2013) identified preferential attachment as a predictor of international investment flows.

Exogenous covariate network configurations. In addition to endogenous network configurations, trade network scholars also consider the role of covariate configurations as drivers of tie formation. These include various *actor covariates*, which are configurations that include nodal attributes, such as more ties surrounding nodes with a particular attribute or the presence of a tie between two actors sharing similar attributes (i.e., a similarity selection effect). For example, both commodity trade and PTA studies have found evidence that wealthier countries tend to form or maintain ties with one another – that is, a wealth-similarity tendency (Manger & Pickup, 2016; Prell & Feng, 2016; Prell et al., 2017) – and, similarly, countries with higher levels of democracy are more likely to form trade agreements with one another – that is, a so-called democracy-similarity effect (Manger & Pickup, 2016). Finally, studies have also shown evidence for actor covariate interaction effects – for example, that countries characterised as big exporters of land-intensive commodities tend to target their exports towards wealthier countries (Prell et al., 2017).

Relations as explanatory covariates. In addition to nodal characteristics, a number of studies reveal the important role played by other kinds of relations in predicting the presence of a tie. For example, the *gravity model* (GM) argues that the presence of trade tie from country i to j is a function of the economic size of countries (e.g., total GDP) and the geographical distance between them, such that senders of goods (i) are attracted to export their goods to larger economies (as proxied by that country's total GDP), but this tendency decreases as geographical distance between i and j increases (Anderson, 2011).

Empirically, scholars have found evidence for the GM model in commodity trade networks (Dueñas & Fagiolo, 2011; Prell et al., 2017; Prell & Feng, 2016), PTA networks (Esteves & Ploeckl, 2016), and networks of foreign direct investment (Koskinen & Lomi, 2013). Another relational covariate is that of alliances, with past research indicating that alliances are a key predictor for the presence of PTA links (Boehmke et al., 2016). Inoue et al.'s (2018) study on PTA and commodity flows shows how the presence of the former kind of relation is a good predictor of the latter. In the context of interfirm studies, research indicates the importance of prior relationships being good predictors of new ties forming (Gulati, 1995a, 1995b; Gulati & Gargiulo, 1999). Finally, Matous & Todo (2016) show that physical proximity is not always a strong predictor of interfirm tie formation.

Focusing on organisations within the same country and controlling for their geographical distance from one another, the authors demonstrate how firms generally preferred trading partners that already had more trading partners among other firms within the country.

The Outcomes of Trade Networks

Until this point, we have summarised studies that consider how to describe and/or explain network structure. Yet many scholars are also interested in understanding how network structure can explain outcomes, either for individual network members or the network as a whole.

Outcomes for individual nodes. A number of studies highlight the impacts trade and trade-related networks have on individual nodes. For example, as shown in Textbox 25.1, a number of studies on international trade from a world-systems perspective have shown how a country's position in a network's core or periphery can explain a number of country-level outcomes. In addition, they show how the structural positions of countries in a PTA network influences whether commodity trade flows develop between those countries (Inoue et al., 2018). Hollway et al. (2020) find that the position of PTAs as brokers between two otherwise disconnected countries increases the likelihood of environmental clauses being introduced. With regards to interfirm networks, research has found that a firm's operational efficiency is positively associated with the overall density of networks, with firms embedded in denser networks being more efficient, as well as with the local clustering surrounding a firm, with more clustering leading to higher efficiency (Basole et al., 2018). A study of automakers in Japan found that firms that had a high number of outgoing links to other firms tended to perform better, suggesting benefits of access to multiple diverse partners for productivity (Matous & Todo, 2017). Other studies imply that densely knit networks are not always desirable for firms because of the cost of redundant relationships (Kim et al., 2011). Schilling and Phelps (2007) show that those firms that are embedded in highly clustered networks and, simultaneously, linked via long paths to non-redundant others, tend to be more innovative than otherwise. Here, the underlying mechanism is seen to be that such firms can access diverse pools of knowledge and build on them within their local, cohesive community of collaborators. Overall, how much redundancy is optimal remains an open question (Shashi et al., 2020).

Outcomes for networks: resilience and vulnerability. A growing number of trade studies consider how structural features of a network can explain why a given network, or node within the network, can absorb or bounce back from an exogenous crisis or shock. In other words, such studies consider how network structure can explain resilience, for the network as a whole or for particular nodes or ties in the network (Hollway, 2022).

For example, research has shown that frequent, clustered interactions can, over time, increase the resilience of an interfirm network to small shocks by diffusing the impact of those shocks across a wider set of actors (Acemoglu et al., 2015). Interfirm networks have also been shown to be highly dynamic, and in this way resilient, in the aftermath of natural disasters, as broken supply links need to be quickly substituted (Pires Ribeiro & Barbosa-Povoa, 2018). Here, the degree of partner substitutability at the micro-level is a crucial source of resilience at the system level (Barrot & Sauvagnat, 2016; Inoue & Todo, 2019; Nuss et al., 2016). In addition, diversifying supply chain partners by creating topologically and geographically long links can also improve interfirm resilience, as such long paths enable firms to reach outside local regions and network cliques in which the impacts of shocks can concentrate.

A number of studies also consider how exogenous shocks can translate into vulnerability, either on the individual nodal level, network level, or both. For example, a network study on the US economy showed how an exogenous shock such as a spike in oil prices can make central sectors – such as plastics and transportation – vulnerable, which in turn impacts the nation's entire economy (Kerschner et al. 2013). Similarly, interfirm studies have shown that highly central firms exacerbate the negative impacts of natural disasters experienced along the supply chain, and that cycles within the interfirm network (as opposed to hierarchical, tree-like structures) can also facilitate the circulation of price shocks within the system and magnify these shocks' propagation (Inoue & Todo, 2019). Finally, they have shown that the robustness of the overall supply network is negatively associated with its average path length – that is, as the average path length between suppliers increases, the network's overall ability to bounce back from a disruption decreases.

These studies on both the vulnerability and resilience of trade networks to exogenous shocks point towards the need for further research on how local or region-specific shocks, such as an earthquake, may impact the global trade network. Such research is forthcoming, given the compilation of international databases that capture boundary-crossing interfirm and intersectoral links. Early studies suggest that international supply chains are more resilient than national or localised ones, as firms operating at global scales may have more opportunities for partner substitution from the global pool when necessary (Kashiwagi et al., 2021).

Questions of Co-evolution

More recently, the literature has moved to consider how networks and attributes may be understood and studied as co-evolutionary processes. For example, studies on PTA networks show how agreements co-evolve with other economic instruments, such as countries' adoption of the gold standard (Esteves & Ploeckl, 2016). Manger and Pickup (2016) use SAOMs to tease apart the co-evolution of trade agreements and countries' democratic behaviour. The authors argued that trade agreements make it more difficult for autocrats to solely distribute rents, and hence trade agreements may serve as channels or pipes of influence for democratisation or democracy consolidation. Manger and Pickup (2016) identify evidence for the causal arrow going in both directions: democracies are more likely to establish trade agreements, but trade agreements also drive (further) democratisation. In terms of the environment, Prell et al. (2017) found evidence for trade ties and land degradation to co-evolve in a vicious feedback loop with one another, where countries exporting more land-intensive commodities tend to form ties with wealthier others and countries with many export ties to wealthier others tend to increase or maintain their high levels of land-intensive exports.

Sometimes co-evolution studies consider how a trade agreement network might co-evolve with another network. For example, Milewicz et al. (2018) use multiplex SAOMs to study how networks of bilateral and plurilateral PTAs co-evolve and, in addition, how these networks co-evolve with additional non-trade issues such as human rights, democracy, environment, corruption, and labour standards. The authors find evidence for pathways of influence between these four networks. Countries' participation in plurilateral PTAs leads to plurilateral PTAs that include non-trade issues and bilateral PTAs that don't, and being in bilateral PTAs that don't include non-trade issues leads to participation in bilateral and plurilateral PTAs that do. Once countries join plurilateral PTAs with non-trade issues though, both types of bilateral PTAs become less likely.

Htwe et al. (2020) also make use of a multiplex SAOM to disentangle how networks of regional trade agreements and bilateral investment treaties co-evolve. They find that countries are more likely to move from bilateral to regional agreements than vice versa, and that countries with many bilateral and regional agreements tend to be attractive bilateral partners. Further, they found that existing regional agreements make more regional agreements less likely. Another set of multiplex ties that continually attracts attention is that of trade, democracy and peace. Democratic Peace Theory is used as a framework to argue that one mechanism by which democratic countries are less likely to go to war, at least with each other, is that they are locked into mutually beneficial trade arrangements, the suspension of which for war would be unattractively costly (Hafner-Burton & Montgomery, 2012). Mon et al. (2019) are interested in the relationship between free trade agreements (FTAs) and political alliances. They also employ a multiplex SAOM to understand how these two types of agreement networks co-evolve. They find that while alliances are likely to lead to FTAs, FTAs do not necessarily lead to alliances and that, while a country's FTA popularity is attractive for both FTAs and alliances, alliance popularity is only attractive for further alliances. Finally, Matous and Todo (2017) tested how network topology and network diffusion co-evolved with organisational performance and found that the restructuring of Japanese automakers' production networks led to improved performance over time, but not the reverse. In other words, their longitudinal analysis suggested that the directly observable association between improved performance and diverse supply chains was not driven by increasing production necessitating expansion of supply networks but that improved performance followed changes in the firms' production networks.

SUMMARY AND FUTURE OUTLOOK

This chapter gave an overview of network studies on international trade at different levels of aggregation. A key aim in conducting this review has been to illustrate how scholars have positioned networks as explanatory, outcome, and/or co-evolutionary variables. We also highlight the different levels of aggregation at which trade network studies occur – that is, country and firm. Network scholars are increasingly investigating trade networks as multilevel, complex systems. Two complementary developments are making multilevel and co-evolutionary work more in common. First, the rise in stochastic models has empowered analysts to answer more complex questions and capture a range of specific complementary and/or competing tendencies through specifying network configurations and their combination. We expect that as computational advances are made for handling large datasets at higher levels of resolution, more studies will explore the interdependencies of trade and trade-related networks, across time, levels, and levels of aggregation. Second, longitudinal trade data is increasingly collected at higher levels of resolution, which not only helps analysts ask questions about co-evolution, but also ask questions about how actors and networks in one level may be embedded and/or influenced by those in another. Taken together, the increased sophistication in network tools and datasets places current trade network scholars in a strong position to further test and explore theoretical concepts on the interdependencies of a global economy and society. As the field progresses, we expect more innovation to take place on a theoretical front, with scholars considering how best to use the data and methods currently available to spur theoretically innovative questions.

REFERENCES

Acemoglu, D., Ozdaglar, A., & Tahbaz-Salehi, A. (2015). Networks, shocks, and systemic risk. NBER Working Paper (20931), 1–36.

Ahuja, G., Polidoro, F., & Mitchell, W. (2009). Structural homophily or social asymmetry? The formation of alliances by poorly embedded firms. *Strategic Management Journal*, *30*(9), 941–958. doi:10.1002/smj.774

Ahuja, G., Soda, G., & Zaheer, A. (2011). The genesis and dynamics of organizational networks. *Organization Science*, *23*(2), 434–448. doi:10.1287/orsc.1110.0695

Alter, K.J., & Meunier, S. (2009). The politics of international regime complexity. *Perspectives on Politics*, *7*(1), 13–24. doi.org/10.1017/S1537592709090033

Anderson, J. E. (2011). The gravity model. *Annual Review of Economics*, *3*(1), 133–160.

Barabási A.-L. & Réka, A. (1999). Emergence of scaling in random networks. *Science*, *286*(5439), 509–512. doi.org/10.1126/science.286.5439.509

Barrot, J.-N., & Sauvagnat, J. (2016). Input specificity and the propagation of idiosyncratic shocks in production networks. *Quarterly Journal of Economics*, *131*(3), 1543–1592. doi:10.1093/qje/qjw018

Basole, R.C., Ghosh, S., & Hora, M.S. (2018). Supply network structure and firm performance: evidence from the electronics industry. *IEEE Transactions on Engineering Management*, *65*(1), 141–154. doi:10.1109/TEM.2017.2758319

Boehmke, F.J., Chyzh, O., & Thies, C.G. (2016). Addressing endogeneity in actor-specific network measures. *Political Science Research and Methods*, 4(1), 123–149.

Bollen, K. (1983). World system position, dependency, and democracy: the cross-national evidence. *American Sociological Review*, 48(4), 468–479. doi.org/10.2307/2117715

Borgatti, S.P., & Foster, P.C. (2003). The network paradigm in organizational research: a review and typology. *Journal of Management*, 29(6), 991–1013. doi.org/10.1016/S0149-2063_03_00087-4

Burns, T.P., Davis, B.L., & Kick, E.L. (1997). Position in the world-system and national emissions of greenhouse gases. *Journal of World-Systems Research*, 3(432), 66.

Breiger, R. (1981). Structures of economic interdependence among nations. In P.M. Blaue & R.K. Merton (Eds.), *Continuities in structural inquiry* (pp. 353–379). Sage.

Carvalho, V.M., Nirei, M., Saito, Y.U., & Tahbaz-Salehi, A. (2020). Supply chain disruptions: evidence from the great East Japan earthquake. *Quarterly Journal of Economics*, 136(2), 1255–1321. doi:10.1093/qje/qjaa044

Chang, E.C.C., & Wu, W.-C. (2016). Preferential trade agreements, income inequality, and authoritarian survival. *Political Research Quarterly*, 69(2), 281–294. doi.org/10.1177/1065912916636688

Clark, R. (2010). World-system mobility and economic growth, 1980–2000. *Social Forces*, 88(3), 1123–1151.

Clark, R. (2012). World-system position and democracy, 1972–2008. *International Journal of Comparative Sociology*, 53(5–6), 367–399. doi.org/10.1177/0020715212470122

Dueñas, M., & Fagiolo, G. (2011). Modeling the international-trade network: a gravity approach. *arXiv*, 1112.2867v1.

Earnest, D.C., & Wilkinson, I.F. (2018). An agent based model of the evolution of supplier networks. *Computational and Mathematical Organization Theory*, 24(1), 112–144. doi:10.1007/s10588-017-9249-1

Esteves, R., & Ploeckl, F. (2016). Gold and trade: an empirical simulation approach. *Conference Proceedings*. 33.

Goto, H., Takayasu, H., & Takayasu, M. (2015). Empirical analysis of firm-dynamics on Japanese interfirm trade network. In Takayasu, H., Ito, N., Noda, I., Takayasu, M. (Eds.), *Proceedings of the International Conference on Social Modeling and Simulation, plus Econophysics Colloquium 2014. Springer Proceedings in Complexity*. Springer.

Granovetter, M. (1985). Economic action and social structure: the problem of embeddedness. *American Journal of Sociology*, 91(3), 481–510. doi:10.2307/2780199

Guan, D., Wang, D., Hallegatte, S., Davis, S.J., Huo, J., Li, S., Bai, Y., Lei, T., Xue, Q., & Coffman, D.M. (2020). Global supply-chain effects of Covid-19 control measures. *Nature Human Behaviour*, 4, 577–587. doi: 10.1038/s41562-020-0896-8

Gulati, R. (1995a). Does familiarity breed trust? The Implications of repeated ties for contractual choice in alliances. *Academy of Management Journal*, 38(1), 85–112. doi:10.2307/256729

Gulati, R. (1995b). Social structure and alliance formation patterns: a longitudinal analysis. *Administrative Science Quarterly*, 40(4), 619–652. doi:10.2307/2393756

Gulati, R., & Gargiulo, M. (1999). Where do interorganizational networks come from? *American Journal of Sociology*, 104(5), 1439–1493. doi:10.1086/210179

Hafner-Burton, E.M., & Montgomery, A.H. (2012). War, trade, and distrust: why trade agreements don't always keep the peace. *Conflict Management and Peace Science*, 29(3), 257–278. doi.org/10.1177/0738894212443342

Hafner-Burton, E.M., Kahler, M., & Montgomery, A.H. (2009). Network analysis for international relations. *International Organization*, 63(3), 559–592. doi.org/10.1017/S0020818309090195

Hearnshaw, E.J.S., & Wilson, M.M.J. (2013). A complex network approach to supply chain network theory. *International Journal of Operations and Production Management*, 33(4), 442–469. doi:10.1108/01443571311307343

Hollway, J. (2021). migraph: tools for multimodal and multilevel network analysis, Version 0.8.13.

Hollway, J. (2022). A framework for resilience of and in international networks. In E. Lazega, T.A.B. Snijders & R. Wittek (Eds.), *A research agenda for social networks and social resilience* (pp. 101–114). Edward Elgar.

Hollway, J., Morin, J.-F., & Pauwelyn, J. (2020). Structural conditions for novelty: the introduction of new environmental clauses to the trade regime complex. *International Environmental Agreements: Politics, Law and Economics*, 20(1), 61–83. doi.org/10.1007/s10784-019-09464-5

Htwe, N.N., Lim, S., & Kakinaka, M. (2020). The coevolution of trade agreements and investment treaties: some evidence from network analysis. *Social Networks*, 61, 34–52. doi.org/10.1016/j.socnet.2019.08.005

Hyun, J., Kim, D., & Shin, S.-R. (2020). The role of global connectedness and market power in crises: firm-level evidence from the Covid-19 pandemic. *Covid Economics: Vetted and Real-Time Papers*, 49, 148–171.

Inoue, S., Ito, N., & Higuchi, T. (2018). Trade structure change in the Asia-Pacific region: network analysis of trade flow and trade agreements. *Japanese*

Journal of Agricultural Economics, 20, 45–50. doi.org/10.18480/jjae.20.0_45

Inoue, H., & Todo, Y. (2019). Firm-level propagation of shocks through supply-chain networks. *Nature Sustainability*, 2(9), 841–847. doi:10.1038/s41893-019-0351-x

Jackson, Matthew O., and Brian W. Rogers. 2005. "The Economics of Small Worlds." *Journal of the European Economic Association*, 3(2–3): 617

Jorgenson, A.K., & Burns, T.P. (2004). Globalization, the environment, and infant mortality: a cross national study. *Humbolt Journal of Social Relations*, 28, 7–52.

Kali, R., & Reyes, J. (2007). The architecture of globalization: a network approach to international economic integration. *Journal of International Business Studies*, 38(4), 595–620.

Kashiwagi, Y., Todo, Y., & Matous, P. (2021). Propagation of economic shocks through global supply chains: evidence from Hurricane Sandy. *Review of International Economics*, 29(5), 1186–1220. doi:doi.org/10.1111/roie.12541

Kerschner, C., Prell, C., Feng, K., & Hubacek, K. (2013). Economic vulnerability to peak oil. *Global Environmental Change*, 23, 1424–1433.

Kick, E.L., & Davis, B.L. (2001). World-system structure and change: an analysis of global networks and economic growth across two time periods. *American Behavioral Scientist*, 44(10), 1561–1578. doi.org/10.1177/00027640121958050

Kim, S., & Shin, E.H. (2002). A longitudinal analysis of globalization and regionalization in international trade: a social network approach. *Social Forces*, 81(2), 445–471.

Kim, Y., Choi, T.Y., Yan, T., & Dooley, K. (2011). Structural investigation of supply networks: a social network analysis approach. *Journal of Operations Management*, 29(3), 194–211. doi:doi.org/10.1016/j.jom.2010.11.001

Kinne, B.J. (2014). Dependent diplomacy: signaling, strategy, and prestige in the diplomatic network. *International Studies Quarterly*, 58(2), 247–259.

Koka, B.R., Madhavan, R., & Prescott, J.E. (2006). The evolution of interfirm networks: environmental effects on patterns of network change. *Academy of Management Review*, 31(3), 721–737. doi:10.5465/amr.2006.21318927

Koskinen, J., & Lomi, A. (2013). The local structure of globalization. *Journal of Statistical Physics*, 151(3–4), 523–548.

Knoke, D., Diani, M., Hollway, J., & Christopoulos, D. (2021). *Multimodal political networks*. Cambridge University Press.

Lee, T., & Bai, B.-I. (2013). Network analysis of free trade agreements. *Korean Journal of International Studies*, 11(2), 263–293. doi:dx.doi.org/10.1016/j.socnet.2010.10.005

Lloyd, P., Mahutga, M.C., & De Leeuw, J. (2009). Looking back and forging ahead: thirty years of social network research on the world-system. *Journal of World-Systems Research*, 15(1), 48–85. doi.org/10.5195/jwsr.2009.335

Madhavan, R., Koka, B.R., & Prescott, J.E. (1998). Networks in transition: how industry events (re) shape interfirm relationships. *Strategic Management Journal*, 19(5), 439–459. doi:10.1002/(SICI)1097-0266(199805)19:5<439::AID-DIA952>3.0.CO;2-2

Mahutga, M.C., & Smith, D.A. (2011). Globalization, the structure of the world economy and economic development. *Social Science Research*, 40(1), 257–272.

Manger, M.S., & Pickup, M.A. (2016). The coevolution of trade agreement networks and democracy. *Journal of Conflict Resolution*, 60(1), 164–191.

Manger, M.S., Pickup, M.A., & Snijders, T.A.B. (2012). A hierarchy of preferences: a longitudinal network analysis approach to PTA formation. *Journal of Conflict Resolution*, 56(5), 853–878.

Matous, P., & Todo, Y. (2016). Energy and resilience: the effects of endogenous interdependencies on trade network formation across space among major Japanese firms. *Network Science*, 4(2), 141–163. doi:10.1017/nws.2015.37

Matous, P., & Todo, Y. (2017). Analyzing the coevolution of interorganizational networks and organizational performance: automakers' production networks in Japan. *Applied Network Science*, 2(1), 5. doi:10.1007/s41109-017-0024-5

Milewicz, K., Hollway, J., Peacock, C., & Snidal, D. (2018). Beyond trade: the expanding scope of the nontrade agenda in trade agreements. *Journal of Conflict Resolution*, 62(4), 743–773. doi.org/10.1177/0022002716662687

Mon, Y.Y., Lim, S., & Kakinaka, M. (2019). Multiplex relations between states: coevolution of trade agreements and political alliances. *Sustainability*, 11(14), 3911. doi.org/10.3390/su11143911

Morin, J.F., Pauwelyn, J., & Hollway, J. (2017). The trade regime as a complex adaptive system: exploration and exploitation of environmental norms in trade agreements. *Journal of International Economic Law*, 20(2), 365–390. doi.org/10.1093/jiel/jgx013

Nair, A., & Vidal, J.M. (2011). Supply network topology and robustness against disruptions: an investigation using multi-agent model. *International Journal of Production Research*, 49(5), 1391–1404. doi:10.1080/00207543.2010.518744

Nemeth, R.J., & Smith, D.A. (1985). International trade and world-system structure: a multiple network analysis. *Review (Fernand Braudel Center)*, 8(4), 517–560.

Nuss, P., Graedel, T.E., Alonso, E., & Carroll, A. (2016). Mapping supply chain risk by network analysis of product platforms. *Sustainable Materials and Technologies*, *10*, 14–22. doi:doi.org/10.1016/j.susmat.2016.10.002

Pires Ribeiro, J., & Barbosa-Povoa, A. (2018). Supply chain resilience: definitions and quantitative modelling approaches: a literature review. *Computers and Industrial Engineering*, *115*, 109–122. doi:doi.org/10.1016/j.cie.2017.11.006

Prell, C., & Feng, K. (2016). The evolution of global trade and impacts on countries' carbon trade imbalances. *Social Networks*, *46*, 87–100.

Prell, C., Feng, K., Sun, L., Geores, M., & Hubacek, K. (2014). The economic gains and environmental losses of US consumption: a world-systems and input-output approach. *Social Forces*, *93*(1), 405–428.

Prell, C., Sun L, Feng K, Myroniuk, TW (2015). Inequalities in global trade: a cross-country comparison of trade network position, economic wealth, pollution and mortality. *PLoS ONE* 10(12): e0144453. doi:10.1371/journal.pone.0144453.

Prell, C., Sun, L., Feng, K., He, J., & Hubacek, K. (2017). Uncovering the spatially distant feedback loops of global trade: a network and input-output approach. *Science of the Total Environment*, *586*, 401–408. doi.org/10.1016/j.scitotenv.2016.11.202

Prew, P. (2010). World-economy centrality and carbon dioxide emissions: a new look at the position in the capitalist world-system and environmental pollution. *Journal of World-Systems Research*, *16*(2), 162–191.

Schilling, M.A., & Phelps, C.C. (2007). Interfirm collaboration networks: the impact of large-scale network structure on firm innovation. *Management Science*, *53*(7), 1113–1126. doi:10.1287/mnsc.1060.0624

Shashi, Centobelli, P., Cerchione, R., & Ertz, M. (2020). Managing supply chain resilience to pursue business and environmental strategies. *Business Strategy and the Environment*, *29*(3), 1215–1246. doi:doi.org/10.1002/bse.2428

Smith, M., & Sarabi, Y. (2022). How does the behaviour of the core differ from the periphery? An international trade network analysis. *Social Networks*, *70*, 1–15. doi.org/10.1016/j.socnet.2021.11.001

Snyder, D., & Kick, E.L. (1979). Structural position in the world system and economic growth, 1955–1970: a multiple-network analysis of transnational interactions. *American Journal of Sociology*, *84*(5), 1096–1126. doi.org/10.1086/226902

Stadtfeld, C., & Amati, V. (2021). Network mechanisms and network models. In G. Manzo (Ed.), *Research handbook on analytical sociology* (pp. 432–452). Edward Elgar.

Uzzi, B., & Lancaster, R. (2003). Relational embeddedness and learning: the case of bank loan managers and their clients. *Management Science*, *49*(4), 383–399.

van de Bunt, G.G., & Groenewegen, P. (2007). An actor-oriented dynamic network approach: the case of interorganizational network evolution. *Organizational Research Methods*, *10*(3), 463–482. doi:10.1177/1094428107300203

Van Rossem, R. (1996). The world system paradigm as general theory of development: a cross-national test. *American Sociological Review*, 61(3), 508–527. doi.org/10.2307/2096362

Wallerstein, I.M. (1974). *The modern world-system*. Academic Press.

Wiedmer, R., & Griffis, S.E. (2021). Structural characteristics of complex supply chain networks. *Journal of Business Logistics*, *42*(2), 264–290. doi:doi.org/10.1111/jbl.12283

Wilhite, A. (2001). Bilateral trade and 'small-world' networks. *Computational Economics*, *18*, 49–64.

PART 3
Concepts and Methods

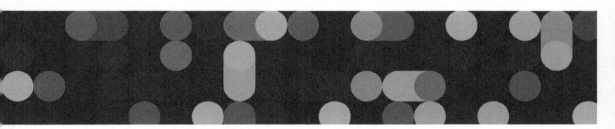

Centrality

Martin G. Everett and Steve P. Borgatti

1 INTRODUCTION

There is very little consensus as to what constitutes a centrality measure beyond the rather vague notion that it is a structural measure of importance. As a consequence, there are already a plethora of measures, with new ones being proposed all of the time. In many instances these so-called 'new measures' have already been proposed by others but in a different context or using a superficially different but equivalent formulation. It is therefore not possible in this chapter to give a comprehensive review of centrality measures and their applications. The paper by Lü et al. (2016) makes a good attempt to do just that and it cites 391 papers. A common approach when proposing a new measure is to focus on some ad hoc concept of importance, develop a measure of this concept and then demonstrate it captures this on a few networks and show that a small number of other measures produce different results, an easy task as there are so many to choose from. As we have no means of assessing what constitutes a centrality measure, the field is inundated with new measures all of the time. This is compounded by the fact that they are often given fanciful names such as influence, prominence, status, power and so on, even though it is an empirical question how a graph-theoretic concept like centrality relates to these variables in any given context.

There have been some attempts to mathematically formalise centrality measures by taking an axiomatic approach. For example, Sabidussi (1966) suggested five properties that every centrality measure should observe. These were things like adding a tie to a node should always increase its centrality; and adding a tie anywhere else in the network should never reduce a node's centrality. Unfortunately, the only measure to pass all five criteria was his own, a form of closeness centrality. More recently, Boldi and Vigna (2014) suggest using three axioms to assess measures. The first two axioms involve how measures perform when changes are made to a graph that initially contains a clique and a cycle. The first axiom is concerned with changes in the relative size of the two components. The second axiom is concerned with adding ties to the cycle component. The third simply states that the addition of an edge increases centrality. Again, of the measures they consider, only a closeness type measure satisfies all three axioms. The fact that well-known and well-used centrality measures such as betweenness, degree and eigenvector do not satisfy these axioms undermines this kind of approach.

The one property that needs to be obeyed by any centrality measure is that isomorphic nodes should always receive the same score. In essence this is a direct consequence of the accepted idea that centrality is a structural measure. Of course, one could envisage measures that go beyond structural properties and include, say, node attributes. In this case we would simply extend the isomorphism concept to include equality of the attributes as well as structural isomorphism.

There are two further properties that are generally accepted to be important for large classes of centrality measures. The first one is that the centre of a star will achieve the highest possible centrality value (Freeman, 1979). It would seem natural to assume that if an individual is directly connected to everyone else and there are no other connections then this individual is in the strongest possible position and should therefore achieve maximum centrality. The assumption here is that being better connected is advantageous. However, if the relation was, say, dislike then being the only person disliked and by everyone would not be a good position. Consequently, centrality measures designed for negative type relations, such as PN centrality (Everett & Borgatti, 2014), should not obey this rule. From this it is clear that the nature of the relation is of importance when considering centrality properties.

The second property is more complex. The open neighbourhood of a node v is the set of all the nodes adjacent to v and is denoted by $N(v)$. If we include v in the set, it is called the closed neighbourhood of v and is denoted by $N[v]$. A node u is said to dominate a node v if $N[u] \supseteq N(v)$, meaning that the open neighbourhood of v is included in the closed neighbourhood of u. A centrality measure c is said to be *neighbourhood preserving* if whenever u dominates v, then $c(u) \geq c(v)$ (Schoch & Brandes, 2016). This implies that, given a graph in which there are some nodes that satisfy neighbourhood inclusion, then the centrality ranking is predetermined. Of the centrality measures commonly used in social networks, the only one that does not obey this property is Bonacich's (1987) beta centrality (also known as Bonacich power), but only when beta is negative. Bonacich suggests using negative beta when being connected to more central actors is a disadvantage and he gives the example of exchange networks (Cook et al., 1983). It is not advantageous to trade with an actor who has many alternatives, especially if you do not yourself have alternatives. We see again that it is the nature of the relation and/or the social context that is important when we consider this property. It should be noted that there exist graphs for which every pair of nodes satisfy neighbourhood inclusion, so the ranking of nodes by almost every centrality measure is completely determined regardless of which measure is used.

It is also possible to have graphs for which no pairs of nodes satisfy the inclusion property, in which case the centrality rankings across measures can be quite independent.

These two properties are therefore best when centrality is applied to graphs representing relations in which being better connected is seen as being advantageous. The star property merely states that in this situation a node at the centre of the star has the maximum possible score. It does not say that this is uniquely true, that is that the only way a node can achieve the highest score is to be at the centre of a star, although this is the case for a number of measures. A simple example where this is not the case would be degree: in a complete graph, for example, every node achieves the highest score. The neighbourhood preserving property helps us understand why rankings are similar for certain classes of graph. Most standard measures have this property and so it is reasonable to expect any new measures proposed to also have this property.

This chapter presents three perspectives on centrality, which we refer to as the 'walk structure perspective', the 'induced centrality perspective' and the 'flow outcomes perspective' (Borgatti & Everett, 2020). In addition, we present a final section on 'data-driven issues'. Our comments should not be seen as competing frameworks but as conceptual ideas that help provide a deeper insight into centrality and bring some semblance of order to a rather chaotic area.

2 THE WALK STRUCTURE PERSPECTIVE

For ease of exposition, we shall first assume that all graphs are simple, undirected and connected. It is a relatively simple matter to extend any of the ideas in the following sections to directed and disconnected graphs. Since the graph is connected, it is possible to get from any node to any other node by a sequence of adjacent edges referred to as walks. This means that any node has the potential to affect any other node in the network. However, the walk structure of the network will determine how much influence a particular node has over the rest of the network, and this is the basis of the walk perspective.

Recall a walk is a collection of adjacent edges such as A-B-C-D-B-C. In this example, we see that the B-C edge has been used twice. A walk in which no edge is repeated is a trail. For example, A-B-C-D-B is a trail. Note that it has a repeated node. A path is a walk in which no node is repeated such as A-B-C-D. Clearly any path is a walk and a trail, and any trail is a walk. The length of a walk is the number of edges it contains, and since walks are unrestricted, they can be of infinite length (unlike paths and trails). A shortest walk between a pair of nodes is called a geodesic path or simply a geodesic. Note there can be more than one geodesic connecting any pair of vertices.

The walk structure perspective says that what a centrality measure measures is the involvement of a node in the walk structure of a graph. The more involvement, the more central. How measures differ is in what kinds of walks they pay attention to – unrestricted walks, trails, paths, geodesics – and what property of the walks they focus on (e.g., their number or their length). The perspective also pays attention to the role of the node in these walks. Are they starting/ending points or interior nodes in the sequence? We shall refer to measures focusing on the former as radial measures and measures focusing on the latter as medial measures.

Let us look at various measures of centrality in light of these different walk properties. Degree is the number of edges incident to a particular node. To view this in terms of the walk structure perspective, we note that an edge is simply a path of length 1. So, degree centrality counts the number of paths of length 1 that emanate from (or terminate at) a node. Note that degree is a radial measure: we are counting paths that emanate from (or terminate at) a node.

Both Sabidussi (1966) and Freeman (1979) define closeness as the sum of graph-theoretic distances from a node to all others, where distance is defined as the length of a geodesic connecting two nodes. The standard closeness measure for node i can be defined as $\Sigma_j d_{ij}$ where d_{ij} is the distance from i to j. Since closeness is an inverse measure of centrality (larger numbers indicate less centrality), an alternative is average reciprocal closeness: $(n-1)^{-1} \Sigma_j d_{ij}$. Both measures of closeness are radial measures like degree but differ from degree in that, instead of counting paths, they assess their typical length. We can see that both degree and closeness make use of length, but in very different ways. Degree uses length to bound the set of paths to be considered (paths of length 1), and then counts them. Closeness uses length to both bound the set of paths (they must be geodesics) and then assess the typical length.

Agneessens et al. (2017) offer a variant of average reciprocal closeness, generalised closeness, that yields a weighted average of distances. This is accomplished by adding a negative exponent to the distances: when the exponent is large, the measure weights short distances more than long ones, as shown in equation (1).

$$c_i(\delta) = \frac{\Sigma_j d_{ij}^{-\delta}}{n-1} \quad (1)$$

When the δ exponent is 1, the measure reduces to closeness measured as average reciprocal distance. Of interest in this context is that, while the measure is clearly about assessing typical length rather than counting paths, Agneessens et al. note that, when the exponent is set to infinity, the formula yields degree centrality. This indicates that our distinction between length and count measures is not always clear-cut and may depend on a parameter.

Betweenness centrality is defined by the formula in equation (2) (Freeman, 1979), where g_{ikj} is the number of geodesic paths from i to j that pass through k and g_{ij} is the total number of geodesics connecting i to j.

$$b_k = \Sigma_{i<j} \frac{g_{ikj}}{g_{ij}} \quad (2)$$

The summation is across all possible pairs i and j. The measure calculates the proportion of shortest paths from anywhere to anywhere that pass through k. In short, the measure defines geodesics as the walks of interest, and then looks at how often k is an interior node in these walks. It is therefore a medial measure of centrality, and the property measured is the share of best paths that k sits on. It includes all of the geodesics that have k as an interior node, but it discounts them in proportion to the number of alternative geodesics between the same pair. In addition, software packages such as UCINET (Borgatti et al., 2002) enable to the researcher to limit the length of geodesics counted, or weight longer paths less. Other betweenness measures have been devised that don't rely on geodesics. For example, Newman (2005) proposes random walk betweenness, which uses all walks, rather than just geodesics.

Another betweenness type measure is flow betweenness (Freeman et al., 1991). The measure is based on the number of edge-independent paths between all pairs of nodes that pass through a given node. The unit of analysis is the set of paths from a source node to a target, which are required to be edge-independent. Thus, the subset of paths used for flow betweenness has the property that they do not share edges. In addition, there is no requirement that the paths be geodesics. This issue is explored further in the section on the flow outcome perspective.

Beta centrality, also known as Bonacich power (Bonacich, 1987) extends the earlier work of Katz (1953) and Hubbell (1965). We shall denote Hubbell's centrality by **h**, Katz's centrality by **k** and Bonacich's beta centrality by **b**. If A is an adjacency matrix and β is non-zero and chosen so that it is smaller in modulus than the reciprocal of the modulus of the largest eigenvalue of A, then the measures can be expressed in matrix form as in equation (3).

$$\mathbf{h} = (I - \beta A)^{-1} \mathbf{1}$$
$$\mathbf{k} = \mathbf{h} - \mathbf{1} \quad (3)$$
$$\mathbf{b} = \mathbf{k} / \beta$$

Under the conditions specified, $(I - \beta A)^{-1}$ can be written as the infinite sum shown in equation (4).

$$(I - \beta A)^{-1} = I + \beta A + (\beta A)^2 + (\beta A)^3 + (\beta A)^4 + (\beta A)^5 \ldots \quad (4)$$

Ignoring the betas, this is a sum of powers of the adjacency matrix. The powers of an adjacency matrix have a meaning. The (i,j)th cell of the A^1 matrix (which is just the adjacency matrix) gives the number of walks of exactly length 1 from i to j. The A^2 matrix gives the number of walks of exactly length 2. The A^3 matrix gives the number of walks of exactly length 3, and so on. This means that, $(I - \beta A)^{-1}$ gives the total number of walks of all lengths from every node to every other, attenuated by β, and if we take the row sums, it counts weighted walks. Hubbell's centrality, then, is a frequency measure of the radial type. It follows from equation (3) that beta centrality and Katz are of the same type. Since as β approaches the reciprocal of the largest eigenvalue beta approaches eigenvector, it follows that eigenvector centrality is also of this type.

Many more measures could be discussed, but it seems reasonable to stop here and present a three-dimensional typology of centrality measures (Borgatti & Everett, 2006). The dimensions are clear. The first dimension is what kind of walks the measure incorporates. The choices given here have been geodesics, paths, trails and unrestricted walks. The second dimension is the node's position along these walks: is it an endpoint or an interior node? We have referred to measures relying on the former as radial and measures relying on the latter as medial. The third dimension is what property of the walks we are assessing: their frequency or their length? For some measures, this distinction is clear-cut. The Hubbell centrality family of measures is more challenging. The scores are the number of walks weighted inversely by their length. Hence, they use both frequency and length, and so are indeterminate in this classification. Table 26.1 presents the typology, with the Hubbell centrality measures occupying a mixed category of length and frequency. The table includes a small number of additional measures (with references) that have not been discussed here but have been placed in areas of the table that would have been empty.

Table 26.1 Three-dimensional typology of centrality measures

Radial measures

	Geodesics	Paths	Trails	Walks
Length	Closeness, Average reciprocal closeness, Generalized closeness	Information (Stephenson & Zelen, 1989)		Immediate effects (Friedkin, 1991)
Length × Freq				Katz, Hubbell, beta, eigenvector
Frequency	Degree	k-reach (Borgatti et al., 2006)	Graph-theoretic power index (Markovsky et al., 1988)	

Medial measures

	Geodesics	Paths	Trails	Walks
Length				
Length × Freq				
Frequency	Betweenness	Flow betweenness (Freeman et al., 1991)		Random walk betweenness

3 THE INDUCED CENTRALITY PERSPECTIVE

An induced centrality is one that can be formulated in terms of the contribution a node makes to a particular whole graph property. If this property can be captured by a single number then this can be found by calculating the change in this number when a node is deleted. In order to satisfy the isomorphism property we restrict our whole graph properties to graph invariants – that is, properties that do not depend on the labelling or representation of the graph. Centralities calculated in this way are also known as *vitalities* (Koschützki et al., 2005); the term 'induced centrality' was suggested by Everett & Borgatti (2010).

Flow betweenness (Freeman et al., 1991), already introduced in the previous section, is a good example of an induced centrality measure. If we think of each edge in our graph as a pipe of unit capacity (over which one unit of material can flow per unit of time), then given a pair of nodes we can calculate the maximum number of units that can flow between them in a single unit of time. This is called the maximum flow and it can be shown that this is equal to the number of edge disjoint paths connecting the two chosen nodes. The total flow in the network is the sum of the maximum flows over all pairs of nodes. The flow betweenness of a node is the change in the total flow of the network when the node is deleted.

Flow betweenness was designed as an induced centrality but other well-known centrality measures can also be formulated as induced centralities. If we use the total number of edges as our graph invariant, then the induced centrality will be degree. However, not all well-known centrality measures can be formulated as induced centrality measures. It is relatively easy to find a graph such that the deletion of two non-isomorphic nodes, say x and y, results in isomorphic subgraphs – that is, G-x is isomorphic to G-y (see Everett & Borgatti, 2010). It follows that any induced centrality measure c must be such that $c(x) = c(y)$ in G. Consequently, if we have a measure that differentiates x from y it cannot be an induced centrality measure. The example in Figure 26.1 taken from Everett and Borgatti shows one such example for closeness.

In Figure 26.1, the closeness type measures assign different scores for x and y, with x obtaining a better score, for example average reciprocal closeness is 0.67 for x and 0.66 for y. (It should be noted that all other standard centrality measures give the same values for x and y.)

Any graph invariant can be used to derive a centrality measure although it is desirable for it to have certain properties. First, the invariant needs to be well defined for all graphs so that deletion of a node does not result in a graph for which the invariant is not defined. Diameter would be an invariant that would not satisfy this condition as node removal may disconnect the graph. Second, it should be sensitive to node removal in the sense that the values can change significantly. The size of the largest clique (the clique number of a graph) would be an example of an invariant that is not sensitive. If the graph had two largest cliques of the same size then the invariant would be totally insensitive. Even if it has just one largest clique the induced centrality would only differentiate clique nodes from non-clique nodes.

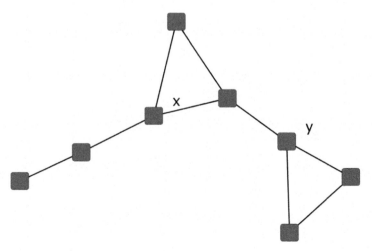

Figure 26.1

Everett and Borgatti (2010) suggest using centrality as the basis for a graph invariant by taking the sum of the centrality scores of all the nodes for a given centrality measure. They then propose using this invariant to obtain an induced centrality which they call *total centrality*. The idea here is that the total centrality measures not only a node's centrality but the centrality it imparts to other nodes in the graph. We now have the original centrality the node possessed (called the *direct centrality*) and the *total centrality*. The difference between the total centrality and the direct centrality is called the *indirect centrality*.

Suppose we use the sum of degree centralities as our invariant. In this case the direct centrality would have the same value as the indirect centrality. This reflects that each edge gives one additional unit of centrality to each of its ends and so this is not very revealing. This is not the case for other centrality measures. In particular, betweenness produces some interesting results. Consider the data collected by Kapferer (1969) on the staff of a mining operation in Africa shown in Figure 26.2 and the centrality scores they obtain in Table 26.2.

We see that pendants Andrew, Henry and Maxwell contribute betweenness to the rest of the network while they have zero betweenness themselves. This is because there are actors on shortest paths between them and other actors. At the other extreme, Abel has a score of 10 for direct betweenness but does not contribute to anyone else's betweenness. The presence of 4 of the actors Godfrey, Soft, Donald and Noah take away betweenness from others, as shown by their negative score. Donald is of particular interest as he removes more centrality from the network than he contributes, resulting in a negative total score.

The induced approach allows us to simply extend the ideas into other contexts. For example, we can use the same approach to define edge centralities. We simply delete edges instead of nodes and do the calculation in the same way as for the node case. In addition, we need not restrict ourselves to a single vertex (or edge). For example, we can delete groups of vertices to obtain group centrality measures (Everett & Borgatti, 1999) to find, say, the centrality of the finance department in an organisation. The same approach could be used if we wanted to take account of a set of invariants rather than just a single invariant. In this case, we can arrange the invariants as a vector and use Euclidean distance or some other inner product as a measure.[1] One key advantage is that this approach allows us to move beyond the standard off-the-shelf measures and base our centrality measure on a graph invariant that fits the research context. This should not be seen in the same light as proposing a new measure, as we assume the chosen graph invariant is something whose properties are understood. In addition, the approach is consistent, so this would not be an entirely new measure.

There is one more important extension of this approach which has become known as the *key player problem*. It was first proposed by Everett and Borgatti (1999) where they called it the *inverse centrality problem* as follows. Given a network find a group of a specified size that has maximal group centrality. The idea was extended by Borgatti (2003, 2006) where he identified two classes of problem that he labelled *key player*

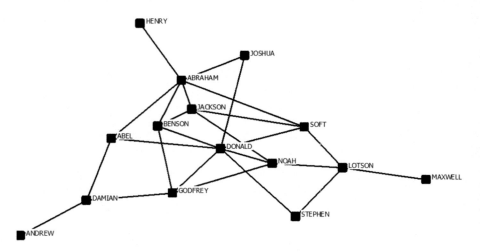

Figure 26.2 Kapferer mining data of uniplex ties

Table 26.2 Total, direct and indirect betweenness of each of the actors in Figure 26.2

Actor	Total	Direct	Indirect
DAMIAN	51	14	38
GODFREY	4	13	−9
SOFT	9	11	−2
LOTSON	47	15	32
JACKSON	13	4	9
JOSHUA	18	1	17
ANDREW	32	0	32
HENRY	24	0	24
ABEL	10	10	0
MAXWELL	30	0	30
ABRAHAM	33	21	12
STEPHEN	19	2	17
NOAH	6	11	−5
BENSON	12	5	7
DONALD	−3	24	−27

positive and *key player negative*. The positive case identifies a subset of actors who are strategically placed to enhance outcomes based on the network structure – for example, in spreading good practice within an organisation. The negative version aims to do the opposite and disrupt the network in some way. An example of that would be to identify a set of individuals in a crime syndicate whose arrest would make the syndicate inoperative. The precise measures that achieve these are not usually the standard ones but ones that are derived with the desired outcome in mind.

4 THE FLOW OUTCOMES PERSPECTIVE

In the justification and application of many centrality measures is the implicit assumption that the measure captures some aspect of something flowing through the network. The flows could be gossip, influence, disease etc., while the outcome captured by the measure could be the time until first arrival, or the certainty of arrival, etc. The flow outcome focuses on the mechanisms and outcomes associated with this flow.

By flow mechanisms we mean the types of trajectory utilised in the flow (such as paths, walks or trails), and how the object that is flowing is duplicated. As examples of these, consider an out-of-print paperback being passed round a book club. The book is passed from member to member, but it is only in one place at one time. In addition, someone would not normally pass the book on to someone they have previously passed the book to. However, another member could pass the book to someone who has already read it, not knowing that it had been passed to that member previously. In this case the book would follow a graph-theoretic trail. Contrast this with the flow of a coin in an economy. The coin will be part of a very long sequence of financial transactions and so could return to someone who has had it before. Indeed, it could happen that the coin was passed from A to B more than once (there would be nothing preventing it). Although unlikely in, say, a large city, this is far more likely in a small remote community. The coin could continue circulating with the same people passing to each other and so it would follow a walk. In this instance a random walk would probably be a better model. In both these cases, the book or the coin are in one place at any one time. This is very different from the content of a Tweet circulating around the Twittersphere via re-Tweet. First, multiple copies of the text will be in existence and these can be passed on to others in the network. Second, someone who receives a Tweet for the second time will usually not re-Tweet it again and so the Tweets will follow trails. Similarly, gossip is copied rather than transferred from person to person. It may also reach a person multiple times, but typically not from the same immediate source. Hence the flow of gossip would also be modelled by trails.

By flow outcomes we mean answers to questions such as: which actor does a coin pass through more often? How long did the book take to get from a given actor to any other randomly chosen actor? How often did each actor receive the same bit of gossip? What are the expected number of re-Tweets to reach a given person? The answers to these questions will depend on the structural position of the node in the network, in other words centrality. Borgatti (2005) explores this idea further using flow outcomes to define a simulation to calculate and verify they give known centrality measures. This approach lays bare the underlying and often unrealistic assumptions of many of the measures.

In particular, Borgatti explores Freeman's closeness and betweenness. To do this he defines a flow mechanism which he calls a package regime in which the packages flow through the network and are only in one place at one time and follow geodesic paths. The first outcome he examines is the time taken to get from a given node to any randomly chosen node in the network assuming that a single step takes a unit of time. This turns out to be the average geodesic distance which is equal to Freeman's closeness divided by $N-1$, where N is the number of nodes. We now make a slight extension to the regime so that if there are a number of alternative geodesics one is randomly selected with uniform probability. We now define an outcome that counts the number of times a package passes through a node. Running a simulation in which this is done a large number of times for every pair of nodes as start and endpoints reproduces betweenness centrality. There are two important points to be made here. The first is that the same regime with different outcomes produces different centrality results. The second point is that it is difficult to think of a real example of flow that follows the package regime. To follow a geodesic not only requires complete knowledge of the network but total control of how the object flows. Consider how a disease flows through a network, it infects direct contacts of infected people and so has multiple manifestations. Assuming that infected individuals develop immunity then it would follow paths but it is highly unlikely these are geodesic.

Borgatti undertakes simulations for a number of mechanisms and betweenness type outcomes on the Padgett and Ansell (1993) Florentine family marriage data. These include the used book, coin and infection regimes already discussed along with some others. Interestingly, with the exception of the package regime which reproduces the betweenness scores, they all place the Medici family with the highest score and the Strozzi family with the second highest. Betweenness and therefore the package regime both keep Medici as the most central but place the Strozzi family in the middle. This is not in keeping with history as the Strozzi family were the most powerful before the rise of the Medici. This indicates that the flow regime inherent in the betweenness model is not consistent with the research context.

We have briefly outlined a few of the possible flow regimes. Table 26.3 gives a brief description of some of the ones we have discussed plus some additional ones.

5 DATA-DRIVEN ISSUES

In discussing the three perspectives we have to a large extent ignored issues related to data. For simplicity we have assumed that the network is a connected binary undirected graph. It should be noted that all three perspectives can be extended to embrace different types of data, often with relative

Table 26.3 Selected flow regimes

Name	Flow	Duplication	Description
Petition	Trail	Single	I have a petition that I pass on to someone else and ask them to sign it but if they have already signed they pass it on to someone else.
Tweet/gossip	Trail	Multiple	I receive a Tweet and re-Tweet but not to someone whom I have already re-Tweeted it to.
Used book	Path	Single	Used book when finished I pass it to a contact who does the same, until someone keeps it. A person does not pass it to someone that has read it.
Disease	Path	Multiple	A disease infects a host, who then infects others. Infected people develop resistance so they can't get it again.
Coin	Walk	Single	A coin moves through the economy until it is lost or retired. It can only be in one place at a time.
Views	Walk	Multiple	My views affect yours, which in turn affect others.
Travel	Geodesic	Single	People travelling prefer to take the shortest route.

ease. Induced centrality needs no modification, as long as we choose graph invariants that are well defined for the type of data we have (and can handle the disconnectedness that may result from removing nodes). For the walk perspective, we have to be careful with measures that assess the length of walks (such as closeness): in disconnected graphs, there is no walk between certain pairs of points and therefore no length to be assessed. For the flow outcome perspective, the main issue is how the data relate to the presumed process governing flow. For example, if the data are valued, do they indicate probabilities that something will flow from A to B? Or perhaps costs? In keeping with the rest of this chapter we give some general approaches and provide specific examples of centrality measures to illustrate the issues.

5.1 Undirected Disconnected Binary Data

From a walk structure perspective, the principal difficulty associated with disconnected graphs lies in measures based on assessing walk length, such as closeness. By definition, a disconnected graph will have pairs of nodes that are not connected by any walk, hence the walk length is undefined. One approach is to assess only the lengths of walks that do exist. Hence, for closeness, we might take the average distance to all reachable nodes. In other words, we calculate the measures within components. This might be of use in certain circumstances, but in general yields a distorted view of a node's centrality. For example, a node forming a connected component of two nodes would have a closeness of 1, making it appear highly central, when in fact the node was highly peripheral. An alternative approach is to assign an arbitrary value to the length of nonexistent walks, such as one plus the diameter of the network. This enables calculations to proceed.

However, this approach would not help us with eigenvector centrality, which in the case of a disconnected graph would assign non-zero scores only to members of the component with the largest eigenvalue (where the scores are calculated separately for each component). All other nodes receive zeros. An ad hoc procedure that can yield plausible scores is to connect all members of each component to all members of every other component by an edge with a tiny edge weight. For instance, Figure 26.3 shows two star-shaped graphs (within which edges have value of 1) joined together such that each intercomponent dyad is assigned an edge

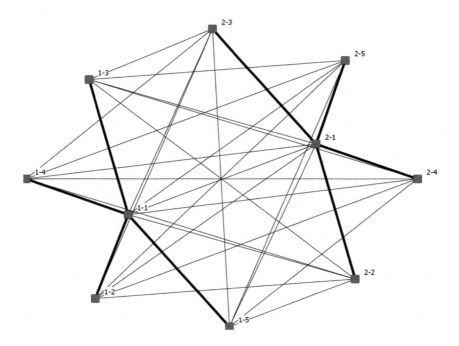

Figure 26.3 Two star-shaped graphs joined. Edges connecting across graphs are assigned an edge weight of 0.1. Edges within each original star have edge weight of 1.0

Table 26.4 Eigenvector scores for combined graph in Figure 26.3

Node	Eigenvector
1–1	0.483
1–2	0.258
1–3	0.258
1–4	0.258
1–5	0.258
2–1	0.483
2–2	0.258
2–3	0.258
2–4	0.258
2–5	0.258

value of 0.1. Table 26.4 shows the resulting eigenvector centrality scores.

Essentially the same considerations apply to induced centralities. If the graph is disconnected, we must ensure that the graph invariant is calculable, either directly or through some artifice such as replacing undefined distances with relatively large values. Note that for induced centralities, it is not just the observed graph that may be disconnected, as the process of removing nodes (or edges) can itself disconnect the graph.

5.2 Directed Binary Data

Betweenness, along with most other medial methods, can be applied to directed data with no particular changes except we now use directed geodesics. We often extend radial measures by having 'in' and 'out' versions of the measure corresponding to incoming and outgoing ties. We would usually interpret these quite differently. On the one hand, if we think about degree in a friendship matrix then actors with high in-degree are popular whereas actors with high out-degree could be seen as gregarious. Closeness would have in-closeness and out-closeness, but if we are using a Freeman type closeness we would also need to make sure the network was strongly connected. On the other hand, average reciprocal closeness would not even require the network to be weakly connected, although too many disconnected ordered pairs of nodes would degrade the quality of the measured scores.

The beta centrality family (Hubbell and Katz together with beta) are usually extended by using the same formulation as in equation 3 but by using both A and A^T (the transpose of A) to get 'in' and 'out' versions. We can do the same with eigenvector to get the left and the right eigenvectors.

There can, however, be problems with eigenvector centrality on directed data. An important property of the undirected version is that in connected networks, there is guaranteed to be a dominant eigenvalue. This is not the case for directed networks and this can cause major issues such as nodes being assigned an arbitrary score. An alternative is to use singular vectors instead of eigenvectors. Every matrix X can be decomposed as the triple product UDV^T, where U is a set of 'out' scores, D is a diagonal matrix of singular values and V is a set of 'in' scores. Choosing the U and V scores associated with the largest singular value, a node has a high U score if it is connected to nodes with high V scores, and vice versa. In network analysis contexts, these U and V scores are known as hubs and authorities (Kleinberg, 1999). Whereas, in eigenvector centrality, a high right-eigenvector score would be obtained by an actor who has outgoing ties to many people who themselves have high right-eigenvector scores, in Hubs and Authorities a node gets a high outscore (hub score) if it has outgoing ties many ties to nodes with high in-scores. Similarly, a node gets a high in-score (authority score) if it has many incoming ties from nodes with high hub scores. For example, a website like Google gets a high hub score to the extent it provides links to popular websites like Wikipedia, which many sites point to. Recently Everett and Schoch (2022) have proposed a similar extension to the beta centrality family as an alternative to using A and A^T.

5.3 Valued Data

The first thing to consider with valued data is to be clear what the values represent. These can be tie strength, frequency of interaction, probabilities, rankings, capacity, costs, distances etc. We typically class these broadly as either similarities (e.g., tie strengths, frequencies of interaction, probabilities, capacities) or dissimilarities (e.g., costs, distances, travel times). Since a simple linear transformation can change dissimilarity data to similarity, we only need to consider similarity data in which higher numbers imply a stronger relationship. Degree can be simply extended by taking the sum or average of all the values incident to a node. Beta centrality can be applied directly without any adjustment and consequently, Hubbell, Katz and eigenvector work as well. Methods that use shortest paths such as closeness and betweenness type measures can be extended quite naturally as we can define optimal paths in a way consistent with the data type. For example, for probability data we can define an optimal path as one where the product of the probabilities associated with the links in the path is maximal. Unfortunately, except in the case of costs or distances this is computationally expensive and so is not the way to proceed. Flow betweenness is a measure that takes this approach but as the edge values are treated as flow capacities it can be difficult to interpret the results. The most common way to treat valued data is to dichotomise the data and then running centrality measures on the binary data. Comparing results for different cut-off values often produces more interpretable results than using the valued data directly. We would take a similar approach if the data was categorical, creating a separate binary graph corresponding to each categorical value.

5.4 Negative Data

If we have negative relations such as 'dislike' then the flow perspective and to a slightly lesser extent the walk perspective do not seem realistic. If Carol dislikes Andy then we don't expect her to pass any information on to Andy except perhaps misinformation or expressions of her dislike for him. If in addition Andy did not like Joe then he would hardly pass on the information that Carol dislikes him. As a consequence, direct ties are interpretable but longer walks do not seem to have a place in any centrality measure. It follows that degree, which only considers immediate ties, is a perfectly acceptable measure (with, of course, the reversal of interpretation this may entail). Someone with high degree of dislike in a friendship network would not be very central. It is unusual to have network data just on negative ties and it is more likely that we have data consisting of both positive and negative ties. Everett and Borgatti (2014) propose a measure they call *PN centrality* which incorporates both positive and negative ties. Their measure incorporates the concept that it is worse to receive a negative tie from someone who receives a lot of positive ties – that is, to be disliked by a popular person. In contrast, it is not too bad to receive a negative tie from someone who receives a lot of negative ties. In other words, being disliked by someone very unlikeable does not harm one's social capital. Their measure is closely related to beta centrality and the undirected version is given in equation (5).

$$PN = \left(1 - \frac{1}{2n-2}A\right)^{-1} 1 \qquad (5)$$

In the equation, A = P − 2N, P is the matrix of positive ties and N is the matrix of negative ties. They also propose directed and valued versions.

5.5 Two-mode Data

Two-mode data (or more generally multimode data), consists of two (or more) different types of nodes associated with each mode. Edges are only possible between modes and not within modes. This type of data and some centrality concepts are discussed in chapter 28 of, this volume. For simplicity we shall initially discuss just two-mode data and very briefly discuss multimode data. There are two fundamentally different approaches to dealing with data of this type.

First, we can use projection to form single mode datasets, for binary data we can form two projections of a two-mode affiliation matrix A, namely AA^T and A^TA. Since these matrices are now symmetric and valued we can only apply methods that work for data of this type – for example, eigenvector centrality or flow betweenness. Some authors have proposed dichotomising the results to accommodate additional centrality methods but this will result in data loss which may compromise the results. Everett and Borgatti (2013) have shown that in nearly all cases using both undichotomised projections does not result in data loss, they call this the *dual projection approach*. Bonacich (1991) had proposed a similar idea but just for eigenvector centrality, Everett (2016) generalises this approach. While this approach is valid in many circumstances the centrality methods that can be used are more limited (they need to apply to valued data). In addition, the projected matrices are not a direct representation of the raw data and this invalidates the perspective we have put forward here. Finally extending to multimode data is not really possible using projections so this technique does not generalise to multimode data. In order to use the perspectives outlined above we suggest the second approach, namely the direct approach.

The direct approach treats the two-mode network in exactly the same as a one-mode network, but for centrality we adjust the normalisation to take account of the fact that within-mode ties are not possible. It is relatively easy to find the normalisation for degree and closeness (Borgatti & Everett, 1997) and betweenness (Everett et al., 2004); we note it is not required for eigenvector as this is usually normalised to a unit length. However, the normalisation is not required at all if the researcher only wants a rank ordering of the nodes within each mode. In this case all one-mode centrality methods are applicable. In addition, the extension to multimode data is unproblematic. Since we are treating the network as if it were a single mode then we can apply all of our perspectives but we do need to take account of the fact that we have multimode data.

The induced perspective does not require any modification beyond making sure the graph invariant is valid for two-mode data. We may wish to have an invariant that takes account of the modes in some way by say having different weightings or even ignoring one of the modes. For example, we may have an invariant that consists of the sum of the distance from every actor to every event.

The walk structure perspective is slightly more problematic. In essence, in most two-mode networks there is an implicit directionality from one mode to the other. Actors go to events; events do not go to actors. However, if we take a very broad concept of influence then it may be possible to use this perspective. An actor participating in an event in some way influences that event, equally well the participation of other actors shapes the event and some of that may be passed on to the actor, so the event, in this case, influences the actor. This may not be the case in general so when considering this perspective it is important to take full account of the type of data being considered.

Finally, the flow perspective is undoubtedly the most problematic. Since usually only one mode has agency then clearly the flows described in Table 26.3 are not possible. As a consequence, the projected matrix of the mode that has agency is probably the only valid approach but as already mentioned this has limited value. It is therefore probably advisable to avoid this perspective when using two-mode data.

6 DISCUSSION

Building on Borgatti and Everett (2020), in this chapter we have tried to bring some cohesion to the topic of centrality rather than give reviews of the large number of centrality measures that are out there. We believe that developers and users of centrality should take into account the ideas presented here. The walk perspective provides a framework in which to place all centrality methods. It is, however, very methods oriented as it focuses on how the measure is constructed. It claims that a node is more central to the extent it participates in the walk structure of the graph. It is simply a typology of measures based on the kinds of walks the measures pay attention to, and what aspect, frequency or length or both they record.

The walk perspective is agnostic about the application. By this we mean it is quite possible to have centrality measures that conform to this perspective but defy interpretation. For example, we could count the number of paths emanating from a node in which adjacent nodes alternate between even and odd degree. Such a measure can be classified by the walk perspective but has no real interpretation as a centrality measure. The induced centrality perspective allows us to measure the contribution of a node to a prescribed graph invariant. This at least gives us a framework in which to interpret the measure provided the measure has a meaningful interpretation in terms of our research context.

The flow perspective is the perspective that relies on meaning by focusing on flow outcomes and is entirely process oriented. It has the advantage that we can use simulation to calculate the measures and therefore we can compare these results with mathematical formulations which claim to be based on the same flow process. In addition, we are able to explore new flow processes which capture what we believe is happening in real data without the need for complex mathematical derivations. It should be noted that this approach is probably not feasible for large complex networks, but nor are a number of graph-theoretic measures.

Finally, the perspectives outlined above need to be cognisant of the type of relational data being analysed. Clearly different types of relation would need different flow models or different graph invariants. In addition, the method may or may not work on directed or disconnected data or we may have valued data, all of which needs to be taken into account.

This chapter is about a deeper understanding of centrality type measures and when they should and should not be used. The issue is about understanding the data, the research questions and precisely what we expect a centrality measure to achieve. It is unfortunately common practice to use a method because it has been used by others, is easily available or simply produces a good result. These are bad reasons and, with so many measures available, trying many different ones and selecting the 'best' is simply bad science. Understanding the measures and when they and are not appropriate is the way forward.

Note

1 Taking the different characteristic magnitudes of different invariants into account, of course.

REFERENCES

Agneessens, F., Borgatti, S.P., & Everett, M.G. (2017). Geodesic based centrality: unifying the local and the global. *Social Networks*, *49*, 12–26.

Boldi, P., & Vigna, S. (2014). Axioms for centrality. *Internet Mathematics*, *10*(3-4), 222-262.

Bonacich, P. (1987). Power and centrality: a family of measures. *American Journal of Sociology*, *92*(5), 1170-1182.

Bonacich, P., & Lloyd, P. (2001). Eigenvector-like measures of centrality for asymmetric relations. *Social Networks*, *23*(3), 191-201.

Bonacich, P., 1991. Simultaneous group and individual centralities. *Social networks*, *13*(2), pp. 155-168.

Borgatti, S.P. (2003). The key player problem. In R. Breiger, K. Carley & P. Pattison (Eds.), *Dynamic social network modeling and analysis: workshop summary and papers* (pp. 241-252). National Academy of Sciences Press.

Borgatti, S.P. (2005). Centrality and network flow. *Social Networks*, *27*(1), 55-71.

Borgatti, S.P. (2006). Identifying sets of key players in a network. *Computational, Mathematical and Organizational Theory*, *12*(1), 21-34.

Borgatti, S.P., & Everett, M.G. (1997) Network analysis of 2-mode data. *Social Networks*, *19*, 243-269.

Borgatti, S.P., & Everett, M.G. (2006). A graph-theoretic perspective on centrality. *Social Networks*, *28*(4), 466-484.

Borgatti, S.P., & Everett, M.G. (2020). Three perspectives on centrality. In R. Light & J. Moody (Eds.), *The Oxford handbook of social networks* (pp. 334-351). Oxford University Press.

Borgatti, S.P., Everett, M.G. and Freeman, L.C. (2002). Ucinet 6 for Windows: software for social network analysis. Analytic Technologies.

Brandes, U. (2008). On variants of shortest-path betweenness centrality and their generic computation. *Social Networks*, *30*(2), 136-145.

Cook, K.S., Emerson, R.M., Gillmore, M.R., & Yamagishi, T. (1983). The distribution of power in exchange networks: theory and experimental results. *American Journal of Sociology*, *89*, 275-305.

Everett, M.G. and Borgatti, S.P., 2013. The dual-projection approach for two-mode networks. *Social networks*, *35*(2), pp. 204-210.

Everett, M. and Schoch, D., 2022. An extended family of measures for directed networks. *Social Networks*, *70*, pp. 334-340.

Everett, M.G. (2016). Centrality and the dual projection approach for two-mode social network data. *Methodological Innovations*, January-December (9), 2059799116630662. doi:10.1177/2059799116630662

Everett, M.G. and Borgatti, S.P., 1999. The centrality of groups and classes. *The Journal of mathematical sociology*, *23*(3), pp. 181-201.

Everett, M.G., & Borgatti, S.P. (2010). Induced, endogenous and exogenous centrality. *Social Networks*, *32*(4), 339-344.

Everett, M.G., & Borgatti, S.P. (2014). Networks containing negative ties. *Social Networks*, 111-120.

Everett, M.G., & Borgatti, S.P. (2019). Dual projection approach to two-mode data. *Social Networks*, *35*(2), 204-210

Everett, M.G., Sinclair, P., & Dankelmann, P. (2004). Some centrality results new and old. *Journal of Mathematical Sociology*, *28*(4), 215-228.

Freeman, L.C. (1979). Centrality in social networks conceptual clarification. *Social Networks*, *1*(3), 215-239.

Freeman, L.C. (1980). The gatekeeper, pair-dependency and structural centrality. *Quality and Quantity*, *14*(4), 585-592.

Freeman, L.C., Borgatti, S.P., & White, D.R. (1991). Centrality in valued graphs: a measure of betweenness based on network flow. *Social Networks*, *13*(2), 141-154.

Friedkin, N.E. (1991). Theoretical foundations for centrality measures. *American Journal of Sociology*, *96*(6), 1478-1504.

Hubbell, C.H. (1965). An input-output approach to clique identification. *Sociometry*, *28*(4), 377-399.

Katz, L. (1953). A new status index derived from sociometric analysis. *Psychometrika*, *18*(1), 39-43.

Kapferer B. (1969). Norms and the manipulation of relationships in a work context. In J Mitchell (ed), Social networks in urban situations. Manchester: Manchester University Press.

Kleinberg, J.M., 1999. Authoritative sources in a hyperlinked environment. Journal of the ACM (JACM), *46*(5), pp. 604-632.

Koschützki, D., Lehmann, K.A., Peeters, L., Richter, S., Tenfelde-Podehl, D., & Zlotowski, O. (2005). Centrality indices. In U. Brandes & T Erlebach (Eds.), *Network analysis: methodological foundations* (pp. 16-61). Springer Science & Business Media.

Lü, L., Chen, D., Ren, X.L., Zhang, Q.M., Zhang, Y.C., & Zhou, T. (2016). Vital nodes identification in complex networks. *Physics Reports*, *650*, 1-63.

Markovsky, B., Willer, D., & Patton, T. (1988). Power relations in exchange networks. *American Sociological Review*, *53*, 220-236.

Newman, M.E. (2005). A measure of betweenness centrality based on random walks. *Social Networks*, *27*(1), 39-54.

Padgett, J.F., & Ansell, C.K. (1993). Robust action and the rise of the Medici, 1400-1434. *American Journal of Sociology*, *98*(6), 1259-1319.

Sabidussi, G. (1966). The centrality index of a graph. *Psychometrika*, *31*(4), 581-603.

Schoch, D., & Brandes, U. (2016). Re-conceptualizing centrality in social networks. *European Journal of Applied Mathematics*, *27*(6), 971-985.

Stephenson, K. and Zelen, M., 1989. Rethinking centrality: Methods and examples. *Social networks*, *11*(1), pp. 1-37.

Structural Cohesion and Cohesive Groups

James Moody and Peter J. Mucha

INTRODUCTION AND BACKGROUND

One of the most interesting features of social networks is they tend to be clumpy – with interactions happening much more often among some subsets of actors than others. Substantively this inhomogeneity reflects natural social groups: in kids' networks these might be peer groups; in organisations, business coalitions; or in national systems, alliances. These sets of actors often capture our most important social activities: these are the people who enforce norms (Axelrod, 1985), influence our behaviour (Friedkin & Cook 1990; Kreager et al., 2011), or otherwise reflect the lived social communities that networks often intend to capture (Freeman, 1992; Friedkin, 2004).

While intuitively common and theoretically salient, social groups are notoriously difficult to identify methodologically, with a multitude of papers describing new approaches for finding groups or communities (for good prior reviews, see, e.g., Porter et al., 2009; Fortunato, 2010; Fortunato & Hric, 2016; Lee & Wilkinson, 2019; Shai et al., 2020). Our intuition is that we face a mismatch between theory and reality. Theoretically, treatments of 'cohesive groups' in social networks tend to be one-dimensional and lead to unrealistic null models. Our theories anticipate sharp boundaries and clear distinctions, but reality is often more nuanced. We think this misfit results from conflating two distinct dimensions that might better be treated separately. On the one hand, groups are characterised by their internal cohesion that captures how difficult it is to separate members of the (sub)network. On the other hand, we expect groups to be socially distinct, implying an implicit boundary maintenance process that delineates 'in' from 'out'. Our theories of groups generally assume high levels of each, when these dimensions might often vary independently.

Even when the theoretical objective is clear(er), however, the methodological problem is non-trivial for at least three reasons. The first is the sheer computational complexity of the task, given the many possible ways to assign nodes to groups; we simply cannot compare every possible solution even with a well-defined metric (indeed, many methods are NP-complete, e.g., Brandes et al., 2008).

Second, for many metrics, there are equivalent solutions that are substantively different, implying we cannot identify a uniquely optimal solution. Consider a bridging node with ties that span two otherwise disconnected cliques: most off-the-shelf methods would require the node to be assigned to one group or the other, or bring both into a single supercluster. Sometimes this is a signal that the method is inappropriate (perhaps we should not be seeking mutually exclusive solutions, even if it's computationally simpler) but often simply reflects the messiness of the world itself: equivalences are features of the world, not problems of the method.

Finally, notions of cohesion are often scale-dependent, with the appropriateness of a given solution depending on the comparison level for a given analysis. We might find a very clear clustering of a large network into a small number of distinct groups, but on examination discover that each group contains its own fractures. Such hierarchical ordering of groups is a puzzle: sets that seem together on one level (the whole network) are fractured at another (within each initial cluster). This last problem has subtly different variants, on the one hand depending on, for example, the number of groups inferred or the nature of null models captured via a resolution parameter (see below), on the other hand reflecting a substantively different order of collective organisation (hierarchical rather than modular).

Our aim in this chapter is to help clarify these distinctions by delineating the two primary dimensions of groups common in the literature and the tools used to measure them. Figure 27.1 provides a simplified rubric that guides this work.

The first dimension is *connectivity*, which refers substantively to the network being 'well-held-together' (Markovsky & Lawler, 1994). Intuitively, we expect cohesive networks to have many relations connecting many pairs; the collective does not depend on any single node (or small subset of nodes) to control or disrupt it. Information can easily pass between all members of a cohesive network. The natural inversion of a cohesive network is anomic or disintegrated, where nodes have few ties to each other and little chance of sharing collective information or identities across the network.

The second dimension is *boundary salience*. A population with salient boundaries has clear differentiation by categories. The most well recognised are ascribed status characteristics (White, 1966), such as race, gender or caste, though social network researchers are often interested in groups without clear external status indicators, such as 'leading crowds' in schools (Coleman, 1961). When boundaries are salient, even if informal, actors likely recognise them and hold relational expectations for behaviours within and between boundaries: mean girls bully the desperate wannabes; and the wannabes on some level expect it (Waters et al., 2004). Pressures towards social balance (Cartwright & Harary, 1956) tend to create homophily within group boundaries as friends come to like the same activities, in some cases becoming equivalent to the group itself (e.g., jocks playing sports, mathletes[1]).

The intersection of these two dimensions defines a space of network archetypes that can easily be misrecognised in empirical work. Standard intuition is that these two dimensions are positively correlated: settings are either anomic – low

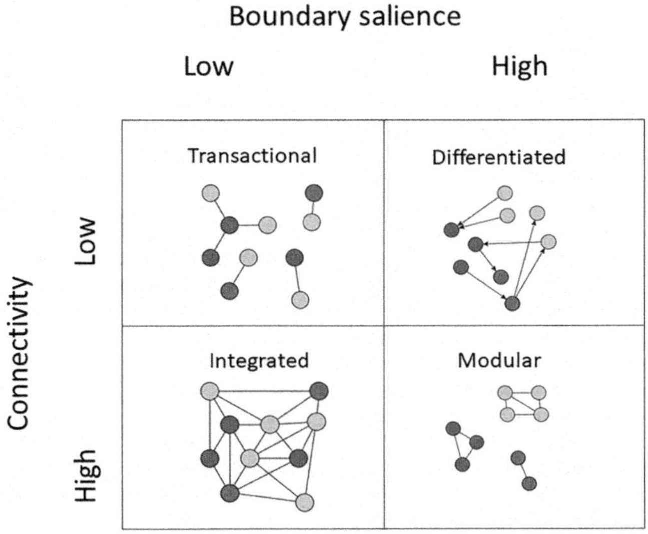

Figure 27.1 **Two dimensions to cohesion and clustering in networks**

connectivity and low boundary salience – or clustered – highly cohesive with strong boundaries. That is, we expect cases to fall along some continuum defined by the diagonal of Figure 27.1. Our intuitive notion of clustered networks often looks like the lower-right quadrant, with clearly defined sets of nodes and minimal contact between sets.

But social settings admit many other topologies. For example, a social system with high categorical differentiation but low (internal) group cohesion is the defining characteristic of kinship exchange systems (White, 1963; Bearman, 1997), where one clan can only marry across clan boundaries to a specific subset of other clans. This generalised exchange system archetype is referred to as 'differentiated' in Figure 27.1, illustrated by the cyclic relationship between the groups (yellow →red→green→yellow).[2] Opposite differentiated networks we find integrated ones that are highly cohesive but have no salient boundaries. The most well known are core–periphery systems composed of a diffuse core that admits a continuous gradient from central to peripheral (Mani & Moody, 2014).

STRUCTURAL COHESION

Node Connectivity

We have worked above with an intuitive notion of cohesion. Here we sharpen the definition by discussing structural cohesion. Structural cohesion was first introduced by Doug White and Frank Harary (2001) and then expanded in Moody and White (2003, p. 103, emphasis original): a group's structural cohesion is equal to *'the minimum number of actors who, if removed from the group, would disconnect the group'*. This concept is known as node connectivity in graph theory (Harary, 1969). Structural cohesion provides a nice operationalisation of Simmel's notion that the 'supra-individual' nature of a collective is the defining characteristic of social life (Simmel, [1908]1950).

A second and equivalent definition of cohesion turns on the relationships between node connectivity and the number of non-overlapping paths connecting pairs in a network. A path in a network is a sequence of adjacent nodes and edges starting with one node and ending with another that does not cross any node/edge multiple times. Two paths are node-independent if they share their starting and ending nodes but no others – they represent alternative routes between source and target. Menger's theorem equates the number of node-independent paths between a pair of nodes to the minimum number of nodes that have to be removed to disconnect the pair. This means we can define an equivalent version of structural cohesion: *a group's structural cohesion is equal to the minimum number of node-independent paths linking each pair of actors in the group*. This is sociologically interesting as it implies that groups with many unique paths connecting everyone in the group are more cohesive, matching our intuition about the ability to share information quickly and robustly among group members. This ability to communicate should lead the group to develop shared ideas and generalised understandings. Figure 27.2 illustrates these points.

Panel 1 and 2 present two networks of equivalent size – eight nodes and ten edges – in which every node is connected to every other node by at least one path. However, removing node 'e' in panel 1 would disconnect the graph, leaving two groups on the 'top' and the 'bottom' of the diagram. That is, the graph is 1-node-connected (note we could have removed 'f' as well, separating out 'd' as an isolate). In panel 2, there is no single node whose removal would disconnect the graph. Instead, we would have to strategically remove pairs ({e f}, {c b} etc.) to disconnect the graph, so the graph is 2-node-connected or a 'biconnected component'.

Note as well that while we can trace a path from node 'a' to 'h' in both cases, in panel 1 all such paths must go through node 'e' – making it a 'cutnode' in this graph – while the other network contains at least one path that avoids 'e': for example, we can highlight paths {a b d f h} and {a c e g h}. These two paths are node-independent; they overlap only on their starting and ending nodes.

In general, a network that has minimum node connectivity k is said to be k-node-connected. Node connectivity is bounded by minimum degree: one cannot be more connected than one has ties since, regardless of where the path would go, independent paths are limited by the number of first-steps on such paths, and thus this is the upper limit on node-independent paths. For sets of nodes, this means that every k-connected set must be at least a k-core (i.e., have degree ≥ k in the subgraph).

Node connectivity is a network-level property – it describes the path structure of the ties within the full graph under consideration. However, we could partition the network by some other feature and subsequently measure the node connectivity of the induced subset. This means that we can use node connectivity as a comparative characteristic for different networks (one school vs another, for example) or sub-parts of a single network.

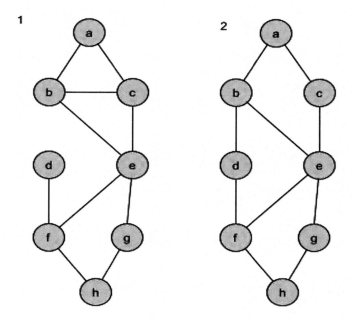

Figure 27.2 Equal volume networks with different node connectivity

Cohesive Blocking

Empirical networks usually admit to internal variation in node connectivity – some parts of a network may be more cohesive than others. We can better describe the cohesive structure of a network by recursively enumerating all k-connected sets and describing how they relate to each other. To do so, one first enumerates all minimum size cutsets and then removes all of the cutsets, assigning each to the relevant sides of their cut. If the induced subgraph is interesting[3] – that is, neither complete nor simply strings of cutnodes – then repeat the procedure on the resulting subgraphs, continuing until no further cutting can be done because you have reached a complete clique or have only isolates left. This procedure ensures that any (k + 1)-connected set embedded within the network will be identified. Since each step takes us deeper into the network, removing the most weakly connected nodes and leaving stronger, more connected sets, we uncover the nested cohesion structure of the network. As an example, consider Figure 27.3.

Figure 27.3 provides a full 'cohesive blocking' of a small example network. The image at the left encircles the induced subsets of the network while the tree at the right enumerates each set and its relation to all the others. The network is 1-connected, with nodes 4 and 13 being the minimum-sized cutsets (since k = 1 these are 'cutnodes'). Removing nodes 4 and 13 results in one 'singleton' cut (node 14) and two bicomponents. We typically ignore the singleton cut and proceed on the bicomponents. The small bicomponent (right branch of the cut enumeration tree) has a size-4 three-clique embedded within it. Since this clique cannot be cut further, this branch ends here. On the other side, the size-12 bicomponent has multiple two cuts along the {9-15-16-17-2} path. Removing non-adjacent pairs of those nodes will disconnect the graph, though most of the cuts result in uninteresting singleton partitions (i.e., removing {15 17} gives two graphs, one of size 3 ({15 16 17}) and one of size 11 (all but 16). After enumerating all of these cuts and examining the resulting induced graphs, one substantive subgraph of size 9 is left. Note this subgraph is also 2-connected, so it has the same node connectivity as the parent graph it was induced from.

The cohesive blocking procedure described above can induce subgraphs that are less connected than their parent subgraphs (indicated in Figure 27.4 by dashed lines on the induced graph). The defining feature is the nested nature of the subgraph – to get to that subset, one had to go through the weakest cuts at the level above. The number of recursions needed to get to a particular subset is its *nestedness* depth, which Moody and White (2003) argue is a reasonable measure of *social*

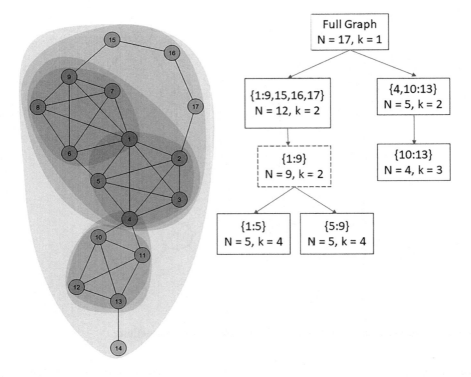

Figure 27.3   Example of cohesive blocking on a network

embeddedness (Granovetter, 1985). The choice to include weaker nested sets reflects the cutting process and thus the 'disconnect' aspect of social cohesion; but it is not unreasonable to focus only on induced graphs that increase *k-connectivity*, in which case the dashed-line box would be removed and one would go directly to the two four components embedded within the overall larger (n = 12) bicomponent, and nestedness is then equivalent to the highest node connectivity set that a node is a member of.

The cohesive blocking routine generally results in two types of induced subgraphs. The first are sets of nodes that calve away from the rest of the graph – separate distinct subsets. These are branching points in the blocking tree and generally correspond to the sorts of subgroups we traditionally think of as 'modular' in Figure 27.1. The other sort are long chains in the blocking structure, representing increasingly cohesive sets nested within each other like Russian dolls – one group is not necessarily distinct, but rather more deeply embedded than the other.

Cohesive blocking provides a full summary of the network connectivity structure, but is difficult to use in subsequent analysis. One solution is to assign nodes to a group based on shared membership in a nested *k* component. In this sense, for example, we might say that all members of either large bicomponent in Figure 27.3 are two distinct groups, with node 4 belonging to both groups. The analyst then needs to determine where in the nestedness tree to break the network, noting that such breaks can result in both overlapping groups (if at a branching point) or a non-exhaustive assignment (i.e., node 14 belongs to neither bicomponent).

Alternatively, one can characterise the network as a whole based on summaries of pairwise cohesion levels. For example, one can determine the highest *k-connected* set all pairs of nodes belong to. In Figure 27.3, for example, the overall for all pairs is 1.9. One can apply a similar summary to individuals (average, min, max) relative to all others (for individual level analysis) or to subgroups induced based on other features. Which summary statistic (mean, median, upper quartile, etc.) best captures the social process at hand is an open question. Any single summary score will almost always average over important divisions – a bowtie network with a single node connecting two large cliques can have a high average score even though the graph as a whole is 1-connected, so there are obvious trade-offs to this approach.

Extensions and Observations

The main advantage of the structural cohesion approach is the clear link between the exact path structure of a network and the sociological notion of cohesion: if our ties bind us together, then structurally cohesive networks are more tightly bound than non-cohesive networks. There are a number of related ideas that have somewhat different implications and are worth spelling out clearly. Most of these alternatives take a feature that is maximised in a graph-theoretic clique and use that dimension as the foundation for the cohesion metric. In most cases, however, these metrics fall victim to a base asymmetry: structurally cohesive groups have these features, but maximising these features does not ensure cohesion. The archetypical case are centralised graphs with single cutnodes (like node e in Figure 27.2) where you have low node connectivity even if other features are high.

For example, consider the difference between node and edge connectivity. Edge connectivity is the number of edges one would have to remove to disconnect a network. This fails as a general feature, when networks are highly centralised, as many ties funnel through a single cutnode. In any social process where nodes control the flow of resources through the network, highly centralised networks introduce unequal control of the flow in the network, leading to bottlenecks, fragmentation and inequality. All k-node-connected networks are at least k-edge-connected; but not all k-edge-connected networks are k-node-connected. Of course, if the social process at play is known to depend more on edges than nodes, then we may be better off focusing on edge connectivity instead. In those cases, we refer the reader to the long literature on min-cut, max-flow problems.

Other alternative metrics aimed at capturing how well the network is 'held together' by the social relations suffer much the same problem. The most common cohesion metric is probably simple density – the proportion of pairs in a network who are connected (simple) or the average strength of relations across pairs (if relation is weighted). Density focuses on volume – all else equal we would expect that having more ties among a set of nodes will result in greater connectivity and ease of resource flow. But this assumes that the network ties are somewhat evenly distributed, as otherwise highly clustered or centralised networks can suffer the sorts of problems illustrated in panel b of Figure 27.2.

A second common measure is average social distance: in a cohesive network each person is socially close to all others (at the limit, directly adjacent as in a clique). This, again, is subject to the dominance effects of high centralisation: networks with very central nodes will have short overall distances between most pairs, but that central node has a dominant role over flow in the network. In some settings, this sort of centralisation is effective – there are clear efficiencies to having centralised nodes that act as routers for distributing information or basic control purposes, for example – but we would argue these are best thought of as *efficient* structures not *cohesive* structures.

A third common measure for cohesion is the proportion of triangles in a network that are closed. Intuitively, this builds on the notion that collections of strong ties form the basis of small groups (Freeman, 1992), and we'd expect that the network as a whole is held together because each connected pair is jointly connected to common thirds. In practice, triadic closure tends to limit group size based on degree as the redundancy implied by common close ties means that relations tend to 'turn in' on others in the same group, creating a direct linkage between the 'held together' and 'distinct' dimensions discussed in Figure 27.1. Cohesion based on transitivity shares the same issues as density and k-cores discussed above: highly cohesive networks tend to be transitive, but highly transitive networks are not necessarily structurally cohesive. Moreover, because there is no distance requirement for node-connectivity, it is possible to have comparatively high k-node-cohesion (k = 3, 4) in very large groups with minimal transitivity. Whether this is a feature or a bug is context dependent. On the one hand, if the social process under investigation allows resources to flow long distances (reputation, information, viruses), then structural cohesion can provide greater efficiency re-linking wider populations with fewer ties. On the other hand, if the setting requires face-to-face reinforcement to be effective, then the distance-limiting features of transitive closure may take precedence.

The main pragmatic barrier to using structural cohesion is computational. The approach provided by Moody and White (2003) combines algorithms by Kanevsky (1990, 1993) and the key step of identifying cutsets runs in $O(2^k V^3)$ (available in SAS/IML and, with some modifications, in iGraph for R). This is often prohibitively computationally expensive for large networks. Sinkovitz et al. (2017) provide a targeted search approach that exploits k-cores (which are fast to find), but forgoes the full blocking approach implied by identifying all cutsets discussed above. Their routine allows enumeration of all k-connected sets on networks with hundreds of thousands of nodes.

Node-connectivity can naturally extend to connectivity through nodes-of-a-class, such as would be found in bipartite networks. Cornwell and Burchard (2019) provide a detailed examination of how graphs are connected through one mode or another and define two-mode node connectivity as the number of nodes in the first mode that would have to be removed to disconnect the second mode. Extending this to the general multilevel network case could be informative, but remains unexplored to the best of our knowledge. Another way one might extend structural cohesion would be to consider paths of particular lengths or that sum to particular weights. These sorts of extensions would lead to somewhat messy and localised versions of a 'cohesive horizon' around focal nodes, but maximal sets that are node-and-distance connected might capture social processes with only localised flow.

PEER GROUPS AND COMMUNITIES

Background

Structural cohesion provides a sociologically principled approach to understanding the connectivity dimension of Figure 27.1, but does not address boundary saliency. Our traditional notions of peer groups (Freeman, 1992) are simultaneously cohesive *and distinct*. When high boundary salience and internal connectivity are combined, we get modular groups: sets of nodes with many ties to each other within groups and few(er) ties between groups. Sociological peer groups are seen as the primary site for social action. Peers share information with each other, react to status updates, enforce norms and generally provide the primary social context within which people orient their behaviour. These groups can be recognised and named within a community formally (youth gangs would be an example) or informally ('the cool kids') but often they are not named, though they might be recognised (Coleman, 1961).

The methodological conundrum of peer groups is that outsiders generally, and data collectors in particular, often lack the information necessary to know which groups are which. This has come to be known generally as the 'community detection'[4] problem, where the goal is to partition the nodes of a network into subsets in a way that optimises a target measure of joint cohesion/distinction.

The ideal-typical modular communities are similar to those in Figure 27.4, which shows four clearly distinct groups, each with very few ties to any other group and many ties within the group. In a standard sociogram, these sorts of groups jump out clearly (left panel); if we represent them as a mixing matrix (right panel) we see that the network is nearly block diagonal, meaning that the blocks on the diagonal have much higher weight than off-diagonal blocks – that is, there is more relational volume within groups than between groups.

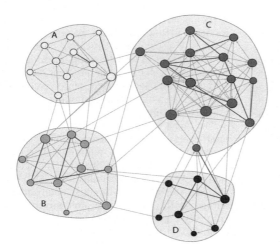

Figure 27.4 Example of a clearly modular network

In most realistic settings, however, the case is not nearly so simple. Consider Figure 27.5 below, which presents eight common clustering algorithms (discussed in detail below) applied to the Gagnon prison network (MacRae, 1960).

This multiplicity of solutions to the community detection problem is expected, analogous to the number of different available methods for unsupervised clustering of point-cloud data. In the presence of unknown mechanisms driving only weakly and potentially overlapping clusters, different algorithmic approaches will often identify different clusters. Some cluster/community labels might be more or less useful than others in a particular application: researchers should ask how particular solutions match their theoretical concerns to evaluate and select them.

Community Detection Methods

Most contemporary strategies for community detection focus on three basic strategies.[5] The first (and most common) is to use some algorithmic

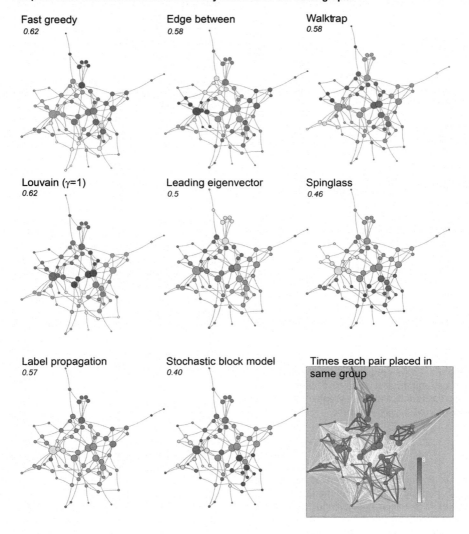

Figure 27.5 Comparison of eight clustering methods on the same real network: colours within panels denote same-community membership

process as a heuristic for optimising a community-relevant descriptive score. The second is to exploit a strong correspondence between the eigenstructure of a network and groups using variants of singular value decomposition. The third considers generative network models to recast community detection as a statistical problem where community membership influences tie probability. A full review of all such methods is beyond the scope of this chapter, but we describe exemplars and highlight some best practices.

Heuristic Sorting Approaches

Heuristic approaches to community detection sort nodes into groups based either on an index of 'groupedness' or a simulated social process that is sensitive to an underlying group structure. Given the complexity of the assignment task, such sorting approaches may not truly maximise the objective function, but instead reflect different strategies to overcome the necessary trade-offs between completeness and computational feasibility in a way that finds a reasonably good partition in a reasonable amount of time. Each of the algorithms we discuss below takes a slightly different approach to this trade-off.

The first step in direct sorting models is to define a score that reflects the group structure of the network which can then be used to judge the fit of any proposed partition. Historically a number of such metrics were developed (e.g., the Freeman segregation index (1972) or the Segregation Matrix Index (Fershtman, 1997)), which intuitively shared the notion that substantive groups are composed of people who have most of their (strong) ties within the group rather than between.

In contemporary work, the *modularity score* is the most common metric used to identify communities.[6] Modularity (Newman & Girvan, 2004) with resolution parameter γ (Reichardt & Bornholdt, 2006) counts the total edge weight within communities relative to a multiple of the expected weight in a random graph model with the same expected degree sequence:

$$\frac{1}{2m}\Sigma_{ij}\left(A_{ij} - \gamma \frac{k_i k_j}{2m}\right)\delta(C_i, C_j)$$

where m is the total weight of edges; k_i is the strength (weighted degree) of node i; A_{ij} is the edge weight between nodes i and j; and δ is an indicator function giving 1 if the pair is assigned to the same community ($C_i = C_j$) and 0 otherwise, thus limiting the sum to within-group node pairs.

The difference within the parentheses ($A_{ij} - \gamma(k_i k_j)/2m$) compares the weight of observed ties in the group compared to that (up to a factor of γ) expected under random mixing. In the original default $\gamma = 1$ formulation, the modularity of a network with only one community is precisely zero by construction, while the modularity of putting each node into its own community (i.e., N communities) gives negative values, and the maximum modularity will be found for some intermediate number of communities. This means that Q can serve as an objective function for partition selection, which was difficult to do with earlier measures. The extent to which one considers the total within-community edge weight relative to the expected random ties is governed by the resolution parameter γ: larger γ values increase the penalty in Q paid by putting node pairs in the same group, typically leading to larger numbers of smaller communities.

Because of the 1/2m normalisation, modularity cannot be larger than one. Then, by comparing the total within-group edge weight against that for a corresponding random graph with the given community labels, one expects Q≈0 for $\gamma = 1$ in the case where the community labels are randomly assigned. As such, it is a common misconception to assume some threshold of Q to immediately imply 'good' clustering into communities. However, it is essential to keep in mind that these special modularity values are relative to a given set of community labels. Importantly, even a random graph without any *a priori* defined community structure may have some partition of nodes into communities with a high value of modularity (Guimerà et al., 2004). Modularity only provides a measure for comparing one set of community labels to another set for the same network; any comparison of the maximum modularity obtained between different networks, or to assess that modularity is 'high' for a given network and thus claim it is strongly clustered, must be performed carefully. For example, one might compare the maximum modularity obtained for a given network against suitable permutations of the network – for example, double edge swaps to explore the space of the associated configuration model (see Fosdick et al., 2018) – and the distribution of maximum modularities computed for each network so obtained.

Early uses of modularity as a score ignored the resolution parameter (which is equivalent to setting it to 1) and much of the initial excitement over modularity was that it 'solved' the number of clusters problem. This, it turns out, is illusory: the number of clusters varies with the resolution parameter, and there is not necessarily a reason to pick $\gamma = 1$ over another value. As an empirical feature, many social networks do admit to scale effects – some small set of resolution values for which there is a largely stable set of returned communities. For example, if one were to cluster faculty in a university based on shared graduate student committees, a coarse division between natural sciences, social sciences and humanities would probably appear for a wide range of small resolution parameter values. But, turning the resolution knob up a bit, one would probably see a stable set of solutions at a higher value reflecting university departments. Importantly, neither of these solutions is wrong – they simply capture sociality at different levels of interaction. We want to emphasise that this is a feature easily *revealed* by tuning the resolution parameter in modularity but is in no way an *artefact* of using the modularity score: many real network settings are naturally clustered at different scales.

A common approach to identifying a good resolution parameter is to calculate communities at multiple different resolution parameters and select points in the parameter space where the identified communities appear to be robust to modest change (see, e.g., Fenn et al., 2009). Figure 27.6 shows the number of communities found by the R-igraph cluster_leiden() function (Traag et al., 2019) for three different networks, demonstrating robust results (plateaus) occur at values above default $\gamma = 1$.[7] The need to undertake some systematic approach becomes even more pressing for community detection in multilayer networks (see Kivela et al., 2014) because of the introduction of at least one additional parameter (typically notated ω) to set the coupling between layers (Mucha et al., 2010). Newman (2016) addressed resolution parameter selection by identifying a fundamental equivalence between modularity maximisation and stochastic blockmodel inference in the special case of a degree-corrected planted partition model, leading to an iterative procedure for finding the γ that self-consistently maximises both modularity and the corresponding likelihood. Pamfil et al. (2019) extended Newman's iterative approach to a variety of multilayer settings. In a different approach, Weir et al. (2017) developed an efficient post-processor to find the convex hull of admissible modularity partitions (CHAMP) for an input collection of community-label partitions, however obtained, to quickly pick out the domains in γ where each partition maximises modularity, thus making it easier to find community features that are robust to changes in γ. The bottom right panel of Figure 27.6 demonstrates this post-processing for the unweighted karate club, finding the community-label partitions corresponding to the line segments along the upper envelope of modularity $Q(\gamma)$, where each line in the diagram corresponds to a single partition of nodes into communities obtained by cluster_leiden(). Recently, Gibson and Mucha (2022) combined the SBM equivalence approach with CHAMP to eliminate the possibility of stochastic fluctuations causing fixed points of the iterative process to go unstable, thus making it easier to find appropriate resolution (and interlayer coupling) parameters.

Once one has a score to optimise, how best to perform the sorting into groups? That is, given a computationally complex optimisation problem, much of the development in community detection has involved coming up with new heuristic search procedures. The earliest models were based on variants of simulated annealing (e.g., UCINET's Factions, de Amorim et al., 1990). Most contemporary approaches use a more targeted search procedure using either a divisive or agglomerative approach. In a divisive approach, one starts with the full network considered as one 'root' community, which is then split by cutting it at its weakest point(s). A commonly used example is Girvan and Newman's (2002) 'edge-betweenness' approach. Edge betweenness is the number of shortest paths between node pairs that cross over that edge. Edges with high betweenness scores generally link parts of the network that are otherwise less linked – that is, they are global bridges. By cutting the network at these points, natural subgroups will fall out. Carried out to its full extent, the process of repeated betweenness calculation and cutting will result in a tree with the whole graph at the root and each node individually at the lowest possible cut level. One way to return a single solution from such a tree is to select the level with highest modularity (Newman & Girvan, 2004).

Agglomerative approaches start with each node assigned to its own community and joins them if doing so improves the objective (e.g., modularity). One generally starts by assigning nodes to some other node they are connected to (with a strong edge weight, if relevant), then joining pairs of nodes that share many neighbours, growing groups until doing so no longer improves fit. Unlike edge betweenness, there is no fixed order to test the joins – particularly early in the process, there are often many equally good assignments so some choices have to be made at random. Much of the effort in these sorts of models is in identifying reasonably good ways to change group assignment, pick which groups to merge and ensuring that doing so doesn't inadvertently walk one into a poor solution.[8] For example, the 'fast greedy' method (Clauset et al., 2004) rapidly increases modularity by merging communities; the Louvain method (Blondel et al., 2008) continues to move one random node at a time between existing

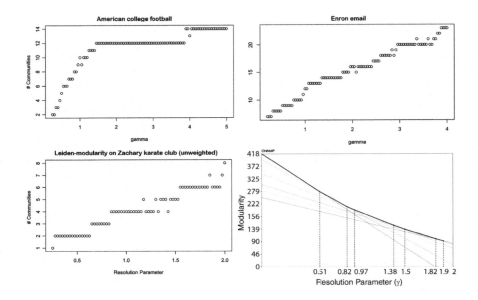

Figure 27.6 Modularity maximisation at different γ resolution parameter values

communities until no further improvement can be found by a single such move and then lifts hierarchically to a smaller graph with nodes corresponding to the communities and repeats; and the recent improvements moving from Louvain to Leiden (Traag et al., 2019) include new checks to ensure that each identified community is a connected component. Ken Frank's KliqueFinder (1995) uses a similar strategy, but optimises the in-group odds ratio for a shared tie.

An alternative heuristic strategy is to allow some process to operate on the network that would itself reveal groups, and then use that result as a proxy for finding groups directly. For example, Moody (2001) reasoned that a peer-influence process should reveal cohesive groups, since within-group ties would push members to hold similar ideas that are distinct from other groups (Friedkin, 1998). This model simulates a peer-influence process over multiple random variables, then clusters nodes based on their resulting scores.[9] Richards' (1995) Negopy program used a similar sorting process based on node IDs as the initialisation stage in its search process, which was then improved on using rule-based sorting techniques. Contemporary methods using this tactic have focused either on a simulated communication process (packet passing methods, such as label propagation (Raghavan et al., 2007)) by following the intuition that peer groups will share more internally to the group than externally, or by simulating random walks on the network, assuming that a random walker will tend to get 'stuck' within communities (Pons & Latapy, 2005).

Eigenvector-based Approaches

Many researchers recognised the qualitative similarity between finding communities in a network and the problem of finding lower-dimensional representations of high-dimensional data objects in general. Intuitively, just as items in a scale should all be more similar to each other than not, peers in a community should all be close to each other (in some sense) in the network. Early approaches (MacRae, 1960; Cairns & Cairns, 1995) used this analogy directly and applied PCA to (some transformation of) the (valued) adjacency matrix. The main advantage of this model was ease of use, but an additional feature is that groups are non-exclusive – nodes with strong ties to multiple groups will have significant loadings on both groups.

This initial simple model has fallen out of favour in recent work (though it still appears sometimes as a starting point for heuristic improvement approaches) in favour of eigenvector-based approaches with more principled mathematical foundations (see, e.g., Chung, 1997). Fiedler (1973) introduced spectral partitioning in terms of the eigenvectors of the (combinatorial) Laplacian matrix.[10] Recently, Priebe et al. (2019) compared and contrasted the types of communities identified via eigendecomposition of the normalised Laplacian matrix versus those identified in the adjacency matrix. In the simplest versions, the elements of a single eigenvector of the corresponding matrix are used to split the network into two parts, and then the process is repeated recursively on each part. Alternatively, a higher-dimensional decomposition may be used to directly partition into multiple parts (as in Priebe et al., 2019). The two obvious advantages of these approaches are the quick performance on large networks and use of a clear mathematical framework that allows developers to build on the large body of work in related spectral methods. Practically, these models (like all methods) work very well if clustering is clear and seem to work well enough when the problem is data reduction on very large networks, where a node misassignment here or there is not too critical. Because the models work on lower-dimensional summaries of the full network, however, some oddities can occur that are easier to control in the node-sorting approaches discussed above – such as ensuring that each community is a connected component.

Stochastic Block Models

The final common approach leverages advances in the statistical models of networks to identify communities. Stochastic block models (SBMs) are generative models, describing a probabilistic process to generate a network with the characteristics defined by the model (Holland et al., 1983; Wang & Wong, 1987; Snijders & Nowicki, 1997; Lee & Wilkinson, 2019). The simplest SBM with K blocks is given by

$$A_{ij}|U_i,U_j \sim Bern\left(U_i^T Q U_j\right)$$

where A is the adjacency matrix, U is an NxK matrix of block membership where $U_{ij} = 1$ if node *i* is a member of block *j* and 0 otherwise, and Q is a KxK matrix defining the probability of ties within and between blocks. If Q is diagonally dominant – for example, Q_{ii} is much greater than Q_{ij} (i ≠ j) – then blocks are ('assortative') communities. While this is the most common use of stochastic blockmodels, one can specify Q in any configuration. Moreover, one need not assume hard boundaries on block membership: mixed membership SBMs allow nodes to have partial membership in multiple groups that sum to 1 (elements of U are continuous rather than binary) or overlapping models where nodes can be in multiple groups simultaneously (Airoldi et al., 2008). In practice, we usually know A but not U, so the goal is to assign nodes to labels in U in a way that maximises the match with the observed data (see Lee and Wilkinson, 2019, for review).

There are multiple implementations of stochastic blockmodels, which can differ both in formal aspects of the model (assumed distributional properties, degree corrections, hard clustering vs soft, inclusion of observed or latent covariates, for example) as well as the search initialisation (often using methods like k-means or spectral clustering for initial group assignments) and model maximisation routines (MCMC, EM likelihood maximisation, etc.). Practically, models often require users to pre-specify the number of clusters searched for (but see Leger, 2016, which maximises within a user-specified range). Importantly, recent advances have improved the computational performance in fitting SBMs (Peixoto, 2014). Substantively, results are often similar to eigenvector approaches and similarly carry no guarantee of connected clusters, unless that is included in a post-processing step. The canonical form of the model does not have any resolution parameter, so users would have to build that in through appropriate information criteria or, more likely in practice, explore stability by forcing lower or higher numbers of communities.

The key advantage of the SBM approach is the core integration with generative statistical modelling frameworks for networks. This integration allows one to build on the formal insights from that literature, including the ability to test graphs against fundamental limits on community detectability (Abbe, 2018), to test alternative models, and include other data-generating features simultaneously. For example, latent network models (Krivitsky et al. 2009) provide the ability to fit latent-space models with clustering, which allows one to better capture natural heterogeneity in latent-space models of networks.

Each of the three approaches to community detection discussed here – heuristic sorts, eigenvalue decomposition and stochastic blockmodels – have deep roots that could each occupy a review in their own right. We emphasise that real-world data is typically too complex to be conclusively modelled with a single technique. Indeed, we want to re-emphasise our analogy to unsupervised clustering of point-cloud data. When data is inherently well clustered, many different algorithms will find the same or highly similar cluster structures. But many real-world cases are less structured, resulting in different algorithms finding differing results. These general observations are intimately connected to *no free lunch theorems* that identify how the improvement of an algorithm across part of an overall problem domain is balanced by diminished performance elsewhere (Peel et al., 2017). That is, in practice, some algorithms might be more or less useful in a specific application.

CONCLUSION

With this chapter we have briefly discussed some of the varied approaches that are available for identifying cohesion and communities in network data, using the two-dimensional rubric of connectivity and boundary salience. We advise users to consider the many different available techniques as a collection of exploratory tools that can be used to try and better understand their data,[11] and to think carefully about how the problem a researcher is asking fits into the two dimensions of Figure 27.1. Is your question primarily about connectivity? If so, cohesive blocking or pairwise connectivity scoring might be most appropriate or techniques that allow for overlapping cluster membership. Is your question primarily about boundary salience? Then you should think carefully about what constitutes boundaries in your setting and attempt to identify the socially active variables that define the boundaries. If your problem is simultaneously about boundaries and connectivity, or if boundaries admit to no clear external label, then consider an ensemble of different community detection routines and explore resolution parameter limits thoroughly. Fundamentally, it is up to researchers to ask themselves how specific community labels might match or contradict their theoretical concerns – only then are we able to substantively understand, evaluate and benefit from these approaches.

ACKNOWLEDGEMENTS

Thanks to Ava Scharfstein for assistance generating figures, Gabriel Varela for detailed comments on earlier drafts and Tom Wolff for help implementing comparative clustering routines. This work is partially supported by the NSF through HNDS-I (BCS-2024271, BCS-2140024) and RAPID (SES-2029790) and support from the James S. McDonnell Foundation.

Notes

1 "You can't join Mathletes, it's social suicide!" (Waters et al., 2004).

2 Colour figures online. We note that there are myriad sorts of generalised structures that can be layered over categories, including many types of hierarchies and chain-generalised exchange systems.

3 Moody and White's (2003) original procedure ignored induced graphs that would result in single nodes or strings of cutsets, as these tend to be uninteresting substantively – i.e., there is little value in inducing a subgraph and further examining it if you already know that its composed solely of cutnodes from the parent graph. Similarly, complete cliques are often substantively interesting but there's no reason to go any further.

4 Terms differ significantly across research traditions here. In sociology and social network analysis 'cohesive peer groups' or 'social cliques' or 'crowds' are commonly used to define socially salient network subgroups. But 'group' and 'clique' have specific different meanings in mathematics and computer science, where much of the recent work in this field has originated, and has instead come under the heading of 'community detection'. Here we generally use the terms 'peer group' and 'community' interchangeably unless the context requires greater specificity.

5 We have collected a set of comparisons in table form here: people.duke.edu/~jmoody77/Cluster-Comparisons.pdf

6 Numerous other such scores exist to be used as objective functions for community detection (see, e.g., the different options available in the leidenalg python package, github.com/vtraag/leidenalg).

7 Football example from Girvan and Newman, 2002. available at www-personal.umich.edu/~mejn/netdata/; Enron email example from R-igraphdata.

8 These sorts of assignment changes and checks are deceptively complicated. One might think it simple to sort nodes to the set where most of their peers are: if ego has mode of peers in group j, make ego's assignment 'j'. But, in practice, assigning one node affects the fit of every other node they are connected to, which leads to a sequence of changes implied by every assignment; a sorting that thus convergences on 'best' is not trivial.

9 In practice, this particular algorithm ends up being quite close to leading eigenvector approaches, so it's probably best to use that instead.

10 The Laplacian matrix is defined as: $L = D-A$; where D is a matrix with (weighted) degrees on the diagonal and 0s elsewhere and A is the adjacency matrix.

11 At the same time, we acknowledge that our perspective is not universally agreed with (see, e.g., Peixoto, 2022, for a very different opinion).

REFERENCES

Abbe, E. (2018). Community detection and stochastic block models: recent developments. *Journal of Machine Learning and Research*, *18*, 1–86.

Airoldi, E.M., Blei, D.M., Fienberg, S.E., & Xing, E.P. (2008). Mixed membership stochastic blockmodels. *Journal of Machine Learning and Research*, *9*, 1981–2014.

Axelrod, R. (1985). *The evolution of cooperation*. Basic Books.

Bearman, P. (1997). Generalized exchange. *American Journal of Sociology*, *102*, 1383–1415.

Blondel, V.D., Guillaume, J.-L., Lambiotte, R., & Lefebvre, E. (2008). Fast unfolding of communities in large networks. *Journal of Statistical Mechanics: Theory and Experiment*, *2008*, P10008.

Brandes, U., Delling, D., Gaertler, M., Gorke, R., Hoefer, M., Nikoloski, Z., & Wagner, D. (2008). On modularity clustering. *IEEE Transactions on Knowledge and Data Engineering* 20:172–88.

Cairns, R.B., & Cairns, B.D. (1995). *Lifelines and risks: pathways of youth in our time*. Cambridge University Press.

Cartwright, D., & Harary, F. (1956). Structural balance: a generalization of Heider's theory. *Psychological Review*, *63*, 277–293.

Chung, F. (1997). *Spectral graph theory*. Vol. 92. CBMS Regional Conference Series in Mathematics. American Mathematical Society. doi.org/10.1090/cbms/092

Clauset, A., Newman, M.E.J., & Moore, C. (2004). Finding community structure in very large networks. *Physical Review E*, *70*, 066111.

Coleman, J. (1961). *The adolescent society*. Free Press.

Cornwell, B., & Burchard, J. (2019). Structural cohesion and embeddedness in two-mode networks. *Journal of Mathematical Sociology*, *43*, 179–194.

de Amorim, S.G., Barthélemy, J.P., & Ribeiro (1990). Clustering and clique partitioning: simulated annealing and tabu search approaches. Research report from Groups d'études et de recherche en analyse des décisions. HEC Montreal, McGill University.

Fenn, D.J., Porter, M.A., McDonald, M., Williams, S., Johnson, N.F., & Jones, N.S. (2009). Dynamic communities in multichannel data: an application to the foreign exchange market during the 2007–2008 credit crisis. *Chaos: An Interdisciplinary Journal of Nonlinear Science*, *19*, 033119–8.

Fershtman, M. (1997). Cohesive group detection in a social network by the Segregation Matrix Index. *Social Networks*, *19*, 193–207.

Fiedler, M. (1973). Algebraic connectivity of graphs. *Czechoslovak Mathematical Journal*, *23*, 298.

Fortunato, S. (2010). Community detection in graphs. *Physics Reports*, *486*, 75–174.

Fortunato, S., & Hric, D. (2016). Community detection in networks: a user guide. *Physics Reports*, *659*, 1–44.

Fosdick, B.K., Larremore, D.B., Nishimura, J., & Ugander, J. (2018). Configuring random graph models with fixed degree sequences. *SIAM Review*, *60*, 315–355.

Frank, K.A. (1995). Identifying cohesive subgroups. *Social Networks*, *17*, 27–56.

Freeman, L.C. (1972). Segregation in social networks. *Sociological Methods and Research*, *6*, 411–430.

Freeman, L.C. (1992). The sociological concept of 'group': an empirical test of two models. *American Journal of Sociology*, *98*(1), 152–166.

Friedkin, N.E. (1998). *A structural theory of social influence*. Cambridge University Press.

Friedkin, N.E. (2004). Social cohesion. *Annual Review of Sociology*, *30*, 409–425.

Friedkin, N.E., & Cook, K.S. (1990). Peer group influence. *Sociological Methods and Research*, *19*(1), 122–143.

Gibson, R., & Mucha, P.J. (2022). Finite-state parameter space maps for pruning partitions in modularity-based community detection. *Scientific Reports*, *12*(1). doi.org/10.21203/rs.3.rs-1551680/v1

Girvan, M., & Newman, M.E.J. (2002). Community structure in social and biological networks. *Proceedings of the National Academy of Sciences of the United States of America*, *99*, 7821–7826.

Guimerà, R., Sales-Pardo, M., & Nunes Amaral, L.A. (2004). Modularity from fluctuations in random graphs and complex networks. *Physical Review E*, *70*, 025101.

Granovetter, M. (1985). "Economic Action and Social Structure: The Problem of Embeddedness." *American Journal of Sociology*, *91*(3), 481–510. http://www.jstor.org/stable/2780199

Harary, F. (1969). *Graph theory*. Addison-Wesley

Holland, P.W., Laskey, K.B., & Leinhardt, S. (1983). Stochastic blockmodels: first steps. *Social Networks*, *5*, 109–137.

Kanevsky, Arkady. (1990). "On the Number of Minimum Size Separating Vertex Sets in a Graph and How to Find All of Them." *Proceedings of the 1st ACM-SIAM Symposium on Discrete Algorithms* :411–21.

———. (1993). "Finding All Minimum-Size Separating Vertex Sets in a Graph." *Networks* 23:533–41.

Kivela, M., Arenas, A., Barthelemy, M., Gleeson, J.P., Moreno, Y., & Porter, M.A. (2014). Multilayer networks. *Journal of Complex Networks*, *2*, 203–271.

Kreager, D.A., Rulison, K., & Moody, J. (2011). Delinquency and the structure of adolescent peer groups. *Criminology*, *49*, 95–127.

Krivitsky, P.N., Handcock, M.S., Raftery, A.E., & Hoff, P.D. (2009). Representing degree distributions,

clustering, and homophily in social networks with latent cluster random effects models. *Social Networks*, *31*, 204–213.
Lee, C., & Wilkinson, D.J. (2019). A review of stochastic block models and extensions for graph clustering. *Applied Network Science*, *4*, 122.
Leger, J. (2016). Blockmodels: A R-package for estimating in Latent Block Model and Stochastic Block Model, with various probability functions, with or without covariates. arXive: https://doi.org/10.48550/arXiv.1602.07587
Leger, J.-B., Barbillon, P., & Chiquet, J. (2021). blockmodels: latent and stochastic block model estimation by a 'V-EM' algorithm. *R Package*. cran.r-project.org/package=blockmodels
MacRae, J. (1960). Direct factor analysis of sociometric data. *Sociometry*, *23*, 360–371.
Mani, D., & Moody, J. (2014). Moving beyond stylized economic network models: the hybrid world of the Indian firm ownership network. *American Journal of Sociology*, *119*, 1629–1669.
Markovsky, B., & Lawler, E.J. (1994). A new theory of social solidarity. In B. Markovsky, J. O'Brien & K. Heimer (Eds.), *Advances in group processes*, vol. 11 (pp. 113–137). JAI Press.
Moody, J. (2001). Peer influence groups: Identifying dense clusters in large networks" *Social Networks* 23:261–283.
Moody, J., & White, D.R. (2003). Structural cohesion and embeddedness: a hierarchical concept of social groups. *American Sociological Review*, *68*(1), 103–127.
Mucha, P.J., Richardson, T., Macon, K., Porter, M.A., & Onnela, J.-P. (2010). Community structure in time-dependent, multiscale, and multiplex networks. *Science*, *328*, 876–878.
Newman, M.E.J. (2016). Equivalence between modularity optimization and maximum likelihood methods for community detection. *Physical Review E*, *94*(5), 052315.
Newman, M.E.J., & Girvan, M. (2004). Finding and evaluating community structure in networks. *Physical Review E*, *69*, 026113.
Pamfil, A.R., Howison, S.D., Lambiotte, R., & Porter, M.A. (2019). Relating modularity maximization and stochastic block models in multilayer networks. *SIAM Journal on Mathematics of Data Science*, *1*, 667–698.
Peel, L., Larremore, D.B., & Clauset, A. (2017). The ground truth about metadata and community detection in networks. *Science Advances*, *3*, e1602548.
Peixoto, T.P. (2014). The graph-tool python library. figshare. doi: 10.6084/m9.figshare.1164194 [sci-hub, @tor]
Peixoto, T.P. (2022). Descriptive vs inferential community detection: pitfalls, myths and half-truths. *arXiv*, 2112 00183. doi.org/10.48550/arXiv.2112.00183
Pons, P., Latapy, M. (2005). Computing Communities in Large Networks Using Random Walks. In: Yolum, p., Güngör, T., Gürgen, F., Özturan, C. (eds) Computer and Information Sciences - ISCIS 2005. ISCIS 2005. Lecture Notes in Computer Science, vol 3733. Springer, Berlin, Heidelberg. https://doi.org/10.1007/11569596_31
Porter, M.A., Onnela, J.-P., & Mucha, P.J. (2009). Communities in networks. *Notices of the AMS*, *56*, 1082–1097 & 1164–1166.
Priebe, C.E., Park, Y., Vogelstein, J.T., Conroy, J.M., Lyzinski, V., Tang, M., Athreya, A., Cape, J., & Bridgeford, E. (2019). On a Two-truths phenomenon in spectral graph clustering. *Proceedings of the National Academy of Sciences*, *116*, 5995–6000.
Raghavan, U.N., Albert, R. & Kumara, S. (2007). Near linear time algorithm to detect community structures in large-scale networks. *Physical Review E*, *76*, 036106
Reichardt, J., & Bornholdt, S. (2006). Statistical mechanics of community detection. *Physical Review E*, *74*, 016110.
Richards, W.D. (1995). *NEGOPY 4.30: manual and user's guide* Simon Fraser University.
Shai, S., Stanley, N., Granell, C., Taylor, D., & Mucha, P.J. (2020). Case studies in network community detection. In R. Light & J. Moody (Eds.), *The Oxford handbook of social networks* (pp. 309–333). Oxford University Press.
Simmel, G. ([1908]1950). The dyad and the triad. In K.H. Wolff (Ed. & Trans.), *The sociology of Georg Simmel*. Free Press.
Sinkovitz, R.S., Moody, J., Oztan, B.T., & White, D.R. (2017). Fast determination of structurally cohesive subgroups in large networks. *Journal of Computational Science*, 62–72.
Snijders, T., & Nowicki, K. (1997). Estimation and prediction for stochastic blockmodels for graphs with latent block structure. *Journal of Classification*, *14*, 75–100.
Traag, V.A., Waltman, L., & van Eck, N.J. (2019). From Louvain to Leiden: guaranteeing well-connected communities. *Scientific Reports*, *9*, 5233.
Wang, Y.J., & Wong, G.Y. (1987). Stochastic blockmodels for directed graphs. *Journal of the American Statistical Association*, *82*, 8–19
Waters, M.S., Michaels, L., Fey, T., Lohan, L., McAdams, R., Meadows, T., Poehler, A., Gasteyer, A., Chabert, L., & Wiseman, R. (2004). *Mean girls*. Paramount.
Weir, W.H., Emmons, S., Gibson, R., Taylor, D., & Mucha, P.J. (2017). Post-processing partitions to identify domains of modularity optimization. *Algorithms*, *10*, 93.

White, D., & Harary, F. (2001). The cohesiveness of blocks in social networks: node connectivity and conditional density. *Sociological Methodology, 31*, 305–359.

White, H.C. (1963). *An anatomy of kinship: mathematical models for structures of cumulated roles.* Prentice-Hall.

White, H.C. (1966). Catnets. Notes on the constituents of social structure. Unpublished manuscript.

Zachary, W.W. (1977). An information flow model for conflict and fission in small groups. *Journal of Anthropological Research, 33*, 452–473.

Multimodal Social Network Analysis

Lorien Jasny

Where one-mode social network data represents ties among one type of nodes, multimodal networks examine relationships within and between separated groups of nodes referred to as 'modes'. The most common use of multimodal data occurs in bipartite networks. A bipartite network consists of two modes or groups of nodes, and each edge in the network has an endpoint in each mode. Thus, ties are between modes and not within a mode. If the first mode has n members and the second mode has m members, then the bipartite matrix A is an $n \times m$ matrix where the i,jth cell corresponds to whether node i of the first mode is tied to node j of the second mode. Unlike one-mode networks, here the diagonal no longer holds any special meaning because the n and m indices represent different nodes rather than identical ones. Multilevel methods can also examine this bipartite matrix as part of a larger social network of $(n+m) \times (n+m)$ where the $n \times n$ and $m \times m$ entries represent the corresponding one-mode matrices (Borgatti & Everett, 1997). In these networks, different kinds of ties can connect nodes of different modes as well as nodes within one mode. The different modes (and connections within) are thought of as levels. This is in contrast (confusingly) with multilevel network methods where the levels are used in hierarchical modelling of multiple networks (Lomi et al., 2016), but are also referred to as multimodal methods (Knoke et al., 2021c).

The analysis of multimodal data is as old as the study of social networks itself. John Hobson's two-mode study of board members of South African companies and how their relationships defined capitalist enterprise in the country marks one of the earliest empirical studies of social networks (Hobson, 2013 [reprint of the 1926 4th ed.] with description in Freeman, 2004). Corporate interlocks have a long history in social network analysis, especially in the investigation of bipartite methods, that continues to the present (Koskinen & Edling 2012; Valeeva et al., 2020). In these networks individuals make up the first mode and the board of different corporations are the second mode. This represents a type of formalised affiliation or *social neighbourhood* that might reflect a variety of different social processes from repeated direct contacts to similar shared experiences. The diversity highlights how difficult it can be to interpret what 'affiliation' relationships mean in practice (Robins & Alexander, 2004). Another classic form of two-mode data is comprised of people and events they attend. The most famous of these is the Davis women dataset (Davis et al., 2009), and the use of bipartite data for actors and events has only increased in popularity with online and big-data sources (Lazer & Radford, 2017; Wang et al., 2019; Isah et al., 2015; Olson & Neal, 2015; Lerner & Lomi, 2020; Shi et al., 2017; Knoke et al., 2021, Chapter 6). Similar to affiliation ties, co-attendance at events does not guarantee that two individuals met or interacted at the event. Beyond these canonical forms of bipartite data, scholars have pushed the boundaries of network analysis by investigating data not traditionally viewed as a social network with two-mode methods. Networks of respondents by policy stance (Leifeld, 2013), beliefs (Boutyline & Vaisey, 2017), musical tastes (Lizardo, 2018) and relational culture (DiMaggio et al., 2018) constitute new ways of exploring social network questions with a variety of methods tailored specifically for these examples (Goldberg, 2011; Leifeld, 2017). In these examples, the two-mode tie is not a proxy for a one-mode social relationship; the individuals in question may never have met nor even know of each other – for example, they might simply agree on a particular policy statement. However, scholars have shown these relational network structures clearly have methodological and theoretical impact. In sum, where multimode data have always been a part of social network analysis, the interest in and applications of multimodal analysis have only continued to grow.

While in many cases the classification for different modes (what is n and what is m) seems obvious, the separation of nodes into the different modes spans a spectrum from analytically tractable but without any inherent meaning to theoretically deeply meaningful. Sexual disease transmission is sometimes modelled as a two-mode network where each gender is a mode and with the assumption of an entirely heterosexual population (meaning no within-mode ties; see Carnegie & Morris, 2012), and alternatively as one-mode network with gender as an attribute and the probability of within-group ties set far lower (Krivitsky & Morris, 2017). Thus, in this network heterosexual and homosexual relationships are modelled as ties within one node type but with gender as an attribute. Thus, the line between theoretically treating different groups as an entirely separate mode or simply as an attribute can blur. In contrast, when exploring socioecological systems (see Bodin, this volume), the types of nodes are so different (e.g., fishers and fish) and, more importantly, relationships between or within the modes are of entirely different forms that it is difficult to imagine a scenario in which all nodes could be considered one and the same. In these latter cases, researchers often struggle with whether to model the network as multimodal or not. However, unlike in the example of networks representing sexual relationships, combining the two modes of humans and fish together has never appeared as a viable modelling option. Thus, the choice to separate nodes into separate modes is sometimes a practical or data-driven one, and sometimes more theoretically driven.

Just as some consideration must be given to determining the node sets, researchers must also carefully consider what the relationships in their networks signify. In many examples, the two-mode relationship is directly measurable as is the case in previous examples of heterosexual relationships and fishermen catching fish. Often, however, these relationships are obfuscated due to the nature of what can be observed or data that can be collected. Co-attendance at an event or co-participation in a club or social grouping can be a (potentially noisy) proxy for direct social interaction or might instead serve as an indication of similar perspectives or circumstances. The two-mode relationship has been theorised to represent a variety of different social relationships:

> [f]irst, some authors argue that individuals' affiliations with events provide direct linkages between the actors and/or between the events. Second, other authors argue that contact among individuals who participate in the same social events provides conditions under which pairwise ties among individuals become more likely. Third, one can view the interaction between actors and events as a social system that is important to study as a whole.
>
> (Wasserman & Faust, 1994, p. 296)

Each of these options have consequences for both the theoretical underpinnings and interpretation of methodological results. Understanding the nature of the specific ties, and how that might affect your research questions, is of course critical. Both the theory and methods of multimodal systems have evolved alongside questions in one-mode network analysis as scholars explore the meanings of established social ties as well as turn to new forms of data collection.

Classically, the only solution for two- or multimode data was to reduce the method down to one single mode. The most popular method for doing so is the one-mode projection that results from matrix multiplication of the two-mode matrix by its transpose (Breiger, 1974). Using the notation developed above, where A is a two-mode matrix $m \mathrm{X} n$, the one-mode projection that focuses on the first mode is AA^T and the second-mode projection is $A^\mathrm{T}A$. The new one-mode matrix is weighted in that the weights correspond to how many alters any given pair of nodes had in common. The diagonal of this matrix is the degree of the respective mode from the original bipartite matrix.

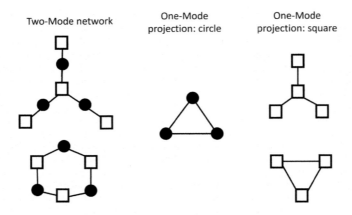

Figure 28.1 Different two-mode matrices with identical one-mode projections

In earlier examinations of two-mode data, often these weights were dichotomised to use classical approaches that were not designed for valued data. This created a sometimes-problematic loss of data in the transformation (Borgatti & Halgin, 2014). Even when the weights are preserved, some data is still lost (Everett & Borgatti, 2013).

Figure 28.1 depicts two different two-mode matrices (left), which correspond to the same one-mode projection (centre) if only the circle mode is considered. It's only when the one-mode projection focusing on the squares is included that the differences between the projections is clear. In the vast majority of empirical cases, incorporating only the one one-mode matrix clearly involves some information loss, but using both one-mode projections – the 'dual-projection' approach – means no loss of information for the majority of empirical cases (Everett & Borgatti, 2013). However, the one-mode projection approach is frequently used when scholars are overwhelmingly more interested in one specific mode and are only interested in the second mode insofar as it connects the first (Robins & Alexander, 2004). In addition to the one-mode projection approach, a variety of other methods use statistical methods to extract important ties among nodes in the one mode from their ties in the second mode (Neal et al., 2022; Shahrezaye et al., 2019; Zhou et al., 2007b; White, 2000). In all of these studies, the authors are cognisant of the impacts of the projection approach on the structure of the resulting network. For example, compared to social networks gathered explicitly as one-mode data, one-mode projections tend to be denser and have higher clustering coefficients (Wasserman & Faust, 1994; Latapy et al., 2008). These differences require changes in the approaches used with traditional social network methods designed for one-mode matrices. Some authors have addressed this by altering standard methods for one-mode matrices to fit the requirements of one-mode projections. Examples include autocorrelation models (Fujimoto et al., 2011), brokerage (Bellotti et al., 2022), community detection (Ling et al., 2022) and permutation models (Jasny, 2012). Overall, the decision to convert two-mode data to one-mode often depends on the context, whether one mode is far more of interest than the second, and whether existing two-mode methods are suitable for addressing the question of interest. The literature is now replete with examples of scholars projecting one-mode data with consideration and attention; while researchers should not automatically think to convert their data from two modes, neither should they reject one-mode applications out of hand.

While the studies above use the second mode as a proxy for the first, more and more frequently the focus and development of multimode analyses are on whole-system approaches. The theory underpinning the full focus on multimodal network structure can be traced to Breiger's classic paper on duality (Breiger, 1974), which expanded Simmel's conceptualisation of identity as a set of overlapping circles of membership (Simmel, [1908]2010). Just as individuals' identities are defined, expanded and constrained by the groups they belong to, the groups' identities are similarly also being negotiated in their networks of interactions (Mohr & White, 2008). This approach to duality challenges the previous interpretation of the second mode as solely a means to understand relationships in the first mode, but rather considers that they are significant and important to understand in their own right. Renewed interest in this interpretation is the motivation behind the recent explosion in methods focused not on reducing multimodal networks to a one-mode network, but instead exploring the full multimodal structure.

The first set of critical methods are simply new ways to visualise multimodal networks. Figure 28.2 shows three very different depictions of the same network data. The left side figure shows a traditional social networks plot with weighted edges (the plot was drawn in the package *network* (Butts, 2008) but similar routines are available in *igraph* (Csardi & Nepusz, 2006)). The centre image shows a Sankey plot (drawn using *networkD3* (Allaire et al., 2017) but similar diagrams are also available in the *bipartite* package (Dormann et al., 2008)). The same network information is conveyed in both, but with very different visual emphases. The first image uses the default layout of a spring-embedded algorithm where nodes that are tied to each other are plotted closer together (Fruchterman & Reingold, 1991), whereas the Sankey plot draws the eye towards who are the biggest senders and receivers. The third image does not show the network ties themselves, but instead is a correspondence plot of the bipartite network data (Faust, 2005; D'Esposito et al., 2014). Here, nodes with more similar ties are plotted closer together. The correspondence analysis reveals structure that is evident in the spring-embedded plot but difficult to determine in the Sankey diagram; events 1 and 6 link Organisations 1 and 2 which are the bridge between the two larger clusters. The cluster on the left in the spring-embedded plot has little structure, which is evident in the overlapping of names in the lower right quadrant of the correspondence analysis, whereas the right cluster has a bit more structure and subsequently is more spread out in the correspondence analysis plot. While this is easy to see in the spring-embedded plot on the left, it would be far more difficult if the network was larger. The Sankey diagram, in contrast, is very good at capturing which events and organisations are more heavily tied to each other with a much greater emphasis on the weights of the ties but it is harder to visualise the clustering or other network structure.

Theory and methods for multimodal networks have co-evolved (Knoke et al., 2021c). Where previously '[m]ethods for studying two-mode affiliation networks ... [were] less well developed than are methods for studying one-mode networks' (Wasserman & Faust, 1994, p. 292), we've seen an explosion in two-mode methods including adaptations for actor-oriented models (Snijders et al., 2013; Koskinen & Edling, 2012), autocorrelation models (Kleinnijenhuis & de Nooy, 2013), blockmodelling (Doreian et al., 2004), brokerage (Jasny & Lubell, 2015), centrality (Faust, 1997; Everett & Borgatti, 2005; Gerdes, 2014; Borgatti & Everett, 1997; Bonacich, 1991), clustering coefficient (Robins & Alexander, 2004; Brunson, 2015; Opsahl, 2013), community detection (Cann et al., 2020; Wang & Liu, 2018; Mucha et al. 2010), exponential random graph models (Wang et al., 2013a; Kevork & Kauermann, 2022; Faust et al., 2002; Agneessens et al., 2004; Skvoretz & Faust, 1999; Pattison & Robins, 2004), key player analysis (Duxbury, 2020), positions (Field et al., 2006) and relational event models (Vu et al., 2015; Quintane et al., 2014). All of these methods have adjusted formula or algorithms to work for a full two-mode structure, where authors have thought through what differences in interpretation must occur when applied to the two-mode graphs. In some cases, the changes to computation are relatively minor. In the example of centrality, one could calculate bipartite indices by changing the ways in which scores are normalised so that they reflect the different maximum possible scores accurately (Borgatti & Everett, 1997; Bonacich, 1991). However, even for these most basic and standard calculations in network analysis, starting from first principles of what the centrality measures should capture, for example whether highly central nodes in the first mode should be connected to highly central nodes in the second mode, can change the interpretation of standard measures in different ways (Faust, 1997). Capturing the spirit of the original measure while adjusting to the multimode data structure is often not straightforward (Brunson, 2015). Similar interpretational differences must be used in some of the statistical models where users need to now differentiate some configurations, for example 2-stars, by whether they contain more nodes in the first or second mode (Skvoretz & Faust, 1999). Combining these counts together by simply using the one-mode term could easily obscure empirical differences. The computation is straightforward and analogous to the one-mode version for most of these models, but deciding how they should be used in two-mode applications, while relatively straightforward, can still vary with context (Wang et al., 2013a).

Although most of the methods just discussed are appropriate for bipartite matrices in which ties are only between modes and not within, new methods for 'multilevel' networks have emerged where ties within each mode as well as between the modes can be analysed conjointly (Wasserman & Iacobucci, 1991; Lomi et al., 2016; Iacobucci & Wasserman, 1990; Lazega et al., 2008; Wang et al., 2013). This is in contrast to another set of multilevel network analyses that instead refer to nested levels of analysis – for example, networks of friendship among children in classrooms nested

THE SAGE HANDBOOK OF SOCIAL NETWORK ANALYSIS

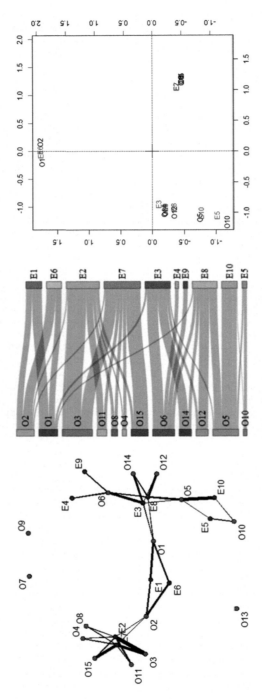

Figure 28.2 Plots of the same two-mode network using a spring-embedded algorithm (left), Sankey diagram (centre) and correspondence analysis (right)

in schools – and is analogous to multilevel modelling in the social sciences more generally (Lazega & Snijders, 2016). Recently, scholars have developed a variety of methods to deal with fully multilevel, multimodal data including stochastic actor-oriented models (SAOMs; see Stadtfeld et al., 2016), autocorrelation models (Bodin et al., 2022), blockmodelling (Žiberna, 2014), conditional uniform graph tests (Bodin & Tengö, 2012), exponential random graph models (ERGM; see Wang et al., 2013b), social selection models (Wang et al., 2016) and visualisation (schochastics 2020). These new approaches to looking at a full ($m+n$) structure where bipartite mXn relationships are considered while simultaneously being embedded with nXn and mXm relations. It represents a fundamental advance for researcher's ability to capture more of the complexity of the social world in a network (Knoke et al., 2021b).

When there are two modes, naturally scholars wonder about pushing the boundaries to include additional different categories of nodes. Networks of three modes or 'tripartite' graphs were first investigated by Fararo and Doreian (1984). Recent additions have included tuples like actors, space and time (Manlove et al., 2018); authors, topics and publication venues (Zhou et al., 2007a); buyers, sellers and brokers (Bonacich et al., 2004); owners, firms and directors (Bohman, 2012); and folksonomies of actors, items and tags (Lambiotte & Ausloos, 2006; Lu et al., 2009; Schmitz et al., 2007; Rafailidis & Daras, 2013). A few methods have been developed for multimodal networks (Ignatov et al., 2017), but most often the analysis is still constrained to projections into two- or one-mode networks due to the lack of methods for full three-mode (and beyond) structures (Knoke et al., 2021b). Most of these examples fall under a tripartite structure where ties are between modes but not within (this is set out explicitly as a rule in Fararo & Doreian, 1984). Others contain hyper-edges where all three modes are linked by the same specific event (e.g., in Bonacich et al., 2004, each sale has one buyer, one seller and one broker). Scholars are still thinking through which of these structures is appropriate to different forms of data, when we can accept some data loss by projecting into one- or two-mode structures, and what fully three-mode methods are necessary.

As an example, consider the data shown in Figure 28.3. This is simulated data, but imagine each black node represents an environmental initiative, and the white nodes represent organisations that fund these initiatives. Ties between initiatives indicate that the sponsors of those initiatives believe that their initiatives mutually support each

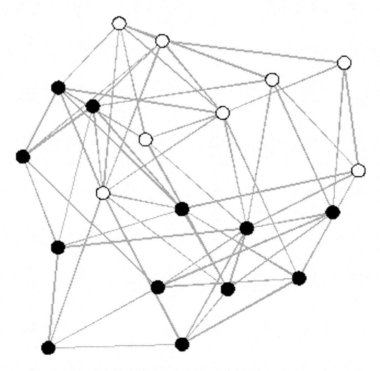

Figure 28.3 A multimodal network of initiatives and funders

other. Ties between initiatives and funders indicate a funding relationship, and ties between funders indicate that these organisations share boardmembers. In a sense, we've already condensed a third mode – these boardmembers – in our dataset. Aside from the tripartite methods mentioned previously, for the most part current analyses still use one-mode projections in cases where otherwise the data structure is simply too complicated. Here, having boardmembers in common represents either a relationship between organisations or merely a similarity between their organisations. The identity of the individual boardmembers is arguably not critical to understanding the relationship between initiatives these organisations support. This assumption must be supported by our understanding of the context – if we believed that support for initiatives depended on the support from one specific boardmember, then we might think about a network between boardmembers and initiatives without the intervening organisation mode. To stress: the choice of modes is entirely dependent on context and understanding who the important nodes are and what are the important relationships to address the research question of interest.

In terms of modelling the network, for example, to use baseline models, ERG models, or an SAOM, we need to first think through whether we want to hold any networks constant. In other words, what are the ties we wish to randomise over, and what should we condition on? For example, in recent work with the fishermen and fish example, we held trophic networks among fish species as constant because we felt that these were unlikely to change over the same period of time as fishermen interacting with each other (Barnes et al., 2022). In our initiatives, organisations and boardmember example, we might think about either conditioning on the network of initiatives to look at questions about funding choices, or we could consider controlling for boardmember interactions to examine a question about initiatives, or we could randomise over all the links simultaneously. Each of these options changes the research question. There is no optimal approach but instead the modelling approach should vary by what is appropriate for the research question and context. If we were interested in predicting ties among initiatives based on having funders in common, we could look at the one-mode projection of the similarity among initiatives by having funders in common and use this projection either in a QAP test or as an edge weight variable in an ERGM or SAOM. In this analysis relationships among the funders don't factor into the answer at all, only the relationships among the initiatives as the dependent variable and the similarity of initiatives by having funders in common (the one-mode projection). By taking the one-mode projection, we're ignoring relationships among funders entirely and we're controlling for funder–initiative links when modelling the relationships between initiatives. The left-hand of Figure 28.4 shows the network among initiatives from Figure 28.3, and on the right-hand side displays the weighted network that results from the one-mode projection of initiatives by funders (plotted on the same coordinates as the left-hand side). We can start to see that there are many differences between the two types of relationships and, indeed, a QAP test would not support any significant correlation between the two.

We could investigate the same question, whether ties between initiatives are related to having funders in common, using a fully multimodal approach without using projections. The motif of interest would be the number of triangles in the full multimodal network with two initiatives and one funder. A significant frequency of this motif would indicate that ties among initiatives are more likely to happen when they have funders in common. We could consider running models conditioning on funder–funder ties and funder–initiative ties, and therefore only simulating the initiative–initiative ties, or we could simulate them all simultaneously. In the latter case, these

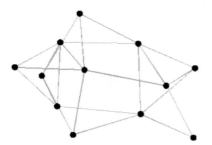 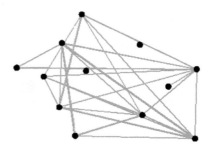

Figure 28.4 One-mode initiative network (left) and projection of initiative-funder network (right)

different kinds of ties should all have different density parameters reflecting the fact that they might change at different rates. More explicitly, in the network in the figure there are seven ties within initiatives, 67 between initiatives and funders and nineteen within initiatives. Even if these numbers were the same, the difference in node type would indicate that, most likely, different generative mechanisms control tie formation with each mode and across modes respectively. Similarly, motifs should specify which type of edge or node is being combined, rather than modelling these jointly. Specifically, it probably wouldn't make much sense to think about a triangle term that combines triangles within initiatives with triangles within funders as well as the two types of triangles that combine node types (one initiative with two funders, and one funder with two initiatives). For this example, there are two triangles within initiatives, two within funders, 41 with two initiatives and one funder, and 108 with two funders and one initiative. Separating out these different kinds of configurations, as well as thinking through the different substantive meanings behind each of these motifs, is a unique aspect of multimodal social network analysis. Researchers must carefully understand which motif or relationship is of interest and how to model this appropriately.

The last few decades have seen a massive growth in the use of multimodal techniques as well as the variety of techniques available and the theory underlying these approaches. Hopefully the next few decades will bring more clarity on a number of open questions. When is it critical to keep to a two-mode (or more) structure and when is a projection appropriate? When are three-mode (or more) networks necessary, and what would methods specific to those data structures look like? Almost all multimode networks currently have undirected ties between modes; what would directionality in a multimodal context look like and can we find cases where it would be theoretically meaningful? We've already seen approaches to multimodal data that incorporate other new approaches for social networks with temporal multimodal methods, methods for large data sets, and more. The exciting prospects for the future are the practical and theoretical insights they bring to all the different fields of social network analysis.

REFERENCES

Agneessens, F., Roose, H., & Waege, H. (2004). Choices of theatre events: P* models for affiliation networks with attributes. *Advances in Methodology and Statistics*, *1*(2), 419–439. doi.org/10.51936/gyae8833

Allaire, J.J., Ellis, P., Gandrud, C., Kuo, K., Lewis, B.W., Owen, J., Russell, K., Rogers, J., Sese, C., & Yetman, C.J. (2017). *NetworkD3: D3 JavaScript network graphs from R* (version 0.4). CRAN.R-project.org/package=networkD3

Barnes, M., Jasny, L., Bauman, A., Ben, J., Berardo, R., Bodin, Ö., Cinner, J., Feary, D., Guerrero, A., Januchowski-Hartley, F.A., & Kuange, J.T. (2022). 'Bunkering down': how one community is tightening social-ecological network structures in the face of global change. *People and Nature*, *4*(4).

Bellotti, E., Czerniawska, D., Everett, M.G., & Guadalupi, L. (2022). Gender inequalities in research funding: unequal network configurations, or unequal network returns? *Social Networks*, *70*(July), 138–151. doi.org/10.1016/j.socnet.2021.12.007

Bodin, Ö., Guerrero, A.M., Nohrstedt, D., Baird, J., Summers, R., Plummer, R., & Jasny, L. (2022). Choose your collaborators wisely: addressing interdependent tasks through collaboration in responding to wildfire disasters. *Public Administration Review*, *82*(6), 1154–1167.

Bodin, Ö., & Tengö, M. (2012). Disentangling intangible social–ecological systems. *Global Environmental Change*, *22*(2), 430–439. doi.org/10.1016/j.gloenvcha.2012.01.005

Bohman, L. (2012). Bringing the owners back in: an analysis of a 3-mode interlock network. *Social Networks*, *34*(2), 275–287. doi.org/10.1016/j.socnet.2012.01.005

Bonacich, P. (1991). Simultaneous group and individual centralities. *Social Networks*, *13*(2), 155–168. doi.org/10.1016/0378-8733(91)90018-O

Bonacich, P., Holdren, A.C., & Johnston, M. (2004). Hyper-edges and multidimensional centrality. *Social Networks*, *26*(3), 189–203. doi.org/10.1016/j.socnet.2004.01.001

Borgatti, S.P., & Everett, M.G. (1997). Network analysis of 2-mode data. *Social Networks*, *19*(3), 243–269. doi.org/10.1016/S0378-8733(96)00301-2

Borgatti, S.P., & Halgin, D.S. (2014). Analyzing affiliation networks. In J. Scott & P.J. Carrington (Eds.), *The Sage handbook of social network analysis* (pp. 417–433). Sage. doi.org/10.4135/9781446294413.n28

Boutyline, A., & Vaisey, S. (2017). Belief network analysis: a relational approach to understanding the structure of attitudes. *American Journal of Sociology*, *122*(5), 1371–1447. doi.org/10.1086/691274

Breiger, R.L. (1974). The duality of persons and groups. *Social Forces*, *53*(2), 181–190. doi.org/10.2307/2576011

Brunson, J.C. (2015). Triadic analysis of affiliation networks. *Network Science*, *3*(4), 480–508. doi.org/10.1017/nws.2015.38

Butts, C.T. (2008). Network: a package for managing relational data in R. *Journal of Statistical Software*, 24(May), 1–36. doi.org/10.18637/jss.v024.i02

Cann, T.J.B., Weaver, I.S., & Williams, H.T.P. (2020). Is it correct to project and detect? How weighting unipartite projections influences community detection. *Network Science*, 8(S1), S145–S163. doi.org/10.1017/nws.2020.11

Carnegie, N.B., & Morris, M. (2012). Size matters: concurrency and the epidemic potential of HIV in small networks. *PLOS One*, 7(8), e43048. doi.org/10.1371/journal.pone.0043048

Csardi, G., & Nepusz, T. (2006). The Igraph software package for complex network research. *Complex Systems*. igraph.org

Davis, A., Gardner, B.B., & Gardner, M.R. (2009). *Deep South: a social anthropological study of caste and class*. University of South Carolina Press.

D'Esposito, M.R., De Stefano, D., & Ragozini, G. (2014). On the use of multiple correspondence analysis to visually explore affiliation networks. *Social Networks*, 38(July), 28–40. doi.org/10.1016/j.socnet.2014.01.003

DiMaggio, P., Sotoudeh, R., Goldberg, A., & Shepherd, H. (2018). Culture out of attitudes: relationality, population heterogeneity and attitudes toward science and religion in the US. *Poetics*, 68(June), 31–51. doi.org/10.1016/j.poetic.2017.11.001

Doreian, P., Batagelj, V., & Ferligoj, A. (2004). Generalized blockmodeling of two-mode network data. *Social Networks*, 26(1), 29–53. doi.org/10.1016/j.socnet.2004.01.002

Dormann, C.F., Gruber, B., & Fründ, J. (2008). Introducing the bipartite package: analysing ecological networks. *Environmental Science*, 8, 4.

Duxbury, S.W. (2020). Identifying key players in bipartite networks. *Network Science*, 8(1), 42–61. doi.org/10.1017/nws.2019.62

Everett, M.G., & Borgatti, S.P. (2005). Extending centrality. In P.J. Carrington, J. Scott & S. Wasserman (Eds.), *Models and methods in social network analysis* (1st ed.) (pp. 57–76). Cambridge University Press. doi.org/10.1017/CBO9780511811395.004

Everett, M.G., & Borgatti, S.P. (2013). The dual-projection approach for two-mode networks. *Social Networks*, 35(2), 204–210. doi.org/10.1016/j.socnet.2012.05.004

Fararo, T.J., & Doreian, P. (1984). Tripartite structural analysis: generalizing the Breiger-Wilson formalism. *Social Networks*, 6(2), 141–175. doi.org/10.1016/0378-8733(84)90015-7

Faust, K. (1997). Centrality in affiliation networks. *Social Networks*, 19(2), 157–191. doi.org/10.1016/S0378-8733(96)00300-0

Faust, K. (2005). Using correspondence analysis for joint displays of affiliation networks. In P.J. Carrington, J. Scott & S. Wasserman (Eds.), *Models and methods in social network analysis* (1st ed.) (pp. 117–147). Cambridge University Press. doi.org/10.1017/CBO9780511811395.007

Faust, K., Willert, K.E., Rowlee, D.D., & Skvoretz, J. (2002). Scaling and statistical models for affiliation networks: patterns of participation among Soviet politicians during the brezhnev era. *Social Networks*, 24(3), 231–259. doi.org/10.1016/S0378-8733(02)00005-9

Field, S., Frank, K.A., Schiller, K., Riegle-Crumb, C., & Muller, C. (2006). Identifying positions from affiliation networks: preserving the duality of people and events. *Social Networks*, 28(2), 97–123. doi.org/10.1016/j.socnet.2005.04.005

Freeman, L.C. (2004). *The development of social network analysis: a study in the sociology of science*. Empirical Press.

Fruchterman, T.M., & Reingold, E.M. (1991). Graph drawing by force-directed placement. *Software: Practice and Experience*, 21(11), 1129–1164.

Fujimoto, K., Chou, C.-P., & Valente, T.W. (2011). The network autocorrelation model using two-mode data: affiliation exposure and potential bias in the autocorrelation parameter. *Social Networks*, 33(3), 231–243. doi.org/10.1016/j.socnet.2011.06.001

Gerdes, L. (2014). Dependency centrality from bipartite social networks. *Connections*, 34(December), 14–28. doi.org/10.17266/34.1.2

Goldberg, A. (2011). Mapping shared understandings using relational class analysis: the case of the cultural omnivore reexamined. *American Journal of Sociology*, 116(5), 1397–1436. doi.org/10.1086/657976

Hobson, J.A. (2013). *The evolution of modern capitalism (Routledge Revivals): a study of machine production*. Reprint of 1926 4th Edition. Routledge. doi.org/10.4324/9780203552063.

Iacobucci, D., & Wasserman, S. (1990). Social networks with two sets of actors. *Psychometrika*, 55(4), 707–720. doi.org/10.1007/BF02294618

Ignatov, D.I., Semenov, A., Komissarova, D., & Gnatyshak, D.V. (2017). Multimodal clustering for community detection. In R. Missaoui, S.O. Kuznetsov & S. Obiedkov (Eds.), *Formal concept analysis of social networks* (pp. 59–96). Lecture Notes in Social Networks. Springer. doi.org/10.1007/978-3-319-64167-6_4

Isah, H., Neagu, D., & Trundle, P. (2015). Bipartite network model for inferring hidden ties in crime data. *Proceedings of the 2015 IEEE/ACM International Conference on Advances in Social Networks Analysis and Mining*, 994–1001. ACM. doi.org/10.1145/2808797.2808842

Jasny, L. (2012). Baseline models for two-mode social network data. *Policy Studies Journal*, 40(3), 458–491. doi.org/10.1111/j.1541-0072.2012.00461.x

Jasny, L., & Lubell, M. (2015). Two-mode brokerage in policy networks. *Social Networks*, *41*(May), 36–47. doi.org/10.1016/j.socnet.2014.11.005

Kevork, S., & Kauermann, G. (2022). Bipartite exponential random graph models with nodal random effects. *Social Networks*, *70*(July), 90–99. doi.org/10.1016/j.socnet.2021.11.002

Kleinnijenhuis, J., & de Nooy, W. (2013). Adjustment of issue positions based on network strategies in an election campaign: a two-mode network autoregression model with cross-nested random effects. *Social Networks*, *35*(2), 168–177. doi.org/10.1016/j.socnet.2011.03.002

Knoke, D., Christopoulos, D., Hollway, J., & Diani, M. (2021a). Agents and events in collective action fields. In D. Knoke, M. Diani, J. Holloway & D. Christopoulos (Eds.), *Multimodal Political Networks* (pp. 134–157). Structural Analysis in the Social Sciences. Cambridge University Press. doi.org/10.1017/9781108985000.007

Knoke, D., Christopoulos, D., Hollway, J., & Diani, M. (2021b). The Potential of Multimodal Political Networks." In D. Knoke, M. Diani, J. Holloway & D. Christopoulos (Eds.), *Multimodal Political Networks* (pp. 197–206). Structural Analysis in the Social Sciences. Cambridge University Press. doi.org/10.1017/9781108985000.010

Knoke, D., Diani, M., Hollway, J., & Dimitris Christopoulos, D. (2021c). *Multimodal Political Networks*. Structural Analysis in the Social Sciences. Cambridge University Press. doi.org/10.1017/9781108985000

Koskinen, J., & Edling, C. (2012). Modelling the evolution of a bipartite network: peer referral in interlocking directorates. *Social Networks*, *34*(3) 309–322. doi.org/10.1016/j.socnet.2010.03.001

Krivitsky, P.N., & Morris, M. (2017). Inference for social network models from egocentrically sampled data, with application to understanding persistent racial disparities in hiv prevalence in the US. *Annals of Applied Statistics*, *11*(1), 427–455. doi.org/10.1214/16-AOAS1010

Lambiotte, R., & Ausloos, M. (2006). Collaborative tagging as a tripartite network. In V.N. Alexandrov, G.D. van Albada, P.M.A. Sloot & J. Dongarra (Eds.), *Computational Science: ICCS 2006*, *3993*, 1114–1117. Lecture Notes in Computer Science. Springer. doi.org/10.1007/11758532_152

Latapy, M., Magnien, C., & Del Vecchio, N. (2008). Basic notions for the analysis of large two-mode networks. *Social Networks*, *30*(1), 31–48. doi.org/10.1016/j.socnet.2007.04.006

Lazega, E., Jourda, M.-T., Mounier, L., & Stofer, R. (2008). Catching up with big fish in the big pond? Multi-level network analysis through linked design. *Social Networks*, *30*(2), 159–176. doi.org/10.1016/j.socnet.2008.02.001

Lazega, E., & Snijders, T.A.B. (2016). Introduction. In E. Lazega & T.A.B. Snijders (Eds.), *Multilevel network analysis for the social sciences: theory, methods and applications* (pp. 1–12). Methodos Series. Springer. doi.org/10.1007/978-3-319-24520-1_1

Lazer, D., & Radford, J. (2017). Data ex machina: introduction to big data. *Annual Review of Sociology*, *43*(1), 19–39. doi.org/10.1146/annurev-soc-060116-053457

Leifeld, P. (2013). Reconceptualizing major policy change in the advocacy coalition framework: a discourse network analysis of German pension politics. *Policy Studies Journal*, *41*(1), 169–198. doi.org/10.1111/psj.12007

Leifeld, P. (2017). Discourse network analysis. In J.N. Victor, A.H. Montgomery & M. Lubell (Eds.), *The Oxford handbook of political networks* (pp. 301–326). Oxford University Press. doi.org/10.1093/oxfordhb/9780190228217.013.25.

Lerner, J., & Lomi, A. (2020). Reliability of relational event model estimates under sampling: how to fit a relational event model to 360 million dyadic events. *Network Science*, *8*(1), 97–135. doi.org/10.1017/nws.2019.57

Ling, L., Li, Y., Long, D., & Wang, Y. (2022). Does syndicating bring syndicating? An exploration targeting ECF based on social structure by complex network analysis. *Social Networks*, *70*(July), 228–239. doi.org/10.1016/j.socnet.2022.02.008

Lizardo, O. (2018). The mutual specification of genres and audiences: reflective two-mode centralities in person-to-culture data. *Poetics*, *68*(June), 52–71. doi.org/10.1016/j.poetic.2018.04.003

Lomi, A., Robins, G., & Tranmer, M. (2016). Introduction to multilevel social networks: Elsevier enhanced reader. *Social Networks*, *44*, 266–268. doi.org/10.1016/j.socnet.2015.10.006

Lu, C., Chen, X., & Park, E.K. (2009). Exploit the tripartite network of social tagging for web clustering. *Proceedings of the 18th ACM Conference on Information and Knowledge Management*, 1545–1548. CIKM '09. ACM. doi.org/10.1145/1645953.1646167

Manlove, K., Aiello, C., Sah, P., Cummins, B., Hudson, P.J., & Paul C. Cross, P.C. (2018). The ecology of movement and behaviour: a saturated tripartite network for describing animal contacts. *Proceedings of the Royal Society B: Biological Sciences*, *285*(1887), 20180670. doi.org/10.1098/rspb.2018.0670

Mohr, J.W., & White, H.C. (2008). How to model an institution. *Theory and Society*, *37*(5), 485–512. doi.org/10.1007/s11186-008-9066-0

Mucha, P.J., Richardson, T., Macon, K., Porter, M.A., & Onnela, J.-P. (2010). Community structure in time-dependent, multiscale, and multiplex networks. *Science*, *328*(5980), 876–878. doi.org/10.1126/science.1184819

Neal, Z.P., Domagalski, R., & Yan, X. (2022). Homophily in collaborations among US House Representatives,

1981–2018. *Social Networks*, *68*(January), 97–106. doi.org/10.1016/j.socnet.2021.04.007

Olson, R.S., & Neal, Z.P. (2015). Navigating the massive world of Reddit: using backbone networks to map user interests in social media. *PeerJ Computer Science*, *1*(May): e4. doi.org/10.7717/peerj-cs.4

Opsahl, T. (2013). Triadic closure in two-mode networks: redefining the global and local clustering coefficients. *Social Networks*, *35*(2), 159–167. doi.org/10.1016/j.socnet.2011.07.001

Pattison, P., & Robins, G. (2004). Building models for social space: neighourhood-based models for social networks and affiliation structures. *Mathématiques et Sciences Humaines. Mathematics and Social Sciences*, *168*(December). doi.org/10.4000/msh.2937

Quintane, E., Conaldi, G., Tonellato, M., & Lomi, A. (2014). Modeling relational events: a case study on an open source software project. *Organizational Research Methods*, *17*(1), 23–50. doi.org/10.1177/1094428113517007

Rafailidis, D., & Daras, P. (2013). The TFC model: tensor factorization and tag clustering for item recommendation in social tagging systems. *IEEE Transactions on Systems, Man, and Cybernetics: Systems*, *43*(3), 673–688. doi.org/10.1109/TSMCA.2012.2208186

Robins, G., & Alexander, M. (2004). Small worlds among interlocking directors: network structure and distance in bipartite graphs. *Computational and Mathematical Organization Theory*, *10*(1), 69–94. doi.org/10.1023/B:CMOT.0000032580.12184.c0

Schmitz, C., Grahl, M., Hotho, A., Stumme, G., Cattuto, C., Baldassarri, A., Loreto, V., & Servedio, V. (2007). Network properties of folksonomies. *Ai Communications*, *20*(December), 245–262.

schochastics (2020). Visualizing multilevel networks with graphlayouts: R-bloggers. 25 April. www.r-bloggers.com/2020/04/visualizing-multilevel-networks-with-graphlayouts/

Shahrezaye, M., Papakyriakopoulos, O., Serrano, J.C.M., & Hegelich, S. (2019). Measuring the ease of communication in bipartite social endorsement networks: a proxy to study the dynamics of political polarization. *Proceedings of the 10th International Conference on Social Media and Society*, 158–165. ACM. doi.org/10.1145/3328529.3328556

Shi, F., Shi, Y., Dokshin, F.A., Evans, J.A., & Macy, W.M. (2017). Millions of online book co-purchases reveal partisan differences in the consumption of science. *Nature Human Behaviour*, *1*(4), 1–9. doi.org/10.1038/s41562-017-0079

Simmel, G. ([1908]2010). *Conflict and the web of group affiliations*. Simon & Schuster.

Skvoretz, J., & Faust, K. (1999). Logit models for affiliation networks. *Sociological Methodology*, *29*(1), 253–280. doi.org/10.1111/0081-1750.00066

Snijders, T.A.B., Lomi, A., & Torló, V.J. (2013). A model for the multiplex dynamics of two-mode and one-mode networks, with an application to employment preference, friendship, and advice. *Social Networks*, *35*(2), 265–276. doi.org/10.1016/j.socnet.2012.05.005

Stadtfeld, C., Mascia, D., Pallotti, F., & Lomi, A. (2016). Assimilation and differentiation: a multilevel perspective on organizational and network change. *Social Networks*, *44*(January), 363–374. doi.org/10.1016/j.socnet.2015.04.010

Valeeva, D., Heemskerk, E.M., & Takes, F.W. (2020). The duality of firms and directors in board interlock networks: a relational event modeling approach. *Social Networks*, *62*(July), 68–79. doi.org/10.1016/j.socnet.2020.02.009

Vu, D., Pattison, P., & Robins, G. (2015). Relational event models for social learning in MOOCs. *Social Networks*, *43*(October), 121–135. doi.org/10.1016/j.socnet.2015.05.001

Wang, D.J., Rao, H., & Soule, S.A. (2019). Crossing categorical boundaries: a study of diversification by social movement organizations. *American Sociological Review*, *84*(3), 420–458. doi.org/10.1177/0003122419846111

Wang, P., Pattison, P., & Robins, G. (2013a). Exponential random graph model specifications for bipartite networks: a dependence hierarchy. *Social Networks*, *35*(2), 211–222. doi.org/10.1016/j.socnet.2011.12.004

Wang, P., Robins, G., Pattison, P., & Lazega, E. (2013b). Exponential random graph models for multilevel networks. *Social Networks*, *35*(1), 96–115. doi.org/10.1016/j.socnet.2013.01.004

Wang, P., Robins, G., Pattison, P., & Lazega, E. (2016). Social selection models for multilevel networks. *Social Networks*, *44*(January): 346–362. doi.org/10.1016/j.socnet.2014.12.003

Wang, X., & Liu, J. (2018). A comparative study of the measures for evaluating community structure in bipartite networks. *Information Sciences*, *448–449*(June), 249–262. doi.org/10.1016/j.ins.2018.03.036

Wasserman, S., & Faust, K. (1994). *Social network analysis: methods and applications*. Cambridge University Press.

Wasserman, S., & Iacobucci, D. (1991). Statistical modelling of one-mode and two-mode networks: simultaneous analysis of graphs and bipartite graphs. *British Journal of Mathematical and Statistical Psychology*, *44*(1), 13–43. doi.org/10.1111/j.2044-8317.1991.tb00949.x

White, D.R. (2000). Manual for statistical entailment analysis 2.0: Sea.Exe. *World Cultures*, *11*(1).

Zhou, D., Councill, I., Zha, H., & Giles, C.L. (2007a). Discovering temporal communities from social network documents. *Seventh IEEE International Conference on Data Mining (ICDM 2007)*, 745–750. doi.org/10.1109/ICDM.2007.56

Zhou, T., Ren, J., Medo, M., & Zhang, Y.-C. (2007b). Bipartite network projection and personal recommendation. *Physical Review E*, *76*(4), 046115. doi.org/10.1103/PhysRevE.76.046115

Žiberna, A. (2014). Blockmodeling of multilevel networks. *Social Networks*, *39*(October), 46–61. doi.org/10.1016/j.socnet.2014.04.002

Blockmodeling, Positions and Roles

Patrick Doreian, Anuška Ferligoj, and Vladimir Batagelj

SOCIAL NETWORKS

A simple social network consists of a set of units, called social actors, with a single relation defined over them. For example, the units could be children and the relation defined as 'plays with'. For a family, the units can be parents and children. One relationship is 'controls' for parents acting towards their children. A more complex network has multiple relations. For the children in a playground, the relations studied could be 'plays with' and 'likes'. An even more complicated network has multiple relations and multiple modes. For a family, the modes are for parents and for children and the relationships studied could include 'controls', 'loves' (and/or 'hates'), 'respects' and 'confides in'. Additional modes (levels) could include multiple generations. In formal organizations with hierarchies, units can be individuals occupying locations at multiple levels with the relations 'reports to', 'seeks work related help from', 'provides work related help to' and 'socializes at breaks.'

Units in a social network can also include groups, organizations, and nations as well as the individuals in these larger and more extensive units. If the units are gangs the relations between them include alliance ties and enemy ties. For organizations, relations can include sending goods or people between organizations, sharing information, or forming alliances. For nations, the relations can include exports to, imports from, providing aid, belonging to military alliances and waging war. Networks can be made up also of objects that have no obvious 'action' identity as actors in the sense of individuals, groups, organizations, or nations. An example is the set of scientific documents for one or more scientific fields. These units include books, articles and research reports. One relation defined over these objects is citation. Almost every scientific document contains references to earlier relevant work and the relational ties are citations of earlier documents by later documents. Patents form a similar set of units where the citations are governed by legal requirements to acknowledge all prior relevant inventions and their patent documents and nothing else. In general, data sets can be created with large networks and multiple types of units. Obviously, the way this is done depends on the size and complexity of the network(s) considered.

Network data can be analyzed in many different ways. There is no single best approach to network clustering. This is a wide-open realm with multiple exciting approaches. One approach is to identify the overall structure of a network and presenting this in a simpler fashion. Blockmodeling does this.

The primary emphasis in this chapter is on generalized blockmodeling (Doreian et al., 2005) which is used for establishing positions, as clusters, in networks and network images that are a simpler version of the overall structure. For the ease of exposition, most of our discussion is focused on simple networks. Given a blockmodel partition, the clusters are labeled positions. The ties between positions and within positions are called *blocks*.

BLOCKMODELING

An early application of blockmodeling ideas is provided in Davis et al. (1941) who presented the Southern Women data as a two-mode table. The modes were women attending events over time and the events attended by the women. The data were reordered according to clusters of women with similar attendance patterns and the events according to which women attended them. See also Freeman (2003) and Everett and Borgatti (2020) for an extended discussion of these data.

One publication dramatically changed the way network analysts viewed the delineation and examination of social network structure. Lorrain and White (1971) introduced the concept of structural equivalence (defined below) as a way of operationalizing both positions and roles in social networks. In doing so, they set the foundations for rigorously studying empirical social structure and examining role systems. The idea was to identify important structural features of networks and link them to the potential roles actors could play. We write further on this below when considering pre-specification of blockmodels. This led directly to the creation of blockmodeling. Breiger et al. (1975) presented a practical algorithm for establishing positions in a network. It was based on a particular way of operationalizing structural equivalence in terms of correlations. Each actor in a network has a set of ties to other actors. This forms a set of locations which can be correlated. This algorithm iteratively uses correlations of locations to identify positions and therefore blocks.

Sailer (1978) provided another way of thinking about blockmodeling. This was later formalized by White and Reitz (1983) with the introduction of regular equivalence as a formal generalization of structural equivalence. Borgatti and Everett (1989) provided a discussion of the class of all regular equivalences for a network. In 1992, the flagship journal of the field, *Social Networks*, devoted a special issue to blockmodeling featuring a variety of approaches that had been created since the early statements helping to define the field. Generalized blockmodeling was created as another systematic approach and secured the foundations of blockmodeling (Doreian et al., 2005). See also Batagelj et al. (1992a, b) for the initial statements outlining this approach. In the following, we do not discuss the details of the various algorithms used for establishing blockmodels. Instead, we focus attention on the core ideas. Our discussion of blockmodeling distinguishes classic blockmodeling and generalized blockmodeling. In doing so, we put the formal/mathematical foundations to one side. The cited documents informing our discussion provide the technical and formal details behind the *mainly* nonmathematical statement provided here. However, some notation is needed here. See also Batagelj (2020) for a general discussion of partitioning networks.

Classic Blockmodeling

Some terms are used to provide a way of describing networks precisely. Actors are represented by *node*s (also known as vertices or units) and social ties between them are represented by *links* (lines, arcs, or edges). A network, denoted N, is comprised of a set of nodes, V, and a set of links, L. Formally, N = (V, L). Some relations are inherently symmetric, for example, co-authoring a scientific paper. For such relations, a link representing a symmetric tie is called an *edge* and the network can be represented as N = (V, E) where E is the set of edges. Such networks are called *undirected networks*. Other social relations are inherently asymmetric. For example, 'parent of' is a relation represented by a directed link that goes from a parent to a child. For networks with only directed links are called *arcs* and the network is written N = (V, A) where A is the set of arcs.

Some relations are defined with an inherent direction but contain symmetric edges. Liking provides an example with an obvious direction – but if one person likes another and the sentiment is reciprocated then, for such a pair, there is a symmetric tie (edge) between them. Other liking ties need not be reciprocated and there is an arc from one person to another. Such a network can be written N = (V, (E, A)) where L = E ∪ A and are no links belonging to both A and E, E ∩ A = ∅. For representing networks with multiple relations, this notation extends naturally to N = (V, (L_1, L_2, ..., L_r)) for a set of r relations. The ideas discussed below apply to all networks but, for ease of exposition, we use single relation networks having no parallel links.

Two nodes are *structurally equivalent* if they are linked in exactly the same way to all other actors in the network. A formal definition can be found in Doreian et al. (2005, p. 172). A set of identified structurally equivalent nodes is called a *position*. If the network has only sets of structurally equivalent nodes, then it is fully consistent with structural equivalence. This means the set of nodes, V, can be partitioned into a set of k clusters, {C_1, C_2, . ., C_k} so that the nodes in a cluster C_i are structurally identical. There are k positions in the network (representing a social structure). This provides a precise operationalization of the term position as being a cluster of nodes. Given, two positions, C_i and C_j, the set of links from all nodes in C_i to all nodes in C_j forms a block. Given k positions there are k^2 blocks and the whole structure is represented by these blocks. Usually, k is much smaller than n (the number of nodes). The structure of the network is represented by a blockmodel or image network where there are only positions (as model nodes) and blocks (model links) – hence the term 'blockmodel'.

White et al. (1976) argue that the representation of a network as a blockmodel image describes a role structure precisely with a clear formulation of positions with the potential to infer the nature of roles. Some pairs of nodes are more likely to be 'almost structurally equivalent' in the sense that their distribution of links is 'almost' the same to other actors. These differences, if small in number, are assumed to not matter much empirically. Put differently, having such small differences implies that the empirical delineation of a blockmodel will not change in large ways for the method being employed. This raises the issue of empirically determining the positions and blocks. While there are many ways of doing this, we confine our attention to those used most frequently. Two of these methods hinge on ways of representing the extent to which pairs of nodes are structurally equivalent.

Burt (1976) proposed an alternative way of operationalizing 'almost structurally equivalent' by using the corrected Euclidean distances between nodes. If two nodes are structurally equivalent, then the corrected Euclidean distance between their locations is 0. 'Almost structurally equivalent' became 'the corrected Euclidean distance is close enough to 0'. The matrix of locations is turned into a matrix of distances which is then subjected to a standard clustering method. Doreian et al. (2005) describe algorithms of the sort suggested by Burt (1976) and Breiger et al. (1975) as 'indirect methods' because the network data are converted into (dis)similarity measures which are clustered using some clustering algorithm. There are three inherent problems with indirect approaches: (1) there are many ways of constructing (dis)similarities not all of which are compatible with an equivalence type; (2) there are many clustering algorithms, the choice of one of them often seems arbitrary; and (3) the methods can be used only in an *inductive* fashion. The third is most consequential as clustering tree diagrams or dendrograms are examined to discern the clusters subsequentially labelled positions. There is no upfront conceptualization beyond the idea of using structural equivalence and analysts accepting what is returned by the clustering algorithm. These problems led Batagelj et al. (1992a, b) to pursue a 'direct approach' to blockmodeling. This was formalized further into 'generalized blockmodeling' (Doreian et al., 1994, 2005) as a general method for partitioning networks into positions and blocks. Their analyses suggest that the direct approach produces better fitting partitions based on equivalence concepts than the indirect approach. Even so, the indirect approach remains useful and can be used more effectively for larger networks than the direct approach (described below) can currently manage.

Generalized Blockmodeling

Generalized blockmodeling (Batagelj, 1997; Batagelj et al., 1992a, b; Doreian et al., 1994, 2005) is a direct approach to network data which, rests on a simple idea. First, rather than thinking about structural equivalence as being approximated by a measure of (dis)similarity, it is more useful to think about the kinds of blocks consistent with structural equivalence, or any kind of equivalence for more general blockmodels. See Doreian et al. (2005, Chapter 6) for a listing of block types and a comparison of blockmodels based on different conceptions of block types.

The direct approach sets up comparisons of an ideal blockmodel based on various definitions of equivalence. Given a definition of equivalence, the ideal blocks are those that are consistent with the equivalence. For structural equivalence only complete (all 1) and null (all 0) blocks are ideal. In general, the empirically established blockmodel approximates an ideal blockmodel. Differences between ideal and empirical blockmodels are easy to construct conceptually. Wherever a 1 appears in a null block there is one type of inconsistency and wherever there is a 0 in a complete block there is another type of inconsistency. All we have to do is count the inconsistencies and seek an empirical partition that minimizes the number of inconsistencies. For this, a clustering problem is formulated with a *criterion function* that represents the sum of all of the inconsistencies from all of the blocks. The clustering problem is to establish a partition into k clusters given that a criterion function is minimized. The only block types for structural equivalence are null and complete blocks. Let A be the number of 1s in a potential null block and B the number of 0s in a potential complete block, the criterion function is $CF = A + B$.

Solving the clustering problem is not easy. While it sounds useful to compare an ideal block with all possible empirical blocks this can be done only for small networks. Some heuristic is needed. Within the generalized blockmodeling problem, a relocation heuristic makes local comparisons of possible ideal and empirical blockmodels. Some number (k) of clusters is chosen and the network nodes are partitioned randomly into k provisional positions. The *neighborhood* for such a partition is made up of other partitions that can be reached by either of the two types of changes. One is simply to move a node from one provisional position to another position. The second is to exchange a pair of nodes between two provisional positions. For each change, the criterion function can be calculated before and after the change. If the criterion function does not decline, then the new partition is discarded. But if it does decline, then the algorithm moves to the new partition. This is repeated until no further reduction of the criterion function is found. Because this is a local optimization method, this must be repeated many times to increase the likelihood of reaching a globally best partition. However, reaching this is not guaranteed.

White and Reitz (1983) generalized the idea of structural equivalence to regular equivalence. Two nodes are *regularly equivalent* if they are linked in equivalent ways to equivalent others. (A formal definition can be found in Doreian et al., 2005, p. 173). White and Reitz (1983) proved that regular equivalence is a proper generalization of structural equivalence. This equivalence was included in the generalized blockmodeling approach with the recognition that regular equivalence permits only two block types: null blocks and blocks that have a 1 in every row and every column of the block. Such blocks are called *1-covered* or *regular* blocks.

Again, a criterion function expressing inconsistencies between ideal and empirical blocks for regular equivalence can be constructed and the local optimization method described above can be used.

Some expanded block types are presented in Doreian et al. (2005, Chapter 7). These new types included row-regular blocks (each row is 1-covered) and column-regular blocks (each column is 1-covered). These were used to partition baboon grooming networks at two points in time where neither structural nor regular equivalence were useful. This general strategy of expanding block types, and hence new types of blockmodels, permits an indefinite expansion of blockmodeling. When different substantive domains are considered, it is likely new block types will be needed. As we see the expansion of blockmodeling in other substantive domains, this is what we observe. We regard these expansions as critically important. Doreian et al. (2005, Chapter 11) present a 'ranked-clusters' blockmodel to study the structure of children's networks and the marriage system for nobility in Ragusa (now known as Dubrovnik) in the 18th and 19th centuries. The analysis was driven by the work of Batagelj (1997). See also Batagelj and Mrvar (2007).

However, with regular equivalence, there is a serious problem. Consider Figure 29.1 which shows a network created by Everett (see Borgatti & Everett, 1989). There is a clear partition using regular equivalence with three positions: [a, c, b, j]; [b. d. g. i]; and [e. f]. At face value, this example presents a compelling case. For the value of regular equivalence as the value of the criterion function is 0. But it is a constructed example. The problem is that empirically, the concept of regular equivalence nearly always fails to provide useful partitions. As Franz Pappi put it 'why does the use of regular equivalence hardly ever work empirically?'[1] He is correct, which raises serious questions. It is, without doubt, a far better conception for partitioning networks in terms of structure and was formulated very well. Could the failure,

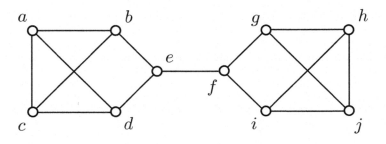

Figure 29.1   The constructed Everett network

thus far, be due to algorithmic shortcomings? If so, better algorithms are needed. But what if the initial conceptualization, despite its brilliance, is the fundamental problem? If it is, this needs to be addressed.

Since the value of a criterion function depends on various factors (e.g., the block types allowed, the network size and network density), the criterion function values obtained for different networks are directly incomparable (Doreian et al., 2005). To address this problem, a *relative fit* (RF) measure was proposed by Cugmas et al. (2021c). It is a measure used to evaluate the extent to which inconsistencies are present in an established blockmodel. These values may be used to select the appropriate blockmodel types and/or the number of clusters. The definition of RF is provided in Cugmas et al. (2021c, pp. 1318–1319). Values of the RF measure can also be of value when fitting different empirical networks to a given specified blockmodel. This is an important development for the empirical application of blockmodeling.

There are some important and useful results stemming from using generalized blockmodeling. First, by setting up a clustering problem with a criterion function that is fully compatible with a type of blockmodel (the criterion function is non-negative and has value 0 exactly when the corresponding partition agree with the assumed equivalence), the criterion function becomes an explicit measure of fit for this blockmodel. Of course, different criterion functions are defined for different types of blockmodel, and each is tailored to the type of blockmodel used. This implies that the values of the criterion function cannot be compared across diverse types of blockmodels and also not for networks of different sizes. The logic of the approach is to formulate models and then fit them to the data using an appropriate criterion function compatible with the blockmodel type. Each blockmodel stands or falls on its own fit to the data.

Second, much can be done by formulating models and fitting them. We often know more about a social network than the applicability of a particular type of equivalence which most often amounts to an expression of ignorance. The more we know, or think we know, about a network, the more we can 'pre-specify' a blockmodel. This is a critical insight. We may know not only the permitted block types but also where some of them are in a blockmodel. (Indeed, we might know where all of them appear in blockmodel.) If we have some knowledge – which can be empirical, or it could have a theoretical foundation – it is useful to pre-specify a blockmodel that uses this knowledge. When this is done, generalized blockmodeling is used in a deductive fashion.

Another element of knowledge is that some nodes belong together in a position or that some pairs of nodes will belong to distinct positions. This kind of knowledge is expressed in the form of constraints on which positions nodes can be placed. The extreme level of knowledge is that we know the structure of the blockmodel image and the positions to which all nodes belong, and this would be expressed in a *completely pre-specified blockmodel*. More likely, pre-specification, if possible, will be partial. Examples of some pre-specified blockmodels are found in Doreian et al. (2005, pp. 233–246).

SIGNED NETWORKS

Signed networks have a set of nodes and a relation whose links can be positive, negative, or null. Such a network can be written N = (V, (P, N, Z)) where P is the set of all positive links, N is the set of all-negative links and Z is the set of all null links. By definition P ∩ N is empty as are P ∩ Z and N ∩ Z, as they are mutually disjoint. Both directed (arcs) and undirected (edges) signed links are possible.

A theoretically driven example of deductive blockmodeling is found with structural balance theory Heider (1946) as formalized by Cartwright and Harary (1956). There are eight possible triples as shown in Figure 29.2. The top row shows four balanced triples – the product of their signs is 1. The bottom row shows four imbalanced triples – the product of their signs is negative. If the signed network has signed links between all pairs of nodes it is complete. A complete signed network is balanced if all of its triples are balanced.

If a signed network is balanced then the nodes can be partitioned into two sets such that all of the positive links are between nodes within clusters and all of the negative links are between nodes in different clusters (Cartwright & Harary, 1956). If the network is not complete in the sense of not having signed ties between all pairs of vertices, the same result holds if it is balanced. Based on the work of Davis (1967) who defined the all-negative triple as balanced, this partitioning idea can be extend to two or more positions such that all of the positive links are within positions and all of the negative links are between positions. Doreian and Mrvar (1996) noted that this implies a particular blockmodel structure with two types of blocks. *Positive blocks* contain only positive or null links and *negative blocks* contain only negative or null links. The implied signed blockmodel

Four Balanced Triples

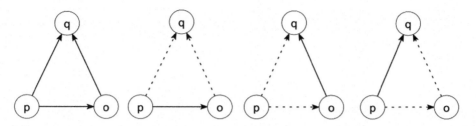

Four Imbalanced Triples

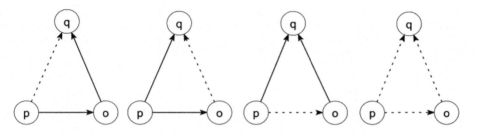

Figure 29.2 Triples for structural balance theory

Note: Solid lines represent positive arcs and dashed lines represent negative arcs.

has positive blocks on the diagonal and negative blocks off the diagonal. Doreian and Mrvar proposed a way of partitioning signed networks that are as close as possible to a partition expected for exact structural balance. The criterion function they proposed counts two types of inconsistencies – positive links in negative blocks and negative links in positive blocks. These inconsistencies can be weighted differently if desired. The relocation algorithm described earlier for generalized blockmodeling is used to solve this clustering problem and is now an integral part of the generalized blockmodeling approach. Examples include women on a college campus (Doreian, 2008), nation states (Doreian & Mrvar, 2015; Traag et al., 2020) and the US Supreme Court decisions (Doreian & Mrvar, 2020).

For signed networks the only block types are all positive blocks and all-negative blocks. Let P be the number of positive ties in what is thought to be a negative block and N the number of negative ties in what is thought to be positive blocks. A simple criterion function is $CF = N + P$. This can be formulated also as $CF = \alpha N + (1 - \alpha) P$ where α lies between 0 and 1. Thus far, signed network partitioning has used $\alpha = 0.5$. However, different values of α can lead to different partitions. Choosing the best value of α is an open problem.

A general criticism of the use of the relocation algorithm in the direct blockmodeling approach is that there is no guarantee that its use will provide the optimal solutions or yields of all of the equally well-fitting partitions for a particular network. Brusco et al. (2011) provide convincing evidence that for 'small problems' (where the number of nodes is less than 30–35) the relocation method does return almost all of the optimal partitions of a signed one-mode network. This was done through comparing the results of the two algorithms using several signed empirical networks regarding the results they produced. However, while the relocation algorithm can manage much larger signed networks, the branch and bound method cannot. Also, the relocation algorithm and the branch and bound algorithm are not identical in terms of the difficulties they encounter with different network features such as size, density of links and the relative proportions of positive and negative links. Brusco et al. (2011) advocate using both algorithms. And the idea of a guarantee, at this time, has not been extended to signed two-mode networks. Potential applications of two-mode signed partitioning of two-mode networks include, in addition to Supreme Court voting patterns, Congressional voting (in the US), voting in other deliberative bodies and voting at the United Nations.

POSITIONS AND ROLES

The paired concepts of positions and roles are staples among social network terms (Ferligoj et al., 2011). The idea of a position is a location in a social structure and a role has a set of expected behaviors thought to be associated with a position. Child is another position that carries age-graded expectations of appropriate conduct by children towards their parents. Expectations of parents and children are coupled into a system of roles. Similarly, in an organization there are locations in some structure, stereotypically, a hierarchy, and roles are coupled to these locations. Expectations include rules for how superiors and subordinates behave in relation to each other. Roles are defined for all levels and positions in the hierarchy and form a coupled system of expectations. Of course, this simple description identifies an idealized form – there can be many variations. Key empirical issues involve delineating positions in social systems, identifying roles that correspond to these positions, the nature of, and extent to which, these roles exist and examining how both role systems and social structures change over time.

Social network analysis provides a set of tools including ways for mapping social structures in ways helping to identify positions and roles. When used for studying social structures over time these tools help analysts understand how social structures and role systems change over time. However, being able to identify process rules generating observed changes over time allows us to examine the evolution of social structures over time. Both network dynamics and network evolution have a place in studying positions and roles. This issue has been tackled in a creative way in terms of the mechanisms generating and maintaining a blockmodel structure over time and the mechanisms for changes in such structures over time. (See Cugmas et al., 2020a; Cugmas et al., 2020b; Cugmas et al., 2021a)

We offer another view of positions and roles based on the work of Doreian and Mrvar (2020) in their exploration of fundamental structures of the US Supreme Court. Figure 29.3 presents an alternative perspective on the roles of actors in

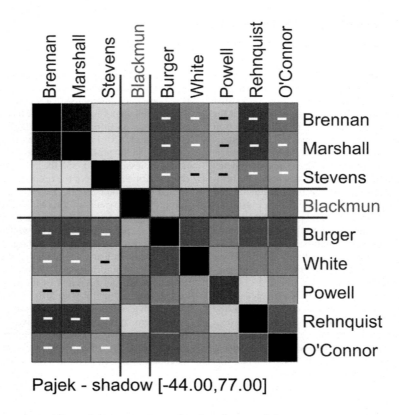

Figure 29.3 A partition of Supreme Court justices into positions

signed social networks. It was created using Pajek (Batagelj & Mrvar, 1998).

It shows a partition of the justices in the sixteenth term of the Burger Court with three clusters. Three liberal justices (Brennan, Marshall and Stevens) are in the first position. Blackmun, a modest liberal, is a singleton in the second position. All of the conservatives occupy the third position. The cells depict the overall net agreements (positive valued items) or net disagreements. Negative net valued disagreements are marked with a minus sign. The magnitudes of the net ties range from –44 to 77 as shown by the Pajek shadow line. The values of the diagonal elements are counts of the number of times a justice was present for a decision. They can be ignored as justices agree with themselves. The darker the shading the more extreme the net agreements or disagreements. The highest level of agreement is between Brennan and Marshall (68). The highest level of disagreement is between Brennan and Rehnquist (–44).

The profile for Blackmun is unusual as he had net positive links with all the other justices. It suggests a new interpretation of the notion of role. Given the conventional split between conservatives and liberals, he was, in this term, involved in a *bridging role* for the liberals and conservatives. Other such examples were identified within this Supreme Court research program for many other terms of the US Supreme Court.

SOME OTHER EXTENSIONS OF GENERALIZED BLOCKMODELING

More examples of ideas and analyses can be viewed as extending generalized blockmodeling ideas in diverse ways that hold promise. There are many such efforts, but we can only cover some of them.

Two-mode and Three-mode Network Arrays

Borgatti and Everett (1992), in the special double issue of *Social Networks* devoted to blockmodeling methods, suggested applying blockmodeling ideas, to multiway network arrays and provided a way of doing so. This moved the approach beyond analyzing single one-mode networks. This extension can also be formulated as a generalized blockmodeling problem where the network is defined by several sets of units and ties between them. Doreian et al. (2005) did this for blockmodeling two-mode networks. The examples they used included the classic Deep South data set (Davis et al., 1941) and Supreme Court voting for a single term. More recently, Batagelj et al. (2007) applied these ideas to three-way network data. In addition to analyzing network data with three distinct types of social objects, they considered two unusual cases. One allowed that the two of the modes were same in a three-way array and the second has all ways the same mode in the three-way array. Krackhardt (1987) office data were used to illustrate this approach. Each of the 22 nodes in this network provided their image of the one-mode relational data for the office. When these 22 perceptions are coupled a full three-way array is created. Even this special case poses severe computational problems for the direct approach that have not been solved. Instead, Batagelj et al. (2007) proposed a dissimilarity measure for structural equivalence for all three cases and adopted an indirect approach. To do this they expressed structural equivalence as an interchangeability condition across modes for three-way networks. This allowed the construction of a compatible dissimilarity measure. Ward's (1963) clustering method was used to obtain the three-dimensional partitioning via hierarchical clustering.

Everett and Borgatti (2020) returned to this topic to couple a variety of ideas including two-mode partitioning, community detection and the notion of dual projections generally, and for our consideration of the Supreme Court signed networks and spectral clustering. See also Jasny (this volume).

Valued Networks

Doreian et al. (2005) confined their attention to binary networks. This was an admitted limitation. As the initial work on blockmodeling dealt with binary networks, extending and adapting this approach to handle valued networks is most important. This task was picked up initially by Batagelj and Ferligoj (2000) and later by Žiberna (2007). He proposed three approaches to generalized blockmodeling valued data by assuming that the values of the links are measured on at least interval scale.

Žiberna (2007) proposed a straightforward generalization of generalized blockmodeling of binary networks to valued blockmodeling by using a threshold parameter; links are assessed in relation to the value of the threshold (without binarizing the network). Patterns within blocks, as signatures of block types, are still examined to identify block types. One problem that emerged is that two blocks with the same pattern of links, but with different values for the links that are present, cannot be distinguished. This implies that such differences in link values cannot be used to locate optimal partitions. This led Žiberna (2008) and Nordlund (2016) to consider another approach called *homogeneity blockmodeling* in which the inconsistency of an empirical block, compared with a corresponding ideal block, is measured by the variability of values within blocks. Ideally, all of the values inside a block are the same which is fully consistent with the idea of blocks being composed of identical links. The homogeneity partitioning establishes blocks with minimum variation in the values of the links within the blocks. While these are present, there is another problem. For binary blockmodeling there is a clear distinction between null blocks and other block types. Yet a null block is homogeneous and cannot be readily distinguished as a special distinctive block type under homogeneity blockmodeling. As a result, while homogeneity blockmodeling is well suited for distinguishing empirical blocks based on link values and finding partitions based on such differences, it is less suited for distinguishing empirical blocks based on block types and finding partitions based on such distinctions. This led Žiberna to consider implicit blockmodeling of valued networks.

While the three approaches to blockmodeling valued relations proposed by Žiberna, all have problems; they are best viewed as important first steps towards establishing better solutions to this class of network partitioning problems. They were proposed, in part, as a response to some results he obtained while examining an obvious strategy for blockmodeling a valued network. Some threshold was selected and used to binarize the network: links at, or above, the threshold are coded 1 while links below the threshold are set to 0. The binarized networks were then treated with the approach advocated by Doreian et al. (2005). We now think that binarizing valued data is a poor data analytic strategy under all circumstances. Consistent with this, Žiberna found this was a poor general strategy because the established partitions can be unstable and can produce different blockmodels depending on the threshold selected. We think he is correct.

Weber and Denk (2007) proposed an approach for valued blockmodeling for input–output relations viewed as networks. Flows between industrial or economic sectors, as an aggregation of flows between businesses, are clearly valued. And the flows that go into national input–output tables can be analyzed also at a 'lower' level with businesses as the units. Regardless of whether data for these flows express the volume of goods and services flowing or their monetary values, it is foolish to even think of these data as binary. So, if blockmodeling is contemplated, it has to deal with valued data whose values can vary greatly. Given that goods and services flow between units, it is natural to think of these data as two-mode data with the rows as transmitters (exporters) and the columns as receivers (importers). Doreian et al. (2005, pp. 265–269) did exactly this for journal-to-journal citation networks. For business-to-business transaction patterns, businesses can remain a part of a trading network or leave, while other businesses can join the trading flows. Studying such economic networks includes evaluating businesses, characterizing the overall structure of these networks along with clustering both nodes and relations. It is possible to identify gaps, both in the form of missing nodes and missing links, in these networks. Additionally, the flows are not simply between pairs of nodes because indirect flows are important and merit attention. While indirect paths of varying length have been considered by network analysts thinking of what flows from one node to another and then onto a third node in social networks is much harder to conceptualize than for economic flow networks.

Another important contribution to this topic was provided by Nordlund and Žiberna (2020). They provided an extensive discussion of treating valued data and provided an invaluable figure (6.2) of a control chart for choosing suitable approaches. They contrast both indirect and direct approaches for blockmodeling in a useful fashion.

DEALING WITH MISSING DATA

Laumann et al. (1983) presented a discussion of the boundary problem for social network analysis. They made it clear that specifying the boundaries of networks must be done with great care to ensure the correct specification of a network. In the context of this argument, there is a major problem for all analyses of social network data which relies on having complete information about the networks studied. See Huisman (2009) for an initial statement regarding missing social network data. But missing data can take many forms. The most problematic, in our view, is when respondents in a studied network refuse to respond or provide no data of any sort. The unfortunate standard response for most analyses is to simply ignore these missing respondents. The result is that the studied network has been shrunk, sometimes considerably, which compromises all subsequent analyses. But, as far as we are concerned, this is a major mistake, endemic to the field; in the data, there are links to those who did not respond. Throwing away such data almost amounts of network analytic crime. The research program of Žnidaršič et al., for example (2017, 2020), reveals that it is possible to reconstruct the network with great accuracy. With the reconstructed network, blockmodeling results most often can be dramatically improved. See also Krause and Huisman, this volume.

STOCHASTIC BLOCKMODELING

The generalized blockmodeling approach, as described above, is explicitly deterministic. A criterion function expressing the score of a clustering problem is minimized to determine the 'best' partition(s) given the criterion function. An alternative strategy is to adopt a probabilistic approach and treat the underlying processes in a stochastic fashion. Mirroring structural equivalence as an underlying conception, two nodes are stochastically equivalent if they have the same probability distribution of their links to other nodes (Holland et al., 1983; Wasserman & Anderson, 1987; Anderson et al., 1992). Using probabilities for links established from the data, positions are populated with stochastically equivalent nodes.

Nowicki and Snijders (2001) developed a Bayesian approach for stochastic blockmodeling. The links can have categorical values and the parameters of their model are estimated by a Markov chain Monte Carlo (MCMC) procedure. Two features of their approach are noteworthy for this discussion: (1) missing data can be managed and (2) given the network data, some nodes may be unclassifiable into a position. Most discussions of blockmodeling quietly ignore the problems of missing data which can have serious consequences (see above). The idea of there being some nodes not belonging to positions was first noted by Burt (1976) in the form of a *residual cluster* and this, too, has been enabled in generalized blockmodeling using the 'do not care' type of blocks.

Airoldi et al. (2007a, b) introduced a family of stochastic blockmodels that combine features of mixed-membership models and blockmodels for relational data in a hierarchical Bayesian framework. They proposed a nested variance inference scheme for this class of models, which is necessary to successfully perform fast approximate posterior inference. Handcock et al. (2007) proposed a new model with latent positions under which the probability of a link between two nodes depends on the distance between them in an unobserved Euclidean 'social space', and the locations of nodes in the latent social space arise from a mixture of distributions, each corresponding to a cluster. They proposed two estimation methods: a two-stage maximum likelihood method and a fully Bayesian method that uses MCMC sampling. They also proposed a Bayesian way of determining the number of clusters that are present by using approximate conditional Bayes factors.

A different approach was made by Peixoto (2020) who wrote about the use of Bayesian inference to extract large-scale modular structures from network data based on a variant of the stochastic blockmodel. Surprisingly, his argument suggests that both network analysis and network partitioning are worthless compared to his approach. If people pay attention to this, the unfolding debate will be lively. See also Peixoto (2014) for an earlier statement.

CONCLUSIONS

There is no doubt that partitioning networks is a most important subject ranging across multiple disciplines with multiple approaches for doing this. The contributions to Doreian et al. (2020a) make this abundantly clear with views from multiple perspectives. We make no claim that blockmodeling is the best such approach, but it has a focus on positions and roles that is absent from most other discussions of partitioning networks. The social scientific importance of considering blockmodeling, positions and roles has to do with their roles in social systems and how they work.

We have noticed that when blockmodeling is applied to empirical networks focused on different substantive domains within distinct disciplines there are often changes in blockmodeling techniques. This suggests that thinking in terms of appropriate block types will lead to new types of blockmodels.

We recognize that much of the work on blockmodeling is static in the sense of focusing on the structure of a network at one point in time. While important, this raises temporal issues regarding blockmodel. Do blockmodel structures change over time? In most cases, yes, they do. Cugmas et al. (2020b) look closely at the stability of scientific citation networks over time. Doreian and Mrvar (2020) did the same for the US Supreme Court. Both of these analyses were descriptive. While being reasonable, something more may be required. A nod in this direction is provided by Schaub et al. (2020) who take network dynamics very seriously.

Note

1. Personal conversation with the first author.

REFERENCES

Airoldi, E.M., Blei, D.M., Fienberg, S.E., & Xing E.P. (2007a). Combining stochastic block models and mixed membership for statistical network analysis. In *Lecture notes in computer science* (pp. 57–74). Springer.

Airoldi, E.M., Blei, D.M., Fienberg, S.E., & Xing, E.P. (2007b). *Mixed membership stochastic blockmodels*. Department of Statistics, Carnegie Mellon University.

Anderson, C.J., Wasserman, S., & Faust, K. (1992). Building stochastic blockmodels. *Social Networks*, 14, 137–161.

Batagelj, V. (1997). Notes on Blockmodeling. *Social Networks*, 19, 143–155.

Batagelj, V. (2020). Clustering approaches to networks. In P. Doreian, V. Batagelj & A. Ferligoj (Eds.), *Advances in network clustering and blockmodeling* (Chapter 3). Wiley.

Batagelj, V., Doreian, P., & Ferligoj, A. (1992a). An optimization approach to regular equivalence. *Social Networks*, 14, 63–90.

Batagelj, V., & Ferligoj, A. (2000). Clustering relational data. In W. Gaul, O. Opitz & M. Schader (Eds.), *Data analysis* (pp. 3–15). Part of a book series *Studies in Classification, Data Analysis, and Knowledge Organization*. Springer.

Batagelj, V., Ferligoj, A., & Doreian, P. (1992b). Direct and indirect methods for structural equivalence. *Social Networks*, 14, 121–135.

Batagelj, V., Ferligoj, A., & Doreian, P. (2007). Blockmodeling of 3-way networks. In P. Brito, G. Cucumis, P. Bertrand & F. de Carvalho (Eds.), *Selected contributions in data analysis and classification* (pp. 151–159). Part of a book series *Studies in Classification, Data Analysis, and Knowledge Organization*. Springer.

Batagelj, V., Ferligoj, A., & Doreian, P. (2020). Bibliometric analysis of the network clustering literature. In P. Doreian, V. Batagelj & A. Ferligoj (Eds.), *Advances in network clustering and blockmodeling* (Chapter 2). Wiley.

Batagelj, V., & Mrvar, A. (1998). Pajek: a program for large network analysis. *Connections*, 21(2), 47–57.

Batagelj, V., & Mrvar, A. (2007). Analysis of kinship relations with Pajek. *Social Science Computer Review*, 26(2), 224–246.

Borgatti, S.P. & Everett, M.G. (1992). Regular blockmodels of multiway, multimode matrices. *Social Networks*, 14, 91–120.

Borgatti, S.P., & Everett, M.G. (1989). The class of all regular equivalences: algebraic structure and computation. *Social Networks*, 21, 183–188.

Breiger, R.L., Boorman, S.A., & Arabie, P. (1975). An algorithm for clustering relational data with applications for social network analysis and comparison to multidimensional scaling. *Journal of Mathematical Psychology*, 12, 328–383.

Brusco, M., Doreian, P., Mrvar, V., & Steinley, D. (2011). Two algorithms for relaxed structural balance partitioning: linking theory, models and data to understand social network phenomena. *Sociological Methods and Research*, 40(1), 57–87.

Burt, R.S. (1976). Positions in networks. *Social Forces*, 55(1), 93–122.

Cartwright, D., & Harary, F. (1956). Structural balance: a generalization of Heider's theory. *Psychological Review*, 63, 277–292.

Cugmas, M., Delay, D., Žiberna, A., & Ferligoj, A. (2020a). Symmetric core-cohesive blockmodel in preschool children's interaction networks. *PLOS One*, 15(1).

Cugmas, M., Ferligoj, A., & Kronegger, L. (2020b). Scientific co-authorship networks. In P. Doreian, V. Batagelj & A. Ferligoj (Eds.), *Advances in network clustering and blockmodeling* (Chapter 13). Wiley.

Cugmas, M., Ferligoj, A., Škerlavaj, M., & Žiberna, A. (2021a). Global structures and local network mechanisms of knowledge-flow networks. *PLOS One*, 16(2).

Cugmas, M., Ferligoj, A., & Žiberna, A. (2021b). Generating global network structures by triad types. *PLOS One*, 13(5).

Cugmas, M., Žiberna, A., & Ferligoj, A. (2021c). The relative fit measure for evaluating a blockmodel. *Statistical methods and applications*, 30(5), 1315–1335.

Davis, A., Gardner, B., & Gardner, M.R. (1941). *Deep South*. Chicago University Press.

Davis, J.A. (1967). Clustering and structural balance in graphs. *Human Relations*, 20, 181–187.

Doreian, P. (2008). A multiple indicator approach to structural balance. *Social Networks*, 30, 247–258.

Doreian, P., Batagelj, V., & Ferligoj, A. (1994). Partitioning networks based on generalized concepts of equivalence. *Journal of Mathematical Sociology*, 19, 1–27.

Doreian, P., Batagelj, V., & Ferligoj, A. (2000). Symmetric-acyclic decomposition of networks. *Journal of Classification*, 17, 3–28.

Doreian, P., Batagelj, V., & Ferligoj, A. (2005). *Generalized blockmodeling*. Cambridge University Press.

Doreian, P., Batagelj, V., & Ferligoj, A. (Eds.) (2020a). *Advances in network clustering and blockmodeling*. Wiley.

Doreian, P., Ferligoj, A., & Batagelj, V. (2020b). Conclusion and directions for future work, In P. Doreian,

V. Batagelj & A. Ferligoj (Eds.), *Advances in network clustering and blockmodeling* (Chapter 14). Wiley.

Doreian, P., & Mrvar, A. (1996). A partitioning approach to structural balance. *Social Networks*, 18(2), 149–168.

Doreian, P., & Mrvar, A. (2009). Partitioning signed social networks. *Social Networks*, 31, 1–11.

Doreian, P. & Mrvar, A. (2015). Structural Balance and Signed International Relations. *Journal of Social Structure*, 16(2) 1–49.

Doreian, P., & Mrvar, A., (2020). Delineating changes in the fundamental structure of signed networks. *Advances in Physics*. doi: 10.3389/fphy.2020.00294

Everett, M.G., & Borgatti, S.P. (2020). Partitioning multimode networks. In P. Doreian, V. Batagelj & A. Ferligoj (Eds.), *Advances in network clustering and blockmodeling* (Chapter 9). Wiley.

Faust, K., & Wasserman, S. (1992). Blockmodels: interpretation and evaluation. *Social Networks*, 14, 5–61.

Ferligoj, A., Doreian, P., & Batagelj, V (2011). Positions and roles. In Scott, J. & Carrington, P.J. & S. Wasserman (Eds.), *The Sage Handbook of social network analysis* (Chapter 29). Sage. 434–446.

Freeman, L.C. (2003). Finding groups: a meta-analysis of the Southern Women data. In R. Breiger, C. Carley & P. Pattison (Eds.), *Dynamic social network modeling and analysis: workshop summary and papers* (pp. 39–79). National Research Council and the National Academies.

Handcock, M.S., Raftery, A.E., & Tantrum, J.M. (2007). Model-based clustering for social networks. *Journal of the Royal Statistical Society: Series A*, 170, 301–354.

Heider, F. (1946). Attitudes and cognitive organization. *Journal of Psychology*, 21, 107–112.

Holland, P.W., Laskey, K.B., & Leinhardt, S. (1983). Stochastic blockmodels: some first steps. *Social Networks*, 5, 109–137.

Huisman, M. (2009). Imputation of missing network data: some simple procedures. *Journal of Social Structure*, 10(1).

Jasny, L. (2023). Multimodal social network analysis. In P.J. Carrington, J. Scott & S. Wasserman (Eds.), *Models and methods for social network analysis*. Sage.

Krackhardt, D. (1987). Cognitive social structures. *Social Networks*, 9, 109–134.

Krause, R., & Huisman, M. (2023). Missing data. In P.J. Carrington, J. Scott & S. Wasserman (Eds.), *Models and methods for social network analysis*. Sage.

Laumann, E.O., Marsden, P.V., & Prensky, D. (1983). The boundary specification problem in network analysis. In R.S. Burt & M.J. Minor (Eds.), *Applied network analysis: a methodological introduction* (pp. 18–34). Sage.

Lorrain, F., & White, H.C. (1971). Structural equivalence of individuals in social networks. *Journal of Mathematical Sociology*, 1, 49–80.

Mrvar, A., & Doreian, P. (2009). Partitioning signed two-mode data. *Journal of Mathematical Sociology*, 33, 196–221.

Nordlund, C. (2016). A deviational approach to blockmodeling of valued networks. *Social Networks*, 44, 160–178.

Nordlund, C., & Žiberna, A. (2020). Blockmodeling networks of valued network. In P. Doreian, V. Batagelj & A. Ferligoj (Eds.), *Advances in network clustering and blockmodeling* (Chapter 6). Wiley.

Nowicki, K., & Snijders, T.A.B. (2001). Estimation and prediction for stochastic block structures. *Journal of the American Statistical Association*, 96, 1077–1087.

Peixoto, T.P. (2014). Efficient Monte Carlo and greedy heuristic for the inference of stochastic blockmodels. *Physical Review E*, 89, 012804.

Peixoto, T.P. (2020). Bayesian stochastic blockmodeling In P. Doreian, V. Batagelj & A. Ferligoj (Eds.), *Advances in network clustering and blockmodeling* (Chapter 11). Wiley.

Reichardt, J., & White D.R. (2007). Role models for complex networks. *European Physical Journal B: Condensed Matter and Complex Systems*, 60, 217–224.

Roffilli, M., & Lomi, A. (2006). Identifying and classifying social groups: a machine learning blockmodeling. In H.-H. Bock, V. Batagelj, A. Ferligoj & A. Žiberna (Eds.), *Data science and classification* (pp. 149–157). Part of a book series *Studies in Classification, Data Analysis, and Knowledge Organization*. Springer.

Sailer, L.D. (1978). Structural equivalence: meaning and definition, computation, and application. *Social Networks*, 1, 73–90.

Schaub, M.T. Delvenne, J.-C., Lambiotte, R., & Barahona, M. (2020) Structured networks and coarse-grained descriptions: a dynamical perspective. In P. Doreian, V. Batagelj & A. Ferligoj (Eds.), *Advances in network clustering and blockmodeling* (Chapter 12). Wiley.

Traag, V., Doreian. P., & Mrvar, A. (2020). Partitioning signed networks. In P. Doreian, V. Batagelj & A. Ferligoj (Eds.), *Advances in network clustering and blockmodeling* (Chapter 8). Wiley.

Ward, J.H. Jr (1963). Hierarchical grouping to optimize an objective function. *Journal of the American Statistical Association*, 58, 236–244.

Wasserman, S., & Anderson, C.J. (1987). Stochastic a posteriori blockmodels: construction and assessment. *Social Networks*, 9, 1–36.

Weber, M., & Denk, M. (2007). Valued blockmodeling for input–output applications. Paper presentated at the Workshop on Blockmodeling, Faculty of Social Sciences, Ljubljana.

White, D.R., & Reitz, K.P. (1983). Graph and semigroup homomorphisms on networks of relations. *Social Networks*, *5*, 193–234.

White, H.C., Boorman, S.A., & Breiger, R.L. (1976). Social structure from multiple networks: I blockmodels of roles and positions. *American Journal of Sociology*, *81*, 730–779.

Žiberna, A. (2007). Generalized blockmodeling of valued networks. *Social Networks*, *29*, 105–126.

Žiberna, A. (2008). Direct and indirect approaches to blockmodeling of valued networks in terms of regular equivalence. *Journal of Mathematical Sociology*, *32*, 57–84.

Žiberna, A. (2020). Blockmodeling linked networks. In P. Doreian, V. Batagelj & A. Ferligoj (Eds.), *Advances in network clustering and blockmodeling* (Chapter 10). Wiley.

Žnidaršič, A., Ferligoj, A., & Doreian, P. (2017). Actor non-response in valued social networks: the impact of different non-response treatments on the stability of blockmodels. *Social Networks*, *48*, 46–56.

Žnidaršič, A., Doreian, P., & Ferligoj, A. (2020). Treating missing network data before partitioning. In P. Doreian, V. Batagelj & A. Ferligoj (Eds.), *Advances in network clustering and blockmodeling* (Chapter 7). Wiley.

Inferential Network Clustering with Hierarchical Bayesian Stochastic Blockmodels

Pierson Browne, Tyler Crick, and John McLevey

Methods and models for network clustering have long been at the core of social network analysis (see Scott et al., this volume). Since the 1970s, network clustering has developed along two deeply intertwined conceptual paths: one focusing on cohesive subgroups and assortative community structure (e.g., see Moody & Mucha, this volume), the other focusing on equivalence, social roles and structural positions (e.g., see Dorien et al., this volume).

Early research on social cohesion sought to identify fully connected subgroups in friendship networks (Festinger, 1949; Luce & Perry, 1949), while later work would focus more on social homophily or heterogeneity among closely connected groups (Friedkin, 1984; Collins, 1988; Erickson, 1988). Increases in the size and complexity of network data have driven the development of many new methods for measuring social cohesion (Wasserman & Faust, 1994), and for scaling up to large networks in reasonable timespans. The well-known and oft-employed Louvain algorithm for optimising modularity (Blondel et al., 2008) and the improved Leiden algorithm (Traag et al., 2019) are noteworthy contributions to this line of work.

The other path, which we are primarily concerned with in this chapter, seeks to cluster nodes based on a structural and/or probabilistic definition of node *equivalence*, such as having identical sets of ties to other nodes. However defined, the concept of equivalence enables researchers to reduce complex networks to simplified representations of the relationships between positions, roles, or *blocks*. We provide a brief high-level overview of this work below; interested readers can find a more detailed account of role theory and positional analysis in Dorien et al. (this volume), which focuses on generalised blockmodelling. In this chapter, we will focus on a probabilistic approach to blockmodelling: the hierarchical Bayesian stochastic blockmodel.

This chapter is organised in two parts. The purpose of the first is to introduce foundational ideas related to (1) equivalence and blockmodelling, (2) Bayesian inference and latent variable models and, finally, (3) the synthesis of these ideas in the form of Bayesian stochastic blockmodels (BSBMs). In the second part of the chapter, we focus on two empirical examples that illustrate some important considerations when developing and interpreting BSBMs.

FOUNDATIONAL IDEAS

Equivalence and Blockmodels

Unlike network clustering methods that are primarily concerned with cohesion and connectivity, blockmodels are ultimately concerned with the concept of *equivalence*. In a classic paper, Lorrain and White (1971) introduced in the idea of 'structural equivalence' as follows:

> a is structurally equivalent to b if a relates to every object x of [the set of nodes] C in exactly the same ways as b does. From the point of view of the logic of the structure, then, a and b are absolutely equivalent, they are substitutable.
> (Lorrain & White, 1971, p. 63)

From the start, this work has been highly influenced by anthropological role theory, specifically the work of S.F. Nadel (1957), who emphasised the inherent complexity of measuring social roles and positions. The overarching goal of early work on blockmodels was to algorithmically reduce complex networks to simplified models of the relationships between structurally distinct social roles, or *positions*. Any possible partition produced by a blockmodel could represent an imperfect proxy of the role structure. White et al. (1976) acknowledge this explicitly in their classic paper: 'the blockmodels of this paper can be said to identify positions, but only in an elementary sense' (p. 734). With Nadel (1957), they contend that data on many types of ties are needed to apprehend social structure, and it is therefore important to consider multiple models (White et al., 1976). Robins (2011) echoes this sentiment, suggesting that although social networks are 'built by social processes that are ongoing and multiple', patterns in network data 'provide evidence from which we may infer something of the social processes that build the network' (p. 484). In short, it is not necessarily the case that structurally equivalent nodes perform the same social roles, and no single blockmodel can hope to capture the totality of a social dynamic within a given network.

The earliest blockmodels used a variety of deterministic approaches to partition empirical networks into clusters of equivalent nodes (Arabie & Boorman, 1982; Arabie et al., 1978; Boorman & White, 1976; Breiger et al., 1975; Light & Mullins, 1979; Wasserman & Faust, 1994; White et al., 1976). However, the requirement that nodes be perfectly interchangeable has proven to be too strict in practice, especially given the complexity of social relationships and the imperfections of data collection and measurement. This led to further innovations in blockmodelling techniques (see Dorien et al., in this volume) as well as more relaxed criteria for equivalence, such as *regular equivalence* (White & Reitz, 1983) and *stochastic equivalence*. The latter is the basis of an approach that has come to be known as the *stochastic blockmodel* (SBM).

Stochastic Equivalence and Blockmodels

Unlike deterministic blockmodels, which require perfect or near-perfect interchangeability between nodes in a block, SBMs partition networks into blocks of *stochastically* equivalent nodes (Anderson et al., 1992; Holland et al., 1983; Nowicki & Snijders, 2001; Snijders & Nowicki, 1997; Wang & Wong, 1987; Wasserman & Anderson, 1987). In an SBM, blocks are organised so as to maximise the likelihood of block membership conditional on hypothesised edge probabilities, and therefore do not need to be perfectly uniform.

For a simple stochastic blockmodel to describe directed network A with N nodes, we need three pieces of information:

1 E, the total number of edges between nodes in A
2 b, a vector of length N containing a block assignment for each node in the network where each $b_n \in \{1...B\}$, where B is the number of distinct blocks
3 p_{rs}, a B-by-B matrix where $r, s \in \{1...B\}$, describing the probability of observing an edge from any node in group r to any node in group s.

Any two nodes in the same block are taken to be stochastically equivalent, which implies that any node in a given block will send ties to other nodes with the same probability as any other node in the same block. This is as true of the interblock edges (p_{rs}, $r \neq s$) which is the probability that a node in one block sends an edge to a node in a different block, as it is of within-block edges (p_{rs}, $r = s$) where a node sends an edge to another node in the same block. It also implies that SBMs can identify blocks in which the nodes do not share any edges with one another, which is not the case for network clustering methods focused on cohesion (e.g., modularity-based algorithms such as Louvain and Leiden).

Fitting an SBM to an observed network requires determining the number of non-empty blocks to use and then partitioning the nodes (b) accordingly. Since the matrix of edge probabilities (p_{rs}) is determined by the block partition (b), each possible permutation of b can be viewed as a possible explanation of the data.[1] Each of these explanations is assigned a likelihood (i.e., a probability that it is the 'correct' explanation), with likelier explanations of the data being assigned more weight than less likely explanations.

While inference about b is often straightforward – though potentially time-consuming and costly in computing power – the choice of B is difficult to make. Early work on SBMs focused on cases where the number of blocks was assumed or known *a priori* (Nowicki & Snijders, 2001; Snijders & Nowicki, 1997). A generalisable approach to determining the most appropriate *B* value for a given network would come later.

Inferential network clustering

So far, we've contrasted cohesion-based approaches to network clustering with positional approaches and offered a high-level comparison of how stochastic equivalence and stochastic blockmodels differ from their deterministic counterparts. Before proceeding any further, let's briefly return to the comparison with cohesion-based network clustering.

With some empirical networks, an SBM may not initially appear to produce results that differ meaningfully from those produced by community detection algorithms based on notions of cohesion rather than equivalence. In fact, certain configurations of the SBM can be coaxed into producing plausible partitions along similar lines as cohesion-based methods (Zhang & Peixoto, 2020). Closer inspection of the two should, however, dispel any notion that they are the same.

Consider the case of a random graph with an arbitrary number of nodes, a number of edges placed between nodes completely at random and whose density falls somewhere between *dense* and *sparse* (such as an Erdős–Rényi graph with a middling *p* (Erdős & Rényi, 1959)). In most such generated networks, traditional modularity-based methods such as Louvain are prone to identifying *communities* from random noise (Peixoto, 2019). Blockmodel-based methods do not. The key point here is that *traditional* community detection algorithms seek to understand networks *as they are observed*, whereas SBMs seek to understand *how networks came to be*, or *how they are generated*. In this sense, we can describe most traditional community detection techniques as *descriptive* (Peixoto, 2021a) and SBMs as *inferential* or *generative*.

Currently, descriptive approaches to network clustering are more widely used than inferential approaches. This is not necessarily a problem, as neither description nor inference enjoys any monopoly on the truth – in network science or otherwise – nor does one predominate over the other in terms of applicability and utility. Descriptive forms of network clustering are invaluable for identifying certain features of an observed network, such as determining which edges are the most vital to community cohesion (e.g., Moody & Mucha, this volume). However, inferential approaches should be used to answer inferential questions, and network analyses concerned with

tie formation and other unobserved generative processes that generate those networks necessarily involve inference (Peixoto, 2021a).

Piexoto (2021a) has proposed a *litmus test* that is helpful in determining whether an inferential approach should be used. The idea is a simple one: after partitioning a network into groups, we learn that our network was generated randomly. Does this alter the utility of our partition? If so, then it is likely that an inferential approach is necessary and descriptive approaches are inappropriate. If not, then it is likely that an inferential approach is not necessary and descriptive approaches are appropriate. In other words, if the generative process that gave rise to the observed network is relevant, then we need an inferential approach; if not, description is likely to be as appropriate, if not more so.

Bayesian approaches to blockmodelling are particularly effective at partitioning networks given some representation of unobserved generative processes and, unlike many other approaches to blockmodelling, can determine the most appropriate number of blocks to account for a given network. Before getting into the details of Bayesian stochastic blockmodels (BSBMs), we'll offer a brief overview of Bayesian inference and latent variable models for readers who are new to Bayesian statistics. Other readers should feel free to skip to the subsequent section.

THE LOGIC OF BAYESIAN INFERENCE AND LATENT VARIABLE MODELS

At its core, the Bayesian approach to inference uses data to update knowledge about one or more unobserved random variables (McElreath, 2020). This is accomplished via Bayes' ubiquitous theorem, which states that the probability of an event *A* conditional on another event *B* is equal to the probability of *B* conditional on *A* multiplied by the unconditional probability of *A* divided by the unconditional probability of *B*. The foregoing can be encapsulated as such:

$$P(A \mid B) = \frac{P(B \mid A)P(A)}{P(B)}$$

While Bayes' theorem is widely accepted and applied across all statistical paradigms and disciplines, Bayesian *inference* distinguishes itself by using probability to describe logically informed states of belief with respect to a given proposition. By way of contrast: the other major statistical paradigm, Frequentism, only permits the use of probability for events that can be sampled from among a population or repeated a theoretically infinite number of times, and thus does not view probability as compatible with statements about hypotheses, propositions, or states of belief (Clayton, 2021).

Readers familiar with Frequentist inference will know that the standard approach to ordinary least-squares (OLS) regression modelling, for example, stipulates that the relationship between a dependent variable (y) and one or more independent variables (X) is governed by a commensurate number of *parameters*. In the simplest case, there is one parameter for each independent variable (β) plus one parameter for the intercept (α), and the value of each is considered *fixed* but unknown. Frequentist doctrine demands this; since parameter values cannot be sampled from, they do not have a frequency. They are true, or they are not. As such, Frequentist tests of statistical significance are configured to assess the plausibility of the observed data assuming the *null* hypothesis (indicating 'no difference' or 'no correlation') is true. If the data is deemed unlikely enough (with the threshold, α, set pre-experimentally), the null is 'rejected' in favour of the data-determined 'alternative' hypothesis.

In the Bayesian paradigm, unobserved random variables in a model are conceptualised as *latent variables*, information about which can be encoded using probability distributions.[2] Rather than treating unobserved variables as fully unknown but with an assumed fixed value (as the Frequentist paradigm does for its parameters), Bayesian inference generally places *weakly informative* distributions over its latent variables and then updates them using observed data.[3] These distributions (known as *priors*, see below) are designed to be consistent with the knowledge researchers have about the latent variables before confronting them (and the rest of the model) with empirical data.

Each of the possible values a latent variable can take can be thought of as an individual 'hypothesis' about the value of that variable (e.g., the hypothesis that $\beta = 0.59$).[4] Bayesian inference seeks to describe the relative plausibility of all such hypotheses (which we'll represent using H) conditional upon a model and observed evidence (the latter of which we'll represent with E). This can be accomplished via Bayes' theorem, which in this setting establishes that the probability of a hypothesis (H) given some evidence (E) is equal to the likelihood of that evidence given some hypothesis, multiplied by the unconditional probability of the hypothesis, divided by the unconditional probability of the evidence. Returning to Bayes' theorem, but with the new symbols subbed in, we get:

$$P(H \mid E) = \frac{P(E \mid H)P(H)}{P(E)}$$

Each of the components in the foregoing expression is individually named:

- *P(H|E)* is the probability of a given hypothesis conditional upon the observed evidence. This is our quantity of interest, and it is known as the *posterior probability* or *inferential probability* (Clayton, 2021).
- *P(E|H)* is referred to as the *likelihood* or *sampling probability* of the data (Clayton, 2021). Likelihood in the Bayesian context is generally identical to that employed in the classical or Frequentist paradigms. It measures the probability of observing the evidence we did observe under the assumption that the hypothesis is true.
- *P(H)* is called the *prior*, and it represents our extant knowledge about the hypothesis *before observing the data*. Bayesian models treat priors as latent variables whose probability distributions are logically determined by the information available to the researcher (Cox, 1946; Jaynes, 2003). While some may baulk at the inclusion of prior information, the use of a prior is essential for producing a posterior probability.
- *P(E)* stands for the unconditional probability of the evidence and is sometimes referred to as the *Bayes denominator* or the *marginal probability of the data*. In many applied settings, this value is difficult to conceptualise and impossible to compute analytically. Fortunately, it only serves to normalise the product in the numerator (ensuring that all posterior probabilities sum to 1), and sampling-based techniques such as MCMC largely obviate the need to know it directly (McElreath, 2020).

The Bayesian use of latent variables confers a great many advantages over the Frequentist adherence to parameter values. For the purposes of this chapter, the most salient advantage is that Bayesian latent variables are never reduced to a single point estimate: at all times, they are configured so as to contain complete descriptions of their probability mass (in the case of discrete variables) or probability density (in the case of continuous variable). This permits Bayesian inference to sustain consideration of multiple plausible values for any given latent variable, weighted proportionally to their posterior probability. The Frequentist approach, conversely, identifies a single value that uniquely maximises likelihood and discards all others.

Latent variables also permit Bayesian models to run as well *forwards* as they do *backwards*. What we mean by this is that any well-specified Bayesian model is as well suited for inferential purposes (backwards) as it is for simulation (forwards).[5] The inferential mode – as discussed above – uses data to update prior distributions over a model's latent variables using the likelihood of the data, which produces a posterior distribution for each latent variable. The simulative mode draws samples from the joint distribution of the model's latent variables to produce a synthetic dataset – this can be done using prior information alone (before observing data), or with the latent variables' posterior distributions.[6]

Some, in fact, have gone as far as to use latent variables as a sort of grand unifying principle, arguing that even observed data is simply a special case of a probability distribution (McElreath, 2020).[7] This view is consistent with the Bayesian paradigm's treatment of measurement error and missing data: the former uses the observed value as a parameter for a distribution representing uncertainty, and the latter treats the missing value as a latent variable with a weakly informative distribution conditioned on observed values from the same case (McElreath, 2020). In this sense, almost all aspects of a Bayesian model – priors, posteriors, data and parameters – take the form of latent variables with differing degrees of uncertainty encoded in their distributions.

The Synthesis: Hierarchical Bayesian Stochastic Blockmodels

Now that we are armed with the foundational ideas motivating blockmodelling and the Bayesian estimation of latent variables, we may proceed to their synthesis. As this is intended to be an accessible introduction, we have opted to minimise the technical details and encourage those interested in developing a deeper understanding of SMB-family models to consult foundational and cutting-edge texts on the subject (e.g., Snijders & Nowicki, 1997; Nowicki & Snijders, 2001; Peixoto, 2019; Zhang & Peixoto, 2020; Peixoto, 2021a).

The Bayesian approach to blockmodelling involves building a generative model and using it to assess the likelihood of the observed network (A) conditional on the range of possible hypotheses about the latent variables (Peixoto, 2019). By constraining our generative model so that it adheres to the observed network's node and inter-block degree counts, the number of latent variables estimated shrinks from several to just one: b.

Fundamentally, we are interested in determining the probability that a given node partition vector b of length N – which partitions the nodes of network A into a number of blocks (B), with each block consisting of stochastically equivalent nodes – was responsible for generating network A. In the now-familiar language of Bayes' theorem, we arrive at the following:

$$P(b \mid A) = \frac{P(A \mid b) P(b)}{P(A)}$$

Where:

- A: an N-by-N adjacency matrix, where each entry A_{ij} indicates the presence or absence of an edge between node i and j (in an undirected network, A is symmetric. In a network without self-loops, the diagonal of A is 0).
- N: the number of nodes in network A.
- B: the number of blocks in a given partition b.
- b: a vector of length N that indexes the nodes in the network, where $b_i \in \{1...B\}$ and $i \in \{1...N\}$. Each permutation of b represents one possible partition of the network.
- $P(b|A)$: the posterior probability, or – equivalently – the probability of a partition b given the observed network A. This is our value of interest.
- $P(b)$: the prior probability of partition b. Since observed network data is generally unique, it makes little sense to introduce information to an BSBM via the prior; the priors, thus, are derived from the observed network.[8]
- $P(A|b)$: the likelihood of observing network A given partition b.
- $P(A)$: the marginal probability of the observed network A. Direct calculation thereof is intractable; the need for knowledge of this value is obviated via sampling.

The likelihood term can be expanded further:[9]

$$P(A \mid b) = P(A \mid e, b) P(e \mid b)$$

where e is a B-by-B matrix and entry e_{rs} contains the number of edges shared between group r and group s.[10]

With the model specified, all that remains is to estimate the posterior probability distribution $P(b|A)$. It should be stressed that BSBMs do *not* identify the single best-fitting partition (b) to the exclusion of all others, but rather provide the probability of all plausible partitions.[11] This is accomplished via Markov chain Monte Carlo (MCMC) sampling, which draws samples from the joint distribution of the model and data proportional to each combination's posterior probability (Peixoto, 2019). An extremely efficient MCMC algorithm for sampling from BSBMs can be found in Peixoto's Python package `graph-tool` (Peixoto, 2014b).

Model selection using minimum description length

As is the case with many other unsupervised learning techniques, BSBMs require users to either pre-specify the number of non-empty blocks (B) or infer the optimal number of blocks from data. Unless an appropriate number of blocks is known *a priori*, pre-specification of B is a fraught endeavour. Setting B too low paves over the nuances of the data, while using a principle such as likelihood maximisation imbues blockmodels with a concerning propensity for overfitting the observed network by favouring excessively large numbers of blocks (Peixoto, 2019).

Standard practice urges the use of information criteria that reward model likelihood (as a measure of overall fit) but punish model complexity to guard against overfitting. Most of the well-known and widely used criteria are not, however, applicable to SBMs. Field mainstays such as the Akiake Information Criterion (AIC) and the Bayesian Information Criterion (BIC) make invalid assumptions about SBM likelihood functions (Peixoto, 2021a). Fortunately, Bayesian posterior probability happens to be a 'universal code' for an information theoretic concept known as *description length* (Grünwald, 2007), which can be exploited to provide a principled choice of B.

A model's description length refers to the amount of information it encodes. It can be measured using a variety of scales, the most common of which is the *bit* or *Shannon* (Shannon, 1948), written using capital sigma (Σ). The concept of Occam's Razor guides information theory towards the principle of *minimum description length* (MDL), which holds that models should balance providing the best possible explanation of the data with the complexity of the model used to do so.[12] Peixoto's (2019) derivation takes the following steps:

We start from the previous equation describing the BSBM's likelihood:

$$P(A \mid b) = P(A \mid e, b) P(e \mid b)$$

Multiplying both sides by P(b) gives us:

$$P(A \mid b)P(b) = P(A \mid e, b) P(e, b)$$

The above step places the *Bayes Numerator* on the left-hand side of the equation, which trivially implies that both sides of the equation above are now proportional to the posterior probability. We can then establish a proportional relationship with description length via the bit/Shannon:

$$P(A \mid b)P(b) = P(A \mid e, b) P(e, b)$$

Which can be rearranged thus:

$$\log_2 P(A \mid e, b) P(e, b) = \log_2(2^{-\Sigma})$$
$$\log_2 P(A \mid e, b) + \log_2 P(e, b) = -\Sigma \log_2(2)$$
$$-\log_2 P(A \mid e, b) - \log_2 P(e, b) = \Sigma$$

The final expression in the above sequence highlights how MDL encodes the trade-off between model complexity and model fit: with higher values of B (more blocks total), the model does a better job of retrodicting the data, which decreases the likelihood term ($-P(A \mid e, b)$), decreasing description length. As B increases, however, so too does the model complexity ($-P(e, b)$), which increases description length.

Because the description length of a model is measured in binary bits/Shannons, it can be thought of as the number of 'yes-or-no' questions one would need to ask to specify and perfectly recreate the observed data in light of the model (MacKay, 2003). The core idea here is that a model with a lower overall description length will have almost certainly done a better job of capturing the *true* model, compared to other models with higher description lengths. In the context of BSBMs, we can think of each different choice of $B \in \{1...N\}$ as representing a different model; MDL provides us with a principled means of determining which model to select. The best choice of B, then, is the one that produces the lowest description length of any $B \in \{1...N\}$.

Most BSBMs can be improved by performing node reassignments via MCMC sampling. The process of reassigning nodes takes advantage of the fully specified Bayesian probability model and its ability to provide full distributions as answers to inferential queries such as our own. Rather than provide the single most likely partition, any BSBM's posterior can be sampled from to recover each node's probability of belonging to each block (for a given B). The end result is a distribution of nodewise block memberships, wherein each node's probability of belonging to a given block is proportional to the likelihood of the partition that assigned the node to the block in question.

Finally, while the BSBM approach described above is effective at avoiding overfitting, it is still prone to underfitting: it can mistake network structure for the product of random noise when the structure is, in fact, inferentially meaningful.

The solution to this conundrum, as proposed by Peixoto (2019), is to situate the node-level BSBM (which has been the focus of our chapter to this point) at the bottom rung of a potentially infinite series of hierarchical BSBM models. In essence, the solution involves modelling the blocks of a node-level BSBM as a network wherein each node represents a block, the edges between which are weighted according to the observed edge counts in the lowest-level model. This 'network of blocks' can itself be partitioned using a higher-level BSBM using similar logic, procedure and model selection techniques as the node-level BSBM.[13] The resulting blocks-of-blocks can themselves be modelled in yet another layer of partitioning, and so on *ad infinitum*. This layered approach to the BSBM permits the effective recovery of nested network structures without sacrificing the model's ability to learn from data in the absence of strongly informative prior information (which would be required to recover complex structure in a single-layer BSBM). Unless otherwise noted, the hierarchical Bayesian stochastic blockmodel will be our model of choice throughout the following empirical analyses.

EMPIRICAL EXAMPLES

In the second part of this chapter, we present two empirical examples that illustrate the use of BSBMs and speak more generally to the use of inferential approaches to network clustering. Our primary goals in this part of the chapter are to (1) illustrate some important considerations when developing a BSBM, (2) clarify what to expect in terms of results and (3) suggest some ways of further interrogating results. To that end, we have selected two networks that differ in useful and interesting ways. The first is constructed from Enron email data, the other from data about disinformation campaigns on Twitter.

The Enron Email Network

Our first example uses a network derived from the ubiquitous Enron email corpus (Klimt & Yang, 2004), which has been used in a wide variety of research contexts, including classification, agent-based models of communication (Matsuyama & Terano, 2008; VanBuren et al., 2009) and social network analysis (Aven, 2015; Corneli et al., 2019; Leskovec et al., 2009).

The versions of the Enron email dataset available from Stanford's SNAP database and from `graph-tool`'s built-in network repository are both undirected and binary (Leskovec et al., 2009), but we consider the network to be directed and weighted. Our reasoning for this is conceptually grounded – in a corporate hierarchy, the direction and volume of email exchanges might be important. The CEO of a corporation, for example, would receive more emails from subordinates than vice versa. We include only the 'core' employees who were implicated in the legal proceedings and for whom complete email data and identifying information is available, forming a more-or-less complete network. For the rest of the employees, there are no records of their emails among each other – only to and from the core, which the Stanford SNAP database terms 'sinks or sources' (Leskovec et al., 2009). The resulting network consists of 149 nodes with 2,582 edges weighted by volume of emails exchanged (total: 65,143).

In what follows, we use the Python package `graph-tool` (Peixoto, 2014b) to develop BSBMs that partition the network into blocks that mirror the actual job titles held by employees. In other words, we will consider the job titles to be a kind of partial 'ground truth' for social roles and see whether our BSBMs can approximate those roles using nothing other than the relational data. However, despite how integral this dataset is reported to be (Hardin et al., 2015; Wilson & Banzhaf, 2009), it lacks definitive metadata about the job titles of the included employees (Diesner & Carley, 2005). We added employee job title information to the dataset ourselves, building on a version of the dataset with other corrections made by Ruhe (2016). From there, we attempted to reconcile as many available versions of the data as we could find. Where there were disagreements between many versions, or remaining vague job titles, we turned to cached online data from the Internet Archive and from Google's web caches. Finally, we used any available LinkedIn profiles of former Enron employees to further enhance the accuracy of the position labels. We also decided to work with the raw emails in the data, rather than choosing any single version of the Enron network to trust.[14]

Figures 30.1–30.4 show results from different BSBMs fit to the Enron email network. Figures 30.1 and 30.2 are based on BSBMs that have not been refined through cycles of MCMC node reassignments. The first uses binary data whereas the second is weighted. Figures 30.3 and 30.4 are refined through MCMC node reassignments. Again, the third is based on binary data and the fourth is weighted. In these figures, and most others in this chapter, we can see the original complex network with circular nodes, labelled with each job title. The hierarchical BSBM is superimposed with square blue nodes, except for Figures 30.4 and 30.5, which we clustered using Traag et al.'s (2019) Leiden algorithm rather than a BSBM for the sake of comparison. The original nodes are positioned and coloured according to their block assignments. In cases where there is more uncertainty about the block assignment, the nodes can be represented as small pie charts that give a rough sense of other plausible block assignments. High resolution colour images are available in the online supplement.

Figure 30.1 shows results for an unweighted BSBM using only Peixoto's (2014a) highly performative clustering heuristic. Inspecting the job titles clustered together in each block, we can identify a number of blocks that look intuitively homogeneous. The CEOs are divided into different clusters, but they share a block one step up the hierarchy. Two of the three blocks in this cluster – the ones with the CEOs and COO – are primarily senior management and executives, while the third has a number of in-house lawyers and more senior management. Figure 30.2 shows results a model that uses edge weights (volume of emails) as a covariate but is otherwise identical.[15] Although there is some consistency with the results in the first model, as well as a fair share of intuitive clustering, the CEO blocks are now clustered with a very large block that includes many traders.

Figures 30.3 and 30.4 show the result of BSBMs that have been refined through a relatively modest 10,000 cycles of MCMC node reassignments, after which we assessed the minimum description length to see whether the model improved.[16] The cycles of reassignment can be tracked and the frequency that a node was placed in a given block provides the marginal posterior distribution, which serves as an estimate of the probability that this was the best choice.

Here, 'best choice' is meant to imply that some latent social dynamic (i.e., not in the model) had the most influence on the observed network. A purely hypothetical explanation might be that certain administrative assistants act as proxies for

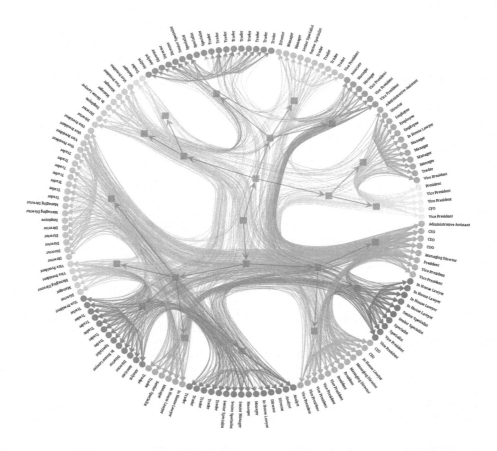

Figure 30.1 The Enron network with job labels, as partitioned using an unweighted BSBM

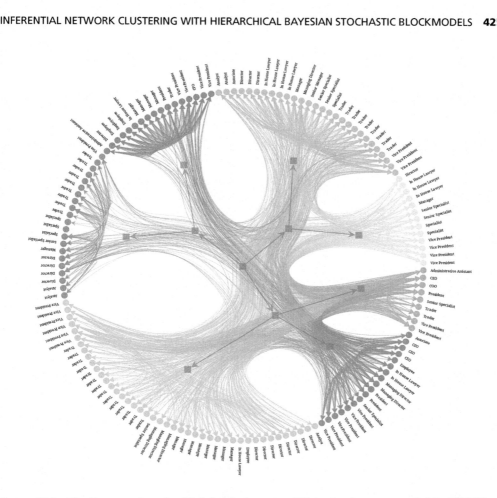

Figure 30.2 The Enron network with job labels, as partitioned using an unweighted BSBM

the CEOs they were grouped with, sending some portion of the emails that the CEOs would have otherwise sent. This could just as easily be driven by social steering of staff barbecue plans as it is by work-related emails. It could also be something as complex as deliberate instruction, meant to make operations appear 'business-as-usual' despite the fraudulent activity happening behind the scenes.

In the refined unweighted SBM shown in Figure 30.3, there are some significant changes that stand out. The two blocks of CEOs and executive management are now clustered together in the hierarchy, with the other executive block now joining a block of primarily non-executive employees. Changes in the refined weighted SBM are less visibly apparent but there is a great deal of information available here for further comparison.

As mentioned previously, we should not be too certain about block assignments where nodes are coloured by pie charts, which indicate the plausibility of some other block assignment. One example is the director on the right side of the unweighted network (see Figure 30.3), who was placed alone in a block, but with the possibility of being assigned to either of the two blocks below. Multiple plausible block assignments like this could mean that an employee has a diverse set of behaviours in the company, that the model or data do a poor job of representing their behaviours, or that more than one model is needed to infer the particular social dynamic where they are more consistent.

Peixoto (2021b) has recently implemented a model clustering function in `graph-tool` that can help researchers get a sense of whether there are different generative stories consistent with the data. For each cluster of models, an overall likelihood contribution to the data can be calculated as a proportion to the other models, out of 100. In the case of the Enron models, only two clusters ever turn up and the second with less than 0.001 likelihood, so is not worth exploring here.

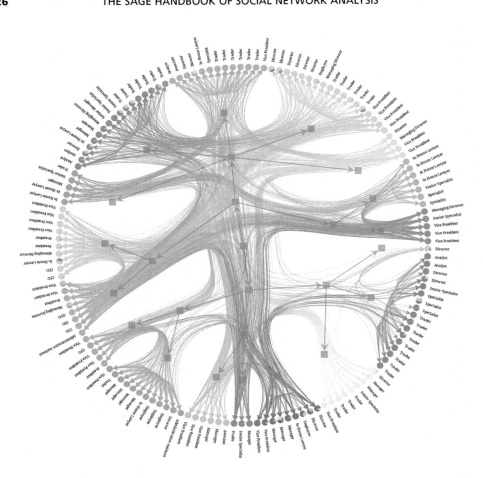

Figure 30.3 The Enron network with job labels, as partitioned using an unweighted BSBM, refined through MCMC

The uncertainty of some of the individual node assignments, often seen in directors and managers, would be a better place to look.

For the sake of comparison, we provide unweighted and weighted assortative cluster results from the Leiden algorithm, using the respective network layouts from the refined SBM models. The results are shown in Figures 30.5 and 30.6, and in Tables 30.1 and 30.2. In both cases, the Leiden algorithm was run with the additional refinement iterations that ensure modularity has been maximised to full model resolution (Traag et al., 2019).

Table 30.1 compares the MDL (i.e., how successfully the model has condensed the information required to recreate the network) for the six analyses so far (four partitioned with BSBMs, two with Leiden). We can see that the three models with edge weights have significantly longer description lengths. This is to be expected because MDL compares different ways of modelling *the same data*. As soon as edge weights or other covariates are added to the network, the data used to represent the model has increased. MDL cannot indicate whether the weighted or unweighted model is preferable. However, for both weighted and unweighted networks, we can see that the SBMs we refined with 10,000 MCMC runs both slightly outperform the unrefined SBMs, and moderately outperform the Leiden algorithm.

We can also evaluate our models using another metric from information theory – mutual information. Mutual information is widely used to evaluate cluster and classification models by comparing the consensus between a ground-truth label of datapoints and the labels produced by a model. There have been a number of variants of mutual information introduced to improve on different aspects of

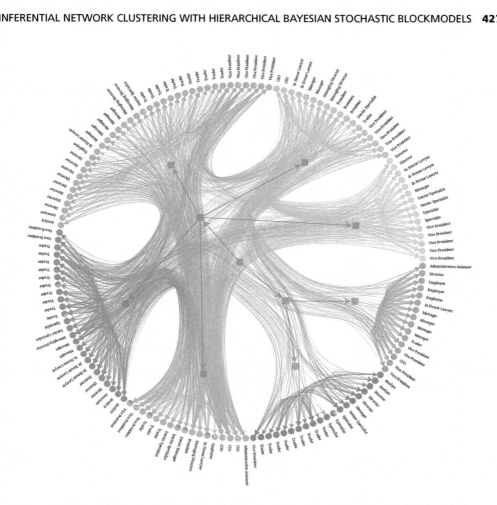

Figure 30.4 The Enron network with job labels, as partitioned using a weighted BSBM, refined through MCMC

the measure, often for different applications. Here, we use Newman et al.'s (2020) *reduced mutual information* (RMI) score, which was developed with particular attention to evaluating community detection methods in networks. We can use RMI to calculate the agreement between any clustering – ground truth or not. Our focus, however, will be on how each model performs relative to the 'Job title' classifications we added to the dataset.

Table 30.2 shows the RMI scores of pairwise comparisons between the six model examples above and the employee job titles, with a score of 1 indicating perfect agreement. Contrary to the MDL measure, the unrefined variants of the SBM perform better here than the refined ones, with the weighted unrefined SBM score doubling the second-best score of the weighted Leiden algorithm.

What explains the apparent contradiction between MDL and RMI? Overfitting is a likely explanation: recall the results of the unrefined weighted SBM (Figure 30.2), where the two executive blocks were clustered with a higher-order block containing many traders. Traders are the most common employee label (there are 35 of them), so placing them together in clusters will disproportionately impact a mutual information score. In this case, the RMI score is 0.44 when placing all of the traders in one group while every other employee is in a second group. In this sense, models that cluster the most common label ('Trader', in this case) together will score well on RMI while not necessarily featuring a comparatively laudable MDL score.

The conceptual caveats here are multiple. We rarely have a ground truth available, but it is also worth stressing the fact that the job titles in this example are only one part of the ground truth – or are, perhaps, a product of a more general ground

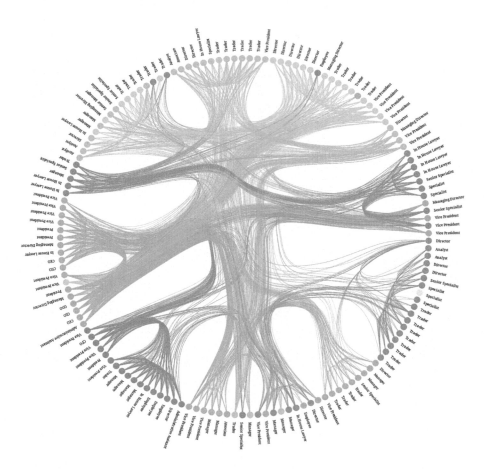

Figure 30.5 The Enron network with job labels, as partitioned using an unweighted Leiden algorithm

truth that jointly gives rise to the observed network structure and the job titles. Various norms of corporate hierarchical structure – such as proscribed efficiency guidelines, proximity and social taboos – are also likely to have been influential. Without more information, the only sure inference to make here is that workplace roles have had some form of influence on who sent emails to whom.

Disinformation on Twitter: IRA Tweets

In our second empirical example, we analyse networks derived from a corpus of Tweets that Twitter determined were the work of Russia's Internet Research Agency (IRA) as part of their election interference research initiative.[17] In 2018, Twitter began releasing datasets of activity by accounts that they had identified as state-backed operations (Roeder, 2018). Data attributed to Russia's infamous IRA was the centrepiece of these releases, containing information on roughly 10 million Tweets from 4,611 accounts.

There are two distinct approaches to forming network edges from Twitter: using metadata (e.g., followers and followees) and using activity data (e.g., mentions, re-Tweets, or replies). In this case, we aggregated all three forms of activity data. Since the full IRA network is too large and complex to give a proper treatment in this brief example, we filter the network to retain only the 1,000 most heavily weighted edges. This leaves 777 nodes in the network, with 555 identified as affiliated with the IRA and 222 accounts not identified as affiliated with the IRA. The combined

INFERENTIAL NETWORK CLUSTERING WITH HIERARCHICAL BAYESIAN STOCHASTIC BLOCKMODELS

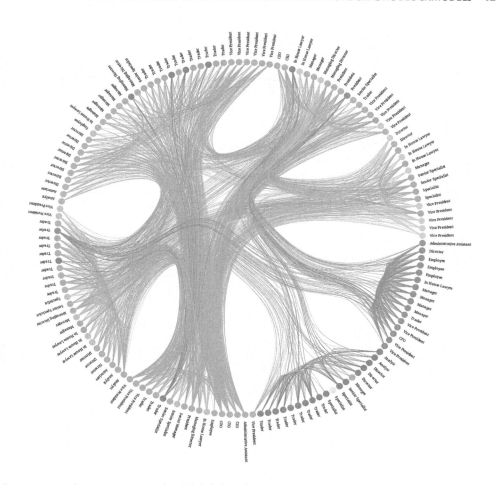

Figure 30.6 The Enron network with job labels, as partitioned using a weighted Leiden algorithm

Table 30.1 Minimum description length (MDL) comparison for the six Enron analyses

	BSBM	BSBM, refined with MCMC	Leiden
unweighted	6350.47	6336.73	6660.11
weighted	16763.89	16754.96	16941.6

weight of these 1,000 edges is 423,911 – so, a lot of activity. This network represents the source and target accounts involved in the heaviest amount of Twitter interaction surrounding the IRA actors. Notably, the data only includes Tweets made by the IRA accounts, forming a directed network that can still be blockmodelled.

Unlike the Enron data, we know next to nothing about the identity of the individuals responsible – it is likely that each IRA worker was responsible for many such accounts. Insofar as Twitter's undisclosed method for detecting state actors can be trusted as accurate, we do know that the Twitter accounts in question were acting under the guidance of some authority. It is also reasonable to assume that the behaviour of these accounts is much more singularly focused than that of corporate employees; if a state-employed Twitter operative wanted to plan a barbeque with their co-workers, they would do it somewhere other than in public Tweets from

Table 30.2 Reduced mutual information (RMI) scores for pairwise comparisons of the six Enron analyses and the employees' official job titles

	Job title	SBM unweighted	SBM weighted	SBM refined unweighted	SBM refined weighted	Leiden unweighted	Leiden weighted
Job title	1						
SBM unweighted	0.004363	1					
SBM weighted	0.042249	0.557893	1				
SBM refined unweighted	−0.01196	0.866441	0.54449	1			
SBM refined weighted	0.01394	0.484362	0.74883	0.482392	1		
Leiden unweighted	−0.00021	0.61373	0.547643	0.595718	0.465708	1	
Leiden weighted	0.020552	0.4696	0.534218	0.478979	0.437218	0.56049	1

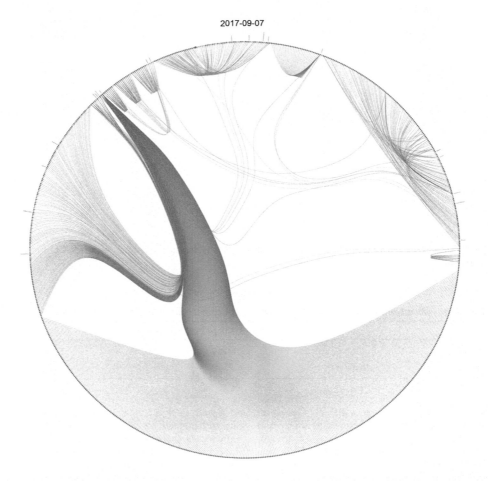

Figure 30.7 Activity in the IRA network at four points in time. Subplots B–D show 12, 20 and 21 December 2015, respectively. Subplot A shows the network on 7 September 2017, when the last IRA Tweet in the dataset was sent

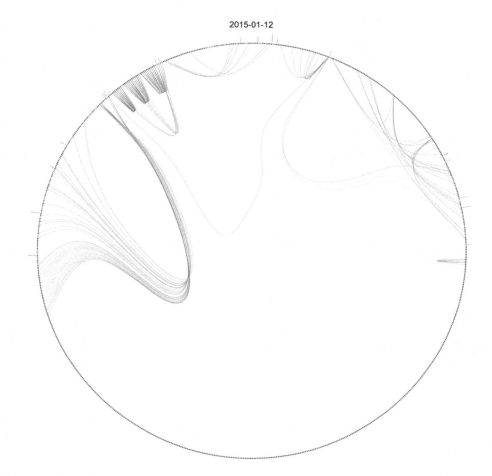

Figure 30.7 Continued

their 'sock puppet' accounts. Given what we know about the generative processes giving rise to this network, one place to start might be to look for evidence of *any* coordination at all.

In the four subplots of Figure 30.7, we show the top 1,000 edges from the IRA network at a few key time points from a day-by-day tie formation animation. These edges are displayed in the animation *when first established*, so although they eventually have the largest edge weights, they are drawn on the day when the edge weight was 1 or more. Source nodes are circled in black if they first interacted with their target on the day of the image. Similarly, in the online colour versions of these figures, the IRA accounts are shown in red, non-IRA in blue and deleted accounts in orange. Edges directed to each of those account categories are coloured in the same scheme.

Subplot A in Figure 30.7 shows the network on 7 September 2017, when the last IRA Tweet in the dataset was sent. The large swath of edges from the bottom occurred primarily in the span of two days. They all originated from the same block of IRA accounts, and they all targeted the same account, *rianru*, which is the account of state-owned Russian news agency RIA Novosti. It would be reasonable to say here that there is evidence of some form of coordinated action. The other blocks display less dramatic but still distinguishable patterns.

On the one hand, the IRA Twitter blockmodel might suggest the presence of marked distinctions between different sets of behaviours, each guided by sets of strategies from senior decision-makers. On the other hand, there is no way to analyse the available data to distinguish between five distinct blocks of Twitter accounts, each

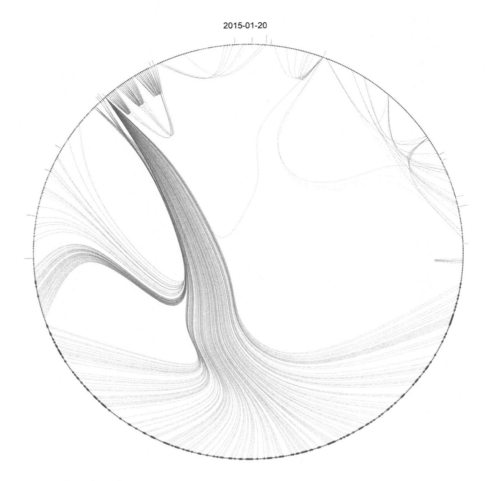

Figure 30.7 Continued

belonging to sets of state employees with official orders and, for example, five state employees each running multiple accounts as they see fit – in other words, we can't easily distinguish top-down coordination from simultaneous autonomous activity. Likewise, the media focus that surrounded online state-backed behaviour during the US election cycle might make it tempting, and legitimately compelling, to conclude that any identified organised behaviour is supportive evidence of foreign influence operations. This conclusion is exactly what Twitter suggested when releasing the data. In reality, disinformation researchers increasingly find that a large portion of online disinformation is targeted domestically (Grace, 2022; Somerville & Heering, 2021).

The network visualisations in Figure 30.8 show an enlarged view of some key distinct patterns in the network. Subplot A shows a small number of IRA accounts targeting Twitter accounts of nondescript origin, and primarily spreading conspiracy theories of the time.[18] The second image shows activity focused on popular US media organisations, like *Mashable*, *The Washington Post* and *Fox News*. In the third image is a mix, with *Al Jazeera*, *Financial Times* and a popular Russia-based satire account as targets. There is a great deal of in-depth analysis that could be undertaken here, but it does seem evident that the activity of these accounts was not solely focused on the US election, especially given the attention paid to RIA Novosti (*rianru*).

Inference about the goals behind these Twitter strategies might be possible, but not without care – how would a *foreign influence* objective be distinguishable from purposefully crafting the *impression* of foreign influence, for other

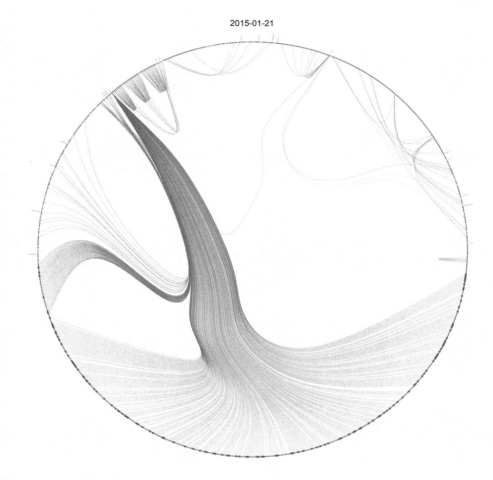

Figure 30.7 Continued

purposes? And how would the intended audience be identified? When 100 accounts send 10,000 Tweets each at the *New York Times*, they are almost certainly not banking on the producers of that newspaper to consider their statements. In still other settings, it turns out that none of these considerations even matter, where the reality is that bots are just tweeting among each other (Common Thread, 2021).

As the two foregoing analyses have made abundantly clear, BSBMs are powerful tools for drawing inferences about the processes that give rise to social structure in networks. What should be equally clear, however, is that researchers must exercise caution when interpreting said inferences. In our analysis of the Enron email network, we saw that BSBMs admirably retrodict some of the structures we might expect to see in a hierarchical network of corporate communications, but were equally made aware of the fact that BSBMs do not necessarily measure any particular kind of 'ground truth' – or if they do, that it may not be the same ground truth researchers expect to draw inferences about. As White et al. (1976), Robins (2011) and Nadal (1957) are wont to emphasise, social roles are complex, embedded and multifaceted: researchers cannot hope to apprehend the totality of a social role through the analysis of one kind of social tie. In our analysis of the IRA disinformation campaign on Twitter, we encountered the pitfalls of ascribing a causal story to the patterns of behaviour hinted at by the results of a BSBM: the same results can be easily reinterpreted to support conclusions that emphasise the foreign influence role of IRA activity, the domestic influence role of IRA activity, or the seemingly impotent bot-on-bot IRA activity.

Figure 30.8 Three different enlarged views of the filtered IRA network

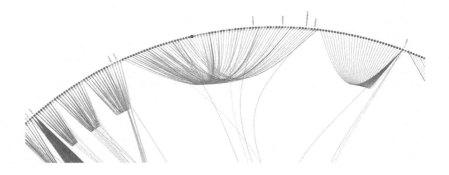

Figure 30.8 Continued

INFERENTIAL NETWORK CLUSTERING WITH HIERARCHICAL BAYESIAN STOCHASTIC BLOCKMODELS   435

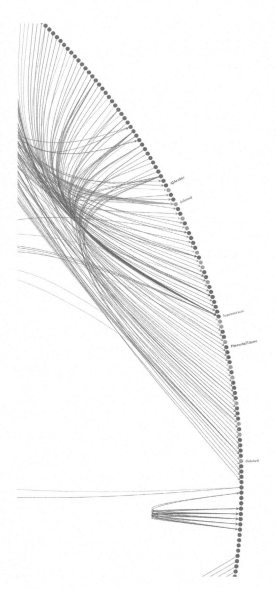

Figure 30.8 Continued

CONCLUSION

In this chapter, we introduced readers to the Bayesian stochastic blockmodel – which is a powerful inferential counterpart to prevailing descriptive approaches to community detection and network clustering – and demonstrated the process of applying and interpreting BSBMs in two very different contexts. As with all unsupervised learning, great care is required when specifying and drawing inferences from the graph partitions we obtain by developing and fitting BSBMs. This is not because SBMs are uniquely prone to misapplication or are otherwise unwieldy. BSBMs open many exciting research opportunities for network scientists by combining decades of insightful work on equivalence, blockmodels and network clustering (see Dorien, this volume) with probabilistic thinking and generative modelling. But, as with all other approaches, we need careful and deliberate analysis to make inferences about meaningful human behaviour.

Notes

1 The permutations of b must respect the model's constraints; in most cases, this means that b cannot contain any empty blocks.
2 It should be noted that Bayesian inference also uses parameters, but generally reserves the moniker for a specific class of model setting that is both fixed and known. Prior probability distributions almost always take the form of parameterised distributions, such as the Gaussian, Poisson, binomial, or exponential distributions. In the context of a model, a Gaussian distribution with $\mu = 1$ (location) and $\sigma = 2$ (scale) represents a perfectly valid prior probability for an unobserved latent variable: in this way, Bayesian models frequently use parameters to describe prior uncertainty, despite the parameters themselves being known and fixed.
3 This is not always the case, as some models/applications are better served by wholly uninformative priors, such as a flat prior, or an improper prior such as Jeffries' prior. Conversely, some models may use strongly informative priors, which may constrain model behaviour (Zondervan-Zwijnenburg et al., 2017).
4 The number of hypotheses contained in a discrete latent variable is countable, whereas the number of hypotheses in a continuous latent variable is un-countably infinite.
5 The term 'well specified', here, is left intentionally ambiguous. Not all prior distributions lend themselves to meaningful output in the simulative mode, and flat/improper priors tend to dramatically limit the utility of a Bayesian model (McElreath, 2020). As such, the merit of Bayesian model simulation depends on good prior specification, a topic that is well beyond the scope of this chapter. Interested readers are encouraged to consult the 'Prior Choice Recommendations' page in the *stan* GitHub repository: github.com/stan-dev/stan/wiki/Prior-Choice-Recommendations

6 Bayesian model invertibility is made more intuitive, we find, when considered in light of the fact that one model's posterior is another model's prior – the only distinction is the amount of information encoded.
7 Namely, one that has all of its probability mass or density on the observed value.
8 For more detail on this aspect of specifying BSBMs, see Peixoto (2019).
9 Since we are only interested in modelling block membership, we are able to greatly simplify our task through the use of a *microcanonical model* (Piexoto, 2019). Borrowed from the field of physics, microcanonical modelling permits models to sort their parameters into those with 'hard' constraints, and those with 'soft' constraints. By treating invariant aspects of the network – such as interblock edge counts – as fixed parameters, we can avoid (potentially intractable) summation and integration signs in our model specification.
10 At this stage, the mathematical model is not yet complete, as the statement of likelihood is not yet directly computable. Since the purpose of this chapter is to introduce readers to BSBMs, we have elided the model's grittier mathematical detail. See Peixoto (2019) for the full specification.
11 One or two explanations of the data may predominate over the others, but a Bayesian model never formally discards any hypothesis with a posterior probability greater than 0.
12 The same principle can be found in the other information criteria briefly discussed in the previous paragraph, AIC and BIC.
13 In what should be a familiar refrain by now, readers who are interested in the technical aspects of Hierarchical BSBMs should consult Peixoto (2019, 2021).
14 Our investigation left us reasonably confident that our corrections were sound, but also surprised us with the discovery of job titles that have not appeared in any other dataset to date. We wound up with only five completely uninformative 'employee' titles remaining, as compared to the best case of 25 in the other datasets that we found. Nonetheless, we by no means claim to have achieved 100 per cent accuracy, given how many other researchers have had a chance to do the same. The authors welcome and encourage any suggested corrections to this dataset. The Enron email corpus is still one of the only public datasets of corporate emails, in a world increasingly rich with such email data – most of the latter will never be seen by academic network analysts.
15 The implementation of BSBMs in Python's `graph-tool` can incorporate as many edge covariates as you like into the Bayesian process, beyond the standard edge weights. Including too many covariates does tend to considerably increase both computation time and the number of blocks. The weighted results for Enron tend to be a bit less visibly intuitive on most model runs, but this might mean that they are better representing some process not determined by job title.
16 This refinement process tends to consistently improve the MDL of a model by some amount, however small, but of course this doesn't tell us whether the model is *good*; it merely tells us that it has outperformed its compatriots.
17 See github.com/fivethirtyeight/russian-troll-tweets/
18 Such as Barack Obama being born in Kenya. More recently, these accounts post about Covid-19 conspiracies.

REFERENCES

Anderson, C.J., Wasserman, S., & Faust, K. (1992). Building stochastic blockmodels. *Social Networks*, 14(1–2), 137–161.

Arabie, P., & Boorman, S. (1982). Blockmodels: developments and prospects. In H.C. Hudson (Ed.), *Classifying social data*. Jossey-Bass.

Arabie, P., Boorman, S., & Levitt, P. (1978). Constructing blockmodels: how and why. *Journal of Mathematical Psychology*, 17(1), 21–63.

Aven, B.L. (2015). The paradox of corrupt networks: an analysis of organizational crime at Enron. *Organization Science*, 26(4), 980–96.

Blondel, V.D., Guillaume, J.L., Lambiotte, R., & Lefebvre, E. (2008). Fast unfolding of communities in large networks. *Journal of Statistical Mechanics: Theory and Experiment*, 2008(10), P10008.

Boorman, S., & White, H. (1976). Social structure from multiple networks. II. Role structures. *American Journal of Sociology*, 81(6), 1384–1446.

Breiger, R.L., Boorman, S.A., & Arabie, P. (1975). An algorithm for clustering relational data with applications to social network analysis and comparison with multidimensional scaling. *Journal of Mathematical Psychology*, 12(3), 328–383.

Clayton, A. (2021). *Bernoulli's fallacy*. Columbia University Press.

Collins, R. (1988). *Theoretical sociology*. Harcourt College.

Common Thread (2021). Four truths about bots. *Twitter*. blog.twitter.com/common-thread/en/topics/stories/2021/four-truths-about-bots

Corneli, M., Bouveyron, C., Latouche, P., & Rossi, F. (2019). The dynamic stochastic topic block model for dynamic networks with textual edges. *Statistics and Computing*, 29(4), 677–695.

Cox, R.T. (1946). Probability, frequency and reasonable expectation. *American Journal of Physics*, 14(1), 1–13.

Diesner, J., & Carley, K.M. (2005). Exploration of communication networks from the Enron email corpus. *SIAM International Conference on Data Mining: Workshop on Link Analysis, Counterterrorism and Security*. Newport Beach, CA, 3–14.

Erdös, P., & Rényi, A. (1959). On random graphs. i. *Publicationes Mathematicae*, 6, 290–297.

Erickson, B.H. (1988). The relational basis of attitudes. In B. Wellman & S.D. Berkowitz (Eds.), *Social structures: a network approach*. Cambridge University Press.

Festinger, L. (1949). The analysis of sociograms using matrix algebra. *Human Relations*, 2(2), 153–158.

Fortunato, S. (2010). Community detection in graphs. *Physics Reports*, 486(3–5), 75–174.

Friedkin, N.E. (1984). Structural cohesion and equivalence explanations of social homogeneity. *Sociological Methods and Research*, 12(3), 235–261.

Grace, P. (2022). Inside Russia's domestic disinformation ecosystem. *Inkstick*. inkstickmedia.com/inside-russias-domestic-disinformation-ecosystem/

Grünwald, P.D. (2007). *The minimum description length principle*. MIT Press.

Hardin, J.S., Sarkis, G., & Urc, P.C. (2015). Network analysis with the Enron email corpus. *Journal of Statistics Education*, 23(2).

Holland, P.W., Laskey, K.B., & Leinhardt, S. (1983). Stochastic blockmodels: first steps. *Social Networks*, 5(2), 109–137.

Jaynes, E.T. (2003). *Probability theory: the logic of science*. Cambridge University Press.

Klimt, B., & Yang, Y. (2004). Introducing the Enron corpus. *International Conference on Email and Anti-Spam*.

Leskovec, J., Lang, K.J., Dasgupta, A., & Mahoney, M.W. (2009). Community structure in large networks: natural cluster sizes and the absence of large well-defined clusters. *Internet Mathematics*, 6(1), 29–123.

Light, J.M., & Mullins, N.C. (1979). A primer on blockmodeling procedure. *Perspectives on Social Network Research*, Elsevier, 85–118.

Lorrain, F., & White, H.C. (1971). Structural equivalence of individuals in social networks. *Journal of Mathematical Sociology*, 1(1), 49–80.

Luce, R.D., & Perry, A.D. (1949). A method of matrix analysis of group structure. *Psychometrika*, 14(1), 95–116.

MacKay, D. (2003). *Information theory, inference and learning algorithms*. Cambridge University Press.

Matsuyama, S., & Terano, T. (2008). Analyzing the ENRON communication network using agent-based simulation. *Journal of Networks*, 3(7), 26–33.

McElreath, R. (2020). *Statistical rethinking: a Bayesian course with examples in r and STAN*. Chapman & Hall.

Nadel, S.F. (1957). *The theory of social structure*. Routledge.

Newman, M.E.J., Cantwell, G.T., & Young, J.-G. (2020). Improved mutual information measure for clustering, classification, and community detection. *Physical Review E*, 101(4). doi.org/10.1103%2Fphysreve.101.042304

Nowicki, K., & Snijders, T.A.B. (2001). Estimation and prediction for stochastic blockstructures. *Journal of the American Statistical Association*, 96(455), 1077–1087.

Peixoto, T.P. (2014a). Efficient Monte Carlo and greedy heuristic for the inference of stochastic block models. *Physical Review E*, 89(1). doi.org/10.1103%2Fphysreve.89.012804

Peixoto, T.P. (2014b). The graph-tool python library. *figshare*. figshare.com/articles/graph_tool/1164194

Peixoto, T. (2019). Bayesian stochastic blockmodeling. In P. Doreian, V. Batagelj & A. Ferlingoj (Eds.), *Advances in network clustering and blockmodeling* (pp. 289–332). Wiley.

Peixoto, T.P. (2021a). Descriptive vs inferential community detection: pitfalls, myths and half-truths. *arXiv*, preprint arXiv:2112.00183.

Peixoto, T.P. (2021b). Revealing consensus and dissensus between network partitions. *Physical Review X*, 11(2). doi.org/10.1103%2Fphysrevx.11.021003

Robins, G. (2011). Exponential random graph models for social networks. In J. Scott & P.J. Carrington (Eds.), *The Sage handbook of social network analysis* (pp. 484–500). Sage.

Roeder, O. (2018). We gave you 3 million Russian troll Tweets: here's what you've found so far. *FiveThirtyEight*. fivethirtyeight.com/features/what-you-found-in-3-million-russian-troll-tweets/

Rosenberg, A., & Hirschberg, J. (2007). V-measure: a conditional entropy-based external cluster evaluation measure. *Proceedings of the 2007 Joint Conference on Empirical Methods in Natural Language Processing and Computational Natural Language Learning (EMNLP-CoNLL)*, Prague, Czech Republic: Association for Computational Linguistics, 410–20. aclanthology.org/D07-1043

Ruhe, A.H. (2016). Enron data. www.ahschulz.de/enron-email-data/

Shannon, C.E. (1948). A mathematical theory of communication. *The Bell System Technical Journal*, 27(3), 379–423.

Snijders, T.A.B., & Nowicki, K. (1997). Estimation and prediction for stochastic blockmodels for graphs with latent block structure. *Journal of Classification*, 14(1), 75–100.

Somerville, A., & Heering, J. (2021). The disinformation shift: from foreign to domestic. *Georgetown Journal of International Affairs*. gjia.georgetown.edu/2020/11/28/the-disinformation-shift-from-foreign-to-domestic/

Traag, V.A., Waltman, L., & Van Eck, N.J. (2019). From Louvain to Leiden: guaranteeing well-connected communities. *Scientific Reports*, 9(1), 1–12.

VanBuren, V., Villarreal, D., McMillen, T.A., & Minnicks, A.L. (2009). Enron dataset research: e-mail relevance classification. Texas State University.

Wang, Y.J., & Wong, G.Y. (1987). Stochastic blockmodels for directed graphs. *Journal of the American Statistical Association*, 82(397), 8–19.

Wasserman, S., & Anderson, C. (1987). Stochastic a posteriori blockmodels: construction and assessment. *Social Networks*, 9(1), 1–36.

Wasserman, S., & Faust, K. (Eds.) (1994). *Social network analysis: methods and applications*. Cambridge University Press.

White, D., & Reitz, K. (1983). Graph and semigroup homomorphisms on networks of relations. *Social Networks*, 5(2), 193–234.

White, H.C., Boorman, S.A., & Breiger, R.L. (1976). Social structure from multiple networks. I. Blockmodels of roles and positions. *American Journal of Sociology*, 81(4), 730–780.

Wilson, G., & Banzhaf, W. (2009). Discovery of email communication networks from the Enron corpus with a genetic algorithm using social network analysis. *2009 IEEE Congress on Evolutionary Computation*, IEEE, 3256–3263.

Zhang, L., & Peixoto, T.P. (2020). Statistical inference of assortative community structures. *Physical Review Research*, 2(4), 043271.

Zondervan-Zwijnenburg, M., Peeters, M., Depaoli, S., & Van de Schoot, R. (2017). Where do priors come from? Applying guidelines to construct informative priors in small sample research. *Research in Human Development*, 14(4), 305–320.

Personal Networks and Egocentric Analysis

Brea Perry, Adam Roth, and Mario Small

INTRODUCTION

Scope

Egocentric analysis is the subset of network research that, rather than examining the network as a whole, is concerned with particular nodes and those nodes' connections. In egocentric analysis, the focal node is termed 'ego' and the nodes to which it is connected, 'alters'. The researcher typically studies not only the connections between ego and alter but also those among the alters themselves. Egocentric research is wide ranging, and this chapter focuses on what is probably the largest and most influential subset of that work.

First, the chapter focuses on egocentric research using primarily one type of data. Egocentric analysts may work with sociocentric or egocentric data. When working with sociocentric data, as in data on all connections among employees in a company, the analyst typically identifies nodes of interest – such as female managers or upwardly mobile employees – and examines the nature, evolution, or consequences of the network of alters surrounding those nodes. A good analyst in such context takes into account that all nodes in the dataset are ultimately connected in a proximate network, and thus examines the data both egocentrically and sociocentrically. When working with egocentric data, as in the connections of a representative sample of Americans, the analyst typically examines the nature, evolution, or consequences of the ego network without concern that each ego may be connected to others. The most important contributions to egocentric analysis as such have been produced by researchers working with egocentric data, and these will be our focus.

Second, the chapter largely focuses on only one kind of unit. Egocentric data may be collected on individuals, organisations, websites, countries, or any kind of entity for which there is interest in focal egos. However, most of the important work has focused on people and their social ties, or what has been termed the 'personal network'. Thus, the personal network will be our focus.

In what follows, we examine the strengths and weaknesses of personal-network, egocentric analysis; assess its early contributions; and discuss its extraordinary resurgence (see McCarty et al., 2019; Perry et al., 2018; Small et al., 2021a). After briefly highlighting a few historical contributions important to today's work, we discuss the relationship between egocentric analysis and three research traditions with which it partly overlaps. We then turn attention to the most important instrument in the collection of egocentric data, the name generator, assessing its advantages and disadvantages. Finally, we assess the recent work on egocentric analysis, which has asked new questions, adopted entirely new perspectives and relied on data well beyond the traditional egocentric dataset. We argue that, because of its unique strengths, egocentric analysis has become one of the most promising areas of growth in social network analysis.

Background

In both sociocentric and egocentric analysis, the history of current research can be traced to works in mid-20th-century anthropology, psychiatry, psychology, sociology and other fields (e.g., Mitchell, 1969), with some formative ideas dating to the late 19th century (Simmel, 1971) and even into antiquity (Aristotle, 1943). A general history of network analysis may be found in Freeman (2004) and a particular history of egocentric analysis in Small et al. (2021b). Two elements of the latter history are important to recount as they provided the conceptual foundation for today's understanding of the personal network and the methodological foundation for much of the current survey work on egocentric studies.

The first element is part of the history of anthropology. Among fieldworkers in the 1950s and 1960s working to systematise the relations and social influence they were observing, a major concern was what Mitchell (1969, p. 12) called 'anchorage', or 'the point of orientation of a social network'. The anthropologists and ethnographer-sociologists of the time were familiar with the work in sociometrics that traced network processes in classrooms and other small contexts. But when studying entire communities – such as the small cities in southern and central Africa that many of the Manchester anthropologists observed – it was impossible for the fieldworkers to trace all possible connections that might influence a person.

As Mitchell put it,

> The sociometrists normally work with a distinct group of subjects – the boys in a scout troop or the children in a classroom. But the problem for the sociologist is more difficult since he is concerned with the behaviour of individuals in a social situation which may be affected by circumstances beyond the immediate context. The person to whom the actor is orienting his behaviour may not be physically present though he would almost certainly be in the individual's personal network.
> (Mitchell, 1969, p. 13)

The researchers out in the field were typically concerned with far more than the behaviour in a single classroom or organisation.

> How far the links of a network need be traced depends entirely upon the field-worker's judgment of what links are significant in explaining the behaviour of the people with whom he is concerned. This implies that normally a network must be traced from some initial starting point: it must be anchored on a reference point.
> (Mitchell, 1969, p. 13)

He continued:

> The point of anchorage of a network is usually taken to be some specified individual whose behaviour the observer wishes to interpret … This has led to the specification of this type of network as ego-centered though the term 'personal network' may be more acceptable.
> (Mitchell, 1969, p. 13)

Deciding where to anchor the observation was important, and the individual was an effective starting point. Thus emerged the personal network tradition.

The second element is part of the history of survey research, where a central figure for what later would become egocentric analysis was Paul Lazarsfeld. As Small et al. (2021b, p. 8) put it,

> Probably his most important study for egocentric analysis was Katz and Lazarsfeld (1955), which attempted to understand how the political opinions of residents of Decatur, IL were affected by social influences. Rather than asking respondents in general terms whether they tended to trust others' views, the authors asked respondents to name those who had an influence on their opinions: 'Do you know anyone around here who keeps up with the news and whom you can trust to let you know what is really going on?' (1955: 140). This kind of question, which later became known as a 'name generator,' was a crucial innovation, as it allowed the authors to know exactly who had been influential.

Asking people to report the names of those who influenced them was a crucial first step. About a decade later, and working with the Detroit Area Study, Laumann did something similar but added a step, which was to ask respondents whether those they were connected to were in turn connected to one another (Laumann, 1973, pp. 264–268). This additional step allowed Laumann to construct a personal network for each survey respondent. This work is the foundation of today's egocentric research survey tradition, where reconstructing individuals' networks, often with more than one name generator, is the most common point of departure.

THE EGOCENTRIC TRADITION

The core belief in egocentric research is that the network of people in an individual's immediate environment shapes their behaviour and well-being. Different researchers focus on different aspects of these relations. Some examine how the nature or structure of the network affect individuals. Others study how people use or activate their network, including how through consultation with or suggestion, support, or nagging from others they make decisions. Part of this work is the study of conflict and competition. Still others examine where personal networks come from and why people have the networks they do.

Egocentric researchers today hail from several different subfields with somewhat different interests. Examining those subfields in relation to egocentric research will prove useful. See Figure 31.1.

Egocentric vs Sociocentric Analysis

Egocentric analysis is ultimately a subset of network analysis, and its most important analytical connections are to sociocentric network research. Sociocentric network research has been primarily concerned with understanding the structure of the whole network, its evolution and its consequences (Brass, 1984; Wasserman & Faust, 1994). Thus, sociocentric data collection has involved selecting a bounded set of actors in a given context (e.g., a classroom, a department in a corporation, a street gang) and recording the ties between all pairs of

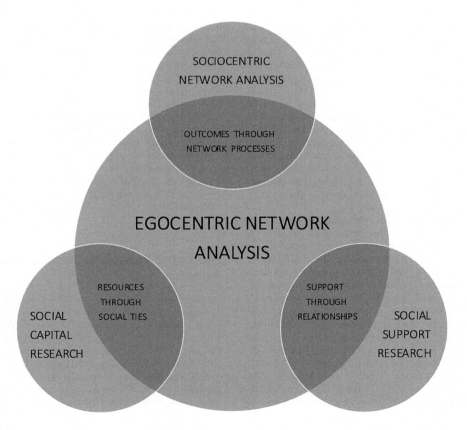

Figure 31.1 The relationship between egocentric network analysis and other research traditions

actors in it. The sociocentric analyst can therefore map the whole network structure, including consequential ties that are present and those that are not. As we have discussed, many researchers use sociocentric data egocentrically. As Borgatti et al. (2013, p. 262) put it, one 'can simply extract the subgraph corresponding to any particular node's first-order neighborhood, which we can call an ego-network'. But the larger egocentric tradition has examined network structure from a different perspective that addresses some of the limitations of sociocentric data.

Whole network data on individuals have two practical and two fundamental problems. The practical one is that such data can be labour-intensive to collect because they require obtaining the connections between each pair of nodes. If individuals are involved, each person must (usually) be asked about the connections to every other person, limiting the size of networks that can be studied and the number of types of relations that can be asked about. For this reason, sociocentric datasets historically have been small (see Wasserman & Faust, 1994). The second practical problem stems from the most common solution to the first. Concerned with the limits of the small samples of yesteryear, many sociocentric analysts today who are concerned with individual behaviour use data collected from companies, often social media companies such as Twitter or Facebook. Because such data collection was not designed by social scientists, the resulting data are often limited in important ways (Grigoropoulou & Small, 2022). For example, they may lack demographic data on individuals or only partially capture an important social concept. With time, increasing data availability and the possibility of merging datasets from separate companies, some of these limitations will probably be redressed.

Nonetheless, two fundamental problems remain. One is that sociocentric data have limited external validity or statistical representativeness (Perry et al., 2018). Because they must involve one bounded set of actors, or one network, generalisation to other networks is difficult. To address this problem, a researcher could randomly select many whole networks (i.e., a sample) from a population of networks to make inferences about networks in general, but resource constraints make this approach impractical except in unusual circumstances. The second is what Laumann et al. (1989) called the 'boundary specification problem' (see Perry & Roth, 2021). Because sociocentric data must be collected on a bounded group, the analyst is forced to assume that relations to individuals outside the group play no role in the behaviour of those inside it. For many questions, that assumption is untenable. For example, an analyst with data on all ties among all students in a school must assume that none of the teachers, parents, or friends in nearby schools affect the network behaviour of the students. Even if an analyst had data on, say, the entire universe of Facebook users, the researcher would need to assume that people not on Facebook – and behaviour of Facebook users outside Facebook – has no impact on the network behaviour of those on Facebook. This problem characterises all sociocentric data, and the degree to which it matters depends on the questions at hand.

Egocentric data address some of these problems. Because probability sampling can be used to select ego respondents, it is possible to make inferences about a population of egos or their networks from a sample. And because researchers need not sample from a given context (such as a school), they do not face the sociocentric boundary specification problem. For example, they can study a sample of Americans and elicit their personal networks in school, at work, and in their neighbourhoods. Egocentric researchers, therefore, often study the implications of being embedded in multiple overlapping social circles (Simmel, 1955).

Egocentric data collected in this fashion have their own disadvantages. One is that all information about networks is elicited from egos, meaning that these are essentially studies of egos' perceptions of their networks, which may or may not be accurate (see Sun et al., 2021). A researcher may then contact the alters to assess the accuracy of ego's reports (see Laumann, 1973), and even to elicit alters' own alters. However, there are logistical limits to how many steps from ego an analyst can go, and the broader social structure from which egocentric networks are derived and in which they are embedded are rarely captured with such data.

Egocentric Analysis vs Social Support Research

Egocentric research shares concerns with research on social support. Both assume that people's well-being is affected by those around them (Cohen & Syme, 1985; House et al., 1988; Lin & Peek, 1999; Pearlin, 1999). Like some egocentric researchers (e.g., Wellman & Wortley, 1990), some social support researchers aim to specify which types of support are available to an individual, who provides them, and under what circumstances. And, both tend to focus on the individual.

Nevertheless, the origins of social support research are in social psychology, while those of egocentric analysis are in structural network research. Consequently, the two perspectives diverge when it comes to structure. The traditional social support perspective is astructural, focusing instead on individuals' perceptions of the functions of social ties and the quality and availability of support resources accessible through relationships (Cohen & Syme, 1985; Coyne & Downey, 1991). In that tradition, social support is conceived as a psychosocial resource (Thoits, 1995), one of a set of tools available in response to stressful situations (Pearlin & Aneshensel, 1986). As such, the social support tradition tends to prioritise close ties (i.e., friends, family members and romantic relationships) and the positive characteristics of relationships, largely ignoring weaker ties and those that are conflictual, burdensome, or otherwise have a negative influence.

Accordingly, the two research traditions also differ considerably with respect to what they measure. Traditional social support research measures the actual or perceived support resources available to individuals. Its support scales are designed to capture one or more latent constructs, usually perceived support from the network as a whole or from subgroups like family or friends. It does not traditionally elicit individual alters through a name generator. As a result, though it provides detailed insight into people's belief in the supportiveness of their interpersonal environments, it is unable to capture how network structure affects support processes and individual well-being.

Egocentric Analysis vs Social Capital Research

Social capital research is comprised of two distinct traditions, one concerned with communities and the other with individuals (Portes, 2000). Research on the social capital of individuals is most relevant to egocentric analysis. That social capital tradition, with origins in the work of Loury (1977), Bourdieu (1985) and Coleman (1988), argues that people secure resources from investment in their social ties (Lin, 1999; Monge & Contractor, 2003). Those resources are diverse in type, and they include high trust, norms of reciprocity or cooperation, access to valuable information and economic opportunities (Granovetter, 1973; Coleman, 1988, 1990; Lin, 1999; Portes, 1998, 2000). Researchers have shown that greater access to and mobilisation of social capital is associated with better jobs, upward mobility, higher salaries and other outcomes.

Egocentric analysts and social capital researchers both see individual well-being as tied to social networks. But while traditionally the former paid attention to the structural characteristics of networks, the latter traditionally focused only on the particular resources (trust, information, etc.) contained in the networks, regardless of their structural characteristics. Today, egocentric analysts borrow liberally from the perspectives of social capital research (e.g., Hampton, 2011; Perry et al., 2021).

Two areas of overlap have come to be especially important. One is the difference between availability and use. Social capital researchers have distinguished 'access to' from 'mobilisation of' social capital (Lin, 1999). The former refers to the social capital resources people gain merely by being embedded in a particular network, as when highly successful managers, because of their connections, receive more unsolicited job offers through their acquaintances. The latter refers to the social capital resources that people secure by expressly turning to their network, as when unemployed people actively turn to those they know in search of a job. Egocentric analysts have pursued analogous lines of work. At times they examine how the characteristics of the personal network (its density, the composition of its members, etc.) are associated with well-being. Others examine the process of mobilisation itself (Small, 2021). This work includes examining which members of their network people cognitively 'activate', or think about, when turning to others for help (Sun et al., 2021).

The second area of overlap involves the design of specific instruments to elicit names for analysis. To understand these, we must first examine in closer detail the most common tool of the egocentric researcher, the name generator (Bidart & Charbonneau, 2011; Bott, 1955; McCallister & Fischer, 1982; Small, 2017). As we shall see, the name generator has been a crucial tool, but also one with several limitations, and social capital researchers have addressed some of these limitations.

ELICITING NETWORKS

The Name Generator

The name generator is the tool most often used for eliciting social networks in egocentric research. Its importance to the resulting analysis is difficult to overstate. The total number of family, friends, friends of friends, co-workers, acquaintances and distal others that could affect a person's decisions, behaviour, support, well-being, or opportunities is far larger than any instrument can elicit, as researchers have found that even the weakest of social connections can be crucial to outcomes like finding a job or receiving social support (e.g., Granovetter, 1974; Small, 2017). Since no generator can capture all of these, the decision of which generator to employ is critical (Marin, 2004; McCarty et al., 2007; Smith & Moody, 2013; Perry & Pescosolido, 2012; Perry et al., 2018; McCarty et al., 2019).

The difficulty of selecting a name generator is magnified by the fact that there are many different types of possible relations an instrument could elicit. The most common types have involved: affect, or alters to whom ego has a particular feeling such as closeness, intimacy, or affinity (e.g., 'who are you close to?'); resource, or alters who provide a particular good or service (e.g., 'who would you borrow money from?'); interaction, or alters who are encountered in a particular period or context (e.g., 'who did you talk to in the last 24 hours?'); roles, or alters who play a given role in ego's life (e.g., 'who are your co-workers?'); and content, or alters who possess a given characteristic of interest (e.g., 'who do you know who is politically conservative?'). Any decision requires excluding a major part of the personal network. As a result, some have argued strongly that addressing such problems calls for multiple generators (Fischer, 1982), but network data can be time consuming to elicit, and the amount of time to reconstruct a total network increases exponentially with the number of names elicited. Thus, most researchers have selected one name generator.

In doing so, researchers have usually followed one of two strategies. Those following a *focused* approach identify a specific research aim and design an elicitation instrument geared to that end. For example, they select an instrument based on the type of relation most relevant to their question, such as the alters ego turned to for information about jobs (Granovetter, 1974) or those whom ego turned to when needing someone to talk to (Small, 2017). In general, focused name generators are powerful when closely aligned with theory but are limited with respect to the scope of research questions that can be answered. Those following an *expansive* approach seek a general name generator that allows for more flexible analysis and the inclusion of weaker and more diverse ties. For example, they might ask respondents to name those they are 'very' and 'somewhat close to' (Wellman et al., 2005). Such strategies tend to produce larger networks.

Regardless of whether their approach is focused or expansive, designers of a name generator have had to confront that ego must be relied on to report on the relation to alters (see Hammer, 1984; Brewer, 2000). Two of the most important challenges are comprehension and recall (see Small & Cook, 2021). 'Comprehension' here refers not only to whether people understand the instrument but also to how they interpret it. For example, in a study of General Social Survey's name generator instrument, Bailey and Marsden (1999) found that when asked whom they talked to about 'important matters', 'many respondents did not find the notion of important matters to be straightforward' (1999, p. 298). Moreover, different people believed the instrument to be eliciting different things, such as who was important to them and whom they talked to regularly. A very different but analogous problem emerges in the context of online surveys, which have become an increasingly popular way of eliciting personal networks. The online format allows for many different ways of presenting an instrument, and the way it is presented has been shown to affect what people report. For example, Vehovar et al. (2008) show that the number of alters reported by a name generator is sensitive to the number of boxes presented on the screen for people to input the elicited names (see also Coromina & Coenders, 2006). Researchers would do well to understand exactly how respondents interpret a given instrument.

The second problem is recall, which can result in both error and bias. Forgetting to name relevant alters is a nontrivial problem, affecting about 20 percent of alters even in more intimate core networks in test-retest conditions in a recent study (Brewer, 2000). Research suggests that people are biased towards recalling more salient alters, such as those they are closest to, those they see or talk to regularly, and those they have known the longest (Brewer, 2000). Forgetting has also been shown to be more prevalent in larger networks that are less densely connected (Bell et al., 2007; Brewer, 2000; Marin, 2004), and when the exchange or interaction relation is less specific and more ambiguous (Bell et al., 2007). Moreover, recall errors can truncate network size and inflate network density, as well as bias aggregated measures of tie strength or function towards more intimacy, support, and frequent interaction (Brewer & Webster, 1999; Marin, 2004; see also Campbell & Lee, 1991). (More on this topic below.)

The most commonly used instrument to elicit a personal network is the 'important matters' name generator from the General Social Survey (GSS). In 1985, the GSS adopted a single name generator from Fischer's (1982) Northern California Community Study (Burt, 1984; Marsden, 1987; McPherson et al., 2006), 'From time to time, most people discuss important personal matters with other people. Looking back over the last six months, who are the people with whom you have discussed an important personal matter?' The idea was to use an expansive, rather than focused, instrument that might have wide application; the resulting network was termed the 'core discussion network'. Its inclusion on the GSS quickly made this name generator a mainstay of research on personal social networks. While the important matters generator was believed to elicit a set of supportive, stable, emotionally close alters that might be predictive of a variety of outcomes, a significant body of research has challenged this assumption (Bearman & Parigi, 2004; Brashears, 2014; Small, 2013, 2017). For example, Small's (2013) research suggests that about half of the important matters network is comprised of alters who are not important to ego, and that people tend to seek discussants who are available when they need to talk or who are relevant to the topics they want to talk about. Moreover, researchers have found that the expansiveness of the instrument has undermined its predictive power. For example, studies attempting to predict health outcomes on its basis have found the instrument weak, particularly in comparison with an instrument that asks whom respondents talk to specifically about health matters (Perry & Pescosolido, 2010; York Cornwell & Waite, 2012).

The Name Interpreter

In most egocentric data collection, name generators are followed by 'name interpreters', or questions about the characteristics or attributes of the alters named. Name interpreters can capture demographic traits (e.g., alter's gender, education, employment status, etc.) or the relational characteristics described earlier, such as affect, role, and interaction relations. As such, they can dramatically improve the power of name generators. For example, rather than limiting the generator to a particular type of relation, the researcher might use a very general name generator and follow up by asking about the specific relations to those alters named. Interpreters capture essential and influential characteristics of alters, such as how the ego and alter are connected. The flexibility in use of name interpreters means that the resulting measures can be predictive of a broad range of outcomes.

Name interpreters require proxy reporting about alters and subjective assessments of relationships that may be biased (Blair et al., 1991; Epley, 2008). The accuracy of proxy reporting depends on the nature of the relationship between ego and alter; more accurate reports have been found for closer alters contacted more frequently (Reysen et al., 2014; Shelley et al., 2006; Triplett, 2013). Reporting accuracy also depends on the nature of the information being elicited. Reports of status characteristics, such as education or marital status, have typically been more reliable than those of attitudes, beliefs or private information (Nelson et al., 1994; Kitts, 2003; Laumann, 1969). Research on abortion, miscarriage, HIV status and related sensitive topics suggests that private or stigmatising information is often shared selectively with like-minded or sympathetic members of social networks (Cowan, 2014; Shelley et al. 1995; Shelley et al., 2006), and that proxy reports of such information tend to be biased towards ego's own worldview (Goel et al., 2010). Conversely, when asked to identify the views of someone whose perspective differs from their own, people often rely on stereotypes (Epley & Caruso, 2008; Goel et al., 2010). Such issues call for caution in the interpretation of name interpreters.

The Network

A crucial step in egocentric network research is the elicitation of ties between alters, a process that allows for the calculation of structural measures of networks. Most often alter–alter ties are recorded by asking about one type of relationship between every pair of alters (e.g., 'Do [NAME1] and [NAME2] know each other well?'). If a large number of alters is produced, the process can be time consuming (Manfreda et al., 2004). There have been several solutions. Often, the researcher is interested in only a small number of alters. For example, the average number of alters produced by the GSS 'important maters' name generator is three, with a maximum of six or seven. Other times, researchers employ information previously elicited from name interpreters. For example, if two alters have previously been reported as siblings of ego, the researcher does not then ask whether those two alters know each other. Such solutions can be implemented in person or programmed into online survey software. As a third alternative, respondents have been presented personal network maps where they can draw lines between visually depicted alters. Finally, some research suggests that selecting a random subset of alters for enquiry – rather than all alters named – can produce high-quality estimates of structural measures (McCarty et al., 2007; Peng et al., 2022).

Position and Resource Generators

While the name generator is a powerful tool for egocentric analysis, it has important limitations for those interested in social capital. One is that, unless it is unusually expansive, it can ignore weak ties known by both social capital and network researchers to be valuable in the context of upward mobility (Granovetter, 1974). One alternative is the *position generator*, which asks respondents whether they know someone in a set of occupations (Lin & Dumin, 1986; Lin, 2002). A typical position generator presents a list of around twenty occupations, ranging in prestige from lower blue-collar (e.g., labourer, server/bartender) to upper white-collar (e.g., lawyer, small business owner). Respondents who know someone in a given occupation are asked a series of follow-up questions (akin to name interpreters) about the alter. These data are used to construct measures of highest accessed prestige and the number and prestige range of positions accessed. Lin developed the position generator to be 'content free', meaning the measures can be used for any substantive application of social capital theory and in cross-national research (Lin et al., 2001; Van der Gaag & Webber, 2008).

Like position generators, *resource generators* are designed to explicitly assess the diversity of distinct kinds of social capital accessible through personal social networks (Van der Gaag & Snijders, 2005). However, in this case, specific resources are measured directly rather than inferring access to resources through alters' occupational prestige. The organisation and administration of the resource generator is like the position generator except that social resources are presented instead of occupations (e.g., 'Do you know anyone who knows how to fix problems with computers?'). If yes, the respondent is asked about their relationship to that alter (typically acquaintance, friend, or family member) to operationalise ability to leverage the resources for their own goals. The resources are then scaled into latent classes of social capital (e.g., political and financial skills social capital; Van der Gaag & Snijders, 2005).

Position and resource generators are very useful for testing theories of social capital, which are an important component of the social network perspective. However, access to social capital (either through alters' occupations or specific knowledge or skills) is only a subset of the range of network functions and mechanisms captured through name generators and of interest to ego-network researchers, making these more restrictive approaches. For example, position generators are less useful for capturing expressive (as opposed to material or instrumental) resources and those that do not depend on labour market participation (Van der Gaag et al., 2008); the efficacy of emotional support is unlikely to be affected by occupation. More broadly, these instruments are narrowly concerned with resource exchange, and thus ignore everything else (e.g., norms and values, misinformation, infectious diseases) that flow through social ties. As such, the egocentric network approach and its primary methodological tools – name generators and interpreters – have proven more flexible and versatile for testing a diverse range of network theories.

NEW DIRECTIONS

The last decade or two have seen a rapid expansion of egocentric network analysis, with multiple conferences, special issues of journals (e.g., *Network Science*; Perry et al., 2020) and multiple volumes (Perry et al., 2018; McCarty et al., 2019; Small et al., 2021a) devoted exclusively to egocentric analysis. In what follows we discuss a sampling of the topics this new work has covered (see also Small et al., 2021a, Part IV).

Strength

The notion of tie strength has long been a feature of the study of personal networks. It played a major role in Granovetter's (1973) argument that weak ties are more likely to be bridges; it was instrumental to what proponents of the GSS name generator believed they captured when asking with whom people discussed important matters (Burt, 1984; Marsden, 1987); and it was thought to be the most supportive type of relation (but see Thoits, 2011; Small, 2017). In recent years, scholars have unpacked both the idea of strength and its implications.

Several have sought to more precisely define 'strength'. Granovetter (1973, p. 1361) had defined 'the strength of a tie [as] a (probably linear) combination of the amount of time, the emotional intensity, the intimacy (mutual confiding), and the reciprocal services which characterize the tie', thereby suggesting that exchange, interactional and affective features combined to characterise an alter as close (see Krackhardt, 1992). A key part of this view is that strength can be understood in a single dimension, typically operationalised as either frequency of interaction or closeness (see Brashears & Quintane, 2018). Granovetter had also offered the oft-repeated rule of thumb that weak ties – which are more likely to be bridges – provide information, while strong ties provide support (Granovetter, 1983).

But Aral and Van Alstyne (2011) showed that this expectation about weak ties was simplistic – weak ties may provide information that is more novel but they also provide less of it, such that there is a trade-off between diversity and bandwidth. Information flow is greater through strong ties; information is more novel through weak ones. Small (2017) showed that the rule of thumb's expectation about strong ties often does not hold – weak ties are effective sources of support, as people are more likely to trust them than expected. Brashears and Quintane (2018), focused again on information transmission, argued expressly that strength contains at least two separate dimensions, '*capacity*, the ability of a tie to transfer information … and *frequency*, the inverse of the average length of time between uses of a tie' (2018, p. 105). The authors show that the two properties, plus *redundancy*, or 'the extent to which the two participants in a tie share common third-parties' (2018, p. 105), separately help account for access to new information. Focused on support, but from a very different perspective, Offer and Fischer (2018) upend the idea that people to whom individuals are close constitute supportive, positive relations. Studying who in their personal networks people find 'difficult', they show that close family members are significantly more likely to be in that category. The work contributes to new research examining negative ties. Collectively, this body of work has questioned the notion of strength as an all-purpose category and more carefully unpacks the dynamics through which information, support and other interpersonal processes operate.

Mobilisation

As we discussed, social capital researchers had identified 'access to' and 'mobilisation of' social capital as different processes (Lin, 1999). The study of mobilisation, however, has been part of several bodies of work which have examined the same notion using different terms, including 'help-seeking behaviour' and the 'activation of social ties' (e.g., Pescosolido, 1992; Smith, 2005; Small, 2017, 2021; Smith et al., 2020). This work has shared a focus on understanding how people decide whether to turn to others, and whom to turn to, when needing information, support, a service, a good, or some other social resource.

Some of the work has centred specifically on the mobilisation decision. Researchers have proposed that people differentiate among alters and decide whom to turn to based on the match between the need and the skills or resources possessed by the alter (Perry & Pescosolido, 2010; 2012; also Wellman & Wortley, 1990; Bearman & Parigi, 2004). Others have argued that people often do not deliberate on the matter, and may at times decide based mainly on opportunity or availability (Small & Sukhu, 2016; Small, 2017, 2021). Other works have shown that cognitive processes affect who people call to mind when deciding they need help, such that both how alters are stored in memory and how recall operates shape the process (Sun et al., 2021; see below). Still others have argued that, rather than examining a single decision, researchers should focus on sets of decisions, given that many conditions for which people need help are recurring or ongoing (Pescosolido, 1992).

One development from research on mobilisation has been methodological. Rather than beginning by mapping the personal network via a name generator, researchers have argued that beginning with either the need for help or with the event are essential to understand mobilisation. Pescosolido (1992) has shown that beginning not with the network but with the pattern of decisions shows that the network of support is broader than often believed and that the features of interaction are more important than typically understood. Small (2017) has shown that if, instead of eliciting the network of those they talk to, respondents are first asked to report the issues for which they have needed someone to talk to, the resulting set of alters – those they actually talked to about those issues – is more likely to include weak ties (see Small, 2021, for an extensive discussion). These works bear a similarity to earlier anthropological work by Boswell (1969), who argued that 'the crisis situation' was the key starting point to understand how social networks are mobilised by those in need.

Cognition

An area that has expanded rapidly focuses on networks, cognition, and the brain (see Brashears & Money, this volume). This research is rooted in human evolutionary theories of the social brain. These suggest that humans' large brains and high intelligence evolved to remember and process increasingly complex social information required to adapt to life in larger social groups (Brashears & Brashears, 2019). While early research in this area claimed that the brain could only hold a finite number of people in memory – and, thus, in a personal network – more recent studies have consistently shown that human social networks exceed this number (Dunbar, 1992; McCarty et al., 2001; Omodei et al., 2017). Researchers have shown that the large capacity is due to compression heuristics, or cognitive schemas that facilitate recall and information processing (Brashears, 2013). Individuals can recall their networks using partial information rather than having to remember every tie (Omodei et al., 2017). Research has provided evidence for a number of compression heuristics. For example, experimental studies have shown that people recall social networks more accurately when networks exhibit triadic closure and affective balance (Brashears, 2013; Brashears & Brashears, 2016).

This research provides important insight into methodological limitations and potential biases in egocentric network research (Perry et al., 2018). Compression heuristics may be especially likely to bias free recall when the name generating task is vague or subject to interpretation, and therefore more cognitively taxing (Omodei et al., 2017). This process would explain why respondents omit fewer alters when the elicitation references specific functions, roles, or contexts or provides a concrete cognitive anchor (Bell et al., 2007). Similarly, it would help explain why respondents are more likely to omit weaker bridging ties (i.e., those that connect ego to a set of actors unconnected to any other alters) or incidental ties (i.e., those that are activated for support or discussion because they happen to be accessible) (Brewer & Webster, 1999; Marin, 2004), even if they perform significant functions (Small & Sukhu, 2016). Taken together, this research suggests that compression heuristics tend to produce observed ego networks that are affectively strong, kin-centred and densely connected. To study social phenomena like diffusion, weak ties, or structural holes, specialised name generators that target unembedded and irregular interaction partners may be necessary.

The last decade has also seen an increase in research combining personal network analysis with neuroscience. Some studies have shown that neural networks influence social learning and behaviour (Noonan et al., 2018; Schmälzle et al., 2017) and, conversely, that social experiences and environments shape brain structure and function (Peer et al., 2021; Sallet et al., 2011). For example, a recent study examined how large egocentric networks are represented in the brain using Facebook data and functional magnetic resonance imaging (fMRI), a technology that measures the amount and location of brain activity (Peer et al., 2021). The authors found that thinking about the structural position of alters in the ego network activated the part of the brain involved in spatial processing, indicating that social and spatial distance may be processed similarly (see also Parkinson et al., 2014). Conversely, the personality traits of alters were coded in the region responsible for social cognitive processing, suggesting that encoding and retrieving information about social networks requires complex cooperation between different parts of the brain (Weaverdyck & Parkinson, 2018). In an experimental study (Schmälzle et al., 2017), researchers examined what happens to brain connectivity when people experience social exclusion, finding increased activity in areas of the brain responsible for understanding the mental states of others. Moreover, people whose brains exhibited more functional connectivity in those regions involved in 'mentalising' had less dense friendship networks (see also Falk & Bassett, 2017; Weaverdyck & Parkinson, 2018).

Context

Although early egocentric research tended to analyse personal networks in a context-less state, people's daily lives do not unfold in a vacuum. They operate in a range of contexts which, in turn, influence their chances at forming and maintaining different types of personal networks. As such, there is a burgeoning body of literature that addresses how multiple contexts, particularly cultural, organisational and spatial contexts, shape personal networks.

We begin with cultural context. The traditional network model in the sociology of culture posits that social networks shape culture (DiMaggio, 1987; Erickson, 1996; Mark, 1998, 2003). This claim finds support in the social contagion literature, which asserts that social behaviours – including beliefs, tastes and preferences – are learned through interactions with others (Centola, 2015; Christakis & Fowler, 2013). However, the traditional network model has been criticised for framing culture as passively transmitted from person to person. Researchers have argued that one's cultural milieu influences their involvement in social relationships (Lizardo, 2006; Vaisey & Lizardo, 2010; see Bourdieu, 1986). For example, a person with 'highbrow' interests (e.g., opera, classical music) may leverage their cultural capital to integrate themselves with an elite crowd by signalling that they belong to the proper social class (Lizardo, 2006; see also McConnell, 2017). The more reasonable view today is therefore not that networks shape culture, but rather that culture and networks shape each other (Emirbayer & Goodwin, 1994, p. 1438). Egocentric research has been crucial to understanding how.

Unlike culture, organisations provide a tangible context in which individuals can form social relationships. Organisational contexts such as workplaces (Doreian & Conti, 2012; Sailer &

McCulloh, 2012), schools (McFarland et al., 2014; Small, 2017), voluntary groups (McPherson & Smith-Lovin, 1987) and childcare centres (Small, 2009) have been shown to be particularly important to personal networks because they bring people into repeated contact with one another (Feld, 1981; Small, 2021). In this sense, organisations contribute to the selection pool of potential alters from whom an individual may eventually draw for his or her personal network (Mollenhorst et al., 2008).

Research on organisational context has paid special attention to how organisational characteristics shape patterns of network formation. For instance, Doreian and Conti (2012) analysed network data from a police academy and found that recruits tended to form friendship ties based on their academy's squad assignment and seating arrangement during formal lectures. Small (2009) studied mothers' involvement at childcare centres, and found that mothers whose children attended centres with more structured opportunities for social interactions (e.g., parent–teacher meetings, field trips) were more likely to develop friendships than mothers in centres with few such opportunities. Small and Gose (2020, p. 89) examined a wide array of studies of organisations involved in low-income populations and found that whether organisations contributed to tie formation depended 'on the degree to which an organization's institutional norms render interaction among participants frequent, long-lasting, focused on others, and centered on joint tasks'. Studies of this kind suggest that personal networks are formed not only in organisations but also by them (Small, 2021).

Research on the role of spatial context in personal networks is longstanding, with an especially large body of work studying how space affects the formation of social ties (see Small & Adler, 2019, for a review). Numerous early network studies noted that people are more likely to form ties when situated in spatially proximate locations (Bossard, 1932; Caplow & Forman, 1950; Festinger et al., 1950; Lawton & Nahemow, 1973). For example, people are more likely to know their nextdoor neighbour than they are to know their neighbour two doors down, three doors down and so on (Sudman, 1988). Others have found that, even with recent advances in communication technology, geographic distance separating individuals across towns, states and even nations dramatically influences the probability of tie formation (Laniado et al., 2018; Spiro et al., 2016).

Although proximity matters, the composition and configuration of space matter as well. Spatial composition refers to the presence of gathering places conducive to social interaction, such as parks, bars, restaurants, libraries and religious centres (Small & Adler, 2019). Such places can not only enable social interaction, but also actively encourage it (Feld, 1981; Klinenberg, 2018; Oldenburg, 1999). Spaces devoid of such places can contribute to social isolation (Klinenberg, 2002; Wilson, 1987). The configuration of space refers to 'the arrangement of physical barriers and pathways that result in the segmentation of a space' (Small & Adler, 2019, p. 120). Researchers in recent years have shown that features of spaces such as the arrangement of offices in a hallway and the position of elevators in a building shape the formation of social relations (e.g., Sailer & McCulloh, 2012).

Research on cultural, organisational, or spatial context has provided a great deal of insight into how the personal network is formed. In doing so, it has relied on many kinds of data, not all of them egocentric in nature. Studies have relied on organisational, not just individual-level data; they have been based on ethnographic observation, not just network elicitation. Today's research on personal networks has often expanded well beyond the confines of egocentric data.

Dynamics

Traditional egocentric studies almost exclusively focused on cross-sectional accounts of personal networks. An increasing number of studies are directing attention to the dynamic and evolutionary nature of personal networks. Researchers have studied several processes contributing to dynamic changes in the personal network. One is social context. Transitions into and out of different social contexts – such as school, workplace and neighbourhood – are likely to cause individuals to form new ties and dissolve old ones (Bidart & Lavenu, 2005; Small et al., 2015; Badawy et al., 2018; Comi et al., 2022). In addition, the adoption of new social roles – such as parent, patient, caregiver – has been shown to induce network changes, as needs and interests shift in response to new responsibilities or expectations (Kalmijn, 2012; Perry & Pescosolido, 2012; Roth, 2020; see also Charles & Carstensen, 2010).

A different body of work has examined turnover in the personal network. While many have documented that individuals add and subtract members from their personal networks through a variety of mechanisms, an interesting finding has shown that the size, structure, and composition of personal networks tends to remain relatively stable even as network members turn over (Wellman et al., 1997; Small et al., 2015; Cornwell et al., 2021). For example, Small et al. (2015) tracked the personal networks of incoming graduate students and found that most tended to substitute old alters with new ones, rather than expanding or shrinking the overall size of their networks. One explanation suggests that every individual has a distinctive 'social signature' that is highlighted by a habitual pattern of social interaction (Saramäki et al., 2014). Individuals may tend to develop archetypal relationships that are unique to their personal history, regardless of who alters are as individuals.

CONCLUSION

The accelerated growth of egocentric network analysis over the past decade foretells a promising future. Traditional methods and questions have given way to new approaches by researchers comfortable with understanding personal networks from methodological perspectives not common to structural analysis; with incorporating ideas from fields such as neuroscience and anthropology; and with asking questions about decision, context, or culture, or space that either had not been asked or had lain dormant for several decades. We believe this work will contribute strongly to the expansion of network analysis well beyond the traditional confines of the field.

REFERENCES

Aral, S., & Van Alstyne, M. (2011). The diversity-bandwidth tradeoff. *American Journal of Sociology*, *117*(1), 90–171.

Aristotle (1943). *On man in the universe*.

Badawy, P.J., Schafer, M.H., & Sun, H. (2018). Relocation and network turnover in later life: how distance moved and functional health are linked to a changing social convoy. *Research on Aging*, *41*(1), 45–84.

Bailey, S., & Marsden, P.V. (1999). Interpretation and interview context: examining the general social survey name generator using cognitive methods. *Social Networks*, *21*(3), 287–309.

Bearman, P.S., & Parigi, P. (2004). Cloning headless frogs and other important matters: conversation topics and network structure. *Social Forces*, *83*(2), 535–557.

Bell, D.C., Belli-McQueen, B., & Haider, A. (2007). Partner naming and forgetting: recall of network members. *Social Networks*, *29*(2), 279–299.

Bidart, C., & Lavenu, D. (2005). Evolutions of personal networks and life events. *Social Networks*, *27*(4), 359–376.

Bidart, C., & Charbonneau, J. (2011). How to generate personal networks: issues and tools for a sociological perspective. *Field Methods*, *23*(3), 266–286.

Blair, J., Menon, G., & Bickart, B. (1991). Measurement effects in self vs proxy responses to survey questions: an information-processing perspective. In P. Biemer, R. Groves, L. Lyberg, N. Mathieowetz & S. Sudman (Eds.), *Measurement errors in surveys* (pp. 145–166). John Wiley & Sons.

Borgatti, S.P., Everett, M.G., & Johnson, J.C. (2013). *Analyzing social networks*. Sage.

Bossard, J.H.S. (1932). Residential propinquity as a factor in marriage selection. *American Journal of Sociology*, *38*(2), 219–224.

Boswell, D.M. (1969). Personal crises and the mobilization of the social network. In J.C. Mitchell (Ed.), *Social networks in urban situations: analyses of personal relationships in central African towns* (pp. 245–296). Humanities Press.

Bott, E. (1955). Urban families: conjugal roles and social networks. *Human Relations*, *8*(4), 345–384.

Bourdieu, P. (1985). The social space and the genesis of groups. *Social Science Information*, *24*(2), 195–220.

Bourdieu, P. (1986). The forms of capital. In J. Richardson (Ed.), *Handbook of theory and research for the sociology of education*, vol. 1 (pp. 81–93). Greenwood Press.

Brashears, M.E. (2013). Humans use compression heuristics to improve the recall of social networks. *Scientific Reports*, *3*(1513).

Brashears, M.E. (2014). 'Trivial' topics and rich ties: the relationship between discussion topic, alter role, and resource availability using the 'important matters' name generator. *Sociological Science*, *1*(27), 493–511.

Brashears, M.E., & Quintane, E. (2018). The weakness of tie strength. *Social Networks*, *55*, 104–115.

Brashears, M.E., & Brashears, L.A. (2016). The enemy of my friend is easy to remember: balance as a compression heuristic. In S.R. Thye & E. Lawler (Eds.), *Advances in group processes*, vol. 6 (pp. 1–31). Emerald.

Brashears, M.E., & Brashears, L.A. (2019). Compression heuristics, social networks, and the evolution of human intelligence. In M.S. Vitevitch (Ed.), *Network science in cognitive psychology* (pp. 97–116). Routledge.

Brass, D.J. (1984). Being in the right place: a structural analysis of individual influence in an organization. *Administrative Science Quarterly*, *29*(4), 518–539.

Brewer, D.D. (2000). Forgetting in the recall-based elicitation of personal and social networks. *Social Networks*, *22*(1), 29–43.

Brewer, D.D., & Webster, C.M. (1999). Forgetting of friends and its effects on measuring friendship networks. *Social Networks*, *21*(4), 361–373.

Burt, R. (1984). Network items and the general social survey. *Social Networks*, 6(4), 293–339.

Campbell, K.E., & Lee, B.A. (1991). Name generators in surveys of personal networks. *Social Networks*, 13(3), 203–221.

Caplow, T., & Forman, R. (1950). Neighborhood interaction in a homogeneous community. *American Sociological Review*, 15(3), 357–366.

Centola, D. (2015). The social origins of networks and diffusion. *American Journal of Sociology*, 120(5), 1295–1338.

Charles, S.T., & Carstensen, L.L. (2010). Social and emotional aging. *Annual Review of Psychology*, 61, 383–409.

Christakis, N.A., & Fowler, J.H. (2013). Social contagion theory: examining dynamic social networks and human behavior. *Statistics in Medicine*, 32(4), 556–577.

Cohen, S., & Syme, S.L. (1985). Issues in the study and application of social support. In S. Cohen & S.L. Syme (Eds.), *Social support and health* (pp. 3–22). Academic Press.

Coleman, J.S. (1988). Social capital in the creation of human capital. *American Journal of Sociology*, 94(suppl), S95–S120.

Coleman, J.S. (1990). *Foundations of social theory*. Belknap Press, Harvard University.

Comi, S.L., Cottini, E., & Lucifora, C. (2022). The effect of retirement on social relationships. *German Economic Review*, 23(2), 275–299.

Cornwell, B., Goldman, A., & Laumann, E.O. (2021). homeostasis revisited: patterns of stability and rebalancing in older adults' social lives. *The Journals of Gerontology: Series B*, 76(4), 778–789. doi: 10.1093/geronb/gbaa026

Coromina, L., & Coenders, G. (2006). Reliability and validity of egocentered network data collected via web: a meta-analysis of multilevel multitrait multimethod studies. *Social Networks*, 28(3), 209–231.

Cowan, S.K. (2014). Secrets and misperceptions: the creation of self-fulfilling illusions. *Sociological Science*, 1, 466–492.

Coyne, J.C., & Downey, G. (1991). Social factors and psychopathology: stress, social support, and coping processes. *Annual Review of Psychology*, 42(1), 401–425.

DiMaggio, P. (1987). Classification in art. *American Sociological Review*, 52(4), 440–455.

Doreian, P., & Conti, N. (2012). Social context, spatial structure and social network structure. *Social Networks*, 34(1), 32–46.

Dunbar, R.I.M. (1992). Neocortex size as a constraint on group size in primates. *Journal of Human Evolution*, 22(6), 469–493.

Emirbayer, M., & Goodwin, J. (1994). Network analysis, culture, and the problem of agency. *American Journal of Sociology*, 99(6), 1411–1454.

Epley, N. (2008). Solving the (real) other minds problem. *Social and Personality Psychology Compass*, 2(3), 1455–1474.

Epley, N., & Caruso, E.M. (2008). Perspective taking: misstepping into others' shoes. In J.A. Suhr (Ed.), *Handbook of imagination and mental simulation* (pp. 297–311). Psychology Press.

Erickson, B.H. (1996). Culture, class, and connections. *American Journal of Sociology*, 102(1), 217–251.

Falk, E.B., & Bassett, D.S. (2017). Brain and social networks: fundamental building blocks of human experience. *Trends in Cognitive Sciences*, 21(9), 674–690.

Feld, S.L. (1981). The focused organization of social ties. *American Journal of Sociology*, 86(5), 1015–1035.

Festinger, L., Schachter, S., & Back, K. (Eds.) (1950). *Social Pressures in informal groups: a study of human factors in housing*. Harper.

Fischer, C.S. (1982). *To dwell among friends: personal networks in town and city*. University of Chicago Press.

Freeman, L. (2004). *The development of social network analysis: a study in the sociology of science*. Empirical Press.

Goel, S., Mason, W.A., & Watts, D.J. (2010). Real and perceived attitude agreement in social networks. *Journal of Personality and Social Psychology*, 99(4), 611.

Granovetter, M.S. (1973). The strength of weak ties. *American Journal of Sociology*, 78, 1360–1380.

Granovetter, M.S. (1974). *Getting a job: a study of contacts and careers*. Harvard University Press.

Granovetter, M.S. (1983). The strength of weak ties: a network theory revisited. *Sociological Theory*, 1, 201–233.

Grigoropoulou, N., & Small, M.L. (2022). The data revolution in social science needs qualitative research. *Nature Human Behaviour*, 6(7), 904–906.

Hammer, M. (1984). Explorations into the meaning of social network interview data. *Social Networks*, 6(4), 341–371.

Hampton, K.N. (2011). Comparing bonding and bridging ties for democratic engagement: everyday use of communication technologies within social networks for civic and civil behaviors. *Information, Communication and Society*, 14(4), 510–528.

House, J.S., Umberson, D.A., & Landis, J.R. (1988). Structures and processes of social support. *Annual Review of Sociology*, 14, 293–318.

Kalmijn, M. (2012). Longitudinal analyses of the effects of age, marriage, and parenthood on social contacts and support. *Advances in Life Course Research*, 17(4), 177–190.

Katz, E., & Lazarsfeld, P.F.. (1955). *Personal influence: the part played by people in the flow of mass communications*. Free Press.

Kitts, J.A. (2003). Egocentric bias or information management? Selective disclosure and the social roots of norm misperception. *Social Psychology Quarterly*, 66(3), 222–237.

Klinenberg, E. (2002). *Heat wave: a social autopsy of disaster in Chicago*. University of Chicago Press.

Klinenberg, E. (2018). *Palaces for the people: how social infrastructure can help fight inequality, polarization, and the decline of civic life*. Broadway.

Krackhardt, D. (1992). The strength of strong ties: the importance of philos in organizations. In N. Nohria & R.C. Eccles (Eds.), *Networks and organizations: structure, form, and action* (pp. 216–239). Harvard University Press.

Laniado, D., Volkovich, Y., Scellato, S., Mascolo, C., & Kaltenbrunner, A. (2018). The impact of geographic distance on online social interactions. *Information Systems Frontiers*, 20(6), 1203–1218.

Laumann, E.O. (1969). Friends of urban men: an assessment of accuracy in reporting their socioeconomic attributes, mutual choice, and attitude agreement. *Sociometry*, 32(1), 54–69.

Laumann, E.O. (1973). *Bonds of pluralism: the form and substance of urban social networks*. John Wiley & Sons.

Laumann, E.O., Marsden, P.V., & Prensky, D. (1989). The boundary specification problem in network analysis. In L.C. Freeman, K. Romney & D. White (Eds.), *Research methods in social network analysis* (p. 87). University Publishing Associates.

Lawton, M.P., & Nahemow, L. (1973). Ecology and the aging process. In C. Eisdorfer & M.P. Lawton (Eds.), *The psychology of adult development and aging* (pp. 619–674). American Psychological Association.

Lin, N. (1999). Building a network theory of social capital. *Connections*, 22(1), 28–51.

Lin, N. (2002). *Social capital: a theory of social structure and action*. Cambridge University Press.

Lin, N., & Dumin, M. (1986). Access to occupations through social ties. *Social Networks*, 8(4), 365–385.

Lin, N., Fu, Y.-c., & Hsung, R.-M. (2001). The position generator: measurement techniques for investigations of social capital. In N. Lin, K. Cook & R. Burt (Eds.), *Social capital: theory and research* (pp. 57–81). Aldine deGruyter.

Lin, N., & Peek, N.K. (1999). Social networks and mental health. In A.V. Horwitz & T.L. Scheid (Eds.), *A handbook for the study of mental health* (pp. 241–258). Cambridge University Press.

Lizardo, O. (2006). How cultural tastes shape personal networks. *American Sociological Review*, 71(5), 778–807.

Loury, G. (1977). A dynamic theory of racial income differences. In P. Wallace & A. LaMond. *Women, minorities, and employment discrimination* (pp. 153–188). Lexington.

Manfreda, K.L., Vehovar, V., & Hlebec, V. (2004). Collecting ego-centered network data via the web. *Metodoloski zvezki*, 1(2), 295.

Marin, A. (2004). Are respondents more likely to list alters with certain characteristics? Implications for name generator data. *Social Networks*, 26(4), 289–307.

Mark, N. (1998). Beyond individual differences: social differentiation from first principles. *American Sociological Review*, 63(3), 309–330.

Mark, N.P. (2003). Culture and competition: homophily and distancing explanations for cultural niches. *American Sociological Review*, 68(3), 319–345.

Marsden, P.V. (1987). Core discussion networks of Americans. *American Sociological Review*, 52(1), 122–131.

McCallister, L., & Fischer, C.S. (1978). A procedure for surveying personal networks. *Sociological Methods and Research*, 7(2), 131–148.

McCarty, C., Killworth, P.D., Bernard, H.R., Johnsen, E.C., & Shelley, G.A. (2001). Comparing two methods for estimating network size. *Human Organization*, 60(1), 28–39.

McCarty, C., Killworth, P.D., & Rennell, J. (2007). Impact of methods for reducing respondent burden on personal network structural measures. *Social Networks*, 29(2), 300–315.

McCarty, C., Lubbers, M.J., Vacca, R., & Molina, J.L. (2019). *Conducting personal network research: a practical guide*. Guilford.

McConnell, W.R. (2017). Cultural guides, cultural critics: distrust of doctors and social support during mental health treatment. *Journal of Health and Social Behavior*, 58(4), 503–519.

McFarland, D.A., Moody, J., Diehl, D., Smith, J.A., & Thomas, R.J. (2014). Network ecology and adolescent social structure. *American Sociological Review*, 79(6), 1088–1121.

McPherson, J.M., & Smith-Lovin, L. (1987). Homophily in voluntary organizations: status distance and the composition of face-to-face groups. *American Sociological Review*, 52(3), 370–379.

McPherson, J. Miller, Lynn Smith-Lovin, and Matthew E. Brashears. (2006). 'Social Isolation in America: Changes in Core Discussion Networks Over Two Decades.' *American Sociological Review* 71(3), 353–375.

Mitchell, J.C. (1969). *Social networks in urban situations: analyses of personal relationships in central African towns*. Manchester University Press.

Mollenhorst, G., Völker, B., & Flap, H. (2008). Social contexts and personal relationships: the effect of meeting opportunities on similarity for relationships of different strength. *Social Networks*, 30(1), 60–68.

Monge, P.R., & Contractor, N. (2003). *Theories of communication networks*. Oxford University Press.

Nelson, L.M., Longstreth, W.T. Jr, Checkoutay, H., van Belle, G., & Koepsell, T.D. (1994). Completeness and accuracy of interview data from proxy respondents: demographic, medical, and life-style factors. *Epidemiology*, 5(2), 204–217.

Noonan, M.P., Mars, R.B., Sallet, J., Dunbar, R.I.M., & Fellows, L.K. (2018). The structural and functional brain networks that support human social networks. *Behavioural Brain Research*, 355, 12–23.

Offer, S., & Fischer, C.S. (2018). Difficult people: who is perceived to be demanding in personal networks and why are they there? *American Sociological Review*, 83(1), 111–142.

Oldenburg, R. (1999). *The great good place: cafes, coffee shops, bookstores, bars, hair salons, and other hangouts at the heart of a community*. Da Capo Press.

Omodei, E., Brashears, M.E., & Arenas, A. (2017). A mechanistic model of human recall of social network structure and relationship affect. *Scientific Reports*, 7(1), 1–8.

Parkinson, C., Liu, S., & Wheatley, T. (2014). A common cortical metric for spatial, temporal, and social distance. *Journal of Neuroscience*, 34(5), 1979–1987.

Pearlin, L.I. (1999). The stress process revisited. In *The structural and functional brain networks that support human social networks* (pp. 395–415). Springer.

Pearlin, L., & Aneshensel, C. (1986). Coping and social supports: their functions and applications. In D. Mechanic & L.H. Aiken (Eds.), *Applications of social science to clinical medicine and health policy* (pp. 417–437). Rutgers University Press.

Peer, M., Hayman, M., Tamir, B., & Arzy, S. (2021). Brain coding of social network structure. *Journal of Neuroscience*, 41(22), 4897–4909.

Peng, S., Roth, A.R., & Perry, B.L. (2023). Random Sampling of Alters from Networks: A Promising Direction in Egocentric Network Research. *Social Networks*, 72, 52–58.

Perry, B.L., McConnell, W.R., Coleman, M.E., Roth, A.R., Peng, S., & Apostolova, L.G. (2021). Why the cognitive 'fountain of youth' may be upstream: pathways to dementia risk and resilience through social connectedness. *Alzheimer's and Dementia*, 18(5), 934–941.

Perry, B.L., & Pescosolido, B.A. (2010). Functional specificity in discussion networks: the influence of general and problem-specific networks on health outcomes. *Social Networks*, 32(4), 345–357.

Perry, B.L., & Pescosolido, B.A. (2012). Social network dynamics in the face of biographical disruption: the case of 'first timers' with mental illness. *American Journal of Sociology*, 18(1), 134–175.

Perry, B.L., Pescosolido, B.A., & Borgatti, S.P. (2018). *Egocentric network analysis: foundations, methods, and models*. Vol. 44. Cambridge University Press.

Perry, B.L., Pescosolido, B.A., Small, M.L., & McCrani, A. (2020). Introduction to the special issue on ego networks. *Network Science*, 8(2), 137–141.

Perry, B.L., & Roth, A.R. (2021). On the boundary specification problem in network analysis: an update and extension to personal social networks. In M.L. Small, B.L. Perry, B. Pescolido & E.B. Smith (Eds.), *Personal networks: classic readings and new directions in egocentric analysis* (pp. 431–443). Cambridge University Press.

Pescosolido, B.A. (1992). Beyond rational choice: the social dynamics of how people seek help. *American Journal of Sociology*, 97(4), 1096–1138.

Portes, A. (1998). Social capital: its origins and applications in modern sociology. *Annual Review of Sociology*, 24(1), 1–24.

Portes, A. (2000). The two meanings of social capital. *Sociological Forum*, 15(1), 1–12.

Reysen, S., Hall, T., & Puryear, C. (2014). Friends' accuracy and bias in rating group identification. *Current Psychology*, 33(4), 644–654.

Roth, A.R. (2020). Informal caregiving and network turnover among older adults. *Journal of Gerontology: Social Sciences*, 75(7), 1538–1547

Sailer, K., & McCulloh, I. (2012). Social networks and spatial configuration: how office layouts drive social interaction. *Social Networks*, 34(1), 47–58.

Sallet, J., Mars, R.B., Noonan, M.P., Andersson, J.L., O'Reilly, J.X., Jbabdi, S., Croxson, P.L., Jenkinson, M., Miller, K.L., & Rushworth, M.F.S. (2011). Social network size affects neural circuits in macaques. *Science*, 334(6056), 697–700.

Saramäki, J., Leicht, E.A., López, E., Roberts, S.G.B., Reed-Tsochas, F., & Dunbar, R.I.M. (2014). Persistence of social signatures in human communication. *Proceedings of the National Academy of Sciences*, 111(3), 942–947.

Schmälzle, R., O'Donnell, M.B.,. Garcia, J.O., Cascio, C.N., Bayer, J., Bassett, D.S., Vettel, J.M., & Falk, E.B. (2017). Brain connectivity dynamics during social interaction reflect social network structure. *Proceedings of the National Academy of Sciences*, 114(20), 5153–5158.

Shelley, G.A., Bernard, H.R., Killworth, P., Johnsen, E.C., & McCarty, C. (1995). Who knows your HIV status? What HIV+ patients and their network members know about each other. *Social Networks*, 17(3), 189–217.

Shelley, G., Killworth, P.D., Bernard, H.R., McCarty, C., Johnsen, E., & Rice, R. (2006). Who knows your HIV status II? Information propagation within social networks of seropositive people. *Human Organization*, 65(4), 430–444.

Simmel, G. (1955). *Conflict and the web of group affiliations*. Free Press.

Simmel, G. (1971). *On individuality and social forms*. Vol. 1907. University of Chicago Press.

Small, M.L. (2009). *Unanticipated gains: origins of network inequality in everyday life*. Oxford University Press.

Small, M.L. (2013). Weak ties and the core discussion network: why people regularly discuss important matters with unimportant alters. *Social Networks*, 35(3), 470–483.

Small, M.L. (2017). *Someone to talk to*. Oxford University Press.

Small, M.L. (2021). How actors mobilize their networks: a theory of decision-making in practice. In M.L. Small, B.L. Perry, B. Pescolido & E.B. Smith (Eds.), *Personal networks: classic readings and new directions in egocentric analysis* (pp. 573–595). Cambridge University Press.

Small, M.L., & Adler, L. (2019). The role of space in the formation of social ties. *Annual Review of Sociology*, 45, 111–132.

Small, M.L., & Cook, J.M. (2021). Using interviews to understand why: challenges and strategies in the study of motivated action. *Sociological Methods and Research*, 1–41.

Small, M., & Gose, L.E. (2020). How do low-income people form survival networks? Routine organizations as brokers. *The ANNALS of the American Academy of Political and Social Science*, 689(1), 89–109.

Small, M.L., Perry, B.L., Pescosolido, B.A., & Smith, E.B. (Eds.) (2021a). *Personal networks: classic readings and new directions in egocentric analysis*. Cambridge University Press.

Small, M.L., Perry, B.L., Pescosolido, B.A., & Smith, E.B. (Eds.) (2021b). Introduction. In M.L. Small, B.L. Perry, B.A. Pescosolido, E.B. Smith (Eds.), *Personal networks: classic readings and new directions in egocentric analysis*. Cambridge University Press.

Small, M.L., Pamphile, V.D., & McMahan, P. (2015). How stable is the core discussion network? *Social Networks*, 40, 90–102.

Small, M.L., & Sukhu, C. (2016). Because they were there: access, deliberation, and the mobilization of networks for support. *Social Networks*, 47, 73–84.

Smith, J.A., & Moody, J. (2013). Structural effects of network sampling coverage I: Nodes missing at random. *Social Networks*, 35(4), 652–668.

Smith, S.S. (2005). Don't put my name on it': social capital activation and job-finding assistance among the black urban poor. *American Journal of Sociology*, 111(1), 1–57.

Smith, E. B., Brands, R. A., Brashears, M. E., & Kleinbaum, A. M. (2020). Social networks and cognition. *Annual Review of Sociology*, 46.

Spiro, E.S., Almquist, Z.W., & Butts, C.T. (2016). The persistence of division: geography, institutions, and online friendship ties. *Socius*, 2, 1–15.

Sudman, S. (1988). Experiments in measuring neighbor and relative social networks. *Social Networks*, 10(1), 93–108.

Sun, H., Brashears, M.E., & Smith, E.B. (2021). On cognition. In M.L. Small, B.L. Perry, B.A. Pescosolido & E.B. Smith (Eds.), *Personal networks: classic readings and new directions in egocentric analysis* (pp. 555–572). Cambridge University Press.

Thoits, P.A. (1995). Stress, coping, and social support processes: where are we? What next? *Journal of Health and Social Behavior*, Extra issue, 53–79.

Thoits, P.A. (2011). Mechanisms linking social ties and support to physical and mental health. *Journal of Health and Social Behavior*, 52(2), 145–161.

Triplett, T. (2013). Can your spouse accurately report your activities? An examination of proxy reporting. *Survey Practice*, 3(1), 1–6.

Vaisey, S., & Lizardo, O. (2010). Can cultural worldviews influence network composition? *Social Forces*, 88(4), 1595–1618.

Van der Gaag, M., & Snijders, T.A.B. (2005). The resource generator: social capital quantification with concrete items. *Social Networks*, 27(1), 1–29.

Van der Gaag, M., Snijders, T.A.B., & Flap, H.D. (2008). Position generator measures and their relationship to other social capital measures 1. In N. Lin & B.H. Erickson (Eds.), *Social capital: an international research program* (pp. 27–49). Oxford University Press.

Van der Gaag, M., & Webber, M. (2008). *Measurement of individual social capital*. Springer.

Vehovar, V., Manfreda, K.L., Koren, G., & Hlebec, V. (2008). Measuring ego-centered social networks on the web: questionnaire design issues. *Social Networks*, 30(3), 213–222.

Wasserman, S., & Faust, K. (1994). *Social network analysis: methods and applications*. Cambridge University Press.

Weaverdyck, M.E., & Parkinson, C. (2018). The neural representation of social networks. *Current Opinion in Psychology*, 24, 58–66.

Wellman, B., & Wortley, S. (1990). Different strokes from different folks: community ties and social support. *American Journal of Sociology*, 96(3), 558–588.

Wellman, B., Hogan, B., Berg, K., Boase, J., Carrasco, J.-A., Côté, R., Kayahara, J., Kennedy, T.L.M., & Tran, P. (2005). Connected lives: the project. In P. Purcell (Ed.), *Networked neighbourhoods* (pp. 161–216). Springer.

Wellman, B., Wong, R.Y.-l., Tindall, D., & Nazer, N. (1997). A decade of network change: turnover, persistence and stability in personal communities. *Social Networks*, 19(1), 27–50.

Wilson, W.J. (1987). *The truly disadvantaged: the inner city, the underclass, and public policy*. University of Chicago Press.

York Cornwell, E., & Waite, L.J. (2012). Social network resources and management of hypertension. *Journal of Health and Social Behavior*, 53(2), 215–231.

Multilevel Network Analysis

Emmanuel Lazega and Peng Wang

INTRODUCTION

Contemporary societies are *organisational societies* (Perrow, 1992), promoting combined individual agency and collective agency by organised entities. In order to measure the extent to which they are linked, one solution is to consider them together: action at the level of individuals and collective action at the level of organisations and institutions can be jointly analysed methodologically by statistically combining microscopic and mesoscopic observations as multilevel network analysis. This provides a renewed understanding of the verticality of actors' positions in social life and a new perspective on the social world (Lazega & Snijders, 2015). Both levels are different and interdependent and multilevel network analysis as a research methodology examines these interdependencies systematically. As superposed levels of agency, they can be examined separately as well as jointly since they are linked by the affiliation of members of one level to collective actors at the higher level. Affiliations can be considered as indicators of deeper processes characterising the 'duality' of individuals and groups (Breiger, 1974) in which the co-constitution of levels are the expression of their vertical interdependencies.

In this chapter we focus on a specific kind of multilevel network analysis that Snijders (2016), in his overview of the 'multiple flavours of multilevel network analyses', identifies as *multilevel network analysis* (MNA) – that is, a framework in which different kinds of actors operate at each level and in which both individual and collective agency takes place at each level. Within-level ties exist between individuals who exchange, but also between organisations that collaborate, and each individual is also affiliated to one or more organisations. Since this method of contextualisation considers several interconnected systems of agency, for cross-sectional data this can be expressed by the multilevel *exponential random graph modelling* (ERGM) approach of Wang et al. (2013b). Each 'level' here is a set of actors, or agents, and the levels are interdependent with respect to the conditions for action and/or outcomes. A hierarchical nesting relation between the levels, which is the traditional basis of statistical multilevel analysis, is not required for the data structure of multilevel networks.

Figure 32.1 is a graph representation of a multilevel network of scientists and their laboratories in their field of research. Lines between blue nodes (squares) represent interorganisational collaborations, and lines between red nodes (circles) represent an interpersonal advice network. Lines

Figure 32.1   Example of visualisations of multilevel networks in French cancer research (2000) used to identify multilevel relational infrastructures

between circles and squares represent cross-level membership of researchers in laboratories.

Statistical methodology was developed to use such datasets from a sociological perspective. Indeed, studying contextual effects on individual behaviour can be misleading with methods (such as linear regression) that look only at individual characteristics (Robinson, 1950; Snijders & Bosker, 2012). For example, a scientist's work influences her/his performance or capacity to obtain funding, but this influence varies depending on the laboratories with which this scientist is affiliated. Hierarchical linear models can account for such contextual effects, where within-laboratory effects are obtained first, then between-laboratories variations are represented by meta-analysis across these effects. This approach is also known as *multilevel analysis of networks* (MAN), in which individuals' actions, beliefs and performances within groups are analysed taking into account their nested collective memberships (Snijders & Bosker, 2012). MAN treats the nested structure as a given exogenous structure, and does not aim to take into account and model the dyadic and higher-order interdependencies between individuals based on their relationships or links between groups. It is not plausible that such groups lack an internal structure, nor that they lack links among each other. Network analyses help in introducing more realistic approximations of the internal structure of these groups and of their interdependencies into the modelling of human and social action. This is where MNA becomes useful which aims at modelling the nested structure as part of the endogenous social process. Lazega et al. (2008) show that it is not enough for a researcher to be central at the individual-level network (a *big fish*) to be recognised. His/her achievements vary depending on whether this scientist operates in a big or small, central or marginal laboratory (a *big pond* or a *small pond*). Position in such multilevel networks can thus be construed as combining both networks in four categories: a *big fish in a big pond* (BFBP), a *big fish in a small pond* (BFSP), etc. In the case in point that will be presented below, the BFBP were the most successful and only the *little fish* (LF) in the big ponds could catch up with them over time. In a different context with different constraints, Bellotti et al. (2016) find that BFSP do better than BFBP.

To test such hypotheses, Wang et al. (2013b) pioneered ERGM specifications for multilevel networks, and demonstrated the features of multilevel ERGMs with simulation studies and modelling examples. Combining multilevel network structure and nodal attributes, Wang et al. (2016a, 2016b) proposed *social selection models* (SSMs) where the existence of multilevel network ties is conditionally dependent on not only the existence of other network ties but also on nodal attributes. They demonstrated that nodal attributes may affect network structures both within and across levels.

By treating network ties as outcome variables, on the one hand, ERGMs and SSMs are designed for modelling the interdependencies among the within and meso level, and how various attributes of nodes at different levels affect tie formation in a multilevel context. On the other hand, *autologistic actor attribute models* (ALAAMs), also known as *social influence models* (Robins & Pattison, 2001b; Daraganova, 2013), treat network structures as exogenous, and model nodal outcomes as a combined result of individual's attributes, network positions, as well as the outcomes of their networked neighbours. Instead of treating individual outcomes as independent observations, ALAAMs allow us to test the interdependencies among the outcomes established by network ties as channels of transmission or influence. In multilevel networks, outcomes can be measured at different levels, and multilevel ALAAMs will enable us to test how individuals' positions in a multilevel network and how attributes or outcomes of nodes at a different level may affect individual outcomes.

In the following section, we review ERGMs and SSMs for multilevel networks, and propose some model specifications for ALAAMs for multilevel networks. Using the French cancer research elite dataset, we demonstrate how these models may answer the following key research questions:

- ERGM: How may within-level network structures affect network structures at a different level through meso-level interactions?
- SSM: How may attributes of nodes at one level affect network structures at a different level?
- ALAAM: How may individuals' outcomes be affected by multilevel network structure and outcomes of others?

THE MODELS

Multilevel Network Representation

The simplest multilevel network consists of nodes from two levels as shown in Figure 32.2. Using the French cancer research elite dataset as an example, one of the levels consists of research laboratories and their formal collaboration ties. We label this collaboration network as (A) which is a collection of collaboration ties $(A = \{A_{ij}\})$ where $(A_{ij} = 1)$ if there is a collaboration between laboratories i and j, otherwise $(A_{ij} = 0)$. The other level consists of researchers and their advice exchange network which is labelled as $(B = \{B_{kl}\})$. Each of the researchers in (B) are members of laboratories in (A). The two-mode affiliation network between researchers and laboratories forms the meso-level network $(X = \{X_{ik}\})$. The overall two-level network (M) consists of the two within-level and one meso-level networks $(M = \{A, B, X\})$. The various nodal attributes (e.g., researcher's gender and age, laboratory's location and size) are labelled by $\left(Y = \{Y_i^A, Y_k^B\}\right)$ where Y_i^A corresponds to attributes of laboratory i, and Y_k^B for researcher k. We use these labels as random variables and their lower cases as instances of the random variables for ERGMs and ALAAMs described below.

ERGM and SSM for Multilevel Networks

Exponential random graph models (ERGMs) model social network tie formation as a result of various social processes arising from the interdependent nature of social ties – that is, the occurrence of one tie may be dependent on the existence of other ties. These social processes are represented by subgraphs, or graph configurations where all ties within each configuration are considered interdependent. Using the various network labels for the multilevel data structure described before, we can express ERGM for multilevel network as

$$\Pr(A=a, B=b, X=x) = \frac{1}{\kappa} \exp \sum_Q \theta_Q z_Q (A, B, X)$$

where

z_Q are graph statistics counting the number of graph configurations of type Q.

θ_Q are model parameters associated with z_Q, where a positive and statistically significant parameter estimate suggests the configuration happens more than one would expect by chance given the rest of the model. Negative parameters mean the opposite.

κ is a normalising constant ensuring a proper probability distribution. κ is intractable even for small networks due to the size of the graph space grows exponentially. The properties and ERGM and estimation of ERGM parameters usually rely on simulations.

From the dyadic independent models to social circuit models (Snijders et al., 2006), Pattison and Snijders (2013) proposed a hierarchy of network tie dependence assumptions guiding the ERGM specification development. These tie dependence assumptions form theoretical bases for constructing ERGM configurations. In single-level networks, such dependencies are usually based on network ties of a single type – for example, the friend of a friend is a friend based on which we can derive a friendship triangle

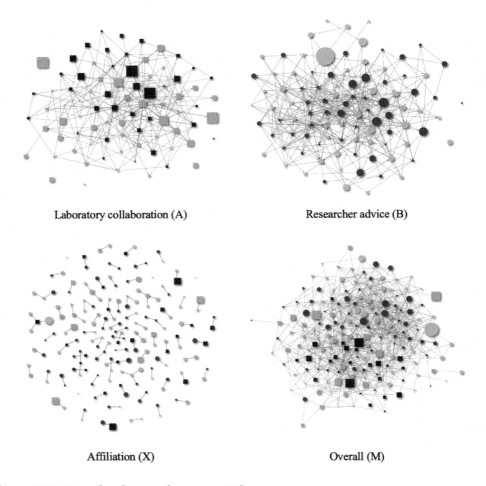

Figure 32.2 A two-level network representation

configuration – or more formally the Markov models (Frank & Strauss, 1986). The most current commonly applied ERGM specifications for one-mode networks are based on social circuit dependence assumption (Snijders et al., 2006). Figure 32.3 presents some ERGM configurations for directed one-mode networks that we use to model within-level network structures.

Extending these tie dependence assumptions to multilevel networks, Wang et al. (2013b) proposed ERGM for multilevel networks with configurations involving both within- and meso-level ties of different types. For example, a cross-level four-cycle follows the social circuit dependent assumption but has two ties from two different levels and two affiliations ties. Figure 32.4 lists a few examples of ERGM configurations for multilevel networks. For the French cancer researcher context, these configurations allow us to test how interlaboratory collaboration and researcher advice exchange may affect each other through cross-level affiliations.

SSMs extend ERGMs by introducing nodal covariates to ERGM graph configurations based on theory and assumptions that social actors with different attributes may have different motivations to form social ties (Robins et al., 2001a); homophily is one such example where people with similar attribute values may be more likely to form ties.

SSMs for multilevel networks can be expressed as

$$\Pr(M = m \mid Y^A = y^A, Y^B = y^B) = \frac{1}{\kappa}\exp\sum_Q \theta_Q z_Q(M, Y^A, Y^B)$$

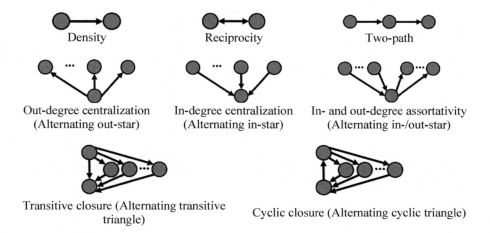

Figure 32.3 ERGM configurations for within-level networks

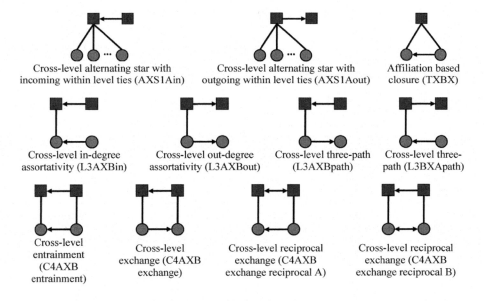

Figure 32.4 ERGM configurations for multilevel networks. Nodes from different levels are represented by different shapes

where attribute values form nodes of different levels serve as covariates, and form part of the graph configurations $z_Q(M, Y^A, Y^B)$. Within each configuration, network tie variables are not only dependent on each other, but also dependent on nodal attribute values. Nodal attributes can have typical forms of binary (e.g., pass or fail of a test), continuous (e.g., age), or categorical (e.g., race). Figure 32.5 lists a few SSM configurations we used in the modelling applications in this chapter. Note that, depending on the types of attribute, these interaction terms can be calculated differently. For example, a positive 'Interaction' effect for binary attribute may suggest homophily – that is, nodes having the attribute are more likely to form network ties – while for continuous attributes, the 'Interaction' statistics are calculated based on the absolute difference between the attribute values of the nodes in the dyad.

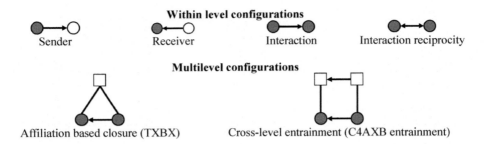

Figure 32.5 Example configurations for social selection models. Attribute values of solid nodes are counted towards the graph statistics

Homophily can then be interpreted from negative parameter estimates for such 'Interaction' effects – that is, the smaller the difference in attribute values, the more likely to form a tie. The same applies to all within- and multilevel configurations. See a more comprehensive list of SSM configurations in Wang et al. (2016a and 2016b).

ALAAM for Multilevel Networks

Auto-logistic actor attribute models share similar model constructs as ERGMs, except that the outcome variables in ALAAMs are binary outcome measures for each individual nodes, and network ties or structures as well as other nodal attributes are treated as predictors for nodal outcomes. Instead of testing how nodal attributes may affect tie formation as in SSMs, ALAAMs are also known as *social influence models* (Robins et al., 2001b) aiming at testing how network structure affects nodal outcomes while taking into consideration the interdependencies among the outcomes established by network ties connections – that is, individual outcomes may be dependent on the outcomes of reachable nodes in the given network.

For a two-level network, let Y^A and Y^B denote the outcome of nodes in level A and B, and Y'^A and Y'^B denote other nodal attributes, ALAAMs for two-level network can be expressed as

$$\Pr\left(Y^A = y^A, Y^B = y^B \mid M = m, Y'^A = y'^A, Y'^B = y'^B\right)$$
$$= \frac{1}{\kappa}\exp\sum_Q \theta_Q z_Q\left(Y^A, Y^B, M, Y'^A, Y'^B\right)$$

where the variables involved in ALAAM graph configurations $z_Q(Y^A, Y^B, M, Y'^A, Y'^B)$ reflect the possible interdependencies among variables $(Y^A, Y^B, M, Y'^A, Y'^B)$ contributing towards nodal outcomes at both levels. Figure 32.6 presents some example ALAAM configurations.

ALAAMs for multilevel networks allow us to test hypotheses for both within- and across-level influence. Using the French cancer researcher data as an example where big fish (BF) and big pond (BP) represent high-performance researchers and laboratories, example hypotheses may include:

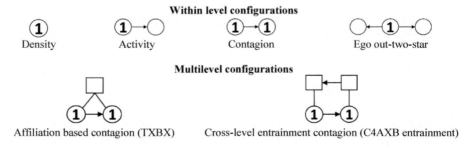

Figure 32.6 Example ALAAM configurations for multilevel networks. Nodes labelled with '1' are nodes having the outcome variable as '1'

- Within the researcher level, seeking advice from BF is more likely to be associated with other BF.
- Within the laboratory level, collaborating with BP is more likely to be associated with other BP.
- Across level, BF are more likely to be members of BP.

For more complex cross-level configuration, using the affiliation-based contagion (TXBX) as an example, we can test whether high research performance is more contagious through advice networks within the same laboratory rather than across different laboratories. We demonstrate some examples of ALAAMs in the application section.

Model Estimation and Selection

Using binary representations of graphs and nodal outcome variables, for a directed network with (n) nodes, the number of possible graphs can be calculated as $2^{n(n-1)}$ while the number of possible nodal level outcomes can be calculated as $2n$ These make the normalising constants (κ) intractable in ERGMs and ALAAMs. The parameter estimations usually rely on simulation-based numerical approximation methods (Snijders, 2002; Handcock et al., 2008; Stivala et al., 2020). These methods typically involve comparisons between the observed graph or outcome attribute statistics and simulated samples from a given set of parameter values. Such comparisons provide directions and scales for updating parameter values with a goal that repeated updates of parameter values will converge and the simulated samples from the converged parameters can reproduce features of the observed data by testing statistics such as *t-ratios*, where (*t-ratio* < 0.1) across all modelled effects suggest a model has converged. For parameter estimation, Snijders (2002) proposed algorithms for Markov chain Monte Carlo (MCMC) maximum likelihood estimations, while Koskinen et al. (2010) and Caimo and Friel (2011) proposed estimation procedures using Bayesian approximations. Stivala et al. (2020) proposed algorithms for estimating large networks with millions of nodes.

Once parameter estimates, hence a converged model, are obtained, the adequacy or model goodness of fit (GOF) of the model can be tested by simulating the converged model, and collecting a greater range of graph statistics beyond the ones included in the model specification, such as the degree distributions, clustering coefficients and geodesic distributions, as representations of the model distribution. Comparing such distributions with the observed statistics using *t-ratios* can serve as the GOF testing statistics, where a t-ratio less than 2.0 suggests the corresponding graph statistic is adequately captured by the model.

These algorithms are implemented in statnet under R (Handcock et al., 2008), or standalone software such as MPNet (Wang et al., 2014) and EstimNetDirected (Stivala et al., 2020). The models presented in this chapter are based on output from MPNet which implements algorithms proposed by Snijders (2002).

For model selection, we use the strategy described in Wang et al., (2016b), where model GOF results serve as guide aiming for the most parsimonious model while providing adequate fit to as many graph statistics as implemented under MPNet.

APPLICATION

This approach to the shaping of the multilevel network across organisational boundaries at the interindividual and interorganisational levels can be illustrated using a case study in the sociology of science, an empirical example of co-constitution without conflation. In this case, the sector of top French cancer researchers – working in an extremely competitive environment – was examined at both the interindividual and the interorganisational levels in 1999–2000. In this context, we identified the systems of superimposed interdependencies, the strategies of the actors who manage these interdependencies, and actors' achievements measured at the individual level. No deterministic order is pre-supposed between multilevel position, strategy and achievements – it is established here by analysis alone. This approach is particularly sensitive to the existence of inequalities between competing actors because these inequalities can render a given strategy more or less 'rewarding' depending on dual positioning as a measurement of opportunity structure.

Data Description

The dataset consists of 97 researchers and their affiliated 82 laboratories. The ties among researchers are defined based on their advice-seeking activities, while the ties defined among laboratories are their collaborations.

Among the 82 laboratories, 36 are in Paris and the rest are in the provinces. The laboratories have between four and 100 staff members, with an average of 28.39 and a standard deviation of 24.05. For social selection models, these two attributes are used as covariates for laboratories.

For ALAAMs, we model what constitute towards BPs. As ALAAMs can only model binary outcomes, we define BPs as laboratories having more than 38 staff or the 75th percentile of the laboratory size distribution.

For researchers, 45 out of the 97 researchers are in Paris, and 50 of them are directors of their laboratories. The researchers' average age is 48.21 with standard deviation of 7.76. Researchers are also categorised by one of seven research areas or specialities. The performance of researchers is calculated based on the average impact factors associated with their publications. Researcher performance is measured based on the impact factors of their publications over five-year periods. Two performance scores are obtained based on the periods 1995–1999 and 2000–2004. We see the former as the past performance with mean at 38.99 and standard deviation of 28.52, and the latter as the current performance with a mean of 39.12 and standard deviation of 28.55. The social selection models presented in this chapter used the current performance as one of the covariates to predict network structure. The ALAAMs, however, used past performance as a covariate to predict the current performance. Again, we use the 75th percentile of the current performance scores, or 51.92 as the cut-off point, where researchers with higher performance scores are seen as BF.

Figure 32.3 presents visualisations of the networks with breakdowns into within-, across- and the overall multilevel structure. The laboratories are represented by blue squares, with darker ones indicating Paris. The size of the laboratory nodes represents laboratory size. The red circles represent researchers with darker-coloured nodes as directors of their laboratories, and size of the researcher nodes represents their current research performance scores.

Modelling Results

We present multilevel ERGM, SSM and ALAAM results for this dataset to demonstrate findings highlighting the cross-level effects.

ERGM: Multilevel structure can explain complicated within-level structure

We extract two models from Wang et al. (2013b) to compare and demonstrate how complicated within-level structure can be explained by multilevel structures. Model 1 in Table 32.1 is an ERGM for the researcher advice network only without considering the multilevel structure, while Model 2 in Table 32.2 presents the multilevel ERGM. The two models have consistent parameter estimates on the negative network density (Arc), the positive tendency for advice ties to be reciprocated (Reciprocity) and the positive tendency for network closure (AT-T). However, in order to obtain a model providing adequate fit to all within-graph statistics, and degree distributions in particular, Model 1 has eight parameters for star-like configurations representing network tie centralisation, while Model 2

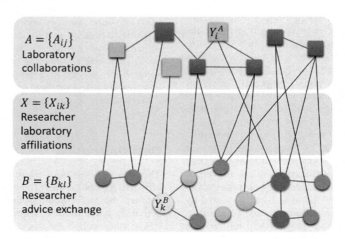

Figure 32.7 Multilevel network among researchers and their affiliated laboratories. Squares represent laboratories, circles represent researchers. For researchers, node size represents performance, darker colour represents directors. For laboratories, node size represents laboratory size, darker colour represents laboratories in Paris

Table 32.1 Within-level ERGM for researcher advice network adapted from Wang et al. (2013b)

Effects	Model (1) para	s.e.	
Arc	−3.213	1.024	*
Reciprocity	3.534	0.213	*
2-out-star	0.358	0.146	*
3-out-star	−0.018	0.009	
2-path	−0.135	0.010	*
AinS(4.00)	0.596	0.159	*
AoutS(4.00)	−0.722	0.599	
AinS(2.00)	−1.164	0.450	*
AoutS(2.00)	0.384	0.787	
AinAoutS(2.00)	−0.233	0.369	
AT-T(2.00)	0.932	0.067	*

contains none of the tie-centralisation effects, which suggests the complicated degree distribution can be explained by the network structures beyond the within-level advice ties.

Although Model 1 provides adequate fits, the model is almost uninterpretable. Model 2, in contrast, provides rich interpretations on the cross-level network structures. The negative (AXS1Aout) effect suggests laboratories with higher numbers of researchers are less likely to seek collaborations with other laboratories, although this effect diminishes once we bring in nodal attributes as discussed below in SSM. The affiliation-based closure effect (TXBX) suggest advice-seeking and common affiliations are promoting one another. Note that as ERGMs and ALAAMs are models for cross-sectional data, the interpretation is not about casual relationships, but more about association, although the results of the underlying dynamic social selection or influence processes are captured by the graph configurations. In this case, we can interpret the positive TXBX effect as researchers are more likely to seek advice within their laboratories, and advice exchange also encourages common affiliations.

The negative L3BXApath cross-level degree assortativity effect suggests the in-degrees of researchers in the advice network is negatively correlated with their affiliated lab's collaboration activity in reaching out to other labs. This may suggest the popular researcher advisors are affiliated with key research labs which do not have the urgency in seeking further collaborations. This effect is also diminished once we include nodal attributes in the SSM.

The cross-level entrainment and exchange effects show interesting dynamics on how 'weak' or non-reciprocal ties may make 'strong' or reciprocal ties at the other level redundant. Both non-reciprocal cross-level entrainment and exchange effects are positive indicators of how the within-level ties are enhancing one another where researchers are more likely to provide or seek advice from others in collaborating laboratories. As ERGMs treat ties as outcomes, the model reflects that advice flow indeed encourages formal collaboration between affiliated laboratories, while formal collaborations may have provided context and resources for the exchange of research advice. However, the cross-level effects become negative as soon as a reciprocal tie is involved. From the laboratories' perspective, mutual collaboration ties may have shared sufficient information or resources that the urge for advice exchange between affiliated researchers is not as immediate. From the researchers' perspective, the reciprocal advice exchange can indicate there is a certain level of interest or lack of knowledge from one another, although the fact that these interests have not yet been translated into formal collaborations suggests collaboration opportunities.

The comparison between Model (1) and (2) shows us how rather complicated within-level network structure can be entirely explained by cross-level effects. The cross-level effects also reveal the dependencies between advice exchange and formal collaborations.

SSM: Within-level network structures can be affected by attributes of nodes at a different level

In SSMs, we bring in nodal attributes as predictors for tie formation. Model (3) in Table 32.2 is extracted from Wang et al. (2016b) as a final SSM for the dataset. The attribute effects in Model (3) suggest that within the advice network, researchers based in Paris are less likely to seek advice (negative Sender effect), but if they do, they tend to seek advice from other researchers in Paris (positive Interaction effect). Researchers tend to seek advice from others of similar age (negative Age Difference effect). Researchers with higher performance are seen as resources of advice (positive Receiver effect), while the negative Performance Difference effect suggests researchers tend to seek advice from others with similar performance. Advice seeking is also more likely to take place within specialities but not exchanged reciprocally (positive Speciality Match effect but negative Speciality Match Reciprocity effects) suggesting a knowledge hierarchy within speciality. The Director attribute does not directly affect advice seeking as

Table 32.2 Multilevel ERGM and social selection model adapted from Wang et al. (2013b; 2016b)

Effects	Model (2) ERGM para	s.e.		Model (3) SSM Para	s.e.	
Laboratory collaboration network {A}						
Arc	−3.831	0.556	*	−3.815	0.574	*
Reciprocity	1.679	0.381	*	1.525	0.413	*
2-path	−0.079	0.029	*	−0.090	0.029	*
Isolates	2.017	0.760	*	2.057	0.769	*
AinS (4.00)	0.640	0.268	*	0.737	0.267	*
AoutS (4.00)	0.320	0.086	*	0.334	0.089	*
AinS (2.00)	−0.889	0.614		−1.039	0.618	
AT-T (2.00)	0.446	0.127	*	0.420	0.13	*
Researcher advice network {B}						
Arc	−4.084	0.118	*	−3.975	0.143	*
Reciprocity	3.313	0.212	*	3.361	0.235	*
AT-T (2.00)	1.085	0.072	*	1.046	0.074	*
AT-C (2.00)	−0.384	0.068	*	−0.360	0.073	*
A2P-U (2.00)	−0.071	0.020	*	−0.083	0.021	*
Paris Sender				−0.386	0.101	*
Paris Interaction				0.569	0.094	*
Age Difference				−0.023	0.006	*
Performance Receiver				0.005	0.002	*
Performance Difference				−0.007	0.002	*
Speciality Match				0.786	0.132	*
Speciality Match Reciprocity				−0.795	0.321	*
Collaboration and affiliation {A, X}						
AXS1Ain (2.00)	0.240	0.131				
AXS1Aout (2.00)	−0.324	0.129	*			
Advice and affiliation {B, X}						
TXBX	1.958	0.275	*	1.945	0.265	*
Cross level interactions {A, B, X}						
L3AXBin	−0.006	0.018		0.004	0.017	
L3AXBout	−0.012	0.008		−0.016	0.01	
L3AXBpath	−0.003	0.010		−0.043	0.016	*
L3BXApath	−0.051	0.015	*	−0.013	0.01	
C4AXB entrainment	0.634	0.104	*	0.524	0.114	*
C4AXB exchange	0.639	0.109	*	0.659	0.108	*
C4AXB exchange reciprocal A	−0.293	0.065	*	−0.256	0.096	*
C4AXB exchange reciprocal B	−0.295	0.136	*	−0.328	0.148	*
Director C4AXB Entrainment				0.840	0.180	*

there is no Sender/Receiver or Interaction within-level effect; however, there is a positive Director C4AXB Entrainment effect suggesting laboratory directors' advice-seeking activities are strongly aligned with the formal collaborations between their affiliated laboratories. Without looking into the multilevel models, one may conclude that laboratory directors do not shape the advice network structure, but the multilevel SSM highlights their advice-seeking activities as having strong impact on the collaboration network at the interlaboratory level. This highlights how "unimportant" nodal attributes at one level may play a significant role in shaping the network at a different level.

The SSM also shows that attributes of laboratories are not as important in the multilevel structure compared to researchers' attributes, as none of the laboratory attribute effects are included in the model, while their corresponding graph statistics are adequately fitted. Although the endogenous structural effect part of the SSM Model (3) is remarkably similar to the ERGM Model (2) both in terms of effect signs and significance, it is worth looking into how the attribute effects may explain the few changes between the two models. First, the negative ERGM AXS1Aout is no longer significant and removed from the SSM. AXS1Aout configuration does not involve advice ties, therefore the negative association of affiliation and outgoing collaboration is more likely to be explained by Director cross-level entrainment effect (while the within-advice attribute effects have less impact, as they do not count towards graph statistics involving collaboration ties). It is the directors' advice-seeking activities that drive the negative AXS1Aout effect. Second, we notice the negative L3BXApath becomes non-significant; instead the negative L3AXBpath becomes significant. When the advice network structure is better explained by the researcher attributes, the cross-level degree assortativity dynamics also change. Instead of popular researchers being less likely to be affiliated with laboratories actively collaborating with other laboratories (negative L3BXApath), it is the other way around, such that it is the popular laboratories in the collaboration network that are less likely to be affiliated with researchers who are actively seeking advice.

ALAAM: individual outcomes can be affected by network structures at a different level

We use the proposed ALAAM to model the association among network positions, researcher performance and laboratory sizes, while taking into account various nodal attributes.

As ALAAMs can only model binary outcomes, we need to choose a cut-off point for continuous outcome variables. The cut-off value usually requires justifications depending on the research context. As an illustrative example, we use the 75th percentile of the original continuous outcome values as the cut-off point. Based on such criteria, researchers are considered as having high performance, or being BF, if their current performance scores are greater than 51.92. For laboratories, we use laboratory size as the outcome variable, and consider a laboratory as a BP if it has more than 38 staff members.

Other nodal attributes are used as predictors for these outcomes, like the attribute covariates used in the SSMs, for researchers; we include their Director statues, whether they are based in Paris, Age, research performance scores from the previous year and their areas of specialities as covariates. For laboratories, we use whether they are in Paris as a covariate.

Table 32.3 Within-level and multilevel ALAAM results

Effects	Model (4) para	s.e.		Model (5) para	s.e.		Model (6) para	s.e.	
Laboratory collaboration network {A}									
Density	−2.312	0.481	*				−1.421	0.541	*
Contagion	0.438	0.132	*				0.473	0.154	*
Researcher advice network {B}									
Density				−4.292	0.912	*	−5.034	0.932	*
Contagion				0.295	0.102	*			
Ego out-2-star				−0.026	0.010	*			
Previous performance				0.084	0.022	*	0.102	0.022	*
Advice seeker within Paris							−0.241	0.113	*
Affiliation network {X}									
Director status							−2.034	0.653	*
Cross level interactions {A, B, X}									
C4AXB-exchange contagion on researcher performance							1.242	0.311	*

Table 32.3 presents a set of three ALAAMs for comparison. Ignoring the meso-level structure, Model (4) and (5) only examine how within-level network ties may serve as channels for social influence. Model (6) considers the overall multi-level structure, and allows the test of cross-level contagion – that is, whether high-performance researchers, or BF, and large laboratories, or BPs, are more likely to be associated with one another through cross-level affiliation.

Model (4) is the ALAAM for BPs, and their associated collaboration network positions. The rather simple model provides adequate fit to 35 attribute statistics, including interaction statistics with the Paris location attribute. The positive contagion effect suggests laboratories that are in collaboration with other BPs are also more likely to be BPs themselves. There is no tendency for BPs to be based in Paris – only eight out of the 36 BPs are in Paris.

Model (5) tests the association between BF and their attributes and positions in the advice network only. The model provides adequate fit to 81 attribute statistics, including attribute interaction statistics. The positive 'Previous performance' effect suggests researchers were more likely to be BF if they had higher previous performance. The Contagion effect suggests research performance is influenced by the performance of advice network partners – that is, researchers who seek advice from BF are also likely to be BF. The negative Ego out-2-star indicates active advice seekers are less likely to be BF. There is no evidence that BF are perceived as sources of advice either, as the model fitted the Receiver and Ego in-2-star statistics. The model also provided good fit to all other researcher attributes, hence none of the location, age, directorship and specialities affected researchers' performance given the effects we see in the model.

Model (6) predicts both laboratory sizes and researcher performance while treating the multi-level network structure as part of the predictors. It provides adequate fit to 232 statistics, including attribute interaction statistics with higher-order graph configurations, such as within- and cross-level triangles and four-cycles.

The within-level effects under Model (6) are largely consistent with Model (4) for the BPs, and our interpretation of the BP contagion effect stays. For BF, however, the previous significant within advice level Contagion and Ego out-2-star effects are no longer required, and they are explained now by the cross-level effects. Researchers' previous performance remains a strong predictor for the current performance. Once we include the multilevel effect, the researchers' location attribute becomes a significant predictor for research performance. The negative effect suggests researchers who are based in Paris that are actively seeking advice are less likely to be BF. In other words, advice seekers in Paris may be more likely to be *small fish*.

The positive cross-level exchange-contagion effect suggests researchers who have been seeking advice from, or providing advice to, other BF in collaborating laboratories are more likely to be BF. And the directions of the laboratory collaboration ties are opposite from the directions of researcher advice-seeking ties which form an advice–collaboration exchange loop. This model provides adequate fit to the cross-level entrainment effects; hence it is only the exchange effect affecting the researchers' performance. From a researcher's perspective, on the one hand, seeking advice from BF whose laboratory is collaborating with the researcher's own laboratory may enhance research performance. From the laboratory's perspective, on the other hand, seeking collaboration from laboratories whose BF researchers are actively seeking advice from its own researchers may enhance research performance.

Comparing Model (6) with Model (5), the positive within-level contagion effect as in Model (5) is no longer significant in affecting research performance, instead the collaborations among laboratories provide context, social settings, resources, and opportunities to enhance researcher performance. In other words, advice seeking ties themselves are not channels of influence unless the affiliated laboratories have formal collaborations in place. Researchers who only seek advice with any BF might not necessarily improve their own performance, unless the BF are indeed from a collaborating laboratory. The success of researchers is associated with both their own and their affiliated laboratories' networks.

It is also worth noting that the director status had no effects within levels in either Model (4) or (5) but becomes significant in affecting laboratory sizes through the cross-level affiliation network. This suggests laboratories are more likely to be BP if their affiliated representatives during the data collection were not the laboratory's directors. This may be because not all researchers, hence directors of all laboratories, were interviewed, and larger laboratories had other representatives than the directors providing survey responses.

Given Model (6) has fitted all statistics related to interactions of the outcome and other attribute covariates, therefore neither Age nor specialities of researchers would have affected researcher performance or laboratory sizes. There is also no evidence for association between high-performance researchers and large laboratories. In other words, BF do not necessarily work in BPs, given other significant effects presented in the model.

Such multilevel network analyses as a methodology can be extended to three or more superposed levels. A case of superposed team level, interindividual level in a profession and interorganisational level among institutions of this profession complexifies collective agency but provides models of cumulative advantage mechanisms, what Lazega and Jourda (2016) call the 'structural wings' of Mertonian, meso-level Matthew effects, with their rich-get-richer-through-borrowing effects. Statistical models for such data formats, including cross-level effects to study these mechanisms and their variety, remain to be designed, implemented and used.

MNA RESEARCH POTENTIAL: COMBINING RELATIONAL CAPITAL OF INDIVIDUALS AND SOCIAL CAPITAL OF COLLECTIVES

Two examples of MNA research provide illustration of how these models (especially MERGMs) are used. The first is in the field of economic sociology; the second is in life-course studies.

Analysing the formation of multilevel networks where the unit of analysis is the pair individual–organisation makes it possible to differentiate between superposed levels of agency where links between individuals can influence links between organisations, as when exchanges of information between two competing individuals in a market (for example, two sellers discussing a common buyer's demand and purchasing power) can lead to contracts signed between the companies employing these three individuals (Brailly et al., 2015; Favre et al., 2016). MERGMs thus tease out some of the relational mechanisms making cooperation between competitors possible (Lazega, 2011; Brailly & Lazega, 2012). More generally, taking the meso level of society seriously requires introducing dynamics into the study of different and superposed systems of interdependencies and collective agency.

The first study looks at network formation at each level of specific markets – that is, trade fairs for television programmes in Eastern Europe and Africa. In this trade fair sellers and buyers of TV programmes (distributors and TV channels) meet once a year to discuss contracts, make deals, keep informed about new films, series and game shows, and observe market evolution. The study of the informal exchange of information between sales representatives and formal deal ties between their companies examines network formation at each level. It shows that these networks are heavily interdependent but that each level has its own specific processes. Tie formation between two organisations takes place in a different context than that between two individuals, and it evolves in a different temporality. For each level, specific structural processes emerge and explain the network morphology. This, however, complexifies the co-evolution of networks and behaviour at both levels separately and jointly. Levels are interdependent and influence each other. Supposing that these levels are nested does not imply that they evolve symmetrically and in sync. As emphasised by Lazega (2015, 2016), the co-evolution of the two levels is complex, dynamic and can be partially disconnected if not asynchronous – thus raising the issue of the costs of synchronisation. Structural organisation of each level as well as the attributes and context explaining tie formation at each level can be different. Brailly (2016) identifies at the interorganisational level a temporality that requires companies to meet regularly at the 'same time next year' in a system that is driven by a core, an 'oligopoly with fringes'. At the interindividual level, sales representatives need to meet 'next time this year' in order to extract more value from their socioeconomic relations in a fragmented and competitive milieu. The long-term deal network between companies influences short-term cooperation ties between individuals, which in return can bring new business opportunities and constraints to their companies.

The potential of this kind of modelling can also be highlighted by combining MNA and life-course research in sociology. The principle of *linked lives* is one of the key tenets of the life-course perspective (Elder et al., 2003; Vacchiano & Spini, 2021), and researchers have long been interested in the influence of these connections on the course of individual lives. What multilevel networks reveal about the life course can be exemplified with research on multilevel networks and status attainment (Vacchiano et al., 2022). MNA thus promises to shed light on how individuals acquire status over time, a question of major interest in life-course research studying cumulative (dis)advantage and social mobility (if any).

Research on social networks and status attainment was already well advanced in the 1990s (Breiger, 1990; Lin, 1999). Networks provide resources, such as information and social support, that facilitate individual action. Accessing and mobilising better resources, conceptualised as relational capital, increases the chances of obtaining, for example, higher paid and more highly skilled jobs. Networks also often mirror ascribed characteristics of individuals (class, gender, ethnicity or human capital), for example through homophily, which exacerbates social inequalities (McPherson et al., 2001). The use of weak ties also increases the chances of networks improving social status (Granovetter, 1973, 1985; Burt, 1992, 2007) by providing individuals with more access to structural opportunities together with fewer constraints. Beyond ascribed and acquired personal characteristics and resources, social resources have also been shown to have an impact on status attainment and social inequalities, namely resources such as information, influence, support, advice or knowledge, to which individuals potentially have access through their contacts. In particular, individuals have access to social resources through mechanisms, such as homophily and transitivity, that link people in similar social positions. These mechanisms make networks a further source of exposure to structural opportunities and constraints (Lin, 1999, 2001).

As seen above in the example of the cancer researchers, individuals embedded in interindividual and interorganisational networks can access, through the latter, resources complementary to their personal resources and their social ties (Breiger, 1974; Lazega et al., 2008; Lazega, 2020; Moliterno & Mahony, 2011). Evidence has emerged from MNA of an additional type of resource that exerts a structural influence on status attainment: resources that derive, under specific conditions, from the organisations to which actors belong and the organisational networks in which they are immersed. Studies by Lazega, Jourda and Mounier (Lazega et al., 2013; Lazega & Jourda, 2016) on cumulative (dis)advantages during academic careers (see Merton, 1968, on this subject) of the researchers whose multilevel networks were examined above show that it is not only personal and social resources that are important for academic success: the centrality and prestige of research laboratories also plays a role. On the one hand, laboratories offer researchers their institutional status, positioning them in the scientific world beyond their individual status (what is called *dual positioning*). This gives researchers complementary access to relational/social capital (through indirect contacts called *dual alters*), which does not depend on their social ties, but on the organisational network of their laboratories – often the networks of their hierarchical or administrative superiors. Dual positioning (whether actors are BFBP, BFSP, LFBP or LFSP) has been shown to matter by providing researchers with a multilevel status, which positions them in the scientific community beyond their personal prestige. This gives them access to complementary resources: infrastructure, reputation and, not least, combined relational/social capital. Indeed, belonging to a BP provides researchers with a wider institutional network, giving them access to resourceful contacts (dual alters), albeit in an indirect way. Access to these indirect contacts is thus a function of affiliation with laboratories of different capacity and power. For example recall that it is researchers with low status in science (LF) who are affiliated with larger labs (BPs) who benefit from the complementary resources of dual alters. Five years after data collection, it is shown that these LFBP are more successful than the LFSP.

Actors navigate their trajectories not only as individuals with their relational capital, but also as members of organisations with their social capital (collective mechanisms) (Lazega, 2020). Based on strong dual positioning, collectively closing multilevel 3-paths provides access to dual alters with complementary resources, which helps some actors (and not others) with an *extended opportunity structure* (Lazega et al., 2013; Lazega & Jourda, 2016) and represent (dis)advantage in competitive social spaces. Lin's social resource theory is developed here with the concept of extended opportunity structure that drives the development of models of status attainment accounting for the structural influence of multilevel networks. In this framework, *vertical linchpins* can give access to dual alters with complementary resources, activating *network lift*. When subordinates are able to borrow the relational capital of their superiors, they can expand their network and reach dual alters who, provided they give access to complementary resources, can create this network lift in terms of performance. Alternatively, when people are weakly active at the next, higher level and others dominate at several levels simultaneously, the latter can exercise power and impose constraint that can end up being taken for granted in the system. In a highly bureaucratised society, it is not rare to see managers exposing subordinates to increasingly open competition, or competing with their subordinates, undermining the latters' activities, networks and projects especially by closing access to dual alters and the extended opportunity structure.

Much remains to be done in understanding the conditions under which this meso-level, extended opportunity structure identified with MERGMs develops social resource theory and provides new avenues of research for combinations of social network analyses and, for example, life-course analyses and understanding of social inequalities.

The challenge here is to understand how social systems at superposed levels co-evolve and how actors at both levels coordinate to generate the socioeconomic structure, with its social processes and (dis)advantages. Other fields of substantive research can benefit from MNA (Glueckler and Doreian, 2016). In political science and sociology, there is something remarkable in the way multilevel relational infrastructures are used in institutional entrepreneurship and institution building processes (Lazega et al., 2016; Lazega, 2018) when they mobilise collegial oligarchies of vertical linchpins simultaneously central and active at different levels of agency. These core cross-level key players concentrate power and punch above their weight in such processes, for example by formulating norms at a higher level and enforcing them at a lower level, thus driving and smoothing adoption processes of regulatory changes. The multilevel character of regulation thus strengthens macro determinants of intrinsically micro- and meso-level processes.

Multilevel models are also used for the study of so-called social-ecological networks (networks comprised of both people-to-people ties and people-to-nature ties) – for example, in supporting resilience to environmental and climate change. Social networks underpin the resilience of human communities to environmental change due to their role in building adaptive capacity (Barnes et al., 2020; Barnes, 2022). Both adaptation and transformation require that social actors and institutions have some level of joint adaptive capacity in order to absorb and shape change. Recent research has begun to disentangle how social networks more specifically relate to adaptation and transformation (Barnes et al., 2020). This work rests on the idea that social-ecological systems can be understood and explicitly modelled as multilevel, social-ecological networks (Bodin et al., 2019). This conceptualisation allows us to consider important relationships in social systems – such as cooperation and communication between key individuals, communities, organisations, or even nations; key linkages in ecological systems – such as trophic food webs, larvae or seed dispersal, or landscape connectivity; and the interactions between these – such as resource extraction, ecosystem service flows, or policy and management actions, including how power manifests in such social-ecological networks and its role in driving adaptation and/or transformation. Multilevel network modelling of this kind is seen as a critical research frontier in this area that can inform the building of more resilient societies and ecosystems to meet the rising tide of dramatic environmental change.

Many policy domains would thus benefit from further applying such an MNA framework. In particular, when each level evolves based on its own dynamics, issues of synchronisation and costs of synchronisation between the temporalities of the levels raise new questions. Some ties at one level remain stable thanks to the fact that other ties at a different level change and create stability from movement at the level of the whole structure (Lazega, 2017). Such dynamic invariants raise, for example, the question of who in society incurs the costs of such synchronisations. Individuals most often incur such costs of synchronisation between levels for the benefit of organisations, an underestimated source of social inequalities for such individuals (Lazega, 2016). To take into account the vertical complexity of a social world in the cohabitation and co-constitution of several levels, it is necessary to further link these levels and their dynamics analytically. An important methodological challenge is to express dynamically the combined and interrelated agency of actors in several actor sets in a multilevel network (Snijders, 2016; Koskinen & Snijders, 2022).

CONCLUSION

Bottom-up and top-down struggles in politics suggest that when a social fact must be observed at analytically different levels of collective action, the analysis of individual agency, relations and skills becomes inseparable from that of organisational agency, structure and culture. To take into account this vertical complexity of a social world in the coordination and co-constitution of several levels, it is necessary to further explore the links between these levels and their dynamics analytically. Analysing superposed levels of collective agency, their synchronisations and unequal costs of such synchronisations (in terms of time and energy spent in complex, collective careers for example) incurred by different levels will lead to new knowledge on social inequalities that are still overlooked in the social sciences. MNA as a method thus helps build a view of how society works that will be useful in the short and long future. With climate change, for example, nationwide policies of management of vital resources will need to synchronise with changes in lifestyles created locally by communities also managing common pool resource institutions (Ostrom, 1990). MNA concepts and methods provide a view of how such interdependent levels of collective agency can co-evolve and coordinate (or not), raising issues of social justice attached to such coordination. These are cutting edge issues that deserve more network analytical research at various levels of society.

More generally, such multilevel actors, forms of agency and processes specify and substantiate dimensions of Breiger's (1974) duality of persons and groups – that is, their co-constitution. Developing MNA dynamics is part of explaining how we all make Breiger's duality happen and how this co-constitution of levels is consequential.

Some of these dynamics evolve beautifully synchronously, others asynchronously. This also extends and relates duality to issues of social justice and inequalities: multilevel networks to somewhere, or to nowhere, are part of duality too.

Social network analysis not only has the conceptual and methodological tools to map these processes, but by its very nature it incorporates in its analyses power asymmetries and structural inequalities in the navigation of social processes in multilevel, nested social contexts. At stake in particular are multilevel solutions to existential problems linked to the transitions that societies face (climate related, ecological, demographic, etc.). How to observe, model and analyse phenomena that are not only characterised by networks of interdependencies between conflicting actors, at one level, but that are also simultaneously dynamic and multilevel raises key issues for the social sciences in endangered societies. Hopefully MNA can help track such phenomena to help manage the dilemmas of collective action that they generate.

REFERENCES

Barnes, M.L. (2022), An integrative network approach for understanding resilience to environmental change. In E. Lazega, T.A.B. Snijders & R.P.M. Wittek (Eds.), *Social Networks and Social Resilience*, Edward Elgar.

Barnes, Michele L., Lorien Jasny, Andrew Bauman, Jon Ben, Ramiro Berardo, Örjan Bodin, Joshua Cinner et al. "'Bunkering down': How one community is tightening social-ecological network structures in the face of global change." People and Nature 4, no. 4 (2022): 1032–1048.

Barnes, M.L., Wang, P., Cinner, J.E., Graham, N.A., Guerrero, A.M., Jasny, L., Lau, J., Sutcliffe, S.R., & Zamborain-Mason, J. (2020). Social determinants of adaptive and transformative responses to climate change. *Nature Climate Change*, 10(9), 823–828.

Bellotti, E. (2012). Getting funded, multilevel networks of physicists in Italy. *Social Networks*, 34, 215–229.

Bellotti, E., Guadalupi, L., & Conaldi, G. (2016). Comparing fields of sciences: multilevel networks of research collaborations in Italian academia. In E. Lazega & T.A.B. Snijders (Eds), *Multilevel network analysis for the social sciences: Theory, methods and applications*, Springer, 213–244.

Bodin, Örjan, Steven M. Alexander, Jacopo Baggio, Michele L. Barnes, Ramiro Berardo, Graeme S. Cumming, Laura E. Dee et al. "Improving network approaches to the study of complex social–ecological interdependencies." Nature sustainability 2, no. 7 (2019): 551–559.

Bodin, Ö., & Tengö, M. (2012). Disentangling intangible social–ecological systems. *Global Environmental Change*, 22(2), 430–439.

Brailly, J. (2016). Dynamics of networks in trade fairs—a multilevel relational approach to the cooperation among competitors. *Journal of Economic Geography*, 16(6), 1279–1301.

Brailly, J., Favre, G., Chatellet, J., & Lazega, E. (2015). Embeddedness as multilevel problem: a case study in economic sociology. *Social Networks*, 44, 319–333

Brailly, J., & Lazega, E. (2012). Diversité des approches de modélisation statistique en analyse de réseaux sociaux multiniveaux. *Mathématiques et sciences humaines. Mathematics and social sciences*, (198), 5–32.

Breiger, R. (1974). The duality of persons and groups. *Social Forces*, 53(2), 181–90.

Breiger, R.L. (Ed.) (1990). *Social mobility and social structure*. Cambridge University Press.

Burt, R.S. (1976). Positions in networks. *Social Forces*, 55, 93–122.

Burt, R. (1992). *Structural holes: the social structure of competition*. Harvard University Press.

Burt, R. S. (2007). Brokerage and closure: An introduction to social capital. OUP Oxford.

Burt, R. S. (2010). Neighbor networks: Competitive advantage local and personal. Oxford University Press.

Caimo, A., & Friel, N. (2011). Bayesian inference for exponential random graph models. *Social Networks*, 33(1), 41–55.

Daraganova, G., & Robins, G. (2013) Autologistic actor attribute models. In D. Lusher, J. Koskinen & G. Robins (Eds.), *Exponential random graph models for social networks: theories, methods and applications* (pp. 102–114). Cambridge University Press.

DiPrete, T., & Eirich, G. (2006). Cumulative advantage as a mechanism for inequality: a review of theoretical and empirical developments. *Annual Review of Sociology*, 32, 271–297. doi:10.1146/annurev.soc.32.061604.123127

Erdös, P., & Rényi, A., 1960. On the evolution of random graphs. Publications of the Mathematical Institute of the Hungarian Academy of Science, 5, 17–61.

Favre, G., Brailly, J., Chatellet, J., & Lazega, E. (2016). Inter-organizational network influence on long-term and short-term inter-individual relationships: The case of a trade fair for TV programs distribution in sub-Saharan Africa. In E. Lazega and T.A.B. Snijders (Eds), *Multilevel network analysis for the social sciences: Theory, methods and applications*, 295–314.

Frank, O., & Strauss, D. (1986). Markov graphs. *Journal of the American Statistical Association*, 81(395), 832–842.

Glückler, J., & Doreian, P. (2016). Social network analysis and economic geography—positional, evolutionary and multi-level approaches. *Journal of Economic Geography*, 16(6), 1123–1134.

Glückler, J., Lazega, E., & Hammer, I. (2017). Exploring the interaction of space and networks in the creation of knowledge: An introduction. *Knowledge and networks*, Springer 1–21.

Granovetter, M. (1973). The strength of weak ties. *American Journal of Sociology*, 78(6), 1360–1380.

Granovetter, M. (1985). Economic action and social structure: the problem of embeddedness. *American Journal of Sociology*, 91(3), 481–510.

Handcock, M.S. (2003). In assessing degeneracy statistical models of social networks. Center for Statistics and the Social Sciences, University of Washington. Working paper no. 39.

Handcock, M.S., Hunter, D.R., Butts, C.T., Goodreau, S.M., & Morris, M. (2008). statnet: software tools for the representation, visualization, analysis and simulation of network data. *Journal of Statistical Software*, 24(1), 1548.

Holland, P., & Leinhardt, S. (1981). An exponential family of probability distributions for directed graphs. *Journal of the American Statistical Association*, 76(373), 33–50.

Koskinen, J.H., Robins, G.L., & Pattison, P.E. (2010). Analysing exponential random graph (p-star) models with missing data using Bayesian data augmentation. *Statistical Methodology*, 7(3), 366–384.

Koskinen, J., & Snijders, T. A. (2022). Multilevel longitudinal analysis of social networks. *arXiv preprint arXiv:2201.12713*.

Lazega, E. (2009). Cooperation among competitors: Its social mechanisms through network analyses. *Sociologica*, 3(1)

Lazega, E. (2015). Mobilités, turnover relationnel et coûts de synchronisation: Comprendre l'action collective par ses infrastructures relationnelles dynamiques et multiniveaux. *Année Sociologique*, 65:391–424.

Lazega, E. (2016). Synchronization costs in the organizational society: Intermediary relational infrastructures in the dynamics of multilevel networks. In E. Lazega & T.A.B. Snijders (Eds), *Multilevel Network Analysis: Theory, Methods and Applications*. Springer. 47–77.

Lazega, E. (2017). Organized mobility and relational turnover as context for social mechanisms: A dynamic invariant at the heart of stability from movement. In Glückler, J., Lazega, E., & Hammer, I. (Eds) *Knowledge and networks*, Springer, 119–142.

Lazega, E. (2018), "Networks and institutionalization: A neo-structural approach" [EUSN 2017 Keynote Address], *Connections*, 37:7–22

Lazega, E. (2020). *Bureaucracy, collegiality and social change: redefining organizations with multilevel relational infrastructures*. Edward Elgar.

Lazega, E., & Jourda, M.-T. (2016). The structural wings of Matthew effects: the contribution of three-level network data to the analysis of cumulative advantage. *Methodological Innovations*, 29. doi.org/10.1177/2059799115622764

Lazega, E., Jourda, M.-T., & Mounier, L. (2013). Network lift from dual alters: extended opportunity structures from a multilevel and structural perspective. *European Sociological Review*, 29, 1226–1238.

Lazega, E., Jourda, M-T., Mounier, L., & Stofer, R. (2008). Catching up with big fish in the big pond? Multi-level network analysis through linked design. *Social Networks*, 30(2), 159–76.

Lazega, E., Mounier, L., Jourda, M.T.S., & Stofer, R. (2006). Organizational vs personal social capital in scientists' performance: a multi-level network study of elite French cancer researchers (1996–1998). *Scientometrics*, 67(1), 27–44.

Lazega, E., & Snijders, T. (Eds)(2015). *Multilevel network analysis for the social sciences: theory, methods and applications*. Springer.

Lazega, E., Jourda, M.-T., & Mounier, L. (2013). Network lift from dual alters: Extended opportunity structures from a multilevel and structural perspective. *European Sociological Review*, 29, pp. 1226–1238.

Lazega, E., Quintane, E. & Casenaz, S. (2016), "Collegial Oligarchy and Networks of Normative Alignments in Transnational Institution Building: The Case of the European *Unified Patent Court*", *Social Networks*, 48:10–22

Lin, N. (1999). Social network and status attainment. *Annual Review of Sociology*, 25, 467–488.

Lin, N. (2000). Inequality in social capital. *Contemporary Sociology*, 29, 785–795.

Lin, N. (2001). *Social capital: a theory of social structure and action*. Cambridge University Press.

Lomi, A., Robins, G. & Tranmer, M. (2016). Introduction to multilevel social networks. *Social Networks*, 44, 266. doi: 10.1016/j.socnet.2015.10.006

Lorrain, F., & White, H.C. 1971. Structural equivalence of individuals in social networks. *Journal of Mathematical Sociology*, 1, 49–80.

Lusher, D., Koskinen, J., & Robins, G. (Eds.) (2013). *Exponential random graph models for social networks: theory, methods, and applications*. Cambridge University Press.

Marsden, P., & Hurlbert, J. (1988). Social resources and mobility outcomes: a replication and extension. *Social Forces*, 66(4), 1038–1059

Matous, P., & Todo, Y. (2015). Exploring dynamic mechanisms of learning networks for resource conservation. *Ecology and Society*, 20(2).

Matous, P., Todo, Y., & Mojo, D. (2013a). Roles of extension and ethno-religious networks in acceptance of resource-conserving agriculture among Ethiopian farmers. *International Journal of Agricultural Sustainability*, 11(4), 301–316.

Matous, P., Todo, Y., & Mojo, D. (2013b). Boots are made for walking: interactions across physical and social space in infrastructure-poor regions. *Journal of Transport Geography*, 31(0), 226–235.

Matous, P., Todo, Y., & Ishikawa, T. (2014). Emergence of multiplex mobile phone communication networks across rural areas: an Ethiopian experiment. *Network Science*, 2(02), 162–188.

McPherson, M., Smith-Lovin, L., & Cook., J. (2001). Birds of a feather: homophily in social networks. *Annual Review of Sociology*, 27(1), 415–444.

Merton, R.K. (1968). The Matthew effect in science. *Science*, 159(3810), 56–63.

Moliterno, T. P., & Mahony, D. M. (2011). Network theory of organization: A multilevel approach. *Journal of management*, 37(2), 443–467.

Ostrom, E. (1990). Governing the commons: The evolution of institutions for collective action. Cambridge university press.

Pattison, P., & Snijders, T. (2013). Modeling social networks: next steps. In D. Lusher, J. Koskinen & G. Robins (Eds.), *Exponential random graph models for social networks: theories, methods and applications* (pp. 287–301). Cambridge University Press.

Perrow, Ch. (1991). A Society of organizations. *Theory and Society*, 20, 725–62.

Rinaldo, A., Fienberg, S., & Zhou, Y. (2009). On the geometry of discrete exponential families with application to exponential random graph models. *Electronic Journal of Statistics*, 3, 446–484.

Robins, G., & Alexander, M. (2004). Small worlds among interlocking directors: network structure and distance in bipartite graphs. *Computational and Mathematical Organization Theory*, 10(1), 69–94.

Robins, G., Elliott, P., & Pattison, P. (2001a). Network models for social selection processes. *Social Networks*, 23(1), 1–30.

Robins, G., Pattison, P., & Elliott, P. (2001b). Network models for social influence processes. *Psychometrika*, 66(2), 161–189.

Robinson, W.S. (1950). Ecological correlations and the behaviour of individuals. *American Sociological Review*, 15, 351–357.

Selznick, P. (1949). *TVA and the grass roots: a study in the sociology of formal organization*. University of California Press.

Snijders, T.A. (2002). Markov chain Monte Carlo estimation of exponential random graph models. *Journal of Social Structure*, 3(2), 1–40.

Snijders, T. A. (2016). The multiple flavours of multilevel issues for networks. In E. Lazega and T.A.B. Snijders (Eds), *Multilevel network analysis for the social sciences: Theory, methods and applications*, Springer, 15–46.

Snijders, T.A.B., & Bosker, R.J. (2012). *Multilevel analysis: an introduction to basic and advanced multilevel modeling* (2nd ed.). Sage.

Snijders, T.A.B., Lomi, A., & Torló, V. (2013). A model for the multiplex dynamics of two-mode and one-mode networks, with an application to employment preference, friendship, and advice. *Social Networks*, 35(2), 265–276. doi: 10.1016/j.socnet.2012.05.005

Snijders, T.A., Pattison, P.E., Robins, G.L., & Handcock, M.S. (2006). New specifications for exponential random graph models. *Sociological Methodology*, 36(1), 99–153.

Stimpson, D.V., Robinson, P.B., Waranusuntikule, S., & Zheng, R. (1990). Attitudinal characteristics of entrepreneurs and non-entrepreneurs in the United States, Korea, Thailand, and the People's Republic of China. *Entrepreneurship and Regional Development*, 2(1), 49–56.

Stivala, A., Robins, G., & Lomi, A. (2020). Exponential random graph model parameter estimation for very large directed networks. *PLOS One*, 15(1), e0227804.

Vacchiano, M., & Spini, D. (2021). Networked lives. *Journal for the Theory of Social Behaviour*, 51(1), 87–103.

Vacchiano, M. Lazega, E., Spini, D. (2022). Multilevel Networks and Status Attainment. *Advances in Life Course Research*, Vol 52, 100479

van Duijn, M.A.J., van Busschbach, J., & Snijders, T. (1999). Multilevel analysis of personal networks as dependent variables. *Social Networks*, 21(2), 1.

Wang, P. (2013) Exponential random graph model extensions: models for multiple networks and bipartite networks. In D. Lusher, J. Koskinen & G. Robins (Eds.), *Exponential random graph models for social networks: theories, methods and applications* (pp. 115–129). Cambridge University Press.

Wang, P., Pattison, P., & Robins, G. (2013a). Exponential random graph model specifications for bipartite networks: a dependence hierarchy. *Social Networks*, 35(2), 211–222.

Wang, P., Robins, G., & Matous, P. (2016a) Multilevel network analysis using ERGM and its extension. In E. Lazega & T.A.B. Snijders (Eds.), *Multilevel network analysis for the social sciences* (pp. 125–143). Springer.

Wang, P., Robins, G., Pattison, P., & Koskinen, J. (2014). MPNet, program for the Simulation and Estimation of (p*) exponential random graph models for multilevel networks. Swinburne

University of Technology and University of Melbourne, Australia.

Wang, P., Robins, G., Pattison, P., & Lazega, E. (2013b). Exponential random graph models for multilevel networks. *Social Networks*, *35*(1), 96–115.

Wang, P., Robins, G., Pattison, P., & Lazega, E. (2016b). Social selection models for multilevel networks. *Social Networks*, *44*, 346–362.

Wasserman, S., & Iacobucci, D. (1991). Statistical modeling of one-mode and two-mode networks: simultaneous analysis of graphs and bipartite graphs. *British Journal of Mathematical and Statistical Psychology*, *44*, 13–44.

Zappa, P., & Robins, G. (2016). Organizational learning across multi-level networks. *Social Networks*, *44*, 295–306.

Exponential Random Graph Models

Johan Koskinen

INTRODUCTION

There are an increasing number of articles, books and book chapters introducing exponential random graph models (ERGMs) that focus primarily on the application, use and interpretation of the model. ERGMs have in fact become so popular that Martin (2020), in a comment on Stivala (2020a, b), claimed that the networks community is moving towards a monoculture of doing everything with ERGMs. He further goes on to suggest that ERGMs aim to become the generalised linear model of network analysis with people unquestioningly and uncritically applying ERGMs, even when these are not fit for purpose. Irrespective of the veracity of his claims, he is correct in pointing out that applying a statistical model in the wrong circumstances without proper heed to what assumptions are implied by the model leads to a 'ritualism' where you force a model to do things it was not designed to do.

The present chapter explains the fundamental principles of the ERGM and how these relate to the many extensions of the model.[1] The core premise of the ERGM is that it is a model for interdependent observations which means that any use of ERGMs needs to consider explicitly what the underlying dependence assumptions are. Furthermore, these dependencies imply a duality in understanding the model: the ERGM is simultaneously a model for tie-variables that are dependent and a model for the whole network. Consequently, the number of observations is either the total number of dyads or one.

In its simplest form, we represent a network as a graph $G(V,E)$ on a fixed set of nodes $V = \{1,\ldots,n\}$ with edge set $E \subseteq \mathcal{N} = \binom{V}{2}$, or, equivalently, as a symmetric binary $n \times n$ adjacency matrix X, whose element X_{ij} is 1 if there is an edge between i and j, and 0 otherwise, $i,j, \in V$.

The purpose of exponential random graph models is to define a statistical model that allocates probability to all possible networks $X \in \mathcal{X} = \{0,1\}^{\mathcal{N}}$, for a fixed set of nodes. This is straightforward to do if we assume that the tie-variables are independent across all pairs of nodes. In that case, a network is just a collection of independent variables characterised by a simple sequence of Bernoulli trials. The independence of ties is, however, an unrealistic assumption and the networks resulting from this process hardly ever share any similarity with the networks we observe in the wild. It is unrealistic because it does not reflect any of the network mechanisms that the literature suggests drive tie-formation, such as cumulative advantage (Merton, 1968; also called the psychosocial effect, Moreno & Jennings, 1938), triadic closure, etc. These 'independence' models, while they tend to have short average path lengths, do not replicate other typical structures of real networks such as skewed degree distributions, clustering, etc. (Robins et al., 2005).

To introduce how we may specify departures from independence in ERGM, we start by considering the implications of independence of ties. First, if tie-variables $X_{12}, X_{13}, \ldots X_{n,n-1}$ are assumed to be independent, then each for each $i,j, \in \mathcal{N}^2$, we have

$$\Pr(X_{ij} = 1) = p_{ij},$$

where $p_{ij} \in (0,1)$ is the tie-probability for the pair ij. By independence the conditional probability that the tie ij will exist, given everything else, is given by

$$\Pr\begin{pmatrix} X_{ij} = 1 \mid X_{12} = x_{12}, \ldots, X_{i,j-1} \\ = x_{i,j-1}, X_{i,j+1} = x_{i,j+1}, \ldots, X_{n,n-1} = x_{n,n-1} \end{pmatrix} = p_{ij}.$$

The interpretation of this is that the state of the rest of the network does *not* inform us about the probability that ij will exist – the probability of this tie remains the same as if we had known nothing about the rest of the network. For example, if we are considering the probability that there is a tie between Elle and Jon, it does not matter if Elle and Jon both are best friends with Colin. Moreover, there is no dependence on the density of the network. Actors i and j may already have ties to all other actors, or to no other actors, the conditional probability that they will have a tie ij is unaffected. We may also consider pairs of tie-variables. Take, for example, two tie-variables of the same node i, say the potential tie to j, and the potential tie to k, X_{ij} and X_{ik}, respectively. By independence, we have that the probability that i has a tie to both j and k is

$$\Pr(X_{ij} = 1, X_{ik} = 1) = p_{ij} p_{ik}.$$

There is consequently nothing that says that both ties being absent (present) is more or less likely than the overall marginal probabilities of the ties being absent (present) individually. The probability for any network $X \in \mathcal{X}$, is given by

$$\Pr(X = x) = \prod_{i<j} \Pr(X_{ij} = x_{ij}) = \prod_{i<j} p_{ij}^{x_{ij}} (1-p_{ij})^{1-x_{ij}}.$$

In particular, if all tie-probabilities are the same $p_{ij} = p$, the model is a homogeneous Bernoulli model[3] (Frank & Strauss, 1986), and the probability for any network becomes

$$\Pr(X = x) = p^{L(x)} (1-p)^{n(n-1)/2 - L(x)},$$

where $L(x) = \Sigma_{i<j} x_{ij}$, and consequently all networks with the same density will be equally likely.

MARKOV GRAPHS

How may we relax the unrealistic assumption of independence of tie-variables? Frank and Strauss (1986) suggested that tie-variables may be independent provided that they are not connected through a node. This is to say, two tie-variables X_{ij} and X_{ik} of the same node i, say the potential tie to j, and the potential tie to k, are not (conditionally) independent (given the rest of the network). They called this the Markov dependence assumption. The implication, using the example above, is that

$$\Pr(X_{ij} = 1, X_{ik} = 1) \neq p_{ij} p_{ik}.$$

Expressed differently, we also see that the conditional probability of ij existing may depend on whether ik exists or not

$$\Pr(X_{ij} = 1 \mid X_{ik} = 1) \neq \Pr(X_{ij} = 1 \mid X_{ik} = 0).$$

Frank and Strauss (1986) formally prove that this dependence assumption is equivalent to a log-linear model with interaction effects. The presence of *both* ij and ik requires the interaction $x_{ij} x_{ik}$. These interaction effects are interactions between tie-variables of the type

$$z_A(x) = \prod_{ij \in A} x_{ij},$$

for subsets $A \subset \mathcal{N}$. An interaction effect of this type is thus a function that indicates whether all tie-variables $x_{ij} = 1$ for ij in the subset A. The interactions enter the probability mass function (pmf) for the network in the linear predictor of the log-linear form

$$\Pr(X = x \mid \theta) = \exp\left\{\sum_{A \in D} \theta_A z_A(x) - \psi(\theta)\right\}, \quad (1)$$

where each subset A in a collection of subsets D, has a statistical parameter θ_A associated with it, and the normalising constant

$$\psi(\theta) = \log\left[\sum_{y \in \mathcal{X}} \exp\left\{\sum_{A \in D} \theta_A z_A(y)\right\}\right], \quad (2)$$

ensures that the distribution sums to one over all networks, $\sum_{x \in \mathcal{X}} \Pr(X = x | \theta) = 1$. The distribution in Eq.(1) is of a so-called exponential family form, which is where the ERGM takes its name from. The pmf in (1) is conditioned on a vector θ of parameters, as each set of parameter values yield different distributions, but we will omit the notational dependence on θ in the sequel when convenient.

Note that the probability of a network x in Eq.(1) depends on functions $z_A(x)$, weighted by their respective parameters. Consequently, if θ_A is positive and the statistic $z_A(x)$ non-zero, then having all tie-variables in A present adds to the (log-) probability of the network. If, on the other hand, θ_A is negative, then having all tie-variables in A present decreases the probability of the network. If θ_A is zero, then the variables in A do not affect the probability of a network at all.

Eq.(1) is in fact more general than the Markov dependence assumption.[4] If Q is a so-called dependence graph on the tie-variables, such that there is an edge between X_{ij} and X_{kh} in Q if and only if X_{ij} and X_{kh} are conditionally dependent given everything else, then the Hammersley–Clifford theorem gives that for the A interaction $\lambda_A(x) = \theta_A z_A(x)$, $\lambda_A(x) \neq 0$ if an only if A is a clique of Q.

Frank and Strauss (1986) proved that for the Markov dependence assumption, only two types of interactions could have non-zero parameters θ_A. The first type is a k-star, where one node i has ties to k other nodes. This forms a star with i in the middle, and k actors at the spokes. This interaction follows intuitively from the Markov dependence assumption as, say, the interaction $x_{ij}x_{ik}$ informs us of whether both or only one of ij or ik exists in the graph (Figure 33.1(b)). If for $A = \{ij,ik\}$, we have a positive parameter θ_A, then, given everything else,[5] we have for example that

$$\Pr(X_{ij} = 1, X_{ik} = 1 | rest) > \Pr(X_{ij} = 1, X_{ik} = 0 | rest),$$

as the probability on the left hand side will have $z_A(x) = x_{ij}x_{ik} = 1$ in the exponent of Eq.(1), but the right hand side will have $z_A(x) = x_{ij}x_{ik} = 0$ in the exponent. The parameter θ_A can thus be said to inform us about how strong the dependence between variables in A is.

The second type of statistic is a triangle, for example $A = \{ij,ik,jk\}$. Intuitively we can see that triangles may have non-zero parameters as x_{ij} and x_{ik} have i in common, x_{ik} and x_{jk} have k in common, but x_{ij} and x_{jk} also have j in common – the edges of the triangle are thus all joined by shared nodes (Figure 33.1(c)). With a positive parameter θ_A for $A = \{ij,ik,jk\}$, graphs where $z_A(x) = x_{ij}x_{ik}x_{jk} = 1$, that is, where the triangle A exists, are thus more likely than graphs where this triangle does not exist, conditionally on the rest of the graph.

Some parameters for some interactions may be set to zero *a priori*, reflecting, for example, the belief that higher-order interactions are not needed. As for most models, and log-linear models in particular, the set of interactions should obey the hierarchy principle. This states that if the k-way interaction is in the model, then every lower-order interaction and main effect is also in the model. Consider for example the triangle interaction $A = \{ij,ik,jk\}$, represented in the model by

$$\theta_A x_{ij} x_{ik} x_{jk}.$$

It is clear that lower-order interactions for this effect are

$$\theta_{ij,ik} x_{ij} x_{ik},$$
$$\theta_{ij,jk} x_{ij} x_{jk}, \text{ and}$$
$$\theta_{ik,jk} x_{ik} x_{jk},$$

as well as the 'main' effects

$$\theta_{ij} x_{ij}, \theta_{ik} x_{ik}, \text{ and } \theta_{jk} x_{jk}.$$

The intuition is that in order to estimate the strength of the interaction A, we need to account for the presence of its constituent elements. The interaction needs to quantify how strong the

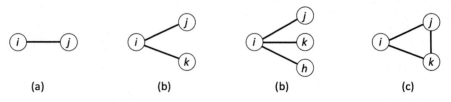

Figure 33.1 Sufficient statistics for the Markov dependence assumption. Sufficient statistics include counts of edges (a), two-stars (b), three-stars (c) and stars up to order *n*–1, as well as counts of the number of triangles (c)

tendency is for the triangle to form over and above the tendency for the individual two-stars to be present.

If we were to have a distinct parameter for all interactions, we would end up with too many parameters. For example, the two-stars have a separate parameter for $A = \{ij,ik\}$ and $A = \{ij,ih\}$, leading to too many parameters and many more parameters than we have tie-variables – each tie-variable would already have its own parameter for the interaction $A = \{ij\}$. Frank and Strauss (1986) remedied this by assuming that all graphs that are isomorphic have the same probability, making the model *permutation invariant*. This translates into the homogeneity assumption, that says that $\theta_A = \theta_{A'}$ for all interactions A and A' that are isomorphic. This means that $\theta_{ij} = \theta_{kh} = \theta_L$ for the edge parameters for all $ij,kh \in \mathcal{N}$. Similarly, a two-star $A = \{ij,ik\}$, $j \neq k$ is isomorphic to any interaction $A' = \{uv,us\}$, $v \neq s$, and we set $\theta_{ij,ik} = \theta_{S_2}$ for all $i \in V$ and $jk \in \mathcal{N}$. For higher-order k-stars, the parameters are set to θ_{S_k}, and for all triangles $\theta_{ij,ik,jk} = \theta_T$. Homogeneity assumptions are common in statistical models in general – in regression models we typically assume that observations are identical up to observable covariates – but for networks it is worthwhile considering the fact that ties are cross-classified by their endpoints. We make the assumption that each node, and each edge, plays by the same rules but whether that assumption holds true or not is ultimately an empirical issue (Koskinen et al., 2018).[6]

The model in Eq.(1) can now be written

$$\Pr(X = x) = \exp\begin{Bmatrix} \theta_L L(x) + \theta_{S_2} S_2(x) + \cdots + \\ \theta_{S_{n-1}} S_{n-1}(x) + \theta_T T(x) - \psi(\theta) \end{Bmatrix},$$

where $L(x)$ is the edge count, $S_2(x) = \Sigma_i \Sigma_{j,k} x_{ij} x_{ik}$ is the number of two-stars, and in general $S_k(x) = \sum_i \binom{x_{i+}}{k}$ is the count of k-stars, and, finally, $T(x) = \sum_{\{i,j,k\} \in} \binom{v}{3} x_{ij} x_{ik} x_{jk}$ is the number of triangles. The probability model that determines the probability of all networks is thus reduced to a weighted sum of counts of the configurations in Figure 33.1.

INTERPRETATION OF MARKOV MODEL

While the Markov dependence assumption on its own has turned out to be insufficient for modelling real networks (see below), it is instructive to consider the substantive interpretations of the model. There is a duality to this interpretation in that the ERGM can either be seen simply as a statistical model for non-independent, binary variables, or as a manifestation of fundamental tie-formation mechanisms. First, in simple statistical terms, the ERGM is a model for $X_{12}, X_{13}, \ldots X_{n,n-1}$ where we assume that there is dependence between the observations. The statistics or configurations account for the fact that some tie-variables are more likely to co-occur than others, something which is captured by their interactions, which are in turn given by the dependence assumption. If, for example, we set the parameters to zero for all interactions other than the singletons, we are explicitly stating that there are no dependencies between ties, and the model reduces to a Bernoulli model. If we allow for dependencies among ties that are connected through a node, the star and triangle statistics simply account for ties being cross-classified by their endpoints and no further behavioural assumptions are needed.

The other side of the duality is that the statistics correspond to meaningful configurations (Moreno & Jennings, 1938) that have been associated with many network mechanisms in the literature. Stars capture the extent to which ties are unevenly distributed in the network, for example, if some people are more popular than others. Merton (1968) proposed cumulative advantage, or the Mathew effect, as the mechanism behind this.[7]

Already Simmel (1902) argued that the triad was fundamentally different from the dyad and various arguments for why we would expect to see triadic closure can be found in the literature (see Granovetter, 1973, for a review). Frank (1980) developed the balance metric

$$\frac{3\tau_3(x)}{3\tau_3(x) + \tau_2(x)},$$

where $\tau_3(x) = T(x)$, and $\tau_2(x)$ is the number of two-paths that are not closed. This motivates the use of triangles and its lower-order interaction, the two-star, as representing a tendency for triads to close and a mechanism of balance. These locally based mechanisms also combine to produce emergent global features (Robins et al., 2005).

The homogeneous Markov model still has too many star parameters both in terms of interpretation and estimation. Snijders et al. (2006) proposed that star statistics be geometrically weighted through imposing the constraint $\theta_{S_k} = -\theta_{S_{k-1}}/\lambda_s$ for a strictly positive constant λ_s. For Markov models, it was often found that parameter estimates alternated between being positive and negative, reflecting the fact that stars are nested in higher-order stars (see Frank & Strauss, 1986). This implies a model that replaces all of the star statistics with a single statistic

$$u_{\lambda_s}^{(s)}(x) = \sum_{k=2}^{n-1} \frac{(-1)^k}{\lambda_s^{k-2}} S_k(x),$$

which means that the degrees are weighted geometrically, with increasingly high degrees getting a decreasing weight (for $\lambda_s > 1$). The alternating star statistic is therefore also called the geometrically weighted degree statistic (see also Hunter & Handcock, 2006). The alternating k-star parameter parameterises the entire degree distribution and the 'shape' of the degree distribution is given by the constant λ_s. As noted in Snijders et al. (2006), if λ_s is considered a free parameter to be estimated, the model is no longer an exponential family model but belongs to the curved exponential family (for modified estimation, see Hunter & Handcock, 2006; Koskinen, 2008).

SOCIAL CIRCUIT DEPENDENCE ASSUMPTION

Early on, it was clear that the Markov model was unstable and that small shifts in the parameters could have dramatic effects on the distribution, resulting in models that place most of their mass on very sparse or very dense networks, occasionally empty or complete graphs (Strauss, 1986; Jonasson, 1999; Häggström & Jonasson, 1999). Markov models were clearly very rarely useful for modelling real networks. Pattison and Robins (2002) suggested that, in addition to dependence through nodes, *dependence through ties* was theoretically motivated. They proposed that tie-variables that did not share a node, might be conditionally dependent conditionally on there existing a path of *realised ties* connecting them. For example, a three-path dependence, where two ties ij and kh, of distinct nodes, could be conditionally dependent should there exist a tie connecting them, $x_{ik} = 1$, $x_{jk} = 1$, $x_{ih} = 1$, or $x_{jh} = 1$. The corresponding interaction would then be a three-path, for example $x_{ij}x_{kh}x_{ik}$. This dependence through ties required a different method for defining dependence assumptions, as the dependence between ties is dependent on the outcomes of other tie-variables. The tie-variables x_{ij} and x_{kh} are conditionally independent if $x_{ik} = x_{jk} = x_{ih} = x_{ik} = 0$ but conditionally dependent otherwise.

Realisation dependence offers a flexible way of defining long-range dependencies between ties that correspond to our intuitions, but the flexibility also means that the model is not as parsimonious as the Markov model. For example, the admissible interactions do not obey the principle of hierarchy. For the three-path dependence, for example, while $x_{ij}x_{kh}x_{ik}$ may be a non-zero interaction, $x_{ij}x_{kh}$ may not be.

Snijders et al. (2006) discovered that realisation dependence could remedy the deficiencies of the Markov models. They suggested a particular form of realisation dependence called the *social circuit dependence assumption*: two tie-variables, X_{ij} and X_{kh}, may be conditionally dependent if $x_{ik} = x_{jh} = 1$ or $X_{ih} X_{jk} = 1$ (Figure 33.2 (b)). The existence of the ties ik and jh provides a social neighbourhood for the interaction of ij and kh. If, for example, i is the supervisor of k, and j is the supervisor of h, then if either the two supervisors start collaborating or the two students start collaboration, then this may increase the likelihood of a collaboration in the other dyad.

Interactions that correspond to the social circuit dependence assumption, include the multiple four-cycles, or independent two-paths, of Figure 33.2 (ii) and (iii), as well as higher-order independent two-paths. When the Markov dependence assumption (Figure 33.2(a)) is assumed in conjunction with the social circuit dependence assumption, the four-cycle with a cord in Figure 33.2 (v) and the independent three-path with a cord in Figure 33.2 (vi) are interactions that account for both dependence through nodes as well as through realised ties. The configurations thus provide a natural extension of the Markov statistics (Figure 33.2 (i) and (iv)) to their elaborations in Figure 33.2 (ii), (iii) and (v), (vi).

The independent two-paths can be labelled according to the number k of shared partners two nodes have. Similarly, the number k of shared partners a directly tied pair has is used to label the order of the triangle. The triangle in Figure 33.2 (iv) is a one-triangle $T_1(x)$, Figure 33.2 (v) is a two-triangle $T_2(x)$, Figure 33.2 (vi) a three-triangle $T_3(x)$, etc. Snijders et al. (2006) used the same principle to reduce the number of parameters for independent two-paths and k-triangles as for the star statistics. Letting θ_{P_k} be the parameter for the independent k-two-path, and θ_{T_k} be the parameter for the k-triangle, they suggested that, for strictly positive λ_P and λ_T,

$$\theta_{P_k} = -\frac{\theta_{P_{k-1}}}{\lambda_P},$$

and

$$\theta_{T_k} = -\frac{\theta_{T_{k-1}}}{\lambda_T}.$$

Generally, this means that higher-order configurations get increasingly less weight in the network (for $\lambda_P > 1$ and $\lambda_T > 1$). For triangles, the

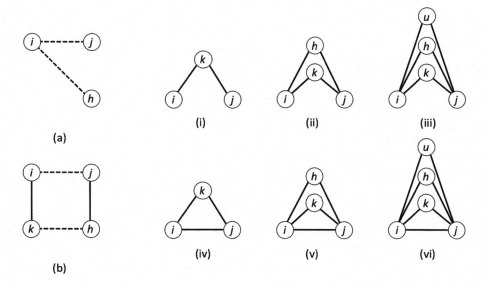

Figure 33.2 Social circuit assumption and statistics. The social circuit dependence assumption model incorporates the Markov dependence assumption, whereby ties are dependent through nodes (a) as well as the four-cycle dependence (b) whereby ties *ij* and *kh* may be dependent if the ties *ik* and *jh* exist (or the ties *ih* and *jk*). Statistics that are concordant with the social circuit dependence are independent two-paths of order one (i), two (ii) and three (ii); and one-triangles (iv), two-triangles (v) and three-triangles (vi). Higher-order two-paths and triangles not depicted here

contribution of shared partners has diminishing returns, whereas in the Markov model, the triangle statistic is additive, in the sense that the contribution of the *k*th shared partner for two nodes *i* and *j*, with $x_{ij} = 1$, is the same independently of *k*. One can think of this as if the pressure on *i* and *j* to be directly tied by having an additional shared partner is the same regardless of whether *i* and *j* already have two or 99 shared partners. Using the parametrisation $\theta_{T_k} = -\theta_{T_{k-1}} / \lambda_T$ instead, we see that the parameter for having 100 shared partners is much smaller than for having three shared partners. This diminishing return on the number of shared partners makes intuitive sense but also has significance for the behaviour of the model as a model for graphs. The Markov model is unstable exactly because you can get radically different types of graphs with the addition of only a few added ties. Consider a graph that has the two-path in Figure 33.2 (i) and compare it to a graph that has the triangle in Figure 33.2 (iv). The difference between these graphs would be one edge and one triangle. Now, consider a graph that has the independent three-two-path of Figure 33.2 (iii) with a graph that has the three-triangle of Figure 33.2 (vi). Again, the graphs would differ only in one edge but now have a difference of three triangles. For the Markov model it is difficult to balance the importance of ties and triangles because the addition of ties can lead to an explosion in the number of triangles (see Snijders et al., 2006, p. 110).[8]

The independent *k*-two-path effect can be written in terms of one parameter θ_P with the statistic

$$u^{(P)}_{\lambda_P}(x) = \binom{n}{2} \lambda_P - \lambda_P \sum_{1 \leq i < j \leq n} \left(1 - \frac{1}{\lambda_P}\right)^{L_{ij}},$$

where $L_{ij} = \sum_{h \neq i,j} x_{ih} x_{jh}$ is the number of two-paths between nodes *i* and *j*. The *k*-triangle effect can be written as a parameter θ_T with the associated statistic

$$u^{(T)}_{\lambda_T}(x) = 3T_1 - \frac{T_2}{\lambda_T} + \frac{T_3}{\lambda_T^2} + \cdots + (-1)^{n-3} \frac{T_{n-2}}{\lambda_T^{n-3}},$$

or alternatively

$$u^{(T)}_{\lambda_T}(x) = \frac{e^\alpha}{e^\alpha - 1} \sum_{i<j} x_{ij} \left(1 - e^{-\alpha L_{ij}}\right),$$

for $\lambda_T = e^\alpha/(e^\alpha - 1)$. The intuition behind the last expression is that each tie has a weight $1 - 1/e^{\alpha L_{ij}}$ that grows with the number of shared partners L_{ij}.

If there are no shared partners, $L_{ij} = 0$, then the contribution is zero as $1 - 1/e^{\alpha \times 0} = 0$.

Dependence Hierarchy

The dependence hierarchy for ERGM introduced in Pattison and Robins (2002) and elaborated in Pattison and Snijders (2013) and Wang et al. (2013a), classifies dependence in ERGM according to four definitions of proximity with different proximity values p. These define the conditions under which two tie-variables X_{ij} and X_{kh} at proximity p are conditionally dependent. The first condition implies the second which implies the third which implies the fourth, and a model is increasingly general for increasing proximity.

Strict inclusion at proximity p means that each of the two nodes i and j is within proximity p of each of the two nodes k and h.

Inclusion relaxes strict inclusion by saying that each of the two nodes i and j is within proximity p of at least one of the two nodes k and h, and, each of the two nodes k and h is within proximity p of at least one of the two nodes i and j.

Partial inclusion relaxes the symmetry of inclusion, by stating that that each of the two nodes i and j is within proximity p of at least one of the two nodes k and h, or, each of the two nodes k and h is within proximity p of at least one of the two nodes i and j.

Distance relaxes the condition further by stating that at least one of nodes i and j is within proximity p of at least one of the two nodes k and h.

On the one hand, inclusion and partial inclusion with $p = 0$ yield the Bernoulli graph. Inclusion with $p = 1$, on the other hand, yields the social circuit dependence assumption but partial inclusion with $p = 1$ results in a model with an edge-triangle statistic (Wang et al., 2022). Markov dependence is obtained from distance with $p = 1$ and the three-path dependence with $p = 0$.

The dependence hierarchy is, in a sense, the unifying theory of ERGM as it not only produces the different dependence assumptions but also relates them to each other. More importantly, the dependence hierarchy is expressed not only in terms of the index set of the adjacency matrix (the nodes) but also in terms of the (partial) structure of a network. As such it captures the essence of White et al.'s (1976) duality of structure and individuals – the network structure affects and constrains the interactions of nodes but these interactions simultaneously make up the structure (Doreian et al., this volume). Note that models that assume independence not only ignore the structure of networks, they also are agnostic to the nodes of the network. A heterogeneous Bernoulli model may assume different probabilities for the tie-variables but there is no reason to refer to it as an ERGM. The heterogeneous Bernoulli model expressed in exponential family form is more commonly known as logistic regression, a model whose properties are well-known. A model such as the so-called β-model (Chatterjee et al., 2011), that introduces heterogeneity in the tie-probabilities, is still a Bernoulli model.

For directed networks, the Markov dependence assumption results in two dyadic interactions: the arc statistic (Figure 33.3(a)) and the reciprocity statistic (Figure 33.3(b)).[9] For each star statistic in the undirected Markov model, the directed Markov model has different interactions depending on the directions of the arcs (see Figure 33.3(i)–(viii) for examples). Similarly, different types of triangles can be distinguished (Figure 33.4(t.i)(t.iv)(t.vii)). Making the social circuit dependence assumption, there is large number of configurations that may have non-zero interactions (see Figure 33.3 and Figure 33.4, and Snijders, 2006, for examples) but Lusher et al. (2013; Section 13.2) provide combination of statistics that typically yield stable models.

EXTENSIONS

ERGMs for undirected graphs have been generalised to models for a wide variety of different types of networks. We briefly present some of configurations that are implied by the Markov and social circuit dependence assumptions along with the associated additional features.

Multiplex Ties

Pattison and Wasserman (1999) extended Markov models to multiplex networks, which was further developed in Lazega and Pattison (1999) and Koehly and Pattison (2005). The ERGM for a multiplex network on relations $\mathcal{R} = \{1,\dots,R\}$ with adjacency matrices $X^{(r)}$ will have statistics of the type $z(x^{(r)})$, interactions for one type of tie, and statistics $z(x^{(r_1)},\dots,x^{(r_p)})$, interactions involving p types of ties $r_1,\dots,r_p \in B \subseteq \mathcal{R}$. For the first type of statistic the univariate undirected or directed statistics are non-zero interactions. For the second type of interaction, the number of statistics grows very quickly with R. For dyadic statistics, we have

$$\sum_{p=2}^{R} \binom{R}{p} = 2^R - (R+1)$$

distinct interactions of the type $x^{(r_1)} x^{(r_1)} \dots x^{(r_p)}$. Combinations of $p > 2$ relations become difficult to interpret and if the principle of hierarchy is to be respected,

EXPONENTIAL RANDOM GRAPH MODELS

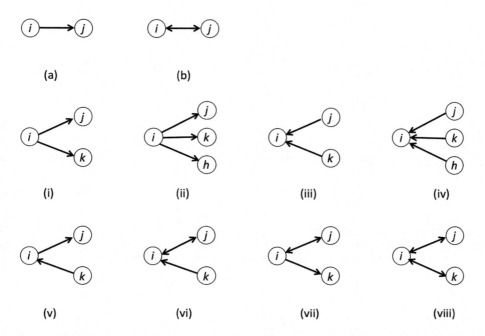

Figure 33.3 Examples of dyadic (a and b) and star statistics (i–viii) of the Markov model for directed networks

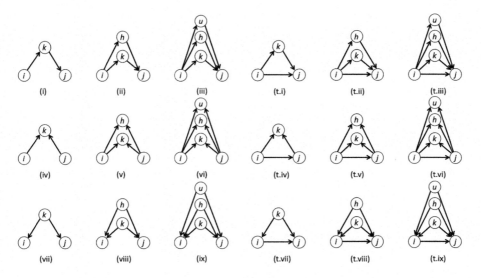

Figure 33.4 Two-paths and triangles for directed graphs. The left-most three columns depict the independent k-two transitive (i–ii), up (iv–vi) and down (vii–ix) paths, for $k = 1,2,3$. The three right-most columns depict the directed k-two transitive (t.i–t.ii), up (t.iv–t.vi) and down (t.vii–t.ix) triangles, for $k = 1,2,3$.

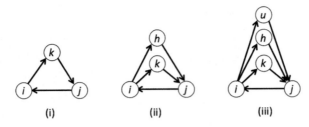

Figure 33.5 Cyclical directed k-triangles, for k = 1,2,3

specifying interactions for relations beyond the pairwise greatly increases the number of model parameters. Krivitsky et al. (2020) proposed a procedure for generating multiplex statistics using *layer logic*. The operations that generate statistics are logical operations for pairwise relations for different types of ties and are not derived out of any specific dependence assumptions. Given the explosion of the number of non-zero interactions for the Markov and social circuit dependence assumptions for $R > 1$, any interaction between different types of ties will have many lower-order interactions. A higher-order interaction, such as a multiplex triangle, cannot be interpreted in isolation and may be the result of a combination of lower-order effects.

For $R = 2$, the dyadic interactions involved are the edge statistics for the two types of ties as well as the interaction between the two types of ties. In general, for multiplex networks, when types of ties are considered pairwise, the Markov dependence assumption gives rise to a number of meaningful statistics, such as the basic entrainment statistic in Figure 33.6(c). Different types of ties may be positively (negatively) correlated, so that the presence of one type of tie is likely to be accompanied by the presence (absence) of another type of tie (see, for example, Agneessens, this volume). This is especially plausible in the case of two types of ties where both reflect a positive relationship such as friendship and support. Different types of ties may also be correlated through nodes in the sense that someone who is very popular or active on one type of relation is also popular or active on other relations. While some of this association may be reflected in entrainment, as in Figure 33.6(a), a general 'gregariousness' may simply be associated with the configuration in Figure 33.6(b). Multiplex closure, such as that represented by Figure 33.6(c), means that one type of tie closes a potentially open two-path for another type of tie.[10]

Analogous to how directed networks yield richer versions of the undirected interactions in a Markov model, directed multiplex configurations admit more complex statistics (Figure 33.7).

Ordered and Valued Ties

Closely related to the case of multiplex ties is when either different type of ties is treated as invariant or numerical. For the first case, assume that we have relations $\mathcal{R} = \{1,...,R\}$ for a reasonably large R, and that we do not really distinguish between interactions $x^{(r_a)}x^{(r_b)}$ for different choices $r_a, r_b \in \mathcal{R}$, then we are really only concerned with the multiplicities of ties – that is, for each dyad we count the number of relations that are active $x^{(1)} + \cdots + x^{(R)}$. For the second case, we may consider ties between individuals to have different strengths or values.

Frank and Strauss (1986) considered random graphs where the tie-variables have colours with range space $\mathcal{R} = \{0,..., R - 1\}$. According to the Hammersley–Clifford theorem, any randomly coloured graph X with dependence structure Q, has probability

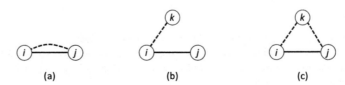

Figure 33.6 Multiplex Markov statistics for undirected graphs. Solid and dashed edges represent different types of ties

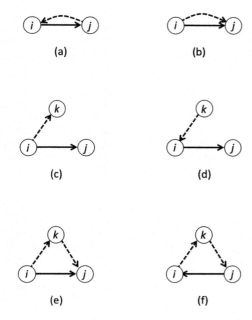

Figure 33.7 Directed Markov statistics for multiplex networks. Solid and dashed arcs represent different types of ties

$$\Pr(X = x) = c^{-1} \exp\left\{ \sum_{A \subseteq \mathcal{N}} \lambda_A(x_A) \right\}, \quad (3)$$

where the interactions λ_A now are functions specific to A, with the constraint that for any $ij \in A$, the sum $\sum_{x_{ij}}^{R-1} \lambda_A(x_A) = 0$; and, $\lambda_A(x_A) = 0$ if A is not a clique of Q. Frank and Strauss (1986) derived the types of statistics for Markov dependence. The dependence graph Q turns out to be the same as for binary networks. However, whereas, for example, the singleton interaction $A = \{ij\}$ can be written $\theta_{ij} x_{ij}$ for a binary network, for coloured edges, $\lambda_{ij}(x_{ij})$ may take different values for different $x_{ij} \in \mathcal{R}$. Even when homogeneity constraints are imposed, the number of parameters to estimate is large. For coloured directed networks – where the binary network has Markov parameters corresponding to asymmetric and mutual dyads – the R-coloured directed graph requires parameters for each of the $R - 1$ assymetric dyads of the type $\{0,r\}$, and $(R - 1)^2/2$ parameters for dyads of the type $\{r_1, r_2\}$, $r_1, r_2 \in \{1,..., R - 1\}$. The number of Markov triangles would be

$$(R^6 + 6R^5 + 12R^4 + 11R^3 + 8R^2 + 4R)/6.$$

If parameters for higher-order stars are assumed to be zero, the number of parameters can be reduced considerably but even for $R = 2$, the number of (homogeneous) parameters are 137, which corresponds to the 138 different triads with three colours (minus 1).

To reduce the number of free parameters, Robins et al. (1999) proposed coding different strengths as different binary networks where $x^{(r)} = 1$ implies that $x^{(r')} = 0$ (or undefined) for all other levels r'. While this modelling framework affords specification of meaningful statistics, it still leads to a formidably long list of interactions even for Markov dependence.

Krivitsky (2012) specified a valued ERGM that has arbitrary functions $\lambda_A(x_A)$ defined for individual edges (and arcs) and functions that are defined for dyads in analogy with reciprocity terms. The understanding of valued networks is underdeveloped in SNA, largely because of the inadequacy of graph theory in describing non-binary networks. A fundamental issue might be that the interpretation of a tie with value 0 is ambiguous – is this an absent tie or is it a tie whose value relative to r is the same as a tie of value s relative to value $r + s$?[11] The intuition of extra-dyadic structures in valued networks is particularly scant. Opsahl and Panzarasa (2009) proposes a number of metrics and Krivitsky (2012) drew on some of these to construct statistics.

For valued ties, models that allow for extra-dyadic dependencies are not automatically coherent and it is not immediately clear what combinations of interactions would satisfy the condition $\sum_{x_{ij}}^{R-1} \lambda_A(x_A) = 0$.

A key premise of the form of Eq. (3) is that the joint distribution may be derived from the conditional distributions of tie-variables, conditional on everything else (Besag, 1974).

When the value of a tie is a count of the number of different types of ties that connect two nodes, the valued graph may be construed as a multigraph. The exponential family form for multigraphs is elaborated by Shafie (2015; Frank & Shafie, 2018). These are well defined in the case of dyad independence, but higher-order dependencies lead to an explosion in the number of non-zero interactions. The challenges with specifying ERGMs for valued graphs mirror the equally challenging theoretical question: what are the research questions that you might ask of valued graphs? ERGMs may be more amenable to the case where, for example, the values represent meaningful counts of transitions between nodes (Block et al., 2022b).

Different Types of Nodes

A two-mode network is a network on two types of nodes, A and B, where ties are only allowed between nodes of different types (see Jasny, this volume). The network on $A \times B$ is thus bipartite and may be represented by a rectangular $|A| \times |B|$ affiliation matrix. As pointed out by Skvoretz and Faust (1999), the Markov dependence assumption for a two-mode network implies statistics that are stars of two types: stars $x_{ih_1} x_{ih_2} \ldots x_{ih_k}$ centred on nodes $i \in A$, and stars $x_{h_1 j} x_{h_2 j} \ldots x_{h_k j}$ centred on nodes $j \in B$. If A is a set of people and B are organisations, and $x_{ij} = 1$ is taken to mean that person $i \in A$ is a member of organization $j \in B$, then the stars represent number of memberships of actors and the number of members of organisations, respectively. They further remarked that the statistics of the Markov model were not adequate for modelling two-mode structures that were of theoretical interest, and added statistics for actor overlaps (later elaborated by Agneessens & Roose, 2008) but without any rationale in terms of dependence assumptions.

Appropriate dependence assumptions for two-mode networks were later developed by Wang (Wang et al., 2009; Wang et al., 2013a) from the set of realisation dependence proposed in Pattison and Robins (2002). The inclusion condition at proximity 1 applied to two-mode networks offers the four-cycle statistic as a direct equivalent of the four-cycle according to the social circuit dependence assumption. The distance condition at proximity 1 further implies a three-path statistic, with terms $x_{ih} x_{jh} x_{ik}$ (Figure 33.8 (a)), which is also a lower-order interaction for the four-cycle (Figure 33.8 (c) and (f)). These two additional interactions capture connectivity and two-mode clustering of the network. The social circuit dependence assumption prescribes two types of multiple independent k-two-paths, depending on whether nodes on the two-paths belong to one mode or the other (compare the difference between Figure 33.8 (d) and (g)).

Wasserman and Iacobucci (1991) derived a dyad-independent log-linear model for the *joint* analysis of two-mode and one-mode networks. Lazega et al. (2008) elaborated the joint representation of *two* types of nodes and *three* types of ties, calling these *multilevel networks* (Lazega and Wang, this volume). While a multilevel network can formally be represented as a (blocked) one-mode network, Wang et al. (2013b) demonstrated that appropriately made dependence assumptions afford homogeneity assumptions that yield configurations (Figure 33.8) that are theoretically important (Lazega and Wang, this volume).

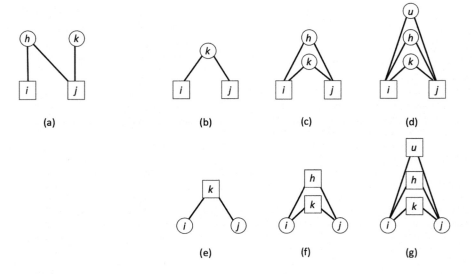

Figure 33.8 Two-mode configurations under a social circuit dependence assumption. The three-path (a) captures reach and connectivity in the network. Stars on either of the two modes, (b) and (e), are Markov statistics that shape the variance of the two-degree distributions. Four-cycles on four nodes are isomorphic (c and f) but multiple four-cycles (d and e) guide the extent to which ones of one type tend to be indirectly connected through k nodes of the other type

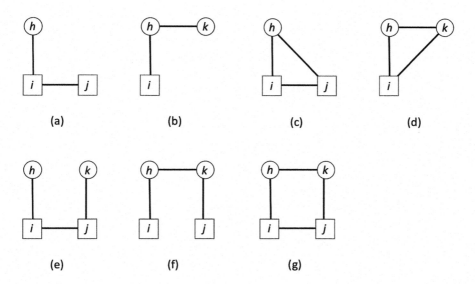

Figure 33.9 Multilevel network configurations

Node Attributes

The p^*-framework (the precursor to ERGM) was designed to analyse networks as logistic regression, specifically with attributes used to model homophily (Wasserman & Pattison, 1996; Moody, 2001). Attributes can, however, also be motivated from first principles.

The homogeneity constraint that sets $\theta_A = \theta_{A'}$ for all A and A' that are isomorphic, greatly reduces the number of parameters to be estimated. We can, however, impose other homogeneity constraints to reflect other factors. For example, assume that we have a categorical attribute vector $Y = (Y_i)$, then we could set $\theta_A = \theta_{A'}$ for all A and A' that are isomorphic and for which the automorphism $\sigma: V \to V$ is such that $Y_i = r$ implies that $Y_{\sigma(i)} = r$. This would mean that we, for example, have one edge parameter for each of the $r^2/2$ possible combinations of (Y_i, Y_j). For stars and triangles, we would similarly differentiate between different-coloured configurations. The number of different types of configurations would be large and for any observed network, many configurations would not be observed (and have zero statistics; see section on degeneracy and model fitting).

Robins et al. (2001) extended the dependence graph Q on X to also include Y in a so-called chain graph, where Y are parent variables of the child variables X, and where there is a directed tie from a parent Y_i to a child variable X_{kh}, if the latter is conditionally dependent on the former given everything else (Figure 33.11). Applying the Markov dependence assumption, there is an arc from Y_i to X_{kh} if and only if the intersection $\{i\} \cap \{k, h\}$ is non-empty. It can be shown that the model can be written

$$\Pr(X = x) = c^{-1} \exp\left\{\sum_{A \subseteq V \times \mathcal{N}} \lambda_A(x_A, y_A)\right\},$$

where $\lambda_A(x_A, y_A)$ is non-zero if and only if A is a clique in the moral graph of the chain graph. These non-zero interactions have two principal forms, statistics that are only functions of tie-variables $\lambda_A(x_A) = \theta_A z_A(x) = \theta_A \prod_{ij \in A} x_{ij}$, and interactions $\lambda_A(x_A, y_A)$ that involve both tie-variables and attribute variables.

For binary attributes, $\lambda_A(x_A, y_A)$ can be written $\theta_A \prod_{kh \in A} x_{kh} \prod_{j \in A} y_j$, which is an interaction of tie-variables and nodal outcomes of relevant nodes. These interactions can be depicted as partially coloured configurations (Figure 33.10). The interaction term

$$z_M(x, y) = \sum_{i,j} x_{ij} y_i = \sum_{i<j} x_{ij}(y_i + y_j) \quad (4)$$

is a count the number of edges that are incident to nodes i with $y_i = 1$ (Figure 33.10 (i.a)). This interaction is a lower-order term for the homophily statistic

$$z_H(x, y) = \sum_{i<j} x_{ij} y_i y_j, \quad (5)$$

a statistic that be represented as counts the configuration in Figure 33.10 (i.b). With a parameter θ_L for $L(x)$, θ_M for (4) and θ_H for the homophily

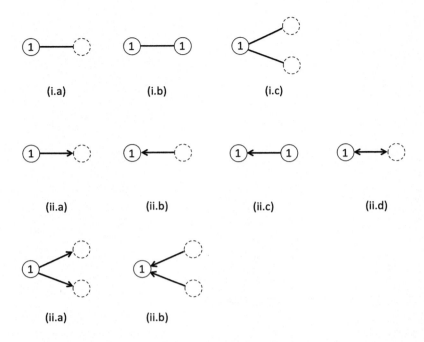

Figure 33.10 Examples of configurations with binary nodal outcomes for undirected (i.a through i.c) and directed networks (ii.a through ii.d, and iii.a through iii.b). A node labelled 1, indicates that y_i is part of the interaction and empty nodes mean that the corresponding variable y_i is not part of the interaction

Table 33.1 Conditional log odds for a tie *ij* in a social selection model with binary attributes Y

		y_j 0	y_j 1
y_j	0	θ_L	$\theta_L + \theta_M$
	1	$\theta_L + \theta_M$	$\theta_L + 2\theta_M + \theta_H$

statistic (5), the contribution of a tie $x_{ij} = 1$ to the linear predictor is given in Table 33.1.

The three parameters θ_L, θ_M and θ_H, thus completely determine the conditional log odds for the three types of dyads. There is a large number of higher-order interactions of tie-variables and attributes such as stars of order two (Figure 33.10 (i.c)) and higher relating to the differences in the variance of the degree distributions of nodes.

Heuristically, it may seem as if higher-order interactions of the types in Figure 33.11 are meaningful. Inspecting the relevant *moral graphs*, we do, however, see that these statistics do *not* follow from the Markov dependence assumption.[12]

For directed networks, the chain graph prescribes dyadic interactions, such as those in Figure 33.10 (ii.a-ii.d), as well as a number of different stars (e.g., Figure 33.11 (iii.a, b); see Lusher et al., 2013, Chapter 8).

For continuous nodal variables, the cliques of the moral graph of the chain graph remain the same as for the dichotomous variables. The specific form of the interactions $\lambda_A(x_A, y_A)$ are, however, not immediately obvious (cp the case of valued ties) but they have generally been taken to be of the form $\lambda_A(x_A, y_A) = \theta_A \prod_{kh \in A} x_{kh} \prod_{i \in A} y_i$. This functional form makes interpretation of sender $\sum_{i,j} x_{ij} y_i$ and receiver $\sum_{i,j} x_{ij} y_i$ statistics straightforward, but it can also be argued that the absolute difference statistic $\sum_{i,j} x_{ij} |y_i - y_j|$ may be preferable to the product $\sum_{i,j} x_{ij} y_i y_j$ for capturing homoplily (Robins et al., 2001).

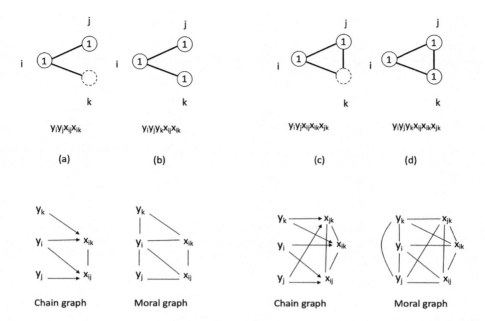

Figure 33.11 Non-Markov statistics for binary attributes and undirected networks. Two-coloured stars with their statistics (a) and (b), and two-coloured triangles with their statistics (c) and (d). Bottom row provides the chain and moral graphs on five variables and six variables, respectively

The framework of Robins et al. (2001) does not apply straightforwardly to dyadic covariates w_{ij}. It is, however, natural to include as dyadic covariates, covariate network and spatial embedding (Daraganova et al., 2012; Sohn et al., 2020; see also Hipp, this volume).

Unobserved Heterogeneity

The homogeneity constraints mean that we assume that the same processes guide tie-formation in all parts of a network but it is plausible that there may be heterogeneity. The first, dyad-independent ERGM of Holland and Leinhardt (1981) assumed that you would directly estimate node-specific activity and popularity, essentially including a dummy variable for each node with the associate parameters α_i for the sender effect and β_i for the receiver effect. The target of inference would then be to estimate α_i and β_i for each node $i \in V$. Wang and Wong (1987) made this model more parsimonious by assuming that α_i and β_i were in fact unobserved variables with a common distribution, the parameters of which were the target of inference. The approach of Wang and Wong (1987) is straightforward to extend to models that are not dyad-independent (as in, e.g., Timishen et al., 2016).

One of the most compelling treatments of structure in networks was presented in White et al. (1976). They suggested that the position of an individual in a network resolved the contradictory perspectives of the individual level and the collective level (Doreian et al., this volume; Browne et al., this volume). If we let position membership be given by an unobserved categorical variable vector $Y = (Y_i)$, we may estimate a blockmodel jointly with ERGM dependencies (Koskinen, 2009). Given any realisation of the positions, $y = (y_i)$, the blockstructure subject to Markov and social circuit dependence, is given by an ERGM with main effects $\theta_r \sum_{i,j} x_{ij} 1\{y_i = r\}$ for each position $r = \{0, \ldots, R-1\}$, and the mixing parameters $\theta_{r,s} \sum_{i,j} x_{ij} 1\{y_i = r, y_j = s\}$ (Koskinen, 2009). Schweinberger and Handcock (2015) proposed a model for the network conditional on y, where the network $X(V_r)$ induced by the nodeset $V_r = \{i \in V: y_i = r\}$ is assumed to follow an ERGM, independently of $X(V_s)$, for all V_s, $s \neq r$. Ties between nodes in different positions can then be assumed to follow a dyad-independent Bernoulli distribution.

If nodes are partitioned into *a priori* sets V_r, and ties are not allowed between nodes in different sets, we can model the networks as (conditionally) independent observations, or parallel networks, on the same ERGM, possibly with some differences in parameters. If parameters are assumed to be identical across networks, conceptually, the ERGM is a model for a blocked adjacency matrix where ties between blocks are constrained to be zero (Koskinen & Lomi, 2013; Stewart, et al., 2019). This could, for example, be the case where the networks are small, such as network structures within small teams (Yon et al., 2021; Agneessens et al., 2022). Another example would be ego-networks where the ego has been removed. In analogy to random effects in multilevel models, the parameters for each network can also be assumed to belong to some common distribution (Koskinen et al., 2015; Slaughter & Koehly, 2016).

Panel Network Data and Longitudinal ERGMs

A particular type of parallel network is panel network data, where a network is observed at discrete points in time (Snijders & Steglich, this volume). Robins & Pattison (2001) suggested that a longitudinal ERGM could be construed by letting the statistics for a network at time t depend on the network at time $t-1$. This was further elaborated by Hanneke et al. (2010), who also proposed that contemporaneous dependencies, like closure, could be construed as lagged effects. These approaches, which could be termed 'network regression', as they regress one network on another (Block et al., 2022a) illustrate the problem with trying to model a network in discrete time. Consider, for example, reciprocity defined through terms $x_{ij}^t x_{ji}^{t-1}$ – that is, a tie is said to be reciprocated if there is a tie at $t-1$ that is reciprocated at time t. This seems a perfectly reasonable way of modelling whether a tie in one direction later leads to a tie in the other direction, but the statistic does in fact not care if the tie ji exists any more. Consequently, you might have a network with no reciprocity but a positive effect for the lagged statistic. Similarly, you can have a network with a high degree of reciprocity but a negative statistic for the lagged statistic. This problem only gets worse for higher-order statistics, like triadic closure.[13]

Desmarais and Cranmer (2012) proposed to alleviate the issue with simultaneity by defining most statistics as non-lagged, for example, using the regular reciprocity terms $x_{ij}^t x_{ji}^t$, but including a *stability term* $\mathbf{1}\{x_{ij}^t = x_{ij}^{t-1}\}$ (originally proposed by Hanneke et al., 2010). As noted in Block et al. (2018), this type of model is a regular ERGM with a covariate network and a multiplex entrainment effect (Figure 33.6(a)). Block et al. (2018) furthermore pointed out that this is not a model that can be interpreted as a longitudinal process as the specification simultaneously assume that the ERGM updating process has reached equilibrium and that the only things that remain stable are the previous network ties – the network does not remember anything about the structure at previous times but each original tie for some reason has a privileged status.

Krivitsky and Handcock (2014) jettisoned the stability term and instead partitioned data into the set $\mathcal{N}_{01}^t = \{ij \in \mathcal{N} : x_{ij}^{t-1} = 0, x_{ij}^t = 1\}$ of tie-variables where a tie has been added and the set $\mathcal{N}_{10}^t = \{ij \in \mathcal{N} : x_{ij}^{t-1} = 1, x_{ij}^t = 0\}$ of tie-variables where a tie has removed. Making the reasonable assumption that different processes may account for the removal and addition of ties, they propose to model ties in $\mathcal{N}_{10}^t$ and $\mathcal{N}_{01}^t$ using different sets of parameters θ^- and θ^+, respectively. They further assume that

$$\Pr\{(X_{ij})_{ij \in \mathcal{N}_{10}^t} = (x_{ij}) ij \in \mathcal{N}_{10}^t | X^{t-1} = x^{t-1}\},$$

and

$$\Pr\{(X_{ij})_{ij \in \mathcal{N}_{01}^t} = (x_{ij}) ij \in \mathcal{N}_{01}^t | X^{t-1} = x^{t-1}\},$$

are independent. This latter property is called *separable*. This separable temporal ERGM thus allows for some limited dependence among outcomes at time t among ties in $\mathcal{N}_{10}^t$ and ties in $\mathcal{N}_{01}^t$, but independence across these sets. Stable ties and null-ties are not modelled and as such, the model focuses on change.

Non-independent observations are inherently difficult to model in discrete time as a change in one observation from one timepoint to the next has different interpretations depending on changes in other observations (Block et al., 2019). The paradox stems from one of the main features of ERGMs, namely that the network is simultaneously a collection of interdependent tie-variables and *one* observation on one network.

Consider modelling a sequence of $\mathcal{N}_{10} = |\mathcal{N}_{10}^t|$ deletions and $\mathcal{N}_{01} = |\mathcal{N}_{01}^t|$ additions of ties as updates according to the conditional probabilities of an ERGM.[14] Without information about the order of these changes, the model would have to treat this order as an unobserved variable. Since the changes are unobserved this also means that some changes may have been reversed – for example, a tie that was created and then deleted. To model this requires that you embed the sequence of changes in continuous time (Snijders & Steglich, this volume). The longitudinal ERGM (Snijders & Koskinen, 2013; Koskinen & Lomi, 2013) assumes that in a given interval $\Delta = (s,t]$, updates of the network are guided by a Poisson process, such that the interarrival time is exponentially distributed, and when an update is done at time $u \in \Delta$ to a tie $X_{ij}(u)$, the value x_{ij} is drawn from the conditional distribution of the ERGM

$$\Pr\left\{X_{ij}(u) = x_{ij} \middle| X_{-ij}(u) = x_{-ij}(u)\right\}.$$

This is a model where the longitudinal process is explicit.[15] In the limit, the longitudinal ERGM loses the memory of the previous timepoint and the model reduces to a cross-sectional ERGM. The model can be estimated jointly for the initial state $X(t_0) = x(t_0)$ and the subsequent timepoints (Koskinen et al., 2015).

ESTIMATION

Estimating the parameters of the ERGM is a challenging task because it is impossible to evaluate the likelihood directly (other than for trivial models or tiny networks).[16] However, we can simulate graphs to explore how probable networks are and to calculate expectations for any given set of parameter values. Sampling from the model can be done using the Metropolis algorithm,[17] which proposes to toggle randomly chosen tie-variables (Corander et al., 1998), or by toggling tie-variables chosen with different weights, as in the tie–no-tie algorithm (Morris et al., 2008), or bigger proposals (Snijders, 2002).

Maximum Likelihood

For a model with statistics $z(X)$ and parameters θ, the maximum likelihood estimate of θ, given data x_{obs}, is the value $\hat{\theta}_{ML}$ that satisfies the likelihood equation[18]

$$E_{\hat{\theta}_{ML}}\{z(X)\} = z(x_{\text{obs}}). \quad (6)$$

In other words, under $\hat{\theta}_{ML}$, networks have the same statistics as our observed statistics *on average*. An iterative scheme for solving the likelihood equation using simulated graphs was first proposed by Dahmström and Dahmström (1993) and later elaborated by Corander et al. (1998). The newer algorithms of Snijders (2002) and Handcock (2003) (see also Hunter & Handcock, 2006) are based on the same principle. Standard errors are obtained from the inverse Fisher information matrix (the square roots of the diagonal elements) and are straightforward to obtain computationally. For independent data their use can be motivated by the large n assymptotics, but large n assymptotics are clearly not relevant for ERGM (Schweinberger et al., 2020). Some simulation studies have, however, demonstrated that these nominal standard errors work as reasonable approximations for testing statistical significance (van Duijn et al., 2009).

Bayesian Inference

In a Bayesian inference framework, the target of inference is to obtain the posterior distribution of parameters, given the observed network. By Bayes theorem, this posterior is given by

$$\pi(\theta | X = x) = \frac{\Pr(X = x | \theta)\pi(\theta)}{\int \Pr(X = x | \theta)\pi(\theta)d\theta}, \quad (7)$$

where $\pi(\theta)$ is the prior distribution for the parameter θ. The posterior distribution completely determines all the uncertainty about θ, after data have been observed, and this is often summarised with the expected values, standard deviations and credibility intervals for the parameters. The expression (7), involves two normalising constants, (2) as well as the denominator in (7), neither of which we can evaluate. Draws from the posterior distribution can still be made using Markov chain Monte Carlo (MCMC), by either approximating (7) (Koskinen, 2004), or introducing auxiliary variables with the same support as X (Koskinen, 2008; Caimo & Friel, 2011). A benefit of the Bayesian approach is that measures of uncertainty are well defined.[19] Setting the prior is, however, hard as it is difficult to state *a priori* what kind of data a set of parameters will produce.

Pseudo-likelihood

There are numerous approximate inference procedures, the most well-known of which is the maximum pseudo-likelihood estimate (MPLE) (Strauss & Ikelda, 1990; Frank & Strauss, 1986; Frank, 1991). Besag (1974) suggested that instead of maximising the likelihood, if dependencies between variables are weak, then maximising the pseudo-likelihood

$$\prod\nolimits_{ij} \Pr\nolimits_{\theta}\left(X_{ij} = x_{ij} \middle| X_{-ij} = x_{-ij}\right),$$

would be a viable alternative. If variables are independent – that is, $\Pr_\theta \left(X_{ij} = x_{ij} \middle| X_{-ij} = x_{-ij} \right) = \Pr_\theta \left(X_{ij} = x_{ij} \right)$ – then the MPLE is the MLE. This is not the case if variables are interdependent, and you will be using data multiple times, both as an outcome to be modelled and as a predictor when conditioning. For most network models, the conditional probability $\Pr_\theta(X_{ij} = x_{ij}| X_{-ij} = x_{-ij})$ differ substantially from the unconditional probability – this is the whole premise of the dependence assumptions we make. Consequently, there is no reason to assume that the MPLE would be good or even usable. The problem is that you never know quite how bad the MPLE is unless you compare it to the actual MLE, but by simulating under these MPLE you will see just how poorly it does. The poor properties of the MPLE for ERGMs have also been demonstrated time and time again (Corander et al., 1998; Snijders, 2002; Corander et al., 2002; Besag, 2001; van Duijn et al., 2009; Lubbers & Snijders, 2007). In fact, any approximation for solving (6) or drawing from (7), needs to be checked using simulation from the model.

Constrained Estimation

Estimating a restricted ERGM is sometimes helpful. For example, density can be treated as a nuisance parameter and the model is then constrained to graphs with a certain number of ties (Corander et al., 1998). This may be useful in the case where models are unstable (see section on degeneracy and model fitting) and the main target of inference is to describe dependencies conditional on the density of the graph – that is, how the available ties are distributed among dyads. For the instance where the degree distribution is very skewed, it may be helpful to 'fix' the degree distribution or the degrees of nodes, and estimate an ERGM conditionally on those constraints. Estimation under constraints amount to restricting the support of the model in the simulation part of the estimation algorithm. If the space of graphs is restricted to a subset $\mathcal{X}_c \subseteq \mathcal{X}$ of graphs, the inference will be conditional on that constraint – that is, that the model is now $\Pr_\theta(X = x | x \in \mathcal{X}_c)$ (Snijders & van Duijn, 2002). For example, we may have a network where ties between certain nodes are impossible or disallowed, in which case $\mathcal{X}_c$ is the space of graphs where such ties are null – structural zeros. This could for example be the collection of alter–alter ties for distinct egonets – ties only exist between alters of the same egos. Another example is when some ties may be present by design and do not make sense modelling. For example, there may be a node u that everyone in a network is forced to report to and while you may want to model the network conditionally on everyone having a tie to u, it does not make sense to explain everyone's tie to u in the same way as their ties to other, normal, actors. The restricted support $\mathcal{X}_c$ would then be all graphs where every node has a tie to u – structural ones. In general, it may be permissible to treat as fixed ties to actors u whenever it is clear that the model that applies to their ties is different from the model for everyone else's ties (Koskinen et al., 2018).

Partially Observed Networks and Large Networks

Dealing with missing data is a difficult problem in general but even more so for social networks (Krause & Huisman, this volume). For ERGMs, let $\mathcal{X}_{obs} \subseteq \mathcal{X}$ define the set of graphs that are constrained to have the same values for the observed tie-variables. If data are missing at random (Krause & Huisman, this volume), then the likelihood is the so-called face likelihood

$$\Pr\left(X_{obs} = x_{obs} | \theta \right) = \sum_{y \in \mathcal{X}_{obs}} \Pr\left(X = y | \theta \right),$$

and inference can be based on the model marginalised with respect to what we have not observed (Handcock & Gile, 2010; Koskinen et al., 2010). This principle also applies to some forms of sampled network data, such as snowball sampled networks. In order for this to apply, and non-sampled tie-variables to be treated as missing data, we need to know the entire population of nodes as well as any relevant nodal and dyadic covariates. Furthermore, even if the population is fully known, likelihood-based inference schemes (Handcock & Gile, 2010; Koskinen et al., 2010) rely critically on simulation of the entire network. If the partially observed population graph is very big, estimating ERGMs for a sample is going to be computationally very costly, if not impossible.

It is tempting to think that inference for an observed network in some sense should generalise to a larger population (for example, Shalizi & Rinaldo, 2013). Apart from the fact that it is well known that if a graph follows an ERGM, then its subgraphs will not follow an ERGM (Snijders, 2010), we do not think that, say, the target of analysing the network in a classroom is in some way to generalise to a network in a classroom with an infinite number of students. Schweinberger et al. (2020) discuss and clarify issues of how and when inference for networks generalise and not (in particular projectivity of ERGMs).

A notable exception to the rule that you cannot draw inference to some unspecified population graph from a sample network is the conditional estimation for snowball sampling proposed by Pattison et al. (2013). They draw on Besag's (1974) coding scheme to define separator sets such that sets of tie-variables are conditionally independent conditionally on these separator sets. Pattison et al. (2013) proved that, under some dependence assumptions, the tie-variables within and between waves S_t and S_{t+1} of a snowball sample are separated from the tie-variables of nodes in waves S_{t+s}, for $s > 1$, by the tie-variables between S_{t+1} and S_{t+2}. The implication is that the ERGM for waves $S_0, ..., S_t$ conditionally on wave S_{t+1}, does not depend on the part of the population graph that is not sampled. Consequently, estimation does not require any knowledge of the population nodes or even the population size.

In general, large networks, in addition to presenting considerable computational challenges, may not necessarily be amenable to ERGMs. The fundamental assumption of most probabilistic network models is that each tie-variable has some probability of being one. From the perspective of one node, you can couch this as there being a chance that there is a tie to each other node in the network. While the probabilities of these ties do not have to be independent (indeed, for ERGMs we assume interdependence) given (the marginal) density, the number of ties of an actor may be bounded but *where* these ties appear is not clear. We can understand a model where an actor could have a tie to, say, 29 other actors – then we can understand why certain ties were realized and others not. In a model where an actor could have a tie to any of the other, say, 9,999 actors, however, it is hard to understand why *these ties* rather than *those ties* exist. For large networks you arguably require other processes to limit the risk-set – that is, the ties that an actor could have ties to. Examples of this could be the combination and intersections of different settings and foci or geography (Daraganova et al., 2012). These settings and contexts may not necessarily be observed, in which case it makes sense to handle this heterogeneity using latent classes as in Schweinberger and Handcock (2015).

Irrespective of the conceptual difficulties of ERGMs for large networks, it may be desirable to have estimation algorithms for estimating ERGMs that are not hampered by large-scale networks. Commonly used approximations include 'stepping' (Hummel et al., 2012) and contrastive divergence (Fellows, 2014). A seemingly related approximate estimation algorithm that does not require simulation of a large network is the algorithm of Byshkin et al. (2018). An alternative approach to approximating the likelihood is to try to break down the network into smaller parts. Stivala et al. (2016) took samples from a network and used the conditional estimation of Pattison et al. (2013) to obtain estimates. These, and other approximations, will give you point estimates and standard errors, but to determine how good these approximations are you require the actual MLEs – something that will involve simulating large networks from the model. A number of approximations for Bayesian estimation have also been proposed (e.g., Bouranis et al., 2017).

COMMON ISSUES

Degeneracy and Model Fitting

The social circuit dependence assumption and the alternating statistics alleviate some of the instabilities of the Markov model (reported above) but do not eliminate these (see Snijders et al., 2006, for illustrations). Schweinberger (2011) provides some precise conditions on the parameters of a social circuit model under which the model is stable.

The exact reason or cause of these instabilities is complex (Schweinberger, 2011) but people often talk about 'degenerate models'. The definition that Handcock (2003) provides for degeneracy identifies the type of networks for which the parameters cannot be estimated. We can consider the estimation equation Eq.(6), that states that the MLE is the value so that the expected (often simulated average) vector of statistics is the same as the observed statistics (degeneracy also affects Bayesian inference, see Koskinen et al., 2010). Now consider the case where a statistic $z_k(x_{\text{obs}})$, say, the number of triangles, is 0. For an average (or an expectation) to be zero, you need some values greater than 0 but also some values less than zero – that is, negative. Since the count of triangles cannot be negative, this means that we can never get an average of 0. The exception would be if all graphs had no triangles but we know that not to be true. The same reasoning applies if the statistic is as large as it possibly could be. There are numerous other examples and we refer the reader to Handcock's (2003) work for further details and results.

There are cases where the likelihood equation (Eq.6) may be satisfied for a set of parameters but where the estimated model places little to no probability on graphs in the neighbourhood of the observed networks. Examples of such instabilities are provided in Snijders et al. (2006). The challenges of estimating ERGMs has led some to believe that all ERGMs are degenerate. That this is not the case is expertly explained in Section 3.1 of Schweinberger et al. (2020).

What is a Good Model?

What counts as a good model? A good model must, first, be well specified in terms of dependencies and have statistics derived from meaningful hypotheses. In particular, insofar as possible, the principle of hierarchy should be satisfied lest your observed patterns are in fact artefacts explained by lower-order statistics. Second, a good model ought to fit data in the sense that the distribution of graphs under the estimated model replicates the observed data. Investigating the implied distribution is straightforward through sampling from the model but there are countless ways of comparing graphs. The fitted statistics are captured by design (Eq.6) but there are many other features of the network that are not explicitly modelled. You would expect a good model to capture the degree distribution (or distributions, for directed networks) and clustering but also global properties such as the geodesic distribution. A criterion is typically that observed features are not *extreme* in the goodness-of-fit (GOF) distribution. 'Extreme' can be interpreted in many ways and is typically used as a shorthand for low-probability events. If you simulate a million networks from your model and none of them have as high a global clustering coefficient as your observed network, then that would suggest that the observed network is extreme in the goodness-of-fit distribution for clustering. If, say, 2.5 per cent of networks have a clustering coefficient that is as great or greater than the observed network, then at least, while unlikely, the statistic is not impossibly large. To report how well the model replicates these features is now commonplace[20] but programs such as MPNet (Wang et al., 2014) also have a much more extensive suite of summaries that are generated by the goodness-of-fit procedure. If a model with few statistics manages to replicate all these features, then we can say that the model is sufficient for explaining the network structure. The question is how many, or which ones, of all the possible summaries of a network that we require a model to replicate.

If one model has a poor fit, with many extreme features, and another model has a good fit, then we may state that one model has a better fit than the other. If, however, both models have an adequate fit, is there a way of quantifying how big the difference is in fit? The improvement in fit in one model may come at the expense of a more complex model, with more statistics, in which case we would expect that fit to be better simply as a result of increased model complexity. If neither model has a good fit, then it does not make sense to measure which one does a less bad job.

Consider a vector $s(x) = (s_1(x), \ldots, s_k(x))^T$ of functions $s_k: \mathcal{X} \to \mathbb{R}$. These functions can be counts of subgraphs or any user-defined set of statistics.[21] Under a fitted model, let

$$\mu_k = E_\theta\left[s_k(X)\right],$$

be the expected count, and

$$\Sigma = E_\theta\left[s(X)s(X)^T\right] - \mu\mu^T,$$

be the variance covariance matrix. Wang et al. (2009) proposed as a single-digit measure of goodness-of-fit, the Mahalanobis distance

$$d_M = \sqrt{\left(s(x_{obs}) - \mu\right)^T \Sigma^{-1}\left(s(x_{obs}) - \mu\right)}.$$

An attractive feature of d_M is that it is not mode-dependent in the sense that the distance is defined for any distribution for networks. Furthermore, an omnibus test like d_M avoids the multiple testing issues that come with investigating the fit of individual statistics s_k. Interpreting d_M is, however, hard. If two models yield different values on d_M, does that mean that the model with a smaller value has a better fit?

The choice of statistics for d_M is arbitrary as there is no set of statistics that completely describes the graph. Shore and Lubin (2015) propose that the network spectrum completely describes the network. The spectrum of a network is the set of (ordered) eigenvalues of the graph Laplacian. The spectral goodness-of-fit that Shore and Lubin (2015) propose is then essentially equivalent to d_M, using the graph spectrum as the statistics. The graph spectrum, like many graph statistics, is invariant in the sense that isomorphic graphs have the same spectrum, but otherwise interpretation of the spectrum is unclear.

Most single-figure GOF measures for standard statistical models attempt to balance the fit of data with the complexity of the model and the number of observations. Formally, we could define the deviance as

$$D(\hat{\theta}, \hat{\pi}) = 2\left\{\log p(x|\hat{\pi}) - \ell(\hat{\theta}; x)\right\},$$

where

$$\ell(\theta; x) = \log \Pr(X = x|\theta),$$

is the log-likelihood, and $p(x|\hat{\pi})$ is the likelihood under the saturated model (which is unity for binary data). For standard models with independent observations, the distribution of the deviance would follow a chi-square distribution. For ERGAMs we have no such result to draw on. The Aikaike information criterion (AIC), which is related to the deviance, takes the form

$$AIC = 2p - 2\ell(\hat{\theta}; x),$$

where p is the number of parameters in the model. While the AIC asymptotically is the Kullack–Leibler divergence $D_{KL}(\hat{\theta}\|p)$ between the model defined by $\hat{\theta}$ and a true model p this has no interpretation in networks – it is not meaningful to analyse a classroom of size 30 and interpret fit in terms of a classroom of an infinite number of students. The penalty p has some appeal in that more complex models are penalised. A closely related measure is the Bayesian information criterion (BIC)

$$BIC = 2p\log(n) - 2\ell(\hat{\theta}; x),$$

which in addition to penalising the number of parameters also includes a penalty for the number of observations. BIC, similar to AIC, can be motivated with reference to asymptotic behaviour but we cannot determine how many observations we have in an ERGM. The deviance information criterion (DIC) instead uses the posterior distribution of the deviance to penalise complexity. While calculating the DIC is more computationally intense than the AIC and BIC, it has been shown to work for the related social influence model (Koskinen & Daraganova, 2022).

With a prior probability $\pi(M_k)$ for model M_k defined by the pmf $p_{M_k}(\theta)$, the posterior probability of the model given data is $p(M_k|x) \propto p(M_k|x) \pi(M_k)$, where $p(x|M_k) = \int p_{M_k}(x|\theta) \pi_{M_k}(\theta) d\theta$. Integrating out parameters can be interpreted as a consistent way of penalising model complexity. This makes it easy to compare the evidence for one model M_k against another M_h irrespective of the prior model probability using the so-called Bayes factor

$$BF_{k,h} = \frac{p(x|M_k)}{p(x|M_h)}.$$

The Bayes factor has great appeal in that it simply compares how likely data are under different model specifications with all the uncertainty about the actual parameter values discounted. Evaluating $p(M_k|x)$ is generally hard, and in the case of ERGMs even more so. A number of algorithms for computing this quantity, under different assumptions with varying computational efficiency have been proposed in the literature (Koskinen, 2004; Caimo & Friel, 2013; Friel, 2013; Everitt et al., 2017; Koskinen & Daraganova, 2022). Second, and more importantly, evaluating $p(M_k|x)$ is only possible with a proper prior distribution $\pi_{M_k}(\theta)$ for the parameters of the model. This prior distribution will have a great impact on the Bayes factor and it is very hard to determine *a priori* what effect it will have (Koskinen, 2004).

The answer to what makes a good model is probably not a quest for the 'best' model but, rather, what is a reasonable model. Generally, we strive towards parsimonious models but this does not mean that we only, say, include parameters that are 'significant'. Some effects need to be included even if we cannot determine if their parameters are zero or not. An effect may have to be included because of the principle of hierarchy – that is, it is a lower-order interaction of tie-variables for some higher-order interaction. An effect may also have to be included because we cannot estimate the other parameters otherwise – the effect may 'stabilise' the model. Robins and Lusher (2013) provide examples of structural models for ERGMs that work in most cases.

Interpretation of ERGMs

We have seen that, in the words of Bannister et al. (2014), ERGMs are hard. Still, the enormous amount of work that has gone into understanding and working with ERGMs, starting with the seminal papers by Snijders (2002) and Corander et al. (1998), have made this modelling framework the method of choice for analysing (cross-sectional) networks, to the point that Martin (2020) finds ERGMs too pervasive. This chapter has tried to illustrate that even if ERGMs nowadays do not seem that hard, understanding them in terms of their underlying dependence assumptions still should not be compromised by routine application of ERGMs. We conclude this chapter by briefly summarising some of the implications that the underlying dependence assumptions have for routine application of ERGMs.

What are We Drawing Inference To?

Standard statistical models often rely on sampling error for the definition of uncertainty. Uncertainty, random terms, etc., are interpreted to stem from the fact that we have observed a sample and not the entire population. This does not make sense for ERGMs as a graph is not a sample and, as discussed earlier, we do not aim to draw inference to a population network (Schweinberger et al., 2020). ERGMs inherently draw inference to an assumed, underlying process. We might even say that inference for ERGMs is *model-based* as opposed to sampling-based.

For graphs, defining the number of observations is not straightforward. For a Bernoulli graph, where the tie-variables are independent we have $n(n-1)/2$ independent observations on a Bernoulli variable. For other dependence assumptions our $n(n-1)/2$ observations are no longer independent. Since the ERGM aims to model the graph, we may even say that we have just one observation on a network. Elsewhere in applied statistics, the importance of the number of observations relates to statistical power, and sample size is the only factor that power is a function of *and* that is also under the control of the researcher. For models with dependent data, such as multilevel models, the relationship between power and sample size is not as straightforward. For networks this relationship is not only intractable but also irrelevant as we cannot choose to increase the size of a network.[22] Nevertheless, asking what the effective sample size is, in the context of ERGMs, may still be of interest in its own right and Kolaczyk and Krivitsky (2015) investigated this in some technical detail for dyad-independent models.

Interpretation of Parameters

How do you interpret the parameter estimates in an ERGM other than whether they are negative, zero, or positive? For a dyad-independent model the ERGM is equivalent to logistic regression, but it is notoriously difficult to interpret the magnitude of the parameters even for logistic regression. To rely on analogies with linear models for interpretation, is increasingly being questioned (see, e.g., Mood, 2010). To discuss this issue, we note first that the parameters θ_A in the canonical form (1) of the model are called the *natural parameters*. For a homogeneous Bernoulli graph the marginal probability of a tie

$$p_{ij} = p = \frac{e^\theta}{1+e^\theta}, \quad (8)$$

is clearly an increasing function of the natural parameter θ but it is not linear. For a model with an exogenous covariate a_{ij} for each dyad, we can similarly write the marginal tie-probability for the in-homogeneous Bernoulli graph as

$$p_{ij} = \frac{e^{\theta_1+\theta_2 a_{ij}}}{1+e^{\theta_1+\theta_2 a_{ij}}}, \quad (9)$$

where, again, for fixed $\theta_2 > 0$ the probability of a tie is an increasing non-linear function of a_{ij}. With more covariates, the effect of one covariate on the probability differs depending on the values of the other covariates.

We can gain some understanding about the model through distinguishing the natural parameters in the canonical parametrisation from the alternative *mean-value parametrisation*, where we, instead of the natural parameters, specify the model in terms of the statistics (Handcock, 2003)

$$\mu(\theta) = E_\theta[s(X)].$$

For the homogeneous Bernoulli graph, the mean-value parameter is simply the number of ties of the graph and the function mapping the natural parameters to the mean-value parameters is $n(n-1)p/2$ (for undirected graphs), where p is given by (8). For (9), the mean-value parameter is $\mu = (\mu_1, \mu_2)^T$, where $\mu_1 = \sum_{i<j} p_{ij}$, and $\mu_2 = \sum_{i<j} a_{ij} p_{ij}$. From the relationship between the natural and the mean-value parameters, we see that the natural parameters completely determine the mean-value parameters (provided the model is not 'degenerate'; Handcock, 2003). Thus, in terms of the magnitude of parameters, we can say that a larger parameter will increase the expected value of the associated expected statistic but we cannot easily say by how much.

The permutation invariance of ERGM is even more obvious from the mean-value parametrisation – the ERGM does not care about where we put a tie in a graph, it only 'cares' about the statistics. As an example, for a binary, monadic covariate $y = (y_i)$, consider a model $p_\theta^M(x \mid y)$ with $L(x)$, covariate effects (3) and (4), and triangles, $T(x)$. According to this model, the two graphs, X and X^*, depicted in Figure 33.12, have the same probability.

While in logistic regression you cannot calculate the change in probability 'everything else equal', it is straightforward to calculate the log odds. For a general ERGM, the log odds for a given dyad will differ depending on what the rest of the network looks like. First, denote by $\Delta_{ij}^+ x$ the matrix x with element x_{ij} set to 1 and denote by $\Delta_{ij}^- x$ the matrix x with element x_{ij} set to 0. The conditional log odds for each variable can be written

$$\log\left[\frac{\Pr(X_{ij}=1 \mid X_{-ij}=x_{-ij})}{\Pr(X_{ij}=0 \mid X_{-ij}=x_{-ij})}\right]$$
$$= \sum_{r=1,\ldots,p} \theta_r \left[s_r(\Delta_{ij}^+ x) - s_r(\Delta_{ij}^- x)\right] = \theta^T \delta^{ij}(x)$$

where $\theta = (\theta_r)$ is the $\theta \times 1$ vector of parameters, and the vector $\delta^{ij}(x) = \left(s_r(\Delta_{ij}^+ x) - s_r(\Delta_{ij}^- x)\right)$ is

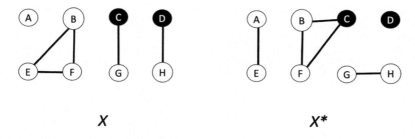

Figure 33.12 Two networks, *X* and *X**, each with eight nodes, five edges, one triangle, eight ties for white nodes and three white-white ties

called the change statistic. From this we see that we can write

$$\Pr(X_{ij} = 1 \mid X_{-ij} = x_{-ij}) = \frac{1}{1+e^{-\theta^T \delta^{ij}(x)}}, \quad (10)$$

something that has been used to sample from the model and but also to understand ERGMs from a game-theoretic perspective (Mele, 2017).

To illustrate the conditioning, consider the conditional probability of the tie *EF*, and the conditional probability of the tie *EA*, given that everything else is as for *X* in Figure 33.12. For model $p_\theta^M(x \mid y)$ with $\theta_T > 0$, the conditional probability of the former will be much higher than for the latter. Unconditionally, however, the ties have the same probability. The conditional log odds for tie-variables are not very useful for interpreting the magnitude of the parameters as we need to know the entire network in order to calculate them. If we calculate conditional log odds for all dyads by conditioning on the rest of the observed network, how would we interpret this? The interpretation would be that this would be the log odds (also expressed in terms of a conditional probability) for the dyad if we observed a network and it looked exactly like our observation. In addition, we would get different conditional log odds for any dyads that did not have identical neighbourhoods and covariates.

It would seem intuitive to somehow try to marginalise over the rest of the network. We can think of this in terms of simulating many networks from the model and calculating the conditional probabilities from the model. Doing this in the correct way we end up with the marginal probabilities $\Pr(X_{ij} = 1)$. What are these and do they help us interpret the parameters?

Residuals and Tie-prediction

For a homogeneous ERGM – that is, an ERGM that does not have any covariates – the marginal tie-probability for each dyad is the expected density. This follows from the permutation invariance of ERGMs. For networks with attribute effects invariance is more complicated. Let $p_\gamma^B(x \mid y)$ be model $p_\theta^M(x \mid y)$ with the triangle parameter set to 0, and the rest set to γ. The former model is thus an in-homogeneous Bernoulli model. Provided that they exist, you can choose the natural parameters γ so that $\mu_{1:3}(\gamma) = \mu_{1:3}(\theta)$. This means that the predicted tie-probabilities are the same for each model. Moreover, if $\hat{\gamma}_{ML}$ are the MLEs from a logistic regression and $\hat{\theta}_{ML}$ are the MLEs obtained from solving (6), then $\mu_{1:3}(\hat{\gamma}_{ML}) = \mu_{1:3}(\hat{\theta}_{ML})$. Ergo, adding structure to the dyad-independent model does not improve, or even change, link-predictions. The estimates for the (first three) mean-value parameters will, of course, be the same for both the logistic regression case and the ERGM. If you condition on density, the natural parameters may even be the same.

A further implication of this property is that residuals, defined as (some function of) the observed value minus the predicted (marginal) tie-probability, are not informative of the fit of the model (Koskinen et al., 2018). These properties also illustrate what it means that the statistics are 'independent' effects. Consider again the graphs in Figure 33.12 and assume that γ_H, θ_H, and θ_T are all positive. The tie *EF* in *X* may be much more likely, given the rest, than *EA* in *X**, under $p_\theta^M(x \mid y)$. The latter has a positive change statistic for both homophily and triangles, whereas the former only contributes positively to the homophily term. Recall, however, that *X* and *X** as a whole are equally likely under $p_\theta^M(x \mid y)$, meaning that the fact that *X* has a homphilous triangle and *X** does not, does not make the graph *X* more likely. The effects are independent in the sense that the ERGM does not care where, say, homophilous ties appear in the graph, nor where triangles appear. Only the total number of homophilous ties and triangles matters. Two dyads *ij* and *kh* that have identical combinations on the covariates – that is,

$y_i = y_k$ and $y_j = y_h$ will have the same (unconditional or marginal) predicted tie-probability, not only under $p_{\hat{\theta}_{ML}}^{\tilde{B}}(x \mid y)$ but also under $p_{\hat{\theta}_{ML}}^{M}(x \mid y)$. If you are only interested in covariate effects, the covariate effects will not change by including structural effects, in the sense that the mean-value parameters for the covariate effects will be the same.

SUMMARY

While there might not be an answer to the question 'ERGMs – good or bad?', this chapter has aimed to demonstrate that what makes ERGMs hard is also what makes them useful and, while all ERGMs are wrong, some ERGMs are indeed useful. ERGMs have proved the only family of (cross-sectional) models that are able to replicate the complexity of observed networks but that does not mean that an ERGM is suitable to every network.

Notes

1. Some sections of the chapter may be suitable as a first introduction to ERGMs, such as Markov graphs, interpretation of Markov model, social circuit dependence, node attributes and the first part of estimation. Other sections, for example dependence hierarchy and unobserved heterogeneity, assume some familiarity or experience with ERGMs. It is instructive to consider different premises of ERGMs by reference to applied studies. Here, rather than selecting particular such studies, we refer the reader to the review of applications by Ghafouri and Khasteh (2020).
2. In the sequel we will write ij as a notational shorthand for the unordered pair $\{i,j\}$ or ordered pair (i,j).
3. Also referred to as an Erdös Rényi graph.
4. The general form of Eq.(1) has been used to model many objects with dependence on a neighbourhood structure (e.g., Kindermann & Snell, 1980), but Frank and Strauss (1986) first derived dependence for graphs.
5. Since interactions are nested this is not always possible.
6. See section on unobserved heterogeneity.
7. The mathematical mechanism is typically attributed to Yule (1925) but Moreno and Jennings (1938) attributed it to Karl Marx's theory of surplus value.
8. Some stability results are provided by Schweinberger (2011).
9. These are the two statistics of the p_1 model (Holland & Leinhardt, 1981).
10. Alternating forms are also implemented in MPNet (Wang et al., 2014).
11. Cp network infrastructure (Koskinen & Lomi, 2013).
12. To accommodate more involved interactions, such as those in Figure 33.11, Robins et al. (2001) proposed, without a detailed proof, that the partial dependence assumptions of Pattison and Robins (2002) may be applied (see Koskinen & Daraganova, 2022, for a detailed derivation for social influence).
13. For an open triad ij, ik at $t - 1$, and a new tie jk at time t, what is the interpretation if ij and ik both have disappeared?
14. Block et al. (2019) investigates dependence over time with reference to how stochastic actor-oriented models and ERGMs consider dependence through time.
15. For undirected network this longitudinal ERGM can be estimated in RSiena (Ripley et al., 2022) using modelType = 6.
16. The normalising constant in Eq. (1) is a sum over *all* possible graphs.
17. The Gibbs sampler is far too inefficient (Snijders, 2002).
18. This is straightforward to obtain through maximising the log-likelihood.
19. If π is a proper, the posterior is proper.
20. Using the GOF function in statnet (Handcock et al., 2018) is, for example, common practice.
21. For coarse statistics s_k, transformations may be needed.
22. For longitudinal data you can increase the number of sampled waves (Stadtfeld et al., 2018).

REFERENCES

Agneessens, F., & Roose, H. (2008). Local structural properties and attribute characteristics in 2-mode networks: p* models to map choices of theater events. *Journal of Mathematical Sociology*, *32*(3), 204–237.

Agneessens, F., Trincado-Munoz, F.J., & Koskinen, J. (2022). Network formation in organizational settings: exploring the importance of local social processes and team-level contextual variables in small groups using Bayesian hierarchical ERGMs. *Social Networks*, August.

Bannister, M.J., Devanny, W.E., & Eppstein, D. (2014). ERGMs are hard. arXiv preprint arXiv:1412.1787.

Besag, J. (1974) Spatial interaction and the statistical analysis of lattice systems. *Journal of the Royal Statistical Society, Series B*, *36*, 192–225.

Besag, J. (2001). Markov chain Monte Carlo for statistical inference. Center for Statistics and the Social Sciences, 9, 24-25.

Block, P., Hollway, J., Stadtfeld, C., Koskinen, J., & Snijders, T. (2022a). Circular specifications and 'predicting' with information from the future: errors in the empirical SAOM–TERGM comparison of Leifeld & Cranmer. *Network Science*, 1–12.

Block, P., Koskinen, J., Hollway, J., Steglich, C., & Stadtfeld, C. (2018). Change we can believe in: Comparing longitudinal network models on consistency, interpretability and predictive power. *Social Networks*, *52*, 180–191.

Block, P., Stadtfeld, C., & Robins, G. (2022b). A statistical model for the analysis of mobility tables as weighted networks with an application to faculty hiring networks. *Social Networks*, *68*, 264–278.

Block, P., Stadtfeld, C., & Snijders, T. A. (2019). Forms of dependence: comparing SAOMs and ERGMs from basic principles. *Sociological Methods and Research*, *48*(1), 202–239.

Bouranis, L., Friel, N., & Maire, F. (2017). Efficient Bayesian inference for exponential random graph models by correcting the pseudo-posterior distribution. *Social Networks*, *50*, 98–108.

Byshkin, M., Stivala, A., Mira, A., Robins, G., & Lomi, A. (2018). Fast maximum likelihood estimation via equilibrium expectation for large network data. *Scientific Reports*, *8*(1), 1–11.

Caimo, A., & Friel, N., (2011). Bayesian inference for exponential random graph models. *Social Networks*, *33*, 41–55.

Caimo, A., & Friel, N. (2013). Bayesian model selection for exponential random graph models. *Social Networks*, *35*(1), 11–24.

Chatterjee, S., Diaconis, P., & Sly, A. (2011). Random graphs with a given degree sequence. *Annals of Applied Probability*, *21*(4), 1400–1435.

Corander, J., Dahmström, K., & Dahmström, P. (1998). Maximum likelihood estimation for Markov graphs. Research report RR1998:8. Department of Statistics, Stockholm University.

Corander, J., Dahmström, K., Dahmström, P., 2002. Maximum likelihood estima- tion for exponential random graph model. In: Hagberg, J. (Ed.), Contributions to Social Network Analysis, Information Theory and Other Topics in Statistics; A Festschrift in Honour of Ove Frank. University of Stockholm, Department of Statistics, Stockholm, pp. 1–17.

Dahmström, K., & Dahmström, P. (1993). ML-estimation of the clustering parameter in a Markov graph model. Research report RR1993:4. Department of Statistics, Stockholm University.

Daraganova, G., Pattison, P., Koskinen, J., Mitchell, B., Bill, A., Watts, M., & Baum, S. (2012). Networks and geography: modelling community network structures as the outcome of both spatial and network processes. *Social Networks*, *34*(1), 6–17.

Desmarais, B.A., & Cranmer, S.J. (2012). Statistical mechanics of networks: estimation and uncertainty. *Physica A: Statistical Mechanics and Its Applications*, *391*(4), 1865–1876.

Everitt, R.G., Johansen, A.M., Rowing, E., & Evdemon-Hogan, M. (2017). Bayesian model comparison with un-normalised likelihoods. *Statistics and Computing*, *27*(2), 403–422.

Fellows, I.E. (2014). Why (and when and how) contrastive divergence works. *arXiv preprint arXiv:1405.0602*.

Frank, O. (1980) Transitivity in stochastic graphs and digraphs, *Journal of Mathematical Sociology*, *7*(2), 199–213

Frank, O. (1991) Statistical analysis of change in networks. *Statistica Neerlandica*, *45*(3), 283–293.

Frank, O., & Shafie, T. (2018). Random multigraphs and aggregated triads with fixed degrees. *Network Science*, *6*(2), 232–250.

Frank, O., & Strauss, D. (1986). Markov graphs. *Journal of the American Statistical Association*, *81*(395), 832–842.

Friel, N. (2013). Evidence and Bayes factor estimation for Gibbs random fields. *Journal of Computational and Graphical Statistics*, *22*(3), 518–532.

Ghafouri, S., & Khasteh, S.H. (2020). A survey on exponential random graph models: an application perspective. *PeerJ Computer Science*, *6*, e269

Granovetter, M. (1973). The strength of weak ties. *American Journal of Sociology*, *78*, 1360–1380.

Handcock, M.S. (2003). Statistical models for social networks: inference and degeneracy. In R. Breiger, K. Carley & P. Pattison (Eds.), *Dynamic social network modeling and analysis: workshop summary and papers* (pp. 1–12). National Academies Press.

Handcock, M.S., & Gile, K. (2010). Modeling social networks from sampled data. *Annals of Applied Statistics*, *4*, pp. 5–25.

Handcock, M.S., Hunter, D.R., Butts, C.T., Goodreau, S.M., Krivitsky, P.N., & Morris, M. (2018). ERGM: fit, simulate and diagnose exponential-family models for networks. Statnet Project. www.statnet.org, R package version 3.9.4.

Hanneke, S., Fu, W., & Xing, E.P. (2010). Discrete temporal models of social networks. *Electronic Journal of Statistics*, *4*, 585–605.

Holland, P.W., & Leinhardt, S. (1981). An exponential family of probability distributions for directed graphs. *Journal of the American Statistical Association*, *76*, pp. 33–65.

Hummel, R.M., Hunter, D.R., & Handcock, M.S. (2012). Improving simulation-based algorithms for fitting ERGMs. *Journal of Computational and Graphical Statistics*, *21*(4), 920–939.

Hunter, D.R., & Handcock, M.S. (2006). Inference in curved exponential family models for networks. *Journal of Computational and Graphical Statistics*, *15*, 565–583.

Häggström, O., & Jonasson, J. (1999). Phase transition in the random triangle model. *Journal of Applied Probability*, *36*(4), 1101–1115.

Jonasson, J. (1999). The random triangle model. *Journal of Applied Probability*, 36(3), 852–867.

Kindermann, R.P., & Snell, J.L. (1980). On the relation between Markov random fields and social networks. *Journal of Mathematical Sociology*, 7(1), 1–13.

Koehly, L.M., & Pattison, P. (2005). Random graph models for social networks: multiple relations or multiple raters. *Models and Methods in Social Network Analysis*, 162–191.

Kolaczyk, E.D., & Krivitsky, P.N. (2015). On the question of effective sample size in network modeling: an asymptotic inquiry. *Statistical Science: A Review Journal of the Institute of Mathematical Statistics*, 30(2), 184.

Koskinen, J.H. (2004). Bayesian analysis of exponential random graphs: estimation of parameters and model selection. Research Report 2004:2. Department of Statistics, Stockholm University

Koskinen, J. (2008). The linked importance sampler auxiliary variable metropolis Hastings algorithm for distributions with intractable normalising constants. MelNet Social Networks Laboratory Technical Report; No. 08-01.

Koskinen J., Caimo, A., & Lomi, A. (2015). Simultaneous modeling of initial conditions and time heterogeneity in dynamic networks: an application to Foreign Direct Investments. *Network Science*, 3(1), 58–77.

Koskinen, J., & Daraganova, G. (2022). Bayesian analysis of social influence. *Journal of the Royal Statistical Society Series A*, 185(4), 1469–2325.

Koskinen, J., & Lomi, A. (2013). The local structure of globalization: the network dynamics of foreign direct investments in the international electricity industry. *Journal of Statistical Physics*, 151(3), 523–548.

Koskinen, J.H., Robins, G.L., & Pattison, P.E. (2010). Analysing exponential random graph (p-star) models with missing data using Bayesian data augmentation. *Statistical Methodology*, 7(3), 366–384.

Koskinen, J., Wang, P., Robins, G., & Pattison, P. (2018). Outliers and influential observations in exponential random graph models. *Psychometrika*, 83(4), 809–830.

Krivitsky, P.N. (2012). Exponential-family random graph models for valued networks. *Electronic Journal of Statistics*, 6, 1100.

Krivitsky, P.N., & Handcock, M.S. (2014). A separable model for dynamic networks. *Journal of the Royal Statistical Society: Series B*, 76(1), 29–46.

Krivitsky, P.N., Koehly, L.M., & Marcum, C.S. (2020). Exponential-family random graph models for multi-layer networks. *Psychometrika*, 85(3), 630–659.

Lazega, E., Jourda, M.T., Mounier, L., & Stofer, R. (2008). Catching up with big fish in the big pond? Multi-level network analysis through linked design. *Social Networks*, 30(2), 159–176.

Lazega, E., & Pattison, P.E. (1999). Multiplexity, generalized exchange and cooperation in organizations: a case study. *Social Networks*, 21(1), 67–90.

Lubbers, M.J., & Snijders, T.A. (2007). A comparison of various approaches to the exponential random graph model: a reanalysis of 102 student networks in school classes. *Social Networks*, 29(4), 489–507.

Lusher, D., Koskinen, J.H., & Robins, G.L. (Eds.) (2013). *Exponential random graph models for social networks: theory, methods, and applications*. Cambridge University Press.

Martin, J.L. (2020). Comment on geodesic cycle length distributions in delusional and other social networks. *Journal of Social Structure*, 21(2.3).

Mele, A. (2017). A structural model of dense network formation. *Econometrica*, 85(3), 825–850.

Merton, R.K. (1968). The Matthew effect in science. *Science*, 159, 56–63.

Mood, C. (2010). Logistic regression: why we cannot do what we think we can do, and what we can do about it. *European Sociological Review*, 26(1), 67–82.

Moody, J. (2001). Race, school integration, and friendship segregation in America. *American Journal of Sociology*, 107(3), 679–716.

Moreno, J., & Jennings, M. (1938) Statistics of social configurations. *Sociometry*, 1(3), 342–374.

Morris, M., Handcock, M.S., & Hunter, D.R. (2008). Specification of exponential-family random graph models: terms and computational aspects. *Journal of Statistical Software*, 24(4), 1548–7660.

Opsahl, T., & Panzarasa, P. (2009). Clustering in weighted networks. *Social Networks*, 31(2), 155–163.

Pattison, P., & Robins, G. (2002). Neighborhood-based models for social networks. *Sociological Methodology*, 32(1), 301–337.

Pattison, P.E., Robins, G.L., Snijders, T.A.B., & Wang, P. (2013). Conditional estimation of exponential random graph models from snowball sampling designs. *Journal of Mathematical Psychology*, 57(6), 284–296.

Pattison, P.E., & Snijders, T.A.B. (2013). Modeling social networks: next steps. In D. Lusher, J.H. Koskinen & G.L. Robins (Eds.), *Exponential random graph models for social networks: theory, methods, and applications* (pp. 287–301). Cambridge University Press.

Pattison, P., & Wasserman, S. (1999). Logit models and logistic regressions for social networks: II. Multivariate relations. *British Journal of Mathematical and Statistical Psychology*, 52(2), 169–193.

Ripley, R.M. Snijders, T.A.B., Boda, Z., Voros, A., & Preciado, P. (2022). Manual for Siena version 4.0.

R package version 1.3.14. www.cran.r-project. org/web/packages/RSiena/
Robins, G., & Alexander, M. (2004). Small worlds among interlocking directors: network structure and distance in bipartite graphs. *Computational and Mathematical Organization Theory*, *10*(1), 69–94.
Robins, G.L., Elliott, P., & Pattison, P.E. (2001). Network models for social selection processes. *Social Networks*, *23*, 1–30.
Robins, G., & Lusher, D. (2013). Illustrations: simulation, estimation and goodness of fit. *Exponential Random Graph Models for Social Networks: Theory, Methods, and Applications*, 167–185.
Robins, G., & Pattison, P. (2001) Random graph models for temporal processes in social networks. *Journal of Mathematical Sociology*, *25*(1), 5–41.
Robins, G., Pattison, P., & Wasserman, S. (1999). Logit models and logistic regressions for social networks: III. Valued relations. *Psychometrika*, *64*(3), 371–394.
Robins, G., Pattison, P., & Woolcock, J. (2005). Small and other worlds: global network structures from local processes. *American Journal of Sociology*, *110*(4), 894–936.
Schweinberger, M. (2011). Instability, sensitivity, and degeneracy of discrete exponential families. *Journal of the American Statistical Association*, *106*(496), 1361–1370.
Schweinberger, M., Krivitsky, P.N., Butts, C.T., & Stewart, J.R. (2020). Exponential family models of random graphs: inference in finite, super and infinite population scenarios. *Statistical Science*, *35*(4), 627–662
Schweinberger, M., & Handcock, M.S. (2015). Local dependence in random graph models: characterization, properties and statistical inference. *Journal of the Royal Statistical Society: Series B*, *77*(3), 647–676.
Shafie, T. (2015). A multigraph approach to social network analysis. *Journal of Social Structure*, 16.
Shalizi, C.R., & Rinaldo, A. (2013). Consistency under sampling of exponential random graph models. *Annals of Statistics*, *41*, 508–535.
Shore, J., & Lubin, B. (2015). Spectral goodness of fit for network models. *Social Networks*, *43*, 16–27.
Simmel, G. (1902). The number of members as determining the sociological form of the group: I. *American Journal of Sociology*, *8*(1902), 1–46.
Skvoretz, J., & Faust, K. (1999). Logit models for affiliation networks. *Sociological Methodology*, *29*(1), 253–280.
Slaughter, A.J., & Koehly, L.M. (2016). Multilevel models for social networks: hierarchical Bayesian approaches to exponential random graph modeling. *Social Networks*, *44*, 334–345.
Sohn, C., Christopoulos, D., & Koskinen, J. (2020). Borders moderating distance: a social network analysis of spatial effects on policy interaction. *Geographical Analysis*, *52*(3), 428–451.
Snijders, T.A.B. (2002). Markov chain Monte Carlo estimation of exponential random graph models. *Journal of Social Structure*, *3*, April.
Snijders, T.A.B. (2010). Conditional marginalization for exponential random graph models, *Journal of Mathematical Sociology*, *34*(4), 239–252.
Snijders, T.A.B., & Koskinen, J. (2013). Longitudinal models. In D. Lusher, J.H. Koskinen & G.L. Robins (Eds.), *Exponential random graph models for social networks: theory, methods and applications* (pp. 130–139). Cambridge University Press.
Snijders, T.A.B., Pattison, P.E., Robins, G.L., & Handcock, M.S. (2006). New specifications for exponential random graph models. *Sociological Methodology*, *36*, 99–153.
Snijders, T.A., & Van Duijn, M.A. (2002). Conditional maximum likelihood estimation under various specifications of exponential random graph models. *Contributions to Social Network Analysis, Information Theory, and Other Topics in Statistics*, 117–134.
Stadtfeld, C., Snijders, T.A.B., Steglich, C., & van Duijn, M. (2018). Statistical power in longitudinal network studies. *Sociological Methods and Research*, *49*(4).
Stewart, J., Schweinberger, M., Bojanowski, M., & Morris, M. (2019). Multilevel network data facilitate statistical inference for curved ERGMs with geometrically weighted terms. Social Networks, 59, 98-119.
Stivala, A. (2020a). Geodesic cycle length distributions in delusional and other social networks. *Journal of Social Structure*, *21*(2.3).
Stivala, A. (2020b). Reply to 'Comment on geodesic cycle length distributions in delusional and other social networks'. *Journal of Social Structure*, *21*(2.3).
Stivala, A., Koskinen, J., Rolls, D., Wang, P., & Robins, R. (2016). Snowball sampling for estimating exponential random graph models for large networks. *Social Networks*, *47*, 167–188.
Strauss, D. (1986). On a general class of models for interaction. *SIAM Review*, *28*(4), 513–527.
Strauss, D., & Ikeda, M. (1990). Pseudolikelihood estimation for social networks. Journal of the American statistical association, 85(409), 204-212.
Thiemichen, S., Friel, N., Caimo, A., & Kauermann, G. (2016). Bayesian exponential random graph models with nodal random effects. *Social Networks*, *46*, 11–28.
van Duijn, M.A., Gile, K.J., & Handcock, M.S. (2009). A framework for the comparison of maximum pseudo-likelihood and maximum likelihood estimation of exponential family random graph models. *Social Networks*, *31*(1), 52–62.

Wang, P., Pattison, P., & Robins, G. (2013a). Exponential random graph model specifications for bipartite networks: a dependence hierarchy. *Social Networks*, *35*(2), 211–222.

Wang, P., Pattison, P., & Snijders, T.A.B. (2022). Exponential random graph models with brokerage-centrality conjugates: exploring organisation characteristics and multilevel brokerage roles in public health systems. In Preparation.

Wang, P., Robins, G., Pattison, P., & Koskinen, J. (2014). MPNet, program for the simulation and estimation of (p*) exponential random graph models for multilevel networks: user manual. Melbourne School of Psychological Sciences, University of Melbourne Australia. sna.unimelb.edu.au/

Wang, P., Robins, G., Pattison, P., & Lazega, E. (2013b). Exponential random graph models for multilevel networks. *Social Networks*, *35*(1), 96–115.

Wang, P., Sharpe, K., Robins, G.L., & Pattison, P.E. (2009). Exponential random graph (p*) models for affiliation networks. *Social Networks*, *31*, 12–25.

Wang, Y.J., & Wong, G.Y. (1987) Stochastic blockmodels for directed graphs. *Journal of the American Statistical Association*, *82*, 8–19.

Wasserman, S., & Iacobucci, D. (1991). Statistical modelling of one-mode and two-mode networks: simultaneous analysis of graphs and bipartite graphs. *British Journal of Mathematical and Statistical Psychology*, *44*(1), 13–43.

Wasserman, S., & Pattison, P. (1996). Logit models and logistic regressions for social networks: I. An introduction to Markov graphs and p. *Psychometrika*, *61*(3), 401–425.

White, H.C., Boorman, S.A., & Breiger, R.L. (1976). Social structure from multiple networks. I. Blockmodels of roles and positions. *American Journal of Sociology*, *81*(4), 730–780.

Yon, G.G.V., Slaughter, A., & de la Haye, K. (2021). Exponential random graph models for little networks. *Social Networks*, *64*, 225–238.

Yule, G.U. (1925). A mathematical theory of evolution, based on the conclusions of Dr J.C. Willis, F.R.S. *Philosophical Transactions of the Royal Society B*, *213*, 21–87.

Network Dynamics

Tom A.B. Snijders and Christian E.G. Steglich

A DYNAMIC APPROACH TO NETWORK ANALYSIS

Dynamic ideas have been pursued in much of social network analysis. Many basic network concepts, such as reciprocation and transitive closure, are fundamentally dynamic because they refer to mechanisms of change (Stadtfeld and Amati, 2021; Steglich and Snijders, 2022). Network dynamics figures prominently in domains ranging from friendship networks (e.g., Selfhout et al., 2010) to inter-organisational networks (e.g., Tasselli et al., 2015) and many others. Since the turn of the millennium, longitudinal network data and methods for analysing them have developed strongly. Some earlier history of longitudinal research about social networks, and of associated statistical models, was briefly reviewed in Snijders (2011).

This chapter treats statistical methods for the analysis of network panel data, i.e., network data collected at two or more points in time, for a constant set of n actors (allowing for some turnover and missingness), where the network can be co-evolving together with other networks or with changing actor attributes (often referred to as 'behaviour'). The network is supposed to be a stochastic digraph, i.e., a structure with binary, random tie variables $X_{ij}(t)$ which can have the value 1 or 0, indicating whether the directed tie $i \to j$ exists at time t; the outcomes are denoted by $x_{ij}(t)$. Extensions to valued networks are also discussed.

Dynamic network models have to represent the feedback processes that are characteristic of networks. As examples, consider some of the processes of tie creation that are traditional in social network analysis: reciprocation (Moreno, 1934), transitive closure (Rapoport, 1953; Davis, 1970), and the Matthew effect ('unto him that hath is given and unto him that hath not is taken away, even that which he hath'; Merton 1968; de Solla Price 1965, 1976; called 'preferential attachment' by Barabási and Albert, 1999). If at some moment t the tie $i \to j$ does not exist, then at some later moment it might be created by reciprocation if currently there is a tie $j \to i$; it might be created by transitive closure if there are two ties arranged in a two-path $i \to h \to j$ (i.e., there currently is an indirect connection from i to j); and it might be created by the Matthew effect if there are many other actors h for which there is a tie $h \to j$ (i.e., currently actor j is highly popular in the sense of having a high in-degree). These examples illustrate that statistical models for network dynamics have to express that the existence of ties will have consequences for the existence, creation, and dissolution of other ties.

Dependence Over Time

For modelling dependence over time, the great majority of published models have used some variation of the Markov property. This property, defined for stochastic processes, expresses (loosely speaking) that the future depends on the past via the present. The earliest proposed longitudinal network models (e.g., Katz and Proctor, 1959; Wasserman, 1987; Robins and Pattison, 2001) postulated that, if data are observations of $X(t_1), X(t_2), \ldots X(t_M)$, then these M consecutive observations constitute a Markov chain.

However, the feedback processes mentioned above may be assumed to operate, unobserved, between the observations. For example, in a group in which the Matthew effect operates, if at time t_1 some node i has a low in-degree and at the next observation t_2 it has a very high in-degree, then it is likely that this has come about by the gradual accumulation of ties directed towards i; the first of these may have been chance occurrences, but once the in-degree was relatively high, it became a self-reinforcing process or cascade (Macy and Evtushenko, 2020). Such a model presupposes that there were changes occurring between the observation moments t_1 and t_2. The most elegant and mathematically tractable way of modelling this is to postulate a *continuous-time Markov process* $\{X(t) \mid t \in t_1 \leq t \leq t_M\}$, in other words, to let the set of time points of the process $\mathcal{T}$ be all real numbers from t_1 to t_M, while still sticking to the panel design for the observed networks: thus it is postulated that the process of network change goes on, unobserved, between the moments of data collection. This was proposed by Sørensen and Hallinan (1976) and Holland and Leinhardt (1977). They also proposed that in this change process, at any instance of time t no more than one tie variable $X_{ij}(t)$ can change. This decomposes the change process into its smallest possible constituents and rules out coordination in the form of the simultaneous creation of a set of ties, as in mutual love at first sight, or the spontaneous split of a group of friends in a quarrel. The actors are dependent because they react to each other (cf. Zeggelink, 1994), not because they coordinate. Mathematically, this is a reasonable requirement as it greatly reduces the complexity of modelling while increasing statistical power.

Dependence Between Ties

The Markov chain model of Katz and Proctor (1959) assumed independent tie variables changing over time according to a Markov chain. However, independence of ties goes against basic ideas of social network analysis. A first relaxation of this assumption is to allow for dependence within dyads. This was done, for longitudinal models, by Wasserman (1979 and other publications), Hallinan (1979) and Leenders (1995 and other publications) for continuous-time Markov processes; and Wasserman (1987 and other publications) for discrete-time Markov processes. These models assume independence between dyads $(X_{ij}(t), X_{ji}(t))$.

This assumption breaks apart the stochastic process into $n(n-1)/2$ independent sub-processes. This helps for tractability, but of the three basic processes mentioned above as examples: reciprocity, transitivity, and Matthew effect, it can represent only the first. Wasserman (1980) proposed the so-called popularity model which assumes independence between rows of the adjacency matrix and represents the Matthew effect, but without reciprocity.

Stochastic models that allow triadic and other higher-order dependencies were proposed for data in the form of rankings – as the Newcomb-Nordlie data – by Snijders (1996), and for data in the form of digraphs by Snijders and van Duijn (1997) and Snijders (2001). General discrete-time autoregressive longitudinal network models were proposed by Robins and Pattison (2001), Hanneke (2010), and Krivitsky and Handcock (2014). These models are described further in this chapter.

Stochastic Models For Network Dynamics

A major reason why stochastic models for network data did not take off before the 1990s is the computational effort needed to estimate their parameters. The dependence structures and feedback processes that characterise network data do not permit the exact analytical calculations that dominated statistical inference before the computer era. Thanks to the diffusion of computational infrastructure, it became possible to estimate plausible models of networks and network dynamics with the more modern tools of simulation-based inference. These techniques rely on the possibility to simulate artificial data in line with the model. A recent overview is given by Fritz et al. (2020).

In this section, we start with presenting two continuous-time Markov process models in more detail: first the LERGM, a tie-oriented model, and then the SAOM, an actor-oriented model. The former is mathematically simpler, the latter closer to most theories in social science. We proceed with a precis of discrete-time exponential random graph models and latent variable models, which also have been used to model network dynamics.

Technically speaking, all models presented are either Markov chains (in discrete time) or Markov processes (in continuous time) on the space of digraphs; or, in a few cases, hidden Markov chains (Cappé et al., 2005). They are defined by probabilistic rules that give a representation of how the network might have evolved from one observation to the next. For discrete-time models, time increases in steps that correspond to the time interval between observation moments; the network observed at a given time point is expressed by autoregressive dependence on the network/s observed at earlier time points. For continuous-time models, time increases gradually in an infinitesimal fashion. Every now and then, at random moments, a change takes place.

Tie-oriented Models in Continuous Time

The Longitudinal Exponential Random Graph Model of Koskinen and Snijders (2013), often referred to as the LERGM, is a dynamic network model allowing quite general dependence structures. The model expresses that there is a process of gradual network change which is unobserved except for its initial and final state, and at random moments in between, ties can be created or dropped, with probabilities depending on the entire state, at that moment, of the network. The changing state remains unobserved until the next observation moment; the process can be simulated because in the simulations the state is known. More precisely, the assumptions are as follows. A random pair (i,j) is chosen, and with some probability (given below) it is decided to change the value of tie variable X_{ij}: create a new tie (change the value 0 to 1), or terminate an existing tie (change 1 to 0). The probability of change can depend on various functions of the network, thus representing the combination of several 'mechanisms', theories, constraints, etc. Technically this is based on the combination of ideas about exponential random graph models (Koskinen, in this volume) with ideas about Markov processes and Gibbs sampling.

As an example, let us consider four theoretical components driving the network dynamics: stochastic tendencies to a given average degree, towards reciprocation, transitivity, and the Matthew effect. These four components will be reflected by the following network statistics:

$L(x) = \sum_{i,j} x_{ij}$ number of ties

$M(x) = \frac{1}{2}\sum_{i,j} x_{ij} x_{ji}$ number of reciprocal dyads

$T(x) = \frac{1}{6}\sum_{i,j,h} x_{ij} x_{jh} x_{ih}$ number of transitive triplets

$S_2(x) = \frac{1}{2}\sum_{i,j,h} x_{ih} x_{jh}$ number of two-in-stars.

If the network dynamics has a tendency to favour changes that increase the value of these four statistics, then this will steer the network process into a direction of, respectively, higher density, more reciprocity, stronger transitivity, or larger in-degree (popularity) differences. To allow differential strengths for the tendency towards the four theoretical components, define the linear combination

$$f(x;\beta) = \beta_1 L(x) + \beta_2 M(x) + \beta_3 T(x) + \beta_4 S_2(x), \quad (1)$$

where the values of the parameters β_k determine the strength of these four tendencies, and x is an arbitrary digraph. The following algorithm defines a change process of so-called *mini-steps*, changing ('toggling') single tie variables $X_{ij}(t)$, dependent on these four statistics according to function $f(x;\beta)$. For observation times t_m and t_{m+1}, sequential application of these mini-steps will bring a network $X(t_m)$ to the next network $X(t_{m+1})$.

Algorithm 1. *Tie-oriented network dynamics.*

For digraphs x, define $x^{(ij+)}$ and $x^{(ij-)}$ as the digraphs which are identical to x in all tie variables except those for the ordered pair (i,j), and for which $x^{(ij+)}$ does have a tie $i \to j$, while $x^{(ij-)}$ does not have this tie. In other words, $x_{ij}^{(ij+)} = 1$ and $x_{ij}^{(ij-)} = 0$.

1 *Choose a random ordered pair (i,j) with equal probabilities, given that $i \neq j$.*
2 *Define $x = X(t)$.*
3 *Define*

$$\pi_{ij} = \frac{\exp(f(x^{(ij+)};\beta))}{\exp(f(x^{(ij+)};\beta)) + \exp(f(x^{(ij-)};\beta))}. \quad (2)$$

With probability π_{ij}, choose the next network to be $x^{(ij+)}$; with probability $1 - \pi_{ij}$, choose the next network to be $x^{(ij-)}$.
4 *Increase the time variable t by the amount Δt, being a random variable with the exponential distribution with parameter ρ.*

This is a model for network dynamics closely related to the exponential random graph model ('ERGM'; Koskinen, in this volume), because the change is taken with the conditional probabilities for X_{ij} given the rest of the digraph in the ERGM with $f(x; \beta)$ as the linear predictor. It follows that repetition of this algorithm for $t \to \infty$ yields a probability distribution of $X(t)$ according to this ERGM. This dynamic algorithm is one of the standard – although inefficient – algorithms to obtain random draws from this model.

A variety of models can be obtained by choices of the parameters β in (1). For $\beta_2 = \beta_3 = \beta_4 = 0$ one obtains a random ('Erdös – Rényi', 'Bernoulli') graph. For $\beta_3 = \beta_4 = 0$ a special case is obtained of the reciprocity model of Wasserman (1979). For $\beta_2 = \beta_3 = 0$ one obtains Wasserman's (1980) popularity model.

Actor-oriented Models in Continuous Time

One of the challenges of network analysis is to incorporate agency in a network model. The call for this by Emirbayer and Goodwin (1994) received responses, among others, from Small (2009), Snijders (2013), and Tasselli and Kilduff (2021). A natural way to combine agency and structure in a statistical model is to use a model for network dynamics where changes of ties are initiated by actors. Such a model can be a good vehicle for expressing and testing social science theories in which the actors have a central role (cf. Udehn, 2002, and Hedström, 2005). Actor-oriented models were proposed by Snijders (1996) for ranked network data and by Snijders and van Duijn (1997) and Snijders (2001) for digraphs. This model type is usually referred to as the Stochastic Actor-oriented Model (SAOM). A general overview is in Snijders (2017), tutorial introductions are in Snijders et al. (2010) and Kalish (2020).

The model expresses again a process of gradual network change, where the network changes without being observed, and the probabilities of change depend on the current (but unobserved) state of the network. At random moments an actor is chosen, and given the opportunity to change one outgoing tie: again this is called a 'mini-step'. The model is specified by a *rate function* $\lambda_i(x; \rho)$, indicating how frequently actor i obtains opportunities for changing an outgoing tie, and an *evaluation function* $f_i(x; \beta)$, determining the probabilities for which tie to change. The latter function may be interpreted as a measure of how attractive network state x is for actor i. The statistical parameters ρ and β are used to reflect the strengths of the various different components included in the rate and evaluation functions. Agency in these models is with the senders of the ties. (For non-directed networks, the definition of agency is more complicated because there are two actors involved in a tie; see Snijders and Pickup, 2017.) The algorithm for a mini-step is as follows.

Algorithm 2. *Actor-oriented network dynamics.*

For digraphs x, define $x^{(ij\pm)}$ as the graph which is identical to x in all tie variables except those for the ordered pair (i,j), and for which the tie variable $i \to j$ in $x^{(ij\pm)}$ is the opposite of this tie variable in x, i.e., $x_{ij}^{(ij\pm)} = 1 - x_{ij}$. For convenience, let $x^{(ii\pm)} = x$.

1. Define $x = X(t)$.
2. For all i, generate independent waiting times Δt_i according to the exponential distribution with parameter $\lambda_i(x; \rho)$. Take the actor i with the smallest value of the waiting time, discarding all other waiting times.
3. For $j \in \{1,\ldots,n\}$, define

$$\pi_{ij} = \frac{\exp(f_i(x^{(ij\pm)}; \beta))}{\sum_{h=1}^{n} \exp(f_i(x^{(ih\pm)}; \beta))}. \quad (3)$$

With probability π_{ij}, choose the next network to be $x^{(ij\pm)}$.

4. Increase the time variable t by the amount Δt_i.

The properties of the exponential function imply that equation (3) can be rewritten as

$$\pi_{ij} = \frac{\exp(f_i(x^{(ij\pm)}; \beta) - f_i(x; \beta))}{\sum_{h=1}^{n} \exp(f_i(x^{(ih\pm)}; \beta) - f_i(x; \beta))}, \quad (4)$$

that is, the probability of a given change depends monotonically on the *increase* (or decrease) in evaluation function that would be generated by this change. This implies that the probability π_{ii} of choosing not to make a change is high for actors i for whom the current state x of the network is near the optimum of the evaluation function $f_i(x; \beta)$.

Model Specification

In the tie-oriented as well as in the actor-oriented model, the researcher has to specify the function $f(x; \beta)$ or $f_i(x; \beta)$, respectively, to specify the model; also the rate function $\lambda_i(x; \rho)$ needs to be specified, but as the data contains no information about individual tie changes this often is specified just as a constant. The model specification should be based on knowledge of the subject matter, theoretical considerations, and the hypotheses to be investigated. We discuss here only the actor-oriented case. An example of discussion of the choice between the tie-oriented and the actor-oriented model is in Koskinen and Lomi (2013).

Like in generalised linear modelling, a convenient class of functions is offered by linear combinations

$$f_i(x;\beta) = \sum_k \beta_k s_{ki}(x), \qquad (5)$$

where the $s_{ki}(x)$ are functions of the network, as seen from the point of view of actor i. These functions are called *effects*. An analogue of (1) for the actor-oriented model is

$$f_i(x;\beta) = \beta_1 \sum_j x_{ij} + \beta_2 \sum_j x_{ij} x_{ji} \\ + \beta_3 \sum_{j,h} x_{ij} x_{jh} x_{ih} + \beta_4 \sum_{j,h} x_{ij} x_{hj}. \qquad (6)$$

These four effects represent, as seen from the point of view of actor i, the number of ties, number of reciprocated ties, number of transitive triplets $\{i \to j \to h, i \to h\}$, and the sum of in-degrees $\sum_h x_{hj}$ of the actors j toward whom i has an outgoing tie. The tie-oriented model with specification (1) and the actor-oriented model with specification (6) define very similar but nevertheless different probability distributions for the network dynamics.

Many other functions of the personal network of actor i may be used as effects $s_{ki}(x)$ in (5). These can be structural effects, depending only on the network x, or effects depending also on covariates. This offers possibilities to express, for example, homophily for actor attributes (McPherson et al., 2001). However, network dynamics may depend on actor attributes according to other mechanisms than homophily. This can be represented by the specifications proposed in Snijders and Lomi (2019). Meeting opportunities can be expressed, for example, by dyadic covariates expressing propinquity. An extensive list of effects is contained in the RSiena manual (Ripley et al., 2023).

The SAOM as an Agent-based Model

The stochastic actor-oriented model may be regarded as a dynamic and stochastic agent-based computational model ('ABM', cf. Macy and Willer, 2002), with an inbuilt connection to empirical observations. There is a difference in the SAOM and ABM traditions in that SAOMs are oriented towards models with an extensive specification leading to a good fit between model and empirical observations and the possibility of testing statistical hypotheses, whereas ABMs are oriented towards more basic models for which it is possible to derive emergent properties and study micro-macro transitions. Examples where the SAOM is used in a way similar to ABMs are Snijders and Steglich (2015) and Prell and Lo (2016). Micro-macro studies using the SAOM were presented by Snijders and Kalter (2020) and by Steglich and Snijders (2022).

Discrete-time Exponential Random Graph Models

Discrete-time Exponential Random Graph ('ERGM') models were proposed, as autoregressive longitudinal extensions of the ERGM (Robins and Pattison, 2001; Lusher et al., 2013). In their general form, they express the probability for a tie to exist at a given observation time as a function depending on the earlier observation of the network included as a binary, dyadic covariate (autoregressive model terms), perhaps other covariates, the ensemble of all tie variables at that same time point (endogenous contemporaneous terms), and their interactions. This implies a very rich portfolio of possible functions to express dependencies over time and between ties. For example, Robins and Pattison (2001) enumerate eight qualitatively different functions representing how the number of transitive triplets could depend on the previously observed network.

Studies that employ discrete-time ERGMs in practice therefore typically rely on further simplifying assumptions, reflected in the model specifications used. The degree to which these additional assumptions are made explicit by the authors unfortunately varies from paper to paper, which makes this literature a bit hard to assess. Many papers employ ad-hoc model specifications without discussing the statistical assumptions that these imply. To illustrate: when no autoregressive model terms are included (e.g., Czarna et al., 2016), the implicit simplifying assumption is made that network observations are independent over time, and the model reduces to a cross-sectional ERGM for independent data sets. By contrast, specifications according to the 'temporal ERGM' in Hanneke et al. (2010) only include the previous observation of the network as a dyadic covariate, with the implicit simplifying assumption that the changes of all tie variables are independent, reducing the model to simple logistic regression. Lerner et al. (2013)

showed that this strong assumption can be reasonable when there are only few changes between observation moments.

Krivitsky and Handcock (2014) proposed the class of 'separable temporal ERGM' ('STERGM') specifications, where the creation of new ties and the dissolution of existing ties are assumed to be conditionally independent processes, both following the ERGM. Whereas the separate modelling of these two processes seems reasonable in many cases, the independence assumption not always is.

The difference between a continuous-time approach and an autoregressive discrete-time approach was discussed by Block et al. (2018). Both approaches postulate that the observed network process is a Markov chain. A major difference is that parameters and their interpretation for discrete-time approaches are dependent on the time duration between waves, which implies for multiple waves that they are based on the assumption of equidistant observations. The parameters of continuous-time models, by contrast, are independent of the time duration between waves, and there is no problem to combine multiple waves with different time distances in between. Another difference is how the dependence between tie variables in $X(t_{m+1})$, given $X(t_m)$, is generated. Continuous-time model represent this dependence as the result of an unobserved sequential process, in which changes depend on earlier changes. Discrete-time models, if they represent this dependence, represent it as contemporaneous dependence where 'everything depends on everything else', although for the STERGM the structure of newly created ties is independent of the structure of terminated ties.

Latent Variable Models

Latent variable models exist in a large variety; see the chapter by Kaur et al. in this volume. They were originally developed for the case of cross-sectional network data. The basic assumption is that there exist latent (i.e., unobserved) actor variables Z such that the probability of a tie between two actors i and j depends on the values Z_i and Z_j. They have been extended to the longitudinal case, which in most cases implies that they are hidden Markov chains (Cappé et al., 2005), i.e., Markov chains conditional on unobserved variables.

For *latent space network models*, the latent variables are vectors in a low-dimensional, often two-dimensional, Euclidean space. The probability of a tie depends on the relative positioning of the actors to each other in that continuous, latent space. Often, this is further specified as dependence on the Euclidean distance between the actors.

Stochastic blockmodels are *latent class network models*, in which Z is categorical, usually with a small number of categories. Covariates can be added to such models.

An example for a latent variable model is the p_2 model (van Duijn et al., 2004). The two continuous dimensions of the latent variable are actors' expansiveness/activity and attractiveness/popularity. Paul and O'Malley (2013) propose an autoregressive discrete-time dynamic model in which the conditional distribution of the network at time t is a p_2 model with covariates expressing triadic effects over time, e.g., transitive closure at time t based on indirect connections at time $t-1$.

Longitudinal latent space models were developed by Sewell and Chen (2015), with the assumption that actors' latent positions follow a Markov chain. A continuous-time longitudinal extension of the stochastic block model was proposed by Matias et al. (2018). A comprehensive review of longitudinal versions of latent variable models (of both kinds) is given by Kim et al. (2018).

The attractiveness of latent variable models for networks is that they give a relatively simple representation of the complexity of networks, using just a few actor variables. This can be fruitful for exploration and description, and provides links to network visualization. However, they cannot express realization-dependence between tie variables: the dependence between contemporaneous tie variables is mediated by the latent variables of the actors, and the actual existence of the ties does not matter[1] once the latent variables are known. This is a severe limitation of the possibilities to represent consequences of the actual existence of ties.

CO-EVOLUTION

This section gives an overview of dynamic data structures that extend the network dynamics discussed above by introducing co-dependent outcome dimensions. These can be changeable variables on the actor level (here generically termed 'behaviour'), on the level of dyads (i.e., other networks between the same actors), or affiliation structures (i.e., networks linking the actors to another set of nodes). Models for such generalised dynamic network data have been developed by extending the SAOM framework.

Co-evolution of networks and behaviour, but also co-evolution of one-mode and two-mode networks, can represent the combination of *social selection* processes, where the one-mode network ties are influenced by the social context, e.g., the behaviour and/or affiliations of friends, and *social influence* processes, where the behaviour and affiliations of actors are influenced by the behaviours and affiliations of those to whom they are tied in the one-mode network. This is elaborated for network-behaviour co-evolution by Steglich et al. (2010) and Veenstra et al. (2013) and for one-mode – two-mode co-evolution by Lomi and Stadtfeld (2014) and Amati et al. (2021).

Dynamics of Networks and Behaviour

Networks are particularly important because of how they are related to individual behaviour and other individual outcomes; see, e.g., Granovetter (1973), Burt (1992), and Lin et al. (2001). Such individual characteristics, however, will also play a role in the explanation of the network dynamics. Thus we encounter the situation where the network and the behaviour – a term that we use here as a shorthand for the relevant changeable characteristics of the actors, which also could be attitudes, performance, etc. – both can be considered as dependent variables, changing interdependently. This is called the *co-evolution* of networks and behaviour.

Standard Actor-oriented Models can represent this co-evolution for behavioural variables that are ordinal discrete, with values 1, 2, etc., up to some maximum value; a binary variable is a special case. Models for continuous behaviour variables were also developed (Niezink et al., 2019). Models for diffusion of innovations are obtained by using a binary variable (1= "non-adopter", 2= "adopter") with the additional constraint that the behavioural variable cannot change from 2 to 1; see Greenan (2015).

Dynamics of Multiple Networks

Another possibility is the co-evolution of multiple networks (Snijders et al., 2013). This could be the 'multiplex' case of one-mode networks for the same actor set, e.g., friendship and advice. When imposing constraints on the permitted combinations of tie variables, it becomes possible to model also valued networks with a small number of categories, such as strong and weak ties (Elmer et al., 2017) or signed networks, where tie values can be positive or negative (Rambaran et al., 2015).

But also the co-evolution of a one-mode together with a two-mode network may be considered, for example, friendship and membership of associations. Two-mode networks could also be defined as affiliations with activities (e.g., sports) or cognitions (e.g., opinions), measured by binary variables (e.g., Fujimoto et al., 2018); we use the word 'affiliation' for the relation represented by a two-mode network.

Actor-oriented Co-evolution Models

Co-evolution of networks and behaviour can be taken together with co-evolution of multiple networks as actor-oriented process models in which all dependent structures (one-mode networks, two-mode networks, behavioural variables, as the case may be) are joined in the dynamic state of the model. The actor orientation implies that changes in these structures are represented as choices made by the actors concerning their outgoing ties and behaviours, depending on the entire context in a dynamic way. The dynamics are modelled again as mini-steps occurring in continuous time, where each mini-step regards only one of the dependent structures. This represents all co-evolution models mentioned above except those where behaviour is represented by a continuous variable (Niezink et al., 2019).

To formulate the process model, suppose that there are $S \geq 2$ co-evolving random structures $X^{(1)},\ldots,X^{(s)}$, where $X^{(s)}$ for each s may be either a $n \times n$ one-mode network, a $n \times m_s$ two-mode network, or a n-dimensional behavioural variable with values $1, 2,\ldots,H_s$. All of these refer to an actor set of n social actors, but the numbers of second-mode nodes m_s and behavioural categories H_s may depend on s. The entire state variable is denoted simply by $X = (X^{(1)},\ldots,X^{(s)})$, with values x.

In the mini-step an actor i will be selected for making a change in $X^{(s)}$ for some s; if the structure is a network the option set will consist of all i's outgoing tie variables $X_{ij}^{(s)}$, and if it is a behaviour the options, representing minimal changes, will be to increase or decrease $X_i^{(s)}$ by one unit, provided this stays within the range; in all cases there is also the option of no change. The set of states reachable in a mini-step by actor i in structure $X^{(s)}$, given that the current state is x^0, is denoted by $\mathcal{A}_i^{(s)}(x^0)$. This is a set of values $x = (x^{(1)},\ldots,x^{(s)})$ which are identical to x^0 for all structures x^r with $r \neq s$; if s is a network, the only difference is at most one entry in row i of its adjacency matrix; if s is a behavioural variable, the only difference is at most a difference of ±1 in one entry in the behaviour for actor i. Furthermore, this set will reflect the constraints mentioned above for ordered networks, if any are relevant.

For each dependent structure there may be different temporalities, different constraints, and different considerations that play a role for the actors' decisions. The model contains separate rate functions $\lambda_i^{(s)}(x;\rho)$ and evaluation functions

$f_i^{(s)}(x;\beta)$ for each dependent structure s. The evaluation function $f_i^{(s)}(x;\beta)$ will depend in the first place on $x^{(s)}$, but its dependence on the other structures x^r defines the cross-dependencies in the co-evolution.

Algorithm 3. *Actor-oriented dynamics of co-evolution.*

1. *Define x^0 as the current state of the combined structures.*
2. *For all s and i, generate independent waiting times Δt_{si} according to the exponential distribution with parameter $\lambda_i^{(s)}(x;\rho)$. Take the pair (s,i) with the smallest waiting time, discarding all other waiting times.*
3. *For this s and i, and for all $x \in \mathcal{A}_i^{(s)}(x^0)$ calculate the ratios*

$$\pi(x) = \frac{\exp(f_i^{(s)}(x;\beta))}{\sum_{y \in \mathcal{A}_i^{(s)}(x^0)} \exp(f_i^{(s)}(y;\beta))}. \quad (7)$$

Determine the next state using probabilities ($\pi(x)$; $x \in \mathcal{A}_j^{(s)}(x^0)$).
4. *Increment the time variable t by the amount Δt_{si}.*

Since for all structures one of the options is not to change anything, a mini-step will not necessarily result in a change of state. The probability of this will be higher, accordingly as the value of the evaluation function of the current state is higher compared to the value of the other reachable states $x \in \mathcal{A}_i^{(s)}(x^0)$.

SOFTWARE

The statistical models for network dynamics mentioned in this chapter are implemented in a variety of R packages (R, 2023). Statistical procedures for the SAOM are implemented in the R package *RSiena* ('Simulation Investigation for Empirical Network Analysis'). An extensive and frequently updated manual is available (Ripley et al., 2023). As basic literature, the best combination is to use Snijders et al. (2010) or Kalish (2020) as tutorials for the methodology, and the recent value of the manual for the requirements on data formats and the operation of the software. There is an extensive website at www.stats.ox.ac.uk/~snijders/siena/ and the software is also available at github.com/snlab-nl/rsiena/wiki. The LERGM for non-directed networks can also be estimated using *RSiena*.

Dynamic Exponential Random Graph Models, including the STERGM, can be estimated using the *statnet* package (Goodreau et al., 2008; Krivitsky et al., 2023; Krivitsky et al., 2003/2022). There is an extensive website at statnet.org. For dynamic latent block models, there is the R package *dynsbm* (Matias and Miele, 2020).

OUTLOOK AND DISCUSSION

The first edition of this book was published in 2011; many of the statistical methods treated in this chapter have been around for one or two decades. A lot has changed over this period. Thanks to a steadily growing community of committed researchers, some developments predicted to occur have, predictably, occurred, and some concerns that were raised in the first edition are concerns no longer.

For one thing, the link between social science theory and longitudinal network modelling is stronger today. The possibility to test quite specific hypotheses about individuals' relational behaviour has sparked theory formation across the social sciences. Researchers have literally *made their theories more elaborate*, to quote Sir Ronald Fisher's famous reply when William Cochran enquired how to make observational studies more likely to yield causal answers (Cox and Wermuth, 2004). These theoretical advances can be found in several hundreds of peer-reviewed publications employing the methods of longitudinal network analysis that we sketched above.

Of the three important dimensions on which, back in the first edition, further progress in statistical modelling for network dynamics was encouraged, the following can be mentioned. The scope of data structures for which these models have been formulated has been considerably extended, as was made clear above. Goodness of fit procedures are available (Lospinoso & Snijders, 2019) and estimation algorithms have been extended. Some progress has been made in extending the SAOM with latent variables, see Schweinberger (2020) and Koskinen and Snijders (2023). It should also be mentioned that there has been great progress in methods for the analysis of time-stamped event streams in both the actor-oriented (Stadtfeld et al., 2017) and the tie-oriented framework (Butts, 2008), with associated R packages *relevent* and *goldfish*. These models were not discussed further because of space constraints.

Of the developments since the appearance of the first edition of this handbook, we think that especially the extension to co-evolution of multivariate and two-mode networks is very promising for empirical social network research. Two-mode networks can be used not only to represent affiliations but also cognitions or activities. This allows representing the relational structure of the social world in much more richness. Several dimensions of relations (friendship, advice, collaboration, etc.) now can be analysed in their mutual dependence, and their joint and separate associations with dynamic actor variables can be investigated. Following a dynamic approach to disentangle selection and influence now is possible not only for networks and behaviour (Steglich et al., 2010) but also for networks and affiliations (Lomi and Stadtfeld, 2014). This also opens possibilities for the analysis of multilevel networks (Lazega and Snijders, 2016), a very promising area.

We mention three issues for which further developments would be fruitful. First, the current version of the SAOM assumes that actors have complete information about the current state of the network, since their probabilities of change may depend on any elements of this state. This is closely related to the restriction of applicability of this model to networks of at most a few hundred actors; applications to larger networks exist but stretch the credibility of the model. Models for larger networks, abandoning the assumptions of complete information, still are *in statu nascendi*. Second, the numerical values of estimated parameters of longitudinal network models are difficult to interpret as their link with the observed data is through the simulations of the model, and thereby indirect. Measures of effect size, or other methods giving a more direct link between parameters in the model and observable quantities, would be valuable to give more body to the conclusions of empirical analyses. Third, the software can be further improved and some of the statistical procedures can be made more efficient.

Note

1 Some latent block models have exceptions to this for reciprocity dependence.

REFERENCES

Amati, V., Lomi, A., Mascia, D., & Pallotti, F. (2021). The co-evolution of organizational and network structure: the role of multilevel mixing and closure mechanisms. *Organizational Research Methods*, 24, 285–318.

Barabási, A.L., & Albert, R. (1999). Emergence of scaling in random networks. *Science*, 286, 509–512.

Block, P., Koskinen, J., Hollway, J., Steglich, C., & Stadtfeld, C. (2018). Change we can believe in: comparing longitudinal network models on consistency, interpretability and predictive power. *Social Networks*, 52, 180–191.

Burt, R.S. (1992) *Structural holes*. Harvard University Press.

Butts, C.T. (2008). A relational event framework for social action. *Sociological Methodology*, 38, 155–200.

Cappé, O., Moulines, E., & Rydén, T. (2005) *Inference in hidden Markov models*. Springer.

Cox, D.R. & Wermuth, N. (2004). Causality: a statistical view. *International Statistical Review*, 72, 285–305.

Czarna, A.Z., Leifeld, P., Śmieja, M., Dufner, M., & Salovey, P. (2016). Do narcissism and emotional intelligence win us friends? Modeling dynamics of peer popularity using inferential network analysis. *Personality and Social Psychology Bulletin*, 42, 1588–1599.

Davis, J.A. (1970). Clustering and hierarchy in interpersonal relations: testing two graph theoretical models on 742 sociomatrices. *American Sociological Review*, 35, 843–852.

de Solla Price, D. (1965). Networks of scientific papers. *Science*, 149, 510–515.

de Solla Price, D. (1976). A general theory of bibliometric and other advantage processes. *Journal of the American Society for Information Science*, 27, 292–306.

Elmer, T., Boda, Z., & Stadtfeld, C. (2017). The co-evolution of emotional well-being with weak and strong friendship ties. *Network Science*, 5, 278–307.

Emirbayer, M., & Goodwin, J. (1994). Network analysis, culture, and the problem of agency. *American Journal of Sociology*, 99, 1411–1454.

Fritz, C., Lebacher, M., & Kauermann, G. (2020). Tempus volat, hora fugit: a survey of dynamic network models in discrete and continuous time. *Statistica Neerlandica*, 74, 275–299.

Fujimoto, K., Snijders, T., & Valente, T. W. (2018). Multivariate dynamics of one-mode and two-mode networks: Explaining similarity in sports participation among friends. *Network Science*, 6, 370–395.

Goodreau, S. M., Handcock, M. S., Hunter, D. R., Butts, C. T., & Morris, M. (2008). A statnet tutorial. *Journal of Statistical Software*, 24(9), 1–26.

Granovetter, M.S. (1973). The strength of weak ties. *American Journal of Sociology*, 78, 1360–1380.

Greenan, C.C. (2015). Diffusion of innovations in dynamic networks. *Journal of the Royal Statistical Society, Series A, 178,* 147–166.

Hallinan, M.T. (1979). The process of friendship formation. *Social Networks, 1,* 193–210.

Hanneke, S., Fu, W., & Xing, E.P. (2010). Discrete temporal models of social networks. *Electronic Journal of Statistics, 4,* 585–605.

Hedström, P. (2005). *Dissecting the social: on the principles of analytical sociology.* Cambridge University Press.

Holland, P.W., & Leinhardt, S. (1977). A dynamic model for social networks. *Journal of Mathematical Sociology, 5,* 5–20.

Kalish, Y. (2020). Stochastic actor-oriented models for the co-evolution of networks and behaviour: An introduction and tutorial. *Organizational Research Methods, 23,* 511–534.

Katz, L., & Proctor, C.H. (1959). The configuration of interpersonal relations in a group as a time-dependent stochastic process. *Psychometrika, 24,* 317–327.

Kim, B., Lee, K.H., Xue, L., & Niu, X. (2018). A review of dynamic network models with latent variables. *Statistics Surveys, 12,* 105–135.

Koskinen, J., & Lomi, A. (2013). The local structure of globalization. *Journal of Statistical Physics, 151,* 523–548.

Koskinen, J. & Snijders, T.A.B. (2013). Longitudinal models. In Lusher, D., Koskinen, J., & Robins, G. (Eds.), *Exponential random graph models* (pp. 130–140). Cambridge University Press.

Koskinen, J.H. & Snijders, T.A.B. (2023). Multilevel longitudinal analysis of social networks. *Journal of the Royal Statistical Society, Series A.* In press.

Krivitsky, P.N. & Handcock, M.S. (2014). A separable model for dynamic networks. *Journal of the Royal Statistical Society, Series B, 76,* 29–46.

Krivitsky, P.N., Handcock, M.S., Hunter, D.R., Butts, C.T., Klumb, C., Goodreau, S.M., & Morris, M. (2003/2022). *Statnet: tools for the statistical modeling of network data.* statnet.org

Krivitsky, P.N., Hunter, D.R., Morris, M., & Klumb, C. (2023). ergm 4: New features for analyzing exponential-family random graph models. *Journal of Statistical Software, 105,* 1–44.

Lazega, E. & Snijders, T.A.B. (2016). *Multilevel network analysis for the social sciences; theory, methods and applications.* Springer.

Leenders, R.T.A.J. (1995). Models for network dynamics: a Markovian framework. *Journal of Mathematical Sociology, 20,* 1–21.

Lerner, J., Indlekofer, N., Nick, B., & Brandes, U. (2013). Conditional independence in dynamic networks. *Journal of Mathematical Psychology, 57,* 275–283.

Lin, N., Cook, K., & Burt, R.S. (Eds.) (2001) *Social capital: theory and research.* Aldine de Gruyter.

Lomi, A., & Stadtfeld, C. (2014). Social networks and social settings: developing a coevolutionary view. *KZfSS, Kölner Zeitschrift für Soziologie und Sozialpsychologie, 66,* 395–415.

Lospinoso, J. A. and Snijders, T.A.B. (2019). Goodness of fit for stochastic actor-oriented models. *Methodological Innovations, 12,* 1–18.

Lusher, D., Koskinen, J., & Robins, G. (2013) *Exponential random graph models.* Cambridge University Press.

Macy, M.W. & Evtushenko, A. (2020). Threshold models of collective behaviour II: The predictability paradox and spontaneous instigation. *Sociological Science, 7,* 628–648.

Macy, M.W., & Willer, R. (2002). From factors to actors: computational sociology and agent-based modelling. *Annual Review of Sociology, 28,* 143–166.

Matias, C., & Miele, V. (2020). *dynsbm: dynamic stochastic block models.* R package version 0.7. CRAN.R-project.org/package=dynsbm

Matias, C., Rebafka, T., & Villers, F. (2018). A semiparametric extension of the stochastic block model for longitudinal networks. *Biometrika, 105,* 665–680.

Niezink, N.M.D., Snijders, T.A.B., & van Duijn, M.A.J. (2019). No longer discrete: modeling the dynamics of social networks and continuous behaviour. *Sociological Methodology, 49,* 295–340.

McPherson, M., Smith-Lovin, L., & Cook, J.M. (2001). Birds of a feather: homophily in social networks. *Annual Review of Sociology, 27,* 415–444.

Merton, R. (1968). The Matthew effect in science. *Science, 159* (3810), 56–63.

Moreno, J.L. (1934) *Who shall survive? A new approach to the problem of human inter-relations.* Beacon House.

Paul, S. & O'Malley, A.J. (2013). Hierarchical longitudinal models of relationships in social networks. *Applied Statistics, 62,* 705–722.

Prell, C., & Lo, Y.-L. (2016). Network formation and knowledge gains. *Journal of Mathematical Sociology, 40,* 21–52.

R Core Team (2023) *R: a language and environment for statistical computing.* R Foundation for Statistical Computing, Vienna. www.R-project.org/

Rambaran, J.A., Dijkstra, J.K., Munniksma, A., & Cillessen, A. (2015). The development of adolescents' friendships and antipathies: a longitudinal multivariate network test of balance theory. *Social Networks, 43,* 162–176.

Rapoport, A. (1953). Spread of information through a population with socio-structural bias: I. Assumption of transitivity. *Bulletin of Mathematical Biophysics, 15,* 523–533.

Ripley, R.M., Snijders, T.A.B., Bóda, Z., Vörös, A., & Preciado, P. (2023) *Manual for SIENA version 4.0.* University of Oxford, Department of Statistics;

Nuffield College. www.stats.ox.ac.uk/~snijders/siena/

Robins, G., & Pattison, P. (2001). Random graph models for temporal processes in social networks. *Journal of Mathematical Sociology, 25,* 5–41.

Robins, G.L. & Pattison, P.E. (2001). Random graph models for temporal processes in social networks. *Journal of Mathematical Sociology, 25,* 5–41.

Selfhout, M., Burk, W., Branje, S., Denissen, J.J.A., Van Aken, M.A.G., & Meeus, W. (2010). Emerging late adolescent friendship networks and big five personality traits: a dynamic social network perspective. *Journal of Personality, 78,* 509–538.

Schweinberger, M. (2020). Statistical inference for continuous-time Markov processes with block structure based on discrete-time network data. *Statistica Neerlandica, 74,* 342–362.

Selfhout-Van Zalk, M.H.W., Burk, W., Branje, S.J.T., Denissen, J., van Aken, M., & Meeus, W. H. J. (2010). Emerging late adolescent friendship networks and big five personality traits: A social network approach. *Journal of Personality, 78,* 509–538.

Sewell, D.K. & Chen, Y. (2015). Latent space models for dynamic networks. *Journal of the American Statistical Association, 110,* 1646–1657.

Small, M.L. (2009) *Unanticipated gains: origins of network inequality in everyday life.* Oxford University Press.

Snijders, T.A.B. (1996). Stochastic actor-oriented dynamic network analysis. *Journal of Mathematical Sociology, 21,* 149–172.

Snijders, T.A.B. (2001). The statistical evaluation of social network dynamics. *Sociological Methodology, 31,* 361–395.

Snijders, T.A.B. (2011). Network dynamics. In J. Scott & P.J. Carrington (Eds.), *The Sage handbook of social network analysis* (pp. 501–513). Sage.

Snijders, T.A.B. (2013). Network dynamics. In R. Wittek, T.A.B. Snijders & V. Nee (Eds.), *The handbook of rational choice social research* (pp. 252–279). Stanford University Press.

Snijders, T.A.B. (2017). Stochastic actor-oriented models for network dynamics. *Annual Review of Statistics and Its Application, 4,* 343–363.

Snijders, T.A.B. & Kalter, F. (2020). Religious diversity and social cohesion in German classrooms: a micro-macro study based on empirical simulations. In V. Buskens, R. Corten & C. Snijders (Eds.), *Advances in the sociology of trust and cooperation: theory, experiments, and field studies* (pp. 525–543). De Gruyter.

Snijders, T.A.B., & Lomi, A. (2019). Beyond homophily: incorporating actor variables in statistical network models. *Network Science, 7,* 1–19.

Snijders, T.A.B., Lomi, A., & Torló, V. (2013). A model for the multiplex dynamics of two-mode and one-mode networks, with an application to employment preference, friendship, and advice. *Social Networks, 35,* 265–276.

Snijders, T.A.B., & Pickup, M. (2017). Stochastic actor-oriented models for network dynamics. In J.N. Victor, M. Lubell & A.H. Montgomery (Eds.), *Oxford handbook of political networks* (pp. 221–247). Oxford University Press.

Snijders, T.A.B., & Steglich, C.E.G. (2015). Representing micro–macro linkages by actor-based dynamic network models. *Sociological Methods and Research, 44,* 222–271.

Snijders, T.A.B., van de Bunt, G.G., & Steglich, C.E.G. (2010). Introduction to stochastic actor-based models for network dynamics. *Social Networks, 32,* 44–60.

Snijders, T. A. B., & van Duijn, M. A. J. (1997). Simulation for statistical inference in dynamic network models. In R. Conte, R. Hegselmann, & P. Terna, (Eds.), *Simulating Social Phenomena,* (pp. 493–512). Springer.

Sørensen, A.B., & Hallinan, M.T. (1976). A stochastic model for change in group structure. *Social Science Research, 5,* 43–61.

Stadtfeld, C., & Amati, V. (2021). Network mechanisms and network models. In G. Manzo (Ed.), *Research handbook on analytical sociology.* Edward Elgar.

Stadtfeld, C., Hollway, J., & Block, P. (2017). Dynamic network actor Markov models: investigating coordination ties through time. *Sociological Methodology, 47,* 1–40.

Steglich, C.E.G. & Snijders, T.A.B. (2022). Stochastic network modeling as generative social science. In K. Gërxhani, N.D. de Graaf & W. Raub (Eds.), *Handbook of rigorous theoretical and empirical sociology,* Research Handbooks in Sociology Series (pp. 73–99). Edward Elgar.

Steglich, C.E.G., Snijders, T.A.B., & Pearson, M. (2010). Dynamic networks and behaviour: separating selection from influence. *Sociological Methodology, 40,* 329–393.

Tasselli, S., & Kilduff, M. (2021). Network agency. *Academy of Management Annals, 15,* 68–110.

Tasselli, S., Kilduff, M., & Menges, J.I. (2015). The microfoundations of organizational social networks: a review and an agenda for future research. *Journal of Management, 41,* 1361–1387.

Udehn, L. (2002). The changing face of methodological individualism. *Annual Review of Sociology, 8,* 479–507.

van Duijn, M.A.J., Snijders, T.A.B., & Zijlstra, B.J.H. (2004). p_2: A random effects model with covariates for directed graphs. *Statistica Neerlandica, 58,* 234–254.

Veenstra, R., Dijkstra, J.K., Steglich, C., & Van Zalk, M.H. (2013). Network–behaviour dynamics. *Journal of Research on Adolescence, 23,* 399–412.

Wasserman, S. (1979). A stochastic model for directed graphs with transition rates determined by reciprocity. *Sociological Methodology, 9*, 392–412.

Wasserman, S. (1980). Analyzing social networks as stochastic processes. *Journal of the American Statistical Association, 75*, 280–294.

Wasserman, S. (1987). The conformity of two sociometric relations. *Psychometrika, 53*, 261–282.

Zeggelink, E.P.H. (1994). Dynamics of structure: an individual oriented approach. *Social Networks, 16*, 295–333.

Relational Event Models

Aaron Schecter and Noshir Contractor

INTRODUCTION

The proliferation of information on human interactions captured in the form of trace data has spurred some to argue that we are living in the computational era of social science (Contractor, 2019; Lazer et al., 2009; Lazer et al., 2020; Pilny & Poole, 2017; Salganik, 2019; Kitts et al., this volume; Wagner et al., 2021). This growth in data has had a particularly profound impact on the analysis of social networks. Because human interactions can be conceptualised as ties or social relationships, Kitts and Quintane (2021) have argued that researchers need to rethink social networks as 'time-situated events linking actors, including interactions such as conversations, meetings, or transactions' (p. 71). They also point towards the increasing amount of technology used to instrument the collection of such data, such as sensor technologies (e.g., Chaffin et al., 2017) and wrangling trace data from various sources like email histories and social media (e.g., Braun et al., 2018). To leverage these data to advance our understanding of human interactions, researchers have developed the relational event model (REM) first proposed by Butts (2008) and Brandes et al. (2009). Indeed, Robins (2015) writes that REMs 'are among the most exciting in recent network methods and we will undoubtedly see further rapid development in the next few years' (p. 196).

Compared to other inferential statistical frameworks such as exponential random graph models (ERGMs) or stochastic actor-oriented models (SAOMs), REM is specifically designed to analyse timestamped sequences of directed interactions between individuals in a network. Importantly, REMs do not require aggregation of data – that is, forming a static network snapshot – which could lead to validity concerns (Howison et al., 2011; Quintane et al., 2014). This characteristic enables researchers to explicitly study how a network unfolds over time, and what patterns of behaviour emerge. Similar to ERGM and SAOM, REM enables researchers to operationalise different social mechanisms (e.g., reciprocity, transitivity) (Contractor et al., 2006) and test their relative strengths. However, REM also enables researchers to examine the temporal dimension of these social processes in the form of sequential structural signatures (Leenders et al., 2016).

This chapter introduces the current research on the relational event model, significant empirical findings and future research directions. The chapter will first provide an overview of the data format, model details and considerations for implementation. Second, the chapter provides an overview of the two main types of sequential statistics used in relational event modelling. Finally, there is an overview of recent empirical applications and a brief discussion of the software tools used to fit REMs.

THE RELATIONAL EVENT MODEL

Relational Event Data

A relational event is defined as a 'discrete event generated by a social actor and directed toward one or more targets' (Butts, 2008, p. 159). For instance, when individual A sends a message to individual B, at time T, the tuple A to B at time T, provides the necessary information required for one relational event. There are many types of relational events. For instance, events can be edits to software repositories (Quintane et al., 2014; Singh et al., 2011), a contribution to a community message board (Faraj & Johnson, 2011), or adoption of a new technology (Aral & Walker, 2014). At its core, an event is a singular instance of some activity, carried out by a human, machine, or the environment at large. Sending a text message, editing code, clicking a link are all events; they occur at a specific point in time and there is a specific entity initiating them. Likewise, a new law passing, a merger being finalised and a natural disaster are also events in the sense that they occur at a specific time, and there is a specific source.

Relational events are encoded as units of data that include, at the minimum, information about the sender, target and time of the event. Additional information such as the type of event (e.g., phone call or text message), weight (Welles et al., 2014), or valence (e.g., positive or negative interaction; Brandes et al., 2009) may be observed and recorded (Marcum & Butts, 2015).

Table 35.1 summarises these attributes and provides an example.

Any of these attributes can be incorporated into a relational event model. For instance, Brandes et al. (2009) determine the weight and valence of events representing diplomatic exchanges. Brunswicker and Schecter (2019) consider the weight of an event as the number of lines of code edited in a software project. DuBois and Smyth (2010) introduce a relational event model to identify different classes of relational events and apply the technique to multiple settings. Alternatively, events may be egocentric (i.e., focused on one individual); Marcum and Butts (2015) use this version of the model to track the behaviours of elderly individuals throughout the course of a day. Despite these examples, most of the extant literature leverages only the core information of the sender, receiver and timestamp.

Model Overview

To derive meaning from REMs, it is important to understand precisely what the model measures. For any process on a network, there is a discrete set of interactions (i.e., relational events) that can occur during a given timeframe. The frequency of each interaction in this set depends on a unique rate of occurrence. Commonplace actions happen more often so they have a higher rate of occurrence, whereas unusual events have a low rate. Further, the rate also determines the time between interactions – a model containing more common interactions will show less time between interactions than a model with more infrequent interactions. This rate variation forms the basis of event history models (Blossfeld & Rohwer, 1995). In event history models, the rate variation is assumed to be the result of certain covariates that are context-specific. For example, how long it

Table 35.1 Characteristics of relational event data

Characteristic	Definition	Illustrative examples
Sender	The entity which originated the event	John sends a text message → John is the sender
Receiver	The entity which is the recipient of the event	Caroline calls Esther → Esther is the receiver
Time	The time at which the event originated	Sarah clicked a link at 7.05pm → the time is 7.05pm
Weight	The relative importance of the event	Richard edits 500 lines of code → the weight of the event is 500
Valence	The tone (positive or negative) of the event	Bob is chastised by his boss → the event has a negative valence
Type	The classification of the event into one or more categories	Mary sends an email, rather than a phone call → the type of event is an email

took for group members to vote in favour of a new bylaw amendment (e.g., an event) might be influenced by a variety of factors like member age, personality, or ideological views. Butts (2008) amended this framework to interpersonal actions, giving rise to the relational event model. Given the social context, the covariates responsible for the variance in interaction rates represent behavioural and cognitive mechanisms that lead individuals to engage in certain events more often than others.

As a sequence of relational events unfolds over time, the likelihood for an action to occur may change. Consequently, the rate of that event should adjust to reflect the influence of past actions. For instance, if two individuals repeatedly communicate with a third party, the propensity for them to communicate with one another may increase. History thus creates the context for the present. The rates of events are continuously updated to reflect the new network structure. This allows someone studying REM to 'understand how past interactions affect the emergence of future interactions, without assuming that they are completely determined by them' (Quintane et al., 2014, p. 533). As such, relational event models are able to capture long-term trends – that is, stability in relationships over time – as well as short-term deviations (Quintane et al., 2013). Long-term trends, measured as accumulating patterns of interaction, represent the path dependence of REMs; the past provides the context for the present. As patterns repeat themselves, they set the stage for certain events to occur in the future. Short-term patterns, such as participation shifts (Gibson, 2005), represent instead myopic actions based only on the present or the immediate past. For instance, individuals may be inclined to respond immediately to a request for information, even if over time they do not have a propensity to form mutual ties. Taken together, these types of behavioural trends can be used to represent a full spectrum of interaction processes in a single model.

Model Details

Relational events must be directed and observed at a specific moment in time. Additionally, relational events may include defining characteristics such as class (or type) weight. Formally, a relational event is a tuple $e_m = (i_m, j_m, k_m, w_m, t_m)$ containing the sender i_m, receiver j_m, type k_m, weight w_m and time m of an event. Let the observed sequence of relational events, E, be defined as $E = \{e_m \mid (i_m, j_m) \in R_{t_m}, 0 < t_1 < \ldots < t_M < T, m = 1, \ldots, M\}$ be a sequence of M strictly ordered relational events that occur between time 0 and time T. The dyad (i_m, j_m) is a member of the set of all potential links, called the risk set $R_{t_m} \subseteq \{(i, j) \mid (i, j) \in D\}$, where D is the set of all possible directed pairs of actors in the network. The risk set can vary such that at time t_m only a subset of events are possible (this could happen if people leave or join the network, for example). Thus, at any given time there could be a different set of potential links. The risk set can also account for two-mode data (Quintane et al., 2014), such as between Facebook users and a thread.

The objective of relational event modelling is to determine the probability of observing a given event sequence E. Building on prior work in survival analysis (Abbott, 1995; Cox, 1972), we can define the hazard rate for an event as $\lambda_{i_m j_m}(t_m)$, which describes the conditional likelihood for the event (i_m, j_m) to occur at time t_m, given that no event has occurred since time t_{m-1}. Further, $S_{i_m j_m}(t_m - t_{m-1})$ is the survival function, which represents the probability that the event (i_m, j_m) has not happened in the time interval $[t_{m-1}, t_m)$. The probability of observing a particular series of events is thus:

$$\mathbb{P}(E) = \prod_{m=1,\ldots M} \left[\lambda_{i_m j_m}(t_m) \times \prod_{(i,j) \in R_{t_m}} S_{ij}(t_m - t_{m-1}) \right]$$

Here, we have the probability that each event in the sequence occurred at a particular time, multiplied by the probability that no other event happened in the time between events. For simplicity we assume that $t_0 = 0$.

Following prior work (e.g., Brandes et al., 2009; Butts, 2008; DuBois et al., 2013a), we operationalise the hazard rate as $\lambda_{i_m j_m}(t_m \mid \theta, E_m) = \exp(\theta' u_{i_m j_m t_m})$, where $E_m \subseteq E$ is the sequence of events up to time t_m, $u_{i_m j_m t_m} \in \mathbb{R}^{P \times 1}$ is a vector of covariates for dyad (i_m, j_m) at time t_m and θ is a P-dimensional vector of intensity parameters that indicate the influence of each statistic on the hazard rate. The vector of covariates $u_{i_m j_m t_m}$ can include measures that describe patterns in the prior sequence of events (i.e., sequential structural signatures), attributes of the individuals and dyads, or environmental factors; a constant term is included to account for the baseline event rate. By operationalising the hazard function as an exponential function, we are effectively imposing a proportional hazards assumption within each time interval (Cox, 1972). This assumption is reasonable for short time intervals but may not hold for longer time periods; see Lerner et al. (2013b) for further discussion. Other hazard functions can be applied where appropriate, but that is outside the scope of this chapter. Using this definition, the full likelihood of a sequence E given a set of parameters θ is equal to:

$$\mathbb{P}(E,\theta) = \prod_{m=1,\ldots M}\left[\exp(\theta' u_{i_m j_m t_m}) \times \sum_{(i,j)\in R_{t_m}} \exp\left(-(t_m - t_{m-1})\exp(\theta' u_{ijt_m})\right)\right.$$
$$\left. \times \sum_{(i,j)\in R_T} \exp-(T - t_m)\left(\exp(\theta' u_{ijT})\right)\right]$$

This expression captures the probability that each event occurred in the sequence at a specific point in time, multiplied by the probability that no other events happened in each observation window, including the time until the final observation point T.

The full relational event model as defined above requires exact timing information. However, in many circumstances the exact timing of events is not known, only the order. In that case, an ordinal version of the relational event model can be applied (Butts, 2008). The partial likelihood function for this case is:

$$\mathbb{P}(E,\theta) = \prod_{m=1,\ldots M}\left[\frac{\exp(\theta' u_{i_m j_m t_m})}{\sum_{(i,j)\in R_{t_m}} \exp(\theta' u_{ijt_m})}\right]$$

This expression is effectively equivalent to a discrete choice or multinomial logit regression model with time-varying covariates. Indeed, some prior work has noted that the ordinal likelihood model can be interpreted as a series of decisions made by actors in a network, where each choice is a single relational event (DuBois et al., 2013a; Stadtfeld & Block, 2017).

Another popular version of REM is the bipartite formulation proposed by Quintane et al. (2014). The bipartite REM is characterised by a modified risk set to account for ties that cannot exist – that is, between nodes in the same class; otherwise, the model logic is the same. Quintane et al. (2014) used the bipartite REM to study patterns of software development. A relational event in their study was any instance of a software developer (sender) interacting with a software bug (receiver). This conceptualisation of relational events as engagement between humans and code has made the REM a useful tool for understanding how software development is organised. For example, Brunswicker and Schecter (2019) used bipartite relational event models to predict developer contributions in an open-source science community.

To conduct statistical inference with relational event models, either in the complete data or ordinal case, the vector of parameters $\hat{\theta}$ that maximise this likelihood function must be determined. The most common approach is to use maximum likelihood estimation (MLE), where the optimal parameters are defined as $\hat{\theta} = argmax_\theta \left(log\, \mathbb{P}(E;\theta)\right)$, where $\mathbb{P}$ is the likelihood function as stated previously. Solving this optimisation problem is straightforward and can be accomplished using several different statistical programs, which will be discussed later in the chapter. Hypothesis testing can be carried out by creating test statistics $z = \frac{\hat{\theta}}{SE(\hat{\theta})}$, where $SE(\hat{\theta})$ is the standard error of the estimated coefficient. The standard errors can be found by taking the inverse of the hessian matrix with respect to the log-likelihood function. The test statistic z approximately follows the standard normal distribution. As an alternative to the frequentist approach, Bayesian estimation can also be used to find the parameters $\hat{\theta}$. The Bayesian approach is particularly popular for extensions to the REM that involve some type of multilevel or latent structure (DuBois et al., 2013a; DuBois et al., 2013b; DuBois & Smyth, 2010).

Complexity and the Need for Sampling with REMs

A key computational hurdle for fitting REMs is calculation of statistics for the risk set at each timepoint (Butts, 2008; Lerner & Lomi, 2019; Vu et al., 2015). For each event, the risk set R_{t_m} is composed of all events that could have occurred at the same time as the observed event, whether they are likely or not. Because the events are dyadic, this means that the risk set contains all the potential dyads that could have existed instead of the true observation. Accordingly, the magnitude of the risk set that must be calculated – and thus the complexity of the REM – is a function of both the number of actors, N, and the number of events, M. For a sequence with N actors, the risk set has cardinality equal to the number of actors N multiplied by N-1 (i.e., no self-loops). Hence, the total size of the risk set for a full sequence is M*(N*(N-1)) potential events.

A key problem with the computation of the risk set is that the number of potential events in a dyadic dataset increases in the order of the square of the number of actors in the dataset. This problem is compounded by the potentially large number of observations needed to identify meaningful effects. Because we would have to calculate the values of statistics for each potential event, this computational problem becomes unmanageable when the number of actors and the number of events become too large (Butts, 2008; Vu et al., 2015). To remedy this issue, random samples of the risk set may be drawn, often using case control sampling (Lerner & Lomi, 2019; Vu et al., 2015). This means that researchers randomly draw a fixed number of potential events from the full risk set and use them to approximate the alternative set. As Schecter and Quintane (2021) demonstrate, such a procedure does not lead to any significant problems with the power, precision, or accuracy of the coefficient estimates. Lerner and Lomi (2019) also find that the REM is relatively stable under random sampling of both the risk set and the event sequence overall.

Goodness of Fit for the REM

Because the relational event model is typically fit using either maximum likelihood estimation or Bayesian methods, likelihood-based measures are typically the most appropriate choice to evaluate fit (Butts, 2008). Common measures reported in studies include the null and residual deviance, the Akaike information criterion (AIC), or Bayesian information criterion (BIC). DuBois et al. (2013b) also suggested using the deviance information criterion (DIC) because of its utility for models generated by Markov chain Monte Carlo simulation, as typically used in Bayesian models. Typically, model improvement is assessed using likelihood ratio tests – that is, improvement in the residual deviance – or by selecting the model with the smallest information criterion value.

While these measures are useful for evaluating model improvement and relative fit, they do not provide any significant insight into how well the REM coefficients replicate the behaviour of the observed sequences. This type of goodness-of-fit measure is common practice for other statistical models of networks like exponential random graph models (Hunter et al., 2008) and stochastic actor-oriented models (Snijders, 2001). To remedy this issue, Brandenberger (2019) proposed a method for evaluating REMs by simulating sequences from the estimated model and comparing them to the original data. A relational event model is considered a good fit if it predicts the actual events and interevent times, within some 'tolerance' (p. 11) constraints, better than a randomly generated sequence.

CREATING RELATIONAL EVENT STATISTICS

There are two common types of effects used in model building for relational events: (1) endogenous and (2) exogenous covariates (Pilny et al., 2016). Endogenous covariates refer to prior patterns in the relational event history up to that point. Often, these are referred to as *network theories of networks* because they are using the presence of ties, or in REM's case, the presence of past structures of relational events, to predict the occurrence of other network interactions (Borgatti & Halgin, 2011). Some of the most common endogenous covariates include factors like reciprocity, closure, brokerage and popularity (Lusher et al., 2013; Robins, 2015). Consider the example of reciprocity. If actor A sends a relational event to actor B, what is the likelihood that B will send a relational event to A next? Exogenous covariates refer to node attributes, environmental conditions, or other external effects (e.g., different time periods; Marcum & Butts, 2015). A wide variety of theories could be drawn upon in these instances. Consider the example of homophily (i.e., birds of a feather flock together). Here, an REM could seek answers to whether actor A might be more likely to send a relational event to actor B because they have something exogenously in common (i.e., age, social identity, attitudes/beliefs, work team, etc.). Finally, endogenous and exogenous covariates can also intersect in a myriad of ways. For instance, Robins and Pattison (2005) review how exogenous and endogenous factors can co-evolve together, particularly to test social influence and social selection models (e.g., do smokers select other smokers as friends or are they influenced by their friends to take up smoking?). For instance, consider the two previously reviewed factors: (1) reciprocity and (2) homophily. One might want to test homophily beyond simple relational event *sending*. Here, REM could be able to test whether or not actor B might *reciprocate* to A (or not) because of some shared homophilous attribute.

The utility of the relational event model is the ability to capture a wide range of sequential patterns, sometimes referred to as sequential structural signatures (SSSs; see Leenders et al., 2016), and use them to predict subsequent interactions. These sequential signatures encompass endogenous patterns, as well as endogenous patterns moderated by exogenous covariates. Importantly, SSSs can be delineated into two types: participation shifts and volume-based. Participation shifts describe simple patterns of myopic or local turn-taking in conversation and are useful for understanding how one event leads to the immediate next event. By contrast, volume-based statistics capture the accumulation of events in certain configurations. These measures are more useful for understanding how the entire past culminates in a particular event. The next sections describe both of these types in greater detail.

Participation Shifts

A simple form of structural signature commonly used in relational event modelling is the participation shift. Participation shifts are patterns based on earlier work by Gibson (2003, 2005) that described turn-taking in small group communication. These patterns have been operationalised in REM as binary variables indicating whether a certain type of event followed another. For example, a participation shift describing *reciprocity* would determine if an event A to B was immediately followed by an event from B to A. Butts (2008) describes several other such statistics and applies them to radio communication. In Table 35.2 a subset of these participation shifts is described.

The first measure, referred to as ABBA, captures a sort of direct reciprocity. A relational event is sent from one individual to another, and the immediate next event is a relational event directed from the receiver back to the sender. This signature is useful for assessing turn-taking in conversation (Gibson, 2005). The second measure, ABBY, is related to the notion of transitivity; a relational event sent from a to b triggers a subsequent message from b to another receiver y. The ABBY participation shift can capture indirect turn-taking or can be used to approximate communication cascades. The participation shifts ABAY and ABXB represent repeated senders and repeated receivers respectively. These measures represent a sort of local centralisation, where consecutive relational events have a specific focus. Finally, the ABXY shift captures a type of turn-usurping behaviour, where the flow of communication jumps from one dyad to another (Butts, 2008; Gibson, 2005). This participation shift is more likely in larger networks with potentially many simultaneous conversations, and thus may not have much substantive significance outside small groups.

Participation shifts have the advantage of being easy to calculate and easy to interpret. Specifically, they are all binary variables taking a value of 1 if consecutive relational events meet a certain criterion, and 0 otherwise. The fitted coefficients also directly relate to how frequently the specific pattern appears over time. However, they are limited in that they are completely myopic; the statistics are only functions of the event immediately prior. Further, participation shifts are most useful in smaller networks where communication is visible to all (such as the radio communication network in Butts, 2008). In that case, turn-taking behaviour has meaning. By contrast, in a much larger network (such as corporate email networks), participation shifts might not capture relevant behaviour, as two consecutive emails may not be related to one another. To remedy these issues, many researchers employ another type of SSS: volume-based statistics.

Table 35.2 Participation shift sequential structural signatures

Pattern	Description	Visualization
AB-BA	Individual a directs a relational event to individual b, and the next observation is a relational event from b to a.	A → B B → A
AB-BY	Individual a directs a relational event to individual b, and the next observation is a relational event from b to a different individual y.	A → B B → Y
AB-AY	Individual a directs a relational event to individual b, and the next observation is a relational event from a to a different individual y.	A → B A → Y
AB-XB	Individual a directs a relational event to individual b, and the next observation is a relational event from a different individual x to b.	A → B X → B
AB-XY	Individual a directs a relational event to individual b, and the next observation is a relational event from x to y, who are both unique individuals.	A → B X → Y

Volume-Based Structural Signatures

As an alternative to participation shifts, volume-based sequential structural signatures are statistics that describe the accumulation of relational events in a particular pattern. Take, for example, the concept of *inertia*. In a network with inertia, the likelihood of A interacting with B at time t is a function of how many messages A has sent B before that time. In other words, the prior volume of interaction impacts the tendency for additional action. Another more complicated measure is *transitivity*. This statistic captures the prior interactions between A and B, as well as the interactions between B and C. Together, these actions can predict the likelihood of A interacting directly with C. In Table 35.3 we describe five common volume-based statistics. *Inertia*, also referred to as persistence (Butts, 2008), is a measure of how often a dyad is repeated over time. In other words, if i sends more events to j, i will become more (less) likely to send subsequent events to j. *Reciprocity* is a measure of how often dyad (i,j) occurs as a function of events sent from j to i previously. Put another way, j sending events to i makes i more (less) likely to respond with a subsequent event. *Activity* describes the tendency for a particular node to initiate a new relational event. In other words, i sending more (less) events in the past makes i more (less) likely to send a new event, regardless of the recipient. Similar to activity, *popularity* represents the tendency for events to be directed towards a particular individual. The more (less) individual j receives events, the more (less) likely they are to receive subsequent events, regardless of the sender. Finally, *transitivity* is a triadic statistic, in that it relates to the likelihood of communication between i and j to prior events between a third-party k (Quintane & Carnabuci, 2016). Essentially, transitivity is a measure of how likely i is to send an event to j if i frequently sent events to k in the past, and k also sent events frequently to j.

A key feature of volume-based SSSs is their ability to capture the path dependent nature of relational event sequences. In other words, the likelihood of an event occurring at time t is a function of not just the last event, but potentially all prior events. Further, volume-based statistics allow for different events to be assessed on a continuum. For example, three actors might initiate relational events at three different rates, based on their prior activity. Such statistics allow for a more nuanced understanding of how communication unfolds.

Table 35.3 Volume-based sequential structural signatures

Variable	Formula	Interpretation	Visualization
Activity	$u^A_{ijt} = \sum_k n_{ikt}$	The likelihood of *i* sending a message to *j* at time *t* is a function of how many messages *i* has sent before time *t*.	
Popularity	$u^P_{ijt} = \sum_k n_{kjt}$	The likelihood of *i* sending a message to *j* at time *t* is a function of how many messages *j* has received before time *t*.	
Inertia	$u^I_{ijt} = n_{ijt}$	The likelihood of *i* sending a message to *j* at time *t* is a function of how many messages *i* has sent to *j* before time *t*.	
Reciprocity	$u^R_{ijt} = n_{kjt}$	The likelihood of *i* sending a message to *j* at time *t* is a function of how many messages *j* has sent to *i* before time *t*.	
Transitivity	$u^T_{ijt} = \sum_k n_{ikt} \times n_{kjt}$	The likelihood of *i* sending a message to *j* at time *t* is a function of how many messages *i* has sent to other individuals *k* and how many times those individuals sent messages to *j* before time *t*.	

Notes: ○ is the sender, ● is the receiver and ⊙ is a third party. Arrows indicate direction of events. Past interactions are represented as solid arrows ⟶ and a future event is represented as a dashed arrow ---▶. The value n_{ijt} is equal to the number of messages sent by i to j up to but not including time t.

Considerations for Weighting Events in REMs

The large size and potentially long time span of relational event datasets requires researchers to use some form of scaling to make the sufficient statistics comparable over time (Brandes et al., 2009; Kitts et al., 2017; Quintane et al., 2014). One approach would be to simply count the number of past relational events on each dyad over the whole event history. This method could be problematic for two reasons. First, some statistics (such as activity or transitivity) could become very large in magnitude, especially compared to constant covariates or participation shifts (which are binary). As a result, the model fitting procedure could become unstable (DuBois et al., 2013b), leading to poor estimates of the REM coefficients. Second, as the magnitudes of the statistics grow, so will the differences across dyads. As a result, it might appear that the relative likelihood of two different events is changing, even though the differences are only due to the accumulation of time. To avoid this issue, researchers can specify their statistics so that their values are independent of how much time or how many events have elapsed since the beginning of the observation window.

An important consideration when using volume-based statistics is thus *how* to assign weights to prior events. Three main forms of scaling are commonly used to control the magnitude of network statistics over time (Brandes et al., 2009; Kitts et al., 2017; Quintane et al., 2014): proportional, exponential decay and sliding window. Proportionate scaling involves dividing the statistic by the sum of the statistic across dyads, yielding fractional values (Butts, 2008; Quintane et al., 2014). This approach ensures all counts are relative to the rest of the network at all points. For instance, the scaled version of activity would be $\Sigma_k n_{ikt} / \Sigma_h \Sigma_k n_{hkt}$. The measure would now be interpreted as the proportion all messages sent before time t by actor i. Alternatively, the exponential decay approach reduces the effect of events over time, so that recent events carry more weight than distant events. For instance, some studies have used a half-life (Brandes et al., 2009; Lerner et al., 2013a), where the half-life is the time until an event has a weight of one half. Other studies have used a sigmoidal function to decrease the weight of prior events (e.g., Kitts et al., 2017). Using decay functions emphasises recent events and represents a sort of diminishing memory in the network (Leenders et al., 2016). Finally, a sliding window approach involves computing the statistics using counts, but only considering events within a certain range. For instance, only events within the last day are counted, or only the last 100 events. While any of these choices can be valid depending on the context, researchers should be aware of the drawbacks of each scaling method (see Schecter & Quintane, 2021).

EMPIRICAL APPLICATIONS OF THE RELATIONAL EVENT MODEL

Relational event models have been applied to a variety of unique empirical contexts, with relational events taking a variety of different forms. A first major application area is the study of communication patterns in teams and organisations, particularly the exchange of text messages, phone calls and emails. Butts (2008) analysed patterns of radio communication among first responders during the 9/11 terrorist attack. Using participation shifts, he found that first responders had a strong tendency to immediately respond to a directed message (ABBA participation shift) and to continue communication chains (ABBY). Quintane et al. (2013) examined short- and long-term patterns of reciprocity and closure in project teams and found that both patterns had a stronger influence on communication in the short-term. In a separate study, Quintane and Carnabuci (2016) tested different triadic brokerage signatures in corporate email communication and found divergent patterns between the short- and long-term time horizons. Schecter et al. (2018) used the relational event model to show how team psychological constructs were linked to the strength of different endogenous structural signatures. For example, the authors found that those who viewed their team as being well coordinated (coordination construct) have a stronger negative tendency towards activity and preferential attachment than have those who do not. In other words, members of the team who believed the team was effective also engaged in decentralised behaviours.

A second application area examines the interactions between humans and various digital artefacts such as software code or online forums. In these studies, the two-mode relational event model is used; relational events are directed from an individual to a task or tool. Studies using relational event models to analyse software development have focused on why developers choose to contribute code to specific software bugs or online apps (Brunswicker & Schecter, 2019; Quintane et al., 2014). These studies have found that development patterns tend to be relatively centralised (a few active developers and a few popular targets), and that individual developers tend to form short-term clusters. Other work has considered contributions to open-source projects like Wikipedia (Lerner & Lomi, 2017, 2018) and identified the emergence of hierarchal relations among contributors. Another study leveraging the two-mode REM approach focused on student engagement in massive online courses (Vu et al., 2015). The authors specifically predicted when students would drop out of the course, what forums they would contribute to and when they would submit quiz responses.

Relational event models have also been used to study a variety of macro-level phenomenon. Examples include hospital patient transfers (Kitts et al., 2017), corporate interlock networks (Valeeva et al., 2020) and financial transactions in the interbank market (Zappa & Vu, 2021). Another common application of REM is to study political collaborations (Brandenberger, 2018, 2019; Lerner et al., 2013a). For instance, Brandenberger (2018) treats the co-sponsorship of a bill as a relational event and uses reciprocity to predict future collaborations. Other work predicts whether two nation states will have positive or negative interactions based on past political relations (Brandes et al., 2009; Lerner et al., 2013a). Relational event modelling has also been used to study more unique contexts, such as patterns of animal networks (Patison et al., 2015; Tranmer et al., 2015). In these studies, the authors use REM to disentangle continuous sensor data tracking when animals are in close proximity to each other – that is, a relational event.

In sum, the relational event model has been applied to a wide array of network data types, including traditional network relations such as communication, two-mode interactions between people and software or tools, interactions between companies or organisations, collaborations and instances of close contact. Across all of these examples, the data structure is still fundamentally the same; timestamped instances of an action between a sender and a receiver, possibly including other information. Further, the studies cited all use fundamentally similar sequential structural signatures such as reciprocity, transitivity, or preferential attachment. As such, the REM is a flexible tool that can be broadly applied across contexts to answer questions about the unfolding of network interactions across a wide spectrum of academic disciplines.

EXTENSIONS TO THE RELATIONAL EVENT MODEL

The basic relational event model as proposed by Butts (2008) has since been extended in several important ways to accommodate various applications. One important area of work involves extending the REM to account for multilevel data. DuBois et al. (2013a) introduced a REM for data that follows a hierarchical structure (e.g., an omnibus REM for multiple event histories). The authors' objective was to pool many observations of independent sequences to conduct inference on behavioural patterns in aggregate. They demonstrated that a hierarchical method could overcome issues of noisy data with potentially short individual sequences. Other work has extended the REM to account for distinct subgroups nested within a broader network by applying stochastic blockmodelling logic (DuBois et al., 2013b). Other research has considered 'pooled' effects for multiple relational event histories (Marcum & Butts, 2015; Vu et al., 2015). These studies each enhance the ability of REM to account for complex interdependencies among social levels, though more work is needed to unify the different approaches.

A second important extension is the relational hyperevent model, which models the occurrence of events from a sender to one or many other receivers (Lerner et al., 2019; Lerner et al., 2021; Lerner & Lomi, 2022). This extension is important because, in many cases, events are not directed at one specific person, but rather a group of people collectively. Consider a person making a statement, in person or via group chat, to a collection of teammates The relational hyperevent model is based on the same likelihood function as the traditional REM, with a hazard rate for each possible event and a survival function for the time between events. The key difference is that the risk set is adjusted to account for events directed at more than one receiver. Specifically, the possible receiver of a relational event is any non-empty subset of the individuals in the network; recipients could be a single individual, a pair of individuals, or even larger groups. Applications of the relational hyperevent model include tracking meetings (Lerner et al., 2021), the spread of disease (Hâncean et al., 2021) and scientific collaboration (Lerner et al., 2019).

SOFTWARE PACKAGES

Researchers have several options for fitting relational event models using statistical software. Perhaps the most common choice is the software package *relevent* (Butts, 2015) in the programming language R which fits the REM using either maximum likelihood or Bayesian estimation techniques.

This package accommodates sequences with complete time information as well as order information only. To accompany the *relevent* package, the *informR* package (Marcum & Butts, 2015) can be used to construct sequence statistics for use in relational event modelling. The *informR* package is particularly useful for creating complex signatures based on participation shift logic – that is, sequences of distinct events following each other directly. An alternative option is the package *goldfish* also in the R programming language (Stadtfeld et al., 2017a). The package *goldfish* is meant to fit dynamic network actor models, which are close analogues of the REM and under certain specifications should yield comparable results on event sequence data (Stadtfeld et al., 2017a, 2017b; Stadtfeld & Block, 2017).

As an alternative to packages designed for relational event modelling, researchers can also leverage the similarities between the REM likelihood function and the Cox regression model (Cox, 1972) with time-varying covariates. If the values of the sequential structural signatures are precomputed for each event, the data structure can be analysed with the R package *survival* (Therneau, 2022) using the coxph function. Further, as noted by Quintane et al. (2014), when only order information, rather than actual timestamp information, is present, the relational event model is equivalent to a conditional logit regression model, which can be estimated using a variety of packages including *survival*. Other researchers have also implemented their own code for conducting relational event analysis, though they are often not widely available.

FUTURE RESEARCH DIRECTIONS

The increasing availability of relational event data spawns many opportunities for future research on REMs, both conceptually and methodologically. Given that REM is a fruitful way of understanding interaction processes, a logical next step is to connect the unveiled patterns to different emergent outcomes. These outcomes may be emergent psychological mechanisms or tangible performance metrics. In either case, future work is needed to establish such connections. The first such extension is the co-evolution of events and states. Current specifications of REM are primarily focused on explaining the dynamic unfolding of relational events based on prior relational events and actor attributes (such as individual demographics) or shared dyadic actor attributes (such as homophily). As such, current implementations' focus on relational events and actor states come at the expense of considering actor events (such as a person exercising or eating) and relational states (such as trust or friendship). As such current implementations of REM do not capture the extent to which relational events (such as communication interactions) can, in turn, influence the unfolding of future relational states of the actors (such as their trust or friendship). Nor are they able to explain the unfolding of future actor states such as the emergence and development of psychological constructs (Carter et al., 2018) or future actor events such as their decision to exercise or eat. Theoretically these processes do not occur in one direction, however; there is a cycle whereby actor and relational states and actor and relational events all co-evolve collectively (Kozlowski, 2015; Zhang & Gable, 2017). There is a continuous process of individuals taking actions based on their underlying beliefs and feelings, and their actions and experiences subsequently reinforce (or change) those same underlying states. This logic is comparable to that of stochastic actor-oriented models (c.f., Snijders, 2001; Snijders et al., 2010) which seeks to explain the co-evolution of actor and relational states but not actor and relational events. Accordingly, a key future direction is to blend the mathematical logic of stochastic actor-oriented models with the relational event model to form a unified co-evolution framework.

The second extension is the connection of REM to network-level outcomes such as team problem-solving effectiveness, commercial success of a product, or downloads for a piece of software. By itself, REM cannot provide a direct inference to such outcomes because it is only capable of predicting specific interaction patterns. Existing work has tried to address this issue in a few ways. For example, one approach is to fit a REM for both high- and low-performing groups (Quintane et al., 2013). Another is to calculate the performance of a *single* relational event by predicting its value, conditioned on the past history (Brunswicker & Schecter, 2019). However, these approaches still cannot connect an entire sequence to an outcome. There are a few potential avenues to solve this problem. First, researchers could use the REM parameter values – for example, the coefficient for inertia for a single team – as independent variables to predict success (Schecter, 2017). Unfortunately, it is not clear whether this approach would yield valid inferential results. Second, performance could be represented as an outcome of some hidden process with partially observable information (e.g., a type of hidden Markov model with relational events as the signal), or as the target variable for a recurrent neural network. Future work can hopefully determine the efficacy of these or other approaches.

Finally, there are a variety of natural extensions to the relational event model that have not been studied or have not been fully developed. For instance, it may be possible to identify clusters in a network based on relational event patterns (DuBois et al., 2013b), or even identify different archetypes of individuals. There is also potential to combine REMs with regression discontinuity models (Bliese & Lang, 2016) to identify different patterns of behaviour before and after some timepoint, or to detect changepoints in the data. Further, the predictive power of the relational event model is not well explored – it is not known under what circumstances the model will accurately predict future events.

REFERENCES

Abbott, A. (1995). Sequence analysis: new methods for old ideas. *Annual Review of Sociology*, *21*(1), 93–113.

Aral, S., & Walker, D. (2014). Tie strength, embeddedness, and social influence: a large-scale networked experiment. *Management Science*, *60*(6), 1352–1370. doi.org/10.1287/mnsc.2014.1936

Bliese, P.D., & Lang, J.W. (2016). Understanding relative and absolute change in discontinuous growth models: coding alternatives and implications for hypothesis testing. *Organizational Research Methods*, *19*(4), 562–592.

Borgatti, S. P., & Halgin, D. S. (2011). On network theory. *Organization science*, *22*(5), 1168–1181.

Blossfeld, H. P., & Rohwer, G. (1995). Techniques of event history modeling: New approaches to causal analysis.

Brandenberger, L. (2018). Trading favors: examining the temporal dynamics of reciprocity in congressional collaborations using relational event models. *Social Networks*, *54*, 238–253. doi.org/10.1016/j.socnet.2018.02.001

Brandenberger, L. (2019). Predicting network events to assess goodness of fit of relational event models. *Political Analysis*, 1–16. doi.org/10.1017/pan.2019.10

Brandes, U., Lerner, J., & Snijders, T.A.B. (2009). Networks evolving step by step: statistical analysis of dyadic event data. *International Conference on Advances in Social Network Analysis and Mining*. 200–205.

Braun, M.T., Kuljanin, G., & DeShon, R.P. (2018). Special considerations for the acquisition and wrangling of big data. *Organizational Research Methods*, *21*(3), 633–659. doi.org/10.1177/1094428117690235

Brunswicker, S., & Schecter, A. (2019). Coherence or flexibility? The paradox of change for developers' digital innovation trajectory on open platforms. *Research Policy*. doi.org/10.1016/j.respol.2019.03.016

Butts, C.T. (2008). A relational event framework for social action. *Sociological Methodology*, *38*(1), 155–200.

Butts, C. (2015). *Package 'relevent'* (1.0-4) [R]. www.r-project.org/pub/R/web/packages/relevent/relevent.pdf

Carter, N.T., Carter, D.R., & DeChurch, L.A. (2018). Implications of observability for the theory and measurement of emergent team phenomena. *Journal of Management*, *44*(4), 1398–1425. doi.org/10.1177/0149206315609402

Chaffin, D., Heidl, R., Hollenbeck, J.R., Howe, M., Yu, A., Voorhees, C., & Calantone, R. (2017). The promise and perils of wearable sensors in organizational research. *Organizational Research Methods*, *20*(1), 3–31. doi.org/10.1177/1094428115617004

Contractor, N. (2019). How can computational social science motivate the development of theories, data, and methods to advance our understanding of communication and organizational dynamics?. In Foucault Welles, B. & González-Bailón, S. (Eds.), *The Oxford Handbook of Networked Communication*. https://doi.org/10.1093/oxfordhb/9780190460518.013.7

Contractor, N.S., Wasserman, S., & Faust, K. (2006). Testing multitheoretical, multilevel hypotheses about organizational networks: an analytic framework and empirical example. *Academy of Management Review*, *31*(3), 681–703.

Cox, D.R. (1972). Regression Models and Life-Tables. *Journal of the Royal Statistical Society. Series B (Methodological)*, *34*(2), 187–220.

DuBois, C., Butts, C.T., McFarland, D., & Smyth, P. (2013a). Hierarchical models for relational event sequences. *Journal of Mathematical Psychology*, *57*(6), 297–309.

DuBois, C., Butts, C.T., & Smyth, P. (2013b). Stochastic blockmodeling of relational event dynamics. *Proceedings of the Sixteenth International Conference on Artificial Intelligence and Statistics*, *31*, 238–246.

DuBois, C., & Smyth, P. (2010). Modeling relational events via latent classes. *Proceedings of the 16th ACM SIGKDD International Conference on Knowledge Discovery and Data Mining*. July, 803–812.

Faraj, S., & Johnson, S.L. (2011). Network exchange patterns in online communities. *Organization Science*, *22*(6), 1464–1480.

Foucault Welles, B., Vashevko, A., Bennett, N., & Contractor, N. (2014). Dynamic models of communication in an online friendship network. *Communication Methods and Measures*, *8*(4), 223-243.

Gibson, D.R. (2003). Participation shifts: order and differentiation in group conversation. *Social Forces*, *81*(13), 35–81.

Gibson, D.R. (2005). Taking turns and talking ties: networks and conversational interaction. *American Journal of Sociology*, *110*(6), 1561–1597.

Hâncean, M.-G., Lerner, J., Perc, M., Ghiță, M.C., Bunaciu, D.-A., Stoica, A.A., & Mihăilă, B.-E. (2021). The role of age in the spreading of Covid-19 across a social network in Bucharest. *Journal of Complex Networks*, *9*(4), cnab026. doi.org/10.1093/comnet/cnab026

Howison, J., Wiggins, A., & Crowston, K. (2011). Validity issues in the use of social network analysis with digital trace data. *Journal of the Association for Information Systems: Atlanta*, *12*(12), 767–797.

Hunter, D., Goodreau, S.M., & Handcock, M.S. (2008). Goodness of fit of social network models. *Journal of the American Statistical Association*, *103*(481), 248–258. doi.org/10.1198/016214507000000446

Kitts, J.A., Lomi, A., Mascia, D., Pallotti, F., & Quintane, E. (2017). Investigating the temporal dynamics of interorganizational exchange: patient transfers among Italian hospitals. *American Journal of Sociology*, *123*(3), 850–910. doi.org/10.1086/693704

Kitts, J.A., & Quintane, E. (2021). Rethinking social networks in the era of computational social science. In R. Light & J. Moody (Eds.), *The Oxford handbook of social networks* (pp. 70–97). Oxford University Press. doi.org/10.1093/oxfordhb/9780190251765.013.24

Kozlowski, S.W. (2015). Advancing research on team process dynamics: theoretical, methodological, and measurement considerations. *Organizational Psychology Review*, *5*(4), 270–299.

Lazer, D., Pentland, A. (Sandy), Adamic, L., Aral, S., Barabasi, A.L., Brewer, D., Christakis, N., Contractor, N., Fowler, J., Gutmann, M., Jebara, T., King, G., Macy, M., Roy, D., & Van Alstyne, M. (2009). Life in the network: the coming age of computational social science. *Science (New York, NY)*, *323*(5915), 721–723. doi.org/10.1126/science.1167742

Lazer, D. M. J., Pentland, A., Watts, D. J., Aral, S., Athey, S., Contractor, N., Freelon, D., Gonzalez-Bailon, S., King, G., Margetts, H., Nelson, A., Salganik, M. J., Strohmaier, M., Vespignani, A., & Wagner, C. (2020). Computational social science: Obstacles and opportunities. *Science*, 369(6507), 1060–1062. doi: 10.1126/science.aaz8170

Leenders, R., Contractor, N., & DeChurch, L. (2016). Once upon a time: understanding team processes as relational event networks. *Organizational Psychology Review*, *6*(1), 92–115.

Lerner, J., Bussmann, M., Snijders, T.A.B., & Brandes, U. (2013a). Modeling frequency and type of interaction in event networks. *Corvinus Journal of Sociology and Social Policy*, *1*, 3–32.

Lerner, J., Indlekofer, N., Nick, B., & Brandes, U. (2013b). Conditional independence in dynamic networks. *Journal of Mathematical Psychology*, *57*(6), 275–283. doi.org/10.1016/j.jmp.2012.03.002

Lerner, J., & Lomi, A. (2017). The third man: hierarchy formation in Wikipedia. *Applied Network Science*, *2*(1), 24. doi.org/10.1007/s41109-017-0043-2

Lerner, J., & Lomi, A. (2018). The free encyclopedia that anyone can dispute: an analysis of the microstructural dynamics of positive and negative relations in the production of contentious Wikipedia articles. *Social Networks*. doi.org/10.1016/j.socnet.2018.12.003

Lerner, J., & Lomi, A. (2019). Reliability of relational event model estimates under sampling: how to fit a relational event model to 360 million dyadic events. *Network Science*, 1–39. doi.org/10.1017/nws.2019.57

Lerner, J., & Lomi, A. (2022). A dynamic model for the mutual constitution of individuals and events. *Journal of Complex Networks*, *10*(2), cnac004. doi.org/10.1093/comnet/cnac004

Lerner, J., Lomi, A., Mowbray, J., Rollings, N., & Tranmer, M. (2021). Dynamic network analysis of contact diaries. *Social Networks*, *66*, 224–236. doi.org/10.1016/j.socnet.2021.04.001

Lerner, J., Tranmer, M., Mowbray, J., & Hancean, M.-G. (2019). REM beyond dyads: relational hyperevent models for multi-actor interaction networks (arXiv:1912.07403). *arXiv*. arxiv.org/abs/1912.07403

Lusher, D., Koskinen, J., & Robins, G. (Eds.). (2013). *Exponential random graph models for social networks: Theory, methods, and applications*. Cambridge University Press.

Marcum, C.S., & Butts, C.T. (2015). Constructing and modifying sequence statistics for relevent using informR in R. *Journal of Statistical Software*, *64*(5), 1–36.

Patison, K.P., Quintane, E., Swain, D.L., Robins, G., & Pattison, P. (2015). Time is of the essence: an application of a relational event model for animal social networks. *Behavioral Ecology and Sociobiology*, *69*(5), 841–855. doi.org/10.1007/s00265-015-1883-3

Pilny, A., Schecter, A., Poole, M. S., & Contractor, N. (2016). An illustration of the relational event model to analyze group interaction processes. *Group Dynamics: Theory, Research, and Practice*, *20*(3), 181.

Pilny, A., & Poole, M.S. (Eds.). (2017). *Group processes: data-driven computational approaches*. Springer. doi.org/10.1007/978-3-319-48941-4

Quintane, E., Conaldi, G., Tonellato, M., & Lomi, A. (2014). Modeling relational events a case study on an open source software project. *Organizational Research Methods*, *17*(1), 23–50.

Quintane, E., & Carnabuci, G. (2016). How do brokers broker? Tertius gaudens, tertius iungens, and the temporality of structural holes. *Organization Science*, *27*(6), 1343–1360.

Quintane, E., Pattison, P.E., Robins, G.L., & Mol, J.M. (2013). Short- and long-term stability in organizational networks: temporal structures of project teams. *Social Networks*, *35*(4), 528–540.

Robins, G. (2015). *Doing social network research: network-based research design for social scientists*. Sage.

Salganik, M.J. (2019). *Bit by bit: social research in the digital age*. Princeton University Press.

Schecter, A.M. (2017). It's about time: theorizing the antecedents and outcomes of dynamic processes in teams and multiteam systems. Doctoral dissertation, Northwestern University.

Schecter, A., Pilny, A., Leung, A., Poole, M. S., & Contractor, N. (2018). Step by step: Capturing the dynamics of work team process through relational event sequences. *Journal of Organizational Behavior*, *39*(9), 1163-1181.

Schecter, A., & Quintane, E. (2021). The power, accuracy, and precision of the relational event model. *Organizational Research Methods*, *24*(4), 802–829. doi.org/10.1177/1094428120963830

Singh, P.V., Tan, Y., & Youn, N. (2011). A hidden Markov model of developer learning dynamics in open source software projects. *Information Systems Research*, *22*(4), 790–807.

Snijders, T.A.B. (2001). The statistical evaluation of social network dynamics. *Sociological Methodology*, *31*(1), 361–395.

Snijders, T.A.B., Van de Bunt, G.G., & Steglich, C.E. (2010). Introduction to stochastic actor-based models for network dynamics. *Social Networks*, *32*(1), 44–60.

Stadtfeld, C., & Block, P. (2017). Interactions, actors, and time: dynamic network actor models for relational events. *Sociological Science*, *4*, 318–352.

Stadtfeld, C., Hollway, J., & Block, P. (2017a). Dynamic network actor models: investigating coordination ties through time. *Sociological Methodology*, *47*.

Stadtfeld, C., Hollway, J., & Block, P. (2017b). Rejoinder: DyNAMs and the grounds for actor-oriented network event models. *Sociological Methodology*, *47*(1), 56–67. doi.org/10.1177/0081175017733457

Therneau, T. (2022). *Survival* (3.3-1) [R].

Tranmer, M., Marcum, C.S., Morton, F.B., Croft, D.P., & de Kort, S.R. (2015). Using the relational event model (REM) to investigate the temporal dynamics of animal social networks. *Animal Behaviour*, *101*, 99–105. doi.org/10.1016/j.anbehav.2014.12.005

Valeeva, D., Heemskerk, E.M., & Takes, F.W. (2020). The duality of firms and directors in board interlock networks: a relational event modeling approach. *Social Networks*, *62*, 68–79. doi.org/10.1016/j.socnet.2020.02.009

Vu, D., Pattison, P., & Robins, G. (2015). Relational event models for social learning in MOOCs. *Social Networks*, *43*, 121–135.

Wagner, C., Strohmaier, M., Olteanu, A., Kiciman, E., Contractor, N. & Eliassi-Rad, T. (2021). Measuring algorithmically infused societies. Nature (2021). doi:10.1038/s41586-021-03666-1

Zappa, P., & Vu, D.Q. (2021). Markets as networks evolving step by step: relational event models for the interbank market. *Physica A: Statistical Mechanics and Its Applications*, *565*, 125557. doi.org/10.1016/j.physa.2020.125557

Zhang, M., & Gable, G.G. (2017). A systematic framework for multilevel theorizing in information systems research. *Information Systems Research*, *28*(2), 203–224. doi.org/10.1287/isre.2017.0690

36

Latent Position Network Models

Hardeep Kaur, Riccardo Rastelli, Nial Friel, and Adrian E. Raftery

Acknowledgement: This publication has emanated from research supported in part by a grant from the Insight Centre for Data Analytics which is supported by Science Foundation Ireland under Grant number 12/RC/2289_P2.

INTRODUCTION

Statistical network analysis has recently emerged as a prominent area of research, with applications in many fields including social sciences, biology, finance and physics. Social networks are used to study actors and the pairwise interactions between them. The formulation of statistical models for such network data plays an important role in describing the network's global topology and in providing interpretable representations of the data. Some of the pioneering work in network analysis dates back to Erdös and Rényi (1959), who introduced the famous Erdös-Rényi model with two connected variants for the generation of random graphs or the evolution of a random network. An initial version of what are called today latent position models was developed soon afterwards by Gilbert (1961), who introduced the so-called *spatially embedded random networks*. The key aspect of these models is that they define a generative framework for the edges of a graph based on the positions of the nodes in a Euclidean space.

Hoff et al. (2002) adapted similar concepts and ideas to the analysis of social networks, by introducing a new framework called the latent position model (LPM) or Latent Space Model (LSM). This work renewed interest in spatially embedded models as a tool for modelling the complex networks arising in many applied fields. As a result, the literature on the topic has increased rapidly, and the LPM has become a widely used statistical model for network analysis. The model has been used in the analysis of corporate governance (Friel et al., 2016), financial risk (Tafakori et al., 2021), trophic food webs (Chiu and Westveld, 2014; Chiu and Westveld, 2011), protein sequence data (Ding et al., 2019), interbank networks (Linardi et al., 2019), trade networks (Ward et al., 2013), social influence (Sweet and Adhikari, 2020; McFowland III and Shalizi, 2021), music contests (D'Angelo et al., 2019), migration flows (Xiao et al., 2022), anomaly detection (Lee et al., 2021), political networks (Ng et al., 2021), conflict networks (Westveld, and Hoff, 2011), flows of controlled substances (Berlusconi, et al., 2017), among others. It has also been used in a variety of other research areas, including neuroscience (Durante et al., 2017; Wilson et al., 2020), item response theory (Jin and Jeon, 2019), mediation analysis

(Liu et al., 2021), education research (Sweet et al., 2013), and epidemiology (Chu et al., 2021).

The literature on LPMs has also been reviewed in previous articles on network analysis, including Rastelli et al. (2016), Salter-Townshend et al. (2012), Matias and Robin (2014), Raftery (2017), Smith et al. (2019), Kim et al. (2018), and Sosa and Buitrago (2021). This chapter provides a review of LPMs and of the recent literature that originated from the seminal paper of Hoff et al. (2002).

NOTATION

Throughout this chapter, we consider data on the relations between a set of nodes $N \in \{1,...,n\}$. The relations are described by the set of edges ε. We denote by $Y = (y_{i,j})_{1 \le i \le j \le n}$ the $n \times n$ adjacency matrix of the observed undirected network, where $y_{i,j}$ is the edge value between the nodes i and j. These edge values are usually binary, discrete or continuous. A collection of dyad-specific covariates may be available. We denote these by $X = (x_{i,j,k})$, where (i,j) is an ordered pair of nodes and $k = 1,...,p$ indexes the covariates. We denote by θ the collection of parameters that do not refer to edges or nodes; we call these the global parameters. We denote by Z the unobserved latent variables, that is the latent positions associated with the nodes. Here z_i represents the unknown position of the corresponding node in a d-dimensional latent space.

LATENT POSITION MODELS

The Original Distance Model and Projection Model

Latent position models (also called latent space models) were introduced by Hoff et al. (2002), for undirected binary networks. This introduced a new family of latent variable models for network data, with the goal of providing a visualisation of a relational dataset through a latent geometric social space. Crucially, the authors introduced an inferential framework to estimate this model for networks of moderate size (of around a few hundred nodes).

The social space introduced by the authors consists of a set of n nodes, each having an unknown position z_i in a d-dimensional latent space, typically $\mathbf{R}^d$. In a Bayesian framework, the positions are assumed to be independent and identically distributed according to a multivariate Gaussian distribution MND(0, Σ). One fundamental property of this model is that, conditionally on the latent positions Z, the relational ties $y_{ij}, \forall\ i,j = 1,...,n$ are independent. In particular, the probability of the presence of a generic edge $y_{i,j}$ is modelled as some function of the latent positions z_i and z_j of the two nodes involved, as shown in Eq 1.

$$\mathbb{P}(Y \mid Z, X, \theta) = \prod_{i<j} \mathbb{P}(y_{i,j} \mid z_i, z_j, x_{i,j}, \theta), \quad (1)$$

where the product is taken over all pairs (i,j), where $i < j$, for $i,j = 1,...,n$.

Thanks to their geometric framework, these models are naturally able to represent common network features such as reciprocity, transitivity, and homophily. In other words, nodes with similar characteristics (i.e., positions) tend to possess higher probability of forming a tie. The similarity of latent characteristics may be defined in different ways: the two approaches proposed by Hoff et al. (2002) are called the *distance model and the projection model*.

3.1.1 Distance model

The latent distance model proposed by Hoff et al. (2002) assumes that each node has an unobserved latent position z_i in a Euclidean latent space, typically in the plane $\mathbf{R}^2$. Then, the closer two nodes' latent positions are to each other, the higher the probability that there is a connection between them. Conversely, the probability of connection decreases as the distance between the nodes increases. The Euclidean distance is most commonly used, but any other distance function may be considered. This framework permits easy visualisation and interpretation of the latent social space. The formulation of Hoff et al. (2002) defines the log odds of a tie between nodes i and j as:

$$\begin{aligned}\eta_{i,j} &= \text{logodds}(y_{i,j} = 1 \mid z_i, z_j, x_{i,j}, \alpha, \beta) \\ &= \alpha + \beta' x_{i,j} - \mid z_i - z_j \mid,\end{aligned} \quad (2)$$

where α and β are real-valued and $|\cdot|$ indicates the Euclidean norm.

This parameterisation is for a logistic regression model with $\theta = (\alpha, \beta)$ where α is an intercept term and β is a vector of coefficients for covariate effects. The distance model is particularly suited for networks with undirected or directed relations exhibiting strong reciprocity.

3.1.2 Projection model

Hoff et al. (2002) postulated the projection model as an alternative to the distance model. This proposes that two nodes have a higher probability of connecting if their respective latent positions are in the same direction ($z'_i z_j > 0$), or conversely, they are less likely to connect if they point in opposite directions ($z'_i z_j < 0$). In other words, two nodes are likely to form a tie if the angle (with respect to the centre of the space) between them is small, and less likely to form a tie if the angle between them is obtuse. The projection model is defined as follows:

$$\eta_{i,j} = \text{logodds}(y_{i,j} = 1 | z_i, z_j, x_{i,j}, \alpha, \beta)$$
$$= \alpha + \beta' x_{i,j} - \frac{|z'_i \cdot z_j|}{|z_j|} \quad (3)$$

The latent effects depend on $\frac{|z'_i z_j|}{|z_j|}$ which is the signed magnitude of the projection of z_i in the direction of z_j. This quantity can be interpreted as the extent of shared characteristics among nodes i and j, multiplied by the activity level of i.

Similarly to the distance model, the projection model provides a latent view of the social space. The latent space, in this case, is more easily thought of in terms of polar coordinates, where the position of a node is interpreted as a direction and a magnitude, indicating the social orientation and sociality effect, respectively. While the distance models naturally yields only symmetric edge probabilities, the projection model can also represent asymmetric edge probabilities, and may thus be more suitable for directed networks. However, it should also be noted that the distance model typically provides a more clear and intuitive representation of the latent space, and arguably more flexibility in representing some network topologies, such as community structures.

Latent Distance Models with Clustering

An extension of the latent space model was proposed by Handcock et al. (2007), who introduced the *latent position cluster model* (LPCM). Their innovation was to model the clustering of highly connected nodes in the network via a latent mixture mode. This model has been extended by others, including Krivitsky et al. (2009), Krivitsky and Handcock (2008), Salter-Townshend and Murphy (2013), Ryan et al. (2017), Gormley and Murphy (2010), Sewell and Chen (2017), Aliverti and Durante (2019). This model integrates the latent space distance models with model-based clustering of the nodes, hence connecting to the literature on stochastic blockmodels (Wang and Wong, 1987; Snijders and Nowicki, 1997).

In the chapter, the latent distance model is given as

$$\text{logodds}(y_{i,j} = 1 | z_i, z_j, x_{i,j}, \beta)$$
$$= \beta'_0 x_{i,j} - \beta_1 | z_i - z_j |. \quad (4)$$

The prior structure is modified by assuming that the latent positions $z_i \in \mathbf{R}_d$ arise from a finite mixture of multivariate normal distributions with G components:

$$z_i \sim \sum_{g=1}^{G} \lambda_g MND_d(\mu_g, \sigma_g^2 I_d),$$

where λ_g is the probability that a node belongs to the g-th group, and $\sum_{g=1}^{G} \lambda_g = 1$. The proposed model captures network features such as transitivity and homophily, but is also capable of representing clustering in a more explicit and natural way.

This work introduces a model-based criterion to select the best number of clusters G and the number of latent dimensions d jointly. The criterion is inspired by the BIC (Bayesian Information Criterion, Fraley and Raftery, 1998) and it combines two principled approximations: one determined by d, the dimension of the latent space and one determined by G, the number of latent clusters or mixture components. While this addresses a gap in the literature by providing a principled approach for model choice, it also emphasises that the method itself (in particular, the BIC) may not be ideal for the selection of the number of dimensions d since the underlying asymptotic approximation result has not been shown to hold in this case.

Latent Distance Models with Node-specific Random Effects

Krivitsky et al. (2009) combined the approaches of Handcock et al. (2007), which involves model based clustering of the latent space positions, and Hoff (2005), which uses actor-specific random effects, into a new model called the Latent Position Cluster Random Effect model (LPCMRE). The proposed model is

$$\eta_{i,j} = \text{logodds}(y_{i,j} = 1 | z_i, z_j, x_{i,j}, \beta)$$
$$= \sum_{k=1}^{p} \beta_k x_{k,i,j} - | z_i - z_j | + \delta_i + \gamma_j, \quad (5)$$

where, in addition to the specification of Handcock et al. (2007), δ_i, γ_j are introduced as actor-specific sender and receiver effects. The purpose of these parameters is to represent different levels of sociality of the nodes, so that a wider variety of degree distributions can be represented.

INFERENCE FOR THE LPM

Estimation

Hoff et al. (2002) considered two main approaches to inference for the LPM. The first is based on maximum likelihood maximisation and it consists of a two-step procedure. In the first step, we compute the maximum likelihood estimator of the pairwise distances between all nodes. The log-likelihood is a convex function of the distances between the actors, so it can be easily maximised using numerical procedures to obtain an estimator. In the second step, the optimal distances are used to derive the actual positions of the nodes in the latent space. The authors proposed performing this step using multidimensional scaling. The two-step procedure does not guarantee that the global maximum of the likelihood is obtained, but empirically it has given good results with low computational demands. This is appealing as the set of inferred positions may be used as a starting point for potentially better, but more computationally intensive procedures.

The second approach proposed by Hoff et al. (2002) is a Bayesian approach based on Markov chain Monte Carlo (MCMC). Prior distributions are specified for the model parameters, and then MCMC is used to obtain approximate samples of the parameters from the posterior distribution. For the distance model, the prior distributions are typically specified as:

$$z_i \overset{iid}{\sim} MVN(0,\Sigma),$$

$$\theta_k \overset{iid}{\sim} N(0,\sigma^2),$$

for some covariance matrix Σ and variance parameter σ^2.

The prior distribution is combined with the likelihood function, namely

$$\mathbb{P}(Y|Z,\theta) = \prod_{i \neq j} \mathbb{P}(y_{i,j}=1|Z,\theta)^{y_{i,j}} \mathbb{P}(y_{i,j}=0|Z,\theta)^{1-y_{i,j}}$$

$$= \prod_{i \neq j} \frac{\exp(y_{i,j}\eta_{i,j})}{1+\exp(\eta_{i,j})}, \qquad (6)$$

to obtain the posterior distribution of the model:

$$\pi(Z,\theta|Y) \propto \mathcal{L}_Y(Z,\theta)\pi(\theta)\pi(Z).$$

The MCMC approach is a standard Metropolis-within-Gibbs algorithm with random walk proposals, where each parameter of the model is sampled in turn from its full conditional distribution. The full conditional distributions for the parameters are not in standard form and are given by:

$$\pi(z_i|Z_{-i},\theta,Y) \propto \pi(z_i)$$
$$\prod_{i \neq j} \mathbb{P}(y_{i,j}=1|Z,\theta)^{y_{i,j}} \mathbb{P}(y_{i,j}=0|Z,\theta)^{1-y_{i,j}}, \qquad (7)$$

$$\pi(\theta_k|\theta_{-k},Z,Y) \propto \pi(\theta_k)\mathcal{L}_Y(Z,\theta), \qquad (8)$$

where the negative subscripts indicate the collection of parameters with the exception of the one negated.

One challenge with LPMs is the high computational complexity, as highlighted by Eq. 7 and Eq. 8. These updates make the number of calculations that are required for the procedure grow with the square of the number of nodes. This quadratic cost is not scalable and it can limit the applicability of the original model.

The MCMC sampling proceeds as follows:

1. Choose an initial guess for all the model parameters Z and θ.
2. For every node $i = 1,\ldots,N$:
   (a) Sample a vector z_i^* from a multivariate Gaussian proposal $q(z_i^* \to z_i)$ which is centred in the current position of this node.
   (b) Calculate the ratio between the full-conditionals $r_z = \dfrac{\pi(z_i^*|Z_{-i},\theta)}{\pi(z_i|Z_{-i},\theta)}$.
   (c) The new proposed values are accepted with probability min$(1,r_z)$, otherwise the current values are retained in the sample.
3. For every node $k = 1,\ldots,K$:
   (a) Sample a new parameter θ_k^* from a Gaussian proposal $q(\theta_k^* \to \theta_k)$ which is centred in the current value of this parameter.
   (b) Calculate the ratio between the full-conditionals $r_\theta = \dfrac{\pi(\theta_k^*|\theta_{-k},Z)}{\pi(\theta_k|\theta_{-k},Z)}$.
   (c) The new proposed value is accepted with probability min$(1,r_\theta)$, otherwise the current value is retained in the sample.

This algorithm generates a Markov chain whose stationary distribution is the posterior distribution sought.

Interpretation of the Posterior Samples

The likelihood defined in Hoff et al. (2002) depends on the latent positions only through the pairwise distances between the nodes. Hence, the model parameters are non-identifiable with respect to any distance-preserving transformations of the latent positions. These transformations include rotations, reflections and translations of the latent positions. In principle, if we focus only on one single configuration of the parameters drawn from the posterior distribution, the non-identifiability issues may be negligible, because a translation, reflection, or rotation of the points would not affect our interpretations of the latent space.

However, in a Bayesian setting, we obtain a posterior sample $\{Z^{(1)}, Z^{(2)}, \ldots\}$, and we are interested in summarising that sample to obtain estimators such as the posterior mean. In this case, applying a transformation (e.g. a translation) to any of the configurations of the sample would directly affect the value of the posterior summaries. Crucially, we have no way to determine whether the latent space was rotated, translated or reflected during the sampling procedure. For this reason, the posterior sample is not identifiable, and we cannot draw meaningful summaries from it.

As a solution to this problem, Hoff et al. (2002) considered Procrustes matching. This approach is based on a comparison of one configuration of points with another via their respective coordinate matrices (we denote these matrices by A and B in this section). In Procrustes matching, a rigid transformation is applied to A to make it as close as possible to the reference B. The matrix A is rotated, reflected and translated to achieve the best match to the reference matrix B, where the best match is defined as the one that minimises the sum of squared distances between corresponding points. This is given by:

$$R^2 = \sum_{i=1}^{n} \sum_{k=1}^{d} (b_{i,k} - a_{i,k})^2.$$

We can set up an optimisation problem by specifying the following transformation of the matrix A:

$$\mathbf{a}'_i = \mathbf{O}'\mathbf{a}_i + \mathbf{T},$$

where $\mathbf{a}_i$ is a vector of coordinates of point i in the matrix A, and O is an orthogonal matrix that induces a rotation and/or reflection and t is a translation vector. Then, the optimal values of **O**, and t can be calculated by minimising the sum of squared distances between points, namely

$$R^2 = \sum_{i=1}^{n} (\mathbf{b}_i - \mathbf{O}'\mathbf{a}_i + \mathbf{t})'(\mathbf{b}_i - \mathbf{O}'\mathbf{a}_i + \mathbf{t}).$$

The optimal values obtained are then applied to the original A configuration leading to the minimum R^2 value (called the Procrustes sum of squares). The computation for the projection model is slightly different from that for the distance model. Since the projection model is not invariant under translation, the optimisation problem involving transformation of matrix A reduces to:

$$\mathbf{a}'_i = \mathbf{O}'\mathbf{a}_i.$$

Thus the modified sum of squared distances is

$$R^2 = \sum_{i=1}^{n} (\mathbf{b}_i - \mathbf{O}'\mathbf{a}_i)'(\mathbf{b}_i - \mathbf{O}'\mathbf{a}_i).$$

The problem of identifiability has been further studied by Shortreed et al. (2006) to extend the work of Hoff et al. (2002). They considered three point estimators for the positions of the nodes, namely, the maximum likelihood estimator, the posterior mode estimator, and the posterior mean estimator (defined after Procrustes matching). They argued that these three estimators may provide inaccurate point estimates of the nodes, since they rely exclusively on the estimated distances to derive the positions. They introduce an original fourth procedure which aims at minimising the Kullback-Leibler divergence between the distribution implied by the fitted positions, and the one implied by the parameters minimising the expected posterior loss. This fourth approach is most commonly used (Handcock et al., 2007; Krivitsky et al., 2009) and is implemented in the **latentnet** R package.

Other Inferential Approaches

The computational complexity of the log-likelihood function in Eq. 6 is on the order of the square of the number of nodes. This is a problem when inferring LPMs, because likelihood-based procedures require a quadratic computing cost, which does not scale well with the size of the data. The full Bayesian approach, on the one hand, based on MCMC is particularly slow and becomes impractical for networks of more than a few hundred nodes. On the other hand, the MLE approach tends to be faster, yet it still requires a quadratic cost and thus it too does not scale well.

A number of papers have specifically addressed this research impasse, by proposing various strategies that can speed up the inferential procedures and thus make the algorithms scale better with large datasets. The variational Bayesian inference procedure proposed by Salter-Townshend and Murphy (2013) proposes to replace the posterior distribution of the model parameters in the Latent position cluster model with a variational posterior. This leads to an approximation that has been widely used in a variety of different settings with latent variables (Jordan et al., 1999; Blei et al., 2017). The advantage of this approximation is that it allows one to characterise the posterior distribution of interest without having to resort to sampling methods like MCMC, which can be much more computationally intensive. However, the approximation error induced is difficult to quantify, and it has been shown that this error can be relevant when assessing the uncertainty around the point estimates provided.

Another approach is considered by Raftery et al. (2012), who introduce a likelihood approximation using case-control sampling. This takes advantage of the fact that the positions of the nodes are primarily regulated by the edges between nodes, rather than by the missing edges. This is especially true in sparse networks, where the few edges that are present give us information on which nodes should be located close to each other. By contrast, the missing edges tend to not provide as much information, so can be thinned out using a case-control sampling strategy. As a consequence, only a fraction of the missing edges are considered in the likelihood calculation, and their contributions are reweighted to make them represent all the missing edges. This approximation yields an unbiased estimate of the likelihood function, while scaling up the procedure to networks of several thousand nodes.

Ryan et al. (2017) extend the distance LPCM by including conjugate priors in the model specification. The key advantage of this approach is that a number of model parameters can be integrated out from the posterior distribution thanks to the conjugacy property. This leads to a marginal posterior which can be characterised through a MCMC sampler. The advantage of this approach is that it can speed up the sampling procedure since many of the model parameters have been integrated out from the posterior. The sampler can explore different models with a different number of latent clusters in one run. This is a key advantage because it allows one to perform model choice on the number of groups without having to fit each of the models individually.

These methodological ideas were introduced for binary graphs, but they have been extended and adopted in a variety of different settings with dynamic and multiview networks. More recently, some other methodological ideas have been considered (Aliverti and Russo, 2021; Rastelli et al., 2018; Spencer et al., 2020; Liu and Chen, 2021) signalling that this research problem remains one of active interest.

AN ILLUSTRATIVE EXAMPLE FOR THE DISTANCE LPM

We now describe a motivating example on an original coauthorship network. The data (collected from Scopus on 17 January 2022) consists of all the bibliographic entries which cite Hoff et al. (2002). A total of 929 articles are part of this dataset, and 1,758 unique authors are involved. From these, we constructed a coauthorship network for all the authors of those papers, where two authors are linked if they coauthored at least one paper. We removed all the authors that published only one paper in total, to focus on the most active authors and to reduce the computational burden. This led to a final undirected binary network of 279 nodes.

We then fit a distance LPM on these data using the R package **latentnet**. We compared a number of models using the BIC criterion, as implemented in **latentnet**. The resulting latent space is shown in Figure 36.1, and a more detailed representation of the results through an interactive plot is available from the authors upon request. A GitHub page is created and anyone requesting more details will be provided information about this page.

The results highlight a strong presence of communities, which reflect the presence of various research groups. Some of the authors tend to have overlapping positions, suggesting strong similarity of research collaborators. Others are positioned in between communities, highlighting that they may have connections with more than one research group or with a more diverse set of collaborators. In Figure 36.2 we show the posterior sample for the intercept parameter, and the distribution of the log-odds for all edges.

These plots show that the latent space plays an important role in determining the presence of edges. The left panel shows that the intercept parameter concentrates around the value 1, signalling a strong effect of the latent space. This is confirmed on the right panel of the same figure, where we can see that the log-odds exhibit large variability, implying edge probabilities that range from 0.00 to 0.38. This means that the model is able to represent the heterogeneity in the data by leveraging the geometric framework induced by the LPM.

In the fitted LPM of Figure 36.1 we can explore the presence of communities by studying how "clustered" the latent space is. However, the LPCM allows one to include this information directly in the modelling, and thus obtain a partitioning of the nodes into groups. For this reason, we also fitted a LPCM with up to 30 groups, and selected the best model using the BIC criterion advocated by Handcock et al. (2007). The results (27 groups) are shown in Figure 36.3. In this case we notice strong agreement between the partitioning of the nodes and the clustering of points in the latent space. The research groups are fairly well captured and they convey an interesting model-based view of the data.

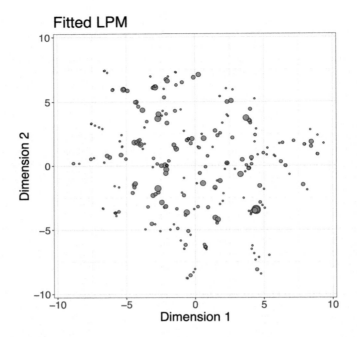

Figure 36.1 Distance LPM fitted on the coauthorship data. Each node represents a different author. The size of a node represents the number of publications in which the author participated

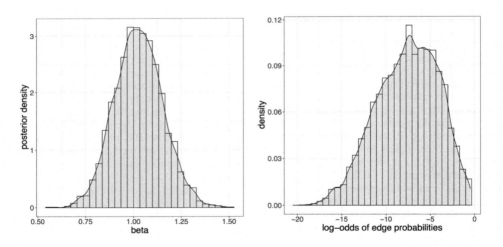

Figure 36.2 The left panel shows the approximate posterior sample for the intercept parameter, called β. The right panel shows instead the η parameters representing the log-odds for the edges appearing. The distribution represents these values across all dyads

In addition, we also provide a third example using the model of Krivitsky et al. (2009). Also in this case we fit the model for different numbers of groups and we select the best fit using BIC. The results for the best model are obtained when only one group is chosen. This is reasonable since the random effects used in the model can explain a substantial part of the

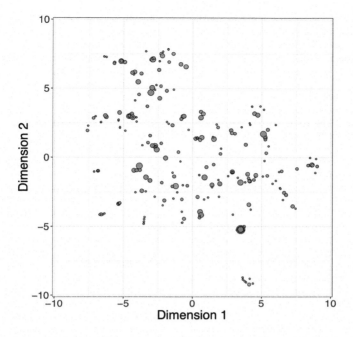

Figure 36.3 Distance LPCM fitted on the co-authorship data. The size of the nodes represent the total number of publications to which the authors participated.

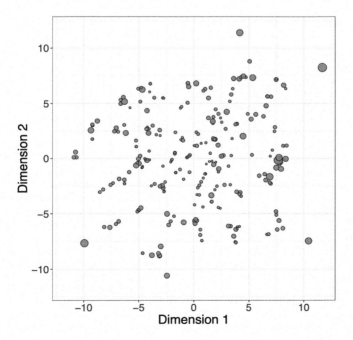

Figure 36.4 Distance LPCMRE fitted on the coauthorship data. The size of the nodes represent their "sociality" random effect parameter

variability in the data, at the expense of the latent space. Nonetheless, the visualisation that the model can offer still includes all the information regarding the model parameters since the sociality of nodes is shown through their size.

In this case, we observe that the sociality is similar for most of the nodes that are positioned in the centre of the latent space. These nodes are well characterised by their latent positions, and the model does not require any random effect to 'correct' their connectivity patterns. Some nodes with a relatively central position also benefit from a high sociality parameter. This represents the fact that some authors will collaborate with diverse research groups and may require the creation of long-distance edges. The sociality parameter addresses this situation, helping to bridge that gap and to create connections regardless of the pairwise distance. However, some of the largest sociality values are observed for nodes in the fringes of the latent space. These authors do not have many connections; for this reason it is difficult to position them centrally or close to other nodes. As a consequence they are pushed to the edge of the latent space. Since, they do have connections to more central nodes, a large sociality parameter can provide a compensation for their loose positioning thus well justifying their observed connections.

STATE OF THE ART

The work of Hoff et al. (2002) has led to a strand of literature that focuses on LPMs and their extensions. In this section, we review some methodological contributions that extend the work of Hoff et al. (2002) in different directions. We organise our exposition by categorising the papers into the type of network data they refer to. However many of the papers are generalisable to multiple contexts and provide novelty in a number of different ways.

LPMs for Multiview Networks

Multiview or multiplex networks are observed when there are multiple relationships among the same set of nodes, hence describing a multirelational network. An example of this framework may be a social network where we observe various types of ties between actors, such as professional ties, family ties or friendship ties. Also, temporal networks are closely connected to multiview networks as they may be seen as a special case where a time dependency is created to connect contiguous network views.

LPMs have been extended to the multiview framework in a number of papers. Gollini and Murphy (2016) introduced the latent space joint model which displays the different relations on the same nodes to be encapsulated in the same latent space. This also introduces a scalable variational approach to speed up the estimation of the latent space model. Another novelty is that they use the squared Euclidean distance instead of the absolute distance in their model.

Instead, Durante et al. (2017) develop an extension of the latent projection model of Hoff et al. (2002) using a novel non-parametric Bayesian approach to model the latent space and the clustering of the nodes. They propose an application to a population of brain connectivity networks, whereby nodes refer to anatomical brain regions and edges refer to the structural interconnections between them. They consider data collected from a number of different samples/individuals, which is where the multiview aspect of their analysis comes from. The application of their model can be seen in a subsequent paper (Durante and Dunson, 2018) in which the model is used to characterise and test for differences in brain connectivity networks. A second paper in a similar direction is Aliverti and Durante (2019).

Salter-Townshend and McCormick (2017) propose a new model for multiview networks which focuses on the interrelation of dyads across different network views. They use a multivariate Bernoulli likelihood whose parameters are determined by multiple latent spaces and by the distances between nodes in different views. The framework permits a model-based assessment of the correlation between the multiple edges, providing a measure of association between the various network views. The price to pay for this additional flexibility, however, is increased computational requirements and a more challenging model-choice task.

D'Angelo et al. (2019) and D'Angelo et al. (2020) introduce a Euclidean distance LPM for multiview networks to model the voting patterns in the Eurovision Song Contest. The authors specify a common latent space to represent the positions of the nodes, but they let the other parameters be different across the various network views. This is a key aspect of the model since it directly allows one to quantify the effect that the latent space can have on the generation of the data. Similarly to Eq. 4, a coefficient for the latent distances approaching zero would mean that the latent distances do not represent a strong effect, and thus the data can be well represented through a homogeneous model. The authors use this aspect of the LPM to determine the effect of the latent space as a way to measure the voting bias of the countries.

Sewell (2019) introduces a new method to analyse cognitive social structures based on the LPM. These data refer to the perception that each node has of the network, so it is related to multiview networks in that the observed data correspond to a collection of networks. He derives an LPM approach which combines the advantages of the latent space visualisation, with additional model parameters which can measure the nodes' biases in perceiving the network.

LPMs for Dynamic Networks

Dynamic or temporal networks refer to networks that evolve over time. Most typically, dynamic networks describe the interactions between the same set of nodes, and are observed through network snapshots that is, at some specific points in time. For this reason, they can be formally represented as a collection of graphs $Y^{(1)},\ldots,Y^{(K)}$. The LPM (Hoff et al, 2002) has been extended to dynamic networks in a variety of ways. Sarkar and Moore (2005) extend it to include time-dynamics in the model parameters. They propose an application to a dataset of friendship relationships and study how these change over time. The proposed model embeds the nodes in the latent space in such a way that the positions of nodes are regularised at each time point to ensure that their positions do not change by much.

Sewell and Chen (2015b) introduced a new model to extend that of Sarkar and Moore (2005). In their framework, the longitudinal network data is modelled via temporal trajectories in a latent Euclidean space. One key novel aspect of this work is that the formulated model introduces a social reach parameter which resembles the nodal random effects of Krivitsky et al. (2009). These parameters aim at representing different levels of activity of the nodes and their sociability, regardless of the latent position.

Friel et al. (2016) define a model for bipartite dynamic networks and apply their method to a network of companies and their directors in Ireland. The model aims at providing a model-based assessment of how appointments of directors to multiple boards may have been associated with financial instability during the 2008 crisis. The authors embed the nodes of bipartite networks into a single latent space, similarly to Gormley and Murphy (2007). They assume that the nodes can move along trajectories, hence capturing the time dependencies in the data. In addition, they note that the data present a strong persistence of edges and non-edges. This refers to dyads that tend not to change their status over time. In order to address this aspect of the data, which is common to many dynamic network datasets, the authors also introduce a regime-switching framework which selects a different intercept parameter based on the previous network realisation. The model captures the heterogeneity shown by the data very well through latent positions and persistence features by modelling the structure of the intercept parameters.

Durante and Dunson (2016) further extend the LPM by allowing the positions of nodes to evolve continuously over time through a nested Gaussian process, which results in time-varying smoothness. The authors incorporate locally adaptive dynamics to study face-to-face dynamic contact network, highlighting the flexibility of their approach in capturing data observed at unequally spaced intervals and structural changes in the nodes' trajectories.

In a similar direction, Rastelli and Corneli (2021) introduce a fully continuous latent position model, which extends the application of LPMs to time-stamped interaction data. They consider and infer the continuous trajectories of the nodes in a two-dimensional latent space, using only their frequency of pairwise connections.

LPMs for Weighted Networks

Weighted networks are characterised by edges that carry additional numerical information. Typically, the edges of these networks carry a real value, for example, representing the intensity or the length of the interaction. Although binary networks are easier to study, weighted networks arise often in practice. Hoff (2005) and Hoff (2021) proposed a general framework that includes various types of latent variable models as special cases, including the distance LPM and the projection LPM. The network variables are considered as the response variables of a regression model and are characterised by a combination of nodal effects, dyadic effects and other types of network-derived information. Westveld and Hoff (2011) mixed extended this framework to model a network of international trade and conflict.

Sewell and Chen (2016) introduce a dynamic weighted network framework. They define the temporal dependencies through a Markovian property, and consider two models for the weights: a Poisson model for count data and a Tobit model for non-negative continuous data. They also consider nodal random effects similarly to Sewell and Chen (2015b), to define a possibly different social reach for each node.

LPMs for Rank Data

Ranked network data can be used to represent rankings of items or entities by the nodes. A bipartite network can be used to represent how a set of nodes rank various items, or the other nodes themselves. Gormley and Murphy (2007) combined the LPM of Hoff et al. (2002) with the Plackett-Luce model (Plackett 1975) to create a new type of LPM which can be used to study bipartite rank networks, and applied their method to the voters' preferences in the 2002 Irish elections.

Sewell and Chen (2015a) further extended the approach of Gormley and Murphy (2007) to account for temporal changes in the networks as well as a social reach effect on the nodes. Their LPM is dynamic in that the nodes move along trajectories, and their positions are used to characterise the various network snapshots at different times. This permits an analysis of the evolution of the latent space, and, thanks to the node-specific parameters, it allows for an assessment of the popularity and stability of individual actors. In both papers, inference is carried out using Bayesian framework and Procrustes matching. As concerns scalability, the methods proposed are particularly demanding since they require an even higher complexity than the original LPM. This points to an important research question for future work in this direction.

Theory of LPMs

The papers we consider in this section are general in that they are not restricted to a particular network type. We first highlight a number of theoretical papers that have studied the LPM framework or some closely connected variants. Rastelli et al. (2016) provide a detailed analysis of the LPM framework by considering some theoretical and empirical aspects that arise from the model structure. They address how the LPM can capture some relevant network features of interest such as clustering, heavy-tailed degree distributions, small world behaviour, and assortative mixing. They also propose a variant of Eq. 2 in which the logistic expression is replaced by a Gaussian kernel. This choice permits a detailed analysis of the theoretical properties of the model, creating a connection to the physics literature on the topic (Newman, 2018).

Smith et al. (2019) focus on the role played by the geometry of the latent space in an LPM. They create a general framework which includes a variety of latent variable models, and they study how switching to a hyperbolic geometry can lead to more flexible network models which can better represent the observed data. In particular, they show that a negative curvature in the space permits more complexity without the need to change any other aspect of the models, hence providing a more parsimonious modelling choice.

Caron and Fox (2017) consider a general latent variable framework, and argue that commonly used frameworks such as the LPM may not be adequate for large networks since they cannot capture sparsity in asymptotic settings. They then propose a new framework based on exchangeable random measures which is capable of maintaining ideal features like network sparsity along with exchange-ability properties.

Extensions of the Projection LPM

The distance LPM and the projection LPM introduced by Hoff et al. (2002) generated two quite separate sets of literature. On the one hand, the distance LPM has been widely applied thanks to its clear representations and easy interpretability. On the other hand, the projection model has been intensely studied due to its tractability and also its similarity to other types of latent factor models. In the projection LPM literature, the work of Hoff (2005) has initiated a research avenue (Hoff, 2007; Hoff, 2011; Hoff, 2021) which has evolved into a flexible and widely applicable framework for network analysis.

Nickel (2008) and Young and Scheinerman (2007) introduce a general latent variable multiplicative structure which is closely connected to the projection model, and call this the Random Dot Product graph model. In its original formulation, the model does not include the logit link for the multiplicative effects. However, this becomes an advantage because it makes the model quite tractable, so a number of network properties can be derived analytically. A number of recent papers extend the random dot product graph and use this framework in network applications applications (Athreya et al., 2021; Passino et al., 2021; Ng and Murphy, 2019; Xie and Xu, 2021; Zhang et al., 2020).

Extensions of the LPCM

The distance LPCM of Handcock et al. (2007) has been especially influential since it inherits the advantages of the basic LPM of Hoff et al. (2002) while gaining more flexibility and interpretability through the clustering structure. This has led to a rich literature about this model and its applications.

Fosdick et al. (2019) introduce a new latent variable network model inspired by the LPCM. They argue that the complexity of networks may be better captured when different statistical models are combined at different levels of resolution. This means that the models may be either stacked into different hierarchical layers, or they may model different aspects of the data. They illustrate their approach by proposing a new model, the latent space stochastic blockmodel, which combines the stochastic blockmodel of Wang and Wong (1987) with the LPM of Hoff et al. (2002). Nodes are clustered into groups following a stochastic blockmodel structure, while the probabilities of connections for nodes belonging to the same group are determined by a group-specific LPM. This effectively creates different resolutions in the model where the inner level, represented by the LPM, can break down and capture the within-group heterogeneous connectivity patterns. The result is a framework that can scale better than that of Handcock et al. (2007) while maintaining the flexibility and interpretability of the LPMs.

Another approach which combines LPMs and clustering is that of Sewell (2020). He considers a clustering framework on the edges rather than on the nodes. This reflects the idea that edges are determined within a particular context they refer to, for example because the nodes interacted within that context. He then introduces a latent space to formalise the presence of these contexts that drive the formation of the edges. As a result, the nodes involved in a particular edge are chosen based on their relative positions with respect to the context of the edge. The methodology can provide latent space representations (as well as clustering) of edges and nodes, hence creating a strong connection with the LPCM. However, differently from the LPCM, the computational complexity of the approach proposed scales with the number of edges in the graph, so it may be particularly suitable for sparse networks.

A dynamic extension of the LPCM is introduced by Sewell and Chen (2017). In this work, the authors consider a dynamic LPM where both the latent positions of the nodes, and their cluster allocations, can change over time. The position of a node is influenced by its previous position and its previous cluster membership. The clustering variables are assumed to have a Markovian structure and depend on their previous value. The authors consider an estimation strategy based on variational inference (for large networks), and another strategy based on MCMC (for smaller networks due to higher computational costs).

Also, they perform model choice using BIC to select the number of clusters, and deviance information criteria (DIC) to select the number of latent dimensions.

Gormley and Murphy (2010) extend the framework of Handcock et al. (2007) to include node covariates. While the LPCM can accommodate edge covariates directly into the edge probabilities through the logit link, the inclusion of a node's information is not as straightforward. Gormley and Murphy (2010) address this gap by proposing a mixture of experts' models as a prior for the latent positions, whereby the nodes' covariates can be used to characterise the group allocation probabilities associated to the nodes. This defines a framework in which covariates can be introduced via the likelihood, and also into the structure of the model, providing more flexibility and possibly a different interpretation of the data.

SOFTWARE

An essential aspect of latent position modelling is the implementation of the methods, which include MCMC, variational methods and other procedures. MCMC estimation of a range of latent position network models is carried out by the R package **latentnet** (Krivitsky and Handcock 2008; Krivitsky et al. 2020). This implements the methodologies outlined in Hoff et al. (2002), Shortreed et al. (2006), Handcock et al. (2007), and Krivitsky et al. (2009). This package has been used to produce the examples in this chapter.

OPEN RESEARCH QUESTIONS

LPMs have had great success in the last two decades thanks to their ability to capture some common network properties, such as transitivity, homophily and clustering. Research on these models is active, and several methodological questions remain open.

One key issue concerns computational efficiency and scalability. While this is a relevant topic throughout network science, it is especially important in the context of LPMs. As mentioned earlier, the original LPM has a quadratic cost which arises from the likelihood calculation. The model requires information from each dyad of the network, and this dyadic information is possibly always different, generating the quadratic cost. While a number of ideas have been proposed, the current approaches can only scale to thousands of nodes, whereas observed datasets can be much larger. This gap highlights the need to define models and methods that can take computational efficiency directly into account, while providing a solid structure for statistical analyses.

Another aspect of the research on LPMs refers to its flexibility in capturing features of interest. A closely related latent variable model, the stochastic blockmodel, can capture both assortative and disassortative behaviours of the nodes. The original LPM falls short in this regard, since the model can capture assortative mixing but it cannot capture disassortative mixing. While social networks tend to often show assortative mixing, other types of networks such as biological networks can exhibit strong disassortative patterns (Newman, 2018). For this reason, variations of the LPM have been recently considered to make the model more flexible in this regard, for example by combining it with the stochastic blockmodel (Fosdick et al., 2019; Ng et al., 2021; Rastelli, 2018).

Another key open research question relates to model choice, and, in particular, to the selection of the dimensionality of the latent space. Most commonly, LPMs are fitted in two latent dimensions, due to easier interpretations and clearer visualisations. However, a number of papers have highlighted how the choice of this parameter, the number of latent dimensions, can be set up as one of model choice. A BIC criterion was introduced by Handcock et al. (2007) to select the number of clusters and the number of latent dimensions jointly. However, the authors note that the asymptotic properties of BIC may not be valid when selecting the number of dimensions. A Deviance Information Criterion (Spiegelhalter et al., 2002) has been used by Friel et al. (2016), D'Angelo et al. (2019), and Sewell and Chen (2017). However, more research on the model choice issue is needed.

REFERENCES

Aliverti, E. and Durante, D. (2019). "Spatial modeling of brain connectivity data via latent distance models with nodes clustering". In: *Statistical Analysis and Data Mining: The ASA Data Science Journal* 12.3, pp. 185–196.

Aliverti, E. and Russo, M. (2021). "Stratified stochastic variational inference for high-dimensional network factor model". In: *Journal of Computational and Graphical Statistics*, pp. 1–10.

Athreya, A., Tang, M., Park, Y., and Priebe, C.E. (2021). "On estimation and inference in latent structure random graphs". In: *Statistical Science* 36.1, pp. 68–88.

Berlusconi, G., Aziani, A., and Giommoni, L. (2017). "The determinants of heroin flows in Europe: A latent space approach". In: *Social Networks* 51, pp. 104–117.

Blei, D.M., Kucukelbir, A., and McAuliffe, J.D. (2017). "Variational inference: A review for statisticians". In: *Journal of the American statistical Association* 112.518, pp. 859–877.

Caron, F. and Fox, E.B. (2017). "Sparse graphs using exchangeable random measures". In: *Journal of the Royal Statistical Society. Series B, Statistical Methodology* 79.5, p. 1295.

Chiu, G.S. and Westveld, A.H. (2011). "A unifying approach for food webs, phylogeny, social networks, and statistics". In: *Proceedings of the National Academy of Sciences of the United States of America* 108.38, pp. 15881–15886. doi: 10.1073/pnas.1015359108.

Chiu, G.S. and Westveld, A.H. (2014). "A statistical social network model for consumption data in trophic food webs". In: *Statistical Methodology* 17.C, pp. 139–160. doi: 10.1016/j.stamet.2013.09.001.

Chu, A.M, Chan, T.W., So, M.K, and Wong, W-K. (2021). "Dynamic network analysis of COVID-19 with a latent pandemic space model". In: *International Journal of Environmental Research and Public Health* 18.6, p. 3195.

D'Angelo, S., Alfò, M., and Murphy, T.B. (2020). "Modeling node heterogeneity in latent space models for multidimensional networks". In: *Statistica Neerlandica* 74.3, pp. 324–341. doi: 10.1111/stan.12209.

D'Angelo, S., Murphy, T.B., and Alfò, M. (2019). "Latent space modelling of multidimensional networks with application to the exchange of votes in eurovision song contest". In: *Annals of Applied Statistics* 13.2, pp. 900–930. doi: 10.1214/18-AOAS1221.

Ding, X., Zou, Z., and Brooks III, C.L. (2019). "Deciphering protein evolution and fitness landscapes with latent space models". In: *Nature Communications* 10.1. doi: 10.1038/s41467-019-13633-0.

Durante, D. and Dunson, D.B. (2016). "Locally adaptive dynamic networks". In: *Annals of Applied Statistics* 10.4, pp. 2203–2232. doi: 10.1214/16-AOAS971.

Durante, D. and Dunson, D.B. (2018). "Bayesian inference and testing of group differences in brain networks". In: *Bayesian Analysis* 13.1, pp. 29–58. doi: 10.1214/16-BA1030.

Durante, D., Dunson, D.B., and Vogelstein, J.T. (2017). "Rejoinder: Nonparametric Bayes Modeling of Populations of Networks". In: *Journal of the American Statistical Association* 112.520, pp. 1547–1552. doi: 10.1080/01621459.2017.1395643.

Erdös, P. and Rényi, A. (1959). "On Random Graphs I". In: *Publicationes Mathematicae Debrecen* 6, p. 290.

Fosdick, B.K., McCormick, T.H., Murphy, T.B., Ng, T.L.J, and Westling, T. (2019). "Multiresolution network models". In: *Journal of Computational and Graphical Statistics* 28.1, pp. 185–196.

Fraley, C. and Raftery, A.E. (1998). "How many clusters? Which clustering method? Answers via model-based cluster analysis". In: *The computer journal* 41.8, pp. 578–588.

Friel, N., Rastelli, R.,Wyse, J., and Raftery, A.E. (2016). "Interlocking directorates in Irish companies using a latent space model for bipartite networks". In: *Proceedings of the National Academy of Sciences of the United States of America* 113.24, pp. 6629–6634. doi: 10.1073/pnas.1606295113.

Gilbert, E.N. (1961). "Random Plane Networks". In: *Journal of the Society for Industrial and Applied Mathematics* 9.4, pp. 533–543.

Gollini, I. and Murphy, T.B. (2016). "Joint Modeling of Multiple Network Views". In: *Journal of Computational and Graphical Statistics* 25.1, pp. 246–265. doi: 10.1080/10618600.2014.978006.

Gormley, I.C. and Murphy, T.B. (2007). "A latent space model for rank data". In: *Lecture Notes in Computer Science (including subseries Lecture Notes in Artificial Intelligence and Lecture Notes in Bioinformatics)* 4503 LNCS, pp. 90–102. doi: 10.1007/978-3-540-73133-7_7.

Gormley, I.C. and Murphy, T.B. (2010). "A mixture of experts latent position cluster model for social network data". In: *Statistical Methodology* 7.3, pp. 385–405. doi: 10.1016/j.stamet.2010.01.002.

Handcock, M.S., Raftery, A.E., and Tantrum, J.M. (2007). "Model-based clustering for social networks (with discussion)". In: *Journal of the Royal Statistical Society. Series A: Statistics in Society* 170.2, pp. 301–354. doi: 10.1111/j.1467-985X.2007.00471.x.

Hoff, P.D. (2005). "Bilinear mixed-effects models for dyadic data". In: *Journal of the american Statistical association* 100.469, pp. 286–295.

Hoff, P.D. (2007). "Modeling homophily and stochastic equivalence in symmetric relational data". In: *arXiv preprint arXiv:0711.1146*.

Hoff, P.D. (2011). "Hierarchical multilinear models for multiway data". In: *Computational Statistics & Data Analysis* 55.1, pp. 530–543.

Hoff, P.D. (2021). "Additive and multiplicative effects network models". In: *Statistical Science* 36.1, pp. 34–50.

Hoff, P.D., Raftery, A.E., and Handcock, M.S. (2002). "Latent space approaches to social network analysis". In: *Journal of the American Statistical Association* 97.460, pp. 1090–1098. doi: 10.1198/016214502388618906.

Jin, I.H. and Jeon, M. (2019). "A Doubly Latent Space Joint Model for Local Item and Person Dependence in the Analysis of Item Response Data". In: *Psychometrika* 84.1, pp. 236–260. doi:10.1007/s11336-018-9630-0.

Jordan, M.I., Ghahramani, Z., Jaakkola, T.S., and Saul, L.K. (1999). "An introduction to variational methods for graphical models". In: *Machine learning* 37.2, pp. 183–233.

Kim, B., Lee, K.H., Xue, L., and Niu, X. (2018). "A review of dynamic network models with latent variables". In: *Statistics Surveys* 12, pp. 105–135. doi: 10.1214/18-SS121.

Krivitsky, P.N. and Handcock, M.S. (2008). "Fitting position latent cluster models for social networks with latentnet". In: *Journal of Statistical Software* 24.5. doi: 10.18637/jss.v024.i05.

Krivitsky, P.N., Handcock, M.S., Raftery, A.E., and Hoff, P.D. (2009). "Representing degree distributions, clustering, and homophily in social networks with latent cluster random effects models". In: *Social networks* 31.3, pp. 204–213.

Krivitsky, P.N., Handcock, M.S., Shortreed, S.M., Tantrum, J., Hoff, P.D., Wang, L., Li, K., Fisher, J., and Bates, J.T. (2020). "Package 'latentnet'". In: Lee, W., McCormick, T.H., Neil, J., Sodja, C., and Cui, Y. (2021). "Anomaly detection in large scale networks with latent space models". In: *Technometrics* just-accepted, pp. 1–23.

Linardi, F., Diks, C., Leij, M. van der, and Lazier, I. (2019). "Dynamic interbank network analysis using latent space models". In: *Journal of Economic Dynamics and Control*. doi: 10.1016/j.jedc.2019.103792.

Liu, H., Jin, I.H, Zhang, Z., and Yuan, Y. (2021). "Social network mediation analysis: A latent space approach". In: *Psychometrika* 86.1, pp. 272–298.

Liu, Y. and Chen, Y. (2021). "Variational Inference for Latent Space Models for Dynamic Networks". In: *arXiv preprint arXiv:2105.14093*.

Matias, C. and Robin, S. (2014). "Modeling heterogeneity in random graphs through latent space models: a selective review". In: *ESAIM: Proceedings and Surveys* 47, pp. 55–74.

McFowland III, E. and Shalizi, C.R. (2021). "Estimating Causal Peer Influence in Homophilous Social Networks by Inferring Latent Locations". In: *Journal of the American Statistical Association*, pp. 1–12.

Newman, M. (2018). *Networks*. Oxford university press.

Ng, T.L.J. and Murphy, T.B. (2019). "Generalized random dot product graph". In: *Statistics & Probability Letters* 148, pp. 143–149.

Ng, T.L.J., Murphy, T.B., Westling, T., McCormick, T.H., and Fosdick, B. (2021). "Modeling the social media relationships of Irish politicians using a generalized latent space stochastic blockmodel". In: *The Annals of Applied Statistics* 15.4, pp. 1923–1944.

Nickel, C.L.M. (2008). "Random dot product graphs a model for social networks". PhD thesis. Johns Hopkins University.

Passino, F.S., Bertiger, A.S., Neil, J.C., and Heard, N.A. (2021). "Link prediction in dynamic networks using random dot product graphs". In: *Data Mining and Knowledge Discovery* 35.5, pp. 2168–2199.

Plackett, R.L. (1975). "The analysis of permutations". In: *Journal of the Royal Statistical Society:Series C (Applied Statistics)* 24.2, pp. 193–202.

Raftery, A.E. (2017). "Comment: Extending the Latent Position Model for Networks". In: *Journal of the American Statistical Association* 112.520, pp. 1531–1534. doi: 10.1080/01621459.2017.1389736.

Raftery, A.E., Niu, X., Hoff, P.D., and Yeung, K.Y. (2012). "Fast inference for the latent space network model using a case-control approximate likelihood". In: *Journal of Computational and Graphical Statistics* 21.4, pp. 901–919. doi: 10.1080/10618600.2012.679240.

Rastelli, R. (2018). "The sparse latent position model for nonnegative weighted networks". In: *arXiv preprint arXiv:1808.09262*.

Rastelli, R. and Corneli, M. (2021). "Continuous Latent Position Models for Instantaneous Interactions". In: *arXiv preprint arXiv:2103.17146*.

Rastelli, R., Friel, N., and Raftery, A.E. (2016). "Properties of latent variable network models". In: *Network Science* 4.4, pp. 407–432. doi: 10.1017/nws.2016.23.

Rastelli, R., Maire, F., and Friel, N. (2018). "Computationally efficient inference for latent position network models". In: *arXiv preprint arXiv:1804.02274*.

Ryan, C., Wyse, J., and Friel, N. (2017). "Bayesian model selection for the latent position cluster model for social networks". In: *Network Science* 5.1, pp. 70–91. doi: 10.1017/nws.2017.6.

Salter-Townshend, M. and McCormick, T.H. (2017). "Latent space models for multiview network data". In: *Annals of Applied Statistics* 11.3, pp. 1217–1244. doi: 10.1214/16-AOAS955.

Salter-Townshend, M. and Murphy, T.B. (2013). "Variational Bayesian inference for the latent position cluster model for network data". In: *Computational Statistics and Data Analysis* 57.1, pp. 661–671. doi: 10.1016/j.csda.2012.08.004.

Salter-Townshend, M., White, A., Gollini, I., and Murphy, T.B. (2012). "Review of statistical network analysis: Models, algorithms, and software". In: *Statistical Analysis and Data Mining* 5.4, pp. 243–264. doi: 10.1002/sam.11146.

Sarkar, P. and Moore, A.W. (2005). "Dynamic social network analysis using latent space models". In: pp. 1145–1152.

Sewell, D.K. (2019). "Latent space models for network perception data". In: *Network Science* 7.2, pp. 160–179. doi: 10.1017/nws.2019.1.

Sewell, D.K. (2020). "Model-Based Edge Clustering". In: *Journal of Computational and Graphical Statistics* 30.2, pp. 390–405. doi: 10.1080/10618600.2020.1811104.

Sewell, D.K. and Chen, Y. (2015a). "Analysis of the formation of the structure of social networks by using latent space models for ranked dynamic networks". In: *Journal of the Royal Statistical Society. Series C: Applied Statistics* 64.4, pp. 611–633. doi: 10.1111/rssc.12093.

Sewell, D.K. and Chen, Y. (2015b). "Latent Space Models for Dynamic Networks". In: *Journal of the American Statistical Association* 110.512, pp. 1646–1657. doi: 10.1080/01621459.2014.988214.

Sewell, D.K. and Chen, Y. (2016). "Latent space models for dynamic networks with weighted edges". In: *Social Networks* 44, pp. 105–116. doi: 10.1016/j.socnet.2015.07.005.

Sewell, D.K. and Chen, Y. (2017). "Latent space approaches to community detection in dynamic networks". In: *Bayesian analysis* 12.2, pp. 351–377.

Shortreed, S., Handcock, M.S., and Hoff, P.D. (2006). "Positional estimation within a latent space model for networks". In: *Methodology* 2.1, pp. 24–33. doi: 10.1027/1614-2241.2.1.24.

Smith, A.L., Asta, D.M., and Calder, C.A. (2019). "The geometry of continuous latent space models for network data". In: *Statistical Science* 34.3, pp. 428–453. doi: 10.1214/19-STS702.

Snijders, T. and Nowicki, K. (Jan. 1997). "Estimation and Prediction for Stochastic Blockmodels for Graphs with Latent Block Structure". In: *Journal of Classification* 14, pp. 75–100. doi: 10.1007/s003579900004.

Sosa, J. and Buitrago, L. (2021). "A review of latent space models for social networks [Una revisión de modelos de espacio latente para redes sociales]". In: *Revista Colombiana de Estadística* 44.1, pp. 171–200. doi: 10.15446/rce.v44n1.89369.

Spencer, N.A., Junker, B., and Sweet, T.M. (2020). "Faster MCMC for Gaussian latent position network models". In: *arXiv preprint arXiv:2006.07687*.

Spiegelhalter, D.J., Best, N.G., Carlin, B.P., and Van Der Linde, A. (2002). "Bayesian measures of model complexity and fit". In: *Journal of the Royal Statistical Society: Series B (Statistical Methodology)* 64.4, pp. 583–639.

Sweet, T. and Adhikari, S. (2020). "A Latent Space Network Model for Social Influence". In: *Psychometrika* 85.2, pp. 251–274. doi: 10.1007/s11336-020-09700-x.

Sweet, T.M., Thomas, A.C., and Junker, B.W. (2013). "Hierarchical Network Models for Education Research: Hierarchical Latent Space Models". In: *Journal of Educational and Behavioral Statistics* 38.3, pp. 295–318. doi: 10.3102/1076998612458702.

Tafakori, L., Pourkhanali, A., and Rastelli, R. (2021). "Measuring systemic risk and contagion in the European financial network". In: *Empirical Economics*. doi: 10.1007/s00181-021-02135-y.

Wang, Y.J. and Wong, G.Y. (1987). "Stochastic blockmodels for directed graphs". In: *Journal of the American Statistical Association* 82.397, pp. 8–19.

Ward, M.D., Ahlquist, J.S., and Rozenas, A. (2013). "Gravity's Rainbow: A dynamic latent space model for the world trade network". In: *Network Science* 1.1, pp. 95–118. doi: 10.1017/nws.2013.1.

Westveld, A.H. and Hoff, P.D. (2011). "A mixed effects model for longitudinal relational and network data, with applications to international trade and conflict". In: *The Annals of Applied Statistics* 5.2A, pp. 843–872.

Wilson, J.D., Cranmer, S., and Lu, Z.-L. (2020). "A Hierarchical Latent Space Network Model for Population Studies of Functional Connectivity". In: *Computational Brain and Behavior* 3.4, pp. 384–399. doi: 10.1007/s42113-020-00080-0.

Xiao, T., Oppenheimer, M., He, X., and Mastrorillo, M. (2022). "Complex climate and network effects on internal migration in South Africa revealed by a network model". In: *Population and Environment*, pp. 1–30.

Xie, F. and Xu, Y. (2021). "Efficient estimation for random dot product graphs via a one-step procedure". In: *Journal of the American Statistical Association*, pp. 1–14.

Young, S.J. and Scheinerman, E.R. (2007). "Random dot product graph models for social networks". In: *International Workshop on Algorithms and Models for the Web-Graph*. Springer, pp. 138–149.

Zhang, X., Xue, S., and Zhu, J. (2020). "A flexible latent space model for multilayer networks". In: vol. PartF168147-15, pp. 11225–11234.

Negative Ties and Signed Networks

Filip Agneessens

INTRODUCTION

Social network relations come in many different forms. Some interpersonal networks, such as liking or friendship ties, have a primarily affective component. Other social relations, such as communication, knowledge sharing and collaboration, are predominately instrumental in nature. These networks are often studied because they are believed to benefit individuals and groups and can be opposed to other kinds of ties, including bullying, dislike, hindrance and conflict. This latter type is usually brought together under the label of *negative* ties, which are typically assumed to be detrimental to the group and its members.

Research focusing on negative relations spans many topics and areas of study. Examples of topics of research include bullying in school classes (van der Ploeg et al., 2020), ambivalent ties among family members (Fingerman et al., 2004), negative gossip among employees (Grosser et al., 2010), conflict among contributors to online platforms (Lerner & Lomi, 2020), and alliances and adversarial relations among nations (Smith et al., 2014).

However, despite an increasing focus on negative ties and signed networks (see, for example, Harrigan et al., 2020; Offer, 2021), studies that incorporate negative networks explicitly remain relatively rare in comparison with the vast number of studies involving positive and instrumental ties (Yang et al., 2019; Neal, 2020; Brooks & Dunkel-Schetter, 2011). Most social network research has traditionally focused on instrumental and positive affect ties because of the benefits that accrue from them (especially within the framework of social capital, e.g., Lin et al., 2001).

This lack of empirical research on negative ties contrasts with both theoretical arguments and existing empirical evidence, which suggest that in many cases negative ties have more impact than their positive counterparts. Negative events not only generate more arousal, but are also likely to lead to more cognitive processing. Therefore, negative relations can have a more profound and longer-lasting impact on those involved, which is referred to as *negative asymmetry* (Labianca & Brass, 2006, p. 600).

One reason for the relative scarcity of social network research involving negative ties might be the difficulty of collecting negative relations. However, another reason might be the lack of a systematic and coherent framework to study negative ties, combined with fewer fit-for-purpose network measures to address such research questions (Everett & Borgatti, 2014). Negative ties might not follow the same logic as positive or neutral ones. For example, most negative relations do not give rise to the same indirect transfer of resources that positive and instrumental ties are often credited with providing.

This chapter provides a non-exhaustive overview of different network measures and methods, which might be helpful for analysing negative and signed networks, and the types of research questions they can answer. In this chapter, we will explore different measures of position for negative and signed networks, discuss suitable whole network measures, consider how to identify subgroups, perform community detection and discuss equivalence and blockmodelling for signed networks).[1] However, we start this chapter with the fundamental question, 'what constitutes a negative tie?'

WHAT ARE NEGATIVE TIES?

Social networks generally capture a relation between two nodes – that is, between a sender and a receiver.[2] The focus of this chapter will be on *interpersonal* relations. However, many of the arguments discussed here also apply when considering negative ties between other types of nodes, such as organisations or countries.

Types of Negative Ties and Positive Ties

Scholars differ in their views about what constitutes a negative tie. However, most tend to contrast negative ties with positive (and sometimes also neutral) ones. One intuitive approach would be to define ties as positive or negative, depending on whether they generate a positive versus negative outcome. For example, being bullied has been found to lead to a decrease in well-being (Sharp, 1995), while being liked tends to increase it (Ladd et al., 1997). From this perspective, it would be obvious to consider liking as a positive tie and bullying as a negative tie due to the outcomes they generate. However, one issue with such an approach is that the same liking ties can become a social liability in specific situations or to certain people. Such a situation is sometimes also referred to as the 'dark side' of social capital or 'opportunity costs' (e.g., Gargiulo & Benassi, 1999). Also, specific types of conflict might, under certain conditions, lead to employees becoming more critical about their initial ideas, thereby allowing them to come up with more innovative ideas and higher performance (Pelled et al., 1999). Similarly, bullying peers can be status-enhancing for the bully (van der Ploeg et al., 2020).

A different way to separate negative ties from positive ties focuses on the inherent aspect of the tie itself and the underlying intent of the sender towards the recipient. This perspective starts from the notion that negative tie research encompasses negative feelings, cognitive judgements and/or behaviours or behavioural intentions directed towards other people (Labianca & Brass, 2006; Yang et al., 2019; Agneessens & Labianca, 2022). How precisely to differentiate positive from negative ties in this tripartite model depends on the type of relation (see Figure 37.1).

Affect. Affect-based network relations focus on the feelings a person has towards others and hence concentrate on the emotional component of how a person relates to someone else (Labianca, 2014). Positive affect-based ties contain a positive emotion, such as liking or loving someone.

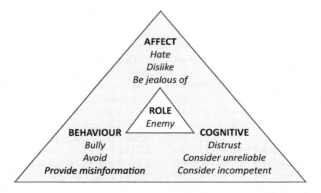

Figure 37.1 Typology of negative ties using the tripartite model: affect, behavioural (intent), cognitive evaluations and role relations (adjusted from Yang et al., 2019)

In contrast, negative affect-based relations involve a negative emotion, such as dislike or hate. We might also consider a third neutral affect-based relation, which refers to being indifferent to a person. Indifference to a person is not the same as not knowing the person. Being indifferent is an active choice resulting from being in contact with that person. Note that the sign of the tie comes from whether there is a positive or negative affect, not its consequences. However, in most cases (but not always), both approaches will lead to the same classification.

Behaviour. A second type of network ties focuses on actual interactions that a person has with others. Behaviour towards others might be defined as positive, negative, or neutral, depending on the actor's intent. Hence, helping and sharing information are generally considered positive ties (even if the help could backfire) because of the person's positive intention. In contrast, hindering or avoiding someone is categorised as a negative tie (Sparrowe et al., 2001) because of its harmful intent, even if it does not negatively impact the recipient. Behavioural ties might also be neutral if there is no positive or negative intent underlying the behaviour.

Cognitive evaluations of others. Cognitive evaluations encompass some evaluation or categorisation of the other. For example, a person might perceive someone to have integrity, competence, or trustworthiness. The negative counterparts would be to consider that the person lacks integrity, is incompetent, or is not trustworthy. Such evaluations tend to be opposites on a one-dimensional scale, where the sign captures the positive or negative evaluation. Vörös and Snijders (2017) considered a range of cognitive judgements, including evaluation of a person's general behaviour ('is shy'), their contact's appearance ('is pretty') and specific characteristics of the alters (e.g., 'has lots of money'). One specific type of cognitive evaluation involves asking a person how they think others in the network relate to each other, referred to as *cognitive social structures* (CSS; Krackhardt, 1987). Such research has increasingly focused on negative ties (Marineau & Labianca, 2021).

Role relations. Besides affect-based ties, behaviour relations and cognitive evaluations, we might consider role relations as a fourth major type of network relation (Borgatti et al., 2022). Role relations are culturally defined ways two people are expected to relate to each other (Nadel, 1957). A role relation often encompasses a combination of affective feelings, behaviour and behavioural expectations and specific judgements of the other. For example, friendship generally involves a positive affective feeling (such as liking the person), behaviour with positive intent (such as helping or spending time together) and positive evaluations (such as trusting the other person) (Fischer, 1982). In contrast, an enemy or nemesis will generate negative feelings (such as dislike or hate), negative behaviour towards each other (such as avoidance or hindrance) and negative evaluations (such as distrust). If the expected behaviour of a friend is broken – for example, because they talked badly behind their friend's back – the friendship relation will be put into question and might be terminated. Some role relations tend to be symmetrical or reciprocal, such as friendship or enmity (i.e., where both can expect the same behaviour and feelings from each other). Other role relations are asymmetrical or antireciprocal, such as the expectations in a mother–child relation or a bully–victim relation.

In practice, not all relations fit perfectly into one of the four categories. For example, a difficult relation generally combines an affective and a behavioural component. However, differentiating between these four types allows the identification of specific processes and theoretical arguments that might only apply to some types of ties.

At the same time, by bringing all these types of relations together under one broader 'umbrella' of negative ties, negative network research can be contrasted with research on positive (and neutral) networks (Labianca, 2014) and highlight some overarching differences between negative and positive ties and a need for a distinct approach.

Negative Ties, Positive Ties and Signed Networks

In many cases, we might consider both positive and negative ties simultaneously. Studies focusing on a combination of positive and negative ties are commonly referred to as *signed network* research. However, studies might differ in how they conceptually relate positive and negative ties with each other.

One form of signed networks focuses on situations where negative ties complement their positive counterparts, meaning that the absence of a negative tie implies the presence of a positive tie and vice versa. One classic example of such a dataset is voting among US Supreme Court justices, where each justice will either support the majority decision on a specific issue or dissent from the decision taken (Doreian & Mrvar, 2020). We will refer to this as a {P|N}-signed network. In this case, it suffices that either the negative or positive ties are collected.

A second version considers positive and negative ties as opposing endpoints of a single dimension with a neutral point in the middle. Studies where a third neutral alternative exists next to the positive and negative options include alliances and adversaries among countries (Smith et al., 2014). We will call this a {P|O|N}-signed network. An example is whether a person considers another person competent versus incompetent, with neutral (neither) in the middle.

The above approaches assume that positive and negative ties exclude each other. In contrast, a third important type of signed network consists of situations where the same person can simultaneously have a positive and negative tie to another person, often referred to as having an ambivalent tie. Examples of network relations where ambivalence might occur are positive and negative gossip (Grosser et al., 2010). We label these {N+P}-signed networks. For affect-based ties, ambivalence might capture having opposing feelings about different aspects or facets of another person (such as liking to hang out with the person but disliking their political views) or opposing evaluations about different aspects (such as trusting them in some situations but not others). However, ambivalence sometimes also might capture having sequential opposing views or behavioural intentions towards another person, such as where a person likes another person one day but dislikes them the next.

The distinction between {P|N}, {P|O|N} and {P+N}-signed networks is particularly relevant because different types of models and measures might apply to some, but not to other types of signed networks. In the rest of this chapter, we will assume for convenience that positive ties have positive effects, while negative ties have detrimental effects for the individual and/or the group.

NODAL-LEVEL MEASURES OF POSITION FOR NEGATIVE AND SIGNED NETWORKS

This section explores different nodal-level measures of position and their theoretical underpinnings. Measures of position can help explain nodal-level outcomes, such as the well-being of people, the grades of schoolchildren and the performance of employees. Popular ways to capture a node's network position include centrality measures (see also Everett & Borgatti, this volume) and measures that incorporate openness and closure in the network structure around a person.

Variants of Degree Centrality for Negative Ties and Signed Networks

One simple measure of centrality entails counting the number of direct connections around a node. Consider a binary network among n nodes stored in a matrix X. A value of 1 for cell x_{ij} means there is a tie from node i to node j, while a 0 represents the absence of a tie. The degree centrality for node i can be calculated as:

$$d_i = \sum_{j=1}^{n} \left(x_{ij} \right) \quad (1)$$

The complementary approach

While degree centrality for positive ties captures someone's access to valuable resources, such resources are unlikely to flow through negative ties. Instead, a high value for degree centrality might indicate exposure to negative behaviour, such as hindrance or bullying (i.e., social liabilities; Labianca & Brass, 2006). Hence, we might want to reverse the values for degree centrality by taking the negative value of the original measure:

$$d_i^{Neg} = -\sum_{j=1}^{n} \left(x_{ij}^{Neg} \right) = \sum_{j=1}^{n} \left(-x_{ij}^{Neg} \right) \quad (2)$$

A more eloquent transformation proposed by Everett and Borgatti (2014) involves subtracting this degree from its theoretical maximum (n-1):

$$d_i^{Neg} = (n-1) - \sum_{j=1}^{n} \left(x_{ij}^{Neg} \right) \quad (3)$$

Note that this is simply a linear transformation of Equation 2. For a {P|N}-signed network, this is equivalent to calculating the degree on the complementary, positive network.

Degree centrality for signed networks

For {P|O|N}-signed or {P+N}-signed networks, we might be interested in simultaneously considering the effect of both positive and negative ties – for example, by adding both in the same regression model to check their relative importance. Alternatively, if we can theoretically assume that both would have the opposite effect, we might want to combine both into a single degree measure by subtracting the value for the negative degree from that of the positive degree.

However, if we assume that a positive and a negative tie might not have the same level of impact (Labianca & Brass, 2006), we could weigh their relative influence (cf. Doreian & Mrvar, 1996):

$$d_i^{Pos,Neg} = \sum_{j=1}^{n} \left((1-\alpha) \cdot x_{ij}^{Pos} - \alpha \cdot x_{ij}^{Neg} \right) \quad (4)$$

where a value close to 0 for α would mean that we primarily give importance to positive ties, while a value close to 1 means that we primarily focus on the negative ties. A value of 0.5 gives equal weight to both.

Another approach starts from the assumption that any real interaction between two nodes will imply that they will either be positively or negatively related to each other, and therefore the presence of a neutral tie implies a non-interaction between those nodes. As a measure of negative degree centrality, we might, in this case, calculate the proportion of all non-neutral ties (i.e., ties that are either positive or negative) involving a node that is negative (Lerner, 2016). Finally, in the case of {P+N}-signed networks, we might instead focus on either ambivalent or negative-only ties (Rook et al., 2012).

Indirect Connections Involving Negative (and Positive) Ties

Nodes might not only impact those alters they are directly linked to, but might also impact others at longer distances. Different theoretical arguments have been developed to explain the processes involving indirect paths for positive ties. However, because negative ties are not generally conducive to the flow of information and other resources, some of these arguments might not directly apply to networks with negative ties. This section proposes five main theoretical arguments for how longer distances might be relevant when studying negative ties and signed networks. The outcomes are summarised in Table 37.1.

Negative ties as 'negative resources'

According to Labianca and Brass's (2006) *social ledger theory*, social networks can provide benefits, but they also create social liabilities. Negative ties are not only likely to create social liabilities for the two people directly involved, but, as their consequences ripple through the network, they can also have detrimental consequences for others further away. However, the extent to which they will impact a person will depend on the distance of the negative tie to that person (Labianca, 2014). The more intermediary actors exist between a person and a negative tie, the more these intermediary actors can 'buffer' the negative effect of such a negative tie and the less it will impact that person. For example, a conflict between two students might have a ripple effect on the working of others in the network, where the impact of this conflict on others depends on how far away these others are from those two students. From this perspective, a negative tie between two people can be considered a type of 'negative resource' which will impact others in a group. Considering a {P|O|N}-signed network, we might use the positive ties to determine how far ego is from those negatively connected dyads in a network. The closer all the negative ties are to ego (based on the positive network), the more ego might be impacted and, therefore, the worse its situation. Hence, one way to capture the effect of negative ties on a node is to calculate the geodesic distance from that node to all the negative ties in the network.

The flow of (mis)information argument

When focusing on resources (such as information or material goods) flowing through a network, a standard method when studying positive networks is to identify the shortest path through which these resources might flow between network members (Borgatti, 2005). However, resources do not generally flow through negative ties. Instead, negative ties (e.g., distrust) often generate avoidance and withholding of information and resources (Harrigan & Yap, 2017). Therefore, the presence of a negative tie may have a similar effect to not being connected at all.

However, in specific contexts, a negative tie between two people might instead lead to them sharing misinformation, while a positive network captures the sharing of information. Therefore, any path in a network that involves at least one negative tie would lead to misinformation – rather than no information – flowing through that path. Note that it might not matter whether a path of distance three involves a single negative tie and two positive ties or whether the path consists of three negative ties. Therefore, we should distinguish between a situation where two nodes:

- are indirectly connected through a positive-only network, in which case ego can receive 'valid' information,
- are indirectly connected through a link that involves at least one negative tie, in which case this will generate misinformation,
- are not linked through any combination of positive and negative ties, in which case no information or misinformation will transfer between the two nodes.

The outcomes of different basic patterns are shown in Table 37.1. Of course, there are potentially multiple ways in which two nodes are connected and we could, in such a case, assess whether at least one positive-only path exists so that a person can obtain the correct information from the source.

Table 37.1 Overview of the effects of direct and indirect paths involving positive and negative ties depending on theoretical approach (where node *a* is ego, node *b* is a direct contact of ego and nodes *c*, *d* and *e* are indirect contacts of ego)

Pattern	A	B	C	D	E	F
Theoretical approach						
Negative ties as negative 'resources'	(+ +)	(+ +)	–	–	–	–
Flow of (mis) information	+ +	+ +	– –	– –	– –	– (or – – –)
Status argument	+ +	+ + +	–	– –	– – –	+ + (or 0)
Attitudinal/ behavioural adjustments	+ +	(+)	(–)	– –	(–)	(+)
Power-dependence	+ +	+	+ + +	– –	– – –	–

Note: Dotted lines represent negative ties, while full lines represent positive ties.

We can easily think of variations to this measure. For example, we could also consider how often a person receives information versus misinformation by calculating the number of positive-only paths as a proportion of all paths, as this proportion could influence the likelihood that this person will believe the (mis)information. Alternatively, we could also take a different perspective and assume that each negative tie adds a slight distortion to the original information. In that case, the number of negative ties in a path would represent the level of distortion happening in that path.

The status argument

A third major approach focuses on the status or popularity a person might gain from their direct and indirect relations with others. The starting point is that having positive ties to others confers status to a person. On the other hand, having negative connections to others can harm a person's status (de Klepper et al., 2017). Such status differences can be transmitted to indirect contacts through 'social osmosis' (Bonacich & Lloyd, 2004). Being positively connected to a person with many positive contacts (and therefore someone with high status) might increase one's own status by proxy (Pattern B in Table 37.1). Hence, being friends with someone who has many friends can increase one's popularity more than being friends with someone who has few friends. Beta centrality follows this basic logic (Bonacich, 1987).

In extension, being positively connected to someone with many negative ties might harm one's status as one inherits the negative status of that person by proximity (Pattern C). In contrast, the same positive tie might increase one's status considerably when it connects to someone with few negative and many positive ties. At the same time, being negatively related to someone directly decreases one's status. This effect will be more damaging if the other person has many positive ties – that is, has a high status or popularity (Pattern E in Table 37.1).

Bonacich and Lloyd (2004) also argue that having a negative connection to someone with many negative ties might increase one's status (Pattern F). However, this last argument might be less self-evident since being disliked by people whom many others dislike might not necessarily make someone popular. However, the measure proposed by Bonacich and Lloyd (2004) relies on the idea that a sequence of two negative ties will lead to a positive indirect effect (that is, the product of two negative values generating a positive value). A variant of this approach was proposed by Everett and Borgatti (2014).

Attitudinal and behavioural adjustments

A considerable amount of network research has centred on the idea that humans tend to adjust their opinions and behaviour towards that of their social contacts. The general argument of social influence is that two people connected through a communication or positive tie are likely to converge in opinion and become similar in behaviour. This specific type of influence is also referred to as social contagion or diffusion (Valente & Vega Yon, 2020). Empirical studies on social contagion include whether a person's own criminal behaviour is affected by that of their peers (Gallupe et al., 2019) and whether members of a team who like each other tend to become similar in their values on social justice and loyalty (Meeussen et al., 2018).

Several mechanisms can explain why people adjust their attitudes and behaviour in the direction of their peers, including social control or social imitation (Mason et al., 2007). One core argument to explain why people tend to converge in their views and attitudes builds on Heider's (1946) *cognitive balance theory*. Two people linked through a positive tie will experience cognitive balance if they are in the same way connected towards a specific object, such as a specific view (e.g., political opinion) or behaviour.

However, if being positively related to someone generates similarity, exposure to views and behaviour by others whom one dislikes might have the opposite effect, meaning that they generate divergence in views, opinions and behaviour. According to balance theory, when two people dislike each other, they will feel discomfort when they have the same relationship with the object. Instead, they might want to take the opposite view or exhibit opposite behaviour (Kitts, 2006). For example, if we consider the effect of a person's resignation on the chances of colleagues leaving, then being friends with someone who resigned might make a focal actor (ego) more likely to resign as well. In contrast, an enemy resigning from a job might increase the chances that ego will stay.

Considering indirect connections in a signed network, on the one hand, a person two steps away from the other will tend to converge if a path consists of two positive or two negative ties (Pattern B and F in Table 37.1). On the other hand, they would diverge if the path combined one positive and one negative tie (an uneven number of negative ties). For example, if the enemy of a friend resigns, this might reduce ego's likelihood of resignation because ego's friend is less likely to resign. In contrast, the enemy of an enemy resigning might increase ego's chance of resigning because it reduces the chances of ego's enemy quitting (consistent with Bonacich & Lloyd, 2004).

Overall, studies provide mixed support for the *negative influence hypothesis* (Kitts, 2006; Takács et al., 2016). In addition, we note that in the above example of social diffusion, we focused on how ego was impacted by people two steps away resigning because the indirect contact's behaviour impacted their direct contact's behaviour, which, in turn, impacted ego's own behaviour (i.e., a sort of 'ripple effect'). One crucial question is whether the indirect link between two people might have any *direct* influence on each other's views or behaviour (see Christakis and Fowler's (2007) *three degrees of separation* argument), or whether the indirect influence that happens is simply due to a ripple effect.

Power-dependence argument

A final approach we will consider here builds on the idea that a (positive) connection might not only bring benefits to those involved (i.e., access) but might also generate dependencies between the two nodes in the dyad (i.e., control). Relying on the power-dependence perspective (Emerson, 1962; Cook et al., 1983), the relative dependence of both nodes in a dyad is affected by the number of alternatives they have. More specifically, node (b)'s dependency on another node (a) is assumed to decrease if (b) has alternative contacts besides (a) for specific resources. Hence, in a context where (b) has many other (positive) connections (besides (a)) while (a) has few alternatives (besides (b)), (b) will be less dependent on (a) than (a) will be on (b). It implies that it is better to link to others with few ties (i.e., prefer to be node (a) in Pattern A rather than in Pattern B in Table 37.1). This idea has been measured using beta centrality, where a negative value for beta is used (Bonacich, 1987).

Considering signed networks, we might think of negative ties as providing threats to a node, while positive ties might provide access but also dependence. For example, Smith et al. (2014) consider the international network of alliances and adversaries due to military conflict. A node's position will be better if it has many allies (direct positive ties) and few adversaries (direct negative ties). A node with many adversaries will need to build alliances to deal with its adversaries. When (a) has a positive connection to someone (b) who has many negative ties (c, d and e) (Pattern C in Table 37.1), this can benefit (a) as (b) will require allies to deal with its adversaries (c, d and e). This need for allies will make (b) more willing to invest in the relation with (a), which increases (a)'s power towards (b) (Marineau et al., 2016). Inversely, when (a) has a negative connection with (b), while (b) has many other negative connections (Pattern F), this will lower the threat of (b) on (a) since (b) needs to deal with many other threats. However, if (b) has many positive connections (Pattern E), then (b) will, of course, be more dangerous for (a).

Hence, from a power-dependence perspective having a positive connection to someone with many positive and few negative ties is less beneficial than having a positive connection to someone with few positive and many negative ties. To capture such power-dependence processes, the Political Independence Index (PII, Smith et al., 2014) relies on a combination of the number of ties at distance d from ego i (P_d) and the number of negative ties at distance d from ego i (N_d):

$$PII_i | \beta, K = \sum_{d=0}^{K} \beta^d \cdot \left(P_d^x - N_d^x \right) \quad (5)$$

where β is the weight given to longer distances.[3]

Structural Holes: Open and Closed Triads

A somewhat different research question, which has received extensive attention in the last decades, is whether it is beneficial to be connected to others who are or are not connected to each other. The seminal work by Burt (1992) has generated a broad debate and given rise to numerous empirical studies and theoretical discussions on the importance of structural holes. The position taken by Burt is that when ego is linked to others who are themselves not connected, this will provide several benefits to the focal person. First, it allows a person to control the information flow between these alters. Moreover, since these alters are not linked to each other, they are more likely to provide access to unique, non-redundant information. Third, the lack of a connection between alters will remove any possibility for coordinated efforts by alters to control ego's actions, reducing the dependency on ego.

Such a structural position will obviously not generate the same beneficial effect when considering negative ties. Instead, using a signed network, we might focus on the disadvantages of being in a structural hole containing negative ties. In particular, we could test whether a positive tie between two people to whom ego is negatively related is more detrimental than an open structure with no positive tie among these two alters. The positive tie among the alters might enable them to build a coalition against ego, which might have a more significant impact than both negative ties in and of themselves (Krackhardt, 1999). Marineau et al. (2016) investigated the effects of such a triadic structural position in an organisational context and found that being in such a structural position harms individual performance.

However, revisiting the original idea of structural holes where there is a positive tie between ego and its connections, we might wonder whether the absence of a tie between others generates the same outcome as the presence of a negative tie. To answer this question, we need to consider the different strategies that brokers might take. If we take the perspective of structural holes as a strategy to keep others apart (i.e., *tertius gaudens*; Obstfeld, 2005), then it might be even more beneficial for ego if their alters are connected through a negative tie than if they have no tie at all. If these alters are negatively related, they are unlikely to coordinate with each other in the future. Moreover, ego can use this to its own advantage by pitting them against each other and ensuring they remain separated.

However, such a negative tie among alters might, in certain circumstances, also work against ego. One potential advantage of being in a structural hole is that ego can benefit from bringing others together who were unconnected before (i.e., *tertius iungens* – the one who brings together; Obstfeld, 2005). Achieving this outcome will be far more difficult if these others are negatively connected. In addition, a negative tie among alters might put a burden on ego to maintain both relations given the cognitive imbalance (Festinger & Hutte, 1954; Marineau et al., 2016; see also the Section on structural balance below). If the alters become aware of the positive relation of ego with the other person, they might be less inclined to provide benefits to ego. They might even force ego to choose between them both, something that an absent tie would not necessarily generate (see also Krackhardt, 1999).

NETWORK-LEVEL PROPERTIES

Because of their inherently different nature, negative networks are often assumed to exhibit very different structures than positive ones. In this section, we consider which network-level properties might be meaningful to consider when dealing with negative ties or signed networks.

Cohesion

One basic network-level concept refers to the cohesion of a network, which is classically captured through measures such as density, connectedness, or compactness (Borgatti et al., 2022, Chapter 10). However, many cohesion measures focus on how easy it is for resources to flow through a network, which is generally antithetical to many negative networks.

One clear exception is density, which denotes the proportion of connections present in a network. When applied to a negative tie network, density might represent the level of antagonistic feelings and noncooperative behaviour present in a group. If a high density for a negative network measures the absence of cohesion, we might consider taking the complement of the negative tie network, as we did for degree centrality. In the case of a {P|N}-signed network, the value for density for the negative tie network is simply one minus the density for the positive network. However, in the case of {P|O|N}-signed networks, it could be interesting to consider both the density for the negative and positive ties simultaneously. Alternatively, if we assume that a neutral tie represents the absence of any interaction between two people (Lerner, 2016), then we might consider calculating the number of negative (or positive) ties in a network as a proportion of the number of ties that are either positive or negative. Finally, in the case of {P+N}-signed networks, we could also be interested in the proportion of ambivalent ties or, alternatively, the percentage of negative-only ties.

Structural Balance

A different, yet related, way of thinking about cohesion for signed networks is to consider the level to which a network exhibits structural balance. Following Heider's classic *cognitive balance theory* (Heider, 1946), Cartwright and Harary (1956) argue that in a signed network, cognitive dissonance will occur when a node is positively connected to two other nodes which are themselves negatively tied to each other (as depicted by Triad C in Figure 37.2). This is referred to as structural balance. For example, a person (a) might have two good friends (b and c) who dislike or are hostile to each other. Such a situation will not only be uncomfortable for the person whose friends are antagonistic to each other, but will also put the other two people into a difficult situation as they will feel uncomfortable about their friend being friends with someone they dislike.

However, negative ties do not always need to result in imbalance. According to Cartwright and Harary's (1956) *structural balance theory*, a triad in which two friends (a and c) have a common enemy (b) does not generate any cognitive dissonance (Triad B in Figure 37.2) and might even strengthen their friendship. Obviously, three people who are friends (Triad A) also give rise to a balanced situation.

A final triad comprises three negative ties among the three nodes (Triad D). Whether such a triad should be considered balanced is an open point of debate (Doreian & Mrvar, 1996). The discussion fundamentally goes back to whether two negative ties should always generate a positive tie (i.e., whether 'the enemy of my enemy is my friend') or whether these three nodes could all three be hostile to each other. Cartwright and Harary (1956) consider Triad D imbalanced, while Davis (1967) takes the opposite view.

These rules have important implications for the overall structure of a {P|N}-signed network.

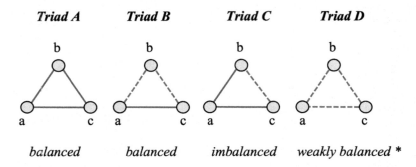

Figure 37.2 Balanced and imbalanced triads in an undirected signed network

*Triad D represents an imbalanced structure according to Cartright and Harary (1956), but is acceptable according to Davis (1967)

Note: Dotted lines represent negative ties, while full lines represent positive ties.

If we follow the original rules about structural balance, meaning that we consider both Triads C and D as imbalanced, then a perfectly balanced network will consist at most of two subgroups (as depicted by Network B in Figure 37.3). In such a network, each subgroup has only positive ties between its members, while only negative links exist between nodes of both subgroups (Cartwright & Harary, 1956).

However, suppose we follow Davis's approach and only consider Triad C problematic. In that case, the resulting signed network can consist of more than two subgroups (Network A in Figure 37.3). Davis (1967) refers to this as *clustering*, while others refer to it as *weak balance* (Aref & Neal, 2020). The basic idea underlying Cartwright and Harary's structural balance approach is that in a network with multiple groups (Network A in Figure 37.3) some of these subgroups would, over time, merge to become allies in order to react to their common enemy (resulting in a structure such as Network B). The question is, in essence, whether we consider a signed network as a multipolar or bipolar structure (Rosecrance, 1966).

Measuring the level of structural balance for {P|N}-signed networks

Structural balance has been a topic of interest in many research areas, including when considering positive and negative ties among children (Yap & Harrigan, 2015), among countries (Doreian & Mrvar, 2015) and among politicians (Aref & Neal, 2020).

Of course, real networks are usually not perfectly balanced. The *extent* to which a network is (im)balanced can be measured by a range of indices (Aref & Wilson, 2018). One straightforward measure involves taking the proportion of all triads in a network that is balanced (Cartwright & Harary, 1956):

$$\text{Triangle Index} = \frac{C_3^+}{C_3^- + C_3^+} \quad (6)$$

where C_3^+ refers to the number of balanced triads in the signed network (the number of Triads A and B from Figure 37.2) and C_3^- refers to the number of imbalanced triads (the number of Triads C and D). Calculating these for the five networks in Figure 37.4, we find that Network A is the only fully balanced network, with Network D being the least balanced.

A different approach to measuring the level of balance relies on counting the number of ties that need to be changed to make a network balanced so that the network splits into two (or more) subgroups. This is known as the *frustration index* (or *line index of balance*; Harary, 1959). For example, Network C (Figure 37.4) only needs one tie {a,e} to switch from negative to positive to become balanced, whereas Network D needs a minimum of three. We will return to this idea when considering blockmodelling.

Measuring the level of structural balance for {P|O|N}-signed networks

The approach of relying on triad counts works well for {P|N}-signed networks. However, relying on triadic configurations alone does not suffice to evaluate the balance of {P|O|N}-signed networks because of the neutral ties in such

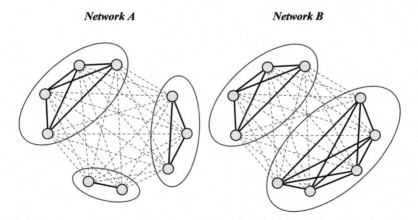

Figure 37.3 Two examples of perfectly balanced {P|N}-signed networks, depending on whether triads with three negative ties (*Triad D*) are allowed (left) or not allowed (right)

Note: Dotted lines represent negative ties, while full lines represent positive ties

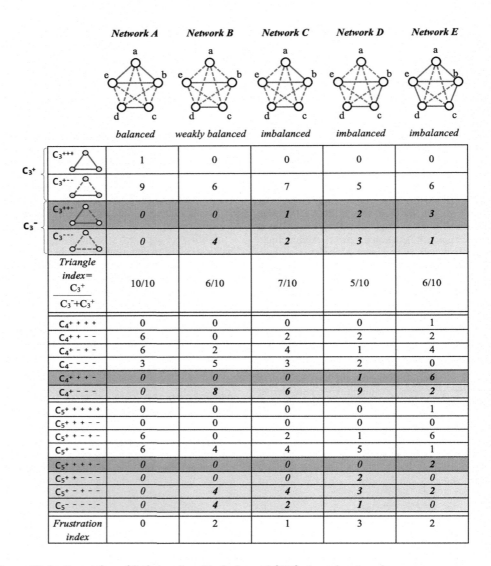

Figure 37.4 Examples of balanced and imbalanced {P|N}-signed networks

Note: Italic, bold values indicate cycles inconsistent with balance (i.e., uneven number of negative ties).

networks. To illustrate this, consider the five {P|O|N}-signed networks in Figure 37.5.

All the networks, except Networks B and C, would seem balanced from a triadic perspective. However, this conclusion is in all of these five cases based on one single triad with no neutral ties. Some scholars have argued that to properly evaluate the balance of a {P|O|N}-signed network, we would need to replace the neutral ties by either a positive or a negative tie and check if we *could* generate a balanced {P|N}-signed network this way. For example, Network A in Figure 37.5 can potentially result in a balanced {P|N}-signed network if we replace the neutral tie {a,d} with a positive tie and the other neutral ties ({a,c},{b,d} and {c,e}) with a negative tie, resulting in two groups {a,d,e} and {b,c}. Network E also has an underlying balanced structure if we make all four neutral ties positive, which would result in a single positively connected group. However, for Network D

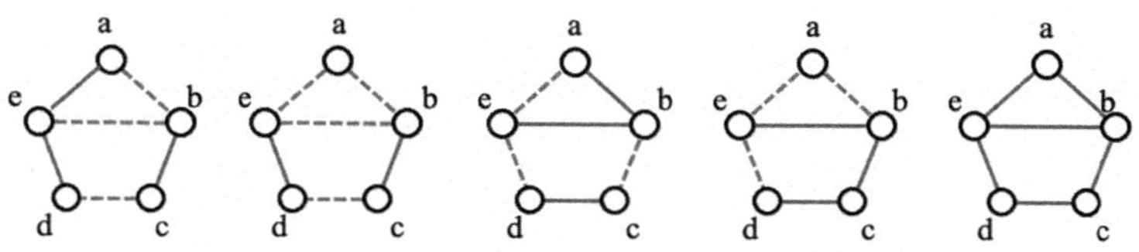

		Network A balanced	Network B weakly balanced	Network C imbalanced	Network D imbalanced	Network E balanced
C_3^+	C_3^{+++}	0	0	0	0	1
	C_3^{+--}	1	0	0	1	0
C_3^-	C_3^{++-}	*0*	*0*	*1*	*0*	*0*
	C_3^{---}	*0*	*1*	*0*	*0*	*0*
Triangle index= $\dfrac{C_3^+}{C_3^- + C_3^+}$		1/1	0/1	0/1	1/1	1/1
$C_4^+ + + +$		0	0	0	0	1
$C_4^+ + - -$		0	0	0	0	0
$C_4^+ - + -$		1	1	1	0	0
$C_4^- - - -$		0	0	0	0	0
$C_4^+ + + -$		*0*	*0*	*0*	*1*	*0*
$C_4^+ - - -$		*0*	*0*	*0*	*0*	*0*
$C_5^+ + + + +$		0	0	0	0	1
$C_5^+ + + - -$		0	0	0	0	0
$C_5^+ + - + -$		1	0	0	0	0
$C_5^+ - - - -$		0	0	0	0	0
$C_5^+ + + + -$		*0*	*0*	*0*	*0*	*0*
$C_5^+ + - - -$		*0*	*0*	*0*	*1*	*0*
$C_5^+ - + - -$		*0*	*1*	*1*	*0*	*0*
$C_5^- - - - -$		*0*	*0*	*0*	*0*	*0*
Balance= $\dfrac{C_k^+}{C_k^- + C_k^+}$		3/3	1/3	1/3	1/3	3/3

Figure 37.5 Examples of balanced and imbalanced {P|O|N}-signed networks

Note: Italic, bold values indicate cycles inconsistent with balance (i.e., uneven number of negative ties).

in Figure 37.5, it is impossible to replace the neutral ties with positive and negative ties and end up with a balanced {P|N}-signed network. Focusing on the four nodes {b,c,d,e}, if we replace the neutral tie {b, d} with a positive tie, the triad {b,d,e} will end up being imbalanced. However, if instead we replace it with a negative tie, the triad {b,c,d} would become imbalanced.

In essence, when we consider a group of four nodes (e.g., {b,c,d,e}), which contains a 4-cycle (e.g., consisting of dyads {b,c}, {c,d}, {d,e} and {e,b}) with only positive and negative values and where an odd number of these four dyads is negative, then there is no possible way to assign either a positive or a negative sign to the two other dyads in the group ({b,d} and {c,e}) so that we end up with four balanced triads. More generally, Cartwright and Harary (1956) have shown that the occurrence of cycles of *any length* in a network, where these cycles have an odd number of negative ties, will be indicative of a network being imbalanced.[4] As an illustration, all the {P|N}-signed networks in Figure 37.4, which contain four-cycles or five-cycles with an odd number of negative ties also contain imbalanced triads. Returning to the {P|O|N}-signed networks in Figure 37.5, we notice that Network D contains both a four-cycle and a five-cycle that has an odd number of negative ties and, therefore, these should be considered imbalanced. Networks A and E do not contain any cycles with an odd number and therefore (as discussed before) have an underlying balanced structure.

Hence, one way to assess the *level of balance* of a {P|O|N}-signed network is by calculating the proportion of imbalanced cycles of all lengths ($k > 2$):

$$\text{Balance} = \frac{\sum_k \left(C_k^+\right)}{\sum_k \left(C_k^+ + C_k^-\right)} \quad (7)$$

where C_k^+ is the number of balanced cycles of length k and C_k^- is the number of imbalanced cycles of length k (which are summed over all $k > 2$).

Weak balance for {P|O|N}-signed networks

The above approach focuses on classic structural balance theory, meaning that Triad D (in Figure 37.2) should be considered a sign of imbalance. If, however, we want to know whether a {P|O|N}-signed network is consistent with the rules of *weak balance*, we should instead check whether a network contains cycles (of any length) with *exactly one* negative tie (Aref & Neal, 2020). For example, Network D in Figure 37.5 contains a four-cycle with one negative tie and therefore is also not weakly balanced, since nodes (d) and (e) should simultaneously be part of the same group and a different group. However, Network B contains no cycles with one negative tie and, therefore, is weakly balanced (as we can generate three groups when we replace all neutral ties with negative ones).

Emergence of balance

Given the basic assumption of balance theory, that nodes aim to reach balance, some scholars have used simulation approaches, such as agent-based modelling, to understand the emergence of balance in networks (Hummon & Doreian, 2003; Stadtfeld et al., 2020). Other studies have tried to empirically test whether and how networks might become balanced over time. Research on signed networks shows that networks do not always converge towards balance in the long run (Yap & Harrigan, 2015; Doreian & Mrvar, 1996; Doreian, 2002; Doreian & Mrvar, 2015). For example, Doreian and Krackhardt (2001) find that some triadic configurations do tend to evolve towards balance. However, they also find that triads with a negative and a positive tie tend to generate a positive, rather than a negative tie.

One issue with studying the evolution of balance is that quite a few analyses examine networks which are fundamentally directed in nature. This means that any triad will consist of six directed ties and that a variety of social processes, such as reciprocity, homophily, transitivity and cyclicality involving a combination of positive and negative ties, might be in play at the same time. These confounding mechanisms make it more difficult to study balance (Aref & Wilson, 2018) and require more complex modelling approaches, such as exponential random graph models (ERGMs) or stochastic actor-oriented models (SAOMs). A discussion of these more complex models is, however, outside the scope of this chapter. Instead, we refer to work by Huitsing and colleagues (2012), Yap and Harrigan (2015), Lerner (2016), Harrigan and Yap (2017) and Toroslu and Jaspers (2022) for some excellent examples. We also suggest consulting Koskinen (this volume), as well as Snijders and Steglich (this volume) for a general introduction to such models.

SUBGROUPS AND BLOCKMODELLING

The previous section focused on capturing properties of the overall network structure. This section deals, instead, with ways to subdivide or partition the nodes in a network. We might be interested in detecting regions (subgroups) in a network where nodes are more tightly connected with each other than in other parts of the network, or, alternatively, we might want to identify subsets of nodes that occupy structurally similar positions in a network.

Subgroups

When we are interested in identifying densely connected subsets of nodes, we can distinguish between two major approaches. One approach starts from single nodes and identifies maximum subsets of nodes that are closely connected to each other according to a specific criterion of cohesion (such as cliques), while a second approach starts with the network as a whole and tries to split the network into a certain number of communities (community detection).

Cliques

A rather straightforward way to identify cohesive subgroups in a network is through the notion of a clique (Luce & Perry, 1949). A *clique* in a positive network is a maximum subset of (at least three) nodes where: (1) everyone is directly connected to each other (which implies that the density in the subgroup is 1.00) and (2) no other nodes are connected to all members of the clique (as otherwise, that node would need to be added to that clique). For example, to identify friendship groups in a network, we might identify subgroups where every member is directly connected through a friendship tie with each other (Krackhardt, 1999). Network A in Figure 37.6 provides an example with two cliques, {a,b,c} and {c,f,g}. Note that nodes can be part of multiple cliques simultaneously.

Identifying dense subgroups is generally not very useful for negative networks. Instead, negative ties can help identify splits between subgroups or can complement the analysis based on positive ties (Agneessens, n.d.).

Taking a complementary approach, a *clique in a negative network* can be identified as the maximal subset of (at least three) nodes, where: (1) there are no negative ties between the members of the clique (a density of 0.00) and (2) all the other nodes in the network have at least one negative tie to one of the nodes of the clique (as otherwise, those other nodes could be added to the clique). Network B in Figure 37.6 depicts the complement of Network A, with no negative ties inside either clique {a,b,c} and {c,f,g} and at least one negative tie from all the other nodes that are not part of the clique.

Both approaches will generate identical outcomes for a {P|N}-signed network. However, in the case of a {P|O|N}-signed network, relying on the negative ties would result in a 'weak' version of cliques, where cliques are based on a combination of neutral and positive ties. Hence, in a {P|O|N}-signed network (e.g., Network C in Figure 37.6), the approach for the positive and for the negative network would provide different results (e.g., nodes {c,e,f,g} in Network C is a clique according to the negative tie approach, but not if we rely on the positive network).[5]

Balanced bicliques

When considering a signed network, we might instead be interested in finding balanced bicliques, similar to the notion of bicliques in two-mode networks (Borgatti et al., 2022). A *balanced biclique* can be defined as the maximal subset of nodes, where these subsets of nodes can be further split into two non-overlapping subgroups, so that (1) all members of each subgroup need to link in a negative way to all members of the other subgroup and (2) all members of the same subgroup are positively linked to each other. Additionally, we usually require both subgroups to have a minimum size of 3.

However, given that negative ties might be quite rare (especially in {P|O|N}-signed networks), we might relax the first criterion and instead require each node of the subgroup to be negatively connected to at least a minimum number of nodes in the other subgroup (while some of the other ties can be neutral).

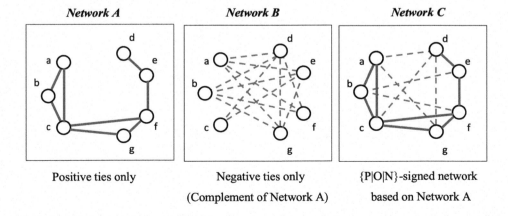

Figure 37.6 An example of clique approaches (positive, negative and {P|O|N}-signed)

Community detection

The general aim of community detection is to divide a network into subsets or communities. Community detection encompasses a wide range of approaches and algorithms (see for example Javed et al. (2018) for an overview). However, the classic and most used approach consists of partitioning the nodes of a network into non-overlapping (i.e., disjointed) subsets in such a way that the density inside the communities (for a positive network) is (relatively) high, while the density between these communities should be sparse (Girvan & Newman, 2002). This logic can be extended to situations dealing with negative ties, where the aim is to find communities, such that the density within communities is relatively sparse and the density between communities is relatively high (Traag & Bruggeman, 2009).

For signed networks, we can combine both and – in line with (the weak version of) structural balance theory – try to maximise the number of positive ties inside each community, while maximising the negative ties between communities, where different weights could be given to the relative importance of each network (Traag & Bruggeman, 2009). This is particularly important when dealing with {P|O|N}-signed networks as Network A in Figure 37.7 illustrates. The figure shows that the optimal partitioning into two sets based solely on the positive network can be different from that based solely on the negative network.

The approach of non-overlapping community detection for signed networks tends to follow the logic of (weak) balance, with each node belonging to only one group. Recent approaches involving overlapping communities (e.g., Chen et al., 2014) have allowed for identifying nodes which are brokers between communities. Finally, we note that the approach of (non-overlapping) community detection has similarities to blockmodelling, which we turn to next.

Structural Equivalence and Blockmodelling

Networks often contain nodes that are in the same, or at least in a very similar, structural position in the overall network. Three different approaches exist to capture such similarities: *structural equivalence*, *automorphic equivalence* and *regular equivalence*, with structural equivalence being the most commonly used type (see also Doreian et al., this volume). Two nodes are exactly structurally equivalent if they are in the same way connected to the rest of the network (Lorrain & White, 1971). Structural equivalence can easily be applied to networks with negative ties (Lorrain & White, 1971) and can help answer research questions, such as whether schoolchildren who bully the same peers (i.e., structurally equivalent) are more likely to be friends with each other or to hold similar beliefs.

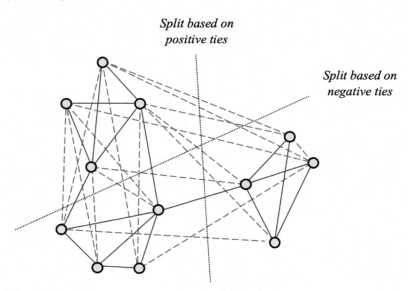

Figure 37.7 Partition of {P|O|N}-signed network into two groups using community detection on positive and negative ties respectively

Structural equivalence is often used as a basis to perform blockmodelling on a network, where nodes are partitioned based on the similar way they relate to the rest of the network (Doreian et al., 2005). Doreian and Mrvar (1996) have proposed blockmodelling techniques which can be applied to {P|N} and {P|O|N}-signed networks.

Following structural balance theory, one obvious way to partition a {P|N}-signed network is to split the nodes into two groups so that it reflects a balanced network – that is, with positive ties inside the groups and negative ties between groups (similar to Network A in Figure 37.3). The nodes are split into two groups in such a way as to minimise mistakes inside the blocks compared to the ideal balanced network (Doreian et al., 1994). An example is provided by the matrix representation of the Network A in Figure 37.8. The nodes in this matrix have been reordered in such a way that all nodes of the same partition are positioned next to

Network A: Blockmodel of a 'bipolar' signed network (with 3 mistakes)

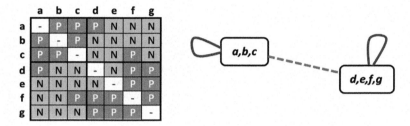

Network B: Blockmodel of a 'multipolar' signed network (with 3 mistakes)

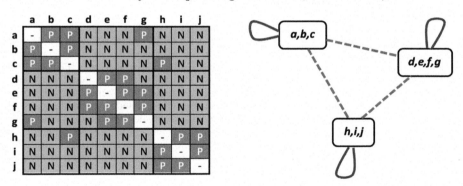

Network C: Blockmodel of a {P|O|N}-signed network

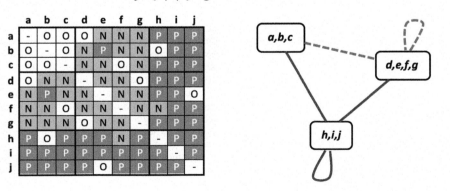

Figure 37.8 Three examples of blockmodelling for signed networks

each other, so that four clear blocks emerge. The two diagonal blocks contain (primarily) positive ties, while the two off-diagonal blocks contain (primarily) negative ties. We can evaluate the fit using a measure such as the frustration index (Doreian & Mrvar, 1996). In the case of Network A, there are a total of three mistakes.

However, blockmodelling can also partition a network into more than two subsets. Following the weak version of balance, we could partition a network into three or more groups, so that positive ties exist in each of the diagonal blocks and negative ties in each of the off-diagonal blocks (e.g., Network B in Figure 37.8). We note that this approach is closely related to the aims of community detection.

However, numerous studies have shown that signed networks might not always fit a strong or weak balanced structure, and blockmodelling can also help identify other solutions (as Lorrain & White (1971, p. 73) propose in their original paper). For example, Doreain and Mrvar (2020) find that splitting the US Supreme Court justices into two groups (conservative and liberal) is too simplistic to represent the patterns of dissent. Instead, they propose models where some of the diagonal blocks might contain (primarily) negative ties and some of the off-diagonal blocks might (primarily) have positive values. Moreover, when dealing with {P|O|N}-signed networks, we might want to differentiate blocks with neutral ties from those with positive or negative ties. Network C (Figure 37.8) shows an example of a network where one diagonal block contains only neutral ties, one only positive ties and one primarily negative ties. In addition, two off-diagonal blocks contain predominantly positive ties (between {a,b,c} and {h,i,j}, and between {d,e,f,g} and {h,i,j}) and one contains primarily negative connections (between {a,b,c} and {d,e,f,g}). The simplified graphical representation next to the matrix provides a clear insight into the overall structure. Considering this structure, the subgroup {h,i,j} could be considered a set of negotiators between the other two subgroups {a,b,c} and {d,e,f,g} (Doreian & Mrvar, 2009).

CONCLUSION

Research on negative ties and signed networks spans a wide range of areas and topics. Negative ties are commonly placed in opposition to positive (and neutral) ties. The prevailing belief is that the social structures of negative ties have their unique social dynamics. This means that most of the standard measures and techniques developed for studying positive ties might be less useful for studying negative networks. This chapter provides a non-exhaustive overview of ways to analyse negative networks.

Similar to their positive counterparts, negative ties tend to belong to one of four types: affect-based, behaviour, cognitive evaluations, or role relations. This distinction can be particularly helpful in order to develop more refined and tailored arguments to explain processes such as structural balance. Specific theories might apply to one type of negative network, but not another. Given the range of types of negative ties, one further avenue for research is how one type of tie might generate another.

One recurring difference with other types of ties is that negative ties do not generally give rise to flow-type processes, at least not in the way positive ties tend to. Nevertheless, negative ties might still be relevant beyond their immediate environment. In this chapter, we offer five ways indirect connections might be important when considering negative ties together with positive ties.

When considering signed networks, it is essential to differentiate between situations where a negative tie is the complement to a positive one – that is, a {P|N}-signed network versus a situation where a third, neutral option is available next to a positive or negative tie. In the latter case, we further distinguish between a {P|O|N}-signed network, where positive ties imply the absence of a negative tie and vice versa, and a {P+N}-signed network where a node can simultaneously have a positive and a negative tie to another node. One issue with the signed network literature is that it does not always specify whether a specific argument or approach applies to all or only some of the three types of signed networks, something we have paid attention to in this chapter.

For signed networks, we also discussed the importance of clarifying the exact meaning of the 'neutral' tie in a specific situation. In particular, does the absence of a positive and negative tie imply the absence of any interaction (and hence exposure) between two nodes, or does it represent a truly neutral tie resulting from (extensive) interaction between two nodes? The answer has important implications for deciding among different measures and how to model a signed network. This issue might be particularly critical in larger networks where not everyone might have had the chance to interact with everybody else.

Another crucial issue is to what extent balance is a central social process in signed networks and what it implies. Structural balance has been a particularly popular area of research in signed graphs, and many measures and methods rely on the assumption that, in an ideal situation, networks will tend to be balanced. However, studies report mixed results regarding how and to what extent networks tend to converge towards balance, which has generated a wide range of points for discussion. One particular issue is what constitutes balance – that is, whether the presence of a triad with three negative ties in a network should be considered a sign of imbalance. To put it differently, should an ideal balanced network consist of only two subgroups, or can it contain more than two subgroups?

Heider's classic argument focuses on affective ties – the idea that a negative affective tie to someone who has a negative affective relation to an object (or a third person) would generate a positive affective relation from ego towards that object (or person). Hence, another issue is what type of relation is being considered. To understand the exact mechanism that might apply in a specific case, scholars might benefit from paying attention to what type of tie they are considering (e.g., whether they are dealing with an affective, behavioural, or evaluative type of relation).

One broader comment is that, by focusing on structural balance, we might become blind to other interesting structural patterns that a signed network might have (Doreian, 2017; Doreian & Mrvar, 2020). This ignorance might be partly due to our choice of techniques and measures. While particular measures and models might be well fitted to test for balance, they might hide other structural patterns present in a network. For example, classic approaches of non-overlapping community detection algorithms tended to find positive ties within and negative ties between subgroups, while recent extensions of blockmodelling have enabled the identification of brokers in signed networks. The measures and approaches discussed in this chapter are far from exhaustive. Instead, this chapter aimed to provide some guidelines of potential approaches to study negative ties, as well as {P|N}, {P|O|N} and {P+N}-signed networks.

Notes

1 Details on many of the measures dealt with in this chapter can be found on filipagneessens.com/negative-ties/
2 In some cases, such as email communication, they might involve multiple recipients simultaneously.
3 See the website for more details.
4 Some argue that the need to consider balance beyond triads in {P|O|N}-signed networks builds on the assumption that cycles bigger than three are also a basis for stress, which is a point of debate (see Deng & Abell, 2010).
5 Everett and Borgatti (2014) suggest a different way of identifying negative cliques. They identify a *negative clique* as the minimal set of nodes, so that the rest of the nodes (that are not members of that clique) have a negative tie to at least one node of the clique. However, they do allow (some) negative ties between members of a negative clique.

REFERENCES

Agneessens, F. (n.d.). Cohesion measures and subgroup analysis for negative and signed networks. Unpublished manuscript.

Agneessens, F., & Labianca, G.J. (2022). Collecting survey-based social network information in work organizations. *Social Networks*, 68, 31–47.

Aref, S., & Neal, Z. (2020). Detecting coalitions by optimally partitioning signed networks of political collaboration. *Scientific Reports*, 10(1), 1–10.

Aref, S., & Wilson, M.C. (2018). Measuring partial balance in signed networks. *Journal of Complex Networks*, 6(4), 566–595.

Bonacich, P. (1987). Power and centrality: a family of measures. *American Journal of Sociology*, 92(5), 1170–1182.

Bonacich, P., & Lloyd, P. (2004). Calculating status with negative relations. *Social Networks*, 26(4), 331–338.

Borgatti, S.P. (2005). Centrality and network flow. *Social networks*, 27(1), 55–71.

Borgatti, S.P., Everett, M.G., Johnson, J.C., & Agneessens, F. (2022). *Analyzing Social Networks Using R*. Sage.

Brooks, K.P., & Dunkel Schetter, C. (2011). Social negativity and health: conceptual and measurement issues. *Social and Personality Psychology Compass*, 5(11), 904–918.

Burt, R.S. (1987). Social contagion and innovation: cohesion versus structural equivalence. *American Journal of Sociology*, 92(6), 1287–1335.

Burt, R.S. (1992). *Structural holes*. Harvard University Press.

Cartwright, D., & Harary, F. (1956). Structural balance: a generalization of Heider's theory. *Psychological Review*, 63(5), 277.

Chen, Y., Wang, X.L., Yuan, B., & Tang, B.Z. (2014). Overlapping community detection in networks with positive and negative links. *Journal of Statistical Mechanics: Theory and Experiment*, 2014(3), P03021.

Christakis, N. A., & Fowler, J. H. (2007). The spread of obesity in a large social network over 32 years. *New England journal of medicine*, 357(4), 370–379.

Cook, K.S., Emerson, R.M., Gillmore, M.R., & Yamagishi, T. (1983). The distribution of power in exchange networks: theory and experimental results. *American Journal of Sociology*, 89(2), 275–305.

Davis, J.A. (1967). Clustering and structural balance in graphs. *Human Relations*, 20(2), 181–187.

de Klepper, M.C., Labianca, G., Sleebos, E., & Agneessens, F. (2017). Sociometric status and peer control attempts: a multiple status hierarchies approach. *Journal of Management Studies*, 54(1), 1–31.

Deng, H., & Abell, P. (2010). A study of local sign change adjustment in balancing structures. *Journal of Mathematical Sociology*, 34(4), 253-282.

Doreian, P. (2002). Event sequences as generators of social network evolution. *Social Networks*, 24(2), 93–119.

Doreian, P. (2017). Reflections on studying signed networks. *Journal of Interdisciplinary Methodologies and Issues in Sciences*, 2.

Doreian, P., Batagelj, V., & Ferligoj, A. (1994). Partitioning networks based on generalized concepts of equivalence. *Journal of Mathematical Sociology*, 19(1), 1–27.

Doreian, P., Batagelj, V., & Ferligoj, A. (2005). *Generalized blockmodeling* (No. 25). Cambridge University Press.

Doreian, P., & Krackhardt, D. (2001). Pre-transitive balance mechanisms for signed networks. *Journal of Mathematical Sociology*, 25(1), 43–67.

Doreian, P., & Mrvar, A. (1996). A partitioning approach to structural balance. *Social Networks*, 18(2), 149–168.

Doreian, P., & Mrvar, A. (2009). Partitioning signed social networks. *Social Networks*, 31(1), 1–11.

Doreian, P., & Mrvar, A. (2015). Structural balance and signed international relations. *Journal of Social Structure*, 16, 1.

Doreian, P., & Mrvar, A. (2020). Delineating changes in the fundamental structure of signed networks. *Frontiers in Physics*, 8, 294.

Emerson, R.M. (1962). Power-dependence relations. *American Sociological Review*, 27, 31–41.

Everett, M.G., & Borgatti, S.P. (2014). Networks containing negative ties. *Social Networks*, 38, 111–120.

Festinger, L., & Hutte, H.A. (1954). An experimental investigation of the effect of unstable interpersonal relations in a group. *Journal of Abnormal and Social Psychology*, 49(4p1), 513.

Fingerman, K.L., Hay, E.L., & Birditt, K.S. (2004). The best of ties, the worst of ties: close, problematic, and ambivalent social relationships. *Journal of Marriage and Family*, 66(3), 792–808.

Fischer, C.S. (1982). What do we mean by 'friend'? An inductive study. *Social Networks*, 3(4), 287–306.

Gallupe, O., McLevey, J., & Brown, S. (2019). Selection and influence: a meta-analysis of the association between peer and personal offending. *Journal of Quantitative Criminology*, 35(2), 313–335.

Gargiulo, M., & Benassi, M. (1999). The dark side of social capital. In R. Leenders & S. Gabbay (Eds.), *Corporate social capital and liability* (pp. 298–322). Springer.

Girvan, M., & Newman, M.E. (2002). Community structure in social and biological networks. *Proceedings of the National Academy of Sciences*, 99(12), 7821–7826.

Grosser, T.J., Lopez-Kidwell, V., & Labianca, G. (2010). A social network analysis of positive and negative gossip in organizational life. *Group and Organization Management*, 35(2), 177–212.

Harary, F. (1959). On the measurement of structural balance. *Behavioral Science*, 4(4), 316–323.

Harrigan, N.M., Labianca, G. (Joe), & Agneessens, F. (2020). Negative ties and signed graphs research: stimulating research on dissociative forces in social networks. *Social Networks*, 60, 1–10.

Harrigan, N., & Yap, J. (2017). Avoidance in negative ties: inhibiting closure, reciprocity, and homophily. *Social Networks*, 48, 126–141.

Heider, F. (1946). Attitudes and cognitive organization. *Journal of Psychology*, 21(1), 107–112.

Huitsing, G., Van Duijn, M.A., Snijders, T.A., Wang, P., Sainio, M., Salmivalli, C., & Veenstra, R. (2012). Univariate and multivariate models of positive and negative networks: liking, disliking, and bully–victim relationships. *Social Networks*, 34(4), 645–657.

Hummon, N.P., & Doreian, P. (2003). Some dynamics of social balance processes: bringing Heider back into balance theory. *Social Networks*, 25(1), 17–49.

Javed, M.A., Younis, M.S., Latif, S., Qadir, J., & Baig, A. (2018). Community detection in networks: a multidisciplinary review. *Journal of Network and Computer Applications*, 108, 87–111.

Kitts, J.A. (2006). Social influence and the emergence of norms amid ties of amity and enmity. *Simulation Modelling Practice and Theory*, 14(4), 407–422.

Krackhardt, D. (1987). Cognitive social structures. *Social Networks*, 9(2), 109–134.

Krackhardt, D. (1999). The ties that torture: Simmelian tie analysis in organizations. *Research in the Sociology of Organizations*, 16(1), 183–210.

Labianca, G.J. (2014). Negative ties in organizational networks. In D. Brass. G. Labianca, A. Mehra, D. Halgin & S. Borgatti (Eds.), *Contemporary perspectives on organizational social networks*. Emerald.

Labianca, G., & Brass, D.J. (2006). Exploring the social ledger: negative relationships and negative asymmetry in social networks in organizations. *Academy of Management Review*, 31(3), 596–614.

Ladd, G.W., Kochenderfer, B.J., & Coleman, C.C. (1997). Classroom peer acceptance, friendship, and victimization: distinct relational systems that contribute uniquely to children's school adjustment? *Child Development*, 1181–1197.

Lerner, J. (2016). Structural balance in signed networks: separating the probability to interact from the tendency to fight. *Social Networks*, *45*, 66–77.

Lerner, J., & Lomi, A. (2020). The free encyclopedia that anyone can dispute: an analysis of the microstructural dynamics of positive and negative relations in the production of contentious Wikipedia articles. *Social Networks*, *60*, 11–25.

Lin, N., Cook, K.S., & Burt, R.S. (Eds.) (2001). *Social capital: theory and research*. Transaction.

Lorrain, F., & White, H.C. (1971). Structural equivalence of individuals in social networks. *Journal of Mathematical Sociology*, *1*(1), 49–80.

Luce, R.D., & Perry, A.D. (1949). A method of matrix analysis of group structure. *Psychometrika*, *14*(2), 95–116.

Marineau, J.E., & Labianca, G.J. (2021). Positive and negative tie perceptual accuracy: Pollyanna principle vs negative asymmetry explanations. *Social Networks*, *64*, 83–98.

Marineau, J.E., Labianca, G.J., & Kane, G.C. (2016). Direct and indirect negative ties and individual performance. *Social Networks*, *44*, 238–252.

Mason, W.A., Conrey, F.R., & Smith, E.R. (2007). Situating social influence processes: dynamic, multidirectional flows of influence within social networks. *Personality and Social Psychology Review*, *11*(3), 279–300.

Meeussen, L., Agneessens, F., Delvaux, E., & Phalet, K. (2018). Ethnic diversity and value sharing: a longitudinal social network perspective on interactive group processes. *British Journal of Social Psychology*, *57*(2), 428–447.

Nadel, S.F. (1957). *The theory of social structure*. Cohen & West.

Neal, J.W. (2020). A systematic review of social network methods in high impact developmental psychology journals. *Social Development*, *29*(4), 923–944.

Obstfeld, D. (2005). Social networks, the tertius iungens orientation, and involvement in innovation. *Administrative Science Quarterly*, *50*(1), 100–130.

Offer, S. (2021). Negative social ties: prevalence and consequences. *Annual Review of Sociology*, *47*, 177–196.

Pelled, L.H., Eisenhardt, K.M., & Xin, K.R. (1999). Exploring the black box: an analysis of work group diversity, conflict and performance. *Administrative Science Quarterly*, *44*(1), 1–28.

Rook, K.S., Luong, G., Sorkin, D.H., Newsom, J.T., & Krause, N. (2012). Ambivalent versus problematic social ties: implications for psychological health, functional health, and interpersonal coping. *Psychology and Aging*, *27*(4), 912.

Rosecrance, R.N. (1966). Bipolarity, multipolarity, and the future. *Journal of Conflict Resolution*, *10*(3), 314–327.

Sharp, S. (1995). How much does bullying hurt? The effects of bullying on the personal wellbeing and educational progress of secondary aged students. *Educational and Child Psychology*, *12*(2), 81–88.

Smith, J.M., Halgin, D.S., Kidwell-Lopez, V., Labianca, G., Brass, D.J., & Borgatti, S.P. (2014). Power in politically charged networks. *Social Networks*, *36*, 162–176.

Sparrowe, R.T., Liden, R.C., Wayne, S.J., & Kraimer, M.L. (2001). Social networks and the performance of individuals and groups. *Academy of Management Journal*, *44*(2), 316–325.

Stadtfeld, C., Takács, K., & Vörös, A. (2020). The emergence and stability of groups in social networks. *Social Networks*, *60*, 129–145.

Takács, K., Flache, A., & Mäs, M. (2016). Discrepancy and disliking do not induce negative opinion shifts. *PLOS One*, *11*(6), e0157948.

Toroslu, A., & Jaspers, E. (2022). Avoidance in action: Negative tie closure in balanced triads among pupils over time. *Social Networks*, *70*, 353-363.

Traag, V.A., & Bruggeman, J. (2009). Community detection in networks with positive and negative links. *Physical Review E*, *80*(3), 036115.

Valente, T.W., & Vega Yon, G.G. (2020). Diffusion/contagion processes on social networks. *Health Education and Behavior*, *47*(2), 235–248.

van der Ploeg, R., Steglich, C., & Veenstra, R. (2020). The way bullying works: how new ties facilitate the mutual reinforcement of status and bullying in elementary schools. *Social Networks*, *60*, 71–82.

Vörös, A., & Snijders, T.A. (2017). Cluster analysis of multiplex networks: defining composite network measures. *Social Networks*, *49*, 93–112.

Yang, S.W., Trincado, F., Labianca, G.J., & Agneessens, F. (2019). Negative ties at work. In D. Brass & S. Borgatti (Eds.), *Social networks at work* (pp. 49–78). Routledge.

Yap, J., & Harrigan, N. (2015). Why does everybody hate me? Balance, status, and homophily: the triumvirate of signed tie formation. *Social Networks*, *40*, 103–122.

Qualitative and Mixed Methods

Betina Hollstein

INTRODUCTION

From the very beginning, network researchers have made use of qualitative data and less standardised approaches to data collection, such as participant observation, qualitative interviews and documents and archival data, as well as interpretative methods of data analysis. Among the very first studies are the classic network investigations by British social anthropologists of networks in African towns, of class structure in small Norwegian island parishes and of the personal networks of couples in their own country (Barnes, 1954; Bott, 1957; Mitchell, 1969). Further, the combination of different approaches such as the integration of qualitative and quantitative data and methods – so-called *mixed-methods studies* – is anything but a recent phenomenon in network research. One thinks of the seminal Hawthorne studies (Roethlisberger & Dickson, 1939), which made use of experiments, participant observation and non-directive interviewing, or of several studies by the Chicago School, or William Foote Whyte's (1943) famous study on the social organisation of a group of 'corner boys' in an Italian neighbourhood in Boston, which combined ethnographic fieldwork and visualisations of the group structure. The concepts developed in these mixed-method studies, such as density, cliques and clusters, and the distinction between formal and informal organisation have become important points of reference in network research.

Although qualitative and mixed-method approaches have long been used in network research, it is only very recently that the contributions of these strategies for the investigation of social networks have been systematically reviewed (e.g., Hollstein, 2011; Domínguez & Hollstein, 2014). Just since the first edition of the *Sage handbook* about a decade ago, we have witnessed a remarkable increase in methodological publications in the area. These include discussions on how qualitative and quantitative approaches can be fruitfully integrated (e.g., Domínguez & Hollstein, 2014; Bellotti, 2015; Bolíbar, 2016; Crossley & Edwards, 2016), and reviews of methodological advancements and innovations such as the increasing use of visual tools in data collection and new combinations of methods (e.g., Rogers & Menjívar, 2014), as well as the systematic inclusion of qualitative and mixed methods in textbooks (e.g., McCarty et al., 2019) and applications of qualitative and mixed methods to most fields of network research.

The fields where qualitative and mixed methods are especially prominent include research on social capital and social support (e.g., Small, 2009;

Smith, 2010; Lumino et al., 2017; Wagner et al., 2018; Chan et al., 2020); networks of migrants and transnational networks (e.g., Scheibelhofer, 2011; Maya-Jariego & Domínguez, 2014; Rogers & Menjívar, 2014; Bilecen & Sienkiewicz, 2015; Bolíbar, 2019; Lubbers et al., 2020); networks in health research (e.g., Karl et al., 2016, Nimmon & Regehr, 2018; Wagner et al., 2018) and life course research (e.g., Bernardi et al., 2014; Hollstein & Wagemann, 2014; Karl et al., 2016; Verd, 2022); networks in education (e.g., Häussling, 2010; Froehlich et al., 2020); social movements (e.g., Mazák & Diviák, 2018); governance networks, political decision-making and policy networks (e.g., Hauck et al., 2016; Hollstein et al., 2017; Lelong et al., 2017; Ahrens, 2018; Wutich et al., 2020); intra- and interorganisational networks (e.g., Häussling, 2014; Wald, 2014; Williams & Sheperd, 2017; Mazák & Diviák, 2018); collaboration networks (e.g., Wald, 2014; Bellotti, 2015) and organisation of work (e.g., Lefrançois et al., 2017); diffusion of innovation (e.g., Avenarius & Johnson, 2014; Manzo et al., 2018) and innovation networks (e.g., Gluesing et al., 2014); and communication networks (e.g., Hepp et al., 2016); social networks and inequality (e.g., Lefrançois et al., 2017; Klärner & Knabe, 2019); and covert networks (e.g., Diviák, 2022).

This chapter reviews the literature in the area with a focus on new applications and methodical advances during the past decade. First, I provide an overview of the contributions of qualitative and mixed-methods for the study of social networks. The subsequent sections focus on procedures of qualitative and mixed-methods network studies – research designs, modes of data collection and analytical strategies – illustrated with recent empirical studies from various fields of social network research.

BENEFITS OF QUALITATIVE AND MIXED METHODS FOR THE STUDY OF SOCIAL NETWORKS

The potential benefits of qualitative and mixed methods in network research are not limited to developing new concepts. Qualitative approaches to data collection and analysis are powerful tools that can enrich the study of social networks in substantial ways. Before outlining these contributions, it is necessary to clarify what is meant by qualitative and mixed methods. *Qualitative methods* refer to a wide range of open and less standardised modes of data collection such as observation techniques, forms of interviewing and the collection of various kinds of documents and archival material, as well as interpretative methods of data analysis. The common denominator of these methods is that they aim at gaining an understanding of social phenomena, the meaning individuals attribute to their actions and the contexts of action (cf. Hollstein, 2011). Qualitative data can be understood as all utterances (actions, verbal utterances, written texts) that allow conclusions to be drawn about the contexts of action, contexts of meaning and references to meaning of the respective utterances (Hollstein, 2011). In contrast to *quantitative data* that usually are presented in the form of numerical data, qualitative data are typically texts or data that have been transferred to texts during the course of analysis – for example, interview transcripts or field notes of ethnographic observations.

Mixed-methods research can be defined as 'research in which a researcher or team of researchers combines elements of qualitative and quantitative approaches (e.g., use of qualitative and quantitative viewpoints, data collection, analysis, inference techniques) for the purpose of breadth and depth of understanding and corroboration' (Johnson & Onwuegbuzie, 2007, p. 123). It is important to note that this combination or integration – referring to a systematic relating or linking of qualitative and quantitative data or strategies of analysis – is a key element in mixed-methods studies (cf., e.g., Tashakkori & Teddlie, 1998; Small, 2011). Were it not for this integrative component, these studies would be no more than the mere addition of qualitative and quantitative analyses.

Clearly positioning network research in the spectrum of empirical methods is not as easy as one might think because network research shares certain characteristics with quantitative methods (e.g., network structures are typically described with numerical data), and shares other characteristics with qualitative methods (e.g., contextuality; also representativity is not applicable without restrictions; cf. Hollstein, 2014; Bellotti, 2015). Drawing on Hollstein's definition (2014), mixed-methods network research is understood as research that meets three criteria. First, both *quantitative, numerical network data* – that is, data describing nodes and relations – and *qualitative textual data* are employed. This does not imply that both types of data must actually be collected, since data may also be converted from one type to another (e.g., Hollstein & Wagemann, 2014; Verd & Lozares, 2014). Yet, structural network data are required so that the 'network' does not remain only a metaphor (Johnson, 1994). Second, in analysing relations and networks, both *quantitative, mathematical strategies* and *qualitative, interpretive strategies* are used. 'While the former are tailored toward analysing the structural dimensions of relationships and networks, the latter are designed to capture practices, meanings, and the social context of relationships and networks' (Hollstein, 2014, p. 11). Finally, during at least one stage of the research process, the data or strategies of analysis are *integrated*, whether at the stage of data collection, data analysis, or interpretation of results (meta-inference) (Hollstein, 2014).

In the study of social networks, qualitative and mixed methods can serve several purposes that are related to formal and substantive aspects of the phenomena under study. These purposes will be briefly described and exemplified, drawing on recent studies from various fields of network research.

Exploring networks

Exploration of previously unexplored social phenomena is the classical task of qualitative, open and inductive approaches. Some phenomena are unexplored because they are new, some are unexplored because they occur only in small numbers or because they have so far escaped the attention of researchers. Also, cases where we expect great variations in networks and meaning of networks call for exploring a broad spectrum of the phenomena (Wald, 2014). Sometimes, exploration is the focus of the entire study – for instance, in the study of Fuller et al. (2011), who investigated the role of personal networks in educational decision-making by interviewing several members of ego-centred personal networks in which the focal person had decided against higher education. Sometimes, exploration is only the first phase before a quantitative investigation, as, for example, when using documents and expert interviews to identify relevant network actors, important topics, events, or forms of interaction (e.g., Wutich et al., 2020). Such explorations can also aid in setting network boundaries, in both whole-network studies and studies concerned with ego-centred networks (McCarty et al., 2019; Marsden & Hollstein, 2022).

Field access: getting in and getting on

Qualitative approaches are not only suitable tools to explore a field of action, they are often also the best – sometimes even the only – way to gain access to the field of research and/or study subjects. Open and less-structured interviews, rather than standardised question–answer formats, have the character of 'normal communication' and can be flexibly adapted to the interviewee and the requirements of the situation. Sometimes such a 'soft' approach is the only way to obtain sensitive network information from certain groups – for example, when investigating subjects greatly pressed for time (politicians, managers); those whose activities are illegal, such as mafia members or drug addicts (e.g., Bellotti, 2015; Chan et al., 2020); or people who are at risk (political activists in authoritarian regimes or potential victims of political repression; e.g., Stys et al., 2022). Recent studies also stress that building trust and rapport with informants is key in studies with vulnerable populations or on sensitive topics (Wagner et al., 2018; Lubbers et al., 2020; Stys et al., 2022; Weissinger, 2022). These studies emphasise that qualitative approaches are important not only in getting access, but throughout the research process.

In addition to these rather formal aspects, two substantive areas can be identified for which qualitative approaches are particularly fruitful.

Network practices

Participant observation, interview techniques and interpretive strategies of data analysis allow researchers to reconstruct the concrete practices, interactions and actions of the subjects in their contexts – that is, their network practices and cultures of 'networking'. What do the exchange relationships of migrants look like (Menjívar, 2000; Maya-Jariego and Domínguez, 2014)? What patterns of cooperation do medium-sized companies in the clothing industry cultivate (Uzzi, 1997), and what forms of interaction do we find in classrooms (Häussling, 2010) or in innovative teams (Gluesing et al., 2014; Wald, 2014)? What cultural practices characterised the 'art of net-working' in the Italian Renaissance (McLean, 1998)? Methods of choice to address such questions include document analysis, observational procedures and open-ended interviews, which social anthropologists have always used (e.g., Barnes, 1954; Mitchell, 1969). Furthermore, ethnographic approaches, observation techniques and open-ended interviews are also used in research on collaboration and innovation networks, new patterns of work and newly emerging roles within global networking organisations (Gluesing et al., 2014).

Network orientations, assessments and interpretations

Moreover, qualitative methods are especially well suited for capturing the actors' systems of relevance, perceptions, interpretations and action orientations. For network research, this aspect is relevant when it comes to actors' overall perceptions and evaluations of the networks in which they are involved. This includes studies on subjective feelings of embeddedness, integration and sense of belonging, such as when integration patterns and network orientations of migrants (Bolíbar, 2019; Lubbers et al., 2020) or commuters (Scheibelhofer, 2011) are investigated. In these studies, individual perceptions, meaning attributions, action orientations and strategies are related to personal egocentric networks. Sometimes only certain relationship types are examined, such as the organisation and meaning of friendship networks (Bellotti, 2015, 2016). Other studies focus on specific relationship performances – for example, the role of personal networks in family formation (Bernardi et al., 2014) or the meaning of 'emotional closeness' (Töpfer & Hollstein, 2022).

Individual perceptions and assessments play a role not only in personal, egocentric networks, but also in networks within and between organisations. This includes studies on the functioning and evaluation of research and innovation networks (Wald, 2014; Häussling, 2014) and the evaluation of the effectiveness of health care systems (Provan & Milward 1995), and also preparatory studies that aim at identifying stakeholders (e.g., Wutich et al., 2020). In these studies, respondents are typically regarded as experts in their field of action.

The following aspects can be best achieved when qualitative and quantitative data and methods are systematically linked. It is through this linking that mixed-method designs create special opportunities for improving data quality and increasing the significance of results.

Data quality

Combining qualitative and quantitative data and methods of analysis can serve as a strategy for validating network data. For instance, in their study of network effectiveness of community mental health systems, Provan and Milward (1995) employed three qualitative strategies to enhance the validity of the data and thus the validity of the results: in-depth meetings with members of the organisations in focus to review questionnaire items and responses to ensure that respondents were interpreting them as the researcher had intended; follow-up by telephone and additional interviewing to collect missing data and to check data that appeared to be inaccurate after comparing questionnaire responses with field notes; and finally, after data were initially analysed, discussion of findings with organisation members ('reality check') to ensure that major conclusions were consistent with members' understandings of system operations (Provan & Milward, 1995). Complementing data from standardised surveys with rich qualitative data can be worthwhile also in studies that rely exclusively on the formal procedures of social network analysis in analysing network data.

Explanatory power and generalisability

Further, perceptive linking of qualitative and quantitative strategies of analysis can enhance the explanatory power and generalisability of results. This outcome is usually achieved by combining breadth (often through survey data) and depth (e.g., through rich qualitative data) to provide a more complete picture of social phenomena. For instance, in his study on 'unanticipated gains', Small (2009) investigated the origins of network inequality in everyday life and developed the concept of *organisational embeddedness perspective*. Combining interviews in childcare centres in several neighbourhoods with survey data on 300 randomly selected childcare centres, he vividly shows how the choice of a certain childcare centre may bear far-reaching consequences for informal support networks (Small, 2009). In another study that also sheds light on the processes of network and support mobilisation, Smith (2010) examines the supportive behaviour of the 'black urban poor' in the context of searching for jobs, and the ways in which social capital is activated. The interviews reveal the reasons why some individuals who possess job-relevant information are reluctant to share such knowledge. Smith then uses survey data to examine the conditions under which the provision of support is more likely. The results show that information is more likely to be given within strong ties and in neighbourhoods with higher socioeconomic status (Smith, 2010). These examples demonstrate that quantitative analyses not only allow a more precise assessment of the *prevalence* of certain patterns of action, they also help in gaining a more complete picture of the *conditions* (institutional settings) under which such patterns have effect (see also Mische, 2009).

Understanding network mechanisms, network effects and network dynamics

These last examples also demonstrate that, with respect to substantive network-related questions, mixed-methods studies can provide empirically sound contributions to current issues, especially concerning the processes and mechanisms, dynamics and consequences of social networks. By producing a more complete picture of the prevalence, conditions and consequences of networks, they provide a more nuanced understanding of social networks and their dynamics, of how and why networks matter and how they change. Other examples are Bernardi et al.'s (2014) study on the influence of personal networks on fertility decisions and Uzzi's (1997) study on cooperation patterns in companies in the clothing industry and the ways these relationships contribute to organisational and economic success. Another recent example is Lelong et al.'s (2017) study on decision-making processes in urban politics. The researchers combined the analysis of actors' networks with an analysis of actors' frames, and by doing so gained new insights into the dynamics that led up to a persistent deadlock in the development of Cologne harbour, and into causes of non-action more generally.

Relating qualitative and structural network data in this way also has theoretical implications. Combining qualitative data on actors' practices and orientations with relational data on relationship and network structures provides a way of linking structure and agency (Hollstein, 2014; Häussling, 2014). Advocates of a relational sociology have been arguing to that effect since the early 1990s (cf. Emirbayer and Goodwin, 1994). We can thus expect empirical studies along such lines to also yield theoretically inspiring insights.

These are the areas where qualitative and mixed-methods approaches can be expected to yield the most promising results. In the remaining parts of this chapter I will focus on how these results can be achieved – on research designs, data collection techniques and analytical strategies in qualitative and mixed-method network studies.

QUALITATIVE APPROACHES TO THE STUDY OF SOCIAL NETWORKS

Qualitative methods employed in social networks studies cover nearly the full spectrum of qualitative methods. Network data are collected by means of ethnographic approaches (e.g., Uzzi, 1997; Avenarius & Johnson, 2014; Häussling, 2014; Maya-Jariego and Domínguez, 2014; Nimmon & Regehr, 2018; Stys et al., 2022), observation techniques (e.g., Mische, 2009; Bellotti, 2015; Häussling, 2010; Gluesing et al., 2014; Lelong et al., 2017) and various forms of interviewing (e.g., Bernardi et al., 2014; Bellotti, 2015; Hepp et al., 2016; Chan et al., 2020; Stys et al., 2022), as well as by making use of various kinds of documents and archival material (e.g., Williams & Sheperd, 2017), including newspaper articles (Edwards & Crossley, 2009; Lelong et al., 2017), biographies (Diviák, 2022), letters (McLean, 1998; Edwards & Crossley, 2009), emails (Gluesing et al., 2014) and media diaries and social network sites (Hepp et al., 2016).

For data analysis, many qualitative studies employ grounded theory as the method of choice (e.g., Bernardi et al., 2014; Hepp et al., 2016), often combined with ethnographic descriptions (e.g., Gluesing et al., 2014). Yet it needs to be emphasised that, depending on the research question and methodological orientation (interactionist, pragmatic, structuralist, or oriented by sociological of knowledge),[1] different interpretative procedures come into question for the analysis of network practices, network interpretations and network processes. Methods of analysis include qualitative content analysis (Lelong et al., 2017; Chan et al., 2020), narrative analysis (e.g., Uzzi, 1997; Hollstein, 2019), frame analysis (e.g., McLean, 1998; Lelong et al., 2017), conversation analysis (e.g., Mische, 2009) and various types of interaction analyses (e.g., Häussling, 2014), as well as qualitative comparative analysis (e.g., Hollstein & Wagemann, 2014).

Most qualitative methods employed for data collection and data analysis in network research are essentially the same as those used in qualitative research on other topics and social phenomena. How the toolkit of qualitative research – observations and ethnography, interviews, documents and archival data – can be employed in network studies is discussed in more detail in Hollstein (2011), including also strategies for data analysis, such as thick descriptions, typologies and the development of models and theories (Hollstein, 2011). In this chapter I confine myself to a few remarks on research design decisions and focus on generic network tools that have been recently developed and advanced, namely qualitative name generators and visual tools used in network data collection.

Research design decisions

Several aspects need to be considered in choosing the methods for data collection and analysis. First of all, it needs to be clarified which of the above-mentioned aspects of relationships and networks are to be investigated. Is it primarily about interactions between actors – that is, about network practices – or are the action orientations and network perceptions of individual actors of primary interest? Depending on whether the focus is more on actual behaviour (e.g., in the study of diffusion processes) or on subjective strategies or the individual's perceptions of relationships (e.g., in the study of the effects of social support), one is more likely to draw on observational data or on the accounts of network actors in interviews or written first-person documents (cf. Hollstein, 2011).

Another key question is the specification of the boundaries of the network (Marsden, 1990). This question is especially pertinent in research on sociocentric or whole networks (Marsden, 1990), but is increasingly discussed also with respect to personal networks (McCarty et al., 2019; Perry & Roth, 2021; Marsden & Hollstein, 2022). Of course, the choice of data collection method also depends on pragmatic considerations such as financial resources and available time. While observations are time-consuming and cost-intensive, archival data are usually much less expensive. For this reason, if they are to be used as a central data collection technique, observations will be focused mainly on narrowly defined questions or small-scale networks. Examples include Häussling's (2010) study of interactional behaviour and network formation in school classrooms and Gluesing et al.'s (2014) shadowing of members in innovative teams. Sometimes only certain data are available, as in studies on covert networks (e.g., Diviák, 2022) or historical networks (Edwards & Crossley, 2009). In the case of secondary analyses, the conditions under which the original data were created must be carefully considered.

Eliciting alters

Questioning subjects on their networks is still the most common method of data collection in both standardised and qualitative network research. Interviews – semi-structured, in-depth, or expert – can be adapted with respect to the research interests. At the same time, interview data are particularly tied to the perspective of the interviewees. This may be desirable when network strategies, orientations and assessments of actors are the focus of research, for instance in studies on subjective evaluations of performance of networks or when the individual perception of integration into personal networks is the focus of research. Yet when actors are to be interviewed as experts on behavioural aspects (e.g., on routines, actors and relationships in organisations), the social location and perspectives of the interviewees have to be considered when selecting interview partners and interpreting their utterances.[2]

An important decision is how open or how structured the questions should be that are asked about the alters and the relationships. With respect to qualitative approaches to the study of networks, Franke and Wald (2006) argue that, as a rule of thumb, questions should be designed as open-ended, the more so the less one knows about a phenomenon, the more important individual actors' strategies and systems of relevance are and the greater impact context factors can be assumed to have. Yet even the most open and unstructured interviews are typically combined with some form of standardised enquiry, especially for obtaining information via name generators and name interpreters (Marsden, 2011; Marsden & Hollstein, 2022). Such method triangulation facilitates the comparability of data across cases, as well as between certain aspects of an individual case.

Some structuration seems to be even more important when researchers are concerned with qualitative panel data (Hollstein, 2021). In this regard, the 'contextual name generator' is worth noting. This data collection tool was developed by Bidart and Charbonneau (2011) in the context of a large, longitudinal, qualitative panel study on the trajectories of young adults. The researchers combined extensive biographical narratives with a two-step name generator. In the first step, questions were asked about 50 contexts that might be relevant for the participants. Generating names in relation to certain contexts with which the alters are associated worked as a 'natural' memory aid (Bidart & Charbonneau, 2011, p. 277). In the second step, more classical name generators were introduced asking for specific resources provided by the alters, but also more open-ended questions were asked on how the relationships evolved over time. The interviews, which lasted between four and ten hours, provided fine-grained data on both a person's global social environment (context-based network) and the specific resource-based network. It also enabled the researcher to reconstruct the development of and changes in networks over time (Bidart & Charbonneau, 2011; Bidart et al., 2020).

Visual tools

When collecting network data, visual tools such as sociograms and network diagrams or drawings are becoming increasingly popular in both qualitative and standardised data collection settings (e.g., Hogan et al., 2007; McCarty et al., 2007; Ryan et al., 2014; Tubaro et al., 2014; Bellotti,

2016; Hepp et al., 2016; Wagner et al., 2018; Maya-Jariego & Cachia, 2019; Gamper & Schönhuth, 2020; Hollstein et al., 2020; Marsden & Hollstein, 2022). A central characteristic of the visualisation is that the sequentiality of the interview situation is complemented by the simultaneity of the pictorial representation of the network. In qualitative and mixed-methods studies, network maps and sociograms constitute strong narration stimuli and can serve as a 'narration generator' that helps to elicit rich network data with detailed accounts of relationship practices and the meaning they have for the interviewees (e.g., Straus, 2002; Ryan et al., 2014; Bernardi et al., 2014; Hollstein et al., 2020). The visual representation promotes communication about relationships in the interview situation, and the simultaneous representation of network members stimulates comparisons between alters. In addition, the conversation can be more easily (re) directed to specific alters. Besides, the graphical representation of networks serves as a cognitive aid helping to maintain an overview of the relationships ('cognitive scaffold', von der Lippe and Gamper, 2017). It allows both interviewer and interviewee to keep track of the relationships discussed and to ensure that alters are collected more completely (Hogan et al., 2007; Hollstein et al., 2020). Furthermore, the visualisation reduces the interviewee burden by making the data collection more engaging and game-like (McCarty et al., 2007; Bellotti, 2016; Maya-Jariego & Cachia, 2019; Gamper & Schönhuth, 2020; Hollstein et al., 2020).

Visual tools may look very different (cf. Hollstein et al., 2020). They range from more standardised instruments, such as the method of concentric circles ('hierarchical mapping technique'; Antonucci, 1986), to 'free-style' drawings, where interviewees are asked to draw their network and are given minimal guidelines for doing so (e.g., Scheibelhofer, 2011). In Antonucci's (1986) method of concentric circles the respondents are asked to enter alters who are important to them and to whom they feel close into three concentric circles. Often, this instrument is combined with follow-up questions on alters and relationships to alters. So-called free drawings are drawn by the interviewees themselves. Free-designs provide information about how the network is cognitively represented (McCarty et al., 2007; Scheibelhofer, 2011). For example, do the respondents draw themselves in and, if so, where do they place themselves – in the centre or standing at the margin? The main basis for the interpretations of the maps is the commentaries by the interviewees (e.g., Scheibelhofer, 2011).

During the data collection, visual tools are handled in different ways (Straus, 2002; Gamper & Schönhuth, 2020): often the sociograms are filled out by the interviewee, sometimes by the interviewer. In earlier studies, data collection was mostly done with paper and pencil, but computers are now increasingly used. There has been good experience with touch screens that are operated by the interviewees themselves, even with elderly participants (Hollstein et al., 2013). In participatory research and low-tech settings, whiteboards, draughts pieces and other figurines are also employed (Schiffer & Hauck, 2010; Stys et al., 2022). Sometimes the sociograms are created in the course of the qualitative interview, sometimes they are used as a starting point and the interview is then conducted on the basis of the sociogram. Mixed approaches are also possible (Bellotti, 2016).

Further methodological research on these tools has just begun, for instance with respect to differences among visual tools regarding manageability, data quality and validity (e.g., von der Lippe & Gamper, 2017; Hollstein et al., 2020). An experimental study provided evidence that the design of a visual tool (structured vs unstructured) can affect the size and composition of the elicited networks (Hollstein et al., 2020). Most respondents tend to prefer concentric circles over other shapes, with some differences in preferences and manageability of tools between participants with low and those with high socioeconomic status (Hollstein et al., 2020).

MIXED-METHODS DESIGNS

In this final section I describe how qualitative and quantitative data and methods can be fruitfully combined and what can be achieved with different mixed-method designs. Mixed-methods research designs differ in various aspects. Creswell and Plano-Clark (2011), for instance, distinguish between differences in the research logic (exploratory or hypothesis-testing), the priority of an approach (is the quantitative or the qualitative part in the foreground?), the sequence of methods (are quantitative and qualitative procedures carried out in parallel or sequentially?) and at which point in the research process the methods are integrated (during data collection, data evaluation, or data interpretation?). These aspects result in a large number of possible research designs. In the following, I discuss the designs most frequently used in mixed-method network research and provide illustrations from recent studies.

Sequential qual-quant design

The so-called sequential exploratory design begins with a qualitative study which is followed by a quantitative study. The quantitative analysis can then be used to determine the *prevalence* of patterns of action, such as network practices, that have been reconstructed in the qualitative study. Or the quantitative analysis can serve to identify the *conditions* of occurrence of the patterns found in the qualitative study. This is how Smith's (2010) above-mentioned study on the supportive behaviour of black urban poor was organised. Another possibility is to combine a qualitative study with a simulation study to analyse possible long-term *consequences*. This approach was used by Rogers and Menjívar (2014), who examined, with agent-based modelling, the consequences of a certain support behaviour on the social networks among economically disadvantaged Salvadoran immigrants. Results of Menjívar's (2000) qualitative study on 'fragmented ties' of poor Salvadoran immigrants living in the San Francisco Bay area served as input for creating a computational model. In this study, Menjívar showed how the failure to reciprocate led to the weakening and dissolution of social ties. The subsequent computer simulation enabled careful tracking of network evolution and analysis of the dynamic behaviour of social networks under different conditions identified in the qualitative study.

Sequential quant-qual design

The so-called sequential explanatory design starts with the collection and analysis of quantitative data, which is then followed by a qualitative study. In this vein, Bearman and Parigi (2004) used open-ended questions to investigate what individuals mean when they say they talk about 'important matters' with other people in the General Social Survey (GSS). Here, the qualitative follow-up served to *deepen* and *illuminate* in greater detail the results of quantitative analysis. Similarly, Bellotti (2015) investigated research collaborations in philosophy using archival data on research funding. She first described the formal structure of these networks and identified mechanisms that facilitated or hindered research funding. She then further explored these mechanisms in a qualitative follow-up study (Bellotti, 2015). In other studies, quantitative analyses provide the ground for the *selection* and *location* of specific cases, which are then examined qualitatively (so-called *mapping*). This can be done by selecting certain cases from a sociocentred network (e.g., Avenarius & Johnson, 2014). Another possibility for localising the cases is multidimensional scaling (MDS; McLean 1997). The criteria for case selection can vary: sometimes the most extreme cases or the 'outliers' are of interest, sometimes just the most typical cases.

Parallel designs

In other studies, quantitative and qualitative strategies are used in parallel (e.g., Provan & Milward, 1995; Uzzi, 1997; Edwards & Crossley, 2009; Small, 2009; Avenarius & Johnson, 2014; Bernardi et al., 2014; Hollstein & Wagemann, 2014; Hepp et al., 2016; Lelong et al., 2017; Bidart et al., 2020). For instance, in their study on the effectiveness of local health networks, Provan and Milward (1995) used data-triangulation in order to *validate* and *confirm* their results. Moreover, parallel designs serve to obtain a *broad, multilayered* and as *comprehensive* as possible understanding of social phenomena, thereby increasing the range and *generalisability* of the results. Here, the aim is not so much convergence as *complementarity*. In parallel designs, the integration of qualitative and quantitative strands often takes place at several stages of the research process. For example, Bernardi et al. (2014) employ such a mixed-methods parallel design to investigate how network effects and social influence affected the fertility behaviour of young adults in West and East Germany. They show how qualitative interviews and standardised methods of collecting network data – network charts, network grids and a network questionnaire – can be applied simultaneously to the same sample. The mixed-methods analysis enables identification of relevant (influential) relationships, as well as their structural characteristics and the ways social influence varies in networks with different structural characteristics.

The study of Gluesing et al. (2014) is an example of a so-called *nested* or *embedded* parallel design. They used a classic ethnographic approach and collected all available data on the communication patterns of the members of innovative teams in globally operating companies. In addition to thousands of emails, the data also included in-depth interviews and observation of the interactions of team members, whom the researchers 'shadowed' for several days. The analysis revealed surprising differences in email use between US and German team members. (The former do most of their communication by email, even if the addressee is in the office next door; German team members, in contrast, would seek out the addressee next door in person; Gluesing et al., 2014). In this study, the observational data helped to *classify* and understand the meaning of email communication.

Finally, parallel designs can also be employed on the basis of qualitative data that are partly converted into standardised, numerical data (so-called *conversion* designs). An example of such a design is Edwards and Crossley's (2009) study on the ego-net of Helen Kirkpatrick Watts, a militant British suffragette. In this historical network study, the authors analysed archival data – letters and newspaper articles – in order to reconstruct the social network of the suffragette and to better understand her involvement in the social movement on the basis of the qualitative data. In another conversion-design study, Hollstein and Wagemann (2014) analyse the effects of social networks on the school-to-work-transition of young adults by using qualitative comparative analysis (QCA; Ragin, 2008), a method that integrates Boolean algebra, fuzzy algebra and qualitative single-case analyses, and that facilitates *systematic case comparisons* and supports the *construction of typologies* that strongly build on the individual cases.

I hope to have demonstrated that this rapidly developing field of qualitative and mixed-methods network studies has important contributions to make to the research into social networks. Among other advantages, these methods offer special tools for addressing challenges faced in network research, namely explication of the problem of agency, linkages between network structure and network actors, and questions relating to network processes and mechanisms, effects and dynamics. Still, the most fruitful results can be achieved when qualitative methods, more standardised methods to describe network structures and quantitative methods of empirical social research are employed in concert.

Notes

1 Theoretical and methodological points of reference are symbolic interactionism (Fine & Kleinman, 1983; McLean, 1998; Lelong et al., 2017) and pragmatism (Bellotti, 2015), relational sociology (Emirbayer & Goodwin 1994; Mische, 2009; Fuhse & Mützel, 2011), the sociology of Georg Simmel (Hollstein, forthcoming), phenomenology, sociology of knowledge (Engelbrecht, 2006), and actor-network theory (cf. Knox et al., 2006; Mützel, 2009; Hepp et al., 2016).

2 Network research has produced an array of findings on factors affecting the accuracy of self-reports; the work in the wake of the seminal Bernard et al. studies (1981) is especially noteworthy in this respect.

REFERENCES

Ahrens, P. (2018). Qualitative network analysis: a useful tool for investigating policy networks in transnational settings? *Methodological Innovations*, *11*(1), 205979911876981.

Antonucci, T.C. (1986). Measuring social support networks: hierarchical mapping technique. *Generations: Journal of the American Society on Aging*, *10*(4), 10–12.

Avenarius, C.B., & Johnson, J.C. (2014). Adaptation to new legal procedures in rural China. In S. Domínguez & B. Hollstein (Eds.), *Mixed methods social networks research* (pp. 177–202). Cambridge University Press.

Barnes, J.A. (1954). Class and committees in a Norwegian island parish. *Human Relations*, *7*(1), 39–58.

Bearman, P.S., & Parigi, P. (2004). Cloning Headless Frogs and Other Important Matters: Conversation Topics and Network Structure. *Social Forces*, *83* (2), 535–557.

Bellotti, E. (2015). *Qualitative networks: mixed methods in social research*. Routledge.

Bellotti, E. (2016). Qualitative methods and visualizations in the study of friendship networks. *Sociological Research Online*, *21*(2), 198–216.

Bernard, H.R., Killworth, P., & Sailer, L. (1981). Summary of research on informant accuracy in network data and the reverse small world problem. *Connections*, *4*(2), 11–25.

Bernardi, L., Keim, S., & Klärner, A. (2014). Social networks, social influence, and fertility in Germany: challenges and benefits of applying a parallel mixed methods design. In S. Domínguez & B. Hollstein (Eds.), *Mixed methods social networks research: design and applications* (pp. 121–177). Cambridge University Press.

Bidart, C., & Charbonneau, J. (2011). How to generate personal networks: issues and tools for a sociological perspective. *Field Methods*, *23*(3), 266–286.

Bidart, C., Degenne, A., & Grossetti, M. (2020). *Living in networks: the dynamics of social relations*. Cambridge University Press.

Bilecen, B., & Sienkiewicz, J.J. (2015). Informal social protection networks of migrants: typical patterns in different transnational social spaces. *Population, Space and Place*, *21*(3), 227–243.

Bolíbar, M. (2016). Macro, meso, micro: broadening the 'social' of social network analysis with a mixed methods approach. *Quality and Quantity*, 50(5), 2217–2236.

Bolíbar, M. (2019). Personal networks and participation: relational mechanisms for the local and transnational civic involvement of immigrants. *Sociological Quarterly*, 60(4), 583–605.

Bott, E. (1957). *Family and social network*. Tavistock.

Chan, G.H., Lo, T.W., Lee, G.K.-W., & Tam, C.H.-L. (2020). Social capital and social networks of hidden drug abuse in Hong Kong. *International Journal of Environmental Research and Public Health*, 17(17), 6231.

Creswell, J.W., & Plano Clark, V.L. (2011). *Designing and conducting mixed methods research* (2nd ed.). Sage.

Crossley, N., & Edwards, G. (2016). Cases, mechanisms and the real: the theory and methodology of mixed-method social network analysis. *Sociological Research Online*, 21(2), 217–285.

Diviák, T. (2022). Key aspects of covert networks data collection: problems, challenges, and opportunities. *Social Networks*, 69, 160–169.

Domínguez, S., & Hollstein, B. (Eds.) (2014). *Mixed methods social networks research: design and applications* (Bd. 36). Cambridge University Press.

Edwards, E., & Crossley, N. (2009). Measures and meanings: exploring the ego-net of Helen Kirkpatrick Watts, militant suffragette. *Methodological Innovations Online*, 4, 37–61.

Emirbayer, M., & Goodwin, J. (1994). Network analysis, culture, and the problem of agency. *American Journal of Sociology*, 99(6), 1411–1454.

Engelbrecht, M. (2006). Netzwerke religiöser Menschen – Die Dynamik von Wissensbeständen und Netzwerken religiöser Traditionen zwischen kollektiver Selbstabgrenzung und individueller Wahl. In B. Hollstein & F. Straus (Eds.), *Qualitative Netzwerkanalyse* (pp. 243–266). VS Verlag für Sozialwissenschaften.

Fine, G.A., & Kleinman, S. (1983). Network and meaning: an interactionist approach to structure. *Symbolic Interaction*, 6(1), 97–110.

Franke, K., & Wald, A. (2006). Möglichkeiten der Triangulation quantitativer und qualitativer Methoden in der Netzwerkanalyse. In B. Hollstein & F. Straus (Eds.), *Qualitative Netzwerkanalyse* (pp. 153–175). VS Verlag für Sozialwissenschaften.

Froehlich, D.E. (2019). Exploring social relationships in 'a mixed way': mixed structural analysis. In D.E. Froehlich, M. Rehm & B. Rienties (Eds.), *Mixed methods social network analysis: theories and methodologies in learning and education*. Routledge.

Froehlich, D.E., Van Waes, S., & Schäfer, H. (2020). Linking quantitative and qualitative network approaches: a review of mixed methods social network analysis in education research. *Review of Research in Education*, 44(1), 244–268.

Fuhse, J., & Mützel, S. (2011). Tackling connections, structure, and meaning in networks: quantitative and qualitative methods in sociological network research. *Quality and Quantity*, 45(5), 1067–1089.

Fuller, A., Heath, S., & Johnston, B. (2011). *Rethinking widening participation in higher education*. Routledge.

Gamper, M., & Schönhuth, M. (2020). Visual network research (VNR): a theoretical and methodological appraisal of an evolving field. *Visual Studies*, 35(4), 374–393.

Gluesing, J.C., Riopelle, K.R., & Danowski, J.A. (2014). Mixing ethnography and information technology data mining to visualize innovation networks in global networked organizations. In S. Domínguez & B. Hollstein (Eds.), *Mixed Methods Social Networks Research* (pp. 203–234). Cambridge University Press.

Grigoropoulou, N., & Small, M.L. (2022). The data revolution in social science needs qualitative research. *Nature Human Behaviour*, 6(7), 904–906.

Hauck, J., Schmidt, J., & Werner, A. (2016). Using social network analysis to identify key stakeholders in agricultural biodiversity governance and related land-use decisions at regional and local level. *Ecology and Society* 21(2), 49.

Häussling, R. (2010). Allocation to social positions in class: interactions and relationships in first grade school classes and their consequences. *Current Sociology*, 58(1), 119–138.

Häussling, R. (2014). A network analytical four-level concept for an interpretation of social interaction in terms of structure and agency. In S. Domínguez & B. Hollstein (Eds.), *Mixed methods social networks research* (pp. 90–118). Cambridge University Press.

Hepp, A., Roitsch, C., & Berg, M. (2016). Investigating communication networks contextually: qualitative network analysis as cross-media research. *MedieKultur: Journal of Media and Communication Research*, 32(60), 20 p.

Hogan, B., Carrasco, J.-A., & Wellman, B. (2007). Visualizing personal networks: working with participant-aided sociograms. *Field Methods*, 19(2), 116–144.

Hollstein, B. (2011). Qualitative approaches. In J. Scott & P.J. Carrington (Eds.), *The Sage handbook of social network analysis* (pp. 404–416). Sage.

Hollstein, B. (2014). Mixed methods social networks research: an introduction. In S. Domínguez & B. Hollstein (Eds.), *Mixed methods social networks research* (pp. 3–34). Cambridge University Press.

Hollstein, B. (2019). What autobiographical narratives tell us about the life course: contributions of qualitative sequential analytical methods. *Advances in Life Course Research*, 41(4).

Hollstein, B. (2021). Promises and pitfalls of qualitative longitudinal research. *Longitudinal and Life Course Studies*, 12(1), 7–17.

Hollstein, B. (forthcoming). Personal network dynamics across the life course: a relationship-related structural approach. *Advances in Life Course Research*.

Hollstein, B., Matiaske, W., & Schnapp, K.-U. (Eds.) (2017). *Networked governance*. Springer.

Hollstein, B., Pfeffer, J., & Behrmann, L. (2013). Touchscreen-gesteuerte Instrumente zur Erhebung egozentrierter Netzwerke. In M. Schönhuth, M. Gamper, M. Kronenwett & M. Stark (Eds.), *Visuelle Netzwerkforschung: Qualitative, quantitative und partizipative Zugänge* (pp. 121–136). transcript.

Hollstein, B., Töpfer, T., & Pfeffer, J. (2020). Collecting egocentric network data with visual tools: a comparative study. *Network Science* 8(2), 223–250.

Hollstein, B., & Wagemann, C. (2014). Fuzzy-set analysis of network data as mixed method. personal networks and the transition from school to work. In S. Domínguez & B. Hollstein (Eds.), *Mixed methods social networks research. design and applications* (pp. 237–269). Cambridge University Press.

Johnson, J. (1994). Anthropological contributions to the study of social networks: a review. In S. Wasserman & J. Galaskiewicz (Eds.), *Advances in social network analysis: research in the social and behavioral sciences* (pp. 113–151). Sage.

Johnson, R.B. & Onwuegbuzie, A.J. (2007). Toward a definition of mixed methods research. *Journal of Mixed Methods Research*, 1 (2), 112–133.

Karl, U., Ramos, A.C., & Kühn, B. (2016). Older migrants in Luxembourg: care preferences for old age between family and professional services. *Journal of Ethnic and Migration Studies*, 43(2), 270–286.

Klärner, A., & Knabe, A. (2019). Social networks and coping with poverty in rural areas. *Sociologia Ruralis*, 59(3), 447–473.

Knox, H., Savage, M., & Harvey, P. (2006). Social networks and the study of relations: networks as method, metaphor and form. *Economy and Society*, 35(1), 113–140.

Lefrançois, M., Saint-Charles, J., & Riel, J. (2017). Work/family balancing and 24/7 work schedules: network analysis of strategies in a transport company cleaning service. *NEW SOLUTIONS: A Journal of Environmental and Occupational Health Policy*, 27(3), 319–341.

Lelong, B., Nagel, M., & Grabher, G. (2017). Political deadlock: a network analysis of decision processes in urban politics. *Yearbook of Swiss Administrative Sciences*, 8(1), 133.

Lubbers, M.J., Verdery, A.M., & Molina, J.L. (2020). Social networks and transnational social fields: a review of quantitative and mixed-methods approaches. *International Migration Review*, 54(1), 177–204.

Lumino, R., Ragozini, G., van Duijn, M., & Vitale, M.P. (2017). A mixed-methods approach for analysing social support and social anchorage of single mothers' personal networks. *Quality and Quantity*, 51(2), 779–797.

Manzo, G., Gabbriellini, S., Roux, V. & Nkirote M'Mbogori, F. (2018). Complex Contagions and the Diffusion of Innovations: evidence from a Small-N Study. *Journal of Archaeological Method and Theory*, 25, 1109–1154.

Marsden, P.V. (1990). Network data and measurement. *Annual Review of Sociology*, 16(1), 435–463.

Marsden, P.V. (2011). Survey methods for network data. In J. Scott & P.J. Carrington (Eds.), *The Sage handbook of social network analysis* (pp. 370–388). Sage.

Marsden, P.V., & Hollstein, B. (2022). Advances and innovations in methods for collecting egocentric network data. *Social Science Research*, 109, 102816.

Maya-Jariego, I., & Cachia, R. (2019). What the eye does not see: visualization strategies for the data collection of personal networks. *Connections*, 39(1), 1–18.

Maya-Jariego, I., & Domínguez, S. (2014). Two sides of the same coin: the integration of personal network analysis with ethnographic and psychometric strategies in the study of acculturation. In S. Domínguez & B. Hollstein (Eds.), *Mixed methods social networks research* (pp. 153–176). Cambridge University Press.

Mazák, J., & Diviák, T. (2018). Transactional activism without transactions: network perspective on anticorruption activism in the Czech Republic. *Social Movement Studies*, 17(2), 203–218.

McCarty, C., Lubbers, M.J., Vacca, R., & Molina, J.L. (2019). *Conducting personal network research: a practical guide*. Guilford.

McCarty, C., Molina, J.L., Aguilar, C., & Rota, L. (2007). A comparison of social network mapping and personal network visualization. *Field Methods*, 19(2), 145–162.

McLean, P.D. (1998). A frame analysis of favor seeking in the renaissance: agency, networks, and political culture. *American Journal of Sociology*, 104(1), 51–91.

Menjívar, C. (2000). *Fragmented ties: Salvadoran immigrant networks in America*. University of California Press.

Mische, A. (2009). *Partisan publics: communication and contention across Brazilian youth activist networks*. Princeton University Press.

Mitchell, J.C. (Eds.) (1969). *Social networks in urban situations. Analyses of personal relationships in central African towns*. Manchester University Press.

Mützel, S. (2009). Networks as culturally constituted processes: a comparison of relational sociology and actor-network theory. *Current Sociology, 57*(6), 871–887.

Nimmon, L., & Regehr, G. (2018). The complexity of patients' health communication social networks: a broadening of physician communication. *Teaching and Learning in Medicine, 30*(4), 352–366.

Perry, B.L., & Roth, A.R. (2021). On the boundary specification problem in network analysis: an update and extension to personal social networks. In M.L. Small & B.L. Perry (Eds.), *Personal networks* (pp. 431–443). Cambridge University Press.

Provan, K.G., & Milward, H.B. (1995). A preliminary theory of interorganizational network effectiveness: a comparative study of four community mental health systems. *Administrative Science Quarterly, 40*(1), 1.

Ragin, C.C. (2008). *Redesigning social inquiry: fuzzy sets and beyond*. University of Chicago Press.

Rice, E., Holloway, I.W., Barman-Adhikari, A., Fuentes, D., Brown, C.H., & Palinkas, L.A. (2014). A mixed approach to network data collection methods. *Field Methods, 26*(3), 252–268.

Roethlisberger, F.J., & Dickson, W.J. (1939). *Management and the worker*. Harvard University Press.

Rogers, B., & Menjívar, C. (2014). Simulating the social networks and interactions of poor immigrants. In S. Domínguez & B. Hollstein (Eds.), *Mixed methods social networks research* (pp. 336–356). Cambridge University Press.

Russell Bernard, H., Killworth, P.D., & Sailer, L. (1981). Summary of research on informant accuracy in network data. *Connections, 4*(3), 11–25.

Ryan, L., Mulholland, J., & Agoston, A. (2014). Talking ties: reflecting on network visualisation and qualitative interviewing. *Sociological Research Online, 19*(2), 1–12.

Ryu, S. (2020). The combination of critical discourse analysis and social network analysis. In M. Huber & D.E. Froehlich (Eds.), *Analyzing group interactions* (pp. 96–106). Routledge.

Scheibelhofer, E. (2011). Potential of qualitative network analysis in migration studies: reflections based on an empirical analysis of young researchers' mobility aspirations. *Migration Letters, 8*(2), 111–120.

Schiffer, E., & Hauck, J. (2010). Net-Map: collecting social network data and facilitating network learning through participatory influence network mapping. *Field Methods, 22*(3), 231–249.

Small, M.L. (2009). *Unanticipated gains*. Oxford University Press.

Small, M.L. (2011). How to conduct a mixed methods study: recent trends in a rapidly growing literature. *Annual Review of Sociology, 37*(1), 57–86.

Small, M.L. (2017). *Someone to talk to* (Bd. 1). Oxford University Press.

Smith, S.S. (2010). *Lone pursuit: distrust and defensive individualism among the black poor*. Russell Sage Foundation.

Straus, F. (2002). *Netzwerkanalysen: Gemeindepsychologische Perspektiven für Forschung und Praxis*. Deutscher Universitäts.

Stys, P., Muhindo, S., N'simire, S., Tchumisi, I., Muzuri, P., Balume, B., & Koskinen, J. (2022). Trust, quality, and the network collection experience: a tale of two studies on the Democratic Republic of the Congo. *Social Networks, 68*, 237–255.

Tashakkori, A., & Teddlie, C. (1998). *Mixed methodology: combining qualitative and quantitative approaches*. Sage.

Töpfer, T., & Hollstein, B. (2022). Reprint of: Order of recall and meaning of closeness in collecting affective network data. *Social Networks, 69*, 194–210.

Tubaro, P., Casilli, A.A., & Mounier, L. (2014). Eliciting personal network data in web surveys through participant-generated sociograms. *Field Methods, 26*(2), 107–125.

Uzzi, B. (1997). Social structure and competition in interfirm networks: the paradox of embeddedness. *Administrative Science Quarterly, 42*(1), 35.

Verd, J.M. (2022). Using a hybrid data collection tool: analysis of youth labour market trajectories integrating quantitative, qualitative and social network data. *International Journal of Social Welfare*, ijsw.12528.

Verd, J.M., & Lozares, C. (2014). Reconstructing social networks through text analysis. In S. Domínguez & B. Hollstein (Eds.), *Mixed methods social networks research* (pp. 269–304). Cambridge University Press.

von der Lippe, H., & Gamper, M. (2017). Drawing or tabulating ego-centered networks? A mixed-methods comparison of questionnaire vs visualization-based data collection. *International Journal of Social Research Methodology, 20*(5), 425–441.

Wagner, K.D., Syvertsen, J.L., Verdugo, S.R., Molina, J.L., & Strathdee, S.A. (2018). A mixed methods study of the social support networks of female sex workers and their primary noncommercial male partners in Tijuana, Mexico. *Journal of Mixed Methods Research, 12*(4), 437–457.

Wald, A. (2014). Triangulation and validity of network data. In S. Domínguez & B. Hollstein (Eds.), *Mixed methods social networks research* (pp. 65–89). Cambridge University Press.

Weissinger, L.B. (2022). Building trust and co-designing a study of trust and co-operation: observations from a network study in a high-risk, high-security environment. *Social Networks*, 69, 136–148.

Whelan, E., Teigland, R., Vaast, E., & Butler, B. (2016). Expanding the horizons of digital social networks: mixing big trace datasets with qualitative approaches. *Information and Organization*, 26(1–2), 1–12.

Whyte, W.F. (1943). *Street corner society: the social structure of an Italian slum*. University of Chicago Press.

Williams, T.A., & Shepherd, D.A. (2017). Mixed method social network analysis: combining inductive concept development, content analysis, and secondary data for quantitative analysis. *Organizational Research Methods*, 20(2), 268–298.

Wutich, A., Beresford, M., Bausch, J.C., Eaton, W., Brasier, K.J., Williams, C.F., & Porter, S. (2020). Identifying stakeholder groups in natural resource management: comparing quantitative and qualitative social network approaches. *Society and Natural Resources*, 33(7), 941–948.

Spatial Analysis of Social Networks

John R. Hipp

INTRODUCTION

A growing area of interest is the linkage of spatial patterns with social networks. The combination of these two areas yields spatial social networks, and is an exciting, developing area of research. Whereas much social network analysis is aspatial, and much existing spatial analysis ignores networks, the marriage of the two is becoming increasingly feasible due to data availability. There is a certain irony in this marriage, as, in fact, many of the analyses that underlie their separate fields are quite similar. Nonetheless, despite the similarity in analytic techniques, the combination of the two fields produces various challenges to researchers.

Of primary importance for spatial networks is propinquity, which is the idea that physical closeness impacts social tie formation. As noted by Daraganova and colleagues (2012, p. 6), 'Physical propinquity effects have been demonstrated to occur for different types of relationship and at multiple levels of analysis.' These strong propinquity effects imply a very strong spatial pattern to the social networks. Nonetheless, even at the time of their writing in 2012 they noted the limited number of explicitly spatial models of networks. With the increasing availability of geographically embedded social network data, this is changing. In this chapter I will present a non-technical overview of some of the areas of research that are exploring spatial social networks in various manners.

METHODS FOR SPATIAL SOCIAL NETWORKS

We can consider spatial analysis and network analysis as special cases under the broader umbrella of relational analysis (Butts & Acton, 2011). As Butts and Acton noted, spatial analysis and network analysis are similar in that they focus on the *relationships* among entities rather than their intrinsic properties. The occasional differences in the two approaches are relatively modest. For example, spatial analysis considers relationships among entities that are a function of physical distance, whereas network analysis typically considers relations to occur based on pair-wise interactions that are a function of structural properties such as reciprocity, transitive closure bias, or Markov dependence.

Scholars in the geography literature are primarily focused on mapping geographic units – polygons – and how they are spatially related to one another.

Nonetheless, there are recent efforts to combine this spatial approach with social networks (Andris, 2016). In this literature, social networks are included as another layer in a *geographic information system* (GIS). This focus on geography differs from social network scholars, who often only incorporate geography based on the physical distance between ties. However, an explicit focus on distance will miss out on how the topology of the landscape can affect movement and social interaction, how physical and administrative boundaries might impact interaction and the spatial fuzziness of a person's location given that residence only accounts for spatial location in part of the day.

Some geographers have defined connections as *social flows* – that is, a connection created when an agent decides to 'move, communicate, or state a relationship between two places' (Andris, 2016, p. 2012). Examples include traffic flows on roads, GPS traces of persons' activity patterns, or more traditional social networks as reported through surveys, etc. (Andris et al., 2018). Nonetheless, visualising these is sometimes difficult for connections that do not follow transportation routes, as they can sometimes leapfrog over locations. Yet another strategy in this literature defines a person's activity pattern (either daily or over some other time period) as an *anthrospace* (Andris, 2016, p. 2015). These activity spaces can then be overlaid in a GIS to describe patterns of movement; however, this strategy cannot be readily extended to a larger analytic sample. Likewise, other spatial analysts have proposed descriptive measures such as the *spatial social network schema*, the *tuning parameter* and the *flattening ratio*, all of which incorporate distance into measures based on topology (Sarkar et al., 2019).

MEASURING DISTANCE BETWEEN TIES BASED ON COMPLETE NETWORKS

One body of research has used data from relatively small-scale geographic areas to collect a complete network and then assess the extent to which social ties are formed based on propinquity. These studies typically assess the strength of the distance decay function. Two of the earliest studies in this area were conducted based on housing of MIT graduate students (Festinger et al., 1950) and students at the University of Minnesota (Caplow & Forman, 1950). By collecting information on where exactly residents lived, and then conducting a survey of the population of residents, these studies using mostly descriptive analyses were able to assess the importance of propinquity.

Furthermore, they were able to assess whether various features of the built environment impacted this tie formation. As one example, Festinger et al. were able to assess the extent to which living near a stairway impacted the formation of social ties.

Other more recent studies have also focused on the effect of propinquity for residents in small-scale communities. For example, a study collecting full network data studied residents in a neighbourhood within Ithaca, NY, and found strong evidence that residents were more likely to form social ties with others on the same block and, among those on the same block, were more likely to form ties with those in housing units closest to their own (Grannis, 2009). Similarly, a study of a newly developed New Urbanist neighbourhood within a mid-sized southern city estimated logistic models and found strong evidence of both propinquity and homophily effects (Hipp & Perrin, 2009). That is, residents were more likely to form ties with others similar to them based on such social characteristics as home value, presence of children, age and marital status. There were also strong propinquity effects, as physical distance reduced the likelihood of weak or strong ties forming even after accounting for these homophily effects. Directly comparing physical distance and social distance, it was found that a 10 per cent increase in home value difference was equivalent to a 5.6 per cent increase in physical distance.

As another way to collect full network data, a study in Nang Rong, Thailand, combined information on the location of dwelling units along with saturated kinship networks of all individuals living in 51 agricultural villages (Verdery et al., 2012). The mostly descriptive analyses in this study demonstrated that extended kin tend to live closer to one another than do unrelated individuals. However, this set of studies does not account for network endogeneity, so in the next section I turn to studies that do adopt such an approach.

ACCOUNTING FOR NETWORK PROCESSES IN COMPLETE NETWORKS

There is a large literature accounting for network endogeneity through exponential random graph models (ERGM) (see Koskinen, this volume). Briefly, the concern is of a direct dependence among the observations – that one observation affects another – or whether the dependence occurs among the errors – exogenous perturbations that are not in the model (Butts, 2008). There is strong overlap between these issues for social network analysis and those used in spatial analysis between geographic locations: effectively, the modelling strategies are the same with sometimes different terminology.

These ERGMs are also sometimes referred to as p* models, and one way they can be incorporated into spatial networks is by accounting for the physical distance between each pair of nodes in the sample. One example used the National Longitudinal Study of Adolescent Health (Add Health) to assess whether physical distance among dyads impacted tie formation (Mouw & Entwisle, 2006). Racial homophily strongly impacted tie formation even after accounting for propinquity. Nonetheless, those living in different block groups, or living farther apart were less likely to report being friends. Thus, students living within 250 metres of one another were 3.1 times more likely to be friends than those living 250–500 metres apart, and 4.5 time more likely than those more than 2 kilometres away (Mouw & Entwisle, 2006, p. 419).

Another paper using ERGMs extended the approach utilised by Butts (2002) and included an interaction function between dyadic distance and tie probability (Daraganova et al. 2012). The authors highlighted that researchers rarely give the actual form of this distance decay function careful consideration. Indeed, Butts and Acton (2011) defined four key characteristics to consider when capturing the shape of this function: (1) monotonicity; (2) baseline probability at the origin; (3) curvature near the origin; (4) tail weight. Although capturing these different portions of the decay function implies using different families of functional forms, studies frequently simply use either an inverse power law or an exponential decay. Daraganova and colleagues tested different functional forms with a snowball sample of working age adults in Australia and found strong spatial effects even when accounting for network endogeneity. They found that the inverse attenuated power law decay function better captured the steep decay they found for nearby ties than did the exponential decay. Furthermore, the model better fitted the actual network when accounting for this spatial effect.

CAPTURING THE NETWORK STRUCTURE FROM THE SPATIAL CONTEXT

Whereas studies showing the importance of physical distance for social network ties are an important component to spatial social network analysis, there are broader features that can also be studied. Doreian and Conti (2012) highlighted the need for social network analysts to also account for how social and spatial contextual features can impact networks. They demonstrated how researchers can use various modelling strategies, including network visualisations, QAP regression, ERGMs, blockmodelling and a framework combining blockmodelling and ERGMs. They defined the social context as 'made up of the human and symbolic features that are intrinsic to situations where social network data are collected' and the spatial context as 'specific features of a context that are located explicitly in geographic space' (Doreian & Conti, 2012, p. 32). This spatial context can extend beyond simple physical distance, and can include various physical boundary effects etc., consistent with how geographers consider spatial networks, and the social and spatial context can actually shape the formation of the observed social network.

Two rural studies also described the spatial context of social networks. One used kin networks across multiple villages in Nang Rong, Thailand, and demonstrated that the social structure of both the relational networks as well as the contexts containing these individuals have important consequences (Entwisle et al., 2007). They found that the network structure covaries with the social context in meaningful ways, which may imply reciprocal effects between them. This same research team combined the same data with spatial information from a GIS to illustrate the movement of tractors and workers between villages (Faust et al., 1999). This descriptive study demonstrated how social networks incorporated into a GIS can be mapped to show their relation to such geographic features as topography, landcover and rivers and roads. Such a strategy can assess whether features such as rivers operate as physical boundaries to movement, or whether nearness or similarity of the villages better explains this movement.

CONSEQUENCES OF NETWORKS FOR DISEASE TRANSMISSION

The physical environment might impact disease transmission through social networks. Thus, combining social networks, the spatial location of persons and disease infectiousness allows assessing how the social network and spatial nearness might operate either in competition, or synergistically, to impact disease transmission. As one example, a study used data from the first 30 days of the 2007 equine influenza outbreak in Australia to describe the dynamics of early epidemic spread (Firestone et al., 2011). Although the study was limited to distance between infected premises as its spatial resolution, it nonetheless highlighted how spatial and social network effects could be studied simultaneously.

A similar technique for studying spatial social networks and disease transmission focused on two bacterial diarrheal diseases in rural Bangladesh using networks based on kinship (Emch et al., 2012). A general challenge for network scholars is considering whether the particular form of ties utilised is appropriate for the research question. In this case, the authors posited that kin ties are most likely to result in shared meals – which are the sites at which such disease transmission is most likely – and also likely to be maintained even if a household moves away. Based on this reasoning, the authors argued that kin ties were the most appropriate to use. Nonetheless, they note that shared meals might also occur for friendship ties and therefore lacking friendship ties limits their ability to properly assess social network effects. Nonetheless, these kin networks improved the performance of the model for explaining disease transmission.

DYNAMIC SPATIAL SOCIAL NETWORKS

Up to now I have been describing cross-sectional studies, and how the network at a point in time can be related to the spatial environment. Nonetheless, there is an implicit dynamic model underlying how the social network and the spatial environment unfold over time. Fewer studies have access to longitudinal data, but these studies can also account for spatial effects. As one example, a study used a three-wave network of 336 Swedish adolescents to assess how physical distance impacted tie formation and tie dissolution (Preciado et al., 2012). They flexibly estimated the distance decay function by using nonparametric logistic regressions. They found that the log-odds of friendship existence, as well as tie formation and dissolution, decrease smoothly with the logarithm of distance. Consistent with their expectations, distance exhibited a stronger effect on tie formation than it did on tie maintenance (or dissolution). Although the slope of this function was steeper for adolescents in different schools compared to those in the same school, the distance effect only appeared significant for tie formation within 1 kilometre, which highlights that distance may have a weaker effect when studying tie formation within an institution such as a school. Their stochastic actor-oriented models (SAOMs) found that nearby distance impacts tie formation and dissolution, and that this effect is independent from the network structure or individual covariates. Furthermore, this distance decay attenuated some of the network dynamic effects.

A US study of adolescent social networks likewise found evidence of a distance decay effect on tie dynamics in a SAOM (Jose et al., 2016). Using Add Health data, this study estimated one model on a single large school, and another on twelve small schools, over three time periods. In addition to the influence and selection processes present for network ties and delinquent behaviour, greater distance between ties reduced tie formation and maintenance. Furthermore, the negative effect of distance on tie formation was three times stronger in the single large school compared to the small schools.

Whereas SAOMs are powerful in that they can model the dynamics of network tie formation and dissolution along with other behaviours by the actors (such as substance use or delinquent behaviour), they do not focus on changes in the presence of nodes. For that reason, a strategy proposed by Almquist and Butts (2014) is an important contribution, and spatial effects can be directly incorporated into their model that uses a logistic function to model node appearance or disappearance. This model allows studying how endogenous group change (with the appearance or disappearance of nodes) is related to interaction dynamics. This statistical model allows moving beyond descriptive strategies, and provides for statistical tests, and has the favourable property of being very scalable for modelling large networks with dynamic nodes.

MEASURING THE SPATIAL DISTRIBUTION OF EGO-NETWORKS

While studies focused on complete network samples are powerful in that they allow accounting for network dynamics while simultaneously assessing the effect of distance on social network ties, they are necessarily quite geographically limited, which limits their ability to generalise their results more broadly. An alternative strategy is to collect a larger, more geographically dispersed, sample to better assess the impact of physical distance on tie formation. The drawbacks to this strategy are the complications in accounting for the local context, and it is extremely challenging to account for network dynamics.

One early study was that of Bib Latané and colleagues using surveys of 552 residents in Boca Raton, 751 people from two elite universities in

Shanghai, China, and social psychologists who had attended a particular conference (Latané et al., 1995). Notably, this study found a strong exponential distance decay function across these samples, with an estimated d value near -1.

Although few studies provide information on the spatial location of both egos and alters in a broad population sample, one such example was the American Social Fabric Study (ASFS) (Butts et al., 2014). Using a spatially stratified egocentric network sample across the western United States, the resulting sample provided a large number of both urban and rural residents, allowing for better generalisation across contexts. One paper using the ASFS data used the age of respondents to predict the average logged distance of their social ties for the rural sample, and found evidence that older residents have social ties that are more spatially dispersed (Smith et al., 2015).

Another study using an egocentric network sample focused on social activity ties (Illenberger et al., 2012). To account for potential ties, the study created 300 bins that were discretised based on total distance, and the widths of these bins were adjusted such that each bin had approximately the same number of inhabitants (based on census data). That is, each bin contained a range of distances and a tie was placed into the appropriate bin depending on the distance to the tie and the range of distances for a particular bin. The authors then divided the number of ties for a respondent in each bin by the population in that bin, to estimate the proportion of existing ties among those available. Using a power law distance decay function, they found a strong distance effect as the probability of an existing tie declined at a d value of approximately -1.4. An interesting finding was that the number of contacts was not related to the density of opportunities nearby: thus rural residents were tied to a higher proportion of eligible ties, rather than having smaller networks.

HOW THE SPATIAL CONTEXT AFFECTS EGO-NETWORKS

Similar to full network studies, egocentric network studies not only can assess how physical distance impacts tie formation or dissolution, but also how features of the spatial context impact the presence of social ties. A nice review of some of this literature is provided by Small and Adler (2019), in which they propose that there are at least three mechanisms through which the spatial context might impact the formation of social ties: (1) spatial propinquity (physical distance), (2) spatial composition (locations that allow social interaction) and (3) spatial configuration (physical barriers and physical routes).

A study using the ASFS explored how various features of the built environment impact the spatial scale of residents' social ties – that is, ties within the local area, the broader city region and a more macro spatial scale for three different types of ties (Boessen et al., 2017a). The evidence that the presence of more bars nearby was associated with having more socialising ties within 5 miles in both the urban and rural samples is consistent with the idea that these bars can serve as 'third places' (Oldenburg, 1999) that enable social interaction and therefore result in more nearby socialising ties. These nearby bars were also associated with more nearby core discussion ties in the rural sample – implying that these may be stronger ties – but not in the urban sample. The presence of more nearby parkland reduced the number of socialising and core discussion ties within 5–50 miles in urban areas, but had no effect on nearby ties. If parks foster *stronger* local ties, rather than a greater *number* of ties, then this could explain this combination of results.

A descriptive strategy for egocentric data is to visually present both the spatial and temporal dimensions of activity patterns. One study utilised activity-travel data and social network information and implemented four visual methods: 3D space-time paths, time windows, 3D activity density surfaces and ring-based visualisation of social networks (Lee & Kwan, 2010). The authors demonstrated how one can visualise people's activities in space-time as well as their social interactions, providing insight into what they termed *sociospatial isolation*.

HOW SPATIAL SOCIAL TIES AFFECT PERCEPTIONS

Beyond measuring the spatial distribution of respondents' social networks, there is a question of the consequences of those ties for perceptions of cohesion with, or attachment to, the neighbourhood or broader community. Whereas there is a rich literature asking respondents to report on the number of social ties they have with fellow residents in their neighbourhood (however defined) and then assessing how this is related to perceptions of cohesion or collective efficacy in the neighbourhood, this strategy effectively assumes that more distant ties are irrelevant. In fact, these more distant ties: (1) may not impact residents' perceptions about the neighbourhood, or (2) may represent a time cost for residents, and therefore *reduce* their sense of attachment to the neighbourhood, or (3) might provide useful information for addressing neighbourhood problems, and therefore *increase* attachment to the neighbourhood.

There is limited research regarding these questions, likely due to the limited data available for testing them. Nonetheless, some recent research has addressed this general question. A challenge is how to incorporate this spatial information. As one example, a study using survey data from a few neighbourhoods in southern California included two variables: one a count of the number of social ties, and the other the average distance (logged) to those ties (Boessen et al., 2014). Although a greater number of what they termed *neighbourhood safety contacts* – alters a respondent would turn to when addressing neighbourhood crime – were associated with greater attachment to the neighbourhood and city, greater average distance to those ties was associated with reduced attachment. A subsequent study using the large-scale ASFS dataset based on the western United States did not simply compute the average distance to a respondent's social ties – since this can obscure the spatial pattern of a respondent's ties – but instead computed counts of the number of ties within different distance bins (Luo et al., 2022). The downside of using discrete distance bins is the arbitrary quality of the size and the number of bins (that is, how much distance is included within a particular bin and the assumption of constancy within bin), and therefore the robustness of the results was confirmed by constructing variables based on a number of different binning strategies and finding similar results. In this study, not only were more local neighbourhood safety ties positively associated with perceived attachment with the neighbourhood and city, but long-distance ties also had a positive relationship with attachment (Luo et al., 2022). This result was robust across both the urban and rural samples – in fact, the spatial distribution of social ties appeared more consequential for attachment in the rural sample than in the urban sample.

Yet another strategy to capture these tie distances is to measure them based on an exponential decay (Hipp et al., 2023). Thus, the distance to each alter from ego was multiplied by the appropriate value of the distance decay function (given a particular beta value) to create this measure. Many versions of this weighted ties measure are created with different beta values. The models are estimated including these measures one at a time and the optimal model is selected based on the lowest Bayesian information criterion (BIC) value, indicating the beta value that best explains the relationship. There was evidence that neighbourhood safety ties showed a much stronger relationship than socialising ties with collective efficacy. The distance decay functions indicated that social ties much further away than the local neighbourhood helped explain perceptions of collective efficacy and a sense of cohesion. Whereas in rural areas social ties from a much broader area were associated with greater collective efficacy, even in urban areas neighbourhood safety ties within 5–10 miles – which are clearly outside any definition of neighbourhood – were associated with more cohesion. Given that the distance decay function does not allow for a possible negative effect from more distant social ties, a measure of long-distance ties was specifically included (and was insignificant). Research has also assessed how the spatial distribution of residents' social ties impact communication networks, and voting preferences and behaviour (Baybeck & Huckfeldt, 2002a, 2002b).

Whereas criminologists have tested whether residents' social ties in the neighbourhood impact their fear of crime, this again presumes that social ties outside the neighbourhood do not matter. A study using the ASFS sample measured distance to social ties based on average distance as well as with discretised distance bins and found that more distant ties indeed reduced residents' reported fear of crime in the neighbourhood. An additional twist is that residents who were socially tied to persons in higher crime neighbourhoods reported *less* fear of crime in the daytime, which may imply a social comparison effect if one lives in a neighbourhood with less crime than one's social ties (Boessen et al., 2017b).

DEFINING NEIGHBOURHOODS BASED ON SPATIAL SOCIAL NETWORKS

Given the importance of social networks for neighbourhoods, some have suggested that the network of ties among residents could be used to actually *define* neighbourhoods (Martin, 2003). That is, in principle if we knew the entire social network of a city we could use some particular clustering technique (sometimes referred to as *community detection algorithms*) to detect locations with relative breaks in the network, implying neighbourhood boundaries given the relative paucity of social ties traversing them. An obvious challenge for such a strategy is the difficulty in collecting a sociometric network for all residents in a city.

As a demonstration of the possible efficacy of this strategy, a paper used data on adolescent social networks in the schools across three rural counties to create such a complete network (Hipp et al., 2012).

By combining adolescent social ties with the spatial distance between adolescents, a valued matrix between adolescents in the county was created, which was factor analysed to detect network neighbourhoods. When assessing various characteristics of their 'neighbourhood', there was greater agreement among residents in the same network neighbourhood compared to those in the same census-defined geographic unit, suggesting that these network neighbourhoods are a more appropriate unit to capture the social environment. Nonetheless, using adolescent networks rather than adult networks limited this to a demonstration study.

Another project used data from billions of phone calls to create a large social network and then assessed how it was related to large geographic units in Great Britain (Ratti et al., 2010). They used a partitioning technique that optimised the network's modularity – that is, it partitioned the area into smaller, non-overlapping regions that maximised the number of ties within them and minimised the number across regions. Their partitioning algorithm yielded geographically cohesive regions that were very similar to official administrative regions, although they also found some novel spatial structures that existed in the social network.

WITHIN-NEIGHBOURHOOD EFFECTS OF SPATIAL NETWORKS

Another body of work has focused on the consequences of social networks that span outside the neighbourhood for the neighbourhood itself. Rather than focusing on the spatial distance of residents' social ties, this literature considers the consequences at an ecological level for the neighbourhood. These ideas were articulated by Sampson in a paper critiquing earlier work viewing neighbourhoods as isolated urban villages, given that resident spatial movement routinely takes them outside their own neighbourhood's boundaries (Sampson, 2004). One empirical example of this perspective is the work of Chris Browning and colleagues (2017) with their concept of ecological networks (eco-networks). Combining the activity pattern literature with the social network literature, their strategy used survey data on where respondents reported going for certain routine activities – that is, the grocery store, school, religious services, childcare, etc. They then placed these patronised locations into particular geographic units, assuming that if two neighbourhood residents spent time within this same geographic location, that this constituted a tie between them. A challenge was choosing the proper geographic units: smaller units increase the likelihood that it is the same location (but can result in too sparse a network to be useful), whereas larger units may not imply any possible social interaction among the residents at the location. The authors used various geographic units, including block groups, and detected robust results. This allowed them to then construct a social network of ties among the residents who responded to the survey in that neighbourhood. They constructed a measure of eco-network intensity based on the two-mode clustering coefficient, and a measure of extensity based on the proportion of residents who shared an ecological location, and found that these measures were associated with changes in neighbourhood collective efficacy.

A variant on the eco-networks strategy is work by Corina Graif and colleagues (2019) that uses commuting flows between neighbourhoods in Chicago as a way to construct network ties. The commuting data came from the Longitudinal Employer Household Dynamics (LEHD) survey, and the study looked at the level of disadvantage of the neighbourhoods that residents commuted to, with the presumption that these connections to less disadvantaged work hubs might actually reduce focal neighbourhood crime.

Another study also used commuting data to form a network of neighbourhoods to explore how these commuting flows might impact the employment outcomes of parolees living in these neighbourhoods (Boessen & Hipp, 2021). The logic was that these commuting patterns captured the economic structure between neighbourhoods, and would likely have consequences for the employment opportunities of the parolees living in the neighbourhood through potential competition in the labour market or through spatial mismatch from jobs. Using LEHD data for parolees in Texas from 2006 to 2010, the analysis created a network of ties between all census tracts in Texas based on commuting ties from home to work, and created measures of out-degree and in-degree for each neighbourhood. Parolees living in neighbourhoods with higher out-degree tended to have less joblessness, whereas those living in neighbourhoods with higher in-degree tended to experience more joblessness, particularly for black and Latino parolees.

Rather than simply using aggregate commuting flows based on administrative data, some research uses GPS information on residents' spatial movements as a way to characterise neighbourhoods. For example, one study used geolocated Twitter data to capture movement of residents and assess how these might result in network ties for gentrifying neighbourhoods in Washington, DC

(Gibbons et al., 2017). A location-based interaction measure of Tweets was created in which presence in the same block group within a one-hour time period constituted a tie. They observed more of these location-based interactions in gentrifying neighbourhoods compared to non-gentrifying ones.

Another prominent example of this strategy is research by a team at Harvard that used geotagged Tweets over eighteen months to first create an estimate of where those tweeting live, and then assessed their activity patterns aggregated to the neighbourhood level (Phillips et al., 2019). Their primary measure of 'structural connectedness' assessed the extent to which neighbourhood residents travelled to all other neighbourhoods in equal proportion. They also constructed a measure capturing the extent to which travels within a city are concentrated in a handful of receiving neighbourhoods. This large-scale study constructed these measures for the 50 largest American cities and found that cities with greater population density, more cosmopolitanism and less racial segregation had higher levels of structural connectedness between neighbourhoods.

DEFINING THE W-MATRIX AROUND NEIGHBOURHOODS

In the literature studying characteristics of neighbourhoods, particularly levels of crime, an empirical challenge is accounting for nearby areas. That is, studies cannot simply assume that neighbourhoods are independent of one another, but rather that there are likely consequences from nearby neighbourhoods. The question then is how to define 'nearby'; this definition is captured in what is referred to as the *W-matrix* – that is, this NxN matrix of all geographic units captures a measure of 'closeness' that is used for constructing measures or in model estimation. The question of defining the proper W-matrix is a challenge that also exists in social network analysis. Researchers often give minimal consideration to what the functional form might be of this W-matrix, with studies often simply assuming a contiguity matrix – in which a focal neighbourhood is only impacted by surrounding neighbourhoods with which it shares a border. Some research instead assumes that some distance decay function such as an inverse distance decay captures 'nearness'. Regardless, there is typically little empirical justification for choosing these particular W-matrices.

Some of the most creative strategies for constructing an appropriate spatial W-matrix come from the literature studying gangs. This literature is perched at the intersection of spatial analysis – given that violence typically occurs between nearby gangs – and social network analysis – given that there can be rivalries between specific pairs of gangs. For example, one study focused on gang violence in Los Angeles using structural equivalence measures, and combined them with spatial analysis in an effort to identify structurally equivalent geographies (Radil et al., 2010). They used a 29x29 gang rivalry matrix, and augmented it with a category of unclaimed territory to yield two 30x30 matrices, one for contiguity and one for gang rivalry. They then used CONCOR – *convergence of iterated correlations* – to compute correlations among the rows and columns. This allowed them to describe the structural relations of these gangs based on both the social network and the spatial distance. Another project using the same data constructed a novel weights matrix for statistical analyses (Tita & Radil, 2011). In this study, a 120x120 matrix of block groups creates a spatial weights matrix, and a location by gang matrix of 120x29 captures gang territory in each block group. After incorporating the 29x29 gang rivalry matrix, the authors were left with a 120x120 matrix identifying block groups that are 'enemies' of one another, which they used in a statistical model with gang crimes as the outcome.

Research using data on gangs in Chicago and Boston modelled fatal and non-fatal shootings (Papachristos et al., 2013). Creating a network based on gang rivalries, the study created social network measures such as reciprocity and transitivity. There was strong evidence in this study that both spatial effects – adjacency of gang turf – and social network effects – prior conflict between gangs – were strong predictors of subsequent gang violence. There was also evidence that reciprocity and status-seeking impacted gang violence. Furthermore, there appeared to be evidence that these spatial and network processes mediated racial effects.

Other studies provide evidence for potential ways to measure the W-matrix, even if they do not do so in their particular study. One example is the literature focusing on youth co-offending networks. In this research, scholars use criminal justice data on those who were arrested committing the same crime, and construct a network based on these 'ties'. These networks typically have spatial information on all the offenders who committed the crime, as well as where the crime occurred. The challenge then is to incorporate this spatial information into the network analyses. One study used official court data from a large US metropolitan area to create a network and then estimated ERGMs to assess whether certain types of neighbourhoods fostered co-offending (Schaefer, 2012).

There was evidence that both social distance and spatial distance impacted these co-offending ties.

SIMULATING SPATIAL NETWORKS ACROSS CITIES

Given the consistent evidence from numerous studies that social ties form based on a distance decay function, some research has incorporated this insight into models that simulate social networks across entire cities. Such a strategy then allows exploring various research questions that would otherwise be of interest to scholars, but typically are not feasible given the difficulty of collecting network data across such a large scale. One simulation example is a study that simply generated nodes randomly in geographical space and then assessed the extent to which a distance step function that gives rise to ties between nodes can capture various generic properties of social networks, such as skewed degree distributions and community structures (Wong et al., 2006). Despite the simple distance function – nearby ties were more likely than further ties (rather than a distance decay function) – the study demonstrated such potential. Another example is a study that built a simulated network based on distance decay estimates and found evidence that their simulation model could reproduce the spatial structure, although it was unable to reproduce other topological characteristics, such as transitivity (Illenberger et al., 2012).

Other research has instead first placed nodes in a spatial pattern that mimics specific cities and then simulated network ties based on a distance decay function. For example, a study simulated such networks based on a stratified sample of micropolitan and metropolitan areas in the US based on a 4x4 design matrix of four levels of population density and four population sizes ranging from approximately 1,000 to 1,000,000 persons (Butts et al., 2011). Using block-level data from the 2000 US Census, the study extrapolatively simulated networks based on two different distance decay functions from the existing literature. There was evidence that geographical variability produced large and distinctive features in the 'social fabric' that overlies these locations based on these simulated networks. Furthermore, several aggregate network properties were well predicted from relatively simple spatial demographic variables.

Although criminological scholars have posited that the actual structure of the network may help residents address neighbourhood problems, studies are typically limited to measuring mean degree from a sample of residents (Bursik, 1999). A study extrapolatively simulated social networks based on where residents live and a distance decay function across five cities (Hipp et al., 2013). The study constructed network measures capturing the hypothesised mechanisms of cohesion and information diffusion and found evidence that several of these network measures were robust predictors of crime at the micro scale of census blocks. In fact, these network measures exhibited stronger relationships with crime than did the more common measures typically used in such studies. It is interesting to note that this study simply simulated the networks based on propinquity, with no consideration of possible homophily effects (given the lack of empirical evidence on the size of homophily effects from spatially based samples), and yet showed promising results. Future studies incorporating homophily effects would be a natural extension of this strategy.

Other research has extrapolatively simulated networks and assessed their relation to the disease transmission of Covid-19. One study of nineteen US cities found that although standard epidemiological transmission models assume spatially uniform local mixing, using realistic social networks based on known spatial features of interpersonal networks demonstrated considerable spatial heterogeneity in the spread of the disease (Thomas et al., 2020). These networks can result in large impacts on local pandemic timing and severity, resulting in severe local outbreaks with a long lag time relative to the aggregate infection curve. Furthermore, this pattern can give rise to considerable variation in how the epidemic can appear to individuals on the ground – mirroring what was actually observed in many locations during the early portions of the pandemic. A follow-up study extrapolatively simulated the network of social ties in San Francisco and showed how these result in disproportionate transmission of Covid-19 across racial/ethnic groups (Thomas et al., 2022). The simulations showed that neighbourhoods with higher levels of structural cohesion were more at risk of the disease, what the authors referred to as the 'flood plain' of the city. Although cohesion commonly has positive consequences for neighbourhood outcomes, it appeared to place these residents at greater risk of this disease, independent of any other features of the neighbourhood.

CONCLUSION

This chapter has discussed spatial analysis of social networks. As one can see, this is an exciting, burgeoning area given the increasing availability of such data. There are a wealth of techniques that researchers can use, and to some extent they depend upon the research question at hand. This is an active research area in which contributions are being made by scholars based within the spatial literature, as well as those operating in the social networks paradigm. Some of the largest challenges are related to simply trying to visually represent these spatial networks. Nonetheless, various statistical techniques are available and more will undoubtedly become available. If there is one key point to highlight, it is that researchers will want to seriously consider distance when accounting for spatial networks, along with how the physical features of the environment can impact these networks, and how this can potentially be impacted, and impact, the social characteristics of these environments. The complexity of these processes ensures the need for much more scholarship in this area going forward.

REFERENCES

Almquist, Z.W., & Carter T. Butts, C.T. (2014). Logistic network regression for scalable analysis of networks with joint edge/vertex dynamics. *Sociological Methodology*, *44*, 273–321.

Andris, C. (2016). Integrating social network data into GISystems. *International Journal of Geographical Information Science*, *30*, 2009–2031.

Andris, C., Liu, X., & Ferreira, J. (2018). Challenges for social flows. *Computers, Environment and Urban Systems*, *70*, 197–207.

Baybeck, B., & Huckfeldt, R. (2002a). Spatially dispersed ties among interdependent citizens: connecting individuals and aggregates. *Political Analysis*, *10*, 261–275.

Baybeck, B., & Huckfeldt, R. (2002b). Urban contexts, spatially dispersed networks, and the diffusion of political information. *Political Geography*, *21*, 195–220.

Boessen, A., & Hipp, J.R. (2021). The network of neighborhoods and geographic space: implications for joblessness while on parole. *Journal of Quantitative Criminology*, February.

Boessen, A., Hipp, J.R., Butts, C.T., Nagle, N.N., & Smith, E.J. (2017a). The built environment, spatial scale, and social networks: do land uses matter for personal network structure? *Environment and Planning B*, *45*, 400–416.

Boessen, A., Hipp, J.R., Butts, C.T., Nagle, N.N., & Smith, E.J. (2017b). Social fabric and fear of crime: considering spatial location and time of day. *Social Networks*, *51*, 60–72.

Boessen, A., Hipp, J.R., Smith, E.J., Butts, C.T., Nagle, N.N., & Almquist, Z. (2014). Networks, space, and residents' perception of cohesion. *American Journal of Community Psychology*, *53*, 447–461.

Browning, C.R., Calder, C.A., Soller, B., Jackson, A.L., & Dirlam, J. (2017). Ecological networks and neighborhood social organization. *American Journal of Sociology*, *122*, 1939–1988.

Bursik, R.J. (1999). The informal control of crime through neighborhood networks. *Sociological Focus*, *32*, 85–97.

Butts, C.T. (2002). Predictability of large-scale spatially embedded networks. In R. Breiger, K.M. Carley & P. Pattison (Eds.), *Dynamic social network modeling and analysis: workshop summary and papers* (pp. 313–323). National Academies Press.

Butts, C.T. (2008). Social networks: a methodological introduction. *Asian Journal of Social Psychology*, *11*.

Butts, C.T., & Acton, R.M. (2011). Spatial modeling of social networks. In T.L. Nyerges, H. Couclelis & R. McMaster (Eds.), *The Sage handbook of GIS and society* (pp. 222–250). Sage.

Butts, C.T., Acton, R.M., Hipp, J.R., & Nagle, N.N. (2011). Geographical variability and network structure. *Social Networks*, *34*, 82–100.

Butts, C.T., Hipp, J.R., Nagle, N.N., Boessen, A., Acton, R.M., Marcum, C.S., & Lickfett, J. (2014). American Social Fabric Study. Survey dataset.

Caplow, T., & Forman, R. (1950). Neighborhood interaction in a homogeneous community. *American Sociological Review*, *15*, 357–366.

Daraganova, G., Pattison, P., Koskinen, J., Mitchell, B., Bill, A., Watts, M., & Baum, S. (2012). Networks and geography: modelling community network structures as the outcome of both spatial and network processes. *Social Networks*, *34*, 6–17.

Doreian, P., & Conti, N. (2012). Social context, spatial structure and social network structure. *Social Networks*, *34*, 32–46.

Emch, M., Root, E.D., Giebultowicz, S., Ali, M., Perez-Heydrich, C., & Yunus, M. (2012). Integration of spatial and social network analysis in disease transmission studies. *Annals of the Association of American Geographers. Association of American Geographers*, *105*, 1004–1015.

Entwisle, B., Faust, K., Rindfuss, R.R., & Kaneda, T. (2007). Networks and contexts: variation in the structure of social ties. *American Journal of Sociology*, *112*, 1495–1533.

Faust, K., Entwisle, B., Rindfuss, R.R., Walsh, S.J., & Sawangdeed, Y. (1999). Spatial arrangement of social and economic networks among villages in Nang Rong District, Thailand. *Social Networks*, *21*, 311–337.

Festinger, L., Schachter, S., & Back, K. (1950). *Social pressures in informal groups*. Stanford University Press.

Firestone, S.M., Ward, M.P., Christley, R.M., & Dhand, N.K. (2011). The importance of location in contact networks: describing early epidemic spread using spatial social network analysis. *Preventive Veterinary Medicine*, 102, 185–195.

Gibbons, J., Nara, A., & Appleyard, B. (2017). Exploring the imprint of social media networks on neighborhood community through the lens of gentrification. *Environment and Planning B: Urban Analytics and City Science*, 45, 470–488.

Graif, C., Freelin, B.N., Kuo, Y.-H., Wang, H., Li, Z., & Kifer, D. (2019). Network spillovers and neighborhood crime: a computational statistics analysis of employment-based networks of neighborhoods. *Justice Quarterly*, 38(2), 344–374.

Grannis, R. (2009). *From the ground up: translating geography into community through neighbor networks*. Princeton University Press.

Hipp, J.R., Boessen, A., Butts, C.T., Nagle, N.N., & Smith, E.J. (2023). "The Spatial Distribution of Neighborhood Safety Ties: Consequences for Perceived Collective Efficacy?" *Journal of Urban Affairs* https://doi.org/10.1080/07352166.2023.2192940

Hipp, J.R., Butts, C.T., Acton, R.M., Nagle, N.N., & Boessen, A. (2013). Extrapolative simulation of neighborhood networks based on population spatial distribution: do they predict crime? *Social Networks*, 35, 614–625.

Hipp, J.R., Faris, R.W., & Boessen, A. (2012). Measuring 'neighborhood': constructing network neighborhoods. *Social Networks*, 34, 128–140.

Hipp, J.R., & Perrin, A.J. (2009). The simultaneous effect of social distance and physical distance on the formation of neighborhood ties. *City and Community*, 8, 5–25.

Illenberger, J., Nagel, K., & Flötteröd, G. (2012). The role of spatial interaction in social networks. *Networks and Spatial Economics*, 13, 255–282.

Jose, R., Hipp, J.R., Butts, C.T., Wang, C., & Lakon, C.M. (2016). Network structure, influence, selection and delinquent behavior: unpacking a dynamic process. *Criminal Justice and Behavior*, 43, 264–284.

Latané, B., Liu, J.H., Nowak, A., Bonevento, M., & Long Zheng, L. (1995). Distance matters: physical space and social impact. *Personality and Social Psychology Bulletin*, 21, 795–805.

Lee, J.Y., & Kwan, M.-P. (2010). Visualisation of socio-spatial isolation based on human activity patterns and social networks in space-time. *Tijdschrift voor Economische en Sociale Geografie*, 102, 468–485.

Luo, X.I., Hipp, J.R., & Butts, C.T. (2022). Does the spatial distribution of social ties impact neighborhood and city attachment? Differentials among urban/rural contexts. *Social Networks*, 68, 374–385.

Martin, D.G. (2003). Enacting neighborhood. *Urban Geography*, 24, 361–385.

Mouw, T., & Entwisle, B. (2006). Residential segregation and interracial friendship in schools. *American Journal of Sociology*, 112, 394–441.

Oldenburg, R. (1999). *The great good place: cafes, coffee shops, bookstores, bars, hair salons, and other hangouts at the heart of a community*. Paragon House.

Papachristos, A.V., Hureau, D.M., & Braga, A.A. (2013). The corner and the crew: the influence of geography and social networks on gang violence. *American Sociological Review*, 78, 417–447.

Phillips, N.E., Levy, B.L., Sampson, R.J., Small, M.L., & Wang, R.Q. (2019). The social integration of american cities: network measures of connectedness based on everyday mobility across neighborhoods. *Sociological Methods and Research*, 004912411985238.

Preciado, P., Snijders, T.A., Burk, W.J., Stattin, H., & Kerr, M. (2012). Does proximity matter? Distance dependence of adolescent friendships. *Social Networks*, 34, 18–31.

Radil, S.M., Flint, C., & Tita, G.E. (2010). Spatializing social networks: using social network analysis to investigate geographies of gang rivalry, territorially, and violence in Los Angeles. *Annals of the Association of American Geographers*, 100, 307–326.

Ratti, C., Sobolevsky, S., Calabrese, F., Andris, C., Reades, J., Martino, M., Claxton, R., & Strogatz, S.H. (2010). Redrawing the map of Great Britain from a network of human interactions. *PLOS One*, 5, 1–6.

Sampson, R.J. (2004). Networks and neighbourhoods: the implications of connectivity for thinking about crime in the modern city. In H. McCarthy, P. Miller & P. Skidmore (Eds.), *Network logic: who governs in an interconnected world?* (pp. 157–166). Demos.

Sarkar, D., Andris, C., Chapman, C.A., & Sengupta, R. (2019). Metrics for characterizing network structure and node importance in spatial social networks. *International Journal of Geographical Information Science*, 33, 1017–1039.

Schaefer, D.R. (2012). Youth co-offending networks: an investigation of social and spatial effects. *Social Networks*, 34, 141–149.

Small, M.L., & Adler, L. (2019). The role of space in the formation of social ties. *Annual Review of Sociology*, 45, 111–132.

Smith, E.J., Butts, C.T., Marcum, C., Hipp, J.R., Almquist, Z., Nagle, N.N., & Boessen, A. (2015). The relationship of age to personal network size, relational multiplexity, and proximity to alters in the western United States. *Journal of Gerontology: Social Sciences*, 70, 91–99.

Thomas, L.J., Huang, P., Yin, F., Luo, X.I., Almquist, Z,W., Hipp, J.R., & Butts, C.T. (2020). Spatial heterogeneity can lead to substantial local variations in Covid-19 timing and severity. *Proceedings of the National Academy of Sciences*, 117.

Thomas, L.J., Huang, P., Yin, F., Xu, J., Almquist, Z.W., Hipp, J.R., & Butts, C.T. (2022). Geographical patterns of social cohesion drive disparities in early Covid infection hazard. *Proceedings of the National Academy of Sciences*, 119.

Tita, G., & Radil, S. (2011). Spatializing the social networks of gangs to explore patterns of violence. *Journal of Quantitative Criminology*, 27, 521–545.

Verdery, A.M., Entwisle, B., Faust, K., & Rindfuss, R.R. (2012). Social and spatial networks: kinship distance and dwelling unit proximity in rural Thailand. *Social Networks*, 34, 112–127.

Wong, L.H., Pattison, P., & Robins, G. (2006). A spatial model for social networks. *Physica A: Statistical Mechanics and its Applications*, 360, 99–120.

Social Network Data Collection: Principles and Modalities*

jimi adams and Miranda Lubbers

INTRODUCTION

Relational questions require relational data and methods. That may seem like a truism that is unnecessary to make explicit, but the social and behavioural sciences are replete with relational theories (Borgatti & Halgin, 2011) and questions that have repeatedly been examined with data that make essentialising assumptions (Emirbayer, 1997) – that is, they rely on *non*-relational data.

There are numerous potential reasons for this disconnect. First, disciplines carry strong methodological norms that do not readily incorporate relational theoretical perspectives, ranging from those that focus on desirable features of data (e.g., the 'large nationally representative samples' that predominate in many corners of sociology; Martin, 2017) to those that prioritise particular analytic dimensions (e.g., the preoccupation with causal identification within some domains of economics and political science; Mogstad & Torgovitsky, 2018) and those that prioritise internal validity or demand experimental control (e.g., in many lab-driven fields; Falk & Heckman, 2009). Each of these cases carries (sets of) strong assumptions that require priorities that are incompatible with network approaches, leaving relational questions to be shoe-horned into available models. Second, some have critiqued social network analysis as being 'only a method' and thus not having the conceptual and theoretical range that demands its development and use across the social sciences in the way that those who see *most* social science as foundationally relational might prefer (Borgatti et al., 2009). Third, as is often the case in scientific fields, theory, data, and analytic capabilities often develop in trajectories that are not well synced with one another, such that the advances in one domain get out well ahead of the others (Lakatos, 1978). Said more positively, we may just be at an opportune point in the life course of social network research when rethinking the approaches to social network data collection is especially needed. Fourth is pragmatic; network data are often demanding to gather, and even more difficult to do well (adams, 2019; McCarty et al., 2019). Therefore, if researchers can get away without those added burdens, they will frequently opt to avoid them.

Despite these potential barriers, we take as given that network research offers a range of unique theoretical, empirical, and other contributions, which

---

*"The authors contributed equally"

warrant well-designed strategies to collect and analyse social network data.[1] Therefore, our focus here is to overview the core principles that have governed many primary strategies for approaching that task[2] and illustrate their utility for a range of social and behavioural scientific questions. We first discuss the general principles of collecting network data, and then elaborate on how those principles have been applied in four strategies of network data collection: experiments, surveys and interviews, observation, and trace data.

GENERAL PRINCIPLES OF NETWORK DATA

As noted above, what makes network research unique is the focus on relationships. Contrasting most social sciences that commonly theorise at the levels of individuals, groups, or their aggregations (e.g., by targeting explanations for the associations between various attributes of whichever of those units are a study's focus), social network research shifts its primary gaze to the relationships *between* those units. This focus on relationships in network research implicates several dimensions that entail unique requirements for data collection. In this section, we outline the importance and strategies for addressing those pertaining to: (1) the definition and interpretation of units involved (both the relationships and the nodes), (2) specifying the rules of inclusion for different network elements in what has been labelled as the network *boundary specification problem* (Laumann et al., 1983), along with (3) how each of these can vary across different relationship dimensions, nodesets (also termed 'modes'), levels, and timescales.

First, the definition and interpretation of units involve conceptualising the *type of relationships* we are interested in, which impacts measurement. We often focus on positive relationships, such as collaboration or friendship, but sometimes negative ties (e.g., conflict, disliking) – or their absence – can be as/more influential than positive ties (e.g., support, liking). We can further distinguish: (1) relatively stable relationships ('states', e.g., dislike, knowing someone) from highly changeable and ephemeral ties ('events', e.g., physical contact, soccer passes, sexual encounters, political discussions), (2) objectively estimable relationships (e.g., financial exchanges, text messages) from those that are perceptually oriented (e.g., trust, 'cognitive social structures'); and (3) other *conceptual* distinctions of the types of relationships that matter (e.g., flows, potential/latent ties, etc.; see Borgatti et al., 2009). Shared across this variety is the *relational* nature of each possibility – turning the analytic lens from the units that comprise a population, and their various characteristics, to the spaces between them and the relationships that fill those spaces. Often our understanding of social dynamics via network ideas requires researchers to account for the patterning of when relationships do *not* form, as much as when they do.

We must also define the *type of nodes* involved in those relationships of interest, which affects sampling. Depending on the research questions, they can be any individual or collective social entity that has relationships with others, such as humans, animals, literary characters, teams, organisations, countries, or words.

Second, and related, we need to define the *boundary on the set of relationships and nodes*: where do we draw the line for which of these belong to the network and which do not? The answer affects both sampling and measurement strategies. Historically, network research has fallen into two groups for addressing this question based on the nodesets: networks in bounded settings such as classrooms, organisations, or neighbourhoods (sociocentric networks, or 'networks in a box', Kadushin, 2011, p. 17)[3] versus networks surrounding focal nodes (egocentric or personal networks; see Small & Perry, this volume). In the first case, we study a 'whole' setting, assuming that everyone who belongs to the setting(s) is a network node, seeking to map the relationships among that presumed 'complete' population. In the second case, we focus on an individual, or more commonly, a sample of individuals, and examine the entities with which each focal node has the relationship(s) of interest. The focal node, its network members, their relationships, and, potentially, the relationships among those network members then form the node's (ego-)network.

Notably, the definition of the tie further delimits the set of nodes in an egocentric network. In theory, every person that individuals know could be identified as a network member, but in practice, researchers often focus on stronger ties (e.g., those they feel closest to or trust most) or more particular relationships governing the substantive research focus, thus generating further boundaries on the network (see Brashears & Money, this volume). Additional restrictions on the nodes – for instance, on the minimum age of network members – or the relationships – for instance, regarding their duration (e.g., support given within the past year) – can make the amount of data more manageable.

Apart from sociocentric and egocentric networks, a third strategy recognises that some phenomena of interest entail blurred boundaries. The nodes are not neatly organised in an institutional or geographical setting, as in sociocentric networks, but neither are they centred on individuals, as in ego-centred networks. These have been labelled *partial networks* (Morris, 2004) or *open system networks* (Kadushin, 2011). When there are no clear *a priori* boundaries, they are often delineated by using some type of network sampling (e.g., Mouw & Verdery, 2012), such that they start with the egocentric networks of a few 'seeds', and then the contacts of these seeds are also invited to participate and so on, until producing a representation of the overall network. Other times, when a partial network is embedded in systems for which digital trace data exist (e.g., social media platforms), the network is created by limiting the geographical area of nodes, the time span of contents, and/or the topics discussed.

Third, networks can be 'multilayered'; they can simultaneously entail more than one type of ties, one type of nodes, or one time point. Research can focus on a single type of relationship or study how different types of relationships interact (e.g., liking and disliking, or advice and information). These are multivariate (or multiplex) networks. Additionally, some studies include two nodesets (or node partitions), such as individuals and organisations, patients and doctors, or Wikipedia entries and editors. This makes the design more complex. If edges can only be formed between nodes of different partitions, the network is called bipartite or two-mode (see Jasny, this volume), such as networks of Wikipedia edits (Keegan & Fiesler, 2017). Even though we only directly observe the connections of people (authors) to entries in this network, we can derive single-mode networks from it, of people who have co-authored Wikipedia entries (people-to-people networks), or networks of entries edited by the same people (entry-to-entry networks). When one type is hierarchically embedded in the other and relationships can be formed between nodes of the same and different levels, we speak of multilevel networks (see Lazega & Wang, this volume).[4] For instance, we may study to what degree individuals working in a set of organisations collaborate with one another, within and between organisations, and whether the formal collaboration ties among organisations shape such interactions. Furthermore, researchers may study relationships at one time point, or longitudinally (in continuous or discrete time; see Snijders, this volume). Especially when investigating event-like relationships, collecting longitudinal data allows us to follow network changes over time, which inform us better about its functioning than a 'snapshot' of the network (see Contractor & Schecter, this volume).

MODES OF DATA COLLECTION

Building on the common principles described above, we now introduce the main methods used for data collection in social network research: experiments, surveys and interviews, observation, and behavioural trace data. We highlight their unique contributions, subtypes, and design decisions – along with some examples.

Experiments

Experiments are ideal for analysing the causal mechanisms underlying social influence or selection processes and have been used for decades for network research (e.g., Bavelas & Barrett, 1951). Other data collection modes mostly show associations between networks and behaviours, but are less suitable for explicitly demonstrating causation.[5] Suppose we observe that highly central people in a collaboration network use more technological devices for their work, such as earphone translators or collaboration software. We may postulate that this is caused by social selection on the variable of interest: people are drawn towards technologically savvy users, which explains their centrality. However, alternative explanations (cf. Shalizi & Thomas, 2011) include social selection on other variables (people are drawn to higher-ranked individuals, who also have the money to buy more gadgets), diffusion (highly central people may receive much more information about the benefits of such devices than less central people, and thus adopt them more often) or adaptation to the same environment (people in similarly central network positions have to manage many social relationships, and doing so is easier with devices). Experiments help determine causal mechanisms and are important tools for theory formation.

The *randomised controlled trial* (RCT) is often seen as the 'gold standard' experimental design. In RCTs, researchers randomly assign individuals to either the experimental or the control condition without telling them which condition they are assigned to, to control potentially confounding variables. The difference between these two conditions is how the independent (explanatory) variable is manipulated. The effect of the independent (predictor) on the dependent (outcome) variable is measured by comparing the treatment to the control groups (through surveys, observation, or trace data). In network experiments, networks can be the independent variable – when studying network effects – or the dependent variable – when studying network formation. Often, the dependent variable is measured at least once pre- and once post-intervention.

We can distinguish four types of network experiments based on their setting (see Table 40.1). First, network experiments have been conducted in semi-controlled, 'natural' environments (field experiments) and fully controlled environments (lab experiments). Field experiments focus on existing network structures and are, therefore, more realistic. Lab experiments tend to construct networks artificially, but they can control confounding variables better. Second, we can distinguish between offline and online experiments for each type. The emergence of online platforms such as Facebook or Amazon Mechanical Turk, and the possibilities of customising aspects of these environments and following behaviours in real time have incited new experimental research.

Let us illustrate each quadrant of Table 40.1 with recent examples using RCT designs. An example of *offline field experiments* (quadrant 1) is Paluck et al.'s (2016) study of the effect of a peer-to-peer anti-conflict intervention in middle schools. The researchers hypothesised that the intervention would reduce conflict behaviour, particularly if the selected peers were highly central in the networks (*social referents*). To test this, they randomly assigned 56 schools to experimental or control conditions. In both conditions, they measured peer networks through a survey at the beginning (before randomisation) and the end of the school year. In the experimental condition, a small portion of students were selected to serve as 'seeds' for the intervention; they met biweekly with trained research assistants to identify conflict behaviours in their school and take a public stance against conflicts. The intervention reduced conflict behaviour substantially, with social referent seeds being most effective.

An illustration of *online field experiments* (quadrant 2) is Bond and colleagues' (2012) study of how political behaviour spreads on Facebook and whether strong ties influence the spread more than weak ties. On the US congressional election day in 2010, they conducted an experiment with all 61 million adult US Facebook users, assigning them randomly to one of three conditions. In the social transmission condition, users received a message shown at the top of their news feed, which encouraged them to vote, displayed a link to information about nearby polling places, presented a button users could click to indicate that they had voted, and showed the IDs of up to six Facebook friends who had already clicked the 'I voted' button alongside the total number of friends who had done so. The second condition similarly encouraged users to vote but did not show the profile pictures or the number of Facebook friends who had voted. Participants in the control condition did not receive any targeted messages. The researchers captured digital trace data of the networks and behaviours, and validated voting behaviours with public voting records. As hypothesised, results showed that social transmission was more effective than encouragement alone, particularly through strong ties.

These first two cases captured 'naturally' occurring networks. In contrast, the following two examples address lab experiments in artificially created networks. An example of *offline lab experiments* (quadrant 3) is Traeger and colleagues' (2020) study of how social robots shape interactions among people (here, networks were the dependent variable). Participants came to an on-site lab and filled in a pre-test survey. Then, they were randomly assigned to groups of three accompanied by a humanoid social robot, the fourth participant. Each group (51 in total) engaged in 30 rounds of a collaborative game. In the vulnerable condition, the robot made vulnerable utterances at the end of each round and admitted its own mistakes; in the neutral condition, it made neutral utterances and did not admit mistakes. In the control condition, the robot was silent. Researchers observed speaking time and directionality, and also measured group perceptions. Participants spoke more with one another (for all three dyads), had more balanced speaking times and perceived their group more positively in the vulnerable condition, showing that robots can effectively alter group behaviour.

Centola's (2010) examination of how network structure affects the spread of behaviours provides an example of *online lab experiments* (quadrant 4). While small-world networks diffuse information or

Table 40.1 Typology of experiments in terms of their setting

Experiments	Offline	Online
Field (semi-controlled; natural)	1. Physical world experiments, intervention studies *Example*: Paluck et al., 2016	2. Experiments (or interventions) on existing online platforms or virtual worlds *Example*: Bond et al., 2012
Lab (fully controlled; artificial)	3. Experiments in an onsite lab *Example*: Traeger et al. 2020	4. Experiments in a virtual lab *Example*: Centola, 2010

germs more rapidly than locally highly clustered networks, Centola hypothesised that this does not hold for complex contagion, when people need contact with multiple adopters to adopt a behaviour. To test this, he constructed a health forum accessible only to invited users. The 1,528 participants were recruited from health-interest websites and created profiles on the platform, then were each randomly assigned to one of two conditions. In one condition, the network had a clustered-lattice structure; in the other, part of the clustered-lattice structure was randomly rewired based on the small-world model. All participants had the same number of contacts in the network (*network buddies*), whose behaviours were visible to them. They could not contact their buddies nor create new ties, so the structure was fixed. Then, a randomly selected participant in each condition was informed about an information-rich health forum website (which Centola also maintained) and encouraged to register. Centola followed the dissemination of this information in real time and found that it spread faster and farther in the clustered-lattice structure than in the small-world structure, confirming his hypothesis.

The range of these network experiments demonstrates the field's diversity. Apart from the setting, the manipulated network element varies across studies: Paluck et al. (2016) manipulated the behaviours of a randomly selected set of nodes (a *peer encouragement design*; Aral, 2016), Traeger et al. (2020) the network context (*settings design*; Aral, 2016), Bond et al. (2012) the information that flows through ties (*mechanisms design*; Aral, 2016) and Centola (2010) the network structure (*structural design*; Aral, 2016). The manipulation creates the exogenous variation needed to establish causality.

Not all network experiments use full-fledged RCT designs, however. Some manipulate a variable to make it measurable or salient but do not use control groups or random assignment. Milgram's (1967) famous small-world experiment is a good example. Milgram asked participants to pass a letter to a target stranger, but only via acquaintances who might either know this person or a person who might know them, and counted the number of intermediaries required for letters that reached the target. Some researchers also cleverly use external events such as a natural disaster to study network formation, comparing it with similar settings where the event did not happen (Phan & Airoldi, 2015) – a natural experiment.

Surveys and Interviews

While perceptions of science often *assume* experimental designs, other designs are more common for studying social networks. Survey and interview-based approaches have a much longer and more detailed history in the social-scientific study of networks (adams, 2019; Marsden, 1990), even in psychology, where experiments are generally highly prioritised (Neal, 2020). Before digging into some of the practicalities of how surveys and interviews have been used to study social networks, it may be helpful to briefly examine why survey and interview methods predominate.

The Thomas and Thomas theorem ('If [people] define situations as real, they are real in their consequences') remains as central to the social sciences today as it was when initially stated in 1928. In part, this is because *perceptions* of social reality can be as important for explaining social and behavioural outcomes as their 'objective' reality. This often leads researchers to prioritise talking to research participants about their social relationships – whether in structured ways through surveys, or more flexible interview techniques. Moreover, some of the most concretely theorised relationships within social networks research (friendship, liking/disliking, esteem, social support) are fundamentally perceptions rather than externally identifiable (Fischer, 1982), thus *necessitating* data collection via surveys or interviews. Finally, even those relationships that have the potential for external validation (e.g., sexual contact, financial exchanges, migration flows) are not always empirically accessible or precisely recordable in the ways researchers desire, thus requiring the use of various proxies for estimating the presence/absence of such relationships (adams, 2019; Kitts, 2014).

As such, whether seeking to collect data on objectively observable ties or perceptions of more subjective relationships, asking respondents has been a foundational strategy for eliciting such data throughout the field's history (adams, 2019; Marsden, 2011; McCarty et al., 2019). Within survey and interview-based strategies, several design considerations require adaptations to the particular needs of *network* data.

In social network surveys, the type of relationship asked about is commonly labelled the type of *name generator* question used (i.e., for what type of relationship are we recording reported partners?). Name generator questions are complemented with a battery of *name interpreter* questions, which are follow-up questions about the characteristics of the named partners (especially in the case of egocentric networks where such information is not gained from the network partners themselves), such as their gender or race, and the relationships with these partners, such as tie strength or duration. In egocentric networks, *name interconnector* questions (Borgatti et al., 2013) may be added that enquire about the perceived relationships *among* a respondent's network partners.

Survey (and interview) researchers are typically quite well attuned to the dual concerns of measurement and sampling considerations as their evaluation and validation are primary concerns in many fields. Evaluations of network data have therefore often taken the form of assessing the agreement between self-reports and external sources of validation (Killworth & Bernard, 1976) or – given the potential for network data to be reported by both partners – comparisons between these multiple reports (adams & Moody, 2007; An, 2022). Generally, these studies find that more precision in questions and higher investment in the behaviour/relationship examined reduces measurement errors and biases.

Measurement considerations have also led studies to examine the overlaps (and divergences) that arise from using different question prompts to elicit network data. For example, Marin and Hampton (2007) showed that a range of commonly employed general name generators elicit different sets of confidants from respondents that overlap only partially. Using a complementary set of multiple name generators that measure the same relational dimension can therefore help reduce measurement bias. Furthermore, researchers have experimented with ways to lower the respondent burden caused by the repetitive questions of name interpreters and interconnectors, by either keeping such questions at a minimum or asking some questions for a sample of ties rather than for all ties (cf. McCarty et al., 2019). Studies have further investigated survey mode and interviewer effects (e.g., An, 2022).

As noted above, because of the boundary specification problem in networks research, the nomination of partners is not *only* a question of measurement, but can also determine the sampling strategy for a study. Particularly in link-tracing (or 'partial') network designs, nominated partners can, in turn, become a device for further sampling from the population of interest, by recruiting them as subsequent study participants. This approach has been formalised in strategies like respondent-driven sampling (Heckathorn & Cameron, 2017) and network sampling with memory (Mouw & Verdery, 2012). These strategies seek to optimise the capacity for statistical inference by specifying particular rules for determining which links are followed to generate a study sample.

Survey network research has a long history and has been conducted in many formats (evolving across time from face-to-face to pencil-and-paper, phone, internet, etc.), with particular adaptations to more secure and private options when the data sought are especially sensitive (Szinovacz & Egley, 1995). While technological advances play some role in shaping those options and preferences, the theoretical and practical enhancements that such developments have fostered are also worth noting.

Network data collection on digital platforms (whether on local laptops or tablets or administered via online portals) illustrates how these developments can accomplish multiple aims at once. Practically, via back-end programming, these approaches encode the data *while they are being collected* in formats that facilitate rapid analysis and minimise (but do not eliminate entirely) the need for data coding and cleaning. Moreover, the potential for interactive approaches within these strategies can reduce respondent burden and enhance respondents' survey experience, which improves the quality of the resulting data (McCarty et al., 2019). One recent example of such digital platforms is Network Canvas, which flexibly elicits a range of respondent attributes, name generators, interpreters and interconnectors – each interactively leveraging these empirically demonstrated benefits (Birkett et al., 2021). For example, in a study of black men who have sex with men and transgender persons, Network Canvas was found to be intuitive and useful for eliciting highly sensitive relational data (Crawford et al., 2021).

Surveys that include network modules draw on many of the demonstrated benefits of survey research in general – including standardised prompts allowing for comparability across respondents and within respondents over time, and capacity for measurement validation and replication across studies. However, as noted earlier, this pursuit of objective measures as the 'gold standard' often belies the importance of social actors' understanding and interpretation of their own relationships to faithfully examining social phenomena. As such, there are both: (1) calls for survey and interview researchers to increasingly (re-) focus on the *meaning* (and not just the structuring) of social relationships (adams, 2019) and (2) other methods with long histories and recent developments that prioritise these aims in their approaches to gathering social network data.

Regarding the first point, social network researchers increasingly use more open, *qualitative interviewing* strategies to enquire about social networks, either alone or in combination with structured network elicitation. In addition to focusing on individuals' understanding and interpretation of their own networks, qualitative interviewing is also suitable for exploring network formation and individuals' agency in networks, and why networks matter in their lives (see Hollstein, this volume). Qualitative interviews can also help validate data obtained with structured interviewing. Regarding the second point, the following sections will elaborate on methods that prioritise both more 'objective' and interpretive elements of measurement.

Observation

While surveys and interviews are the most common modes of social network data collection, they are not always the best choice. For instance, they are not viable for research with subjects that cannot read or reflect on relationships, such as young children (e.g., Martin et al., 2005) or animals (e.g., Mann et al., 2012; Rushmore et al., 2013). Furthermore, surveys may not capture behaviours reliably. For instance, humans are typically good at recalling routinised interactions but easily forget more fleeting or less recent interactions (e.g., Killworth & Bernard, 1976). In addition, behaviours are situated in contexts, and when abstracted from these contexts, *accounts* of behaviour are often inconsistent with behaviour (Jerolmack & Khan, 2014). Observation may be a better alternative in these cases when the ties are observable interactions or transactions.

Like surveys, observation has been used since the origins of social network research. For instance, Bott (1928) and Hagman (1933) observed social interactions among preschool children. Each day, Bott chose one child in the group and recorded its interactions with the other children. Hagman compared her observation of children's interactions with the children's recall of the same interactions – a forerunner of informant accuracy studies (e.g., Killworth & Bernard, 1976).

As with surveys and interviews, we can distinguish between structured (or systematic) and unstructured (ethnographic) observation. For *systematic observation*, researchers face partially the same decisions regarding the network boundary problem as in surveys. First, they must define the ties they want to observe. For instance, what counts as an interaction among children, regarding content, time, or directionality? When a child plays alongside another but not *with* them, does it count as an interaction? Second, researchers must define who belongs to the network. For instance, they can observe interactions among preschool children in the classroom and thus sample whole classes, but if they are more interested in unstructured play, they could also sample children and study their ego-centred networks on playgrounds or playdates. For animals, researchers often delineate a geographical area or follow a community and adopt a threshold for the minimal number of sightings needed before the animal counts as belonging to the focal population. Researchers must also decide what other aspects of the interactions to observe (e.g., type, contact duration).

These decisions ultimately depend on the research questions, as well as on equipment, available time and team size.

Researchers relying on observation need to design measurement procedures that lower the complexity of observing a group of people over a prolonged period. Given the sheer volume of simultaneously occurring interactions, they must make choices in what to record, often by sampling on nodes and/or time. For nodes, they may focus on either one subject at a time (*focal sampling*; see the example of Bott at the start of this section) or the entire group (*all occurrence sampling*). For time, they may record networks continuously for a specific duration (*sequence sampling*) or observe the subject or group at set intervals (i.e., *scan sampling*), among other possibilities. For instance, Rushmore et al. (2013) observed a wild chimpanzee community in Uganda for nine months. Each morning, they randomly selected a chimpanzee and followed them for ten hours, scanning their company every 15 minutes. Given earlier primate research, they conceptualised being at a distance of up to 50 metres as contact, and up to 5 metres as close contact. In research among preschoolers, Martin et al. (2005) combined two procedures. On the one hand, they cycled through a randomly ordered list of names, observing each child for 10 seconds before continuing with the next name on the list. They paused for 5 minutes at the end of the list and then started again, recording the focal child's company, behaviours and affective expressions. On the other hand, they used focal observations centering 10 minutes on the same child to observe its actions and the responses of its interaction partners. Coding protocols are typically completed for each subject-time unit and are as structured as surveys.

Technological advances have dramatically augmented the possibilities of systematic observation. Wearable sensors and tracking devices are increasingly used to record interactions, amplifying the details researchers can capture. While we elaborate digital trace data below, here we address how researchers have strategically deployed them in observational designs. For instance, Mastrandrea et al. (2015) had students of one French high school wear sensor-containing badges, which captured when pairs of students were within 1–1.5 metres of one another, facing one another for at least 20 seconds. From those observations, the researchers inferred contact, recording more than 67,000 contact events in one week. Comparing these data with contact diaries completed by the same students, they found that the sensors reflected short contacts much better than the diaries, although the latter accurately presented the network's backbone. Tracking devices log the exact location of individuals at all times and, when given to a bounded group, they capture who is within range of whom at what times. Animal social network researchers have similarly used GPS trackers, sometimes enhanced with accelerometers or heartbeat monitors, and radiofrequency identification detection systems (Smith & Pinter-Wollman, 2021).

Researchers examining human networks have also used mobile phone apps (e.g., Keil et al., 2020). These include professional conference apps (de Vaan & Wang, 2020), which track the location of each conference attendee and allow them to contact each other on the app. Some mobile phone apps allow researchers to ask participants at set times (using alarms) to enter the names of the people with whom they interact and further information about these interactions, such as type of contact, duration and quality. They are a viable alternative to pen-and-paper contact diaries (Fu, 2007). While these technological advances augment the granularity of observation data, they can be costly and involve technological challenges (e.g., battery life), and not all capture the nature or context of interactions, although combining them with human observation can offset this last challenge (Smith & Pinter-Wollman, 2021).

Unstructured (ad libitum) and *ethnographic observation* have also long been used to study social networks (e.g., Loomis, 1941), either alone or complementing interview and survey data. Ethnographers tend to focus on communities, and relationships are integral to communities. Their long-term immersion in a field allows ethnographers to gain trust within the community and observe relationships and interactions naturally onsite, in real time and in changing conditions. In contrast to structured observation, ethnographers may not predefine who belongs to the network or what constitutes a tie. Furthermore, they do not use predetermined protocols but record what they believe is most relevant for their research questions, in a more free-flowing format. Nonetheless, as in structured observation, they cannot observe everything. Ethnographers' attention is also focused on their research questions, but, more broadly, they pay attention to events or behaviours among individuals, across situations, and over time – behaviours that affirm their hypotheses but also those that challenge them. They observe how the behaviours or events are situated in the physical and cultural context, and how informants' perceptions of them (*emic*) deviate from the ethnographer's interpretation (*etic*). This open, typically inductive focus engenders the element of surprise, allowing for discovering unforeseen network patterns and practices.

As a recent example, Torres (2019) interviewed older adults in a New York City neighbourhood about their core discussion ties while also observing her participants in coffee shops and other neighbourhood sites during five years of fieldwork. Ethnographic observation showed that many ties defied the strong tie–weak tie binary. Torres called these ties 'elastic' – they were both strong, providing social support, and weak, as the participants kept their distance by gossiping or not recalling their acquaintances' names. These novel insights could only be gained with an inductive, multipronged, exploratory approach.

When encounters among informants increasingly occur online, ethnographers have also entered digital spaces, using virtual or digital ethnography or *netnography*, often complementing ethnography in physical sites. Digital ethnography is related to digital trace data (discussed below) but focuses more on how virtual communities emerge, the contents of interactions, their meaning and the formation of identities in such groups. In some cases, digital ethnography is complemented with network visualisation. For instance, Cottica et al. (2020) used semantic networks (see González-Bailón & Shugars, this volume) to analyse the contents of discussions in an online forum, and Akemu and Abdelnour (2020) visualised email exchanges in an organisation (trace data) among workers seated in different areas in the organisation (*ethnographic observation*).

Ethnographic observation has received comparatively less attention in social network scholarship, but it has been vital to understanding networks (Lubbers & Molina, 2021). It has detected culturally salient relationship categories and their basic properties and explored individual agency in networks (i.e., networking practices or relational work), long-term network dynamics, and networks' embeddedness in larger contexts. Ethnography is, however, a highly intensive mode of data collection for both researchers and participants, in stark contrast to the mode we will discuss next.

Behavioural Trace Data

Many of the principles underpinning ethnographic observational approaches to gathering social network data have also motivated the recent proliferation of more passively collected 'bread crumb' varieties of network data, especially those available through digital platforms (see, e.g., Salganik, 2019). Thus, the fourth mode of data collection we address is harvesting the traces of human behaviours, or as Paxton and Griffiths (2017, p. 1631) called them, 'wild' data. With their proliferation, behavioural trace data have become a rich resource for network researchers. Many of these data are timestamped (i.e., event-based, longitudinal data) and some are geolocated.

We can again distinguish between data about offline and online behaviours. *Trace data about offline behaviours* can be extracted from (offline or online) historical archive records (e.g., Bloch et al., 2022), population register data (Van der Laan et al., 2022), newspaper archives for discourse and policy networks (Nagel & Satoh, 2019), epidemiological contact tracing data for Covid-19 contagion (Hâncean et al., 2020), Scopus or Web of Science records for co-authorship (Akbaritabar & Barbato, 2021), policy event descriptions (Pal & Spence, 2020), or national statistics for networks of flows among countries (Danchev & Porter, 2018), to name but a few options. Many of these data sources are digitised, facilitating research (see, e.g., McLevey & McIlroy-Young, 2017). Furthermore, several authors have proposed automated extraction methods, for instance, using *natural language processing* (Bloch et al., 2022), decreasing some burdens of the task, though increasing others.

Trace data on online behaviours have become abundant. The website 'internet live stats',[6] curated by the Real Time Statistics Project, gives an instant idea of the thousands of Tweets, Instagram and tumblr posts sent, skype calls made and YouTube videos viewed, and the millions of emails sent globally *in just a single second*. Many of these data contain relational information, as people like, respond to, or re-Tweet, for instance. Other online communities (e.g., gaming communities, crowdfunding sites) also continuously produce digital trace data on networks, which researchers can study (Bainbridge, 2007).

When using trace data, it is crucial to know the system that has generated the data thoroughly to ensure construct validity and reliability: what does the system afford users to do (and not do), how do users adopt the system, have the algorithms or use changed over time, how does the system archive interactions? Furthermore, researchers must still specify the network boundaries, even if this occurs implicitly. For example, node and edge types are sometimes determined by the type of data, but researchers need to clearly determine boundaries on the set of nodes they include in their analysis. While trace data may be sociocentric, the networks are often so large that researchers limit the set by defining, for instance, geographical, temporal, or topic-related boundaries (González-Bailón et al., 2014).

Despite their abundance, these data also come with some caveats that must be addressed. A disadvantage of trace data is that important sociodemographic attributes and outcome variables are often unavailable. Furthermore, it may be difficult to gauge how representative data are of larger populations of ties or nodes. In addition, extracting unambiguous network data from records can be labour-intensive, depending on the type of data. The documents have typically not been created for research and, in many cases, relations are embedded in texts (with qualitative meaning), and the contents may be unclear, difficult to code systematically, prone to errors, or contain missing data. It may also be challenging to disambiguate nodes, as some users have multiple accounts, and some accounts are operated by bots. Thus, while behavioural trace data are promising for collecting data on large-scale, naturally occurring networks, their cleaning and validation need substantial work (termed 'entity resolution'; Young et al., 2016).

FINAL CONSIDERATIONS

We focused on the main modes and types of social network data collection, ignoring less conventional modes such as contact diaries (Fu, 2007). We have not discussed mixed-methods designs, which combine multiple modes of data collection simultaneously or sequentially (e.g., quantitative methods followed by qualitative methods, or vice versa; e.g., Small, 2011). Promising possibilities for mixing data include 'data linkage', where, for instance, survey participants are asked to give their social media accounts and consent to their analysis, and combining 'big' and 'thick' data – that is, digital trace data with in-depth interviews with selected nodes. This illustrates how data collection is a highly creative puzzle involving the choice of modes, their combination and the many smaller design decisions with myriad possibilities. We have sought to highlight the principles governing choices among these possibilities.

A final consideration concerns the ethical challenges of collecting social network data (Tubaro et al., 2021). Like all social science data, social network data need to be collected with the highest care for ethics, ensuring respect for participants (e.g., confidentiality, informed consent, special protection of vulnerable research participants), beneficence (minimising risks and maximising benefits), and justice in the social distribution of research risks and benefits. Each data collection mode comes with its own challenges, each described at length in general methodology books. A particular though not unique[7] challenge for social network analysis is the collection of data about network members who have *not* given explicit consent to their collection. In sociocentric networks, individuals who did not give their consent are often not placed on rosters of names from which respondents pick their nominations. This omission introduces methodological problems, as the group's network structure may not be adequately represented if persons are missing from the analysis (see Krause & Huisman, this volume); whether they are highly central or peripheral in the network changes the group's network structure considerably. In egocentric networks, we are typically not interested in identifying network members, but rather in understanding their attributes, the characteristics of the relationships the respondent has with them and the relationships they have with one another. In this case, researchers often reduce ethical problems by asking respondents to use nicknames or initials when nominating network members, rather than their full names. When network members are not personally identifiable, network data become attributes of the respondents (their perceptions of their personal networks), and anonymising respondent data is then sufficient for ensuring confidentiality of network members.

ACKNOWLEDGMENTS

Miranda Lubbers is grateful for the funding of the Catalan Institution for Research and Advanced Studies (ICREA Acadèmia).

Notes

1 If you need more convincing, we point you to conceptual and theoretical chapters elsewhere in this volume (e.g., Prell et al.) or the application to topic(s) of your particular interest below.
2 Coincidentally, one approach we discuss in detail below – ethnographic observation – is among the most primed to incorporate relational conceptualisations into 'standard' research design approaches.
3 While these are frequently referred to as 'whole' or 'complete' networks, the boundary specification and/or data collection practicalities often enforce limitations on how complete they truly are.
4 If the higher-level groups do not have relationships among them, they are also called *multilevel networks*, but in that case the higher-level groups are not nodes.
5 Survey and observation researchers can take certain measures to strengthen their designs in this respect: they can collect additional data to control for the most plausible alternative explanations, longitudinal data, or add qualitative questions to have respondents explain the observed behaviour in their words. While such measures make a stronger case for causation, they may still not provide definitive evidence.
6 www.internetlivestats.com/
7 Surveys enquiring about household members, or students rating their teachers, involve similar problems.

REFERENCES

adams, j. (2020). *Gathering social network data*. Sage.
adams, j., & Moody, J. (2007). To tell the truth: measuring concordance in multiply reported network data. *Social Networks*, 29(1), 44–58.
Akemu, O., & Abdelnour, S. (2020). Confronting the digital: doing ethnography in modern organizational settings. *Organizational Research Methods*, 23(2), 296–321.
Akbaritabar, A., & Barbato, G. (2021). An internationalised Europe and regionally focused Americas: a network analysis of higher education studies. *European Journal of Education*, 56(2), 219–234.
An, W. (2022). You said, they said: a framework on informant accuracy with application to studying self-reports and peer-reports. *Social Networks*, 70, 187–197.
Aral, S. (2016). Networked experiments. In Y. Bramoullé, A. Galeotti & B.W. Rogers (Eds.), *The Oxford handbook of the economics of networks* (pp. 375–411). Oxford University Press.
Bainbridge, W.S. (2007). The scientific research potential of virtual worlds. *Science*, 317(5837), 472–476.
Bavelas, A., & Barrett, D. (1951). An experimental approach to organizational communication. *Personnel*, 27, 386–397.
Birkett, M., Melville, J., Janulis, P., Phillips II, G., Contractor, N., & Hogan, B. (2021). Network Canvas: key decisions in the design of an interviewer assisted network data collection software suite. *Social Networks*, 66, 114–124.
Bloch, A., Vasques Filho, D., & Bojanowski, M. (2022). Networks from archives: reconstructing networks of official correspondence in the early modern Portuguese empire. *Social Networks*, 69, 123–135.
Bond, R.M., Fariss, C.J., Jones, J.J., Kramer, A.D.I., Marlow, C., Settle, J.E., & Fowler, J.H. (2012). A 61-million-person experiment in social influence and political mobilization. *Nature*, 489(7415), 295–298.

Borgatti, S.P., Everett, M.G., & Johnson, J.C. (2013). *Analyzing social networks.* Sage.

Borgatti, S.P., & Halgin, D.S. (2011). On network theory. *Organization Science, 22*(5), 1168–1181.

Borgatti, S.P., Mehra, A., Brass, D.J., & Labianca, G. (2009). Network analysis in the social sciences. *Science, 323*(5916), 892–895.

Bott, H. (1928). Observation of play activities in a nursery school. *Genetic Psychology Monographs, 4,* 44–88.

Centola, D. (2010). The spread of behavior in an online social network experiment. *Science, 329*(5996), 1194–1197.

Cottica, A., Hassoun, A., Manca, M., Vallet, J., & Melançon, G. (2020). Semantic social networks: a mixed methods approach to digital ethnography. *Field Methods, 32*(3), 274–290.

Crawford, N.D., Josma, D., Harrington, K.R.V., Morris, J., Quamina, A., Birkett, M., & Phillips II, G. (2021). Using the think-aloud method to assess the feasibility and acceptability of Network Canvas among black men who have sex with men and transgender persons: qualitative analysis. *JMIR Formative Research, 5*(9), e30237.

Danchev, V., & Porter, M.A. (2018). Neither global nor local: heterogeneous connectivity in spatial network structures of world migration. *Social Networks, 53,* 4–19.

de Vaan, M., & Wang, D. (2020). Micro-structural foundations of network inequality: evidence from a field experiment in professional networking. *Social Networks, 63,* 213–230.

Emirbayer, M. (1997). Manifesto for a relational sociology. *American Journal of Sociology 103*(2), 281–317.

Falk, A., & Heckman, J.J. (2009). Lab experiments are a major source of knowledge in the social sciences. *Science, 326*(5952), 535–538.

Fischer, C.S. (1982). *To dwell among friends: personal networks in town and city.* University of Chicago Press.

Fu, Y.-C. (2007). Contact diaries: building archives of actual and comprehensive personal networks. *Field Methods, 19*(2), 194–217.

González-Bailón, S., Wang, N., Rivero, A., Borge-Holthoefer, J., & Moreno, Y. (2014). Assessing the bias in samples of large online networks. *Social Networks, 38,* 16–27.

Hagman, E.P. (1933). The companionships of preschool children. *University of Iowa Studies in Child Welfare, 7,* 10–69.

Hâncean, M.-G., Perc, M., & Lerner, J. (2020). Early spread of Covid-19 in Romania: imported cases from Italy and human-to-human transmission networks. *Royal Society Open Science, 7,* 200780.

Heckathorn, D.D., & Cameron, J. (2017). Network sampling: from snowball and multiplicity to respondent-driven sampling. *Annual Review of Sociology, 43,* 101–119.

Jerolmack, C., & Khan, S. (2014). Talk is cheap: ethnography and the attitudinal fallacy. *Sociological Methods and Research, 43*(2), 178–209.

Kadushin, C. (2011). *Understanding social networks: theories, concepts, and findings.* Oxford University Press.

Keegan, B., & Fiesler, C. (2017). The evolution and consequences of peer producing Wikipedia's rules. *Preprint SocArXiv* 10.31235/osf.io/28sgr

Keil, T.F., Koschate, M., & Levine, M. (2020). Contact logger: measuring everyday intergroup contact experiences in near-time. *Behavior Research Methods, 52*(4), 1568–1586.

Killworth, P.D., & Bernard, H.R. (1976). Informant accuracy in social network data. *Human Organization, 35*(3), 269–286.

Kitts, J.A. (2014). Beyond networks in structural theories of exchange: promises from computational social science. *Advances in Group Processes, 31,* 263–298.

Lakatos, I. (1978). *The methodology of scientific research programmes.* Vol. 1. Cambridge University Press.

Laumann, E.O., Marsden, P.V., & Prensky, D. (1983). The boundary specification problem in network analysis. In R.S. Burt & M. Minor (Eds.), *Applied network analysis: a methodological introduction* (pp. 18–34). Sage.

Loomis, C.P. (1941). Informal groupings in a Spanish-American village. *Sociometry, 4*(1), 36.

Lubbers, M.J., & Molina, J.L. (2021). The ethnographic study of personal networks. *Etnografia e Ricerca Qualitativa, 14*(2), 185–200.

Mann, J., Stanton, M.A., Patterson, E.M., Bienenstock, E.J., & Singh, L.O. (2012). Social networks reveal cultural behaviour in tool-using dolphins. *Nature Communications, 3*(1), 980.

Marin, A., & Hampton, K.N. (2007). Simplifying the personal network name generator: alternatives to traditional multiple and single name generators. *Field Methods, 19*(2), 163–193.

Marsden, P.V. (2011). Survey Methods for Network Data. In J. Scott & P.J. Carrington (eds.) *The Sage Handbook of Social Network Analysis* (Pp. 370–388). Sage.

Marsden, P.V. (1990). Network data and measurement. *American Review of Sociology, 16,* 435–463.

Martin, J.L. (2017). *Thinking through methods: a social science primer.* University of Chicago Press.

Martin, C.L., Fabes, R.A., Hanish, L.D., & Hollenstein, T. (2005). Social dynamics in the preschool. *Developmental Review, 25*(3–4), 299–327.

Mastrandrea, R., Fournet, J., & Barrat, A. (2015). Contact patterns in a high school: a comparison between data collected using wearable sensors, contact diaries and friendship surveys. *PLOS One*, *10*(9), e0136497.

McCarty, C., Lubbers, M.J., Vacca, R., & Molina, J.L. (2019). *Conducting personal network research: a practical guide*. Guilford Press.

McLevey, J., & McIlroy-Young, R. (2017). Introducing metaknowledge: software for computational research in information science, network analysis, and science of science. *Journal of Informetrics*, *11*(1), 176–197.

Milgram, S. (1967). The small-world problem. *Psychology Today*, *1*(1), 60–67.

Mogstad, M., & Torgovitsky, A. (2018). Identification and extrapolation of causal effects with instrumental variables. *Annual Review of Economics*, *10*, 577–613.

Morris, M. (2004). *Network epidemiology: a handbook for survey design and data collection*. Oxford University Press

Mouw, T., & Verdery, A.M. (2012). Network sampling with memory: a proposal for more efficient sampling from social networks. *Sociological Methodology*, *42*(1), 206–256.

Nagel, M., & Satoh, K. (2019). Protesting iconic megaprojects: a discourse network analysis of the evolution of the conflict over Stuttgart 21. *Urban Studies*, *56*(8), 1681–1700.

Neal, J.W. (2020). A systematic review of social network methods in high impact developmental psychology journals. *Social Development*, *29*(4), 923–944.

Pal, L.A., & Spence, J. (2020). Event-focused network analysis: a case study of anti-corruption networks. *Policy and Society*, *39*(1), 91–112.

Paluck, E.L., Shepherd, H., & Aronow, P.M. (2016). Changing climates of conflict: a social network experiment in 56 schools. *Proceedings of the National Academy of Sciences*, 113(3), 566–571.

Paxton, A., & Griffiths, T.L. (2017). Finding the traces of behavioral and cognitive processes in big data and naturally occurring datasets. *Behavior Research Methods*, *49*(5), 1630–1638.

Phan, T.Q., & Airoldi, E.M. (2015). A natural experiment of social network formation and dynamics. *Proceedings of the National Academy of Sciences*, *112*(21), 6595–6600.

Rushmore, J., Caillaud, D., Matamba, L., Stumpf, R.M., Borgatti, S.P., & Altizer, S. (2013). Social network analysis of wild chimpanzees provides insights for predicting infectious disease risk. *Journal of Animal Ecology*, *82*(5), 976–986.

Salganik, M.A. (2019). *Bit by bit: social research in the digital age*. Princeton University Press.

Shalizi, C.R., & Thomas, A.C. (2011). Homophily and contagion are generically confounded in observational social network studies. *Sociological Methods and Research*, *40*(2), 211–239.

Small, M.L. (2011). How to conduct a mixed methods study: recent trends in a rapidly growing literature. *Annual Review of Sociology*, *37*, 57–68.

Smith, J.E., & Pinter-Wollman, N. (2021). Observing the unwatchable: integrating automated sensing, naturalistic observations and animal social network analysis in the age of big data. *Journal of Animal Ecology*, *90*(1), 62–75.

Szinovacz, M.E., & Egley, L.C. (1995). Comparing one-partner and couple data on sensitive marital behaviors: the case of marital violence. *Journal of Marriage and Family*, *57*(4), 995–1010.

Torres, S. (2019). On elastic ties: distance and intimacy in social relationships. *Sociological Science*, *6*, 235–263.

Traeger, M.L., Sebo, S.S., Jung, M., Scassellati, B., & Christakis, N.A. (2020). Vulnerable robots positively shape human conversational dynamics in a human-robot team. *Proceedings of the National Academy of Sciences*, *117*(12), 6370–6375.

Tubaro, P., Ryan, L., Casilli, A.A., & D'Angelo, A. (2021). Social network analysis: new ethical approaches through collective reflexivity. *Social Networks*, *67*, 1–8.

van der Laan, J., de Jonge, E., Das, M., Te Riele, S., & Emery, T. (2022). A whole population network and its application for the social sciences. *European Sociological Review*, online first. doi.org/10.1093/esr/jcac026

Young, A.M., Rudolph, A.E., Su, A. E., King, L., Jent, S., & Havens, J.R. (2016). Accuracy of name and age data provided about network members in a social network study of people who use drugs: Implications for constructing sociometric networks. *Annals of Epidemiology*, *26*(11), 802–809.

Missing Network Data

Robert W. Krause and Mark Huisman

A problem when conducting network research is that the object of study, usually people or organisations formed by people, is not always willing or capable to fully cooperate with the researcher, leading to no or incomplete information about the participant (or organisation). Incomplete information, or missing data, are often seen as nuisance by researchers, and often treated as such – that is, missing data are mostly ignored. Participants who dropped out of the study are excluded from the analysis or, if at all, only mentioned in the overall response rate. This treatment at best only lowers the power of the statistical analysis and at worst introduces biases into the results.

MISSING DATA MECHANISMS

There are several options available for the treatment of missing data. Rubin (1976) made it clear that it is of fundamental importance to consider the probability distribution of the missingness for an appropriate treatment of missing data in statistical modelling. Rubin defined three types of mechanisms for this probability distribution, which have been translated to the network data context by Huisman and Steglich (2008). Let I be the indicator matrix of whether a tie variable is observed or missing, with $I_{ij} = 1$ if x_{ij} is observed and $I_{ij} = 0$ if x_{ij} is missing. Further we use the convention that u represents the observed part of the data ($I_{ij} = 1$) and v represents the unobserved part of the data ($I_{ij} = 0$). Thus the network x can be reassembled from u and v. With a given network we can define an observation model for $I, f(I \mid x, \zeta)$, which is a probability model for what is and is not observed, depending on the network x and some statistical parameter ζ. Given this specification, three types of mechanisms are defined taking into account the dependencies between the missing and observed data.

First, data are *missing completely at random* (MCAR) if the probability of them to be missing is independent of any observed variable and also independent of the missing values themselves, $f(I \mid u, v, \zeta) = f(I \mid \zeta)$. A special case of MCAR can arise when survey methods set a limit to the out-degree of a node (e.g., by asking to name *three* friends in your class). Any respondent giving the maximum allowed answer has, strictly speaking, missing data on all other outgoing ties, because the respondent might have nominated any additional number of friends if they had been allowed to. This is usually disregarded by researchers, and the remaining tie variables are set observed to no-ties.

Second, data are called *missing at random* (MAR) if the probability of being missing is independent of the missing value itself, but is dependent on other observed variables (e.g., men are less likely to fill out the network questionnaire, assuming gender is a completely observed attribute), $f(I \mid u, v, \zeta) = f(I \mid u, \zeta)$. For non-network data, treatment methods have been developed which yield unbiased estimates under these two mechanisms (for an overview, see Schafer & Graham, 2002), therefore they are often referred to as *ignorable missing data*. With the right treatment the fact that data is missing can be ignored.

The third mechanism is data *missing not at random* (MNAR). Data are MNAR if the probability of being missing is related to the missing values themselves (e.g., isolates are less likely to participate in a network study), $f(I \mid u, v, \zeta)$. Missing data related to specific tie variables can follow complex patterns. For instance, i's probability to drop out of the study can be related to nodal attributes of specific alters j with attribute k_j (e.g., being linked to someone who is not participating might increase the probability for drop-out). Missing data mechanisms may also be related to structural embeddedness (e.g., being in a triad makes participants less likely to participate). In both examples the probability of a tie variable being missing depends most crucially on the tie variable itself but also on other (tie) variables. Data being MNAR can cause severe biases in network statistics and parameters of network models (Krause et al., 2020).

While knowing the true missing data mechanism is necessary for the most accurate treatment, it is impossible in real data. By definition, one would need to know the missing values themselves to differentiate MNAR from M(C)AR. This is only possible in rare occasions, for example, when data were collected which had to be discarded for, say, ethical reasons (e.g., participant retracts participation from the study). Then one could theoretically know the responses that the missing node would have given. However, even in such a case, one would not be allowed to use that data to test if the missing tie variables are MNAR. The problem gets further aggravated by the fact that missing data within a larger dataset are hardly ever consistently following any one mechanism. For instance, some employees in the company did not fill out the survey because they were on vacation (MCAR), others have little time because of the demanding role they perform in the company (MAR) and others yet refuse to participate because they dislike most of their co-workers, feel isolated from them and do not want to disclose their perception of the company network (MNAR). Thus, no single mechanism would be at work in this company. Research on missing (network) data thus usually focuses on artificially created missing data in observed (e.g., Smith et al., 2017) or simulated networks (e.g., Krause et al., 2020). Any such results should be seen as optimal cases which are not directly transferable to real missing data. Such research can, however, provide boundaries of potential biases and gives researchers an idea whether and which actions might be necessary given the data, design, research question and hypothesised missing data mechanism.

What is one to do now, knowing that the missing data mechanism is crucial for correct treatment, but that it will always remain unknown? First of all, the often-echoed phrase 'The best treatment for missing data is not to have any', while unhelpful after the data collection, is especially true in networked data. Before diving into the topic of how to treat missing data, researchers should spend more time preventing the occurrence of missing data. Methods to prevent data from becoming missing include building trust that the data will not be used against the participant and provides benefits for the participant or the network as a whole, providing incentives, educating the participants (and, where necessary, especially their legal guardians) about the research, its goals, benefits and possible risks to avoid drop-out due to false or missing information on the participant's side. Sending reminders and providing multiple opportunities to fill out the survey can especially alleviate data that is MCAR (e.g., sickness or vacation). Further, securing the support from the relevant authority figures (e.g., headmaster, teacher, CEO, HR) will provide organisational help and can facilitate higher response rates. For more information on collecting network data see adams and Lubbers, this volume.

However, even data collected with the most care are likely to have some holes in them. The larger the group the more likely it is that some members will not participate. For non-network data tests can be utilised to differentiate between MAR and MCAR (e.g., simple t-tests to test differences between responders and non-responders on data available for both, or Little's MCAR Test, Little 1988. These tests typically test if any variable in the dataset can predict the occurrence of missing data ($I_{ij} = 1$) for a given variable. If a predictor in, for instance, a logistic regression with I as the dependent variable, is significant, then it can be assumed that the data are at least MAR and not MCAR (the probability for data to be missing is at least dependent on one observed variable). In the network world, for instance, one could compute the observed in-degree of a node (i.e., summing all observed incoming tie variables and thus implicitly imputing missing incoming tie variables with 0) and use this measure to predict the occurrence of missing outgoing tie-variable data. Nodal attributes and other network statistics could equally be utilised. However, it still remains impossible to verify if the data is MNAR or not. Further, as has been shown by several studies (e.g., Smith et al., 2017; Krause et al., 2020), network measures tend to be biased even when data are MCAR. Thus, while investigating the missing data mechanism should be a standard procedure when handling (network) data with missings, it does have a smaller impact on the analysis step than in non-network data. Even if data are MCAR or MAR (the more favourable mechanisms), one should still employ the advanced missing data handling algorithms we will discuss below.

Lastly, one should always invest some time in exploring potential sources of data being MNAR. Are we investigating a sensitive topic? Are participants likely to drop out/not participate because of their relations? Do the demographic statistics and the network overall match with what we can know about the population (e.g., previous studies or data provided by HR, municipality, or school)? If data are suspected to be MNAR, the optimal course of action would be to first try to acquire the missing data, when possible. Given that this is sometimes not an option or fails to fill (all) the holes, one should try to conduct sensitivity analysis (Daniels & Hogan, 2008). In short, the goal of the sensitivity analysis is to investigate how *sensitive* the results are to the assumption of data being M(C)AR. For example, suppose a small bias is included in an imputation algorithm (more on imputation later) which leads to lower overall out-degree of missing nodes. After imputation, one proceeds as usual with the planned analysis. The results can then be compared to an analysis under M(C)AR. If no meaningful differences arise, then one can have some confidence that even if nodes with lower out-degree were more likely to be missing, this does not introduce a meaningful bias in the results. However, advanced treatments for missing network data are a relatively young field and, at the time of writing, hardly any work has been done on providing tutorials, scripts, or guidelines for sensitivity analysis for social networks. A complicating factor is that there are always a large set of possible MNAR mechanisms to explore. More work is necessary to provide both reliable guidelines and simple enough tools to employ them. While many network researchers often explore their missing data and evaluate if they have any evidence for MAR or MNAR, the vast majority does not mention these explorations in their work.

MISSING DATA TYPES

While missing data mechanisms describe the probability distribution of the missing data, missing data types describe how the missingness is distributed over the dataset – that is, the network. In cross-sectional network research two types of missing data are usually distinguished: *actor non-response* (also referred to as *unit non-response*) and *tie non-response* (also referred to as *item non-response*; Huisman & Steglich, 2008). Actor non-response occurs when all outgoing tie variables of an actor are missing, $\sum_{j=1}^{n} I_{ij} = 0$. In tie non-response only some, but not all tie variables of an actor are missing, $0 < \sum_{j=1}^{n} I_{ij} < n-1$. The terminology of 'non-response' implies that data is collected via self-reports of network actors and stems from classical survey research. With self-reports actor non-response is the most likely type of missing data distribution. However, other data collection methods, for instance *link-tracing* or *snowball sampling*, might lead to tie non-response.

In tracing methods, for instance, missing data occurs between those nodes at the periphery of the network. If one follows multiple seed nodes for k steps each, then any tie variable between nodes only reached in the last (k^{th}) step are missing. For instance, one might select Adam as seed node and follow Adam's ties three steps deep. Adam is connected to Charlie, who in turn is connected to Donna, who lastly is connected to Erik. Further, Adam is connected to Charlotte, who in turn is connected to Daniel, who's trace end with Erica. Because we did not investigate to whom Erik or Erica are tied (beyond Donna and Daniel respectively), by design we have missing data on the tie variable between the two of them.

Another type of missing data, related to link-tracing methods but also very prevalent in criminal networks (see Ouellet, this volume) or other networks generated by data mining are *missing nodes*. This means that not just the connections of a node are missing, but the researcher is unaware of the presence of the node itself in the network. In link-tracing methods this happens either when the node is too many steps away from the seed node, or when the network is separated into several disconnected components with seed nodes not covering every component (isolated nodes would form a component of 1).

In criminal networks, where networks are often formed by co-participation in crimes or co-arrests, nodes might be missing because they were not caught by the authorities and there might not even have been any evidence that more than the known number of suspects were involved (Bright et al., 2021; Diviák, 2019). Additionally, entire subsets of the network might be missing because the crime itself was never reported or discovered. A very strict reading of such co-arrest data could thus claim that any not-observed tie variable between any two nodes is actually missing data because having no evidence that two people have jointly committed a crime is not the same as them not having committed a crime. This likewise applies to data collected from, for instance, newspapers about politicians or celebrities. Just because there has not been an article about members of certain parties talking to each other does not mean that they have not. To put it in the common saying, 'Absence of evidence is not evidence of absence.' While such an approach would certainly be statistically correct, it would also be futile. Incomplete and partially inaccurate data can still be used to make relevant inferences about networks. However, researchers should always be aware that they might be missing certain links (or even nodes) and treat their results with appropriate caution. Data from multiple sources and especially qualitative data from members of the network can help to grasp how big potential problems are.

A further problem in criminal networks is the *spotlighting* effect (Smith & Papachristos, 2016; Diviák et al., 2022), that those under investigation might either know they are under surveillance and thus reduce their activities, leading to more missing ties and nodes, or that the intense surveillance will uncover especially many ties for the primarily surveiled nodes. This will make them appear more central than they would be in the completely observed network because others, having more missing data, will have fewer confirmed ties.

This can similarly be translated to networks that are constructed from interviews or surveys of a subset of the population. Like snowball sampling they only cover a part of the network and some of the tie variables remain missing, while entire segments of the network remain completely unknown, including their nodes. While data collected in such a way can be extremely useful in answering research questions (see, for instance, the work by Krivitsky & Morris, 2017), any reconstruction of the supposed whole network needs to consider the sampling procedure and limit the conclusions to the observed part of the data. Methods have been developed to estimate general network features (Frank & Carrington, 2007) or even complex network models based on sampled data (Pattison et al., 2013; Stivala et al., 2016).

EFFECTS OF MISSING DATA

The effects of missing data on descriptive network statistics, cliques and block structures (for blockmodels, see Doreian et al., this volume) depend on the amount of missing data, on the network structure, on the descriptive statistic (or block algorithm) in question and how the missing data are treated. Note that there is no effect of missing data but only effects of missing data treatments. One always has to make a decision about missing data, otherwise the result will always be *unknown*.[1] The default treatments for networks are list-wise or pair-wise deletion, or imputation of unconditional means, meaning imputation of no-ties ($x_{ij} = 0$), as most social structures are sparse (density < .5) and no-tie being the most likely value. For these treatments some combinations of statistic and overall network structure are more robust to missing data than others. Larger and more centralised networks are usually more robust against missing data (Smith & Moody, 2013). Measures based on in-degree are found to be overall more reliable (Costenbader & Valente, 2003; Smith & Moody, 2013; Smith et al., 2017). A notable difference between network and non-network data can be seen under the MCAR mechanism. While sample estimates of means, variances and model parameters are usually unbiased for non-network data under MCAR with list-wise deletion, the same does not apply to network data. There can be considerable biases in model parameters and descriptive statistics, even if data are missing *completely at random* (Huisman & Steglich, 2008; Smith & Moody, 2013; Huisman, 2009; Krause et al., 2020). For a detailed overview of how missing data can affect your specific measure of interest, we suggest exploring the existing literature: for effects on descriptive statistics, Smith and Moody (2013), Smith et al. (2017), Huisman (2009), Krause et al. (2020); for effects on estimated parameters of ERGMs, Gile and Handcock (2006), Krause et al. (2020); and SAOMs, Huisman and Steglich (2008), Krause et al. (2018); for the effects of missing data on block models, Žnidaršič et al. (2017).

MISSING DATA TREATMENTS

Researchers have several options for handling missing data in networks which can broadly be separated into three categories:[2] deletion, likelihood-based estimation and imputation (for a general overview of missing data handling, see Schafer & Graham, 2002). Deletion methods reduce the network to a fully observed subsample (list-wise deletion of actors; Huisman & Steglich, 2008) or ignore the missing data for some, but not all statistical calculations (pair-wise deletion, e.g., incoming ties of nodes with missing outgoing information are counted for calculation of the out-degree of the observed sender but not when calculating the reciprocity or transitivity of the network). Deletion methods are commonly used and the default for most statistical programs; they are very common because they are straightforward in their application and explanation. However, they do not perform well in most situations, because they discard too much information (Huisman & Steglich, 2008; Huisman, 2009; Žnidaršič et al., 2012; Krause et al., 2020). In non-network data, cases are usually presumed to be independent (or conditionally independent when conditioning on some higher level, such as school classroom or company), thus removing participants with missing values will not affect the overall outcome of the model under MCAR. However, removing actors from a network will also remove information about the remaining actors because incoming ties of the removed actors are outgoing ties of observed actors. These remaining actors will be left with a lower out-degree compared to what was actually observed. Further removal of nodes can affect more complex structures like brokerage or transitive triads. Despite these limitations deletion can be a sufficiently adequate missing data treatment if only a small number of nodes is affected.

To avoid loss in statistical power, researchers sometimes recruit more participants, until the desired sample size is obtained. In some cases this is easily feasible, only requiring some minor investments in recruiting new participants. In other cases, though possible, recruiting more participants can become very expensive (e.g., medical trials or neuroscientific studies), or very difficult (e.g., studies of rare diseases or disorders, indigenous secluded people, or high-profile organisations). For other studies it can, however, be impossible to recruit new people. In, for instance, a study following a cohort of people over multiple years (e.g., Dijkstra et al., 2015) one cannot simply add new people and enquire retrospectively about experiences and contacts they had years, or even decades, ago, at least not with any reliability comparable to the data collected in the original sample.

Likelihood-based methods estimate the model parameters from the marginal distribution of the observed data. Under M(C)AR this will lead to approximately unbiased estimates in larger samples, given that the employed model is correct (Schafer & Graham, 2002). Likelihood-based estimation methods are available for various families of network models: for the *exponential random graph model* family (ERGM; Koskinen, this volume) see Robins et al. (2004); Gile and Handcock (2006); Handcock and Gile (2007, 2010); Koskinen et al. (2010); for the family of *stochastic actor-oriented models* (SAOM; Snijders, this volume) see Snijders et al. (2010). However, these methods are by definition model based, and thus cannot aid the estimation of nonparametric models or help with the calculation of network (e.g., transitivity) or nodal (e.g., centrality) descriptive statistics.

Imputation methods replace the missing values with plausible guesses (Rubin, 1987; Schafer & Graham, 2002). We will provide an overview of some (simple) methods later in this chapter. The methods differ in the amount of information they use for the replacement of the missing values. Stochastic imputation methods use draws from probability distributions to replace missing values. These methods can be used for multiple imputation, where multiple imputed datasets are generated based on a conditional probability model. This set of imputed datasets are analysed separately leading to a distribution of model parameters. These are then combined to obtain parameter estimates and standard errors. For the calculation of the standard errors both the average within imputation variance (the uncertainty given the observed data) and the between imputation variance (the uncertainty due to missing data and imputation) are taken into account.

Both single and multiple imputation allow model estimation with all observed information, as well as, the calculation of descriptive statistics. While both provide unbiased parameter estimation under MCAR, only multiple imputation is able to provide unbiased estimates of standard error, both under MCAR and MAR, given the imputation model is correctly specified. For non-network data, likelihood-based estimation and multiple imputation are considered the state of the art (Schafer & Graham, 2002) and the same applies for network data (Krause, 2019).

The problem of missing network data becomes a double-edged sword when likelihood-based methods or multiple imputation are used as missing data treatments. The distinction between missing data in network studies and missing data in non-network studies is best highlighted for the case of actor non-response, where some nodes provide no information. On the one hand, non-responding actors (i.e., missing outgoing network nominations) not only create missing data for the non-responding node, but also create missing data for the incoming ties of some (in case of partial non-response) or all (in case of complete non-response) other nodes in the network. The true in-degree for all actors becomes unknown, because the non-responding actors could have send ties to any or all other actors. Similarly, network-wide measures (e.g., centralisation, transitivity, reciprocity) also are unknown and can only be estimated based on the observed data. This makes missing data in networks seemingly more severe, and induces biases in network measures even under MCAR.

However, networks provide a data structure in which missing data can be better treated, if the right methods are employed. First, for undirected networks it is sufficient if only one side provides information about the relation (if $x_{ij} = 1$ then $x_{ji} = 1$; if I trade with you, you necessarily have to be trading with me). In such cases, missing data only occur for the relations between two missing nodes, or if – for legal, ethical, or methodological reasons – information can only be used if both sides provide a response about the relationship. Directed networks, however, do not have this straightforward solution for missing data. Still, if some members of the network do not provide any information about their contacts (no outgoing ties are observed), there is information about these missing participants because others in the network could provide information about their relations to the missing nodes (incoming ties are observed – if the data collection allowed for such nominations). Unlike for regular panel data, the participants in a network are not randomly sampled and independent of each other. Their interdependencies constitute the subject of the analysis and can be leveraged to better handle missing data. Thus, also for directed networks, complete non-response by some members of the network does not mean that no information is available about them, which in contrast would be the case in non-network data. Both, likelihood- and imputation-based procedures try to leverage this available information about missing nodes.

LIKELIHOOD-BASED METHODS

We will not dive deeper into likelihood-based methods in this chapter. They are the default for most of the common statistical programs. For ERGM estimation, they are by default implemented in the ergm() function of the ergm R-package (Hunter et al., 2008; R Core Team, 2021), available for Bayesian ERGM estimation in the bergmM() function of the Bergm R-package (Caimo & Friel, 2014), and available in the Pnet software (Wang et al., 2009). For an example of such an application of Bergm on missing data see for instance Estévez et al. (2022). While the default treatment for SOAMs does not rely on likelihood estimation (Huisman & Steglich, 2008), likelihood-based estimation (and thus missing data handling) is available with maximum-likelihood estimation (Snijders et al., 2010), including Bayesian estimation (Koskinen & Snijders, 2022). However, all of these methods assume that the data are M(C)AR and that the estimation model is specified correctly. When missing data occurs, even though treatments are readily available, one should investigate potential avenues for the data being MNAR. As of yet, none of these methods provide functionality to handle data MNAR, however, even when MNAR is assumed. The results provided with likelihood-based estimation are generally more reliable than results obtained by using simpler treatments, like deletion.

IMPUTATION METHODS

All imputation methods strive to replace the missing data with plausible guesses so that a complete dataset with the planned sample size is obtained. The imputation methods differ in how much information they use to obtain these plausible guesses and how many guesses are made (single vs multiple imputation). We will discuss some available imputation methods for network data according to the four general classes of imputation models as highlighted by Schafer and Graham (2002).

Imputation of Unconditional Means

First, *imputation of unconditional means* is a simple procedure where each missing value is replaced with the mean over the observed cases of that variable. Although the means of variables are preserved, variances and covariances (relations between variables) are often severely biased. Rounding the mean values, in case of binary or categorical data, even adds more error to the imputed values. Although the added variability is random, it is better to keep rounding to a minimum (Graham, 2009).

For binary tie variables, the total mean value equals the network density d. Rounding the density (using a threshold of 0.5) results in filling in zeros (0) in sparse networks ($d < 0.5$) and ones (1) in dense networks ($d > 0.5$). In the former case, missing ties are treated as absent, in the latter they are treated as present. The imputation of zeros is called *null tie imputation* by Žnidaršič et al. (2012) and is sometimes even used in dense networks.

Imputation from Unconditional Distributions

Second, *imputing from unconditional distributions* can alleviate the problem of underestimating the variances due to imputing means by using the observed (empirical) distribution of responses to impute the missing scores. In one class of procedures, called hot-deck procedures, these distributions are simulated by (randomly) selecting an observed 'donor case' from the same dataset, and replacing the missing values with the observed scores of that donor (e.g., Sande, 1982). Although such procedures preserve univariate distributions of variables (i.e., means and variances), relations are still biased.

Hot-deck imputation

Hot-deck imputation in networks uses completely observed donor nodes to replace all ties of the missing actor (actor non-response), or the missing ties of an incomplete actor (tie non-response). Donor actors can either be randomly selected, or by using observed attribute values or structural properties of the network (so called *nearest neighbours*), or both. Huisman (2009) gives an example of the latter option where nodes are matched on in-degree and attribute values. Instead of finding only one donor actor (the 'best' donor), a set of donors can be selected from which one is randomly chosen. Alternatively, the mean of the donors can be used for the imputation (Žnidaršič et al., 2017).

Imputation by preferential attachment

Barabási and Albert (1999) proposed *preferential attachment* as a simple model for the growth of networks, which was used by Huisman and Steglich (2008) as an imputation model. The model assumes that the probability that a new tie $x_{ij} = 1$ will emerge between actors i and j is proportional to the current number of neighbours (i.e., in-degree) of actor j. This means that the probability that an actor (observed or missing) will link to another is dependent on the connectivity of others. Huisman and Steglich (2008) propose a two-step imputation procedure based on random draws from out-degree distributions and random draws using preferential attachment probabilities to impute missing data caused by actor non-response. Huisman (2009) investigates this method also for tie non-response. While using more information than the methods discussed so far, it is still a rather simplistic model of network structure.

Imputation of Conditional Means

Third, *imputations of conditional means* use a formal model that accurately captures the association between a missing item and observed items. For non-network data, linear (regression) models are used to predict the conditional means of the missing items. These procedures result in more accurate predictions of the missing scores and yield unbiased estimates of means under MAR, but underestimate variances and generally overestimate covariances. Alternatively, instead of computing the overall variable mean, one can impute a group-specific mean – that is, condition the mean on the membership of some group to obtain, on average, a more accurate imputation than unconditional mean imputation.

In the network setting, the density used to determine the imputation of a 0 or a 1 could be calculated based on some observed characteristic (e.g., age). Another option, is using the observed in-degree ('average popularity') or the mean of the observed outgoing ties of nodes with missing tie variables ('average activity'). The latter method can obviously not be used in the case of actor non-response. The former method results in imputing the modal value of the incoming ties and is called *imputation based on model in-degree values* by Žnidaršič et al. (2012).

Reconstruction

Another network specific imputation method is *reconstruction*, introduced by Stork and Richards (1992). In reconstruction, the missing outgoing tie variables of non-respondents are replaced with observed incoming ties to these actors – that is, missing tie variable x_{ij} is replaced with the observed value of x_{ji}. This results in symmetric networks between respondents and non-respondents. Additional steps are required for tie variables between non-respondents. For these, random imputation by single draws from the density (Huisman & Steglich, 2008; Huisman, 2009; Krause et al., 2020) or modal in-degree values

(Žnidaršič et al., 2012) can be used. Reconstruction is only an imputation method when applied to directed networks; for undirected networks it is identical to using the available responses from observed nodes. Note that reconstruction can be regarded as hot-deck imputation, defining the donor actor as the second actor in the dyad whose incoming tie is not observed.

Imputation from Conditional Distributions

Last, *imputing from conditional distributions* yields, when done properly, means, variances and covariances which are unbiased, or have at least largely reduced bias compared to other imputation methods. The conditional distribution of the missing values is simulated using imputation models similar to those of the previous category (imputing conditional means), conditional on the observed variables in the model. The missing scores are replaced by random draws from these distributions. In the practice of empirical research, this procedure usually amounts to imputing regression predictions with an added error term, randomly drawn from the normal or t distribution. In general, multiple imputation procedures fall in this class of imputations methods (Schafer & Graham, 2002; Graham, 2009).

Link prediction

All the simple methods presented above have in common that they are not model based. Although some depend on properties of the observed network (e.g., reciprocity in the case of reconstruction), they do not use statistical models to relate observed and unobserved responses. Imputation methods that use such models (the conditional methods, in the classification of Schafer & Graham, 2002) are the link-prediction methods based on stochastic blockmodels proposed by Guimer'a and Sales-Pardo (2009); methods based on latent factor models proposed by Hoff (2009); methods based on ERGMs proposed by Koskinen et al. (2010) and Gile and Handcock (2006); methods based on Kronecker graph models proposed by Kim and Leskovec (2011); and methods based on SAOMs by Krause et al. (2018).

Especially ERGMs and SAOMs can be well utilised to provide imputations for missing ties, either as part of the analysis using the respective model (Koskinen et al., 2010; Koskinen et al., 2013; Krause et al., 2018; Krause & Caimo, 2019; Krause et al., 2020) or as a first (imputation) step before a consecutive (different) analysis (Hipp et al., 2015; Wang et al., 2016).

Multiple Imputation

Using the (conditional) distributions of the missing values allows us to draw multiple times from these distributions to replace the missing values more than once. The proper steps of this procedure, introduced by Rubin (1987), are as follows. First, an imputation model is specified, then for each missing value m imputations are obtained from the distribution derived from the imputation model by repeatedly predicting the missing variables (either by drawing the parameters of the imputation model from a Bayesian posterior distribution of the model parameters or by obtaining a distribution of model parameters via bootstrapping). This results in m completed datasets. Second, the planned analysis is performed on each of the m completed datasets separately (e.g., the regression model is run for each of the m imputations). Third, the results are combined using Rubin's rules (Rubin, 1987; see Schafer & Graham, 2002, for a more detailed introduction).

Multiple imputation methods can be (and often are) used to obtain more reliable estimates of model parameters under missing data. In this way, they are similar to likelihood methods and if the correct models are used, both will asymptotically give the same result, assuming the data are M(C)AR. An advantage of multiple imputation is that it can also be used to obtain imputed data for other future analyses (e.g., data imputed with ERGM can be used to then run a block model or calculate centrality scores, which in turn can then be used as variable in a regression model).

Several multiple imputation procedures are available for networks either centred around the ERGM or the SAOM family. Methods and algorithms have been developed for imputation with ERGMs (Wang et al., 2016; Hipp et al., 2015), imputation with Bayesian ERGMs (Koskinen et al., 2010; Krause et al., 2020; Krause & Caimo, 2019) and imputation with Bayesian and non-Bayesian SAOMs (Krause et al., 2018; Krause et al., 2019a; Krause et al., 2019b). While the exact specifications and their data requirements of these procedures differ (e.g., most SAOM procedures are designed for longitudinal network data), the principle is the same. First, a reasonable model, ERGM or SAOM, is defined for the data. Second, the model is estimated on the observed data (Wang et al., 2016; Hipp et al., 2015; Koskinen et al., 2010; Krause et al., 2018; Krause et al., 2019a; Krause et al., 2020; Krause & Caimo, 2019; Krause et al., 2019b). Third, this model is then used to obtain multiple imputations for the missing tie variables by fixing all observed tie variables to their observed values and letting the missing tie variables change according to the model with the observed structure (see Krause et al., 2018, for more detail on the fixing of observed tie variables in longitudinal imputation). If the planned analysis (model) is the same as this imputation procedure, then the likelihood-based Bayesian procedures do not require an additional step (Koskinen et al., 2010; Krause et al., 2019b). However, the non-Bayesian approaches require that the initially planned model is now applied separately to all of the *m* (now complete) network datasets. As a last step, Rubin's rules are applied to obtain the final parameter estimates and their standard errors. For examples of such procedures see, for instance, Hipp et al. (2015) or de Lange et al. (2022). Imputation with ERGMs requires to first estimate a model (e.g., with the ergm() function of the ergm package in R) and then using the estimated model to impute the missing tie variables (e.g., by using the simulate.ergm() function in R). Likewise, imputations with SAOMs first require the estimation of a SAOM (usually with the siena07() function of the RSiena package in R) and then imputing the missing ties with the estimated model (again by using the siena07() function of the RSiena package in R). Imputations with Bayesian ERGM can be generated jointly with the estimation of a Bayesian ERGM (e.g., as implemented in the bergmM() function of the Bergm package in R).

All of these methods can be applied to one-mode and two-mode networks, and options for multiplex data are also available. ERGM imputation is also possible for signed and count graphs (Bergm imputation for such data is so far not implemented).

DISCUSSION AND FUTURE DIRECTIONS

Missing network data is unfortunately often unavoidable and simple treatments such as collecting more data or deletion methods are either not possible (one cannot just increase the network system in size) or are likely to lead to (severe) biases. However, in recent years new advanced treatments are available to handle missing network data both for more accurate model estimation and to obtain reliable imputations that can be used for other analyses. Likelihood-based estimation and the multiple imputation procedures described can be considered the gold standard for missing data treatment in binary networks. There is less work on weighted networks; however, work by Žnidaršič et al. (2017), while not relying on a statistical model, shows promise to alleviate severe biases.

While missing data treatments for non-network data have been explored for over 50 years now, there is far less known for network data. While many of the advances outside networks can be readily applied (e.g., Rubin's rules for combining multiple imputations) others are not easily transferable (e.g., deletion under MCAR can lead to biases in networks). We want to list, in no particular order, a few important areas that require investigation to provide all SNA researchers with improved methods to handle missing data: sensitivity analyses to investigate the (potential) impacts of MNAR; missing attribute data and how network connections can be used to impute missing attributes of nodes (see Krause et al., 2019a, for first steps in this direction); statistical models for signed and weighted graphs; investigating the number of required imputations for multiple imputation procedures.

Note

1 For instance, while the mean of the vector $a =$ (1, 2, *'Missing'*) seems to be $\bar{a}=1.5$, it is actually unknown, after all, the missing value could be any number. Only if it is 1.5 will $\bar{a}=1.5$. This might seem like a pedantic exercise but it is important to realise that one *always* makes a decision about missing data.
2 The usual fourth category for missing data treatments, re-weighting, is not readily applicable in network research because the statistics of the observed sample, and thus also statistics of subgroups (e.g., network members of a certain age, gender, race) are likely to be biased already and thus re-weighting those will simply extend this bias.

REFERENCES

Barabási, A., & Albert, R. (1999). Emergence of scaling in random networks. *Science*, *286*(5439), 509–512.

Bright, D., Brewer, R., & Morselli, C. (2021). Using social network analysis to study crime: navigating the challenges of criminal justice records. *Social Networks*, *66*, 50–64.

Caimo, A., & Friel, N. (2014). Bergm: Bayesian exponential random graphs in R. *Journal of Statistical Software*, *61*(2), 1–25.

Costenbader, E., & Valente, T.W. (2003). The stability of centrality measures when networks are sampled. *Social Networks*, *25*, 283–307.

Daniels, M.J., & Hogan, J.W. (2008). *Missing data in longitudinal studies: strategies for Bayesian modeling and sensitivity analysis.* Chapman and Hall/CRC.

de Lange, E., Milner-Gulland, E., & Keane, A. (2022). Effects of social networks on interventions to change conservation behavior. *Conservation Biology, 36*(3), e13833.

Dijkstra, J., Kretschmer, T., Pattiselanno, K., Franken, A., Harakeh, Z., Volle- bergh, W., & Veenstra, R. (2015). Explaining adolescents' delinquency and substance use: a test of the maturity gap: the snare study. *Journal of Research in Crime and Delinquency, 52*(5), 747–767.

Diviák, T. (2019). Key aspects of covert networks data collection: problems, challenges, and opportunities. *Social Networks, 69,* 160–169.

Diviák, T., van Nassau, C., Dijkstra, J., & Snijders, T.A.B. (2022). Dynamics and disruption: structural and individual changes in two Dutch jihadi networks after police interventions. *Social Networks, 70,* 364–374.

Estévez, J.L., Kisfalusi, D., & Takács, K. (2022). More than one's negative ties: the role of friends' antipathies in high school gossip. *Social Networks, 70,* 77–89.

Frank, O., & Carrington, P. (2007). Estimation of offending and co-offending using available data with model support. *Journal of Mathematical Sociology, 31*(1), 1–46.

Gile, K., & Handcock, M. (2006). Model-based assessment of the impact of missing data on inference for networks. CSSS working paper no. 66. Working Paper Series, University of Washington, Seattle.

Graham, J. (2009). Missing data analysis: making it work in the real world. *Annual Review of Psychology, 60,* 549–576.

Guimerá, R., & Sales-Pardo, M. (2009). Missing and spurious interactions and the reconstruction of complex networks. *Proceedings of the National Academy of Sciences, 106*(52), 22073–22078.

Handcock, M., & Gile, K. (2007). Modeling social networks with sampled or missing data, CSSS working paper no. 75. *Journal of Statistical Software.*

Handcock, M., & Gile, K. (2010). Modeling social networks from sampled data. *Annals of Applied Statistics, 4,* 5–25.

Hipp, J., Wang, C., Butts, C., Jose, R., & Lakon, C. (2015). Research note: Tte consequences of different methods for handling missing network data in stochastic actor based models. *Social Networks, 41,* 56–71.

Hoff, P. (2009). Multiplicative latent factor models for description and prediction of social networks. *Computational and Mathematical Organization Theory, 15*(4), 261–272.

Huisman, M. (2009). Imputation of missing network data: some simple procedures. *Journal of Social Structure, 10,* 1–29.

Huisman, M., & Steglich, C. (2008). Treatment of non-response in longitudinal network studies. *Social Networks, 30,* 297–308.

Hunter, D., Handcock, M., Butts, C., Goodreau, S., & Morris, M. (2008). ergm: a package to fit, simulate and diagnose exponential-family models for networks. *Journal of Statistical Software, 24*(3), 1–29.

Kim, M., & Leskovec, J. (2011). The network completion problem: inferring missing nodes and edges in networks. *Proceedings of the 2011 SIAM International Conference on Data Mining* (pp. 47–58). SIAM.

Koskinen, J., Robins, G., & Pattison, P. (2010). Analysing exponential random graph (p-star) models with missing data using Bayesian data augmentation. *Statistical Methodology, 7*(3), 366–384.

Koskinen, J., Robins, G., Wang, P., & Pattison, P. (2013). Bayesian analysis for partially observed network data, missing ties, attributes and actors. *Social Networks, 35,* 514–527.

Koskinen, J., & Snijders, T.A.B. (2022). Multilevel longitudinal analysis of social networks. *arXiv.* Preprint arXiv, 2201.12713.

Krause, R. (2019). *Multiple imputation for missing network data.* PhD thesis, University of Groningen.

Krause, R., & Caimo, A. (2019). Multiple imputation for Bayesian exponential random multigraph models. *International Workshop on Complex Networks,* 63–72.

Krause, R., Huisman, M., & Snijders, T.A.B. (2018). Multiple imputation for longitudinal network data. *Italian Journal of Applied Statistics, 30,* 33–57.

Krause, R., Huisman, M., Steglich, C.E.G., & Snijders, T.A.B. (2020). Missing data in cross-sectional networks: an extensive comparison of missing data treatment methods. *Social Networks, 62,* 99–112.

Krause, R., Iashina, A., Huisman, M., Steglich, C.E.G., & Snijders, T.A.B. (2019a). Multiple imputation of missing ties and actor attributes. Dissertation, Chapter 5.

Krause, R., van Rijsewijk, L., Huisman, M., Steglich, C.E.G., & Snijders, T.A.B. (2019b). Multiple imputation of missing ties and actor attributes. Dissertation, Chapter 6.

Krivitsky, P., & Morris, M. (2017). Inference for social network models from egocentrically sampled data, with application to understanding persistent racial disparities in HIV prevalence in the us. *The Annals of Applied Statistics, 11*(1), 427–455.

Little, R.J. (1988). A test of missing completely at random for multivariate data with missing values. *Journal of the American Statistical Association, 83*(404), 1198–1202.

Pattison, P., Robins, G., Snijders, T.A.B., & Wand, P. (2013). Conditional estimation of exponential random graph models from snowball sampling designs. *Journal of Mathematical Psychology*, *57*(6), 284–296.

R Core Team (2021). *R: a language and environment for statistical computing*. R Foundation for Statistical Computing.

Robins, G., Pattison, P., & Woolcock, J. (2004). Missing data in networks: exponential random graph (p*) models for networks with non-respondents. *Social Networks*, *26*, 257–283.

Rubin, D. (1976). Inference and missing data. *Biometrika*, *63*, 581–592.

Rubin, D. (1987). *Multiple imputation for nonresponse in surveys*. Wiley.

Sande, I.G. (1982). Imputation in surveys: coping with reality. *American Statistician*, *36*(3a), 145–152.

Schafer, J., & Graham, J. (2002). Missing data: our view of the state of the art. *Psychological Methods*, *7*, 147–177.

Smith, C., & Papachristos, A. (2016). Trust thy crooked neighbor: multiplexity in Chicago organized crime networks. *American Sociological Review*, *81*(4), 644–667.

Smith, J., & Moody, J. (2013). Structural effects of network sampling coverage I: Nodes missing at random. *Social Networks*, *35*, 652–668.

Smith, J., Moody, J., & Morgan, J. (2017). Network sampling coverage II: The effect of non-random missing data on network measurement. *Social Networks*, *48*, 78–99.

Snijders, T.A.B., Koskinen, J., & Schweinberger, M. (2010). Maximum likelihood estimation for social network dynamics. *Annals of Applied Statistics*, *4*(2), 567.

Snijders, T.A.B., van de Bunt, G.G., & Steglich, C.E.G. (2010). Introduction to actor-based models for network dynamics. *Social Networks*, *32*, 44–60.

Stivala, A., Koskinen, J., Rolls, D., Wang, P., & Robins, G. (2016). Snowball sampling for estimating exponential random graph models for large networks. *Social Networks*, *47*, 167–188.

Stork, D., & Richards, W.D. (1992). Nonrespondents in communication network studies. *Group and Organisation Management*, *17*, 193–209.

Wang, C., Butts, C., Hipp, J., Jose, R., & Lakon, C. (2016). Multiple imputation for missing edge data: a predictive evaluation method with application to Add Health. *Social Networks*, *45*, 89–98.

Wang, P., Robins, G., & Pattison, P. (2009). *Program for the Simulation and Estimation of Exponential Random Graph (p*) Models*. Pnet.

Žnidaršič, A., Doreian, P., & Ferligoj, A. (2012). Absent ties in social networks, their treatments, and blockmodeling outcomes. *Metodoloski Zvezki*, *9*, 119–138.

Žnidaršič, A., Ferligoj, A., & Doreian, P. (2017). Actor non-response in valued social networks: the impact of different non-response treatments on the stability of blockmodels. *Social Networks*, *48*, 46–56.

Scientific Software for Network Analysis

Pierson Browne, Adam Howe, Yasmin Koop-Monteiro, Yixi Yang, and John McLevey

INTRODUCTION

This chapter serves as a practical introduction to scientific software tools commonly used in social network analysis, and network science more generally. Rather than review the vast and diverse software landscape,[1] we focus on helping newcomers to the field get started with analysing network data for the first time. To that end, we introduce three software tools: UCINet with NetDraw, R with the `sna` library, and Python with the `NetworkX` package.[2]

UCINet is a proprietary menu-based, or GUI (*graphical user interface*), program that runs on Windows. While there are other excellent GUI tools available for analysing network data,[3] we have selected UCINet primarily because it has a long history in social network analysis, starting in the early 1980s when Lin Freeman collected, documented and circulated a variety of network analysis programs written in different programming languages by other researchers. Those programs were eventually translated into a single BASIC program (UCINet 3) by 1987, and then replaced by a new network analysis program developed by Steve Borgatti, which would become UCINet 4. This chapter uses a version of UCINet 6 released in 2022.

While GUI programs are still widely used in network analysis, most recent technical developments in network analysis methodology (see Scott et al., this volume) are first, and sometimes only, available in programming languages such as R and Python. These software tools are becoming indispensable in contemporary network analysis, with some even winning awards from INSNA (e.g., `STATNET` (Handcock et al., 2008) and `rSiena`(Ripley et al., 2011)). Moreover, programming languages offer many advantages over GUIs, such as facilitating greater reproducibility, transparency and auditability (McLevey et al., 2021; McLevey, 2021).

For each software tool, we guide readers through the process of loading network data, visualising networks, generating descriptive statistics, calculating centrality measures and data-driven approaches to detecting subgroups.[4] Throughout, we will use data from the Copenhagen Networks Study (Sapiezynski et al., 2019; Stopczynski et al., 2014),[5] which is comprised of digital records from more than 700 participating university students collected over a period of four weeks during an academic term. This dataset contains an attribute list with students' gender (which the researchers coded as male, female, or not specified) and four edge-lists containing information on students' Facebook friendship ties, phone call ties, SMS messaging ties and face-to-face interactions captured via Bluetooth (i.e., 'proximity events', in which two students were close enough for their devices to scan each other). Apart from Facebook friendships, the observed ties are temporal – the phone calls, SMS messages and Bluetooth connections edgelists all contain timestamps, measured in the number of seconds elapsed since the beginning of the study.

GRAPHICAL USER INTERFACES

UCINet with NetDraw

UCINet (Borgatti et al., 2002) is a Windows-based GUI for social network analysis. It contains a broad range of network analysis tools, including centrality analysis, subgroup and positional analyses, network correlation and regression, and 'p1' (stochastic dyad) models. UCINet also includes an integrated network visualisation program called NetDraw that allows users to create simple network visualisations. As previously mentioned, UCINet has a long history in social network analysis and remains one of the most popular GUIs for network analysis today (Huisman & Duijn, 2011; Knoke & Yang, 2019).

As a GUI-based environment, all UCINet routines are organised into sub-menu items within the *File, Data, Transform, Tools, Network, Visualize, Options* and *Help* drop-down menus. The buttons below the menu ribbon are shortcuts to popular sub-menu items.

Given that using UCINet necessarily involves frequent navigation of the drop-down menus, this section will employ a shorthand: top-level menu items will appear at the left-hand side, followed by a rightward-facing arrow and either another menu or the desired item. Consider the following:

Network → Centrality → Multiple Measures

The above, by way of an example, should be interpreted as an instruction to first select the 'Network' drop-down, followed by the 'Centrality' sub-menu found therein, before finally selecting the 'Multiple Measures' item found within the 'Centrality' sub-menu.

In what follows, we use UCINet 6 for Windows (Version 6.739) to demonstrate basic data loading and analysing processes.

Data Preparation and Loading

There are several straightforward methods for loading data into UCINet. One easy approach involves importing either network data or attribute data (or both) in matrix format via an Excel file (using *Data → Import Excel*) or pasting the data directly into the UCINet DL editor (by selecting *Data → Data editors → DL editor*). It is also possible to load data in the form of edgelists, which help save disk space if the network is sparse. To record tie strength using an edgelist, a third column can be added next to each node pair to specify the strength of the tie. To record multirelational ties, additional columns in an

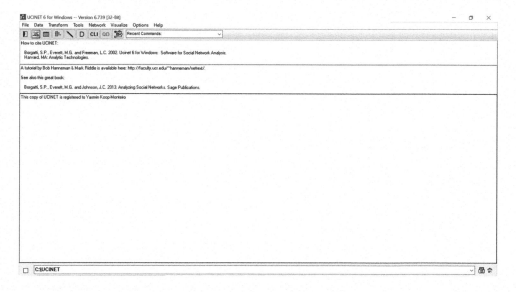

Figure 42.1 View of UCINet program window

edgelist can specify various relationships between pairs of nodes.

Using the *Transform* and *Data* menu items, researchers can manage the data as needed to transpose, symmetrise, dichotomise and normalise the data, impute missing values, combine relations and so on. For example, one popular data manipulation approach involves projecting a two-mode affiliation matrix to a one-mode matrix (e.g., turning student–Facebook group memberships into co-memberships) using *Data → Affiliations* (two-mode to one-mode) and choosing *sums of cross-products (overlaps)* as the data conversion method.

To load the Copenhagen student network data, we can copy and paste each edgelist (Edgelist1 data format) and attribute list (Matrix data format) in the DL editor.[6] Next, we click *Save* and select a name and file location for each file. Once saved, UCINet generates two copies of each file (a *.##d* file containing the data and a *.##h* file containing the metadata), either of which can be opened in UCINet. Edgelists are automatically saved as matrices in UCINet. Additionally, we can create a 'same gender' matrix (1 = gender match, 0 = no match) from the gender attribute data using *Data → Attribute to matrix* and choosing 'exact matches' as the similarity metric.

Visualising Networks

Visualising a network in UCINet is quick and easy with NetDraw, which can be launched using *Visualize → NetDraw*. The first step is to load network data into NetDraw by navigating to *File → Open file*. Attribute data can be brought into NetDraw in the same way. Then, using the Properties menu, researchers can assign unique properties to nodes and ties (such as colour, size, symbol and line thickness) based on node attributes and tie strength or direction.

To visualise the phone calls network (which is valued and directed), we first load the data and save it as 'calls.##h'. We can then select *File → Open → UCINet dataset → Network* and choose the *calls.##h* file.

Next, we can open gender attribute data (*File → Open → UCINet dataset → Attribute data* and select the gender attribute file). To set node colour according to gender (e.g., green for male, orange for female, grey for unknown) we can use *Properties → Nodes → Symbols → Color*.

We can then set node size according to degree centrality. Centrality measures can be calculated in NetDraw directly using *Analysis → Centrality Measures*.[7] To set node size according to in-degree,

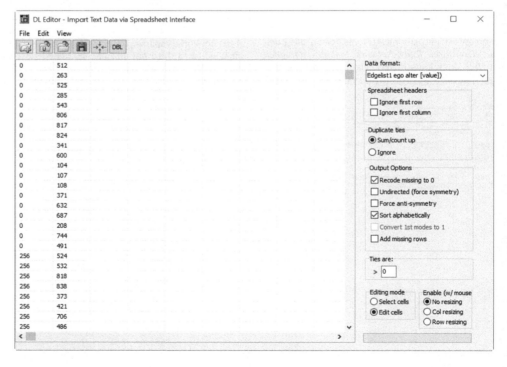

Figure 42.2 View of DL Editor with Facebook edgelist data from the Copenhagen Networks Study

SCIENTIFIC SOFTWARE FOR NETWORK ANALYSIS

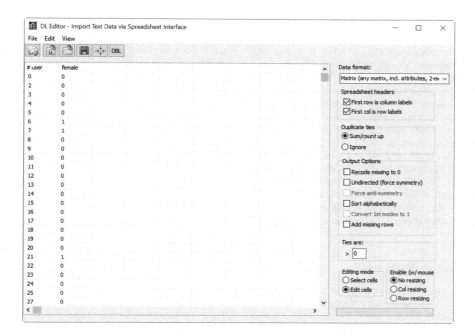

Figure 42.3 View of DL Editor with gender attribute data from the Copenhagen Networks Study

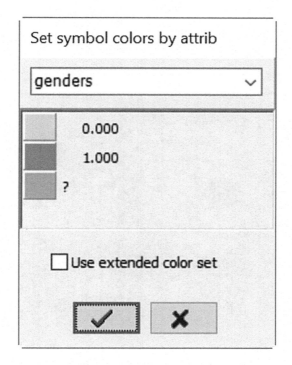

Figure 42.4 Assigning node colour by gender attribute

we use *Properties → Nodes → Size → Attribute-based* and select in-degree as the desired attribute. We can also set edge thickness according to tie strength using *Properties → Lines → Size → Tie Strength*.

The resulting visualisation, shown in Figure 42.5, is fairly busy, but is a useful foundation for exploring the network. For example, node 401 is the largest node in the network, which indicates that participant 401 received calls from the largest number of people in this study. To inspect 401's ego-network, we can right-click on 401 and select *Egonet*. We can also view 401's attributes by right-clicking and selecting *Attributes*. To display the edge weights, we can click on the edge weight shortcut located in the ribbon below the drop-down menu (it has an image of a tie with a number above it to signal an edge weight).

Descriptive Statistics

UCINet offers various statistics to help understand a network's characteristics (Borgatti et al., 2018; Hanneman & Riddle, 2005; Prell, 2012). Degree centralisation (e.g., Freeman, 1978), for example, can be found using *Network → Whole networks & cohesion → Multiple whole-network measures*. Other useful descriptive statistics include whole-network measures of cohesion, such as the overall density of the network, the degree of network closure, and the average path distance between two nodes (Burt, 1980; Wasserman & Faust, 1994); all can be accessed using *Network→ Whole networks & Cohesion measures→ Multiple whole-network measures*. Researchers can also use *Tools Univariate statistics* to calculate different measures (including the mean, standard deviation, minimum and maximum values) for the rows and columns of a matrix. The Facebook friend network, for example, has degree centralisation 0.107, density 0.20, transitivity 0.244 and an average path length of 2.98 (meaning it takes an average of two to three 'hops' for one node to reach another node in the network).

Centrality Analysis

UCINet offers a wide variety of centrality measures to assess a node's structural position in a network (under *Network → Centrality*), including degree (Freeman, 1978), eigenvector (Bonacich, 1972), beta/power (Bonacich, 1987) and betweenness (Freeman, 1978) centrality. Details about each of these measures can be found in the *Help* file or by searching within the help menu item.

To get multiple measures of centrality for the Facebook friendship network (which is binary and undirected), we can use *Network → Centrality → Multiple measures*. This generates a text file with centrality measures for all 800 nodes in the Facebook friendship network.

Results can be exported to an Excel file for further analysis (this can be done with *Data → Export → Excel*). For example, within Excel (or

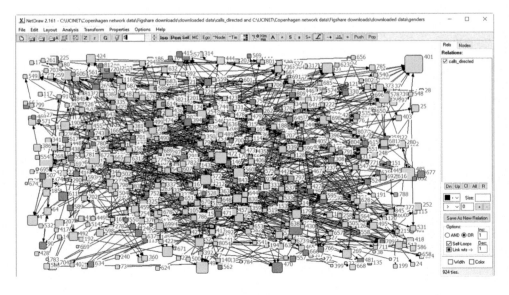

Figure 42.5 Phone calls network with node colour and size showing gender and in-degree centrality

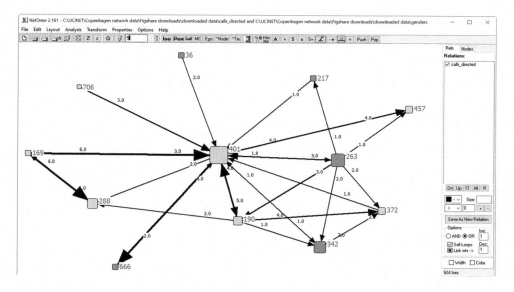

Figure 42.6 Node 401's ego-network (link weights represent the number of incoming and outgoing calls between 401 and his alters)

some other spreadsheet software), we can sort the columns listing the different centrality measures from highest to lowest (and vice versa) to see which nodes have the highest and lowest centrality scores.

The results show that node 485 has the highest degree centrality in this network, with 101 Facebook friendship ties to other students in this study. Node 485 also obtained the highest eigenvector and beta centrality in this network, which suggests that 485 has popular alters (Facebook friends) and a higher degree of influence on other students in this network. Node 13, however, received the highest betweenness centrality score and thus has the largest number of Facebook friendship ties to other study participants that are themselves unconnected. Node 13 could therefore serve as a bridge between these unconnected alters.

Subgroup Analysis

UCINet offers multiple ways to detect densely connected substructures in a network. To assess the number of cliques (Luce & Perry, 1949; Wasserman & Faust, 1994; Scott, 2017) in the Facebook friendship network, we can use *Network → Subgroups → Cliques*. The minimum clique size consists of three nodes, but because this is a large network, we will increase the minimum clique size to reduce the volume of output and focus only on larger groups. In this case, we will increase the minimum clique size to thirteen, but this is an arbitrary decision and simply for illustration. This returns a text file indicating that seven cliques with size thirteen were identified. By examining the resulting output file, we observe several overlapping memberships in various cliques, with nodes 49, 74, 96, 104, 173, 190, 217, 401 and 817 sharing overlapping memberships in all seven cliques.

UCINet is also capable of organising nodes into unique blocks within a core–periphery structure (Borgatti & Everett, 2000), in which core actors interact primarily with other core actors and periphery actors also primarily interact with core actors. This can be done using *Network → Core/Periphery*. Likewise, UCINet's continuous core–periphery model can assign a 'coreness' value to each node in a network based on their closeness to the maximally connected core (*Network → Core-Periphery → Continuous*).

Looking at the Bluetooth network (which is a valued and undirected graph measuring 'proximity events' between students), the results of the continuous core–periphery model reveal that node 48 has the highest coreness value in the network (with a value of 0.168) and is closest to being in the network core. However, the model correlation is quite weak (0.183), indicating that the core–periphery model is not a good fit for the Bluetooth network data.[8] This lack of a clear core–periphery structure in the Bluetooth network makes sense given the expected spatial dynamics of a large student network. Social factors and behavioural patterns (like friendships or repeated seating arrangements during lectures) can, for example, lead students to (more or less) evenly cluster into smaller subgroups of nodes that are most frequently in close contact with one another (as opposed to a core–periphery structure where most students are often only spatially proximate to a few members of the core group).

UCINet has been a popular software choice for networks researchers since the 1980s. Like other popular GUI software, it is capable of handling reasonably large datasets (Gary, 2018; Huisman & van Duijn, 2011) and offers many options for descriptive, positional and subgroup analysis (including the centrality measures, core–periphery models and clique analysis described in the previous subsections). Beyond this, UCINet can perform some simple inferential statistical analyses, including *multiple regression quadratic assignment procedures* (MRQAP) (see Krackhardt, 1987; Dekker et al., 2007), via the Tools →Testing Hypotheses sub-menu items. However, the accessibility gains that come with a GUI come at a cost, such as making transparency, reproducibility and auditability more challenging. UCINet users are also limited to the methods and models that are currently implemented in the software, whereas programming environments allow researchers to implement new methods and models, and to work with multiple specialised software packages at the same time. In the following sections, we'll demonstrate how one can use packages for the programming languages R and Python for network analysis.

PROGRAMMING LANGUAGES

Over time, inferential approaches to network analysis have become increasingly prominent (e.g., Cranmer et al., 2020; Scott et al., this volume). Many important advances in this area – including *exponential random graph models* (ERGMs; Koskinen, this volume), *stochastic actor-oriented models* (SOAMs; Snijders & Steglich, this volume), *latent position models* (LPMs; Kaur et al., this volume), *relational event models* (REMs; Schecter & Contractor, this volume) and *Bayesian stochastic blockmodels* (BSBs; Browne et al., this volume), among others – are not available in GUI software like UCINet, but vibrant scientific communities have formed around their implementation in R and Python packages. Similarly, recent conceptual advances in network analysis – including those associated with the development of computational social science (Kitts et al., this volume), socioecological systems (Bodin, this volume), sociosemantic networks (Shugars & González-Bailón, this volume), culture and science (Lizardo, this volume; Kang & Evans, this volume), contagion and diffusion (Centola, this volume), network interventions (Valente, this volume) and multimodal (Jasny, this volume) and multilevel networks (Lazega & Wang, this volume) typically require bespoke data cleaning and modelling that is best done with a programming language (McLevey et al., 2021). Below, we provide introductions to R and Python, both of which are widely used in contemporary network analysis.

R with sna

R is a free/open-source programming environment developed for statistical computing (R Core Team, 2021). R is based on a command line interface, but there are a number of *integrated development environments* (IDEs) available, the most popular of which is RStudio, which enables users to iteratively develop, execute and debug R code (RStudio Team, 2020). R is widely used in many research fields, including network analysis. In this section, we focus on the utility of one key social network analysis packages within R: sna (Butts, 2008).

Data Preparation and Loading

First, the sna package and all of its dependencies can be installed by calling the `install.packages()` function, with the name of the package specified inside the parentheses surrounded by quotation marks, and the dependencies option set as `True`:

```
install.packages('sna', dependencies=True)
```

Once the installation has concluded, the sna package can be loaded into R using the `library()` function, albeit without the quotation marks this time.

```
library(sna)
```

We'll start by loading the Bluetooth data from the Copenhagen Networks Study, stored in a comma-separated value (*.csv*) file.[9] We do this by using the built-in R function `read.csv()`.[10] We'll also provide R with column names and store the resulting dataframe as an object called `bt_data`:

```
bt_data <- read.csv('bt_symmetric.csv',
  col.names = c(
  'timestamp',
  'user_a',
  'user_b',
  'rssi'))
```

We can inspect the first six rows of the resulting dataframe by calling the `head()` function.[11]

```
head(bt_data)
```

	timestamp	user_a	user_b	rssi
1	0	0	−1	0
2	0	1	−1	0
3	0	2	−1	0
4	0	3	−2	−88
5	0	5	−1	0
6	0	6	−1	0

The first column 'Timestamp' indicates when the Bluetooth connection was established, taking the form of an integer that counts the number of seconds elapsed since the beginning of the study. The two middle columns 'user_a' and 'user_b' indicate the ID number of the individuals whose devices connected. A value of -1 or -2 indicates that no connection was made, or that the device connected with didn't belong to someone participating in the study. The final column stands for *received signal strength indicator*, which is a signal strength indicator that we won't be using in this section.

The dataframe we're left with represents the entirety of the Bluetooth data collected during the whole study period – far more than we need to work with in this section. To whittle it down to more manageable dimensions, we can utilise the `subset()` function, which allows us to specify which rows and columns we'd like to keep. We'll specify that we only want rows whose timestamps belong to the first 12 hours of the study (which is 43,200 seconds), and the only columns we want to keep are the two 'user' columns. Then we remove the old dataframe and view the top six rows of the new one:

```
# Create an edgelist consisting of connections from the first 12 hours
bt_edgelist <- subset(bt_data,
  timestamp <= 43200,
  select = c('user_a', 'user_b')
)

# Remove old dataframe
rm(bt_data)
# View the top six rows of 'bt_edgelist'
head(bt_edgelist)
```

	user_a	user_b
1	0	−1
2	1	−1
3	2	−1
4	3	−2
5	5	−1
6	6	−1

Our last data processing task involves removing the ineligible users (-1 and -2) from the dataframe. In this case, we will also remove all duplicate rows.

```
# Remove any 'users' with negative ID numbers
bt_edgelist <- bt_edgelist[bt_edgelist$user_a >= 0, ]
bt_edgelist <- bt_edgelist[bt_edgelist$user_b >= 0, ]

# Remove duplicate rows from the dataframe
bt_edgelist <- bt_edgelist[!duplicated(bt_edgelist), ]
```

Finally, we'll pass the dataframe to the `network()` function from the `sna` package to create a network object, which we will call `g`. In the `network()` function we specify that the dataframe is in edgelist format and that the resulting network is undirected. We then delete the dataframe:

```
# Create an undirected network from 'bt_edgelist'.
g <- network(bt_edgelist,
    matrix.type = 'edgelist',
    directed=FALSE
    )

# Delete 'bt_edgelist' from memory, as it is no longer needed.
rm(bt_edgelist)
```

With this, all the necessary data has been loaded and pre-processed; we may now proceed to visualise and explore the network.

Visualising Networks

A useful initial step in most network analysis workflows involves quickly plotting the network, which we will do using the `gplot()` function. We will set aside a more detailed discussion of visualisation, including setting colours and sizes by node attributes, until the subgroup analysis section. We use the `set.seed()` function to ensure the layout of the graph does not change across R sessions, and use the `par()` function to ensure the graphical output pane in R is set to a single plot area (i.e., one row and one column):

```
set.seed(2)
par(mfrow = c(1,1))
gplot(g, usearrows = FALSE, vertex.cex = 2)
```

Descriptive Statistics and Exploratory Analysis

We'll continue with a high-level view of the network by reviewing some common network summary statistics. The `sna` package provides simple procedures for doing so. In fact, we can generate a printout of common statistics by calling the network object itself:

```
g
```

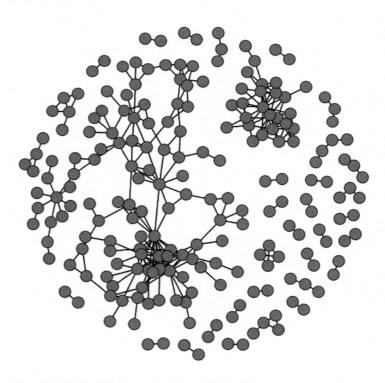

Figure 42.7 Visualisation of the example Bluetooth network

This will produce the following printout:

```
Network attributes:
 vertices = 213
 directed = FALSE
 hyper = FALSE
 loops = FALSE
 multiple = FALSE
 bipartite = FALSE
 total edges= 317
 missing edges= 0
 non-missing edges= 317
Vertex attribute names:
 vertex.names
No edge attributes
```

Among other things, this enables us to quickly see that our undirected network has 213 nodes and 317 edges.[12]

We can also use functions from the sna package to calculate whole-network statistics. The network's density, for example, can be calculated using the gden() function:

```
# Calculate network density
gden(g, mode='graph')

[1] 0.01404022
```

The method for calculating many whole-network and nodal statistics can differ based on whether the network is directed (digraph) or undirected (graph). Here, we set mode = 'graph' since our example network is undirected.

Centrality Analysis

The sna package contains functions that calculate various centrality measures. For now, we'll focus on degree, eigenvector and betweenness centrality. The functions for each are as follows:

- degree centrality: degree()
- eigenvector centrality: evcent()
- betweenness centrality: betweenness()

To calculate one of the centrality measures, call the corresponding function and pass the network (g) as the first argument, along with an additional argument: gmode = 'graph'. Additionally, for eigenvector and betweenness centralities, it is often convenient to rescale the results such that they range from 0 to 1 – we'll accomplish this by dividing the resulting vector by the maximum value present. In the code block below, we calculate each centrality measure and save the results in their respective variables:

```
# Calculate Degree Centrality
deg <- degree(g, gmode = 'graph')

# Calculate Eigenvector Centrality
eig <- evcent(g, gmode = 'graph')

# Rescale Eigenvector Centrality so that the maximum is 1
eig <- eig/max(eig)

# Calculate Betweenness Centrality
btwn <- betweenness(g, gmode = 'graph')

# Rescale Betweenness Centrality so that the maximum is 1
btwn <- btwn/max(btwn)
```

For the sake of convenience, we'll combine the three centrality scores into a dataframe using the cbind() function and assign the result to an object called centralities:

```
# Combine the centrality scores into a single dataframe
centralities <- cbind(deg, eig, btwn)
```

As with most of the dataframes we create in this section, we'll verify that the result is behaving how we expect it to by examining the first six rows using the head() function:

```
head(centralities)
```

This dataframe could also be saved to disk as a .csv file using the `write.csv()` function. This isn't a strictly necessary part of our workflow, but it will allow us to load the centrality scores later without having to recalculate them:

	deg	eig	btwn
1	1	5.919215e-141	0.000
2	1	1.937978e-07	0.000
3	1	5.919215e-141	0.000
4	15	9.425547e-01	0.287074444
5	6	3.308802e-10	0.001809735
6	7	3.950270e-10	0.001488315

```
# Save the centralities dataframe to disk
write.csv(centralities, file='centralities.csv')
```

Finally, we can add the centrality measures to our network object as node attributes. In the following code block, the `%v%` operator tells R that we are adding what comes after the operator as a vertex attribute to network `g`, and that the attribute should be named according to the string that appears between the `%v%` and `<- operators`:

```
# Add each of the centrality scores to the network as vertex attributes
g %v% 'deg' <- deg
g %v% 'eig' <- eig
g %v% 'btwn' <- btwn
```

Subgroup Analysis

The simple network visualisation we created at the start of this analysis in R (see Figure 42.7) reveals two large components, along with many dyads and triads. In order to examine these structures in more detail, we can use the `component()` and `kcores()` functions from the `sna` package. Let's start with components:

```
# Calculate components and store results in 'cd'
cd<-component.dist(g, connected = 'weak')
```

R stores information from the component detection algorithm within the `cd` object that we created. We can access that information using R's $ operator, which is used to extract information from any R object. For example, we can extract information about the sizes of all identified components, which the algorithm saves within the `cd` object using the label `csize`. We're primarily interested in the largest components, so we'll take the results from `cd$size`, sort them in descending order and pass the result to the `head()` function, which will provide us with the sizes of the six largest components in the network:

```
head(sort(cd$csize, decreasing = True))
[1] 107 26 5 4 4 4
```

We can also determine how many components are in our network by passing `cd$size` to R's built-in `length()` function, which tells us that the network has 34 components:

```
length(cd$size)
[1] 34
```

Next, we add each node's component membership to the network as a vertex attribute called `component`:

```
# Add the component membership to the network as a vertex variable
g %v% 'component' <- cd$membership
```

Now that we have stored that information in the network object, we can use it to easily modify our network visualisations. In this case, we'll use vertex colours to indicate component membership, and vertex sizes set to correspond to various centrality measures.[13] To accomplish this, we create a `colours` object that corresponds to the list of component memberships.[14]

SCIENTIFIC SOFTWARE FOR NETWORK ANALYSIS   621

The `par(mfrow = c(1,3))` tells R that we want to print three graphs in a single row. Then we plot the network three times, once for each of the degree measures:

```
# Add 1 to the vector of component memberships and store as 'colours'
colours = get.vertex.attribute(g,'component')+1

# Ensure that the following 3 visualizations will be plotted
together
par(mfrow = c(1,3))

# Draw 3 plots, one for each of the centrality measures
set.seed(2)
gplot(g,
  vertex.cex = log(get.vertex.attribute(g,'deg') + 1),
  vertex.col = colours,
  usearrows = FALSE)
title('Degree', line = -4)
set.seed(2)
gplot(g,
  vertex.cex = log(get.vertex.attribute(g,'eig')+1)*5,
  vertex.col = colours,
  usearrows = FALSE)
title('Eigenvector', line = -4)
set.seed(2)
gplot(g,
  vertex.cex = log(get.vertex.attribute(g,'btwn')+1)*5,
  vertex.col = colours,
  usearrows = FALSE)
title('Betweenness', line = -4)
```

Now we can see the relationship between network components and centrality measures. The degree centrality for nodes in the two largest components is larger than for nodes in smaller components, as one might expect. There are a few nodes with high eigenvector centrality in a dense portion of the largest component, and the nodes that seem to link the two portions of the largest component together have the largest betweenness centralities.

We can also use the `component` attribute to extract different subnetworks. Here we use the `get.inducedSubgraph()` function to extract the subnetwork of the largest component (component #1) and save it as the network object `subnet`. The summary of the network confirms the number of vertices (107) matches the size of component #1:

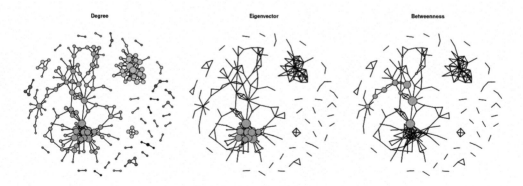

Figure 42.8 Visualisation of example Bluetooth network showing component membership (node colour) and three common degree measures (node size)

```
# Return a subgraph of our network consisting of nodes in component 1
subnet <- get.inducedSubgraph(g, v=which(g %v% 'component'==1))
subnet

Network attributes:
 vertices = 107
 directed = FALSE
 hyper = FALSE
 loops = FALSE
 multiple = FALSE
 bipartite = FALSE
 total edges= 193
 missing edges= 0
 non-missing edges= 193
Vertex attribute names:
 component vertex.names
No edge attributes
```

Next, we plot the subnetwork of component #1 using the `gplot()` function:

```
# Plot the subgraph of component 1
set.seed(2)
gplot(subnet,
  usearrows = FALSE,
  vertex.cex = 2)
```

Another way to explore the community structure in a network is using k-cores analysis (Borgatti et al., 2022; Seidman, 1983). For this portion of the analysis we use the component #1 subnetwork, as it will be easier to interpret without the many extra dyads and triads. First, we use the `kcores()` function to determine the k-core membership of each vertex in the subnetwork, saving the results in an object called `kcoSub`. We can then graph the subnetwork, setting the vertex colour based on k-core membership. At the same time, we will calculate degree centralities for the nodes in the subnetwork and use these to scale the size of the nodes in the visualisation. We'll also include the k-core value of each node as a numerical label to help interpret the results:

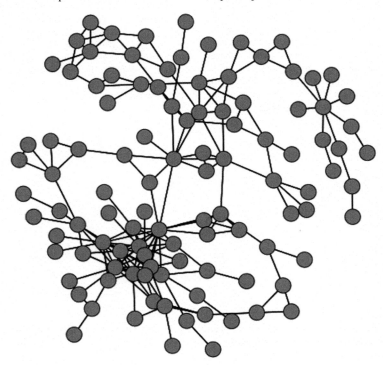

Figure 42.9 Visualisation of component #1 subgraph from the example Bluetooth network

```
# Extract k-cores from subnet and view first 6 values
kcoSub <- kcores(subnet, mode='graph')
head(kcoSub)
```

47	69	101	179	244	263
1	5	3	2	2	5

```
# Calculate the degree centrality of each vertex in subnet
subDeg <- degree(subnet, gmode = 'graph')
subnet %v% 'deg' <- subDeg
set.seed(2)
gplot(subnet,
  vertex.col = kcoSub+1,
  vertex.cex = log(get.vertex.attribute(subnet,'deg'))+1,
  usearrows = FALSE,
  label = kcoSub,
  label.cex = .5)
```

The plot reveals that the subnetwork contains five k-cores, each denoted by a different colour. The k-core associated with purple appears to occupy a particularly dense region of the network – these nodes are part of k-core 5. We'll extract and graph this k-core network; to do so, we create a new network called g_kco, which only contains nodes that have a kcoSub value of 5. This k-core network has eleven vertices and 80 edges:

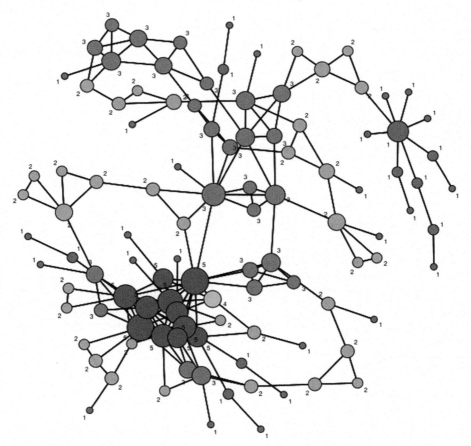

Figure 42.10 Visualisation of component #1 subgraph from example Bluetooth network showing k-core membership (node colour) and degree (node size)

```
# Create a sub-subgraph consisting of vertices in k-core 5
g_kco <- as.network(subnet[kcoSub==max(kcoSub), kcoSub==max(kcoSub)])
g_kco

Network attributes:
 vertices = 11
 directed = TRUE
 hyper = FALSE
 loops = FALSE
 multiple = FALSE
 bipartite = FALSE
 total edges= 80
 missing edges= 0
 non-missing edges= 80
Vertex attribute names:
 vertex.names
No edge attributes
```

We'll conclude by plotting this k-core network. Since this is a small network, we can safely enlarge the node size (using the `vertex.cex` argument). The result is arguably the 'core-of-the-core' of the network:

```
set.seed(2)
gplot(g_kco,
 usearrows=FALSE,
 label = get.vertex.attribute(g_kco,'vertex.names'),
 label.cex = .5,
 vertex.cex = 2,
 label.pos=5)
```

In this section we used the `sna` R library to conduct an analysis of the Bluetooth data from the Copenhagen Networks Study. `sna` is part of a larger suite of R packages that comprise `statnet`, which is an award-winning comprehensive collection of R packages for network analysis.

Python with NetworkX

Python is a general-purpose open-source programming language (van Rossum, 1995). Its ease of use, flexibility and expansive package environment have cemented it as one of the most commonly used languages for a broad range of data collection, machine learning and data analysis tasks (McLevey, 2021; Sayeth Saabith et al., 2019; Srinath, 2017; Stančin & Jović, 2019). For the purposes of this section, we have chosen to focus on `NetworkX`, a Python package with utilities for processing, visualising, manipulating and analysing networks (Hagberg et al., 2008b; Hagberg et al., 2008a).

Data Preparation and Loading

In addition to using `NetworkX` for network analysis, we'll use the packages `matplotlib.pyplot` for visualisation and `pandas` for data processing.[15] We'll start by loading all the required packages:

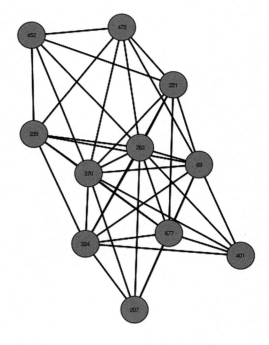

Figure 42.11 Visualisation of k-core #5 subgraph from component #1 subgraph of example Bluetooth data

```
import matplotlib.pyplot as plt
import networkx as nx
import pandas as pd
```

Next, we'll read the SMS data from the Copenhagen Networks Study and store it as a dataframe called `sms_df`:

```
sms_df = pd.read_csv('../copenhagen_data/sms.csv')
sms_df.head()
```

Running `sms_df.head()` prints the first five observations in our dataset:

	timestamp	sender	recipient
0	18	370	512
1	37	512	370
2	126	370	512
3	134	0	512
4	312	137	136

As with the R example above, we'll whittle the data down to a more manageable size, this time by isolating the first week of messages using the timestamp data. Since the timestamp column of our dataframe tracks when an SMS message was sent (in seconds elapsed since the beginning of the study), we can use it to isolate the first week of messages:

```
# Isolate first week of SMS messages and drop 'timestamp' column
sms_df_week_1 = sms_df.loc[sms_df['timestamp'] < 604800,
 ['sender', 'recipient']]
```

The above code makes use of the `pandas` dataframe `loc[]`, which allows us to specify index-based conditions for the rows (before the comma) and columns (after the comma) to subset the data we want. Next, we'll load it into `NetworkX` using the `from_pandas_edgelist()` function. By setting the `create_using` argument to `nx.Digraph`, we've indicated to `NetworkX` that the resulting network is directed:

```
# Create directed network from SMS dataframe, where 'sender' -> 'recipient'
sms_net = nx.from_pandas_edgelist(sms_df_week_1,
   source='sender',
   target='recipient',
   create_using=nx.DiGraph )
```

We'll also load the gender attribute data using `pandas`:

```
# Load gender data from 'genders.csv' and
# inspect the first and last five rows
gender = pd.read_csv('../copenhagen_data/genders.csv')
gender
```

	user	female
0	0	0
1	2	0
2	3	0
3	4	0
4	5	0
...	...	...
782	840	0
783	841	1
784	845	0
785	846	0
786	847	1

From the data preview above, we can see that there is not a perfect one-to-one match between the dataframe's index and its user ID column (*# user*). We can get around this by instructing *pandas* to re-index the dataframe using the '*# user*' column via the `set_index()` method. We'll do so, and then export the resulting dataframe as a dictionary, which consists of key-value pairs,[16] that we'll use to add the gender information to our network as node attributes:

```
# Re-index the gender dataframe
# and export values as a python dictionary
gender_dict = gender.set_index('# user').to_dict(orient='index')

# Add gender values to network as node attributes
nx.set_node_attributes(sms_net, gender_dict)
```

We can confirm that the above code worked by subscripting the list of nodes in our network (using square brackets), which causes NetworkX to return information about the retrieved node's attributes. For example, for the first two nodes (node 370 and 512) in the edgelist, we can retrieve their gender using:

```
print(sms_net.nodes[370])
print(sms_net.nodes[512])
```

```
{'female': 0}
{'female': 1}
```

Before moving on, it would be a good idea to ensure that all the nodes in our network are now in possession of a gender value. We can do this by using set subtraction (part of the Python basic library) to see if any members of our network are absent from the gender dataframe:

```
# Get set of nodes in network but not in the gender dataframe
missing_gender = set(sms_net.nodes) - set(gender['# user'])
missing_gender
```

```
{1,
31,
56,
109,
143,
166,
175,
202,
257,
312,
322,
331,
454,
458,
605,
688,
748,
843}
```

These nodes are not represented in the gender dataframe. We'll assign a value of -1 for these nodes to indicate that gender is not specified:

```
# Set gender values of nodes with missing gender data to -1
nx.set_node_attributes(sms_net, {n:{'female':-1} for n in missing_gender})
```

Visualising Networks

The NetworkX package includes a suite of visualisation tools that are built on top of the Matplotlib visualisation library. To demonstrate how one might use these features, we'll extract and then plot the largest component in sms_net:

```
# Create list of components of network
# Sort by length and return the largest
giant_component = max(nx.weakly_connected_components(sms_net), key=len)

# Create a subgraph consisting of nodes from the giant component
giant_subgraph = sms_net.subgraph(giant_component)
```

When we plot the network, we'll colour the nodes according to their gender attribute. We'll accomplish this by creating a dictionary of colours that correspond to each gender value, and then create a list containing the appropriate colour for each node's given gender value:

```
# Define colours
colors = {0:'limegreen', 1:'tab:cyan', -1:'silver'}

# Create list of colours of length equal to the number of nodes in the network
gender_generator = nx.get_node_attributes(giant_subgraph, 'female').values()
node_colors = [colors[c] for c in gender_generator]
```

The `draw_networkx()` function alone is capable of visualising the network if called with the network as the only argument. However, we'll improve on the visualisation by passing the following arguments to the function:

- `pos`: for this network, the `kamada_kawai_layout()` produces a less cluttered and more consistent layout than the default layout algorithm;
- `node_size`: increasing the node size aids visibility on a large canvas;
- `node_color`: the gender-based colours we specified above are supplied here;
- `with_labels`: removing node labels helps to limit visual clutter.

Finally, we'll use some code drawing on the `matplotlib` library to further clean up the visualisation:

```
# Plot the giant component
fig = plt.figure(figsize=(15, 15))

nx.draw_networkx(giant_subgraph,
  pos = nx.kamada_kawai_layout(giant_subgraph),
  node_size = 200,
  node_color = node_colors,
  with_labels = False,
)

# Add black outlines to each node
ax= plt.gca()
ax.collections[0].set_edgecolor('#000000')

# Remove unsightly box around graph
for spine in plt.gca().spines.values():
    spine.set_visible(False)
```

For those interested in exploring the giant component of the SMS network in more detail, the `pyvis` package produces interactive visualisations that can be manipulated and reconfigured by hand. If the `pyvis` package has been installed, the following code block can be used to launch an interactive visualisation in-browser or in a Jupyter Notebook (Granger & Perez, 2021; Beg et al., 2021):

```
# OPTIONAL: For interactive graphs
from pyvis.network import Network

sms_pyvis = Network('700px', '700px', notebook=True)
sms_pyvis.from_nx(sms_net)
sms_pyvis.show('sms.html')
```

Descriptive Statistics

Now that we have a visual sense of the giant component, we'll zoom back out to examine the entire SMS network. The `sms_net` object contains a series of useful attributes and methods that can be leveraged for information about the network. The `nodes` attribute, for instance, returns a list of all the nodes in the network. Supplying this information to Python's built-in `len()` function gives you the number of nodes in the network:

```
# Determine number of nodes in network
len(sms_net.nodes)
405
```

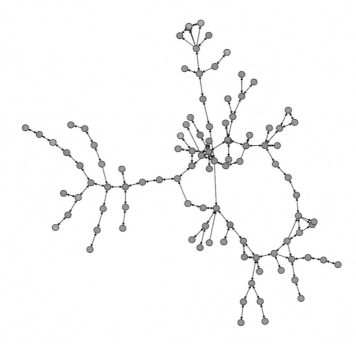

Figure 42.12 A plot of the largest component from the first week of the Copenhagen Networks Study's SMS data

The same goes for edges:

```
# Determine number of edges in network
len(sms_net.edges)
609
```

```
# Get degree counts
counts = nx.degree_histogram(sms_net)
counts

[0, 42, 195, 35, 73, 12, 28, 11, 4, 2, 2, 0, 0, 0, 1]
```

Using `matplotlib`, we can covert the counts into a histogram, where each bin corresponds to a node's combined in- and out-degree:

```
fig = plt.figure(figsize=(7, 7), frameon=False)
for spine in plt.gca().spines.values():
   spine.set_visible(False)
bins = range(0, len(counts))
plt.bar(x=bins, height=nx.degree_histogram(sms_net))

plt.xlabel('Degree')
plt.ylabel('Count')
plt.show()
```

`NetworkX` also contains functions for producing whole-network statistics such as density or average shortest path length. For example, we

`NetworkX` also contains a wide variety of functions for exploring and analysing networks. The `degree_histogram()` function, for instance, returns a list of combined in- and out-degree counts:

can easily compute the density of the large subgraph we visualised in the previous subsection (Figure 42.12):

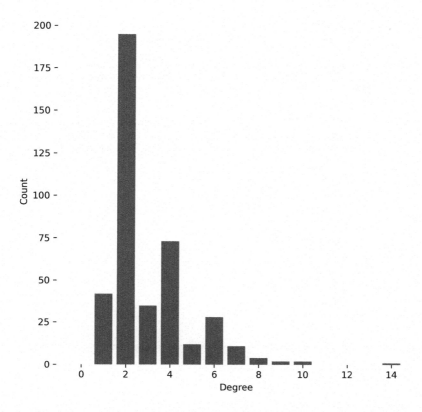

Figure 42.13 A histogram of the degree counts from the nodes contained in the first week of the Copenhagen Networks Study's SMS data

```
# Density of 'giant_subgraph', rounded to 5 significant figures
round(nx.density(giant_subgraph), 5)
0.0197
```

NetworkX cannot calculate average shortest path length (ASPL) on the whole network because it consists of many separate components, and thus the path length for some dyads is infinite. We can, however, assess the ASPL on the largest component:

```
# ASPL of 'giant_subgraph', rounded to 2 figures.
round(nx.average_shortest_path_length(giant_subgraph), 2)
6.38
```

Centrality Analysis

NetworkX features an extensive library of methods for calculating various measures of centrality (Everett & Borgatti, this volume). The full list of NetworkX centrality methods can be found in the package's documentation.[17] For the purposes of this chapter, we'll stick to the usual suspects: degree, in-degree, out-degree, eigenvector and betweenness. Starting with degree centrality:

```
# Calculate the degree centrality of each node in the SMS network
deg = nx.degree_centrality(sms_net)
```

Now that we've calculated the degree centrality for each node in the network, we can use the resulting Python dictionary as the basis for a new centralities dataframe:

```
# Create a dataframe and add degree centrality as a column
sms_centralities = pd.DataFrame.from_dict(deg, orient='index', columns=['deg'])
sms_centralities
```

	deg
370	0.0049505
512	0.0247525
0	0.0049505
137	0.00990099
136	0.0049505
...	...
441	0.00990099
552	0.0049505
416	0.0049505
70	0.00247525
129	0.0049505

We can follow a similar process to calculate each of the remaining centrality measures and add them to our centralities dataframe:

```
# Calculate remaining centrality measures and store in centralities
dataframe
eig = pd.Series(nx.eigenvector_centrality(sms_net))
sms_centralities['eig'] = pd.Series(eig)

bet = pd.Series(nx.betweenness_centrality(sms_net))
sms_centralities['bet'] = bet

in_deg = pd.Series(nx.in_degree_centrality(sms_net))
sms_centralities['in_deg'] = in_deg

out_deg = pd.Series(nx.out_degree_centrality(sms_net))
sms_centralities['out_deg'] = out_deg

sms_centralities
```

	deg	eig	bet	in_deg	out_deg
370	0.0049505	0.0194126	0	0.00247525	0.00247525
512	0.0247525	0.061966	0.0096594	0.0123762	0.0123762
0	0.0049505	0.0194126	0	0.00247525	0.00247525
137	0.00990099	0.19865	0.00107486	0.0049505	0.0049505
136	0.0049505	0.0622308	0	0.00247525	0.00247525
...	...	...	...	...	...
441	0.00990099	7.86541e-10	0	0.0049505	0.0049505
552	0.0049505	7.70929e-24	0	0.00247525	0.00247525
416	0.0049505	7.70929e-24	0	0.00247525	0.00247525
70	0.00247525	2.4543e-18	0	0.00247525	0
129	0.0049505	7.07689e-11	0	0.00247525	0.00247525

Subgroup Analysis

As we've done in previous sections, we'll demonstrate subgroup analysis by isolating a k-core. In the case of NetworkX, we can do this using the k_core() function. We'll tell NetworkX to find k-cores where *k* = 4. Again, this is an arbitrary decision made for the purposes of illustration:

```
# Find k-core for 'k' = 4
sms_kcore = nx.k_core(sms_net, k=4)
```

We can visualise the extracted k-cores using the same approach we've employed throughout this section:

```
# Assign colours to nodes in k-core
k_col = [colors[c] for c in nx.get_node_attributes(sms_kcore,
'female').values()]

# Plot k-core
fig = plt.figure(figsize=(15, 15))

nx.draw_networkx(sms_kcore,
 pos = nx.nx_pydot.pydot_layout(sms_kcore, prog='fdp'),
 node_size = 200,
 node_color = k_col,
 with_labels = False,
 )

# Add black outlines to each node
ax= plt.gca()
ax.collections[0].set_edgecolor('#000000')
# Remove unsightly box around graph
for spine in plt.gca().spines.values():
 spine.set_visible(False)
```

At the outset of this section, we made the decision to render the SMS data as a directed graph, where the act of sending an SMS message was distinct from the act of receiving one. While there are many advantages to using directed graphs, the choice to do so carries some computational disadvantages. NetworkX's core–periphery algorithm – periphery() – cannot be called using a directed network. In a similar vein, NetworkX uses a fast, efficient algorithm for finding cliques in undirected networks; it can be accessed via the function find_cliques(). This approach is incompatible with directed networks such as ours, and we're consequently forced to use a slower recursive alternative. The added processing time isn't of any concern for us, as our network is small enough to trivialise the increase. On larger networks, however, this could pose a problem. Recursive clique detection can be performed using the find_cliques_recursive() function:

```
# Find cliques using the recursive algorithm and assess length of resulting list
sms_cliques = list(nx.find_cliques_recursive(sms_net))
len(sms_cliques)
```

301

Our clique-finding exercise returned many cliques – almost as many as there are nodes in the network. This is because we asked NetworkX to find *all* cliques, which would provide us with all maximally connected subnetworks in the network: any group of two nodes that share a mutual edge would have been included. Let's narrow down the list of cliques to include only those with three or more members:

```
# Create new clique list consisting only of cliques with 3 or more members
sms_cliques_3 = [set(c) for c in sms_cliques if len(c) >= 3]
sms_cliques_3
```

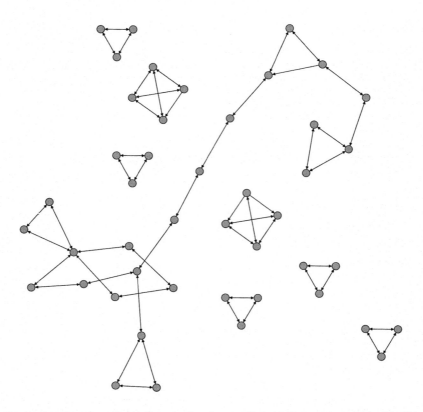

Figure 42.14 Visualisation of the first twelve hours of Copenhagen Networks Study's Bluetooth data, showing the network's k-cores, where $k = 4$

```
[{3, 49, 357},
{4, 221, 344},
{4, 266, 424},
{8, 419, 557},
{12, 13, 492},
{39, 257, 331},
{39, 331, 707},
{95, 551, 640},
{100, 177, 743},
{133, 237, 299},
{146, 176, 611},
{163, 164, 304, 494},
{266, 424, 785},
{267, 269, 403},
{283, 441, 530},
{292, 325, 427},
{339, 379, 584}]
```

Our network contains seventeen cliques with three or more members. These results are of a size that one might visually inspect them for any overlaps, but since we're using a programming language, we can easily automate the process. Using a list comprehension with two for-loops, we can iterate over every pair of cliques to see if any of the nodes belong to more than one clique:

```
# Use list comprehension to determine nodes
# that appear in more than one clique
[set.intersection(a, b)
for i,a in enumerate(sms_cliques_3)
for j,b in enumerate(sms_cliques_3)
if i > j and set.intersection(a, b)
]
[{4}, {39, 331}, {266, 424}]
```

From the foregoing, we can see that nodes 4, 39, 331, 266 and 424 belong to multiple cliques.

As in the case of `sna` for R, this section on network analysis with Python barely scratches the surface of what is possible. Much more can be done with `NetworkX`, as well as other Python network science packages such as `iGraph` (also available for R, see igraph.org) and `graph-tool` (Peixoto, 2014).

CONCLUSION

In this chapter, we provided readers with a practical introduction to three of the software environments that are widely used for social network analysis: UCINet with NetDraw, R with `sna`, and Python with `NetworkX`. All are excellent starting points, but they comprise a small fraction of the packages available for social network analysis. Readers who prefer to use GUIs may wish to look into other tools, such as Visone (Brandes & Wagner, 2004), Pajek (De Nooy et al., 2018), ORA (2014), or Gephi (Heymann & Le Grand, 2014).

For those interested in further exploring the R package environment for network analysis, we recommend looking further into the `statnet` suite (which includes the `sna` library used here), which has an extensive toolkit for exploring, analysing, modelling, simulating and visualising networks (see Krivitsky et al., 2003/2022). Another powerful network science library for R is `RSiena`, which implements SAOMs for longitudinal network analysis with at least two waves on panel data (Ripley et al., 2022; Snijders & Steglich, this volume). RSiena can be used to study the evolution of unweighted, directed or non-directed networks, including one-mode networks, two-mode networks and multivariate networks.

Finally, we recommend that readers interested in Python look into the `graph-tool` package (Peixoto, 2014). While using `graph-tool` users to have a slightly higher degree of technical sophistication (see McLevey, 2021; an accessible introduction); it is very computationally efficient and implements an array of cutting-edge methods for generative network science, Bayesian inference and stochastic blockmodelling (Browne et al., this volume). It can also produce stunning network visualisations. These characteristics alone make the learning investment for using `graph-tool` worthwhile.

Notes

1. Almost 30 years before this volume went to press, Wasserman and Faust (1994) reviewed 27 different software tools. The software landscape has changed a lot since then, but it remains large and diverse.
2. For the sections on R and Python, some basic programming experience on the part of the reader is assumed. Programming experience is unnecessary for the UCINet sections.
3. Such as Pajek (De Nooy et al., 2018), Visone (Brandes & Wagner, 2004) and ORA (Carley, 2014), to cite just a few examples.
4. As with Prell and Schaefer's (this volume) general introduction to social network analysis, we deliberately set aside more complex network methods and models in this chapter.
5. The data used in this chapter can be found at: doi.org/10.6084/m9.figshare.7267433.v1
6. For the Bluetooth network, make sure to remove edges that list -1 and -2 as the second node since these are empty scans and scans of non-participating devices, respectively.
7. The process for calculating centrality measures in NetDraw is distinct from the process used in UCINet proper; the process in UCINet will be covered in the pertinent subsection below.
8. As Borgatti and Everett note, the 'coreness measure is only interpretable to the extent that the model fits' (Borgatti & Everett, 2000, p. 393).
9. Note that R can load many other data formats, including Excel spreadsheets.
10. The example below assumes that *bt_symmetric.csv* is stored in R's current working directory. If that isn't the case, you can either change R's

current working directory using the `setwd()` function or change the filepath to point to where the Bluetooth data is stored.
11 The `head()` function is a built-in part of R's standard library; it can be used on a wide variety of different objects.
12 Throughout this chapter, 'edge' and 'tie' will be used interchangeably, as will 'vertex' and 'node'.
13 We add 1 to the degree measures to account for nodes that may have degrees of zero, which would effectively exclude these nodes from the plot. We take the logarithm of the degree measures (and in the case of 'eig' and 'bet', multiply this by 5) to adjust the size difference between the smallest and largest degree nodes, thus making the graph easier to visually interpret.
14 The *+1* in the code adjusts the colour palette.
15 As with R, you want to ensure that all the necessary packages are installed before attempting to run the code presented below. The code examples in this section depend on the following packages: `matplotlib`, `networkx`, `pandas` and `scipy`. The `graphviz`, `pygraphviz` and `pydot` packages are required for some of the visualisations but are unnecessary for all other code examples.
16 Key-value pairs in a dictionary are analogous to the word-definition pairs found in traditional language dictionaries.
17 See networkx.org/documentation/stable/reference/algorithms/centrality.html

REFERENCES

Beg, M., Taka, J., Kluyver, T., Konovalov, A., Raga-Kelley, M., Thiéry, N.M., & Fangohr, H. (2021). Using Jupyter for reproducible scientific workflows. *Computing in Science and Engineering*, 23(2), 36–46.

Bonacich, P. (1972). Factoring and weighting approaches to status scores and clique identification. *Journal of Mathematical Sociology*, 2, 113–120.

Bonacich, P. (1987). Power and centrality: a family of measures. *American Journal of Sociology*, 92(5), 1170–1182.

Borgatti, S., & Everett, M. (2000). Models of core/periphery structures. *Social Networks*, 21(4), 375–395.

Borgatti, S., Everett, M., & Freeman, L. (2002). Ucinet for Windows: software for social network analysis. *Harvard, MA: Analytic Technologies*, 6, 12–15.

Borgatti, S., Everett, M., & Johnson, J. (2018). *Analyzing social networks* (2nd ed.). Sage.

Borgatti, S., Everett, M., Johnson, J. & Agneessens, F. (2022). *Analyzing social networks using R*. Sage.

Brandes, U., & Wagner, D. (2004). Analysis and visualization of social networks. In M. Jünger & P. Mutzel (Eds.), *Graph Drawing Software* (pp. 321–340). Springer.

Burt, R.S. (1980). Models of network structure. *Annual Review of Sociology*, 6(1), 79–141. doi: 10.1146/annurev.so.06.080180.000455

Butts, C.T. (2008). Social network analysis with SNA. *Journal of Statistical Software*, 24, 1–51.

Carley, K. (2014). ORA: a toolkit for dynamic network analysis and visualization. www.casos.cs.cmu.edu/events/summer_institute/2015/reading_list2/pubs/2014ORAaToolkit.pdf

Cranmer, S., Desmarais, B., & Morgan, J. (2020). *Inferential network analysis*. Cambridge University Press.

De Nooy, W., Mrvar, A., Batagelj, V. (2018). *Exploratory social network analysis with Pajek: revised and expanded edition for updated software*. Cambridge University Press.

Dekker, D., Krackhardt, D., & Snijders, T.A.B. (2007). Sensitivity of MRQAP tests to collinearity and autocorrelation conditions. *Psychometrika*, 72(4), 563–581. doi: 10.1007/s11336-007-9016-1

Freeman, L.C. (1978). Centrality in social networks. *Social Networks*, 1(1968), 215–239.

Gary, R.D. (2018). UCINet. In B.B. Frey (Ed.), *The Sage encyclopedia of educational research, measurement, and evaluation* (pp. 1747–1751). Sage.

Granger, B., & Pérez, F. (2021). Jupyter: thinking and storytelling with code and data. *Computing in Science and Engineering*, 23(2), 7–14.

Hagberg, A.A., Schult, D.A., & Swart, P.J. (2008a). Exploring network structure, dynamics, and function using NetworkX. In G. Varoquaux, T. Vaught & J. Millman (Eds.), *Proceedings of the 7th Python in Science Conference* (pp. 11–15). SciPy.

Hagberg, A., Swart, P., & Chult, D.S. (2008b). *Exploring network structure, dynamics, and function using NetworkX*. Los Alamos National Lab. (LANL).

Handcock, M.S., Hunter, D.R., Butts, C.T., Goodreau, S.M., & Morris, M. (2008). statnet: software tools for the representation, visualization, analysis and simulation of network data. *Journal of Statistical Software*, 24(1), 1548.

Hanneman, R.A., & Riddle, M. (2005). *Introduction to social network methods*. University of California, Riverside. faculty.ucr.edu/~hanneman/nettext/

Heymann, S., & Le Grand, B. (2014). Chapter six exploratory network analysis: visualization and interaction. *Complex Networks and their Applications*, 174.

Huisman, M., & van Duijn, M.A.J. (2011). A reader's guide to SNA software. In J. Scott & P.J. Carrington (Eds.), *The Sage handbook of social network analysis* (pp. 578–600). Sage.

Knoke, D., & Yang, S. (2019). *Social network analysis*. Sage.

Krackhardt, D. (1987). QAP partialling as a test of spuriousness. *Social Networks*, 9, 171–186.

Krivitsky, P.N., Handcock, M.S., Hunter, D.R., Butts, C.T., Klumb, C., Goodreau, S.M., & Morris, M. (2003/2022). *statnet: software tools for the statistical modeling of network data*. statnet.org

Luce, R.D., & Perry, A.D. (1949). A method of matrix analysis of group structure. *Psychometrika*, 14(2), 95–116.

McLevey, J. (2021). *Doing computational social science: a practical introduction*. Sage.

McLevey, J., Browne, P., & Crick, T. (2021). Reproducibility, transparency, and principled data processing. In U. Engel & A. Quan-Haase (Eds.), *Handbook of computational social science*. Routledge.

Peixoto, T.P. (2014). The graph-tool Python library. *figshare*. figshare.com/articles/graph_tool/1164194

Prell, C. (2012). *Social networks analysis: history, theory and methodology*. Sage.

R Core Team (2021). *R: a language and environment for statistical computing*. R Foundation for Statistical Computing. www.R-project.org/

Rachel Darley, G. (2018). UCINet. In B.B. Frey (Ed.), *The Sage encyclopedia of educational research, measurement, and evaluation*. Sage, 1747-1751.

Ripley, R.M., Snijders, T.A., Boda, Z., Vörös, A., & Preciado, P. 2011. *Manual for RSIENA*. University of Oxford, Department of Statistics, Nuffield College.

RStudio Team (2020). *RStudio: integrated development environment for R*. RStudio, PBC. www.rstudio.com/

Sapiezynski, P., Stopczynski, A., Lassen, D.D., & Lehmann, S. (2019). Interaction data from the Copenhagen Networks Study. *Scientific Data*, 6(1), 1–10.

Sayeth Saabith, A.L., Fareez, M.M.M., & Vinothraj, T. (2019). Python current trend applications: an overview. *International Journal of Advance Engineering and Research Development*, 6(10).

Scott, J. (2017). *Social network analysis* (4th ed.). Sage.

Seidman, S.B. (1983). Network structure and minimum degree. *Social Networks*, 5(3), 269–287. doi: 10.1016/0378-8733(83)90028-X

Snijders, T.A.B. (2017). Stochastic actor-oriented models for network dynamics. *Annual Review of Statistics and Its Application*, 4, 343–363.

Srinath, K.R. (2017). Python: the fastest growing programming language. *International Research Journal of Engineering and Technology*, 4(12), 354–357.

Stančin, I., & Jović, A., (2019). An Overview and comparison of free Python libraries for data mining and big data analysis. *42nd International Convention on Information and Communication Technology, Electronics and Microelectronics (MIPRO)*, IEEE, 977–982.

Stopczynski, A., Sekara, V., Sapiezynski, P., Cuttone, A., Madsen, M.M., Larsen, J.E., & Lehmann, S. (2014). Measuring large-scale social networks with high resolution. *PLOS One*, 9(4), e95978.

van Rossum, G. (1995). *Python tutorial*. Centrum voor Wiskunde en Informatica (CWI).

Wasserman, S., & Faust, K. (1994). *Social network analysis: methods and applications*. Cambridge University Press.

Index

ABBA participation shift, 518, 520
Abbott, A., 37, 58
ABBY participation shift, 518, 520
activity recognition, 46–48
actor attributes, 26
actor-oriented co-evolution models, 507–508
actor-oriented models in continuous time, 504
actors, 20
    interaction with each other, 78
    as relations among social categories, 35–36
    social categories as relations amonsg, 35–36
adaptive capacity, 83–84
adding/deleting nodes, 289
adverse childhood experiences, 328
Advocacy Coalition Framework (ACF), 95, 98, 100–101
affect, 543–544
affective relation, 20
agency, 64–65
agent-based models, 505
aggregation
    trade relations and levels of, 350–351
Ahnert, Ruth, 256, 259, 260
Ahnert, Sebastian, 256, 259, 260
Akaike Information Criterion (AIC), 422, 517
Al Jazeera, 432
all occurrence sampling, 593
Alshamsi, A., 47
alter, 20
alteration strategy
    adding/deleting nodes, 289
    egocentric network interventions, 290
    link addition/deletion, 289
    network interventions, 289–290
    rewiring, 289–290
Amazon Mechanical Turk, 590
American Social Fabric Study (ASFS), 579–580
Annales d'histoire économique et sociale, 257–258
anthrospace, 576
ANTMN (analysis of topic model networks), 139
Aristotle, 205
arousal affect, 46
artefacts
    cultural, 207–208
    scientific, 227, 232–233
assimilation, 179–180
associative diffusion model (ADM), 192
attitudinal and behavioural adjustments, 548

atypicality, and cultural holes, 196–197
autologistic actor attribute models (ALAAMs), 80, 457, 460–462
    individual outcomes and network structures, 465–467
    for multilevel networks, 460–461
automorphic equivalence, 556

balanced bicliques, 555
Bank of England, 344
Barabási, A.-L., 4, 66, 228
Barkey, Karen, 58
Barnes, John, 2
Barnes, M.L., 104
Barnes, R.C., 343
Bayesian inference, 419–423
Bayesian inference framework, 489
Bayesian information criterion (BIC), 422, 517, 580
Bayesian stochastic blockmodels (BSBMs), 417
    disinformation on Twitter, 428–435
    empirical examples, 423–435
    Enron email network, 423–428
    IRA Tweets, 428–435
Bayesian stochastic blockmodels (BSBs), 616
Bayes Numerator, 422
Bearden, Jim, 3, 342
Bearman, Peter, 56, 58, 230, 569
behaviour, 544
behavioural trace data, 594–595
behaviour change, 267–278
    centrality, 269–270
    path length, 268
belief homophily, 101
belief networks, 205–207
Berelson, Bernard, 269
Bhaskar, Roy, 64
bibliometric analysis, 93
binary data
    directed, 372
    undirected disconnected, 371–372
'binary metaphorical' approach, 98
bipartite/affiliation network. *See* two-mode networks
Black Lives Matter (BLM) movement, 146
Blair, Ann, 256
Blau space, 189
blockmodeling, 27, 62, 405–408
    classic, 405–406
    generalized, 406–408, 411–412

positions and roles, 410–411
   stochastic, 413
   structural equivalence and, 556–558
blockmodels, 10
   equivalence and, 417–419
   stochastic equivalence and, 418–419
blocks, 405, 417
Bonacich, Philipp, 56
Boorman, Scott, 56
Borgatti, Steve, 610
Bott, Elizabeth, 2
Bott, Helen, 1
boundary salience, 377–378
boundary specification problem, 588
Bourdieu, Pierre, 3, 65, 310, 311
Breiger, R.L., 33, 56, 59, 147
bridging groups. *See* social clusters
bridging individuals, 286
Burt, Ronald, 3, 56

Carley, Kathleen, 56, 62, 189
Carley's constructural model, 189
Cartwright, D., 408, 550–551, 554
categorical imperative and cultural holes, 194
catnet, 34, 61–62
Centola, Damon, 38, 132
centrality, 269–270
   complex, 276–277
   data-driven issues, 370–374
   discussion, 374
   flow outcomes perspective, 369–370
   induced centrality perspective, 367–369
   limits of, 273–275
   overview, 363–364
   walk structure perspective, 364–366
centrality analysis, 614–615, 619–620, 629–630
Cheng, S., 33
Chicago, 58–59
Chicago School, 562
citation networks, 229–230
   cluster-level, 95–96
   detected communities in, 94
classic blockmodeling, 405–406
climate change
   and local fishing community, 83–85
   and social-ecological networks, 83–85
cliques, 555
   in negative network, 555
cluster analysis, 35–36
clustering, 551
   latent distance models with, 528
co-authorship networks, 227–229
Cochran, William, 508
co-evolution, 355–356, 506–508
   actor-oriented co-evolution models, 507–508
   dynamics of multiple networks, 507
   dynamics of networks and behaviour, 507

cognition
   egocentric analysis, 447–448
   evolution of minds, 213–214
   neural representations of social information, 214–216
   in social networks, 216–220
cognitive balance theory, 548, 550
cognitive evaluations, 544
cognitively activated network, 217
cognitive networks, 205–207
cognitive relation, 20
cognitive social structures (CSS), 544
cohesion, 245–246, 550
cohesive blocking, 379–381
Coleman, J., 310, 311, 313, 315–318, 443
Coleman, J.S., 164
collaborative governance, 100–101
collective identities, 61–62
collective learning, 92
collective level
   social capital at, 314–315
collective social capital
   measuring, 317
Columbia University, 56–57
common-pool resources (CPRs), 102
community detection, 556
   algorithms, 580
   methods, 383–384
comparative networks, 99–100
complete networks, 20, 23–24, 120
complex centrality, 276–277
complex contagions, 270–273
compression heuristics, 218
computational hermeneutics, 59
computational social science (CSS)
   computer-mediated networks, 48–50
   face-to-face networks, 46–48
   and social networks, 44–50
computer mediated communication (CMC), 135
computer-mediated networks, 48–50
conceptualisation of social support, 322–324
conceptual networks, 205–207
CONCOR (convergence of iterated correlations), 582
configurations, 20
   in social network, 80
connections, 20
Connections, 19
constructural imagery, 189–192
constructuralism, 189–190, 197–198
   Carley's constructural model, 189
   Mark's network ecology model (NEM), 189–190
contentious politics, 147
context, and egocentric analysis, 448–449
continuous time
   actor-oriented models in, 504
   tie-oriented models in, 503–504
continuous-time Markov process, 502
conversational agency, 64

conversion designs, 570
convolutional neural networks (CNNs), 236
co-offending networks, 247–248
Cooper, Patrick Ashley, 344
cooperation, 92–93
Copenhagen Networks Study, 616, 625
Coppola, Francis, 315
corporate networks
    comparative perspectives, 339–342
    duality of interlock networks, 342–343
    interlocks in semi-periphery, 340–341
    key issues, 342–345
    network dynamics, 343–344
    new directions, 345
    overview, 336–337
    power structure research and network analysis, 337–339
    spatiality, 344–345
    temporality, 343
    transnational networks, 341–342
    transnational perspectives, 339–342
Corporations, classes and capitalism (Scott), 340
Covid-19 pandemic, 118, 233, 275, 278, 297–298, 300, 304, 583, 595
credibility, and social spreading, 271
crime
    cohesion, 245–246
    co-offending networks, 247–248
    digital networks, 249–250
    gangs, 245–246
    neighbourhood networks, 246–247
    and networks, 243–250
    networks within criminology, 243–244
    peer effects and delinquency, 244–245
    police networks, 249
    prison networks, 248–249
    social organisation of, 245
    subgroups, 245–246
critical path analysis (CPA), 93, 97, 112–115
cross-cutting ties, 268
Crossley, Nick, 3, 63–64
cultural artefacts, 207–208
cultural betweenness, 207
cultural brokers, 195
cultural consumption networks, 195–196
cultural holes, 198
    agent-centric approaches to study of, 193–195
    and atypicality, 196–197
    and categorical imperative, 194
    culture-centric approaches to study of, 195–197
    as model for cultural networks, 193
    vs. structural holes, 194–195
    in text networks, 196
cultural holes imagery, 189, 192–197
cultural matching, 191
cultural matching model (CMM), 191
cultural networks, 62–63, 188
    analysis, 59

overview, 202–203
    and semantic, 203–204
    social construction of, 208–209
    theoretical background, 204–205
culture, 62
    constructural imagery, 189–192
    cultural holes imagery, 189, 192–197
    network, 62
    overview, 188–189
culture-centric approaches
    categorical diversity, 196–197
    cultural consumption networks, 195–196
    cultural holes in text networks, 196
    to study of cultural holes, 195–197
culture conversion model (CCM), 190–191
culturosocial structure, 193

dark network, 136
data. *See also* network data
    for actor attributes, 26
    -gathering strategies, 25
    negative, 373
    network, 27–28
    organising, 26
    preparation and loading, 611–612, 616–618, 624–626
debates within study of interlocks, 338–339
degeneracy and model fitting, 491–492
degree centrality, 27
    complementary approach, 545
    for negative ties, 545–546
    for signed networks, 545–546
delinquency, and peer effects, 244–245
Democratic Peace Theory, 356
density, 27, 62
    network, 80, 119, 121, 132, 206, 219, 229, 299, 301, 343, 352, 408, 444, 550, 605–606
    and network centralisation, 27
    population, 247, 582–583
dependence
    hierarchy, for ERGM, 480
    over time, 502
    between ties, 502
description length, 422
descriptive statistics, 121, 614, 618–619, 627–629
deviance information criterion (DIC), 517
diffusion, 123
    network, 267–278
digital activism networks, 300–301
digital ethnography, 594
digital friendship ties/networks, 298–299
digital networks, 249–250
    and SNA, 298–301
    and social media, 297–305
digraph, 27
DiMaggio, Paul, 56, 59
direct centrality, 368
directed/asymmetrical network, 20

directed binary data, 372
discourse network analysis, 156
discourse networks, 138–139
discrete-time exponential random graph (ERGM) models, 505–506
disease transmission
 consequences of networks for, 577–578
disinformation on Twitter, 428–435
distance LPM, 531–534, 536
distance model, 527
distributions
 conditional, 606
 unconditional, 605
diversity, 181
 categorical, 196–197
 ethnoracial, 181
domains, 62
Domhoff, G. William, 337
Drucker, Johanna, 260, 262, 264
duality of interlock networks, 342–343
duality principle, 36, 59
dual positioning, 468
dual projection approach, 373
Dugas, Gaetan, 275
Duke University, 60
Durkheim, Emile, 35, 322
dyad, 27
dyadic conversion, 191
dynamic approach to network analysis, 501–506
Dynamic Exponential Random Graph Models, 508
dynamic networks
 LPMs for, 535
dynamics
 egocentric analysis, 449–450
 of multiple networks, 507
 of networks and behaviour, 507
dynamic spatial social networks, 578

ecological node, 78–79
eco-networks, 246–247
Edelstein, Dan, 259
edge-betweenness approach, 385
edge connectivity, 381
edgelists, 26, 610–612
edges, 20, 61, 405, 526–527, 531–532, 534–537
ego, 10, 20, 24–25, 119, 439, 444–445, 548–549
ego-centred networks, 589
egocentric analysis
 background, 440–441
 cognition, 447–448
 context, 448–449
 dynamics, 449–450
 egocentric tradition, 441–443
 eliciting networks, 443–446
 mobilisation, 447
 new directions, 446–450
 scope, 439–440
 vs. social capital research, 443

vs. social support research, 442–443
 vs. sociocentric analysis, 441–442
 strength, 446–447
egocentric network interventions, 290
egocentric tradition, 441–443
 egocentric analysis *vs.* social capital research, 443
 egocentric analysis *vs.* social support research, 442–443
 egocentric *vs.* sociocentric analysis, 441–442
ego-networks/egocentric networks, 10, 20, 24, 256
 spatial context affecting, 579
 spatial distribution of, 578–579
ego network studies, 24
eigenvector-based approaches, 386–387
eliciting networks, 443–446
elite networks, 133–134
Emirbayer, M., 3, 55
emotional excitement, 271
endogenous network configurations, 353
Enron email network, 423–428
entities, 20
environmental governance research, 77
environmental policy network analysis
 core research themes, 98–104
 overview, 92–93
 scholarship, 93–98
equivalence
 blockmodels and, 417–419
 stochastic, 418–419
 structural, 556–558
Erdős-Renyi model, 526
Erickson, Bonnie, 56
Erikson, Emily, 59
estimation
 exponential random graph models (ERGMs), 489–491
 LPM, 529
ethnic inequality, 178–182
 and contact, 178–182
 as function of migration, 178–182
 and tolerance, 178–182
ethnic relations
 ethnic inequality, 178–182
 inter-group contact, 176–178
 overview, 175–176
 understanding, through network analysis, 175–183
ethnoracial diversity, 181
Euler, Leonhard, 9
Europe, 56, 60, 167, 180
 ancient, 255
 Eastern, 340, 467
 household solar panel installations in, 271
 mediaeval, 255
 Novo Nordisk Foundation in, 226
European Research Council (ERC), 226
event-driven focus, 24
event relations, 20
exogenous covariate network configurations, 354

experiment(s)
    Milgram's, 591
    as mode of data collection, 589–591
    offline field, 590
    offline lab, 590
    online field, 590
    online lab, 590
exploratory analysis, 618–619
exponential random graph models (ERGMs), 11, 28, 137–138, 455, 505, 513, 554, 576–577, 603, 606–607, 616
    Bayesian inference framework, 489
    common issues, 491–496
    constrained estimation, 490
    degeneracy and model fitting, 491–492
    dependence hierarchy for, 480
    different types of nodes, 483–485
    drawing inference, 493–494
    estimation, 489–491
    extensions, 480–489
    good model, 492–493
    interpretation of, 493
    interpretation of Markov model, 477–478
    interpretation of parameters, 494–495
    Markov graphs, 475–477
    maximum likelihood, 489
    for multilevel networks, 457–460
    multilevel structure, 462–463
    multiplex ties, 480–482
    node attributes, 485–487
    ordered and valued ties, 482–483
    overview, 474–475
    panel network data and longitudinal, 488–489
    partially observed networks/large networks, 490–491
    pseudo-likelihood, 489–490
    residuals and tie-prediction, 495–496
    social circuit dependence assumption, 478–480
    unobserved heterogeneity, 487–488
extensions
    of LPCM, 536–537
    of the projection LPM, 536
    to relational event model, 521

Facebook, 48–49, 135, 152, 192, 271–272, 290, 298–300, 304, 442, 515, 590, 612, 614–615
face-to-face networks, 46–48
feminism, 163
Financial Times, 432
Firth, Robert, 207
Fischer, Claude, 3
Fisher, Sir Ronald, 508
flattening ratio, 576
flavour network, 36
flow(s)
    of (mis)information argument, 546–547
    social categories from, 33
flow models, 21–22

flow outcomes perspective, 369–370
focal sampling, 593
Fox News, 432
Frank, Ken, 386
Frank, O., 11, 475–477, 482–483
Franke, K., 567
Franklin, Benjamin, 257
#FreeAJStaff movement, 301
free drawings, 568
Freeman, L.C., 4, 56
friendship
    and interethnic contact, 180–181
    racial friendship segregation, 182
    and support, 180–181
frustration index (line index of balance), 551
Fuhse, J., 37, 38
full/whole networks, 20
fully articulated socialecological network model, 79

gangs, 245–246
Garfield, Eugene, 229
Gates Foundation, 226
Gaudet, Hazel, 269
gender. *See also* women
    in business/organisations, 168–169
    co-evolution of, 169–170
    defined, 162
    discrimination, 233
    inequalities, 162–163
    overview, 162–163
    and schools, 165–167
    in scientific networks, 233
    as social construction, 163–165
    and social networks, 162–171
gendered personal networks, 167–168
generalised conversion, 191
generalised conversion model (GCM), 191–192
generalised conversion value, 190
generalized blockmodeling, 406–408
    dealing with missing data, 412–413
    other extensions of, 411–412
    three-mode network arrays, 411
    two-mode network arrays, 411
    valued networks, 411–412
General Social Survey (GSS), 444–445
genetic ancestry testing (GATs), 181
geographic information system (GIS), 576–577
geometrical abstraction, 1
Gibson, David, 64
Giuliani, Rudolph, 35
The Godfather, 315
Goodman, L.A., 33
goodness of fit (GOF)
    Mahalanobis distance, 492
    for the REM, 517
    spectral, 492
Google, 275–276
Gould, Roger, 56

Graif, Corina, 247, 581
Grandjean, Martin, 256, 259, 260
Granovetter, Mark, 2, 56, 268, 298
graphical user interfaces, 611–616
    centrality analysis, 614–615
    data preparation and loading, 611–612
    descriptive statistics, 614
    NetDraw, 611
    subgroup analysis, 615–616
    UCINet, 611
    visualising networks, 612–614
graph theory, 9
gravity model (GM), 354
Great Depression, 344
group dynamics, 2
GUI (graphical user interface), 610
Guilbeault, D., 38

Hanna, Michael, 38, 39
Harary, F., 408, 550–551, 554
Hawthorne studies, 562
health
    communities, 299–300
    and social support, 326–329
health behaviours/outcomes
    overview, 116–117
    research and SNA/T, 118–122
    and social networks, 117–118
health interventions
    and SNA/T, 124–125
    and social networks, 124–125
Helen Kirkpatrick Watts, 570
heterosexuality, 37, 167
heuristic sorting approaches, 384–386
Hierarchical Bayesian Stochastic Blockmodels, 421–423
Hilferding, Rudolf, 337
Hobson, John, 392
holism, 57
Homans, George, 2
homogeneity blockmodeling, 412
homophily, 20, 23, 50, 66, 122, 191
    belief, 101
    and partisan identity, 137
    political, 137
    racial and ethnic, 176, 182
hooking up, 37
hot-deck imputation, 605
Hudson's Bay Company (HBC), 344
hypergraph representation of scientific networks, 233–234
hypothesis testing, 28

Identity and Control (White), 34, 57, 61, 63
idiographic approaches, 156
Ikegami, Eiko, 59
imputation
    from conditional distributions, 606
    of conditional means, 605
    hot-deck, 605

    multiple, 606–607
    by preferential attachment, 605
    from unconditional distributions, 605
    of unconditional means, 604–605
imputation methods, 604–607
    imputation from conditional distributions, 606
    imputation from unconditional distributions, 605
    imputation of conditional means, 605
    imputation of unconditional means, 604–605
    multiple imputation, 606–607
indirect centrality, 368
indirect connections
    involving negative ties, 546–549
    involving positive ties, 546–549
individual networks, 131–133
    diffusion mechanisms, 132
    networks and participation, 131–132
individual social capital, 310–311, 316–317
    measuring, 316–317
individual strategy
    bridging individuals, 286
    low-threshold adopters, 286
    marginals, 286
    network interventions, 284–286
    opinion leader interventions, 284–286
induced centrality perspective, 367–369
induction strategy
    network interventions, 287–289
    network outreach, 287–288
    optimal leader–group matching, 288–289
    respondent-driven sampling (RDS), 287
    word of mouth (WOM), 287
inferences, 28
    for the LPM, 529–531
inferential network clustering, 419
The Inner Life of Empires (Rothschild), 258
Institutional Collective Action Framework, 98, 100–101
institutions, 312
integrated development environments (IDEs), 616
interactionist theories, 164
interaction rituals, 190
interactions, 63–64
interdisciplinarity, 232
interest intermediation, 99
interethnic contact, 180–181
    and friendship, 180–181
    and support, 180–181
interethnic relationships, 182
inter-group contact
    ethnic relations, 176–178
    name generators, 176–177
    network structure and content, 176–178
    position generators, 177–178
interlocking directorships, 336
interlock networks, duality of, 342–343
interlocks
    debates within the study of, 338–339
    in the semi-periphery, 340–341

International Network of Social Network Analysis, 20
international trade networks
    explaining networks/network structure, 353–354
    outcomes of trade networks, 354–355
    questions about network topology, 352
    questions of co-evolution, 355–356
    structure and causality, 351–356
    summary/future outlook, 356
    trade network studies, 351–356
    trade relations and levels of aggregation, 350–351
interorganisational collaboration, 124
interpersonal sentiments, 47
interpretation
    of ERGMs, 493
    of Markov model, 477–478
interventions. *See also specific interventions*
    egocentric network, 290
    network, 282–293
    opinion leaders, 284–286
    selection, 290–291
    word of mouth (WOM), 287
interviews
    expert, 564
    as mode of data collection, 591–593
    non-directive, 562
    open/less-structured, 564
    qualitative, 250, 562, 568–569, 592
    stakeholder, 77
    structured, 24
    unstructured, 567
inverse centrality problem, 368
investment, 311–312
IRA Tweets, 428–435
issue networks, 99

Jeidels, Otto, 336–337
Jennings, Helen Hall, 19
Johnson–Lindenstrauss theorem, 234
Jones, C., 37
journal impact factor (JIF), 229
Journal of Historical Network Research, 262
Journal of Immunology, 232
Journal of Public Administration and Theory (JPART), 98
Journal of Social Structure, 19

Kassabova, Biliana, 259
Katz, Elihu, 269–270
Kaufman, J.
    generalised conversion model (GCM), 191–192
key player problem, 368
Kitts, J.A., 49
KliqueFinder, 386
knowledge economy, 231
Krohn, M.D., 244

large networks, 490–491

Latané, Bib, 578–579
latent position cluster model (LPCM), 528, 531, 536–537
    extensions of, 536–537
Latent Position Cluster Random Effect model (LPC-MRE), 528, 533
latent position models (LPMs), 526–528, 616
    with clustering, 528
    distance, 531–534, 536
    distance model, 527
    for dynamic networks, 535
    estimation, 529
    interpretation of posterior samples, 529–530
    for multiview networks, 534–535
    with node-specific random effects, 528
    other inferential approaches, 530–531
    projection model, 527–528, 536
    for rank data, 536
    theory of, 536
    for weighted networks, 535
latent position network models
    illustrative example for distance LPM, 531–534
    inference for LPM, 529–531
    latent position models, 527–528
    notation, 527
    open research questions, 537–538
    overview, 526–527
    software, 537
    state of the art, 534–537
latent space models. *See* latent position models
latent space network models, 506
latent variable models, 419–423, 506
Laumann, E., 24, 56
layer logic, 482
Lazarsfeld, Paul, 269–270, 440
Lazega, E., 34
Lee, Nancy, 2
legitimacy, and social spreading, 271
Lemercier, Claire, 259
Lerner, J., 36, 517
Levine, Joel, 2–3
Lévi-Strauss, Claude, 2
Lewin, K., 1
Lewis, K.
    generalised conversion model (GCM), 191–192
likelihood-based methods, 604
Lin, Nan, 3
link prediction, 606
links, 20, 153
link-tracing sampling, 601
Lizardo, O., 35, 59, 194
    cultural matching model (CMM), 191
    culture conversion model, 190–191
location-aware technology, 46–48
Locke, John, 257
Lockwood, David, 34
Lomi, A., 36, 517

Longitudinal Employer Household Dynamics (LEHD) survey, 581
longitudinal ERGMs, 488–489
Lorber, J., 37
Lorrain, F., 33
low-threshold adopters, 286
Lundberg, George, 2

macro-level social capital, 310
Madagascar, 81–83
map analysis, 37
marginals, and individual strategy, 286
Mark, N.P., 189–190
Markov chain Monte Carlo (MCMC), 461, 529–531
    procedure, 413
    simulation, 517
Markov graphs, 475–477
Markov model, 477–478
Marsden, P.V., 33
Mashable, 432
matrix representations, 26
Matthew Effect, 23, 501
maximum likelihood estimation (MLE), 516
maximum pseudo-likelihood estimate (MPLE), 489–490
Mayo, Elton, 2
means
    conditional, 605–606
    unconditional, 604–605
mean-value parametrisation, 494
Measuring Culture project, 60
membership categorisation devices, 39
meso-level networks, 150–152
methodological individualism, 57
micro-level social capital, 310
micromobilisation
    ego-network-model of, 149
    and social networks, 147–150
Midura, Rachel, 259
migration, 179–180
    and ethnic inequality, 178–182
Milgram, Stanley, 4, 591
Milgram's experiment, 591
Mills, C. Wright, 337
minds
    evolution of, 213–214
    social brain hypothesis, 213–214
minimum description length (MDL), 422
    model selection using, 422–423
Mische, A., 3
missing at random (MAR) data, 600–601, 603
missing completely at random (MCAR) data, 599–601, 603–604, 607
missing data
    dealing with, 412–413
    effects of, 602–603
    mechanisms, 599–601
    treatments, 603–604
    types of, 601–602

missing network data, 599–607
    effects of missing data, 602–603
    imputation methods, 604–607
    likelihood-based methods, 604
    missing data mechanisms, 599–601
    missing data treatments, 603–604
    missing data types, 601–602
missing nodes, 412, 601, 604
missing not at random (MNAR) data, 600–601, 604, 607
Mitchell, Clyde, 2
mixed methods
    benefits of, 563–566
    data quality, 565
    explanatory power and generalisability, 565
    exploring networks, 564
    field access, 564
    network dynamics, 565–566
    network effects, 565–566
    network mechanisms, 565–566
    network orientations/assessments/interpretations, 564–565
    network practices, 564
    overview, 562–566
    for study of social networks, 563–566
mixed-methods designs, 568–570
    parallel designs, 569–570
    sequential qual-quant design, 569
    sequential quant-qual design, 569
mixed-methods research, 563
mixed-methods studies, 562
MNA research potential, 467–469
mobilisation
    cultural capital, 190
    egocentric analysis, 447
mobilised network, 217
models. *See specific models*
modes of data collection, 589–595
    behavioural trace data, 594–595
    experiments, 589–591
    observation, 593–594
    surveys and interviews, 591–593
modularity, 384
modularity score, 384
Mohr, John, 33, 62–63
Mokken, Rob, 3
Montesquieu, 35
Moreno, Jacob, 1, 19
motifs, 80
Mullins, Nick, 2
multidimensional scaling, 11
multiform heterogeneity, 36
multigroup network, 21
multilevel exponential random graph models (ML-ERGM), 80, 87
multilevel network analysis (MNA), 455–456, 469–470
    ALAAM for multilevel networks, 460–461
    application, 461–467
    data description, 461–462

ERGM and SSM for multilevel networks, 457–460
model estimation and selection, 461
modelling results, 462–467
models, 457–461
multilevel network representation, 457
overview, 455–457
research potential, 467–469
multilevel network representation, 457
multilevel networks, 484
ALAAM for, 460–461
ERGM for, 457–460
SSM for, 457–460
multilevel structure, and within-level structure, 462–463
multimodal networks, 21
multimodal social network analysis, 392–399
multiple imputation, 606–607
multiple networks, 28, 34
dynamics of, 507
hierarchical modelling of, 392
multiple regression quadradic assignment procedures (MRQAP), 616
multiplex community affiliation clustering (MCAC), 134
multiplex relationships, 119
multiplex ties, 480–482
multiview networks, and LPMs, 534–535
Muñoz, Trevor, 261
Mützel, S., 37

Nadel, S.F., 418
Nadel, Siegfried, 2, 10
name generators, 25, 176–177, 443–445
name interpreter questions, 25
name interpreters, 445
Namier, Lewis, 255
National Longitudinal Study of Adolescent Health (Add Health), 177, 577
National Science Foundation (NSF), 226
natural language processing (NLP), 207, 595
natural parameters, 494
negative asymmetry, 542
negative blocks, 408
negative data, 373
negative influence hypothesis, 548
negative networks
nodal-level measures of position for, 545–549
negative relation, 20
negative resources, 546
negative ties, 543–545
attitudinal and behavioural adjustments, 548
flow of (mis)information argument, 546–547
indirect connections involving, 546–549
as negative resources, 546
network-level properties, 549–554
open and closed triads, 549
power-dependence argument, 548–549
status argument, 547
structural holes, 549

types of, 543–544
variants of degree centrality for, 545–546
Negopy program, 386
neighbourhood networks, 246–247
neighbourhoods
defining, based on spatial social networks, 580–581
safety contacts, 580
W-matrix around, 582–583
netdoms, 62
NetDraw, 610, 611
netness, 34, 62
netnography, 594
network(s), 445. *See also specific types*
co-evolution of, 169–170
constructural imagery, 189–192
co-offending, 247–248
and cooperation, 92–93
and crime, 243–250
of cultural artefacts, 207–208
cultural holes imagery, 189, 192–197
culture and interaction (NCI), 55
density, 80, 119, 121, 132, 206, 219, 229, 299, 301, 343, 352, 408, 444, 550, 605–606
endogeneity, 23
as explanandum, 23
as explanans, 22–23
as institutional arrangement, 99–100
as method, 100–101
outcomes for, 354–355
for programme implementation, 292–293
as questions and answers, 259–262
resilience and vulnerability, 354–355
of scientists, 230–231
social capital in structure of, 312–314
of social relations, 2
topologies, 23
network accountability, 164
network analysis, 3, 181
and (de)colonial project, 182–183
defined, 92
dynamic approach to, 501–506
environmental policy, 92–104
ethnic relations and, 175–183
historical, 255–264
power structure research, 337–339
scientific software for, 610–633
network boundary, 24–25
network buddies, 591
Network Canvas, 592
network contingency of social support, 324–326
network culture, 62
network data, 27–28. *See also* data
degree centrality, 27
density, 27
dyad, 27
triad censuses, 27
network diffusion, 267–278

centrality, 269–270
complex contagions, 270–273
path length, 268
simple contagions, 270–273
network dynamics
  actor-oriented models in continuous time, 504
  co-evolution, 506–508
  corporate networks, 343–344
  dependence between ties, 502
  dependence over time, 502
  discrete-time ERGM models, 505–506
  dynamic approach to network analysis, 501–506
  latent variable models, 506
  model specification, 504–505
  outlook and discussion, 508–509
  SAOM as agent-based model, 505
  software, 508
  stochastic models for, 502–503
  tie-oriented models in continuous time, 503–504
network ecologies, 189–190
network ecology model (NEM), 189–190
network function
  defined, 21
  models of, 21–22
network-identified peer opinion leaders, 291–292
network interventions, 282–293. *See also* interventions
  alteration strategy, 289–290
  evidence on effectiveness of, 291–292
  individual strategy, 284–286
  induction strategy, 287–289
  intervention selection, 290–291
  overview, 282–283
  segmentation strategy, 286–287
  taxonomy of, 283–284
network-level properties, 549–554
  cohesion, 550
  structural balance, 550–554
network management, 99–100
network outreach, 287–288
Network Science, 4, 19
Network Science Society, 20
Networks of corporate power, 340
network structures and individual outcomes, 465–467
network topology, 352
NetworkX, 624–629
new public management (NPM), 99
New School for Social Research, 57
New York Times, 433
nodal attributes, 26
nodal-level measures
  and negative networks, 545–549
  and signed networks, 545–549
node attributes, 485–487
node connectivity, 378–379, 382
nodes, 20, 61
  adding/deleting, 289
  bridging, 286
  different types of, 483–485

ecological, 78–79
Euclidean distances between, 406
and position, 406
social, 78
-specific random effects, 528
structurally equivalent, 405–406
nomothetic approaches, 156
Northern California Community Study, 444
notation, and latent position network models, 527
novelty, 232
Novo Nordisk Foundation, 226
null tie imputation, 605

obesity, and peer social networks, 122–123
observations
  ethnographic, 594
  as mode of data collection, 593–594
  structural cohesion, 381–382
officer networks, 249
offline field experiments, 590
offline lab experiments, 590
Okhmatovskiy, Ilya, 340
'oligarchic bank hegemony,' 340
1-covered or regular blocks, 407
one-mode analysis, 10
one-mode networks, 21
online field experiments, 590
online lab experiments, 590
online links, 48–50
open and closed triads, 549
open system networks, 589
opinion leaders
  interventions, 284–286
  network-identified peer, 291–292
optimal leader–group matching, 288–289
ordered and valued ties, 482–483
organisational embeddedness perspective, 565
organisational societies, 455
Ostrom, Elinor, 99, 102

Padgett, J.F., 36, 56, 58
panel network data, 488–489
Pappi, Franz, 407
parallel designs, 569–570
Park, B., 33
Parsons, Talcott, 56
partially observed networks, 490–491
partial networks, 589
participation shifts, 518
partisan identity
  and homophily, 137
path length, 268
Pattison, P.E., 34
peer effects, and delinquency, 244–245
peer groups and communities, 382–388
  background, 382–383
  community detection methods, 383–384
  eigenvector-based approaches, 386–387

heuristic sorting approaches, 384–386
stochastic block models (SBMs), 387–388
perceived emotional support, 328
personal networks/local networks, 20, 24, 119, 439–450
gendered, 167–168
women, 168
personal political networks, 132–133
phenomenological individualism, 57
Physical Review E, 4
PN centrality, 373
police networks, 249
political and policy networks
coordination and organising, 134–137
discourse networks, 138–139
elite networks, 133–134
individual networks, 131–133
overview, 130–131
policy networks, 137–138
Polletta, Francesca, 58
polycentricity, 102–104
Porter, John, 337
positional-attribute focus, 24
position and resource generators, 445–446
position generators, 25, 177–178
positive blocks, 408
positive relation, 20
positive ties, 544–545
attitudinal and behavioural adjustments, 548
flow of (mis)information argument, 546–547
indirect connections involving, 546–549
power-dependence argument, 548–549
status argument, 547
types of, 543–544
potential network, 217
Powell, W.W., 36
power-dependence argument, 548–549
power structure research and network analysis, 337–339
preferential attachment, 353, 605
preferential trade agreement (PTA) networks, 351
priming, 219
prison networks, 248–249
programming languages, 616–633
centrality analysis, 619–620, 629–630
data preparation and loading, 616–618
descriptive statistics, 618–619
exploratory analysis, 618–619
Python with *NetworkX,* 624–629
R with sna, 616
subgroup analysis, 620–624, 631–633
visualising networks, 618
projection LPM, 536
projection model, 527–528
property rights, 312
Prosopographia Imperii Romani, 255
psychological geography, 1–2
publics, 65
Putnam, Robert, 3, 310
Python, 624–629

qualitative interviewing strategies, 592
qualitative methods
benefits of, 563–566
data quality, 565
defined, 563
explanatory power and generalisability, 565
exploring networks, 564
field access, 564
network dynamics, 565–566
network effects, 565–566
network mechanisms, 565–566
network orientations/assessments/interpretations, 564–565
network practices, 564
overview, 562–566
for study of social networks, 563–566
qualitative textual data, 563
quantitative data, 563
questions about network topology, 352
Quintane, E., 49

race
relational sociology of, 38–39
racialisation of neighbourhoods, 181–182
Radcliffe-Brown, Alfred, 2
radio frequency (RFID) sensors, 46
randomised controlled trial (RCT), 589–590
rank data, and LPMs, 536
rapid automatic keyword extraction (RAKE), 94
Rawson, Katie, 261
realised network, 217
Real Time Statistics Project, 595
reciprocity, 519
reciprocity assumptions, 312
reconstruction, 605–606
reduced mutual information (RMI) score, 427
regular equivalence, 418, 556
relation(s)
defined, 20
as explanatory covariates, 354
forms of, 20
social categories from, 33
relational event data, 514
relational event models (REMs), 28, 616
creating relational event statistics, 517–520
empirical applications of, 520–521
extensions to, 521
future research directions, 522–523
goodness of fit for, 517
model details, 515–516
model overview, 514–515
overview, 513–514
relational event data, 514
sampling with, 516–517
software packages, 521–522
relational event statistics
creating, 517–520
participation shifts, 518

volume-based structural signatures, 519
  weighting events in REMs, 520
relational hyperevent models (RHEM), 36
relational norms, 45
relational realism, 57
relational sociology, 3, 55–66
relationship-interpreter questions, 25
reputational focus, 24
research design decisions, 566–567
research questions
research questions, formulating, 22–23
residuals and tie-prediction, 495–496
resilience, 354–355
resource generator, 25
respondent-driven sampling (RDS), 287
restricted conversion value, 190
rewiring networks, 289–290
RF measure, 408
Rice, Yael, 256
Ritter, E.R., 343
Roe v. Wade, 2
role relations, 44–45, 544
Rosental, Paul-André, 259
Rothschild, Emma, 258–259, 262
Russia's Internet Research Agency (IRA), 428
Rutgers University, 60
R with sna, 616
Ryan, Yann Ciarán, 259

Santa Barbara, 59–60
Santoro, M., 34
scan sampling, 593
schools
  and gender, 165–167
  interethnic contact and friendships, 182
  and social networks, 165–167
scientific artefacts, 227
  heterogeneous networks of, 232–233
  novelty, 232
scientific data, 226
scientific networks, 225–236
  analysing complex, 230–233
  analysing simple, 227–230
  entities and identities in, 226–227
  gender in, 233
  hierarchical, 235–236
  hypergraph representation of, 233–234
  neural embedding for large-scale, 234–235
  overview, 225–226
  people and social institutions, 226–227
  scientific artefacts, 227
  scientific data, 226
  and social domains, 233
scientific software
  graphical user interfaces, 611–616
  for network analysis, 610–633
  programming languages, 616–633

scientists
  networks of, 230–231
  science of team science, 230–231
Scott, John, 34, 65, 340
Seeley, J.L., 37
segmentation strategy
  groups, 286–287
  network interventions, 286–287
  positions, 287
semantic network
  and cultural networks, 203–204
  overview, 202–203
  social construction of, 208–209
  theoretical background, 204–205
sensor technology, 46–48
sentiment-related sensor research, 46
sentiments, 44
sequence sampling, 593
sequential explanatory design, 569
sequential exploratory design, 569
sequential qual-quant design, 569
sequential quant-qual design, 569
sequential structural signatures (SSSs), 517–519
sexual relationships, 167
signed networks, 408–409, 544–545
  degree centrality for, 545–546
  network-level properties, 549–554
  nodal-level measures of position for, 545–549
  variants of degree centrality for, 545–546
Simmel, Georg, 1, 212, 322
simple contagions, 270–273
Skype, 274
SNAP database, 423
Snijders, Tom, 11
snowball sampling, 601
social brain hypothesis, 213–214
social capital, 3, 123
  as 'capital,' 316
  collective, 314–315, 317
  conclusion/future directions, 318
  dark side of, 315–316
  declining in contemporary societies, 318
  general measurement issues, 317–318
  individual, 310–311, 316–317
  measurement of, 316–318
  overview, 309
  phenomenon, 309–310
  and social movement, 150
  in structure of a network, 312–314
  theoretical accounts of, 310–315
social capital research, 443
social categories, 61–62
  actors as relations among, 35–36
  challenges, 38–40
  emergence of, 37–38
  as infrastructure for networks, 34–35
  as relations among actors, 35–36
  from relations and flows, 33

and social networks, 32–40
    weakening of, 36–37
social circuit dependence assumption, 478–480
social clusters, 276
social construction
    gender as, 163–165
    of semantic and cultural networks, 208–209
social contagion, 123
social coordination, 271
social determinants of health (SDOH), 116
social-ecological interdependencies, 76–77, 78
social-ecological networks, 102–104
    analysing, 79–81
    applications, 81–88
    constructing, 77–79
    ecological components, 85–87
    multilayered, 80
    overview, 75–77
social embeddedness, 380
social fields, 65
social flows, 576
social geometry, 1
social influence, 123
social influence models, 457, 460
social influence theory, 22
social information
    neural representations of, 214–216
social institutions, 226–227
social integration, 123
social interactions, 163
social isolation, 123
social learning, 92
social ledger theory, 546
social media, 48–50
    and digital networks, 297–305
    ethical considerations and dilemmas, 303–304
    methodological considerations and challenges, 301–303
    network ties, 153
    overview, 297–298
    and SNA, 298–301
    and social movements, 152–153
social morphology, 2
social movement organisations (SMOs), 150–151, 154
social movements
    analytical considerations, 155–157
    defined, 147
    methodological considerations, 153–155
    overview, 146–147
    thinking relationally about, 147
    and virtual networks, 152–153
social neighbourhood, 392
social network analysis and theory (SNA/T), 116–117, 212, 297–298
    central ideas in, 9–11
    context, 19–20
    development of, 1–9
    and digital networks, 298–301

health communities, 299–300
and health interventions, 124–125
and health research, 118–122
and social media, 298–301
social network data collection, 587–596
    general principles of network data, 588–589
    modes of data collection, 589–595
social networks, 324, 404–405
    cognition in, 216–220
    and computational social science, 44–50
    defined, 20
    eliciting alters, 567
    and ethics, 28–29
    and gender, 162–171
    and health behaviours/outcomes, 117
    and health interventions, 124–125
    mechanisms and functions linked to health, 123–124
    and micromobilisation, 147–150
    network, 27–28
    qualitative and mixed methods, 563–566
    qualitative approaches to study of, 566–568
    research design decisions, 566–567
    research designs, 23
    and schools, 165–167
    and social categories, 32–40
    spatial analysis of, 575–584
    structures, 121, 122
    studying, 24
    theorising, 21
    types relevant to health, 117–118
    visual tools, 567–568
Social Networks, 3–4, 8, 19, 180, 405, 411
social node, 78. *See also* actors
social organisation of crime, 245
social pain, 216
social referents, 590
social relations, 84
social relations focus, 24
social ritualization, 164
social selection models (SSMs), 456
social support, 123, 182, 299
    conceptualisation of, 322–324
    definition and typology, 322–324
    distinction and network contingency of, 324–326
    and health, 326–329
    overview, 322
    research, 442–443
Society and Natural Resources, 98
sociocentric analysis
    egocentric vs, 441–442
sociocentric social networks, 120
sociogram, 2
sociological peer groups, 382
sociomatrix, 9
sociometry, 1–2
sociospatial isolation, 579
Socrates, 205
software

latent position network models, 537
network dynamics, 508
relational event models, 521–522
Somers, Margaret, 56
spatial analysis of social networks, 575–584
spatial distribution, 181–182
　　of ego-networks, 578–579
spatiality, and corporate networks, 344–345
spatially embedded random networks, 526
spatial networks
　　within-neighbourhood effects of, 581–582
spatial social networks
　　accounting for network processes, 576–577
　　consequences for disease transmission, 577–578
　　defining neighbourhoods based on, 580–581
　　distance between ties and complete networks, 576
　　dynamic, 578
　　methods for, 575–576
　　network structure, 577
　　simulating, across cities, 583
　　spatial context and ego-networks, 579
　　spatial distribution of ego-networks, 578–579
　　spatial social ties affecting perceptions, 579–580
　　within-neighbourhood effects of, 581–582
　　W-matrix around neighbourhoods, 582–583
spatial social network schema, 576
spatial social ties, and perceptions, 579–580
specific form of governance, 99
spotlighting effect, 602
SSM
　　for multilevel networks, 457–460
　　within-level network structures, 463–465
Stark, David, 56, 58
state relations, 20
statistical methods, 121
status argument, 547
stochastic actor-oriented models (SAOMs), 28, 137, 504, 513, 554, 578, 603–604, 606–607, 616
　　as an agent-based model, 505
stochastic block models (SBMs), 387–388, 413, 418, 506
stochastic equivalence, 418–419
stochastic models for network dynamics, 502–503
stochastic network models, 28
Stokman, Frans, 3
story, 61
Strauss, D., 11, 475–477, 482–483
strength, and egocentric analysis, 446–447
Strogatz, Steven, 4
structural balance
　　emergence of balance, 554
　　measuring for -signed networks, 551
　　measuring for -signed networks, 551–554
　　weak balance for -signed networks, 554
structural balance theory, 550
structural cohesion, 378–382
　　cohesive blocking, 379–381
　　extensions and observations, 381–382
　　node connectivity, 378–379

structural equivalence, 62, 556–558
structural expectations, 45
structural holes
　　vs. cultural holes, 194–195
structural holes theory, 22
structuralism, 56
structurally equivalent nodes, 405–406
structural position, 270
Stuhler, O., 33
subgroup analysis, 615–616, 620–624, 631–633
subgroups, 245–246, 554–556
　　balanced bicliques, 555
　　cliques, 555
　　community detection, 556
support
　　and friendship, 180–181
　　and interethnic contact, 180–181
surveillance capitalism, 263
surveys as mode of data collection, 591–593
switchings, 63
Syme, Ronald, 255

telecommunication, 48–50
temporality, and corporate networks, 343
tie-oriented models in continuous time, 503–504
ties, 20
　　dependence between, 502
　　multiplex, 480–482
　　ordered and valued, 482–483
Tilly, Charles, 34, 56–58
tolerance
　　and ethnic inequality, 178–182
total centrality, 368
total quality management (TQM), 273
trade networks
　　outcomes of, 354–355
　　as a world system, 352–353
trade network studies
　　asking questions about structure and causality, 351–356
　　classifying, 351–356
trade relations and levels of aggregation, 350–351
transactions, 63
transitivity, 353, 519
transnationalism, 179–180
transnational networks, 341–342
triad censuses, 27
Tucson, Arizona, 59
tuning parameter, 576
Twitter, 25, 48–49, 131–135, 152–154, 272, 274, 298, 300–305, 442
　　disinformation on, 428–435
　　IRA Tweets, 428–435
two-mode data, 373–374
two-mode networks, 10, 21

UCINet, 610, 611, 615–616
UCINet 3, 610

UCINet 4, 610
UCINet 6, 610
undirected disconnected binary data, 371–372
undirected networks, 405
undirected/symmetrical network, 20
University of Chicago, 58–59
University of Notre Dame, 60
unobserved heterogeneity, 487–488
unstructured (ad libitum) and ethnographic observation, 594
US General Social Survey (GSS), 190

Vaisey, S.
    cultural matching model (CMM), 191
valence affect, 46
valued data, 372–373
vegetation cluster, 80
vertices, 20
virtual ethnography, 594
virtual networks
    and social movements, 152–153
visualising networks, 612–614, 618, 626–627
visual tools
    social networks, 567–568
vitalities, 367
volume-based structural signatures, 519
vulnerability, 354–355

Wald, A., 567
walk structure perspective, 364–366

Warner, Lloyd, 2
The Washington Post, 432
Watts, Duncan, 4
weak balance, 551
weak culture, 191
Weber, Max, 310–311, 316
Web of Science, 8
Web of Science (WoS) database, 93
weighted networks, and LPMs, 535
weighting events in REMs, 520
Weil, André, 2
Wellman, Barry, 3, 56
White, Harrison, 2, 10, 32, 33, 35, 37, 56–57
William Foote Whyte, 562
Windolf, Paul, 340
within-level network structures, 463–465
within-neighbourhood effects of spatial networks, 581–582
W-matrix around neighbourhoods, 582–583
women. *See also* gender
    homophilous ties, 168–169
    in leadership positions, 169
    personal networks, 168
word of mouth (WOM) intervention, 287
World Health Organizations (WHO), 116
world systems perspective (WSP), 352–353

Yale University, 59

Žiberna, A., 411–412